THE ROUTLEDGE RESEARCH COMPANION TO MODERNISM IN MUSIC

Modernism in music still arouses passions and is riven by controversies. Taking root in the early decades of the twentieth century, it achieved ideological dominance for almost three decades following the Second World War, before becoming the object of widespread critique in the last two decades of the century, both from critics and composers of a postmodern persuasion and from prominent scholars associated with the 'new musicology'. Yet these critiques have failed to dampen its ongoing resilience. The picture of modernism has considerably broadened and diversified, and has remained a pivotal focus of debate well into the twenty-first century. This Research Companion does not seek to limit what musical modernism might be. At the same time, it resists any dilution of the term that would see its indiscriminate application to practically any and all music of a certain period.

In addition to addressing issues already well established in modernist studies such as aesthetics, history, institutions, place, diaspora, cosmopolitanism, production and performance, communication technologies and the interface with postmodernism, this volume also explores topics that are less established; among them: modernism and affect, modernism and comedy, modernism versus the 'contemporary', and the crucial distinction between modernism in popular culture and a 'popular modernism', a modernism of the people. In doing so, this text seeks to define modernism in music by probing its margins as much as by restating its supposed essence.

Björn Heile is Professor of Music (post-1900) at the University of Glasgow. He is the author of *The Music of Mauricio Kagel* (Ashgate, 2006), the editor of *The Modernist Legacy: Essays on New Music* (Ashgate, 2009), co-editor (with Martin Iddon) of *Mauricio Kagel bei den Darmstädter Ferienkursen für Neue Musik: Eine Dokumentation* (2009) and co-editor (with Peter Elsdon and Jenny Doctor) of *Watching Jazz: Encountering Jazz Performance on Screen* (2016), plus many other publications on new music, experimental music theatre and jazz. Among other projects, he is trying to write a book on the global history of musical modernism.

Charles Wilson was Senior Editor for twentieth-century composers on the second edition of the *New Grove Dictionary of Music and Musicians*, and currently lectures at the School of Music, Cardiff University. He served as Editor-in-Chief (2009–12) of the journal *Twentieth-Century Music*. His research focuses on the relationship between historiography and practice (both personal and institutional) in the art music of the twentieth and twenty-first centuries.

THE ROUTLEDGE RESEARCH COMPANION TO MODERNISM IN MUSIC

Edited by Björn Heile and Charles Wilson

LONDON AND NEW YORK

First published 2019
by Routledge
2 Park Square, Milton Park, Abingdon, Oxon OX14 4RN

and by Routledge
711 Third Avenue, New York, NY 10017

Routledge is an imprint of the Taylor & Francis Group, an informa business

© 2019 selection and editorial matter, Björn Heile and Charles Wilson;
individual chapters, the contributors

The right of Björn Heile and Charles Wilson to be identified as the authors
of the editorial material, and of the authors for their individual chapters,
has been asserted in accordance with sections 77 and 78 of the Copyright,
Designs and Patents Act 1988.

All rights reserved. No part of this book may be reprinted or reproduced or
utilised in any form or by any electronic, mechanical, or other means, now
known or hereafter invented, including photocopying and recording, or in
any information storage or retrieval system, without permission in writing
from the publishers.

Trademark notice: Product or corporate names may be trademarks or
registered trademarks, and are used only for identification and explanation
without intent to infringe.

British Library Cataloguing in Publication Data
A catalogue record for this book is available from the British Library

Library of Congress Cataloging in Publication Data
Names: Heile, Björn. | Wilson, Charles, 1968–
Title: The Routledge research companion to modernism in music/edited
by Björn Heile and Charles Wilson.
Description: Abingdon, Oxon ; New York, NY : Routledge, 2019. |
Includes bibliographical references and index.
Identifiers: LCCN 2018005543 | ISBN 9781472470409 (hardback) |
ISBN 9781315613291 (ebook)
Subjects: LCSH: Modernism (Music) | Music – History and criticism.
Classification: LCC ML193. R66 2018 | DDC 780.9/04 – dc23
LC record available at https://lccn.loc.gov/2018005543

ISBN: 978-1-4724-7040-9 (hbk)
ISBN: 978-1-315-61329-1 (ebk)

Typeset in Bembo
by Apex CoVantage, LLC

Bach musicological font developed by © Yo Tomita

Printed in the United Kingdom
by Henry Ling Limited

CONTENTS

List of figures		*viii*
Music examples		*ix*
List of contributors		*xi*
Acknowledgements		*xv*

Introduction   1
Björn Heile and Charles Wilson

PART 1
Foundations   **31**

1   The birth of modernism – out of the spirit of comedy   33
James R. Currie

2   What was contemporary music? The new, the modern and the
contemporary in the International Society for Contemporary
Music (ISCM)   56
Sarah Collins

3   Institutions, artworlds, new music   86
Martin Iddon

4   Modernism and history   108
David J. Code

5   Musical modernity, the beautiful and the sublime   133
Edward Campbell

Contents

PART 2
Positions 153

6 Reactive modernism 155
J. P. E. Harper-Scott

7 Musical modernism, global: comparative observations 175
Björn Heile

8 Musical modernism and exile: cliché as hermeneutic tool 199
Eva Moreda Rodríguez

9 Modernism: the people's music? 216
Robert Adlington

10 Modernism for and of the masses? On popular modernisms 239
Stephen Graham

11 Times like the present: de-limiting music in the twenty-first century 258
Charles Wilson

12 The composer as communication theorist 287
M. J. Grant

13 How does modernist music make you feel? Between subjectivity and affect 307
Trent Leipert

PART 3
Practices 325

14 Between modernism and postmodernism: structure and expression in
John Adams, Kaija Saariaho and Thomas Adès 327
Alastair Williams

15 Foundations and fixations: continuities in British musical modernism 353
Arnold Whittall

16 The Balinese moment in the Montreal new music scene as a regional
modernism 379
Jonathan Goldman

17 *Vers une écriture liminale*: serialism, spectralism and *écriture* in the
transitional music of Gérard Grisey 400
Liam Cagney

Contents

18 Contemporary opera and the failure of language   427
    Amy Bauer

19 'Es klang so alt und war doch so neu!': modernist operatic culture
    through the prism of staging *Die Meistersinger von Nürnberg*   454
    Mark Berry

20 The modernism of the mainstream: an early twentieth-century
    ideology of violin playing   475
    Stefan Knapik

Index   497

FIGURES

6.1   Francis Poulenc, *Trois mouvements perpétuels*, no. 1, diatonic pitch-space
networks for (a) bars 1–2, (b) bars 5–7, (c) bars 12–13 and (d) bars 14–15   166

6.2   Poulenc, *Trois mouvements perpétuels*, no. 1, voice-leading graph   168

6.3   Two hearings of bars 10–11: (a) as a minor-mode variant of the basic idea,
(b) as a flickering between B♭ major and G♭ major   169

16.1   Excerpt from Claude Vivier's notebooks written during his stay in Bali
(December 1976–March 1977)   387

17.1   Reproduction of a section of Gérard Grisey's notes on Karlheinz
Stockhausen's *Stimmung*   416

18.1   'Solo de solitude', from Claude Vivier, *Prologue pour un Marco Polo*   436

18.2   Text of the duet between the Duchess and her lover in Salvatore Sciarrino,
Luci mie traditrici, Scene 3   442

19.1   Richard Wagner, *Die Meistersinger von Nürnberg* (dir. Harry Kupfer, Staatsoper
Unter den Linden, Berlin). *Festwiese* scene (Act 3, scene 5), with staired
centrepiece visible.   460

19.2   *Die Meistersinger* (dir. Kupfer, Staatsoper Unter den Linden, Berlin). Eva offers
the *Festwiese* garland to Walther (Act 3, scene 5)   461

19.3   *Die Meistersinger* (dir. Stefan Herheim, Salzburger Festspiele, 2013). Act 1,
scene 1, with Hans Sachs's writing desk having expanded to become the
interior of Nuremberg's Katharinenkirche   463

19.4   *Die Meistersinger* (dir. Herheim, Salzburger Festspiele, 2013). Act 2, scene 7:
the *Prügelfuge*, with busts (left to right) of Goethe, Wagner and Beethoven at
the front of the stage   465

MUSIC EXAMPLES

6.1	Arnold Schoenberg, String Quartet no. 2, second movement, bars 165–76	156
6.2	Alfred Schnittke, *Stille Nacht*, bars 21–30	164
6.3	Francis Poulenc, *Trois mouvements perpétuels*, no. 1, basic idea, bars 1–2	166
6.4	Poulenc, *Trois mouvements perpétuels*, no. 1, bar 24	167
6.5	Poulenc, *Trois mouvements perpétuels*, no. 1, comparison of bars 1–2 and 10–11	167
14.1	John Adams, *Harmonielehre* (1985), Part I: piano part, bars 578–92	331
14.2	Kaija Saariaho, *Lichtbogen* (1986), bars 160–63	338
14.3	Thomas Adès, *Asyla*: first movement, bars 1–4	342
15.1(a)	James Clarke, *Untitled no. 2*, bars 1–2 (solo piano and strings only)	360
15.1(b)	Clarke, *Untitled no. 2*, ending	361
15.2(a)	Clarke, String Quartet no. 3, bars 1–2, 5–7	363
15.2(b)	Clarke, String Quartet no. 3, bars 74–78	365
15.3(a)	Clarke, *Untitled no. 7*, bars 45–51	366
15.3(b)	Clarke, *Untitled no. 7*, bars 154–56	367
15.4(a)	Morgan Hayes, *Shirley and Jane*, bars 1–9	370
15.4(b)	Hayes, *Shirley and Jane*, bars 158–65	371
15.5	Hayes, *Elemental 1*	374
16.1	Gilles Tremblay, *Oralléluiants* (1974–75), rehearsal figure 60	385
16.2	Claude Vivier, *Pulau dewata* (1977), end	387
16.3	Cantus firmus melody from José Evangelista, *Ô Bali* (1989), measured version	389
16.4	Evangelista, *Ô Bali*, bar 160: harmony derived from adjacent notes of cantus firmus	389
16.5	John Rea, *Médiator*, 2'42"–3'24"	392
17.1	Opening of 'Le Souffle' from Gérard Grisey, *Vagues, Chemins, le Souffle*, featuring a resonance chord	410
17.2	First page of the score of Gérard Grisey, *D'eau et de pierre*	412
18.1	Piet's drunken aria. György Ligeti, *Le Grand Macabre*, revised version, Scene 1	431

ix

Music examples

18.2	*Zwiefacher* of the black and white minister. Ligeti, *Le Grand Macabre*, Scene 3	433
18.3	Gepopo's second aria. Ligeti, *Le Grand Macabre*, Scene 3	434
18.4	Salvatore Sciarrino, *Luci mie traditrici*: comparison of the prologue and three intermezzos	440
18.5	Descending tetrachord that pervades David Lang, *The Difficulty of Crossing a Field*	444

CONTRIBUTORS

Robert Adlington holds the Queen's Anniversary Prize Chair of Contemporary Music at the University of Huddersfield. He is author of books on Harrison Birtwistle, Louis Andriessen and avant-garde music in 1960s Amsterdam, and editor of volumes on 1960s avant-garde music and music and communism. He has published articles on Luigi Nono, Luciano Berio, new music theatre and musical temporality. He is writing a new book provisionally entitled *Musical Models of Democracy*.

Amy Bauer is Associate Professor of Music at the University of California, Irvine. She received her PhD in music theory from Yale University, and has published articles in *Music Analysis, Journal of Music Theory, Contemporary Music Review, Indiana Theory Review* and *Ars Lyrica*, and book chapters on the music of Ligeti, Messiaen, Chávez, Lang, the television musical, and the philosophy and reception of modernist music and music theory. Her books include *Ligeti's Laments: Nostalgia, Exoticism and the Absolute* (Ashgate, 2011), and the collections *György Ligeti's Cultural Identities* (co-edited with Márton Kerékfy, Routledge, 2017) and *The Oxford Handbook of Spectral and Post-Spectral Music* (co-edited with Bryan Christian, forthcoming).

Mark Berry is Reader in Music History at Royal Holloway, University of London. He has written widely on musical and intellectual history from the late seventeenth century to the present day. The author of *Treacherous Bonds and Laughing Fire: Politics and Religion in Wagner's 'Ring'* (Ashgate, 2006), *After Wagner: Histories of Modernist Music Drama from 'Parsifal' to Nono* (Boydell & Brewer, 2014) and *Arnold Schoenberg: A Critical Life* (to be published by Reaktion in 2018), he is presently writing a study on Schoenberg and intellectual biography and co-editing the *Cambridge Companion to Wagner's 'Der Ring des Nibelungen'*. He regularly reviews concert and opera performances for his blog, Boulezian, which experience has led to a more focused academic interest in the staging of operas and its relationship to historical musicology. His work on Wagner has won the Prince Consort Prize and Seeley Medal.

Liam Cagney received a PhD from City University of London in 2016 for a historiographical study of the early emergence of French spectral music, a study he is currently developing into a monograph. Recent publications include a chapter on Irish art music since 2000 for *The Invisible Art: A Century of Music in Ireland 1916–2016* and a chapter on Tristan Murail for *The Oxford*

Handbook of Spectral and Post-Spectral Music. He is a regular contributor to *Gramophone* and the *Irish Times,* and is co-founder of the podcast *Talking Musicology,* which was nominated in 2017 for a *Classical:NEXT* Innovation award. He was shortlisted for the 2017 White Review Short Story prize for a piece of prose about Kanye West.

Edward Campbell is Senior Lecturer in Music at the University of Aberdeen and co-director of the university's Centre for Modern Thought. He specializes in contemporary European art music and aesthetics, including historical, analytical and aesthetic approaches to European modernism, the music and writings of Pierre Boulez, contemporary European opera, and the interrelation of musical thought and critical theory. He is the author of the books *Boulez, Music and Philosophy* (Cambridge University Press, 2010) and *Music after Deleuze* (Bloomsbury, 2013), and the co-editor of *Pierre Boulez Studies* (Cambridge, 2016). He is currently editing *The Cambridge Stravinsky Encyclopedia* for publication in 2019 and working on a monograph provisionally titled *East-West Encounters in Music in France since Debussy.*

David J. Code is Reader in Music at the University of Glasgow, School of Culture and Creative Arts. He previously taught at Stanford University, on a Mellon Postdoctoral Fellowship, and at Bishop's University in Québec. His research into the work of Claude Debussy, Stéphane Mallarmé and Igor Stravinsky has appeared in such periodicals as the *Journal of the American Musicological Society, Journal of the Royal Musical Association, 19th-Century Music, Journal of Musicology* and *Representations.* In 2010 he contributed a biography of Claude Debussy to the Reaktion Press 'Critical Lives' of major modernist figures. Recently, he has also published articles on the music in the films of Stanley Kubrick, and is currently planning a series of monographs under the working title 'An Ear for the Movies: Musicality in the Work of Major Directors'. He has received substantial funding for his work from the Arts and Humanities Research Council as well as the British Academy and Royal Society of Edinburgh.

Sarah Collins is a Lecturer in Musicology at the University of Western Australia. She has been a Visiting Fellow at Harvard University, a Marie Skłodowska-Curie Research Fellow at Durham University, and a postdoctoral fellow at the University of New South Wales. She has had articles published in the *Journal of the Royal Musical Association, Twentieth-Century Music, Music & Letters, Musical Quarterly* and elsewhere, and she is the author of *The Aesthetic Life of Cyril Scott* (Boydell Press, 2013). She is a co-editor, with Paul Watt and Michael Allis, of the *Oxford Handbook of Music and Intellectual Culture in the Nineteenth Century* (Oxford University Press, forthcoming) and the reviews editor of the *Journal of the Royal Musical Association* and the *RMA Research Chronicle.*

James R. Currie, Associate Professor at the University at Buffalo (State University of New York), is a writer and performance artist who teaches classes on music history and music and philosophy in the Department of Music. Most notably, he is the author of the widely read article 'Music After All' (*Journal of the American Musicological Society,* 2009) and the monograph *Music and the Politics of Negation* (Indiana University Press, 2012), and his work has focused around critical questions concerning the political imbrications of academic practice in the era of late postmodern capitalism.

Jonathan Goldman is Associate Professor of Musicology in the Faculty of Music of the Université de Montréal. His research focuses on modernist and avant-garde music in a regional perspective. His book *The Musical Language of Pierre Boulez* (Cambridge University Press, 2011) won an Opus Prize for book of the year. He edited a multi-authored volume on Quebec composers (*La création musicale au Québec*, PUM) in 2014 and another on creative process (*Texts and Beyond*, UT Orpheus) in 2016. Yet another multi-authored volume, *The Dawn of Musical Semiology* (University of Rochester Press, 2017), co-edited with Jonathan Dunsby, was published in honour of Jean-Jacques Nattiez. Jonathan Goldman was Editor of the contemporary music journal *Circuit: musiques contemporaines* from 2006 to 2016 and Music Editor of the *Routledge Encyclopedia of Modernism* (2016). His articles have appeared in journals such as *Perspectives of New Music*, *American Music*, *Music Analysis*, *Tempo* and *Filigrane*.

Stephen Graham is a Lecturer in Music at Goldsmiths, University of London, where he specializes in twentieth and twenty-first century music and culture, looked at through theoretical lenses. His book on underground and fringe experimental musics, *Sounds of the Underground*, was published by University of Michigan Press in May 2016. He has had articles or chapters published on fringe avant-gardes (*Perspectives of New Music*, 2010), Justin Timberlake (*American Music*, 2014), and *The X Factor* and reality television (*Popular Music*, 2017). He is currently working on pieces on independent music publishing and the 'unpop' avant-garde of the 1970s and 1980s, late style in popular music and a larger project on the evolving nature of the music degree in the United Kingdom.

M. J. Grant is a musicologist whose work focuses on the sociology and anthropology of music. Her many writings on modernist music include the monograph *Serial Music, Serial Aesthetics: Compositional Theory in Post-War Europe* (Cambridge University Press, 2001). At present, her research focuses on music and collective violence, especially in the case of war and torture. She has held a number of research and teaching posts in Germany, including a junior professorship at the University of Göttingen and a fellowship at the Käte Hamburger Center for Advanced Study in the Humanities 'Law as Culture' in Bonn. She is currently Teaching Fellow in Music at the University of Edinburgh.

J. P. E. Harper-Scott is Professor of Music History and Theory at Royal Holloway, University of London. He has published extensively on music of the nineteenth and twentieth centuries, with a particular focus on twentieth-century British music and theories of musical modernism. He has produced five books, including three on Elgar and one on Walton, and his sixth, *Ideology in Britten's Operas*, will be published by Cambridge University Press in 2018.

Björn Heile is Professor of Music (post-1900) at the University of Glasgow. He is the author of *The Music of Mauricio Kagel* (Ashgate, 2006), the editor of *The Modernist Legacy: Essays on New Music* (Ashgate, 2009), co-editor (with Martin Iddon) of *Mauricio Kagel bei den Darmstädter Ferienkursen für Neue Musik: Eine Dokumentation* (2009) and co-editor (with Peter Elsdon and Jenny Doctor) of *Watching Jazz: Encountering Jazz Performance on Screen* (2016) and many other publications on new music, experimental music theatre and jazz. Among other projects, he is trying to write a book on the global history of musical modernism.

Martin Iddon is a composer and musicologist. His musicological research has largely focused on new music in post-war North America and West Germany. His books *New Music at Darmstadt* and *John Cage and David Tudor* are published by Cambridge University Press. His music is published by Composers Edition and a portrait CD, *pneuma*, was released on Another Timbre in 2014. He is Professor of Music and Aesthetics at the University of Leeds.

Contributors

Stefan Knapik is a London-based writer and cellist. He completed his doctorate at Magdalen College, Oxford, on early twentieth-century ideologies of violin playing (2012) and has published his research in *19th-Century Music* and *Music & Letters*. He has previously taught at Oxford University and at Cardiff University. He currently performs on the London scene in a wide variety of contexts, and in 2016 formed the London Cello Quartet.

Trent Leipert completed a PhD in Music History and Theory at the University of Chicago with a dissertation on the composition of the subject as subject of composition in contemporary music and multimedia. His research examines the relationship between subjectivity and affect in contemporary composition, intermedia and post-punk. He teaches in the Department of Media, Art, and Performance at the University of Regina.

Eva Moreda Rodríguez is Lecturer in Music at the University of Glasgow and the author of the monographs *Music and Exile in Francoist Spain* (Ashgate, 2015) and *Music Criticism and Music Critics in Early Francoist Spain* (Oxford University Press, 2016), as well as a number of chapters and journal articles focusing on the political and cultural history of Spanish music throughout the twentieth century. Her work has received funding from the Music & Letters Trust, the Carnegie Trust for the Universities of Scotland and the Lilly Library, University of Indiana, among others. She is keen to disseminate the music of Spanish exiled composers in Spain and beyond, and has written CD liners and programme notes, as well as maintaining the site Spanish Music in Exile (http://musicinexile.wordpress.com) and giving the occasional performance of Spanish art song.

Arnold Whittall is Professor Emeritus of Music Theory and Analysis at King's College London and General Editor of the Cambridge University Press *Music since 1900* series. His latest book is *The Wagner Style* (Plumbago Press, 2015). He is continuing his extended series of essays on 'British Music after Britten' in the *Musical Times*, and has contributed to many recent symposia, including *Transformations of Musical Modernism* (Cambridge University Press, 2015), *Pierre Boulez Studies* (Cambridge, 2016) and *The Dawn of Music Semiology: Essays in Honor of Jean-Jacques Nattiez* (University of Rochester Press, 2017).

Alastair Williams is Professor of Music at Keele University. His research interests are in modernism and modernity, Austro-German traditions and subjectivity in music. He is the author of *New Music and the Claims of Modernity* (Ashgate, 1997), *Constructing Musicology* (Ashgate, 2001) and *Music in Germany since 1968* (Cambridge University Press, 2013), and a contributor to the *Cambridge History of Twentieth-Century Music* (Cambridge, 2004). He has also published in a wide range of journals. He has received funding from the Arts and Humanities Research Council and the British Academy. Furthermore, he has served on the Arts and Humanities Research Council Peer Review College and is a member of the advisory panel of the journal *Music Analysis*.

Charles Wilson was Senior Editor for twentieth-century composers on the second edition of the *New Grove Dictionary of Music and Musicians*, and currently lectures at the School of Music, Cardiff University. He served as Editor-in-Chief (2009–12) of the journal *Twentieth-Century Music*. His research focuses on the relationship between historiography and practice (both personal and institutional) in the art music of the twentieth and twenty-first centuries.

ACKNOWLEDGEMENTS

We would like to thank first and foremost all our authors for their imaginative and erudite contributions. Volumes of this type never proceed entirely according to plan, and we gratefully acknowledge their patience over a longer time frame than was initially envisaged. But the unanticipated has its boons as well. Much of the pleasure of this project has been in the surprising and exhilarating intellectual turns it has taken: texts that transcended expectations in their range and coverage, proposals bounced back to us in a scarcely recognizable but infinitely more interesting form, and simply bold ideas and striking formulations that have forced us to think again. We shall be glad if the process has been even a fraction as rewarding for others as it has been for us.

We owe a particular debt to Heidi Bishop for the initial suggestion of a *Research Companion to Modernism in Music* and for leading it smoothly from the Ashgate to the Routledge stable. Annie Vaughan has patiently overseen the production process, for which she deserves enormous thanks, as does Paula Clarke Bain, who provided an exceptionally thorough index for the volume. We are grateful to Matthew Lush and Igor Leão Maia for their expert help with music examples. Our academic colleagues at Glasgow and Cardiff have been generous in their encouragement and support: we would like to single out, at the former, John Butt and, at the latter, David Beard, Robert Fokkens, Danijela Špirić-Beard and, especially, Kenneth Gloag, whose postmodernism preceded our modernism in true Lyotardian fashion, but who sadly did not live to see this volume reach completion.

INTRODUCTION

Björn Heile and Charles Wilson

To an observer in the last decade of the twentieth century it might have seemed implausible that a newly minted *Research Companion to Modernism in Music* would be needed in the second decade of the twenty-first. Back then, critical debates on modernism, not to mention modernist practices in music and elsewhere, were finding themselves increasingly subject to challenge. It was almost as if modernism, styled first as a breaker then as a maker of taboos, had itself become taboo. In music composition the late work of established (and invariably white male) modernist figures – among them Harrison Birtwistle, Pierre Boulez, Elliott Carter, György Ligeti and Iannis Xenakis – continued to garner attention. Modernism retained much of its authority too in music theory and analysis and in the rapidly burgeoning field of source studies on twentieth-century music. But in both the 'new' musicology and critical theory more generally, the fall from grace seemed unmistakable. In his book *A Singular Modernity* of 2002, Fredric Jameson reeled off the putative charge sheet: phallocentrism (and, with it, logocentrism); authoritarianism; repressiveness; 'the teleology of the modernist aesthetic as it proceeded on triumphalistically from the newer to the newest'; the 'cult of the genius or seer'; and, last but by no means least, the 'non-pleasurable demands made on the audience or public'.[1] More recently, however, the pendulum has swung in the other direction.

Within music studies, the critique voiced (or ventriloquized) by Jameson has mostly come from the 'new musicology' of the 1990s, which tended to focus on three of modernism's implicit claims: those of autonomy, authority and exclusivity. In each of these areas powerful challenges have been laid, but also compelling defences mounted. In terms of autonomy, it is now widely accepted that modernist music has rarely been either politically neutral or immune from the influence of the commercial market, let alone Pierre Bourdieu's 'market of symbolic goods'.[2] Yet that same ideal of autonomy, however tarnished and compromised, has also often prevented music from merely affirming the political or socioeconomic status quo, producing some powerful instances of resistance – in popular music too, where the dominance of the commercial monopoly of the entertainment industry constantly threatens to become hegemonic.[3] In terms of authority (or authoritarian tendencies), the idea of modernism as an 'imperative', a direction that composers felt inwardly or outwardly compelled to follow, has generated widespread controversy and debate, whether in discussions of specific institutions such as the BBC or Darmstadt,[4] or wider contexts, such as that of serialism in America.[5] It might be pointed out too that a number of composers who in the 1970s proclaimed their freedom from the shackles of musical modernism have since either absorbed aspects of modernist construction into their music (John Adams, for example) or continued to rely (albeit covertly) on them (Arvo Pärt).[6] And, setting aside supposedly reluctant or intimidated composers, the idea that modernist music necessarily imposes itself on reluctant or intimidated listeners has itself been challenged recently by literature that extols the (at times overtly sensual) 'pleasure of modernist music'.[7]

In terms of modernism's claims to exclusivity, critics have pointed to its discriminatory tendencies, whether patriarchal, ethnocentric or elitist.[8] Indeed, as a child of the 'age of extremes',[9] modernism's representations of gender and sexuality, race and ethnicity, and class and popular culture are, although rarely as universally and straightforwardly negative as asserted by its detractors, at times troubling even for its advocates. Ben Earle has recently launched a challenge against 'commentators who find [in modernism] consoling signs of such liberal values as pluralism, compromise, cooperation and cultural exchange', arguing that it is instead 'inextricably bound up with desires for historical priority, for the domination of perceived inferiors, for exclusion and/or estrangement of the work of others', before concluding that 'modernism is essentially anti-liberal.'[10] Earle's account cannot be easily dismissed, but it arguably describes the particular strand of modernism that he is engaged with – one that is, in one way or another, bound up with fascism – more accurately than others (even if Earle scrupulously avoids equating modernism and fascism or dissolving one into the other). Although it would be wrong to deny or belittle the existence of such tendencies, it is equally problematic to suggest that they are representative of the diversity of positions and currents that can legitimately be considered modernist. For instance, recent critics have noted both the particularity of gendered responses to modernism, and its appropriation in popular cultures of the world.[11] Finally, to demonize discrimination and exclusivity per se would be a mistake. Producing any kind of artwork requires exclusions and discriminations, and there may be a strong case at times for what Gayatri Chakravorty Spivak has called a 'strategic essentialism', whereby a certain type of cultural (musical, stylistic) identity is strongly or even aggressively asserted in order to preserve rare and distinctive forms of (musical) expression or avoid the levelling consequences of stylistic homogeneity.[12] However much modernism in general may be adaptable to different territories and cultural milieus, it seems unreasonable to require any modernist work in particular to be all things to all people.

This notion of modernism's singularity and monolithic nature has been challenged by such notions as hybrid modernisms, peripheral modernisms, moderate modernisms and occult modernisms, making it questionable whether one should continue to speak of modernism in the singular at all.[13] But to go much further down this road of fragmentation and pluralization would seem nominalistic and ultimately unproductive. The very fact that modernism can be recognized across such diverse terrains suggests that the concept retains sufficient coherence to be graspable in its essential impulses, even when its cultural manifestations differ.

The picture of modernism has therefore broadened and diversified considerably in the decade and a half since Jameson reported the 'unspoken consensus' on modernism's 'no longer desirable' features. It now extends not only beyond the traditional cultural centres of Western Europe and North America but also beyond modernism's well-established home ground in high-art culture – towards popular culture, commercial culture and advertising.[14] Not long after Jameson's critique, one of us (Björn Heile) was able to observe in the introduction to another collection of essays the striking re-emergence of modernism as a topic of research and discourse in musicology, accompanied by the equally striking eclipse of its erstwhile adversary, postmodernism, as a critical concept.[15] Both these developments have continued apace in the intervening years and even some former critics of modernism have subtly changed their perspective.[16] There has been further significant recent research on musical modernism, while, despite some notable contributions,[17] postmodernism still awaits its reawakening as a topic of academic discussion.

Introduction

The attempt to situate the modernist project within wider social and historical contexts has had, above all, the effect of drawing attention to what Christopher Chowrimootoo has called the tension between modernism's 'unequivocal ideals' and its often 'ambivalent practice'.[18] Additionally, responses to modernism that were previously considered ambiguous, reluctant or equivocal have been subject to re-evaluation. Just as in literature the 'new modernist studies has extended the designation "modernist" [...] to [...] cultural producers hitherto seen as neglecting or resisting modernist innovation',[19] so definitions of musical modernism have broadened to include repertoire that was previously typically regarded to lie outside its purview. In the space of just over twenty years, Sibelius, Elgar, Nielsen, Britten, Walton, Bridge and others have been claimed for modernism,[20] in the process endowing the term with an increased currency, even a prestige, that would have seemed out of place – or rather out of time – just a couple of years earlier, when any association with modernism was likely to damage the prospects of any composer, living or dead, awaiting (re)discovery and canonization.

In actual fact, the work that is frequently cited as the instigator of this extended definition of modernism, James Hepokoski's monograph on Sibelius's Fifth Symphony, appeared back in 1993, but it is fair to say that it acquired a different status with the publication of Arnold Whittall's *Musical Composition in the Twentieth Century*,[21] with its proclamation of 'moderate modernism' and the subsequent books by J. P. E. Harper-Scott, Daniel Grimley and others.[22] Furthermore, Hepokoski followed Carl Dahlhaus in distinguishing between '"musical modernism", which flourished between 1889 and 1914 as a self-contained period in music history' and the 'new music' (*Neue Musik*) of the succeeding generation.[23] In that sense, Hepokoski's association of Sibelius with modernism (in Dahlhaus's more narrow sense) was uncontroversial, even if his advocacy of what he calls 'the seemingly more accessible, comfortable Fifth' Symphony (compared to the 'dissonant, austere' Fourth) was perhaps more surprising.[24] Moreover, Dahlhaus's original term *musikalische Moderne* does not neatly translate into 'musical modernism', as Hepokoski implies (*Moderne* is closer to 'modernity' than 'modernism', and what was traditionally understood as 'musical modernism' in English is more akin to Dahlhaus's *Neue Musik*). Nevertheless, once the association between Sibelius and 'modernism' had been established, it seems to have stuck, enabling, for instance, the blunt title of Harper-Scott's book *Edward Elgar, Modernist* (the kind of formulation that both Dahlhaus and Hepokoski would presumably have shied away from). In his essay in the present volume, Harper-Scott's distinction between 'faithful' modernism and 'reactive' and 'obscure' responses to it enables the debate to progress. At the same time, Mark Berry's caution about declaring Rachmaninoff non-modernist illustrates the extent to which the attribution has become loaded. Is there anything or anyone that is decidedly non-modernist, and would such an attribution automatically diminish the composer in question and their work?

Theories of modernism in music, modernist music and musical modernism

Musical modernism seems forever in need of a theory to account for its existence. The fact that modernist music often faced hostility from audiences and critics, and remains contentious to this day, is perhaps a reason for this, but by no means the only one. On the one hand modernism, more even than related concepts such as the Baroque, Classicism and Romanticism, has the problem that it is used both as a periodizing term and to describe a movement or tendency whose manifestations can be grounded chronologically but not limited to a defined period. (One might cite as an analogy the persistence in certain quarters of the *stile antico* church styles characteristic of the late Renaissance into the late eighteenth century.) Ultimately, therefore, modernism is perhaps better defined in the Foucauldian or post-Foucauldian terms of an 'episteme', defined by Stephen Paul Miller as 'an era's prevailing mind-set, its epistemological horizons',[25] even though, as Jameson stresses, abandoning periodization altogether is far easier said than done.[26]

But while modernism resembles earlier epistemes in this key respect, there remains an inescapable sense that it is, in another sense, unprecedented. Modernism describes a movement or tendency during a period of unparalleled diversity, in which it competed with different directions and an ever-increasing share of older music within the sphere of classical or art music, while the latter in turn increasingly lost ground to jazz and popular music. Certainly earlier ages saw competing musical directions and trends, and classical composition was never the only show in town, but the rapidly diversifying cultural marketplace brought about by modernity, notably through new production and distribution technologies, such as amplification, recording and broadcasting, changed the nature of the game.[27]

It is customary at a point such as this for us to lay our cards on the table and to come up with a definition of musical modernism and a corresponding theory to account for it. This is a daunting task, not only due to the inherent complexities of the issue but also the myriad of competing theories that have been formulated in the past. Furthermore, the contributors to this volume give voice to a considerable range of views. We believe that this diversity of views is a strength not a weakness, and we have not aimed for ideological or theoretical cohesion. We don't view it as our task to sum up (yet again) and synthesize the existing theories of musical modernism, nor to come up with a completely new idea that would supersede them (if only!). We can, however, give some indication of the contribution to the wider debate surrounding musical modernism we aim to make with this volume.

One immediate clarification would seem to be in order. The title of this book refers to 'modernism in music'; in this introduction we have, seemingly interchangeably, written about 'musical modernism' and 'modernist music'. The terms are indeed nearly but not completely synonymous. The expression 'modernism in music' places the emphasis on a general cultural and artistic phenomenon (modernism) that finds its specific expression in music, and it thereby invites comparison between modernist expressions in the different art forms and draws attention to their presumed kinship. It is therefore a more capacious category than 'modernist music', for there may be modernist attributes or modernist aspects in music that we may nonetheless balk from classifying as modernist. A number of contributions in this book come to mind for which this distinction seems pertinent, whether they concern popular music (in Stephen Graham's contribution) or Offenbach's operettas (in James Currie's). Furthermore, 'modernism in music' covers not only composition, but also performance, which is discussed here by Stefan Knapik and, with respect to operatic productions, Mark Berry. 'Musical modernism', finally, falls somewhere between the two terms. It emphasizes specifically musical manifestations of modernism, thereby relating it to modernisms in the other arts, while at the same time homing in on the specifically musical.

To elucidate how we understand modernism in music, we turn to a text that has been seminal in discussions of literary modernism but is rarely mentioned in musical contexts, Virginia Woolf's 1924 essay 'Character in Fiction' (also widely known under the title 'Mr Bennett and Mrs Brown').[28] In it, Woolf makes what she calls the 'disputable assertion' that 'on or about December 1910 human character changed'.[29] On this basis, she distinguishes between 'the Edwardians' – she mentions H. G. Wells, Arnold Bennett and John Galsworthy – and 'the Georgians', represented by E. M. Forster, D. H. Lawrence, Lytton Strachey, James Joyce and T. S. Eliot. The charge she levels at the Edwardians is not only that their literary conventions and styles are staid and outdated, but that they are no longer true to the new realities. As she puts it: 'All human relations have shifted – those between masters and servants, husbands and wives,

Introduction

parents and children. And when human relations change there is at the same time a change in religion, conduct, politics and literature.'[30] And, one would like to add, music.

In other words, Woolf here rehearses the argument that, in various permutations, has dominated theories of modernism ever since: modernism as an artistic response to the social changes wrought by modernity. In many respects, her account is admittedly sketchy, presumably due to the limitations presented by the form of the public lecture in which it was originally aired, although the emphasis she places on the revolution in gender relations goes well beyond most classic accounts of social modernity and artistic modernism. In any case, the origin of this linkage between social change and artistic response is hard to find, presumably since in its most basic form it is arguably a commonplace. Nevertheless, it resonates with Max Weber's ideas on the social conditions for artistic expression in, for instance, *The Rational and Social Foundations of Music* (although Woolf is unlikely to have encountered this work, published posthumously just a few years earlier).[31] Weber did not live long enough (and maybe lacked sufficient specialist interest) to comment in detail on musical modernism, although Eduardo de la Fuente cites an evocative letter to his wife, in which Weber records his impressions of seeing Richard Strauss's *Salome*.[32] In his published work he similarly sketched the intimate although often ambiguous connection between the excitement of city life and incipient modernist art and music in terms that have lost little of their immediacy (and have reminded many of his friend Georg Simmel):

> [I]f we ask whether what is called modern *technology* in the ordinary meaning of the word does not stand in some relationship with formal-aesthetic values after all, then in my opinion we must undoubtedly answer *yes* to this question, in so far as very definite formal values in our modern artistic culture could only be born through the existence of the *modern metropolis*: the modern metropolis, with its railways, subways, electric and other lights, shop windows, concert and catering halls, cafes, smokestacks, and piles of stone, the whole wild dance of sound and colour impressions that affect sexual fantasy, and the experiences of variations in the soul's constitution that lead to a hungry brooding over all kinds of seemingly inexhaustible possibilities for the conduct of life and happiness. Partly as a protest, a specific means of fleeing from this reality: the highest aesthetic abstractions, the deepest forms of dream, or the most intense forms of frenzy; and partly as an adaptation to this reality: apologies for its own fantastic and intoxicating rhythms.[33]

What proved most influential for future generations was Weber's idea of the 'disenchantment' (*Entzauberung*) of modernity, the devaluation of religious belief and mysticism through the process of rationalization in Western (and not only Western) society that, more than any social and historical condition, required a specific artistic response. This proved critical for the Frankfurt School: 'disenchantment' is a key term in Theodor W. Adorno and Max Horkheimer's *Dialectic of Enlightenment*.[34] It would be fanciful to suggest that Woolf's impressionistic account of the relation between social modernity and artistic modernism provided the blueprint for the aesthetics of the Frankfurt School. One key difference is that for someone like Adorno the aesthetics of shock, rupture and fragmentation, which he regarded as essential for modernism, were not just *expressions* of the experience of the alienation of modernity, but functioned as a form of *criticism* that was ultimately intended to lead to its overcoming. Woolf's agenda differs, in that her depiction of the social changes she witnessed is, in common with Weber's, not as negative and pessimistic as Adorno's. As Peter Childs has put it, 'artistic reactions and responses [to the breakdown of socio-cultural relations and aesthetic representation] have bifurcated into the largely celebratory and [. . .] the primarily condemnatory, apocalyptic and despairing' (although he neglects to mention the many, including Woolf, who remained ambivalent or torn between these poles – arguably also a characteristic modernist position).[35] Indeed, Weber hinted at a similar point in his distinction between 'protest [and] fleeing from reality' and 'adaptation to this reality' in the quotation above. In any case, there are some significant shared themes in the perceptions of artistic modernism articulated here, outlining a critical tradition – not necessarily expressly Marxist but typically at least running in parallel with Marxist thought – that remains influential to the present day. Note, for instance, the homage paid to Weber and Weberian themes in T. J. Clark's magisterial *Farewell to an Idea*, which regards modernism as co-dependent with socialism,[36] or the importance placed on Weber, Adorno and the Frankfurt School in a popular (and particularly clear and astute) introduction such as that by the aforementioned Childs.[37] Finally, the tradition finds its apogee and possible transcendence in Seth Brodsky's recent *From 1989* (which, not surprisingly, draws on Clark).[38]

Within this tradition – as in most critical traditions that have seriously engaged with modernism – it is practically a given that responding adequately to the experience of modernity makes obligations. We have mentioned shock, rupture and fragmentation as characteristic expressions. Ezra Pound famously summarized the modernist artistic ethos in the pithy slogan: 'make it new!' Although there have been relatively quiet, harmonious and moderate forms of modernism, one tenet unites most if not all proponents of artistic modernism: the means of expression have to be adequate to the spirit of the age and to what is being expressed. For this reason, modernist artists and composers developed a highly self-reflective and critical approach towards style and technique and tended to view inherited traditions with suspicion. This is not to say that they necessarily discarded or negated all traditional elements, but that they typically subjected them to critical scrutiny. Adorno's insistence on the *historischer Materialstand* ('historical state of the material') may be dogmatic and petty minded, but it points to an issue that was and remains crucial for modernist theory and practice.[39] Few would regard Woolf as dogmatic, but it is there in her 'Character in Fiction' too:

> [The Edwardian writers] have developed a technique of novel-writing which suits their purpose; they have made tools and established conventions which do their business. But those tools are not our tools, and that business is not our business. For us those conventions are ruin, those tools are death.[40] [. . .] The Georgian writer had to begin by throwing away the method that was in use at the moment.[41]

In other words, according to Woolf, the new experience of living in modernity cannot be adequately expressed using the techniques and materials of the realist novel. She does in fact question the relation between representation and reality, when she asks: 'What is reality? And who are the judges of reality?' Similar arguments can be and have been made about figurative painting or diatonic tonality in music.

Rather than a detailed critique of Woolf's theory of modernity, our intention here is to focus on three hypotheses that her essay appears to raise: 1) the notion of a moment of fundamental break or rupture, whether that moment is a relatively localizable point in time (Woolf's December 1910), a moment whose character or quality of experience extends over a longer period, or an epistemic break that is enacted repeatedly in different contexts at different times;[42] 2) the nature of the historical divide, whether it constituted a true break with tradition or a more continuous development within it, and what it is about modernist art – and modernist music – that might justify reading it in such a way; 3) the shift in human character, human sensibility or even human nature that might have motivated such a break.

Introduction

1) Regarding the first of these points, that of the originary break, Woolf is both astonishingly precise and at the same time vague: 'on or about December 1910'. Curiously, she gives no reason for the date, but the catalyst appears to have been Roger Fry's seminal exhibition *Manet and the Post-Impressionists*.[43] Despite the apparent arbitrariness of the date, however, it is surely as good as any to posit an epistemic break – and that is what a number of commentators have interpreted Woolf as doing (including some who venture scarcely beyond the one quotation). In his ambitious cultural survey of the twentieth century, *Modern Times, Modern Places*, Peter Conrad quotes it in the context of a chapter symptomatically entitled 'Doomsday and After'. A few years either side of Woolf's decisive watershed, 1908 saw Schoenberg's String Quartet no. 2 Op. 10 with its 'air from other planet', namely atonality. Further important works, such as the Three Piano Pieces Op. 11 (1909), the Five Pieces for Orchestra Op. 16 and the monodrama *Erwartung* Op. 17 (1909), followed in quick succession. Around the same time, Stravinsky's Diaghilev ballets *Firebird* (1910), *Petrushka* (1911) and *The Rite of Spring* (1913) inaugurated Parisian modernism. Bartók's First String Quartet was composed in 1908–09 and his *Allegro barbaro* for piano in 1911. In Russia, Scriabin's *Prometheus* dates from 1908–10 and his Piano Sonatas nos. 6 and 7 from 1911–12. On the other side of the Atlantic, finally, Charles Ives's Third Symphony and *Central Park in the Dark* fall into the same period.[44] Of course these works had important predecessors, and the notion that they sprang forth fully formed from nowhere is nothing but an historian's convenient narrative fiction. Still, the temporal proximity of these manifestations is remarkable considering that they occurred in geographically and culturally distant places and arose from quite different traditions. A connection can be made here to Dahlhaus's distinction between the *musikalische Moderne* of 1889–1914 and the flowering of *Neue Musik* from 1914 onwards, although the key date 1914 seems to have been chosen for its political not its musical significance.[45]

Nonetheless, watersheds, when meaningful at all, are only part of the story. We are dealing still with an epistemic consciousness – the opening (to invoke Miller once more) of an 'epistemological horizon' which then becomes available over a longer period. Some, indeed, see that horizon opening up far earlier. As David Code reminds us in his contribution to this book, Pierre Boulez names Claude Debussy's *Prélude à l'après-midi d'un faune* (1894), thereby coinciding with Dahlhaus, but locating modernism firmly in Paris (whereas Dahlhaus associated it with Richard Strauss).[46] Arnold Whittall goes even further back to late Beethoven.[47] In literary studies, particularly outside the English-speaking world, it is common to associate modernism's first flowering (pun intended) with Baudelaire's *Les fleurs du mal* (Flowers of Evil, 1857); indeed, Baudelaire was also responsible for the coining of the term *modernité*. It is to Baudelaire that Walter Benjamin and, mostly in response to the former, Theodor W. Adorno turned in their influential conceptions of modernism (and, as David Code reminds us in his contribution to this volume, so did Pierre Boulez).[48] If there is a prize for the earliest date, it may have to go to the art historian T. J. Clark, who proposed – with a precision surpassing even Virginia Woolf – 25 Vendémiaire in Year 2 (16 October 1793, according to the French Republican Calendar), the day on which Jacques-Louis David's painting *The Death of Marat* was unveiled.[49] Clark's suggestion appears positively orthodox compared to James Currie's proposing of Jacques Offenbach's *Orphée aux enfers* (1858) as the inauguration of musical modernism in this book.

Just as some posit the break earlier, others situate it later. Taruskin subtly relocates it from around 1910 to the objectivity of the neo-classicism of the 1920s, declaring that '[t]he history of twentieth-century music as something esthetically distinct from that of the nineteenth century begins not at the fin de siècle, then, but here, in the 1920s', specifically with Stravinsky's Octet.[50] In his view, expressionism is essentially a continuation of the 'maximalism' of late romanticism.[51]

For our purposes, the stylistic changes around 1910 are significant and should not be dismissed, although that is not to deny that they may signal larger developments that are more gradual in nature and of earlier origin.

2) A similar, related debate concerns the issue of the nature of the historical divide: the question of when it happened is inevitably bound up with what it constituted. Here, Woolf's testimony is ambiguous. On one hand, the contrast she sets up between 'the Edwardians' and 'the Georgians' has all the hallmarks of a generational struggle such as they occur in practically every age. On the other, a change in human character or sensibility must surely herald an epochal break. Most of the authors cited in the previous section seem to support this latter view: it goes without saying that sudden revolutions can be more precisely dated than gradual evolutions. That said, Taruskin's point about the continuity of 'maximalism' is clearly designed to undermine traditional chronologies of musical modernism, even if he posits a later epochal break. In a related way, Ian Pace notes that the idea of a rupture in Western art music – whether in 1890 or around 1918 – 'makes sense in the context of a German-dominated view of nineteenth-century musical history driven by antagonism between Wagner and Brahms. But with a greater focus upon nineteenth-century French, Italian, and Russian musical traditions in particular [...] many of the most apparently radical early twentieth-century developments in music sit within longer traditions without too much difficulty.'[52] Once again, conceptions of modernism are inseparable from the chosen focus. As on most questions, the authors in this volume take subtly different positions on this matter; overall, however, they share the belief that if modernism did not constitute a historical rupture, it certainly marked an important turning point. Significantly, it is Harper-Scott, one of those responsible for the extension of the concept of modernism to composers and repertoires previously regarded as separate from it, who signals his commitment to 'the radical core of the modernist event', speaking further of the 'radical split between pre-modernist and modernist music'. Indeed, the challenge of his work rests on his claim that there is indeed a radical element inherent in the work of such figures as Elgar, William Walton and others.[53] To use his work as evidence of the continuity of musical modernity means therefore to miss the thrust of Harper-Scott's argument. In wider music historiography, the way modernism is being framed appears to have undergone a similar change. While most textbooks on twentieth-century and modern(ist) music (the terminology varies subtly) tend to stress modernism's innovative and revolutionary credentials, an apparently more recent trend seeks to integrate it more or less seamlessly in the longer history of musical modernity. This idea has been given impetus by Karol Berger and John Butt, although its application to the historiography of musical modernism has been mostly down to Julian Johnson.[54] According to Johnson:

> It is not only possible to see Modernism as part of a bigger picture but necessary, and the usual divisions are not only problematic but increasingly meaningless if we are to understand music more fully as part of modern thought, sensibility, and experience. [...]
>
> It is unsurprising that from this broader view of musical modernity, the category of Modernism has become excessively fraught. [...] Whereas the aesthetics of Modernism used to divide musical sheep and goats into conservative and progressive camps, recently we have found it more interesting to explore the co-existence and interaction of diverse stylistic practices, which, on closer inspection, begin to show some remarkable similarities. Elgar, Nielsen, Sibelius, Mahler, or Vaughan Williams can all be heard as Modernist composers once the category is understood in relation to the aesthetic mediation of social modernity, rather than exclusively through technical and stylistic terms to do with atonality or metrical asymmetry. This implicitly resists a dominant conception of music history in terms of a progressive turnover of styles and practices,

Introduction

packaging up the past in neat bundles as it cuts through the field of the future like some great Hegelian combine-harvester.

Indeed there is no one way in which to mediate social modernity: even the notorious polarization of Schoenberg and Stravinsky in Adorno's *Philosophie der Neuen Musik* is an acknowledgement of that. But to go from there in order to suggest that any conceivable mediation of modernity is therefore modernist might seem, to many, a step too far. It is nonetheless a step that Johnson proceeds to make:

> The closer one looks, the more the boundaries expand. If Modernism is not defined through specific technical attributes, then the term reaches back to include Wagner, Berlioz, Chopin, late Beethoven. If, instead, self-critical reflection upon musical language becomes the defining feature of a Modernist attitude, what of the ironic self-consciousness that defines so much of the later eighteenth century, from Haydn's quartets to Mozart's *Così fan tutte*? The category of Modernism thus begins to flow back across Romanticism into Classicism itself, and in doing so it dissolves its own boundaries as anything specific to the twentieth century. It begins to make far more sense (and appears far more interesting) to see the period from the mid-eighteenth to the late-twentieth century in a single span rather than repeating a linear history according to the usual subdivisions.[55]

It would appear as if his rhetoric gets somewhat ahead of itself here. Karol Berger and Anthony Newcomb, cited approvingly by Johnson, remark somewhat similarly that it is now 'possible to see the modernism of the twentieth century as a chapter in a much longer story, the story of musical modernity'.[56] But they do not then proceed, as Johnson does, to dissolve twentieth-century modernism completely into modernity. We may wish to expand or question boundaries, but it makes sense to retain not only distinctions between concurrent movements and tendencies but also some sense of their chronological emergence, whether that occurred in rapid succession or unevenly over a more protracted timespan. Likewise, although we do not wish to define modernism solely through 'specific technical attributes', these matter, as does what Johnson revealingly calls '*mere* style history' (our emphasis). It may be possible to argue that most or all music in the period discussed by Johnson is engaged in the 'aesthetic mediation of social modernity', but for that very reason this observation is of limited value. What matters is *how* it does so, and, as was discussed above, in modernism this crucially tends to involve an alignment of the means of expression ('mere style' included) with what is being represented or expressed. Mozart's *Così fan tutte* undeniably offers a 'mediation of social modernity', but surely that does not make it a work of modernism any more than the roughly contemporary English canvases of Joseph Wright of Derby (1734–97), despite their frequent choice of industrial and technological subject matter. The same might be said of the early twentieth-century novels of John Galsworthy, with which Virginia Woolf takes issue in 'Character in Fiction', and which address the societal transformations wrought by modernity but without a corresponding transformation of language or expression. A self-conscious and refractory manipulation of those means of expression would appear to be an element indispensable to modernism, as opposed to earlier manifestations of musical modernity. Many modernist composers saw themselves as breaking with tradition (gleefully or regretfully or sometimes both) and as standing at the dawn of a new age. So did audiences and other observers. The modernist impulse is inseparable from a reaction *against* aspects of the past that were seen as discredited and of the present that seemed complacent. This rift has still not healed. Again, one's perspective depends on one's focus: while the music of Mahler, Debussy, Sibelius, Poulenc, Shostakovich or Britten does not usually face any hostility in the concert hall (Stravinsky and Bartók are borderline cases), the music of Schoenberg, Varèse and Boulez does and in all likelihood will continue to do so for the foreseeable future, and this fact is not just a technical detail. Pointing this out does not imply that there are no overarching similarities between these groups of composers or that they were not all engaged in the aesthetic mediation of social modernity at some level, but the characteristic differences in the way they did so should not be minimized. Likewise, while it is essential to put modernist rhetoric under critical scrutiny, modernism's critical and problematic relation to the past and tradition remains one of its crucial features.

To be fair, in the introduction to *Transformations of Musical Modernism*, co-written by Johnson with Erling E. Guldbrandsen, the emphasis shifts slightly. While modernism is still placed in a larger historical continuity and viewed primarily through aesthetic categories, its specific identity is put into sharper relief.[57] Likewise, in that book modernism is explicitly conceived of as an ongoing phenomenon ('alive and kicking as a musical force'),[58] whereas Johnson's *Out of Time* struck a rather valedictory note, seeming to suggest that not only modernism but musical modernity and, with it, Western art music as we know it has come to an end. This is implicit in his opening gambit setting out to trace the history between Galileo looking at the sky with his newly invented telescope and the American astronaut Bill Anders looking down from space in 1968 in his famous photograph 'Earthrise', and it is made explicit on the following pages, which are devoted to a discussion of end times, evidenced by works ranging from Beckett's *Endgame* (1957) to Lars von Trier's *Melancholia* (2011).[59] Johnson's cultural pessimism is shared by T. J. Clark and Richard Taruskin, whose *Oxford History* is predicated on the idea that the end of the 'literate tradition' at its basis is 'foreseeable' and indeed nearing its 'culminating phase'.[60] In other words, Taruskin and Johnson do see a rupture in historical continuity – only it occurs *after* not *before* or *through* modernism. Modernism is figured as the endpoint.[61] In this book, Arnold Whittall sounds a similar note.

3) Woolf's essay 'Character in Fiction' is notable yet further for its suggestion that the ruptural event of modernism responds to changes in human sensibility or even, more radically, human nature in itself. No other explanation quite captures what we earlier called the 'imperative' many composers evidently felt when they abandoned the safety of established conventions (e.g. tonality, pulse, rhythm, recognizable textural models, conventional forms based on repetition, standardized instrumentation, traditional genres and media) to explore, in Pierre Boulez's words (based on a painting by Paul Klee), the 'edge of fertile land'.[62] To avoid misunderstanding, however, this imperative is of a psychological, not historical or sociological, kind: we argue that composers *experienced* a need, not that there objectively ever was a need for a particular kind of music. (At the same time, this subjective sense of an imperative should not be trivialized: if we take them at their word – and there is no reason why we shouldn't – composers did not act wilfully or frivolously.)[63] And continuously open to debate and reinterpretation is the question of what this 'abandonment of convention' meant to individual composers. In this volume J. P. E. Harper-Scott helpfully reconfigures Schoenberg's fabled 'emancipation of the dissonance' as rather the emancipation of the pitch class from a fixed symbolic identity as a scale degree, in doing so astutely shifting the emphasis from *poiesis* to *esthesis*, from the tonal landscape itself to the ability of listeners to orient themselves within that landscape.

Woolf's diagnosis of a change in human nature is a particular provocation for conservatives, who view human nature as essentially immutable.[64] Small wonder, then, that it was by and large conservatism that most consistently and tenaciously opposed modernism. This is hardly surprising given the premium placed on innovation in most forms of modernist art and music or the results this produced, which often challenged established traditions; yet, following Woolf,

Introduction

it could be argued that the idea of a change in human character is likewise irreconcilable with conservatism.

In this context, it is worth remembering that, in his *Oxford History of Western Music*, Richard Taruskin repeatedly refers to José Ortega y Gasset's call for the 'Dehumanization of Art' (as a radical form of a change in human character) as a way of explicating musical modernism. To be fair, Taruskin originally introduces Ortega to characterize French modernism in contradistinction to German forms, and he also makes it clear that, in Ortega's usage, dehumanization has 'nothing to do with robots or concentration camps'.[65] Nevertheless, there is a sense in which the disturbing present-day connotations of 'dehumanization' are used to discredit musical modernism as a whole by association (he is cited some twenty times, often extensively), and Taruskin wastes little time in reminding readers that Ortega was 'one of the architects of Spanish fascism and a sworn enemy of democracy' (linking him to Stravinsky's admiration for Mussolini).[66] This last point is demonstrably false. While Ortega's elitism militates against current notions of cultural democracy (which are in turn often based on unreflected ideas of egalitarianism), his actual political views were impeccably democratic. According to Benjamin Steege's account,

> [a]lthough he had initially praised the 1923 military coup by the aristocrat Miguel Primo de Rivera, Ortega turned against the ensuing dictatorship and fully embraced Republicanism, was equally alarmed by mass movements on the left and the right, and can ultimately be considered 'conservative' only in the sense of the 'conservative liberal'. Prior to his 1936 self-exile to Buenos Aires, he briefly held office as member of a party supporting socialist republican policies.[67]

Arguably more important than Ortega's own political affiliation, though, is the meaning and relevance of the term 'dehumanization'. Steege finds 'the slogan of dehumanization [. . .] undoubtedly sensationalistic'. As he explains:

> It [dehumanization] was not a call for mechanization. It did not mean removing human agency from the process of aesthetic production. Nor did it mean denying individual, subjective responses to art works. Nor, finally, did Ortega imagine dehumanization to be a matter of simply de-emphasizing the characteristic objects of a human lifeworld, or even traces of the human form itself. The slogan, in short, did not mean so much the elimination of the human as a historical being as it meant a shift of focus away from experience as habitually lived by that being and towards aspects of the world taken at a moment removed from the flux of everyday practice and feeling.[68]

In a similar vein, Chandler Carter speaks of Ortega's term as signifying a 'depersonalized aesthetic' or an 'aesthetic of detached objectivity' and emphasizes that 'for Ortega, the modernist aesthetic that Stravinsky exemplified merely rejected the overt emotionalism of nineteenth-century art in a return to the sounder artistic principles of eighteenth-century classicism',[69] cautioning that '[a]s much as it offends contemporary liberal ideals, the modernist movement to depersonalize art should not be lumped casually with the extremist ideologies of its age.'[70]

Maria João Neves likewise sees 'the attribute "dehumanization"' as being at risk of devaluing 'the meaning of what is precisely at stake. The philosopher got caught up in contradictions as pointed out by Ciríaco Morón: "How can Ortega call art dehumanized which in his own words is a new way to feel existence?"'[71] In other words, what Ortega seems to have wanted to draw attention to is a new aesthetics, one that responds to or maybe better addresses itself to a new sensibility ('a new way to feel existence'). While the term 'dehumanization' may at least have

11

some superficial appeal when applied to works such as Stravinsky's Octet (one of Taruskin's chief examples), Ortega's other preferred composer was Debussy, and, as David Code argues forcefully in his contribution to this volume, it is very hard to tar the composer of *Pelléas et Mélisande* and countless *mélodies* (among many other deeply humanist works) with the same brush.

Ortega y Gasset was only one of many writers and theorists associated with the rise of artistic modernism in its various forms, and his views are no more representative than those of others (compare, for instance, Paul Bekker or the aforementioned Max Weber). The reason he remains of interest does not lie in his elitism or the somewhat reductionist nature of his dichotomy between the old Romanticism (or 'realism' as he mostly called it) and the new art or, for that matter, in the term 'dehumanization' itself, but rather in his insights into the way in which modernism is intimately associated with what, for want of a better word, we would like to call a 'new sensibility'. And, despite their many differences, it is at this point that Ortega and Woolf meet. That is not to say that Woolf's diagnosis of a 'change in human character' equates to the 'outward concentration' – as opposed to 'inward concentration' (*concentración hacia afuera* and *concentración hacia adentro* or *Außen-* and *Innenkonzentration*) – that Ortega, strongly influenced by Germanic phenomenology, demanded.[72] Yet both, like many others at the time, clearly sensed that the customary coupling of social, political and technological change on the one hand and new expressive means on the other was not sufficient to 'explain' the rupture of modernist art, and that a third, mediating factor needed to be considered, namely human subjectivity itself. Maybe this also explains some of modernism's utopian character, since the old sensibilities, tastes and habits refused to go away so easily (although, considering its many guises in the different art forms, it is important to realize that modernism as a whole has by no means been as universally unpopular as is sometimes claimed).

This, in essence, is what we believe drove and continues to drive modernist composers and musicians: to create music that addresses itself to the experience of modernity. Such a statement does not imply a preference for any of the different forms and varieties of modernism: maximalist and expressionist or minimalist, detached and playful; early, high or late; French, German, American or other; avant-gardist or moderate; popular or esoteric etc. Modernity is typically assumed to consist of a number of more or less interrelated features, and artistic responses to them can in turn take a number of forms.

Aspects of modernism in music

Modernism in music, then, is a diverse phenomenon, encompassing a variety of in some cases contrasting positions; there are many ways of responding creatively to the experience of life in modernity. Consider, for example, the 'bifurcations' between the embrace of social and technological change and the rejection of or escape from them mentioned previously. Although there are some core principles shared by most modernist composers, such as a belief in innovation (although not necessarily in progress), it is generally not fruitful to think of modernist music as a stylistically or aesthetically coherent category, with a number of bullet points that can be said to be shared by composers and repertoires. It makes more sense to think of musical modernism as a series of family resemblances, whereby different members of the family may share certain features but none is common to all of them, and where distant members may be connected by a chain of resemblances without sharing a single feature in common.

Take two of the features that are often seen as defining for modernity: secularization and the increasing role of technology. It is immediately apparent that, in line with the comments by Weber and Childs cited above, composers who are normally regarded as modernist (a certain circularity between people on the one hand and characteristic features is an inevitable element

Introduction

in all classificatory endeavours) have taken a number of contrasting positions and that no homogeneous and coherent 'party line' emerges. While it is possible to construct a canon of secular modernists, a significant number of modernist composers were not only inspired by various religious or spiritual ideas, but these often acted as the chief motivation for their art: this can be said, for instance, of Scriabin, Messiaen, Stockhausen, Jonathan Harvey, Mark Andre (Marc André) and Galina Ustvolskaya. For others, such as Schoenberg, Stravinsky, Wolfgang Rihm, Dieter Schnebel and, as pointed out in this volume by Liam Cagney, Gérard Grisey, religion provided an important impulse at least during parts of their respective lives (and a similar argument could be made about John Cage, depending on how one defines 'religion'). This is not to mention religious composers on the margin of musical modernism, such as Arvo Pärt, John Tavener, James MacMillan, Krzysztof Penderecki, Henryk Górecki, Sofia Gubaidulina, Giya Kancheli and Pēteris Vasks. Thus, nothing could be further from the truth than to suggest that the supposed secularization of modernity – in itself a very complex and contradictory phenomenon – finds its direct expression in the disappearance of religion in modernist composition. On the contrary, many composers, musicians and audiences – but, again, by no means all – seem to have looked to music as a refuge from the alienation and disenchantment of modernity and as a source of re-enchantment, an attitude that it is difficult to reconcile with certain principles of modernism but that is evidently not incompatible with it.[73] At the same time, it is noteworthy that the vast majority of the compositions concerned (certainly of the first group of composers) are non-liturgical, so the role of organized religion in patronage appears to continue to decline. This is not to say that churches and other institutions do not continue to support music-making and composition, but even when modernist theology was at its height, attitudes to modernism in music were marked by caution at best.

A similarly complex picture emerges when considering technology. On one hand, as M. J. Grant shows in her contribution to this volume, composers and musicians have always embraced the latest innovations – recording, broadcasting, digital technologies etc. – and used them creatively. Thus, to cite only the most obvious example, the development of electronic and computer music is an essential component of any history of musical modernism. On the other hand, it is perhaps even more remarkable how stubbornly composers have stuck to a model of production and distribution that has been obsolete for about a century, from the perspective of media technology: writing scores (often using pen and paper) to be played by musicians on traditional instruments (sometimes led by a conductor) in live performance – with recording or broadcasting as optional secondary manifestations of the work. Contrast this with popular music, where technologies of production and distribution largely determine the nature of the music. A dependence on recording, broadcasting and amplification is arguably a defining feature of popular music (even forms which reject these technologies, such as 'unplugged' acoustic music, are negatively dependent on what they react to).[74] In comparison with many forms of popular music, then, it is striking how *limited* the influence of technological change on much modernist music has proven to be.

Such a judgement does not, however, take into account what effects the experience of technology and its impact on human subjectivities and sensibilities had on the nature of the music itself, irrespective of the use of technological tools. Raising this issue almost inevitably provokes mention of Russolo's *intonarumori* and such works as Honegger's *Pacific 231*, Mosolov's *Iron Foundry* or Antheil's *Ballet mécanique*. But their conscious, direct and somewhat simplistic attempts to depict technology in tone-painting may only be the tip of the iceberg of musical responses to technological developments, which may be complex, subtle and often unconscious: indeed, if we assume – again, rather as Weber does in the earlier quotation – that our daily use and experience of technology has inevitably had an effect on our entire consciousness and sensibilities, it must have had an effect on the products of our imagination too – but possibly in ways we would not be able to clearly identify. Note, for instance, that T. S. Eliot didn't hear pre-modern primitivity in the *Rite of Spring*, but 'the scream of the motor-horn, the rattle of machinery, the grind of the wheels, the beating of iron and steel, the roar of the underground railway, and other barbaric noises of modern life'.[75]

About this book

This book does not attempt to provide a comprehensive survey of existing literature on musical modernism. By contrast, without discarding previous research, we (the editors) have sought to re-think its subject and develop innovative critical approaches. Instead of presenting contributors with narrowly defined briefs, which might have resulted in an emphasis on reviewing existing literature, we encouraged them to develop novel and in some cases untested ideas and critical frameworks. While we started with a number of topics, the intention was never that these would comprehensively cover the whole territory represented by modernism in music. Although some of the resulting chapters clearly represent authoritative discussions of a given topic, others far exceeded their ostensible subject, and some topics failed to attract an interested author. By that point, however, the idea of a territory parcelled out into discrete, if contiguous areas had been largely superseded by that of a series of multivalent and variously intersecting and overlapping essays. The book's structure, then, emerged out of the explicit and implicit debates between authors, and may be based on issues of approach, method and critical tradition, as much as subject matter – and that seems fitting for a subject that is defined discursively as much as stylistically or chronologically. What makes music modernist, after all, is not solely that it was composed or performed at a certain time and place and that it conforms with certain stylistic norms, but the stance it takes: towards tradition, culture, society and its own role within them.

In keeping with such a view of musical modernism, the contributions to this book do not follow any form of 'party line'. Once again, the image of family resemblances may suggest itself. There is a fairly broad spectrum of opinion on such issues as moderate or (relatively) conservative modernism, for example. Although no one directly opposes J. P. E. Harper-Scott's advocacy of 'reactive modernism', it is noteworthy that Edward Campbell, M. J. Grant, Liam Cagney and Amy Bauer choose predominantly (but not exclusively) examples from more avant-garde traditions (in the sense in which the term is mostly understood in music historiography, rather than that proposed by theorists of the avant-garde such as Peter Bürger).[76] Although postmodernism, Alastair Williams's topic, is usually viewed as a distinct issue, there are significant similarities between the examples discussed by him and Harper-Scott and the methods and strategies used to investigate them. Following the self-positioning of many of its leading proponents, such as John Adams or George Rochberg, musical postmodernism has mostly been viewed as a response to the high modernism of the post-war avant-gardes, but maybe it could just as legitimately and plausibly described as a continuation of the moderate modernisms of previous eras (just as the renewed interest in moderate modernism may be a reflection of the influence of postmodernism). Indeed, one of Harper-Scott's examples, Alfred Schnittke, is often categorized as postmodernist. It will come as little surprise that, in his chapter, Arnold Whittall, one of the pioneers of the study of moderate modernism, is fairly even-handed in his appreciation of both innovative and responsive traditions and aspects.

A similar picture emerges regarding the tension between the popular (including but not limited to popular music) and the recondite or elitist. It may come with the territory that Robert Adlington and Stephen Graham both chart overlaps, congruences, alliances and allegiances between musical modernism and the popular, although Graham adds a distinct note of caution

Introduction

when he suggests that modernism's embrace of the popular may be a one-sided affair that disregards popular culture's essence. Similarly, while Eva Moreda Rodríguez appears to make a pitch for what one may want to call 'The New Modernism Studies'™ (free from all associations with elitism, sexism, classism and racism) by consigning the idea of modernism's elitism firmly to the world of cliché, other authors, such as Whittall, seem to at least implicitly assume that musical modernism and popular culture are separate spheres; one, Mark Berry, uses the term 'popular' exclusively in scare quotes (which does not necessarily rule out the existence of an authentic popular culture not requiring similar typographical acts of distanciation).

As already alluded to, there is a similar spectrum of views regarding the definition and date of origin of modernism. While it is unlikely that many contributors would wholeheartedly agree with every aspect of our account here, it probably represents a reasonable approximation of the tenor emerging. In terms of methodological approaches, the nature and subject matter of the book privileges historical and critical accounts of often broad developments or general issues, but there is no shortage of detailed analytical observations on individual works in the contributions by Harper-Scott, Whittall, Williams, Amy Bauer, Jonathan Goldman and Charles Wilson.

When it comes to critical approaches, although more recent contributions provide important additions and in some cases correctives, the continuing hold of the work of Theodor Adorno may come as a surprise (it certainly did to the editors). A clear majority of the contributions (thirteen overall) at least mention Adorno and many discuss his writings in detail. It would be problematic to jump to conclusions about any theoretical dependence of the musicology of modernism on work that has come under significant criticism, however. The longest and most detailed engagement with Adorno's work, in David Code's chapter, consists of a vehement attack not only on him but also, remarkably, on his most prominent and vociferous critic within musicology: Richard Taruskin. A number of other contributors, such as Björn Heile, are to various extents also critical of Adorno's work. It is nevertheless fair to say that, were the contents of this collection to be viewed as in any way representative, Adorno would remain the leading theorist of musical modernism. Indeed, it is their shared appreciation of his work that unites the two authors that in some other respects are perhaps furthest apart from one another: Mark Berry and Stephen Graham. It is in fact Graham, writing about a field of which Adorno was famously dismissive, who mounts perhaps the most spirited defence against what he describes as the 'caricatured version of Adorno, not wholly inaccurate but nevertheless reductionist, [that] sees him as an irremediably sour figure fixated on *Kulturindustrie* standardization and "new music" authenticity', maintaining that his 'arguments about mass culture are far more layered than we might expect given the impression we get of him as a humbugging naysayer from figures such as Charles Rosen and Lukács'.

Compared to the critical theory of Adorno and others, musicological research proper appears to have had a less direct influence on the authors represented here. Although it may no longer come as a surprise, it should be regarded as anomalous that no such thing as a standard historical account of musical modernism appears to have emerged – or at least one that would be identifiable as the work of one author, not as the cumulative result of a collective body of scholarship.

Another figure whose prominence may surprise is Pierre Boulez, who plays a significant role in the contributions by David Code, Liam Cagney, Mark Berry and others. Whether the widespread appreciation for his work as a musical thinker and writer, composer and conductor in this collection is representative of wider trends is hard to say. If so, the fluctuations in his reputation may mirror those of modernism as a whole, for which he was often, rightly or wrongly, regarded as a standard-bearer. Even so, considering that, as outlined previously, the rehabilitation of modernist studies tended to go hand in hand with a re-definition of modernism in music, placing greater emphasis on moderate traditions, not to mention issues such as race, class, gender and sexuality, this apparent re-appreciation of a much-maligned representative of 'hard-core modernism' is an interesting development. What emerges clearly is the subtlety and profundity of Boulez's thought and work (at least once one looks beyond some of the rhetoric, notably of his early writings), which, during the pitched ideological battles, perhaps neither side had quite appreciated. Only the future will show whether these are indeed early signs of a posthumous re-evaluation of Boulez's work.

One of the guiding ideas for the book was to pursue a strategy suggested by Harper-Scott in his *The Quilting Points of Musical Modernism* and view modernism in music from the perspective of its 'constitutive outside'.[77] Harper-Scott does not explain the term further. Its origins are somewhat unclear, but it seems to have been coined by Derrida and subsequently taken up by Ernesto Laclau and Chantal Mouffe, Judith Butler, Stuart Hall and others. To provide something like a definition, Hannah Richter quotes Laclau and Mouffe, who argue that 'in the absence of ontological grounding, identity constitution must take place against a "radical outside, without a common measure with the inside"'.[78] Whether a term from political philosophy about collective identity formation can be directly applied to definitions of musical modernism appears doubtful, considering too that the present account is less overtly political than Harper-Scott's. The following thoughts should therefore perhaps be understood as being loosely inspired by the example set by Harper-Scott and the tradition he has referred to, rather than as a theoretically reflective approach to the concept.

There can be little doubt, however, that modernism defined itself or was defined at least as often by what it excluded than by what it included. Although modernism may not have been as exclusive, negative and resistant to affirmation as is often claimed, this aspect of Andreas Huyssen's diagnosis cannot be denied entirely.[79] For this reason, it makes sense to view modernism from the outside or from its margins, rather than to try to define it solely by its supposed essence. In other words, one way of asking the question 'what is modernism in music?' is by asking 'what is it not?'

Accordingly, a number of contributions stake out the limits or margins of musical modernism, in a chronological and historical, geographical and cultural, aesthetic, social, political or conceptual sense, and they debate a number of themes that are typically viewed as falling outside its remit or as being antithetical to it. Thus, James Currie discusses comedic modernism, J. P. E. Harper-Scott reactive modernism, Stephen Graham popular modernism, Robert Adlington political modernism, Björn Heile modernism at the peripheries, Trent Leipert modernism and feeling, and Alastair Williams postmodernism. It is easy to see that these terms are often regarded as oxymoronic or that they refer to common binarisms. Musical modernism is typically regarded as serious if not humourless, based on innovation (and therefore standing in antithetical relation to conservatism), elitist, autonomous and based in a small number of centres in (predominantly Western) Europe and North America, emphasizing the cerebral over the emotional and antagonistically related to postmodernism. Our intention here is not so much to refute those views in an exercise in revisionism, but rather to problematize them in order to clarify modernism's elusive nature.

It is impossible to list all the intersections and resonances between different contributions, and readers are invited to draw their own network of connections, but one strand that may be worth highlighting concerns what one may call the geography of musical modernism. These contributions question the implicit universalism of standard accounts of musical modernism to ask not only *when* it happened and what it involved but *where* it happened. Thus, Eva Moreda Rodríguez focuses on the importance of exile for the development of modernist music, Björn Heile charts the global diffusion of musical modernism, Charles Wilson interrogates the 'locatedness' of contemporary music and Jonathan Goldman homes in on a specific regional culture

Introduction

in Quebec. Indeed, one could argue that Liam Cagney's account of the emergence of spectralism and Arnold Whittall's of recent developments in British music belong in the same context as Goldman's. Due to the centrality of France and, to a lesser extent, Britain to most accounts of twentieth-century music history, these aspects are usually foregrounded as central to the development of modernist music as such, whereas the interest in Balinese gamelan among Quebecois composers would more likely be regarded as a regional peculiarity, if it is seen as worthy of mention at all (despite two relatively prominent names among the composers in question). It is worth asking, however, whether spectralism is inherently more significant and has therefore been able to contribute to keeping France, and in particular Paris, at the centre of developments, or whether, conversely, it was the centrality of Paris and its powerful institutions that propelled spectralism to international pre-eminence. Needless to say, these kinds of questions can be asked about any number of comparable examples – and it is important that we do ask them, rather than taking the reductive syntheses of standard historiographical accounts, with their succession of style labels, composer names and work titles, at face value.

★★★

The section on 'Foundations' unites contributions that discuss the preconditions for or origins or fundamental properties of musical modernism. Consequently, the chapters in this section predominantly concern aspects that are widely shared between different varieties of modernist composition and music-making, from both synchronic and diachronic perspectives. In a dizzying essay ranging from Jacques Offenbach to Bugs Bunny, via Poulenc, Cage, Webern and Ligeti, among others, James Currie draws attention to the penchant for comedy – intentional and unintentional – that runs like a thread through modernist music, but that, unlike for instance in literature, has been commonly overlooked in favour of an insistence on modernist high seriousness. Currie's contribution goes beyond an amusing account of modernist moments of musical comedy; rather, he suggests 'that the comic proclivities of modernist musical production be thought of as having provided audiences with new models for being in the world', arguing further that

> Modernist comedy came to offer bearings within the strange shifting landscape left exposed in the wake of the demise of confidence in more normative constructions of the human that had prevailed up to that point. The comforting notion that the human could be scripted as an individual being in which principles of thinking (reason) and feeling (emotion) balance themselves out in consonant counterpoint to larger social forms no longer rang true. And faced with this false note, modernists set about experimenting with other somewhat post-humanist notions: conceiving the human as a pre-rational, de-individuated collective being, as in primitivist works, such as Stravinsky's *Rite of Spring*; or as a kind of machine, as in Futurism; or as an animal, in Janáček's *The Cunning Little Vixen* (1921–23); or having passed over into the being of objects, as in Ravel's *L'enfant et les sortilèges* (1925); or, in Cage, as the Buddhist nothing at the centre of nature.

As this quotation may suggest, Currie also alerts us to the ambiguity of comedy: while it is often subversive, it is also dangerously evasive, sweetening the pill but only so as to allow us to continue as normal. It may therefore be altogether less subversive than it likes to pretend. As he puts it: 'we cannot take comfort in the mere assertion, far too prominent in postmodern musicology, that by simply pooh-poohing modernist high seriousness we will put ourselves on the side of the angels'.

Sarah Collins debates the (literal and figurative) negotiations about the notion of the contemporary in an institution that, probably more than any other, had the opportunity to define musical modernism: the International Society for Contemporary Music. It is largely a story of failure. The term chosen by the Society was not the modern or modernist, or, as in its German name, the new, but the 'contemporary', which represented what Collins calls a 'soft consensus', an aesthetic relativism that 'has the effect of undercutting the critical impulse that is required to engender historical change'.

The focus on institutions is continued and enlarged in Martin Iddon's chapter. Rather than creating a conventional list of the institutions that have proved crucial in the formation of musical modernism, Iddon outlines institutional theory. For instance, he distinguishes between 'three ways in which one might conceive how an institution interacts with human activity: rational choice institutionalism, historical or normative institutionalism, and social institutionalism', interspersing his account with case studies illustrating the effects of theoretical concepts in actual institutions, such as the Darmstadt International Summer Courses, the Warsaw Autumn festival or the Donaueschinger Musiktage. As he argues, musical modernism's relation with institutions was and is often complex and fraught. While it depended on them, it was also ideologically opposed to institutionalization, prioritizing the *sui generis* and *nonpareil* which, by their nature, evade the stable categories institutions tend to rely on:

> It is, though, precisely in the areas where artworlds [in Howard Becker's sense] reject – cannot make sense of – objects which present themselves as candidates for appreciation, but do not meet the grade, that one finds the point at which institutional theory loses its explicatory power and the point at which aesthetic theory must take over. In this sense, the transgressive, the *unacceptable*, is more important than ever.

David Code focuses on history, distinguishing between '"music History (capital H)" and "music history (small h)" – taking the former to mean an approach rooted in some notion of universal historical laws, and the latter an approach driven by relations to contingent, particular historical events', and associating the former ('History') primarily with Adorno and the latter ('history') with Taruskin. Taking issue with both, particularly in the ways in which each accounts for the music of Debussy (or fails to do so), he proposes a reconsideration of the thought of Pierre Boulez, who, in Code's words, 'proved a more open-minded listener than either Adorno or Taruskin to the human possibilities of modernist music'. Specifically, he follows Boulez in his appreciation of Baudelaire: 'What does [modernism] consist of?' asks Boulez. 'It is difficult to answer very precisely. "Modernism", says Baudelaire, "is the transitory, the fugitive, the contingent, one half of art, of which the other half is the eternal and the immutable".'

The section is brought to a close by Edward Campbell, who is concerned with the aesthetic qualities of modernist music. According to him:

> Musical modernity needs concepts in terms of which we can discuss new music and with which we can make meaningful connections with thought and with the other arts. To this extent the crisis in new music as a crisis of incomprehension on the part of the listening public may be in part to do with the seeming disconnectedness of the music from other areas of human thought and creativity.

The concepts he alights on are the beautiful and the sublime, and he subsequently discusses their applicability to and reconceptualization in the compositional work of Raphaël Cendo, Claude Debussy, Morton Feldman, Brian Ferneyhough, Sofia Gubaidulina, Georg Friedrich Haas,

Introduction

Helmut Lachenmann, Wolfgang Rihm, Arnold Schoenberg, Karlheinz Stockhausen, Jörg Widmann and Bernd Alois Zimmermann, alongside or across philosophical reflections from Burke and Kant to Adorno, Lyotard and Vladimir Jankélévitch, among others. In doing so, Campbell reconsiders the continuing relevance of these traditional concepts for a critical understanding of musical modernism.

The section on 'Positions' comprises individual and in some cases contentious arguments about specific aspects of musical modernism. As a further differentiation of the idea of 'moderate modernism', J. P. E. Harper-Scott develops his concept of 'reactive modernism', which he distinguishes from 'faithful modernism' on one side and 'obscure responses' to what he describes as 'the essential trauma of modernity' on the other. Understanding modernism as an 'event' according to the philosophy of Alain Badiou, Harper-Scott analyses how Alfred Schnittke's *Stille Nacht* and the first of Poulenc's *Trois mouvements perpétuels* 'can be said to return again and again to the moment', *of* the disjunction itself, the point when the sd/pc [scale degree/pitch class] monad is broken up', thereby marking Schoenberg's 'emancipated dissonance' in the compulsive manner characteristic of reactive modernism.

Björn Heile investigates the global diffusion of musical modernism, studying its adoption and development in four different countries – Argentina, Mexico, Finland and Japan – from a comparative perspective. In this way, he uncovers specificities but also underlying commonalities in the ways different national and regional cultures responded to the challenges posed by musical modernity. Adopting the perspective of critical cosmopolitanism, he argues that cultural influence was at least partly reciprocal: not only were distant musical cultures affected by modernist music, but 'modernism [at the centre] would not have become what it did without its encounters with others in far-flung corners of the globe'.

Eva Moreda Rodríguez continues the reflection on the places and displacements of musical modernism, arguing that the alienation often associated with modernism can be seen to be intimately connected with the experience of exile shared by many of its protagonists. Focusing in particular on the largely neglected experiences of Spanish Republican exiles, such as Jaume Pahissa, Salvador Bacarisse, Rosa García Ascot and Rodolfo Halffter, she examines the clichés surrounding common understandings of modernism and exile, concluding that the experience of exile, like that of modernism, is far more diverse than is typically assumed. Nevertheless, the one general conclusion she permits herself is that 'displacement meant for many composers a re-examination of their commitment to a modernist project and a revisitation of the tools and devices they had confidently used thus far to develop it'. In other words, what unites modernism and exile is that they radically question assumed certainties (including those seemingly offered by modernism itself).

Taking his cue from Rachel Potter's distinction between democratic and authoritarian tendencies of modernism, Robert Adlington argues that the democratic tradition of musical modernism is often overlooked or misunderstood. His wide-ranging discussion of who 'the people' are that democratic musicians should 'serve' ends on an interesting note: following Rancière, he calls for an 'anti-hegemonic' practice. In the absence of an 'original "people" [or] an original popular will', there is the potential to act as 'a figure of the people' by asserting 'pockets of autonomy' from established power, based on the presupposition of equality. 'In this conception', he concludes, 'even the most stridently exclusive modernism, to the extent that it truly resists prevailing forms of normativity, may be understood as comprising the people's music'.

In a similar way to Adlington, Graham is interested in popular modernisms, discussing numerous examples of popular music that fulfil his criteria of 'criticality; a challenge to normal procedures; and affects of estrangement, shock and alienation' as well as existing critical approaches

Björn Heile and Charles Wilson

to these repertoires. Ultimately, however, he is sceptical whether the deterministic search for popular modernism does justice to popular music's inherent qualities and values:

> Attempts at loading up popular music with modernist credentials, however much they might make sense in specific examples, risk weakening popular music by playing into outmoded hierarchies of cultural value. Modernism as a concept is alive and well. But it will always be anchored in a particular period of time and a particular set of aesthetic and cultural values. Popular music has, despite its hegemonic commercial and social presence, perhaps struggled to gain the kind of cultural prestige that rightfully infuses modernist art. The way to secure that prestige is potentially not to reach for labels like modernist but instead to look at popular music's own processes and idioms and develop critical languages of value in response. Popular modernism seems to me to be a useful term to some degree. But even better would be a self-sufficient conception of the popular that could comfortably incorporate both criticality and commercialism.

In his contribution, Charles Wilson leads the contested concept of the contemporary, traced by Sarah Collins from the founding years of the ISCM, into the twenty-first century, analysing the discourse of de-limitation around four key notions in contemporary music – access, medium, location and subjectivity – and drawing on three recent compositions: Anna Clyne's *Night Ferry* (2011), James Bulley and Daniel John Jones's *Living Symphonies* (2014) and Alvin Curran's *Vindobona Blues* (2005). As he concludes:

> There seems little doubt that contemporary music as both institution and practice has sought to break with many of the 'bad old' values associated with modernism: its exclusivism and elitism, its restrictions as to medium and mediation, its locatedness and ethnocentricity and its weddedness to the idea of the stable, authorial human subject. And yet [...] the transcendence of such limits is not quite effortless or straightforward. Not all de-bordering is liberating, and not all transgression necessarily transgressive.

Consequently, instead of aiming for the flat, undifferentiated *chronos* of 'presentism', he argues that the liberating potential that modernism has sought may lie in *kairos*, the 'propitious moment', which always suggests an urgency or necessity. In other words,

> all creative activity [...] is predicated on precisely that notion that there is something to do and that now is the time to do it. Such a sense of the timeliness of the present – timely by virtue of its very fragility and transience – rehabilitates both past and future and offers what the current phase of our 'unending modernity' might profitably recapture.

Concentrating primarily on the post-WWII avant-gardes, M. J. Grant charts the influence of communication technologies and theory on composers, pointing out how by 'pushing the boundaries of the "musical" through electronic and other means, they so radically called into question many of the assumptions and conventions that had arisen around musical practice and the "nature" of music'. The significance of these developments was by no means limited to music-structural matters, as is sometimes argued. On the contrary, as Grant emphasizes,

> [d]escribing composers as communication theorists also implies something about the relationship of their work to the social. [...] Reflections on how humans relate to the

Introduction

sounding world around them and to each other through the ordering of sound and movement were [. . .] fundamental to the work of many musical modernists.

True to the values of the avant-garde, in doing so 'composers [did] not merely reflec[t] the social world but also th[ought] through alternatives to the status quo.'

Trent Leipert likewise interrogates a common myth about musical modernism, its supposed 'impersonal' quality and lack of an affective, emotional or expressive dimension. Taking his cue from affect studies, he adopts the distinctions proposed by Eric Shouse: 'Feelings are *personal* and *biographical*, emotions are *social* and affects are *prepersonal*.' According to Leipert, the issue is not that modernist music does not speak to these aspects, but that it is predominantly invested in feeling, the most problematic and least explored of these categories. Despite these difficulties, Leipert traces feeling in the music and thought of Tristan Murail and Iannis Xenakis. He concludes with a reflection on the problematic status of the late modernist subject. Following Alain Badiou and in particular Gianni Vattimo, he encourages us to 'accept th[e] strangely sustained condition of permanent decline [of the subject]', rather than

urging a conservative resistance to the diminishment of metaphysical concepts or a postmodern exuberance in their elimination. [. . .] Just as the subject persists, however problematically, feeling, as a point between pre-subjective affect and socially expressed emotion, also reveals itself as a concept that is both challenging and necessary – a way to understand forms of *attachment* to the subject and what these attachments might mean.

One way of experiencing these forms of attachment to the subject may be late modernist music.

The final section, on 'Practices', is dedicated to discussions of the creative endeavours of particular individuals and groups. Alastair Williams argues that, '[a]lthough postmodernism as a historical moment has now passed, it survives as a pressure that operates within modernism to ensure that innovation and communication work together [. . .] [and] to expand its range of expression'. Demonstrating how postminimalism (particularly in the work of John Adams), spectralism (as realized by Kaija Saariaho), the interest in historical reference represented by the work of Thomas Adès, and related developments in other fields such as critical musicology and historically informed performance practice are all 'products of the way in which postmodernism has succeeded in recasting modernism over recent decades', he concludes that, rather than replacing modernism, these postmodernist discourses and practices have 'brought out a suppressed side of it and helped it to expand and to mutate'.

Arnold Whittall uses his chapter as an opportunity to reflect on his own career of over forty years of thinking, researching and writing about many of the phenomena discussed in this book. As he points out, however, the term 'modernism' was rarely used in musicology during the 1960s and 1970s, and he attributes his own interest in it to the influence of literary studies, notably Malcolm Bradbury and James McFarlane's *Modernism: 1890–1930*.[80] After an introduction to influential positions in British musical modernism, represented by Michael Finnissy and Thomas Adès, he focuses on more recent contributions in the work of James Clarke and Morgan Hayes. In this context, the comparison between Whittall's and Williams's discussions of Adès is instructive: while for Williams Adès is squarely associated with postmodernism, Whittall appears to have no difficulty aligning him with modernist traditions, presumably in line with his longstanding interest in moderate modernism, reserving the term postmodernism – or rather 'genuine postmodernism' – to what he describes as the 'John Adams phase', which opens up 'certain affinities with the otherwise very different stylistic and technical qualities of minimalism and spectralism'. If this last point is not, after all, so far away from the observations of Williams, who similarly described Adams's postminimalism and Saariaho's spectralism side by side, this should not come as a surprise considering that, as we have seen, Williams regards postmodernism as a corrective *within* modernism, rather than as an opposed tendency.

It should not be concealed here that Whittall's long observation of the scene leads him to a pessimistic conclusion:

> It remains to be seen for how long new examples of genuinely modernist music will appear alongside [. . .] more immediately accessible compositions: but in the context of a performance culture which has not thus far brought the more challenging examples of modernism composed since 1900 into the mainstream, a pessimistic prediction seems justified.

Jonathan Goldman focuses on the kind of specific regional practice that has not commonly been covered in general surveys of modernist music: the interest in Balinese gamelan of a range of late twentieth-century composers in Quebec, including Gilles Tremblay, Claude Vivier, José Evangelista and John Rea. Relating the global dimension of cross-cultural representation in all its complexity to the local sociocultural and political specificities of Quebec with its secessionist movement, he argues that this work should be seen in the context of other twentieth-century composers' encounters with non-Western music as a significant aspect of 'late modernism' (Metzer), 'transformed modernism' (Williams) or 'second modernity' (Mahnkopf), distinct from but not necessarily opposed to postmodernism.

Whereas Goldman focused on a small group of composers in Quebec, Liam Cagney turns his attention to almost contemporaneous developments on the other side of the Atlantic, in Paris, where another, similarly close-knit group of composers developed a style that would prove influential internationally (and here the similarities could be said to end): spectralism. Homing in on the formative years of Gérard Grisey, in particular, Cagney corrects many common misconceptions. Not only did its pioneers Hugues Dufourt and Grisey originally reject the term 'spectralism', they also pursued more wide-ranging re-conceptualizations in the whole arena of musical thought than the technical procedures of composing with harmonic spectra, which the term has predominantly come to signify. Furthermore, although the spectralists often distanced themselves from serialism, Cagney demonstrates how many of their ideas and practices grew out of an engagement with (post-)serialism as well as with the myriad of styles and approaches that emerged in its wake. As he argues, spectralism thus conceived can best be understood through the French concept of *écriture*, which combines the two aspects of 'constructivist compositional tool-kit and [. . .] regulative metaphysical system'. As he puts it, '*écriture* encapsulates the inevitable tension in Grisey's compositional outlook between fluidity and fixity, between a music of transience and difference and a discourse of structure and identity'.

The inclusion in this volume of an essay on spectralism is justified by its centrality in the development of modernist music, as one of the key stylistic movements to emerge from the late twentieth century. As we have seen, however, Williams claims part of its legacy for postmodernism, a position that appears to be supported by Whittall. And indeed Cagney's own account illustrates how spectralism emerged from a remarkably pluralist engagement with a diverse set of styles and approaches, from the legacy of serialism in Pierre Boulez's work from the late 1960s and early 1970s, through the example of Dutilleux, the stochastic music of Xenakis and the electroacoustic experiments of Jean-Étienne Marie, to the spirituality of Stockhausen's *Stimmung* and the (proto-)minimalism of La Monte Young – an eclecticism that is indeed akin to postmodernism, even if Grisey's achievement lay in fusing these diverse influences into a

Introduction

coherent and arguably original and innovative musical language, in a fashion that is more clearly associated with modernist principles.

Opera has frequently been sidelined in accounts of musical modernism. The reasons for this neglect are not hard to find: audiences are commonly conservative and institutions wary of the risk and expense of putting on new, untested and challenging work. At an aesthetic level, opera presents the twin challenges of musical language and dramaturgic conception, which are not always aligned, particularly in the twentieth and twenty-first centuries: while some operas have 'accompanied' traditional plots and dramatic conceptions with (more often moderately) modernist music, others have experimented with innovative dramatic ideas set to fairly traditional music. It is comparatively rare that musical language and dramaturgic conception are inherently related, but that seems a requirement from a modernist perspective. In her contribution, Amy Bauer discusses the relations that bind music, philosophy and language, before analysing five contemporary operas – György Ligeti's *Le Grand Macabre*, Claude Vivier's *Prologue pour un Marco Polo*, Helmut Lachenmann's *Das Mädchen mit den Schwefelhölzern*, Salvatore Sciarrino's *Luci mie traditrici* and David Lang's *The Difficulty of Crossing a Field* – as 'five completely different operatic attempts at foregrounding the failure of language as representation'. According to her, 'the challenge of modernism is met head on in these works by musicalizing language, turning it into a particularity that must be experienced, a task for which opera is uniquely suited'. Accordingly, the five operas point towards 'a new operatic practice that engages fully with a modernist aesthetic'.

Opera is also the focus of Mark Berry's chapter. However, he is not primarily interested in composition but operatic production, focusing in particular on stagings of Richard Wagner's *Die Meistersinger von Nürnberg* by Harry Kupfer, Stefan Herheim, David Bösch and David McVicar. What, in Berry's view, makes Kupfer's, Bösch's and, in particular, Herheim's productions modernist is their willingness 'to criticize and interrogate' the work, by virtue of which they remain paradoxically true to it, something that McVicar's production signally fails to do. It is through its critique – including, one might add, its auto-critique – that modernism retains a hope of emancipation, in contradistinction, once again, with McVicar's emphasis on anti-critical 'entertainment', which aligns his approach with conservatism and postmodernism.

As Berry's contribution has demonstrated, modernism in music does not only concern composition, but is often said to have had a similarly significant impact on performance practice, including the performance of the historical repertoire. The nature and effect of that influence is far from certain, however. Just as it would be problematic to reduce modernist composition to one particular style or compositional technique – whether dodecaphony or neo-classicism, for example – so it is untenable to equate modernist approaches to performance with simple injunctions of *espressivo* and *rubato* playing or Stravinskyan insistence on impersonal execution instead of (inter)subjective interpretation. As Stefan Knapik shows in his chapter, the influence of modernism on performance practice issued from different philosophical traditions and took a variety of forms. His particular focus is early twentieth-century violin treatises, which were heavily influenced by vitalism, a philosophical movement that he describes as integral to modernist thought. As he argues:

> Far from offering fewer constraints than those implicit in the practices of the Early Music movement, not to mention their representation by Taruskin, the vitalistic traditions of mainstream classical performance turn out to have been just as didactic and prescriptive, only in a different way. And in that different way – in particular their elevation of the ascetic, austere and essentially self-serving image of the artistic genius – they constitute what is arguably an equally important part of modernism's legacy to performance practice.

Notes

As these examples have shown, the debates about the meaning of modernism in music are unlikely to go away any time soon. Furthermore, rather than being merely semantic disputes about labels, terms and their definitions, these debates go to the heart of musical culture, what we value in and about music, and how we, as composers, musicians, critics, musicologists, teachers, students and listeners, can contribute to its continued flourishing into the future. The book is intended to further advance those debates, opening them up, instead of closing them down.

Notes

1 Fredric Jameson, *A Singular Modernity* (New York: Verso, 2002), 1.
2 Pierre Bourdieu, 'The Market of Symbolic Goods', in *The Field of Cultural Production: Essays on Art and Literature*, ed. Randal Johnson and trans. Richard Nice (Cambridge: Polity Press, 1993), 112–44; Georgina Born, *Rationalizing Culture: IRCAM, Boulez, and the Institutionalization of the Musical Avant-Garde* (Berkeley and Los Angeles: University of California Press, 1995).
3 See, for instance, Max Paddison, 'Adorno, Popular Music and Mass Culture', in *Adorno, Modernism and Mass Culture* (London: Kahn & Averill, 2004), 81–105.
4 See Leo Black, *BBC Music in the Glock Era and After* (Woodbridge: Boydell & Brewer, 2010); Paul Attinello, Christopher Fox and Martin Iddon, eds., 'Other Darmstadts', special issue, *Contemporary Music Review* 26, no. 1 (2007); Martin Iddon, *New Music at Darmstadt: Nono, Stockhausen, Cage, and Boulez* (Cambridge: Cambridge University Press, 2013); see also Iddon's contribution to this volume.
5 See Joseph N. Straus, 'The Myth of Serial "Tyranny" in the 1950s and 1960s', *Musical Quarterly* 83, no. 3 (1999), 301–43, and Anne C. Shreffler's response, 'The Myth of Empirical Historiography: A Response to Joseph N. Straus', *Musical Quarterly* 84, no. 1 (2000), 30–39.
6 On John Adams, see Alastair Williams's contribution to this volume; on Pärt, see David Clarke, 'Parting Glances: David Clarke Reappraises the Music and the Aesthetics of Arvo Pärt', *Musical Times* 134 (1993), 680–84.
7 Arved Ashby, ed., *The Pleasure of Modernist Music: Listening, Meaning, Intention, Ideology* (Rochester, NY: University of Rochester Press, 2004).
8 See Susan McClary, 'Terminal Prestige: The Case of Avant-Garde Music Composition', *Cultural Critique* 12 (1989), 57–81.
9 Eric J. Hobsbawm, *The Age of Extremes: A History of the World, 1914–1991* (London: Michael Joseph, 1994).
10 Ben Earle, *Luigi Dallapiccola and Musical Modernism in Fascist Italy* (Cambridge: Cambridge University Press, 2013), xii–xiii.
11 See, inter alia, Ellie M. Hisama, *Gendering Musical Modernism: The Music of Ruth Crawford, Marion Bauer, and Miriam Gideon* (Cambridge: Cambridge University Press, 2006), and Martin Scherzinger, '"Art" Music in a Cross-Cultural Context: The Case of Africa', in *The Cambridge History of Twentieth-Century Music*, ed. Nicholas Cook and Anthony Pople (Cambridge: Cambridge University Press, 2004), 584–613. See also Stephen Graham's contribution to this volume.
12 See Gayatri Chakravorty Spivak, 'In a Word: Interview', in *Outside in the Teaching Machine* (London: Routledge, 1993), 3–4; Georgina Born, 'Introduction: V. Techniques of the Musical Imaginary', in *Western Music and Its Others: Difference, Representation, and Appropriation in Music*, ed. Georgina Born and David Hesmondhalgh (Berkeley: University of California Press, 2000), 42.
13 See, inter alia, Patricia A. Morton, *Hybrid Modernities: Architecture and Representation at the 1931 Colonial Exposition, Paris* (Cambridge, MA: MIT Press, 2003); Dilip Parameshwar Gaonkar, ed., *Alternative Modernities* (Durham, NC: Duke University Press, 2001).
14 See, for example, Mary E. Davis, *Classic Chic: Music, Fashion, and Modernism* (Berkeley and Los Angeles: University of California Press, 2006).
15 Björn Heile, 'Introduction: New Music and the Modernist Legacy', in *The Modernist Legacy: Essays on New Music* (Aldershot: Ashgate, 2009), 1–10.
16 The most conspicuous case in point is Susan McClary, a recent essay of whose revisits some of her earlier positions in 'Terminal Prestige'. See her 'The Lure of the Sublime: Revisiting the Modernist Past', in *Transformations of Musical Modernism*, ed. Erling E. Guldbrandsen and Julian Johnson (Cambridge: Cambridge University Press, 2015), 21–35.
17 Pride of place has to go to Kenneth Gloag, *Postmodernism in Music* (Cambridge: Cambridge University Press, 2012).

Introduction

18 Christopher Chowrimootoo, 'Reviving the Middlebrow, or: Deconstructing Modernism from the Inside', *Journal of the Royal Musical Association* 139, no. 1 (2014), 187–93.

19 Douglas Mao and Rebecca L. Walkowitz, 'Introduction: Modernisms Bad and New', in *Bad Modernisms*, ed. Mao and Walkowitz (Durham, NC: Duke University Press, 2006), 1.

20 See James Hepokoski, *Sibelius: Symphony No. 5* (Cambridge: Cambridge University Press, 1993); J. P. E. Harper-Scott, *Edward Elgar, Modernist* (Cambridge: Cambridge University Press, 2006); Daniel M. Grimley, *Carl Nielsen and the Idea of Modernism* (Woodbridge: Boydell Press, 2010); Christopher Chowrimootoo, '"Britten Minor": Constructing the Modernist Canon', *Twentieth-Century Music* 13, no. 2 (2016), 261–90; J. P. E. Harper-Scott, *The Quilting Points of Musical Modernism: Revolution, Reaction, and William Walton* (Cambridge: Cambridge University Press, 2012); Ben Earle, 'Modernism and Reification in the Music of Frank Bridge', *Journal of the Royal Musical Association* 141, no. 2 (2016), 335–402.

21 Arnold Whittall, *Musical Composition in the Twentieth Century* (Oxford: Oxford University Press, 1999); see also Whittall, *Exploring Twentieth-Century Music: Tradition and Innovation* (Cambridge: Cambridge University Press, 2003) and 'Individualism and Accessibility: The Moderate Mainstream, 1945–75', in *The Cambridge History of Twentieth-Century Music*, ed. Cook and Pople, 364–94.

22 It is telling in this context that, in his *Edward Elgar, Modernist*, Harper-Scott quotes Hepokoski and Whittall (and no one else) on page 1, although he takes issue with the latter.

23 Hepokoski, *Sibelius*, 2–3. See also the discussion of Dahlhaus's distinction between *musikalische Moderne* and *Neue Musik* in Sarah Collins's contribution to this book.

24 Ibid., 1.

25 Stephen Paul Miller, *The Seventies Now: Culture as Surveillance* (Durham, NC: Duke University Press, 1999), 28. The episteme is discussed by Foucault in Michel Foucault, *The Archaeology of Knowledge* (London: Tavistock Publications, 1972), 191. Kenneth Gloag cites and discusses these references in his article 'Situating the 1960s: Popular Music – Postmodernism – History', *Rethinking History* 5, no. 3 (2001), 397–410.

26 The first of Jameson's 'four maxims of modernity' reads tellingly 'We cannot not periodize' (*A Singular Modernity*, 29).

27 See Leon Botstein, 'Music of a Century: Museum Culture and the Politics of Subsidy', in *The Cambridge History of Twentieth-Century Music*, ed. Cook and Pople, 40–68; Michael Chanan, *Repeated Takes: A Short History of Recording and Its Effects on Music* (London: Verso, 1995).

28 Virginia Woolf, 'Character in Fiction' (1924), in *Selected Essays*, ed. David Bradshaw (Oxford: Oxford University Press, 2008), 37–54. The text was first read as a paper at the Heretics (Cambridge) and appeared as 'Character in Fiction' in *The Criterion* (edited by T. S. Eliot) in July 1924. It was then issued in book form as *Mr. Bennett and Mrs. Brown* (London: Hogarth Press, 1924), a title that Woolf had in fact already used for an earlier and shorter text, published in *The Nation and Athenaeum* in December 1923 (*Selected Essays*, 32–36). The British Library has digitized a copy of the Hogarth Press publication at http://www.bl.uk/collection-items/mr-bennett-and-mrs-brown-by-virginia-woolf (accessed 15 May 2017).

29 Ibid., 38.

30 Ibid.

31 Max Weber, *The Rational and Social Foundations of Music*, ed. and trans. Don Martindale, Johannes Riedel and Gertrude Neuwirth (Carbondale: Southern Illinois University Press, 1958).

32 Eduardo de la Fuente, *Twentieth Century Music and the Question of Modernity* (New York: Routledge, 2010), 57.

33 Max Weber, 'Remarks on Technology and Culture', *Theory, Culture & Society* 22, no. 4 (2005), 29; see also Fuente, *Twentieth Century Music and the Question of Modernity*, 62.

34 Max Horkheimer and Theodor W. Adorno, *Dialectic of Enlightenment: Philosophical Fragments*, ed. Gunzelin Schmid Noerr and trans. Edmund Jephcott (Stanford, CA: Stanford University Press, 2002).

35 Peter Childs, *Modernism* (London: Routledge, 2000), 17.

36 T. J. Clark, *Farewell to an Idea: Episodes from a History of Modernism* (New Haven, CT, and London: Yale University Press, 1999), 6–8.

37 Childs, *Modernism*.

38 Seth Brodsky, *From 1989, or European Music and the Modernist Unconscious* (Oakland: University of California Press, 2017), 252–58. As Brodsky points out himself, his book is more based on Žižek and Lacan than Adorno and even *keeps* Adorno out (ibid., 252), though that is hardly a sufficient explanation for a dizzying, complex, potentially paradigm-changing and inherently unsummarizable book. Nevertheless, the centrality of 'radical negativity' (ibid.) to the book and hence its indebtedness to the critical theory of the Frankfurt School remains apparent, if in often oblique ways.

39 Adorno introduced the idea of the historical state of the material in his *Philosophy of New Music* (Minneapolis and London: University of Minnesota Press, 2006) and developed it further in his *Aesthetic Theory* (London: Athlone Press, 1997). See also, inter alia, Max Paddison, *Adorno's Aesthetics of Music* (Cambridge: Cambridge University Press, 1997), 151–52; Andrew Bowie, *Adorno and the Ends of Philosophy* (Cambridge: Polity Press, 2013), 138; and David Code's critical discussion in this volume.

40 Woolf, 'Character in Fiction', 48.

41 Ibid., 49–50.

42 The three possibilities outlined here correspond roughly to the three definitions of the word 'moment' given in the online *Oxford English Dictionary* (accessed 9 July 2017): a) 'A very short period or extent of time'; b) 'A period of time (not necessarily brief) marked by a particular quality of experience or by a memorable event'; c) 'A particular stage or period in a course of events or in the development of something; a turning point; a historical juncture'.

43 See David Bradshaw's comment in Woolf, *Selected Essays*, 226.

44 The chronology of Ives's compositions is famously complicated, but for our purposes it is sufficient that his work undergoes a similarly momentous change around the same time as that of his contemporaries.

45 Carl Dahlhaus, *Nineteenth-Century Music* (Berkeley and Los Angeles: University of California Press, 1989), 332–38. Cf. also the discussion of myths of origin in Fuente, *Twentieth Century Music and the Question of Modernity*, 31–39.

46 Pierre Boulez, *Stocktakings from an Apprenticeship* (Oxford: Clarendon Press, 1991), 267. Paul Griffiths has followed Boulez in this regard; *A Concise History of Modern Music from Debussy to Boulez* (London: Thames & Hudson, 1978). Cf. M. J. Grant's contribution to this volume.

47 Whittall, *Exploring Twentieth-Century Music*, 189. In his contribution to this volume, Whittall has qualified this further: 'Even if, as is often argued, the earliest phase of musical modernism belongs to the post-classical romanticism of the nineteenth century, its fullest, high-modernist manifestation as post-tonal music has occurred in the years since 1900' (354).

48 See Walter Benjamin, *The Writer of Modern Life: Essays on Charles Baudelaire* (Cambridge, MA: Harvard University Press, 2006); Adorno, *Aesthetic Theory*. Adorno did not dedicate an essay (never mind a book) to Baudelaire as such, but the fact that the poet is cited twenty-seven times in *Aesthetic Theory*, covering much of the book, suggests the role that he played in Adorno's thinking.

49 Clark, *Farewell to an Idea*, 15.

50 Richard Taruskin, *Music in the Early Twentieth Century*, vol. 4 of *The Oxford History of Western Music* (New York: Oxford University Press, 2011), 448.

51 Ibid., 5–6.

52 Ian Pace, review of *Luigi Dallapiccola and Musical Modernism in Fascist Italy*, by Ben Earle, *Music & Letters* 98, no. 1 (2017), 156–57.

53 Harper-Scott, *Edward Elgar, Modernist*; Harper-Scott, *The Quilting Points of Musical Modernism*.

54 Karol Berger, *Bach's Cycle, Mozart's Arrow: An Essay on the Origins of Musical Modernity* (Berkeley: University of California Press, 2007); Karol Berger, Anthony Newcomb and Reinhold Brinkmann, eds., *Music and the Aesthetics of Modernity: Essays* (Cambridge, MA: Harvard University Department of Music, 2005); John Butt, *Bach's Dialogue with Modernity: Perspectives on the Passions* (Cambridge: Cambridge University Press, 2010); Julian Johnson, *Out of Time: Music and the Making of Modernity* (New York: Oxford University Press, 2015).

55 Johnson, *Out of Time*, 7–8.

56 Berger and Newcomb, preface to *Music and the Aesthetics of Modernity: Essays*, 1.

57 Erling E. Guldbrandsen and Julian Johnson, eds., *Transformations of Musical Modernism* (Cambridge: Cambridge University Press, 2015).

58 Ibid., 2.

59 Johnson, *Out of Time*, 1–3.

60 Taruskin, preface to *Music in the Early Twentieth Century*, xii; see also James R. Oestreich and Richard Taruskin, 'Classical Music: Debriefing; A History of Western Music? Well, It's a Long Story', *New York Times*, 19 December 2004, http://query.nytimes.com/gst/fullpage.html?res=9B05E0D81630F93AA2 5751C1A9629C8B63.

61 Interestingly, Johnson studiously avoids the term 'postmodernism', which does not occur once in the book, although he at one point mentions 'post-modernity' only to add '(a term most often avoided today)' (Johnson, *Out of Time*, 3).

Introduction

62 Pierre Boulez, 'At the Edge of Fertile Land (Paul Klee)', in *Stocktakings from an Apprenticeship*, ed. Paule Thévenin and trans. Stephen Walsh (Oxford: Clarendon Press, 1991), 158–72.

63 See, for example, the essays and statements collected in Daniel Albright, ed., *Modernism and Music: An Anthology of Sources* (Chicago and London: University of Chicago Press, 2004).

64 Andy Hamilton, 'Conservatism', in *The Stanford Encyclopedia of Philosophy*, ed. Edward N. Zalta, Fall 2016 (Metaphysics Research Lab, Stanford University, 2016), https://plato.stanford.edu/archives/fall2016/entries/conservatism/.

65 Taruskin, *Music in the Early Twentieth Century*, 60.

66 Ibid., 476.

67 Benjamin Steege, 'Antipsychologism in Interwar Musical Thought: Two Ways of Hearing Debussy', *Music & Letters* 98, no. 1 (2017), 77.

68 Ibid., 81.

69 Chandler Carter, 'The Rake's Progress and Stravinsky's Return: The Composer's Evolving Approach to Setting Text', *Journal of the American Musicological Society* 63, no. 3 (2010), 569.

70 Ibid., 572.

71 Maria João Neves, 'The Dehumanization of Art: Ortega y Gasset's Vision of New Music', *International Review of the Aesthetics and Sociology of Music* 43, no. 2 (2012), 370–71.

72 Steege, 'Antipsychologism in Interwar Musical Thought', 78.

73 See Helga de la Motte-Haber, ed., *Musik und Religion*, 2nd ed. (Laaber: Laaber-Verlag, 2003), 215–66; Catherine Pickstock, 'Quasi una sonata: Modernism, Postmodernism, Religion, and Music', in *Resonant Witness: Conversations Between Music and Theology*, ed. Jeremy S. Begbie and Steven R. Guthrie (Grand Rapids, MI: Eerdmans, 2011), 190–214.

74 Mark Katz's idea of the 'phonograph effect' is an excellent way to conceptualize the different relations to technology. See Mark Katz, *Capturing Sound: How Technology Has Changed Music*, rev. ed. (Berkeley and London: University of California Press, 2010).

75 Quoted in Albright, *Modernism and Music*, 12.

76 Peter Bürger, *Theory of the Avant-Garde* (Manchester: Manchester University Press, 1984).

77 Harper-Scott, *The Quilting Points of Musical Modernism*, 4.

78 Hannah Richter, 'Beyond the "Other" as Constitutive Outside: The Politics of Immunity in Roberto Esposito and Niklas Luhmann', *European Journal of Political Theory*, 15 July 2016.

79 Andreas Huyssen, *After the Great Divide: Modernism, Mass Culture, Postmodernism* (Bloomington: Indiana University Press, 1986).

80 Malcolm Bradbury and James Walter McFarlane, eds., *Modernism: 1890–1930* (Harmondsworth, UK: Penguin Books, 1976).

Bibliography

Adorno, Theodor W. *Aesthetic Theory*. Edited by Gretel Adorno and Rolf Tiedemann. Translated by Robert Hullot-Kentor. London: Athlone Press, 1997.

———. *Philosophy of New Music*. Translated by Robert Hullot-Kentor. Minneapolis and London: University of Minnesota Press, 2006.

Albright, Daniel, ed. *Modernism and Music: An Anthology of Sources*. Chicago and London: University of Chicago Press, 2004.

Ashby, Arved, ed. *The Pleasure of Modernist Music: Listening, Meaning, Intention, Ideology*. Rochester, NY: University of Rochester Press, 2004.

Attinello, Paul, Christopher Fox and Martin Iddon, eds. 'Other Darmstadts'. Special issue, *Contemporary Music Review* 26, no. 1 (2007).

Benjamin, Walter. *The Writer of Modern Life: Essays on Charles Baudelaire*. Cambridge, MA: Harvard University Press, 2006.

Berger, Karol. *Bach's Cycle, Mozart's Arrow: An Essay on the Origins of Musical Modernity*. Berkeley: University of California Press, 2007.

Berger, Karol, Anthony Newcomb and Reinhold Brinkmann, eds. *Music and the Aesthetics of Modernity: Essays*. Cambridge, MA: Harvard University Department of Music, 2005.

Black, Leo. *BBC Music in the Glock Era and After*. Woodbridge: Boydell & Brewer, 2010.

Born, Georgina. *Rationalizing Culture: IRCAM, Boulez, and the Institutionalization of the Musical Avant-Garde*. Berkeley and Los Angeles: University of California Press, 1995.

————. 'Introduction: V. Techniques of the Musical Imaginary'. In *Western Music and Its Others: Difference, Representation, and Appropriation in Music*, edited by Georgina Born and David Hesmondhalgh, 37–58. Berkeley: University of California Press, 2000.

Botstein, Leon. 'Music of a Century: Museum Culture and the Politics of Subsidy'. In *The Cambridge History of Twentieth-Century Music*, edited by Cook and Pople, 40–68.

Boulez, Pierre. *Stocktakings from an Apprenticeship*. Edited by Paule Thévenin. Translated by Stephen Walsh. Oxford: Clarendon Press, 1991.

————. 'At the Edge of Fertile Land (Paul Klee)'. In *Stocktakings from an Apprenticeship*, 158–72.

Bourdieu, Pierre. 'The Market of Symbolic Goods'. In *The Field of Cultural Production: Essays on Art and Literature*, edited by Randal Johnson and translated by Richard Nice, 112–44. Cambridge: Polity Press, 1993.

Bowie, Andrew. *Adorno and the Ends of Philosophy*. Cambridge: Polity Press, 2013.

Bradbury, Malcolm, and James Walter McFarlane, eds. *Modernism: 1890–1930*. Harmondsworth, UK: Penguin Books, 1976.

Brodsky, Seth. *From 1989, or European Music and the Modernist Unconscious*. Oakland: University of California Press, 2017.

Bürger, Peter. *Theory of the Avant-Garde*. Translated by Michael Shaw. Manchester: Manchester University Press, 1984.

Butt, John. *Bach's Dialogue with Modernity: Perspectives on the Passions*. Cambridge: Cambridge University Press, 2010.

Carter, Chandler. 'The Rake's Progress and Stravinsky's Return: The Composer's Evolving Approach to Setting Text'. *Journal of the American Musicological Society* 63, no. 3 (2010): 553–640.

Chanan, Michael. *Repeated Takes: A Short History of Recording and Its Effects on Music*. London: Verso, 1995.

Childs, Peter. *Modernism*. London: Routledge, 2000.

Chowrimootoo, Christopher. 'Reviving the Middlebrow, or: Deconstructing Modernism from the Inside'. *Journal of the Royal Musical Association* 139, no. 1 (2014): 187–93.

————. '"Britten Minor": Constructing the Modernist Canon'. *Twentieth-Century Music* 13, no. 2 (2016): 261–90.

Clark, T. J. *Farewell to an Idea: Episodes from a History of Modernism*. New Haven, CT, and London: Yale University Press, 1999.

Clarke, David. 'Parting Glances: David Clarke Reappraises the Music and the Aesthetics of Arvo Pärt'. *Musical Times* 134 (1993): 680–84.

Conrad, Peter. *Modern Times, Modern Places*. London: Thames & Hudson, 1998.

Cook, Nicholas, and Anthony Pople, eds. *The Cambridge History of Twentieth-Century Music*. Cambridge: Cambridge University Press, 2004.

Dahlhaus, Carl. *Nineteenth-Century Music*. Translated by J. Bradford Robinson. Berkeley and Los Angeles: University of California Press, 1989.

Davis, Mary E. *Classic Chic: Music, Fashion, and Modernism*. Berkeley and Los Angeles: University of California Press, 2006.

Earle, Ben. *Luigi Dallapiccola and Musical Modernism in Fascist Italy*. Cambridge: Cambridge University Press, 2013.

————. 'Modernism and Reification in the Music of Frank Bridge'. *Journal of the Royal Musical Association* 141, no. 2 (2016): 335–402.

Foucault, Michel. *The Archaeology of Knowledge*. London: Tavistock Publications, 1972.

Fuente, Eduardo de la. *Twentieth Century Music and the Question of Modernity*. New York: Routledge, 2010.

Gaonkar, Dilip Parameshwar, ed. *Alternative Modernities*. Durham, NC: Duke University Press, 2001.

Gloag, Kenneth. 'Situating the 1960s: Popular Music – Postmodernism – History'. *Rethinking History* 5, no. 3 (2001): 397–410.

————. *Postmodernism in Music*. Cambridge: Cambridge University Press, 2012.

Griffiths, Paul. *A Concise History of Modern Music from Debussy to Boulez*. London: Thames & Hudson, 1978.

Grimley, Daniel M. *Carl Nielsen and the Idea of Modernism*. Woodbridge: Boydell Press, 2010.

Guldbrandsen, Erling E., and Julian Johnson, eds. *Transformations of Musical Modernism*. Cambridge: Cambridge University Press, 2015.

Hamilton, Andy. 'Conservatism'. In *The Stanford Encyclopedia of Philosophy*, edited by Edward N. Zalta, Fall 2016. Metaphysics Research Lab, Stanford, CA: Stanford University, 2016. https://plato.stanford.edu/archives/fall2016/entries/conservatism/.

Introduction

Harper-Scott, J. P. E. *Edward Elgar, Modernist*. Cambridge: Cambridge University Press, 2006.

———. *The Quilting Points of Musical Modernism: Revolution, Reaction, and William Walton*. Cambridge: Cambridge University Press, 2012.

Heile, Björn. *The Modernist Legacy: Essays on New Music*. Aldershot: Ashgate, 2009.

Hepokoski, James. *Sibelius: Symphony No. 5*. Cambridge: Cambridge University Press, 1993.

Hisama, Ellie M. *Gendering Musical Modernism: The Music of Ruth Crawford, Marion Bauer, and Miriam Gideon*. Cambridge: Cambridge University Press, 2006.

Hobsbawm, Eric J. *The Age of Extremes: A History of the World, 1914–1991*. London: Michael Joseph, 1994.

Horkheimer, Max, and Theodor W. Adorno. *Dialectic of Enlightenment: Philosophical Fragments*. Edited by Gunzelin Schmid Noerr. Translated by Edmund Jephcott. Stanford, CA: Stanford University Press, 2002.

Huyssen, Andreas. *After the Great Divide: Modernism, Mass Culture, Postmodernism*. Bloomington: Indiana University Press, 1986.

Iddon, Martin. *New Music at Darmstadt: Nono, Stockhausen, Cage, and Boulez*. Cambridge: Cambridge University Press, 2013.

Jameson, Fredric. *A Singular Modernity*. New York: Verso, 2002.

Johnson, Julian. *Out of Time: Music and the Making of Modernity*. New York: Oxford University Press, 2015.

Katz, Mark. *Capturing Sound: How Technology Has Changed Music*. Rev. ed. Berkeley and London: University of California Press, 2010.

Mao, Douglas, and Rebecca L. Walkowitz, eds. *Bad Modernisms*. Durham, NC: Duke University Press, 2006.

McClary, Susan. 'Terminal Prestige: The Case of Avant-Garde Music Composition'. *Cultural Critique*, no. 12 (1989): 57–81.

———. 'The Lure of the Sublime: Revisiting the Modernist Past'. In *Transformations of Musical Modernism*, edited by Guldbrandsen and Johnson, 21–35.

Miller, Stephen Paul. *The Seventies Now: Culture as Surveillance*. Durham, NC: Duke University Press, 1999.

Morton, Patricia A. *Hybrid Modernities: Architecture and Representation at the 1931 Colonial Exposition, Paris*. Cambridge, MA: MIT Press, 2003.

Motte-Haber, Helga de la, ed. *Musik und Religion*. 2nd ed. Laaber: Laaber-Verlag, 2003.

Neves, Maria João. 'The Dehumanization of Art: Ortega y Gasset's Vision of New Music'. *International Review of the Aesthetics and Sociology of Music* 43, no. 2 (2012): 365–76.

Oestreich, James R., and Richard Taruskin. 'Classical Music: Debriefing; A History of Western Music? Well, It's a Long Story'. *New York Times*, 19 December 2004. http://query.nytimes.com/gst/fullpage.html?res=9B05E0D81630F93AA25751C1A9629C8B63.

Pace, Ian. Review of *Luigi Dallapiccola and Musical Modernism in Fascist Italy*, by Ben Earle. *Music & Letters* 98, no. 1 (2017): 163–67.

Paddison, Max. *Adorno's Aesthetics of Music*. Cambridge: Cambridge University Press, 1997.

———. 'Adorno, Popular Music and Mass Culture'. In *Adorno, Modernism and Mass Culture*, 81–105. London: Kahn & Averill, 2004.

Pickstock, Catherine. 'Quasi una sonata: Modernism, Postmodernism, Religion, and Music'. In *Resonant Witness: Conversations Between Music and Theology*, edited by Jeremy S. Begbie and Steven R. Guthrie, 190–214. Grand Rapids, MI: Eerdmans, 2011.

Richter, Hannah. 'Beyond the "Other" as Constitutive Outside: The Politics of Immunity in Roberto Esposito and Niklas Luhmann'. *European Journal of Political Theory*, 15 July 2016.

Scherzinger, Martin. '"Art" Music in a Cross-Cultural Context: The Case of Africa'. In *The Cambridge History of Twentieth-Century Music*, edited by Cook and Pople, 584–613.

Shreffler, Anne C. 'The Myth of Empirical Historiography: A Response to Joseph N. Straus'. *Musical Quarterly* 84, no. 1 (2000): 30–39.

Spivak, Gayatri Chakravorty. 'In a Word: Interview'. In *Outside in the Teaching Machine*, 1–24. London: Routledge, 1993.

Steege, Benjamin. 'Antipsychologism in Interwar Musical Thought: Two Ways of Hearing Debussy'. *Music & Letters* 98, no. 1 (2017): 74–103.

Straus, Joseph N. 'The Myth of Serial "Tyranny" in the 1950s and 1960s'. *Musical Quarterly* 83, no. 3 (1999): 301–43.

Taruskin, Richard. *Music in the Early Twentieth Century*. Vol. 4 of *The Oxford History of Western Music*. New York: Oxford University Press, 2011.

Weber, Max. *The Rational and Social Foundations of Music*. Translated and edited by Don Martindale, Johannes Riedel and Gertrude Neuwirth. Carbondale: Southern Illinois University Press, 1958.

Björn Heile and Charles Wilson

———. 'Remarks on Technology and Culture'. *Theory, Culture & Society* 22, no. 4 (2005): 23–38.
Whittall, Arnold. *Musical Composition in the Twentieth Century*. Oxford: Oxford University Press, 1999.
———. *Exploring Twentieth-Century Music: Tradition and Innovation*. Cambridge: Cambridge University Press, 2003.
———. 'Individualism and Accessibility: The Moderate Mainstream, 1945–75'. In *The Cambridge History of Twentieth-Century Music*, edited by Cook and Pople, 364–94.
Woolf, Virginia. *Selected Essays*. Edited by David Bradshaw. Oxford: Oxford University Press, 2008.

PART 1

Foundations

1

THE BIRTH OF MODERNISM – OUT OF THE SPIRIT OF COMEDY

James R. Currie

The attempt to summarize something as geographically pervasive as comedy within something as temporally extensive as the historical time covered by musical modernism could easily come across as being prey to hubris. Since in comedy one of the fates of those seduced by hubris is to be reduced to comedy's great paradigm – of a king slipping up on a banana peel and landing on his arse – the attempt therefore runs the risk of becoming comic itself. More than any other, comedy is the genre that appears in the plural: both in-and-of itself, through its characteristic tendency towards stylistic mixture and diversity, but also in terms of the wide range of variations produced in the genre through the strong attendance it gives to the highly specific temporal and geographical configurations in which it is brought into being. In the words of Laurent Berlant and Sianne Ngai, comedy is a 'vernacular form', and thus, '[w]hat we find comedic (or just funny) is sensitive to changing contexts'.[1] There are comedies, not comedy. The point is almost empirical, easily registered in the difficulty we can have in accessing the nuance of humour when learning another language, or how oddly lame the jokes appear of other countries and times past. As Henri Bergson wrote in his justly famous 1900 essay on laughter: 'how often has the remark been made that many comic effects are incapable of translation from one language to another, because they refer to the customs and ideas of a particular social group!' Indeed, for Bergson there is even a hint of the sinister about this, for '[h]owever spontaneous it seems, laughter always implies a kind of secret freemasonry, or even complicity, with other laughers, real or imaginary'.[2] In a lighter vein, we might simply say that comic works are homebodies, relishing neither foreign vacations nor time travel except as a source of material for comic working. The comic is seemingly allergic to grand narratives. It is a kind of hilarious gravitational force that precludes transcendent flight, forcing subjects to remain anchored to their material limitations, broadly conceived, and to learn somehow to live with humour within human finitude.

As such, comedy has often made a good fellow traveller for postmodern discourse, which is similarly anti-metaphysical and insistent in its demands that the particularity of specific contexts and their histories should preside over our understanding of human cultural endeavours. It is therefore unsurprising how easily comedy has come to be lauded by postmodern musicologists.[3] But if postmodernism and comedy go well together, so do modernism and comedy too, and since modernism has so regularly functioned as postmodernism's determinative antagonist, particularly in musicological discourse, then comedy is perhaps a less clear indicator of allegiances than some might once have hoped. The conjunction of modernism and comedy, whilst historically interesting in and of itself, is also thus an expedient location from which to disturb some of the presumptions that have prevailed in musicology for the past quarter-century. And although this theme is not the presiding focus of the following essay, its provocation is an abiding pressure throughout. To that degree, my speculations can be thought of as a contribution to our increasingly complex understanding of our modernist inheritance at a moment when, faced with the extraordinary challenges of our contemporary moment, the certainties that our postmodern worldview had once seemed to offer now wither.

As a starting point, we can note how well postmodernism's comic ethos matches up with broad patterns that emerged into discourse in the middle of the nineteenth century, when the proclivities and contentions that were to become characteristic of modernist modalities first started to sprout. Both, after all, exhibit a strongly anti-transcendental agenda that is frequently communicated by means of comedy. For postmodern thinking, fuelled by the negative examples provided by the totalitarian projects of the twentieth century, this agenda is part and parcel of its across-the-board radical democratic critical tendency, which sees the transcendent as the means by which power shores up its forces and thus works to exclude rather than embrace.[4] With regard to the mid-nineteenth century, the antipathy towards the transcendental position develops in the wake of the 1848 revolutions amidst the profound questioning of Romanticism and the culture and politics of the first half of the nineteenth century that arose in the bathos following that moment of political failure.[5] Criticism of Romanticism was, of course, as old as Romanticism itself. The common post-1848 claim was that Romanticism must now be rejected since, crudely put, it was but a form of transcendental escapism, and thus too distracted by gazing at the stars to be able to forge a credible politics on the ground at a moment of crisis. But this was something that early on Romanticism had already self-reflexively woven into the texture of its own discourse by means of, among other things, the fragment and its own particular brand of irony. Irrespective of precedent, however, the strategic flourishing of anti-Romantic sentiment at the mid-century point resulted in a strongly materialist swerve which tended to sacrifice transcendental and metaphysical claims to the exigencies of a kind of positivistic pragmatism, and whose broadly defined artistic impulse came under the aegis of realism and its various analogies. As is well known, in visual arts, for example, the painter's gaze started to turn away from the epic horizons of Romanticism, beyond which utopia might one day emerge, and to redirect its attention back towards the everyday of modern life, as in the paintings of Manet and, in the comic vein, in the caricatures of Daumier. In the novel we see plots increasingly driven by a sense that the motor of causality in human affairs is of a broadly scientific bent – sociological, psychological, economic – a tendency epitomized in Zola's famous assertion in *Le roman expérimental* (1880) that his novels should be thought of more as a scientific experiment. Romantic notions of musical transcendence did, of course, remain a powerful force in European musical culture in the second half of the nineteenth century, particularly in German-speaking lands.[6] But even in Germanic musical discourse there likewise developed a competing materialist strain. When in other countries, notably in France, that strain became all-consuming then, as with postmodernism, comedy was often not far behind.

Take, for example, the first full-length operetta, Jacques Offenbach's magnificent *Orphée aux enfers* (*Orpheus in the Underworld*), premiered in 1858 in Paris at the Théâtre des Bouffes-Parisiennes. This is a comic assault that takes no prisoners, sacrificing anything in its path that claims truth can only be grasped by floating above the odour and texture of contemporary life. If Zola could refer to his novels as scientific experiments then, following the lead of Siegfried Kracauer in his famous *Jacques Offenbach and the Paris of His Time* of 1937, we can think of Offenbach here as a kind of satirical journalist. With all the hilarity of a bruiser in drag as an ingénue, Offenbach's masterpiece dons the garb of antiquity and of European opera's hallowed mythological origins, and taking hefty swipes en route at, among others, the corny acting at the Comédie Française and, beloved of the French, Gluck's *Orphée et Eurydice*, it enacts an extraordinarily damning portrait of Napoleon III, the early years of the Second Empire in France, and the bourgeoisie's complicity with his reign and resulting self-betrayal of their own radical political past. At the very beginning of his virtuosic analysis of the 1851 coup d'état that led to Louis Napoleon being declared emperor in 1852, Karl Marx famously wrote in *The Eighteenth Brumaire of Louis Bonaparte* (1851–52) that 'Hegel observes somewhere that all the great events and characters of world history occur twice, so to speak'. Adopting the formula of a stand-up comedian telling a joke, he then concludes: 'He forgot to add: the first time as high tragedy, the second time as low farce.'[7] In Marx's essay, the triumph of Louis Napoleon, a distant nephew of Napoleon Bonaparte, is but a pitiful re-enactment of the events by which Napoleon himself gained power in November of 1799 during the Revolution. Offenbach's operetta is the unofficial musical based on Marx's thesis, for here music history, like its political counterpart, happens twice: first time as opera, second time as operetta.[8]

As with certain strains in postmodernism, there is the sense in Offenbach's operetta that modern life is, in part, one of worn out, enervated historical repetition, a costume drama of flimsy garments that either fails fully to cover up the obscenities of the contemporary or is simply all there is to the contemporary.[9] In broad daylight we are robbed of our belief in the eternal validity of the truths of the past. The epic theatre of history collapses, leaving the masterpieces of Western culture to roam aimlessly along the hall of funhouse mirrors left in its wake – which, interestingly, were invented during this period by Charles Frances Ritchel.[10] What is of note for our purposes is less that Offenbach, via the mode of satire, uses comedy in order to enact this disenchantment. As Kracauer points out, by 1858 satire of antiquity was a French tradition stretching back at least two hundred years, and was particularly in vogue in the early years of the Second Empire.[11] Rather, it is that by employing comedy to do so, Offenbach repeatedly sidesteps despair and heads straight to the party, most obviously in the infamous 'can-can', the 'Infernal Galop' from Act 2 scene 2.[12]

In terms of the lofty ethical and spiritual claims made for high art, the conceptualization of music brought to the stage in this work is extraordinarily raw. Everything about the art is shown to be instrumental, void of possibility of redemption into aesthetic autonomy. It is as if musical material were simply a tool available in order to get something done. Orpheus is recast as a virtuoso concert violinist. Yet in comparison with the myth, where his musical gifts are imbued with the possibilities of transcending the boundary between life and death, when we first encounter him in Act 1 the practice of his art functions predominantly within an inane psychic economy: a means to the end of the narcissistic validation that he thereby receives from his audiences. No longer the mysterious and somewhat mute shade, Eurydice is now a crass and highly vocal Philistine, unmoved by the music of her husband – who evidently leaves her unmoved in other departments too, since she is having an affair. Rather than the redemptive medium through which humans seek to transcend the barriers separating themselves from each other and the world, music here reinforces divisions, shoring up the dam of the individual against the threat of being swept away by oceanic feelings. In the hilarious 'Duo du Concerto' of Act 1, when Orpheus starts to play his hour-and-a-quarter-long violin concerto at Eurydice, she first finds it boring, and then agonizing. It is as if the basic distinction between what should be music and what is noise has been transgressed. Music is here mere stuff, like a rock: something that might leave one either indifferent or, should someone think to smash it against one's skull, damaged. And yet rather than leaving us feeling bereft, the effect of Offenbach's masterpiece is almost joyous. Music is simply us, in all our limitation and self-serving mess – this is what the piece seems to tell. And we give that message a standing ovation.

However many striking similarities of outlook we might admit between Offenbach's genius in the mid-nineteenth century and the postmodern appreciation of the comic, these interrelated ideas – of Offenbach as an incipient modernist, and that the roots of European musical modernism might be found in the comic proclivities of post-1848 culture – might still give pause. In defence, there are a number of things we could remind ourselves of here. For example, in many historical accounts of other art forms, Paris around the turn of the 1860s is precisely the time and place where the controversies that will come to preoccupy modernism start to raise their heads. On the one hand, the great city was, in Walter Benjamin's phrase, the 'Capital of the Nineteenth Century'; and yet Benjamin's uncompleted magnum opus on the Paris Arcades, the famous *Passagen-Werk*, also argues that it was where the capitalist crises of twentieth-century political and cultural life, with all their reverberations throughout artistic modernism, have their origin.[13] Theodor Adorno was to make a similar two-way historical diagnosis of the second half of the nineteenth century in his *In Search of Wagner*.[14] The fact that the realism characteristic of the culture of that age was precisely what so much modernist artistic polemic then reacted against is, in this regard, somewhat moot. After all, modernist criticism of realism frequently proceeded not from a rejection of realism as a goal for art per se, but from passing judgement on realism's failure to be real enough. As the philosopher Alain Badiou has stated in a now well-known phrase from his widely read *The Century*, the twentieth century and its modernist art can be understood as driven first and foremost by a 'passion for the real'.[15] And so if we still in fact do continue to resist opening up our historical understanding of modernism to its mid-nineteenth-century origins, and in turn perhaps to comedy too, then that is perhaps because we fall prey to representing modernism in terms of modernism's own self-representations – or at least to what we have tended to assume modernism's own self-representations to have been. The centrally organizing fantasy here would be modernism's belief in the radically clean break it makes with the past; that its creative acts occur, as it were, *ex nihilo*, and that, oedipally, it had, in Linda Hutcheon's phrase, 'to reject historicism and to pretend to a parthenogenetic birth fit for the new machine age'.[16] Or, as Carl E. Schorske wrote back in the early 1980s at the beginning of his justly famous study of *fin-de-siècle* Vienna,

> In the last one hundred years [. . .] 'modern' has come to distinguish our perception of our lives and times from all that has gone before, from history as a whole, as such. Modern architecture, modern music, modern philosophy, modern science – all these define themselves not *out* of the past, indeed scarcely *against* the past, but in independence of the past.[17]

To a degree, this is of course something of a reduction of the vexed discourses with the past that embroiled modernism as it sought to conceptualize its actions.[18] But as, for example, Richard Taruskin's extraordinary work on Stravinsky and his relationship to the Russian tradition attests, it has nevertheless been revelatory to read composers against the grain when they profess that there has been no precedent for their actions.[19]

Offenbach, of course, is far from completely absent from modernist recognition, and so his characteristically materialist, mid-nineteenth brand of comedy was available as an influence. He was, to take but one example, of great import to Karl Kraus and his particular brand of cultural criticism, and Kraus's influence on Schoenberg and his generation in Vienna is not to be underestimated.[20] Kraus would perform Offenbach's operettas in his famous one-man performances and readings, singing all the parts to a piano accompaniment.[21] The appeal to Kraus and his followers lay in part in Offenbach's use of satire and parody seemingly as a means of unmasking the hypocrisy underlying the surface appearance of the social and political life of his times. And

Modernism – out of the spirit of comedy

it is interesting, as an aside, to speculate regarding the degree to which Offenbach, via Kraus, may have fuelled Schoenberg's own strong proclivities towards acerbic musical parody in the flagrant psychotic comedy of *Pierrot lunaire*, or the brittle neo-classical *froideur* of the Op. 25 Piano Suite, or later in the excruciatingly hollow E-flat major 'tonality' of the end of the *Ode to Napoleon Buonaparte*, to name but three examples.[22] But if such lines of influence kept open the possibility of a precedent for modernist musical discourse in mid-nineteenth century comedy, they nevertheless did so in part by means of a certain misreading of comedy's political force, at least with regard to Offenbach. For as Carl Dahlhaus once put it, 'the notion that Offenbach was a "subversive" whose music harbors portents of "revolution" is, if not sheer myth, at least grossly naïve'.[23] It may well be, as Kracauer wrote, that *Orpheus in the Underworld* 'laid bare the foundations of contemporary society and gave the bourgeoisie an opportunity to see themselves as they really are'.[24] But it was nevertheless ultimately a roaring financial success, and it seems credible to argue that the bourgeoisie, rather than reeling from the smart, took great pleasure in the entertainment provided by the spectacle of their own brutal disenchantment. Even Louis Napoleon himself gave the work his seal of approval when, in April 1860, he agreed to attend a gala at the Théâtre-Italien only on the condition that Offenbach's *Orpheus* would be on the programme. Apparently he was delighted.

The case of Offenbach's *Orpheus in the Underworld* thus presents us with a certain paradox that regularly makes its pressure felt with regard to the function of comedy in musical modernism. On the one hand, comedy here provides access to an arsenal of materialist ammunition that can then be aimed at Romantic musical metaphysics; but it simultaneously also engenders a kind of entertaining pleasure that can douse the incendiary potential of its own putative content. There is, of course, little to suggest that Offenbach had any significant problem with the effectivity of his political satire ultimately being trumped by the musical pleasures of comic entertainment. Success at the box office was in most instances sufficient validation, and Offenbach's savvy understanding of how musical pleasures could override political repercussions was probably crafted into the work itself as a selling point.

In this regard, one of Offenbach's most important twentieth-century heirs is the notoriously 'apolitical' Richard Strauss who, on 5 June 1916, in a famous letter to his librettist Hugo von Hofmannsthal, declared:

> I am ultimately now the only composer who has humor and wit and a marked paro-distic talent. Yes, I feel the downright calling to be the Offenbach of the twentieth century ... Starting with *Der Rosenkavalier* is our way: its success proves it.[25]

The content of most of Strauss's operatic works from *Der Rosenkavalier* onwards, which so frequently turn to comedy, seems studiously to avoid the potential for political controversy and biting cultural critique that Offenbach's works, with such virtuosity, simultaneously encourage and circumvent. But like Offenbach, Strauss nevertheless presents us with pervasive and oddly non-judgemental appreciations of how easily distracting musical attractiveness can be in comparison to content or to the seemingly correct emotive claims and allegiances to which we should be compelled by history, politics and ethics. As Edward Said notes of Strauss's later music, for example, it 'makes none of the emotional claims it should [. . .] [I]t is smoothly polished, technically perfect, worldly, and at ease *as music* in an entirely musical world.'[26] And with a nod towards Adorno's critique of Strauss, Said admits that, considering the 'appalling depredations of Germany during the war', this can be 'downright embarrassing'.[27] Such embarrassments, we might argue, were perhaps there with Strauss from the beginning, even in the gory angst of *Salome* – a work that is only comic when viewed perversely as camp grotesque, from whence it becomes hilarious. As with Offenbach, with *Salome* one senses a knowingness regarding how a conflict of interests between musical sensations and putative literary contents and meanings might be put to work at the box office. Based on the play by Oscar Wilde, which was banned by the British Lord Chamberlain for its depiction of Biblical characters, Strauss's operatic setting, by comparison, mostly created a somewhat titillating scandal that was part and parcel of its not insignificant appeal to contemporary audiences. The very success of *Salome* is, to a degree, a magnificent joke, and so is as much a part of the history of musical modernism's relationship to comedy as are comic works of musical modernism themselves.[28]

To the degree that music so easily manages to override content, making it perfectly normal for us to be transported by a song whose words we have completely misheard, or to swoon to a recording of an opera whose plot we may be less informed about than the TV advertisement by which we recognize it, then perhaps music per se is inadvertently comic – or so, at the very least, are the pretentions and delusions it inspires in the humans by whom it is employed. It is certainly worth noting that not only is musical modernism characterized by a preponderance of works whose content is comic, but that starting in the mid-nineteenth century there is a marked increase in music itself constituting such comic content in musical works, particularly in works of a more Dada orientation. The apotheosis of this tendency is perhaps to be found in one of the great unacknowledged jokes of twentieth-century music, Cage's *4'33"* of 1952. Rather than a somewhat po-faced Zen experiment in silence, the famous stunt might productively be reconceptualized in terms of Cage's own beloved Satie and Dada, or even Eugène Ionesco and the absurdist drama of that time: a pianist sits down at the keyboard to play and then absolutely nothing happens.[29] Further, if music is something of a joke, then one of the conclusions that modernists were to draw from this was that we should think about reconceiving the art form in more modest, pragmatic terms. Comedy is thus not only an obvious component of things like Satie's *musique d'ameublement*, or the interest pervasive in European musical modernism in jazz, café and dance music and popular forms, which frequently, and problematically from the perspective of race, gender and class, manifested itself in comic terms.[30] It could also be a significant fellow traveller to *Gebrauchsmusik* and other more utilitarian endeavours.

Indeed, like their postmodern heirs, many musical modernists wanted to lighten things up on all sorts of levels of expression, style and technique.[31] The increasing contemporary perceptions that the culture of the late nineteenth and early twentieth century was in a state of decadent ill-health led to a similarly pervasive sense of claustrophobia and the necessity of a cure, as epitomized in the writings of Friedrich Nietzsche, whose philosophy was to go viral in cultural debates at the turn of the twentieth century. For example, in 1888 in *The Case of Wagner*, faced with the sickness he perceived in Wagner's art, Nietzsche humorously invokes the supposed last words of Goethe ('Licht! Mehr Licht!') and exclaims: 'I feel the urge to open the windows a little. Air! More air!'[32] The call for clarity, cleanliness and a certain transparency of affect and effect can be heard echoing all the way from the middle of the nineteenth century at least through to the neo-classical discourses of the years between the wars, and comedy was often scripted as a privileged means by which these goals were to be achieved. In the early 1880s, in *Thus Spoke Zarathustra*, Nietzsche has his eponymous hero pronounce: 'I would only believe in a god who knew how to dance. And when I saw my devil, there I found him earnest, thorough, deep, somber: it was the spirit of gravity – through him all things fall. Not by wrath does one kill, but by laughing. Up, let us kill the spirit of gravity!'[33] Throughout the period on the more local level of biography, we repeatedly see composers striving to break out of the constrictions of stylistic deadlocks and their attendant historical baggage precisely through such means, indifferent to gravity or fond of humour, or indeed both.

Modernism – out of the spirit of comedy

For example, at the very end of his life, Verdi found himself in the predicament of feeling that he had been left behind by culture while simultaneously wanting on some level to remain engaged with forging a music appropriate for Italy as it started to face the pragmatic realities of its increasingly rapid modernization.[34] His means of negotiating this problematic was his final opera, *Falstaff* (1893), his only comic opera since the early failure of *Un giorno di regno* (King for a Day, of 1840). It is a work that in its pervasive atmosphere of parody and ironic distance breaks with the centrality in the Italian operatic tradition of the nineteenth century for forging dramatic empathy with characters by means of elevated lyric outpouring. To the degree that in the second half of the nineteenth century Verdi himself had been perceived as the embodiment of this tradition, his use of comedy at this point not only allowed Italian opera partially to unmoor itself from its past, but in a sense allowed Verdi to exit himself too. This is late-style humour at its best – the ageing composer accessing comic vitality, throwing off the trappings of a creative life, opening up the possibilities of a world of new compositional possibilities and thus refusing the weighty melancholy that insists that the last works should somehow bring definitive, funereal punctuation.

Or take Schoenberg, who first announces his departure to atonality in the last movement of the Second String Quartet Op. 10 (1908) by means of a soprano setting of Stefan George's 'Entrückung' (Rapture), a poem whose first lines immediately invoke a change in gravitational force: 'Ich fühle luft von anderem planeten' ('I feel the air of another planet'). Such Nietzschean overtones are then sounded more fully in the poem's final stanza: 'Ich steige über schluchten ungeheuer, / Ich fühle wei ich über letzter wolke / In einem meer kristallnen glanzes schwimme' (I rise up over monstrous ravines, / I feel as if I were swimming over the last cloud / In a shimmering crystal sea).[35] Having clinched the deal with atonality and thus learned how, invoking Nietzsche's words once more, to kill the spirit of gravity, Schoenberg is then free to put a significant compositional wager on comedy, most emphatically first in the expressionist derangements of *Pierrot lunaire*, and then with relative consistency through to the end of his life.

Schoenberg's pattern of a transformation in the perception of gravity somehow preceding, or at least cohabiting with, a defection towards the comic is also replicated in the earlier years of György Ligeti's career. Admittedly, Ligeti's compositional practice from the very beginning was strongly orientated towards the comic, and throughout his career he tended to keep audiences in the discomfort of a certain ambiguity as to whether the music was meant to be funny or not. One could, for example, take the case of the 1958 electronic work *Artikulation*, which audiences often found funny and which Kagel said sounded like Ligeti talking in Hungarian. Nevertheless, Ligeti first makes an established name for himself among the composers of the European avant-garde with such serious micropolyphonic classics as the 1961 *Atmosphères*, which, with its kaleidoscopic landscape of vast clouds of sound, investigates and invokes a gaseous world in which the human's normal relationship to gravity barely registers. Indeed, such weight-defying investigations at the limits of the human remained a preoccupation of Ligeti's modes of inspiration throughout his artistic life. In conversation with Péter Várnai, talking of a particular moment of polarized tessitura in the 1966 Cello Concerto, Ligeti states that his goal was 'to create the impression of a vast soap-bubble that may burst at any moment'.[36] And later, in his short essay on his 1988 Piano Concerto, he writes that

> if this music is played correctly – by which I mean at the correct speed and with the correct accentuation within individual layers – it will after a time 'take off' like an airplane: the rhythmic events, being too complex to be followed in detail, simply begin to hover.[37]

James R. Currie

But in the early 1960s, the possibility for Ligeti that the success of his micropolyphonic works might legitimate his reputation within the status quo seems to have inspired a certain terror. And, as Richard Toop writes, 'far from hastening to follow up on the success of this work, he seems to have gone out of his way to undermine any idea of himself as "the next great composer"'.[38] Like Verdi at the end of his life, immured in the monument of Italian opera and seeking a breath of comic fresh air as escape, Ligeti at the point of his 'first maturity' sees a trap hiding in the offer to take his place at the table. He thus keeps the danger at bay through a series of works whose proclivities are endlessly available to comedy, such as the pieces immediately following which came out of his idiosyncratic relationship to the Fluxus movement – *Trois Bagatelles for David Tudor* (1961), *Die Zukunft der Musik* (1961) and *Poème symphonique* (1962)[39] – and then *Aventures* (1962) and *Nouvelles Aventures* (1962–65).

If culture and composers' own practices were to be revivified by making them float by means of laughter, for modernists that did not, however, always imply that the great import assigned to culture by the Romantics, particularly musical culture, was now but a balloon ripe for popping. If many modernists were perhaps happy to use figures of comedy in order to create some distance between themselves and the metaphysical seriousness of Romantic musical aesthetics or anything else that threatened to entrap through weight, a sense of ambivalence regarding the ease with which comedy can leap into bed with flippancy and inane entertainment was never far away. As Zarathustra states, right before the passage quoted above: 'Who among you can laugh *and be elevated at the same time?*'[40] Zarathustra's laughter is thus a far cry, for example, from that espoused by Mikhail Bakhtin in his celebrated *Rabelais and His World*. It is not some carnivalesque inversion of the hierarchy, whereby cultural authority is reduced to the level of what Bakhtin calls the 'lower bodily stratum', where we become happy as pigs in shit. Zarathustra's laughter and, by implication, certain forms of modernist musical comedy work rather through recognition of the strategic value of a seeming paradox: that one way of preserving the possibility of the continuing life of serious culture is by *making recourse* to comedy. As Nietzsche later writes about Zarathustra in *Ecce Homo*, it is only with the spirit who 'plays naively' and

> confronts all solemnity in gesture, word, tone, eye, morality, and task so far, as if it were their most incarnate and involuntary parody [...] that *great seriousness* really begins, that the real question mark is posed for the first time, that the destiny of the soul changes, the hand moves forward, the tragedy *begins*.[41]

And the potential truth value of this paradoxical economy, in which play and parody are the price to be paid for great seriousness and tragedy, is given validation by its appearance in locations far-flung from the assumed normal orbit of Nietzsche's influence.

Francis Poulenc's superb 1944 setting of Guillaume Apollinaire's surrealist *Les mamelles de Tirésias*, for example, is a work that seems to be all about bursting the balloon of serious culture. Indeed, balloon bursting constitutes the opera's best-known image. Having announced her feminist intention to liberate herself from her husband, Thérèse then further liberates herself from her breasts too, which transpire to be two balloons, one red, one blue, that float away from her chest on strings before she explodes them with a cigarette lighter, at which point they then flop to the floor like flaccid rubber scrotums. Thérèse's initially Nietzschean act of defiance in relation to the gravity of her own body is undermined by her then immediately wielding the material weight of comedy. As a result, Nietzschean flights of fancy, which perhaps delude us into thinking that, like the Overman, we might leap from high peak to high peak above the cloud line, are bluntly cut short.

Modernism – out of the spirit of comedy

However, in a series of conversations broadcast on the radio in 1953–54 with Claude Rostand, Poulenc stated that, far from being mere parody, 'I consider *Les mamelles* as my most authentic work, along with *Figure humaine* and the *Stabat*'.[42] From the perspective of the relationship between Poulenc's biography and music, we might take a lead from Christopher Moore's excellent research and view the complex slipperiness that Poulenc introduces here into the relations between his categories as evidence of the continuing effects of the queer aesthetics of camp and its social double speak that Moore sees as defining of Poulenc's practice in the 1920s.[43] Poulenc asks us, for example, to consider the funeral scene for the two drunks, Presto and Lacouf. Like most stage drunkards, Presto and Lacouf are pure slapstick, and as characters they barely constitute a sketch, exerting next to no genuine force on the causal momentum of the plot. Without rhyme or reason, they enter in Act 1 scene 4 to a hilarious music-hall polka, get into a duel at the drop of a hat, even though they are supposedly fast friends, and manage to kill each other over a ridiculous disagreement as to whether they are in Zanzibar (which in Poulenc's work is an imaginary town between Monte Carlo and Nice) or Paris. But when in the immediately following scene Thérèse reads the announcement of their death in the newspaper, it unleashes a music of extraordinary gentle beauty, completely absent of inverted commas and nudges and winks, that steadily gathers all of the characters into its embrace in a manner not unlike that of the Countess's act of forgiveness at the end of Mozart's *The Marriage of Figaro*. As Poulenc commented, at this point 'you could very easily replace the words with a liturgical text without great scandal, I think'.[44] Like the Mozart, which similarly invokes religious music by subsuming the different characters into a texture of hymn-like unity, it is as if the busy preoccupation that Poulenc's characters uphold with their roles in the surreal madcap of the rest of the drama has momentarily been put here on hold, and as the chorus members carry the bodies of the drunks offstage in a funeral procession, a moment of sublime temporal stasis opens up.

Such apparent incongruities are, of course, of the essence of many of our assumptions regarding comedy.[45] But continuing with the potential for a queer reading, we might consider the following thought-provoking passage of Moore's:

> Poulenc's musical and dramatic disguises periodically draw undue attention to their own incongruity. Indeed, there are moments in the composer's works when his elaborate musical makeup cannot entirely hide the expressive reality of the queer subjectivity it is attempting to cover up. Such moments of 'failed seriousness' are apparent in Poulenc's music during instances of particularly acute emotional abandon, when the intensity of the expressive register actually *undermines* theatricality and, paradoxically, points to an underlying and irrepressible authenticity.[46]

And so maybe what happens at the funeral of Presto and Lacouf is that costumes momentarily slip off the shoulder, revealing that *Les mamelles* is in fact a tragic work trying to 'pass' in comic drag. For Daniel Albright, in a revelatory discussion of Poulenc's masterpiece, this moment is interpreted in terms of a logic of difference and so 'by extensive development of frivolous music-hall numbers [...] Poulenc created exactly that clear system of differentiation that permits the funeral music to register as funereal.' Continuing, he posits that 'it is arguable that the funeral in *Les mamelles de Tirésias* is graver, more anguished, than anything in [Poulenc's] *Stabat Mater*, simply because the *Stabat Mater* is so thoroughgoingly sad that its wrenching chromaticisms lose force, lacking much contrasting material to wrench away from'.[47] But if, for certain modernists, the historical predicament of their times meant that comedy had become perhaps the only frame in which authentic expression could come into focus, for others such a contextual preservation strategy for the vulnerability of seriousness in the modern age was still too open to possible infection. As we will continue to see, comedy is often too prone to making things dialectically unstable to be fully trustworthy, and faced with that risk some composers sought a solution to the question of authentic expression in a logic of absolute seriousness.

Active at much the same time as Poulenc, Anton Webern epitomizes such a stance of unconditional humourlessness. Through a compositional process of unrelenting condensation, the lyric impulses of Webern's musical utterances are distilled down to a point of such concision that anything extraneous to the seriousness of the intent boils off, leaving fragments of an almost ball-bearing-like density, seemingly impenetrable to comic perversion. Since a certain spin on Webern's example became the paradigm at Darmstadt in the 1950s, it is then unsurprising how extraordinarily humourless the European avant-garde party line tended to be at that time and why ultimately it spawned a small virus of comic antagonists, such as Mauricio Kagel and the already mentioned Ligeti. Of course, in the wake of the devastations of World War II, the earnestness of the party line was easily validated by literal-minded reasoning: serious music for serious times. But if Poulenc's *Les mamelles de Tirésias* is a comic lure that ultimately traps us in a serious expression, then it is just as fair to assert that Webern and Darmstadt constitute a rigorous discipline of seriousness that can inadvertently strike us as ridiculous. And that is true whether one is attracted to this music (as I am) or not. Although there can be something exasperatingly philistine about the giggles that difficult modernist music can still inspire in audiences, it is nevertheless the case that one can easily be caught off guard into cartoonish modes of perception, finding oneself hallucinating Looney Tunes when a chesty low contralto is accompanied by the avian squawk of an E-flat clarinet in a Webern song, or imagining strings hilariously snapping out of the body of a grand piano like broken springs from a mattress in Boulez's *Structures 1a*. The hilarity that modernist musical earnestness has so frequently inspired during the course of its reception is thus as much part of the history of musical modernism's engagement with comedy as are more clearly identifiable examples of comic music per se.

But the comic infection that seriousness can so easily catch – and vice versa, as Poulenc attests – speaks to a broader point about the immanent instability of all positions. On one hand, this is an ahistorical philosophical point, available just as easily in Socrates tormenting his interlocutors in a Platonic dialogue as it is in Hegel's dialectical drama in *The Phenomenology of Spirit*, or the infinite metonymic dispersals of Derridean *différance*. But if it has often been the case philosophically that forms of identification and conceptualization are vulnerable to transformation and upheaval, this philosophical point then verges towards an almost unavoidable truth about lived experience during the times usually identified with musical modernism. For as the forces of modernity started exponentially to expand and metastasize as they reached the twentieth century, the world increasingly became characterized by dizzying cross-fertilizations that resulted in a global condition of radical, insomniac restlessness and instability in which we are still thoroughly enmeshed. Since instability is also a common marker of the comic, we might then reason that to talk in one breath of the age of modernism and comedy is to waste one's resources on a tautology, since the formal features of one are to all extents and purposes isomorphic with those of the other. Modernism, we might argue, is but the cultural symptom of a fundamentally comic modernity, and so the history of musical modernism can quite literally amount to the recounting of a joke. Take, for example, the case of the extraordinary relationship and correspondence (May 1949–August 1954) between Cage and Pierre Boulez. Here the mathematical seriousness of Boulez's explorations in integral serialism finds itself in bed with the Buddhist humour of Cage rolling dice; total control concludes in chance operations, thus giving birth to an unintended conflation of opposites, which, as Freud reminds us, is the source of all good jokes.

Modernism – out of the spirit of comedy

For those still beholden unto postmodern musicology's desire to pull the rug out from under what they perceive as the oppressive legacies that modernist musical cultures have bequeathed unto us, then to talk openly about the ridiculousness of modernist musical seriousness is to allow for postmodernism's own Nietzschean moment of opening the windows and letting in a bit of air. Nietzsche, after all, has been as regularly on the menu for postmodernism as he was for modernism. But postmodern discourse has perhaps too hastily identified with its desires in this regard. No doubt, to appropriate the famous words from one of Peter Porter's poems, 'the cost of seriousness will be death', and it is for these reasons that later in the poem it is asserted: 'Which is why the artist must play'.[48] And no doubt one of the great tragic ironies of the twentieth century is that it was precisely in this age of such staggering carnage and violence that the question of how to respond appropriately, and of how to inhabit seriousness, reached a certain crisis of confidence too. Yeats diagnosed the predicament with alarming precision as early as 1919 in 'The Second Coming', writing that 'The ceremony of innocence is drowned; / The best lack all conviction, while the worst / Are full of passionate intensity'.[49] But if the prevalence of comedy is, as I suggest, one of the symptoms of this crisis, its ineradicable supplement is silence and suicide. Adorno's famous assertion that '[t]o write poetry after Auschwitz is barbaric', and, moreover, that to do so is perhaps even fatal for poets themselves, is played out in horrifyingly literal terms in the suicides of writers who were Holocaust survivors, such as Paul Celan and Primo Levi.[50] And in Adorno's corpus, the validity of the inextricable bond between the horror of the concentration camps and the impotence and complicity of serious poetry faced with that broken reality is registered by the admiration he continued to uphold to the end of his life for Samuel Beckett, in whose work impossibly sad silences are to be found in the very cavity of the mouth that laughs.[51] Without an understanding of this vexed dialectic that the twentieth century brought to such a head between comedy and death, the pleasure taken in comic debasement becomes highly vulnerable to the *form* of cruelty. Comedy, after all, can indeed be exceedingly brutal. It exhibits a strikingly reliable tendency for co-opting laughter as a means of neutralizing the impact on our conscience of the violence that is perpetrated against others, inuring us to the valid reasons why others might indeed refuse to laugh, and thereby inuring us to their pain too.[52] The comic recourse that postmodern musicological squeamishness makes when faced with examples of modernism's non-negotiable seriousness thus quickly reaches its ethical and political limitations. The real problem has not been seriousness per se, but *how and when* to be serious, and in this regard we might pause on Slavoj Žižek's own critique of postmodern academic thought, which, in one of its moments, plays on Yeats's memorable lines.[53] Perhaps what we need today is rather a situation in which the worst lack all conviction whilst the best are full of passionate intensity.

In the twentieth century, one of the most extraordinary musical judgements to have been passed on comedy's complicity with cruelty comes from Nina Simone – a 'best' of passionate intensity if ever there was one. I refer to her famous 1964 protest song, 'Mississippi Goddam', written in response to the Mississippi murder of Megdar Evers and the death of four African American children in the 16th Street Baptist Church bombing in Birmingham, Alabama. As with Poulenc, her point is deathly serious, but we are seduced into engaging with it by means of comic bait. The song begins as if we were about to hear a bit of amusing music-hall shtick. Vamping on the spot to a mechanically inane oom-pah, Simone cracks an absurdist joke to loosen everyone up: 'This is a show tune, but the show hasn't been written for it yet.' In the recording of Simone's famous 1964 performance of this song in Carnegie Hall,[54] at a time when the song was unknown and had only been performed in public once before at the Village Gate in Greenwich Village, the audience laughs, as if settling down into their seats. Comedy puts everyone at ease; things are in place, just as they should be. But as the song proceeds, the inexorable vamping undergoes a kind of inverse transmogrification into a terrifying, predatory *perpetuum mobile*, and the music-hall banter becomes increasingly infected by ever more excoriating forms of furious address unambiguously directed at the audience. Through an accumulating refusal of compromise, this finally culminates in a proclamation: that 'this whole country is full of lies', and that 'you're all gonna die and die like flies'. At this point of excess, where the rage reaches a magnitude threatening to the very confines of the song's basic formal articulation, Simone snatches the whole thing away, as if it had merely been the chimera of some mad witch, and we return once more to the safety of the opening's comic vamping, which now, of course, seems repellent. It is as if we find ourselves with a knife in our hands and a seemingly innocent throat that we are being asked to slit. Indeed, the gothic melodrama of my image is not unwarranted, since the laughter that this music had initially inspired at the opening now literally gets stuck in *our* own throats, as the physical symptom of our guilt. Death by comedy: for Simone during the era of the civil rights movement, that perhaps seemed like a valid form of execution.

If Simone makes comic complicity the very topic of her song, it has also often been the theme in the reception of modernist musical works, as is captured nicely by the reception of Bertolt Brecht and Kurt Weill's *Die Dreigroschenoper* (*The Threepenny Opera*). As Stephen Hinton has shown, the reception of this work has been dogged since its earliest days by the following nagging question: 'how could a work of subversive tendency and high artistic merit attract such widespread public acclaim?'[55] In a letter written to Adorno soon after the première, Ernst Bloch, for example, noted that it is curious 'how the "gaiety" masks what is *épatant*. No-one boos, the house is sold out every night.' He then adds: 'even the *Friederike* audience is happy'.[56] *Friederike* refers to a piece of Franz Lehár's, and Bloch's invocation of it suggests that for certain critical intellectuals in 1928 operetta audiences were assumed to be incapable of digesting shocking political critique in the theatre. The question of operetta is also raised by Elias Canetti in his recollections of Berlin at the time of the first performances. As he states, 'An opera it was not, nor a send-up of opera, as it had originally been' – in other words, in John Gay's eighteenth-century *The Beggar's Opera*, on which *The Threepenny Opera* was modelled. Canetti continues: 'it was, and this was the one unadulterated thing about it, an operetta'.[57] Like Bloch, Canetti also works with the assumption that operetta audiences tend to seek consolation rather than confrontation. He talks of 'the saccharine form of Viennese operetta, in which people found their wishes undisturbed'. But for Canetti, the success of the work lay in the fact that Viennese light entertainment had been put into play with 'a Berlin form, with its hardness, meanness and banal justifications', which, he importantly concludes, 'people wanted no less, probably even more, than all that sweetness'. As a result, Canetti's assessment of the success of *The Threepenny Opera* is oddly similar to our diagnosis of the success of *Orpheus in the Underworld*, seventy years earlier: 'If it is the job of satire to castigate people for the injustice they represent and commit, for the misdeeds which turn into predators and multiply, then here, on the contrary, everything was glorified that one would otherwise shamefully conceal.'[58] So even if the precedent of Offenbach and mid-nineteenth century comic musical modes are not openly acknowledged or realized here, it can nevertheless be said that they are thoroughly active in practice.

If it is not important whether culture sustains a critical vigilance vis-à-vis its audiences, then there is nothing here to perturb. A modernist interest in comedy has merely provided one means of successfully forging a bond with an audience, and from the vantage of postmodern academic thought, that would usually be something to be celebrated. It would challenge the notion that '[m]odernism constituted itself through a conscious strategy of exclusion, an anxiety of contamination by its other: an increasingly consuming and engulfing mass culture'.[59] It would give salutary evidence of a bridge across what Andreas Huyssen famously termed 'the Great Divide', that modernist discourse from the mid-nineteenth century onwards conceptualized in order

Modernism – out of the spirit of comedy

to shore up a categorical distinction between the world of high art and that of mass culture. If indeed the potential origins of aspects of musical modernism in mid-nineteenth-century comic forms has tended to have been kept from acknowledgement, then that suggests that there have been those with a vested interest in keeping the discursive power inherent in that history from being activated. And there is no doubt that the vested interests of particular musical individuals, communities, institutions and musical practices have sometimes found camouflage in the seemingly universal validity of modernism's official claims. This said, this chapter nevertheless has no intentions of making a judgement one way or the other, since the sometimes spurious distinction between high art and mass culture can just as easily be a means of distracting from perhaps more far-reaching levels of analysis and critique. And so true to its comic proclivities, this chapter proceeds from the paradoxical position of a jolly pessimism. Regarding high art versus mass culture? Well, they've both got a lot of blood on their hands.

In this instance, what is perhaps more interesting than evaluating whether comic modernist works triumph or burn as a result of their popular appeal is the nature of the audience response itself and how that might be understood. In the case of Offenbach and Brecht/Weill, this response easily contradicts basic expectations regarding human narcissism, since the unflattering image that the comic mirror reflects back to those sitting before it in the theatre produces pleasure rather than the flinch of a wounding recognition. A traditionally conservative conclusion to be drawn would be that such indifference to criticism is the indicator of moral decline. And such a conclusion is not always unwelcome. After all, as I was originally writing this, Donald Trump stood as the Republican nominee for president of the United States of America – a man whose extraordinary cynical indifference to his own moral standard is not unrelated to a certain grotesque comic aptitude on his part and the evident appeal this engenders in those enamoured of him. As I finish editing, he is now the president. Not completely unlike characters in Offenbach and Brecht/Weill, Trump's is a performance that says 'I am crass, self-serving, racist, sexist, philistine and without moral sentiment'. And for a certain proportion of the American population who continue to support him, the response is sometimes: 'Great! We are too!' Maybe the ancient and enduring critique of comedy – that it trains us in the art of enjoying and thus imitating moral ugliness – is therefore not without wisdom.[60] If commentators such as Arpad Szakolczai are correct in noting an increasing 'commedification' of all aspects of the public sphere and an accompanying transformation of politics into farce, then certainly the ancient debate remains topical.[61] What is limited about the conservative line for our purposes, however, is that it does not make room for consideration of the pragmatic reasons *why* such an indifference to one's own shortcomings might start to seem necessary and attractive, rather than just being a symptom of lack of moral vigour, however much that can *also* be the case.

Certainly the appeal of indifference and its relationship to comedy circulates during classic periods of modernist activity. Bergson, in 1900 in his already mentioned *Laughter*, notes 'the *absence of feeling* which usually accompanies laughter'. As he continues: 'Indifference is its natural environment, for laughter has no greater foe than emotion.'[62] For Bergson, such thoughts were more charming than alarming, sustenance for an easy image of Apollonian utopia: 'In a society composed of pure intelligences there would probably be no more tears, though perhaps there would still be laughter; whereas highly emotional souls, in tune and unison with life, in whom every event would be sentimentally prolonged and reechoed, would neither know nor understand laughter.'[63] His conclusion is one that would continue to echo strongly, particularly in Parisian musical culture and the discourses of what we have come to call neo-classicism between the two world wars: 'To produce the whole of its effect, then, the comic demands something like a momentary anesthesia of the heart. Its appeal is to intelligence, pure and simple.'[64] If Bergson's marvellous conceptualization of comic indifference is, nevertheless, perhaps a little fey, another landmark essay of the period, the 1903 'The Metropolis and Mental Life' by the great German sociologist Georg Simmel, gets us closer to material pragmatics. For Simmel, one of the main challenges posed to the individual by modern social forms is how it can resist 'being levelled' and 'swallowed up in the social-technological mechanism'.[65] The modern metropolis, in which modernist art was predominantly produced, and which provided it with so much inspiration, nevertheless is a place that exacerbates the quota and rapidity of stimulation to such a degree that its inhabitants have to develop significant new skills in order to adapt and survive. And so 'the metropolitan type – which naturally takes on a thousand individual modifications – creates a protective organ for itself against the profound disruption with which the fluctuations and discontinuities of the external milieu threaten it'.[66] Because, according to Simmel, emotions are not quick enough to be up to the task, the metropolitan type therefore recalibrates itself, not completely unlike Bergson's laughers, towards a more intellectual mode. And the most characteristic psychic phenomenon of this modality for Simmel is the 'blasé outlook', whose essence 'is an indifference toward the distinctions between things'.[67] Since for the metropolitan there is no time for indulging in nuances and the specificity of the emotional reactions they engender, comedy, by definition, is its preferred mode. With roots stretching back to carnival, comedy is, after all, a great leveller of distinctions. This is borne out by the way jokes conventionally proceed by making a short circuit between two seemingly distinct things, so that a king becomes a pauper, or an idiot a university professor, the nuance of their specificities now, as it were, seen *sub specie indifferentiae*.

Evidence of an affinity for this kind of pragmatic indifference to nuance and distinction can be found all over the place in twentieth-century musical modernism, even in locations that are not, at first glance, immediately comic in and of themselves. For example, in Stravinsky's famous 1924 statement about his Octet, the assertion that the piece 'is not an "emotive" work' is then immediately elaborated by the statement that 'I have excluded from this work all sorts of nuances', and that, as a result, it cannot 'admit the introduction of the element of "interpretation" in its execution without risking the complete loss of its meaning'.[68] Admittedly, tone in Stravinsky can be difficult to gauge, a fact exacerbated by Stravinsky's virtuosic ability, musically and personally, to don masks. The potential joke lurking around Stravinsky's 'Mon Octuor' essay lies in the flagrant contrast in which its dictatorial 'objective' tone stands in relationship to the jolly, often very funny, musical antics of the Octet itself. Moreover, if the Octet is littered with stylistic references to a whole plethora of other musics, then so too the 'Mon Octuor' essay, which parodically co-opts the stylistic pose of modernist aesthetic manifestos and early twentieth-century logical philosophy, such as Wittgenstein's *Tractatus* (1921), in which argument proceeds by means of an unsentimental assertion of separate bullet points rather than the more continuous 'expression' of accumulating paragraphs. But the essay's latent humour should not distract us from a more far-reaching intimation, that Stravinsky is here conceptualizing the Octet *itself* as a kind of metropolitan being in Simmel's sense. If we acknowledge the threat posed to the city dweller who tries to feel all the distinctions by which he is bombarded, then likewise for Stravinsky a 'work created with a spirit in which the emotive basis is the nuance is soon deformed in all directions'. An emotive work risks being overtaken by others, notably performers; such music 'soon becomes amorphous, its future is anarchic and its executants become its interpreters'.[69] And so to protect itself from being so consumed, the Octet puts a wager on a certain autonomy to be purchased through the currency of indifference. Comedy is the stylistic symptom born of that pragmatic exchange.

Traces of Stravinsky's tendency towards conflating artistic order with an implied social order make their pressure felt strongly at such moments, bringing us close to the man who was attracted to Mussolini and fascism. Nevertheless, distasteful as this might be, my invocation of

Modernism – out of the spirit of comedy

Simmel should remind us that the question of how realistically the human is to sustain itself within late modernity's overawing complexities is a very real question whose answers remain vexed and uncomfortable. Assumptions that the right course of action in ethics and politics is always transparent, and that any straying from what has been deemed the only path of good is simply wrong, inform us of very little apart from the smugness of our ethical and political narcissism. In the same way that the convolutions of modernity sometimes lead, as we have seen, to modernists seeking seriousness anamorphically from the displaced vantage of the comic, then likewise, the very real challenges posed by modernity to the reality and conceptualization of the human as a social being has led to perfectly valid concerns coming into focus perversely, through the vantage of possibly repellent political ideologies. Once more, this bespeaks not only the ahistorical philosophical fact of the slippage inherent in any conceptualization and its application, but also this fact's exacerbation by the ongoing metastases of modernity itself.

Within the context of these concerns, I therefore suggest that the comic proclivities of modernist musical production be thought of as having provided audiences with new models for being in the world. Modernist comedy came to offer bearings within the strange shifting landscape left exposed in the wake of the demise of confidence in the more normative constructions of the human that had prevailed up to that point. The comforting notion that the human could be scripted as an individual being in which principles of thinking (reason) and feeling (emotion) balance themselves out in consonant counterpoint to larger social forms no longer rang true. And faced with this false note, modernists set about experimenting with other somewhat posthumanist notions: conceiving the human as a pre-rational, de-individuated collective being, as in primitivist works, such as Stravinsky's *Rite of Spring*; or as a kind of machine, as in Futurism; or as an animal, in Janáček's *The Cunning Little Vixen* (1921–23); or having passed over into the being of objects, as in Ravel's *L'enfant et les sortilèges* (1925); or, in Cage, as the Buddhist nothing at the centre of nature. Or, as I assert, as a comic being. Coming into view in the middle of the nineteenth century in works such as Offenbach's *Orpheus in the Underworld* and the audience practices such works drew upon and brought into being, modernism's comic being is one who practises a certain discipline of indifference towards the representation and reflection of its own moral and political shortcomings. Narcissistic identification with one's potential goodness is here replaced with identification with one's capacity for taking pleasure in the very ability to survive. And it is perhaps testament to the fraught conundrums of the twentieth century that one of the great paragons of such comic being came in the form of a speaking rabbit with crossdressing proclivities and an accent from Brooklyn, New York, the Mecca for all foreigners, exiles and immigrants: Bugs Bunny.

If modernity is a condition in which, in Marx's famous words from *The Communist Manifesto*, 'all that is solid melts into air', in which forces of communication and capital drive their way through localized forms of home and belonging, imposing complex new demands of adaptation on the beings who are trying to sustain their lifeworlds, then Bugs Bunny is a quintessential figure of modernity. Like a migrant worker, this rabbit exists in a condition of constant vagrancy. With each new episode he pops up in a new location where he must then attempt to survive; yet each new attempt is hounded by forces that seek his annihilation. The conclusion of each episode marks the beginning once more of his exile; the next episode is but a temporary and tenuous cessation of his unstable, nomadic life. If Bugs Bunny were to view his own existence emotionally he would, in Stravinsky's words, be 'deformed in all directions', traumatized. And so, as if he has been reading Simmel and Bergson, Bugs' most memorable and identifying reaction is a sign of indifference, of a blasé attitude, and of his fundamental anaesthesia of the heart. Faced with the shifting array of challenges with which his life presents him, the rabbit responds periodically with the same blank seen-it-all-before tag: 'What's up, doc?'

James R. Currie

This is meaningless punctuation, barely more than a fermata or quick breath snatched amidst the *perpetuum mobile* of the kinaesthetic gesticulation that constitutes the raison d'être of these otherwise oddly under-achieving narratives. In this sense it is more music and refrain than language and discourse. And as such it *is* funny. But if the medium is the message, and phlegmatic always the tone of the Rabbit's address, then the catchphrase courts an existential bleakness. A question is usually an intersubjective provocation; when the addressee responds, the social is activated. But in Bugs Bunny cartoons, when the question 'What's up, doc?' is posed, no one answers. Either it is never heard, as if at that moment all others disappear and the rabbit were alone, or at the moment when the rabbit speaks the question he himself disappears and becomes inaudible, the question merely echoing in some private interiority inaccessible to the other inhabitants of the diegesis. In either case, for the brief moment of its enunciation, the endless murderous chase in which Bugs Bunny finds himself pursued is put on hold; it is as if the indifferent affect of his catchphrase acts like a talisman and casts some minor spell. When the murderous other disappears, or when you the prey disappear from that other's perception, you are then safe. The blasé indifference with which the spell must be intoned may well be a puerile trick, like a child covering its eyes in order to hide. But in the world of Bugs Bunny, it works; it buys time. And from the short circuit that is made across the contrast between what had been our low expectations and the undeniable evidence of the trick's effectiveness, we laugh. This laughter, however, is close to the world of Samuel Beckett, since the price that has been paid for the indifference of 'What's up, doc?' to work is isolation: the rabbit is only safe for the moment in which he can create a virtual reality in which he is alone and no one else exists.

If Bugs Bunny were only this, the appeal of his comic indifference as a pragmatic tool for surviving modernity would be minimal. Even if one could develop the skills for making the spell of 'What's up, doc?' last longer, it is not clear that one would want to. As we have seen, 'What's up, doc?' courts isolation. But it also implies boredom, the blankness of its tone a prefigurement of the hoped-for answer: 'What's up?' 'Nothing's up!' Such indifference is a bargain made with meaninglessness for the sake of safety; it is the light humour of the quotidian in which no news is good news. And it is full of risk. For at any moment the forms that keep the peace might break: your pension fund might be annulled; a change in administration might rob you of your health insurance; a flood, tornado or oil company might destroy your domicile; or a human deranged by lack of home or finance or meaning might attack you for the small change in your wallet, or for no reason at all other than sheer unsupported rage. And then where will you be? Certainly too alone to have the luxury of practising arts of indifference!

It is interesting, thus, to note that Bugs Bunny, presented with the threat to his own life, is only anecdotally concerned to get away from the danger. Predominantly he seeks to see what opportunities are available for play, and more than once those opportunities are provided by music. Once more, to quote Porter, '[t]he cost of seriousness is death [. . .] which is why the artist must play'. In the 1950 cartoon *The Rabbit of Seville*, Bugs Bunny, fleeing for his life from pursuit by the ever trigger-happy Elmer Fudd, takes refuge in an open-air theatre where a performance of *The Barber of Seville* is about to take place. Bugs quickly out-manoeuvres Elmer. But instead of then cashing in on the advantage to make a break for it, he remains on site to torment the dumb Elmer through a series of outrageously virtuosic (mal)appropriations of Carl Stalling's condensed version of Rossini's overture, which, apart from a brief snippet of Mendelssohn's famous wedding march, constitutes the music. The ensuing intertextual mayhem finally concludes when, having undergone a split-second mock marriage to an Elmer in bridal drag, Bugs pushes Elmer off from high up in the flys and he lands in a wedding cake on which is written: 'The Marriage of Figaro'.

Modernism – out of the spirit of comedy

It is, of course, much to our advantage that Bugs sticks around to entertain us, but the question still remains as to why he doesn't just escape. In an incredibly touching *sui generis* essay, 'Improvisation in Homage to Stravinsky', the great Czech novelist Milan Kundera proposed that there was a link between Stravinsky's exilic status and his 'neo-classical' stylistic play. 'Without a doubt, Stravinsky, like all the others, bore within him the wound of his emigration; without a doubt, his artistic evolution would have taken a different path if he had been able to stay where he was born.' He then continues:

> In fact, the start of his journey through the history of music coincides roughly with the moment when his native country ceases to exist for him; having understood that no country could replace it, he finds his only homeland in music; this is not just a nice lyrical conceit of mine, I think it is an absolutely concrete way: his only homeland, his only home, was music, all of music by all musicians, the very history of music; there he decided to establish himself, to take root, to live; there he ultimately found his only compatriots, his only intimates, his only neighbors, from Pérotin to Webern; it is with them that he began a long conversation, which ended only with his death.[70]

When you can no longer go home, you have to stick around and play with what's available. This is as true for Stravinsky as it is for Bugs Bunny, who is something of a neo-classicist too, at least in *The Rabbit of Seville* and the 1957 *What's Opera, Doc?* But in the ongoing condition of modernity, with its forces of profound destabilization from which nobody can any more be guaranteed immunity, it is increasingly true for everyone. None of us are going home. Comedy, with its extraordinary aptitude for rapidity, and the lightness of touch with which it can manage to engage with what it encounters, makes for a most useful tool in this regard. And we might argue that in its ability to act as an anti-inflammatory for the heart, it thereby suggests how we might walk away with fewer scars than if we had found ourselves prone to acts of emotional gravity and so tripped up in our play.

Ultimately, the appeal of a Bugs Bunny, and perhaps of neo-classicism and modernist musical comedy in general, is that they offer us, amidst a fundamentally benighted contemporary human reality, productive fictions for how such survival might be achieved. Certainly these fictions come with hefty responsibilities; like any instruments, we must have a vision of what music we wish to make from them and for whom, and hence commit to the discipline of developing techniques to bring that performance into being. In this regard, Donald Trump is as much a comic genius as Francis Poulenc. Certainly, we cannot take comfort in the mere assertion, far too prominent in postmodern musicology, that by simply pooh-poohing modernist high seriousness we will put ourselves on the side of the angels. Such equations would only make sense if the radical destabilizations that are now the *sine qua non* of our condition and of the continuing forces of modernity itself had somehow never come to pass; and if postmodern musicology is in the business of trading in such wares, then it is more pre-modern than anything else, and thus a very dangerous, pseudo-medieval fantasy indeed. Certainly, modernist musical comedy in its dialectical sophistication, as I have sought to show, quickly gives the lie to such too easy identifications. For comedy is only as good as we are at wielding it. Anything more is simply grace, theological humour, which is perhaps the only time we get to laugh for free.

Notes

1 Lauren Berlant and Sianne Ngai, 'Comedy Has Issues', *Critical Inquiry* 43 (2017), 234.
2 Henri Bergson, *Laughter: An Essay on the Meaning of the Comic*, trans. Cloudesley Brereton and Fred Rothwell (Rockville, MD: Arc Manor, 2008), 11.

3 In musicology, one of the strongest proponents of this kind of postmodern comic ethics and politics was Wye Jamieson Allanbrook, who would frequently implore us to take guidance for dealing with the troubles of our own time from the jostling, democratic comic play that she so lovingly articulated in Mozart's stylistic language. With Allanbrook, analytic musical observations about comedy were thus often in close proximity to prescriptions about worldview: for example, 'With comic flux – the mixture of stylistic modes – comes a democracy of thematic material not possible in the monoaffective style of the Baroque'. See Allanbrook, 'Theorizing the Comic Surface', in *Music in the Mirror: Reflections on the History of Music Theory Literature for the 21st Century*, ed. Andreas Giger and Thomas J. Mathiesen (Lincoln: University of Nebraska Press, 2002), 203.

4 For an elaboration and critique of this kind of postmodern mode within musicology see my 'Music After All', *Journal of the American Musicological Society* 62 (2009), 145–203, and the preface ('A No-Music') to my *Music and the Politics of Negation* (Bloomington: Indiana University Press, 2012), xi–xviii.

5 For an excellent overview of anti-Romantic sentiment after 1848 and its repercussions on musical discourse see Sanna Pederson, 'Romantic Music under Siege in 1848', in *Music Theory in the Age of Romanticism*, ed. Ian Bent (Cambridge: Cambridge University Press, 1996), 57–74.

6 The classic articulation of the survival of Romantic music aesthetics in the generally anti-Romantic environment of the second half of the nineteenth century is Carl Dahlhaus's 'Neo Romanticism', in *Between Romanticism and Modernism*, trans. Mary Whittall (Berkeley: University of California Press, 1989), 1–18.

7 Karl Marx, 'The Eighteenth Brumaire of Louis Bonaparte', trans. Terrell Carver, in *Marx's 'Eighteenth Brumaire': (Post)modern Interpretations*, ed. Mark Cowling and James Martin (London: Pluto Press, 2002), 19. For more on the dialectical complexities of Marx's employment of comedy and on the powerful webs of literary and theatrical allusion in 'The Eighteenth Brumaire', see Martin Harries's excellent 'Homo Alludens: Marx's Eighteenth Brumaire', *New German Critique* 66 (1995), 35–64.

8 For an interesting investigation of the dialogue between past and present in Offenbach's oeuvre see Mark Everist, 'Jacques Offenbach: The Music of the Past and the Image of the Present', in *Music, Theatre, and Cultural Transfer: Paris, 1830–1914*, ed. Annegret Fauser and Mark Everist (Chicago: University of Chicago Press, 2009), 72–98.

9 The roots of postmodern forms of historical pastiche in earlier forms of modernism have been acknowledged since early on in the debates about the meaning and political valence of the postmodern. For example, in *Postmodern: The Architecture of the Postindustrial Society* (New York: Rizzoli, 1983), 35, Paolo Portoghesi reminds us that '[t]hose who fear a wave of permissiveness [in postmodernism's relationship to the past] would do well to remember that the ironic use of the quotation and the archeological artifact as an *objet trouvé* are discoveries of the figurative avant-garde of the twenties that have landed on the island of [postmodern] architecture sixty years late'. It has been rarer, however, to trace such roots back into modernism's immediate prehistory during the age of realism.

10 For an examination of the valence of the idea of the mirror for postmodern musical discourse, see my 'Postmodern Mozart and the Politics of the Mirror', in *Mozart Studies*, ed. Simon P. Keefe (Cambridge: Cambridge University Press, 2006), 214–42.

11 Siegfried Kracauer, *Jacques Offenbach and the Paris of His Time*, trans. Gwenda David and Eric Mosbacher (Cambridge, MA: Zone Books and MIT Press, 2002), 206.

12 The one notable exception in *Orphée* is John Styx's lament, 'Quand j'étais roi de Béotie' ('When I was King of Boetia'), whose affect, at least for Kracauer, 'is the sadness of one to whom the present means nothing, the past everything' (Kracauer, *Jacques Offenbach*, 208).

13 Still the most formidable of introductions to this aspect of Benjamin's work is Susan Buck-Morss's *The Dialectics of Seeing: Walter Benjamin and the Arcades Project* (Cambridge, MA, and London: MIT Press, 1989).

14 An excellent analysis of Adorno's crossed historical trajectories is to be found in Andreas Huyssen's 'Adorno in Reverse: From Hollywood to Richard Wagner', in *After the Great Divide: Modernism, Mass Culture, Postmodernism* (Bloomington, IN: Indiana University Press, 1986), 16–43.

15 Although, for Badiou, this is not without dialectical convolutions: 'I think the crucial point (as Hegel grasped long ago with regard to the revolutionary Terror) is this: the real, conceived in its contingent absoluteness, is never real enough not to be suspected of semblance. The passion for the real is also, of necessity, suspicion. Nothing can attest that the real is the real, nothing but the systems of functions wherein it plays the role of the real. All the subjective categories of revolutionary, or absolute, politics [. . .] are tainted by the suspicion that the supposedly real point of the category is actually nothing but semblance.' Alain Badiou, *The Century*, trans. Alberto Toscano (Cambridge: Polity Press, 2007), 52–53.

Modernism – out of the spirit of comedy

16 Linda Hutcheon, 'The Politics of Postmodernism: Parody and History', *Cultural Critique* 5 (1986–87), 185.

17 Carl E. Schorske, *Fin-de-Siècle Vienna: Politics and Culture* (New York: Vintage Books, 1981), xvii.

18 Among the many works that address this topic with regard to music, I would note Joseph N. Straus, *Remaking the Past: Musical Modernism and the Tonal Tradition* (Cambridge: Cambridge University Press, 1990), and more recently Tamara Levitz, *Modernist Mysteries:* Perséphone (Oxford: Oxford University Press, 2012).

19 Richard Taruskin, *Stravinsky and the Russian Traditions: A Biography of the Works through* Mavra, 2 vols (Berkeley: University of California Press, 1996). Taruskin has also, of course, approached the issues from the opposite position as well, arguing that it is precisely when the claim is being made regarding a direct connection to the past that what we are really dealing with is a masking of the present. See his superb 'The Pastness of the Present and the Presence of the Past', in *Authenticity in Early Music: A Symposium*, ed. Nicholas Kenyon (Oxford: Oxford University Press, 1988), 137–207.

20 For example, see Alexander Goehr, 'Schoenberg and Karl Kraus: The Idea behind the Music', *Music Analysis* 4 (1985), 59–71, and Allan Janik and Stephen Toulmin, *Wittgenstein's Vienna* (New York: Simon and Schuster, 1973).

21 Walter Benjamin, 'Karl Kraus Reads Offenbach', in *Walter Benjamin – Selected Writings*, vol. 2, part 1: *1927–1930* (Cambridge, MA: Harvard University Press, 2005), 110–12, Georg Knepler, *Karl Kraus liest Offenbach: Erinnerungen, Kommentare, Dokumentationen* (Berlin: Henschelverlag, 1984), and Edward Timms, 'Karl Kraus's Adaptations of Offenbach: The Quest for the Other Sphere', *Austrian Studies* 13 (2005), 91–108.

22 Admittedly, such speculations do not immediately resonate with Schoenberg's more typical scripting of Offenbach. As with Gershwin, Offenbach for Schoenberg is usually viewed in terms of the possibilities of an authentic popular music. So, for example, in the 1926 'New Music, Outmoded Music, Style and Idea', Schoenberg writes that 'there are a few composers, like Offenbach, Johann Strauss and Gershwin, whose feelings actually coincide with those of the "average man in the street". To them it is no masquerade to express popular feelings in popular terms. They are natural when they talk thus and about that.' Arnold Schoenberg, *Style and Idea: Selected Writings of Arnold Schoenberg*, ed. Leonard Stein and trans. Leo Black (London: Faber and Faber, 1975), 124. However, since such sentiments are also congruent with other aspects of Kraus's admiration for Offenbach, the connection remains feasible.

23 Carl Dahlhaus, *Nineteenth-Century Music*, trans. J. Bradford Robinson (Berkeley and Los Angeles: University of California Press, 1989), 228.

24 Kracauer, *Jacques Offenbach*, 206.

25 Translated by Leon Botstein in his 'The Enigmas of Richard Strauss: A Revisionist View', in *Richard Strauss and His World*, ed. Bryan Gilliam (Princeton, NJ: Princeton University Press, 1992), 3.

26 Edward Said, *On Late Style: Music and Literature Against the Grain* (New York: Vintage Books, 2006), 46.

27 Ibid., 45.

28 For a succinct account of some of the paradoxes (comic and otherwise) of Strauss's *Salome* success, see Alex Ross, *The Rest Is Noise: Listening to the Twentieth Century* (New York: Picador, 2007), chapter 1 ('The Golden Age: Strauss, Mahler, and the Fin de Siècle'), 3–35.

29 Considering how often comedy makes its pressure felt in Cage's artistic activities, it is relatively surprising that the topic of his potentially comic ethos has rarely been addressed directly and systematically. Taruskin's damning and provocative 'No Ear for Music: The Scary Purity of John Cage' argues ultimately that the comedy, whimsy and identification with Satie were the opposite of humour – a kind of terrifying control-freakism. Taruskin's piece first appeared as a review in *New Republic*, 15 March 1993, and was then reprinted in *The Danger of Music and Other Anti-Utopian Essays* (Berkeley: University of California Press, 2009), 261–79. Also of interest is Andre Mount's 'John Cage, Experimental Art Music, and Popular Television', *Music and the Moving Image* 3, no. 4 (2011), 31–56, which deals with Cage's televised performances and their humour, intentional and otherwise.

30 'Golliwog's Cakewalk' from Debussy's *Children's Corner* (1908) is a good case in point. Framed by the ragtime stylistic associations of the opening and closing sections, the middle portion of the composition presents hilariously lubricated quotations of the venerable opening of Wagner's *Tristan und Isolde* that are prefaced and punctuated by the most slapstick of circus antics, and whose oiliness makes them slide expressively towards the slightly seedy stylistic demimonde of a musical Montmartre. And yet the composition also totters questionably between celebrating, on the one hand, the triumph of popular and African American musics at the expense of Wagnerian pretentions, while, on the other, keeping such musics in a subjected position through the tacit assumption that the reduction of Wagner to their

level would, by definition, constitute an insult. For some interesting observations on the dialectics of the cakewalk in Debussy's piece, see Jody Blake's classic *Le tumulte noir: Modernist Art and Popular Entertainment in Jazz-Age Paris, 1900–1930* (University Park, PA: Pennsylvania State University Press, 1999), esp. 31, and also Michael J. Puri, 'The Passion of the Passacaille: Ravel, Wagner, *Parsifal*', *Cambridge Opera Journal* 25, no. 3 (2013), particularly 286–87; on the cakewalk, see Davinia Caddy, 'Parisian Cake Walks', *19th-Century Music* 30 (2007), 288–317; for a well-known examination of the relationship between Debussy and Wagner see Robin Holloway, *Debussy and Wagner* (London: Eulenburg, 1979).

31 Lightness as an aesthetic value has also prevailed within postmodern discourse, as is most touchingly attested by, among many other instances, the postmodern novelist Italo Calvino's celebration of the quality in the first of his Charles Eliot Norton Lectures, simply entitled 'Lightness', which he gave at Harvard University, 1985–86, and which were later posthumously published as *Six Memos for the Next Millennium* (New York: Vintage Books, 1993), 3–29.

32 Friedrich Nietzsche, *The Birth of Tragedy and The Case of Wagner*, trans. Walter Kaufmann (New York: Vintage Books, 1967), 165.

33 Friedrich Nietzsche, *Thus Spoke Zarathustra: A Book for All and None*, ed. Adrian Del Caro and Robert B. Pippin and trans. Adrian Del Caro (Cambridge: Cambridge University Press, 2006), 29.

34 My remarks here have been greatly influenced by Emanuele Senici's superb 'Verdi's *Falstaff* at Italy's Fin de Siècle', *Musical Quarterly* 85, no. 2 (2001), 274–310.

35 For more on Schoenberg, atonality, and the idea of floating, see Lydia Goehr, 'Adorno, Schoenberg, and the *Totentanz der Prinzipien* – in Thirteen Steps', *Journal of the American Musicological Society* 56, no. 3 (2003), 595–636.

36 György Ligeti, *György Ligeti in Conversation with Péter Várnai, Josef Häusler, Claude Samuel, and Himself* (London: Eulenburg Books, 1983), 53.

37 Cited in Martin Scherzinger, 'György Ligeti and the Aka Pygmies Project', *Contemporary Music Review* 25, no. 3 (2009), 237.

38 Richard Toop, *György Ligeti* (London: Phaidon, 1999), 80.

39 On the comic potential of the *Poème symphonique*, I am grateful to Nicholaus Emmanuel for his unpublished paper presented at the 2015 meeting (Louisville, KY) of the American Musicological Society: 'Meaningless Mechanicized Situations of Disrelation: Ligeti's *Poème Symphonique* as a Comic Reflection of Modernity'. On Ligeti and the Fluxus movement see Eric Drott, 'Ligeti in Fluxus', *Journal of Musicology* 21, no. 2 (2004), 201–40.

40 Nietzsche, *Thus Spoke Zarathustra*, 28. My emphasis.

41 Friedrich Nietzsche, *On the Genealogy of Morals and Ecce Homo*, trans. Walter Kaufmann and R. J. Hollingdale (New York: Vintage Books, 1989), 299.

42 Francis Poulenc, *Entretiens avec Claude Rostand* (Paris: René Juilliard, 1954), 143.

43 Christopher Moore, 'Camp in Francis Poulenc's Early Ballets', *Musical Quarterly* 95, nos. 2–3 (2012), 299–342.

44 Poulenc, *Entretiens*, 151.

45 See, for example, Michael Clark, 'Humor and Incongruity', in *The Philosophy of Laughter and Humor*, ed. John Morreall (Albany, NY: SUNY Press, 1987), 139–55.

46 Moore, 'Camp in Francis Poulenc's Early Ballets', 303.

47 Daniel Albright, *Untwisting the Serpent: Modernism in Music, Literature, and Other Arts* (Chicago: University of Chicago Press, 2000), 304.

48 Peter Porter, *The Cost of Seriousness* (Oxford: Oxford University Press, 1978).

49 W. B. Yeats, *Selected Poetry*, ed. A. Norman Jeffares (London: Macmillan, 1962), 100.

50 The famous line, which Adorno returned to later in *Negative Dialectics*, originally appeared in the 1949 essay 'Cultural Criticism and Society', in *Prisms*, trans. Samuel and Shierry Weber (Cambridge, MA: MIT Press, 1983), 34.

51 For example, see Adorno, 'Trying to Understand *Endgame*', *Notes to Literature: Volume 1*, trans. Shierry Weber Nicholsen (New York: Columbia University Press, 1991), 241–76.

52 For example, Mladen Dolar writes that 'Laughter is a condition of ideology. It provides us with the distance, the very space in which ideology can take its full swing. It is only with laughter that we become ideological subjects, withdrawn from the immediate pressure of ideological claims to a free enclave. It is only when we laugh and breathe freely that ideology truly has a hold on us – it is only here that it starts functioning fully as ideology, with the specifically ideological means, which are supposed to assure our free consent and the appearance of spontaneity, eliminating the need for the non-ideological means of outside constraint.' Cited in Alenka Zupančič, *The Odd One In: On Comedy* (Cambridge, MA: MIT Press, 2008), 4.

Modernism – out of the spirit of comedy

53 Slavoj Žižek, *Violence: Six Sideways Reflections* (London: Profile Books, 2008), 72–73.
54 *Nina Simone in Concert*, LP, Philips mono/stereo PHM 200-135/PHS 600-135 (1964).
55 Stephen Hinton, *Kurt Weill: The Threepenny Opera* (Cambridge: Cambridge University Press, 1990), 181.
56 Ibid.
57 Ibid., 192.
58 Ibid.
59 Huyssen, *After the Great Divide*, vii.
60 In the *Republic*, Socrates, for example, states that 'surely we don't want our guardians to be too fond of laughter either. Indulgence in violent laughter commonly invites a violent reaction.' Plato, *The Republic*, trans. Desmond Lee, 2nd rev. ed. (Harmondsworth, UK: Penguin Books, 1987), 144.
61 Arpad Szakolczai, *Comedy and the Public Sphere: The Rebirth of Theatre as Comedy and the Genealogy of the Modern Public Arena* (New York: Routledge, 2013).
62 Bergson, *Laughter*, 10.
63 Ibid., 10.
64 Ibid., 11.
65 Georg Simmel, 'The Metropolis and Mental Life', in *On Individuality and Social Forms: Selected Writings*, ed. Donald N. Levine (Chicago: University of Chicago Press, 1971), 324.
66 Ibid., 326.
67 Ibid., 329.
68 Quoted in Piero Weiss and Richard Taruskin, 'The New Objectivity', in *Music in the Western World: A History in Documents*, ed. Piero Weiss and Richard Taruskin (New York: Schirmer Books, 1984), 459.
69 Ibid., 459.
70 Milan Kundera, 'Improvisation in Homage to Stravinsky', in *Testaments Betrayed*, trans. Linda Asher (London and Boston: Faber and Faber, 1995), 97–98.

Bibliography

Adorno, Theodor W. 'Cultural Criticism and Society'. In *Prisms*, translated by Samuel Weber and Shierry Weber, 17–34. Cambridge, MA: MIT Press, 1983.
———. 'Trying to Understand *Endgame*'. In *Notes to Literature: Volume 1*, edited by Rolf Tiedemann and translated by Shierry Weber Nicholsen, 241–76. New York: Columbia University Press, 1991.
Albright, Daniel. *Untwisting the Serpent: Modernism in Music, Literature, and Other Arts*. Chicago: University of Chicago Press, 2000.
Allanbrook, Wye Jamieson. 'Theorizing the Comic Surface'. In *Music in the Mirror: Reflections on the History of Music Theory Literature for the 21st Century*, edited by Andreas Giger and Thomas J. Mathiesen, 195–216. Lincoln: University of Nebraska Press, 2002.
Badiou, Alain. *The Century*. Translated by Alberto Toscano. Cambridge: Polity Press, 2007.
Benjamin, Walter. 'Karl Kraus Reads Offenbach', trans. Rodney Livingstone. In *Walter Benjamin: Selected Writings*, vol. 2, part 1: *1927–1930*, edited by Michael W. Jennings, Howard Eiland and Gary Smith, 110–12. Cambridge, MA: Harvard University Press, 2005.
Bergson, Henri. *Laughter: An Essay on the Meaning of the Comic*. Translated by Cloudesley Brereton and Fred Rothwell. Rockville, MD: Arc Manor, 2008.
Berlant, Lauren, and Sianne Ngai. 'Comedy Has Issues'. *Critical Inquiry* 43 (2017): 233–49.
Blake, Jody. *Le tumulte noir: Modernist Art and Popular Entertainment in Jazz-Age Paris, 1900–1930*. University Park, PA: Pennsylvania State University Press, 1999.
Botstein, Leon. 'The Enigmas of Richard Strauss: A Revisionist View'. In *Richard Strauss and His World*, edited by Bryan Gilliam, 2–32. Princeton, NJ: Princeton University Press, 1992.
Buck-Morss, Susan. *The Dialectics of Seeing: Walter Benjamin and the Arcades Project*. Cambridge, MA, and London: MIT Press, 1989.
Caddy, Davinia. 'Parisian Cake Walks'. *19th-Century Music* 30 (2007): 288–317.
Calvino, Italo. 'Lightness'. In *Six Memos for the Next Millennium*, 3–29. New York: Vintage Books, 1993.
Clark, Michael. 'Humor and Incongruity'. In *The Philosophy of Laughter and Humor*, edited by John Morreall, 139–55. Albany, NY: SUNY Press, 1987.
Currie, James. 'Postmodern Mozart and the Politics of the Mirror'. In *Mozart Studies*, edited by Simon P. Keefe, 214–42. Cambridge: Cambridge University Press, 2006.
———. 'Music After All'. *Journal of the American Musicological Society* 62 (2009): 145–203.

———. 'A No-Music'. In *Music and the Politics of Negation*, xi–xviii. Bloomington: Indiana University Press, 2012.

Dahlhaus, Carl. 'Neo Romanticism'. In *Between Romanticism and Modernism*, translated by Mary Whittall, 1–18. Berkeley: University of California Press, 1989.

———. *Nineteenth-Century Music*, translated by J. Bradford Robinson. Berkeley and Los Angeles: University of California Press, 1989.

Drott, Eric. 'Ligeti in Fluxus'. *Journal of Musicology* 21, no. 2 (2004): 201–40.

Everist, Mark. 'Jacques Offenbach: The Music of the Past and the Image of the Present'. In *Music, Theatre, and Cultural Transfer: Paris, 1830–1914*, edited by Annegret Fauser and Mark Everist, 72–98. Chicago: University of Chicago Press, 2009.

Goehr, Alexander. 'Schoenberg and Karl Kraus: The Idea behind the Music'. *Music Analysis* 4 (1985): 59–71.

Goehr, Lydia. 'Adorno, Schoenberg, and the *Totentanz der Prinzipien* – in Thirteen Steps'. *Journal of the American Musicological Society* 56 (2003): 595–636.

Harries, Martin. 'Homo Alludens: Marx's Eighteenth Brumaire'. *New German Critique* 66 (1995): 35–64.

Hinton, Stephen. *Kurt Weill: The Threepenny Opera*. Cambridge: Cambridge University Press, 1990.

Holloway, Robin. *Debussy and Wagner*. London: Eulenburg, 1979.

Hutcheon, Linda. 'The Politics of Postmodernism: Parody and History'. *Cultural Critique* 5 (1986–87): 179–207.

Huyssen, Andreas. *After the Great Divide: Modernism, Mass Culture, Postmodernism*. Bloomington: Indiana University Press, 1986.

Janik, Allan, and Stephen Toulmin. *Wittgenstein's Vienna*. New York: Simon and Schuster, 1973.

Knepler, Georg. *Karl Kraus liest Offenbach: Erinnerungen, Kommentare, Dokumentationen*. Berlin: Henschelverlag, 1984.

Kracauer, Siegfried. *Jacques Offenbach and the Paris of His Time*. Translated by Gwenda David and Eric Mosbacher. Cambridge, MA: Zone Books and MIT Press, 2002.

Kundera, Milan. 'Improvisation in Homage to Stravinsky'. In *Testaments Betrayed*, translated by Linda Asher, 97–98. London and Boston: Faber and Faber, 1995.

Levitz, Tamara. *Modernist Mysteries: Perséphone*. Oxford: Oxford University Press, 2012.

Ligeti, György. *György Ligeti in Conversation with Péter Várnai, Josef Häusler, Claude Samuel, and Himself*. London: Eulenburg, 1983.

Marx, Karl. 'The Eighteenth Brumaire of Louis Bonaparte', translated by Terrell Carver. In *Marx's 'Eighteenth Brumaire': (Post)modern Interpretations*, edited by Mark Cowling and James Martin, 19–111. London: Pluto Press, 2002.

Moore, Christopher. 'Camp in Francis Poulenc's Early Ballets'. *Musical Quarterly* 95, nos. 2–3 (2012): 299–342.

Mount, Andre. 'John Cage, Experimental Art Music, and Popular Television'. *Music and the Moving Image* 3, no. 4 (2011): 31–56.

Nietzsche, Friedrich. *The Birth of Tragedy and The Case of Wagner*. Translated by Walter Kaufmann. New York: Vintage Books, 1967.

———. *On the Genealogy of Morals and Ecce Homo*. Translated by Walter Kaufmann and R. J. Hollingdale. New York: Vintage Books, 1989.

———. *Thus Spoke Zarathustra: A Book for All and None*. Edited by Adrian Del Caro and Robert B. Pippin. Translated by Adrian Del Caro. Cambridge: Cambridge University Press, 2006.

Pederson, Sanna. 'Romantic Music under Siege in 1848'. In *Music Theory in the Age of Romanticism*, edited by Ian Bent, 57–74. Cambridge: Cambridge University Press, 1996.

Plato. *The Republic*. Translated by Desmond Lee. 2nd rev. ed. Harmondsworth, UK: Penguin Books, 1987.

Porter, Peter. *The Cost of Seriousness*. Oxford: Oxford University Press, 1978.

Portoghesi, Paolo. *Postmodern: The Architecture of the Postindustrial Society*. New York: Rizzoli, 1983.

Poulenc, Francis. *Entretiens avec Claude Rostand*. Paris: René Juilliard, 1954.

Puri, Michael J. 'The Passion of the Passacaille: Ravel, Wagner, *Parsifal*'. *Cambridge Opera Journal* 25, no. 3 (2013): 285–318.

Ross, Alex. *The Rest Is Noise: Listening to the Twentieth Century*. New York: Picador, 2007.

Said, Edward. *On Late Style: Music and Literature Against the Grain*. New York: Vintage Books, 2006.

Scherzinger, Martin. 'György Ligeti and the Aka Pygmies Project'. *Contemporary Music Review* 25, no. 3 (2009): 227–62.

Schoenberg, Arnold. *Style and Idea: Selected Writings of Arnold Schoenberg*. Edited by Leonard Stein. Translated by Leo Black. London: Faber and Faber, 1975.

Schorske, Carl E. *Fin-de-Siècle Vienna: Politics and Culture*. New York: Vintage Books, 1981.

Senici, Emanuele. 'Verdi's *Falstaff* at Italy's Fin de Siècle'. *Musical Quarterly* 85, no. 2 (2001): 274–310.

Simmel, Georg. 'The Metropolis and Mental Life'. In *On Individuality and Social Forms: Selected Writings*, edited by Donald N. Levine, 324–39. Chicago: University of Chicago Press, 1971.

Straus, Joseph N. *Remaking the Past: Musical Modernism and the Tonal Tradition*. Cambridge: Cambridge University Press, 1990.

Szakolczai, Arpad. *Comedy and the Public Sphere: The Rebirth of Theatre as Comedy and the Genealogy of the Modern Public Arena*. New York: Routledge, 2013.

Taruskin, Richard. 'The Pastness of the Present and the Presence of the Past'. In *Authenticity in Early Music: A Symposium*, edited by Nicholas Kenyon, 137–207. Oxford: Oxford University Press, 1988.

———. *Stravinsky and the Russian Traditions: A Biography of the Works through* Mavra. 2 vols. Berkeley: University of California Press, 1996.

———. 'No Ear for Music: The Scary Purity of John Cage'. *New Republic*, 15 March 1993. Reprinted in *The Danger of Music and Other Anti-Utopian Essays*, 261–79. Berkeley: University of California Press, 2009.

Timms, Edward. 'Karl Kraus's Adaptations of Offenbach: The Quest for the Other Sphere'. *Austrian Studies* 13 (2005): 91–108.

Toop, Richard. *György Ligeti*. London: Phaidon, 1999.

Weiss, Piero, and Richard Taruskin, eds. *Music in the Western World: A History in Documents*. New York: Schirmer Books, 1984.

Yeats, W. B. *Selected Poetry*. Edited by A. Norman Jeffares. London: Macmillan, 1962.

Žižek, Slavoj. *Violence: Six Sideways Reflections*. London: Profile Books, 2008.

Zupančič, Alenka. *The Odd One In: On Comedy*. Cambridge, MA: MIT Press, 2008.

2

WHAT WAS CONTEMPORARY MUSIC?

The new, the modern and the contemporary in the International Society for Contemporary Music (ISCM)

Sarah Collins

> What could the substitution of the two small words, *modern* and *contemporary* – which had hitherto appeared to be interchangeable – contain that would prove so explosive?[1]

> All music that is temporary is contemporary.[2]

In 1955, Hans Keller described the concept of 'contemporary music' as 'largely illusory'.[3] His reasoning was as follows: all periods in music history have witnessed a conflict between an emerging epoch and an established or ageing epoch; this conflict arises from the very fact that epochs are contemporary to each other during the period of transition; so the idea of 'contemporary music' at any one time is merely an empty construct marked by the politics of two epochs vying for the authority of timeliness. Keller's examples focus on instances of non-contemporaneous intersections: J. S. Bach was considered out of date by his younger contemporaries, only to be admired later by modernists; the musical techniques associated with the development of atonality and serialism can be seen in the works of Mozart;[4] and Brahms was as much a 'contemporary' of Schubert as he was of Schoenberg.[5] For Keller, then, chronological categories tell us very little about musical developments, and the category of 'contemporary music' is one such category. In this type of account, the 'contemporary' is ineffective as a descriptive term, in that it cannot possibly encompass the extensive array of music being composed at any one time, and it is ineffective as a 'critical yardstick', because neither the sheer fact of newness nor public accolade (which might arguably indicate a closeness to 'contemporary life') are adequate measurements of value. In the absence of any real content, then, the term became simply a defensive gesture on behalf of a particular style of music to which the public had grown apathetic, and about which the critical discourse was woefully inadequate: 'The good old times fight the bad old times; and the good young times fight the bad old times; and everybody blames somebody. The only people who really profit by this state of transition are the bad composers.'[6]

The problem Keller identified extends beyond his immediate era of course, and he no doubt would have been bemused to read the first issue of the *Contemporary Music Review* in 1984 – a special issue on the 'musical thought' of IRCAM, which was implicitly presented as being representative of the 'new spirit' of 'contemporary music'.[7] Perhaps mindful of concerns similar to those articulated by Keller earlier, the guest editor Tod Machover took pains to assure the reader that IRCAM was not stylistically partisan, emphasizing the

> diversity of musical outlook [which] reflects quite clearly the current situation of contemporary music, where no single ideology is pre-dominant and where, in the best of cases at least, talent and message are valued more than adherence to this week's latest stylistic fashion.[8]

Tellingly, Machover went on to attribute this diversity to the 'neutrality of technology, which offers powerful tools for exploration and creation but does not orient the composer in any particular musical direction'.[9] Needless to say, the use of technology in artistic production is no more 'neutral' than the concept of the 'modern' itself,[10] and while the journal's originating aim to encourage critical discourse on new music was certainly in line with Keller's own ambitions, it clearly succumbed, at least in this inaugurating issue, to the precise dangers that he had outlined in relation to the category of 'contemporary music' three decades earlier – namely that *the 'contemporary' has a pretence of neutrality while in fact being intensely ideological.*

The ideology underpinning the general application of the phrase 'contemporary music' has undoubtedly favoured the progressive and the international, so that while there have been different periodizations of 'contemporary music' – with its beginnings usually made to coincide with various historical events or broader cultural trends after WWII – there does seem to have been a certain consistency in the types of musical developments to which it has been applied. For example, for Max Paddison the term 'contemporary music' implied a type of 'advanced' or 'progressive' music, and referred to such music composed after WWII,[11] and this was clearly also the perspective of the *Contemporary Music Review* in its early issues. And indeed in an article published around the same time, in the older journal *Perspectives of New Music*, Boulez himself used the term to refer to a type of music that audiences claimed to be incomprehensible, together with Foucault who positioned it within a history of art that self-consciously reflects upon its own language, structures and materials.[12] The lineage of the type of application described by Foucault and Boulez can be traced once again to that journal's first issue which, despite the emphasis in the title on 'New Music', declared itself a forum for the discussion of 'contemporary music'.[13] The first issue, in 1962, included contributions from Stravinsky, Krenek, Stockhausen, Babbitt, Carter and others, joining in one forum the discussion of developments from '12-tone music' to 'electronic music'. Similarly, when Rose Rosengard Subotnik described the 'challenge of contemporary music' in an essay of 1987, the challenges she described were those of a certain type of music that could be seen as a late-century continuation of, or response to, the compositional developments associated with Continental musical modernism.[14] This view has been further reinforced by recent reconceptions of musical modernism as an ongoing tradition.[15] The general usage of the phrase 'contemporary music', then, could see it apply with fairly equal efficacy to phenomena such as the 'second modernity' of 1980 described by Claus-Steffen Mahnkopf; the 'transformed' modernism of the 1970s described by Alastair Williams; or the second 'year zero' of 1945, followed by a renewed high modernism until the early 1970s, as described by Arnold Whittall.[16] Allowing for the differences in periodization, as well as the problematic entanglements of 'late' modernism, postmodernism and the transformed modernisms thereafter, it might be ventured that there is a general understanding of 'contemporary music' as referring to particular avant-garde musical developments after WWII, and implying a special association with the idea of the 'new' and the 'modern'.

Yet, as Keller implied, 'contemporary' is not a property of a certain type of music, but rather it is a form of temporalization, involving an activity of bringing different things into relation.[17]

Like all totalizing concepts – such as 'society', 'culture' or indeed 'twentieth-century music' or 'World Music' – the category of the contemporary has been highly malleable. It has not only been applied to progressive or experimental developments, but has also been utilized by reactionary forces, and in other areas of the arts, such as in the controversial change in name of the Boston 'Museum of Modern Art' to the 'Institute of Contemporary Art' in 1948. In a statement about the name change that became known as the 'Boston Manifesto', the organization described the term 'modern' as applying to art that had 'run its course' and had 'become both dated and academic'.[18] Modern art (and in particular the type of abstract art supported by its one-time parent institution MoMa) had become 'a cult of bewilderment' that 'rested on the hazardous foundations of obscurity and negation, and utilized a private, often secret, language which required the aid of an interpreter', and its tendencies towards dominance through mystification should be undermined by a move towards the more 'wholesome and permissive' category of the contemporary.[19] This change in name was highly politicized in the post-WWII American context, and the discourse that surrounded the change clearly drew on Cold War associations between artistic abstraction, Continental elitism and communism in McCarthy era politics. The content of the category of the 'contemporary', then, is strictly relational, depending very much on differing responses to the question: contemporary to what? And according to whom? Or, as Giorgio Agamben has put it, 'of whom and of what are we contemporaries?'[20]

In what follows, I will examine an earlier episode in the history of the category of the 'contemporary', from the British perspective of the International Society of Contemporary Music (ISCM) during the inter-war period. My purpose here is not to confirm the truism that all historical periods are experienced as contemporary to those living at the time. Rather, it is to suggest that while the specific limitations and tendencies associated with the category of the contemporary have been made to emblematize the historical conditions of the late twentieth century and the types of questions about art that arose from them, these tendencies were in fact already part of the discourse on the relationship between the modern, the new and the contemporary for decades prior, during a period of quite different historical conditions. Recognizing this genealogy also invites us to explore the link between recent critiques of the 'contemporary' and earlier anxieties associated with musical modernism.

After an examination of the various critiques of the category of the 'contemporary' I will draw these into a discussion of the particular challenges faced by the ISCM from the early 1920s until the mid-1940s. During this period there was a great deal of uncertainty about whether the organization would support all contemporary musical tendencies, or just progressive tendencies – an uncertainty which resulted in a disjunction between the ISCM's claims of aesthetic neutrality on the one hand and its members' own aesthetic alignments on the other. This period also saw a disjunction between the ISCM's aim to transcend national boundaries and remain politically neutral, while at the same time being structured in such a way as to foster competition between national sections in their bid for representation at the international festivals. It is my contention that these two types of disjunction were interrelated, allowing us to trace specifically how, during the inter-war period, the category of the 'contemporary' in music was made to lend its chimera of neutrality to the politics of internationalism. This discussion will show that there has been, and perhaps continues to be, a structural similarity between the problems associated with the notion of the 'contemporary' and those associated with the notion of the 'international', in such a way as to make the category of the 'international contemporary' an impossibility in both conceptual and practical terms, and in any case undesirable according to its own aims.

I focus on the British perspective of the ISCM for two reasons. First, because the British section played a particular role in the establishment and early administration of the organization: its first president was the British music scholar Edward Dent (who was important in the organization's early history for other reasons as well),[21] and the initial headquarters of the ISCM were in London. The British section also played a particular role in formulating the society's commitment to 'contemporary' music, in contrast to the more explicitly delineated category of *Neue Musik* supported by the Austrian and German sections. This difference reflected a significant point of confusion in the aims of the ISCM, and one that was never fully resolved, as we will see. The other reason for limiting our scope to the British perspective in what follows, rather than reaching for a broader survey, is that British music culture had a very particular relationship with the works of the Continental avant-garde, or with what might be thought of, by the time of the inter-war period, as an emerging 'canon' of musical modernism. There is often a 'narrative of belatedness' that emerges from discussions of the British reception of musical modernism in this sense, reinforcing the idea that it seemed to approach modernism as something that was not quite organic to its own culture.[22] This means that the idea of 'contemporaneity' – or something being 'of its time' – meant something quite specific in the British context.

By examining the British perspective of the ISCM, we see how the 'contemporary' became an inherently defensive posture. The contemporary was local and located – it was not international or ideal – and it was often only those who perceived themselves to be peripheral in relation to a centre, or belated in relation to something or somewhere more timely, who advocated the contemporary. The ISCM example shows how the category of the 'contemporary' has historically represented a desire to reduce the power of a dominant value system by democratizing the field, yet in its pursuit of neutrality and pluralism it refuses to name that which it is positioned against, making it vulnerable to ideological manipulation.[23] I will argue that the problems that have come to be associated with the term 'contemporary music' in fact have their origins in the inter-war response to pre-war modernism – a response whose underlying attitude of 'lateness' itself mirrors the 'non-historical fixity'[24] of post-WWII discourse on art.

The 'contemporary'

One of the reasons why the category of the contemporary has come to have a natural association with various historical moments after 1945,[25] in music as well as in the other arts, is that it seems to offer a way of describing a prevailing mentality of 'coming after' – of being post-war, post-modern, post-art and eventually, of course, post-history. One might also add – as Terry Smith has done in describing the conditions of possibility for 'contemporary art' – postcolonial, post-Cold War, post-ideological, transnational, de-territorialized, diasporic, and global.[26] Indeed, the idea that the contemporary has had an association with post-ness is enshrined in Smith's definition of the contemporary as 'multiple ways of being with, in, and out of time, separately and at once, with others and without them', leading to the conclusion that 'after the era of grand narratives, they may be all that there is. Indeed – who knows? – aftermath may last forever.'[27] In other words, the contemporary has come to demarcate a post-historical moment that implies neither a connection with an old nor the beginning of a new.

The category of the contemporary also depends upon an intensification of the process of globalization – a process through which it becomes increasingly possible to talk about some kind of shared 'contemporary' sensibility across borders. This link between the contemporary and globalization once again reinforces the impression that the category applies best to the post-WWII context. The concept might be said to have increasing legitimacy as the process of globalization intensifies, because as interconnectedness increases so does the possibility that more people come under the impression that they are living in something of a common time (the 'now') and a common place (the 'world').[28] On this point, Peter Osborne has argued that the contemporary is not only a historical fiction, but also a 'geopolitical fiction', noting that despite there being no 'actual shared subject-position from the standpoint of which [the contemporary's] relational totality could be lived as a whole', it pretends as if there were, projecting a temporal unity over a range of disjunctions in the experience of time and nowness.[29] This projected unity was particularly problematic in the context of colonialism, because the 'now' was measured from the perspective of the colonizer, and by this measure the contrasting 'now' of the colonized seemed early and primitive – it seemed, in this sense, non-contemporaneous. Osborne claimed that this fiction of temporal unity has indeed been increasingly supported by global interconnectedness, and that the idea of the global has been made possible by the reduction of culture to capital and exchange value. Commenting on a January 2010 issue of *e-flux*, which noted how the 'contemporary' had replaced the 'modern' to describe the art of today, Richard Meyer exhibited a similar concern:

> with this shift, out go the grand narratives and ideals of modernism, replaced by a default, soft consensus on the immanence of the present, the empiricism of now, of what we have directly in front of us, and what they have in front of them over there.[30]

Digital media also plays a role in this globalizing process of course, making Meyer's comment about the neutrality of technology similar to the kind of 'soft consensus of the immanence of the present' that the category of the contemporary seems to offer.

Given that part of the problem with the contemporary is that it presents the 'world' or 'globe' as a 'projected unity', both spatially and temporally, it is unsurprising that many of the criticisms that have been made of the concept bear a striking similarity to those levelled against internationalism. So just as Osborne's colonizers enforced their own version of the contemporary upon the colonized, so too does the 'soft consensus' required of internationalism seem to assume a common basis of equivalence (or a common exchange value) for the discussions involved to take place. Bruno Latour has highlighted this problem as being one of not recognizing the 'threat of multiple worlds'. He noted in particular that the idea that religion can be separated out from peace negotiations amounts to just this kind of assumption:

> When men of good will assemble with their cigars in the Habermas Club to discuss an armistice for this or that conflict and they leave their gods on hooks in the cloakroom, I suspect that what is under way is not a peace conference at all.[31]

As Latour implies here, any attempt to paper over the crucial non-equivalences makes such a soft consensus a chimera.

In a related sense, the problems associated with the category of the contemporary more broadly have come to be seen as emblematic of the overarching 'value pluralism' of postmodernism, whereby differing accounts of reality are accorded equal merit, or become equalized on the plane of capital. Accordingly, the category of the contemporary is open to just the same type of critique as has been levelled at value pluralism more generally, such as by David Clarke in relation to what he termed the 'Elvis-and-Darmstadt' realization, when one discovers the 'historically synchronous but aesthetically incongruous moments in twentieth-century music'.[32] Clarke criticized John Rockwell's book *All American Music* in that it conveys no tensions in the pluralist culture of high and low, simply 'celebrating a "happy babble of overlapping dialogues"'.[33] For Terry Smith, similarly, a definition of contemporary art as merely any art occurring in the present time was in no way useful: 'this pluralist happymix is illusory'.[34] Although Clarke was describing the values and ideology underlying the postmodern disavowal of the high-low divide in music historiography, the point holds true for the issue of contemporaneity more broadly, and his critique of the liberal humanist impulse to accord equal validity to instances of difference is relevant also to the consideration of the problem of the contemporary.[35] And in an even more recent iteration of this concern, the American art critic and theorist Hal Foster commented in his latest book that the 'paradigms' by which he investigates contemporary art

> imply that art is not merely a matter of disconnected projects. Put more strongly, [. . .] even if art is not driven toward any teleological goal, it still develops by way of progressive debate, and this means – why not say it? – that there is art that is more (and less) salient, more (and less) significant, more (and less) advanced. It sounds only fair to assume that artists can choose freely from a repertoire of subjects, themes, and forms, and that as a consequence all work is equal in interest or importance. To me that freedom is more like whateverness, and that equality is more like indifference.[36]

Pluralism also evokes belatedness, in that its emergence heralded, in Arthur Danto's famous phrase, 'the end of art' – namely the historical moment when everyday objects could be displayed in a gallery and considered art, at which point there ceased to be any special claim that could be made by the aesthetic.[37] In other words, value pluralism was implicated in the creation of a condition of post-ness in art.

From these strands of critique we can sketch three characteristics of the contemporary (conceived as an activity of temporalization, as opposed to a compositional technique or style):

1   The contemporary has an association with lateness, or a sense of coming after, though it fails to address the crisis of legitimation that attends belatedness.
2   The contemporary has an association with value pluralism, and is therefore incapable of advocating a viable alternative mode of being.
3   The contemporary has an association with the international in that it is a projected unity, yet it has no means of forging alliances across national boundaries. The contemporary is, in this sense, a 'soft consensus', which has the effect of undercutting the critical impulse that is required to engender historical change.

I will now turn to exploring how these three characteristics – as well as the types of critique that have attended them in the post-WWII context – were explicitly put at issue in the early history of the ISCM, during a period in which the categories of the new, the modern and the contemporary were anything but synonymous.

What's in a name? The new, the modern and the contemporary

In the period when the ISCM was first established in the early 1920s, 'atonal' music was quickly becoming the iconic modernist technique with which composers had to reckon, one way or another, if they were to signal their timeliness. In this context, there was an initial discussion about whether the Society would support all forms of music composed recently, or whether it would favour progressive music.[38] As Egon Wellesz recalled, it was in the winter of 1922 that he was approached by Rudolf Réti – representing a group of Viennese composers whom Dent described as 'mostly the pupils of Schönberg'[39] – with the idea of an international music festival at Salzburg. Dent surmised that Réti's idea was inspired by a series of modern chamber music concerts in Donaueschingen that had taken place in August 1921, with a second series planned for July 1922. Dent claimed that this series, involving Hindemith, Krenek, Hermann Scherchen and others, was the first instance of concerts devoted entirely to modern music after WWI, opening the way for the idea of an international festival of modern music. Out of the initial idea and the discussions of Réti and his Viennese colleagues, just such a festival took place a week after the end of the Donaueschingen series, in August 1922 in Salzburg, and the ISCM was formed at a meeting immediately following the festival.

Given the context for the ISCM's establishment, and the figures involved in the initial idea, it seemed likely that the organization would be founded on principles in line with the prevailing aesthetic tendencies of the initiating group, yet as discussions about the name, structure and remit of the organization progressed, a more non-partisan aim gradually gained dominance. This drive towards being non-partisan was reflected to an extent in the decision to locate the headquarters of the ISCM in London, which was seen as a more neutral option by all, at least according to Dent. Dent insisted that the suggestion of London as the ISCM's headquarters was not made by the British group, but rather reflected the incapacity of the Austrian and German sections to overcome local politics, both professional and stylistic:

> we had all taken for granted that the only centre could be Vienna, as the whole movement had been started there. But we had reckoned entirely without the bitter jealousy between Vienna and Berlin, a hostility far intenser than any remnant of Franco-German war-hatred. Berlin would not tolerate Vienna as a centre, and we all felt that neither Berlin nor Paris were appropriate at the moment. Neither Switzerland, Belgium or Holland were considered acceptable; the Americans solved the problem by proposing London, which was agreed to unanimously, with the solitary exception of Réti. I felt a very genuine sympathy with him. The Americans were very properly determined to make Europe realize that America – and not merely the United States – was a musical continent, and they felt that London was the most convenient link between the two worlds.[40]

Despite the invocations of neutrality, then, it is clear that the choice of London was a part of an unspoken agenda to dilute the dominance of the Austro-German sections of the Society.

The internal politics surrounding discussions about the aesthetic remit of the organization were also reflected in the different titles attributed to the organization across its different founding national sections. In English, the Society's title was International Society for Contemporary Music; the French section also agreed along similar lines, with Société Internationale pour la Musique Contemporaine; but in German the title was Internationale Gesellschaft für Neue Musik.[41] Needless to say, the divergence could have been easily mitigated by the German section agreeing to 'Internationale Gesellschaft für zeitgenössische Musik', or the British section agreeing to 'International Society for New Music'. The other option, of course, would have been to use the word 'modern', as in Gesellschaft zur Förderung der modernen Musik. The implications of these differing titles seemed deliberate enough to prompt Adorno to speculate that the proliferation of the use of the term 'neue Musik' to indicate a certain type of music was in fact due to the German title of the ISCM, an organization that he viewed as aiming to

> foster every trend in music which was making efforts to distance itself from the New German school, from Impressionism and from the vestiges of other nineteenth-century tendencies. Just how adventitious that name was is revealed by the English title of the very same organization, the International Society for Contemporary Music (ISCM), which replaces the polemical 'new' with the neutral, chronological 'contemporary'.[42]

The types of historiographical politics bound up with translation of the terms used in the various titles of the organization can be seen very clearly even in the comparatively more recent case

What was contemporary music?

of the English translation of Carl Dahlhaus's use of the term 'Neue Musik' – with a capital 'N', indicating more than mere chronological newness – in his text *Die Musik des 19. Jahrhunderts* (1980), translated into English as *Nineteenth-Century Music* in 1989 by J. Bradford Robinson. Matthew Riley has traced the ambiguities created by the English translation of Dahlhaus's book, noting that while Dahlhaus used the term 'Neue Musik' to describe the stylistic developments now associated with the modernist canon – namely radical developments in music after 1910, including those associated with the Second Viennese School, Stravinsky, and early developments in serialism – he used the term 'musikalische Moderne' to describe an earlier period of musical radicalism that was distinct in character, from the 1890s to just before WWI, involving the works of Strauss and the early works of Schoenberg. The nuances involved in this shift in periodization and the ideological leanings that underpinned it had implications for the translation:

> since this 'Neue Musik' approximates rather closely the traditional English-language textbook meaning of 'modernism' or 'modern music', Robinson has still more problems of translation. He tries several phrases for 'Neue Musik', including 'contemporary music', 'modern music', 'twentieth-century modern music' and 'modern twentieth-century music', thus obscuring Dahlhaus's clear distinction between 'musikalische Moderne' and 'Neue Musik', and, still more importantly, obscuring the basic stability of the category 'Neue Musik' in Dahlhaus's thinking. Even using the English phrase 'early modernism' for 'musikalische Moderne', as some writers have done, significantly distorts Dahlhaus's meaning. That he might have referred to Richard Strauss's music of the 1890s as 'frühe Neue Musik' [early new music] is unthinkable. But from Robinson's translation one gets the impression that there is a progressive movement in twentieth-century composition called 'modernism' or 'modern music' that begins in 1889. This point matters. One of the German commentators on Dahlhaus, Walter Werbeck, observes that 'Moderne' is a good label for the period around 1900 precisely because of its 'value-free neutrality'. I'd suggest that, in English, the term 'modern*ism*' is not value-free or neutral.[43]

That the task of translation here might involve searching for a 'value-free term' is a crucial point, because this is just what the ISCM purportedly wished to do by using the term 'contemporary music' in 1922, at least from the perspectives of the British and French sections. By contrast, the use of the term *Neue Musik* in the German title indicated their more explicit distance from inter-war neo-classical tendencies and, more controversially, from the use of modal inflections derived from folk music, which some viewed as being more accessible to audiences. For example, in reflecting upon the criticisms of the twelve-tone technique in 1947, Schoenberg noted that while he could happily ignore criticisms that proceeded from the 'pre-Wagnerian horror of dissonances' and the 'more romantic and sentimental reproach of cerebrality', it did concern him that there were many younger composers opting for modal harmonies in order to avoid chromaticism, a shift which seemed to him to be the wrong type of progress: 'what contemporary music based on modal principles I have heard sounded to me more a melodic mannerism than an expression of new tonal configurations'.[44]

Anton Haefeli observed that the different title of the organization was more than a semantic issue – rather, it reflected the confusion of 'aesthetic convictions' ('ästhetischen Bekenntnisse') among its members.[45] Haefeli pointed to a document titled 'The Objectives of the ISCM' from 1923, in which Dent wrote that the guiding principle of those who founded the Society was indeed to pursue 'groundbreaking trends in music', yet Haefeli also noted that this remit was never officially defined by the General Assembly of the ISCM, because what constituted 'groundbreaking trends' was felt to be different in different countries, and in any case it was thought that those who were committed to it could discern its 'spirit' in its different iterations. In a later declaration at the ISCM festival in Prague, in 1935, the General Assembly seemed to offer some formality to this ambiguous observation, with the equally ambiguous and somewhat circular idea that the organization would promote music that 'conformed to the spirit of the organization'.[46] And by 1937 the ISCM declared its 'goals' as being to

> foster meritorious contemporary music without prejudice as to the composer's nation, race, political opinions, or religion; to protect and lend support to new or particularly challenging research streams; to represent and safeguard in the best way possible the shared interests of contemporary composers.
>
> The expression 'modern music' must be defined by each national section regarding its own activities. For the Society as a whole, the decision must be given by the General Assembly of Delegates.[47]

The idea that the separate national sections were to decide what constituted 'modern music' according to their national contexts seems to undercut the value of the term 'contemporary', which for Dent, at least, was a category that could transcend the cultural nationalisms that drove major international conflict. On a practical level, the 'contemporary' provided an apparently non-partisan category that seemed to offer an equalization of the playing field and to ensure that emerging composers, regardless of their nationality or style, would have an international forum in which to present their new work. Dent wrote of the difficulty in seeking out the most 'cosmopolitan' musicians for the international jury for each ISCM festival – by which he meant jury members who could assess the submitted compositions without overt national or stylistic bias.[48]

For Dent, another important aim of promoting 'contemporary music', in the sense of music by living composers (as opposed to what he called 'dead art', though more descriptively than pejoratively), was to create support for a continuing community of composers, regardless of national affiliation, and provide them with opportunities for their works to be performed. Supporting a contemporary musical culture was in this way designed to support international cohesion for very practical reasons, and Dent's argument against anyone who avoided contemporary music because it was not guaranteed of being 'good' was that:

> It is not a question of its being better music or worse music. Contemporary music, like any other form of contemporary art, is the *expression of our own time*, and if we took a real interest in it, it would mean the linking-up of more and more members of the community in sympathy of aspirations.[49]

So here we see Dent invoking the idea that the realization that 'we' inhabit a shared present moment (namely '*our*' own time) will result in a shared set of aspirations and reduce partisan conflicts. This statement may have made sense in 1921 when he wrote it, but, as we will see, the question of *whose* version of the contemporary constituted an expression of '*our*' collective time became an increasingly contested issue in the 1930s.

The Constitution (now embodied in the 'Statutes') of the ISCM has continuously specified that the purpose of the organization has been to promote contemporary music with no regard for nationality or politics, and although there was a preponderance of 'new music' or progressive music in the organization's early festivals, because of the overriding strength of the Austrian and German sections in the 1920s, Dent himself at least was very keen to maintain a non-partisan aesthetic policy. This posture was reinforced by associates of Dent such as Egon Wellesz, who later wrote in a clearly defensive tone that:

> It would be wrong to connect any single movement in modern music exclusively with the aims of the ISCM; the aim of the society must be to give a universal view of the tendencies in music at the moment of a festival. Otherwise it would lose its contact with the new developments in music and would have to be replaced by another society to represent the spirit and aims of a new generation of composers.[50]

Later in the same article Wellesz admits that the society, 'above all in the twenties, favoured works of an experimental character', though he claims that these were still the *nuove Musiche* of our time, and in promoting this kind of music, the International Society 'took the place of the Italian courts of the early seventeenth century, which encouraged Caccini, Peri, Monteverdi and their contemporaries'.[51] Similarly, Rollo Myers sought to reinforce this aspect of aesthetic neutrality in the first and only issue of the ISCM's own journal, *Music Today*, published in 1947. In his editorial introduction Myers declared the Society's success in its aim to

> [bring] to light music of all shades and tendencies by contemporary composers, both known and unknown, and selected on their merits by Juries of musicians of international standing [so that] the ISCM would seem to have fully justified its existence.[52]

In reality, of course, the Society's origins and founding members made it particularly sympathetic to progressive music during the 1920s at least, and the fact that it was structured as a federation of national sections, all competing for the selection of their works by an international jury, meant that a section was more likely to have works performed if it included in its submission the work of established composers, who were more competitive against the submissions of other national sections.

A concrete example of the Society's refusal to waver from its avowed position of aesthetic and political neutrality has been described in detail by Anne Shreffler.[53] In brief, the 1935 annual festival of the ISCM was to be held at a town in then Western Czechoslovakia called Karlsbad (now Karlovy Vary, in the Czech Republic). Karlsbad had a large population of ethnic Germans, some of whom supported the political agenda of the German nationalists and others who were sympathizers of the Nazi regime. Karlsbad was part of the Sudetenland area of Czechoslovakia, which was annexed by Nazi Germany three years later in 1938 as part of the Munich agreement of the Western allies to try to appease Hitler. The problem for the ISCM in 1935 was that there had been increasing public support in Karlsbad for the Sudeten German Party, which indeed gained 60% of the Sudeten German vote in the parliamentary elections of 1935. Preparations for the festival had been proceeding smoothly, but only a few months before the event was to take place, the city authorities published a notice in the newspaper to the effect that the festival had been cancelled. In Shreffler's account, the cause of the cancellation was specifically linked to the gain in support for the Sudeten German Party, which was backed by the National Socialists and which had an explicit interest in complying with Nazi aesthetic ideology. In this context, a music festival containing a large number of atonal and twelve-tone works by composers who included Jewish German emigrants fleeing persecution suddenly seemed like a less attractive prospect. The programme for the festival was to include the world premiere of Anton Webern's Concerto for Nine Instruments Op. 24, Arnold Schoenberg's Variations for Orchestra Op. 31, and Alban Berg's Symphonic Pieces from *Lulu*. There were also works by other exiled composers such as Eisler, Scherchen, Heinrich Jalowetz, Rudolf Kolisch, Wladimir Vogel and Eduard Steuermann.[54]

The organizers scrambled to have the festival moved to Prague, but the Czech Philharmonic Orchestra were on summer vacation and would not be back in time, and there were a number of other 'practical obstacles' to it being held in Prague.[55] Then Hanns Eisler, who had been exiled from Austria and was living in Moscow working for the Comintern's International Music Office, offered the possibility of holding the festival in the Soviet Union, with costs, orchestra and venues provided. Dent, acting on behalf of the ISCM, turned down Moscow's offer, and made renewed diplomatic moves to 'appeal to the artistic, national and international prestige of Czechoslovakia'.[56] The Czech government responded well to these appeals and became involved, with a representative of the prime minister coordinating discussions between artistic organizations and finally agreeing to host the festival in Prague after all. The orchestral musicians even came back a week early from their summer leave to play in the festival. Outlining the political stakes involved in the decision to host the festival, Shreffler noted that:

> The political pressures on the Czech government were clear. To allow the festival to be snatched up by the USSR after being rejected by the Sudeten Germans of Karlsbad would look too much like fleeing into the arms of Moscow.[57]

Given this tense political context, the type of music performed at the festival and the emigrant status of some of the composers whose music was to be performed would have been viewed as an intentional affront to the aesthetic ideology of the Nazis, even though the ISCM was avowedly a non-political organization. It was certainly read this way when Karlsbad rejected the festival, and it also appeared this way in relation to another festival that was run at precisely the same time – the festival of the Nazi-backed Permanent Council for the International Cooperation of Composers, whose president was Richard Strauss. The Permanent Council had been set up the year before in 1934, a move that was viewed by some as a direct challenge to the authority of the ISCM.[58] While the ISCM was thought to be 'democratically' run, with all sections being involved in electing the international jury for each festival, the Permanent Council was run in a dictatorial style by Strauss, who had sole power of appointment of other members of the organization.[59] Furthermore, the Permanent Council wished to move the focus from the 'contemporary' to the role of music in cultivating and reflecting national character.[60]

The upshot of these various political and aesthetic pressures was that the ISCM was forced into undertaking some soul-searching in 1935 about what its aesthetic and political parameters were going to be, and whether it was going to condemn the actions of the Permanent Council, and the Nazi regime that backed it, and commit itself explicitly to supporting progressive music as part of this open condemnation. At the Prague festival the General Assembly of the ISCM did not pass a proposed resolution to condemn the rival festival of the Permanent Council, but it did make the first statement in its history that might be viewed as overtly political. Shreffler, citing Haefeli, explains:

> The proclamation, written in French (the official language of the Society), states that the ISCM's primary aim is to defend the cause of 'the most vital' (les plus vivantes) modern music. [. . .] Furthermore no discrimination on the basis of nationality, race or religion would be tolerated as long as the creative work conformed to the spirit of the organization.[61]

This statement allowed the ISCM to tacitly reject Hanns Eisler's calls for the Society to support the Popular Front of the Soviets against Fascism on the one hand, while also avoiding

What was contemporary music?

Ernst Krenek's calls for the organization to explicitly reject social and commercial commitment by embracing only the most progressive music. And it was not only Eisler and Krenek who had adjured the ISCM to articulate its position more clearly: critics such as Michel-Dimitri Calvocoressi, writing for the *Musical Times* and quoting from André de Blonay in the *Schweizerische Musikzeitung*, argued that '[t]he ISCM must work its own salvation [sic], by pursuing a liberal, firm, yet tactful policy, and all those who believe in spiritual independence for artists must help'.[62]

At the ISCM festival in Paris, two years after the Prague festival at which the society committed itself to the most 'vital' trends in contemporary music though failed to explicitly condemn the actions of the Nazi regime, the General Assembly seemed to go ever so slightly further in this direction by passing a resolution to include in Article 3 of the Statutes the words

> The ISCM aims at furthering contemporary music, regardless of creeds, politics or nationality, especially the inaccessible and problematic tendencies, whilst guarding the interests of the living composers.

This remark seemed to draw the Society more explicitly away from the doctrine of Socialist Realism, and from the commercial spheres. Its aim, then, seemed to be about protecting the type of music that was not pleasing to audiences – or, in other words, the type of music that 'needed' protecting. Crucially though, as Anne Shreffler has pointed out in a footnote, the phrase 'especially the inaccessible and problematic tendencies' only appeared in the German translation of the ISCM Statutes, not in the English, French or Italian versions, serving only to continue the nationally determined 'aesthetic convictions' regarding *Neue Musik* and 'contemporary music' that had beset the organization since its inception.[63]

While these divisions reflect a clear absence of consensus within the organization on matters of crucial importance to the remit of the ISCM itself, it is true that the German section had withdrawn from the society in 1933, and there were bans on the membership of occupied countries from 1938 to 1941. When the German section applied for re-entry into the ISCM in 1947, the ISCM meeting of delegates did finally carry a motion that marked out a more overt policy, at least in relation to one form of state intervention:

> The ISCM is willing to consider the application for the admission of a German Section when the German musicians shall have succeeded in forming one in accordance with the ISCM Statutes. It is understood that the principle of the exclusion of Nazis will be followed.[64]

Yet this statement was still only confined to the question of whether the German section could re-enter the organization. The broader question of whether the Society would actively reject any form of state or politically motivated intervention into the work or lives of musicians was at this time, it would seem, never clearly enshrined in the Statutes at a more general level.[65] In this way, the ISCM struggled with the broader problem of the supposedly 'neutral' category of the 'contemporary', suggesting that while a non-partisan stance may have been highly constructive in some contexts (such as in democratizing and internationalizing the field), it became increasingly problematic as the political environment became gradually more polarized. I will turn now to discussing the nature of the problems presented by the operation of the category of the 'contemporary' in this context.

Sarah Collins

The lateness of the contemporary, and the legitimation crisis

The contemporary is the untimely.[66]

I mentioned at the outset that the problem of the contemporary in the ISCM drew our attention to the sense of belatedness that characterized the milieu from which the organization was initiated. The cause of this belatedness was captured by Raymond Williams in one of his final public lectures. The lecture was titled 'When was Modernism?', capturing the retrospective mode that he was seeking to historicize. Williams explicitly addressed this aftermath position, calling it the 'non-historical fixity of *post*-modernism', and attributing it to the failure of modernism's dissident stance through its tendency towards border crossing, or its internationalist agenda:

> What quite rapidly happened is that modernism lost its antibourgeois stance, and achieved comfortable integration into the new international capitalism. Its attempt at a universal market, trans-frontier and trans-class, turned out to be spurious. Its forms lent themselves to cultural competition and the commercial interplay of obsolescence, with its shifts of schools, styles and fashions essential to the market. The painfully acquired techniques of significant *dis*connection are relocated, with the help of the special insensitivity of the trained and assured technicists, as the merely technical modes of advertising and the commercial cinema. The isolated, estranged images of alienation and loss, the narrative discontinuities, have become the easy iconography of the commercials.[67]

The situation described here by Williams was undoubtedly driven by the increasing institutionalization of modernist art after WWI, and the fashionable status of some of its central protagonists – factors which fuelled a latent scepticism about the level of sincerity in modernist art. One of the consequences of the self-awareness of this problem in the early twentieth century was what might be termed, after Jürgen Habermas, a 'legitimation crisis', which Steven Connor also described in terms of 'the fact that there no longer seems to be access to principles which can act as criteria of value for anything else'.[68] The crisis of legitimation is of course consequent upon the claims to autonomy and alienation of modernist art itself and the cultural and institutional forms that supported it,[69] yet it also springs directly from the realization that the meaning or significance of present experiences can only be grasped in retrospect, with the passing of time, and that any attempt at contemporary self-understanding is doomed to be hopelessly idiosyncratic. Or as Connor put it:

> in trying to understand our contemporary selves in the moment of the present, there are no safely-detached observation-posts, not in 'science', 'religion', or even in 'history'. We are in and of the moment that we are attempting to analyse, in and of the structures we employ to analyse it.[70]

The problem of the belatedness of knowledge in relation to experience became a persistent preoccupation for some British artists in the inter-war period, leading to this period being theorized as 'late modernism', at least with respect to literature.[71] While 'late modernism' in music is, like the 'contemporary', a label generally applied to a post-WWII period, I will argue elsewhere that a fuller recognition of how the preoccupation with lateness operated upon the British music consciousness of the inter-war period reveals a close alignment with the kinds of concerns that have been so persuasively identified in the literary sphere.[72] Philip Rupprecht has also noted how belatedness was a longstanding feature of the British response to musical modernism more generally.[73]

Recognizing that a sensibility of lateness and a crisis of legitimation were noteworthy characteristics of the inter-war British cultural sphere provides an additional context for the types of concerns that undergirded the initial formation of the ISCM. During this period, questions about the basis for a critic's authority became a common trope of British music criticism, as did calls for reform to criticism based on whatever authority was decided upon – be it the critic's special sensibility, or their level of specialization, or recognition by the profession or the readership. With the idea of the rational progressive development of music having been largely discredited during the pre-war years, many in the inter-war period worried at the absence of a consensual set of values with which to distinguish genuine change from mere novelty. Indeed, in a striking pre-figuring of Keller's pithy comment that 'all music that is temporary is contemporary',[74] some of the language that was used against the idea of contemporaneity itself in the inter-war period directly linked it with an absence of sincerity, almost by definition:

> It appears a little absurd when a work written twenty-five years ago is tacitly discarded because a different manner is in fashion. The point of view treats music as something ephemeral, which to-day is and to-morrow lights the kitchen fire, a point of which is fatal to artists, whether they are the makers of art or the receivers of it. It is the great invader of sincerity. [. . .] Sincerity may be evidenced by the refusal of fashion. There are no rules for finding it, but there is a safe rule for missing it, and that is over-eagerness for the very latest thing.[75]

In a similar expression of the belatedness of the idea of the 'contemporary', in an article about the ISCM festival in 1938 in London, Ernest Newman vented his frustration at the claims of the contemporary associated with the Society. He wrote that clearly the phrase 'contemporary music' did not mean simply recent music – it implied something specific about style – but yet that there was such a plurality of approaches to tradition and innovation in the Society's programmes that it was unclear what the parameters of the 'contemporary' were. For Newman, contemporary composers contradicted each other about the extent to which, for example, music should contain themes, be melodic, use a twelve-tone row, or use quarter-tones. Despite this plurality, Newman sensed that there was in fact a distinction that was pervasively made between what should and should not count as progress. Diverging from the usual trope of questioning the sincerity and transience of contemporary music, Newman instead cast the confusion specifically in terms of an ageing modernism. He contrasted the youthful audiences at the Proms with the more typically 'elderly gentleman' of the ISCM directorate

> still not only running round and shouting 'rah! Rah!' with the boys but trying to persuade himself and us that he is one of the boys and to hell with Time, and obviously suffering more and more, as the years go on, from the infirmities of reversionary adolescence, the waters of pity well up in my perhaps too sympathetic heart. I grieve to think of the strain he is putting on his poor old feet and his ageing arteries. And perhaps the saddest part of it all is that some of the real boys just laugh at them, and decline to go wood-crafting with these gallant survivals as scout leaders.[76]

The crisis of legitimation, which of course pre-figures the kinds of problems with cultural pluralism outlined by David Clarke and others, mentioned above, can be construed more broadly in discussions of 'contemporary music' in Britain in the 1920s and 1930s. For example, an anonymous critic writing about the new series of BBC 'Concerts of Contemporary Music' in *The Times* on 25 November 1933 asked, 'How long does music remain contemporary?' The concert included Schoenberg's Three Piano Pieces Op. 11 and 'five [sic] shorter and easier pieces, Op. 19', both of which called up for the critic the

> memories of the long-past pre-War days when we picked them out carefully on the piano and felt very up to date in taking these first steps in what was then called 'modern' music. 'Contemporary' is, we believe, a post-War term. Still it must be admitted that no one then played these pleasing trifles as Mr. Eduard Steuermann played them last night, with his caressing, old-world, romantic touch, and his infinite faith in the rightness of wrong notes.

The concert also included Schoenberg's *Pierrot Lunaire*, which, while written in the same period, the critic notes

> did not come to this country until the term 'contemporary' had been invented. It is dated by the *fin de siècle* morbidity of its theme and the conscious eccentricity of the setting for a voice which neither quite speaks nor quite sings. [. . .] It came just when he had shed the ponderous post-Wagnerian manner of his early works, and before he had become so theory-ridden as to lose his power of invention.[77]

These comments are characteristic of a wider sense in British music criticism that the 'contemporary' could suggest a type of music that was stylistically and thematically different from 'modernist' music, and that it has a temporal demarcation after WWI, seen as a time that looked back retrospectively on a bygone modernism of pre-War days. In other words, the 'contemporary' as a 'post-war term' was a phenomenon that was perceived as coming after modernism, and was of uncertain value just as the objects of modernism had become merely quaint – as products of a 'reversionary adolescence'. So while the term 'contemporary' was of course used in relation to music before WWI – with the earliest appearances in the 1860s and more substantive considerations of the idea appearing in the 1890s[78] – the term began to be used to refer to a *particular type* of music only after WWI, in this sense reinforcing the idea that it was a 'post-War term' that had a special association with the idea of coming after. So when a critic like Newman used the term in the early 1920s, the application was to praise Bartók for being truly new, rather than merely fashionably new like others whose work merely extended pre-War modernist developments.[79] He also used the term to refer to music that seemed untimely or not aligned with current tendencies or sentiments (e.g. the 'divorce that undoubtedly exists [. . .] between contemporary music and contemporary life').[80] These types of usage typify the increasingly delineated application of the term after WWI, suggesting that it was not, even at this early time, the neutral or inclusive term that certain figures in the ISCM intended it to be.

Risk and antithesis

He who cannot take sides should keep silent.[81]

While the argument to retain the notion of the 'contemporary' in the ISCM was a clear rejection of limiting the scope of their programmes to *Neue Musik*, it also reflected a certain crippling self-consciousness on the part of the organization, resulting in an inability to mark out

What was contemporary music?

its position on what would become integral questions related to its activities, such as the relationship between contemporary music and society more generally; contemporary composers' responsibility (or otherwise) to their audience; and the relationship between contemporary music and contemporary politics. These are questions that would be answered very differently in the case of contemporary music and *Neue Musik* respectively, so the lack of clarity in this regard had far broader implications.

To extrapolate this point I turn to Adorno's famous essay of 1955 titled 'The Aging of the New Music', which laments the trajectory of 'New Music' in the period that concerns us, and particularly in the 1930s and 1940s. Not unlike Benjamin with his concern that a critic should not fail to 'take sides', Adorno worried over what he called the 'danger of the dangerless'.[82] In this essay, Adorno laments the systemization of the twelve-tone technique whereby musical material became the servant of a system for its own sake – resulting in what he called the 'arbitrariness of a radicalness for which nothing is any longer at stake'.[83]

> Without stakes in a double sense: neither emotionally, because through the inhibition vis-à-vis such chords and the happiness in them their substance [sic], their power of expression, their relation to the subject has been lost; nor in actuality, for almost no one gets excited anymore about the twelve-tone technique that is served up at all music festivals. [. . .] Twelve-tone technique cannot be conceived without its antithesis, the explosive power of the musically individual, which even today still lives in Webern's early works. Twelve-tone technique is the inexorable clamp that holds together what no less powerfully strives to break apart. If it is employed without being tested against such contrary forces, if it is employed where there is nothing counteracting it to be organized, then it is simply a waste of energy.[84]

One of the primary 'antitheses' that Adorno was thinking of, of course, was the tonal system, and he went on to write that for New Music to have any meaning at all, this meaning was only found in its *relation* to what it was designed to negate. He wrote that 'meaning is itself historical'. In other words, without reference to what is being rejected by the new, there is no meaning in it, only empty rationalization; there is no authenticity, 'no longer any musical frontier' to define the 'boundary of listening' which once fuelled what he called the 'inner compulsion' of New Music.[85]

Adorno goes even further, saying that what is lost in this absence of antithesis and the rejection of expression in favour of rationalization is the 'element of transfiguration, the ideological element of expression',[86] and he saw this problem as having been evident in new music as early as 1927. This loss of antithesis under the pose of ideological neutrality meant a forfeiture of New Music's 'aesthetic substance and coherence'.[87]

In a later essay titled 'Music and New Music' Adorno specifically targeted the ISCM to support his claim that the critical impulse of New Music had been dangerously neutralized by attempts to make it 'self-contained and unrelated to what had gone before and what continues to fill the opera houses, concert halls and the ether', a strategy that 'tends to erect a wall around the music itself and to neutralize it instead of promoting its cause'.[88] This criticism referred to events such as the ISCM festivals, which were indeed made up of a week of concerts of only contemporary music. The criticism of this method, as opposed to interjecting contemporary music into concerts of established repertoire, was not Adorno's alone. In 1946, when the ISCM was preparing to re-group after a number of years of being dormant due to WWII, there were questions raised from both inside and outside the organization about whether it still had a continuing relevance, or rather, whether contemporary music any longer needed a separate forum to support it. For example, of the 1946 Festival in London, Alan Frank observed how:

> the growing pains of the 'new music' are past, its language has become more stable and universal. Composers today are again writing music qua music, and not qua essays in experimental idioms and techniques. Many musicians argue therefore that societies such as the ISCM (and its London Branch, the Contemporary Music Centre) are no longer necessary. Their work was completed when contemporary music no longer needed a spearhead. Today the segregation of such music (they assert) is an anachronism and has no artistic justification.[89]

Similarly Edward Clark conceded that the 'redistribution of composers all over the world' made the post-WWII situation very different from the post-WWI scenario, and acknowledged that the society would have to think about 'what role it was going to play in the restoration efforts'.[90]

While the factors identified by Clark undoubtedly played an important role in the ISCM's lessening significance, many of these and other changes – such as the maturing of the modernist style, the dispersal of artists in exile, and the intervention of new avenues for publication and new publics – would also have described the situation of writers and poets, yet comparable organizations in the literary sphere, such as PEN (a group established in 1921 to support international cooperation between poets, essayists and novelists), continued to play an extremely active role after WWII, attaining consultative status to the United Nations in 1949 as 'representatives of writers of the world' and associate status in UNESCO, participating in discussions about the establishment of Universal Human Rights, and pursuing advocacy initiatives such as the International Writers in Prison Committee in 1960. Even today, PEN International evidently still consider themselves to be a 'non-political' organization, and their current structure and public engagement is cast as explicitly arising from their long and influential history.[91] By contrast, while the present-day ISCM does indeed still run international festivals of new music (the most recent of its annual meetings, now called 'World Music Days', was held in Vancouver, Canada, in 2017, and the one before in the remote South Korean town of Tongyeong in 2016), it has not chosen to prioritize a corollary programme of advocacy on behalf of persecuted composers and performers, nor does it emphasize the significant role the organization played in the cultural politics of the inter-war period.[92]

Adorno lighted upon a problem that lay at the very heart of the ISCM itself when he noted that the English title of the organization replaced the polemical 'New' (or the *Neue Musik* in the German title of the organization) with what he described as the more 'neutral, chronological' category of the 'contemporary', as noted above. For Adorno, the contemporary was a flaccid marker of distinction, which with its focus only on the recent, rather than the new, sought to detach new music from its history and therefore to dilute its 'strangeness'. This point about a lack of antithesis – which might be seen as the 'problem' of the contemporary more generally – is perhaps more familiar to the art history and criticism of the 1970s onwards. Indeed the argument sounds very much like the 'end of art' scenario described by Danto, as noted above. Danto draws a distinction between *modern* art on the one hand, which viewed itself as rejecting tradition and carrying history forward in new directions, and the idea of *contemporary* art on the other hand, which, in contrast,

> has no brief against the art of the past, no sense that the past is something from which liberation must be won, no sense even that it is at all different as art from modern art

What was contemporary music?

generally. [. . .] [T]he basic perception of the contemporary spirit was formed on the principle of a museum in which all art has a rightful place, where there is no *a priori* criterion as to what that art must look like.[93]

According to Danto, this 'contemporary spirit' indicated the end of art because the condition of something being art was its connection to some kind of historical narrative and sense of relation. Adorno's criticism of the ageing of new music was exactly this: that it no longer saw itself as part of, or a rejection of, a historical narrative and therefore had lost the function of critique and negation – modern art had become, therefore, *merely* contemporary. Danto's idea that the end of art is heralded by the sole subject of art becoming 'what is art?' resonates with Adorno's critique of rationalization in an ageing new music, where the system itself is the only signifier of meaning. In these arguments we see the 'contemporary' being distinguished from both the 'modern' and the 'new' in a way that laments the loss of a critical impulse.

There was an attempt to examine related issues at the 1938 ISCM festival in London, at a Congress on 28–29 May at Queen Mary Hall, Bloomsbury, titled 'Music and Life'. The discussion was chaired by Edwin Evans and was attended by composers, publishers, performers and music critics, as well as a presenter who aimed to represent 'the Unknown Listener'.[94] Subsequent to the discussion it was reported that

> the problem was to elucidate the attitude of the public towards modern music, and a considerable measure of agreement was found for the view that people would only accept what was truly familiar. [. . .] The approach to the subject was made by three music publishers (Mr. Soffor OUP, Mr. Hawkes of Boosey's, and Mr. Gibson of Chester's), who represent the main channel of communication between composer and the public. They agree that on any long view the present position was encouraging.[95]

It was noted at the Congress that children do not seem as resistant to the new as adults, and that 'amateurs' should be encouraged to perform new music (at which point in the discussion Sir Donald Tovey 'obliged to demonstrate Three Blind Mice sung in whole tones').

> What constituted contemporary music was discussed at the following session, to which half a dozen of our younger composers contributed. Opinion was divided whether it should be defined technically by the dethronement of tonality, as was proposed by Mr. Alan Bush, or whether it was a question not so much of method as of spirit. Professor Wellesz urged that the word 'modern' should be used for technical innovations and 'contemporary' kept for works procured by modern social conditions. Mr. Lennox Berkeley defined it as 'representative of the age in which we live' and Miss Harriet Cohen made the good point that a big thing like the 12-tone system would hardly come into existence without some social necessity behind it.[96]

The Congress included a session on 'Contemporary Music and the General Public' (which Alan Frank summarized in terms of the recognition that 'you cannot get away from the fact that what is known as contemporary music has no link whatsoever with the ordinary public, who, to put it bluntly, will not touch it with a barge-pole'),[97] followed by a session on 'What is 'Contemporary Music?' Frank noted in his report of this second session that while audiences enjoyed the music of Sibelius, they did not consider him 'contemporary', and concluded that what was meant by contemporary music, then, was what 'was described in the course of the Congress by Dr. Vaughan Williams as "this wrong-note stuff", and by the Unknown Listener as "misery music"'.[98] Nevertheless

> Dr. Malcolm Sargent, in perhaps the most brilliant and what seemed to be the most generally disliked speech of the whole Congress, went one farther when he insisted that the essence of the finest music of whatever period is always the same. He objected to so much talk about the new music expressing the 'spirit of the contemporary age', its sociological implications, and so on. Why worry about this? If music is good, its message speaks for itself, and there is nothing to say afterwards. If it is not good, no apologies, however ingenious, can persuade us otherwise. This point of view of Dr. Sargent's naturally caused some consternation.[99]

These discussions evince the very real entanglements of the contemporary with the sensibility of lateness (or, in Sargent's argument, of untimeliness) and the problems of legitimation. The ISCM's inability to fashion a coherent position in relation to these problems meant that its category of the contemporary was open to just the same type of ossification that Adorno discerned in the ageing of New Music. To the extent that the category of the 'international contemporary' in music was rhetorically positioned against national partisanship (and, less explicitly perhaps, against Austro-German cultural dominance) in the first instance, and then later had the potential to be positioned against the reactionary aesthetics of Nazism and Soviet Socialist Realism, it certainly did not lack opportunities for antithesis – even after WWII, when it was very much a part of the politics of Cold War polarization.[100] The ISCM's 'stagnation',[101] despite these opportunities, conveys the long-term limitations of aesthetic relativism, and likewise perhaps the 'soft consensus' of the version of liberal internationalism that equalizes difference and fails to account for the non-equivalence of 'multiple worlds'. The value of staking out a position of neutrality and bipartisanship in response to conflict are not at issue here, and this meritorious position involves, by necessity, a degree of compromise. Yet the discussions surrounding the structure, aims and activities of the ISCM present a more nuanced counter to the largely emancipatory rhetoric that surrounded the 'contemporary' during the period under discussion, and suggest that there were other alternatives available.

The impossibility of an 'international contemporary'

There was a tension from the very outset between the international aims of the ISCM and its structure as a federation of national sections. This divergence between aims and structure exemplified the tension between an older vision of a 'cosmopolitan' internationalism that construed world citizenship as the means to global peace, with individuals and groups being recognized as world citizens by a world government (through global democracy), and the alternative view that world peace can best be secured by respecting the sovereignty and self-determination of nations (rather than the individuals within them) using a federal structure of international cooperation.[102] This tension within the ISCM paralleled the confusion between its non-partisan aesthetic aims on the one hand, and its underlying desire to promote progressive music as the legitimate version of the 'contemporary' on the other. This problem is not simply an instance of the difference between theory and practice (a criticism that has been applied to inter-war internationalisms more generally), but rather it relates to a latent incongruity in the notion of an 'international contemporary' itself. As a projected unity that, as Peter Osborne has observed, manifests itself as a 'speculative collectivity of the globally transnational', the contemporary registers more at the level of cosmopolitanism, rather than internationalism. This misalignment

What was contemporary music?

was compounded in the context of the ISCM, because not only was it a federation of national sections, but those national sections were effectively made to compete for pre-eminence in the eyes of an international jury, as we have seen.[103] This structure was enshrined in the organization's initial Constitution, which was hastily drawn up by Dent and Edwin Evans during the lunch hour of the initial meeting just after the Salzburg festival of 1922, and agreed to by the gathered group that same afternoon:[104]

> We decided to make the Society a federation of national societies already existing, like the Contemporary Music Centre in London and the *Verein für Privat-Aufführungen* in Vienna; each national section would be autonomous and responsible for its own local activities and finances, but would pay an annual contribution to the central funds. Each section would send a delegate to the general council, and these would elect a jury to choose the festival programmes.[105]

The impact of this policy on the ability of the ISCM to meet its aims over the course of the next two decades was noted by critics, with one article in *The Times* in 1942 describing the 'harm' done to the state of contemporary music by the ISCM through its problematic constitution and 'method', which served only to 'neutralize' any benefits that the organization may have brought:

> While the aim was international unity in the cause of art, the works and the performers to play them were selected on strictly national lines by national committees. This produced a competition between the nations for representation [which was] apt to degenerate into contests of the oddities.[106]

The extent to which the ISCM's structure undercut the aims of its self-proclaimed cosmopolitan members can be seen in the nostalgic adherence to a narrative of harmonious international cooperation in the organization's later years – a narrative that perhaps best described the potential of the ideals of the ISCM, rather than its actuality. Egon Wellesz held a somewhat rosy-eyed view of the international, describing the ISCM festivals as instances of harmonious interaction for the purpose of forwarding a common cause, namely the promotion of the 'music of our time'.[107] Rollo Myers similarly evoked the 'atmosphere of international good-fellowship which it has always been the aim of the ISCM to promote throughout the world', holding to the initial vision, even after WWII, that the ISCM 'is strictly non-partisan, and does not represent any particular "school" or tendency; nor is it intended to appeal only to a musical *élite*'.[108] And even despite Dent's detailed account of the very real tensions created by personal and national jealousies at the early festivals in his retrospective of 1947, his rendering was not completely devoid of the nostalgia for the potential of international fraternity:

> the two things which stood out in all our minds were that here was a great demonstration of music that looked forward to the future, and also a demonstration of international friendly co-operation. The ill-feeling engendered by the war was completely forgotten; Frenchmen, Englishmen, Germans and Australians could all sit down together and take part in playing the same piece of music.[109]

It is not my contention that these rosy accounts were undermined by the national tensions that Dent and others were faced with in the reality of organizing the festivals. Indeed, tensions and negotiations were to be expected, and Dent's navigation of the various national sensibilities involved, his exceptional linguistic abilities, and his herculean efforts in building the trust of the various national sections and mediating between them were truly incredible. Even from the outset, in the trial international music festival in Salzburg in 1922 (out of which the ISCM was formed), there were already some 'petty dissensions' attributed to 'Central European particularism, which measured with some jealousy the portions of programme-space allotted to each section', and Dent was praised in this context for 'keeping the discussion on the international plane whenever there was a tendency to deviate into national channels'.[110]

Of more interest here is that the aspirations of the ISCM seemed in fact to be undermined by its own structure, and specifically the role of the international jury in seeking out representatives of the 'international contemporary' in music for the festivals, while at the same time acknowledging that the 'contemporary movement' received different national expressions. Indeed it seems telling that in the same journal issue as Myers's and Dent's published accounts of the ability of the *international contemporary* to transcend borders appeared articles describing the various *national* expressions of the 'contemporary', among them 'Music of the New World', 'New Soviet Music' and 'The Contemporary Movement in Hungary'.

There had been some discussion about whether the festivals should include representative works from each member nation, to be merely curated by a programme committee, rather than an international jury selecting which works would be performed (a process which sometimes resulted in some member nations having no representative works being presented in a particular festival). This was a particular bugbear of the Italian section that eventually resulted in their withdrawal from the ISCM altogether.[111] In the early 1950s there was a proposal to adopt mandated national representation,[112] though it was also acknowledged that the policy of representation would potentially serve to concretize the idea of the 'contemporary spirit' as a national spirit or a spirit of the people – nationally determined – rather than an expression of a 'common' contemporary, or a shared space and time. This point clearly remained an issue after WWII, with the ISCM's Presidential Council in 1954 stressing the importance of 'adopting standards less on the basis of sectional representation and more on a basis of quality':

> The relation between sections and Central Office has in general been good. But we have still the impression that most sections regard the Society and their section as two things only loosely related to each other and do not realize that the sections, added together, *are* the Society, and not Central Office.[113]

Conclusion

The story of the ISCM reflects the difficulties in navigating the problems associated with the category of the contemporary. Its initial mandate, at least from the British perspective, was to create a forum for the promotion of a contemporary music culture that was not limited to the avant-garde, yet its inability to adequately articulate either an aesthetic or a political antithesis during the inter-war period – regarding aggressive forms of cultural nationalism, for example – against which its equalizing and democratizing aims were positioned meant that the idea of the contemporary had no shared content or meaning, and it became merely a designation of different national expressions of the 'now'. While the ISCM festivals themselves were certainly and by all accounts very collegial, and effective in creating a shared sense of contemporaneity in a social sense among young composers, musically and politically the organization remained hamstrung by the fact that its structure encouraged competition between the national sections, which undermined its avowedly 'cosmopolitan' aims.

What was contemporary music?

It must be emphasized that highlighting these tensions is in no way intended to diminish either the historical or current value of the organization itself, nor is it to be construed as an argument against international cooperation. By the same token, while the discussion of cultural pluralism in the foregoing may evoke a sense of doubt, my intention has simply been to draw parallels between the different registers of critique that have come to bear on the category of the 'contemporary'. Equally, the foregoing might be said to have not taken adequate account of the differences between how the 'contemporary' has applied to art, music and literature: for example, while some types of contemporary art in the second half of the twentieth century might be accused of being prone to commercial replication, this is less the case for contemporary music of course, which suffered (or enjoyed, depending on your point of view) a far more contested relationship with the public during that period, though less so perhaps in the case of minimalist and post-minimalist developments in North America. Despite these differences, however, the vulnerability to commercial replication is only one expression of the problem that the 'contemporary' has a pretence of ideological neutrality, and there have been many other expressions of this problem explored here in relation to music.

Far from passing judgement on the ISCM, or seeking in any way to undermine the undeniable merits of international cooperation, tolerance of diversity and social inclusion, this analysis is intended simply to demonstrate the severe limitations (and perhaps even dangers) of the category of the contemporary. In its appearance of neutrality (i.e. without ideology) and its nowness (i.e. without history), the contemporary elides any productive antithesis, and without the antagonism of risk that comes from staking out a position of antithesis, it surrenders its potential to result in new forms of listening, or to present new forms of international cooperation.

Notes

I would like to thank Karen Arrandale, Astrid Kvalbein, Giles Masters and Arnold Whittall for their insightful comments on early drafts of this chapter.

1 Serge Guilbaut, 'The Frightening Freedom of the Brush: The Boston Institute of Contemporary Art and Modern Art, 1948–1950', in *Dissent: The Issue of Modern Art in Boston*, exhibition catalogue (Boston: Institute of Contemporary Art, 1985), 61; quoted in Richard Meyer, *What Was Contemporary Art?* (Cambridge, MA: MIT Press, 2013), 324n15.
2 Hans Keller, '"Contemporary" Music', *Musical Times* 96 (1955), 132.
3 Ibid., 131.
4 Specifically, Keller wrote that the opening of the development section in the finale of Mozart's second G minor Symphony was 'not only [. . .] anti-tonal, unfolding its succession of ten different notes like a note-row, but – far more important technically – it is in fact composed (as I hope to demonstrate in a forthcoming analysis) according to a strict, if unconscious, serial method. These circumstances in themselves do not, of course, make the passage particularly valuable; they just make it uncontemporary' (ibid.).
5 On this point, Keller compared Schoenberg's essay 'Brahms the Progressive' with Furtwängler's claim that Brahms's harmony of the 1890s echoed Schubert's in the 1820s.
6 Keller, '"Contemporary" Music', 132.
7 See the inaugural editorial by Nigel Osborne, 'Editorial', *Contemporary Music Review* 1, no. 1 (1984), i–ii.
8 Tod Machover, 'A View of Music at IRCAM', *Contemporary Music Review* 1, no. 1 (1984), 1–10.
9 Ibid., 1–2.
10 For an exploration of the types of ideology that have underpinned these and similar claims of the musical avant-garde in both the early and later twentieth century, see Georgina Born, *Rationalizing Culture: IRCAM, Boulez, and the Institutionalization of the Musical Avant-Garde* (Berkeley and Los Angeles: University of California Press, 1995), and Anne C. Shreffler, 'Ideologies of Serialism: Stravinsky's *Threni* and the Congress for Cultural Freedom', in *Music and the Aesthetics of Modernity*, ed. Karol Berger and Anthony Newcomb (Cambridge, MA: Harvard University Department of Music, 2005), 217–45.

11 See Max Paddison and Irène Deliège, eds., *Contemporary Music: Theoretical and Philosophical Perspectives* (Farnham: Ashgate, 2010).

12 Michel Foucault and Pierre Boulez, 'Contemporary Music and the Public', trans. John Rahn, *Perspectives of New Music* 24, no. 1 (1985), 6–12.

13 Arthur Berger and Benjamin Boretz, 'Editorial Note', *Perspectives of New Music* 1, no. 1 (1962), 4–5.

14 Rose Rosengard Subotnik, 'The Challenge of Contemporary Music' (1987), in *What Is Music? An Introduction to the Philosophy of Music*, 2nd ed., ed. Philip Alperson (University Park, PA: Pennsylvania State University Press, 1994), 359–96.

15 See for example Erling E. Guldbrandsen and Julian Johnson, eds., *Transformations of Musical Modernism* (Cambridge: Cambridge University Press, 2015), and David Metzer, *Musical Modernism at the Turn of the Twenty-First Century* (Cambridge: Cambridge University Press, 2009).

16 Claus-Steffen Mahnkopf, 'Neue Musik am Beginn der Zweiten Moderne', *Merkur*, nos. 594–95 (1998), 864–75, and Alastair Williams, 'Ageing of the New: The Museum of Musical Modernism', in *The Cambridge History of Twentieth-Century Music*, ed. Nicholas Cook and Anthony Pople (Cambridge: Cambridge University Press, 2004), 535; both cited in Metzer, *Musical Modernism at the Turn of the Twenty-First Century*. See also Arnold Whittall, '1909 and After: High Modernism and "New Music"', *Musical Times* 150 (2009), 5–18.

17 Indeed Keller noted how 'co-temporary' was the preferred term in eighteenth-century English, emphasizing more readily perhaps the relational nature of the concept (Keller, '"Contemporary" Music', 131).

18 From a statement released by the Boston Institute of Contemporary Art titled '"Modern Art" and the American Public', 17 February 1948, repr. in Guilbaut, 'The Frightening Freedom of the Brush', 61; quoted in Meyer, *What Was Contemporary Art?* 194.

19 '"Modern Art" and the American Public', 17 February 1948, repr. in Guilbaut, 'The Frightening Freedom of the Brush', 52; quoted in Meyer, *What Was Contemporary Art*, 33 and 191.

20 Giorgio Agamben, 'What Is the Contemporary?' in *What Is an Apparatus and Other Essays*, trans. David Kishik and Stefan Pedatella (Stanford, CA: Stanford University Press, 2009), 39.

21 Indeed Egon Wellesz went so far as to claim that from the day that Dent was 'unanimously elected' as the inaugural president of the ISCM in 1922 until the London Festival in 1938, 'the course of the ISCM was directed by him'; 'E. J. Dent and the International Society for Contemporary Music', *Music Review* 7 (1946), 206. While Wellesz's account is clearly exaggerated, there is little doubt of the pivotal nature of Dent's role in the early formation of the ISCM, not only in terms of his skills in diplomacy, mediation and languages, which allowed him to navigate the various personal sensitivities and professional politics between the national sections, but also in terms of shaping the vision and structure of the Society. The initial Constitution for the ISCM was written by Dent together with Edwin Evans (who was at that time the chairman of the London Contemporary Music Centre, which became the headquarters of the ISCM). Dent was president from the Society's inception until 1938, at which point Evans assumed the role, though Dent stepped in again in 1946 to reconstruct the society after WWII, because Evans had become too ill to continue.

22 See Matthew Riley, ed., *British Music and Modernism, 1895–1960* (Farnham: Ashgate, 2010); Philip Rupprecht, *British Musical Modernism: The Manchester Group and Their Contemporaries* (Cambridge: Cambridge University Press, 2015).

23 David Clarke has also described this kind of tendency as being inherent to liberalism's approach to cultural pluralism; see his 'Elvis and Darmstadt, or: Twentieth-Century Music and the Politics of Cultural Pluralism', *Twentieth-Century Music* 4, no. 1 (2007), 3–45. In more extreme terms, it has been referred to as the 'malady of tolerance' by Isabelle Stengers in *Cosmopolitique, Vol. I: La guerre des sciences* (Paris: La Découverte; Les Empêcheurs de penser en rond, 1996), quoted (presumably in translation) by Bruno Latour in 'Whose Cosmos, Which Cosmopolitics? Comments on the Peace Terms of Ulrich Beck', *Common Knowledge* 10, no. 3 (2004), 456.

24 Raymond Williams referred to 'the non-historical fixity of *post*-modernism' in one of his last public lectures, on 17 March 1987 at the University of Bristol – a lecture which was subsequently reconstructed from the notes of Fred Inglis and published as 'When was Modernism?' *New Left Review* I/175 (1989), 52 (original emphasis).

25 Notwithstanding the rather different way in which we might think of 'contemporaneity' as an 'unspoken value' of pre-Enlightenment musical culture. See, for example, William Weber, 'The Contemporaneity of Eighteenth-Century Musical Taste', *Musical Quarterly* 70, no. 2 (1984), 175–94.

26 Terry Smith, 'Contemporary Art and Contemporaneity', *Critical Inquiry* 32, no. 4 (2006), 693.

27 Terry Smith, *What Is Contemporary Art?* (Chicago: University of Chicago Press, 2009), 6.

28 Indeed Smith, following Alberro, links the emergence of the category of the 'contemporary' almost entirely to globalization, globalized capitalism and the ubiquity of digital media; see Smith, *What Is Contemporary Art?*

29 Peter Osborne, 'Global Modernity and the Contemporary: Two Categories of the Philosophy of Historical Time', in *Breaking Up Time: Negotiating the Borders between Present, Past and Future*, ed. Chris Lorenz and Berber Bevernage (Bristol, CT: Vandenhoeck & Ruprecht, 2013), 80. Also see Peter Osborne, 'The Fiction of the Contemporary: Speculative Collectivity and Transnationalism in The Atlas Group', in *Aesthetics and Contemporary Art*, ed. Armen Avanessian and Luke Skrebowski (Berlin: Sternberg, 2011), 101–23.

30 Meyer, *What Was Contemporary Art?* 14–15.

31 Latour, 'Whose Cosmos, Which Cosmopolitics?' 456.

32 Clarke, 'Elvis and Darmstadt', 8.

33 John Rockwell, *All American Music: Composition in the Late Twentieth Century* (New York: Knopf, 1983), 5; quoted in Clarke, 'Elvis and Darmstadt', 10.

34 Smith, 'Contemporary Art and Contemporaneity', 683.

35 On this point, Clarke draws from Kofi Agawu and Satya P. Mohanty, who both variously reject the unifying claims of Enlightenment rationality, though still seek to 'recover our commonality' in order to undermine the alienating effects of foregrounding difference. See Kofi Agawu, 'Contesting Difference: A Critique of Africanist Musicology', in *The Cultural Study of Music: A Critical Introduction*, ed. Martin Clayton, Trevor Herbert and Richard Middleton (New York and London: Routledge, 2003), 227–37; and Satya P. Mohanty, 'Us and Them: On the Philosophical Bases of Political Criticism', *Yale Journal of Criticism* 2, no. 2 (1989), 1–31.

36 Hal Foster, *Bad New Days: Art, Criticism, Emergency* (London: Verso, 2015), 1–2.

37 See Arthur C. Danto, *After the End of Art: Contemporary Art and the Pale of History* (Princeton, NJ: Princeton University Press, 1997).

38 Indeed, even after WWII, critics such as Henry Boys responded to criticisms that the first post-war ISCM festival contained too much music of the established modernist composers – such as Schoenberg, Webern, Bartók, Stravinsky, Hindemith, Krenek and Prokofiev – by arguing that the persistence of these figures in the festivals in fact demonstrated that contemporary music had attained a certain stability of style. For Boys, then, these established modernists 'still represent the main tendencies of contemporary music, the types of choice which are open to the younger composers', and thus provide 'valid and durable standards'; Henry Boys, 'London Festival of the International Society for Contemporary Music', *Tempo*, no. 1 (1946), 18.

39 Edward Dent, 'Looking Backward', *Music Today* 1, no. 1 (1947), 7.

40 Ibid., 9–10.

41 For an excellent discussion of the internal politics behind this divergence in the title of the Society, see Anton Haefeli, *Die Internationale Gesellschaft für Neue Musik (IGNM): Ihre Geschichte von 1922 bis zur Gegenwart* (Zürich: Atlantis Musikbuch-Verlag, 1982), especially chapter 7: 'Neue oder zeitgenössische Musik? Zum Programm und zur Wirkungsgeschichte der IGNM'.

42 Theodor W. Adorno, 'Music and New Music' (1960), in *Quasi una fantasia: Essays on Modern Music*, trans. Rodney Livingstone (London: Verso, 1998), 249.

43 Matthew Riley, '*Musikalische Moderne*: Dahlhaus and After', paper presented at *Elgar and Musical Modernism Conference*, Gresham College, 14 December 2007. I would like to thank Matthew Riley for generously supplying a print copy of this paper, to ensure accuracy of quotation.

44 Arnold Schoenberg, response to 'Open Forum: Variations on a Theme – Music's Future, Tonal or Atonal?' *Music Today* 1, no. 1 (1947), 133.

45 Haefeli, *Die Internationale Gesellschaft*, 262.

46 Anne C. Shreffler, 'The International Society for Contemporary Music and Its Political Context (Prague, 1935)', in *Music and International History in the Twentieth Century*, ed. Jessica C. E. Gienow-Hecht (New York and Oxford: Berghahn, 2015), 58–92.

47 Reproduced in Haefeli, *Die Internationale Gesellschaft* (emphasis added).

48 'During the long period of my presidency I gradually learned who were the really international-minded musicians of the Western world; I learned too the characteristics of the various nations. It was curious that although "modern music" starts from Debussy and Ravel, the Central Europeans seemed to be almost completely ignorant of French music and its makers or interpreters. The most cosmopolitan in their appreciations, as far as I could judge, were the Americans and the English'; see Edward Dent, 'Introduction', typescript introduction for a book provisionally titled *Music Between Two Wars*, to

celebrate the twenty-first anniversary of the founding of the International Society for Contemporary Music (unpublished), 1943, Rowe Music Library, King's College, University of Cambridge, *GB-Ckc*, EJD/1/1/1/2.

49 Edward J. Dent, 'The World of Music: The Contemporary Music Centre', *The Illustrated London News*, 1 October 1921, 432 (emphasis added).

50 Wellesz, 'E. J. Dent', 206–7.

51 Ibid., 208.

52 Rollo H. Myers, 'Foreword by the Editor', *Music Today* 1, no. 1 (1947), 3.

53 Shreffler, 'The International Society'.

54 Ibid., 65.

55 Ibid., 64.

56 Ibid.

57 Ibid., 65.

58 See Pamela M. Potter, 'Strauss and the National Socialists: The Debate and Its Relevance', in *Richard Strauss: New Perspectives of the Composer and His Work*, ed. Bryan Gilliam (Durham, NC, and London: Duke University Press, 1992), 104; and Anton Haefeli and Reinhard Oehlschlägel, 'International Society for Contemporary Music', *Grove Music Online. Oxford Music Online* (Oxford University Press), http://www.oxfordmusiconline.com/subscriber/article/grove/music/13859 (accessed 29 September 2015).

59 This view of the Permanent Council's purposes and structure was contested by Herbert Bedford (co-Secretary) in a letter to the editor of the *Musical Times* in early 1936 in response to intimations made by Calvocoressi about the Permanent Council. Bedford retorted that while Calvocoressi (drawing from André de Blonay) claimed that the Permanent Council had been set up in opposition to the ISCM, 'with the object of pursuing a thoroughly Hitlerian policy in music, Richard Strauss being the Führer who appoints the delegates of all countries, and of securing a triumph for the reactionary tendencies now rife in Germany', Bedford insisted that he had 'observed no sign of even individual ill-feeling' against the ISCM. He maintained that, 'with the exception of [Strauss's] nomination of the German and English members, each delegate of the Conseil Permanent represents either his own national society of composers or its equivalent', and that the Council's aim was simply the 'defence of *droit moral*'. Herbert Bedford, 'The Permanent Council for the International Co-operation of Composers', *Musical Times* 77 (1936), 159.

60 As Ernst Krenek pointed out in a strident critique of the Council, their view of the 'international' was synonymous with the derogatory terms 'Neutöner' or 'Atonaliker' (quoted in Shreffler, 'The International Society', 69).

61 Shreffler, 'The International Society', 77, citing Haefeli, *Die Internationale Gesellschaft*, 197.

62 M. D. Calvocoressi, 'Music in the Foreign Press', *Musical Times* 76 (1935), 1099.

63 Shreffler, 'The International Society', 87n75.

64 Minutes of the Assembly of Delegates of the International Society for Contemporary Music, Copenhagen, 2 June 1947, 7. The meeting was presided over by Dent, and recorded by the secretary Edward Clark, with the President's Council comprising Alois Hába, Francis Poulenc, Douglas Moore and Paul Sanders. There were seventeen national sections represented at the meeting. I wish to thank Astrid Kvalbein for generously sharing these minutes, which were among materials from her archival research in the Royal Library, National Library of Denmark and Copenhagen University Library. Kvalbein's work on Pauline Hall and the Norwegian section of the ISCM can be found at http://mugi.hfmt-hamburg.de/en/Artikel/Pauline_Hall (accessed 26 July 2016) and https://brage.bibsys.no/xmlui/handle/11250/172651 (accessed 26 July 2016).

65 And this, despite influential members of the organization being clearly of the view that it should be. For example, Edward Clark in 1947 tried to bolster the society's reputation by arguing for its political relevance. He refers to the Society's Prague declaration (1935) and argues that in promoting new music the ISCM 'opposed fascism as the negation of culture'; see Edward Clark, 'A Festival of Contemporary Music', *The Listener*, 4 July 1946, 29. Nevertheless, as secretary of the organization, Clark clearly had an interest in maintaining the argument for the continuing relevance of the ISCM in the post-WWII context.

66 Roland Barthes summarizing Nietzsche, cited without original reference in Giorgio Agamben, 'What Is the Contemporary?' 40.

67 Williams, 'When Was Modernism?' 51. Original emphasis. Indeed others, such as Agamben (following Nietzsche and Barthes), ascribe the positive value of untimeliness to the contemporary: 'contemporariness does not simply take place in chronological time: it is something that, working within

What was contemporary music?

chronological time, urges, presses, and transforms it. And this urgency is the untimeliness, the anachronism that permits us to grasp our time in the form of a "too soon" that is also a "too late"; of an "already" that is also a "not yet"' (Agamben, 'What Is the Contemporary?' 47). The final comment here of existing between the 'too late' and the 'not yet' echoes Hans Keller's sentiment described at the outset as the problem with the category of the contemporary, though for Agamben this sensibility of being in transition is what makes a critical awareness of the present possible.

68 Steven Connor, *Postmodernist Culture: An Introduction to Theories of the Contemporary*, 2nd ed. (Oxford: Blackwell, 1997), 8.

69 For example Subotnik described how 'the contemporary aesthetic [namely modernism, in this context] has refined the relativistic aspects of historicism to such an extreme that it has negated the hopes of contemporary music as a whole for historical vindication as a standard repertory and locked it into a self-contradiction. [. . .] [I]n effect, the contemporary aesthetic has loaded relativism, a supposedly value-free position, with a complex value system of its own' (Subotnik, 'The Challenge of Contemporary Music', 274–75).

70 For Connor, this is the 'terminal self-consciousness' that typifies the postmodernist moment (*Postmodernist Culture*, 5).

71 See for example Tyrus Miller, *Late Modernism: Politics, Fiction and the Arts Between the World Wars* (Berkeley: University of California Press, 1999) and Jed Esty, *A Shrinking Island: Modernism and National Culture in England* (Princeton, NJ: Princeton University Press, 2003). The term has referred to a slightly different period in the sphere of architecture; see Charles Jencks, 'Postmodern and Late Modern: The Essential Definitions', *Chicago Review* 35, no. 4 (1987), 31–58.

72 See Sarah Collins, *Lateness and Modernism: Untimely Ideas about Music and Literature between the Wars* (Cambridge: Cambridge University Press, forthcoming).

73 Rupprecht, *British Musical Modernism*.

74 Keller, '"Contemporary" Music', 132.

75 'Sincerity in Music', *The Times*, 20 January 1923, 6.

76 Ernest Newman, 'Reflections after the Feast – I: What Is "Contemporary Music"', *Sunday Times*, 3 July 1938, 7.

77 '"Contemporary" Music', *The Times*, 25 November 1933, 10.

78 For example see 'Contemporary Music', *Musical Times and Singing Class Circular* 36 (1895), 27–28, reporting on a lecture give at the London Institution on 29 November 1895 by Sir Joseph Barnby on the topic, which sought to link musical style with the broader intellectual climate, or 'mental attitude', of the time – 'Modern music was the reflection of the subtle undercurrents of emotion which marked an analytical age' (ibid., 27) – and the national temperament: 'England was more practical, more logical, more restrained'.

79 E.N. [Ernest Newman], 'Music of the Week', *Sunday Times*, 5 September 1920, 4.

80 Ernest Newman, 'The World of Music: A Stocktaking', *Sunday Times*, 6 November 1921, 7.

81 Walter Benjamin, 'Critic's Technique in Thirteen Theses', in 'One Way Street', *Walter Benjamin: Selected Writings*, vol. 1: *1913–1926*, ed. Marcus Bullock and Michael W. Jennings (Cambridge, MA: Harvard University Press, 1996), 460.

82 Theodor Adorno, 'The Aging of the New Music' (1955), in *Essays on Music*, ed. Richard Leppert and trans. Susan H. Gillespie (Berkeley and Los Angeles: University of California Press, 2002), 181.

83 Ibid., 185.

84 Ibid., 185–86.

85 Ibid., 190–91.

86 Ibid., 191.

87 Ibid., 181.

88 Theodor W. Adorno, 'Music and New Music', 250.

89 Alan Frank, 'The ISCM Festival', *Musical Times* 87 (1946), 233. Ernest Newman made a similar point, commenting on the performance of Hindemith's String Quartet in E flat (1943) at the 1946 London festival: 'Here at last was a fine musician, getting down, without any grimacing, any posturing, any shouting of slogans, any waving of banners, to the simple business of saying something worth saying, and saying it with complete mastery'; 'The Contemporary Music Festival', *Sunday Times*, 14 July 1946, 2. Henry Boys also noted new 'stabilities of style' in contemporary music in that same post-war festival ('London Festival', 18). Yet Frederick Goldbeck, writing in the ISCM's own journal in 1947, saw this supposed stability as an overwhelming failure in contemporary music culture: 'The bewilderment of picking ideas at a moment when there are no more definite sides to be picked, the old dichotomy

tradition-rebellion being now meaningless. A sense of frustration: it is unpleasant enough to be cut off from the straightforward means of expression that were at the disposal of the golden period, and to have to deny oneself the possibility of catching up with any of these periods – with some, national or other, "wish-it-were" and "might-have-been" tradition – or with the timeless spirit of folklore. The fear of writing "ugly" music. The fear of being modern, and the fear of not being modern [. . .] contemporaries are terrified at their failure to find anything either to yield to or to fight against. Instead of challenging public and critics, they never stop challenging and censuring themselves. [. . .] [T]he spell of dissonance has faded, and everything has to be reconsidered again and again'; 'Music and Tradition', *Music Today* 1 (1947), 113–14.

90 In addition to these factors, the Society's reduced significance after WWII has been attributed to the emergence of other influential international initiatives such as the international summer school in Darmstadt, and the intervention of new technologies into new music composition that made the support of large-scale performance forces less essential to ensuring the performance of new works. There was also a renewed commitment by a number of broadcasting organizations in Europe to support the performance over radio of contemporary music.

91 See, for example, the professionally produced pamphlet 'The PEN Story', in the 'Our History' section of their current website http://www.pen-international.org/our-history/ (accessed 26 July 2017), a publication complete with timeline, photographs and rousing quotations from current and former members.

92 The official website of the ISCM today includes a one-line history: 'Since our founding in 1922, our network has grown to include more than 60 organizations in over 50 countries, on every continent', http://www.iscm.org/about/about-iscm (accessed 26 July 2017). The society did have communication with UNESCO in the late 1940s, as evidenced in the minutes to their annual meetings, and it is true that today the ISCM is one among many current affiliates of the International Music Council, in the company of others such as the International Association of Music Information Centres, the International Federation of Chopin Societies and the International Music Managers' Forum. However, it is not clear when the ISCM last posted an activity report to the IMC.

93 Danto, *After the End of Art*, 5.

94 This was reported by 'Feste', 'Ad Libitum', *Musical Times* 79 (1938), 658–61.

95 'Music and Life Congress', *The Times*, 30 May 1938, 21.

96 Ibid.

97 Alan Frank, 'Music and Life, 1938', *Musical Times* 79 (1938), 461.

98 Ibid.

99 Ibid.

100 Thank you to Anne Shreffler for many insightful discussions on this point.

101 A term used by Haefeli in describing the state of the organization after 1945; see his *Die Internationale Gesellschaft*.

102 Robert Fine described this division as the difference between international law – which 'upholds the internal and external sovereignty of nations and regulates relations between states on this basis [. . . guaranteeing] the integrity of states based on the right of national self-determination and the principle of non-interference in the internal affairs of other states' – and 'cosmopolitan law', which 'reaches both inside and outside states [. . . recognizing] individuals and groups in civil society, as well as states, as legal personalities' and therefore seeking to 'impose limits on how states can behave toward the people who live within their territories'; 'Taking the "Ism" Out of Cosmopolitanism', *European Journal of Social Theory* 6, no. 4 (2003), 452. See also Daniel Laqua, ed., *Internationalism Reconfigured: Transnational Ideas and Movements between the Wars* (London and New York: I. B. Tauris, 2011), 5–6.

103 For more on this topic see Martin Thrun, '"Feste und Proteste": Über das nationale Prinzip der Organisation der "Internationalen Gesellschaft für Neue Musik" nach 1922', in *Nationale Musik im 20. Jahrhundert: Kompositorische und soziokulturelle Aspekte der Musikgeschichte zwischen Ost- und Westeuropa*, Konferenzbericht Leipzig 2002, ed. Helmut Loos and Stefan Keym (Leipzig: Gudrun Schröder Verlag, 2004), 457–70. Thank you to Giles Masters for drawing my attention to this essay.

104 Later ratified in December 1922 at a meeting of delegates from eight countries (Austria, Czechoslovakia, Denmark, France, Germany, Great Britain, Holland and Switzerland) in London; see Dent, 'Looking Backward', 9–11.

105 Quoted in Jennifer Doctor, *The BBC and Ultra-Modern Music, 1922–36: Shaping a Nation's Tastes* (Cambridge: Cambridge University Press, 1999), 74.

106 'Contemporary Music: Standards Readjusted', *The Times*, 17 July 1942, 6.

107 Wellesz, 'E. J. Dent', 208.

108 Rollo H. Myers, 'Foreword by the Editor', 3–4.

109 Dent, 'Looking Backward', 9.

110 Edwin Evans, 'The Salzburg Festival', *Musical Times* 63 (1922), 629. See also Haefeli, who effectively details how the issue with the name of the society was a direct result of the different notions of the contemporary and the new in the different national sections (*Die Internationale Gesellschaft*, 268–70).

111 Even as early as 1923, Casella had denounced the international jury's apparent neglect of the submissions by Italian composers; see Dent, 'Looking Backward'. See also the minutes of the 1939 meeting of the ISCM in Warsaw, where a letter was read out from Casella which announced the section's withdrawal from the ISCM, on account of 'La place insuffisante faite à notre école depuis plusieurs années par le jury'. The minutes record that 'the secretary was instructed to reply to Signor Casella regretting the decision of the Italian Section but stating that complete liberty of action had always been conceded to the Jury and that the Delegates considered this to be a paramount condition of the Society's policy'; see page 2 of the Minutes of the 18th Conference of Delegates, Warsaw, 1939, President Edwin Evans (who was too ill to attend the meeting), President's council (1939/40: Béla Bartók, Zbigniew Drzewiecke, Darius Milhaud, Carleton Sprague Smith; Secretary: Edward Clark). At the 1946 meeting, Luigi Dallapiccola proposed to the meeting that it accept a newly formed Italian section (8), but the delegates were concerned about Casella's involvement. The delegates only accepted Dallapiccola's proposal after he agreed to a 'thorough cleansing of its membership' to omit Casella, although in the following year's meeting there was a reference to the sad loss of 'three of [the ISCM's] most distinguished members, the composers Manuel de Falla, William [sic] Pijper, and Alfredo Casella' (Minutes of the Assembly of Delegates, Copenhagen, 1947, President Edward J. Dent; President's council Alois Hába, Francis Poulenc, Douglas Moore, Paul Sanders; Hon. Secretary Edward Clark). I wish to thank Astrid Kvalbein for the copy of the minutes.

112 See 'The ISCM – A Proposal', *Musical Times* 94 (1953), 171–72. The anonymous author wrote that, for the ISCM, 'contemporary' used to mean music of the day whatever the style, but in 1953 it has a tendency towards the avant-garde. This concern was acknowledged by the ISCM, which proceeded to establish a 'committee of direction' for the society. The committee was charged with the responsibility of considering the proposal that each national section should be guaranteed representation in every festival, or at least on a three-year rotation, and that the international jury should be replaced by a programme-building committee.

113 Report of the Presidential Council to the Assembly of Delegates of the International Society for Contemporary Music, Mt. Carmel Haifa, June 1954 (original emphasis).

Bibliography

Adorno, Theodor W. 'Music and New Music' (1960). In *Quasi una fantasia: Essays on Modern Music*, translated by Rodney Livingstone, 249–68. London: Verso, 1998.

———. 'The Aging of the New Music' (1955). In *Essays on Music*, edited by Richard Leppert and translated by Susan H. Gillespie, 181–202. Berkeley: University of California Press, 2002.

Agamben, Giorgio. 'What Is the Contemporary?' In *What Is an Apparatus and Other Essays*, translated by David Kishik and Stefan Pedatella, 39–54. Stanford, CA: Stanford University Press, 2009.

Agawu, Kofi. 'Contesting Difference: A Critique of Africanist Musicology'. In *The Cultural Study of Music: A Critical Introduction*, edited by Martin Clayton, Trevor Herbert and Richard Middleton, 227–37. New York and London: Routledge, 2003.

Alberro, Alexander. 'Questionnaire on "The Contemporary"'. *October*, no. 130 (2009): 55.

Bedford, Herbert. 'The Permanent Council for the International Co-operation of Composers'. *Musical Times* 77 (1936): 159.

Benjamin, Walter. 'One Way Street'. In *Walter Benjamin: Selected Writings*, vol. 1: *1913–1926*, edited by Marcus Bullock and Michael W. Jennings, 444–88. Cambridge, MA: Harvard University Press, 1996.

Berger, Arthur, and Benjamin Boretz. 'Editorial Note'. *Perspectives of New Music* 1, no. 1 (1962): 4–5.

Born, Georgina. *Rationalizing Culture: IRCAM, Boulez, and the Institutionalization of the Musical Avant-Garde*. Berkeley and Los Angeles: University of California Press, 1995.

Boys, Henry. 'London Festival of the International Society for Contemporary Music'. *Tempo*, no. 1 (1946): 18–20.

Calvocoressi, M. D. 'Music in the Foreign Press'. *Musical Times* 76 (1935): 1098–99.

Clark, Edward. 'A Festival of Contemporary Music'. *The Listener*, 4 July 1946, 29.

Clarke, David. 'Elvis and Darmstadt, or: Twentieth-Century Music and the Politics of Cultural Pluralism'. *Twentieth-Century Music* 4, no. 1 (2007): 3–45.

Collins, Sarah. *Lateness and Modernism: Untimely Ideas about Music and Literature between the Wars*. Cambridge: Cambridge University Press, forthcoming.

Connor, Steven. *Postmodernist Culture: An Introduction to Theories of the Contemporary*. 2nd ed. Oxford: Blackwell, 1997.

'Contemporary Music'. *Musical Times and Singing Class Circular* 36 (1895): 27–28.

'"Contemporary" Music'. *The Times*, 25 November 1933, 10.

'Contemporary Music: Standards Readjusted'. *The Times*, 17 July 1942, 6.

Danto, Arthur C. *After the End of Art: Contemporary Art and the Pale of History*. Princeton, NJ: Princeton University Press, 1997.

Dent, Edward J. 'The World of Music: The Contemporary Music Centre'. *The Illustrated London News*, 1 October 1921, 432.

———. 'Looking Backward'. *Music Today* 1, no. 1 (1947): 6–25.

Doctor, Jennifer. *The BBC and Ultra-Modern Music, 1922–36: Shaping a Nation's Tastes*. Cambridge: Cambridge University Press, 1999.

Esty, Jed. *A Shrinking Island: Modernism and National Culture in England*. Princeton, NJ: Princeton University Press, 2003.

Evans, Edwin. 'The Salzburg Festival'. *Musical Times* 63 (1922): 628–31.

'Feste'. 'Ad Libitum'. *Musical Times* 79 (1938): 658–61.

Fine, Robert. 'Taking the "Ism" Out of Cosmopolitanism'. *European Journal of Social Theory* 6, no. 4 (2003): 451–70.

Foster, Hal. *Bad New Days: Art, Criticism, Emergency*. London: Verso, 2015.

Foucault, Michel, and Pierre Boulez. 'Contemporary Music and the Public', translated by John Rahn. *Perspectives of New Music* 24, no. 1 (1985): 6–12.

Frank, Alan. 'Music and Life, 1938'. *Musical Times* 79 (1938): 461.

———. 'The ISCM Festival'. *Musical Times* 87 (1946): 233–35.

Goldbeck, Frederick. 'Music and Tradition'. *Music Today* 1 (1947): 110–16.

Guldbrandsen, Erling E., and Julian Johnson, eds. *Transformations of Musical Modernism*. Cambridge: Cambridge University Press, 2015.

Haefeli, Anton. *Die Internationale Gesellschaft für Neue Musik (IGNM): Ihre Geschichte von 1922 bis zur Gegenwart*. Zürich: Atlantis Musikbuch-Verlag, 1982.

Haefeli, Anton, and Reinhard Oehlschlägel. 'International Society for Contemporary Music'. In *Grove Music Online: Oxford Music Online*. Oxford: Oxford University Press. http://www.oxfordmusiconline.com/subscriber/article/grove/music/13859 (accessed 29 September 2015).

'The ISCM – A Proposal'. *Musical Times* 94 (1953): 171–72.

Jencks, Charles. 'Postmodern and Late Modern: The Essential Definitions'. *Chicago Review* 35, no. 4 (1987): 31–58.

Keller, Hans. '"Contemporary" Music'. *Musical Times* 96 (1955): 131–32.

Laqua, Daniel, ed. *Internationalism Reconfigured: Transnational Ideas and Movements between the Wars*. London and New York: I. B. Tauris, 2011.

Latour, Bruno. 'Whose Cosmos, Which Cosmopolitics? Comments on the Peace Terms of Ulrich Beck'. *Common Knowledge* 10, no. 3 (2004): 450–62.

Machover, Tod. 'A View of Music at IRCAM'. *Contemporary Music Review* 1, no. 1 (1984): 1–10.

Mahnkopf, Claus-Steffen. 'Neue Musik am Beginn der Zweiten Moderne'. *Merkur*, nos. 594–95 (1998): 864–75.

Metzer, David. *Musical Modernism at the Turn of the Twenty-First Century*. Cambridge: Cambridge University Press, 2009.

Meyer, Richard. *What Was Contemporary Art?* Cambridge, MA: MIT Press, 2013.

Miller, Tyrus. *Late Modernism: Politics, Fiction and the Arts between the World Wars*. Berkeley: University of California Press, 1999.

Mohanty, Satya P. 'Us and Them: On the Philosophical Bases of Political Criticism'. *Yale Journal of Criticism* 2, no. 2 (1989): 1–31.

'Music and Life Congress'. *The Times*, 30 May 1938, 21.

Myers, Rollo H. 'Foreword by the Editor'. *Music Today* 1, no. 1 (1947): 3–5.

Newman, Ernest. 'Music of the Week'. *Sunday Times*, 5 September 1920, 4.

————. 'The World of Music: A Stocktaking'. *Sunday Times*, 6 November 1921, 7.

————. 'Reflections after the Feast – I: What Is "Contemporary Music"'. *Sunday Times*, 3 July 1938, 7.

————. 'The Contemporary Music Festival'. *Sunday Times*, 14 July 1946.

Osborne, Nigel. 'Editorial'. *Contemporary Music Review* 1, no. 1 (1984): i–ii.

Osborne, Peter. 'The Fiction of the Contemporary: Speculative Collectivity and Transnationalism in The Atlas Group'. In *Aesthetics and Contemporary Art*, edited by Armen Avanessian and Luke Skrebowski, 101–23. Berlin: Sternberg, 2011.

————. 'Global Modernity and the Contemporary: Two Categories of the Philosophy of Historical Time'. In *Breaking Up Time: Negotiating the Borders between Present, Past and Future*, edited by Chris Lorenz and Berber Bevernage, 69–86. Bristol, CT: Vandenhoeck & Ruprecht, 2013.

Paddison, Max, and Irène Deliège, eds. *Contemporary Music: Theoretical and Philosophical Perspectives*. Farnham: Ashgate, 2010.

Potter, Pamela M. 'Strauss and the National Socialists: The Debate and Its Relevance'. In *Richard Strauss: New Perspectives of the Composer and His Work*, edited by Bryan Gilliam, 93–114. Durham, NC, and London: Duke University Press, 1992.

Riley, Matthew. '*Musikalische Moderne*: Dahlhaus and After'. Paper presented at *Elgar and Musical Modernism* conference, Gresham College, 14 December 2007.

Riley, Matthew, ed. *British Music and Modernism, 1895–1960*. Farnham: Ashgate, 2010.

Rockwell, John. *All American Music: Composition in the Late Twentieth Century*. New York: Knopf, 1983.

Rupprecht, Philip. *British Musical Modernism: The Manchester Group and Their Contemporaries*. Cambridge: Cambridge University Press, 2015.

Schoenberg, Arnold. Response to 'Open Forum: Variations on a Theme – Music's Future, Tonal or Atonal?' *Music Today* 1, no. 1 (1947): 132–34.

Shreffler, Anne C. 'Ideologies of Serialism: Stravinsky's *Threni* and the Congress for Cultural Freedom'. In *Music and the Aesthetics of Modernity*, edited by Karol Berger and Anthony Newcomb, 217–45. Cambridge, MA: Harvard University Department of Music, 2005.

————. 'The International Society for Contemporary Music and Its Political Context (Prague, 1935)'. In *Music and International History in the Twentieth Century*, edited by Jessica C. E. Gienow-Hecht, 58–92. New York and Oxford: Berghahn, 2015.

'Sincerity in Music'. *The Times*, 20 January 1923, 6.

Smith, Terry. 'Contemporary Art and Contemporaneity'. *Critical Inquiry* 32, no. 4 (2006): 681–707.

————. *What Is Contemporary Art?* Chicago: University of Chicago Press, 2009.

Stengers, Isabelle. *Cosmopolitique, Vol. I: La guerre des sciences*. Paris: La Découverte; Les Empêcheurs de penser en rond, 1996.

Subotnik, Rose Rosengard. 'The Challenge of Contemporary Music' (1987). In *What Is Music? An Introduction to the Philosophy of Music*. 2nd ed., edited by Philip Alperson, 359–96. University Park, PA: Pennsylvania State University Press, 1994.

Thrun, Martin. '"Feste und Proteste": Über das nationale Prinzip der Organisation der "Internationalen Gesellschaft für Neue Musik" nach 1922'. In *Nationale Musik im 20. Jahrhundert: Kompositorische und soziokulturelle Aspekte der Musikgeschichte zwischen Ost- und Westeuropa*. Konferenzbericht Leipzig 2002, edited by Helmut Loos and Stefan Keym, 457–70. Leipzig: Gudrun Schröder Verlag, 2004.

Weber, William. 'The Contemporaneity of Eighteenth-Century Musical Taste'. *Musical Quarterly* 70, no. 2 (1984): 175–94.

Wellesz, Egon. 'E. J. Dent and the International Society for Contemporary Music'. *Music Review* 7 (1946): 205–8.

Whittall, Arnold. '1909 and After: High Modernism and "New Music"'. *Musical Times* 150 (2009): 5–18.

Williams, Alastair. 'Ageing of the New: The Museum of Musical Modernism'. In *The Cambridge History of Twentieth-Century Music*, edited by Nicholas Cook and Anthony Pople, 506–38. Cambridge: Cambridge University Press, 2004.

Williams, Raymond. 'When Was Modernism?' *New Left Review* I/175 (1989): 48–52.

3

INSTITUTIONS, ARTWORLDS, NEW MUSIC

Martin Iddon

The following chapter takes a slightly unusual form. The main body of the text sketches a theory first of institutions in general, drawing from work principally in economics, sociology and political science, and considering the competing, and sometimes complementary, claims of rational choice institutionalism, historical or normative institutionalism and social institutionalism, before placing the artworld theories of, among others, Arthur Danto, George Dickie and Howard Becker – which is to say institutional theories of art – into the context of this larger theoretical frame. Within the main body of the text, then, there is no mention of new music at all; it is exclusively theoretical. However, the text is periodically punctuated by insertions mainly paraphrasing or commenting on writings which examine the institutions of post-war music in Europe. Each of these exemplifies in practical terms the playing out of the theoretical point being raised in the text at that point, such that it is possible to see in an, I trust, immediate way the direct relevance positions ostensibly so apparently distant from and, in some respects, alien to mainstream musicology might have for understanding the structures which allow (new) music to take place, as well as helping to understand the limits of such approaches.

★

In explaining what he means by a category mistake, Gilbert Ryle outlines the following situation:

> A foreigner visiting Oxford or Cambridge for the first time is shown a number of colleges, libraries, playing fields, museums, scientific departments and administrative offices. He then asks 'But where is the University? I have seen where the members of the Colleges live, where the Registrar works, where the scientists experiment and the rest. But I have not yet seen the University in which reside and work the members of your University.' It has then to be explained to him that the University is not another collateral institution, some ulterior counterpart to the colleges, laboratories and offices which he has seen. The University is just the way in which all that he has already seen is organized. When they are seen and when their co-ordination is understood, the University has been seen. [...] He was mistakenly allocating the University to the same category as that to which the other institutions belong.[1]

Institutions, artworlds, new music

At the heart of Ryle's well-known thought experiment lies, as a side product, an instructive demonstration of the nature of institutions, what they are and how they function, even if not in the way suggested, on first examination, by the thought experiment itself.

From the perspective of more recent theories of institutionalism – broadly what has been termed the new institutionalism and after, as well as some earlier, related writers, such as Karl Polanyi – Ryle has things, at least in part, the wrong way round: the visiting foreigner is quite correct that he has not seen the University. The University – or, to be more precise, the *institution of* the University – is not a thing that he, as an outsider, even *could* encounter. As should become clear in what follows, Ryle is perfectly correct in his statement that the University is precisely the way in which all its elements are arranged from the perspective of someone who, as an insider, understands, perhaps intuitively, the co-ordination of those elements. He is right, too, that this does not, as such, belong to the same category as offices, departments, libraries and so on (or not if those are regarded as physical buildings), nor is the University a 'collateral' or 'ulterior' counterpart, save in very particular ways, which may be explained by what some new institutionalists might regard as Ryle's own category mistake in expanding upon just this point:

> For while the Church and the Home Office are institutions, the British Constitution is not another institution in the same sense of that noun. So inter-institutional relations which can be asserted or denied to hold between the Church and the Home Office cannot be asserted or denied to hold between either of them and the British Constitution. 'The British Constitution' is not a term of the same logical type as 'the Home Office' and 'the Church of England'.[2]

To be sure, there are important distinctions which might be made between the Home Office and the British Constitution and, indeed, one might go so far as to agree that, properly considered, these two are not terms of the same logical type. Yet it is not necessarily the case that it is on the territory of the 'institutional' that the distinctions may be sought. Indeed, precisely the commonalities between the two members of this pair may help to expose more clearly what might be meant when speaking of institutions in general, especially noting that the British Constitution – as distinct from the constitutions of, say, India or the United States of America or, for that matter, most of the world's countries – is not codified in any single document, instead comprising multiple forms of documentation of differing status, legal judgements and, in part, convention. Karl Polanyi rejects an attempt to describe (for his purposes, economic) processes in ways which might make Ryle's distinction hold – where the human or material existence of the Home Office, in terms of its buildings or the people who work in them and the network of relationships that develops between those elements, distinguishes it from the British Constitution – since:

> reduced to a mechanical, biological and psychological interaction of elements that economic process would possess no all-round reality. It contains no more than the bare bones of the processes of production and transportation, as well as of the appropriative changes. In the absence of any indication of societal conditions from which the motives of the individuals spring, there would be little, if anything, to sustain the interdependence of the movements and their recurrence on which the unity and the stability of the process depends.[3]

In the sense that Polanyi describes an institution, it might very well be thought, then, that his concern is with that which might be held to be the common ground between such institutions as seemingly distinct as, precisely, the Home Office and the British Constitution, namely the ways in which they define conditions of actions, the 'rules of the game' of the social, thus providing a unifying medium between individuals and society. Though Polanyi is still concerned above all with the economic, his description might usefully stand for institutional thinking more broadly:

> The instituting of the economic process vests that process with unity and stability; it provides a structure with a definite function in society; it shifts the place of the process in society, thus adding significance to its history; it centers interest on values, motives and policy. Unity and stability, structure and function, history and policy spell out operationally the content of our assertion that the human economy is an instituted process.[4]

Institutions, in this sense, then – whether or not they may be to all intents and purposes coterminous with a certain set of buildings, a certain geographical location, or a certain, perhaps specialized or specialist, group of individuals – are, in truth, things which give rise to how individuals might act within particular (institutional) contexts. Thinking about institutions thus, there are perhaps three ways in which one might conceive of how an institution interacts with human activity: rational choice institutionalism, historical or normative institutionalism, and social institutionalism. The last two of these three are, certainly, complementary and, moreover, there are certain aspects of the first – especially according to a particular way of framing both 'rationality' and 'decision' – which require consideration and integration into institutional theory more broadly.

Regular participants at the Darmstadt New Music Courses might note that the physical buildings associated with the courses change, sometimes quite significantly. Over the terms of office of the past two directors, important venues have included the Georg-Büchner-Schule, the Lichtenberg-schule, the Mornewegschule, the Bessunger Knabenschule, the Musikakademie and the Schaderstif-tung. Looking back further over the history of the courses, many other places have been significant, perhaps most famously the hunting lodge at Kranichstein and the Marienhöhe. Even though concert venues in the city are relatively few and far between, these too can change a great deal: the same courses as noted above have tended to use a combination of the Orangerie, Centralstation, the Staatstheater, the Sporthalle at Böllenfalltor, the Darmstadtium, the Kunsthalle, 603qm at the Technische Universität Darmstadt, as well as spaces within the (predominantly school) buildings used for teaching and lecturing. But even the most seemingly central of these can become marginal, and many are only relatively rarely utilized. Moreover, according to this sort of building stock version of institutions, during the courses themselves no one involved goes to the administrative heart of the institution, the Internationales Musikinstitut Darmstadt building itself, which is, not least, often on the *wrong* outskirts of the city for convenience. In any case, there is relatively little consistency in the physical spaces used.

Even though there are many familiar faces to regular participants, the participant body changes radically from course to course. Likewise, though a particular director of the courses may have tutors who are used regularly – whether because they are particularly valued for their contribution to the courses or because they express a particular aesthetic stance the director feels it is important to represent – the tutors, too, are far from consistent. What remains constant across the years – or what changes at a radically slower pace – is the way in which the courses function: the particular relationship between lectures, seminars, one-to-one tutorials, workshops and concerts, on the one hand, and the social milieu of the courses more broadly understood on the other. Despite the radical inconsistencies in sites and individuals, participants nevertheless still always attend the same courses.

Martin Iddon, 'The Dissolution of the Avant-Garde, Darmstadt 1968–1984' (PhD diss., University of Cambridge, 2004).

———, 'Trying to Speak: Between Politics and Aesthetics, Darmstadt 1970–1972', *Twentieth-Century Music* 3, no. 2 (2006), 255–75.

———, *New Music at Darmstadt: Nono, Stockhausen, Cage, and Boulez* (Cambridge: Cambridge University Press, 2013).

Within rational choice institutionalism, the institution itself provides only a regulative role: 'institutions are an intervening variable capable of affecting an individual's choices and actions but not determining them'.[5] This is to say, apart from any other consideration, the preferences – the desires and goals – of individuals according to such a theory are exogenous, originating outside the institution which is the sphere of action, in which 'institutions are important as features of a *strategic context*, imposing constraints on self-interested behaviour'.[6] According to Hayek's well-known dictum, 'man is as much a rule-following animal as a purpose-seeking one'.[7] Essentially, rational choice institutions are populated with neo-classical economic actors:

> choices are made by individuals, who are assumed to be selfish, only interested in maximizing their own welfare – or at most that of family members. In doing so, all individuals are seen to make rational choices, namely, they choose the most cost-efficient way to achieve a given goal.[8]

Nevertheless, the rationality of such actors is, at best, bounded. As Ha-Joon Chang defines the rather large set of issues with the harder-edged version of rational choice theory:

> The list of non-rational behaviour is endless. We are too easily swayed by instincts and emotion in our decisions – wishful thinking, panic, herd instinct and what not. Our decisions are heavily affected by the 'framing' of the question when they shouldn't, in the sense that we may make different decisions about essentially the same problem, depending on the way it is presented. And we tend to over-react to new information and under-react to existing information; this is frequently observed in the financial market. We normally operate with an intuitive, heuristic (short-cut) system of thinking, which results in poor logical thinking. Above all, we are over-confident about our own rationality.[9]

In the field of artistic judgements, one might be rather relieved by such objections. Nevertheless, there is good reason for scepticism regarding the rationality of individuals and the decisions they make beyond the territory of aesthetics. Daniel Kahneman distinguishes between two selves: the fast-thinking, intuitive Humans (or System 1), whose judgements are made almost instantly, and the slower, contemplative Econs (or System 2), who theorize and judge carefully, taking whatever steps possible to constrain and control the fast, but irrational, reflexes of the Humans.[10] As

Kahneman explains, '[w]hen all goes smoothly, which is most of the time, System 2 adopts the suggestions of System 1 with little or no modification. You generally believe your impressions and act on your desires, and that is fine – usually.'[11]

In this sense, even if the Econ-self of a person is properly rational, the Human-self is, arguably, not, where rationality is defined as logical consistency: 'a rational person can prefer being hated to being loved, so long as his preferences are consistent'.[12] Habermas quotes Richard Norman in explaining some of the surprising results of this in the area of taste:

> To want simply a saucer of mud is irrational, because some further reason is needed for wanting it. To want a saucer of mud because one wants to enjoy its rich river-smell is rational. No further reason is needed for wanting to enjoy the rich river-smell, for to characterize what is wanted as 'to enjoy the rich river-smell' is itself to give an acceptable reason for wanting it, and therefore this want is rational.[13]

As Habermas explains it, the key factor in such activities being recognized as rational is that actors 'use predicates such as "spicy", "attractive", "strange", "terrible", "disgusting", and so forth, in such a way that other members of their lifeworlds can recognize in these descriptions their own reactions to similar situations'.[14] Habermas does, to be sure, acknowledge that art, which is to say aesthetic experience, in particular represents a privileged sphere in which otherwise aberrant, idiosyncratic judgements can be made without the censure of irrationality being the consequence of their distance from common cultural understanding. Through this sort of recasting of rationality, Habermas arrives at a position which comes close to that of social institutionalism, in which the institutional rules and norms are so deeply embedded that thinking outside of them is exceptionally unusual. Chang recognizes something similar when he argues that '[t]he limited choice set may also be [...] because we have been taught to limit the range of what we want and what we think may be possible through the socialization process and deliberate manipulation of our preferences'.[15] Precisely this version of rationality is one that will be encountered again below in the examination of the place of so-called rational myths in institutions.

By contrast, in opposition to Chicago School-style libertarianism, Kahneman stresses that Humans 'often need help to make more accurate judgments and better decisions, and in some cases policies and institutions can provide that help',[16] thus approaching a historical institutionalist perspective, which would suggest that individuals act in accordance with a set of norms which, rather than being unspoken, impose obligations: people do what they 'ought' to. Koelbe oversimplifies, but perhaps not a great deal, when he says that

> [t]o the historical institutionalists, institutions play a determinant role since they shape the actions of individuals but are at times affected by collective and individual choices. To the sociologists, institutions are themselves dependent upon larger 'macro level' variables such as society and culture, and the individual is a largely dependent and rather unimportant variable.[17]

As Thelen and Steinmo define it, in its simplest terms

> historical institutionalism represents an attempt to illuminate how political struggles 'are mediated by the institutional setting in which [they] take place'. In general, historical institutionalists work with a definition of institutions that includes both formal organizations and informal rules and procedures.[18]

Institutions, artworlds, new music

Actors according to such a view are, unsurprisingly, quite different from the Econs of rational choice theories, though perhaps still some way from the complex Humans of everyday life. Part of the reason for this may lie in the imbrication of institutional theory and economics or political science: 'historical institutionalists tend to see political actors not so much as all-knowing, rational maximizers, but more as rule-following "satisficers"'.[19] These political actors, then, have an intimate understanding of 'good enough'. Yet what follows from this sort of perspective is that not only do real people not consider what would maximize their self-interest with every decision they take, they do not even necessarily *know* what would be most advantageous for them. Instead, the historical institutionalist position is that 'most of us, most of the time, follow societally defined rules, even when so doing may not be directly in our self-interest'.[20] As Thelen and Steinmo go on to argue, it is not even the case that singular routes lead to desired goals, *even presuming* that a rational actor might have such clarity regarding their self-interested aims. This suggests that full-blooded historical institutionalism requires a healthy dose of game theory in order to make sense of how actors, institutions and events are intertwined.[21]

In such an institutional context, the institution necessarily shapes the activity of individuals because, though individuals bring certain desires and goals into an institutional milieu, these exogenous goals are shaped by the institution. Some goals are simply not achievable within certain institutional contexts, which is to say that 'institutions shape the goals political actors pursue and the way they structure power relations among them, privileging some and putting others at a disadvantage'.[22] Legitimated (and, for that matter, legitimate) power is, as W. Richard Scott opines, 'normatively regulated power'.[23] 'What we do around here' is always, then, an expression of power, whether active enforcement or passive conformity is the mode in which that power is deployed. Once an actor enters an institutional context

> organizational position [. . .] influences an actor's definition of his own interests, by establishing his institutional responsibilities and relationship to other actors. In this way, organizational factors affect both the degree of pressure an actor can bring to bear on policy and the likely direction of that pressure.[24]

Georgina Born's description of IRCAM in the mid-1980s shows composers and music technologists operating in full 'satsificing' mode, both with full knowledge of the ways in which the institutional demands of IRCAM actively force a reshaping of private goals *and* in ways which seem to be (unnoticed) implicit consequences of being involved with IRCAM. In the first case, Born spoke to a psychoacoustician regarding the development of the Formes software, who acknowledged the challenges of having to negotiate between a private desire to carry out development which 'becomes a much richer domain and generates knowledge, in the sense of coming to know how to create a system as well as gaining an end goal' with the demands of the artistic aspects of IRCAM personified as Boulez – to have working tools ready for use whenever a composer may need them. The issue was summarized by another member of the musicians' group: 'We need to translate all these ideas into "*les categories de Pierre*"' (Born, 214–15). As the director of the Chants/Formes project more charitably described it: 'If you present [a technology] to Boulez that's not in a musical context, he's not interested, even if it's a very deep and interesting thing. [. . .] Boulez is interested in having real musical output' (ibid., 140). Here there is slippage from an active understanding that there exist local 'rules and regulation' to which one must subscribe in order to 'get things done'

> towards the normalization of that in the seemingly more reasonable idea that, as a musical institution, it makes sense that a *musical* output should be placed first and foremost, notwithstanding the possibility that *better* musical outputs might be achieved by taking the longer, technical route. This possibility becomes gradually invisible or only expressible in the light of an understanding that 'musical significance' takes priority.
>
> Georgina Born, *Rationalizing Culture: IRCAM, Boulez, and the Institutionalization of the Musical Avant-Garde* (Berkeley and Los Angeles: University of California Press, 1995).

As Jepperson puts it, '[i]nstitutions are not just constraint structures; all institutions simultaneously empower and control'.[25] Exogenous goals do not somehow magically become endogenous goals according to such a view. Institutional analysis does not claim that institutions *produce* these goals, but they do set the limits of the possible; they 'constrain and refract politics but they are never the sole "cause" of outcomes'.[26] They structure how, in a Marxist analysis, for instance, class conflict takes place, but do not — at any rate not on their own — give rise to the possibility of that conflict. As Hall summarizes it:

> Institutions emerge from this analysis as critical mediating variables, constructed by conscious endeavor but usually more consequential than their creators intended. They are not a substitute for interests and ideas as the ultimate motors of political action, but they have a powerful effect on which interests and ideas will prevail.[27]

Though Culkin was summarizing McLuhan's description of the operation of media, it is no less true in this context to observe that '[w]e shape our tools and thereafter they shape us'.[28]

The distinction between historical and social models of institutions may be ultimately quite finely drawn. As March and Olson argue, '[m]uch of the behavior we observe in political institutions reflects the routine way in which people do what they are supposed to do'.[29] What one is 'supposed' to do evidently contains a double meaning: 'The rules may be imposed and enforced by direct coercion and political or organizational authority, or they may be part of a code of appropriate behavior that is learned and internalized through socialization or education.'[30] As such one should be wary, as Habermas cautions, of eliding the two, permitting 'no distinction between cultural values and the institutional embodiment of values in norms',[31] noting too that, for himself at least, social institutionalism essentially thus describes something that is both less and more than institutions as such, rather more showing the ways in which institutions exist within and are inflected by broader cultural formations:

> Institutions are supposed to issue from processes of reaching understanding among acting subjects (and to solidify as objective meaning complexes in relation to them) in a way similar to that in which, on Popper's view, problems, theories, and arguments issue from cognitive processes. With this model we can, it is true, explain the conceptual nature and the relative independence of social reality, but not the specific resistance and *coercive* character of established norms and existing institutions through which societal formations are distinguished from cultural.[32]

As such, '[e]very process of reaching understanding', which is to say every institutional formation, 'takes place against the background of a culturally ingrained preunderstanding'.[33] In

Institutions, artworlds, new music

a sense, the relationship Habermas is proposing between the cultural and the social returns to his thoughts regarding how rationality might, more broadly, be understood. The normative elements of a situation are thus distinguishable – if certainly not always distinguished – from the factual elements. Thus, there is a distinction to be made, for Habermas, between the social currency (*Geltung*) and the validity (*Gültigkeit*) of an argument.[34] As Habermas puts it:

> If arguments are valid, then insight into the internal conditions of their validity can have a rationally motivating force and a corresponding effect. But arguments can also have an influence on the attitudes of addressees independently of their validity – when they are expressed in external circumstances that guarantee their acceptance.[35]

These circumstances, then, relate to '*institutional differentiations of a general conceptual framework* for argumentation as such'. This sort of reflexivity is expressed on the personal level, too, since – recalling the questions of taste noted above – one would

> call a person rational who interprets the nature of his desires and feelings [*Bedürfnisnatur*] in the light of culturally established standards of value, but especially if he can adopt a reflective attitude to the very value standards through which desires and feelings are interpreted.[36]

Aesthetic judgement, in this sense, represents a paradigmatic case of the relationships between desires and cultural values, in the sense that 'arguments that serve to justify standards of value do not satisfy the conditions of discourse' where 'the adequacy of value standards, the vocabulary of our evaluative language generally, is made thematic'.[37] These evaluations, Habermas claims, bring an individual to encounter 'a work or performance in such a way that it can be perceived as an authentic expression of an exemplary experience, in general as the embodiment of a claim to authenticity'.[38] In more general terms, Habermas would have it that discourses essentially recommend that an idea be accepted as a generalizable norm; in the case of aesthetic determinations, 'grounds or reasons serve to guide perception and to make the authenticity of a work so evident that this aesthetic experience can itself become a rational motive for accepting the corresponding standards of value'.[39] In this sort of way, Habermas suggests, institutional norms are ideas which proceed *from* cultural values, such that they become more or less indistinguishable in an everyday sense from reasonable (which is to say, rational) grounds for action. Just as '[i]nstitutional patterns shape behavior such that some courses are perceived as natural and legitimate',[40] so institutional negotiation of cultural values *produces* these patterns in the first place. As such, one might recall the passage from I. C. Jarvie, quoted by Habermas, which captures the simultaneously soft/hard nature of the territory which is thus constructed and, indeed, relates to individual wishes and desires:

> People living in a society have to find their way around it, both to accomplish what they want and to avoid what they do not want. We might say that they construct in their minds a conceptual map of the society and its features, of their own location among them, of the possible paths which will lead them to their goals, and of the hazards along each path. The maps are in a way 'softer' than geographic maps – like dream maps they create the terrain they are mapping. Yet in a way this is a harder reality: geographical maps are never real but sometimes reflect real terrains, yet social maps *are* terrains to be studied and mapped by other people.[41]

Charles Wilson, in his examination of the self-construction of György Ligeti's compositional identity, explicitly sets out to demonstrate the way in which 'composers' public statements, through the uniquely authoritative status accorded them by scholars, have played an essential role in propping up [the] image of the heroically independent creator' (Wilson, 6). As Wilson stresses, despite a wide range of theoretical positions which insist upon the essential embeddedness of individuals within cultures (and, indeed, the common sense view that, 'inspiration' notwithstanding, artistic production does not spring absolutely *ex nihilo*), the image of 'innumerable "isolated" and "autonomous" creators both legitimates and is legitimated by the still widespread "pluralist" paradigm of contemporary culture', while 'the image of "the artist as individual" becomes a valuable promotional tool to [the] market, co-optable by the very forces it once set out to resist' (ibid., 6). In the specific case examined by Wilson, Ligeti deploys the existing notion of the artist as heroically resisting the demands of mainstream and specialist culture alike in his public pronouncements on his work, describing what he does as 'neither "modern" nor "postmodern" but something else', avoiding a return to 'tonality or to expressionism or all the "neo" and retrograde movements which exist everywhere' and using 'certain complex possibilities in rhythm and new possibilities in harmony which are neither tonal nor atonal'. According to his own view, 'I wanted to find my own way and I finally found it' (Ligeti, in ibid., 7). Wilson rightly observes that even this 'neither-nor-ness' is a longstanding reflection of mainstream culture, whether that deplored by Roland Barthes or embedded in the stance of Gustave Flaubert (ibid., 7–8). More pertinently still, Ligeti's development as a composer is deeply intertwined with the communities in which he worked – especially, early in his career, with the Cologne circle from which he is studiously careful to distance himself – while his critique of Boulez's *Structure Ia* essentially reiterates Boulez's own repudiation of the piece, albeit with greater analytical richness, and 'Metamorphoses of Musical Form' retreads matter discussed by Stockhausen in his Darmstadt 'Musik im Raum' presentation (ibid., 10). Nevertheless, as Wilson shows, just this image of heroic individuality then permeates discussions of Ligeti, strongly inflecting the critical commentary surrounding his work. Perhaps even more strikingly, just the same narrative of some sort of individualistic breaking with serial orthodoxy has been applied to Luciano Berio, Bruno Maderna, Luigi Nono and many others (ibid., 11). This norm – the myth of the lone composer – becomes indistinguishable from a 'natural and legitimate' view of what composers, almost necessarily, do.

Charles Wilson, 'György Ligeti and the Rhetoric of Autonomy', *Twentieth-Century Music* 1, no. 1 (2004), 5–28.

Though Habermas is unconvinced that Jarvie's model allows for a distinction between precisely cultural values and the institutional embodiment of such values in norms, nevertheless it helps to emphasize the symbolic-mythical aspects of institutions, which are profoundly intertwined with such an interaction between values and norms. Friedland and Alford, in similar vein, have called for a recognition of institutions as 'simultaneously material and ideal, systems of signs and symbols, rational and transrational'. Of course, the persistence of institutions over time is accounted for, at least in part, by the 'taken for granted-ness' of repeated institutional structural features.[42] Yet, just as institutions are 'supraorganizational patterns of human activity by which individuals and organizations produce and reproduce their material substance and organize time and space', they are also 'symbolic systems, ways of ordering reality, and thereby rendering

Institutions, artworlds, new music

experience of time and space meaningful'.[43] These systems are pervasive. Friedland and Alford emphasize some of the everyday encounters one might have with them:

> This does not mean that when one buys, makes love, votes, or prays that property, love, democracy, or God really exists or really obtains as a result of those behaviors. It means that the behaviors make sense to those who enact the behavior only in relation to those transrational symbolic systems and that those symbolic systems only make sense in terms of the behavior. To believe that 'the people rule', 'a nation decides', 'love conquers all', 'the market is efficient', is no more rational than to hold that 'God watches over us all'.[44]

These sorts of beliefs are what might be characterized, in institutional terms, as 'rational myths'. Like those mentioned by Friedland and Alford, Meyer and Rowan describe universalism, contracts, restitution and expertise as rational myths which have been 'generalized to diverse occupations, organizational programs, and organizational practice', but go further to stress, vitally, that '[t]hese myths may originate from narrow contexts and be applied in different ones'.[45] Meyer and Rowan hypothesize that 'organizations which incorporate institutionalized myths are more legitimate, successful, and likely to survive'.[46] Although this may seem paradoxical, the currency of institutional norms trumps the validity of cultural realities to the extent that, Meyer and Rowan believe, the legitimacy of such myths is self-reinforcing. In short, then, a rational myth is an institutional practice which represents a certain (tacitly coercive) expression of norms which are believed to lead to a certain outcome, *even if* the evidence does not support such 'progress' towards results, while still increasing the legitimacy of the activity. On a broader level, this indicates too a tendency towards institutional isomorphism, which is to say the repetition in fresh contexts of that which already exists elsewhere, even though this does not *necessarily* include a repetition of that which is ostensibly successful.[47]

At the Eighth Meeting of the Związek Kompozytorów Polskich (ZKP; Polish Composers' Union) in June 1955, Tadeusz Baird proposed the foundation of the Warsaw Autumn, specifically proposing that it be modelled according to the example of the Prague Spring Festival (Jakelski, 10). Yet, in the end, it was the language of cultural revival (ibid., vi) and international exchange borrowed from the foundational myths of, amongst other post-war institutions, the Darmstadt New Music Courses which grounded the festival (ibid., 64–65), even though, in the case of Warsaw Autumn, it was the idea of being a bridge between East and West which prevailed, rather than the centrality Darmstadt implicitly claimed for itself (ibid., 71–83). As the festival developed, Józef Patkowski – founder of the Experimental Studio of Polish Radio – defended the Darmstadt model: 'Many of the most free-thinking musicians and theoreticians participate in Darmstadt, [. . .] [n]o-one dictates anything, it is possible to be very critical about the music produced there' (ibid., 40). Aspects of the programmes of the Warsaw Autumn were, in some cases conspicuously, similar to contemporaneous programmes at Darmstadt: David Tudor's visit in 1958 essentially reproduced his Darmstadt programme (John Cage, Bo Nilsson, Karlheinz Stockhausen and Christian Wolff were represented). Between 1956 and 1961, Stockhausen featured in the form of *Klavierstück XI*, *Gesang der Jünglinge*, *Zeitmaße* and *Zyklus*, while Boulez was represented by the *Livre pour quatuor*, the Second Piano Sonata, the *Sonatine* for flute and piano, the first book of *Structures* and *Improvisation sur Mallarmé* (ibid., 10), the Warsaw

> Autumn also presenting Bartók, Berg, Schoenberg, Stravinsky and Webern. Notwithstanding the concerns of, for instance, Wiktor Weinbaum, Director of the Music Group at the Ministerstwo Kultury i Sztuki (MKiS; Ministry of Culture and Art) that not all the interests of ZKP members were being represented, by 1963 it had become official policy to send 'observers to international festivals (Darmstadt) so they can select the most attractive musical works presented there, and bring them back for performance at our festival' (ibid., 76). Lutosławski's riposte to Weinbaum that all those trends that had 'some vitality' were represented is notable (ibid., 35–36).
>
> Of course, the observation that the world of new music is a comparatively small one is reasonable, such that overlaps in presentation are inevitable. It is true too that, with tight budgets and funders to be accountable to, festival directors must be, at least comparatively, cautious. It is also assuredly not the case that the Warsaw Autumn did not *also* have its own distinctive programming. But these aspects do not detract from the underlying point that the programmes of one festival often imitate those at another and, by doing so, increase the institutional legitimacy of the music performed.
>
> Lisa Jakelski, 'The Changing Seasons of the Warsaw Autumn: Contemporary Music in Poland, 1960–1990' (PhD diss., University of California, Berkeley, 2009).

The transmission of rational myths helpfully demonstrates at least some of the ways in which institutions persist over time. Transmission might occur synchronically or diachronically equally well. What matters, Zucker proposes, is that '[t]he actor doing the transmitting simply communicates them as objective fact, and the actor receiving them treats them as an accurate rendition of objective fact'.[48] Even though Meyer and Rowan are surely right that, '[i]n institutionally elaborated environments, organizations also become sensitive to and employ external criteria of worth',[49] Zucker's insistence that 'increasing objectification and exteriority will increase transmission' is no less significant,[50] which is to say that generalizability is prized axiomatically, but also that this process, too, is self-reinforcing:

> Continuity of the transmission process will also increase institutionalization. The more the history of the transmission process is known, the greater the degree of continuity the actors assume. The history of transmission provides a basis for assuming that the meaning of the act is part of the intersubjective common-sense world. As continuity increases, the acts are increasingly objectified and made exterior to the particular interaction. The act is clearly repeatable, not tied to a unique actor or situation.[51]

The grounding of rules in some sort of event is vital. There must be a sense that 'something happened' to cause institutional norms to have formed in the way that they have. As such, 'we see rules as reflecting historical experience in a way that ordinarily makes the rules, but not the experience, accessible to individuals who have not themselves lived through the experience'.[52] Because of this embedded process of transmission, the norm takes on a validity of its own, while 'the specific experiential justifications for specific rules are likely to be irretrievable'.[53] Hayek's description captures both the practice and the belief:

> [an individual] is successful not because he knows why he ought to observe the rules which he does observe, or is even capable of stating all these rules in words, but because his thinking and acting are governed by rules which have by a process of selection

Institutions, artworlds, new music

been evolved in the society in which he lives, and which are thus the product of the experience of generations.[54]

It is, then, in just this way that institutions become what they are: the rational myth – its acceptance and normalization – is a paradigmatic example of how institutions form and remain recognizably the same over time: 'institutions are those social patterns that, when chronically reproduced, owe their survival to relatively self-activating social processes'.[55] In this sense, institutional norms do not only determine what an institution *is*, but also contribute to its longevity: 'routine reproductive procedures support and sustain the pattern, furthering its reproduction – unless collective action blocks, or environmental shock disrupts, the reproductive process'.[56]

> Though he was doubtless there at the event (and had received plenty of polite refusals or late cancellations from Pierre Boulez regarding participation at Darmstadt at other times), when, in a description published in 1962, the first director of the Darmstadt New Music Courses, Wolfgang Steinecke, came to recall 1952's so-called *Wunderkonzert* – ostensibly a foundational event of the nascent Darmstadt School – he exaggerated the event out of all proportion: he added to the programme Boulez's *Structures*, which was not performed, implied that Maderna's first version of *Musica su due dimensioni* was not regarded as a failure, and ignored the broadly catastrophic (in performance terms) presentation of Stockhausen's *Kreuzspiel* (Iddon 2013, 82). It would be some years later before any of the four composers Steinecke mentioned – alongside Boulez, Maderna and Stockhausen was Luigi Nono – had sufficient cultural 'clout' for them to go so far as to outline 'a new thematic, which was of particular significance for the stylistic development within the framework of the generation of the music', as Steinecke claimed. Nonetheless, even *had* all four composers had their music performed, and performed well, what they were *doing* was quite distinct. In a sense, Steinecke was writing nothing more than what – according to how history had turned out – *ought* to have happened. It is only one, if one of the most prominent, examples of how the rational myth of ultra-orthodox serial Darmstadt pervades the discourse around the events of the new music courses, even though the cultural reality of the situation was significantly more fluid. The strength of this myth is indeed such that not only has it been repeated in multiple contexts, but also large numbers of composers – some of whom were present during the foundational years of the early 1950s – have gone to some lengths (as have their defenders and promoters) to define at least parts of their careers specifically in *opposition* to it, as in the cases of Berio, Boulez, Kagel, Ligeti and even Maderna, who moved to and lived in Darmstadt, having an almost everyday interaction with the institution.
>
> Martin Iddon, *New Music at Darmstadt: Nono, Stockhausen, Cage, and Boulez* (Cambridge: Cambridge University Press, 2013).

Nevertheless, though institutions persist over time, in order to do this – and do this successfully – change is inevitable, and vital. As March and Olsen note, the repetition of procedures in routine situations might be taken to imply that novel situations call for invention, but, in truth, the institutional approach tends, instead, to be to mould the unexpected into the shape of the existing system: 'the most standard organizational response to novelty is to find a set of routines that can be used.'[57] Such ways of considering institutional change might be thought to map most neatly onto the model of 'punctuated equilibrium' proposed by Stephen Krasner, according to which 'institutions are characterized by long periods of stability, periodically "punctuated" by

97

crises that bring about relatively abrupt institutional change, after which institutional stasis again sets in'.[58] In broad terms, this is certainly a helpful starting point and describes many, if not most, situations. Yet, of course, such changes, even if approached by the attempt to integrate the novel into the extant procedures for dealing with events, necessarily in turn cause alterations in those procedures. As they change, so too do the rules and routines designed for the *general* approach to the world, a world which now encompasses this *specific* novelty. Furthermore, as noted above, even assuming rationalist self-interested Econs to populate the world, there is likely to exist more than one potential route to bring about desired goals. As such, the operations of individuals within the institutional framework themselves bring about contradictions. For there to be more than one path to an end, one might expect too that, along with the order institutional norms bring, such regulations are already rife with contradiction. As such the intersection of institutions which contain inevitable degrees of ambiguity in their functioning, alongside individuals themselves doubtless less rigid and fixed than rational choice theories would imply, necessarily produces 'deviation as well as conformity, variability as well as standardization'.[59]

Considering these more finely nuanced issues, Thelen and Steinmo suggest that there are at least four ways in which institutions encounter and deal with change. Though their examples are focused on the sphere of political science, they are no less germane more broadly:

1   A change in the broader social or cultural context means that an institution which was previously marginal takes on a more central role (or vice versa);
2   Such changes can cause *existing* institutions to find their purpose altered in order to adapt to the new environment, especially where 'new actors' enter existing institutional contexts;
3   Equally, such changes can cause a shift in the strategies adopted by 'old actors' within the existing institutions, as those actors adapt their goals to the changing exogenous environment;
4   Actors adjust goals in accordance with changes in the institution itself, rather than exogenous changes, whether they 'occur in moments of dramatic change (institutional breakdown or institutional formation of the sort that Krasner's model of punctuated equilibrium highlights)' or as a 'result of more piecemeal change resulting from specific political battles or ongoing strategic maneuvering within institutional constraints'.[60]

Between 1970 and 1974, the Darmstadt New Music Courses were radically remodelled, even though the shifts were not necessarily felt to be as great as they were until the more 'press-friendly' leadership of the 1980s and 1990s made pains to *present* the courses afresh. As well as the broad cultural sense, especially among a younger generation in the wake of the 1968 *événements*, that authority not only could but in fact should (or must) be challenged, the local West German context meant that in institutions where *Mitbestimmung* (co-determination) rights had not been achieved such rights were being urgently pursued by those not at the head of these institutions. In the light of this, a group of composers, performers and journalists demanded democratization of the courses, both in terms of the involvement of participants with activities and also in the introduction of measures to attract a more diverse participant body (Iddon 2006, 261–63). An even more local – but no less pressing – factor was a financial crisis in the city budget, Darmstadt itself, as ever, being the major financial backer of the courses (ibid., 267). As a result, the courses moved to a biennial pattern and brought in a call for pieces, with the result that the end of the courses would come to rotate around studio concerts of new pieces, largely premieres, written by participant composers, performed by

Institutions, artworlds, new music

participant instrumentalists, such that, from 1972 onwards, the Kranichsteiner Musikpreis was won by one or more composers and performers at each edition of the courses (ibid., 264). The purpose of coming to Darmstadt thus changed: young composers and performers came, in part, both to be performed and, as the prestige of the Kranichsteiner award increased, to receive institutional approbation for their work. This change of focus provided a space for younger composers to take centre stage, whether as Helmut Lachenmann did in running the first Composition Studio in 1972, or by winning the Kranichsteiner Musikpreis as Wolfgang Rihm did in 1978. Arguably too, the diversity made it possible for New Complexity and spectralism, initially in the hands of Brian Ferneyhough and Gérard Grisey respectively, to flourish. As a result of these changes, even though there remained grumbling until the then-director, Ernst Thomas, left the role at the beginning of the 1980s, the institution managed to retain its broad shape and authority, even though its mode of operation had shifted to some degree. By contrast, Karlheinz Stockhausen was less able to adapt: his 1974 courses remained as authoritarian as ever and, following further participant protests, he found himself uninvited from 1976 onwards, with a single return visit in 1996 (Iddon 2008).

Martin Iddon, 'Trying to Speak: Between Politics and Aesthetics, Darmstadt 1970–1972', *Twentieth-Century Music* 3, no. 2 (2006), 255–75.

————, 'Pamphlets and Protests: The End of Stockhausen's Darmstadt', in *Musikkulturen in der Revolte: Studien zu Rock, Avantgarde und Klassik im Umfeld von '1968'*, ed. Beate Kutschke (Stuttgart: Franz Steiner, 2008), 55–65.

There are, unsurprisingly, significant correlations between the generalist descriptions of institutions above and what Arthur Danto termed the artworld, which refers variously, as George Dickie summarizes it, to 'the rich structure in which particular works of art are embedded', '*the institutional nature of art*' and 'the broad social institutions in which works of art have their place'.[61] In this context, Danto noted that '[t]o see something as art requires something the eye cannot descry – an atmosphere of artistic theory, a knowledge of history of art: an artworld'.[62] To be sure, Danto does not approach a solution to the version of Meno's paradox which inevitably ensues in the case of the artwork, perhaps best captured by Heidegger: 'What art is should be inferable from the work. What the work of art is we can come to know only from the essence of art.'[63] This is to say that one can, logically speaking, know nothing of art, because to know of art in general, one would have first to know specific artworks, but in order to recognize an artwork *as* an artwork, one would have to have a conception of what art is. Danto – like Dickie and Becker after him – is much more pragmatic in this respect. For Danto, the idea of an artwork which *precedes* the world which gives birth to it, and which bears it, is untenable in any practical sense. His position in general is to inveigh

> against the isolation of artworks from the historical and generally causal matrices from which they derive their identities and structures. The 'work itself' thus presupposes so many causal connections with its artistic environment that an ahistorical theory of art can have no philosophical defense.[64]

Dickie's solution is to claim that 'every work of art must have some minimal *potential* value or worthiness', which is to say that there must be, even if nebulously, a threshold of 'art content', which accounts for the base level of what Dickie refers to as 'the classificatory sense of "work of art"', while wanting to preserve the distinction between this and the evaluative sense of the same expression (an evaluative sense which, as noted above, Habermas claims is the privileged territory of aesthetics proper).[65] As Dickie puts it, then, for his purposes, what matters is not, as such, that

> [t]he institutional theory of art may sound like saying, 'A work of art is an object of which someone has said, "I christen this object a work of art."' Rather the question revolves around the way in which that status is conferred: just as the christening of a child has as its background the history and structure of the church, conferring the status of art has as its background the Byzantine complexity of the artworld.[66]

The artworld itself, then, is fairly clearly recognizable as a sort of institution in the terms outlined earlier. Dickie describes the theatre precisely as 'as an established way of doing and behaving', which 'occurs on both sides of the "footlights": both the players and the audience are involved and go to make up the institution of the theater'.[67] The roles of all of these individuals within the theatrical artworld are established by its historical traditions, which is to say its institutional norms. What is presented in a theatre, Dickie says, is art because it is presented within an institution where theatrical art happens, within the theatre-world framework.[68] The institution of the theatre, then, *is* the sum of these practices. As just that sum, institutional theory offers a reminder – against the tempting romanticism of everyday images of artistic production – that in order to be in the world *as* art, a great many people are required, carrying out a great many tasks. In the case of painting, which Howard Becker takes to be paradigmatic of art at its most solitary (without the more obvious labour required for the production of films, concerts, plays or operas), there remain all manner of activities intertwined with the act of putting paint to canvas:

> Painters [. . .] depend on manufacturers for canvas, stretchers, paint, and brushes; on dealers, collectors, and museum curators for exhibition space and financial support; on critics and aestheticians for the rationale for what they do; on the state for the patronage or even the advantageous tax laws which persuade collectors to buy works and donate them to the public; on members of the public to respond to the work emotionally; and on the other painters, contemporary and past, who created the tradition which makes the backdrop against which their work makes sense.[69]

Becker sagely adds that it is not necessary 'even that [these people] be alive at the same time'.[70] These individuals 'keep the machinery of the artworld working and thereby provide for its continuing existence'.[71] Though Dickie notes that '*every person* who sees himself as a member of the artworld is thereby a member',[72] he also goes on to observe that entry into the artworld is *also* determined by a knowledge of 'the rules of the game', which is to say that, in order to be a fully fledged participant in an institution, one must both *know* and *conform* to the norms which give rise to and support the continuation of that institution:

> All of these roles are institutionalized and must be learned in one way or another by the participants. For example, a theater-goer is not just someone who happens to enter a theater; he is a person who enters with certain expectations and knowledge about what he will experience and an understanding of how he should behave in the face of what he will experience.[73]

It is not here, then, a question of not caring to belong to any club that would have one as a member. In order to be a member of this sort of club, one would, in a sense, *already* have to be

Institutions, artworlds, new music

a member, since membership *is* the internalization and reproduction of a certain set of institutional norms.[74]

> As Björn Heile notes, for the most part Mauricio Kagel has been viewed, much like Ligeti, as a sort of 'internal dissident' within the post-war avant-garde, part of the Cologne circle, but critical of its orthodoxy and dogma (Heile, 16). While that view certainly has some merits – and Heile is doubtless right that the more scientific pronouncements of that scene would surely have been at odds both with Kagel's intellectual background and with his sense of the absurd – the way in which Kagel *became* part of that circle is assuredly no less significant. As Heile describes it, Kagel was, following his arrival, both 'keen to belong and to learn' and to 'mimic the typical soundworld of integrally serial works of the late '50s even where they are not actually serially constructed' (ibid., 17). His 'visiting card', the 1957 revision of his 1953 sextet, *looks* like a post-1951 piece of European multiple serialism, stereotypical almost to the point of parody and rich with polymetric passages, different time signatures for different parts, quarter-tones and multiple playing techniques. Kagel's own commentary speaks of the vertical and horizontal use of 'a series of 21 durations', resulting in 'chords of rhythms'. Other aspects of his language are redolent of the exegeses of the time: the String Sextet is made up of a '"constellation of timbres, rhythms, bowings and dynamic levels" which "permeate" the composition [...] pointing to a tentative serialization of these parameters' (ibid., 18–19). Yet the polymetric structures appear first in the revision, undertaken after Kagel had arrived in Germany from Argentina and encountered the post-war avant-garde: 'one might be forgiven for suspecting that one reason why Kagel introduced polymetres was to make his piece look more complex and difficult than it really was. After all, the actual rhythms were not affected by the revision, and they are not all that difficult' (ibid., 19). A restructuring of the form similarly moved the sextet from a conventional 'dramatic first and a slow second movement' form into one which became 'highly episodic with frequent dramatic ruptures between seemingly self-contained sections' (ibid., 20). Notwithstanding his implicit claims for sophisticated serial underpinnings, Kagel 'appears to invent rows as he goes along, more or less at random' and, while 'stress[ing] technical and structural issues, [...] is silent on the source for his rhythms'. In sum, in order to gain acceptance, Heile asserts that Kagel 'may well have pretended to be a more orthodox serial composer than he was' (ibid., 17).

> Björn Heile, *The Music of Mauricio Kagel* (Aldershot: Ashgate, 2006).

All these individuals are, then, what Becker terms 'integrated professionals' (as, for that matter, are the artists themselves) and, with their integration into the institution of the artworld, it becomes *necessary* that the institution continue to reproduce itself, which is to say to *continue to present* artworks of the sort that *it presents*: this activity is a major part of the 'relatively self-activating social processes' of the artworld. Notably, as Becker observes, this requires precisely that the available art meet the available space for presentation in order to validate the integrity and sustainability of the artworld institution. In short, 'the aesthetic current in a world will certify as sufficiently good to be displayed roughly the amount needed to fill the display opportunities'.[75] In broad terms, this means that artistic institutions tend towards treating artists as interchangeable. To use Becker's examples, if one cannot have a Picasso, then a Matisse will do just as well: 'anyone who wants to exhibit "Twenty New American Photographers" or publish "Ten New British Poets" will always be able to fill those slots'.[76] In saying this, Becker is not making the claim that artworlds have no interest in making judgements about quality – notwithstanding Dickie's 'minimum aesthetic value' – but rather that, even though those involved with an artworld both can and do make judgements of taste, artworlds are concerned with larger numbers of artists than the very best for at least two reasons. First, more idealistically, as might be clear from Thelen and Steinmo's outlining of changes within institutions – as relevant to the institutions of artworlds as any other – what is perceived of as having greatest validity in the moment, such that it may later transpire that a supported artist who was initially marginal (either to the institution or to the world at large) becomes central. Though artworld participants may make judgements of taste, they are not so confident in the validity of those judgements over time as all that. Second, more cynically, if an artworld concerned itself with only the very greatest of artwork – especially only the very greatest as presently judged by that present set of integrated artworld professionals – then the institutions of that artworld would necessarily fail since 'we would shut our galleries eleven months out of the year, open Carnegie Hall every now and then, and publish many fewer books'.[77] Not only would that mean that those involved would lose their jobs – a pressing reason for continuity, nonetheless – but the institution would then simply not be in a position to present the very finest of work, since 'you cannot maintain those organizations with such sporadic use'.[78]

Nevertheless, in its decisions about what and who will be presented, even in this larger frame, an artworld necessarily defines the boundaries of what will be acceptable *as* art but also *who* can be accepted as a member of the artworld. It is here too that Becker sees those outer limits of the frame of the institution with respect to artworks, recalling Thelen and Steinmo's note, for them in the context of institutional change but not less significant here, that 'institutions explain everything until they explain nothing'.[79] To be sure, Becker relies upon Dickie's 'enfranchised group of persons who serve, so to speak, as trustees for the generalized *musée imaginaire*, the occupants of which are the artworks of the world'.[80] Following Dickie's claim that an object which cannot *be appreciated* as art cannot *be* art at all, there are limits and constraints upon these custodians who cannot 'by fiat declare just anything a work of art'.[81] Ted Cohen, arguing in part that Duchamp's *Fountain* ought not so unambiguously to be declared an artwork under Dickie's conditions, maintains that, among other items, objects which could not meet the threshold for appreciation might include 'ordinary thumbtacks, cheap white envelopes, the plastic forks given at some drive-in restaurants'.[82] Yet Danto feels that Cohen is, implicitly at least, relying upon standards which look for the beautiful – in its traditional elision with the good – in a problematic way since 'in fact aesthetic values compass [. . .] negative considerations; we are repelled, disgusted, even sickened by certain works of art'.[83]

Broadly speaking, for the audience at the audience at the 1954 Donaueschinger Musiktage, what John Cage and David Tudor presented did not constitute music. Responses ranged from 'shouting, laughter, and general confusion', through comparisons to Charlie Chaplin and Buster Keaton, to the whole event being dubbed 'childish sensationalism' (Iddon 2013, 161). Yet swathes of the artworld of European new music found ways to come to accommodate both Americans. Tudor was comparatively straightforward: because of his performances of music which *was* recognizable as music from the European perspective – and because at the time he seemed to be performing European musics beyond the range of most of his contemporaries – even those who were sceptical about Tudor's repertoire choices found it possible to accommodate him in their worldview (ibid., 171–84). There was even some sort of reversal, or rethinking, of earlier critiques such that discussions of indeterminate music were impelled by the thought that only the brilliance of a performer like

Tudor would turn them from lead into gold (ibid., 259–60, 263). As such, Cage's position was always more complex. For some, his work would essentially never be acceptable and he was thus ejected from the orderly artworld of post-war new music forthwith (ibid., 300–303). For others, however, it became necessary *not* to change the standards by which it was possible to recognize what constituted new music as such, but rather to reshape Cage into a figure whose work *did* mirror ideas which the Europeans already had, whether it was Stockhausen's attempt to show that Cage's notations for the *Solo for Piano* necessarily indicated that Cage had 'properly' composerly desires and that those desires mapped onto (almost) the same sorts of notational ambiguity that Stockhausen had worked out in *Zyklus* (ibid., 240–42) or, by contrast, Heinz-Klaus Metzger's several attempts to turn Cage into a leftist European-style class warrior, where the freedoms of Cage's score map onto emancipated labour – the conductor's part in the *Concert for Piano and Orchestra*, in which the conductor's arm performs variable clock time, doubtless an arch comment on workers clocking on and off, therefore – and where letting the notes be themselves represents a (by turns, violent and Zen) 'slap in the face of every traditional European aesthetic concept' (ibid., 225–28).

Martin Iddon, *New Music at Darmstadt: Nono, Stockhausen, Cage, and Boulez* (Cambridge: Cambridge University Press, 2013).

Perhaps, at most, from the sort of perspective offered here, one might go so far as to agree with Danto that 'unappreciable objects would be those which would not support the claim that every object can be viewed practically *or* aesthetically. These objects cannot be psychically distanced.'[84] In this sense, the institution provides the framework for the making of aesthetic judgements, providing the rules *according to which* aesthetic determinations take place. Moreover, the impetus for institutional norms to reproduce themselves in social practices means that artworks which meet *existing* thresholds of recognizability as art are more likely to find (present) acceptance. This is certainly not to say that the unfamiliar *cannot* be acceptable – far from it. Rather, the integration of the unfamiliar into the institution requires either precisely that the reception of unfamiliar artworks force that work into the shape of something which becomes more-or-less familiar, thus transforming the work in the process of its reception, or flexing those norms (or even producing new norms) in order to account for this unfamiliar object which is, nevertheless, certainly a part of the world, thus altering the future shape of the institution itself. Even so, as Becker observes, there can be a fine line between acceptance and rejection: 'the organizations of an art world exclude many people whose work closely resembles work accepted as art'.[85] He is convinced that the reasons for acceptability or otherwise must 'lie not in the work but in the ability of an artworld to accept it and its maker', since 'art worlds frequently incorporate at a later date works they originally rejected'.[86] It is, though, precisely in the areas where artworlds reject – cannot make sense of – objects which present themselves as candidates for appreciation, but do not meet the grade, that one finds the point at which institutional theory loses its explicatory power and the point at which aesthetic theory must take over. In this sense, the transgressive, the *unacceptable*, is more important than ever.

Notes

1 Gilbert Ryle, *The Concept of Mind* (London: Hutchinson, 1949), 16.
2 Ibid., 17–18.
3 Karl Polanyi, 'The Economy as Instituted Process' (1957), in *The Sociology of Economic Life*, ed. Mark Granowetter and Richard Swedberg (Boulder, CO: Westview, 1992), 34.

4 Ibid. Polanyi is clear, too, that even where he speaks of the economy, non-economic institutions – he names religion and the state – are no less important than 'monetary institutions or the availability of tools and machines themselves that lighten the toil of labor' (ibid.).

5 Thomas A. Koelbe, 'The New Institutionalism in Political Science and Sociology', *Comparative Politics* 27, no. 2 (1995), 232.

6 Kathleen Thelen and Sven Steinmo, 'Historical Institutionalism in Comparative Politics', in *Structuring Politics: Historical Institutionalism in Comparative Analysis*, ed. Sven Steinmo, Kathleen Thelen and Frank Longstreth (Cambridge: Cambridge University Press, 1992), 7.

7 Friedrich Hayek, *Law, Legislation and Liberty: Rules and Order* (Chicago: University of Chicago Press, 1973), 11.

8 Ha-Joon Chang, *Economics: The User's Guide* (London: Pelican, 2014), 173.

9 Ibid., 198–99. As Chang stresses, superficially rational choice theory is 'a parable of individual *freedom*' since economic actors can procure whatever they may desire, so long as they have the means to afford it, with an 'inseparable' link being drawn within many varieties of free market economics between this liberty to choose as a consumer and an individual's broader political liberty (ibid., 174–75). Nevertheless, as Chang later observes, the limits of human rationality arguably make individuals more, rather than less, significant 'because we admit that individuals are products of society that we can appreciate more the free will of those who make choices that go against social conventions, prevailing ideologies or their class backgrounds' (ibid., 199).

10 See Daniel Kahneman, *Thinking, Fast and Slow* (London: Penguin Books, 2011), esp. 20–25 and 408–18.

11 Ibid., 24.

12 Ibid., 411.

13 Richard Norman (1971), quoted in Jürgen Habermas, *The Theory of Communicative Action: Reason and the Rationalization of Society*, trans. Thomas McCarthy (London: Heinemann, 1984), 16.

14 Habermas, *The Theory of Communicative Action*, 16–17.

15 Chang, *Economics*, 200.

16 Kahneman, *Thinking, Fast and Slow*, 411.

17 Koelbe, 'The New Institutionalism', 232.

18 Thelen and Steinmo, 'Historical Institutionalism in Comparative Politics', 2, quoting G. John Ikenberry. The limits of the political might be conceived of quite broadly. Even writing from the discipline of political science, Thelen and Steinmo cast a wide net, suggesting that 'in general, institutionalists are interested in the whole range of state and societal institutions that shape how political actors define their interests and that structure their relations of power to other groups' (ibid.). Such a view seems, to me at least, thus to include any form of institution at all, to the degree that all cultural institutions are also, perforce, societal institutions.

19 Ibid., 8.

20 Ibid.

21 Ibid., 9.

22 Ibid., 2.

23 W. Richard Scott, 'Unpacking Institutional Arguments', in *The New Institutionalism in Organizational Analysis*, ed. Walter W. Powell and Paul J. DiMaggio (Chicago: University of Chicago Press, 1991), 176.

24 Peter Hall, *Governing the Economy* (Oxford: Oxford University Press, 1986), 19.

25 Ronald L. Jepperson, 'Institutions, Institutional Effects, and Institutionalism', in *The New Institutionalism*, ed. Powell and DiMaggio, 146.

26 Thelen and Steinmo, 'Historical Institutionalism in Comparative Politics', 2–3.

27 Peter A. Hall, 'The Movement from Keynesianism to Monetarism: Institutional Analysis and British Economic Policy in the 1970s', in *Structuring Politics*, ed. Steinmo, Thelen and Longstreth, 109.

28 John Culkin, quoted in Lance Strate, 'Studying Media *as* Media: McLuhan and the Media Ecology Approach', in *Transforming McLuhan: Cultural, Critical, and Postmodern Perspectives*, ed. Paul Grosswiler (New York: Peter Lang, 2010), 73.

29 James G. March and Johan P. Olsen, *Rediscovering Institutions: The Organizational Basis of Politics* (New York: Free Press, 1989), 21.

30 Ibid., 21–22.

31 Habermas, *The Theory of Communicative Action*, 81.

32 Ibid.

33 Ibid., 100.

34 Ibid., 29.

Institutions, artworlds, new music

35 Ibid.
36 Ibid., 20.
37 Ibid.
38 Ibid.
39 Ibid.
40 Walter W. Powell, 'Expanding the Scope of Institutional Analysis', in *The New Institutionalism*, ed. Powell and DiMaggio, 192.
41 I. C. Jarvie, *Thinking about Society: Theory and Practice* (Dordrecht: D. Reidel, 1986), 28–29.
42 See Scott, 'Unpacking Institutional Arguments', 179.
43 Roger Friedland and Robert R. Alford, 'Bringing Society Back In: Symbols, Practices, and Institutional Contradictions', in *The New Institutionalism*, ed. Powell and DiMaggio, 242–43.
44 Ibid., 250.
45 John W. Meyer and Brian Rowan, 'Institutionalized Organization: Formal Structure as Myth and Ceremony', in *The New Institutionalism*, ed. Powell and DiMaggio, 48.
46 Ibid., 61.
47 See Paul J. DiMaggio and Walter W. Powell, 'The Iron Cage Revisited: Institutional Isomorphism and Collective Rationality in Organizational Fields', in *The New Institutionalism*, ed. Powell and DiMaggio, 72. Those readers who work in tertiary education may well have encountered precisely such uses of 'successful' business practices in the university environment, even though questions of, for instance, profitability do not obviously seem to have very much to do with pedagogy or research. Nor, by contrast, do businesses in broad terms have the same concerns with longevity as those that seem, to me at least, to characterize the work of a university: there are fewer than 6000 companies in the world older than 200 years, over half of which are located in a single country, Japan. Roughly 90% of these companies are small – and, as such, antithetical to 'growth' in a capitalist sense – and employ fewer than 300 people.
48 Lynne G. Zucker, 'The Role of Institutionalization in Cultural Persistence', in *The New Institutionalism*, ed. Powell and DiMaggio, 87.
49 Meyer and Rowan, 'Institutionalized Organization', 51.
50 Zucker, 'The Role of Institutionalization in Cultural Persistence', 87.
51 Ibid.
52 March and Olsen, *Rediscovering Institutions*, 38.
53 Ibid.
54 Hayek, *Law, Legislation and Liberty: Rules and Order*, 11.
55 Jepperson, 'Institutions, Institutional Effects, and Institutionalism', 145.
56 Ibid.
57 March and Olsen, *Rediscovering Institutions*, 34.
58 Thelen and Steinmo, 'Historical Institutionalism in Comparative Politics', 15.
59 March and Olsen, *Rediscovering Institutions*, 38.
60 Thelen and Steinmo, 'Historical Institutionalism in Comparative Politics', 16–17.
61 George Dickie, *Art and the Aesthetic* (Ithaca, NY: Cornell University Press, 1974), 29.
62 Arthur Danto, quoted in ibid., 29.
63 Martin Heidegger, 'The Origin of the Work of Art' (1936), in *Basic Writings*, ed. David Farrell Krell and trans. Albert Hofstadter (London: Routledge, 2009), 144.
64 Arthur C. Danto, *The Transfiguration of the Commonplace: A Philosophy of Art* (Cambridge, MA: Harvard University Press, 1981), 175.
65 Dickie, *Art and the Aesthetic*, 42–43.
66 Ibid., 49.
67 Ibid., 30.
68 Ibid. Dickie notes too that play texts constitute a part of literature in their unperformed guises and, as a result, are recognizable as artworks of a different kind in the literary artworld. As much as the artworld itself is a matrix, there is also a matrix of artworlds that intersect one with another.
69 Howard Becker, *Art Worlds* (Berkeley: University of California Press, 1982), 13.
70 Ibid.
71 Dickie, *Art and the Aesthetic*, 35–36.
72 Ibid. My italics.
73 Ibid.
74 For more detailed criticism of the notion that anyone who sees themselves as a member of an artworld *is* a member of that artworld, see Becker, *Art Worlds*, 150–53.

75 Ibid., 230.

76 Ibid., 231.

77 Ibid.

78 Ibid.

79 Thelen and Steinmo, 'Historical institutionalism in Comparative Politics', 15.

80 Danto, *The Transfiguration of the Commonplace*, 91–92.

81 Ibid.

82 Ted Cohen, 'The Possibility of Art: Remarks on a Proposal by Dickie', *Philosophical Review* 82, no.1 (1973), 78. In truth, Cohen is also trying to show that the problems of giving minimum threshold status to candidates for aesthetic appreciation reveal underlying flaws in Dickie's basic position.

83 Danto, *The Transfiguration of the Commonplace*, 92. Arguably, Danto deploys some sleight of hand in this critique. For right or wrong, Cohen seems to be talking about aesthetic value, while Danto lets his argument slide instead into one about aesthetic values. At the very least, they seem to me to be talking at cross purposes.

84 Ibid., 91–92. Even this is hardly an unproblematic stance, of course. The idea that aesthetic distance has to do with 'proper' approaches to judgement is no less historically grounded than many of the other approaches Danto and others rightly see as involved in particular contexts. Moreover, many more recent forms of immersive art, particularly in, say, the work of Punchdrunk or Blast Theory, offer direct challenges to Danto in ways not dissimilar to the clash which motivates Cohen's encounter with Duchamp. Neither is the practical/aesthetic distinction made by Danto a universal, since it would seem unlikely to have been recognized in this form, at least, by the Ancient Greeks, as outlined in, among other places, Giorgio Agamben, *The Man without Content*, trans. Georgia Albert (Stanford, CA: Stanford University Press, 1999).

85 Becker, *Art Worlds*, 227.

86 Ibid.

Bibliography

Agamben, Giorgio. *The Man without Content*. Translated by Georgia Albert. Stanford, CA: Stanford University Press, 1999.

Becker, Howard. *Art Worlds*. Berkeley: University of California Press, 1982.

Born, Georgina. *Rationalizing Culture: IRCAM, Boulez, and the Institutionalization of the Musical Avant-Garde*. Berkeley and Los Angeles: University of California Press, 1995.

Chang, Ha-Joon. *Economics: The User's Guide*. London: Pelican, 2014.

Cohen, Ted. 'The Possibility of Art: Remarks on a Proposal by Dickie'. *Philosophical Review* 82, no. 1 (1973): 69–82.

Danto, Arthur C. *The Transfiguration of the Commonplace: A Philosophy of Art*. Cambridge, MA: Harvard University Press, 1981.

Dickie, George. *Art and the Aesthetic*. Ithaca, NY: Cornell University Press, 1974.

DiMaggio, Paul J., and Walter W. Powell. 'The Iron Cage Revisited: Institutional Isomorphism and Collective Rationality in Organizational Fields'. In *The New Institutionalism*, edited by Powell and DiMaggio, 63–82.

Friedland, Roger, and Robert R. Alford. 'Bringing Society Back In: Symbols, Practices, and Institutional Contradictions'. In *The New Institutionalism*, edited by Powell and DiMaggio, 232–63.

Habermas, Jürgen. *The Theory of Communicative Action: Reason and the Rationalization of Society*. Translated by Thomas McCarthy. London: Heinemann, 1984.

Hall, Peter A. *Governing the Economy*. Oxford: Oxford University Press, 1986.

———. 'The Movement from Keynesianism to Monetarism: Institutional Analysis and British Economic Policy in the 1970s'. In *Structuring Politics*, edited by Steinmo, Thelen and Longstreth, 90–113.

Hayek, Friedrich. *Law, Legislation and Liberty: Rules and Order*. Chicago: University of Chicago Press, 1973.

Heidegger, Martin. 'The Origin of the Work of Art' (1936). In *Basic Writings*, translated by Albert Hofstadter and edited by David Farrell Krell, 139–212. London: Routledge, 2009.

Heile, Björn. *The Music of Mauricio Kagel*. Aldershot: Ashgate, 2006.

Iddon, Martin. 'The Dissolution of the Avant-Garde, Darmstadt 1968–1984'. PhD diss., University of Cambridge, 2004.

———. 'Trying to Speak: Between Politics and Aesthetics, Darmstadt 1970–1972'. *Twentieth-Century Music* 3, no. 2 (2006): 255–75.

Institutions, artworlds, new music

———. 'Pamphlets and Protests: The End of Stockhausen's Darmstadt'. In *Musikkulturen in der Revolte: Studien zu Rock, Avantgarde und Klassik im Umfeld von '1968'*, edited by Beate Kutschke, 55–65. Stuttgart: Franz Steiner, 2008.

———. *New Music at Darmstadt: Nono, Stockhausen, Cage, and Boulez*. Cambridge: Cambridge University Press, 2013.

Jakelski, Lisa. 'The Changing Seasons of the Warsaw Autumn: Contemporary Music in Poland, 1960–1990'. PhD diss., University of California, Berkeley, 2009.

Jarvie, I. C. *Thinking about Society: Theory and Practice*. Dordrecht: D. Reidel, 1986.

Jepperson, Ronald L. 'Institutions, Institutional Effects, and Institutionalism'. In *The New Institutionalism*, edited by Powell and DiMaggio, 143–63.

Kahneman, Daniel. *Thinking, Fast and Slow*. London: Penguin Books, 2011.

Koelbe, Thomas A. 'The New Institutionalism in Political Science and Sociology'. *Comparative Politics* 27, no. 2 (1995): 231–43.

March, James G., and Johan P. Olsen. *Rediscovering Institutions: The Organizational Basis of Politics*. New York: Free Press, 1989.

Meyer, John W., and Brian Rowan. 'Institutionalized Organization: Formal Structure as Myth and Ceremony'. In *The New Institutionalism*, edited by Powell and DiMaggio, 41–62.

Polanyi, Karl. 'The Economy as Instituted Process' (1957). In *The Sociology of Economic Life*, edited by Mark Granowetter and Richard Swedberg, 29–51. Boulder, CO: Westview, 1992.

Powell, Walter W. 'Expanding the Scope of Institutional Analysis'. In *The New Institutionalism*, edited by Powell and DiMaggio, 183–203.

Powell, Walter W., and Paul J. DiMaggio, eds. *The New Institutionalism in Organizational Analysis*. Chicago: University of Chicago Press, 1991.

Ryle, Gilbert. *The Concept of Mind*. London: Hutchinson, 1949.

Scott, W. Richard. 'Unpacking Institutional Arguments'. In *The New Institutionalism*, edited by Powell and DiMaggio, 164–82.

Steinmo, Sven, Kathleen Thelen and Frank Longstreth, eds. *Structuring Politics: Historical Institutionalism in Comparative Analysis*. Cambridge: Cambridge University Press, 1992.

Strate, Lance. 'Studying Media *as* Media: McLuhan and the Media Ecology Approach'. In *Transforming McLuhan: Cultural, Critical, and Postmodern Perspectives*, edited by Paul Grosswiler, 67–80. New York: Peter Lang, 2010.

Thelen, Kathleen, and Sven Steinmo. 'Historical Institutionalism in Comparative Politics'. In *Structuring Politics: Historical Institutionalism in Comparative Analysis*, edited by Steinmo, Thelen and Longstreth, 1–32.

Wilson, Charles. 'György Ligeti and the Rhetoric of Autonomy'. *Twentieth-Century Music* 1, no. 1 (2004): 5–28.

Zucker, Lynne G., 'The Role of Institutionalization in Cultural Persistence'. In *The New Institutionalism*, edited by Powell and DiMaggio, 83–107.

4
MODERNISM AND HISTORY

David J. Code

'I personally recall that world, which you can only imagine was preferable to this one,' she said. 'Eras are conveniences, particularly for those who never experienced them. We carve history from totalities beyond our grasp. Bolt labels on the result.'
— *William Gibson,* The Peripheral *(2014)*[1]

Thus it is the evolution – the fate – of our own thinking that we have seen, for good or ill, inscribing itself into those studies that were intended, above all, to scrutinize a recent past.
— *Pierre Boulez,* Penser la musique aujourd'hui *(1963)*[2]

Any inquiry into 'modernism and history' that begins with the hope of securely framing modernism *in* history will quickly discover the acuity of the image, in my first epigraph, of contingent constructs carved from an ungraspable totality. For even if we sidestep the thorny question of modernism's elusive historical origins – to which we find numerous, widely disparate answers across specialist and non-specialist literatures alike – what might seem at first like a more secure ending boundary for a distinctly modernist historiography also proves, on closer inquiry, a 'convenience' of differing value for different commentators. Within an accessible 1997 evaluation of the discipline of history around the millennium, for example, Richard J. Evans, while accepting that some of the publications he describes as postmodern 'would probably not be accepted as such by their authors', nonetheless finds the label a useful shorthand for his impression that 'something important has happened to history in the last twenty years or so. The great overarching narratives such as Marxism and modernization theory have collapsed.'[3] But with a little further investigation, we find that even this most widely accepted determinant of a (loosely located) late 'boundary moment' for modernist approaches to history – that is, the break in postmodernity from any sense of a single, universal 'master narrative' – may not quite suffice to fix modernism within a stable and discrete historical era.

For one intriguing instance, written rather closer to that era's supposed 'collapse', Marshall Berman begins the rich study of 'the experience of modernity' he published in 1982 under the Marxian title *All That Is Solid Melts into Air* by suggesting, in the face of some 'bleak' implications he saw in early postmodern theory, that 'remembering the modernisms of the nineteenth century can give us the vision and courage to create the modernisms of the twenty-first'.[4] No

Modernism and history

doubt those for whom a 'postmodern' turn came, instead, with palpable promises of liberation from the many oppressive aspects of modernism's master narratives might well see in such a notion of 'modernisms of the twenty-first century' (which brings to mind the 1980 essay by Jürgen Habermas: 'Modernity – an Incomplete Project?') a wholly misguided 'futuristic nostalgia' (as it were) for cultural proclivities better consigned, after Leon Trotsky, to 'the dustbin of history'.[5] These two cases alone, at any rate, might suffice to suggest that any delineation of 'modernism in history' can itself only be inextricably *historical* – the product of ongoing debates within a contentiously shared 'era'. One practical way to approach the web of contingencies and conveniences that inevitably arises for an essay of this nature is to take Evans's sense of 'postmodernism in its more constructive modes' as a summons to preface any selection of exemplary cases in modernist music historiography with an 'open acknowledgement of the historian's own subjectivity'.[6]

To that end, I will begin by recalling, on one hand, the suggestion in Carl Dahlhaus's 1983 study *Foundations of Music History* that the idea of a quasi-coherent 'generation' may be one of the more robust historiographical constructs, and on the other, the remainder of that complete sentence in my first epigraph: 'Eras are conveniences, *particularly for those who never experienced them*'.[7] For if that postmodern 'boundary moment' has any substance at all, it seems crucial to acknowledge that someone of my generation actually 'never experienced' modernism in its 'high' or 'classic' form. Of course the situation has never been simple – indeed a bit more retrospection brings the suspicion that those of us born in the 1960s have always experienced a thoroughly hybrid perspective on musical modernism and whatever came after.[8]

At risk of indulging the 'pseudo-dialectical' thinking that Richard Taruskin, in the polemical preface to his *Oxford History of Western Music*, has strenuously challenged in Dahlhaus's *Foundations*, I find that one useful heuristic framing of this hybrid perspective arises from a recognition, at its widest extremes, of a relatively clear opposition between 'music History (capital H)' and 'music history (small h)' – taking the former to mean an approach rooted in some notion of universal historical laws, and the latter an approach driven by relations to contingent, particular historical events. No argument is needed to identify the philosopher Theodor W. Adorno, high priest of 'negative dialectics', as by far the most influential practitioner of the former. On the other hand, Taruskin affirms his allegiance to the latter when stating his determination to discard the 'tenets of neo-Hegelian art history' in favour of an 'investigation of the actual causes of aesthetic and stylistic evolution, which are to be found within rather than outside the histories of social and political affairs'.[9]

Taking these two influential voices as exemplary case studies for inclinations apparent, to lesser degrees, across wide spans of literature, in what follows I will offer a brief sketch of their stated methodological aims, followed by a selective assessment of their treatment of a few specific moments in modern music history. Further exemplifying the 'subject position' (as we now say) informing this chapter, I will give particular focus, in the latter phases, to the different accounts of one of my own specialist interests, the music of Claude Debussy – whose longstanding centrality to modern music historiography has found its most startlingly specific formulation in Pierre Boulez's famous claim (in a 1958 encyclopedia article) that modern music 'awakens' in a single piece, the 1894 *Prélude à l'après-midi d'un faune*.[10]

Finally, in partial mitigation of the pseudo-dialectical structure that arises from the juxtaposition of Adorno's 'History' with Taruskin's 'history', I will set up some closing thoughts by turning back – as a free-floating 'third term' rather than a neo-Hegelian 'synthesis' – to some further writings of Boulez himself. If his most infamous remarks now exemplify an authoritarian side of high modernism whose passing nobody could possibly mourn, others, I find, still offer surprising sidelights on the question of cultural bias that seems endemic to modernist music historiography. No doubt Boulez's extravagant claim for his most illustrious modern French forebear can be deemed, in part, a further instance of the same bias. But at least he was able to admit that his nomination of 'Mallarmé, Debussy and Cézanne' as an initiatory constellation 'at the root of all modernity' could seem somewhat chauvinistic (*autarcique*).[11] And his passing invocation of Baudelaire, elsewhere, captures an alternative dialectical framing of 'modernity' that has often been elided in other appropriations of this earlier compatriot, which arguably retains much potential to inform ongoing reflection about modernism and history far beyond the boundaries of France alone.

Adorno

From the present perspective, the fact that the belated postmodern turn in Anglo-American musicology of the late 1980s and early 1990s occurred at the very time when Adorno's work was achieving new and increasingly overweening prominence appears a slightly anomalous feature of the historiographical landscape.[12] How, we might be tempted to ask, could this high modernist critic extraordinaire – post-Hegelian priest of 'critical theory', quick to damn all concessions to the 'false consciousness' of the 'culture industry'; influential participant in avant-garde cenacles like the Darmstadt *Ferienkurse*, whose death in 1969 irrevocably bound him to the era *before* most postmodern breakthroughs – claim such status amidst what seem, in any judicious assessment, exactly contrary critical currents?

One simple answer: as an early champion, Rose Rosengard Subotnik, put it in the preface to an important 1991 essay collection, the discovery of Adorno promised a 'reintroduction of moral questions' into a music academy then almost wholly in thrall to 'empirical' or 'analytic' methods, usually assumed (like the musical subject matter to which they were largely applied) to operate wholly free from ideological or political taint.[13] But if it is easy enough, now, to understand how refreshing Adorno's extravagantly poetic, morally invested 'Continental' approach must have seemed to many scholars who, chafing within those positivistic limits, were also keen to challenge their ideological neutrality, it is hard not to sense an unsettling tension between the demandingly austere, Frankfurt School notion of musical 'truth value' and the radically more relativistic 'ethnomusicological' orientation also hailed, across the same generation, for its potential to transform disciplinary practices of musicology.[14]

What is most striking in a present re-reading of the work that emerged alongside Subotnik's during the Anglo-American heyday of Adorno's writing (meaning roughly the decade or two from the early 1990s well into the millennium) is the sheer determination of many champions to reaffirm his continuing relevance long after the waning of his direct aesthetic influence, even while granting the substance and significance of much trenchant critique that had also come, over the same years, from many quarters.[15] At one level, the phenomenon bespeaks a quasi-religious reverence best exemplified in a sweeping assertion Subotnik quotes, at one point, from Donald Kuspit: 'To truly do justice to Adorno – to object to him – one must completely submit oneself to him, commit oneself completely to his method, live with it and comprehend its effect on life.'[16] For those loath to submit in this fashion, more productive lines of thought can be glimpsed behind a little terminological echo that crops up in a milder version of the same claim, as offered by British Adornian Max Paddison:

> In order to counteract the tendency to become fixated on the individual (and exaggerated) elements which make up his argument, it is important that Adorno be read in the light of his own method, while at every point (and he is constantly changing perspective) the connection has also to be made with the context of his theory as a whole.[17]

Modernism and history

Whatever we think of the mystagogical demand to connect 'every point' of his writing with his 'theory as a whole', the confidence with which Paddison, like Kuspit, refers to Adorno's 'method' invites an inquiry of more practical value for these retrospective reflections on 'modernism and history'.

What, then, is the Adornian method? Two or three core tenets, it appears, are most often emphasized as essential to the approach widely celebrated under the banner of 'critical theory'. First of all, Adorno and Adornians tend to insist that the method rests, at basis, on immanent critique of musical works, developed as freely as possible from covert or unexamined presupposition. Second, we are given to understand that this is a thoroughly dialectical method – which means a few things at once. On the broadest level, it proposes an intricately mediated relation between art and society, wherein each evolves, independently, in thrall to the Hegelian 'objective spirit of history' – and wherein any 'authentic' art must continually strive (and fail) to realize a utopian obligation that places it, by definition, in critical relation to contemporary commodity culture. On the local level of argument, meanwhile, the method requires unending vigilance against reductively monolithic formulations of any given historical concept (thesis) that neglect its inextricable interpenetration by its co-defining opposite (antithesis). Finally, many critics emphasize, as a third strength of the immanent and dialectical method so defined, the ostensible transparency of its own ideological stance, and thus its openness to self-critique.[18]

If the outlines of the method seem clear enough, it is surprising to find how often even avowed Adornians readily grant serious shortfalls in its execution. On the question of immanent critique, for example, Paddison candidly concedes that Adorno's 'so-called "immanent analyses" of musical works are disappointingly traditional on a technical level, and do not convincingly bridge the gap between technical analysis and philosophical interpretation'.[19] As for the famous dialectical sensibility, on the other hand, what Paddison indulgently characterizes as a 'rather extreme application of Max Weber's concept of rationalization' comes into starker focus against the background of Berman's truly dialectical framing of modernity:

> There is a mode of vital experience – experience of space and time, of the self and others, of life's possibilities and perils – that is shared by men and women all over the world today. I will call this body of experience 'modernity'. To be modern is to find ourselves in an environment that promises us adventure, power, joy, growth, transformations of ourselves and the world – and, at the same time, that threatens to destroy everything we have, everything we know, everything we are.[20]

Adorno's complete effacement of one side of this 'mode of vital experience' ('adventure, power, joy, growth') under doom-laden mantras about the 'horror of history' finds incisive diagnosis in one of Berman's footnotes: 'In [Georg] Simmel – and later in his youthful followers Georg Lukács, T. W. Adorno, and Walter Benjamin – dialectical vision and depth are always entangled, often in the same sentence, with monolithic cultural despair'.[21]

Such monolithic despair inevitably imparts a distinct slant to Adorno's views on the kind of art that can possibly be deemed 'authentic'. To assert – in a typical instance – that 'new music [. . .] has taken all the darkness and guilt of the world on itself' leaves little room for any new music that seeks to embrace, however fleetingly, modern modes of 'adventure' and 'joy'.[22] Just as typical is the fuzziness about the human creative acts that conceivably drive this obligatory opposition to history's horrors and acceptance of the world's guilt. Attributions of agency to the art and music themselves, rather than to anyone who actually *makes* such things, is characteristic of a historiography that locates the 'spirit of History', again and again, in ostensibly objective 'tendencies of the material' rather than in any conscious choices on the part of human subjects.[23] To be sure, Adorno occasionally grants a secondary role to creative subjectivity: 'in immanent reciprocation', we read in *Philosophy of New Music* (1947), 'directives are constituted that the material imposes on the composer and that the composer transforms by adhering to them'.[24] But just as common are the many passages that efface human agency entirely under an anthropomorphic framing of grand abstractions: 'music concedes the legitimacy of history and therefore history would like to quash it'.[25]

It is hardly surprising to find that the contrasting 'small h' approach to music history plays a more negligible role in this method. But it is worth noting one puzzling wobble. If anything is clear in Adorno's modernist historiography, it is the pre-eminent status of Schoenberg's atonal phase – which he is still celebrating in the late essay 'Vers une musique informelle' (1961) as the moment when new music came closest to matching Beethoven's earlier near-attainment of music's utopian potential.[26] But similar clarity is notably absent from his account of twelve-tone technique. Beyond his comfortable acceptance, at one point, of the 'didactic' implications in Ernst Krenek's comparison of twelve-tone composition with Palestrina style, and his direct anticipation, at another, of Boulez's famously invidious contrast between Schoenberg and Webern, Adorno allows himself a more fundamental slippage when, after first describing the technique, in *Philosophy of New Music*, as a product of the music's 'proper gravitational vector', he asserts in 'Vers une musique informelle' that '[w]hat stopped the development of the "free musical style", as Alois Hába termed it over thirty years ago, was not anything inherent in the music, as Schoenberg may well have imagined, but sociological and ideological factors'.[27] Such haziness about internal and external explanation, touching so central a development in Adorno's favoured music-historical lineage, seems hard to put down, forgivingly, to a rich vein of contradiction.

To turn to my chosen music-historical test case is to find a similar haziness permeating Adorno's few remarks about Debussy. The key passage in *Philosophy of New Music* proceeds entirely as a gloss on a familiar interdisciplinary cliché:

> Listening must re-educate itself in order to hear Debussy correctly, not as a process of damming up and release but as a juxtaposition of colours and flashes, as in a painting. The succession merely displays what, in terms of its own meaning, is simultaneous in the way of an eye that wanders over a canvas.[28]

We recognize the casual endorsement of the well-worn 'Impressionist' trope, whose longstanding and widespread acceptance in scholarly and public accounts of Debussy alike may make it all too easy to absorb, as well as Adorno's further claim that 'the development of painting's productive forces [in France] so prevailed over those of music that the latter involuntarily sought refuge in great painting'.[29] What is missing from this odd image of French music seeking shelter in a more developed art form, however, is any acknowledgement that the 'Impressionist' trope itself has only ever been a pure artefact of reception, with little solid basis in immanent musical detail or documented creative affinity.

As a matter of historical fact it was Schoenberg, not Debussy, who at a key point in his development engaged in substantive aesthetic exchanges with an actual painter, Wassily Kandinsky, about the new aesthetic challenges now in view with the advent of atonality and abstraction. (Indeed the exchange hinged, in part, on questions of spatiality in the two art forms – later a key term in Adorno's critique both of Debussy and Stravinsky.)[30] The complete absence of any

Modernism and history

similar documented interest on Debussy's part has been succinctly noted, back in 1966, by Polish musicologist Stefan Jarocinski:

> Contrary to what has often been alleged, there is nowhere to be found in [Debussy's] articles, his correspondence, or even in the recollections of those who knew him best, the slightest proof that Impressionist painting had influenced him to any extent. On the contrary, [. . .] he repudiated the term Impressionism when applied to his music, and employed it himself only in an ironic sense.[31]

No doubt it is still possible for those of a critical-theoretical bent to invoke an authentic, 'involuntary' resonance (to borrow Adorno's term) between disparate artistic materials at similar stages in their respective Histories. But the obvious question arises: why would such affinity obtain primarily, if not solely, between Debussy's music and a painterly style that had flourished in the hands of artists exactly one generation older, rather than with any of the many, wildly variegated 'post-Impressionist' styles actually in constant, febrile development as he attained compositional maturity in the late 1880s and 1890s?[32]

In truth, although a deeply interdisciplinary sensibility is often deemed another strength of Adorno's method, it is clear that his sensitivity to actual – immanent – developments in French painting of this time was patchy at best. When, for instance, he invokes 'the passage from impressionism to pointillism in painting' to exemplify a sweeping claim that progress in artistic procedures involves 'a movement towards increasing logical elaboration', he merely demonstrates, once more, the opportunistic selectivity of this 'History'.[33] For the 'pointillism' of Georges Seurat and Paul Signac et al. was only one of numerous post-Impressionist styles, among which many freer approaches (e.g. that of Paul Gauguin, Vincent van Gogh and Paul Cézanne) were to prove at least as influential – recall Boulez's proto-modernist triumvirate – on subsequent generations.[34] And beyond any quibbling about the most appropriate interdisciplinary affinities (which often becomes something of a mug's game), Adorno's casual resort to this central painterly trope of Debussyan reception spawns a blatant disregard for the full range of immanent musical facts. To claim, for example, that in Debussy '[t]here is no "end": the piece stops like a painting one has turned away from', is to ignore a whole lineage of actual Debussy pieces – from *Pour le piano* (1894–1901), through *La mer* (1903–5) to all three late chamber sonatas (1915–17) – whose blazingly rhetorical conclusions render such interdisciplinary generalizations patently absurd.

It would be easier to deem Debussy a relatively minor deaf spot in Adorno's criticism were it not that the painting trope also proved pivotal – as in the supposedly parallel development from Impressionism to cubism – to his more extensive treatment of Stravinsky.[35] There is little need to engage in detail here with the infamous 'Stravinsky and the Restoration' section of *Philosophy of New Music* – characterized even by Robert Hullot-Kentor, in the preface to his 2006 translation, as 'easily the most reviled and automatically dismissed of anything [Adorno] wrote'.[36] But a slightly broader view might serve to test the 'self-critical' strengths occasionally celebrated in this method. For Adorno returned to Stravinsky years later, in the 1962 essay 'Stravinsky: A Dialectical Portrait', which some acolytes have found an exemplary instance of self-critical reflection.[37]

That reading seems strange on the face of it given Adorno's bald assertion, early in this essay, that 'I see no reason to retract anything that I wrote in 1947'.[38] He proceeds to frame, hypothetically, a 'not implausible objection' he imagines others could direct at his original critique, and a (hypothetical) 'plea for the defence' of Stravinsky he thinks they may be tempted to offer – which includes the (still hypothetical) charge against him that he imagines they could raise: that 'I violated my own most cherished principles of criticism' (meaning the commitment to immanent analysis). But he answers all such hypotheses with one of his most imperious affirmations of a non-negotiable 'fact' about music:

> As a temporal art, music is bound to the fact of succession and is hence as irrevocable as time itself. By starting it commits itself to carrying on, to becoming something new, to developing. What we may conceive of as musical transcendence, namely the fact that at any given moment it has become something and something other than what it was, that it points beyond itself — all that is no mere metaphysical imperative dictated by external authority. It lies in the nature of music and will not be denied.[39]

Damning Stravinsky's temporal processes in this light, he transmutes what is indeed an undeniable fact — music must 'carry on' in time — into an arbitrary, monolithic insistence that only one way of 'carrying on' (i.e. 'developing', in the Beethovenian and Schoenbergian sense central to his own education) can ever count as historically 'authentic'.

Hardly a robust instance of self-critique, 'Stravinsky: A Dialectical Portrait' thus proves a particularly blatant instance of the thoroughgoing Austro-German bias widely acknowledged by Adorno's champions and detractors alike. But familiar and unignorable as this bias may be, his most forgiving readers tend to understate the parochial narrowness of the critical purview it supports. When observing, for example, that Adorno 'seemed to be so identified with his own cultural heritage and its aesthetic values that he was quite blind to the different terms of reference of any non-European let alone non-Western culture', Paddison blithely skates past his more shocking blindness (or deafness) to the music created not in some distant, exotic culture — or even by someone born at a moderate geographical remove, like Stravinsky — but by a composer native to Germany's closest Western European neighbour.[40] We must no doubt grant (with Paddison) that Adorno was 'constantly changing perspective' — and further exploration will find, for example, that 'Vers une musique informelle' contradicts even the 'cardinal fact' that serves to damn Stravinsky in 'A Dialectical Portrait'. ('It is nowhere laid down that modern music must a priori contain such elements of the tradition as tension and resolution, continuation, development, contrast and reassertion.')[41] Similarly, the few references to Debussy in the posthumously published *Aesthetic Theory* have lost all clichéd associations with painting. But while nobody would demand dogmatic rigidity as a critical obligation, it is hard not to wonder, in the face of such radical shifts of opinion, what can be said to survive as a solid core of this music-historical method.

The suspicion that, much like the music prophetically evoked in 'Vers une musique informelle', Adorno's method remains a promissory note towards some as yet unrealized, truly immanent, dialectical and self-critical project only deepens when we read this further frank acknowledgement from Subotnik:

> Through a complex process of mediation, which Adorno does not pretend to understand or elucidate adequately, a process involving the artist's early ways of perceiving reality (through childhood assimilation of societal structures) and the contemporaneous state of artistic materials, techniques and technology (all, like form, stemming from outside the imagination), the essential tendencies of a given historical moment become translated into the formal aspects of great art.[42]

In other words, Adorno 'does not pretend to understand or elucidate adequately' even the fundamental question — 'how are we to say that X and Y are related in Z fashion?' — that, by her own account, had first drawn Subotnik out from the narrowly analytic academic confines

Modernism and history

within which she had written a traditional 'life and works' dissertation and towards this Continental alternative.[43] Paddison's sense, in the mid-1990s, that 'Adorno's Critical Theory continues to make us uncomfortable with received notions of music as splendidly autonomous and somehow entirely separate from society and the everyday' can only seem terribly outdated now, after a few decades of 'cultural musicology'.[44] Perhaps there is more lasting substance in Alastair Williams's narrowly methodological claim, a year or so later, that without such a critical theory (inchoate as it is) 'modernism's challenging of traditional aesthetics, its pull away from integration and its quest for theoretical understanding could be understood only by a pale explanation of technique'.[45] But the choice seems too stark. Technique, in music as in all other arts, has generally been a means to various human ends. Surely there are better approaches to the endlessly fascinating relation between the two than a repeated refurbishment of a mid-twentieth-century model whose narrow cultural bias has long proved inadequate even to a pluralistic sense of Western art music, let alone everything else.

Taruskin

When Taruskin, in the polemical preface reprinted at the start of every volume of his *Oxford History*, deems the work of Adorno 'preposterously overrated' and damns all the postmodern 'new musicologists' as 'Adornians to a man or woman', he clearly stakes a claim to be offering just such a better alternative.[46] But even without undertaking the thorough investigation needed to determine just which particular Adornian sins can be fairly attributed to any of the disparate scholars occasionally bundled together (happily or not) under the label 'new musicology', a careful assessment of the vast survey that follows finds that it, too, proves riven by tensions arising from partly incompatible historiographical paradigms. In this case, in fact, unlike the postmodern reception of the arch-modernist Adorno, the instability seems built into the very foundations.

For one thing (to borrow again from Evans's millennial reflections), as a 'multi-volume and "authoritative" synoptic history', the *OHWM* seems a distinctly belated contribution to a genre whose very 'idea' already seemed 'out of date' to many historians back in 1997.[47] This pervasive tinge of anachronism only deepens with Taruskin's distinctly postmodernistic prefatory claim that, rather than the 'music itself', the 'mediating discourse' will be the main subject of his historical 'story' (in his most extreme formulation: 'the discourse, so often slighted in the past, is in fact the story').[48] The claim sits uneasily with the relatively traditional, 'narrative' approach he then, by his own description, adopts for this 'attempt at a true history'.[49] If a key question about the relation between historical discourses and the worldly truths they purport to describe (as has been widely debated after the postmodern turn) seems casually elided here, we might also wonder just how well Taruskin's determination to root such a narrative primarily in 'reception', of the kind that can give rise to 'social contention', really holds up across all the highly technical, enthusiastically erudite music analyses that give the *OHWM* much of its considerable bulk.[50]

Beyond this rebarbative preface alone, the account of musical modernism in Taruskin's last volumes rests on methodological foundations elaborated more extensively in a couple of earlier essays. The first of these, given as a lecture back in 1989 and reprinted with a reflective commentary of 2008, challenges what Taruskin sees as the standard telling of nineteenth- and twentieth-century music history, described in the *OHWM* as part of the broader 'neo-Hegelian' and 'linear' tale that 'the arts steadily progress toward a state of ever more perfect autonomy'.[51] This is not the only one of his sallies against hidebound tradition that carries a strong whiff of the straw man. As he well knows, even arch-progressivists like Adorno and Boulez saw some eras as diversions from the longer-range 'arc of History'; apart from his new dating, to *c*1923, of the 'true break' between nineteenth- and twentieth-century musical worlds (which can only ever be arbitrarily imposed), his proposed 'zigzag' alternative – i.e. two progressively maximal-izing 'zigs' in alternation with two anti-progressive 'zags', one in the interwar years, the other at the postmodern turn – does not appear as radically unfamiliar as he seems to think.[52] What is more distinctive is the pair of terms by which he purports to bring the messy variety of musical culture under each vector of this jagged 'superperiodization'.

Ironically, the key terms in question, as first presented in the essay 'The Poietic Fallacy' of 2004 and scattered throughout the *OHWM*, could well be said to infuse this story of musical modernism with the same quasi-dialectical thinking Taruskin finds so execrable in Dahlhaus. Borrowing the well-known distinction between *poiesis* (artistic creation) and *esthesis* (audience reception) first introduced to music by semiotician Jean Molino, he defines the 'fallacy' he labels with the first term as 'the conviction that what matters most (or, more strongly yet, that all that matters) in a work of art is the making of it, the maker's input'.[53] As he sees it, the enthralment of most previous stories about modernism to this 'poietic fallacy' accounts in large part for the oft-noted alienation of 'new music' from a wide audience. This charge, in turn, drives his deter-mination to focus this 'true' story, instead, on *esthesis* – and thus to write 'a view of "serious" music that takes adequate account of its function as a communicative medium'.[54]

As an aside, we might note how this programme simplifies the actual practice of 'History with a capital H' – within which the agency of 'the maker' often proves quite elusive and ambig-uous. Much more important, however, is the ease with which the quasi-dialectical opposition of *poiesis* and *esthesis* elides a crucial 'third term'. Noting that Molino's original formulation had also included 'a *niveau neutre*, a neutral level, that analysed the structure of the message itself', Taruskin suggests that this third or middle term was discarded 'once it was realized that analysis itself was an esthesic function'.[55] The realization may indeed be irrefutable. But the problem-atic label '*niveau neutre*' aside, it hardly follows that the musical phenomena themselves simply do not exist, in their material and sonorous facticity, before analysis takes place. We may never be able to analyse music in a value-neutral way, but we can easily describe its constituent facts falsely (say, by taking *forte* for *piano*, flute for fiddle, fugue for aria). To believe otherwise is to accept a discursive extreme in postmodern historiography that has been thoroughly debunked (in my reading of Evans) through several late-century debates – and that clearly holds little real attraction for Taruskin, given his frequent appeals to historical 'fact' to contradict the discursive misrepresentations of others.[56]

If, all claims to some higher truth aside, the *OHWM* inevitably deploys both facts and dis-courses selectively to buttress prior musical and historical investments, the elaboration of its 'zig-zag' linear historiography illustrates, above all, the perils of over-schematic musical periodization. Recalling his commitment to tracing the causes of stylistic evolution in the social and political realm, it will come as no surprise to find the First World War identified as the main cause of the first 'zag'. Long seen to mark a turn to greater objectivity in all the arts, this worldwide cataclysm now comes under Taruskin's quasi-dialectical scheme as the cause of what he calls 'the "poietic" bias (the emphasis on the "making" of the composition rather than on its "effect") that increasingly characterized advanced composing-practice after the Great War'.[57] But what emerges most vividly from the discursive context surrounding this idea of a new 'poietic bias' – apart from a sense that its human source seems to float, disconcertingly, between composers and later analysts – is the sheer, unruly variety of the music actually created in this 'period'.

Perhaps the clearest instance of the instability inherent in any such attribution of a broad stylistic change to a single social and political cause is the discussion, on a single page, of three closely contemporaneous operas by Paul Hindemith. Two, we read, 'maintained prewar "maxi-malist" styles (the first "post-Strauss," the second "post-Debussy")', while the third 'showed signs of postwar irreverence for high artistic values'.[58] Are we to understand the war as the cause of

Modernism and history

both of these stylistic choices, or just the typical 'postwar' one? Perhaps the case of Hindemith, at least, seems relatively easy to resolve – given Taruskin's sense of increasing emphasis rather than clear caesura – with a look ahead to the greater 'objectivity' of his later *Gebrauchsmusik*. But the puzzle of causality becomes more pressing in the account of Alban Berg, a figure at the heart of the neo-Hegelian lineage propounded by Adorno (his one-time student). For Taruskin, Berg's music offers a rare case of dialectical synthesis:

> His expressive aims remained traditionally humanistic, concerned with the representa-
> tion, and possible transmission, of subjective feelings like erotic love (in the *Lyric Suite*),
> or grief and consolation (in the Concerto). It was to these ends that Berg sublimated
> the intellectual curiosity that attracted him to technical tours de force. His obsession
> with motivic and harmonic asymmetries acted as a useful counterfoil to his represen-
> tational bent, enabling his music to be at once eclectic and economical in a way that
> interests analysts, and giving his music, to a perhaps greater degree than that of the
> other early Viennese atonalists, strong appeal on both the poietic and esthesic planes.[59]

Suggestive as this description of a distinctive compositional accomplishment might be, it seems difficult to explain such a rich admixture of 'expressive aims' and 'intellectual curiosity' – in two works written in 1926 and 1935, respectively – as the result of a single socio-historical event.

For all the scorn Taruskin pours on the 'pseudo-dialectical "method"' he finds in *Foundations of Music History* (and deceptively distils to a crude question: 'Is art history the *history* of art, or is it the history of *art*?'), Dahlhaus's thoughts on the 'problems of social history' actually remain directly relevant to the questions that arise from this 'superperiodization', which inevitably throws up works (and entire *oeuvres* – say, by Erich Wolfgang Korngold or Edgard Varèse) that prove exceptions, in various ways, to the 'debunking, materialist, objective, and antimetaphysical spirit of postwar disillusion'.[60] Rather than having to say, with a temporal locution typical of *Zeitgeist* historiography, that the 'decadence' of Korngold's 'sumptuous expressionist drama' (e.g. *Das Wunder der Heliane*, 1926) was 'a little old-fashioned in the age of *neue Sachlichkeit*', it would be better to accept that the 'age' itself has only ever been a discursive 'convenience' (see again my epigraph) – its label 'bolted on' to a 'totality' better seen in light of Dahlhaus's gloss on leading *annales* historian Fernand Braudel:

> The structures [. . .] that coexist at any given time, interacting to constitute or deter-
> mine an historical circumstance, differ from each other not only in respect of their age,
> i.e. how far back they extend into the past and the timespan allotted to them, but also
> in the rate at which they alter. The historian Fernand Braudel spoke of the various
> 'rhythms' of coexisting structures, ranging from the geographic conditions of a culture
> to the styles of its art. And, to use a musical metaphor, there is cause to doubt whether
> the overlapping tempos can be reduced to a common underlying metre (though some
> feel that the succession of generations gives a certain 'natural rhythm' to the history of
> art). There is, strictly speaking, no such thing as 'Time' in the singular but only 'times'
> in the plural, the times of overlapping structures in conflicting rhythms.[61]

From this perspective, indeed, Taruskin's ostensibly event-driven superperiodization could seem, in its more forced applications, just as polemically selective a construct as Adorno's ostensibly immanent 'objective historical spirit'.[62]

The possibility that 'les extrèmes se touchent' here can be supported with a closer look at Taruskin's objections to the 'capital H' tale he roundly rejects. In a crucial passage of his preface,

David J. Code

he identifies the 'vice' that 'vitiated' the work of Adorno (and rapidly aged that of the 'new musicologists') as the assumption 'that the meaning of artworks is fully vested in them by their creators, and is simply "there" to be decoded by a specially gifted interpreter'. He continues:

> [This] is, all pretenses aside, still an authoritarian discourse and an asocial one. It still grants oracular privilege to the creative genius and his prophets, the gifted interpreters. It is altogether unacceptable as a historical method, although it is part of history and, like everything else, deserving of report. The historian's trick is to shift the question from 'What does it mean?' to 'What has it meant?' That move is what transforms futile speculation and dogmatic polemic into historical illumination.[63]

What is strange here is the uncritical assumption that the interrogative shift so described will automatically prevent the historian from granting 'oracular privilege' to some other 'authoritarian discourse' in service of a different, externally based but no less dogmatic polemic. More bluntly: the 'historian's trick', as Taruskin puts it, remains incomplete so long as his new question lacks a crucial qualifier: 'What has it meant. . . *and to whom?*'

As it happens, this missing qualifier proves particularly damaging to the account of Debussy in Volume 4 of the *OHWM*. For a start, it appears that Taruskin, while deciding to relieve this composer of the 'Ur-modernist' status he was happy to affirm in a review written back in 1989, has also had second thoughts about his 'Impressionism' – a cliché he once treated with apt circumspection, but now (in an exact reversal of Adorno) accepts with little more than a dutiful caveat.[64] He gives no evidentiary justification for this change of mind – indeed none, to my knowledge, exists. It could be that he has simply found, over the years, that the parallel with a supposedly 'objective' style of painting (as it has often been understood) fits well with the claims about a modernist 'dehumanization of art' famously propounded in a 1925 essay by Spanish philosopher José Ortega y Gasset, which he first draws into his story alongside the early 'French modernists' Debussy and Satie and grants fully oracular privilege through many subsequent chapters (see also the introduction to this volume).

Whatever 'historical illumination' Ortega might bring to later, more appropriate episodes, Taruskin's wholesale adoption of his dehumanized hearing of Debussy perfectly illustrates how a prior commitment to authoritarian discourse can enforce a selective disregard for historical and musical facts. It would be hard, for example, to pack more bias and inaccuracy into this single paragraph:

> One finds representations aplenty in [Debussy's] music of the sea, of the wind, of gardens in the rain and balconies in the moonlight, but of humans few unless viewed *en masse* and from afar ('Fêtes' [. . .]), or unless mythical (fauns, sirens), artificial ('Golliwogg', his daughter's Negro doll [. . .]), or already embodied in art ('Danseuses de Delphes' [. . .] the first of the *Préludes*, which title evokes not the dancers themselves but the Greek vase on which they are painted).[65]

Even the initial nod to a few 'nature' titles (*La mer*, 'Jardins sous la pluie') sidesteps a whole contemporary discourse about the interpenetration of artistic representations with the experience of their human perceivers – as in Mallarmé's stated ideal: 'peindre non la chose, mais l'effet qu'elle produit'.[66] The reference to humans 'en masse and from afar' in 'Fêtes' coolly suppresses the fact that the march episode in question only *begins* at 'distant' *pianissimo* – but then approaches, through fifty-four bars of crescendo, to a vividly proximate *fortissimo* with full brass and percussion. Taruskin gives no justification for deeming Debussy's 'mythical' figures any less

Modernism and history

'human' in symbolic implication than, say, the Rhine maidens and dwarves (et al.) in Wagner's *Ring*, nor for assuming that the stately rhythms of 'Danseuses de Delphes' should be heard to evoke an inert image – what, in truth, would *that* sound like? – rather than the hieratic, choreographed gestures it surely brought to mind.[67]

Against any suggestion that such selective hearing and description remains open to interpretation, I would note the starker omission, here, of all the more overtly 'human' Debussy *Préludes* – from the well-known 'La fille aux cheveux de lin', through 'La sérénade interrompue' (presumably played and heard, and interrupted, by *someone*), to 'La danse de Puck' and 'Minstrels'. (If some such pianistic characterizations are mediated by literary 'artifice', so too, of course, were many in Schumann or Liszt.)[68] But this slight widening of the lens does not yet capture the even broader elision behind Taruskin's blithe Ortegan assertion 'but of humans few'. To focus only on the instrumental music, in service of this polemical generalization, is to ignore or efface the human implications in all of Debussy's vocal music – notably including the several dozen *mélodies* that embodied (often in the triptych form that stands as his signal contribution to the 'song cycle' genre) the most overt and disparate expressions of poetic personae and imagery across his whole career.[69]

This last point brings to mind a telling remark in Gary Tomlinson's 2007 review of the *OHWM*. Beyond challenging the way that Taruskin, posing as a privileged 'medium' of music history, 'appears to want to sustain the illusion that his story was conveyed to him by the traces of the past he examines', Tomlinson also notes a stale air of scholarly familiarity clinging to much of the repertoire selected for close attention.[70] Radical historiographical posturing aside, he suggests, the decisions about what and what not to include (about which Taruskin expresses shocking complacency) seem to him largely to re-enshrine a pre-existing canon of 'the sum of the efforts of historical musicologists across much of the twentieth century'.[71] We have already glimpsed the insidious effects of such investment in the vagaries of prior musicological interest: it will be forever impossible to free Debussy from the Impressionist cliché so long as we find historical 'truth value' in the mere fact that so many scholars have been happy to repeat it. But a more unsettling line of concern can emerge, I think, by considering two other, interrelated questions.

First of all: *why* have the *mélodies*, one of the genres in which Debussy wrote most often, been granted so little importance in standard music histories that Taruskin can readily overlook their significance for a full understanding of his art? And second, *why* is it that Ortega found it so easy to project the 'dehumanization' he heard in 1920s Stravinsky back to Debussy, whose radically different motivations should be abundantly clear from the scattering of the word 'expressif' through scores that also bear countless more precisely human indications, from 'joyeux' to 'passionément' to 'comme un tendre et triste regret'?

Some answers may emerge with a bit more thought about the missing qualifier in that 'historian's trick' ('What has it meant . . . and to whom?'). Given that Ortega wrote very little of substance about music, many musicologists will likely first encounter his remarks on Debussy and Stravinsky in the *OHWM*.[72] In this context, his Latinate name may all too easily suggest a healthy Mediterranean perspective – as in Friedrich Nietzsche's late rejection of Wagnerian 'diseases' for the refreshing clarity of Georges Bizet – behind his hearing of French and Russian modernism.[73] The truth is quite the opposite. Ortega's intellectual and aesthetic proclivities were in fact thoroughly and passionately Germanic. Their deepest roots lie in the neo-Kantian philosophy he studied in Marburg – a town to which he later attributed 'half of my hopes and nearly all of my intellectual discipline'.[74] Famously characterized as 'the man who liked to think of himself as a twentieth-century Goethe', he was granted a prominent speaking role at the poet's 1949 bicentenary.[75] And this 'Germanism', which he saw as the essential

119

David J. Code

ingredient for Spain's claim to a fully European destiny, found ample illustration, for example, in the marked predominance he gave to German writers in a series of translations for The Library of Twentieth-Century Ideas, and in the name of his only son: Miguel Germán.[76]

This pronounced 'Germanist' leaning seems to me to impinge directly on the distorted account of Debussy's music Taruskin offers under Ortega's oracular guidance. For if Adorno was so in thrall to Austro-German 'development' that he could not hear any other approach to musical time as authentic, Taruskin takes from Ortega an equally narrow sense of musical expression, which can only have originated in the discourse that has, over decades, consistently located the pinnacle of such expression in the compositional lineage of German Idealism. It is only from this unacknowledged, monolithic perspective, I suggest, that it has proven so easy for both to ignore all those *expressif* indications (and sounds) – because Debussy's music expresses 'passion' and 'tenderness' and the like by other means than those long heard to define Western musical 'expression' *tout court*.[77]

The towering irony here – Taruskin, so polemically opposed to Teutonic music-historical imperialism, imports into his hearing of Debussy a Germanic bias that differs only in kind from Adorno's – rests on a larger, even more basic point. Ortega's idea of 'dehumanization', like anyone else's proposed distinction between acts and creations more or less characteristically human, could only ever be inextricably culturally contingent.[78] Some reinforcement of this point, were it needed, can readily be found in a baldly relativistic invocation of the same idea that appeared, just a few years before Ortega's essay, in a controversial publication by an eminent native Germanist. In this passage from his *Reflections of a Nonpolitical Man* (1918), Thomas Mann first answers one peevish question only to end with another:

> What is, then, this development, this progress I have been speaking of? Well, to indicate what it is about, I need a handful of shamelessly ugly, artificial words. It is about the politicization, literarization, intellectualization, and radicalization of Germany. *It aims at her "humanization" in the Latin-political sense, and her dehumanization in the German one.* It aims, to use the favourite word, the battlecry and hosanna of civilization's literary man, at the *democratization* of Germany, or, to summarize everything and to bring it over a common denominator: it aims at her de-Germanization. And I should have a part in all this mischief?[79]

In short, Ortega's ostensibly universal and objective characterization appears here, in words written during the shell-shocked aftermath of the Great War, as a contingent and contested emergence from centuries of debate over the relative values of French *civilisation* and German *Kultur*.

This long, internecine struggle clearly complicates any monolithic conception of Western (or even Western European) culture. And some of its more precise relevance for musicological reflections on 'modernism and history' might start to emerge with a slight step beyond the boundaries of Western Europe. As Taruskin points out, the music of Hungarian composer Béla Bartók gave Adorno – who mischaracterized it, with that of the Czech Leoš Janáček, as the 'product of a rural or agrarian society' – yet one more occasion to exercise his 'smug ethnocentric bias'.[80] But the same music inspires Taruskin himself to what seems, in a long view, suspiciously like a blatant double standard. Back in 1989 he caricatured Debussy, primarily on the basis of his writings rather than his music, as someone who demanded 'an absolute demarcation between popular culture and high culture'.[81] Perhaps this 'elitist' charge largely falls away from the *OHWM* because it is impossible to maintain in the same pages as the little example from 'Golliwog's Cakewalk'. Even so, there remains a telling disjunction between Taruskin's dogged riffs on the 'dehumanized' Debussy and the complex, multi-dimensional humanity he grants the younger composer: 'Bartók was torn, like all educated Magyars, both between the universal and the particular and between the elite and the popular.'[82]

Even without the suppressed charge of elitism, we might well wonder how *this* Bartók could have felt, on discovering Debussy's 'dehumanized' music, a similar 'impact on his development to his discovery of peasant song itself'. Maybe we are to understand the impact solely in terms of, say, 'the prevalence of seventh chords [. . .] often moving in parallel à la Debussy' – as in Taruskin's account of the *Music for Strings, Percussion and Celesta* (1936).[83] But (to borrow one of his own terms of critique) the paired reference to Debussy and 'peasant song' carries subtler human implications than such shallow 'techno-essentialism' can allow.[84] For when Bartók recalled the revelation modern French music had brought to a whole generation of Hungarians hitherto in thrall to Germanic models, he specifically highlighted the different approach to song he found in Debussy, attributing it to his 'facility to reach back to the declamation of the ancient French language'.[85] He thus identified one inspirational model for his own new, *parlando rubato* style of lyrical expression (as in the middle movement of *Music for Strings*) – which he drew, in significant part, from the distinct accentuations and inflections of his own native tongue.

The unacknowledged cultural relativism lurking behind that deceptively universal claim of 'dehumanization' thus comes into focus, from this perspective, as a deafness to different ideals of musical lyricism. Debussy's *mélodies* all too easily fall away from a story told in Ortega's thrall, because their acute sensitivity to the declamatory nuances of the French language places them at a marked remove from the more melody-dominated song tradition inherited from a different, deceptively universal ideal of *Volkstümlichkeit*.[86] No doubt the question remains as to why it has also proven so easy, within this radically selective hearing, to efface all the *expressif* aspects of the instrumental music as well. But leaving this further query for another time, I think the surprisingly similar bias here exposed in Adorno and Taruskin might best serve as a pivot towards concluding reflections if we note, in marked contrast, the more finely relativistic perspective offered on this very issue by Boulez – a figure often charged with quite the opposite historiographical impulses.

Within a passing reference to the long debate over the relative value of 'pure vocality, in the conventional sense' and song that 'reproduces as faithfully as possible the inflections of spoken language', Boulez proposes, at one point, a suggestive parallel between 'the antinomy of Italian opera and French opera' during the mid-eighteenth century *Querelle des bouffons* and that of 'Wagner and Debussy' much later.[87] We can question the complete accuracy of this parallel while leaving the basic point intact. In the eighteenth century, as in the early twentieth, the debate was never really about how and how not to be 'human' – it was rather about the particular forms of human expression various hearers were willing to validate from their own cultural perspective. On this point at least, Boulez proved a more open-minded listener than either Adorno or Taruskin to the human possibilities of modernist music.

Conclusion: Boulez (. . . und Baudelaire ist auch dabei)

'Open-minded' is perhaps not the first adjective that comes to mind for a figure who first enters the *OHWM* under a charge of 'violence' and 'frantically coercive rhetoric'.[88] Taruskin is referring, of course, to the most infamous of all neo-Hegelian music-historical decrees – as pronounced by Boulez not once but twice, in slightly different forms. The later version, in the essay 'Possibly. . .' of May 1952, is the most plainly coercive: 'any musician who has not experienced – I do not say understood, but fully experienced – the necessity of dodecaphonic language is USELESS. For his entire work falls short of the needs of his time'.[89] But in a different essay published a few months earlier, 'Schoenberg is Dead' (given the date, the very title – as Taruskin remarks – a 'shocking provocation'), the similarly intransigent assertion that 'any composer is *useless* who does not pursue the path of serialism' brings, with its continuation, a wry aside: '(which does not mean that every composer will be useful in the contrary case)'.[90]

The addition may seem trivial – but it actually amounts to a frank admission that Boulez's coercive bombast rests, at basis, not on any pressing regard for 'the needs of the time' but on an irreducibly subjective notion of what he himself, on the authority of his own undoubtedly extraordinary gifts, deigns to find artistically useful. Such slippage from a notionally universal sense of historical responsibility to a narrowly self-congratulatory solipsism has perhaps been all too common across much of modernist historiography. It is relatively easy, for instance, to trace back (in a couple of close variants) into my chosen proponents of 'History' and 'history'.

Consider, for a start, Adorno's 1950 response to early criticism of his *Philosophy of New Music*:

> As a consequence of the philosophy for which I am responsible, [they say], I have implicitly applied to music a concept of objective spirit that asserts itself over and above the heads of individual artists as well as beyond the merits of individual works. *This concept is as foreign today to everyday consciousness as it is self-evident to my own spiritual experience.*[91]

On the other hand, Taruskin answers Charles Rosen's critique of the last volume of the *OHWM* (which adduces Cold War tensions as a cause of just about everything in late twentieth-century musical culture) with a similar appeal to subjective experience – now of a worldly, not spiritual, nature:

> I believe it is fair to say that the Cold War gave Americans a far greater scare than any of the actual wars our armies fought overseas. (And not even the Civil War threatened massive civilian casualties.) How could anyone's psychic equilibrium remain undisturbed? (Mine was definitely unbalanced: *I could never take seriously plans or promises that had to do with anything that lay more than a few days in the future.*) How could the artistic expressions of such psyches fail to reflect that disturbance?[92]

In reply, Rosen urbanely deflates this solipsistic hyperbole. 'For me, by contrast', he writes, 'the cold war years were a time of hope and looking forward. I got a Ph.D., made my first recordings and my New York debut, and obtained a two-year Fulbright fellowship to work in Paris.'[93] He leaves us to fill in the blanks: however much Taruskin might dramatize his Cold War memories to support an extravagant historiographical conceit, a glance at his publication list will find that he, too, managed to fulfil at least a few long-term plans amidst those unbalancing world-historical disturbances.[94]

He would have done better to recall his own cautions against over-simplistic accounts, for example, of the experience of the composer Karl Amadeus Hartmann under the Nazis. 'One's tendency in retrospect', he writes in the *OHWM*, 'is to imagine life under totalitarianism in terms of stark choices and moral extremes. Real-life conditions are seldom so clear-cut.'[95] Directly relevant to his own totalizing sense of Cold War culture, this more nuanced view – which permits him the eminently sensible acknowledgement that 'people are inconstant and inconsistent' – can also help forestall any over-hasty 'demonization' of Boulez as a quasi-totalitarian enforcer of post-Webernian serial doctrine. In fact, a brief comparative glance to Boulez's words, alongside Taruskin's and Adorno's, on two brilliant ballet scores of 1913 – Debussy's *Jeux* and Stravinsky's *Le sacre du printemps* – can begin to suggest who was the more catholic listener to serial and non-serial music alike.

Dutiful caveats forgotten, Taruskin saves his laziest concession to painterly cliché for *Jeux*, which he deems the 'ultimate masterpiece of "impressionism"' based on a few generalities about

Modernism and history

'harmonic and coloristic subtlety', *piano* dynamics and 'kaleidoscopically shifting motivic patterns'.[96] Boulez, by contrast, finds the unique temporal unfolding of this quicksilver work the stimulus to a new, post-architectural formal metaphor:

> One must experience the whole work to have a grasp of its form, which is no longer architected, but *braided* [*tressée*]; in other words, there is no distributive hierarchy in the organization of 'sections' (static sections: themes; dynamic sections: developments) but successive distributions in the course of which the various constituent elements take on a greater or lesser functional importance.

The passage may bear a techno-essentialist odour, but the inspired poetic image (think of all the hair symbolism in Debussy) nonetheless invites a more temporally imaginative hearing than any impressionistic overview. Still, a yet wider gulf opens between Adorno and Boulez on Stravinsky. Adorno's non-dialectical hearing leads ultimately to a disdainful sniff: 'There is something intrinsically amiss with Stravinsky's music; "il y a quelque chose qui ne va pas".'[97] By contrast, in the early pages of his essay 'Stravinsky Remains', Boulez poses a reflective question about the interrelation of stylistic strengths and weaknesses:

> It is undeniable [...] that Stravinsky possesses, to a lesser degree, the sense of development – that is, of sonorous phenomena undergoing constant renewal. Maybe we will judge this a weakness – and indeed it is; but might I be allowed to think that this is also one of the principal sources of that rhythmic force that he found necessary to deploy in order to face up to the difficulty of writing?[98]

He then makes good on Adorno's omission by providing a lengthy and detailed immanent analysis of *Le sacre*, focused above all on the rhythmic dimension so easily denigrated under the other's ethnocentric bias.[99]

While fans of the dialectic may thus be tempted to hail, in Boulez, a mid-century synthesis of Austro-German and Franco-Russian – i.e. Webernian and Stravinskyan – modernist streams, I will take two different, more broadly suggestive aspects of his writings as openings to my concluding reflections. The first concerns the thoroughly Eurocentric bias apparent both in Adorno's 'critical theory' and Taruskin's *OHWM*.[100] Boulez, whose appreciation of intra-European cultural divisions has been noted above (and whose prominence within a once-imperial power inevitably implies considerable Eurocentric privilege), occasionally offers glimpses, as well, of a yet broader cultural relativism. It may be hard, after the influential challenges of Edward Said and his followers, to read even the most laudatory reference to 'musics of the Near and Far East' as wholly free of patronizing 'orientalism' (not to say crass generalization).[101] But when Boulez, in an essay titled after Paul Klee, 'À la limite du pays fertile', recognizes that the 'non-harmonic character' of 'Hindu music' allows it, at once, a greater intervallic and rhythmic complexity than much Western art music, he arguably registers genuine respect for different orders of creative accomplishment.[102] And in his elaborations on the similar musical openness once shown by Debussy, he pushes beyond such *poietic* concerns to touch on musical *esthesis* as well.

The key passage in 'La corruption dans les encensoirs' opens with an apologetic note of over-familiarity, then nods in passing to the crucial point:

> We have elaborated quite enough, by now, on the surprise and impact caused in Debussy, during the 1889 Exposition, by the Annamite theatre, the Javanese dancers, and the sonority of the gamelan. Paradoxically, it is the shock of *a tradition codified*

differently, but just as powerfully, as the tradition of the West, that precipitates the rupture of the new music with the traditional European elements: we might well ask whether it was not the sheer ignorance that such other conventions could exist that provoked such powerful impressions of liberty.

As the highlighted phrase makes clear, Boulez understands the revelation of non-Western musics to lie not only in their 'richer scales', more 'supple rhythms', or 'totally different' instruments. Rather, as he puts it, 'it was above all the poetics [*la poétique*] of these far Eastern musics that enforced their corrosive influence'. The close kinship of his *poétique* with Taruskin's *poiesis* must not confuse the point. For when Boulez invokes, alongside Debussy, the painters Van Gogh and Klee and the poet Paul Claudel – all forced, by various exotic encounters, towards a scepticism about the 'supremacy of [European] culture' – he clearly implies that the issue was not just one of technical means, but of the equally powerful expressive and representational effects such artists were able to sense (however dimly) in methods radically different from those whose supremacy had long gone unquestioned.[103]

The familiarity of the story of 'Debussy and the exotic', which has only deepened since Boulez's essay, should not defuse the profound historiographical questions it raises. For if the notion of a 'universal History' – in the Hegelian sense of my 'capital H' – has by some accounts proven an uncomfortable import even for the closest neighbours of the Germanic context from which it first arose, how much more problematic must it seem when forced outward, through and beyond the furthest outposts of Europe's former colonies?[104] In fact, in a further striking irony, the clearest illustration of the perils of 'conceptual imperialism' that lurk behind such careless extensions of Eurocentric claims about musical history and experience alike can be found in the very paragraph in which Taruskin most pointedly challenges the presumed 'universality' of the German tradition. Compare his first sentence with the last two:

> Since Wagner's time, the German art of music had brought to a pitch of perfection the most consummately developed technique ever devised for representing the idealized experience of subjective feeling in tones. Philosophers and psychologists who have reflected upon the methods, highly manipulative in several meanings of the word, by which composers in the German tradition achieved this representation, have tended to fall under its spell. They have attributed universality to a local, highly specialized idiom. They have cast it in essential terms, as the culminating realization of music's intrinsic or 'absolute' properties.[105]

It is bizarre to find that closing challenge to others' presumptions of 'universality' so soon after Taruskin's own ringing claim for the 'supremacy' – recall Boulez – of German music's expressive idiom ('the most consummately developed technique ever devised'). How could anyone support such a claim, given that none of us will ever attain a fully '-emic' receptivity (as the anthropologists might have it) to the 'subjective feeling', idealized or otherwise, on offer through the world's unencompassable variety of musical techniques?

The second guiding thread I will draw from Boulez, finally, might offer a way to balance the marked tilt towards debunking critique that has characterized this essay so far with a more positive – though necessarily provisional – programme for further thought about 'modernism and history'. Again, the key passage appears in 'Corruption in the Censers':

> What does [modernism] consist of? It is difficult to answer very precisely. 'Modernism', says Baudelaire, 'is the transitory, the fugitive, the contingent, one half of art, of which the other half is the eternal and the immutable'.[106]

Modernism and history

This paraphrase of Baudelaire's famous 1863 essay 'The Painter of Modern Life' may, again, breathe a deceptive air of familiarity. But in truth, the slightly misleading nature of Boulez's excerpt proves exemplary of a widespread tendency, in later reception, to read the essay too simply – as if Baudelaire did indeed locate modernism solely in that one, 'contingent' half of art, rather than in the dialectical interplay between this 'fugitive' element and a countervailing urge towards the 'eternal'.[107] Maybe, after the waning of imperialistic 'Histories' and 'histories' alike, this subtler, dual sense of the modernist aesthetic could still prove of lasting diagnostic (if never prescriptive) value for further historical stories about modernism and its successors.[108]

The exemplary aesthetic range that allowed Baudelaire to include both the little-known sketch artist Constantin Guys and a composer as monumentally influential as Wagner in his pantheon of modernist art can suggest the catholic inclusivity this diagnostic conceit might allow. In other words, if it permits us to ask – not from a *poietic* or *esthesic* point of view, but in full appreciation of the endlessly rich interplay between the two – how finely any art whatsoever captures the most fugitive social, technological or personal concerns of its modern moment, it might also invite us to weigh whether, and if so how, it refracts such contingencies through any of the various concepts human cultures have occasionally invested with eternal value: number or nature; the nation or the folk; the mythic, the ancestral or the sacred. We need not insist on such interplay in all cases, for the Baudelairean dialectic encompasses its own extremes – say, at one end, the non- or anti-art movements whose attempted subversion of all established sanctions of lasting value distinguishes them from more institutional modernisms as a true 'avant-garde', and at the other, perhaps, such rigorously conventional products as can be found within the more stringent reaches of the neo-classical and serial Stravinsky.[109]

It would be tempting to suggest that the same dialectic could even prove illuminating for musical encounters well beyond the postcolonial periphery of Europe, were that not just to court a different kind of conceptual imperialism. For apart from his oracular insights into Parisian modernity, Baudelaire also claims a prominent place, of course, in the history of Western exoticism – indeed, one all too exemplary for its overlap with a closely related proclivity for masculinist, objectifying erotic fantasy. To choose him as my valedictory guide, then, makes it all the more pressing to acknowledge, once more, the 'subject position' that has led me, in this chapter, to re-enshrine (even in challenging it) the authoritarian and individualistic historiographical perspective of a white, male, Eurocentric triumvirate – Adorno, Taruskin, Boulez – whose claim to speak, from their own subjective experience, for all of 'modernism and history' has long been open to challenge from a widely diverse range of other perspectives.

Maybe that choice of representative voices now seems a sad concession to Dahlhaus's dispiriting (and fatalistic) suggestion that 'the canon upon which music historiography is based is transmitted by tradition: historians do not compile it so much as encounter it'.[110] But it might, more generously, be taken to reflect a (perhaps belated) need to reckon with those domineering voices at the current stage in 'the evolution of my own thinking' (see my second, Boulezian epigraph). Maybe such a reckoning still holds some slight value even for historians much further along with the revisionist projects necessary to secure various 'Others' – from Emily Dickinson, Gertrude Stein and Virginia Woolf through Berthe Morisot, Suzanne Valadon and Sonia Delaunay to Louis Armstrong, Thelonious Monk and John Coltrane – an honoured place alongside Boulez's three *Belle époque* Frenchmen in the shifting constellations of 'modernism and history'. It is with an eye to those more diverse vistas (and beyond, to farther-flung modernisms as yet unchampioned) that we could indeed grant the final word to Baudelaire, in the iconic last lines of his great poem 'Le voyage':

> Nous voulons, tant ce feu nous brûle le cerveau,
> Plonger au fond du gouffre, Enfer ou Ciel, qu'importe?
> Au fond de l'Inconnu pour trouver du *nouveau*!

David J. Code

[We wish, the fire so burns in our brain,
To dive deep into the abyss, Hell or Heaven, who cares?
Into the depths of the Unknown to find something *new!*][111]

Notes

1 William Gibson, *The Peripheral* (London: Penguin Books, 2014), 282.
2 Pierre Boulez, *Penser la musique aujourd'hui* (Paris: Éditions Gonthier, 1963), 14. Unless otherwise noted, all translations from the French are my own.
3 Richard J. Evans, *In Defence of History*, rev. ed. (London: Granta, 2000), 291.
4 Marshall Berman, *All That Is Solid Melts into Air: The Experience of Modernity* (London: Verso, 1982), 36.
5 See Jürgen Habermas, 'Modernity – An Incomplete Project?' in *The Anti-Aesthetic: Essays on Postmodern Culture*, ed. Hal Foster (Port Townsend, WA: Bay Press, 1983), 3–15; and Bertrand M. Patenade, *Stalin's Nemesis: The Exile and Murder of Leon Trotsky* (London: Faber and Faber, 2009), 193–94, 352.
6 Evans, *In Defence of History*, 248.
7 Gibson, *The Peripheral*, 282 (emphasis added); Carl Dahlhaus, *Foundations of Music History*, trans. J. B. Robinson (Cambridge: Cambridge University Press, 1983), 142. Dahlhaus attributes this idea to Wilhelm Pinder.
8 For instance, in my own memory (or reconstruction) of the 1970s and 1980s, even as a new pop music canon began congealing around much-mythologized 'revolutionary' accomplishments of the 1950s and 1960s, much university music education remained rooted in the 'classical' canon – whose ancestry in modernism's 'pre-origins' Lydia Goehr was to theorize only a few years later in *The Imaginary Museum of Musical Works: An Essay in the Philosophy of Music* (New York: Oxford University Press, 1992). But I also recall the North American version of the music history curriculum I encountered starting to draw on alternative ventures like John Rockwell's *All American Music: Composition in the Late Twentieth Century* (New York: Knopf, 1983), whose call for catholicity of taste offered an opening towards the broader perspectives already long debated, in other contexts, under the rubric of postmodernism.
9 Richard Taruskin, *The Oxford History of Western Music*, 6 vols., rev. ed. (Oxford: Oxford University Press, 2010), vol. 4, xx. Cited hereafter as *OHWM*.
10 Pierre Boulez, *Relevés d'apprenti*, ed. Paule Thévenin (Paris: Éditions du Seuil, 1966), 336. Cited hereafter as *RA*.
11 Boulez, 'La corruption dans les encensoirs', *RA*, 33. There is no exact translation of Boulez's adjective, which invokes a discourse of national self-sufficiency.
12 See, inter alia, Rose Rosengard Subotnik, *Developing Variations: Style and Ideology in Western Music* (Minneapolis: University of Minnesota Press, 1991); Max Paddison, *Adorno's Aesthetics of Music* (Cambridge: Cambridge University Press, 1993) and *Adorno, Modernism and Mass Culture: Essays on Critical Theory and Music* (London: Kahn & Averill, 1996); Alastair Williams, *New Music and the Claims of Modernity* (Aldershot: Ashgate, 1997); Michael Spitzer, *Music as Philosophy: Adorno on Beethoven's Late Style* (Bloomington: Indiana University Press, 2006); and Robert Hullot-Kentor's new translation of Adorno's *Philosophy of New Music* (Minneapolis and London: University of Minnesota Press, 2006), cited hereafter as *PNM*.
13 Subotnik, *Developing Variations*, 40.
14 For example in ibid., 14.
15 See, for example, the later chapters of Paddison, *Adorno, Modernism, and Mass Culture*, which address important critiques from, for example, Simon Frith, Richard Middleton and Trevor Wishart. Williams tackles the objections of Habermas and Dahlhaus in *New Music and the Claims of Modernity*, 18 and 37.
16 Subotnik, *Developing Variations*, 39. The reference is to Donald Kuspit, 'Critical Notes on Adorno's Sociology of Music and Art', *Journal of Aesthetics and Art Criticism* 33, no. 3 (1975), 322.
17 Paddison, *Adorno, Modernism and Mass Culture*, 83.
18 I glean these core principles from a reading of all the works cited thus far.
19 Paddison, *Adorno, Modernism, and Mass Culture*, 69. See also Subotnik, *Developing Variations*: 'where Adorno does indulge in long passages of technical musical discussion [. . .] his criticism tends to be uninspired' (49).
20 Paddison, *Adorno, Modernism, and Mass Culture*, 115, and Berman, *All That Is Solid Melts into Air*, 15.
21 Berman, *All That Is Solid*, 28n.

Modernism and history

22 *PNM*, 102.

23 For example, *PNM*, 176n3.

24 *PNM*, 32.

25 Ibid., 87.

26 Theodor W. Adorno, 'Vers une musique informelle', in his *Quasi una fantasia: Essays on Modern Music*, trans. Rodney Livingstone (London: Verso, 1992), 273.

27 *PNM*, 151; 'Vers une musique informelle', 274.

28 *PNM*, 138.

29 Ibid., 141.

30 See *Arnold Schoenberg, Wassily Kandinsky: Letters, Pictures, and Documents*, ed. Jelena Hahl-Koch and trans. John C. Crawford (London: Faber and Faber, 1983).

31 Stefan Jarocinski, *Debussy: Impressionism and Symbolism*, trans. Rollo Myers (London: Eulenburg, 1976), 91.

32 Here I should note the problematic nature of the 'generational' conceit I have taken from Dahlhaus. In fact, both Cézanne and Mallarmé were of the same generation as leading Impressionists Claude Monet and Alfred Sisley (all born *c*1840); Debussy referred, at a few points, to older artists Pierre Puvis de Chavannes and Gustave Moreau (both born in the 1820s); different artistic *oeuvres* rarely evolve in lockstep for any long period of time. But Adorno's sense of music sheltering under a 'more developed' art surely implies some sort of up-to-date affinity with, say, the most recent explorations of figures born from the late 1840s to the 1860s, including Paul Gauguin and Vincent Van Gogh, Georges Seurat and Paul Signac, Pierre Bonnard and even Henri Matisse (b. 1869).

33 *PNM*, 63.

34 For a contemporary source that strongly reinforces this point, see the influential early essays of the young 'Nabi' painter Maurice Denis (1870–1943), as later collected in his *Théories, 1890–1910, du symbolisme et de Gauguin vers un nouvel ordre classique* (Paris: Rouart et Watelin, 1920).

35 *PNM*, 141. See also this typical inter-artistic generalization: 'The inspiration of Stravinsky's idiosyncratic attack on culture in the name of culture could be traced back to the strand of sensuousness in Debussy and Ravel, or in comparable figures in painting, such as the late Renoir and perhaps even the decorative elegance of Matisse' (164). Clearly Adorno has not spent much time considering specific paintings like Matisse's *Baigneuses avec une tortue* (1907–8), whose tortured psychology (and sheer weirdness) puts it well beyond most notions of 'decorative elegance'.

36 *PNM*, 173n30. Strangely, Hullot-Kentor nonetheless finds in this essay a useful critique, before the fact, of postmodernism.

37 See, for example, Paddison, 'Stravinsky as Devil: Adorno's Three Critiques', in *The Cambridge Companion to Stravinsky*, ed. Jonathan Cross (Cambridge: Cambridge University Press, 2003), 192–202.

38 Theodor W. Adorno, 'Stravinsky: A Dialectical Portrait', in his *Quasi una fantasia*, 145–75, 147.

39 Ibid., 150. On page 199 of 'Stravinsky as Devil', Paddison simply drops Adorno's hypothetical framing of the prior remarks in order to read them as straight 'self-criticism'.

40 Paddison, *Adorno, Modernism, and Mass Culture*, 113.

41 Adorno, 'Vers une musique informelle', 282.

42 Subotnik, *Developing Variations*, 19.

43 Ibid., xvii. Later, Subotnik refers to the 'complex system of structural analogues' between music and society by which Adorno tries 'to maintain some semblance of interconnectedness and meaning in modern culture' (ibid., 49). The hedging language no doubt reflects her recognition that such 'analogues' and isomorphisms (e.g. between 'polyphony' and the actions of individuals in a free society, or between 'static' musical temporality and a historically non-progressive culture, see *PNM*, 18 and 40) rarely if ever rise above the lowest of 'low hermeneutics', as later critiqued by Carolyn Abbate in her 'Music: Drastic or Gnostic?' *Critical Inquiry* 30, no. 3 (2004), 505–36.

44 Paddison, *Adorno, Modernism, and Mass Culture*, 132.

45 Williams, *New Music and the Claims of Modernity*, 37.

46 *OHWM*, xiii.

47 Evans, *In Defence of History*, 175.

48 *OHWM*, xv.

49 Ibid., xi.

50 The question becomes acute at the many points where Taruskin deems some music or other 'an analyst's delight' (or the like) – as if his own version of that delight can be presumed the same for everyone. The limits of that presumption become clear when, for example, he acknowledges 'the arduousness and

David J. Code

tediousness' of his analysis of Boulez's *Structures Ia* (1951) and suggests that 'the reader is forgiven for skimming'. *OHWM*, e.g. vol. 4, 320 and vol. 5, 36.

51 See Taruskin, '*Et in Arcadia Ego*; or, I Didn't Know I Was Such a Pessimist until I Wrote This Thing', in his *The Danger of Music and Other Anti-Utopian Essays* (Berkeley and Los Angeles: University of California Press, 2009), 1–24 (cited hereafter as *DM*). In his 2008 commentary, he writes 'although I now find the account far too schematic and insufficiently nuanced [. . .] it does provide the general framework around which I have structured my detailed treatment of *The Oxford History of Western Music* (though without the zigzag terminology)' (*DM*, 19).

52 See Dahlhaus's admission that it is hard to conclude 'whether the "nineteenth century" in European music history ended in 1889, 1908, or 1924 (i.e. whether the deciding factor was the advent of modernism, the transition to atonality, or the collapse of expressionism)', *Nineteenth-Century Music*, trans. J. Bradford Robinson (Berkeley and Los Angeles: University of California Press, 1989), 335. See also Adorno: 'since the heroic decade, the period around World War I, it has as a whole been a history of decline, of involution to the traditional' (*PNM*, 9). Boulez refers at one point to 'that indescribably disjointed period 1920–30', and he asserts the historiographical point even more plainly in his encyclopedia entry on 'Counterpoint': 'the essays in linear writing that proliferated madly between 1914 and 1940 [. . .] are of an appalling poverty, while also originating from a completely false historical point of view'; see his 'Moment de Jean-Sébastien Bach', *RA*, 9–25, 12, and 'Contrepoint', *RA*, 286–94, 291.

53 Taruskin, 'The Poietic Fallacy', in *DM*, 301–29, 305. The essay's title reflects its debt to a 'scurrilous little tract' (*OHWM*, xvi) by David Hackett Fischer, *Historians' Fallacies: Toward a Logic of Historical Thought* (New York: Harper & Row, 1970). Readers might wish to see how many such 'fallacies' they can spot in the *OHWM* itself (I stopped once my list included 'the Baconian fallacy', 'the fallacy of declarative questions', 'the fallacy of the insidious generalization', 'the fallacy of narration', 'the fallacy of causation' and 'the fallacy of the universal man'). While the more insidious of such things are no doubt best avoided, others make me wonder whether Fischer's contentious term 'fallacy' might occasionally be replaced with the gentler 'compromise', given that every historian will have to 'select, measure, and classify' what they study (as Dahlhaus observes in *Foundations*), and present it, if not necessarily in a traditional narrative, at least in some similarly arbitrary discursive form.

54 Ibid., 329.

55 Ibid., 305.

56 See Evans: 'As historians, we clearly cannot recover a single, unalterably "true" meaning of a dispatch simply by reading it; on the other hand, we cannot impose any meaning we wish to on such a text either. We are limited by the words it contains, words which are not, contrary to what the postmodernists suggest, capable of an infinity of meaning. [. . .] The fact is, as Dominick LaCapra sensibly remarks, that historical research is a dialogue between two kinds of significances – the historian's and the document's' (*In Defence of History*, 106). Perhaps predictably, one of the debates he discussed focused on the Holocaust: 'Auschwitz was not a discourse. It trivializes mass murder to see it as a text. The gas chambers were not a piece of rhetoric' (ibid., 104). The stakes may be lower for music, but the historians' responsibility to a reality beyond their own discourse is surely the same. For one of many instances where Taruskin affirms this point himself – and also, incidentally, reinstates *poiesis* over *esthesis* – see his challenge to erroneous discourse about the 'arch-Romanticism' of Pyotr Chaikovsky: 'in fact no nineteenth-century composer retained a more thoroughly eighteenth-century outlook on his craft' (*OHWM*, vol. 4, 141).

57 *OHWM*, vol. 4, 686.

58 Ibid., 528. The works in question are *Mörder, Hoffnung der Frauen* (1919), *Sancta Susanna* (1922) and *Das Nusch-Nuschi* (1921).

59 *OHWM*, vol. 4, 719.

60 Although his chapter title – 'The Significance of Art: Historical or Aesthetic?' – opens him to challenge in light of Fischer's 'Fallacy of Question Framing' (see above), Dahlhaus never puts this question so crudely in his text. The italics Taruskin borrows appear in a declarative sentence: 'Music history fails either as *history* by being a collection of structural analyses of separate works, or as a history of *art* by reverting from musical works to occurrences in social or intellectual history cobbled together in order to impart cohesion to an historical narrative' (*Foundations*, 19–20). In this form, it more clearly reflects its origin, with all of these historiographical reflections, in the practical difficulties encountered in writing *Nineteenth-Century Music*. It also seems, rather than a 'senseless binarism' (as Taruskin puts it), a practical opening to evaluative questions still fruitfully addressed to any work of music history – from Subotnik's 'life and works' PhD thesis to the *Oxford History* itself.

61 Dahlhaus, *Foundations*, 141–42.

Modernism and history

62 It also gives rise to some strange contradictions. For example, at one point we read of the widespread 'ban on pathos' after the Great War, which led to a change in performance style 'of all European classical music, regardless of age or origin'. But a few pages later, we find that the exclusion of strings from a concerto accompaniment of 1923–24 'was characteristic of Stravinsky at this time. Strings were too "humanoid" and "expressive" for his taste (especially as they were played then, with lots of throbbing vibrato and lots of *portamento* or sliding pitch)' (*OHWM*, vol. 4, 475 and 491). If the 'ban' in question was indeed caused by the war, surely we need some explanation for its delayed enforcement.

63 *OHWM*, xiii.

64 In the 1989 review of an edition of Debussy's letters, titled 'The First Modernist', Taruskin notes 'many misleading attempts to pigeonhole him as an impressionist or a symbolist' (*DM*, 199). In the *OHWM*, after an account of 'Nuages' (*Nocturnes*, 1899) largely in thrall to the Impressionist cliché – and graced by a reproduction of Monet's *Impression, Sunrise* (1872) – he admits that 'drawing connections between Debussy and the impressionist painters was itself an exercise in impressionism, ringed with caveats (including the composer's expressed discomfort with the idea)' (vol. 4, 86).

65 *OHWM*, vol. 4, 78. I excise some identifying details that seem unnecessary here.

66 Letter to Henri Cazalis of 30 October 1864, in Stéphane Mallarmé, *Oeuvres complètes*, ed. Henri Mondor and Georges Jean-Aubry (Paris: Gallimard, 1945), 307. For a more public and famous variant of the same idea see the 'definition' proposed by Émile Zola in his 1866 article 'Les Réalistes du Salon': 'a work of art is a corner of creation seen through a temperament'; Émile Zola, *Écrits sur l'art*, ed. Jean-Pierre Leduc-Adine (Paris: Gallimard, 1991), 125.

67 In truth, the inspiration is usually attributed to a sculptural fragment, not a vase.

68 Similarly, like many Romantic forebears Debussy summons an imaginary landscape in the prelude 'Les collines d'Anacapri' by evoking the music of its human populace, through pervasive tarantella rhythms and a broad tune marked 'Comme une chanson populaire'.

69 See my 'The Song Triptych: Reflections on a Debussyan Genre', *Scottish Music Review* 3 (2013), http://www.scottishmusicreview.org/index.php/SMR/article/view/44 (accessed 18 August 2017). Taruskin does include a lengthy discussion of *Pelléas et Mélisande*, whose references to Debussy's sense of the intense 'humanity' of Maurice Maeterlinck's play seem hard to reconcile with his Ortegan conceit.

70 Gary Tomlinson, 'Monumental Musicology', *Journal of the Royal Musical Association* 132, no. 2 (2007), 349–74, esp. 353 and 356.

71 Ibid., 350. Taruskin asserts that 'Inclusion and omission imply no judgment of value here. I never asked myself whether this or that composition or musician was "worth mentioning", and I hope readers will agree that I have sought neither to advocate or denigrate what I did include'; see *OHWM*, xi. The fact that he opts to devote a few pages to the little Satie-esque 'Sarabande' from *Pour le piano*, and then say almost nothing about much more substantial works like the faun *Prélude* or *La mer*, clearly shows how impossible it is to separate questions of inclusion and omission from those of judgement and value.

72 See, for example, this dry observation in Franz Niedermayer, *José Ortega y Gasset*, trans. Peter Tirner (New York: Frederick Ungar, 1973): 'The Charleston and jazz music worried him; Ortega has frequently succumbed to the temptation of writing music criticism' (ibid., 53).

73 See Friedrich Nietzsche, *Der Fall Wagner: Ein Musikanten-Problem* (Leipzig: C. G. Neumann, 1888).

74 Quoted in Niedermayer, *José Ortega y Gasset*, 21.

75 See Rockwell Gray, *The Imperative of Modernity: An Intellectual Biography of José Ortega y Gasset* (Berkeley and Los Angeles: University of California Press, 1989), 206 and 332, and also Niedermayer, *José Ortega y Gasset*, 75. Niedermayer later quotes a characterization of Ortega by 'the brilliant Basque Eugenio Imaz' as 'the man from Málaga who fancied he had a German soul' (ibid., 115).

76 According to Niedermayer, of the 'several hundred volumes' in this collection, 'about seventy-five percent' were by Germans (ibid., 44).

77 Here, then, is some wider intellectual-historical context for Tomlinson's apt critique: 'Debussy's turn away from Germanic, post-Wagnerian orchestration cannot easily fit into the narrative of an Ortegan dehumanization that Taruskin pursues. His orchestration, that is, was anti-Germanic, like his unglued harmony; but instead of pointing away from emotionalism it carved out a new brand of affective warmth, distinct from German approaches – one that would be exploited, soon and repeatedly, not only by later French composers but also in film scores' ('Monumental Musicology', 356).

78 Inflammatory as it may be to admit it, the model that springs insistently to mind here is Wagner's anti-Semitic dismissals of Felix Mendelssohn.

79 Thomas Mann, *Reflections of a Nonpolitical Man*, trans. Walter D. Morris (New York: Ungar, 1987), 46–47. The first emphasis added.

80 *OHWM*, vol. 4, 421.

81 Taruskin, 'The First Modernist', *DM*, 200.

82 The piano piece 'Golliwog's Cakewalk' (from *Children's Corner*, 1908) is only the most famous of Debussy's many riffs on popular culture, which extended from the 'music hall' preludes 'Minstrels' and 'Général Lavine, Eccentric' through the Dickensian caricature 'Hommage à S. Pickwick, esq. P. P. M. P. C.' to numerous pieces based on French folk song or the rhythms of Spanish and Italian folk dance. For Bartók, see *OHWM*, vol. 4, 444.

83 Both remarks are in *OHWM*, vol. 4, 380.

84 Taruskin takes the term 'techno-essentialist' from Christopher Williams, to criticize the theoretical approach to music as 'a machine made of notes' (*OHWM*, vol. 4, 195). He often courts the same criticism himself, not least by treating Debussy's 'Nuages' primarily as an example of formal organization by symmetrical pitch structures, rather than an instance of suggestively unfolding orchestral poetry.

85 Béla Bartók, *Essays*, ed. Benjamin Suchoff (London: Faber and Faber, 1976). The quoted words are in 'Hungarian Peasant Music', 304–15, 306; see also the reference to the 'musical recitation' found in *Pelléas* and 'some of [Debussy's] songs which were based on the old French *recitativo*', in 'Harvard Lectures', 354–92, 386. On the 'absolute hegemony of German music' in Hungary before 'Debussy appeared', see 'The Influence of Debussy and Ravel in Hungary', 518.

86 To bring this point into relief, recall the reports of Ludwig Wittgenstein's fondness for whistling the tunes of Schubert's *Lieder* along with someone else's piano accompaniment. The same wordless exercise would be pointless (and ridiculous) for the vast majority of Debussy's mature *mélodies*. See e.g. Scott Messing, *Schubert in the European Imagination*, vol. 2 (Rochester, NY: University of Rochester Press, 2007), 79.

87 Boulez, 'Trajectoires: Ravel, Stravinsky, Schoenberg', in *RA*, 241–64, 257.

88 *OHWM*, vol. 5, 19.

89 Boulez, 'Éventuellement. . . ', in *RA*, 147–82, 149.

90 Boulez, 'Schoenberg est mort', in *RA*, 265–72, 271.

91 *PNM*, 165. Emphasis added.

92 Richard Taruskin, 'Afterword: Nicht blutbefleckt?' *Journal of Musicology* 26, no. 2 (2009), 282–83. Emphasis added.

93 Charles Rosen, 'Music and the Cold War', *New York Review of Books*, 7 April 2011, 42.

94 According to the *New Grove*, Taruskin published his first article in 1970, and finished his Columbia PhD in 1975 – well within the years overshadowed by the doctrine of 'mutually assured destruction' and (grimly) enlivened by a great deal of 'nuclear apocalypse' pop culture; Paula Morgan, 'Taruskin, Richard', *Grove Music Online*, *Oxford Music Online*, Oxford University Press, http://www.oxfordmusiconline.com/subscriber/article/grove/music/47125 (accessed 21 September 2017).

95 *OHWM*, vol. 4, 772.

96 Ibid., 567.

97 Adorno, 'Stravinsky: A Dialectical Portrait', 150.

98 Boulez, 'Stravinsky demeure', in *RA*, 75–145, 77–78.

99 As always, one can admire the thoroughness and insight of such an analysis while questioning some its particular methods. For a study that offers a different account than Boulez of a very small span of *Le sacre*, while challenging the equally monolithic interpretations (in very different terms) of Adorno and Taruskin, see my 'The Synthesis of Rhythms: Form, Ideology, and "The Augurs of Spring"', *Journal of Musicology* 24, no. 1 (2007), 112–66.

100 Alongside Tomlinson's critique of this aspect of the *OHWM* in his 'Monumental Musicology' (esp. 366–68) see also Susan McClary, 'The World According to Taruskin', *Music & Letters* 87, no. 3 (2006), 408–15, where she challenges his neglect even of such significant Western music as most of 'that produced or deeply influenced by African Americans' (ibid., 412).

101 The reference is to Edward Said, *Orientalism* (New York: Pantheon, 1978) and the whole subsequent literature it spawned, notably including Said, *Culture and Imperialism* (London: Chatto and Windus, 1993).

102 Boulez, '*À la limite du pays fertile*', in *RA*, 205–21, 210. Needless to say, the artistic respect comes without any truly ethnomusicological sense of music and its sustaining cultures.

103 The whole preceding paragraph is redacted from 'La corruption dans les encensoirs', *RA*, 38. There is some irony in the fact that Debussy's recognition of these alternatives only arose through his experience of the self-congratulatory colonialist enterprise of the Expositions Internationales.

104 For one suggestive source for the idea that cultural differences extended to disparate historiographical inclinations see Gertrude Stein's little novel, *Paris France* (New York: Charles Scribner's Sons, 1940), 11–12 and 38–39.

Modernism and history

105 Taruskin, 'The Golden Age of Kitsch', *DM*, 245–60, 250. This essay is puzzling to read against Taruskin's 'zigzag' superperiodization. When he explains the decline of opera in the early twentieth century with a single word, 'talkies', and then elaborates by noting that '[f]ilm, in short, could keep the promise of romanticism, and preserve its flame more effectively than opera, which had been the romantic art par excellence' (ibid., 246–47), the question must surely arise: what did the volcanic emergence, in the 1930s, of the century's most influential and 'romantic' audiovisual entertainment medium have to do with the supposedly ironic and objective 'spirit of the age'?

106 Boulez, *RA*, 37.

107 See, for example, T. J. Clark, *The Painting of Modern Life: Paris in the Art of Manet and His Followers* (Princeton, NJ: Princeton University Press, 1984); T. J. Clark and Anne M. Wagner, *Lowry and the Painting of Modern Life* (London: Tate Publishing, 2013); and the catalogue of the 2007 exhibition at the Hayward Gallery, London and the Castello de Rivoli, Museum of Contemporary Art, Turin, *The Painting of Modern Life: 1960s to Now*, ed. Ralph Rugoff (London: Hayward Publishing, 2007). In the essay itself, see the early claim that '[t]he beautiful is made up of an eternal and invariable element, of which the quantity is extremely difficult to determine, and of a more relative and circumstantial element which will be, so to speak, one after the other or all at once, the fashions, morals and passions of the present epoch'. Later, Baudelaire further underlines that first, 'eternal and invariable' element when praising Constantin Guys for his demonstration of the principles necessary 'in order that all *modernity* is worthy to become antiquity'. Charles Baudelaire, *Oeuvres complètes*, ed. Claude Pichois (Paris: Gallimard, 1975), vol. 2, 683–724, 685 and 695.

108 For a more recent echo of the same sort of dialectical image, see Michel Foucault's characterization of the modern (post-Nietzschean and -Mallarméan) human being as an 'empirico-transcendental doublet' in the later chapters of *Les mots et les choses: une archéologie des sciences humaines* (Paris: Gallimard, 1966).

109 On the first of these extremes see for example Peter Bürger, *Theory of the Avant-Garde*, trans. Michael Shaw (Minneapolis: University of Minnesota Press, 1984), and Taruskin, 'Optimism Amid the Rubble', *DM*, 37–42, 39.

110 Dahlhaus, *Foundations*, 97. To be fair, on the same page he also acknowledges that '[f]or an historian to "receive" a predetermined canon [. . .] in no way excludes the possibility of his criticising that canon'.

111 'Le voyage' is the final poem of *Les Fleurs du Mal* (Baudelaire, *Oeuvres complètes*, 129–34, 134).

Bibliography

Abbate, Carolyn. 'Music: Drastic or Gnostic?' *Critical Inquiry* 30, no. 3 (2004): 505–36.

Adorno, Theodor W. *Quasi una fantasia: Essays on Modern Music*. Translated by Rodney Livingstone. London: Verso, 1992.

———. *Philosophy of New Music*. Translated by Robert Hullot-Kentor. Minneapolis and London: University of Minnesota Press, 2006.

Bartók, Béla. *Essays*. Edited by Benjamin Suchoff. London: Faber and Faber, 1976.

Baudelaire, Charles. *Oeuvres complètes*. Edited by Claude Pichois. 2 vols. Paris: Gallimard, 1975–76.

Berman, Marshall. *All That Is Solid Melts into Air: The Experience of Modernity*. London: Verso, 1982.

Boulez, Pierre. *Penser la musique aujourd'hui*. Paris: Éditions Gonthier, 1963.

———. *Relevés d'apprenti*. Edited by Paule Thévenin. Paris: Éditions du Seuil, 1966.

Bürger, Peter. *Theory of the Avant-Garde*. Translated by Michael Shaw. Minneapolis: University of Minnesota Press, 1984.

Clark, T. J. *The Painting of Modern Life: Paris in the Art of Manet and His Followers*. Princeton, NJ: Princeton University Press, 1984.

Clark, T. J., and Anne M. Wagner. *Lowry and the Painting of Modern Life*. London: Tate Publishing, 2013.

Code, David. 'The Synthesis of Rhythms: Form, Ideology, and "The Augurs of Spring"'. *Journal of Musicology* 24, no. 1 (2007): 112–66.

———. 'The Song Triptych: Reflections on a Debussyan Genre'. *Scottish Music Review* 3 (2013). http://www.scottishmusicreview.org/index.php/SMR/article/view/44 (accessed 18 August 2017).

Dahlhaus, Carl. *Foundations of Music History*. Translated by J. B. Robinson. Cambridge: Cambridge University Press, 1983.

———. *Nineteenth-Century Music*. Translated by J. Bradford Robinson. Berkeley and Los Angeles: University of California Press, 1989.

Denis, Maurice. *Théories, 1890–1910, du symbolisme et de Gauguin vers un nouvel ordre Classique*. Paris: Rouart et Watelin, 1920.

Evans, Richard J. *In Defence of History*. Rev. ed. London: Granta, 2000.

Fischer, David Hackett. *Historians' Fallacies: Toward a Logic of Historical Thought*. New York: Harper & Row, 1970.

Foucault, Michel. *Les mots et les choses: une archéologie des sciences humaines*. Paris: Gallimard, 1966.

Gibson, William. *The Peripheral*. London: Penguin Books, 2014.

Goehr, Lydia. *The Imaginary Museum of Musical Works: An Essay in the Philosophy of Music*. New York: Oxford University Press, 1992.

Gray, Rockwell. *The Imperative of Modernity: An Intellectual Biography of José Ortega y Gasset*. Berkeley and Los Angeles: University of California Press, 1989.

Habermas, Jürgen. 'Modernity – An Incomplete Project?' In *The Anti-Aesthetic: Essays on Postmodern Culture*, edited by Hal Foster, 3–15. Port Townsend, WA: Bay Press, 1983.

Hahl-Koch, Jelena, ed. *Arnold Schoenberg, Wassily Kandinsky: Letters, Pictures, and Documents*. Translated by John C. Crawford. London: Faber and Faber, 1983.

Jarocinski, Stefan. *Debussy: Impressionism and Symbolism*. Translated by Rollo Myers. London: Eulenburg, 1976.

Kuspit, Donald. 'Critical Notes on Adorno's Sociology of Music and Art'. *Journal of Aesthetics and Art Criticism* 33, no. 3 (1975): 321–27.

Mallarmé, Stéphane. *Oeuvres complètes*. Edited by Henri Mondor and Georges Jean-Aubry. Paris: Gallimard, 1945.

Mann, Thomas. *Reflections of a Nonpolitical Man*. Translated by Walter D. Morris. New York: Ungar, 1987.

McClary, Susan. 'The World According to Taruskin'. *Music & Letters* 87, no. 3 (2006): 408–15.

Messing, Scott. *Schubert in the European Imagination*. 2 vols. Rochester, NY: University of Rochester Press, 2006–7.

Morgan, Paula. 'Taruskin, Richard'. *Grove Music Online. Oxford Music Online*. Oxford University Press. http://www.oxfordmusiconline.com/subscriber/article/grove/music/47125 (accessed 21 September 2017).

Niedermayer, Franz. *José Ortega y Gasset*. Translated by Peter Tirner. New York: Frederick Ungar, 1973.

Nietzsche, Friedrich. *Der Fall Wagner: Ein Musikanten-Problem*. Leipzig: C. G. Neumann, 1888.

Paddison, Max. *Adorno's Aesthetics of Music*. Cambridge: Cambridge University Press, 1993.

———. *Adorno, Modernism and Mass Culture: Essays on Critical Theory and Music*. London: Kahn & Averill, 1996.

———. 'Stravinsky as Devil: Adorno's Three Critiques'. In *The Cambridge Companion to Stravinsky*, edited by Jonathan Cross, 192–202. Cambridge: Cambridge University Press, 2003.

Patenade, Bertrand M. *Stalin's Nemesis: The Exile and Murder of Leon Trotsky*. London: Faber and Faber, 2009.

Rockwell, John. *All American Music: Composition in the Late Twentieth Century*. New York: Knopf, 1983.

Rosen, Charles. 'Music and the Cold War'. *New York Review of Books*, 7 April 2011, 40–42.

Rugoff, Ralph, ed. *The Painting of Modern Life: 1960s to Now*. London: Hayward Publishing, 2007.

Said, Edward. *Orientalism*. New York: Pantheon, 1978.

———. *Culture and Imperialism*. London: Chatto and Windus, 1993.

Spitzer, Michael. *Music as Philosophy: Adorno on Beethoven's Late Style*. Bloomington: Indiana University Press, 2006.

Stein, Gertrude. *Paris France*. New York: Charles Scribner's Sons, 1940.

Subotnik, Rose Rosengard. *Developing Variations: Style and Ideology in Western Music*. Minneapolis: University of Minnesota Press, 1991.

Taruskin, Richard. 'Afterword: Nicht blutbefleckt?' *Journal of Musicology* 26, no. 2 (2009): 274–84.

———. *The Danger of Music and Other Anti-Utopian Essays*. Berkeley and Los Angeles: University of California Press, 2009.

———. *The Oxford History of Western Music*. 6 vols. Rev. ed. Oxford: Oxford University Press, 2010.

Tomlinson, Gary. 'Monumental Musicology'. *Journal of the Royal Musical Association* 132, no. 2 (2007): 349–74.

Williams, Alastair. *New Music and the Claims of Modernity*. Aldershot: Ashgate, 1997.

Zola, Émile. 'Les Réalistes du Salon'. In *Écrits sur l'art*, edited by Jean-Pierre Leduc-Adine, 120–25. Paris: Gallimard, 1991.

5

MUSICAL MODERNITY, THE BEAUTIFUL AND THE SUBLIME

Edward Campbell

Theodor Adorno, noting the difficulty of creating new art that can be beautiful in a truthful way, eschewed any response to musical modernity that would move quickly beyond bewilderment, anxiety and insecurity to something easily assimilable as traditionally beautiful. For Jean-François Lyotard the arts for the last century have no longer been concerned primarily with the beautiful but rather with a renewed concept of the sublime and, in making this distinction, he distinguishes properly artistic work from cultural activities. This dissociation of the beautiful from the modern in Adorno and Lyotard contrasts strikingly with Helmut Lachenmann's revalorization of the beautiful and his distinction of 'humanity's legitimate and profoundly rooted demand for art as the experience of Beauty, and its false satisfaction and alienation in the form of art "fodder" manufactured by the bourgeoisie and preserved in a society of repressed contradictions'.[1]

Recognizing the problematic that is worked out in these three positions, this chapter explores the problem of the beautiful in modernity as set out by Adorno, following Schoenberg's theoretical reflections on the question. From there I look to the fundamental polarity that emerges between the post-tonal view of Lachenmann, for whom there is the possibility of a 'rescued' concept of the beautiful, and that of Lyotard for whom the modern is uniquely the moment of the sublime. Alongside a recognition of the continued importance of the work of Burke and Kant, whose philosophical positions are the most paradigmatic in such discussions, alternative theorizations of the sublime by Jacques Derrida, Jean-Luc Nancy and Barbara Claire Freeman are considered in passing as well as Vladimir Jankélévitch's work on the ineffable and the 'saturated phenomena' theorized by Jean-Luc Marion. In addition to this range of philosophical positions, the work of a number of modernist composers – including Raphaël Cendo, Claude Debussy, Morton Feldman, Brian Ferneyhough, Sofia Gubaidulina, Georg Friedrich Haas, Helmut Lachenmann, Wolfgang Rihm, Arnold Schoenberg, Karlheinz Stockhausen, Jörg Widmann and Bernd Alois Zimmermann – is considered in relation to the beautiful and/or the sublime.

Adorno and the problem of beauty

While Adorno struggled with the question of beauty in relation to musical modernity, it was not always so, and he was capable, certainly in his early years, of recognizing beauty in new music. In a letter to Alban Berg dated 28 June 1926 discussing the music of Anton Webern, towards which he had ambivalent feelings, he writes: 'the song "Welt der Gestalten" from op. 4,[2] or the second movement from op. 5, or the 5th bagatelle from op. 9, truly contain some of the purest, most beautiful lyricism that there is'.[3] In his later writings, however, beauty is not at all clear-cut or unproblematic. In the incomplete and posthumously published *Aesthetic Theory* he states that 'the definition of aesthetics as the theory of the beautiful is so untruthful because the formal character of the concept of beauty is inadequate to the full content [*Inhalt*] of the aesthetic. [. . .] [T]he concept of beauty is but one element'.[4] Beyond his criticisms of the Platonic and Kantian notions of the beautiful in art, he reflects on the problem of beauty in relation to new music, citing Schoenberg, for whom 'Chopin was fortunate: He needed only to compose in F-sharp major, a still unexploited key, for his music to be beautiful'.[5] For Adorno, certainly after 1945, any idea of authentic beauty seemed at odds with both the actual development of art and the totalitarian catastrophes in the context of which that art had developed. Consequently, the 'criterion of success is the ability of art to appropriate into its language of form what bourgeois society has ostracized'.[6]

Furthermore, the facile dismissal of modern art as ugly is, for Adorno, all too literal in its reading of new work, failing to hear it or read it in terms of what has previously been held to be taboo and 'what has not yet been socially approved'. What Adorno refers to as 'spiritualization in new art prohibits it from tarnishing itself any further with the topical preferences of philistine culture: the true, the beautiful, and the good'.[7] In the essay 'Music and New Music' from 1960, he writes

> There are no words for the noble, the good, the true and the beautiful that have not been violated and turned into their opposite – just as the Nazis could enthuse about the house, its roof resting on pillars, while torture went on in the cellars. The positive values have degenerated into a mere device to prevent anyone reflecting on the fact that none of them has been made real in practice. Anyone who is truly concerned about them feels unable to express them in words and feels compelled to deconstruct them when others venture to do so.[8]

In this way, Adorno rejects rigid structures and posits the desirability of conceptual fluidity if art is to relate to actuality. It is an aesthetic theory that must begin from below, not from above, not from a systematic idea of art, as in Hegel, but from the work itself. In his book on Mahler he wishes to know why a given artwork deserves to be described as beautiful,[9] and in the essay 'The Aging of the New Music' (1955), discussing the shock experienced by the first listeners to Stravinsky's *Rite of Spring* and Berg's *Altenberg Lieder*, he states that this

> cannot simply be attributed to unfamiliarity and strangeness, as the good-natured apology would have it; rather, it is the result of something actually distressing and confused. Whoever denies this and claims that the new art is as beautiful as the traditional one does it a real disservice; he praises in it what this music rejects so long as it unflinchingly follows its own impulse.[10]

Finally, in a radio conversation with Stockhausen from 1960, Adorno speaks of the place of negativity in musical thinking:

> Those who reproach us for not taking account of the human in music obstinately defend, one can be sure of it, the institutional framework in which habitual music unfolds. In contrast, the human voice really makes itself heard in what does not conform to this institutional frame, in what risks being denounced by this framework as

inhuman, as lacking in love, as not thinking of man. [. . .] [A]rt which is sincere with regard to man and truth is precisely that which does not allow itself to advertise a product to the world such as it is, in harmony with it, representing it in such a way to make believe that everything is for the best and that, at this moment as always, the human is immediately perceptible. [. . .] [T]he most profound reason for resistance against new music is that this moment of truth of negativity reminds men that their pretended positivity is only apparent and false.[11]

Schoenberg and beauty

Prior to Adorno's reflections, Schoenberg had already been grappling with the question of the beautiful in the context of new music. While he declared 'my music is not lovely',[12] his artist friend Wassily Kandinsky was perhaps more far-sighted in recognizing that the composer was 'almost alone in severing himself from conventional beauty'. Indeed, for the artist, Schoenberg was 'endeavouring to make complete use of his freedom and [had] already discovered gold mines of new beauty in his search for spiritual harmony'.[13]

Schoenberg's writings contain a number of references to the beautiful, and he suggests that just as the music of Wagner, Mahler, Strauss, Reger and Debussy was once found to be dissonant or even incomprehensible, 'what at first appeared harmonically incoherent, wild, confused, arbitrary, eccentric and hideous is today felt to be beautiful'.[14] Even Hindemith and Krenek, if only 'in their best moments', are judged to have produced beautiful music.[15] On the subject of twelve-tone composition, while dissonance and consonance are attributed less to their degree of beauty than to the extent of their comprehensibility,[16] he acknowledges the problematic recurrence of a 'nostalgic longing for old-time beauty' which needs to be calmed.[17]

In the *Theory of Harmony* Schoenberg reflects at greater length on the question of beauty, declaring that laws determining beauty are not prescribed by aesthetics, which merely works towards abstracting such principles from 'the effects of art'.[18] Against the judgements of theorists he argues that beauty is a matter for individual listeners and not something experienced in the same way by everyone.[19] He rejects the notion that the creation of beauty is the artist's aim, positing instead that art is produced by a necessity which only afterwards may be discussed in terms of beauty.[20] While, historically speaking, composers have at times produced music which aestheticians found ugly, Schoenberg is in no doubt that the creator is always right.[21] The artist has no need of beauty, and is satisfied with having 'expressed himself' in the knowledge that future listeners will recognize this unintentional beauty even if the present generation cannot. Nuancing this further, he distinguishes between genuine beauty, which is perceived by the listener in response to the creative work, and a sterile beauty amounting to the pursuit of strict rules and forms. Where the listener looks for beauty, the artist strives for integrity. Consequently, nothing is either beautiful or ugly in itself, and music may be said to be either beautiful or ugly 'according to who is handling it, and how'. It is familiarity which effects the sensation of beauty: since 'the ear is often slow-witted', it is not easy to adapt to the new, and those with the most sophisticated notion of traditional beauty are often the most intransigent in accepting anything not in keeping with it.

Lachenmann and the beautiful

Adorno's dissociation of the beautiful from the modern and Schoenberg's severance of any concern for the beautiful from the artist contrast strikingly and rather paradoxically with Helmut Lachenmann's later revalorization of the beautiful.

Edward Campbell

In the article 'The "Beautiful" in Music Today' (1980), Lachenmann articulates a renewed idea of the beautiful, noting that for the 1950s musical avant-garde, the generation of Boulez and Stockhausen, 'beauty was not merely out of place; it was downright suspect'.[22] He distinguishes, however, between a genuine and deep-rooted need for beauty in art and the false satisfaction of this need in the form of art 'fodder'. While beauty was dismissed by the avant-garde, for Lachenmann it survived in its 'socially accepted form as reified categories'.[23] The musical parameterization in the serial music of the 1950s and an 'implicit denial of the Beautiful reified as the Comfortable and Familiar' failed and resulted in the emergence of the generation of Ligeti, Penderecki and Kagel, who introduced new freedom into their works, in which the tonal elements excluded by the serialists were now tolerated. In Lachenmann's view this represented a 'veiled regression', which was followed in the 1970s by an 'open regression' to a reified concept of beauty. He judges that by 1980 all avant-gardists, except his former teacher Luigi Nono, had lost their early vigour, while the new tonal composers were championing a return to 'the bourgeois concept of beauty in the same reactionary form it had at the end of World War II, if not before'. Looking to the later development of the serial composers, and perhaps thinking also of Kandinsky's earlier statement, he remarks that the transformation in the work of many of the post-war generation turned the one-time 'prospectors for gold' into mere 'jewellers'.[24]

In the light of all of this, Lachenmann defined his goal as one of rescuing beauty 'from the speculations of corrupt spirits, and the cheap pretensions of avant-garde hedonists, sonority-chefs, exotic-mediationists and nostalgia-merchants'.[25] To do this a composer must 'take account of the "aesthetic apparatus" – that is, the sum total of categories of musical perception as they have evolved throughout history to the present day; of the "instrumentarium" which comes with them'; of playing techniques and notation as well as institutions and markets, all of which embody 'the ruling aesthetic needs and norms'. In accepting this challenge, he notes that the renewed concept of the beautiful, which will be different for every composer, must be a negotiation between the composer's personal expressive will and the aesthetic apparatus.[26] The concept of the beautiful needs to be purged through the prism of 'the real contradictions of social expectations', and the result has to establish itself not by confirming but rather by illuminating what previously has been reified.

Lachenmann's stance led him to open conflict with fellow composer Hans Werner Henze in 1983. Accused by Henze of composing a 'musica negativa', Lachenmann penned an open letter to his fellow composer in which he rejected musical naïveté along with 'disposable expressivity', the notion of adding a little atonality to an essentially nineteenth-century tonal palette.[27] Defending himself, Lachenmann claims that he is branded an

> ascetic, sulking preacher with moralizing finger raised in the desert of choked scratching noises [. . .]. My emergency definition of beauty as 'rejection of convention' becomes instead, in the distorting mirror of idiocy, 'rejection of pleasure'. Convention and pleasure as one: here the petits bourgeois are unmasked.[28]

Henze is criticized as having failed to really engage with tradition and, while Henze claims that he has taken a radical view, for Lachenmann this 'is betrayed by complacent technique', which is too close to the 'mediascape and purée of culture which is nearly choking us'.[29] Since Henze's music 'merely helps itself to traditional materials (instead of developing them further)',[30] Lachenmann opposes his use of 'off-the-shelf products from the supermarket of tradition',[31] accusing him of 'unscrupulously' exploiting traditional musical material rather than allowing it to reflect.[32] Ultimately, for Lachenmann, there is no such thing as 'expressive spontaneity', and

Musical modernity, the beautiful and the sublime

a composer cannot draw innocently from tradition or avoid engaging with the multiplicity of connotations already associated with particular sounds.[33]

Interestingly, beauty finds a place in the work of Lachenmann's teacher and friend Luigi Nono, and the Italian composer's scenic action *Al gran sole carico d'amore* (1974, rev. 1977) is a multi-levelled, multi-sourced, polyglot, homage-cum-elegy to a century of failed revolutions from the Paris Commune and the civil war in France in 1871, the failed Russian revolution of 1905, political and industrial conflict in Turin in the 1950s, the storming of the Moncada barracks in Cuba in 1953, the failed guerrilla struggle of Che Guevara and Tania Bunke in Bolivia in 1967 and the Vietnam war. All these events ended with the defeat of the revolutionary side, with which Nono identified himself. Early in the work Nono sets words by Che Guevara, 'beauty is not contrary to the revolution', simultaneously with words by communard Louise Michel: 'Love for my fellow human beings is the only breathable air for my infinite and generous heart, drunk with solidarity.' For Jürgen Flimm, Guevara's statement 'hangs like a banner over the works of Luigi Nono', and it may well also be decisive for Lachenmann's standpoint.[34]

As Elke Hockings puts it, by the late 1960s, for Lachenmann, tonality had become the 'incarnation of human ignorance'. Where the question in 1969 was how to free oneself from a tonality that seemed obsolete, by 1979 Lachenmann had to acknowledge that tonality 'always catches up on you' and that the task had consequently become one of understanding the tonal implications inherent within the material.[35] He came to realize the impossibility of trying to prevent the shadows of the musical past from appearing in his work.[36] Even with the serial music of the 1950s the

> use of the tempered scale already implies a tonal effect [. . .] traditional playing techniques: crescendo, sforzato, linear evolution, tremolo, a clash of cymbals, orchestral silence [. . .] [are all] clichés ruled by tonal thought which, in the framework of tonality, function completely in relation to harmonic-melodic development.

In addition to this, the new music produced its own catalogue of rhetorical figures: ways of beginning or finishing, dramatic percussion flourishes, trembling ostinatos, formal sforzatos, multiphonics or clusters as well as a number of figures stemming from the nineteenth-century symphonic vocabulary or from 'serial figuration'. Consequently, a composer cannot appropriate traditional elements for composition without emptying them of conventional meanings and associations.

The title of Lachenmann's *Ausklang* for piano and orchestra from 1984–85 'can refer both to the final notes or beats of a piece of music and the fading-out of a single sound'.[37] Lachenmann's piece consequently luxuriates in the sounding out of piano sounds and the imaginary reverberations they set off in the orchestra. While, as we will see later in the chapter, this concern with sounding out, especially as it relates to sound at the threshold of its phenomenal existence, may be understood as inhabiting the territory of the sublime, the composer's intense concentration on the production of novel musical gestures results in music which most certainly redefines what we count as beautiful. Lachenmann says that *Ausklang*, of all his pieces, is the one in which the solo instrument most radically turns towards familiar sounds, melodic fragments and virtuosity. The virtuosic solo part includes many nineteenth-century pianistic clichés, including arpeggios, chromatic runs, glissandos and so on. Furthermore, tonal chords are placed unexpectedly in otherwise relatively dissonant contexts, tonal and whole-tone harmonies are used, and glissandos are heard over silently depressed chords to produce a very personal sound world within which remembered fragments from existing musical history nevertheless appear.

Of course within contemporary music there are moments that are patently identifiable in terms of conventional beauty. Lachenmann's fellow composer and friend Wolfgang Rihm has no compunction in juxtaposing music that is flagrantly modernist in aesthetic alongside passages that cut deeply into the DNA of the German Romantic tradition: in *Fremde Szenen I–III* (1982–84), for instance, Rihm composes with great freedom, working between music that is characteristically modern and sections where he parodies Schumann and occasionally Beethoven, both melodically and rhythmically, but always beautifully, while never losing himself.[38]

In a similar way, Rihm's student Jörg Widmann also works at times within the canons of the conventionally beautiful, but this 'beauty' is never unchallenged and often oscillates between conventional beauty and a range of more experimental sounds akin to those found in Lachenmann and others. Widmann has spoken of 'the tremendously difficult nature of beauty' and of his search for 'new beauty'.[39] Henze, with whom Widmann studied between 1993 and 1996, responded to his music by saying 'with you it is either too beautiful or too ugly', something which is exemplified in Widmann's *Lied* for orchestra (2003, rev. 2009), an extended Schubertian meditation in which conventionally, indeed hyper-beautiful melodic lines are combined, twisting and turning unexpectedly to create a harmonic labyrinth with tonal and coloristic changes, with microtonal inflections, sudden crescendos, moments at the threshold of audibility, pauses and tonal clusters. Indeed, Widmann also includes the performance instruction 'dangerously beautiful' ('gefährlich schön') in the score (bar 163, page 23). The work caused Widmann some problems with certain fellow composers at the time, who were outraged that such a work could be written in the twenty-first century.[40] Douglas Cooksey, reviewing an Edinburgh International Festival performance of the work in 2005, described it as 'melodic and accessible one moment but punctuated by moments of shocking violence at others, delicate pizzicatos shattered by a single gong stroke, the violins frequently playing softly at the stratospheric limits of their range'.[41] In this way, Widmann's *Lied* seems to play on the cusp of the beautiful and the sublime, oscillating between the deliriously beautiful and aspects of sound which, in their strained quietness, striking violence or interior intensity, suggest the possibility of an uncapturable beyond.

Another composer who explores this kind of ambiguity is Sofia Gubaidulina, who wrote in 1978 that 'the ideal relationship between traditional and modern compositional techniques is for the composer to be in complete command of all methods – new as well as traditional – but in such a way as not to emphasize either one over the other'.[42] The conventionally beautiful is manifest in places in her *Offertorium – A Musical Offering* for violin and orchestra (1980, rev. 1982 and 1986). David Murray, for example, writes of Gubaidulina's penchant for *Affekt*, and how the later sections of *Offertorium* are lyrically meditative, using diatonic modes, elements of 'nostalgic pastiche' and insinuations of Russian Orthodox chant, the solo violin concluding the piece with a continuous, sweetly ascending melodic line which sounds after it has played over darker, more ominous figures in the orchestral part.[43] As with the music of Widmann, it would, however, be mistaken to characterize Gubaidulina's music as focused above all on beauty and – as Claire Polin observes with reference to *Seven Words* for cello, bayan and strings (1982), a work which features tone clusters, 'limited melody and rhythmicized clusters' – 'she does not always write what to some appear as beautiful or even meaningful music'.[44] Again, with *Allelujah* (1990) for mixed chorus, large orchestra and soloists,

> a two-note motif ends and is altered by a blaring orchestral chord. [. . .] The material is spun out [. . .] while the orchestra and choir brutalize it with a thick white cloud of 'noise'. In a sense, what was beautified before becomes 'uglified' now.

Modernity and the sublime

In stark contrast to Lachenmann's challenge that we rethink the beautiful and his aesthetic of a newly constituted beauty, Jean-François Lyotard theorizes that modernity is no longer a period in which the arts are at all concerned with the beautiful. To take just one example of a position that is developed a number of times in his writings, Lyotard states in the essay 'After the Sublime, the State of Aesthetics' that the arts for the last century have no longer been concerned primarily with the beautiful but rather with a renewed concept of the sublime and, in marking this separation, he distinguishes properly 'artistic work' from 'cultural activities'.[45]

After Longinus's early introduction of the term, the sublime was much used in the late eighteenth and early nineteenth centuries, appearing frequently in the aesthetic writings of philosophers and writers Burke, Kant and Diderot and the painters Reynolds, Delacroix, Friedrich and Turner. It proved valuable in helping articulate the Romantic experiences of awe, terror, grandeur, infinity, eternity and divinity, experiences which in their imprecision and irrationality went beyond the order of an aesthetics based on the beautiful. In the visual art of the twentieth century, the sublime was at the heart of the work first of Kazimir Malevich (1879–1935), Wassily Kandinsky (1866–1944) and Piet Mondrian (1872–1944) and later of Barnett Newman (1905–70), Mark Rothko (1903–70), Clyfford Still (1904–80) and Jackson Pollock (1912–56). Robert Rosenblum writes of the connectedness of the painters of the Romantic sublime with those of the abstract sublime, Newman, Rothko, Still and Pollock, in terms of their shared concern with 'boundlessness' and the 'threshold of [...] shapeless infinities'. For Rosenblum, Newman's painting *Vir heroicus sublimis* places us in the presence of 'a void as terrifying, if exhilarating, as the arctic emptiness of the tundra' and 'in its passionate reduction of pictorial means to a single hue (warm red) [...] it likewise achieves a simplicity as heroic and sublime as the protagonist of its title'. In this way, Newman, Still, Rothko and Pollock, while using elementary means, nevertheless succeed in creating intriguingly complex works suggestive of the mysterious now when art emerges.[46]

Contemporary thought is rich in having produced a panoply of notions of the sublime, with alternative conceptualizations from Lyotard, Derrida, Nancy, Marion and others and, following Simon Morley's categorization, the contemporary sublime has been related to the unpresentable, transcendence, nature, technology, terror, the uncanny and altered states. While focusing in particular on the work of Lyotard, I will also look at some of these other, complementary conceptions of the sublime in order to make a number of connections with aspects of musical modernity.

In 'The Sublime and the Avant-Garde', following Barnett Newman's essay 'The Sublime is Now' (1948) and his art pieces *Vir heroicus sublimis* and *Here I, Here II, Here III*, Lyotard re-theorizes the sublime as a 'here and now', something which cannot be shown, presented or named, a sensation of time, an occurrence in the now which consciousness cannot formulate. Recognizing that in music one sound normally follows another, he raises the perhaps forgotten 'possibility of nothing happening, of words, colours, forms or sounds not coming', an outcome he describes as the 'misery of the musician with the acoustic surface, the misery the thinker faces with a desert of thought'. The sublime of the now is found in waiting, with the attendant risk that nothing may happen and the suspense, anxiety but also pleasure or even joy that this can summon; in other words, it elicits an interior contradiction. For Lyotard, Newman's sublime breaks with Burke and Romantic art except for the fact that it holds to the indispensable imperative of the sublime as that 'of bearing expressive witness to the inexpressible'.[47]

Adapting Lyotard's text slightly, Newman's sublime may be said to inhere in the fact that 'here and now there is this [composition/sound], rather than nothing'. Like the Kantian sublime, this irruption entails forgoing any all-knowing rationality while acknowledging that the coming into being of the sound or composition was unforeseeable, the result of no necessity and in fact contradictory. Indeed, for Lyotard, the sublime may be the singular aesthetic means of characterizing the modern, testifying to the unbridgeable gulf between thought and reality. When noting the shift from taste and purposiveness (beauty) to the sublime and its disruption of the harmony of the faculties, the artist becomes 'the involuntary addressee of an inspiration come to him from an "I know not what"'.[48] It is a statement redolent of Stravinsky's most likely disingenuous description of himself as 'the vessel through which *Le Sacre* passed'.[49]

In a mélange of Burke and Kant, Lyotard acknowledges that the sublime can be a mixture of pleasure and pain or a pleasure which results from pain, entailing a disconnection between the faculties where a sound or whatever else 'can only be thought, without any sensible/sensory intuition as an Idea of reason'.[50] Imagination is unable to produce a representation answering to the Idea, hence the dislocation, pain, pleasure and tension. He recognizes at the same time that 'the edge of the break, infinity, or the absoluteness of the Idea can be revealed in what Kant calls a negative presentation' and the Jewish law prohibiting images is cited as a pre-eminent example. Consequently, Lyotard is able to affirm that the sublime of the avant-garde was already present embryonically in Kant's aesthetic. The 'Is it happening?' so important for Newman, while missing from Kant's theorization, is found in Burke in the suspension of the threatening terror that allows a different sort of pleasure. Drawing on Burke, Lyotard lists the privations of darkness, solitude, silence, emptiness and death, the suspension of which lead to delight. The sublime now becomes 'a matter of intensification', and the arts, whatever their materials, pressed forward by the aesthetics of the sublime in search of intense effects, can and must give up the imitation of models that are merely beautiful, and try out surprising, strange, shocking combinations. Shock is, *par excellence*, the evidence of (something) *happening*, rather than nothing, suspended privation.[51]

Lyotard is undoubtedly correct in recognizing that Burke and Kant adumbrated a range of possibilities for creative experimentation that were explored later by the artists and musicians of the avant-garde. Where the painters Manet, Cézanne, Braque and Picasso most likely did not read Burke or Kant, we know that Haydn read Burke, Wagner read Schopenhauer and Mahler read Kant. Burke, unlike Kant, addresses the world of sound and the sublime explicitly in terms of 'excessive loudness', 'strength of the sound', 'a sudden beginning, or sudden cessation of sound of any considerable force', low, intermittent, confused, uncertain, inarticulate sounds, or sounds that imitate the sounds of animals in pain or danger. Indeed, for Burke, the sonic manifestations capable of summoning the sublime are 'almost infinite'.[52]

For Lyotard, it is pivotal that the composer works with all kinds of combinations of materials to allow an event to happen. In doing so, there is no place for models, since the sublime work attempts 'to present the fact that there is an unpresentable', a tendency Merleau-Ponty points to in Cézanne, who takes hold of and communicates something of perception at its point of origin. Following Adorno, Lyotard finds political value in the sublime, in that 'neo-romantic, neo-classical and symbolic forms imposed by the cultural commissars and collaborationist artists' all attempt to block the irruption of the event and the welcoming of the now. Closer to Lachenmann's reconstituted notion of beauty, the event is at the same time not that of the '*petit frisson*, the cheap thrill, the profitable pathos, that accompanies an innovation', since the 'Is it happening?' of the sublime is much less certain, is not presumptuous and arises from the ensuing privation.[53]

New music and the sublime

Prior to the more recent theorizations of the sublime by Lyotard and others, the philosopher Vladimir Jankélévitch had already explored some of the music of the first half of the twentieth century in terms of the related concept of the 'ineffable'. In *Music and the Ineffable* (1961), he tells us that 'the mask, the inexpressive face that music assumes voluntarily these days, conceals a purpose: *to express infinitely that which cannot be explained*'. Again,

> the musical mystery is not 'what cannot be spoken of', the untellable, but the *ineffable* [. . .] and the ineffable [. . .] cannot be explained because there are infinite and interminable things to be said of it: such is the mystery of God, whose depths cannot be sounded, the inexhaustible mystery of love, both Eros and Caritas, the poetic mystery par excellence.[54]

Ineffability 'provokes bewilderment': 'one delves without end [. . .] into this heartening plenitude of meanings' and it is 'explicable into infinity'. A difference from Lyotard's sublime might be the distance Jankélévitch identifies between 'a negative that is unsayable to a positive that is ineffable'.[55] He states that 'musical rapture is an escape from immanence – but it also does not breach that wall; it merely makes an opening, similar to the opening cleared within our human condition by an innocent, highly fragile emotional caritas'.[56]

For Jankélévitch, 'music, gradually exhausting all possible combinations of sounds, tends inexorably toward silence'. Music, 'a melodious construction, magic duration, an ephemeral adventure, and brief encounter – is isolated, between beginning and end, in the immensity of nonbeing'. Liszt's late works are 'invaded by silence' in which 'nothingness, like the encroaching sand, invades the melody, desiccates its verve'.[57] Debussy, meanwhile, 'seeks to grasp the liminal moment when silence becomes music'. At the beginning of *La mer*, for example, 'a clamor arises from the enigmatic depths where music is improvising itself into being', while elsewhere Debussy's music 'gives access to terminal nothingness. Making infinite gradations in the nuances of imperceptibility.'[58] In such passages Jankélévitch anticipates Lyotard and others in recognizing important aspects of the sublime in the music of early modernism.

While Jankélévitch for the most part avoids discussion of the Austro-German musical tradition, there is no doubt that the sublime is also to be found there. Despite a general lack of reference to the sublime in Schoenberg's theoretical texts, his great opera *Moses und Aron* is strongly indicative of the inexpressible in its concern with God's ineffability. Where the unfaithful Israelites want a tangible God, Moses, refusing to provide any description of God, reveals the Deity as 'unique, eternal, omnipresent, invisible and unrepresentable', just as Jankélévitch later identified the mystery of God as ineffable. Something of God's ineffableness or sublimity is equally apparent in the vocal part for bass given to Moses, which is set in *Sprechgesang*. So entirely Other and ungraspable is the Deity that it cannot be fixed within the confines of musical pitch or melody, and Moses' speech song is Schoenberg's faltering attempt to find sound capable, as Lyotard would have it, of presenting the fact of unpresentability. Furthermore, the fact that Schoenberg, despite completing the first two acts of the work by 1932, did not complete the third act again seems strongly emblematic of the unpresentability at the heart of the work, and is perhaps indicative of the absence of limit, the parergon set out by Derrida as a marker of the sublime.

In 'Sacred Fragment: Schoenberg's Moses und Aron', an essay from 1963, Adorno reflects on Schoenberg's twelve-tone opera from a number of aspects relevant to the sublime. For Adorno, as for the entire Jewish tradition, God who is the Absolute defies the understanding of finite beings. Desiring to name him through some kind of felt necessity, they in fact betray him, and the philosopher judges that Schoenberg must have realized that the 'absolute metaphysical content' he was dealing with would thwart and prohibit the work's completion while he at the same time refused to set his sights any lower. More generally, Adorno judges that significant artworks are those that 'aim for an extreme; they are destroyed in the process and their broken outlines survive as the ciphers of a supreme unnameable truth'. Of *Moses und Aron*, he suggests the likelihood that it was never completed for the simple reason that it was impossible to do so, despite the fact that this was an unintended outcome. Going further, Schoenberg does not feign the presence of the Absolute in the work, and 'the absolute which this music sets out to make real, without any sleight of hand, it achieves as its own idea of itself'.[59] The fact that Moses does not sing is Schoenberg's way of satisfying the ban on images of God, while the central challenge is to produce the musical and dramatic means with which 'to represent the idea of the sacred'.[60] Ultimately, however, the significance of the work goes beyond the theological sphere, since Schoenberg has in fact made present one of art's great antinomies. He negates the Hegelian presupposition that 'elusive content is to be captured by chaining it to the subject matter which, according to tradition, it once inhabited'. The real achievement for Adorno is what Schoenberg managed to do with the work, its inherent difficulties notwithstanding, as he faced the paradoxical question of 'the possibility of the impossible'. Focusing on the work's great technical complexity, in terms of the sheer number of notes, its polyphony and abundance of simultaneous events, Adorno suggests that 'the density of the construction becomes the medium in which the ineffable can manifest itself without usurpation', and he writes also of a 'compositional saturation' which at the same time avoids monotony.[61]

Staying with the Austro-German tradition and with opera, the sublime appears very differently in Bernd Alois Zimmermann's opera *Die Soldaten* from 1965. In this case, the viewer/listener is arguably overwhelmed by the scale of the orchestral forces, with sixteen singing roles, ten speaking roles, a hundred orchestral players including percussion, tubular bells, marimbaphone, vibraphone, piano, harpsichord, celesta and organ. As the original score was deemed unplayable, Zimmermann had to revise it in 1963–64 but, beyond its instrumentation, the multimedia in the work includes film screens, projectors, tape recorders and loudspeakers, and incorporates the sounds of marching and screams. Zimmermann uses musical styles from different historical periods and combines traditional and contemporary forms to create a kind of collage. As with Berg's *Wozzeck*, each scene is constructed from a traditional musical form – strophe, chaconne, ricercar, toccata and so on – alongside which jazz rhythms, Bach chorales, a folk song ('Rösel aus Hennegau') and the *Dies irae* are assembled and juxtaposed.[62]

For Philippe Albèra, Zimmermann 'seeks to give form in his music to "sporadic flux and without rules for ideas and moods, images, flashes of thought" which "turn in a spiral in the subconscious and unconscious" and which repulse one another in whirling agitation (Journal 7 March 1946)'.[63] Albèra's account of *Die Soldaten* shows clearly why it operates in the territory of the sublime. The work

> carries in itself all the weight of history and condenses its entire evolution up to that point. The end of the opera shows the implacable logic of the annihilation which touches humiliated, alienated and finally depersonalized individuals; it brings with it the entire world, adding an apocalyptic dimension absent from Lenz's piece, and where one perceives without difficulty the traces left by the experience of the war, as well as the contradictory desire to represent it while exorcising it. Such contradictions are thematized in the music.[64]

Albèra picks up on the 'Babelian multiplicity of musical languages and forms' employed by Zimmermann, which are 'concentrated in a moment of eternity thanks to the absolute structure which governs the whole'. Beyond the opera, Zimmermann's monumental *Requiem for a Young Poet* (1967–69) is judged by Albèra 'a bitter declaration of individual impotence', of sounding 'like the failure of his own creative purpose' and ultimately of 'engulfing the individualities

Musical modernity, the beautiful and the sublime

which had dreamed of taking possession of it'. Linking the two works, he suggests that *Die Soldaten* 'seems to have precipitated the composer in a sort of rush to the abyss, as if he had opened Pandora's Box, through a subject which awakened all the traumas of the war'.[65] Much earlier, in an article from 1953–54, in which he explored a rationale for musical composition, Zimmermann responded that its purpose was 'to communicate an obscure order, or to express otherwise, to render the ungraspable graspable. This is, at the deepest level, the antinomy of compositional creation and its secret.'[66] While such citations might arguably be indicative of nothing more than an early reliance on Romantic commonplaces, it is nevertheless possible to note a foretaste of Lyotard's sublime in both Zimmermann's concern with the presentation of the unpresentable and the capacity of the artwork to testify to a trauma which cannot itself be adequately presented, but whose existence can be inferred. As Kiene Brillenburg Wurth notes, this focus on the traumatic horrors of the twentieth century, such as two World Wars, the Holocaust and Hiroshima/Nagasaki, questions the sublime of the Enlightenment and suggests that the entire humanist project has failed. It bears witness to the impossibility of overcoming and being reconciled with 'events that (still) defy imaginative and also conceptual grasp'.[67]

Beyond the angst of Zimmermann's works, Stockhausen's *Stimmung* for six vocalists and six microphones (1968) arguably explores less threatening aspects of unpresentability. Composed in just intonation, the piece works through the second, third, fourth, fifth, seventh and ninth overtones of a fundamental pitch class of B♭, and is 'the first major Western composition to be based entirely on the production of vocal harmonics'.[68] As Stockhausen notes:

> specific *overtones* – indicated by a series of numbers from 2 to 24 and by series of voice sounds taken from the phonetic alphabet – must emerge as strongly as possible [. . .]. One listens to the inner self of the sound, the inner self of the harmonic spectrum, the inner self of a vowel, *the inner self.*[69]

In doing all of this, Stockhausen enters into the inner life of the sound and opens an aspect of sonic experience not usually apparent to perception, a world of microscopic sonic atoms which intensifies our sense of sound, almost like entering into the inner life of a painted canvas as we come to see the multiple aspects of red or blue, no longer a unified point on a colour or pitch spectrum, but a micro-world suddenly opened up and creating the sensation that there is further to go, if we only could. To this extent, it is arguably the case that the works of the spectral composers Tristan Murail and Gérard Grisey equally carry us into the realm of the sublime, suggesting, as they seem to, that they have taken us to the very origins of sound phenomena in spectral form, beyond which lies some unreachable noumenal world of sound itself.

Continuing to explore this much more understated pole of sublimes, which seems to broach the very threshold of silence and in which the sublime, after Newman and Lyotard, is the 'now', a highly contingent moment of expectation and anxiety, Morton Feldman writes in a short essay titled 'Philip Guston: The Last Painter': 'Years ago there was a game Philip Guston and I used to play. We were the last artists. Remember Alexander Pope's "Art after art goes out, and all is night"?' He continues

> During those years we all talked constantly about an imaginary art in which there existed almost nothing. [. . .]
> More than a philosophic toy, 'nothing' is a crucial point of arrival and departure for being the last artists. It is obvious that we don't begin with nothing, less obvious that after years of working one arrives at very little.
> [. . .]

> We live from moment to moment, an invisible gestalt shaping the form of our lives.
> In art we exist from poem to poem, from painting to painting. We are confronted
> with the fact, or rather it is more in evidence, that we have very little to bring, extremely
> little to say. We experience 'nothing', then, not unlike the medieval Kabalists, who
> understood it as that ultimate place where it becomes possible to speculate about God.
> Whatever insight was found was expressed metaphorically.[70]

In addition to this aesthetic fascination with almost nothing and the great simplicity of means in Feldman's later works, there are also works of great length, for example the String Quartet no. 2 (1983), which is one continuous piece extending over six hours, or *For Philip Guston* for flute, percussion and piano (1984), which lasts for four hours and is extremely slow and quiet. Such pieces are daunting challenges for performers and listeners alike and can strike a note of panic in the mind of the participant who must face the certainty that once the piece begins there is no escape.

In a different way, the music of the new complexity composers, for example of Brian Ferneyhough, poses great challenges for performers. In one passage of Ferneyhough's *Time and Motion Study III* (1974) for sixteen solo voices, percussion and electronics, the singers have 'to interpret five or six rhythmicized lines of instructions simultaneously'.[71] Indeed, Ferneyhough acknowledges that some of his works 'approach or (in the case of *Unity Capsule*) deliberately overstep the limits of the humanly realizable'.[72] When Joël Bons claims that performers of Ferneyhough's pieces 'can realize only 50 to 80% of the score', Ferneyhough does not disagree. He challenges performers 'to come to terms with their own natural limits, and thereby transcend them' as they 'consistently overstep the bounds of the humanly possible'.[73] At the extreme, he creates 'a notation which deliberately sets out to offer *a practical surfeit of information* at any particular juncture'. While his goal is to underline 'the indissoluble links binding hierarchically (ideologically) grounded selection procedures with the ultimate sonic result', there can be no doubt that the experience exhibits aspects of the sublime, at least for performers.[74] It is most likely the case that performances of the complex music of composers such as Ferneyhough stands in line with virtuosic music of the past which, for Wurth, 'invoke[s] a technological sublime *avant la lettre*: a sublime that does not revolve around the indeterminacy associated with the infinite'.[75]

The childhood experiences of Georg Friedrich Haas in the mountainous province of Vorarlberg in Austria, on the Swiss border, seem to have marked him as a composer. Rather than captivating him with a sense of the landscape's natural beauty, it seems that the mountains were menacing for Haas and that he felt hemmed in by the narrow, sun-starved valley. Like Stockhausen and the spectralists, Haas explores the inner life of sounds with the use of microtonality. His Third String Quartet 'In iij. Noct.' (2001), lasting around fifty minutes, is performed 'in complete darkness': 'the musicians can see neither their music nor their fellow performers, and are seated as far apart from one another as possible – for example they might be seated around the audience in the four corners of the auditorium'.[76] Audience members, in at least one performance, have been required to sign a document clearing the performers of liability while providing details for an emergency contact.[77] For Alex Ross, 'the music [often] borders on noise: the strings emit creaks and groans, clickety swarms of pizzicato, shrill high notes, moaning glissandos. At other times, it attains an otherworldly beauty, as the players spin out glowing overtone harmonies', and he concludes that Haas 'is an esoteric Romantic, dwelling on the majesty and terror of the sublime'.[78]

Closely related to the sublime is philosopher Jean-Luc Marion's concept of 'saturated phenomena', an idea which emerges from his phenomenological first principle of givenness, whereby 'a phenomenon only shows *itself* to the extent that it first gives *itself*'.[79] For Marion,

Musical modernity, the beautiful and the sublime

some phenomena are so overflowing in their givenness that the intentional acts directed towards them are overwhelmed, engulfed, saturated and 'all horizons are shattered'.[80] The concept is developed at length in the book *In Excess: Studies of Saturated Phenomena* (2002), in part in relation to the event, the idol, flesh, the icon and the name, the idol considered in relation to 'the radiance of painting'. While Marion does not develop his ideas in relation to music, the emergence of three composers, Franck Bedrossian, Raphaël Cendo and Yann Robin, for whom saturation is a crucial principle is in itself striking, their music being termed 'saturated music'.

All three composers focus in their own distinctive ways on the notion of the saturation of sound phenomena. Bedrossian and Cendo both gave papers on the topic at a colloquium on sound excess ('l'excès du son') at the Centre de Documentation de la Musique Contemporaine (CDMC) in 2008. It seems that these were the first public pronouncements to be made on the subject of the saturation of sound and of the musical phenomenon, which can be 'excess of energy', as well as of materials and of meaning.[81]

Cendo draws attention to Xenakis, who 'thought excess in a recurrent way' in a piece such as *Tracées* (1987) for large orchestra, where he superposed 'complex sounds' in the sense of 'cracked sounds [*fendus*], multiphonics with or without the addition of the voice, clusters and crushed sounds [*écrasés*]'.[82] As for his own work, Cendo writes of working with '"destroyed" material' and 'extreme saturation, this feeling of a total destruction and the will to set up this rubble as absolute beauty!' He describes *Rokh* for flutes, violin, cello and piano (2011–12) as exploring a great deal of material which is worked upon in each of the three movements, with 'Rokh I' alternating 'moments of total saturation and infinitesimal moments that are static or rustling' and where 'the elements multiply, giving rise to very dense and turbulent sound material' with 'extreme gestural writing' that is energetic and seemingly unpredictable in movement. 'Rokh II' explores 'very dense material that is always at the threshold of audibility'. Finally, 'Rokh III' 'compacts [...] all the elements of the piece at a rate that is at the limit of the achievable. Time speeds up and the raw elements of the first movement return, this time multiplied and superimposed'.[83]

Concluding remarks

The discussion of the beautiful and the sublime in this chapter should not result in the labelling of individual composers or works as inhabiting exclusively one or other world. Consideration of the compositions of Lachenmann, Gubaidulina, Widmann and Rihm in relation to a reconstituted notion of beauty does not preclude the likelihood that their works also present aspects of the sublime which have not been explored here. The frequent shifts from gestures that are conventionally beautiful to moments of disintegration, destruction and of noise testify to the futility of reductionism.

While the problem of conventional beauty within modernity persists, it is clear that Lyotard's stark opposition of beautiful and sublime is not the only option, and Lachenmann offers the possibility of reconstituting beauty in unforeseen ways. It is perhaps significant that Rolf Hind names Ennio Morricone as Lachenmann's favourite composer, noting that he is fond of Morricone's score for Sergio Leone's great film *Once Upon a Time in the West*, music that is easily recuperable in terms of the conventionally beautiful.[84] Over and against those who would wish to adopt his ideas in a reductionist way, for Lachenmann, composers can play even with the conventionally beautiful, but they need to understand what they are doing.

The sublime has never been one thing, and the notion of a plurality of perspectives is not new. Wurth sets out with great clarity some of the multiple historical understandings of the sublime that have proliferated since the eighteenth century. She considers these varying conceptions in terms of their narrative structure, noting in particular how some accounts from the

145

eighteenth century operate on the basis of 'unresolved simultaneity rather than an alternation of pain and pleasure'.[85] The Romantic concept of *Sehnsucht*, 'the inherent inability of the self to coincide with itself in a continuity of past and present', is presented by Wurth as 'an ironic commentary on the Kantian sublime as infinite', since 'what constantly interrupts the thrust forward toward resolution of the latter is the counteractive pull of a dislocated past'.[86] Where in Burke pain is succeeded and replaced by pleasure and where in Kant the failure of the imagination is replaced by reason in a plot-like structure, this is not the case with *Sehnsucht*, in which pain and pleasure are continually implicated, paradoxically and simultaneously present without release.[87] There is no transformation or breakthrough here as in Kant, and Wurth suggests that *Sehnsucht* is 'an ironic mode of the sublime' in which limits are explored but not overcome,[88] just as in Schopenhauer's sublime liberation and frustration are experienced simultaneously.[89]

In a similar way, beyond Lyotard, Jacques Derrida, reading Kant, challenges the supposed opposition between the beautiful and the sublime and instead bases their difference on the question of limit. In *The Truth in Painting* (1978), Derrida introduces the Greek word 'parergon', meaning 'outside the work', 'in relation to the frame, to speculate on the meanings of something that is neither outside nor inside the work, neither a part of it nor absolutely extrinsic to it'.[90]

For Derrida, while the form of the beautiful comes about through the 'presence of a limit', the sublime is found 'in an "object without form" and the "without-limit" is "represented" in it or on the occasion of it, and yet gives the totality of the without-limit to be *thought*'.[91] Consequently, 'if art gives form by limiting, or even by framing, there can be a *parergon* of the beautiful [. . .]. But there cannot, it seems, be a *parergon* for the sublime'. The sublime is incapable of any satisfactory presentation, hence the question as to how something unpresentable can present itself and the suggestion that the sublime 'inadequately presents the infinite in the finite'. Restated, 'the inadequation of presentation is presented'. While in semiotic terms the beautiful may be understood as 'signifying finitude' and the sublime as 'signified infinity', Hegel sets out from the 'thought of sublimity' in distinction to Kant, who begins with that presentation which is 'inadequate to this thought, of the sublime'. For Derrida, both philosophers 'reflect the line of cut or rather the *pas* crossing this line between finite and infinite as the proper place of the sublime and the interruption of symbolic beauty'.[92]

In contrast, for Jean-Luc Nancy 'the sublime is a feeling, and yet, more than a feeling in the banal sense, it is the emotion of the subject at the limit. The subject of the sublime, if there is one, is a subject who is moved'.[93] Again, it is '*the sensibility of the fading of the sensible*'. As with Derrida, the key notion here is that of the 'limit'. Nancy expands:

> Stretched to the limit, the limit (the contour of the figure) is stretched to the breaking point, as one says, and it in fact does break, dividing itself in the instant between two borders, the border of the figure and its unlimited unbordering. Sublime presentation is the feeling of this striving at the instant of rupture, the imagination still for an instant sensible to itself although no longer itself, in extreme tension and distension ('overflowing' or 'abyss').[94]

As with Lyotard and Derrida, Nancy's sublime presents the non-presentable, since 'the unlimitedness that affects the exposed feeling of the sublime cannot be presented to it, that is, this unlimitedness cannot become present in and for a subject'. The 'without-name is named, the inexpressible is communicated: *all is presented – at the limit*. But in the end, and precisely at the limit itself, where all is achieved and where all begins, it will be necessary to deny presentation its name.'[95]

Musical modernity, the beautiful and the sublime

Finally, Barbara Claire Freeman distinguishes between a masculine sublime which 'seeks to master, appropriate or colonize the other' and a feminine sublime which 'involves taking up a position of respect in response to an incalculable otherness', stating that 'a politics of the feminine sublime would ally receptivity and constant attention to that which makes meaning infinitely open and ungovernable'.[96]

Derrida, Nancy and Freeman are not the only theorists to reconsider the sublime in the face of modernity and beyond, but it is important to present something of their views, if only to show that Lyotard's reading is not the only available one. While more detailed discussion of how Lyotard's view differs from those of Derrida, Nancy and Freeman might lead to different conclusions in terms of music, this is beyond the scope of the current chapter. Their contrasting positions offer interesting perspectives and variations which enlarge the range of possible manifestations of the sublime in musical modernity and offer directions for further work.

While the better-known accounts in Burke and Kant evidently do not exhaust the working of the sublime, Burke's disjunction of fear and wonder and Kant's mathematical and dynamic sublimes continue to have significant revelatory power in the context of new music and visual art. But beyond this, the modern sublime, which can be so many things, seems much more multivalent in its suggestiveness and is capable of articulating something of what fascinates in such works. Where Lyotard distinguishes the sublime of modernity from its Romantic precursor, for Wurth this distinction is ultimately unconvincing.[97] Acknowledging that Lyotard is unconcerned with the transcendence of Romantic understandings, she argues that the immanent sublime, which he locates uniquely in the modernist concern with the fundamental materiality of the arts, for example in Wagner, Schoenberg and beyond, is present also in previous music.[98] Furthermore, she argues that the music and writings of John Cage anticipate Lyotard's location of the sublime in the moment, the now.[99] Whatever the validity of these remarks, it seems clear that Lyotard's reconstituted sublime seems particularly well matched to the immanent materiality of a great deal of musical modernity, even if the break with the Romantic concept might not be as stark as he thinks.

We might also wonder if there are not compositional, performative and listening sublimes. Following Lyotard, it would seem that the composer, open to the musical event, faces that sublime moment of the Now when something may or may not happen. At this point we may think of composers such as Sibelius or Ives who suddenly stopped composing when the muse seemed to leave them and the sublime came up short. Similarly, Ferneyhough's music may be sublime in its overload of information for the performer and perhaps in a different way for the listener, though, at the same time, it would be a mistake to equate musical complexity and sublimeness, since complexity alone is no guarantor of the sublime and may in fact register nothing more than incomprehension or banal annoyance.

There is also the question of the extent to which the same composition can exhibit elements of both the beautiful and the sublime, successively or simultaneously; Widmann's *Lied*, for example. According to Wurth, Wagner's great essay on Beethoven from 1870 'puts the categories of the beautiful and the sublime in a continuous spectrum, positing the latter as the ultimate realization of the former (and, conversely, the former as an initiation into the latter)'.[100]

It may be that Kant's mathematical and dynamic sublimes are as valid for the new as they were for the music of the classical period. Where Elaine Sisman finds the mathematical sublime in the final movement of Mozart's Jupiter Symphony,[101] we may think equally of the proliferating heterophonies or the multi-prismatic solos of Boulez's *Répons*, in which sounds are transformed and projected around the auditorium in real time, but where the detail is beyond the reach of the most acute perception. Similarly, the Burkean or even Kantian dynamic sublime recognized in

Haydn's 'Representation of Chaos' from *The Creation* finds its late twentieth-century corollary in the complex micropolyphonic pitch spaces of Ligeti's *Atmosphères*, *Lux Aeterna* and *Lontano*, assisted by the visual opulence of Stanley Kubrick's cosmic vistas. But beyond this, the modern sublime, which can be so many things, seems much more multivalent in its suggestiveness.

Musical modernity needs concepts in terms of which we can discuss new music and with which we can make meaningful connections with thought and with the other arts. To this extent the crisis in new music as a crisis of incomprehension on the part of the listening public may be in part to do with the seeming disconnectedness of the music from other areas of human thought and creativity. Consequently, Adorno, Lachenmann and Lyotard, in quite different ways, help direct us through some of the difficulties of new music. Schoenberg was already aware of the fickle nature of the beautiful and was wise enough to separate it from the intentionality of the composer, locating it in the experience of the critical listener. Adorno theorizes the falseness and danger of presenting unreflective beauty in a brutal age and Lachenmann teaches us to be cognizant of the dangers of the conventional, the unreflective, the connotations inherent in socialized sounds and the need to use sounds and to create beauty in fresh ways. While Lachenmann's reconstituted beauty opens up the sonic horizon to a great variety of new sounds, Lyotard gives new aesthetic direction to the debate with the suggestion that music is capable of revealing the presence of the unpresentable. In the work of all three, Adorno, Lachenmann and Lyotard, we have a clear sense of the social and political importance of music and the need for engagement with music and its materials. In this respect, newly constituted beauty and a new multivalent sublime enable modern music to connect with our culture and to resonate with the experience of life in the early twenty-first century. To this degree the problem of the beautiful and the sublime in new music is nothing other than the quest for musical authenticity, itself a compromised term in need of careful handling.

Notes

1 Helmut Lachenmann, 'The "Beautiful" in Music Today', *Tempo*, no. 135 (1980).
2 The song is titled 'Eingang' and is the first of five songs to texts by Stefan George.
3 Theodor W. Adorno and Alban Berg, *Correspondence: 1925–1935*, ed. Henri Lonitz and trans. Wieland Hoban (Cambridge and Malden, MA: Polity Press, 2005), 60.
4 Theodor W. Adorno, *Aesthetic Theory*, ed. Gretel Adorno and Rolf Tiedemann and trans. Robert Hullot-Kentor (Minneapolis: University of Minnesota Press, 1997), 50–51.
5 Ibid., 16.
6 Ibid., 93.
7 Ibid.
8 Theodor W. Adorno, *Quasi una fantasia: Essays on Modern Music*, trans. Rodney Livingstone (New York and London: Verso, 1998), 265. The last sentence in the original reads: 'Wem es darum geht, darf sie nicht mehr in den Mund nehmen und muß sie demontieren, wo man sie ihm entgegenhält'; Theodor W. Adorno, *Musikalische Schriften I–III: Klangfiguren, Quasi una fantasia*, ed. Rolf Tiedemann (Frankfurt: Suhrkamp, 1978), 2: 490.
9 Theodor W. Adorno, *Mahler: A Musical Physiognomy*, trans. Edmund Jephcott (Chicago: University of Chicago Press, 2013); see also Anne Boissière, *Adorno: la vérité de la musique moderne* (Villeneuve d'Ascq: Presses Universitaires du Septentrion, 1999), 26.
10 Theodor W. Adorno, *Essays on Music*, ed. Richard D. Leppert (Berkeley and Los Angeles: University of California Press, 2002), 181.
11 Karlheinz Stockhausen and Theodor W. Adorno, 'La résistance à l'encontre de la nouvelle musique', trans. Carlo Russi, *Contrechamps* 9 (1988), 141–42.
12 Detlev Claussen, *Theodor W. Adorno: One Last Genius* (Cambridge, MA: Harvard University Press, 2009), 387.
13 Wassily Kandinsky, *Concerning the Spiritual in Art*, trans. Michael T. H. Sadler (New York: Dover, 1977), 16–17.

Musical modernity, the beautiful and the sublime

14 Arnold Schoenberg, *Style and Idea: Selected Writings of Arnold Schoenberg*, ed. Leonard Stein (Berkeley and Los Angeles: University of California Press, 1975), 285.

15 Ibid., 294.

16 Ibid., 216.

17 Ibid., 248–49.

18 Arnold Schoenberg, *Theory of Harmony*, trans. Roy E. Carter (Berkeley and Los Angeles: University of California Press, 1983), 9.

19 Ibid., 10.

20 Ibid., 30.

21 Ibid., 325–26.

22 Lachenmann, 'The "Beautiful" in Music Today', 20.

23 Ibid., 21.

24 Helmut Lachenmann, *Écrits et entretiens*, ed. Martin Kaltenecker (Geneva: Contrechamps, 2009), 196.

25 Lachenmann, 'The "Beautiful" in Music Today', 22.

26 Ibid., 24.

27 Martin Kaltenecker, 'H. L.', in *Helmut Lachenmann*, programme book for Festival d'Automne à Paris, 1993.

28 Helmut Lachenmann, 'Open Letter to Hans Werner Henze', trans. Jeffrey Stadelman, *Perspectives of New Music* 35, no. 2 (1997), 192.

29 Ibid., 196.

30 Ibid., 189–90.

31 Helmut Lachenmann, 'On Structuralism', *Contemporary Music Review* 12, no. 1 (1995), 93.

32 Lachenmann, 'Open Letter to Hans Werner Henze', 190.

33 Ibid., 191.

34 Raf Pimlott and Jürgen Flimm, 'Al gran sole carico d'amore', *59 Productions*, 2009, http://59productions. co.uk/project/al-gran-sole-carico-damore/ (accessed 8 August 2017).

35 Elke Hockings, 'Helmut Lachenmann's Concept of Rejection', *Tempo*, no. 193 (1995), 8–9.

36 Kaltenecker, 'H. L.'

37 Peter Niklas Wilson, 'Seeking Refuge by Means of Attack', CD liner notes for *Ausklang/Tableau* (Col Legno WWE 1CD 31862, 1994).

38 See Alastair Williams, 'Swaying with Schumann: Subjectivity and Tradition in Wolfgang Rihm's *Fremde Szenen I–III* and Related Scores', *Music & Letters* 87, no. 3 (2006), 379–97.

39 Graham Lack, 'At Fever Pitch: The Music of Jörg Widmann', *Tempo*, no. 231 (2005), 29–31.

40 Conversation with the composer in Edinburgh on 1 September 2005.

41 Douglas Cooksey, 'Edinburgh International Festival – Bamberg Symphony/Nott (5)', *Classical Source*, September 2005, http://classicalsource.com/db_control/db_concert_review.php?id=2833 (accessed 2 April 2015).

42 Michael Kurtz, *Sofia Gubaidulina: A Biography*, trans. Christoph K. Lohmann (Bloomington: Indiana University Press, 2007), 138.

43 David Murray, 'Record Review', *Tempo*, no. 171 (1989), 29.

44 Claire Polin, 'The Composer as Seer, but Not Prophet', *Tempo*, no. 190 (1994), 16.

45 Jean-François Lyotard, *The Inhuman: Reflections on Time*, trans. Geoffrey Bennington and Rachel Bowlby, 1st ed. (Stanford, CA: Stanford University Press, 1992), 135.

46 Robert Rosenblum, 'The Abstract Sublime', *Art News* 59, no. 10 (1961), 38–41, 56, 58.

47 Lyotard, *The Inhuman*, 89–93.

48 Ibid., 96.

49 Igor Stravinsky and Robert Craft, *Expositions and Developments* (Berkeley and Los Angeles: University of California Press, 1981), 148.

50 Lyotard, *The Inhuman*, 98.

51 Ibid., 100.

52 Edmund Burke, *A Philosophical Enquiry into the Origin of Our Ideas of the Sublime and Beautiful*, ed. Adam Phillips (Oxford: Oxford University Press, 1998), 75–78.

53 Lyotard, *The Inhuman*, 101–7.

54 Vladimir Jankélévitch, *Music and the Ineffable*, trans. Carolyn Abbate (Princeton, NJ: Princeton University Press, 2003), 71–72.

55 Ibid., 72–73.

56 Ibid., 127.

Edward Campbell

57 Ibid., 131–34.
58 Ibid., 144.
59 Adorno, *Quasi una fantasia*, 226–29.
60 Ibid., 239.
61 Ibid., 243–45.
62 DVD Booklet for *Die Soldaten*, ArtHaus Musik, 1989, 15–16.
63 Bernd Alois Zimmermann, *Écrits*, ed. Philippe Albèra (Geneva: Contrechamps, 2010), 9.
64 Ibid., 15.
65 Ibid., 16–18.
66 Ibid., 140.
67 Kiene Brillenburg Wurth, *Musically Sublime: Indeterminacy, Infinity, Irresolvability* (New York: Fordham University Press, 2009), 150; see also Gene Ray, *Terror and the Sublime in Art and Critical Theory: From Auschwitz to Hiroshima to September 11* (New York: Palgrave Macmillan, 2005).
68 Gregory Rose and Helen Ireland, CD liner notes for *Stimmung* by Karlheinz Stockhausen (Hyperion CDA66115, 1987), 2.
69 Karl Heinrich Wörner, *Stockhausen: Life and Work* (Berkeley: University of California Press, 1973), 65–66.
70 Morton Feldman, *Give My Regards to Eighth Street: Collected Writings of Morton Feldman*, ed. B. H. Friedman (Cambridge, MA: Exact Change, 2000), 37–38.
71 Brian Ferneyhough, *Collected Writings*, ed. James Boros and Richard Toop (Amsterdam: Harwood Academic Publishers, 1995), 215.
72 Ibid., 319.
73 Ibid., 232–33.
74 Ibid., 4–5.
75 Wurth, *Musically Sublime*, 117.
76 'Georg Friedrich Haas: "In iij. Noct."', http://www.universaledition.com/composers-and-works/georg-friedrich-haas-278/works/in-iij-noct-10484 (accessed 19 October 2015).
77 Mark Swed, 'Music Review: Georg Friedrich Haas' Revelatory Romp in the Dark', *Los Angeles Times Blogs: Culture Monster*, 20 April 2010, http://latimesblogs.latimes.com/culturemonster/2010/04/georg-friedrich-haas-revelatory-romp-in-the-dark.html.
78 Alex Ross, 'Darkness Audible', *The New Yorker*, 22 November 2010, http://www.newyorker.com/magazine/2010/11/29/darkness-audible (accessed 10 August 2017).
79 Jean-Luc Marion, *In Excess: Studies of Saturated Phenomena*, trans. Robyn Horner and Vincent Barraud (New York: Fordham University Press, 2002), 30.
80 Robyn Horner and Vincent Barraud, 'Translator's Introduction', in ibid., ix.
81 Pierre Rigaudière, 'La saturation, métaphore pour la composition ?' *Circuit: musiques contemporaines* 24, no. 3 (2014), 37–40.
82 Ibid., 39–40.
83 Raphaël Cendo, 'Le dessin sous-jacent', CD liner notes for *Rokh* (Stradivarius STR 33926, 2012), my translation.
84 Rolf Hind, 'Helmut Lachenmann: Everything Counts', *The Guardian*, 14 October 2010, sec. Music, http://www.theguardian.com/music/2010/oct/14/helmut-lachenmann-rolf-hind.
85 Wurth, *Musically Sublime*, 8.
86 Ibid., 17–18.
87 Ibid., 49–69.
88 Ibid., 71.
89 Ibid., 83.
90 Jacques Derrida, *The Truth in Painting*, trans. Geoff Bennington and Ian McLeod (Chicago: University of Chicago Press, 1987), 127.
91 Ibid.
92 Ibid., 131–34.
93 Quoted in Simon Morley, ed., *The Sublime* (Cambridge, MA, and London: MIT Press, 2010), 47.
94 Quoted in ibid., 48.
95 Ibid., 50.
96 Quoted in ibid., 65.
97 Wurth, *Musically Sublime*, 106.
98 Ibid., 114.

99 Ibid., 127.

100 Ibid., 85.

101 Elaine R. Sisman, *Mozart: The 'Jupiter' Symphony* (Cambridge: Cambridge University Press, 1993), 9–20; 79.

Bibliography

Adorno, Theodor W. *Musikalische Schriften I–III: Klangfiguren, Quasi una fantasia*. Edited by Rolf Tiedemann. Frankfurt: Suhrkamp, 1978.

———. *Aesthetic Theory*. Edited by Gretel Adorno and Rolf Tiedemann. Translated by Robert Hullot-Kentor. Minneapolis: University of Minnesota Press, 1997.

———. *Quasi una fantasia: Essays on Modern Music*. Translated by Rodney Livingstone. New York and London: Verso, 1998.

———. *Essays on Music*. Edited by Richard D. Leppert. Translated by Susan H. Gillespie. Berkeley and Los Angeles: University of California Press, 2002.

———. *Mahler: A Musical Physiognomy*. Translated by Edmund Jephcott. Chicago: University of Chicago Press, 2013.

Adorno, Theodor W., and Alban Berg. *Correspondence: 1925–1935*. Edited by Henri Lonitz. Translated by Wieland Hoban. Cambridge and Malden, MA: Polity Press, 2005.

Boissière, Anne. *Adorno: la vérité de la musique moderne*. Villeneuve d'Ascq: Presses Universitaires du Septentrion, 1999.

Burke, Edmund. *A Philosophical Enquiry into the Origin of Our Ideas of the Sublime and Beautiful*. Edited by Adam Phillips. Oxford: Oxford University Press, 1998.

Claussen, Detlev. *Theodor W. Adorno: One Last Genius*. Cambridge, MA: Harvard University Press, 2009.

Cooksey, Douglas. 'Edinburgh International Festival – Bamberg Symphony/Nott (5)'. *Classical Source*, September 2005. http://classicalsource.com/db_control/db_concert_review.php?id=2833.

Derrida, Jacques. *The Truth in Painting*. Translated by Geoff Bennington and Ian McLeod. Chicago: University of Chicago Press, 1987.

Feldman, Morton. *Give My Regards to Eighth Street: Collected Writings of Morton Feldman*. Edited by B. H. Friedman. Cambridge, MA: Exact Change, 2000.

Ferneyhough, Brian. *Collected Writings*. Edited by James Boros and Richard Toop. Amsterdam: Harwood Academic Publishers, 1995.

Hind, Rolf. 'Helmut Lachenmann: Everything Counts'. *The Guardian*, 14 October 2010, sec. Music. http://www.theguardian.com/music/2010/oct/14/helmut-lachenmann-rolf-hind.

Hockings, Elke. 'Helmut Lachenmann's Concept of Rejection'. *Tempo*, no. 193 (1995): 4–14.

Horner, Robyn, and Vincent Barraud. 'Translator's Introduction'. In *In Excess*, edited by Jean-Luc Marion, ix–xx.

Jankélévitch, Vladimir. *Music and the Ineffable*. Translated by Carolyn Abbate. Princeton, NJ: Princeton University Press, 2003.

Kaltenecker, Martin. 'H. L.' In *Helmut Lachenmann*. Programme book for Festival d'Automne à Paris, 1993.

Kandinsky, Wassily. *Concerning the Spiritual in Art*. Translated by Michael T. H. Sadler. New York: Dover, 1977.

Kurtz, Michael. *Sofia Gubaidulina: A Biography*. Translated by Christoph K. Lohmann. Bloomington: Indiana University Press, 2007.

Lachenmann, Helmut. 'The "Beautiful" in Music Today'. *Tempo*, no. 135 (1980): 20–24.

———. 'On Structuralism'. *Contemporary Music Review* 12, no. 1 (1995): 93–102.

———. 'Open Letter to Hans Werner Henze'. Translated by Jeffrey Stadelman. *Perspectives of New Music* 35, no. 2 (1997): 189–200.

———. *Écrits et entretiens*. Edited by Martin Kaltenecker. Geneva: Contrechamps, 2009.

Lack, Graham. 'At Fever Pitch: The Music of Jörg Widmann'. *Tempo*, no. 231 (2005): 29–35.

Lyotard, Jean-François. *The Inhuman: Reflections on Time*. Translated by Geoffrey Bennington and Rachel Bowlby. 1st ed. Stanford, CA: Stanford University Press, 1992.

Marion, Jean-Luc. *In Excess: Studies of Saturated Phenomena*. Translated by Robyn Horner and Vincent Barraud. New York: Fordham University Press, 2002.

Morley, Simon, ed. *The Sublime*. Cambridge, MA, and London: MIT Press, 2010.

Murray, David. 'Record Review'. *Tempo*, no. 171 (1989): 29–35.

Pimlott, Raf, and Jürgen Flimm. 'Al gran sole carico d'amore'. *59 Productions*, 2009. http://59productions.co.uk/project/al-gran-sole-carico-damore/.

Polin, Claire. 'The Composer as Seer, but Not Prophet'. *Tempo*, no. 190 (1994): 13–18.

Ray, Gene. *Terror and the Sublime in Art and Critical Theory: From Auschwitz to Hiroshima to September 11*. New York: Palgrave Macmillan, 2005.

Rigaudière, Pierre. 'La saturation, métaphore pour la composition?' *Circuit: musiques contemporaines* 24, no. 3 (2014): 37–50.

Rosenblum, Robert. 'The Abstract Sublime'. *Art News* 59, no. 10 (1961): 38–41, 56, 58.

Ross, Alex. 'Darkness Audible'. *The New Yorker*, 22 November 2010. http://www.newyorker.com/magazine/2010/11/29/darkness-audible.

Schoenberg, Arnold. *Style and Idea: Selected Writings of Arnold Schoenberg*. Edited by Leonard Stein. Berkeley and Los Angeles: University of California Press, 1975.

———. *Theory of Harmony*. Translated by Roy E. Carter. Berkeley and Los Angeles: University of California Press, 1983.

Sisman, Elaine R. *Mozart: The 'Jupiter' Symphony*. Cambridge: Cambridge University Press, 1993.

Stockhausen, Karlheinz, and Theodor W. Adorno. 'La résistance à l'encontre de la nouvelle musique'. Translated by Carlo Russi. *Contrechamps* 9 (1988): 121–42.

Stravinsky, Igor, and Robert Craft. *Expositions and Developments*. Berkeley and Los Angeles: University of California Press, 1981.

Swed, Mark. 'Music Review: Georg Friedrich Haas' Revelatory Romp in the Dark'. *Los Angeles Times Blogs: Culture Monster*, 20 April 2010. http://latimesblogs.latimes.com/culturemonster/2010/04/georg-friedrich-haas-revelatory-romp-in-the-dark.html.

Williams, Alastair. 'Swaying with Schumann: Subjectivity and Tradition in Wolfgang Rihm's *Fremde Szenen I–III* and Related Scores'. *Music & Letters* 87, no. 3 (2006): 379–97.

Wörner, Karl Heinrich. *Stockhausen: Life and Work*. Berkeley: University of California Press, 1973.

Wurth, Kiene Brillenburg. *Musically Sublime: Indeterminacy, Infinity, Irresolvability*. New York: Fordham University Press, 2009.

Zimmermann, Bernd Alois. *Écrits*. Edited by Philippe Albèra. Geneva: Contrechamps, 2010.

PART 2

Positions

6

REACTIVE MODERNISM

J. P. E. Harper-Scott

Art may tell a truth
Obliquely

– *Robert Browning,* The Ring and the Book, *XII, 855–56*

Most scholarship on what Arnold Whittall has called the 'moderate mainstream' of musical composition since 1900[1] has tended either to presume that its techniques are conservative, and so to allow it no part in the narrative of musical modernism, or on the contrary to insist that it is modernist, but without precisely explaining how modernist aesthetics are to be rewritten in order to accommodate the new style.[2] The traditional sub-Adornian binary of progressive and reactive, modernist and not, has proven itself to be a blunt instrument with which to investigate the majority of musical composition in the last century, and if the complex relation between the music of composers such as Britten, Stravinsky and Shostakovich and that of their contemporaries is to be satisfactorily understood, it is necessary to arrive at a new theoretical understanding of the event of modernism and of the technical consequences of subjective responses to that event.[3]

While retaining a focus on the radical core of the modernist event, but without reducing all artistic production to a binary opposition of radical and conservative, this chapter will argue for an aesthetic, intellectual and political middle ground for 'reactive' music, between the poles of a 'faithful' modernism which confidently asserts the possibility of a new, post-tonal artistic configuration, and an 'obscure' response to modernism which utterly rejects the abandonment of tonality and willingly submits to the aesthetic blandishments of the pure commodity. Reactive music's willingness to partially embrace the new enables it, in however attenuated a fashion, to advance the cause of the artistic revolution, and to enter into a profound engagement with its historical situation in a world constantly being reshaped by late capitalism. Replacing the traditional binary with a more flexible three-part model of aesthetic responses not only opens up a roomier intellectual space for serious music which retains a distance from the avant-garde but also enables a more sophisticated understanding of the history of music in relation to the economic and ideological developments of the twentieth century.

A work which stands prominently on the boundary between faithful and reactive modernism is one which famously seems to cross the border from pre-modernist to modernist musical

155

Example 6.1 Arnold Schoenberg, String Quartet no. 2, second movement, bars 165–76
© Universal Edition, Vienna. All rights reserved

aesthetics: Schoenberg's Second String Quartet. In the scherzo, Schoenberg famously quotes and distorts the Viennese street-ballad, 'O du lieber Augustin' (see Example 6.1). Forces of integration and disintegration tug disconcertingly against one another. Against the second violin's first four-bar melody, the cello provides two promising V–I gestures in two-bar phrases. The non-diatonic notes E♭ and A♭ give the bass line a slightly stumbling gait but do not much muddy the diatonic footprint of the phrase. The viola's canonic repetition of the melody, at pitch, starting in the fourth bar, is a further reassuringly traditional gesture. But both metre and harmony have a disintegrative quality. The first violin's three-bar phrase length cuts across the four-bar melodic phrase, and although its second three-bar phrase coincides with the arrival of the viola's canonic entry, the V–I motion in the cello is one bar out of phrase with this new statement. Overall, despite hints of regularity, the metre is splintered and disorientating. The harmony is even more perplexing: while bar 165 can be parsed as projecting a D major/minor harmony, and bar 168 seems to be only a little murkier in its presentation of D major, that tonality is not in any sense conventionally supported. An implied V7/G in bars 166–67 and 169, if such it is, would relegate this putative 'tonic' to 'dominant' status. But it seems more responsive to the effect of the music to judge the harmonies to be serendipitous rather than planned: incidental harmonies do emerge from the contrapuntal interplay, but they are not completely reflected back onto that counterpoint (as would be the case in common-practice tonality) to give the horizontal counterpoint a vertical, harmonic dimension. Striking in this passage is how appositely Schoenberg realizes the glib message of the quoted song: 'O, du lieber Augustin, alles ist hin' ('Oh, you dear Augustin, everything is broken'). This nonspecific sense of malfunction or disrepair is not just captured by Schoenberg: it is monumentalized as an aesthetic credo. The tonal past is irrecoverably broken, *even when tonality seems somehow to linger*. And this is, in simple form, the first proposition of reactive modernism, which might be roughly stated: 'tonality is broken, but the new world can be accommodated to existing conditions, to create a post-tonal music that is less unpalatable than the revolutionary examples'.

Passages such as this cannot be understood either as 'modernist' or 'non-modernist', 'progressive' or 'conservative' on the old binary models. Two different aesthetic principles, one faithful and one reactive, are held in dialectical equilibrium. The familiar melody, and the relic of tonality, does not step temporally backwards over the radical split between pre-modernist and modernist music: both the non-tonal and the tonal elements in this music must be understood as having already accepted the new musical reality. This particular dialectical configuration, which I shall exemplify in this chapter, is what I call reactive modernism. It is an aesthetic as inescapably modernist as its contemporary aesthetic of faithful modernism: both are shaped by, and are a subjective response to, the same kernel of an emancipatory truth claim. In order to grasp both the musical qualities of reactive modernism and the means by which it carries forward the revolution of faithful modernism, the following sections trace two circuits through questions of the historical and aesthetic character of this musical style. The first circuit deals abstractly with problems in historiography, aesthetics and ideology; the second sharpens the focus on the difference between faithful and reactive subjects by gazing at them through the lens of psychology.

The subjects of musical modernism: history, aesthetics and the event

Any attempt to understand modernism requires a simultaneous attention to history and aesthetics, and both of these categories are problematic. Recent theorists of history such as Frank Ankersmit, Keith Jenkins, Alan Munslow and Hayden White have argued persuasively that there is a conundrum at the heart of history writing.[4] A written history is fictive, which is to say that it is a form of writing, an act of imagination which recasts the past in narrative form. The past, however, does not have a form. This structural disjunction between history writing and its empirical object raises a considerable epistemological question: how can we be sure that a written history corresponds in some way to the facts of history? What philosophers call 'the correspondence theory of truth' codifies the traditional understanding of how the truth of a statement is established. Simply expressed, the theory is that 'x is true if and only if x corresponds to some fact' and therefore 'x is false if and only if x does not correspond to some fact'. It might seem obvious that a historical claim is true if and only if a historical statement corresponds to some fact, but the constitutive structural difference between the facts of the past (which are *actual*) and narratives of those facts (which are *fictive*) ensures that history is a more vexatious enterprise than novel-writing:

> Because the 'before now' doesn't have in it a shape of its own, because the 'before now' doesn't have in it 'events' that have, as it were, the shape of narratives, there is nothing

against which we can check our imagined narrative orderings to see if they 'correspond', for there is literally nothing for them to correspond to.[5]

For many historiographers, such as Hans Ulrich Gumbrecht, the historian's role in creating the history rises in importance relative to the facts that are being interpreted – and by conscious design: since a historian's claim is that the past, while real, cannot be directly interpreted, the 'objective historian' imagined by modernism must be replaced by a 'subjective' one whose own voice, normally a writerly one, is foregrounded as a means of underlining the impossibility that there could ever be any authoritative, objective statement about history.[6] While accepting the basic premise of postmodern historiography, that there is no means of establishing a correspondence between the empirical facts of history and the narrative form of history writing, I suggest that a history with a claim to representing the past accurately can still be written. Because while there can be no mapping of empirical data onto fictive narrative, there is more to history than empirical data. In addition to the empirical data there are *events*, in a sense of the word I take from the philosopher Alain Badiou.[7] And these events, as I will show, also shape the development of aesthetics, thus linking the music historian's two concerns.

Such things as the storming of the Bastille or the signing of the Treaty of Frankfurt are empirically verifiable facts. But the *event* is something else. The facts of a given historical situation are finite. We could envisage a list of such data in abstract form, where facts are represented by letters (a, b, c), which can be listed for a very long time (. . .) before terminating eventually in the last remaining fact (z) which is the last of the set: $\{a, b, c \ldots z\}$.

Where does the event fit with this abstract model? Badiou argues that an event differs radically from the finite facts which are 'in' a situation. An event is a manifestation in any historical or aesthetic situation (or, indeed, any other kind of situation) of a *truth*, and a truth is not only 'outside' the situation but is infinite: it is not exhausted by a particular expression, not articulable in only one language, not limited to a single historical appearance, but universally and infinitely available to all people, in all times and places. It is instructive to grasp the idea abstractly before fleshing it out with aesthetic examples. The event can be compared roughly to a human mind. Say that the definition of my mind is that it is the set of things about which I can form an impression. This includes notebooks, roast chicken, love. . . , and my mind. Written abstractly, with letters again being used to represent things (with M indicating my mind itself), this set of things would be: $M = \{a, b, c \ldots M\}$.

Clearly, to define the human mind in this way entails an infinite regress, because the last element in the set of things about which my mind can form an impression is my mind itself – which is the set of things about which I can form an impression, the last element of which is my mind – which is the set of things . . . (and so on, infinitely). The event, like the mind, is infinite, and therefore not part of the situation, but it also counts as one of the empirical facts of the situation: so it has a paradoxical quality, albeit one that is readily understood (and it means that the Badiouvian event is no more eerie an idea than the human mind). The abstract form of the event has a similarly paradoxical form because in any given situation, say France in 1789, there are all the really existing empirical facts (a man called Robespierre, a prison called the Bastille) which one can count finitely – and there is also the event. This element does not have a *purely* empirical existence, because while it appears in France in 1789, it is not *only* to be found there – it is, as I have already said, available at all times and in all places. In this historic instance it took the particular form of a call to liberty which had already been made by Spartacus in 73BC and by the Roundheads during the English Civil War, and would be made again by the Bolsheviks in 1917 and the crowds on either side of the Berlin Wall in 1989. The elements of an event (E) are thus all of the empirical contents of the situation, plus the event: $E = \{a, b, c \ldots E\}$.

To read the history of music in any particular period by the light of this evental model, we need to understand the make-up of the body of works which carried the nominated truth into a new artistic configuration. For this, it is necessary to understand the only three conceptually possible subjective responses in a given situation, all of them contemporary with the event, which go by the names *faithful subject, reactive subject* and *obscure subject*.[8]

The faithful subject

This 'revolutionary' subject:

1   discerns a truth in some kind of *trace* (a statement, a maxim, a codification, an aesthetic principle...)
2   forms part of a *body* (an army, a set of scientific theories, a collection of musical works) which is committed to the instantiation of the evental truth
3   is an operation which produces a new *present* (a state in the world) in which the truth will have been manifested

The present is the distinctive creation of the faithful subject. In science the present will be a new enlightenment, manifested as a theory that can account for the new truth; in artworks it is a new intensity of expression, an artistic configuration enriched by the inbreaking of new possibilities for mediating expression and form. The faithful subject is revolutionary because it exhibits a high degree of 'fidelity' to the truth. The subordination of a body of artworks to the faithful production of a present from the trace of a truth can lead to ridicule or rejection (Beethoven's late quartets, Schoenberg's free atonal music after 1908, Stockhausen's *Gesang der Jünglinge* ...). But more often than not it is met in the situation by a moderate reaction, a realistic response in the form of the second subjective operation.

The reactive subject

This 'realistic subject':

1   denies that the truth which it discerns in the trace is realistic
2   distances itself from the faithful subject as a means of denying the reality of the discerned truth
3   is an operation which produces an *extinguished present* (a state in the world a little 'less unpalatable' than the revolutionary one) in which the truth is accommodated to existing modes of understanding

The reaction does not come as an attempted reinstatement of the old and the abolition of the new; the reaction denies but it does not destroy, and it remains productive. The reactive subject is the majority response to an event: if in music the faithful subject is embodied in works which declare a new world of artistic communication, the reactive subject is embodied in works which adopt some of the new expressive possibilities but accommodate them to existing formal archetypes. The reactive subject of musical modernism might recognize the expressive value of the emancipation of dissonance as something which can enable a response to a contemporary new subjective necessity; but tonality, the handed-down form from the Baroque to the Romantic periods, is not (as in the case of the faithful subject) reconstructed from the bottom up, emerging from the nature of the musical material itself. In reactive modernism there is a heightened freedom of dissonance treatment at all structural levels, but not an emancipation of dissonance. A piece might, for instance, prolong a dissonant 'tonic', or incorporate elements of serialism. These are examples of what Badiou calls *reactionary novelties*, the inventions of the reactive subject which offer new forms of resistance to the faithfully produced present. As evidence of the resistance to revolution, one can observe the traditional architecture of tonality returning somehow to strap the whole into place: the exigencies of the form, the pre-existing functional background of the configuration that held sway before the event, are the principal features of this extinguished present. The new expressive intensity of the faithful subject is therefore directly referenced, perhaps on the surface of the music, only to be set aside, differentiated from the goals of the piece, so that the body of works does not submit to the same dangerous advocacy of the radical new present, and the reactive subject may enjoy some of the chic of progressiveness without any of the attendant dangers of losing an audience in the concert hall. But what is absolutely crucial about the reactive subject is that, although ostensibly 'accessible' and 'moderate', it carries within itself the truth claim of the faithful subject. The truth claim is negated, but in order to be negated, it has first to be presented. Reactive modernism therefore is a parallel presentation of the truth claims of the revolutionary event, in musical terms the emancipation of dissonance. Far from being a rejection of the musical revolution, as is usually supposed, reactive modernist music furthers the aesthetic revolution – with all its radically progressive ideological burden – of faithful modernism. The only artistic response which denies these truth claims, and which should be firmly separated from the reactive subject, is the third and final subjective possibility.

The obscure subject

This 'ideological subject':

1   affirms and endorses that there is a hegemonic Body of supreme, transcendent power (a tradition, a city, a state, a god...)
2   flatly denies both that there is any validity at all in the trace and that it is legitimate for anybody to affirm such a trace
3   is an operation which examines and destroys the new present brought into being by the faithful subject

The obscure subject conceives the creation of the present as altogether impossible, base, fallacious, and unacceptable for intellectual or moral reasons. Structurally it is recognized by its blank refusal of the present. In order to appeal to an uncontaminated, pre-evental form of appearance, the obscure subject proposes a pure and transcendent Body, that is to say a Body conceived as if it were natural and eternal, morally neutral, obviously 'right', and not a product of history or cultural relations of power.

In artistic terms the obscure subject manifests as iconoclasm in service of the governing ideology; it conceives of the body of faithful works as formalist abominations: 'We go from the pagan statues hammered by the Christians to the gigantic Buddhas blown up by the Taliban, via the Nazi auto-da-fes (against "degenerate" art) and, more inconspicuously, the disappearance into storage facilities of what has fallen out of fashion.'[9] The great physical violence of these famous iconoclastic gestures should not becloud the subtler metaphysical violence of the related final idea, which was elsewhere expressed pungently by Heidegger in a vision of artworks reduced to their pure material basis, lifeless and ignored: 'Beethoven's quartets lie in the publisher's storeroom like potatoes in a cellar.'[10] For in modernity, the obscure subject's principal goal has, time and again, been the maintenance of the influence of capital and the centuries-long

Reactive modernism

process that has led us close to the commodification of everything: this is its fundamental ideological commitment, however much it may vary the means of achieving it. Thus one finds the obscure subject not only in the development from nineteenth-century 'trivial music' to twentieth-century 'popular music', or in the historically parallel shift in focus from sheet music to sound recording as the favoured commodity form, but also in the mechanization of compositional process (a rationalization in keeping with capitalist developments in the broader economy and culture of Europe), and in certain areas of critical writing on music. One cannot simplistically speak of a division between high and low, art and popular styles (though there is some truth in the generalization), since the post-1900 obscure subject's rejection of a subjectively reclaimed diatonic tonality in favour of a conventional presentation of utterly familiar, undemanding, saleable and ephemeral music (this last quality being vital for capitalist circulation) can equally be perceived in the work of 'art' composers or in instrumental genres that were important to art composition. Hence the playfully iconoclastic commodification of Wagner in Fauré's and Messager's *Souvenirs de Bayreuth*, or the deliberate accessibility of minimalism, an aesthetic so patently rationalized, and so at odds with the needs of subjective expression, that it might be the perfect artistic expression of post-Fordism.

Like the reactive subject, the obscure subject is inconceivable without the revolutionary event. The reassertion of a transcendent and incorruptible aesthetic state from before the event requires that there be a revolutionary upstart to quash. Minimalism requires classic modernism as its external delimiter; commercial pop requires art music as its 'stuffy' and 'snooty' poor relation on record-shop shelves. By denying it with such force, the obscure subject still outlines an empty space – a point on a map marked 'here be dragons' – in which those who wish to seek it can find the truth embodied in the faithful subject.

In what follows, I shall give precise aesthetic definitions, linked to specific details in individual pieces of music, for several of the means by which reactive modernist music articulates its denial of the truth claims of the modernist event. In this way, the reactive subject's subconscious nurturing of that event, so to speak its sugar-coating of the expressionist extreme, will become clear. The examples given here by no means offer an exhaustive introduction to the manifestations of reactive modernism, but they should provide a technical introduction that can serve as a basis for recognizing the reactive subject when it is discovered elsewhere.

A crucially important caveat must be noted here. The three 'subjects' of musical modernism should not be mistaken either for composers or for pieces of music. The three subjects are logical possibilities for a response to an event. Naturally, a listener is likelier to find manifestations of faithful subjectivity in the late work of Schoenberg than they are in the late work of Philip Glass. But the reactive subject is not entirely absent from the music of Schoenberg: where his music accommodates emancipated dissonance to some kind of implicit or explicit tonal framework (as in 'Saget mir, auf welchem Pfade' in *Das Buch der hängenden Gärten*, or in the 'O du lieber Augustin' episode in the Second String Quartet), he produces a reactive subjectivity. These three subjects can, in fact, manifest anywhere at any time, and a benefit of the model is that it prevents a dilettantish slotting of composers or their works into any particular aesthetic box. Such dilettantism is a cordial friend of commercial or intellectual value judgement because it enables statements such as 'This work is worth more because it is by a composer of unimpeachable modernist reputation', and so on. The outcome of the abstract nature of the modernist subjects is that there is no pantheon of modernist composer gods. There are only pieces of music which, from time to time, and in a different balance, manifest three different kinds of modernist subjectivity. *Pace* Adorno, Schoenberg is not a faithfully modernist composer, and Stravinsky is not a reactively modernist one. All that the model affords is that from time to time passages in their music form part of the *body* of faithful or reactive modernist subjectivity. Everyone is in, and everyone is out, because what matters is not biographical personalities and individual works, the empirical facts of music history, but truth, the finitely presented infinity of an event.

Modernism and trauma

It should now be clear that what Whittall calls *moderate modernism*, and which I am here more precisely defining as *reactive modernism*, is not simply a milder form of the 'classic' early modernism of Schoenberg et al. While that assumption is not wholly untrue, it is too imprecise to enable music criticism to understand the historical position or contribution of what, after all, not only constitutes the majority of art music composition in the twentieth century but has also been judged by performers and listeners to be the most appealing and the most representative music of that period. The democratic importance of this music is significant enough for it to merit significantly more sustained attention than it has sometimes received. But there is more to it than that. As what we might call 'the constitutive outside' of faithful modernism, which is to say the musical aesthetic which lies between that of music most often called 'modernist' and the various mass-market products of the culture industry (pop and its proliferating subgenres, jazz, film music, minimalism etc.), it is difficult to fit faithful modernism into a history which seems – from the judgement of the majority of musical actors, if not professional musicologists – to deny it a home at all. In short, without a rigorous understanding of reactive modernist music, modernism in music remains a largely mysterious phenomenon. Without reactive modernist music, the chances of absorbing the truth claims of faithful modernism are significantly impaired. In any case, the *psychology* of both faithful and reactive forms of modernism is essentially identical. And as a way into discovering what is distinctive, and simultaneously the same, about faithful and reactive modernism, building a psychoanalytic picture, step by step, can be a useful heuristic tool.

Both faithful and reactive aesthetics are responses to the essential trauma of modernity (i.e. the period after the French Revolution); they simply articulate their trauma differently.[11] Their shared trauma is the cultural realization, after Freud, that the Self is not whole but fragmented, that human life in modernity is (to borrow some formulations of Adorno) a 'damaged life', whose conflicted parts are 'torn halves of an integral freedom, to which however they do not add up'.[12] Self-reflexive subjectivity is not new to the music or art of modernity; it is found already in Machaut and troubadour poetry.[13] What changed around 1789 was the sense that subjectivity as determined externally (by fate or feudal obligations) was replaced by the new possibility that subjectivity could be created immanently, through the agency of the individual. In the Enlightenment the main tool of this agency was taken to be rationality, as a principle organizing both internal and external reality, individuals and their society.

In the Baroque and Classical styles which comprise music's collective response to eighteenth-century Enlightenment rationality, halves still add up to wholes. The musical opposition, and eventual reconciliation, of tonic and dominant in so-called common-practice tonality is the *locus classicus* of positive dialectics in pre-modernist music. The resultant musical form, in which dialectical poles are resolved into a new synthesis, is a potent analogue of the Enlightenment belief in the reliable, emancipatory function of rationality, and the possibility – verging on certainty – of achieving a unity within the human spirit at both individual and social levels. Again and again this assuasive pattern was repeated in works which danced and sang exultantly of the boon of rationality. But soon after 1789, in the works of Beethoven, Schubert, and others, the tonic/dominant polarity came into question. The dominant began to lose its 'natural' role as the mirror of the tonic soul. To give just one example from many in Beethoven, the arbitrariness of the dominant's role as 'official Other' to the tonic is shown up by the merest lip-service he pays to it at the end of the exposition in the first movement of the Ninth Symphony (a perfunctory

Reactive modernism

slippage from the B♭ secondary key area onto the 'proper' dominant), and at the start of the reca-pitulation (where a ♭VI–i cadence, B♭–D minor) has to serve as a 'perfect cadence'. And even the tonic, the Self of traditional tonality, can seem to become merely another murkily defined tonal mirage among many, in some of Schubert's recapitulations.[14]

Throughout the nineteenth century, the dialectic took a turn towards the negative. By the early years of the twentieth century, the example of the emancipation of the dominant from its pre-modern function could be applied to the entire hierarchical pitch space of music. Not only was the dominant no longer the official Other, but free motion in post-tonal (and later twelve-tone) space rejects the idea that there can be an Other – or even a Self – at all. The rejection of the oppositional concepts of consonance and dissonance, encapsulated most famously in Schoen-berg's declaration of the 'emancipation of dissonance', is the first radical declaration in music history of the irreconcilability of difference, of the making-whole of a fragmented subjectivity.[15]

The faithful modernism of the emancipated dissonance (in the early twentieth century) and of various post-serial emancipations of the musical idea itself (in the later twentieth century) is the subject of other chapters in this volume. In this chapter my focus is on reactive mod-ernism, which is characterized by a kind of broken tonality which returns again and again to the traumatic loss of wholeness that pre-modernist music was able to rely on and reconstruct by the simple act of repetition. Repetition is, indeed, the musical mark of the reassuring old Enlightenment belief in the iterability, throughout the human race, of the rational, subjective self-construction that romantic heroes, intellectuals and artists were held to exemplify. And it is in the iterability of cadential structures, which give punctuation to the rational argument of tonal music, that the productive failure of reactive music is sometimes most obviously seen.

I have already noted that, in tonality, the dominant which wrenches tonal music away from its tonic centre can be reconciled with it through a perfect authentic cadence, i.e. the coming to rest on a 'closed' space between bass and melody, a root-position chord I surmounted by a $\hat{1}$. This motion from tonic to dominant can be endlessly repeated, in traversals from the smallest to the largest scale – from simple binary forms through sonata structures to the capacious space of an entire operatic act. When repetition seems to 'fail', as in exceptional cases such as the conclu-sion of Mozart's *Musikalischer Spaß*, the exception (here, of course, a comic one) proves the rule: the joke is funny because we know that it is ludicrous to think that a cadence could fail. In musi-cal modernism, by contrast, the characteristic attitude to repetition takes on the character of the psychoanalytic encounter with a traumatic event. In both the therapeutic and musical situations, repetition is an inescapable part of returning to and 'working through' that trauma when simple repetition has proved incapable of bringing comfort and reassurance.

Case study 1: Schnittke

An unanticipated breakdown in the calmative quality of traditional musical repetition occurs at the end of the first melodic presentation of Schnittke's *Stille Nacht* (1978). Outwardly, the piece has all the accoutrements of tonality and convention: a key signature (G major), a time signature (3/4), an Italian tempo marking (Lento), a classical-seeming repeat mark (albeit with a note that is not played on the first run through), and above all a very familiar and singable diatonic tune. Phrase lengths are regular, coming in pairs of two bars, and the harmony has a childlike simplicity, all tonic, dominant and subdominant. But when Gruber's 'Silent Night' melody reaches the point where it should have its first perfect authentic cadence, there is a quiet catastrophe (see Example 6.2). What should be a resolution to an octave G in the violin appears as an augmented octave G–G♯. This wholly unexpected dissonance attracts an imme-diate response from the piano, which plays a low C♯. It is as if this is an attempt to normalize

163

Beim ersten Mal spielt das Klavier erst ab dem Zeichen ✛; bei der Wiederholung von Anfang an.
[The first time through, the piano plays from the sign ✛; on the repeat it plays from the beginning onwards.]

Example 6.2   Alfred Schnittke, *Stille Nacht*, bars 21–30
© With kind permission. Musikverlag Hans Sikorski GmbH & Co. KG, Hamburg

the chromatic intruder, perhaps by leading via a D to a perfect authentic cadence, with the 'wrong' G–G♯ sonority 'corrected' to an octave G. (The tonal logic here would be: the G♯ can tonicize C♯, which is merely the third of chord V of V.) But the C♯ goes nowhere: instead it merely tolls forty times, with an increasingly gelid unconcern for the encroaching nightmare that develops above it.

On the repeat, the formerly sweet tonality remains soured. A listener without a score might hope that the phrase will reach a proper perfect authentic cadence, but the once-affirmatory character of the traditional repeat marking now works against, rather than for, integration: the distended octave remains, and it carries forward into the second thematic presentation, starting at bar 27, where the piano melody is accompanied by skeletal, pizzicato violin arpeggios from G to G♯ (with D/D♯ clashes on dominant, and C/C♯ clashes on subdominant harmonies). All these repetitions of the unproductive, knell-like bass and of the sharp-and-natural root of each childlike chord constitute a process of elevating the little disturbance of bar 23 – a moment that could have been explained away and resolved back into tranquillity, but was not – into an authentic trauma of reactive modernist tonality. By bar 39 melodic repetition, too, breaks down: the piano omits the repetition of phrase three ('Round yon virgin, mother and child'), while the bass continues to toll C♯ and the violin provides its mutated subdominant and tonic harmonies. In the third presentation of the theme, the piano carries the mutated arpeggios (now inverted) and the violin has a form of the tune which regularly raises or lowers individual notes by one octave, to create angular leaps that further distort the profile of the melody. As before, the piano omits the repetition of its third phrase (now an accompaniment phrase). Finally, in a six-bar coda, the piano plays two iterations of the G/G♯ arpeggio while the violin plays *ppp diminuendo*

Reactive modernism

scordatura glissandos that sink to a D below the instrument's normal lowest G. In this final iteration of what should be a ringing open string tone, the piece makes one final break with unified identity, now at the level of the expected G–D–A–E tuning of the solo instrument itself.

This disturbing little piece instantiates several traumatic encounters with tonality which are characteristic of reactive modernism. The process begins with an 'emancipation' of an elementary tonal gesture, the cadence. The form of the cadence is retained, but the content of it has been changed. We still hear a putative resolution to the first scale degree, but 1̂ 'is' no longer the pitch class G – or rather *not only* the pitch class G. It 'is' *both G and G♯*. Schnittke has opened a rift between the tonal sign of the scale degree and the physical materiality of the pitch class: an emancipated dissonance, a G♯, has been reconciled as well as it ever could be to pre-existing tonal order. But the encounter leaves a traumatic 'remainder' that the piece cannot fully account for. This disjunction between the handed-down form, tonality, and the historical demands of the musical materials, which call for an emancipation of Enlightenment functions, is the *echt*-reactive experience. Where repetition of such an aberrant element in Beethoven (e.g. the C♯ in the *Eroica*) or Wagner (the resolution of the often-repeated *Tristan* chord in the last bars of *Tristan und Isolde*) would eventually lead to a more or less comfortable and comforting kind of synthesis, in reactive modernist music such promises would feel fake not only to the musical style but to the twentieth century's distinctive critical understanding of subjectivity. In this piece, everything flows from that single traumatic encounter of the new, which grows through its constant repetition to become a dominating psychological dynamic. To put it in Freudian terms, we encounter here a return of the repressed, a musical manifestation of the death drive.[16]

Case study 2: Poulenc

The first of Poulenc's *Trois mouvements perpétuels* of 1918, another ostensibly very simple piece, exhibits with particular clarity several of the characteristic operations of the reactive modernist subject in the first half of the twentieth century. Although this piece is brief and relatively straightforward, it shows how the reactive and obscure subjects represent fundamentally opposed responses to the modernist event. Analysis of its translucent musical processes therefore enables a concrete demonstration – on a more practical scale than would be possible in more complex pieces – of the reactive subject's traversal of its aesthetic territory.

The perpetual movement of the piece's title is in this case the left-hand accompaniment, first heard in the movement's basic idea in bars 1–2 (see Example 6.3). With the exception of the final bar, this accompaniment figure, which presents a B♭ major quasi-Alberti bass pattern, is played without variation throughout the movement. Motivically, every short-breathed, two-bar melody in the piece is derived from the opening idea, so that the opening bars provide a source for almost all the music in the piece. Figure 6.1 shows how simple inversions and combinations of the falling diatonic steps in bars 1–2 are used to generate the melodies in bars 5–7 and 14–15, and even the bare dyads – major ninths – in bars 12–13. Whether heard as four falling steps (-4) followed by three falling steps (-3), or a combination of -3, -1 and -3 (shown in Figure 6.1(a)), the components of the melody are varied to lend motivic unity to all but the last bar.[17] As these snatches of melody come and go, shifting place above the immutable bass line, the piece spends most of its length composing out a lucid but quite plain prolongation of its tonic triad (see Figure 6.2). If the tonal middleground seems comprehensible, attention to detail complicates matters. The last bar, bar 24, immediately stands out as having an enigmatic relation both to the tonic and to the motivic unity otherwise on display in the movement (see Example 6.4).[18] Taken as a whole, the harmony is a combination of a chord of B♭ and a seventh chord on D major. This

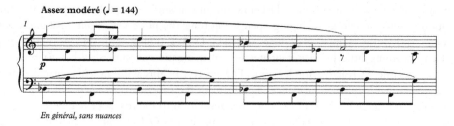

Example 6.3 Francis Poulenc, *Trois mouvements perpétuels*, no. 1, basic idea, bars 1–2

© Copyright 1918. Chester Music Limited. All Rights Reserved. International Copyright Secured. Printed by permission of Chester Music Limited

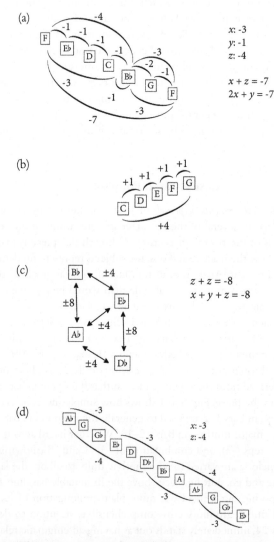

Figure 6.1 Francis Poulenc, *Trois mouvements perpétuels*, no. 1, diatonic pitch-space networks for (a) bars 1–2, (b) bars 5–7, (c) bars 12–13 and (d) bars 14–15

Example 6.4 Poulenc, *Trois mouvements perpétuels*, no. 1, bar 24

© Copyright 1918. Chester Music Limited. All Rights Reserved. International Copyright Secured. Printed by permission of Chester Music Limited

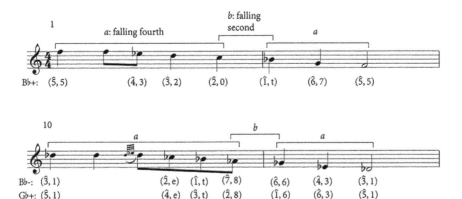

Example 6.5 Poulenc, *Trois mouvements perpétuels*, no. 1, comparison of bars 1–2 and 10–11

© Copyright 1918. Chester Music Limited. All Rights Reserved. International Copyright Secured. Printed by permission of Chester Music Limited

decorative overspreading of the final tonic chord seems to demand an explanation, and while it is not hard to find one, this answer to the riddle of the final bar soon opens up questions about other parts of the piece.

In established nineteenth-century chromatic practice, which is an obvious source for Poulenc's apparently 'conservative' musical language in this piece, D is closely related to B♭ via what neo-Riemannian theory calls an *LP* transformation: the B♭ is dropped a semitone to A (the *Leittonwechsel* transformation, *L*), and the F is raised a semitone to F♯ (the *Parallel* transformation, *P*). Major and minor chords on B♭, D and F♯ are all, in fact, closely related by simple chromatic transformations, a fact which illuminates the strong implication that beats 2 and 3 of this bar (and the grace notes to the final beat) are arpeggiating an F♯-minor chord. The only time the opening two-bar melody is heard off-tonic is in bars 10–11, where, as shown in Example 6.5, it is transposed down a major third into G♭ major.

Although bars 10–11 slightly vary the melody, in both cases we hear a melody formed of motives *a*, *b*, and *a* again. In the first instance the melody falls $\hat{5}$–$\hat{5}$ in B♭; in the second instance it falls $\hat{5}$–$\hat{5}$ in G♭. So, bars 10–11 are a real transposition, T(e, − 4), of bars 1–2.[19] But that is only if we attend to the melody on its own. In a contrapuntal context, this transposed melody on top of the never-changing accompaniment figure gives bars 10–11 as a whole the harmonic flavour of B♭ minor, so that the same melodic notes are heard in their contrapuntal–harmonic context as descending $\hat{3}$–$\hat{3}$ in B♭ minor. If we attend to the melody, we hear G♭ major; if we attend to

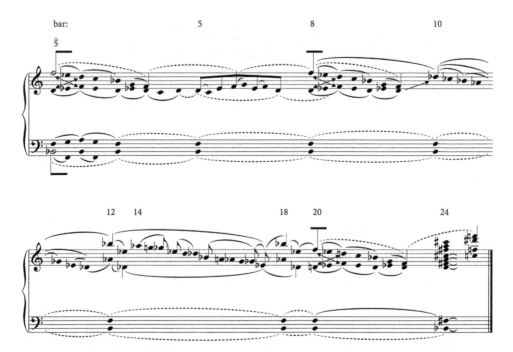

Figure 6.2 Poulenc, *Trois mouvements perpétuels*, no. 1, voice-leading graph

the melody plus accompaniment, we hear B♭ minor. It would be easy, and is in fact normal, to describe this effect as 'bitonality', the presentation of two keys simultaneously. But that does not quite capture what is heard in bars 10–11. It is not true that the melody is in G♭ while the accompaniment is in B♭ minor; that would indeed be bitonality. Instead, there is a clear sense that the melody is heard *both* in G♭ *and* in B♭ minor, because it is possible to hear it simultaneously as a real transposition of the bars 1–2 basic idea *and* a tonal transposition into B♭ minor. Consequently, it is possible to hear each note as if it has a double scale degree function. D♭ is *both* $\hat{3}$ in B♭ minor *and* $\hat{5}$ in G♭ minor. The Schenkerian graph of Figure 6.2 reflects the fact that the counterpoint creates a tonal 'normalization' by reading the melody here as generating modal mixture within the tonic B♭, by prolonging a melodic D♭ which then skips, in bar 12, to a B♭ which completes a $\hat{5}$–♭$\hat{3}$–$\hat{1}$ arpeggiation of the B♭ (minor) triad.

But this gesture of normalization, on which the orthodox bias of Schenkerian method shines a useful light, exercises a force which leaves a kind of 'remainder' that tonality cannot quite contain. Although musical lines of course have no agency, we might say metaphorically that the melody 'wants' to make a *PL* shift to G♭ major but the harmony 'wants' to make the melody appear to be in B♭ minor, albeit with a flattened $\hat{2}$ and $\hat{7}$. Figure 6.3(a) shows how, on this reading, scale degrees $\hat{6}$, $\hat{7}$, $\hat{2}$ and $\hat{3}$ are lowered by a semitone on the pitch class axis to create this harmonic effect. (The seven notes of the melody in bars 1–2 are numbered x^1 to x^7; the seven notes of the melody in bars 10–11 are numbered y^1 to y^7.) But the quality that might lead some to call this moment 'bitonal' is not captured by this hearing, since it is in the essence of the bitonal comportment to music to hear two keys simultaneously between parts (e.g. melody and bass). But in this case *the melody itself* is in two keys at once – the first (G♭ major) generated by its identity as a real transposition, the second (B♭ minor) generated by its harmonic context. Although the pitch levels remain constant, their scale degree quality can consequently be heard to 'flicker' between two positions, as shown in Figure 6.3.

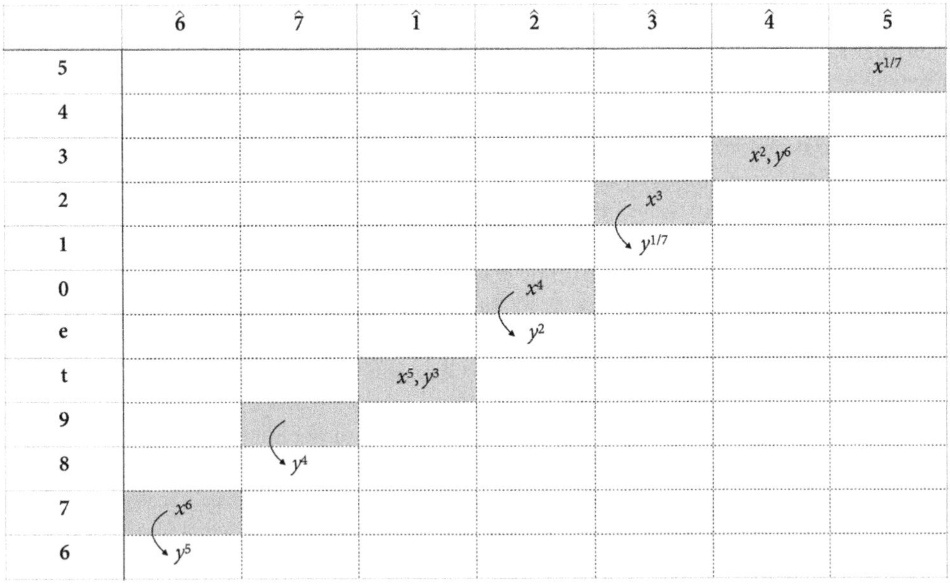

(a)

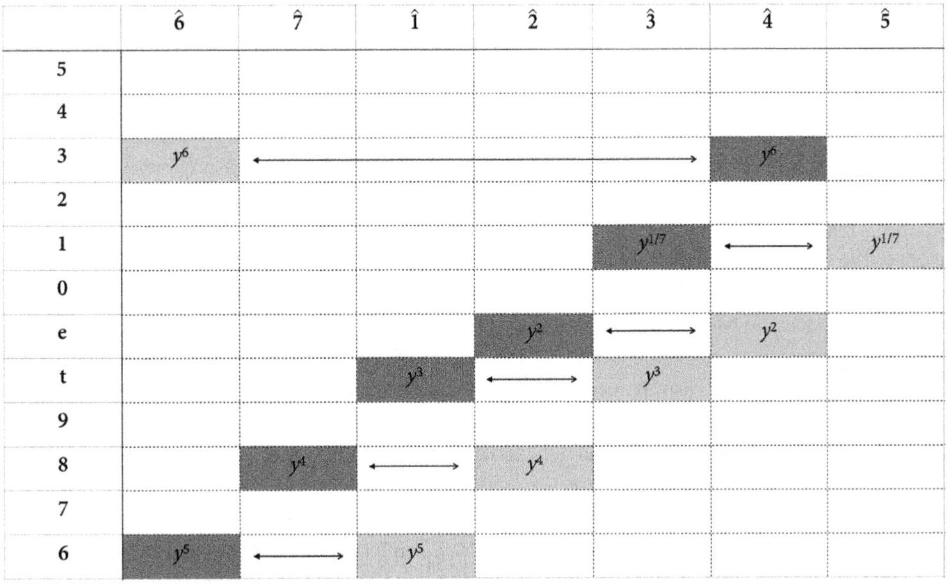

(b)

Figure 6.3 Two hearings of bars 10–11: (a) as a minor-mode variant of the basic idea, (b) as a flickering between B♭ major and G♭ major

If we were to hear both the transposition and the harmonic context, it would be difficult to hear the D♭, for instance, as either $\hat{5}$ or $\hat{3}$: like the duck-rabbit illusion, it would be heard as both and neither at the same time.

In short, tonality in these bars appears somehow self-contradictory in a way that is characteristic of reactive modernism. In tonal music written before the event of modernism, real transposition of the kind seen in bars 10–11 would effect a modulation to a new key, because the unity of scale degree function and pitch class identity is in principle, in the common-practice style, locked firmly together. It is part of the ideology – i.e. the structuring of musical ideas – in common-practice tonality that each scale degree can have one and only one pitch class associated with it. This is such a strong, transparent, and apparently instinctive association that listeners would be forgiven for missing that this conjunction of material (pitch class) and symbolic (scale degree) qualities of musical notes is an entirely arbitrary effect of the tonal system. By this means, judgements of consonance and dissonance can be effectively regulated, and 'tension' can be pacifically 'resolved'. If the pitch D♭ occurs in a B♭-minor context in pre-eventual tonality, that pitch is parsed as $\hat{3}$. Ideologically, the yoking of scale degree (sd) to pitch class (pc) creates a powerful symbolic glue that ensures a reliable functioning of a musical order. In principle, there is no reason why scale degree and pitch class should not float free of each other, but tonality combines them into a monad. Its insistence that it is 'natural' for a pitch class to have a scale degree role can be seen as a musical correlate of a rationalized ordering of society in which individuals have a knowable function in the social whole. Such gluing together of a name (a pitch class, a person) and a function ($\hat{3}/\hat{5}$, ruler/subject) has an effect, in music and in society, of enforcing a totality.

Understood in this way, what faithful modernism calls *emancipation of the dissonance* is thus revealed more precisely to be an *emancipation of the pitch class* from the shackles of a fixed sd/pc symbolic system. Its rejection of tonality dissolves the glue holding together the sd/pc monad, so that pitch classes lose their function: the former whole has been fragmented, and is incapable of being reconstructed. In this emancipation, the scale degree itself disappears as a meaningful musical symbol, and tonality is lost. It is thus, precisely, the dismissal of the scale degree, not the increase in the permissibility of dissonance per se, which constitutes the modernist revolution: the old *order* has been overturned, even if the same material actors (the twelve tuned pitches of the Western scale) remain in place to inhabit the new world. In reactive modernism, the emancipating dissolution of the sd/pc ideological glue is only partly realized. Reactive modernism accepts the revolutionary principle that the sd/pc monad has been ruptured, and that pitch classes can exist independently of tonal function; but it does not accept the corollary of this rupture, namely that the function of the scale degree has also been abolished. It is the retention of the scale degree function, even when its ideological coupling with pitch classes has been broken, that gives reactive modernism its particular late-tonal character. The pitch class is emancipated, but only up to a point: the old system of scale degree function is not wholly abandoned.[20]

In this *Mouvement perpétuel*, the particular manifestation of reactive subjectivity is seen especially in two features. The first is the way that real transposition, instead of effecting a new association of sd/pc monads (e.g. a switch from a B♭ to a G♭ scale, each with seven pitch classes strictly conjoined with seven scale degrees), fails to complete a switch between keys and instead 'flickers', duck-rabbitlike, between them. The second is in the breakdown of the processes of parsimonious voice leading from tonic B♭ to and from its third-related keys: in bar 24, the superimposition of two such hexatonically related chords (B♭ and F♯ minor) are simply superimposed, their sd/pc monads not exchanging positions with each other but competing for symbolic space. The negative dialectics of reactive modernism – the fact that its musical 'objects [pitch classes] do not go into their concepts [scale degrees] without leaving a remainder'[21] – can assume manifold forms, but whether it is an uneasy synthesis of note rows and tonal functions in Britten, an enriched tonic sonority (for instance, with an added seventh) in Sibelius or Walton, or what might strike a lay listener as 'wrong-note' harmonies in Shostakovich or Stravinsky – all these cases bespeak an often extreme tension between the reactive claims of a tenacious tonality and the emancipatory abolition of the sd/pc ideology.

Conclusion

How do these abstract musical details relate to what I earlier called 'the essential trauma of modernity'? The beginnings of an answer can be found in a Badiouvian reading of the clinical component of trauma recovery by three Dutch psychoanalysts, Gregory Bistoen, Stijn Vanheule and Stef Craps, who unpick the significant similarities between traumatic reaction and Badiou's theory of the event:

> What typifies a traumatic reaction, and what is re-asserted by this theory of the event, is that the traumatic event cannot be entirely grasped from within the interpretative background that is present at the moment of its occurrence. [. . .] The information that a trauma supposedly delivers is basically unknowable from within the pre-existent world in which it emerges.[22]

The therapeutic discovery of psychological meaning does not flow directly from the naming of a traumatic event, such as the moment of being abandoned by a parent or (in a musical sense) the naming of the emancipation of dissonance. The meaning of the signs cast into the world by an event such as a trauma or an artistic revolution cannot be straightforwardly or immediately grasped, because 'both an event and its signifiers are indiscernible and undecidable from within the here and now of the yet-to-be-modified world. As far as the established knowledge-regime is concerned, the name of an event is nothing more than a gibberish "empty signifier" with no referent.'[23] What does *emancipated dissonance* mean, without a body of faithful and reactive modernist works to work out its implications? The meaning of an event, insofar as it can be partly encoded in language, will only emerge after the event, so to speak 'in the future anterior, when the new world has been fully actualized'.[24] And the same is true of a traumatic reaction, where 'recovery is not the result of the direct verbalization of the undigested experience, but rather of the creation of a new context that allows for it to be read'.[25]

Modernism is compelled to repeat the traumatic encounter with the fragmentation of common-practice musical subjectivity, the decentring of the longstanding sd/pc monad, and the eradication of concepts such as 'home', 'security' and 'totality'. In faithful and reactive modernism alike, the repetition compulsion reveals time and again the failure of musical repetition to achieve the old certitudes of totality. If faithful modernism can be said to adhere closely to the moment *after* the radical disjunction, reactive modernism can be said to return again and again to the moment *of* the disjunction itself, the point when the sd/pc monad is broken up. As in psychic trauma, the return of the repressed does not itself achieve a transformative breakthrough. It is only as the new musical world is populated with an increasingly substantial body of faithful and reactive modernist pieces, all of which (unlike the obscure response to modernism) repeatedly confront the traumatic core of modernist musical language, that a meaning can clarify and a truth can emerge. And, unified as they are in their acknowledgement of the essential traumatic rupture of modernity, both faithful and reactive modernism are essential, vigorous artistic materializations of the human struggle to reach a new, and potentially emancipatory, view of its fractured subjectivity. Faithful modernism is a powerful witness to the transformations of modernity, but it is time for the traumatic awakening of the reactive subject of musical modernism to be given the attention it deserves.

Notes

1 Arnold Whittall, *Musical Composition in the Twentieth Century* (New York and Oxford: Oxford University Press, 1999).
2 Recent developments in thinking on such music have tended to focus on Scandinavian or British music. See, for instance, Daniel M. Grimley, *Carl Nielsen and the Idea of Modernism* (Woodbridge: Boydell, 2010), James A. Hepokoski, *Sibelius, Symphony No. 5* (Cambridge: Cambridge University Press, 1993) and J. P. E. Harper-Scott, *Edward Elgar, Modernist* (Cambridge and New York: Cambridge University Press, 2006).
3 Adorno's views on the aesthetics of modernism had hardened into an untypically (for him) crude binary by the time of his canonic position statement, *Philosophie der neuen Musik* (1949), but in a short, unpublished 1928 essay, his concept of 'stabilized music' comes closer to the concept of the reactive I outline in this chapter. See Theodor Adorno, 'Die stabilisierte Musik', in *Musikalische Schriften V*, ed. Rolf Tiedemann, *Gesammelte Schriften* (Frankfurt: Suhrkamp, 2003).
4 See F. R. Ankersmit, *Historical Representation* (Stanford, CA: Stanford University Press, 2001), F. R. Ankersmit, *Meaning, Truth, and Reference in Historical Representation* (Ithaca, NY: Cornell University Press, 2012), Keith Jenkins, *Re-thinking History* (London: Routledge, 1991), Keith Jenkins, *Refiguring History: New Thoughts on an Old Discipline* (London: Routledge, 2003), Keith Jenkins and Alun Munslow, eds., *The Nature of History Reader* (London: Routledge, 2004), and one of the founding texts of postmodern historiography, Hayden V. White, *Metahistory: The Historical Imagination in Nineteenth-Century Europe* (Baltimore and London: Johns Hopkins University Press, 1973).
5 Jenkins and Munslow, *The Nature of History Reader*, 3. The postmodernist musicologist Lawrence Kramer makes a similar point less translucently: 'The claims of interpretation are both testable and contestable in relation to history, practice, logic, and reflection on the symbolizing process. But they are not account-able to the means or ends of empiricism because they address objects of knowledge of a different order than those of empiricism, objects to which empirical methods can at best be applied poorly'; Lawrence Kramer, *Interpreting Music* (Berkeley and London: University of California Press, 2011), 30.
6 See Hans Ulrich Gumbrecht, *In 1926: Living at the Edge of Time* (Cambridge, MA, and London: Harvard University Press, 1997). Among recent musicology which consciously follows Gumbrecht's model, see Thomas Irvine, 'Normality and Emplotment: Walter Leigh's "Midsummer Night's Dream" in the Third Reich and Britain', *Music & Letters* 94, no. 2 (2013), 295–323.
7 See particularly Alain Badiou's books *Theory of the Subject*, trans. Bruno Bosteels (London: Continuum, 2009), *Being and Event*, trans. Oliver Feltham (London and New York: Continuum, 2005) and *Logics of Worlds: Being and Event, 2*, trans. Alberto Toscano (London and New York: Continuum, 2009).
8 See Badiou, *Logics of Worlds*, 45–89, for the fullest general exposition of the metaphysics of these subjects.
9 Ibid., 73.
10 Martin Heidegger, 'The Origin of the Work of Art', in *Off the Beaten Track*, ed. Julian Young and Kenneth Haynes (Cambridge: Cambridge University Press, 2002), 3.
11 The obscure response to musical modernism is also conditioned by the same trauma, but its denial is extremely powerful.
12 Theodor W. Adorno, *Aesthetics and Politics* (London: Verso, 2010), 123. Adorno, however, denies the possibility of 'the middle-term between Schönberg and the American film', the reactive subject that is the focus of this chapter. 'Reflections from damaged life' is the subtitle of Theodor W. Adorno, *Minima Moralia*, trans. E. F. N. Jephcott (London and New York: Verso, 2005).
13 See, for instance, Sarah Kay, *Subjectivity in Troubadour Poetry* (Cambridge: Cambridge University Press, 1990), and Judith Ann Peraino, *Giving Voice to Love: Song and Self-Expression from the Troubadours to Guillaume de Machaut* (New York and Oxford: Oxford University Press, 2011).
14 See Nicholas Marston, 'Schubert's Homecoming', *Journal of the Royal Musical Association* 125, no. 2 (2000), 248–70.
15 My focus in this chapter is largely on pitches and scale degrees. This is not because other elements of music – rhythm, timbre, dynamics, and so on – are of little importance, but because the semiotics of the other musical parameters do not have anything like the same totalizing effect: a symphony cannot be ended simply by a return of string sonority or a sequence of crotchets. Pitch exercises such a control, and it is in the parameter of pitch that musical encoding of modernity's interrogation of the possibilities of emancipation can be most clearly seen. Current musicological worries about a focus on pitch emerge from an antipathy towards the varieties of faithful modernism which focus strongly on it, rather than from a persuasive sense that pitch is not the principal factor in determining the identity of most musical pieces.

Reactive modernism

16 See Sigmund Freud, *Beyond the Pleasure Principle, Group Psychology, and Other Works*, ed. James Strachey et al., vol. XVIII, The Standard Edition of the Complete Psychological Works of Sigmund Freud (London: Vintage Books, 2001).

17 Labelling these motivic gestures x (-3), y (-1), and z (-4), we see that bars 5–7 are an inversion of $x + y$, bars 14–15 are heard either as $x + x + z$ or $z + x + x$, and the chords in bars 12–13 are verticalizations of $x + y + z$ (with the contour of the 'melody' in their two voices being provided by z).

18 Its diatonic steps (+4, +2, +5, +2, +5) break the established patterns of the movement so far, with this new emphasis on +2 and +5. The rest of the movement has operated by simple additions within the network afforded by x, y and z. While it is possible to explain these new intervals as $-2y$ and $-y + -z$, such an explanation brushes the experiential difference of this bar under the tidy theoretical carpet. The motives in bars 5–7 and 14–15 *sound* as if they are derived from bars 1–2, and even the ninths in bars 12–13 sound like slightly exaggerated intervallic summaries of the descending melodic octaves we have already heard four times so far. Bar 24, by contrast, does not sound like a new form of the basic melodic idea at all: it sounds like an arpeggiation of a strange new chord whose constituent intervals bear no immediately apparent relation to the contexts opened up by the piece so far.

19 I take this notation, along with much of the theoretical orientation concerning transformation in this case study, from Steven Rings, *Tonality and Transformation* (New York and Oxford: Oxford University Press, 2011). 'T' indicates a transposition, and the elements in the parenthesis respectively indicate the change to the scale degree (e means 'identity' in Rings's notation, i.e. no change at all in scale degree, so that $\hat{5}$ remains $\hat{5}$) and to the pitch class (which moves down four semitones in this transposition).

20 Music which constitutes an obscure response, by contrast, will use tonality as if the emancipation proclamation had never been made, and the sd/pc monad could still function as before. The obscure response proclaims a non-fragmented tonality, declaring that a pre-existing, transcendent tonal Body can restore order to the musical present. The political implications of the faithful – reactive – obscure trajectory, which are a broad cultural analogue of the communist – social democratic – neoliberal logic of political economy in the last century, are unfolded at length in J. P. E. Harper-Scott, *The Quilting Points of Musical Modernism: Revolution, Reaction, and William Walton* (Cambridge: Cambridge University Press, 2012), especially chapter 4.

21 This is a definition of negative dialectics given by Adorno in *Negative Dialectics* (London: Routledge, 1973), 5.

22 Gregory Bistoen, Stijn Vanheule and Stef Craps, 'Badiou's Theory of the Event and the Politics of Trauma Recovery', *Theory & Psychology* 24, no. 6 (2014), 839.

23 Ibid., 840.

24 Ibid.

25 Ibid., 841.

Bibliography

Adorno, Theodor W. *Negative Dialectics*. London: Routledge, 1973.

———. 'Die stabilisierte Musik'. In *Musikalische Schriften V*. Edited by Rolf Tiedemann, 721–28. Frankfurt: Suhrkamp, 2003.

———. *Minima Moralia: Reflections from Damaged Life*. Translated by E. F. N. Jephcott. London and New York: Verso, 2005.

———. *Aesthetics and Politics*. London: Verso, 2010.

Ankersmit, F. R. *Historical Representation*. Stanford, CA: Stanford University Press, 2001.

———. *Meaning, Truth, and Reference in Historical Representation*. Ithaca, NY: Cornell University Press, 2012.

Badiou, Alain. *Being and Event*. Translated by Oliver Feltham. London and New York: Continuum, 2005.

———. *Logics of Worlds: Being and Event, 2*. Translated by Alberto Toscano. London and New York: Continuum, 2009.

———. *Theory of the Subject*. Translated by Bruno Bosteels. London: Continuum, 2009.

Bistoen, Gregory, Stijn Vanheule and Stef Craps. 'Badiou's Theory of the Event and the Politics of Trauma Recovery'. *Theory & Psychology* 24, no. 6 (2014): 830–51.

Freud, Sigmund. *Beyond the Pleasure Principle, Group Psychology, and Other Works*. The Standard Edition of the Complete Psychological Works of Sigmund Freud, edited by James Strachey, Anna Freud, Alix Strachey and Alan Tyson. Vol. XVIII. London: Vintage Books, 2001.

Grimley, Daniel M. *Carl Nielsen and the Idea of Modernism*. Woodbridge: Boydell, 2010.

Gumbrecht, Hans Ulrich. *In 1926: Living at the Edge of Time.* Cambridge, MA, and London: Harvard University Press, 1997.

Harper-Scott, J. P. E. *Edward Elgar, Modernist.* Cambridge and New York: Cambridge University Press, 2006.

———. *The Quilting Points of Musical Modernism: Revolution, Reaction, and William Walton.* Cambridge: Cambridge University Press, 2012.

Heidegger, Martin. 'The Origin of the Work of Art'. In *Off the Beaten Track*, edited by Julian Young and Kenneth Haynes, 1–56. Cambridge: Cambridge University Press, 2002.

Hepokoski, James A. *Sibelius, Symphony No. 5.* Cambridge: Cambridge University Press, 1993.

Irvine, Thomas. 'Normality and Emplotment: Walter Leigh's "Midsummer Night's Dream" in the Third Reich and Britain'. *Music & Letters* 94, no. 2 (2013): 295–323.

Jenkins, Keith. *Re-thinking History.* London: Routledge, 1991.

———. *Refiguring History: New Thoughts on an Old Discipline.* London: Routledge, 2003.

Jenkins, Keith, and Alun Munslow, eds. *The Nature of History Reader.* London: Routledge, 2004.

Kay, Sarah. *Subjectivity in Troubadour Poetry.* Cambridge: Cambridge University Press, 1990.

Kramer, Lawrence. *Interpreting Music.* Berkeley and London: University of California Press, 2011.

Marston, Nicholas. 'Schubert's Homecoming'. *Journal of the Royal Musical Association* 125, no. 2 (2000): 248–70.

Peraino, Judith Ann. *Giving Voice to Love: Song and Self-Expression from the Troubadours to Guillaume de Machaut.* New York and Oxford: Oxford University Press, 2011.

Rings, Steven. *Tonality and Transformation.* New York and Oxford: Oxford University Press, 2011.

White, Hayden V. *Metahistory: The Historical Imagination in Nineteenth-Century Europe.* Baltimore and London: Johns Hopkins University Press, 1973.

Whittall, Arnold. *Musical Composition in the Twentieth Century.* New York and Oxford: Oxford University Press, 1999.

7

MUSICAL MODERNISM, GLOBAL

Comparative observations

Björn Heile

[W]ithin the limits of plausible argument, the most instructive comparisons [...] are those that surprise. No Japanese will be surprised by a comparison with China, since it has been made for centuries, the path is well trodden, and people usually have their minds made up already. But a comparison of Japan with Austria or Mexico might catch the reader off her guard. [...]

The point being that good comparisons often come from the experience of strangeness and absences.

– Benedict Anderson[1]

The aim of this chapter is to imagine musical modernism as a global phenomenon, beyond the largely unquestioned Eurocentrism of dominant accounts. This undertaking proves both impossible and necessary. Impossible, since such a totalizing claim cannot be fulfilled, and the number of relevant issues, theories, discourses, phenomena and case studies is incalculable. Furthermore, more perhaps than other art forms, modernist music has a knack of hiding the traces of its cultural-geographic particularity behind a universalist façade: it seems to have no place – or, where it does make recourse to 'local colour' or colludes in nationalist discourses, these attempts are often regarded as superficial, inessential or inauthentic. Necessary because that last point speaks to a revealing anxiety: musical modernism is defined as much by what lies outside (literally, in a geographic sense), by what is excluded and by what is repressed as by what is taken for granted and no longer questioned. Its apparent placelessness and universality is one of the most intriguing mysteries surrounding modernist music, one that is in need of interrogation.

Something like this global perspective proposed here was envisioned almost exactly thirty years ago by Bruno Nettl, who argued that '[d]uring the last hundred years, the most significant phenomenon in the global history of music has been the intensive imposition of Western music and musical thought upon the rest of the world.'[2] It is telling that such a vision of a 'global history of music' has taken place within ethnomusicology but not within (historical) musicology, even though, as Nettl points out, Western music is the predominant historical agent. For the most part, musicology remains curiously uninterested in the geographic dissemination and limits of music of Western origin, and its remarkable expansion is rarely considered to be an integral part of its history. There are relatively simple reasons for this lacuna: although there has been no shortage of alternative propositions, the dominant tradition in music historiography has largely depicted Western music history as a succession of genius composers and their masterworks, with primacy accorded to the development of musical style and compositional technique. Furthermore, music historiography is primarily interested in time, not space or cultural geography, an emphasis strengthened by the division between historical musicology and ethnomusicology (and part of my wider effort could be understood as the attempt to link the two or think across their division).[3] Geographical variations were acknowledged – the different national styles of the Baroque or the nationalisms of the late nineteenth and early twentieth centuries come to mind – but they were generally viewed as local differentiations within an overarching general history.

Nettl's idea of a 'global history of music' has its perhaps most influential counterpart in Franco Moretti's concept of 'world literature', which Moretti has contrasted with the traditional concentration on national literatures, arguing that the latter are artificial constructs which obscure the real diffusion of concepts and ideas. In a widely read article in *New Left Review*, for instance, he has analysed common patterns in the adoption of the Western novel in different countries and cultures (primarily Japan, India and Brazil).[4] This 'bird's-eye view' of larger patterns, such as the adoption of forms and genres, necessitates a practice of 'distant reading' which Moretti has pitted against the recent dominance of close reading in literary studies.[5] In similar ways, I will here focus primarily on the subject matter traditionally associated with the social history of music, such as institutions, rather than the criticism and analysis of individual compositions. There are obviously significant differences between literature and music that prevent any direct application of Moretti's ideas to music, chief among them the fact that literature can relatively easily cross borders in translation, whereas, despite claims of it being a 'universal language', music tends to be more integrally linked to its place of origin and is therefore materially foreign in distant places. Nevertheless, Moretti's zeal in emphasizing comparative approaches and commonalities across different cultures, languages, nations and regions and his commensurate critique of the exclusive focus on national traditions is inspiring for musicology, which appears to lurch between universalism and nationalism without a developed method of comparison that recognizes the entanglement of national, regional and global histories, and the conceptual framework he has developed provides a useful starting point.

In contradistinction to literary criticism and many other cognate fields,[6] musicology has yet to fully recognize the global nature of musical modernism, which has long outgrown its origins in the West. It is worth pointing out in this context that the global diffusion of musical modernism does not only concern the binary relation between 'the West and the rest' as it were, but that, prior to (or simultaneously with) its dissemination in Asia, the Middle East and Africa, Western classical music 'conquered' or, more neutrally, 'spread to' or 'was adopted in' Central, Eastern and Northern Europe and the Americas (note too that its diffusion in its supposed heartlands in Central and Western Europe is also uneven, with some areas best considered as semi-peripheries). In other words, the dissemination of Western art music largely mirrored that of Western modernity as a whole, but, as so often, such a sweeping claim obscures the particularities of the process of adoption and adaptation and the specific experiences, ideas and objectives of the agents involved. Modernity is not a monolithic entity, a 'thing', but a complex and not necessarily coherent conglomeration of ideas, institutions and practices, which is rarely adopted wholesale and in one fell swoop, but typically partially and over a significant period of time.

To be sure, there are various national, regional or local histories of music which include music of Western origin, either as an exclusive focus or in relation to other forms of music, but these are not usually considered part of a general history of music. Recent years have also seen a greater interest in cultural geography (broadly conceived) in the study of Western classical music, particularly musical modernism, and the present chapter has to be seen in this context.[7] What is still lacking, however, is a comparative dimension which does not only concern the musical development of a chosen locale in isolation but also the relations between different places, between the centre and the periphery and between different peripheries. As Nettl, among others, has shown, while the adoption or partial adoption of Western music or aspects thereof occurred in specific ways in every country or region, there are also instructive commonalities; moreover, the particularities can only really be seen for what they are in the light of comparisons with other histories. In the second part of this chapter, I will therefore present short case studies exploring the adoption of (previously) Western modernism in different parts of the world: Argentina, Mexico, Finland and Japan – very different places that share one crucial feature: they have all emerged as centres of musical modernism. What I am interested in, then, are the shifting relations between different centres, peripheries and semi-peripheries.

My objective is not only to provide a fuller account of the history of modernism in music by adding the story of its global dissemination and thereby enlarging its coverage with the addition of further composers and pieces, but also to explore the extent to which musical modernism as we (already) know it is at least partly *the result* of this dissemination. In other words, I propose that modernism would not have become what it did without its encounters with others in far-flung corners of the world. It follows that musical modernism is not exclusively Western: it is undoubtedly the product of modernity, but the latter should not be equated with Western culture. In the social sciences, the notion of multiple and different modernities has long been widely accepted and modernity is therefore no longer understood as a uniquely Western achievement or, more neutrally, characteristic.[8] Similarly, it makes sense to understand musical modernism as a feature of modernity more than of Western culture: composers, performers and their audiences do not become Westerners as a result of or precondition for their involvement with musical modernism. By contrast, these practices are more or less unthinkable without the affordances of modernity. Furthermore, although cultural influence in its most manifest forms mostly spread from the (Western) centres to the (non-Western) peripheries, the direction of cultural transfer is not immutable and the former did not remain entirely unaffected. In what follows I will present some theoretical and methodological approaches, before outlining the aforementioned case studies and arriving at a number of tentative conclusions, interpreting the global diffusion of musical modernism in the light of recent thinking in cosmopolitan studies.

Entangled histories: musical modernism, colonialism and postcolonialism

Any study of the global dimension of musical modernism has to contend with the fact that it is inextricably connected with the history of Western hegemony. There are no two ways about it: if it hadn't been for the political, technological, economic, cultural and bluntly military dominance of the West during recent centuries, during the age of empire as much as its continuing aftermath, Western music would not have been adopted so widely (Nettl's use of the word 'imposition' in the above quotation is telling in this regard). Its dissemination has little or nothing to do with its intrinsic qualities and a lot if not everything with its intimate association with power. Colonialism, one of the darkest chapters in the history of the world and perhaps the most symptomatic expression of Western hegemony, is of crucial importance here, although it is not the only context in which Western music impacted on the rest of the world and continues to do so.

Studies of the imposition (and here that word is undoubtedly apposite) of Western music under colonialism have often stressed its intimate association with power, rather than regarding it as an innocent or even beneficial side effect of empire. For example, David Irving's work on colonial Manila, Geoffrey Baker's on colonial Cuzco, Rachel Beckles Willson's on Palestine, Kofi Agawu's on Africa and Nettl's synoptic overview illustrate the extent to which music was deeply implicated in the colonizing project and frequently used as a tool to exert power and control.[9] David Irving has described this process particularly clearly and unflinchingly (although the other studies cited here and many more often contain remarkably similar passages; they are almost a staple of recent ethnomusicological writing):

> [C]onflict between cultures – brought about largely by colonialism – has had a ruinous impact on the musics of the world, causing many traditions to disappear altogether, especially in territories that were conquered by European nations and incorporated into colonial empires. Musical practices played important roles in this conflict, for in the early modern world there was arguably no music that was not constitutive of societies' ideological values and a signifier of deep cultural symbolism. Every act of musical performance was inextricably intertwined with religious or political cultural systems or imbued with expressions of social or ethnic identities. The musics of many non-European peoples (often inseparable from specific ritual practices) declined or were eradicated amidst the imposition of new cultural systems by European colonial empires, for these musics and their associated practices were frequently considered incompatible with or irreconcilable to the cultural frameworks of the hegemonic societies that supplanted the social structures of indigenous populations.
>
> Of course, some early modern European empires actively attempted to incorporate subjugated peoples into their own colonial societies. In many colonies, especially the so-called settlement colonies, sustained intercultural encounters between indigenous populations and European settlers often entailed the imposition of Europe's strict forms and rules on local musics. Through musical display and musical pedagogy, there was a concerted and conceited attempt by dominant ruling groups to effect the integration of subjugated peoples' musical tastes, involving the subtle transformation or outright manipulation of musical styles and aesthetics, made actively or passively in the hope of achieving some form of social cohesion.[10]

Following Edward Said, Irving uses the term 'counterpoint' both literally and figuratively, arguing that '[t]o early modern Europeans, counterpoint represented a means by which sound and society could be rationalized, and in this sense it became a formidable agent of colonialism.'[11]

Irving's description concerns the imposition of Western music during colonization in the early modern period. Needless to say, the experience of countries and regions that remained formally independent is somewhat different, although they were often likewise subject to Western hegemony, including in musical matters. In any case, modernist composition is typically the product of a later stage during the nineteenth and twentieth centuries, often coinciding with decolonization, and it requires a developed infrastructure of orchestras, conservatoires, instrument builders, publishers, broadcasters, record companies and, in some cases, opera houses, some of which became emblems of modern statehood almost on a par with flags, currencies, passports and national museums. The founding of conservatoires provides a particularly good (if partial and incomplete) insight into the diffusion of Western-style music pedagogy (variously dedicated to Western classical music or both Western and indigenous music): Rio de Janeiro (1847), Boston (1853), Mexico City (1866), Tokyo (1879), Havana (1885), Buenos Aires (1893), Melbourne (1895), Stellenbosch (South Africa, 1905), Istanbul (1917), Shanghai (1927), Beirut (1920s), Baghdad (1936), Cairo (1959) etc. (Moretti's predilection for maps seems apt in this

Musical modernism, global

context.)[12] It is also worth pointing out that regional and national cultures of Western classical music do not necessarily follow the European model (which itself is far from monolithic) in every detail. According to Bonnie C. Wade, for example, Japan boasts a very lively culture of choirs, wind bands and domestic piano-playing as well as a number of professional and amateur symphony orchestras, but a comparatively less developed culture of chamber music, at least at professional level.[13]

While this later phase in the adoption in Western music and modernist composition may no longer be the result of direct colonial imposition, it often directly follows on from it, and, even in non-colonized cases, it epitomizes continuing cultural inequality. Furthermore, in most cases, Western art music remains primarily, but not necessarily exclusively or inevitably, associated with the 'Westernized' and urbanized elites. There is, therefore, no cause for triumphalism.

At the same time, however, it would be too simple to denounce Western music as an agent of imperialism and advocate its erasure from all places outside the West. History isn't easily reversible. As Arjun Appadurai has put it, '[f]or the former colony, decolonization is a dialogue with the colonial past, and not a simple dismantling of colonial habits and modes of life'.[14] Furthermore, I cannot deny that I am personally writing from the perspective of a white middle-class male brought up and educated in Germany and Great Britain (although I don't expect or hope that all my readers will share my perspective), and, from this perspective, to ask or expect non-Western people to drop Western music in favour of 'their own' is hardly less evidence of a colonialist mind set than encouraging or forcing them to drop 'their own' music in favour of 'ours'. Millions have invested heavily in this music, have come to love it and empathize deeply with it, whether as composers, musicians or listeners, and who am I to suggest that it is not 'theirs' (when, in some sense, it was often 'we' who first brought it to 'them')? Furthermore, as the above quotation from Appadurai indicates, in many parts of the world the long history of Westernization and hybridization means that there is no pure, authentic indigenous music to go back to, nor a clear dividing line between colonizers and subalterns, imposed Western and indigenous culture, including music.[15] For better or worse, our histories are 'entangled', and our historiography has to reflect this.

The notion of entangled histories emphasizes the relations between different traditions, cultures and areas, and the reciprocity of their impacts on one another; it thus seeks to correct the emphasis on autonomy in traditional historiographies with their focuses on nation, tradition or culture.[16] In a nutshell, I believe that musical modernism has to be recognized as at least in part a product of entangled histories, more than of the autonomous and internal development of the Western classical tradition. From this perspective, the simultaneity of the global diffusion of Western music on one side and of the – however partial or stereotyped – appropriation of non-Western elements by Western composers is not coincidental. They are two sides of the same coin, different results of cultural contact, marked by asymmetrical power relations.

Nor, and this is one of the key messages of this contribution, should we assume that the adoption of Western music is necessarily an act of acquiescence and subservience. In many other fields, postcolonial approaches have shown how the colonizer's tools can be turned against them. To name just two examples, Homi Bhabha has demonstrated how the presumed authority of colonial discourse is undermined from within through mimicry, and John Thieme has analysed how postcolonial authors are 'writing back' by usurping and thereby contesting canonical English texts.[17] Its abstract nature and the legacy of the idea of autonomy mean that Western classical music has rarely been similarly overtly politicized. Nevertheless, there is no reason to take for granted that music of Western origin can only be used in an affirmative manner. Certainly, Irving argues that, in the case of colonial Manila, indigenous people exercised resistance not only by hanging on to their traditional musical practices, but also by actively appropriating those of the colonizers, thereby challenging their supremacy, and Baker makes similar points about Cuzco.[18] In modernism, these kinds of strategies are arguably widespread. For instance, Steven Nuss argues that in his *Essay for String Orchestra* (1963), Toshiro Mayuzumi, one of the most internationally successful Japanese composers of his generation, while eschewing overt reference to Japaneseness and apparently embracing Western modernism, '[through the] consistent use of the [Western] instruments, form-suggestive titles, and conventional ensemble groupings of Western art music [clearly attempted] to take what he saw as the West's insidious (musical) colonialism and flip it on its head'.[19] In the piece, Mayuzumi made reference to the Noh drama *Tsurukame*, which is largely a panegyric of the emperor, which Nuss regards as evidence of a distinctly right-wing perspective:

> *Essay* as recomposed *Tsurukame* is heard [...] not just as an exoticizing piece of deliberate Japaneseness but as a subtle, yet powerful call for emperor worship: a specific political statement meant to call Japan back from the brink of what Mayuzumi and others saw as the abyss of psychological and cultural westernization.[20]

This may be an isolated case and, at least if we follow Nuss's interpretation, admittedly one of very dubious political character, but the political motivations of non-Western composers have rarely been considered (and may more often than not be concealed), so Mayuzumi's strategy of using the musical tools of the West to oppose it may be far from unique.

To illustrate some of the ways in which Western musical modernity took root outside the West, I propose a perhaps counterintuitive analogy: the indigenization of cricket as analysed by Appadurai in the case of India. As he points out, the sport was deeply infused with Victorian values and was introduced to India as a tool of colonization, intended to reinforce hierarchies of race, class and gender and 'as a means for the moral disciplining of Orientals'.[21] In many respects, cricket was and remains Britain's most successful colonial export, more eagerly embraced by subject populations than most other aspects of its culture. But the natives soon challenged the superiority of the colonizers, literally and metaphorically. As Appadurai puts it,

> it is not the case that an Anglophone class drama was simply reproduced in India, but that in the circulation of princes, coaches, army officials, viceroys, college principals, and players of humble class origin between India, England, and Australia a complex imperial class regime was formed, in which Indian and English social class hierarchies were interlinked and cross-hatched to produce, by the 1930s, a cadre of non-elite Indians who felt themselves to be genuine cricketers and genuinely 'Indian' as well.[22]

Although the specifics are significantly different, this process of decolonization and indigenization also took place in other parts of the Empire, notably the Caribbean (the 'West Indies' in cricketing terms). In cricket, the former metropolis has been provincialized. At a time when, as Nicholas Cook has put it, '"Western" music has become a global currency in the same way as the hamburger, and one sometimes has the impression that the "art" tradition flourishes more in East Asia, Israel, and parts of South America than in its former heartlands',[23] is it too fanciful to suggest that Western music too has been indigenized? It, too, may be of Western origin but it does no longer 'belong to' people in Europe and North America; as I suggested above, it is best seen as an aspect of musical modernity, more than Western culture (although we have to give it some sort of name, so the term '*Western* music' is difficult to avoid). Thankfully, music is not primarily a competitive sport (although it often feels like one and there is no shortage of contests), but the long list of first-rate composers, performers and programmes, such as the Venezuelan

Musical modernism, global

music education programme El Sistema,[24] from all over the world demonstrates that the West has long lost its supremacy. Appreciating this means having to relinquish many habits of thought. One of those is the association of musical understanding with profound enculturation: we like to assume that Western classical music is deeply rooted in the culture, intimately connected to other art forms, such as literature and the visual arts, intellectual history, such as philosophy or religion and theology, and that an active awareness of these traditions enriches our appreciation. The fact that millions who may, for example, have a better understanding of calligraphy than the Dutch masters, of Confucius than Kant and Buddhism than the Bible evidently find deep satisfaction, meaning and fulfilment in this music challenges such notions (although it does not entirely invalidate them – just as it does not lend credence to universalism).

Furthermore, the idea of a global musical modernity problematizes notions of 'trans-culturalism' or 'cross-culturalism', which have become normative in discussions of musical modernism outside the West. Note, for instance, how the conceptual framework established by Yayoi Uno Everett in a largely admirable contribution, with its plethora of terms, including 'intercultural synthesis', 'crossover', 'cross-cultural readings', 'fusion', 'cross-fertilization' and 'syncretism' is, apparently despite her intentions to the contrary, predicated on the existence of a gap between two distinct and readily identifiable cultures, which needs to be bridged – and her contribution was evidently intended to be programmatic for the collection which it introduces, and indeed the remaining contributions largely follow her ideas.[25] As so often in these cases, what is meant by 'Western music' (a term encompassing more than a thousand years of historical development, with a similar geographical, generic and stylistic diversity) remains rather diffuse. In most cases discussed by Everett, what we're left with are instruments, the tuning system, institutions such as the orchestra, notation, and the roles of composer, performer and (possibly) conductor. To be sure, these are significant Western innovations exported to East Asia, but they say little about musical style, whereas the other side of the equation tends to be far more stylistically specific (which rather neatly corresponds to Moretti's argument that peripheral literatures tend to combine Western forms with indigenous contents).[26] Considering that these Western institutions and traits were introduced to Japan as long ago as during the Meiji Restoration (1868–1912), do we really have to resort to the idea of 'trans-culturalism' and attendant 'East-meets-West' rhetoric every time a Japanese composer writes a composition for symphony orchestra, an institution that has a longer history in East Asia than in Scandinavia?[27] To be sure, the Western symphony orchestra raises different associations in Japan than the shō or shakuhachi (although for most Japanese the latter two are possibly stranger than the former), but these kinds of asynchronicities and collisions are characteristic of the experience of modernity as such and not unique to intercultural contact or conflict. It is probably true, however, that, as Alejandro L. Madrid argues, at modernity's peripheries these sorts of contradictions are more apparent than at the centres[28] – which is precisely what lends the study of the peripheries such urgency.

What is striking is that, in almost all cases, the adoption of the performance culture of Western classical music, together with the requisite institutional and educational infrastructure, is relatively quickly followed by an embrace of composition, and that, more often than not, notions of modernism assumed some kind of regulative or exemplary function (which does not necessarily mean that it was embraced wholeheartedly and uncritically). We are commonly so accustomed to this fact that we no longer regard it as surprising. Yet there is no compelling reason why composers adopted what they seem to have regarded as an international norm (or at least one norm among the possibilities in circulation). As Madrid puts it, 'achieving modernity became the primary political goal of the elites that dominated peripheral societies, as shown in the variety of policies implemented throughout their histories to stimulate processes of modernization', and this seems to have included modernist composition.[29] How this process of negotiation occurred in different places and contexts has yet to be studied in detail, and it is here that a comparative dimension is particularly useful. As will be illustrated, there appear to be certain patterns, such as the importance of bridge-builders who travel to study at one of the musical centres (in conservatories, with private tutors, at institutions such as the Darmstadt International Summer Courses or festivals) or, conversely, visitors from those centres (facilitating such exchanges has been one of the most widespread and apparently successful methods adopted by national governments to support the arts). The function of international organizations such as the International Society for Contemporary Music (ISCM) should likewise not be underestimated. Despite its flaws and later (relative) decline, the ISCM was an important force in the world of contemporary music, particularly in the 1920s and 1930s, and its annual 'New Music Days' represented a unique forum, specifically for participants from the peripheries (although, as so often, their perspectives are rarely acknowledged in the literature).[30] Another commonality consists of conflicts between nationalist and conservative factions and universalist or internationalist innovators (although the correlations between nationalism and conservatism and universalism and progressive or avant-gardist ideas are by no means a given), which are typically linked to wider debates about cultural politics. In the following, I want to briefly outline key developments in Argentina, Finland and Japan, with some additional observations on Mexico and mainland China.

Case studies: musical modernism in the peripheries?

Argentina

Argentina is often regarded – not least by its inhabitants – as the most European nation in Latin America (which is more than a little affront to its not insignificant populations of indigenous, Asian or African descent). Like Argentina as a whole, its capital Buenos Aires, which dominates the rest of the country culturally, politically and economically, played a comparatively minor role during the colonial period, and its character is more marked by the massive waves of predominantly European immigration during the nineteenth and early twentieth centuries. Nevertheless (or maybe *because* of this), the *criollo* identity (the culture of predominantly rural Hispanic settlers), in particular the gaucho legends based in the pampas, retain a special place in the Argentine imagination. As a result of European immigration, Buenos Aires became a centre of musical life rivalling the North American and European metropoles (Carlos Kleiber, Michael Gielen, Daniel Barenboim and Martha Argerich all hail from the city). Although there were significant precursors, Alberto Williams (1862–1952) is often regarded as the founding father of Argentine classical composition. His training is exemplary for pioneering composers from the peripheries: after his initial education in Buenos Aires, he travelled on a government grant to Paris to study with César Franck. On his return, he took an extended trip to Buenos Aires province (despite its relative proximity to the capital, the centre of the pampas and the gaucho tradition) to study local folk music.[31] In the following, he pioneered a nationalist style, introducing the tunes and in particular the dance rhythms, above all the milonga, associated with the gauchesco tradition into a broadly European Romantic (later neoclassically infused) style. From the 1930s onwards, this tradition was continued primarily by Juan José Castro, who was particularly active as an internationally renowned conductor. He too had spent time in Paris, studying with d'Indy among others, and his work was featured at the ISCM Festival in 1931.[32]

The year 1929 saw the founding of the Grupo Renovación dedicated to promoting modernist composition by Juan José Castro, his brother José Maria Castro, Juan Carlos Paz and others. It was linked to the significant magazine *Sur*, run by the formidable Victoria Ocampo (and among whose contributors counted Jorge Luis Borges) and broadly associated with the political left, a significant point during the 'infamous decade' of military rule and political instability as well as the repercussions of the Spanish Civil War and later WWII, which were strongly felt in Argentina.[33] It later became the Argentine sub-section of the ISCM, and its international links were strengthened by a much-reported visit by Igor Stravinsky in 1936.[34] For his part, Juan Carlos Paz, one of the Grupo's co-founders and another student of d'Indy, pursued a radically different path from 1934 onwards, when he discovered dodecaphony and renounced nationalism and the appropriation of folk music in favour of the international avant-garde, an all but unique position among Latin American composers at the time.[35] In 1937, Paz founded the Conciertos de la Nueva Música, which was later transformed into the Agrupación Nueva Música. Where the Grupo favoured largely neo-classical tendencies, the Agrupación was more devoted to the avant-garde (including but not exclusively serialism). In many ways his counterpart was Alberto Ginastera, who had largely assumed the mantle of the nationalist, neo-classical tradition, and occupied many influential positions until his public opposition to Juan Perón led to his dismissal and eventual departure for the United States. The Argentine new music scene during the early 1950s was polarized between Alberto Ginastera on one side and Paz on the other.[36]

The case of Paz and the Agrupación illustrates the importance of international links: Paz had a wide international network of contacts and his books demonstrate that he was extremely well informed about the latest developments.[37] In addition, the group included Michael Gielen (who would later on pursue a stellar career as a conductor in Germany), who was the nephew of Eduard Steuermann, Schoenberg's favourite pianist, with whom he corresponded regularly. Furthermore, the Brazil-based Hans-Joachim Koellreutter was a frequent guest in Buenos Aires, reporting from his experiences at the Darmstadt International Summer Courses and the Milan Twelve-Tone Congress of 1949 (thereby demonstrating the intersection between global and regional networks). Finally, particular importance has to be attached to the visits by Pierre Boulez, as pianist and music director for the theatre company Renaud-Barrault in 1950 and 1954, mirroring Stravinsky's visit before WWII.[38] What this example demonstrates is both the difficulty of pursuing the idea of a cosmopolitan modernism on the periphery and the paradoxical strengths drawn from this position. Despite the reliance on a relatively small number of contacts and mediators, groups such as the Agrupación were in many ways more international than their counterparts at the centres, since they tended to take a more active interest in what happened around them and in a variety of places (Paz was equally well informed about American experimentalism as European serialism, for instance), and they often felt freer to appropriate what seemed useful to them, rather than feeling a priori beholden to specific traditions.

A new era began with the founding in 1962 of CLAEM (Centro Latinoamericano de Altos Estudios Musicales) under the auspices of the Instituto di Tella, with Ginastera as director.[39] In leading the Centre and inviting guests, Ginastera proved to be far more open and visionary than his own rather narrow and conservative tastes may suggest; in 1964, he also opened an electronic music studio (directed by the Peruvian composer César Bolaño until 1967, by the Argentine Francisco Kröpfl thereafter), despite his own dislike of electronic music.[40] The Centre hosted leading international lights such as Luigi Dallapiccola, Luigi Nono, Iannis Xenakis and Aaron Copland, but it had an even greater impact in bringing together and energizing the (previously quite disparate) Latin American avant-garde. Unfortunately, the Centre was forced to close in 1970 due to the increasing political instability during the so-called Argentine Revolution. Despite continuing political and economic instability, Argentina has developed and maintained a vibrant and mostly fiercely internationalist culture of modernist composition.

Björn Heile

Mexico

Where the musical development in Argentina was affected by political instability with frequent periods of dictatorship and authoritarian rule, Mexico experienced cultural near-paralysis under the long period of one-party rule from 1929 to 2000. The preceding revolution (1910–29) is, however, notable for its direct effect on the arts, including music, in particular for promoting a nationalist style. Although musical nationalism was hardly a new or unique idea, its implication in the revolutionary struggles gave it a particular urgency. More importantly, it received a thorough theoretical foundation through the decisive influence of the philosopher and politician José Vasconcelos, who, in his *The Cosmic Race*, developed the ideas of *indigenismo* and *mestizaje*, which he propagated as minister of education (1921–24) among other positions (his brief tenure belying the towering influence he exerted not only in Mexico but for successive generations of Latin American politicians and intellectuals).[41] These ideas found their most immediate expression in some of the works of Carlos Chávez, arguably the most influential Mexican composer of his (or possibly any other) generation. Where earlier nationalist composers, such as Manuel Ponce, like their counterparts throughout much of Latin America, primarily oriented themselves towards the *criollo* heritage of the Hispanic settlers, in many (although by no means all) of his works Chávez sought to evoke the pre-Conquest Aztec culture.[42] Although a new generation of scholars dispute the common claim that Vasconcelos commissioned Chávez's seminal ballet *El fuego nuevo* (1921), there is little doubt that, at least for a time, Chávez was very close to Vasconcelos and that he was able to exert direct political influence even after Vasconcelos's tenure, which is otherwise almost unheard of in the history of musical modernism.[43] Chávez also stands out in developing far more substantial ties to the United States than to Europe. Although he visited Europe, his impressions were predominantly negative, whereas he repeatedly travelled to New York, where he established particularly close bonds with Edgard Varèse and various relevant associations, including the International Composers' Guild.[44] The most immediate parallel here is to Ginastera, who was likewise influenced by Pan-American ideas but who was more drawn to Copland and his circle than to Varèse. Not unlike their Argentine counterparts, most Mexican composers reacted against nationalism in the 1960s, leading to a mature cosmopolitan culture (dodecaphony had been introduced by Rodolfo Halffter in 1953). A composer such as Julio Estrada, for example, is as much a part of the international new music circuit as of the leading institutions of his native country (as professor at the University of Mexico) and equally at home in advanced computer and mathematical models of music theory as in acting as editor of a ten-volume history of Mexican music.

Finland

To include Finland, one of the most advanced economies in the world and a member of the European Union, in this section may seem counterintuitive. Despite the towering stature of Sibelius, it should not be forgotten, however, that the country joined musical modernity quite late: both the Helsinki Philharmonic Society (the first such orchestra in the Nordic countries) and the Helsinki Music Institute (renamed Sibelius Academy in 1939) were founded in 1882.[45] It is also important to realize that Europe or 'the West' are not monolithic categories and that there is no simple binary between centre and periphery. Despite the heroic efforts of early modernists, such as Aarre Merikanto (1893–1958) during the 1920s and 1930s, Finland remained a musical backwater until at least the 1960s.[46] It is certainly revealing that up to and including international stars, such as Magnus Lindberg, Esa-Pekka Salonen and Kaija Saariaho, most if not all major Finnish composers spent their formative years abroad.

Musical modernism, global

Much of the credit for introducing Finland to musical modernism has to go to Erik Bergman (1911–2006).[47] As was almost mandatory at the time, Bergman's earliest compositions were in a nationalist Romantic style. Clearly unsatisfied, he went to study with Heinz Tiessen in Berlin from 1937 to 1939 and again in 1942–43. That he went to Nazi Germany (at one point at the height of the war!) has to be viewed with some suspicion, although options may have been limited for Finns at the time and Tiessen himself was firmly associated with the political left. In 1952, Bergman started to experiment with dodecaphony, a technique that he apparently did not encounter during his studies in Berlin, but only discovered later, mostly in books rather than actual compositions. He was the first Finnish composer to adopt the technique (the simultaneity with Halffter's work in Mexico is remarkable and only partly coincidental) at a time when the work of the Second Viennese School was completely unknown in Finland – which is a good indication of how isolated the country was. To develop his grasp of twelve-tone technique, he went to Switzerland in 1954 to study with Wladimir Vogel, another student of Tiessen's, and he also visited the Darmstadt International Summer Courses in 1957, following which he (relatively briefly and cautiously) adopted integral serialism, before also embracing aleatory technique. His evident attempt to keep up with the most advanced developments is complemented by a deep interest in non-Western music, which led him on extensive travels across much of the world, during which he acquired a sizeable collection of instruments, some of which he learned to play. The strand of his compositions which adopt aspects and materials from non-Western music, in which he was a pioneer, contrasts and intersects with those exploring Western modernist techniques. Later in his life, he also returned closer to home, turning his attention to his environment, particularly the Arctic: as I have described it elsewhere, it would appear as if the encounter with the other enabled him to see the strangeness of the self through the eyes of the other.[48]

Again not unlike in other parts of the globe, it was during the 1960s that Finland opened up to modernism, encountering both the Second Viennese School and the post-WWII serial avant-garde almost simultaneously, not least due to the mediation of figures such as Bergman. That period was again short-lived, however,[49] and it was not before the 1980s that the famous generation of composers connected with the Korvat Auki (Ears Open) association and linked to the ensemble Avanti!, such as Lindberg, Salonen and Saariaho, firmly established Finland among the leading centres of musical modernism, and they often paid tribute to Bergman for having paved the way – despite the latter's long tenure at the Sibelius Academy, not as a teacher, however: most of the younger composers studied with Paavo Heininen and some with Einojuhani Rautavaara.[50] This was by no means simply a natural process of generational succession, but was accompanied by heated debates. The term composers associated with Ears Open reserved for the operas of the so-called Finnish Opera Boom of the 1970s – 'fur-cap operas' – illustrates the nature of the debate.

It is revealing that Bergman himself never acquired an international reputation on a par with that of his more traditional and nationalist contemporary Rautavaara, just as, in Argentina, Paz's international reception never rivalled that of Ginastera. Although there could be specific reasons or differences in the (perceived or real) inherent quality of the work accounting for the limited international success of modernist composers from the peripheries, it seems likely that their work militates against prevalent stereotyped expectations which associate the other with exoticism (an issue to which I shall return).

Japan

In Japan, music was seen as a prime agent of the desired Westernization during the Meiji Restoration (1868–1912). As a consequence, Western music was introduced in schools, and legions of composers busied themselves writing or simply adapting Western-style children's songs (*shoka*); as in so many other regions, other agents introducing Western music were the military and the Protestant Church. While earlier Japanese composers mostly imitated European Romantic models, Kosaku Yamada (1886–1965), a graduate of the Berlin Hochschule für Musik, was the first to explore modernist techniques. His opposite was Kiyomi Fujii (1899–1944), who collected and studied traditional Japanese music, particularly folk songs, which he emulated in his own compositions, albeit scored for Western instruments. As Judith Ann Herd puts it, Yamada's and Fujii's 'perspectives regarding East and West eventually led to the establishment of the dual factions found in Japanese modern music today'.[51] Although these can be characterized as the opposition between Western modernism and nationalist traditionalism, the relations between these elements were (and are) complex and in flux. The year 1930 saw the founding of the Federation of Newly Rising Composers, which incorporated both nationalist and modernist composers, and which in 1935 became the Japanese section of the ISCM.[52] It is worth noting that the vast majority of nationalists made use of Western instruments or techniques, just as most Western-style modernist composers explored some aspects of their Japanese heritage; needless to say, many changed their positions over time. Witness, for instance, Toshiro Mayuzumi's Pan-Asianism (mentioned before),[53] the various attempts at intercultural fusion in the work of Toru Takemitsu[54] or the engagements with both the international avant-garde and Japanese traditional music undertaken by Toshio Ichiyanagi,[55] to name but some of the most internationally renowned figures. It is telling that both Takemitsu and Ichiyanagi felt emboldened to fully explore their native heritage only on extended travels abroad (in both cases encouraged by John Cage). A similar phenomenon can be observed in the work of Toshio Hosokawa, who only learned to appreciate Japanese traditional music, specifically *gagaku*, the music for the Imperial court, when studying with the Korean exile Isang Yun in Berlin in the late 1970s.[56] Although his work is clearly based on the modernist techniques associated with the German avant-garde, at the level of aesthetics he is inspired by Zen Buddhism, calligraphy and the idea of *ma* (which Wade translates as 'pregnant nothingness').[57]

Differences and similarities

These case studies from very different parts of the world share a number of remarkable similarities. What links the musical pioneers in different countries is that they spent formative years abroad at one of the centres of musical modernism, mostly in France and Germany, although in later years also in the United States. Many of them subsequently worked as bridge-builders and mediators, often introducing their compatriots abroad, while also introducing their home publics to the most recent international developments by inviting leading international composers. The roles played by Takemitsu in Japan and Ginastera in Argentina are exemplary in this regard. A similar point can be made about the importance of Chou Wen-chung for younger Chinese composers, although, due to the continuing censorship and government control of the arts in the People's Republic, Chou had to concentrate his efforts in the United States, where he co-founded the Center for US-China Arts Exchange at Columbia University, which became an important rallying point for the 'New Wave' of composers from China, including Tan Dun.[58] Erik Bergman's work can also be mentioned in this context, even though he was not primarily active as a teacher or organizer and administrator. But not all connections were and are of an exclusively bilateral nature: consider, for example, the roles played by Koellreutter for the new music scene in Argentina (and presumably other Latin American countries) or that of Isang Yun for Japan and other Asian countries. Furthermore, the example of integrating traditional music with modernist techniques provided by Béla Bartók inspired generations of composers

Musical modernism, global

worldwide.[59] Finally, international organizations such as the ISCM and, from 1973, the Asian Composers League and, in a different way, the Darmstadt International Summer Courses, have played an important role in providing forums for the definition of musical modernism on a global scale and for the negotiation between different positions.

Another striking commonality concerns the debates between nationalist and, variously, internationalist, universalist or avant-gardist camps and positions. The latter are often (but not always) identified with serialism, whose dissemination provides an interesting insight into the diffusion of musical modernism more widely (without wishing to fetishize one particular technical development). By contrast, nationalist aesthetics are typically aligned with broadly late Romantic or, in a later phase, neo-classical styles. The irony here is that, while, ideologically, nationalism emphasizes cultural distinctiveness, its expression on the level of musical language tended to be, if anything, more globally diffused and codified than serialism or any other more decidedly advanced and internationalist idioms. It is indeed remarkable how interchangeable nationalist compositions from widely different parts of the globe often appear. The most obvious exception in this instance is Chávez, whose music typically avoids post-Romantic or neo-classical clichés. This is in keeping with a cultural-political discourse that was in many ways more subtle and complex than that of comparable countries and where, in the wake of Vasconcelos's indigenism, the simple identification of nationalism with conservatism does not hold – as is also suggested by Chávez's friendship with Varèse (indicating too that Chávez's work should not be simply equated with nationalism). Broadly speaking, where nationalist positions remained widely dominant during the 1920s and 1930s, from the 1960s onwards internationalist modernism gained footholds in most regions. The pithy position taken by the Brazilian composer Marlos Nobre – 'I am Brazilian; I write music; I do not write Brazilian music'[60] – may well be common at the turn of the twenty-first century, but it would have been a radical view throughout much of the preceding century. While there are significant differences between these debates in various countries and regions which deserve detailed scrutiny, it is clear that a comparative perspective presents a bigger picture and helps to contextualize the specificities in each particular case. The common concentration on individual national or regional histories in isolation cannot explain the significant parallels between them.

Revealingly, however, composers associated with nationalist aesthetics tend to be more successful internationally than their internationalist counterparts. This is apparent from a comparison between Ginastera and Paz in Argentina or Rautavaara and Bergman in Finland. In respect of Japan, Wade has similarly observed that '[d]eliberations on the Japaneseness of this and that music continue – mostly on the part of Western observers', citing Anthony Palmer, who charged Minoru Miki with 'striking out upon the murky waters of hybridization, always of questionable fruitfulness', while praising Takemitsu for 'remain[ing] Japanese' (which, apparently, is self-evidently positive).[61] Lau has made a closely related point about the New Wave of Chinese composers, who he argues are willingly capitalizing on the orientalist expectations harboured by their Western audiences.[62] Finally, Saavedra and Madrid have argued that the widespread identification of Chávez with nationalism is reductive, which similarly suggests an over-enthusiasm among North American and European audiences for exotic elements to the detriment of other aspects.[63] According to Carol A. Hess, this emphasis on difference is, as far as the United States is concerned, a result of Cold War politics and the policy of supporting military dictators in the name of anti-communism.[64] This argument is indeed plausible (if somewhat reductive), although it overlooks the fact that the tendency described is hardly restricted to US-American views of Latin American music but symptomatic of European and North American perceptions of music from the peripheries more widely. There is a clear pattern of exoticist expectations, whereas universalist or avant-gardist conceptions are typically undervalued since they are perceived as mere imitations of trends from the centre and hence as inauthentic or of little interest. There is also a distinct possibility that the admission of modernist composition from the peripheries on equal terms would undermine the primacy of the centre. Bhabha's idea of mimicry, according to which colonialism was based on difference and hence could not allow the possibility that colonial subjects may be fundamentally like the colonizers, is instructive in this regard: the recognition of difference guaranteed by the code of the exotic puts the other in its place.

Elusive reciprocity: has the global diffusion of musical modernism affected its essence?

While there is thus little doubt that the global diffusion of musical modernism had an effect on the peripheries, any reciprocity is more difficult to assess. It is less clear that the peripheries had a similar impact on the centre or that the nature and meaning of musical modernism at the centre changed significantly as a result of its expansion. On one hand, it is hard to believe that the concurrence between the rise of musical modernism and the height of imperialism is entirely coincidental and that modernism remained completely unaffected by colonialist thought and practice to which, as we have seen, it owed its own global dissemination. Fredric Jameson has made a related point about literary modernism, namely that it had a lot more to do with colonialism than is commonly thought; its supposed apolitical character and formalism should be regarded as a response to a lack, created by the invisibility of the economic structures which lay in the colonies.[65] On the other hand, correlation famously does not equal causation, and it is certainly telling that, with the glaring exception of Paris, musical modernism is less concentrated in the centres of empire than its counterparts in literature and the visual arts (London, for instance, is of marginal importance in modernist music, whereas Vienna remained a major centre long after its political decline).

For Moretti, the imbalance between centre and periphery (whereby forms typically travel from the centre to the periphery but very rarely in the opposite direction and hardly ever from one periphery to the other) is expected and reveals little more than the differentials in power and resources.[66] For most postcolonial thought, by contrast, the idea of reciprocity, that, in some form, the experience of empire and its underpinning ideology must affect modernist thinking and its artistic expressions, which we have already observed in Jameson (who can otherwise hardly be connected with postcolonialism), is essential.[67] This line of thought is developed by Edward Said in *Culture & Imperialism*, in which he reveals the extent to which 'processes of imperialism occurred [. . .] by the authority of recognizable cultural formations, by continuing consolidation within education, literature, and the visual and musical arts', concluding that 'imperialism has monopolized the entire system of representation'.[68] Imperialism's all-encompassing and totalizing nature means that it is paradoxically hidden, and Said's achievement in *Culture & Imperialism* is in demonstrating how canonical works of Western (mostly English) literature are subtly informed by its submerged presence. But, significantly, Said's work is equally about the 'response [by subject populations] to Western dominance which culminated in the great movement of decolonization all across the Third World'.[69] In music studies, Said's challenge has been taken up by Erlmann and Irving, who have both emphasized the reciprocity of their work – Erlmann by stressing that South Africa impacts on the West, just as the West influences South Africa; Irving by highlighting the 'contrapuntalism' (a term derived from Said's use of 'counterpoint') between 'the perspectives of both the elite and the subaltern'.[70]

Musical modernism, global

The abstract nature of musical modernism complicates a straightforward adoption of Said's approach. As he has explained:

> narrative is crucial to my argument here, my basic point being that stories are at the heart of what explorers and novelists say about strange regions of the world; they also become the method colonized people use to assert their own identity and the existence of their own history.[71]

Modernist music is not 'about empire' in this sense; nor, to be frank, does it reveal much about the perspective of the subaltern (but its value may lie precisely in complicating the binarism between colonizer and subaltern). It is certainly tempting to argue that the use of non-Western materials in Western composition, from Debussy's gamelan evocations through the *Weltmusik* ideas of the post-war avant-gardes to recent attempts at intercultural fusion, should be seen as the flipside of the global diffusion of Western music. Just how crucial the discovery of non-Western music was for modernist composition is difficult to gauge, since this question quickly leads to counter-factual speculation (e.g. what would Debussy have done, had he not discovered gamelan music?), but the most likely answer is that the impact was much more than superficial (as is sometimes argued) but not nearly as fundamental as the reciprocal effect of the introduction and imposition of Western music around the world. But the asymmetry is of an even more fundamental sort: overwhelmingly, it was not musical modernism from the peripheries that had an impact at the centre but traditional music (or what was thought to be traditional music); to this day, the influence of composers from non-Western countries in the West remains marginal, and is typically restricted to figures who have spent at least part of their career in the West, a situation that almost certainly owes much more to access to resources and publicity than talent or the vibrancy of the musical culture concerned.

A further argument can be made that aspects of the very ideology of modernist music are subtly informed by the cultural logic of imperialism. The idea of progress in the use of materials and techniques, coupled with the very notion of centres of innovation which are 'ahead of' the peripheries, reveals a folding of time into space akin to the 'time-lag' separating the colony from the metropolis as theorized by Bhabha. The (in)famous footnote in Adorno's *Philosophy of New Music*, in which he excludes the 'extra-territorial' music 'from the periphery' ('agrarian regions of Southern Europe') of Janáček and Bartók from the 'developmental tendency of occidental music',[72] fits into this context as does Schoenberg's alleged remark about the discovery of dodecaphony 'ensur[ing] the supremacy of German music for the next hundred years'.[73] Although the explicit link established here between the *Materialstand* (the objective state of the material) and geography or nationality may not necessarily be directly caused by imperialism, empire is its most symptomatic expression, and it may not be too far-fetched to suggest that empire's deep roots in the European imagination have had an effect on most if not all conceptions of place and time, and notions of innovation and historical progress. Despite all these points, it has to be conceded that any argument about the effects of the geographic expansion of musical modernism and colonialism more widely on the nature of modernist music and thought remains currently tentative and that they can probably not be compared to the impact musical modernity had on the peripheries. What *is* certain, however, is that both aspects – the global expansion of musical modernism *and* the impact it had on its nature including at the centre – are important aspects of the history, aesthetics and theory of modernism in music that demand to be investigated.

Björn Heile

Local–global, particular–universal: cosmopolitanism as procedural ethics

How, then, do we reconcile the conflicts between musical nationalists and universalists that are such a characteristic feature of musical modernism in the peripheries (and not only there)? How do we ensure that composers feel empowered to embrace both their local, national or regional heritage and what is or is perceived to be an international language, and how do we guard against a reception predicated on difference and exoticist expectations on one hand or mimicry and inauthenticity on the other? It seems clear to me that, to return to the cases cited above, there is no better reason to demand from Miki that his music should be Japanese than there would be to demand that the music of Brian Ferneyhough should be British, or that of Helmut Lachenmann German. Likewise, Nobre has as much right to claim Western modernism as his own as do Ferneyhough or Lachenmann. In this context, it is worth noting that the reference to a specific local tradition is not necessarily the preserve of non-Western composers: note, for instance, the idea of *lokale Musik* ('local music') in the work of the German composer Walter Zimmermann or similar conceptions in the work of the British composer Michael Finnissy (as in his *English Country Tunes*) or, in a slightly different mode, the American John Luther Adams.[74] These deliberate turns to the small scale, local and particular seem akin to Deleuze and Guattari's idea of a 'minor literature', one that eschews all claims to a dominant position (something Deleuze and Guattari found realized in the work of Franz Kafka, whose writing undermined the function of German as the national language of a powerful empire).[75] These gestures cannot on their own redress the systemic injustices and imbalances between 'the West and the rest' in the world of music or elsewhere, but neither are they irrelevant.

Answering the questions explored in this chapter means recognizing that they are badly phrased: there cannot be a final, conclusive reconciliation between nationalist and universalist positions, nor can we resolve the competing claims between local and global, particular and universal once and for all. But neither do we have to resign ourselves to complete relativism. A way forward (rather than 'the answer') lies in the procedural ethics offered by cosmopolitanism.[76] It is important here to differentiate between the concept of cosmopolitanism as framed in recent debates in the social sciences and humanities and its everyday meaning. Here, cosmopolitanism should be understood as an ethical corrective to the unregulated process of globalization, without falling prey to the siren songs of nationalism.[77] In the words of Anthony Appiah, cosmopolitanism 'begins with the simple idea that in the human community, as in national communities, we need to develop habits of coexistence: conversation in its older meaning, of living together, association'.[78] There are two principles to this: '[o]ne is the idea that we have obligations to others, obligations that stretch beyond those to whom we are related by the ties of kith and kind, or even the more formal ties of a shared citizenship', and 'the other is that we take seriously the value not just of human life but of particular human lives, which means taking an interest in the practices and beliefs that lend them significance'.[79] Cosmopolitan ethics is therefore normative but not foundational; it is about '*developing* habits of coexistence and conversation'; in other words about the *processes* of negotiation and mediation, without dictating or predicting the *outcome* of this process.[80] It is this approach which may enable us to move beyond the unhelpful binarism between nationalist and universalist perspectives. It is necessary here to clear up some common misunderstandings about cosmopolitanism mostly associated with the everyday use of the term, namely that it is essentially Western or that it is primarily associated with privilege and multinational corporations. For instance, James Clifford has argued that 'the project of comparing and translating different travelling cultures need not be class- or ethnocentric', looking, for instance, at the experiences of Pakistani labourers in Gulf countries.[81]

Musical modernism, global

Most significant for our purposes is cosmopolitanism's conflicted stance towards universalism and diversity or relativism. Although Daniel Chernilo, for instance, has defended certain conceptions of universalism from a cosmopolitan perspective (though his heavy qualification should be noted),[82] most cosmopolitan thinkers reject such an association, stressing on the contrary that, in the words of Ulf Hannerz, cosmopolitanism 'includes an aesthetic stance of openness towards divergent cultural experiences, a search for contrasts rather than uniformity', whereas universalism assumes sameness.[83] Likewise, Bhabha has associated cosmopolitanism with Julia Kristeva's notion of a 'right to difference in equality',[84] and Fred Dallmayer has proposed a 'hermeneutics of difference' which would negotiate between Enlightenment and modernist ideas of universalism on one hand and postmodernist and postcolonial notions of identity politics on the other.[85] In a similar way, most proponents are at pains to stress that forming allegiances with distant others does not mean repudiating local ties. Indeed, several commentators have called for 'rooted cosmopolitanism' or, like Bhabha, 'vernacular cosmopolitanism'.[86] Denigrating the local and particular in favour of the distant and universal is therefore not a cosmopolitan position. The cosmopolitan does not make a categorical distinction between local allegiances and those with distant others.

On this basis, Zimmermann's and Finnissy's positions may be more compatible with cosmopolitan principles than radical nationalist or universalist perspectives. What a cosmopolitan approach to global musical modernism is intended to achieve is to do justice to the achievements of all composers and musicians, those from the peripheries and semi-peripheries as much as those from the centres, those more inclined to follow local, national or regional traditions as much as those who are beholden to universalist or internationalist conceptions.

Notes

1 Benedict Anderson, 'Frameworks of Comparison', *London Review of Books*, 21 January 2016, 18.
2 Bruno Nettl, *The Western Impact on World Music: Change, Adaptation, and Survival* (New York: Schirmer Books, 1985), 3.
3 This is hardly the first such attempt; indeed there has been a surge of publications crossing the divide, perhaps the most influential of which is Nicholas Cook, 'We Are All (Ethno)musicologists Now', in *The New (Ethno)musicologies*, ed. Henry Stobart (Lanham, MD, and Plymouth: Scarecrow Press, 2008), 48–70. It is fair to say, however, that overcoming disciplinary boundaries proved harder in practice than in theory.
4 Franco Moretti, 'Conjectures on World Literature', *New Left Review* 1 (2000), 54–68.
5 Franco Moretti, *Distant Reading* (London: Verso, 2013).
6 See also, among others, Peter Brooker and Andrew Thacker, eds., *Geographies of Modernism: Literatures, Cultures, Spaces* (London and New York: Routledge, 2005); Mark A. Wollaeger and Matt Eatough, eds., *The Oxford Handbook of Global Modernisms* (New York and Oxford: Oxford University Press, 2012).
7 This interest has taken a variety of forms and has come from different fields, so the list here is as heterogeneous as it is incomplete: Max Paddison, 'Centres and Margins: Shifting Grounds in the Conceptualization of Modernism', in *Rethinking Musical Modernism*, ed. Dejan Despic and Melita Milin (Belgrade: Serbian Academy of Sciences and Arts, 2008), 65–81; Tamara Levitz (convenor), 'Musicology Beyond Borders?' *Journal of the American Musicological Society* 65, no. 3 (2012), 821–61; Dana Gooley (convenor), 'Cosmopolitanism in the Age of Nationalism, 1848–1914', *Journal of the American Musicological Society* 66, no. 2 (2013), 523–49; Brigid Cohen, *Stefan Wolpe and the Avant-Garde Diaspora* (Cambridge: Cambridge University Press, 2012); Brigid Cohen, 'Limits of National History: Yoko Ono, Stefan Wolpe, and Dilemmas of Cosmopolitanism', *Musical Quarterly* 97, no. 2 (2014), 181–237; Christian Utz, *Komponieren im Kontext der Globalisierung: Perspektiven für eine Musikgeschichte des 20. und 21. Jahrhunderts* (Bielefeld: Transcript Verlag, 2014).
8 See Dilip Parameshwar Gaonkar, ed., *Alternative Modernities* (Durham, NC: Duke University Press, 2001); Arjun Appadurai, *Modernity at Large: Cultural Dimensions of Globalization* (Minneapolis and London: University of Minnesota Press, 1996). These accounts are contested by others, however, most vociferously by Fredric Jameson in his *A Singular Modernity* (New York: Verso, 2002).

Björn Heile

9 See D. R. M. Irving, *Colonial Counterpoint: Music in Early Modern Manila* (New York: Oxford University Press, 2010); Geoffrey Baker, *Imposing Harmony: Music and Society in Colonial Cuzco* (Durham, NC, and London: Duke University Press, 2008); Rachel Beckles Willson, *Orientalism and Musical Mission: Palestine and the West* (Cambridge: Cambridge University Press, 2013); V. Kofi Agawu, *Representing African Music: Postcolonial Notes, Queries, Positions* (New York and London: Routledge, 2003); Nettl, *The Western Impact on World Music*, 7–11.

10 Irving, *Colonial Counterpoint*, 2–3.

11 Ibid., 3. Said's idea of counterpoint is developed in his *Culture & Imperialism* (London: Vintage Books, 1994).

12 Some of these institutions were preceded by similar private, public, military or ecclesiastical music schools or university music departments. 'Conservatory' can be a flexible concept. Astonishingly, there does not appear to be a study of the global diffusion of the conservatory model.

13 Bonnie C. Wade, *Composing Japanese Musical Modernity* (Chicago: University of Chicago Press, 2014), 114–15.

14 Arjun Appadurai, 'Playing with Modernity: The Decolonization of Indian Cricket', in *Modernity at Large: Cultural Dimensions of Globalization* (Minneapolis and London: University of Minnesota Press, 1996), 89.

15 Cf., among others, Baker, *Imposing Harmony*, 5. It is worth pointing out here that there are significant differences in the experience of Western domination in different parts of the world. Postcolonial theory, with its tendency towards binary distinctions between colonizer and subaltern, is dominated by scholars and activists from the Indian sub-continent, Africa and the Middle East. Latin America and East Asia, which were and still are extremely important cultural meeting grounds for the diffusion of music of Western origin, had rather different histories in this respect.

16 On the notion of entangled histories, see Wolf Lepenies, *Entangled Histories and Negotiated Universals: Centers and Peripheries in a Changing World* (Frankfurt: Campus Verlag, 2003); Jorge Cañizares-Esguerra, 'Entangled Histories: Borderland Historiographies in New Clothes?' *American Historical Review* 112, no. 3 (2007), 787–99. A good introduction is provided by Annette Werberger, 'Überlegungen zu einer Literaturgeschichte als Verflechtungsgeschichte', in *Kulturen in Bewegung: Beiträge zur Theorie und Praxis der Transkulturalität* (Bielefeld: Transcript Verlag, 2012), 109–41; an impressive (ethno)musicological example is Veit Erlmann, *Music, Modernity, and the Global Imagination: South Africa and the West* (New York and Oxford: Oxford University Press, 1999).

17 Homi K. Bhabha, *The Location of Culture* (London: Routledge, 1994), 121–31; John Thieme, *Postcolonial Con-Texts: Writing Back to the Canon* (London: Continuum, 2001).

18 Irving, *Colonial Counterpoint*, 3–4; Baker, *Imposing Harmony*, 2.

19 Steven Nuss, 'The Politics of Toshiro Mayuzumi's Essay for String Orchestra', in *Locating East Asia in Western Art Music*, ed. Yayoi Uno Everett and Frederick Lau (Middletown, CT: Wesleyan University Press, 2004), 86–87. Cf. also Wade, *Composing Japanese Musical Modernity*, 115–16.

20 Nuss, 'The Politics of Toshiro Mayuzumi's Essay for String Orchestra', 117.

21 Appadurai, 'Playing with Modernity: The Decolonization of Indian Cricket', 94.

22 Ibid., 96.

23 Nicholas Cook, 'Introduction: Trajectories of Twentieth-Century Music', in *The Cambridge History of Twentieth-Century Music*, ed. Nicholas Cook and Anthony Pople (Cambridge: Cambridge University Press, 2004), 9.

24 El Sistema has recently come under criticism: cf. Geoffrey Baker, *El Sistema: Orchestrating Venezuela's Youth* (New York: Oxford University Press, 2014); Gustavo Borchert, 'Sistema Scotland: A Critical Inquiry into the Implementation of the El Sistema Model in Raploch' (MMus thesis, University of Glasgow, 2012), http://theses.gla.ac.uk/4044. Its merits are not the issue here, though.

25 Yayoi Uno Everett, 'Intercultural Synthesis in Postwar Western Art Music: Historical Contexts, Perspectives, and Taxonomy', in *Locating East Asia in Western Art Music*, ed. Everett and Lau, 1–21.

26 Moretti, 'Conjectures on World Literature', 64–65.

27 It is worth quoting Kofi V. Agawu on the problematic emphasis on origins (in his case focusing on Africa): 'How long will we continue to talk about this or that feature as originating in this or that foreign culture? For example, what sense does it make, after a century and a half of regular, continuous, and imaginative use, to describe the guitar as a "foreign" instrument in Africa, or a church hymn as representing an alien musical language, or a perfect cadence as extrinsic?' (*Representing African Music*, 148). He goes on to point out that the same point would have to be made about Beethoven's Violin Concerto, since the violin is of middle-Eastern, not European origin.

Musical modernism, global

28 Alejandro L. Madrid, *Sounds of the Modern Nation: Music, Culture, and Ideas in Post-Revolutionary Mexico* (Philadelphia: Temple University Press, 2008), 7.

29 Ibid.

30 For the history of the ISCM see Anton Haefeli, *Die Internationale Gesellschaft für Neue Musik* (Zurich: Atlantis-Verlag, 1982). Haefeli has little to say on non-Western members, although the appendices give a clear impression of the organization's reach. Furthermore, his accounts of 'internationalism' (73–87), the ISCM's contested apolitical stance (190–232) and the debates about the meaning of 'contemporary' (262–85) – which, in the organization's German title, is replaced with 'neu' ('new') – are instructive in this regard. Cf. Sarah Collins's contribution to this volume.

31 Gerard Béhague, *Music in Latin America: An Introduction* (Englewood Cliffs, NJ, and London: Prentice-Hall, 1979), 108–10.

32 Susana Salgado, 'Castro', *Grove Music Online, Oxford Music Online*, Oxford University Press, http://www.oxfordmusiconline.com/subscriber/article/grove/music/44159.

33 'Omar Corrado: música culta y política en Argentina entre 1930 y 1945', http://www.latinoamerica-musica.net/historia/corrado/musica1930-45.html (accessed 7 August 2015).

34 Omar Corrado, 'Stravinsky y la constelación ideologica argentina en 1936', *Latin American Music Review* 26, no. 1 (2005), 88–101.

35 Béhague, *Music in Latin America*, 245–46. For more detail on Paz see Omar Corrado, *Vanguardias al sur: la música de Juan Carlos Paz* (Bernal: Universidad Nacional de Quilmes, 2012).

36 Esteban Buch, 'L'avant-garde musicale à Buenos Aires: Paz contra Ginastera', *Circuit: musiques contemporaines* 17, no. 2 (2007), 11–33; Christina Richter-Ibáñez, *Mauricio Kagels Buenos Aires (1946–1957): Kulturpolitik–Künstlernetzwerk–Kompositionen*, 1st ed. (Bielefeld: Transcript Verlag, 2014), 82–83; Pamela Jones, *Alcides Lanza: Portrait of a Composer* (Montreal: McGill-Queen's University Press, 2007), 34–35.

37 Juan Carlos Paz, *Introducción a la música de nuestro tiempo* (Buenos Aires: Editorial Sudamericana, 1971); Juan Carlos Paz, *La música en los Estados Unidos* (México: Fondo de Cultura Económica, 1980); Juan Carlos Paz, *Arnold Schönberg: o, El fin de la era tonal* (Buenos Aires: Editorial Nueva Visión, 1958).

38 See Richter-Ibáñez, *Mauricio Kagels Buenos Aires (1946–1957)*, 93–98 and 155–61 for further details on Pierre Boulez's visits.

39 On CLAEM, see Hernán Gabriel Vázquez, 'Historia, actividad y recepción crítica del CLAEM', in *Catálogo completo del Festival La Música en el Di Tella, Resonancias de la modernidad*, ed. José Luis Castiñeira de Dios (Buenos Aires: Secretaría de Cultura de la Presidencia de la Nación, 2011), 15–22.

40 'Los músicos del Di Tella: una reunión cumbre', *Clarin.com*, http://www.clarin.com/espectaculos/musica/musicos-Di-Tella-reunion-cumbre_0_498550150.html (accessed 6 August 2015).

41 José Vasconcelos, *La raza cósmica: misión de la raza iberoamericana* (Madrid: Aguilar, 1967). See also Ilan Stavans, *José Vasconcelos: The Prophet of Race* (New Brunswick, NJ: Rutgers University Press, 2011).

42 It is worth noting, however, that both Alejandro L. Madrid and in particular Leonora Saavedra go out of their way in arguing that Chávez's work should not be limited to one particular ideology or style, just as the political and aesthetic debates in Mexico at the time were richer than terms such as 'nationalism' or 'indigenism' may imply.

43 According to Madrid, the claim that Vasconcelos commissioned Chávez was made by Roberto García Morillo in his *Carlos Chávez: vida y obra*, 1st ed. (México: Fondo de Cultura Económica, 1960), 19. It is repeated by Robert Parker, 'Chávez, Carlos', *Grove Music Online, Oxford Music Online*, Oxford University Press, http://www.oxfordmusiconline.com/subscriber/article/grove/music/05495. It is disputed by Saavedra in her 'Of Selves and Others: Historiography, Ideology, and the Politics of Modern Mexican Music' (PhD diss., University of Pittsburgh, 2001); see Madrid, *Sounds of the Modern Nation*, 52–53.

44 Leonora Saavedra, 'Carlos Chávez's Polysemic Style: Constructing the National, Seeking the Cosmopolitan', *Journal of the American Musicological Society* 68, no. 1 (2015), 99–150.

45 Kalevi Aho et al., *Finnish Music* (Keuruu: Otava, 1996), 36–37.

46 Tim Howell, *After Sibelius: Studies in Finnish Music* (Aldershot and Burlington, VT: Ashgate, 2006), 29–56.

47 On Bergman, see my 'Erik Bergman, Cosmopolitanism and the Transformation of Musical Geography', in *Transformations of Musical Modernism*, ed. Erling E. Guldbrandsen and Julian Johnson (Cambridge: Cambridge University Press, 2015), 74–96.

48 See ibid.

49 Aho et al., *Finnish Music*, 97–102.

50 Ibid., 138–41.

51 Judith Ann Herd, 'Western-Influenced "Classical" Music in Japan', in *The Ashgate Research Companion to Japanese Music*, ed. Alison Tokita and David W. Hughes (Aldershot and Burlington, VT: Ashgate, 2008), 367.

52 Shigeo Kishibe et al., 'Japan', *Grove Music Online, Oxford Music Online*, Oxford University Press, http://www.oxfordmusiconline.com/subscriber/article/grove/music/43335.

53 Herd, 'Western-Influenced "Classical" Music in Japan', 373.

54 Wade, *Composing Japanese Musical Modernity*, 116–18.

55 Yayoi Uno Everett, *Toshi Ichiyanagi*, Oxford Bibliographies: Music (New York: Oxford University Press, 2013).

56 Basil Rogger, ed., 'Roche Commissions 2010: Toshio Hosokawa', 45, http://www.roche.com/roche-commissions_10_toshiohosokawa.pdf (accessed 10 August 2015).

57 'Interview with Toshio Hosokawa', *Revista Sonograma Magazine*, http://sonograma.org/2011/01/interview-with-toshio-hosokawa/ (accessed 9 August 2015); Yoko Narazaki, 'Hosokawa, Toshio', *Grove Music Online, Oxford Music Online*, Oxford University Press, http://www.oxfordmusiconline.com/subscriber/article/grove/music/49743. Wade associates *ma* with Takemitsu's early work; see her *Composing Japanese Musical Modernity*, 116.

58 Chou Wen-chung, 'Wenren and Culture', in *Locating East Asia in Western Art Music*, ed. Everett and Lau, 209–20; Frederick Lau, 'Fusion or Fission: The Paradox and Politics of Contemporary Chinese Avant-Garde Music', in *Locating East Asia*, 22–39. A brief note about conventions for Japanese and Chinese names: in this chapter, Japanese names are given with given names before the family name and Chinese names with the family name first. The composers mentioned in this chapter are primarily known in English by the names adopted here, and it would unnecessarily confuse readers to adopt different conventions.

59 Yayoi Uno Everett and Frederick Lau, eds., *Locating East Asia in Western Art Music* (Middletown, CT: Wesleyan University Press, 2004), xx, 32, 130, 210; Wade, *Composing Japanese Musical Modernity*, 39, 11, 189, 198.

60 Quoted in Malena Kuss, ed., *Music in Latin America and the Caribbean: An Encyclopedic History* (Austin: University of Texas Press, 2004), xii.

61 Wade, *Composing Japanese Musical Modernity*, 135–36.

62 Lau, 'Fusion or Fission'.

63 Madrid, *Sounds of the Modern Nation*; Saavedra, 'Carlos Chávez's Polysemic Style'.

64 Carol A. Hess, *Representing the Good Neighbor: Music, Difference, and the Pan American Dream* (New York: Oxford University Press, 2013). Gerard Béhague's influential work, cited repeatedly in this contribution, could be seen as an example of the tendency Hess describes. Béhague makes nationalism the central focus and organizing rationale of his work, in ways that seem not wholly dictated by the subject matter (Béhague, *Music in Latin America*, x).

65 Fredric Jameson, *Modernism and Imperialism* (Derry: Field Day Theatre Company, 1988).

66 Moretti, *Distant Reading*, 111–14.

67 These two positions are not necessarily contradictory but mostly incompatible. They operate largely on different planes.

68 Said, *Culture & Imperialism*, 12 and 25.

69 Ibid., xii.

70 Erlmann, *Music, Modernity, and the Global Imagination*; Irving, *Colonial Counterpoint*, 7.

71 Said, *Culture & Imperialism*, xiii.

72 Theodor W. Adorno, *Philosophy of New Music* (Minneapolis and London: University of Minnesota Press, 2006), 176.

73 Schoenberg's remark has been handed down by Josef Rufer and its authenticity has to be questioned. Whether the association between stylistic innovation and national supremacy is Schoenberg's or Rufer's, it is certainly not uncharacteristic of the time. It is quoted in Hans H. Stuckenschmidt, *Arnold Schoenberg* (New York: Schirmer, 1978), 277.

74 For Zimmermann's idea of *lokale Musik*, see his 'Lokale Musik', in *Insel Musik* (Cologne: Beginner Press, 1981), 203–12, http://home.snafu.de/walterz/biblio/lokale_musik.pdf, and 'Nische oder das Lokale ist das Universale', in *Weltmusik*, ed. Peter Ausländer and Johannes Fritsch (Cologne: Feedback Studio Verlag, 1981), 127–51, http://home.snafu.de/walterz/biblio/nische.pdf; Ian Pace and Michael Finnissy, 'Interview between Ian Pace and Michael Finnissy on English Country Tunes, February 2009', *Notations* 1 (2009), 13–16, https://ianpace.wordpress.com/2014/12/03/interview-between-ian-pace-and-michael-finnissy-on-english-country-tunes-february-2009/. The difference in John Luther Adams's

Musical modernism, global

case is that his music is more concerned with the nature and geography of a specific area, more than its music or culture, but what unites the approaches is their emphasis on place.

75 Gilles Deleuze and Félix Guattari, *Kafka: Toward a Minor Literature* (Minneapolis and Oxford: University of Minnesota Press, 1986).

76 Parts of the following section have already appeared in my 'Erik Bergman, Cosmopolitanism and the Transformation of Musical Geography'. It will be apparent, however, that the context in the present chapter is quite different. The two publications are in many ways complementary, the earlier one on Erik Bergman focusing on a concrete example, the present on a general account. The emphasis on critical cosmopolitanism provides the glue connecting the two.

77 Gerard Delanty, 'The Idea of Critical Cosmopolitanism', in *Routledge Handbook of Cosmopolitan Studies*, ed. Gerard Delanty (Abingdon: Routledge, 2012), 38–46.

78 Anthony Appiah, *Cosmopolitanism: Ethics in a World of Strangers*, 1st ed. (New York: W. W. Norton, 2006), xix.

79 Ibid., xv.

80 On proceduralism in cosmopolitan ethics see Gerard Delanty, *The Cosmopolitan Imagination: The Renewal of Critical Social Theory* (Cambridge: Cambridge University Press, 2009), 96–98; James D. Ingram, *Radical Cosmopolitics: The Ethics and Politics of Democratic Universalism* (New York: Columbia University Press, 2013), 84–102.

81 Quoted in Pnina Werbner, 'Anthropology and the New Ethical Cosmopolitanism', in *Routledge Handbook of Cosmopolitan Studies* (Abingdon: Routledge, 2012), 156. See also Carol Appadurai Breckenridge, Sheldon Pollock, Homi K. Bhabha and Dipesh Chakrabarty, eds., *Cosmopolitanism* (Durham, NC, and London: Duke University Press, 2002); Fuyuki Kurasawa, 'A Cosmopolitanism from Below: Alternative Globalization and the Creation of a Solidarity without Bounds', *European Journal of Sociology/Archives Européennes de Sociologie* 45, no. 2 (2004), 233–55; Pnina Werbner, 'Global Pathways: Working Class Cosmopolitans and the Creation of Transnational Ethnic Worlds', *Social Anthropology* 7, no. 1 (1999), 17–35.

82 Daniel Chernilo, 'Cosmopolitanism and the Question of Universalism', in *Routledge Handbook of Cosmopolitan Studies*, ed. Gerard Delanty (Abingdon: Routledge, 2012), 47–59.

83 Ulf Hannerz, 'Cosmopolitans and Locals in World Culture', *Theory, Culture & Society* 7, no. 2 (1990), 237–51.

84 Bhabha, *The Location of Culture*, xvii.

85 Fred Reinhard Dallmayr, *Beyond Orientalism: Essays on Cross-Cultural Encounter* (Albany, NY: SUNY Press, 1996), xi.

86 Werbner, 'Anthropology and the New Ethical Cosmopolitanism'; Homi K. Bhabha, 'Unsatisfied: Notes on Vernacular Cosmopolitanism', in *Text and Nation*, ed. Laura Garcia-Morena and Peter C. Pfeifer (London: Camden House, 1996), 191–207.

Bibliography

Adorno, Theodor W. *Philosophy of New Music.* Translated by Robert Hullot-Kentor. Minneapolis and London: University of Minnesota Press, 2006.

Agawu, V. Kofi. *Representing African Music: Postcolonial Notes, Queries, Positions.* New York and London: Routledge, 2003.

Aho, Kalevi, Pekka Jalkanen, Erkki Salmenhara and Keijo Virtamo. *Finnish Music.* Keuruu: Otava, 1996.

Anderson, Benedict. 'Frameworks of Comparison'. *London Review of Books*, 21 January 2016.

Appadurai, Arjun. *Modernity at Large: Cultural Dimensions of Globalization.* Minneapolis and London: University of Minnesota Press, 1996.

———. 'Playing with Modernity: The Decolonization of Indian Cricket'. In *Modernity at Large*, 89–113.

Appiah, Anthony. *Cosmopolitanism: Ethics in a World of Strangers*. 1st ed. New York: W. W. Norton, 2006.

Baker, Geoffrey. *Imposing Harmony: Music and Society in Colonial Cuzco.* Durham, NC, and London: Duke University Press, 2008.

———. *El Sistema: Orchestrating Venezuela's Youth.* New York: Oxford University Press, 2014.

Beckles Willson, Rachel. *Orientalism and Musical Mission: Palestine and the West.* Cambridge: Cambridge University Press, 2013.

Béhague, Gerard. *Music in Latin America: An Introduction.* Englewood Cliffs, NJ, and London: Prentice-Hall, 1979.

Bhabha, Homi K. *The Location of Culture.* London: Routledge, 1994.

Björn Heile

————. 'Unsatisfied: Notes on Vernacular Cosmopolitanism'. In *Text and Nation*, edited by Laura Garcia-Morena and Peter C. Pfeifer, 191–207. London: Camden House, 1996.

Borchert, Gustavo. 'Sistema Scotland: A Critical Inquiry into the Implementation of the El Sistema Model in Raploch'. MMus thesis, University of Glasgow, 2012. http://theses.gla.ac.uk/4044.

Breckenridge, Carol Appadurai, Sheldon Pollock, Homi K. Bhabha and Dipesh Chakrabarty, eds. *Cosmopolitanism*. Durham, NC, and London: Duke University Press, 2002.

Brooker, Peter, and Andrew Thacker, eds. *Geographies of Modernism: Literatures, Cultures, Spaces*. London and New York: Routledge, 2005.

Buch, Esteban. 'L'avant-garde musicale à Buenos Aires: Paz contra Ginastera'. *Circuit: musiques contemporaines* 17, no. 2 (2007): 11–33.

Cañizares-Esguerra, Jorge. 'Entangled Histories: Borderland Historiographies in New Clothes?' *American Historical Review* 112, no. 3 (2007): 787–99.

Chernilo, Daniel. 'Cosmopolitanism and the Question of Universalism'. In *Routledge Handbook of Cosmopolitan Studies*, edited by Gerard Delanty, 47–59. Abingdon: Routledge, 2012.

Chou Wen-chung. 'Wenren and Culture'. In *Locating East Asia in Western Art Music*, edited by Everett and Lau, 209–20.

Cohen, Brigid. *Stefan Wolpe and the Avant-Garde Diaspora*. Cambridge: Cambridge University Press, 2012.

————. 'Limits of National History: Yoko Ono, Stefan Wolpe, and Dilemmas of Cosmopolitanism'. *Musical Quarterly* 97, no. 2 (2014): 181–237.

Cook, Nicholas. 'Introduction: Trajectories of Twentieth-Century Music'. In *The Cambridge History of Twentieth-Century Music*, edited by Nicholas Cook and Anthony Pople, 1–17. Cambridge: Cambridge University Press, 2004.

————. 'We Are All (Ethno)Musicologists Now'. In *The New (Ethno)Musicologies*, edited by Henry Stobart, 48–70. Lanham, MD, and Plymouth: Scarecrow Press, 2008.

Corrado, Omar. 'Stravinsky y la constelación ideologica argentina en 1936'. *Latin American Music Review* 26, no. 1 (2005): 88–101.

————. *Vanguardias al sur: la música de Juan Carlos Paz*. Bernal: Universidad Nacional de Quilmes, 2012.

Dallmayr, Fred Reinhard. *Beyond Orientalism: Essays on Cross-Cultural Encounter*. Albany, NY: SUNY Press, 1996.

Delanty, Gerard. *The Cosmopolitan Imagination: The Renewal of Critical Social Theory*. Cambridge: Cambridge University Press, 2009.

————. 'The Idea of Critical Cosmopolitanism'. In *Routledge Handbook of Cosmopolitan Studies*, edited by Gerard Delanty, 38–46. Abingdon: Routledge, 2012.

Deleuze, Gilles, and Félix Guattari. *Kafka: Toward a Minor Literature*. Minneapolis and Oxford: University of Minnesota Press, 1986.

Erlmann, Veit. *Music, Modernity, and the Global Imagination: South Africa and the West*. New York and Oxford: Oxford University Press, 1999.

Everett, Yayoi Uno. 'Intercultural Synthesis in Postwar Western Art Music: Historical Contexts, Perspectives, and Taxonomy'. In *Locating East Asia in Western Art Music*, edited by Everett and Lau, 1–21.

————. *Toshi Ichiyanagi*. Oxford Bibliographies: Music. New York: Oxford University Press, 2013.

Everett, Yayoi Uno, and Frederick Lau, eds. *Locating East Asia in Western Art Music*. Middletown, CT: Wesleyan University Press, 2004.

Gaonkar, Dilip Parameshwar, ed. *Alternative Modernities*. Durham, NC: Duke University Press, 2001.

García Morillo, Roberto. *Carlos Chávez: vida y obra*. 1st ed. México: Fondo de Cultura Económica, 1960.

Gooley, Dana, convenor. 'Cosmopolitanism in the Age of Nationalism, 1848–1914'. *Journal of the American Musicological Society* 66, no. 2 (2013): 523–49.

Haefeli, Anton. *Die Internationale Gesellschaft für Neue Musik*. Zurich: Atlantis-Verlag, 1982.

Hannerz, Ulf. 'Cosmopolitans and Locals in World Culture'. *Theory, Culture & Society* 7, no. 2 (1990): 237–51.

Heile, Björn. 'Erik Bergman, Cosmopolitanism and the Transformation of Musical Geography'. In *Transformations of Musical Modernism*, edited by Erling E. Guldbrandsen and Julian Johnson, 74–96. Cambridge: Cambridge University Press, 2015.

Herd, Judith Ann. 'Western-Influenced "Classical" Music in Japan'. In *The Ashgate Research Companion to Japanese Music*, edited by Alison Tokita and David W. Hughes, 363–81. Aldershot and Burlington, VT: Ashgate, 2008.

Hess, Carol A. *Representing the Good Neighbor: Music, Difference, and the Pan American Dream*. New York: Oxford University Press, 2013.

Musical modernism, global

Howell, Tim. *After Sibelius: Studies in Finnish Music.* Aldershot and Burlington, VT: Ashgate, 2006.

Ingram, James D. *Radical Cosmopolitics: The Ethics and Politics of Democratic Universalism.* New York: Columbia University Press, 2013.

'Interview with Toshio Hosokawa'. *Revista Sonograma Magazine.* http://sonograma.org/2011/01/interview-with-toshio-hosokawa/ (accessed 9 August 2015).

Irving, D. R. M. *Colonial Counterpoint: Music in Early Modern Manila.* New York: Oxford University Press, 2010.

Jameson, Fredric. *Modernism and Imperialism.* Derry: Field Day Theatre Company, 1988.

———. *A Singular Modernity.* New York: Verso, 2002.

Jones, Pamela. *Alcides Lanza: Portrait of a Composer.* Montreal: McGill-Queen's University Press, 2007.

Kishibe, Shigeo, David W. Hughes, Hugh de Ferranti, W. Adriaansz, Robin Thompson, Charles Rowe, Donald P. Berger, et al. 'Japan'. *Grove Music Online. Oxford Music Online.* Oxford University Press. http://www.oxfordmusiconline.com/subscriber/article/grove/music/43335.

Kurasawa, Fuyuki. 'A Cosmopolitanism from Below: Alternative Globalization and the Creation of a Solidarity without Bounds'. *European Journal of Sociology/Archives Européennes de Sociologie* 45, no. 2 (2004): 233–55.

Kuss, Malena, ed. *Music in Latin America and the Caribbean: An Encyclopedic History.* Austin: University of Texas Press, 2004.

Lau, Frederick. 'Fusion or Fission: The Paradox and Politics of Contemporary Chinese Avant-Garde Music'. In *Locating East Asia in Western Art Music,* edited by Everett and Lau, 22–39.

Lepenies, Wolf, ed. *Entangled Histories and Negotiated Universals: Centers and Peripheries in a Changing World.* Frankfurt: Campus Verlag, 2003.

Levitz, Tamara, convenor. 'Musicology Beyond Borders?' *Journal of the American Musicological Society* 65, no. 3 (2012): 821–61.

'Los músicos del Di Tella: una reunión cumbre'. *Clarin. Com.* http://www.clarin.com/espectaculos/musica/musicos-Di-Tella-reunion-cumbre_0_498550150.html (accessed 6 August 2015).

Madrid, Alejandro L. *Sounds of the Modern Nation: Music, Culture, and Ideas in Post-Revolutionary Mexico.* Philadelphia, PA: Temple University Press, 2008.

Moretti, Franco. 'Conjectures on World Literature'. *New Left Review* 1 (2000): 54–68.

———. *Distant Reading.* London: Verso, 2013.

Narazaki, Yoko. 'Hosokawa, Toshio'. *Grove Music Online. Oxford Music Online.* Oxford University Press. http://www.oxfordmusiconline.com/subscriber/article/grove/music/49743

Nettl, Bruno. *The Western Impact on World Music: Change, Adaptation, and Survival.* New York: Schirmer Books, 1985.

Nuss, Steven. 'The Politics of Toshiro Mayuzumi's Essay for String Orchestra'. In *Locating East Asia in Western Art Music,* edited by Everett and Lau, 85–118.

'Omar Corrado: Música culta y política en Argentina entre 1930 y 1945'. http://www.latinoamerica-musica.net/historia/corrado/musica1930-45.html (accessed 7 August 2015).

Pace, Ian, and Michael Finnissy. 'Interview between Ian Pace and Michael Finnissy on English Country Tunes, February 2009'. *Notations* 1 (2009): 13–16.

Paddison, Max. 'Centres and Margins: Shifting Grounds in the Conceptualization of Modernism'. In *Rethinking Musical Modernism,* edited by Dejan Despic and Melita Milin, 65–81. Belgrade: Serbian Academy of Sciences and Arts, 2008.

Parker, Robert. 'Chávez, Carlos'. *Grove Music Online. Oxford Music Online.* Oxford University Press. http://www.oxfordmusiconline.com/subscriber/article/grove/music/05495.

Paz, Juan Carlos. *Arnold Schönberg: o, El fin de la era tonal.* Buenos Aires: Editorial Nueva Visión, 1958.

———. *Introducción a la música de nuestro tiempo.* Buenos Aires: Editorial Sudamericana, 1971.

———. *La música en los Estados Unidos.* México: Fondo de Cultura Económica, 1980.

Richter-Ibáñez, Christina. *Mauricio Kagels Buenos Aires (1946–1957): Kulturpolitik – Künstlernetzwerk – Kompositionen.* 1st ed. Bielefeld: Transcript Verlag, 2014.

Rogger, Basil, ed. 'Roche Commissions 2010: Toshio Hosokawa'. http://www.roche.com/rochecommissions_10_toshiohosokawa.pdf (accessed 10 August 2015).

Saavedra, Leonora. 'Of Selves and Others: Historiography, Ideology, and the Politics of Modern Mexican Music'. PhD diss., University of Pittsburgh, 2001.

———. 'Carlos Chávez's Polysemic Style: Constructing the National, Seeking the Cosmopolitan'. *Journal of the American Musicological Society* 68, no. 1 (2015): 99–150.

Said, Edward W. *Culture & Imperialism.* London: Vintage Books, 1994.

Salgado, Susana. 'Castro'. *Grove Music Online. Oxford Music Online*. Oxford University Press. http://www.oxfordmusiconline.com/subscriber/article/grove/music/44159.

Stavans, Ilan. *José Vasconcelos: The Prophet of Race*. New Brunswick, NJ: Rutgers University Press, 2011.

Stuckenschmidt, Hans H. *Arnold Schoenberg*. New York: Schirmer, 1978.

Thieme, John. *Postcolonial Con-Texts: Writing Back to the Canon*. London: Continuum, 2001.

Utz, Christian. *Komponieren im Kontext der Globalisierung: Perspektiven für eine Musikgeschichte des 20. und 21. Jahrhunderts*. Bielefeld: Transcript Verlag, 2014.

Vasconcelos, José. *La raza cósmica: misión de la raza iberoamericana*. Madrid: Aguilar, 1967.

Vázquez, Hernán Gabriel. 'Historia, actividad y recepción crítica del CLAEM'. In *Catálogo completo del Festival La Música en el Di Tella, resonancias de la modernidad*, edited by José Luis Castiñeira de Dios, 15–22. Buenos Aires: Secretaría de Cultura de la Presidencia de la Nación, 2011.

Wade, Bonnie C. *Composing Japanese Musical Modernity*. Chicago: University of Chicago Press, 2014.

Werberger, Annette. 'Überlegungen zu einer Literaturgeschichte als Verflechtungsgeschichte'. In *Kulturen in Bewegung: Beiträge zur Theorie und Praxis der Transkulturalität*, 109–41. Bielefeld: Transcript Verlag, 2012.

Werbner, Pnina. 'Global Pathways: Working Class Cosmopolitans and the Creation of Transnational Ethnic Worlds'. *Social Anthropology* 7, no. 1 (1999): 17–35.

———. 'Anthropology and the New Ethical Cosmopolitanism'. In *Routledge Handbook of Cosmopolitan Studies*, 153–65. Abingdon: Routledge, 2012.

Wollaeger, Mark A., and Matt Eatough, eds. *The Oxford Handbook of Global Modernisms*. New York and Oxford: Oxford University Press, 2012.

Zimmermann, Walter. 'Lokale Musik'. In *Insel Musik*, 203–12. Cologne: Beginner Press, 1981. http://home.snafu.de/walterz/biblio/lokale_musik.pdf.

———. 'Nische oder das Lokale ist das Universale'. In *Weltmusik*, edited by Peter Ausländer and Johannes Fritsch, 127–51. Cologne: Feedback Studio Verlag, 1981. http://home.snafu.de/walterz/biblio/nische.pdf.

8

MUSICAL MODERNISM AND EXILE

Cliché as hermeneutic tool

Eva Moreda Rodríguez

Exile and musical modernism have at least this in common: generalizations, stereotypes and clichés about them abound. This is not entirely surprising: they are both complex, multifarious phenomena, and they are also two of the most influential forces to have shaped twentieth-century music. It is therefore understandable that they arouse fascination and stimulate commentators to make sense of them. To that end, stereotypes, clichés and generalizations can sometimes appear helpful. They almost invariably contain a grain of truth and yet at the same time remain general enough to sustain the illusion that they can help us make sense, once and for all, of phenomena such as exile and/or musical modernism. When dealing with most clichés and generalizations, it is easy to come up with a name, a musical work or a fragment of writing that can be cited to prove the point. Of course, in most cases it is equally easy to come up with other examples to refute that same point, or turn it on its head.

Let us look at some of these clichés and assess the extent to which they allow us to make sense of the concepts at issue. Where exile is concerned, we might find it portrayed as a rift, or as a gateway to hitherto unthinkable opportunities (another property of clichés is that they sometimes contradict each other). Exile, we are told, is always transformative. Exile and its associated financial and administrative complications force musicians to take on work they would never had accepted otherwise, which makes such work unrepresentative of the musician's creative voice. Exile leaves one living in two places at the same time. The footsteps of exile are always present in the exile's music; everything the exile does must be regarded through the lens of displacement.

Musical modernism likewise comes with its own set of generalizations and clichés. We may have heard, for example, that musical modernism is predominantly white, male and middle class; that musical modernism is all about the autonomy of the work (preferably the concert work). Musical modernism neglects the popular, the amateur, the easily accessible. Musical modernism is elitist. The preferred language of expression in musical modernism is the twelve-tone row and serialism – that is, the most inaccessible, least ingratiating of all possible languages. There is also a third set of clichés concerning the intersection of modernism and exile, albeit one perhaps more prominent in literary than in musical modernism: many mid- to late twentieth-century accounts of literary modernism have focused heavily on displacement, among them such first-hand memoirs as Ernest Hemingway's symptomatically titled *A Moveable Feast*.[1]

Even if most, if not all, of these clichés contain an element of truth, they work pervasively to shape our thinking and smooth out the complexities – the detail – in a landscape which is, by definition, enormously complex and full of nuance. Clichés and generalizations typecast individuals and musical works: for example, writing about Kurt Weill, Stephen Hinton has pointed out that narratives of Weill's success and fulfilment in the United States pretty much regard him as a collection of typologies rather than an individual (a German Weill with a particular set of characteristics versus an American Weill with a different set of characteristics). Such typecasting, in Hinton's opinion, prevents us from truly making sense of Weill's career and music, because 'typecasting appears to preclude change and development, and Weill clearly did change and develop'.[2] Similarly, Michael Beckerman has warned about the dangers of applying pre-established categories with inadequate critical scrutiny: the category 'composers in exile', for example, can predispose us to expect certain behaviours in exiled composers that are at odds either with the historical reality or the ways in which exiled composers perceived the dynamics they inhabited.[3]

Scholars of musical modernism and of music and exile have already gone a long way towards debunking the clichés and generalizations surrounding both phenomena, sometimes separately, sometimes in association. Nevertheless, either because they contain a grain of truth, or perhaps because they somehow promise to make sense of modernism and exile – in finding common ground between them, or a master narrative that could encompass them both – such clichés and generalizations remain operative, at times in subtle ways. One example concerns the Spanish Republican exile during and shortly after the Spanish Civil War (1936–39), which included a number of composers committed to renewing Spanish music during the 1920s and the mid-to-late 1930s. During their displacement in a variety of European and Latin American countries, some of these exiled composers turned to writing music for the screen. Julián Bautista arrived in Argentina in 1940 and soon found himself receiving numerous commissions from the local film industry. Rodolfo Halffter, in Mexico, collaborated with another prominent Spanish exile, Luis Buñuel, in *Los olvidados* and *Nazarín*. In Cambridge, Roberto Gerhard wrote the music for the feature film *This Sporting Life*, and received further commissions of incidental music for the Royal Shakespeare Company and other British institutions. Nevertheless, Spanish musicology has hardly engaged with such music. A reason for this may be that Spanish-language studies of music and the moving image have only started to develop relatively recently in comparison with equivalent studies in the English language. Nevertheless, here too there may be certain clichés, generalizations and prejudices at work: namely, the dichotomy between 'high-brow' or serious modernist work and 'low-brow' or commercial commitments that the exiles were, somehow unbecomingly, forced to accept.[4]

This chapter aims to contribute to the ongoing questioning and debate that surrounds the intersection between musical modernism and exile, and to ask how we can make sense of both these phenomena and draw general conclusions while preserving nuance and detail. Indeed, to say that, faced with two contradictory clichés, the answer lies somewhere in the middle would be a cliché in itself – for example, if we were to say that exile is neither an absolute tragedy nor a gateway to new opportunities but something in between. It is my contention that examining clichés of exile through the lens of musical modernism, and vice versa, can help articulate a response to them that is more nuanced than 'meeting in the middle' and more conducive to a context-sensitive understanding of people, musical works and music-making. I shall examine three clichés (one relating to exile, the other two relating to musical modernism), provide examples and counterexamples relating to all three, and discuss whether we can reuse or qualify the cliché in some way to make sense of the multiplicity of issues raised by both modernism and exile.

Cliché no. 1: the discontinuity of exile

Edward Said famously described exile as an 'unhealable rift'.[5] His is but one of the many definitions of and perspectives on exile which focus on the fragmentation and discontinuity that it allegedly brings. As Leon Botstein has pointed out, scholarship on victims of exile 'has emphasized [. . .] the varying trajectories of their careers, the disappearance of careers, and the emergence of new careers'.[6] Underlying such approaches is the notion that exile breaches a continuity or congruity of some sort, and that such a break can produce one of two distinct outcomes: it can lead to a sense of loss, with the exile being unable to recover from the impact of leaving his or her past life behind; or it can lead to the opening up of multiple employment and creative opportunities which the exile laps up eagerly.[7]

On a general level, it seems right – even obvious – to assume that exile is likely to have a major impact on those affected by it. But to put exile in the centre can sometimes act as a barrier to a nuanced and critical understanding of an exile's biography and oeuvre. Andrea Bohlman and Florian Scheding have pointed out that the successive displacements of Hanns Eisler have 'fashioned, obscured and faded his portrait as a composer', because the succession of places in which he lived are used as anchors both to narrate the composer's biography and to make sense of his music. In a way, Bohlman and Scheding argue, we tend to understand Eisler as a succession of Eislers: the Austrian Eisler, the American Eisler, the GDR Eisler.[8] Diachronic approaches, they point out, are ignored.

Although it has been less prominent in migration studies than exile from Nazi Germany, the Spanish Republican exile presents similar problems to scholars. A case comparable to Eisler's is that of Salvador Bacarisse, a composer born in Madrid in 1898. Bacarisse, a socialist, had served as vice-president of the Consejo Central de la Música (Central Music Council) of the Spanish Republican government during the Spanish Civil War and was hence forced into exile in France when the war ended in 1939. While in France, thanks to his friendships with Spanish performers, Bacarisse had works performed in Francoist Spain as early as the 1950s, and towards the end of the decade his name started to be mentioned in histories of Spanish music published in Spain. Such studies, from the late 1950s to the present, portray Bacarisse as a composer whose creative energy, commitment to modernism and ability to promote modernism in Spain were cut short by his displacement, which turned him into a more conservative composer – or, in Tomás Marco's words, led to his 'becoming stuck' – in exile.[9]

An examination of Bacarisse's biography and oeuvre yields a certain amount of evidence to support the argument that exile had a decisively negative impact on his career. Most of the historical accounts dwell on his *enfant terrible* status in his early career: his Opus 1, the symphonic poem *La nave de Ulises*, was awarded the prestigious Premio Nacional de Música (National Prize for Music) in 1922, but it could not be given its first performance at the time; the musicians of the Orquesta Filarmónica de Madrid refused to play it because they considered the work to be too audacious. Bacarisse's modernist credentials were reinforced both by his membership of the Grupo de los Ocho (Group of Eight), a loose association of composers in the late 1920s and 1930s who borrowed from the French avant-garde,[10] and by his music criticism, in which he sternly confronted those styles and composers he considered old-fashioned and conservative.[11]

Similarly, there are several aspects of Bacarisse's life and works after he left Spain that support the notion that exile meant discontinuity and rupture with his modernist past. In Paris, his involvement with local musical life was minimal beyond contact with other Spanish exiles. Besides, the works he wrote while in exile would have been unlikely to cause the same kind of controversy as those he composed in Madrid, since in Paris he stuck mostly to tonality, integrating within it a range of stereotypically Spanish stylistic features. These traits, exemplified in his most successful work from this period, the guitar Concertino, have sometimes been read as an expression of Bacarisse's nostalgic feelings for his home country.

The historiography of Spanish music, therefore, has split Bacarisse into two, just as Eisler has been split into the various Eislers: on the one hand the pre-Civil War, modernist and revolutionary Bacarisse; on the other, the exiled, nostalgic, conservative Bacarisse. This again can be regarded as typecasting, and although this model offers one way to make sense of Bacarisse's music, at the same time it neglects certain other threads that might cause us to explain his later works in a different way – not merely as the product of nostalgia but as stemming, rather, from values and beliefs that remained consistent throughout his life. In particular, Bacarisse's interest in Spanish musical traditions and heritage was not a result of his exile, and his understanding and use of those traditions had nothing to do with the *españolismo* (clichéd and superficial Spanish musical nationalism) ascribed to him by some.[12]

Where the first of these two issues is concerned, there is ample evidence that Bacarisse's interest in Spanish traditional music and culture predates his displacement. When asked in an interview from the early 1960s about his settings of Spanish literature from the Middle Ages to the Baroque, Bacarisse explained his choice of texts as a literary preference and not as a return (*retorno*, highly reminiscent of the French *retour*), implying that he had not gone back to Spanish classical literature after exile, but rather that it had been an interest of his throughout his life, a point that he proceeded to illustrate with a number of examples.[13]

On the second count, Bacarisse's interest in Spanish traditions and their expression in music, far from being simply a product of nostalgia, can be regarded to a significant extent as reflecting his political commitment, which developed and evolved considerably during his exile. Bacarisse's advocacy of modernist music back in Spain had been informed by his left-wing beliefs: for him, supporting new music went hand in hand with promoting art music and access to music education among the Spanish population. A similar commitment to the education of the masses is also apparent in the writings Bacarisse produced while in exile: he became concerned that what the Franco regime was promoting as true Spanish music among the Spanish population consisted of the 'lesser' genres of urban popular music, such as *cuplé, zarzuela, revista* and so on.[14] Although Bacarisse's views on such genres may seem, from our perspective, inflexible, simplistic and even uninformed, the crucial point is that he retained even in exile his commitment to contributing to the musical life and education of his country – and, what is more, that this commitment encouraged self-reflection on Spanish identity and its expression in music, as is evident from Bacarisse's writings, his interviews[15] and works as diverse as *Pasodoble* (taken from his withdrawn one-act opera *Toreros*), *24 preludios*, the guitar Concertino or the piano concertos. Rather than speaking of rupture or rifts, we might invoke Lydia Goehr's concept of 'doubleness', a condition that 'exists in practices of thought and activity that invoke two-sided, mediating, or conflicting ideals, productions, and conditions'.[16] Indeed we might extend it in recognition of the fact that some of the conflicting ideals, productions and conditions to which Goehr refers are equally applicable to modernism.

Establishing continuity to make sense of an exile's music, however, does not mean trying to present an exile's trajectory as always linear and cohesive, or assuming that the exile perceived it as such; in this regard, we might extend Lydia Goehr's 'doubleness' and speak instead of 'multipleness', in order to reflect the possibility that there might exist more than two sides and that the exile might weigh the various sides differently at particular stages of his or her life. Rosa García Ascot, a pianist, composer and colleague of Bacarisse's in the Grupo de los Ocho, provides a good example of this in the joint autobiography she published with her husband, Jesús Bal y Gay, in 1990.[17] One could well imagine that exile impacted García Ascot decisively. When the Civil War started, she and her husband were living in Cambridge (England), where Bal y Gay

Musical modernism and exile

was teaching Spanish at the university. In 1938, since they did not wish to return to Spain, Bal y Gay accepted membership of the Casa de España in Mexico City, whereas García Ascot spent a year in Paris studying with Nadia Boulanger and was reunited with her husband in Mexico in 1939. She lived in exile for twenty-six years before returning to Madrid in 1965. Nevertheless, in the opening lines of her autobiography, García Ascot does not seem to ascribe particular significance to the years she spent in Mexico over her other experiences of displacement (most of which were non-forced). She writes that:

> Throughout my life, I have been a very keen traveller. Sometimes out of personal choice, sometimes because of life's obligations and very often for pleasure, for inner need. Apart from Barcelona, Tortosa, Madrid and Granada, France, Cambridge, London, Paris, Mexico, Europe and then Mexico again looking forward to the definitive return to Spain.[18]

The paragraph, however, should not be read as a mere list – a succession of places to which García Ascot was connected and felt similar levels of attachment. The subsequent pages of her autobiographical account indeed clarify that, as happily mobile as she may have been, she did not have a detached, neutral relationship to place. On the contrary, place was crucial in her understanding of Spanish modernism and her position within it. The above sentences convey the sense that all the places she mentions are hierarchically organized with respect to Spain, which is presented as the ultimate destination of her journeys; on the next page, indeed, she describes herself as 'Spanish to the bone'.[19] There is no sense, however, that García Ascot felt particularly attached to a specific place in Spain – unlike, say, Adolfo Salazar, who, like García Ascot, was born and grew up in Madrid and in his letters from exile repeatedly expressed his nostalgia in terms of returning to Madrid specifically.[20] What we do get instead is a strong sense of García Ascot's connection to the history of Spanish music and, in particular, Spanish modernism, through her mention of several key places. García Ascot's mother had family connections in Barcelona and Tortosa, but, beyond that, both places were also crucial in García Ascot's training: Felipe Pedrell, a musical nationalist typically regarded as the father of Spanish musicology, was himself from Tortosa, as García Ascot reminds the reader later on in the account.[21] He was also a friend of her parents and advised them on their daughter's early musical education. As for Barcelona, García Ascot travelled there frequently an as adolescent to take piano lessons with Enrique Granados, another prominent figure of the Spanish nationalist school. The fourth city on the list, Granada, situates her in the genealogy of Spanish modernism without distancing her from Spanish nationalism, since it was there that she started piano and composition lessons with Manuel de Falla, who introduced her to the works of Debussy and Ravel.[22]

Madrid, which appears in third place in the list, is not only García Ascot's birthplace: it also confirms her position in the aforementioned genealogy. It was in Madrid that she joined the Grupo de los Ocho, most of whose members were from Madrid as well. The various back-and-forth moves between these places documented by García Ascot in her autobiography very often hint again at her allegiance to modernism as both performer and composer; for example, she mentions that in September 1935 she was in Granada for about ten days consulting with Falla on her own Piano Concerto[23] and rehearsing his own Harpsichord Concerto.

What García Ascot's autobiographical narrative shows is that modernism as a community can have its own sites of memory. This is true of Spanish modernism in García Ascot's case, but the conclusion could be applied to both modernism more broadly and to other communities within modernism, national or otherwise. The mere existence, development and perpetuation of such sites of memory depend, to a great extent, on the constant movement and displacement of individuals and works to and from those places. For example, García Ascot's stays in Granada and Madrid did not merely provide her with an orientation in terms of place: recognizing and studying such sites of memory as pivotal places, sometimes literally and sometimes more symbolically, can help articulate readings of the exiles' lives that rely neither on the illusion of absolute coherence and continuity nor on discontinuity, but rather make productive use of the connections between places themselves and between individuals and places, and also of the ways in which the exiles themselves regarded those connections and operated within them.

Cliché no. 2: high brow versus low brow

Another trope that appears frequently in writings about exiled composers and musicians is that – having arrived in a foreign land with few to no contacts, not to mention other complications (illness, old age) sometimes thrown into the mix[24] – they are forced to accept jobs, tasks and commissions they would not otherwise have taken. Although such considerations are sometimes coupled with a certain sense of indignation that well-known, talented composers had to condescend to write commercial music, in recent years the tendency has been to take a less prejudiced approach to such 'low-brow' and sometimes 'low-prestige' activities. The result has been an improved understanding of the ways in which such activities allowed the exiles to develop their creative practice in different directions or to interact with a variety of other practitioners and audiences. The best example is perhaps the growing body of literature on the film music that Central European expatriates wrote for Hollywood,[25] but there are others. Florian Scheding, for instance, has examined the opportunities that the 1940s London scene offered to Central European exiles: these included, among others, programming and arranging for the BBC, teaching at Morley College, and performing or writing music for cabaret.[26] These and other studies, rather than differentiating between high-brow and low-brow, tend to focus on how the different activities exiles were engaged in fed off each other: Malcolm Gillies takes Bartók's focus on folk music research during his years in America as a starting point for an examination of his late compositions, not with a sense of loss or regret that Bartók showed less of an interest in composition during this time, but rather concluding that 'all [his compositions], to a greater or lesser extent, evidence the editorial, if not quasi-compositional, hand of others'.[27]

But there is a second, related area to which less attention has been paid: in fact, examining the different types of musical activity the exiles undertook not only changes our perception of what 'high-' and 'low-brow' might be; it also, in many cases, changed the exiles' own perception too. The exiles' own view of their trajectories must certainly be taken into account if we want to make sense of the diverse and sometimes non-linear nature of their careers beyond the 'high-brow'/'low-brow' dichotomy. For example, Claudia Maurer Zenck has examined the ways in which Ernst Krenek established hierarchies and drew lines between need and ambition:

> He was inclined to accept Weill's turn to Broadway musicals because this step seemed an absolute need for the colleague of olden days. Had Bartók given evidence of such a necessity or of an artistic reorientation, he would have respected what, in their absence, seemed to him to be concessions.[28]

Krenek's distinctions between 'absolute need' and 'concessions' may come across as petty and arbitrarily rigid. We may ask ourselves, for example, when need ceases to be need, or whether, under the terms of Krenek's classification, it is acceptable for a composer to make concessions to commercialism not in order to avoid starvation but simply in order to maintain the same comfortable standard of living he had enjoyed in Europe. To pursue answers to such questions

Musical modernism and exile

in themselves might ultimately be inane and futile; more productive would be to acknowledge the fact that exiled composers would have asked themselves similar questions at different points in their experience of displacement, and that their changing understanding of the boundaries between high-brow and low-brow, between selling out and self-expression, can help us make sense of their music.

The Spanish Republican exile provides another instructive example in the person of Catalan composer Roberto Gerhard. Gerhard studied with Arnold Schoenberg in Vienna and then in Berlin from 1923 to 1928. Back in Barcelona after his studies in Central Europe, Gerhard did not immediately adopt twelve-tone technique in a systematic way, but he did remain in touch with his former teacher. He brought Schoenberg twice to Barcelona (in 1931 and 1932) and he co-organized the festival of the International Society for Contemporary Music there in 1936; at the festival, Anton Webern conducted the first performance of Alban Berg's Violin Concerto. Gerhard stayed in Barcelona throughout the Civil War and served as an adviser to the Catalan government (Generalitat de Catalunya), working together with members of the Consejo Central de la Música after it moved to Barcelona (along with the Republican government itself) in November 1937. He finally left Spain for Paris in 1939 and then settled in Cambridge in 1940 on a short-term fellowship at King's College, after which he stayed in the city as a freelance composer and arranger.

After a gap of eight years due to the vicissitudes of the Spanish Civil War and then the Second World War, Gerhard and Schoenberg started to correspond again in 1944. What we read in Gerhard's first letter to Schoenberg after this impasse is not only a summary of Gerhard's musical activities after he settled in Cambridge, but also a pretty detailed impression of how Gerhard perceived the various opportunities available to him.[29] Gerhard referred matter-of-factly to the various commissions he had received from artistic and broadcasting institutions: writing about the arrangements of Spanish *zarzuela* he had completed for the BBC, he fondly described the genre as 'late 19th-century operetta stuff of a certain Hispano-offenbachian type'. He also claimed that, thanks to these arrangements, he had improved his skills at orchestration. He also mentioned his ballets and music for the radio, among which he highlighted *Adventures of Don Quixote* and explained, not without a hint of pride, that it had not been well received ('the music seems to have made something of a stir here, and I gather the BBC received some nasty letters from listeners') – perhaps implicitly elevating the ballet's first performance to the category of the stereotypical modernist scandal. One of the last paragraphs in Gerhard's letter, however, suggests that he did indeed establish a hierarchy between his concert works and such commissions, no matter how instructive or entertaining he found them:

> I must say that [my wife] is, as she always was, quite determined to divorce me should I ever cease endeavouring to become a 'serious' composer. This is the reason, I suppose, why I have written a String Quartet, a Symphony and now a second violin concerto.[30]

Gerhard, however, insisted in his letter that he was grateful that England had offered him, for the first time in his life, the opportunity to live entirely off composing and arranging music, 'a thing which not so long ago I couldn't help regarding as one of [my wife's] perversities'. Indeed, before going into exile, Gerhard had been forced to hold a variety of music-related jobs simultaneously: he worked as a music librarian and researcher at the Biblioteca Nacional de Catalunya, taught at Barcelona's Escola Municipal de Música, wrote music criticism and translated German-language books on music theory and history. In past decades, scholarship on Gerhard tended to focus on his concert works from the mid-1950s onwards; authors paid little attention to the commissions he had fulfilled in Britain before that,[31] and on some occasions were downright dismissive of them.[32] The latest scholarship on Gerhard has partially addressed this imbalance;[33] integrating Gerhard's own perspectives on his output can further help to challenge the boundaries and understand the cross-fertilization between his incidental and his concert music, his experimental and his less experimental output.

Cliché no. 3: autonomy versus identity

My last point concerns not one but two seemingly irreconcilable clichés, one surrounding modernism and one surrounding exile. The former refers to the autonomy of the work of art, which has long been upheld as a central tenet of musical modernism. The latter has to do with displacement's supposed ability to exacerbate the expressive potential of music: national, political and racial identities, put to the test by the vagaries of exile, are supposed to make their way inevitably into the music, which thus becomes anything but autonomous.[34] There are, indeed, numerous examples in both the German and the Spanish exiled community that support the point that displacement can result in a heightened sense of identity precisely at a point when one's identity is most at risk: Max Paddison, for example, has examined how Adorno, himself one of the more ardent proponents of the autonomy of the work of art, had to come to terms with issues regarding his own identity only when he went into exile, because the intellectual context Adorno had taken for granted in Germany (and which he had not previously perceived as part of his own 'identity') was radically different from what he found in America.[35]

We may start to qualify the latter cliché by admitting that one does not need to experience exile in order to find one's sense of identity challenged and to decide to express such tensions in music. But, on the other hand, there are a few identity-challenging scenarios that recur almost as a matter of course when examining the life stories of exiles: from the complications of having to establish one's national identity administratively and bureaucratically,[36] to the temptation to play up or play down one's national identity in the host country (with Roberto Gerhard, for example, using flamenco in his UK ballet commissions during the 1940s, even though he was not Andalusian, but Catalan) and, further, to the questioning of one's political beliefs and identities in changing political circumstances.

An example of an exile facing all three of these types of difficulty is provided by Ernst Krenek's speech at the annual festival of the International Society for Contemporary Music in London in 1938. Addressing the assembly, he expressed the hope that his Austrian nationality would make it easier for him to live in exile:

> It was the quality of universalism in the Austrian composer which had given Austria its place in music through the centuries. Perhaps this very quality might make it a little less hard for the Austrian than for others to make his home all over the world.[37]

Krenek's very participation at the festival posed for him and the rest of the organization questions of identity and belonging, even at the most mundane and bureaucratic level, that would possibly not have arisen had he not been in exile. Officially he was not, and could never be, a delegate, since Austria was no longer an independent country and was therefore not entitled to maintain an ISCM section. Moreover, Krenek, though representing Austria, had not set foot in the country since 'the events of March' and he, together with the other Jewish members of the Austrian ISCM committee, had resigned 'to avoid making difficulty'.[38]

Both the alleged autonomy of the musical work in modernism and the heightened expressive powers that music supposedly acquires because of displacement have already been questioned separately by scholars of modernism and scholars of exile. As one of the former, Gianmario

Musical modernism and exile

Borio has pointed out that Nono's work (like that of other canonical modernist composers) cannot be understood in a manner independent from his interaction with and commitment to his environment, both political and otherwise.[39] In parallel, scholarship of recent years has greatly increased our understanding of how identity can be expressed through different and sometimes diametrically opposed musical languages; what is posited as autonomous at a certain point in history may later acquire connotations that turn it into a vehicle for the expression and construction of identity, as is demonstrated by Severine Neff in her discussion of Schoenberg's Second Chamber Symphony. Schoenberg started composing the symphony in 1903 and resumed work on it 1939. In consequence, 'Schoenberg, that quintessential Modernist, was confronted directly with a prototypical issue of contemporary composition: what is the underlying sense of writing tonal music after the atonal and twelve-tone revolutions that he himself initiated and brought to fulfilment?'[40] Neff warns against the dangers of interpreting the symphony as a product of nostalgia and assuming that Schoenberg wished, as it were, to go back in time. Instead, she argues that, as well as Schoenberg's experience of exile, the Second Chamber Symphony illuminates the notion that tonal and non-tonal music do not exist in a dichotomy but can, for many composers, be complementary.[41]

The supposedly heightened expressive content with which exile imbues music has also been qualified or questioned by scholars. The mere idea that music can be used as a tool to express exile identity – or conflicts of identity brought about by exile – becomes problematic as soon as one asks *who* the recipient of such expressive behaviour may be: Sally Bick points out that, even though the work of an exile may be rich in references to exile, the composer does not necessarily intend that all members of the audience will be able to decode such references.[42]

While not denying the possibility that exile might prompt composers to express in music their feelings concerning displacement, scholars have tried to counteract reductive understandings of this process. Rachel Beckles Willson, for example, has compared the development of different composers in exile in order to devise a more nuanced model: shock and creative crisis at the beginning are followed by self-reflective crisis management and nostalgia in a second stage, then the construction of a new compositional voice in the third stage – a model that she herself admits needs qualification.[43] And if identity can be expressed through different and sometimes diametrically opposed musical languages, the corollary is that at least some composers will be open to and familiar with a range of styles and techniques they can switch between for different purposes, and they will also be, at least in some cases, looking at new ways of imbuing existing styles with new meanings. For example, Brigid Cohen has analysed Stefan Wolpe's engagement with a variety of languages (jazz, maqam) in an attempt to arrive at the 'human tongue' – an interest in the primitive or the elemental, which again is a feature found in various branches of modernism.[44] Although there is a clear continuity between Wolpe's work and thinking pre- and post-exile, displacement influenced him in terms of both the questions he wanted to explore in his music and the specific languages he chose for that purpose, whether encountered in his employment at Black Mountain College or through his collaborations with jazz musicians.

Of course, it is not necessary for a composer to go into exile in order to realize the versatile expressive possibilities of specific languages and styles: Laura Silverberg, for example, has examined how, while atonality and specifically twelve-tone technique were associated in the West with 'abstract, supposedly "apolitical" modernism', they saw a remarkable flourishing in the 1960s in the GDR, as if to show that 'modernist techniques had a rightful place in socialist new music'.[45] Exile, however, by exposing the displaced person to both new styles and techniques and new challenges regarding the definition of one's own identity, may make this process particularly fruitful. Bick, for example, has explored the implications of Eisler's use of a 'high-modernist style' (i.e. twelve-tone technique) in film music as opposed to autonomous concert works,[46] and Roberto Gerhard similarly used twelve-tone technique in his incidental music for the theatre. Bohlman and Scheding have examined another work in which Eisler makes use of twelve-tone technique, the *Reisesonate* for violin and piano, and they conclude that twelve-tone technique can, in Eisler's own words, be both 'the enemy of fascism' (because dodecaphonism means at the same time dissonance and reason) and a marker of nostalgia (Eisler harking back to his pre-war studies with Schoenberg).[47] Again with reference to Eisler, James Parsons focuses on another allegedly key aspect of modernism: the focus on construction and the unity of the work. To do so, he examines how Eisler's *Hollywooder Liederbuch* contradicts the notion of the song cycle as a perfect unity.[48] Parsons considers the structural irregularities in the work to constitute not a flaw but an expressive decision. When the piece comes to an end, 'Eisler at last declares his cycle's objective: how one is to be at home with one's self when one's former home is no longer is at hand. How should one remember a Heimat transformed by war, "beyond those streaks of red"?'[49]

If the clichés mentioned at the beginning of this section concerning modernism and exile have been problematized separately by commentators, so has the combination of both. Danuser, for example, has discussed the notions of 'autonomy' and 'identity' in the context of modernism not as mutually exclusive but as complementary. Danuser argues that Stravinsky, Schoenberg and Bartók were part of an older generation of modernists who believed in the autonomy of the work of art, although Schoenberg himself underwent while in exile a 'transformation of the artistic identity' which was 'his own response to the problem of preserving identity'.[50] On the other hand, Danuser argues, the younger composers born around 1900 (Weill, Hindemith, Krenek, Eisler) engaged with 'the paradigm of artful functional music'.[51] For some, the distinction is not as clear-cut: Bartók has repeatedly been depicted as a composer uniquely able 'to reconcile the claims of formal musical modernism with the cultural politics of identity and subjective musical particularity'.[52]

In the remainder of this section, I shall discuss another intersection between modernism, exile and the expression of identity: by focusing again on several Spanish Republican exiles, I shall illustrate how, throughout their careers, they never saw commitment to modernism and loyalty to their own national and political identity as mutually exclusive. Indeed, they regarded both as inextricably linked, and the extent of such a connection was, in most cases, made obvious by exile: in the absence of the tried-and-tested devices such composers had relied upon to formulate their dual commitment to the modernist project and to national/political identity, they found themselves forced to find new ways of reconciling both – sometimes successfully, sometimes unsuccessfully.

My first case study concerns Jaume Pahissa, who was born in Barcelona in 1880 and died in exile in Buenos Aires in 1969. In early twentieth-century Barcelona, Pahissa was a major figure of Catalan *modernisme* – a term which is not exactly synonymous with English-language modernism, either musical or otherwise, nor with Spanish literary *modernismo*. Catalan *modernisme* did share with these other movements a concern with innovation, but what was unique was its focus on architecture, design and the decorative arts: Antoni Gaudí, who designed the Sagrada Família church in Barcelona, was one of its foremost representatives, and Pahissa himself started an architecture degree before he decided to focus on music. The specific nature of Catalan *modernisme* is highly context sensitive and, in some respects, can even be considered expressive of Catalan national identity. Although we may not find many explicit references to Catalan folklore or history in *modernisme*, the focus on urban and industrial development ties in well with the development of Catalan identity since the mid-nineteenth century: indeed, such development had been effected at the hands of the bourgeoisie and always with the idea that Catalonia was leading industrial development ahead of other Spanish regions.

Musical modernism and exile

The music Pahissa wrote during his period of *modernisme* also speaks of a compromise between the need to write music suitable for a world undergoing rapid modernization and the ambition to do so in a way that was expressive of national, regional or local difference. Pahissa ticks many of the boxes we currently associate with modernism: he believed that tonality had been exhausted after Wagner, and like Schoenberg he devised, after years of experimentation, a system to replace it, which he called intertonality.[53] Pahissa's experiments with intertonality also tick a second box, that of the 'modernist scandal': in 1926, his *Suite intertonal*, in which he first applied intertonality systematically to a large-scale piece, was met with controversy on the occasion of its first performance in Barcelona, with the press reporting that several members of the audience complained energetically, while others supported Pahissa. The press itself was divided, and the criticisms are again reminiscent of those faced by major modernist figures such as Schoenberg and Stravinsky: on the one hand, lack of emotion; on the other, a worthy theoretical effort which, in some critics' opinion, was unlikely to prove a significant influence on other composers.[54]

As was the case with architectural *modernisme*, though, Pahissa's commitment to renewing music was not divorced from his milieu, but rather profoundly context sensitive and perceived as such by his fellow Catalan citizens. This recognition is exemplified by the books *La música catalana contemporània: Visió de conjunt* (1960) and *Història de la música catalana* (1969), both written by composer Manuel Valls at a time when Catalan cultural nationalism and opposition to the Franco regime and centralist Spanish nationalism were thriving again. Both books assume that Catalan art music is separate from Spanish art music, hence Valls's efforts to establish the uniqueness of Catalan musical identity and its status within Western culture.[55]

Valls argued that Catalan art music as such had come into being at around the time when Catalonia acquired its sense of nationhood, or, in Valls's words, acquired 'self-awareness as a national entity able to accomplish spiritual enterprises'.[56] Far from a 'blood-and-soil'-type nationalism or an overreliance on traditional values, though, Valls presented a varied list of 'impulses' which had, in his opinion, shaped Catalan national identity and music, the most relevant of which, he argued, was the role of the artisans and the bourgeoisie. Significantly, he also mentioned Wagnerism among such impulses.[57] Wagner's operas were indeed more popular in Catalonia than they were in the rest of Spain; more generally, Catalan composers tended to show a greater affinity with Austro-German music (including not only Wagner, but also Richard Strauss and the Second Viennese School) than composers from Madrid. Pahissa's experiments with chromaticism and his attempts to advance music beyond Wagner were therefore regarded by Valls as representative of his commitment to Catalan music. In both books, Valls named Pahissa as a composer who had not managed to produce a high-quality oeuvre of his own but who was nevertheless interesting for having kept Catalan music alive after Wagnerism and introduced a variety of trends and styles that the new generation would then perfect.[58]

In exile, however, Pahissa's career took a rather different turn, and one reminiscent of Zemlinsky's trajectory: that of a middle-aged composer who goes into exile having attained considerable prestige in his native environment and is unable either to continue cultivating his highly context-specific music or to pursue music in a manner adapted to his new context. Indeed, Pahissa soon found out that his prestige in Barcelona was not easily transferable to Buenos Aires. He complained about his fate in a bitter letter of 1959 to Guido Valcarenghi of Ricordi Americana, writing that: 'It is 22 years since I was buried in this well which is Buenos Aires, away from the musical world. My career ended after I left Europe'.[59]

Pahissa never attained his goal of finding stable employment in the field of music while in exile and instead found himself juggling a number of music-related jobs: private teaching and voice coaching, composing and arranging for the amateur music market (work that he published

209

Eva Moreda Rodríguez

through Ricordi Americana) and, perhaps more importantly, writing books on music for the general public, the best-known of which is probably his biography of Manuel de Falla, who also spent the last years of his life in Argentina. Pahissa's career and output in Argentina hardly resemble those we would expect of a modernist composer, and this is probably why Valls, who continued to emphasize the narrative of music history as progress, hardly referred to Pahissa's career in exile or to his significance for Catalonia as a mature composer. He simply mentioned that Pahissa had established himself as a teacher in Argentina[60] and that he had reverted to post-Romanticism rather than maintaining his profile as a modernist.[61]

The second example I wish to discuss concerns the revival of Spanish early music among the Spanish exiled community. Far from constituting an organized revival movement, exiled Spanish composers developed their interest in early music independently from one another. At the same time, in most cases we can interpret their interest as complementing, rather than conflicting with, the notion of a modernist project in exile.

Some of the exiles had indeed engaged with Spanish early music before they left Spain: Rodolfo Halffter, for example, did so as a composer, adapting French neo-classicism to the Spanish context (his 1928 *Sonatas de El Escorial* are reminiscent of Scarlatti, whom the Grupo de los Ocho regarded as a Spanish composer due to his lengthy residence in Spain). Jesús Bal y Gay worked as a researcher of sixteenth-century music at the Centro de Investigaciones Históricas in Madrid, whereas Roberto Gerhard occupied himself with eighteenth-century music at the Biblioteca Nacional de Catalunya. After exile, their engagement with Spanish early music changed. Halffter, for one, all but abandoned neo-classicism in favour of serialism. This, however, does not mean that Spanish early music completely disappeared from his horizon: in the later decades of his career, he repeatedly claimed to be inspired by the austerity and economy of means that he saw in Spanish early music.[62] Back in Spain, many of his critics agreed.[63] Bal y Gay, meanwhile, who was unable in Mexico to access primary sources for his research on early Spanish music, turned to writing on topics he could research more easily, and hence produced articles on Mexican music and books on Chopin and Debussy.[64] Nevertheless, Spanish early music was still an important part of his life: it was in exile that Bal y Gay took up composition in earnest, and his first work of significance was the neo-classically inspired *Serenata para orquesta de cuerda* (1942). Roberto Gerhard, on the other hand, alongside his career as a freelance composer, still found time to undertake research into eighteenth-century music on the side: shortly after he arrived in Cambridge, he uncovered a manuscript of some of Joan Baptista Pla's sonatas at the library in King's College and prepared an edition.[65] He also let some of the inspiration, if not the music directly, influence his compositions, such as the opera *La Dueña* (1945–49).

Others turned to Spanish early music in exile out of necessity rather than choice. Adolfo Salazar, a critic utterly committed to the introduction of musical modernism (of the Franco-Russian persuasion) in Spain and a mentor to members of the Grupo de los Ocho in the 1920s and 1930s, had initially been dismissive of research into early Spanish music, which he considered worthwhile only if used to illuminate the present and promote the advancement of Spanish contemporary music.[66] In exile, however, he found himself forced to write books on a variety of music topics – including, for example, a book on Don Quixote in music – in order to earn a living in Mexico. Pahissa, who in Barcelona had not shown any particular interest in early music, published three sets of two settings for mixed chorus while in Argentina (*Dos motetes, Dos madrigales, Dos canciones*). Each set consisted of a Spanish early music piece transcribed by himself, followed by his own pastiche-style composition. Interestingly, two out of the six pieces in the three sets explore themes of displacement and difference: Pahissa's own motet (*Quomodo sedet sola*) is a setting of the opening lines of the Lamentations of Jeremiah, which describe

Musical modernism and exile

the desertion and desolation of Jerusalem after the destruction of the temple and the exile to Babylon,[67] whereas the first of the *Dos canciones* is an arrangement of *Tres morillas*, a well-known song from the Cancionero de Palacio, which refers to three Muslim women who are forced to convert to Christianity after their native city of Jaén falls into Christian hands.

When considered alongside other examples from the Spanish exile, Pahissa's engagement with Spanish early music reveals itself not simply as nostalgia but rather as a living reality that permitted the articulation of feelings about exile and/or the ways in which displacement had effected a different kind of commitment to modernity. On the one hand, we have Gerhard using his research on eighteenth-century music partly as a source of income and partly to regain a degree of presence in Francoist Spain, at the same time establishing himself in the British theatrical world by composing *La Dueña*. On the other hand, we have Bal y Gay going back in time not once but twice: not only to the music of the Spanish eighteenth century, but also to the years preceding the Civil War, during which time his colleagues and acquaintances were cultivating the neo-classically inspired style that he himself did not experiment with until he went into exile.

Conclusion

Our examination of the clichés presented at the start of this chapter – undertaken using a variety of examples, some better known than others – might leave readers with the simple impression that all clichés are true up to a point but none are universally applicable. This would, in itself, be another cliché, and not a terribly productive one if our aim is to make sense of phenomena as broad as modernism, exile and their intersections. If we are to draw any general conclusion from the examples I have discussed, it would probably be that displacement meant for many composers a re-examination of their commitment to a modernist project and a revisitation of the tools and devices they had confidently used thus far to develop it. At the same time, their acquisition of new tools or the reformulation of their commitment to modernism was often effected in a way that took place into account (whether their place of origin or their place of migration). The detailed examination and comparison of individual stories and works serves only to complicate and multiply the nuances of what may end up resembling only superficially our received wisdom on modernism, exile and their intersections.

Notes

1 Bridget T. Chalk, *Modernism and Mobility: The Passport and Cosmopolitan Experience* (New York: Palgrave Macmillan, 2014), 4.

2 Stephen Hinton, 'Hindemith and Weill: Cases of "Inner" and "Other" Direction', in *Driven into Paradise: The Musical Migration from Nazi Germany to the United States*, ed. Reinhold Brinkmann and Christoph Wolff (Berkeley and Los Angeles: University of California Press, 1999), 263.

3 Michael Beckerman, 'Jezek, Zeisl, Améry, and the Exile in the Middle', in *Music and Displacement: Diasporas, Mobilities and Dislocations in Europe and Beyond*, ed. Florian Scheding and Erik Levi (Lanham, MD: Scarecrow Press, 2010), 44–46.

4 See, for example, Leticia Sánchez de Andrés, 'Roberto Gerhard's Ballets: Music, Ideology and Passion', in *The Roberto Gerhard Companion*, ed. Monty Adkins and Michael Russ (Farnham: Ashgate, 2013), 196.

5 Edward Said, *Reflections on Exile and Other Essays* (Cambridge, MA: Harvard University Press, 2000), 73.

6 Leon Botstein, 'Reinventing Life and Career: The Perils of Emigration', *Musical Quarterly* 90, no. 3 (2007), 309.

7 Brinkmann discusses the prevalence of both these tropes in the literature about exiled composers, with Schoenberg and Weill at both ends of the continuum. See Reinhold Brinkmann, 'Reading a Letter', in *Driven into Paradise*, ed. Brinkmann and Wolff, 11–13.

8 Andrea F. Bohlman and Florian Scheding, 'Hanns Eisler on the Move: Tracing Mobility in the *Reisesonate*', *Music and Letters* 96, no. 1 (2015), 77.

Eva Moreda Rodríguez

9 Tomás Marco, *La música de la España contemporánea* (Madrid: Publicaciones Españolas, 1970), 11. The historiographical works I am referring to here include: Federico Sopeña, *Historia de la música española contemporánea* (Madrid: Rialp, 1958), 251 and 258; Manuel Valls, *La música española después de Manuel de Falla* (Madrid: Revista de Occidente, 1962), 113; Tomás Marco, *Spanish Music in the Twentieth Century* (Cambridge, MA: Harvard University Press, 1993), 108; Christiane Heine, 'Salvador Bacarisse (1898–1963) en el centenario de su nacimiento', *Cuadernos de música iberoamericana* 5 (1998), 43.

10 Other members of the Grupo de los Ocho include Julián Bautista, Rosa García Ascot, Ernesto and Rodolfo Halffter, Juan José Mantecón, Gustavo Pittaluga and Fernando Remacha. Bautista, García Ascot, Rodolfo Halffter and Pittaluga also went into exile.

11 Christiane Heine, 'La crítica musical de Salvador Bacarisse en *Crisol* y *Luz* (1931–1934)', in *Los señores de la crítica: Periodismo musical e ideología del modernismo en Madrid (1900–1950)*, ed. Teresa Cascudo and María Palacios (Sevilla: Doble J, 2011), 195–254.

12 Heine, 'Salvador Bacarisse en el centenario de su nacimiento', 68; [unsigned], 'Noticiario musical', *Blanco y negro*, 7 September 1963, 102.

13 Interview (undated, possibly early 1960s) with Bacarisse at Radio France, reprinted in programme notes to concert on the occasion of the donation of works by Salvador Bacarisse, Fundación Juan March, 9 March 1988.

14 Salvador Bacarisse, 'La cultura, la democracia y la música', *Cultura y democracia* 2 (1950), 14.

15 Interview (undated) with Bacarisse at Radio France (see above note 13).

16 Lydia Goehr, 'Music and Musicians in Exile: The Romantic Legacy of a Double Life', in *Driven into Paradise*, ed. Brinkmann and Wolff, 68.

17 Jesús Bal y Gay and Rosa García Ascot, *Nuestros trabajos y nuestros días* (Madrid: Fundación Banco Exterior, 1990).

18 Ibid., 25.

19 Ibid., 26.

20 See, for example, letter from Adolfo Salazar to Ernesto Halffter, 26 August 1943; reprinted in *Adolfo Salazar: Epistolario, 1912–1958*, ed. Consuelo Carredano (Madrid: Publicaciones de la Residencia de Estudiantes, 2008), 588; letter from Adolfo Salazar to Ernesto and Alicia Halffter, 15 March 1940, reprinted in ibid., 478–80.

21 Bal y Gay and García Ascot, *Nuestros trabajos y nuestros días*, 26

22 Ibid., 37.

23 García Ascot's Piano Concerto has not survived; indeed, most of her music was lost during the Spanish Civil War.

24 Malcolm Gillies, 'Bartók in America', in *The Cambridge Companion to Bartók*, ed. Amanda Bayley (Cambridge: Cambridge University Press, 2011), 190–201.

25 Sally Bick, 'A Double Life in Hollywood: Hanns Eisler's Score for the film *Hangmen Also Die* and the Covert Expression of a Marxist Composer', *Musical Quarterly* 93, no. 1 (2010), 90–143; Ben Winters, *Erich Wolfgang Korngold's* The Adventures of Robin Hood: *A Film Score Guide* (Lanham, MD: Scarecrow Press, 2007); Ben Winters, 'Swearing an Oath: Korngold, Film and the Sound of Resistance?' in *The Impact of Nazism on 20th-Century Music*, ed. Erik Levi (Vienna: Böhlau, 2014), 61–76.

26 Florian Scheding, '"Problematic Tendencies": Émigré Composers in London, 1933–1945', in *The Impact of Nazism*, ed. Erik Levi (Vienna: Böhlau, 2014), 247–72; Florian Scheding, '"I Only Need the Good Old Budapest": Hungarian Cabarets in Wartime London', in *Twentieth-Century Music and Politics: Essays in Memory of Neil Edmunds*, ed. Pauline Fairclough (Farnham: Ashgate, 2012), 211–30.

27 Gillies, 'Bartók in America', 196.

28 Claudia Maurer Zenck, 'Challenges and Opportunities of Acculturation: Schoenberg, Krenek, and Stravinsky in Exile', in *Driven into Paradise*, ed. Brinkmann and Wolff, 185.

29 Letter from Roberto Gerhard to Arnold Schoenberg, 2 December 1944, Arnold Schoenberg Centre, http://archive.schoenberg.at/letters/search_show_letter.php?ID_Number=10786.

30 It is this second violin concerto, composed between 1942 and 1945, that is today known as Gerhard's Violin Concerto. The concerto he wrote at the beginning of his exile is thought to be lost.

31 See, for example, Julian White, 'National Traditions in the Music of Roberto Gerhard', *Tempo*, no. 184 (1993), 2–13; Allan F. Moore, 'Serialism and Its Contradictions', *International Review of the Aesthetics and Sociology of Music* 26 (1995), 77–95.

32 Tomás Marco, *Música española de vanguardia* (Madrid: Guadarrama, 1970), 30; Sánchez de Andrés, 'Roberto Gerhard's Ballets', 99.

33 For example, Llano's study of Gerhard's ballets: Samuel Llano, 'Exile, Resistance and Heteroglossia in Roberto Gerhard's *Flamenco*', in *Stages of Exile: Spanish Republican Exile Theatre and Performance*, ed. Helena Buffery (Oxford and New York: Oxford University Press, 2011), 107–24.

34 See also Goehr, 'Music and Musicians in Exile', 76.

35 Max Paddison, 'Adorno and Exile: Some Thoughts on Displacements and What It Means to Be German', in *Music and Displacement*, ed. Scheding and Levi, 135–36.

36 Chalk, *Modernism and Mobility*, 18. Chalk focuses on how such challenges affected writers and were reflected in literary works; similar perspectives could be applied to music.

37 Minutes of the delegates' meeting at the International Society for Contemporary Music, London 1938, unpublished. Fons Robert Gerhard (Institut d'Estudis Vallencs, Valls, Catalonia), 13_07_10.

38 Ibid.

39 Gianmario Borio, 'Musical Communication and the Process of Modernity', *Journal of the Royal Musical Association* 139, no. 1 (2014), 178–83, 180–82.

40 Severine Neff, 'Cadence after Thirty-Three Years: Schoenberg's Second Chamber Symphony, Op. 38', in *The Cambridge Companion to Schoenberg*, ed. Jennifer Shaw and Joseph Auner (Cambridge: Cambridge University Press, 2010), 209.

41 Ibid., 210.

42 Bick, 'A Double Life', 112.

43 Rachel Beckles Willson, 'A New Voice, a New 20th Century? An Experiment with Sándor Veress', *Tempo*, no. 62 (2008), 40.

44 Brigid Cohen, 'Boundary Situations: Translation and Agency in Wolpe's Modernism', *Contemporary Music Review* 27, no. 3 (2008), 337.

45 Laura Silverberg, 'Between Dissonance and Dissidence: Socialist Modernism in the German Democratic Republic', *Journal of Musicology* 26, no. 1 (2009), 44–45.

46 Bick, 'A Double Life', 118.

47 Bohlman and Scheding, 'Hanns Eisler on the Move', 91–92.

48 James Parsons, 'Hanns Eisler's *Hollywooder Liederbuch* and "The New Stuff of Life"', in *The Impact of Nazism*, ed. Levi, 91–111.

49 Ibid., 106.

50 Hermann Danuser, 'Composers in Exile: The Question of Musical Identity', in *Driven into Paradise*, ed. Brinkmann and Wolff, 163.

51 Ibid., 158.

52 Leon Botstein, 'Out of Hungary: Bartók, Modernism, and the Cultural Politics of Twentieth Century Music', in *Bartók and His World*, ed. Peter Laki (Princeton, NJ: Princeton University Press, 1995), 4. See also David Cooper, 'Bartók's Orchestral Music and the Modern World', in *The Cambridge Companion to Bartók*, ed. Bayley, 45.

53 Pahissa's intertonal theory was based on dissonance: the 'perfect' or 'pure' chord was considered to be a chord composed of two semitones and a whole tone (for example: C, C♯, D). A second, 'less harsh', category of dissonant chord was that based upon the interval of a fourth (for example: D, G, C). Other chords were formed on diminished and augmented fourths. Pahissa described intertonality as 'the continuation, the evolution, the overcoming of tonality'. See Jaume Pahissa, *Los grandes problemas de la música* (Buenos Aires: Poseidón, 1945), 117.

54 Xosé Aviñoa, *Jaume Pahissa: Un estudi bibliogràfic i crític* (Barcelona: Biblioteca de Catalunya, 1996), 128–30.

55 Manuel Valls, *La música catalana contemporània: Visió de conjunt* (Barcelona: Selecta, 1960), 14.

56 Manuel Valls, *Història de la música catalana* (Barcelona: Tàber, 1969), 133.

57 Ibid.

58 Valls, *La música catalana contemporània*, 75; Valls, *Història de la música catalana,* 133.

59 Letter from Jaume Pahissa to Guido Valcarenghi, 7 June 1959; reprinted in Aviñoa, *Jaume Pahissa*, 233–34.

60 Valls, *Història de la música catalana*, 183–84.

61 Valls, *La música catalana contemporània*, 90.

62 Marco Aurelio Carballo, *De Quijotes y Dulcineas* (Mexico City: Conaculta, 2014), 198.

63 See, for example, on the Third Piano Sonata, Enrique Franco, 'Varia creación de cámara y homenaje a Óscar Esplá', *Arriba*, 24 October 1967, 23; Antonio Iglesias, 'Halffter y Narcís Bonet, en el Ateneo', *Informaciones*, 23 October 1967, 23.

Eva Moreda Rodríguez

64 Jesús Bal y Gay, *Chopin* (Mexico City: Fondo de Cultura Económica, 1959); Bal y Gay, *Debussy* (Mexico City: Fondo de Cultura Económica, 1962).
65 See also Eva Moreda Rodríguez, 'Early Music in Francoist Spain: Higini Anglès and the Exiles', *Music and Letters* 96, no. 2 (2015), 223–26.
66 María Cáceres-Piñuel, '"Una posturita estética que no representa sino un frenazo": El discurso crítico de Subirá en torno al neoclasicismo (1929–1936)', in *Los señores de la crítica*, ed. Cascudo and Palacios, 261–64.
67 'Quomodo sedet sola civitas plena populo! Facta est quasi vidua domina gentium; princeps provinciarum facta est sub tributo.' ('How doth the city sit solitary that was full of people! How is the mistress of the peoples become as a widow: the Princes of provinces made tributary!')

Bibliography

Aviñoa, Xosé. *Jaume Pahissa: Un estudi bibliogràfic i crític*. Barcelona: Biblioteca de Catalunya, 1996.

Bacarisse, Salvador. 'La cultura, la democracia y la música'. *Cultura y democracia* 2 (1950): 13–18.

Bal y Gay, Jesús. *Chopin*. Mexico City: Fondo de Cultura Económica, 1959.

——. *Debussy*. Mexico City: Fondo de Cultura Económica, 1962.

Bal y Gay, Jesús, and Rosa García Ascot. *Nuestros trabajos y nuestros días*. Madrid: Fundación Banco Exterior, 1990.

Bayley, Amanda, ed. *The Cambridge Companion to Bartók*. Cambridge: Cambridge University Press, 2011.

Beckerman, Michael. 'Jezek, Zeisl, Améry, and the Exile in the Middle'. In *Music and Displacement*, edited by Scheding and Levi, 43–54.

Beckles Willson, Rachel. 'A New Voice, a New 20th Century? An Experiment with Sándor Veress'. *Tempo*, no. 62 (2008): 36–41.

Bick, Sally. 'A Double Life in Hollywood: Hanns Eisler's Score for the film *Hangmen Also Die* and the Covert Expression of a Marxist Composer'. *Musical Quarterly* 93, no. 1 (2010): 90–143.

Bohlman, Andrea F., and Florian Scheding. 'Hanns Eisler on the Move: Tracing Mobility in the *Reisesonate*'. *Music & Letters* 96, no. 1 (2015): 77–98.

Borio, Gianmario. 'Musical Communication and the Process of Modernity'. *Journal of the Royal Musical Association* 139, no. 1 (2014): 177–204.

Botstein, Leon. 'Out of Hungary: Bartók, Modernism, and the Cultural Politics of Twentieth Century Music'. In *Bartók and His World*, edited by Peter Laki, 3–63. Princeton, NJ: Princeton University Press, 1995.

——. 'Reinventing Life and Career: The Perils of Emigration'. *Musical Quarterly* 90, no. 3 (2007): 309–18.

Brinkmann, Reinhold. 'Reading a Letter'. In *Driven into Paradise*, edited by Brinkmann and Wolff, 3–20.

Brinkmann, Reinhold, and Christoph Wolff, eds. *Driven into Paradise: The Musical Migration from Nazi Germany to the United States*. Berkeley and Los Angeles: University of California Press, 1999.

Cáceres-Piñuel, María. '"Una posturita estética que no representa sino un frenazo": El discurso crítico de Subirá en torno al neoclasicismo (1929–1936)'. In *Los señores de la crítica*, edited by Cascudo and Palacios, 255–78.

Carredano, Consuelo, ed. *Adolfo Salazar: Epistolario, 1912–1958*. Madrid: Publicaciones de la Residencia de Estudiantes, 2008.

Carballo, Marco Aurelio. *De Quijotes y Dulcineas*. Mexico City: Conaculta, 2014.

Cascudo, Teresa, and María Palacios, eds. *Los señores de la crítica: Periodismo musical e ideología del modernismo en Madrid (1900–1950)*. Sevilla: Doble J, 2011.

Chalk, Bridget T. *Modernism and Mobility: The Passport and Cosmopolitan Experience*. New York: Palgrave Macmillan, 2014.

Cohen, Brigid. 'Boundary Situations: Translation and Agency in Wolpe's Modernism'. *Contemporary Music Review* 27, no. 3 (2008): 323–41.

Cooper, David. 'Bartók's Orchestral Music and the Modern World'. In *The Cambridge Companion to Bartók*, edited by Bayley, 43–61.

Danuser, Hermann. 'Composers in Exile: The Question of Musical Identity'. In *Driven into Paradise*, edited by Brinkmann and Wolff, 155–71.

Franco, Enrique. 'Varia creación de cámara y homenaje a Óscar Esplá', *Arriba*, 24 October 1967, 23.

Gerhard, Roberto. 'Letter to Arnold Schoenberg'. 8 December 1944, Arnold Schoenberg Center.

Gillies, Malcolm. 'Bartók in America'. In *The Cambridge Companion to Bartók*, edited by Bayley, 190–201.

Goehr, Lydia. 'Music and Musicians in Exile: The Romantic Legacy of a Double Life'. In *Driven into Paradise*, edited by Brinkmann and Wolff, 66–91.

Heine, Christiane. 'Salvador Bacarisse (1898–1963) en el centenario de su nacimiento'. *Cuadernos de música iberoamericana* 5 (1998): 43–75.

———. 'La crítica musical de Salvador Bacarisse en *Crisol* y *Luz* (1931–1934)'. In *Los señores de la crítica*, edited by Cascudo and Palacios, 195–254.

Hinton, Stephen. 'Hindemith and Weill: Cases of "Inner" and "Other" Direction'. In Brinkmann and Wolff, eds., *Driven into Paradise*, 261–78.

Iglesias, Antonio. 'Halffter y Narcís Bonet, en el Ateneo'. *Informaciones*, 23 October 1967, 23.

Levi, Erik, ed. *The Impact of Nazism on 20th-Century Music*. Vienna: Böhlau, 2014.

Llano, Samuel. 'Exile, Resistance and Heteroglossia in Roberto Gerhard's *Flamenco*'. In *Stages of Exile: Spanish Republican Exile Theatre and Performance*, edited by Helena Buffery, 107–24. Oxford and New York: Oxford University Press, 2011.

Marco, Tomás. *La música de la España contemporánea*. Madrid: Publicaciones Españolas, 1970.

———. *Música española de vanguardia*. Madrid: Guadarrama, 1970.

———. *Spanish Music in the Twentieth Century*. Cambridge, MA: Harvard University Press, 1993.

Maurer Zenck, Claudia. 'Challenges and Opportunities of Acculturation: Schoenberg, Krenek, and Stravinsky in Exile'. In *Driven into Paradise*, edited by Brinkmann and Wolff, 172–93.

Moore, Allan F. 'Serialism and Its Contradictions'. *International Review of the Aesthetics and Sociology of Music* 26 (1995): 77–95.

Moreda Rodríguez, Eva. 'Early Music in Francoist Spain: Higini Anglès and the Exiles'. *Music & Letters* 96, no. 2 (2015): 209–27.

Neff, Severine. 'Cadence after Thirty-Three Years: Schoenberg's Second Chamber Symphony, Op. 38'. In *The Cambridge Companion to Schoenberg*, edited by Jennifer Shaw and Joseph Auner, 209–25. Cambridge: Cambridge University Press, 2010.

'Noticiario musical'. *Blanco y negro*, 7 September 1963, 102.

Paddison, Max. 'Adorno and Exile: Some Thoughts on Displacements and What It Means to Be German'. In *Music and Displacement*, edited by Scheding and Levi, 135–53.

Pahissa, Jaume. *Los grandes problemas de la música*. Buenos Aires: Poseidón, 1945.

Parsons, James. 'Hanns Eisler's *Hollywooder Liederbuch* and "The New Stuff of Life"'. In *The Impact of Nazism*, edited by Levi, 91–111.

Said, Edward. *Reflections on Exile and Other Essays*. Cambridge, MA: Harvard University Press, 2000.

Sánchez de Andrés, Leticia. 'Roberto Gerhard's Ballets: Music, Ideology and Passion'. In *The Roberto Gerhard Companion*, edited by Monty Adkins and Michael Russ, 79–105. Farnham: Ashgate, 2013.

Scheding, Florian. '"I Only Need the Good Old Budapest": Hungarian Cabarets in Wartime London'. In *Twentieth-Century Music and Politics: Essays in Memory of Neil Edmunds*, edited by Pauline Fairclough. Farnham: Ashgate, 2012.

———. '"Problematic tendencies": Émigré composers in London, 1933–1945'. In *The Impact of Nazism*, edited by Levi, 247–72.

Scheding, Florian, and Erik Levi, eds. *Music and Displacement: Diasporas, Mobilities and Dislocations in Europe and Beyond*. Lanham, MD: Scarecrow Press, 2010.

Silverberg, Laura. 'Between Dissonance and Dissidence: Socialist Modernism in the German Democratic Republic'. *Journal of Musicology* 26, no. 1 (2009): 44–84.

Sopeña, Federico. *Historia de la música española contemporánea*. Madrid: Rialp, 1958.

Valls, Manuel. *La música catalana contemporània: Visió de conjunt*. Barcelona: Selecta, 1960.

———. *La música española después de Manuel de Falla*. Madrid: Revista de Occidente, 1962.

———. *Història de la música catalana*. Barcelona: Tàber, 1969.

White, Julian. 'National Traditions in the Music of Roberto Gerhard'. *Tempo*, no. 184 (1993): 2–13.

Winters, Ben. *Erich Wolfgang Korngold's* The Adventures of Robin Hood: *A Film Score Guide*. Lanham, MD: Scarecrow Press, 2007.

———. 'Swearing an Oath: Korngold, Film and the Sound of Resistance?' In *The Impact of Nazism*, edited by Levi, 62–76.

9

MODERNISM

The people's music?

Robert Adlington

Not for the first time, then, artistic isolates with massive agendas have moved to heal the wound of popular indifference by broadcasting that popular victory has already been won. Did any modernist manifesto neglect to indicate that its handful of exiled signatories spoke from the destined mountaintop of aesthetic history and in the ultimate interest of twentieth-century humanity?[1]

Preliminaries: kinds of modernism

In her book *Modernism and Democracy*, the literary historian Rachel Potter explores the articulation within modernist studies of 'two genealogies of modernism' in early twentieth-century Anglo-American literature.[2] The first is marked by hostility to a mass public and everyday life, and specifically by suspicion towards liberal and democratic values. Writers such as Ezra Pound and T. S. Eliot proposed that progressive artists should assume a legislative role, forming a new sovereign class in opposition to the debased and discredited laws of the popular commercial sphere. The second genealogy of modernism champions democracy and the popular voice. In modernist studies, this genealogy is associated especially with women writers such as Virginia Woolf, Gertrude Stein and Mina Loy, who sought to identify progressive literary styles with less authoritarian values, including the foregrounding of self-expression and individual freedom. Having postulated her two genealogies, Potter is quick to problematize them, noting that they are oversimplified and unhelpful in comprehending the subtly different and evolving attitudes of writers to changing ideas of democracy in the early twentieth century. Yet she is not alone in discerning these divergent tendencies within modernism. Raymond Williams – whose penetrating analyses of the politics of modernism I will return to in several places in this chapter – notes how the critique offered by modernists could 'go either way [. . .] [towards privileging] art as a sacred realm above money and commerce [. . .] [or towards] the revolutionary doctrines [. . .] of art as the liberating vanguard of popular consciousness'.[3] For Richard Sheppard, modernism encompassed both 'right-wing nostalgia' for 'an ideal, hieratic past', and 'left-wing utopianism' that strove for 'an ideal, socialist future'.[4] Hubert van den Berg traces a similar pattern in the evolution of the idea of the artistic avant-garde, within which the motifs of uncompromising leadership and dedicated service intermingle, sometimes to the point of uncomfortable contradiction.[5]

Modernism: the people's music?

Recent musicology has tended to focus upon the first reading of modernism, highlighting its hostility to the popular sphere. Peter Franklin, for instance, proposes that modernism offers a late manifestation of Romanticism's antipathy to mass consumer taste and the trends of the market, asserting instead the need for 'a new kind of cultural power, of cultural aristocracy'.[6] Franklin here follows Andreas Huyssen's well-known reading of modernism as a phenomenon that constituted itself through 'a conscious strategy of exclusion, an anxiety of contamination by its other: an increasingly engulfing mass culture'.[7] For many present-day commentators on musical modernism, any broader impulse of social critique behind this 'strategy of exclusion' rapidly evaporated to leave behind a club of inaccessibility, exemplified in Arnold Schoenberg's assertion that 'if it is art, it is not for all', and Milton Babbitt's advocacy of composition as a specialist field comparable to advanced mathematics or theoretical physics.[8] Richard Taruskin has argued that 'the legacy of fascism is an inherent [. . .] facet of the anti-democratic legacy of modernism', a conclusion adduced from the 'contempt of liberalism and democracy' shown by Stravinsky's sympathy for Mussolini, Schoenberg's 'fealty to a rigid social hierarchy', and Webern's welcoming of the Nazis to Vienna.[9] Ben Earle similarly remarks upon the 'heroic self-image' of modernist artists, whose claims for transcendence above quotidian realities map neatly onto the aspirations of mid-century fascism.[10] For Earle, modernism 'is inextricably bound up with desires for historical priority, for domination of perceived inferiors, for exclusion and/or estrangement of the work of others. [. . .] Modernism itself is essentially anti-liberal'.[11]

The danger of views such as these becoming accepted orthodoxy in current musicology is that they risk allowing us to forget the presence within the classic modernist movements of a democratizing or popular-revolutionary urge. Italian Futurists, for instance, rejected the view of art as an 'inviolable and sacred world', proclaiming instead that 'we will sing of great crowds excited by work, by pleasure, and by riot [. . .] [and] of the multi-coloured, polyphonic tides of revolution in the modern capitals'.[12] In the early years of the Bolshevik republic, Constructivists similarly 'declared unconditional war on art' on the basis that 'the means and qualities of art are not able to systematize the feelings of a revolutionary environment'; instead, the goal was 'to summon the masses to creative activity'.[13] Tristan Tzara described the early Dada performances at the Cabaret Voltaire as 'new art to the greatest number of people', highlighting how the variety of nationalities and staged activities on show represented 'the joy of the people';[14] German Dadaists, meanwhile, demanded 'the international revolutionary union of all creative and intellectual men and women on the basis of radical Communism'.[15] Weimar modernism, in turn, developed in critical response to the erstwhile 'isolation of the artist'; in the words of Walter Gropius, 'lack of all vital connection with the life of the community led inevitably to barren esthetic speculation.'[16] The post-1945 neo-avant-garde extended the concern of Futurism and Dada to abolish the separation of art from everyday life through the experimental activities of the *dérive* and the happening. In the sixties and seventies, new waves of progressive and experimental cultural activity were given direction by the New Left's critique of forms of cultural oppression and control, and by the popular protests of 1968.

Did none of this touch musicians? Of course it did. For every aristocrat of the senses or *Kunstführer* associated with musical modernism, there was a poet of the proletariat or socially engaged visionary willing to argue that modernism was the people's music. The house composers of the Futurist movement ridiculed the 'idiotic religious excitement' of bourgeois concert audiences, and strove instead to render 'the musical soul of the masses' through the musical transcription of 'street-cars, internal-combustion engines, automobiles, and busy crowds'.[17] Nikolai Roslavets, a leading figure in Moscow's musical life following the 1917 revolution, intended his experimental 'New System of Tone Organization' to give rise to what he called '"head smashing" works for the proletariat'.[18] A concern for 'the people' was by no means the exclusive property of the left: Alfredo Casella, the Italian fascist regime's 'unofficial composer',[19] argued at one and the same time for a music of 'dynamism', 'boldness', 'architectonic sense' and 'absence of rhetoric', and for the creation of 'theatres modern in every way, which will welcome at the cheapest prices a totally new public, one no longer laden with prejudices like the haggard aristocratic-bourgeois phalanx that still turns up at La Scala'.[20] After the fall of Mussolini, the same conjunction of aesthetic adventurousness and popular motivation was voiced by Casella's harshest critics, who linked his muscular neo-classicism with totalitarianism, and argued instead that (in the words of Luigi Nono) to be 'an activist musician, not *above* but *in* the class struggle as it exists' required 'the use of the musical language at its most advanced stage'.[21] The equation of liberatory music and politics was clearer still in the Black Arts Movement of mid-1960s New York, where free jazz musicians legitimized their innovative music as a 'reflection of the Negro people as a social and cultural phenomenon', whose 'purpose ought to be to liberate America aesthetically and socially from its inhumanity'.[22] Free improvisers similarly saw their musical experimentation as the product of a situation where 'the existing forms are incapable of serving the needs of people';[23] 'we believed', claimed Musica Elettronica Viva's Alvin Curran, 'that the new direction in music would have a transformative effect on society.'[24]

Despite the urgency and frequency with which such claims have been prosecuted, the notion that a radically unfamiliar mode of artistic expression can act in the interests of a broad populace remains counterintuitive to many. It is the central purpose of this chapter to understand how such a claim could be sustained. But first, a possible objection needs to be addressed: are all the musicians just cited legitimate examples of musical modernism? Jim Samson's contention that modernism qualifies as an 'essentially contested concept', whose very existence is predicated upon debates about its meaning, acts as a reminder that there is unlikely to be general agreement on this question.[25] Debates over definitions of musical modernism have intensified in recent years, with the term deployed in relation to an increasingly diverse range of musical practices, prompting angry disputes about what can or cannot count as 'modernist'.[26]

To circumvent these endless wrangles, I propose to focus upon what these musicians do all have in common – namely, the perception of creating a music that resists hegemonic models, whose innovation upturns perceived fundamentals of compositional order and expressive code, defying the musical 'common sense' of culture at large. We can see this 'anti-hegemonic' instinct clearly expressed in Helmut Lachenmann's insistence upon the 'negation of inherited norms', or in Eddie Prévost's 'refusal to bend to the contours of the superstructures of authority', to cite just two examples.[27] It may manifest itself in different ways: as withdrawal or estrangement of meaning; as aggressive assault on conventions and norms; as detached, speculative experiment; as reversion to unmediated instinct and spontaneity. It may follow the prescription of Gramscian 'counterhegemony' in seeking to establish an alternative dominant worldview, or it may be aimed at the dissolution of all constraining social ideology. Importantly, it is a perspective not necessarily coterminous with modernism, in any of its existing definitions. For instance, the 'anti-hegemonic' may well encompass music identified as one of modernism's unstable others, be it 'avant-garde', 'experimental', or 'postmodern'.[28] Conversely, it may exclude moderate 'modernist' repertoire whose disquieting aspect is not yet divorced from mainstream expressive conventions to the extent that it confounds conventions of musical reception.[29] Further, perceived as a critical alternative to cultural mainstreams, anti-hegemonic music is a category that depends upon a particular view of the prevailing hegemony or hegemonies to be reacted against. Emphasis may variously be placed on popular culture or on the canon of high art; upon an ever-same cultural stasis, or the way that the cultural mainstream is ever-changing, meaning that what is perceived as harshly antagonistic one day may become accepted commodity or cultural

Modernism: the people's music?

heritage the next. The term 'anti-hegemonic' defines a clear creative attitude, but which music gets included within the category remains open to debate.

The musicians mentioned above undoubtedly held quite different views on this last point, but what unified them was the desire to posit alternatives to mainstream norms on behalf of, rather than in opposition to, a broader populace. In their view, hegemonic culture reflected the interests of a social elite – however defined – and worked to oppress that elite's benighted subjects. The innoculatory effects of mass culture were now regarded not as indication of debased popular taste but rather as a cynical tool wielded by others to bolster established power. In offering a progressive alternative to mainstream culture, so the argument went, anti-hegemonic music could serve as a democratic force, indicating fields of future possibility for oppressed populations.

Of course, such a stance brings a paradox: it states that serving the popular cause requires critically confronting, or indeed comprehensively rejecting, the premises of a dominant cultural mainstream which is ostensibly sustained by the preferences of that very populace. How can one claim that a music that declines to affirm widespread norms be imagined to do so in the popular cause? Wasn't a primary characteristic of modernism precisely 'the property of being hard to sell to large numbers of people'?[30] What communal goals can be sought by texts which are, in Leonard Diepeveen's words, 'not cooperative'?[31] The failure of such music to appeal to the constituency it was intended to benefit has sometimes been acknowledged even by its practitioners, as in the case of African American free jazz, which some of its proponents eventually accepted had 'lost almost all contact with black listeners' by the end of the 1960s.[32] As we will see in the following section, other progressive artists, including figures such as Brecht and Nono, argued that their experimental works could and did appeal to a broad audience (in their case, workers specifically) but that institutional factors and performance conventions typically impeded such unproblematic communication. Commentators have tended to be sceptical of such claims, in the absence of independent verification.[33] In any case, the challenge to conventions of reception implicit in the business of being 'anti-hegemonic' in itself poses an obstacle to asserting a popular identification. So on what bases, then, could the claim be made that such music is, nonetheless, for 'the people'?

Communalizing the 'not cooperative': the options

The idea that musical and social revolution go hand in hand – that 'the New Music [. . .] should be music adequate for a new society', to quote Christian Wolff – has been a commonplace throughout the twentieth century.[34] Indeed, it was a view as self-evident to its proponents as the contrary stance – that the needs of the people are best served by accessibility and familiarity – was (and is) to the past century's realists and populists. There were however many variants to the basic idea, variously emphasizing such aspects as rupture, negative critique, and anticipation of a different future. The following discussion surveys some of these, providing a preliminary mapping of different arguments regarding the perceived proximity of anti-hegemonic music-making and the popular cause. As we will see, a recurrent theme is the ease with which the putatively 'democratic' modernist slips into being an 'elitist' modernist – pointing to the vagueness of the distinction between the two positions.

A core strategy was to forge a simple rhetorical association with the principle of revolution. The equation of artistic and political advance had been mooted in progressive circles since at least the 1820s, but it gained new currency from the wave of peasant, proletariat and nationalist uprisings that culminated in the 1917 Bolshevik Revolution in Russia and the 1918–19 November Revolution in Germany. These events encouraged new artistic movements to reach for the kind of revolutionary rhetoric quoted towards the start of this chapter, casting themselves as overthrowing the *ancien régime* of individualism and aestheticism in favour of down-to-earth ideologies of primitivism, labour and machines. This certainly implied no necessary investment in the political programmes of revolutionary movements (although the German Dada and Bauhaus movements did come to espouse a kind of Leninism in the 1920s). Artists were more frequently motivated by an essentially aesthetic attraction to the idea of revolution; the shock, social antagonism and 'violent assault on existing conventions' being realized in the political sphere provided a suitably controversial model for artistic iconoclasts to emulate.[35] As Raymond Williams has noted, this aesthetic appropriation could profoundly misrepresent the revolutionary process: in the Futurist formulation, for instance, fetishization of anarchy and riot replaced strict party organization, and the model of the polyphonic carnival was substituted for 'the single track of proletarian revolution'.[36]

Anti-hegemonic musicians have been equally willing to couch their experiments in revolutionary terms, although the degree to which a specifically political connotation was intended has varied between them. When John Cage declared (in 1939) that 'percussion music is revolution', the intended association between compositional and political fields was left relatively open.[37] When, a couple of decades later, Pierre Boulez likened his compositional thought to 'the state of "permanent revolution"', or Bill Dixon named a festival 'October Revolution in Jazz', the association with radical politics was more explicit, because of the overt reference to Marxist theory and the events of 1917.[38] A similar desire to appropriate the kudos of political progressivism may be perceived in Percy Grainger's and Dane Rudhyar's contemporaneous assertions of the 'democratic' nature of their musical innovations, and even in Schoenberg's resonant call, in 1926, for the 'emancipation of the dissonance'.[39]

By no means all invocations of revolution by progressive musicians signalled sympathy for the cause of popular rule, however. Schoenberg is a case in point. In his *Harmonielehre* (1911) he allowed that a new approach to tonality could replace 'the laws of the autocrat' with a 'self-directed' domain which 'following its own dictates, [will] make for itself laws consistent with its nature'. Yet the revised edition of 1921 added that 'this new order will soon begin to resemble the old, until it becomes completely equivalent to the old [. . .] for order is as much God's will as change'.[40] This and further textual additions making clear that 'art has nothing to do with revolution' were added in part as a defensive response to conservative critics' characterization of Schoenbergian atonality in terms of 'Bolshevik anarchy'.[41] Further evidence of leading modernists' hostility to mass politics can be found in Stravinsky's comprehensive rejection, in his *Poetics*, of 'the prestige of revolution', and his equation of revolution with chaos.[42] Others aligned themselves with an idea of revolution whose inhumanity and violence appeared only to presage a new kind of domination, as in George Antheil's description of his *Ballet mécanique* (1925): 'All efficiency. NO LOVE. Written without sympathy. Written cold as an army operates. Revolutionary as nothing has been revolutionary.'[43]

More substantive claims for proximity to a popular cause emerge when musicians move beyond purely rhetorical invocations of rupture and violent change to position their anti-hegemonic music as a form of contestation – in other words, as a critique of 'how things are'. This 'critical stance towards contemporary culture' (to quote composer and essayist Claus-Steffen Mahnkopf)[44] may be traced back to what some scholars have regarded as the founding crises of modernism – namely the processes of urbanization, industrialization and rationalization that represented a 'cultural cataclysm' to many early twentieth-century artists for the threat they posed to the most fundamental tenets of liberal humanism.[45] This history helps to remind us that social criticism is arguably a facet of both genealogies of modernism delineated by Rachel Potter: the key difference is whether the criticism is an expression of hostility towards the masses themselves, or is (as it were) levied against powerful forces on their behalf. It is not always easy to distinguish between the two.

Modernism: the people's music?

This is clear if we turn to the 'critical composition' of post-war German composers such as Nikolaus A. Huber, Helmut Lachenmann and Mathias Spahlinger. The work of these figures hardly constitutes a unified school of composition, but it manifests a shared interest in the 'socially emancipatory implications' of a systematic interrogation of accepted musical practices.[46] The origins of the idea of critical composition may be traced to the antiauthoritarian critique of the German student movement in the late 1960s;[47] in Huber's and Spahlinger's cases, it was an approach additionally informed by a personal commitment to Marxism. Sensitivity to the constraining force of social ideology drove approaches to composition aimed at 'offering as much resistance to the inherited categories of communication as is demanded by the contradictions and unfreedom embodied in them'.[48] Specifically, critical composers aimed at a 'negation of norms', which could apply to the domains of musical material, performance techniques or concert convention, in order to achieve what Lachenmann termed the 'freedom of the non-standardised (so to speak, the freedom of the "oppressed")'.[49] But who is gaining freedom from whom, in this 'exclusion' of habits 'preformed in society'?[50] 'The prerequisite for critical composition', Huber noted, 'is critical listening',[51] and whilst the collaboration that this implies promised for Huber a welcome breach of the divide between composer and audience, it rests on an assumption: namely, the listener's preparedness to (as Lachenmann put it) 'allow himself to be provoked and infected' in order to recognize 'that experience of freedom [...] as a precondition for human thinking per se'.[52] This would seem to imply the stance of 'detachment and disinterestedness' that Pierre Bourdieu argued was dependent upon cultural competencies granted only to those with particular social and educational backgrounds.[53] Arguing (with Marx) for the 'full and free development of every individual' is one thing; assuming it as a present possibility for listeners in general is quite another. The claims of critical composition to constitute a democratizing force – as opposed to another retreat of the elite, the very 'anxiety of contamination' described by Huyssen – hang entirely upon the unproven availability of the required modes of reflectively analytical listening to a wider audience.

'Critical' composers have sought to shore themselves up against accusations of elitism by identifying other, more specific targets for their oppositional stance. One of these is 'the bourgeoisie' – or, to adopt more modern parlance, the comfortable middle classes – a target that has united anti-hegemonic artists of very different creative and political hues. Indeed, the claim to be anti-bourgeois – to 'ignore and circumvent [it], or [...] increasingly shock, deride and attack [it]' – is read by Raymond Williams as a defining characteristic of modernist art.[54] One could confidently expect fully signed-up Marxists to take critical aim at the bourgeoisie – and indeed the writings of composers as varied as Eisler, Nono, Cardew and Spahlinger are rich with such attacks. But critique of the bourgeoisie was also voiced by anti-hegemonic musicians with less well-advertised political affiliations. An early Fluxus manifesto announced the desire to 'purge the world of bourgeois sickness', a goal pursued through the group's radical assault upon the performance conventions of established artistic institutions.[55] Indeed, it is common for any subversion of concert hall convention – of the sort encountered in the theatre pieces of Kagel and Ligeti, for instance – to be regarded as an attack on bourgeois values specifically. Alternatively, musical or dramatic devices can be deployed to mock the musical tastes of the bourgeoisie, as in the early theatrical works of Peter Maxwell Davies with their parodies of hymns and foxtrots.

The question that arises here is the extent to which an anti-bourgeois stance may be deduced as simultaneously a pro-proletariat, pro-popular and/or pro-democratic one. Marxist orthodoxy regards the bourgeoisie as being in unyielding conflict with the masses, suggesting that to attack bourgeois taste was implicitly to express solidarity with those who are exploited by the bourgeoisie – regardless of whether the exploited groups had any interest in or identification with the mode of critique. The logic is faulty, however, in so far as the self-same bourgeois (or parts of it, at least) have long accepted the theatre and the concert hall as places where such attacks may occasionally be expected and even welcomed as a token of their tolerance and curiosity. Indeed, shocking the bourgeois has been described by more than one author as a characteristically bourgeois pursuit.[56] (Georg Lukács wrote memorably about the 'ultra-radicals' in art 'who imagine that their anti-bourgeois moods [. . .] have transformed them into inexorable foes of bourgeois society.')[57] Raymond Williams also notes how modernism's attacks on the bourgeoisie have more often resembled the 'aristocratic complaint' that the bourgeoisie were 'vulgar, hidebound, moralistic and spiritually narrow', than they have given voice to the viewpoint of an exploited majority.[58]

Preferred by some anti-hegemonic musicians as the principal target for their contestatory practice is the socio-economic edifice of capitalism, manifested today in the global creative industries and their tendency (in the words of Anthony Iles) to 'trap, fix, shape and automate our very powers of perception and affectability'.[59] How could such opposition act in support of the masses that (seemingly gladly) consume the very cultural products manufactured by these industries? The argument hangs on the thesis, well-worn in leftist critical theory, that 'popular culture' is a misnomer, in so far as it is the outcome, not of a genuinely free expression of public preference, but of a profit-producing mechanism predicated on force-feeding and central control. The composer James Dillon, for instance, has argued that 'if you talk about popular today you're talking about mass audiences and a mass mindset, which is the tail-end of propaganda and advertising campaigns and massive forms of indoctrination through subliminal means of technology.'[60] From this analysis arises the perception that radically different forms of cultural expression may serve the purposes of humanity precisely by offering a critical diagnosis of life under capitalism. This may be achieved either mimetically – depicting modernity as it actually is, 'staging the brutality and grime of life' beneath the illusory veils of consumerism and entertainment culture[61] – or may take the path of critical autonomy advocated by Adorno, in which the unflinching engagement of an artist with historically sedimented 'material' forges a truthful image of the relation, perilously imbalanced under late capitalism, between individual and social forces.

However, music created on either of these models – as bleak dystopia or rigorous exercise of technique – faced the problem of its extreme marginalization, rendering (as even Adorno recognized) its emancipatory effects largely mute. More effective acts of resistance to capitalism arguably arose from kinds of engagement with mass culture, rather than total rejection of it. In the case of mid-century jazz the critique of the culture industry arose from musicians working within it – and it was precisely the social injustices confronting African American musicians that, in the words of Ronald Radano, helped them 'resist hegemonic co-optation' by the forces of capitalism.[62] Black jazz musicians of the 1940s came to resent the entertainment function assigned to their performances, regarding it as a form of stereotyping intrinsically connected to the racial discrimination they suffered in other areas of life. Bebop responded to this dissatisfaction by aspiring to the complexity and autonomy from social function associated with musical modernism, in a conscious attempt to 'to dispel the stereotypical image of shuffling, smiling Negro entertainers, who provided danceable beats and recognizable melodies for segregated audiences'.[63] In this effort, the 'prestige of autonomy' could serve a liberatory function for those ordinarily excluded from the 'higher' reaches of culture.[64]

Other progressive jazz musicians sought to reclaim the 'popular' from the 'commercial' rather than treat the two as inseparable, thus countenancing an engagement with vernacular culture, albeit subjected to various characteristically modernist processes of defamiliarization. Members of the Chicago jazz collective AACM, for instance, were committed to 'the dissemination of "great Black music" [. . .] on our own terms, without the intervention of the normal industry

Modernism: the people's music?

manipulations'.[65] This cause required the deployment of noise, parody and fragmentation to highlight the problematic cultural histories underpinning popular music's circuits of appropriation and transmission, and it played too on the long-established avant-garde perception that popular forms, for all their mediation by commerce, carried oppositional potential within the institutionalized artworld.[66] In Radano's words, 'the abstract, nontonal sound world of modernism' was deployed by AACM in order actively to 'recast its dominant styles into a personal musical vocabulary that placed the black musical legacy at the forefront'.[67] Such experimental ventures were regarded as entirely consistent with the social activism within marginalized communities in which AACM musicians were also heavily invested.

Nowhere is the resistance to capitalist commodification more energetically asserted than in discourses around free improvisation. This music's defiance of commodity form has multiple aspects. First, free improvisation's insistence on 'living in the here and now' means that, for some of its champions, 'it can't be bought and sold by capitalism'; there is no fixed object to be endlessly reproduced and fetishized.[68] Second, its frequently jarring and amorphous sounding qualities are seen as refusing the modes of consumption favoured by the record industry.[69] Third, in collective improvisation individual contributions are often difficult to disentangle from the whole, marking a communal rather than individualistic ethos; Eddie Prévost has consequently declared that the free improviser 'refuses to own or to be owned'.[70] Comparable claims have been made for contemporary noise music, in particular that its explorations of feedback, overloaded circuitry, and other aggressively amplified electronic sound defy mass reproduction.[71]

Such claims need to reckon with the familiar story of progressive art's entanglement with the market capitalism that it has frequently been imagined to oppose. The centrality to both modernist artists and commerce of certain shared values – the injunction to 'make it new'; the entrepreneurialism; the concern for publicity – suggests how innovative artistic practice was as much the product of the twentieth century's newly adventurous consumer culture as its nemesis. (Peter Franklin notes how within the 1960s musical avant-garde 'the barriers and targets for the corporate project of bourgeois-shocking outrage were reached and surpassed almost with the relish and efficiency of target-driven financial and managerial services.')[72] This commonality of values increases the precariousness of alternative forms of creativity in the face of creeping commodification, especially in a post-Fordist economic landscape where niche interests are targeted for market expansion, non-conformism and difference are valuable brand attributes, and 'disruptive innovation' is considered a core business strategy.[73] From this arises many theorists' conviction that 'aesthetic innovation and experimentation' is today 'integrated into commodity production generally'.[74] Modernism, we are told, has become capitalism's 'preferred cultural style', finally realizing the avant-garde goal of the collapse of art into life – only in the form of abject surrender rather than triumphant colonization.[75] Certainly, it would be foolish to assert that any genre of anti-hegemonic music entirely resists commodification: concert tickets are sold; CDs are made; online circulation and publicity are routed via global technology corporations. Set alongside this reality, it is worth recognizing the very limited contribution that anti-hegemonic musics are likely to make to the processes of capital accumulation, either for the musicians themselves or for the capitalist networks and modes of exchange upon which they depend.[76] Nor does the ever more complete subsumption of social life by capitalism fully erase distinctions between mainstream and marginalized cultures; the oft-asserted impossibility of a revolutionary overthrow of capitalism does not fully disable projects of resistance to hegemonic norms, nor does it prevent the positing of communitarian over individualistic economic models.

At this juncture we can turn from accounts of anti-hegemonic music that lay stress upon its negative critique of the forces of oppression, to a different explanation of its popular mandate: namely, that it offers a positive articulation of alternative subjectivities. The case of noise music is again useful here. For some of its practitioners, noise carries the potential to disinter levels of subjectivity that have been engulfed by the shaping processes of modernity.[77] Whether it is the jolt provided by a blast of amplified feedback, or a more meditative openness to 'let sounds be themselves', noise has been claimed to offer 'the articulation of a thwarted condition'[78] – with no special initiation process required. The sense that this represents a casting back to primordial, forgotten levels of being is mirrored in the explanations of some free improvisers, among whose declared goals is to 'make music as if for the first time' or 'as if there had never been any music before'.[79] The common idea here may be understood in the terms by which Kristeva explained the disruptive and destabilizing impact of modernist literature: the 'phenotext' of codified meaning may be 'disturbed, ruptured and undercut' by the 'genotext', which is produced by the materiality of language and 'articulates the drives and desires of a pre-linguistic subjectivity'.[80] The result is what might be termed a somatic modernism. It is no accident that several writers have associated musical modernism with the Lacanian concept of 'jouissance', which Kristeva borrowed to encapsulate the loss of a coherent sense of self in the face of the genotext.[81] In Lacan's usage, jouissance is usually understood as denoting a mingling of pleasure and pain – an 'excessive, perverse, murderous' pleasure, to quote Jean-Michel Rabaté.[82] Arved Ashby's reference to 'the bottomless well of possibility' produced by some anti-hegemonic music's abandonment of conventional syntax in favour of the raw materialities of sound nicely captures the combination of excitement and destabilizing anxiety that such experiences may produce. (The complex relation of anti-hegemonic music to pleasure will be returned to in the following section.)

But if the retrieval of a lost subjectivity provides one way to account for the function of a radically different music, it is a trope that has jostled alongside something like the opposite argument: that a new music corresponds to the emergence of a new citizen, one characteristic of a changed or future society. This argument builds upon the post-Romantic claim that modernism's difficulty was to be explained by the distinctively modern consciousness – be it tortured, liberated, multi-layered or otherwise complex – of its creators, only now the argument was turned to the wider popular consciousness being forged by revolutionary processes. As Brecht asserted in 1938, a revolutionary situation enables the masses to 'shed their dehumanization and thereby men become men again – but not the same men as before'.[83] This brings us up against the very notion of a prevailing hegemony to be resisted or countered. In Gramsci's definition, hegemony represented the ideology of a ruling order that was accepted as 'common sense' by the greater part of those who were ruled. To challenge a hegemonic bloc therefore required challenging aspects of one's own understanding of 'how things are', and not simply an assertion of existing tastes or an alternative popular culture.

How, then, to argue that the masses were ahead of – or resistant to – prevailing musical tastes? Communist composers were prepared to regard the proletariat as either already having attained this new, altered consciousness, or being well on the path to so doing. Luigi Nono's defence of his interest in and relationship with factory workers during the 1960s hung on the argument that they and he shared significant common ground through their involvement with advanced technology. Factory workers' labour required (in Nono's view) mastery of technology, an experience that entailed a 'progress of consciousness' in advance of the rest of society. This in turn demanded a mode of musical communication 'exceeding convention and habit', one readily produced in the environs of the electronic studio.[84] The basis of new compositions in recordings of factory sounds was a logical extension of Nono's 'certainty that avant-garde music could become the true musical culture of the workers, advanced from the point of view of art just as politically'.[85] Nono liked to claim that factory workers found electroacoustic pieces like his *La fabbrica illuminata* easier to comprehend than standard concert music because of this advanced consciousness.[86]

Modernism: the people's music?

Other musical Marxists placed the emphasis on the proletariat to come. Nikolai Roslavets, writing in the 1920s, was influenced by Trotsky's perception that a truly proletarian culture could not be expected in the immediate aftermath of revolution. Accordingly, his belief that it was his innovative compositional techniques, rather than 'peasant folk song and traditional forms', that provided 'the building blocks of truly revolutionary music' was predicated on a vision of the proletarian taste of the future, rather than the present.[87] In such a perspective, the distinction between taking the lead from the proletariat on the one hand, and prescribing its path on the other, was hazy at best. The didactic element of revolutionary modernism emerged even more sharply in the manifestos of other figures. Brecht advocated an 'aggressive concept of what is *popular*', one that he sought to advance in his own works, and which included being 'intelligible to the broad masses [...] assuming their standpoint' but also, importantly, 'correcting it'.[88] Such thinking re-emerges in the 1970s in ventures like Louis Andriessen's 'socially critical' Orkest De Volharding;[89] following Hanns Eisler's dictum that a composer's responsibility was to engage with society precisely in order 'to clarify the consciousness of the most advanced class, the working class',[90] Andriessen was committed both to 'taking the audiences' needs and tastes as a starting point', but also the 'need to develop and criticise them at the same time'.[91]

Improvisatory experimental musics since the 1960s have shown elements both of the conviction that a new popular consciousness already exists, and that it needed to be developed and disseminated. Groups such as AMM, Musica Elettronica Viva and Het Leven were motivated significantly by a desire for greater self-liberation on the part of the musicians themselves, sometimes to the extent of not publicly announcing performances at all.[92] This might seem to mean an abandonment of a broader audience – and thus risk a return to the haughty 'private societies' of earlier musical modernisms. But this risk could be rhetorically circumnavigated by conceiving of performers as (in Eddie Prévost's words) 'mandated delegates', 'laying out a kind of blueprint for new kinds of human relationships' on behalf of others who chose to attend as an audience.[93] And a logical extension of this stance could be to invite public participation, in recognition of the perception that 'the people' themselves – or at least some of them – were 'on the move'. This was the step taken by Musica Elettronica Viva at the end of the 1960s, whose devised improvisation pieces *Zuppa* (1968) and *Soundpool* (1969) permitted anyone to join in.[94] The sonic obscurity of this music was, as it were, given social sanction by the 'democratic' manner of its production, which aimed at a demystification of the codes of creative practice and a symbolic levelling of participatory involvement. As the anti-hegemonic effort shifted from kinds of sounds to kinds of performance practice – a 'turn towards social relations', as Anthony Iles has put it[95] – so could new bases be found for proclaiming the proximity of musical experiment to a broader community.

Two persistent challenges: difficulty and difference

Anti-hegemonic musicians have thus sought to articulate the popular claims of their unpopular music in contrasting ways: as a prompt to reject 'unfree' modes of thought; as critique of the bourgeoisie and of capitalism; as auguring the rediscovery of lost subjectivities and/or the formation of new ones. In the rhetoric of many individual musicians, multiple justifications may intermingle, reflecting the strain involved in adopting a stance that at face value seems untenable. As the foregoing account illustrates, the 'democratic' genealogy of modernism encompasses positions that more properly belong in the 'elitist' camp.

This fact hasn't prevented many of these same arguments from continuing to surface on the pages of favoured present-day conduits for adventurous musicians such as *Musiktexte* and *The Wire*. In assessing the chances for such position-taking, I want to identify two key challenges which continue to be inadequately addressed in the manifestos and practice of democratically minded anti-hegemonic musicians. In thinking through these issues in detail, there is much to be learnt about the aspirations and effects of anti-hegemonic music-making.

The first concerns the nature of the experience afforded by anti-hegemonic music, and specifically the question of the relation of practitioners' experience to that of those others in whose cause they claim to be acting. Modernism's claim to subversion has often been seen as predicated on its refusal of the enjoyment associated with bourgeois art or commercial culture, on the insistence (in other words) upon an alternative to pleasurable consumption. Whilst modernism's opponents decry its 'agony', its supporters often prize precisely the 'non-pleasurable demands made on the audience or public' or 'the incompatibility [. . .] with pleasure'.[96] We have already seen versions of this attitude in the idea that modernist music stands in opposition to capitalist culture and the pleasurable modes of engagement encouraged therein. The refusal of pleasure can be driven variously by the desire to strike an attitude of radical alienation, or by the determined pursuit of technical rigour (in rebuttal of the surface banalities of the culture industry). With regard to the two genealogies of modernist music, this stance of antagonism may be interpreted as serving either of two contrary social ends: as a snub to the mindless, consumerist masses; or as a tool to highlight their oppression and to stoke them into revolutionary action.

But are things so simple? Relevant here is an argument advanced with characteristic force by Richard Taruskin, which focuses upon what he perceives as the underlying hypocrisy of modernists' critique of pleasure. For Taruskin, the supposed distinction between the elevating function of art and the 'entertainment' provided by popular culture is illusory: a voluntary engagement with culture (whether 'high' or 'low') is always motivated by pleasure, albeit that such pleasure may take different forms.[97] The art/entertainment binary thus maps no real difference in motivation for engagement with cultural products, but rather a desire to mark as superior the particular pleasures of a cultural elite. From this vantage point, modernism's insistence on an alternative to pleasure is simply an intensification of an argument made on behalf of art in general since the advent of Romanticism.

In reality, both sides of this debate are compromised by reductive thinking. Modernists such as Adorno – Taruskin's argument is specifically mounted against Adorno and his latter-day followers – have been content to conclude that popular culture is a blandly homogeneous sphere of passive consumption partly because of their disinclination to attribute agency to those who engage with this culture, meaning that such engagement is simplistically read as a precipitate of the familiar conventions underpinning popular cultural forms.[98] Taruskin, on the other hand, is too ready to regard modernism's critique of entertainment as a denigration of pleasure in general.[99] Modernists have by no means always drawn this equation.[100] Schoenberg, for one, prevaricated on the matter. In 1937 he famously stated his willingness to suspend pleasure in order better to undertake 'the duty of developing my ideas for the sake of progress in music, whether I liked it or not'.[101] But nine years later he noted that 'just as obvious as that music is not created to please, is that fact that music *does* please', adding that any composer 'creates in the first place for his own pleasure'.[102] One may identify a wide array of attitudes to pleasure among anti-hegemonic musicians. At one extreme we may place Nicolaus A. Huber's curation of 'lifeless anti-sounds' in his ensemble piece *Harakiri* (1971) – sounds which, in Beate Kutschke's words, 'do not invite being listened to and enjoyed'.[103] At the other, we find the collective improvisation of MEV's *Soundpool* (1969), designed to guide the performers away from an everyday 'environment where painful noise is being produced by other human beings' and towards 'valleys of pleasure in which all are able to hear each other and harmony becomes possible'.[104] In between, there are anti-hegemonic musicians focused upon goals that do not necessarily sit neatly on the dichotomous spectra linking pleasure and its imagined others:

things such as provoking active reflection, challenging established values and modes of perception, aiming to productively unsettle, or to arouse the destabilizing 'jouissance' alluded to earlier in this chapter. Many of these musicians might well accept Taruskin's contention that the pursuit of such goals affords creative satisfaction, whilst rejecting his insinuation that such satisfaction can be considered straightforwardly interchangeable with pleasure, 'the agreeable' or 'an intensity of delight'.[105]

The strength of Taruskin's argument resides not so much in the assertion of the primacy of pleasure within all voluntary musical engagement, as in his highlighting the disparities that frequently separate the experiences of modernist musicians and those of their wider audiences. Taruskin's implication is that modernists frequently enjoy the music they claim is to be disliked; they find easy what is being offered as intrinsically difficult. It is a theme explored at length in Leonard Diepeveen's book *The Difficulties of Modernism*. Diepeveen regards difficulty not as an intrinsic property of particular works (as some modernists have contended) but as 'a cultural *situation*, the smooth management of which gives a person entry into high culture'.[106] Modernists who proclaimed difficulty as an intrinsic facet of their artistic output possessed the professionalized skills to domesticate difficulty, to bring it within acceptable limits – their difficulty, in other words, was very different from the visceral, bewildering experience of the untutored reader or listener. 'Difficulty's apologists', Diepeveen contends,

> didn't adequately acknowledge the messiness of difficulty and its social situation, particularly that difficulty *is* about power and about failure: a work is difficult because some person or group of persons doesn't understand it, and further, this group that doesn't understand the difficult work recognizes that others *do* claim to understand it.[107]

In Taruskin's account, this disparity between specialist musicians' and general audiences' experience of anti-hegemonic music is only compounded by the efforts of sympathetic commentators (and sometimes the musicians themselves) to wish away the difficulty experienced by ordinary listeners, resulting in what Taruskin calls 'coercive rhetoric, a hard sell'.[108]

Such a disparity in experience is of course the very essence of elite modernism – whether or not it is framed in terms of the rejection of pleasure. The elite modernist finds value in the greater novelty, nuance, spiritual depth or structural sophistication of modernist art in part precisely because of their rarefied standing, their dependence upon special understanding. But it is a much more problematic stance to maintain for those wishing to ascribe anti-hegemonic music with a popular mission or broader social cause, because of the way it reinscribes the Romantic idea of art as 'a realm of occult or forbidden knowledge'.[109] It is a conception evidently built on a logic of subjection – a narrative of mastery. 'If atonal atrocities begin to personify and communicate the technocratic ethos – i.e. experts manipulating ideas and materials', Eddie Prévost has argued, then 'bourgeois life senses not threat but renewal.'[110]

How might things be different? The notion of art as a transformative force, one that brings about change, necessarily attributes to the artist some kind of privileged vantage point: to deny a gap of insight and outlook between artist and audience would seem to deny all possibility for the forging of new creative visions – including anti-hegemonic ones that seek to unmask the prevailing 'common sense' as anything but. The challenge for a democratic anti-hegemonic musician is to locate a space between, on the one hand, the occult practice largely impervious to the public gaze, and on the other, engaging in superficial novelty that leaves dominant practices untouched. Adorno's notion, cryptically advanced in the final sentence of his essay 'Vers une musique informelle', that 'the aim of every artistic utopia today is to make things in ignorance of what they are' offers a hint of what this might mean.[111] An anti-hegemonic music only sets aside the hypocrisies and 'bad faith' identified by Taruskin when the discomfort and disorientation that may be felt by an audience is equally present to its practitioners;[112] where the alternative pleasures it may afford are as attainable by the wider group as by the musicians who strive to act on its behalf. Something of the kind is articulated by improviser and noise artist Mattin, when he talks of 'actively distributing one's vulnerability [. . .]. The goal is to create an unprecedented situation – strange for everybody, without a didactic or presupposed agenda.'[113] Without this potential for common experience, the socially oriented visionary becomes difficult to distinguish from the hermetic high priest, advocating a direction for humanity that only the initiated few may ever pursue.

The second key challenge confronting the project of a 'people's modernism' is social difference. Specifically, what are the consequences for cultural progressives of the recognition of the situatedness and multiplicity of worldviews and values among contemporary audiences? Historically, modernism's political potency tended to be articulated through homogenizing claims: that there exists a single undifferentiated mass public; that this public consumes an undifferentiated popular culture, taking an enjoyment from it that is comparably undifferentiated; that modernism proposes a single alternative direction, as a necessary liberation from cultural oppression. Whether or not that liberation is available purely to the visionaries who create it, or to 'the people' at large, is the issue separating elite and 'democratic' modernists. But the suppositions of early modernists about the uniformity of the masses – as in the rhetorical flourishes of Futurists, Constructivists and Dadaists cited at the start of this chapter – became increasingly hard to sustain as the twentieth century progressed. As Jeremy Gilbert has succinctly outlined, the 'general liberalisation of advanced capitalist societies [. . .] expanded the personal freedom of their citizens and allowed many new sets of demands to emerge', producing 'a proliferation of demands, positions and identities' that made it 'difficult for coherent yet clearly antagonistic communities of interest to emerge'.[114] Thus, through the second half of the century, distinct, previously marginalized groups came to the forefront of social conflict, replacing the assumed singularity of a mass proletariat with a multiplicity of differing standpoints and social and political agendas.

This development presents a challenge to any anti-hegemonic musician. For what within this diversified social situation can be assumed as the status quo, the 'common sense', the usual? How may one aspire to jolt listeners from the 'taken-for-granted' when nothing, perhaps, can any longer be taken for granted? Does there any longer exist a single hegemonic culture to be reacted against? The emergence of a pluralistic cultural field had the paradoxical effect that, in Jim Samson's words, 'the notion of an avant-garde, spearheading us into the future, has become itself a conservative – even anachronistic – idea, an idea predicated on the assumption, illusory but immensely powerful, of a single culture.'[115] Critics of modernism have emphasized the capacity of different social constituencies to find subversive meanings and significance in music rejected by modernists. For instance, Susan McClary points to the disparity between what she sees as modernists' characteristic preoccupation with structural autonomy (with its disavowal of personal identities and the sensuous), and the commitment of other musical communities to music's interaction with 'forms of sedimented cultural memory' and 'the experiences of the body'.[116] For Georgina Born, comparably, Adorno's focus upon 'the interaction between composer's subjectivity and musical text' fails to do full justice to music's 'plural and distributed materiality', which compels an especially active role to meaning generation on the part of a situated listener.[117] From such ineradicable differences in perspective arise the likelihood that one person's edifice of cultural hegemony may be another's force of resistance or liberation; one person's stupefying din is another's enlivening provocation.

Of course this demographic pluralization hasn't stopped musicians desiring to contest perceived mainstreams. On the contrary, the past fifty years have seen an explosion of musics conceived as markers of various marginal and/or dissenting identities. Awareness of social differ-ence has frequently coupled with a sensitivity to dominant cultural forms and a desire to explore alternatives, producing musico-social movements fundamentally concerned with asserting the affective rights of a particular group within society, rather than making a claim for the liberation of society as a whole. The 'self-liberation' desired by free improvisers at the end of the 1960s, mentioned at the end of the last section, provides a good example, inseparable as it frequently was from visions of an alternative worldview and lifestyle. The role of an anti-hegemonic music as an integral aspect of the identity of a particular community became increasingly prevalent in the 1970s and 1980s, with the emergence of death and black metal, industrial, noise and other 'under-ground' and experimental micro-genres, each beneficiaries of a social and technological context that enabled more active expression of resistance to convention through creative experiment.[118] Relevant here, also, are artists working outside the cosmopolitan centres traditionally associ-ated with modernism, whose relationship to the specific contexts and situations of their region are of growing interest within the 'new modernist studies'.[119] These grassroots modernisms – if they may so be termed, indicating the way in which each 'claims to speak the truth of its audience's situation'[120] – begin to break down some of the oppositions historically touted by modernism's advocates and critics alike: they present a music that takes issue with society as it is, but from a communal rather than fiercely individualistic context; whose venturesomeness is integrally linked to ways of life and behaviours, rather than autonomous of social practice; which asserts a visionary inviolability yet claims no universal relevance or superior legitimacy for all.

Does this development mark the end for a revolutionary musical modernism that serves humanity as a whole? Raymond Williams's categories of 'alternative' and 'oppositional' cul-ture, first elaborated in 1973, are useful here. Both designate 'that which is not corporate; [. . .] practices, experiences, meanings, values which are not part of the effective dominant culture.'[121] The 'alternative', however, corresponds specifically to 'the individual and small-group solutions to social crisis' that began to emerge in the late 1960s: adopting the stance of 'disregarding or despising' dominant culture, an alternative culture 'simply finds a different way to live and wishes to be left alone with it'.[122] The 'oppositional', on the other hand, 'finds a different way to live and wants to change the society in its light', demanding solutions which ultimately involve revolutionary action. Williams's binary echoes the vigorous debates on the left during the late 1960s and early 1970s – waged between old left, New Left and the counterculture – about the respective significance of attitudinal and political liberation in the post-war world. As his word-ing suggests, he judged the 'alternative' to be of secondary importance to the 'oppositional'. But Williams was writing in 1973, at arguably the very last moment when one might legitimately have hope for the coming to consciousness of a mass revolutionary class in Western Europe. The question that remains for those who harbour aspirations for transforming society through anti-hegemonic cultural practice is how it may be possible to transcend the particularities of individual experience and subject position to reach – whether through negation, provocation, visceral assault, destabilizing pleasure, or re-sensitization to the world and its discontents – a broader 'people'.

Conclusion: figuring the people

These challenges are unlikely to cause progressive musicians to desist from proclaiming such goals as 'societal progress' and 'serving man' any time soon.[123] Such assertions at least continue to remind us of the inadequacy of the view that all radically different music is socially detached in both intention and effect. The 'democratic' genealogy of modernism mooted by Rachel Potter appears to be alive and well in the field of music-making. However, as we have seen, it is not

Robert Adlington

untouched by elements of conceptual confusion and contradiction. In particular, 'democratic' and 'authoritarian' tendencies (to borrow Potter's characterization) are not always as easily separable as the rhetoric surrounding them might suggest.

One final question relating to this last point deserves brief appraisal. Namely: what is meant by 'society' and 'man' in such manifesto statements as those just cited? Who, in other words, are 'the people'? The endeavours of most of the musicians who have been considered in this discussion are not fully understood without seeking an answer to this question. Here, there is space only to note briefly two concerns that may arise from positing such an entity, as well as to entertain one final option for construing the 'popular' claims of anti-hegemonic music-making. Constructions of 'the people' have served the ends of politicians, philosophers and artists for centuries. But they carry risks. Elizabeth G. Traube notes how the idea of 'the people' has frequently functioned as 'Reason's domestic Other' – in other words, a local equivalent to the exoticized 'primitive' populations often celebrated by anthropologists for their organic traditions and cultural autonomy. To name 'the people', Traube suggests, is to invoke 'a "discourse of alterity" that distances what it studies from the fictional self it constructs. [. . .] An effect of the dichotomizing is to emphasize differences between the cultures of observers and observed.'[124] To this extent, the democratic modernist's romanticization of the people (like that of many populists and realists) is merely the essentializing flipside of the elitist's vilification. But what about those artists whose invocations of 'the people' explicitly assert a first-person identification – an 'us', rather than a 'you' or 'them'? Here the question is how to distinguish between, on the one hand, faithful representation of a community, and on the other, a kind of cultural ventriloquism in which popular identity is constructed in the service of demagoguery. Political theorists have frequently observed how populists' appeals to 'the people' become a tool for attaining unchallenged power that privileges unanimity and authority over accountability and difference of opinion.[125]

From such concerns emerges a case for anti-hegemonic musicians to set aside considerations of their imagined audiences or constituencies, and focus instead upon their democratic contribution as subversive or disruptive actors. For Jacques Rancière, there is no 'original "people", nor an original popular will'; rather there is the potential to act as 'a figure of the people' by asserting 'pockets of autonomy' from established power – 'a strong movement of action which embodies a power which is the power of everybody and anybody'. The 'power of the people', in Rancière's conceptualization, 'is not the power of the population or of the majority, but the power of anyone at all, the equality of capabilities to occupy the positions of governors and of the governed'.[126] Anti-hegemonic music-making suits itself to Rancière's depiction of the 'power of anybody' because of the way that, by definition, it exists outside – as a 'part which has no part' – of the dominant hegemony. None of this resolves the dilemmas, noted at the outset of this chapter, regarding what is hegemonic and what is not. But it offers a conception of popular action that, as Rancière himself points out, 'does not belong to any particular group, to any particular vanguard', and whose presupposition is the assertion of equality, rather than a connection with a larger populace. In this conception, even the most stridently exclusive modernism, to the extent that it truly resists prevailing forms of normativity, may be understood as comprising the people's music.

Notes

I am grateful to Stephen Graham, Neil Smith and the editors of this volume for offering insightful comments on earlier drafts of this chapter.

1 William J. Maxwell, 'Ralph Ellison and the Constitution of Jazzocracy', *Journal of Popular Music Studies* 16, no. 1 (2004), 40–57.

Modernism: the people's music?

2　Rachel Potter, *Modernism and Democracy: Literary Culture 1900–1930* (Oxford: Oxford University Press, 2006), 1–4. Potter's reading is presented as a response to Michael Levenson's classic study *A Genealogy of Modernism* (Cambridge: Cambridge University Press, 1986).

3　Raymond Williams, *The Politics of Modernism: Against the New Conformists* (London: Verso, 1989), 34.

4　Richard Sheppard, *Modernism – Dada – Postmodernism* (Evanston, IL: Northwestern University Press, 2000), 80–81.

5　Hubert F. van den Berg, 'Avant-Garde: Some Introductory Notes on the Politics of a Label', in *Sound Commitments: Avant-Garde Music and the Sixties*, ed. Robert Adlington (New York: Oxford University Press, 2009), 15–33.

6　Peter Franklin, 'Modernismus and the Philistines', in 'Round Table: Modernism and Its Others', ed. Laura Tunbridge, *Journal of the Royal Musical Association* 139, no. 1 (2014), 186.

7　Andreas Huyssen, *After the Great Divide: Modernism, Mass Culture, Postmodernism* (Bloomington: Indiana University Press, 1986), vii. Franklin, however, does not follow Huyssen in positing the historical avant-garde as offering a critical mediation between modernism and mass culture. Scholarly investigation of the entanglements of modernism and mass culture is surveyed in Douglas Mao and Rebecca L. Walkowitz, 'The New Modernist Studies', *PMLA* 123, no. 3 (2008), 744–45. On the specific case of music, see the chapter by Stephen Graham in the present volume.

8　Arnold Schoenberg, 'New Music, Outmoded Music, Style and Idea' (1946), in *Style and Idea: Selected Writings of Arnold Schoenberg*, ed. Leonard Stein (London: Faber and Faber, 1975), 124; Milton Babbitt, 'Who Cares if You Listen?' *High Fidelity* 8, no. 2 (1958), 38–40 and 126–27.

9　Richard Taruskin, 'The Dark Side of the Moon', *New Republic*, 5 September 1988, 32–34. The first of these claims is worded slightly differently in the reprint of this essay ('the legacy of fascism is an inseparable [...] facet of the lofty legacy of modernism'): see *The Danger of Music and Other Anti-Utopian Essays* (Berkeley: University of California Press, 2009), 212. For a reading of literary modernism as proto-Fascist, see Tom Gibbons, 'Modernism and Reactionary Politics', *Journal of Modern Literature* 3, no. 5 (1974), 1140–57.

10　Ben Earle, *Luigi Dallapiccola and Musical Modernism in Fascist Italy* (Cambridge: Cambridge University Press, 2013), 221 and 230.

11　Ibid., xii–xiii.

12　Luigi Russolo, cited in ibid., 4; Filippo Tommaso Marinetti, cited in *Art in Theory 1900–2000: An Anthology of Changing Ideas*, ed. Charles Harrison and Paul Wood (Oxford: Blackwell, 2003), 148.

13　Alexei Gan and KOMFUT, cited in *Art in Theory*, ed. Harrison and Wood, 344 and 333.

14　Tristan Tzara, cited in Marius Hentea, *Ta Ta Dada: The Real Life and Celestial Adventures of Tristan Tzara* (Cambridge, MA: MIT Press, 2014), 67.

15　Richard Huelsenbeck, cited in *Art in Theory*, ed. Harrison and Wood, 259.

16　Walter Gropius, cited in ibid., 310.

17　Luigi Russolo, cited in *Modernism and Music: An Anthology of Sources*, ed. Daniel Albright (Chicago: University of Chicago Press, 2004), 179; Francesco Pratella, cited in David Ohana, *The Futurist Syndrome* (Brighton: Sussex Academic Press, 2010), 71.

18　Nikolai Roslavets, cited in Amy Nelson, *Music for the Revolution: Musicians and Power in Early Soviet Russia* (University Park, PA: Pennsylvania State University Press, 2004), 64.

19　Francesco Parrino, 'Alfredo Casella and "The *Montjoie!* Affair"', *Repercussions* 10, no. 1 (2007), 97.

20　Casella, cited in Earle, *Luigi Dallapiccola*, 93 and 173.

21　Luigi Nono, 'Une lettre de Luigi Nono: "Je suis un musicien militant"' (1971), in *Écrits*, ed. Laurent Feneyrou (Geneva: Éditions Contrechamps, 2007), 347; Luigi Nono, 'La musica è uno strumento di lotta: Intervista di Gabor Hallasz' (1975), in *Scritti e colloqui*, ed. Angela Ida De Benedictis and Veniero Rizzardi (Lucca: Ricordi, 2001), 2: 217.

22　Archie Shepp, cited in Bernard Gendron, 'After the October Revolution: The Jazz Avant-Garde in New York, 1964–65', in *Sound Commitments*, ed. Adlington, 226.

23　Edwin Prévost, *No Sound Is Innocent* (Matching Tye: Copula, 1995), 101.

24　Amy C. Beal, '"Music Is a Universal Human Right": Musica Elettronica Viva', in *Sound Commitments*, ed. Adlington, 110.

25　Jim Samson, 'Either/Or', in *Rethinking Musical Modernism*, ed. Dejan Despić and Melita Milin (Belgrade: Serbian Academy of Sciences and Arts, 2008), 23–24. On the difficulties of defining modernism, see also Richard Sheppard, 'The Problematics of European Modernism', in *Theorizing Modernism*, ed. Steve Giles (London: Routledge, 1993), 1–4.

26 See, for instance, *British Music and Modernism, 1895–1960*, ed. Matthew Riley (Aldershot: Ashgate, 2010), which advocates a newly expanded definition, and the contrasting opinions voiced in the comments responding to the online version of Tunbridge, ed., 'Round Table: Modernism and Its Others', posted at http://www.rma.ac.uk/students/?p=1585. Such expansiveness has been seen as characteristic of 'new modernist studies'; see Mao and Walkowitz, 'The New Modernist Studies'.

27 Helmut Lachenmann, 'The "Beautiful" in Music Today', *Tempo*, no. 135 (1980), 23; Prévost, *No Sound Is Innocent*, 98.

28 Peter Bürger and Andreas Huyssen are among those who distinguish between modernism and the avant-garde.

29 A further implication is the exclusion of neo-tonal neo-classicism, offered by Richard Taruskin among others as constituting the most significant stylistic and aesthetic rupture in twentieth-century composition; see his *Music in the Early Twentieth Century*, vol. 4 of *The Oxford History of Western Music* (Oxford: Oxford University Press, 2005), 467. Setting aside Stravinsky's own vocal rejection of modernism – see Tamara Levitz, *Modernist Mysteries:* Perséphone (New York: Oxford University Press, 2012), 174–75 – the approach taken in this essay is determined by the way in which hegemonic models are reinscribed as well as lightly parodied in Stravinsky's neo-classical music, an aspect recognized in Hanns Eisler's description of neo-classicism as 'the musical style of "good society"', mimicking 'the inscrutable mask of a big banker'; *A Rebel in Music: Selected Writings* (New York: International Publishers, 1978), 164–65.

30 Mao and Walkowitz, 'The New Modernist Studies', 744.

31 Leonard Diepeveen, *The Difficulties of Modernism* (New York: Routledge, 2003), 163.

32 Iain Anderson, *This Is Our Music: Free Jazz, the Sixties, and American Culture* (Philadelphia: University of Pennsylvania Press, 2007), 149. Stephen Graham makes a similar point in his *Sounds of the Underground: A Cultural, Political and Aesthetic Mapping of Underground and Fringe Music* (Ann Arbor: University of Michigan Press, 2016), 199.

33 On Brecht see the editorial 'Presentation II', in *Aesthetics and Politics: Theodor Adorno, Walter Benjamin, Ernst Bloch, Bertolt Brecht, Georg Lukács*, ed. Ronald Taylor (London: Verso, 1977), 66. On Nono see Timothy S. Murphy, 'The Negation of a Negation Fixed in a Form: Luigi Nono and the Italian Counter-Culture 1964–1979', *Cultural Studies Review* 11, no. 2 (2005), 108.

34 Beate Kutschke, 'Aesthetic Theories and Revolutionary Practice: Nikolaus A. Huber and Clytus Gottwald in Dissent', in *Sound Commitments*, ed. Adlington, 78.

35 Williams, *The Politics of Modernism*, 57.

36 Ibid., 52.

37 John Cage, 'Goal: New Music, New Dance', in *Silence: Lectures and Writings* (Cambridge, MA: MIT Press, 1961), 87.

38 Pierre Boulez, 'Putting the Phantoms to Flight', in *Orientations: Collected Writings*, ed. Jean-Jacques Nattiez and trans. Martin Cooper (London: Faber and Faber, 1986), 71; Benjamin Piekut, *Experimentalism Otherwise: The New York Avant-Garde and Its Limits* (Berkeley: University of California Press, 2011), chapter 3.

39 Percy Grainger, 'Democracy in Music' (1931), in *Grainger on Music*, ed. Malcolm Gillies and Bruce Clunies Ross (Oxford: Clarendon Press, 1999), 217–22; Dane Rudhyar, 'Dissonant Harmony – A New Principle of Musical and Social Organization' (1928), online at Rudhyar Archival Project website, http://www.khaldea.com/rudhyar/dissonantharmony.html; Arnold Schoenberg, 'Opinion or Insight' (1926), in *Style and Idea*, 258–63. In his article 'Emancipation of the Dissonance' Robert Falck reveals that the term had a significant prehistory before Schoenberg used it; see *Journal of the Arnold Schoenberg Institute* 6, no. 1 (1982), 106–11.

40 Arnold Schoenberg, *Theory of Harmony*, trans. Roy E. Carter (London: Faber and Faber, 1978), 152. This English edition marks the differences between the original German editions.

41 See *A Schoenberg Reader: Documents of a Life*, ed. Joseph Auner (New Haven, CT: Yale University Press, 2008), 165.

42 Igor Stravinsky, *Poetics of Music in the Form of Six Lessons*, trans. Arthur Knodel and Ingolf Dahl (Cambridge, MA: Harvard University Press, 1942), 9–13.

43 George Antheil, cited in Carol J. Oja, *Making Music Modern: New York in the 1920s* (New York: Oxford University Press, 2003), 80–81.

44 See the editor's foreword to *Critical Composition Today*, ed. Claus-Steffen Mahnkopf (Hofheim: Wolke, 2006), 8.

45 Sheppard, *Modernism – Dada – Postmodernism*, 6–7.

Modernism: the people's music?

46 Rainer Nonnemann, 'The Dead End as a Way Out – Critical Composition: A Historical Phenomenon?' in *Critical Composition Today*, ed. Mahnkopf, 89.

47 Ibid.

48 Lachenmann, 'The "Beautiful" in Music Today', 22.

49 Helmut Lachenmann, 'Zur Frage einer gesellschaftskritischen (-ändernden) Funktion der Musik', in *Musik als existentielle Erfahrung: Schriften 1966–1995*, ed. Josef Häusler (Wiesbaden: Breitkopf & Härtel, 1996), 98.

50 Lachenmann, cited in Alex Ross, *The Rest is Noise: Listening to the Twentieth Century* (London: Fourth Estate, 2007), 527.

51 Nicolaus A. Huber, 'Critical Composition', *Contemporary Music Review* 27, no. 6 (2008), 567.

52 Lachenmann, 'Zur Frage'.

53 Pierre Bourdieu, 'Introduction' to *Distinction: A Social Critique of the Judgement of Taste*, trans. Richard Nice (New York: Routledge, 1984), 4. Bourdieu has been criticized for the one-dimensional picture he gives of the tastes of those lacking these specific competencies, although this criticism doesn't deny the existence of sharp socially determined differences in modes of aesthetic reception; see Georgina Born, 'The Social and the Aesthetic: For a Post-Bourdieuian Theory of Cultural Production', *Cultural Sociology* 4, no. 3 (2010), 177–78.

54 Williams, *The Politics of Modernism*, 53. See also Peter Gay, *Modernism: The Lure of Heresy* (New York: Norton, 2007), 5–7.

55 Cited in Hannah Higgins, *Fluxus Experience* (Berkeley: University of California Press, 2002), 76. Higgins notes, however, the unease of some Fluxus figures regarding such attacks (see 75–80).

56 Earle, *Luigi Dallapiccola*, 132; see also Williams, *The Politics of Modernism*, 55.

57 Georg Lukács, 'Realism in the Balance', in *Aesthetics and Politics*, ed. Taylor, 36.

58 Williams, *The Politics of Modernism*, 54.

59 Anthony Iles, 'Introduction', in *Noise and Capitalism*, ed. Anthony Iles and Mattin (Gipuzkoa: Arteleku, 2009), 11.

60 Dillon, cited in Igor Toronyilalic, 'Theartsdesk Q&A: Composer James Dillon', *The Arts Desk*, 31 October 2010, http://www.theartsdesk.com/classical-music/theartsdesk-qa-composer-james-dillon.

61 Graham, *Sounds of the Underground*, 190.

62 Ronald M. Radano, *New Musical Figurations: Anthony Braxton's Cultural Critique* (Chicago: University of Chicago Press, 1993), 19.

63 Guthrie P. Ramsey, *Race Music: Black Cultures from Bebop to Hip-Hop* (Berkeley: University of California Press, 2004), 106.

64 Ibid., 109; see also Ingrid Monson's invocation of 'Afro-Modernism', in *Freedom Sounds: Civil Rights Call out to Jazz and Africa* (New York: Oxford University Press, 2007), 71.

65 Don Moye, cited in Ajay Heble, *Landing on the Wrong Note: Jazz, Dissonance, and Critical Practice* (New York: Routledge, 2000), 67.

66 Thomas E. Crow famously referred to the avant-garde's use of popular cultural elements as 'a message from the margins'; see his *Modern Art in the Common Culture* (New Haven, CT: Yale University Press, 1998), 28.

67 Radano, *New Musical Figurations*, 108.

68 Ben Watson, *Derek Bailey and the Story of Free Improvisation* (London: Verso, 2004), 4 and 3.

69 Prévost, *No Sound Is Innocent*, 181.

70 Ibid., 182. It is worth noting that overt individualism is by no means absent from all improvisation; see Robert Adlington, *Composing Dissent: Avant-Garde Music in 1960s Amsterdam* (New York: Oxford University Press, 2013), chapter 3.

71 Csaba Toth, 'Noise Theory', in *Noise and Capitalism*, ed. Iles and Mattin, 32.

72 Franklin, 'Modernismus and the Philistines', 186.

73 David Cottington, *The Avant-Garde: A Very Short Introduction* (Oxford: Oxford University Press, 2013), 94–95.

74 Fredric Jameson, *Postmodernism: Or, the Cultural Logic of Late Capitalism* (London: Verso, 1991), 4–5.

75 John Xiros Cooper, *Modernism and the Culture of Market Society* (Cambridge: Cambridge University Press, 2004), 31; Peter Bürger, *Theory of the Avant-Garde*, trans. Michael Shaw (Minneapolis: University of Minnesota Press, 1984), 54.

76 Chapters 4 to 6 of Graham, *Sounds of the Underground* give extensive attention to the economics of underground music. Graham emphasizes the financial precarity of many underground musicians.

77 A related argument is that noise enables a suspension of subjectivity and access to an 'anti-self'; see GegenSichKollektiv, 'Anti-Self: Experience-Less Noise', in *Reverberations: The Philosophy, Aesthetics and Politics of Noise*, ed. Michael Goddard, Benjamin Halligan and Paul Hegarty (London: Bloomsbury, 2012), 193–206.

78 Iles, 'Introduction', 11.

79 Prévost, *No Sound Is Innocent*, 123; Alvin Curran, 'On Spontaneous Music', *Contemporary Music Review* 25, nos. 5–6 (2006), 485.

80 Graham Allen, *Intertextuality* (London: Routledge, 2000), 50.

81 For instance, see Arved Ashby, 'Introduction', in *The Pleasure of Modernist Music: Listening, Meaning, Intention, Ideology* (Rochester, NY: University of Rochester Press, 2004), 4; Graham, *Sounds of the Underground*, 225–41; J. P. E. Harper-Scott, *The Quilting-Points of Musical Modernism: Revolution, Reaction, and William Walton* (Cambridge: Cambridge University Press, 2012); Toth, 'Noise Theory', 27.

82 Jean-Michel Rabaté, *Jacques Lacan: Psychoanalysis and the Subject of Literature* (Basingstoke: Palgrave Macmillan, 2001), 27.

83 Bertolt Brecht, 'Against Georg Lukács', in *Aesthetics and Politics*, ed. Taylor, 69.

84 Luigi Nono, '*Die Ermittlung*: un'esperienza musicale teatrale con Weiss e Piscator' (1966), in *La nostalgia del futuro: Scritti scelti, 1948–1986*, ed. Angela Ida De Benedictis and Veniero Rizzardi (Milan: Saggiatore, 2007), 131.

85 Michela Garda, 'Da Venezia all'Avana: Nono, la politica e le tradizioni musicali', in *Presenza storica di Luigi Nono*, ed. Angela Ida De Benedictis (Lucca: LIM, 2011), 43.

86 Nono, 'Il musicista nella fabbrica' (1966), in *Scritti e colloqui*, 1: 207–8. Similar arguments that the proletariat were naturally inclined to works based on the noises of machines characterized the constructivism of the early Soviet era; see Nelson, *Music for the Revolution*, 56.

87 Roslavets, cited in Nelson, *Music for the Revolution*, 63–64.

88 Brecht, 'Against Georg Lukács', 81.

89 Louis Andriessen, 'Brief History of De Volharding' (1972), in *Louis Andriessen: The Art of Stealing Time*, ed. Mirjam Zegers (Todmorden: Arc, 2002), 135.

90 Eisler, *A Rebel in Music*, 116.

91 Andriessen, 'Brief History of De Volharding', 136.

92 Prévost, *No Sound Is Innocent*, 28.

93 Ibid., 121–22. The claim that free improvisation contests the kinds of relationships characteristic of capitalism has however been disputed; see Mattin, 'Improvisation and Communisation' (2013), http://www.mattin.org/essays/Improvisation_and_Communisation.html.

94 Beal, 'Music Is a Universal Human Right', 108–10.

95 Iles, 'Introduction', 15.

96 Henry Pleasants, *The Agony of Modern Music* (New York: Simon and Schuster, 1955); Fredric Jameson, *A Singular Modernity: Essay on the Ontology of the Present* (London: Verso, 2013), 1; Earle, *Luigi Dallapiccola*, 132.

97 Richard Taruskin, 'The Musical Mystique: Defending Classical Music against Its Devotees', in *The Danger of Music*, 340–41.

98 On this, see Tia DeNora, *After Adorno: Rethinking Music Sociology* (Cambridge: Cambridge University Press, 2003), 21–34.

99 Harper-Scott reads this focus on pleasure as revealing Taruskin's commitment to 'the circuits of Capital' and the promise of consumerist enjoyment; see *The Quilting-Points of Musical Modernism*, 14–15.

100 As has been clearly demonstrated in literary studies by Diepeveen, *The Difficulties of Modernism*, and Laura Frost, *The Problem with Pleasure: Modernism and Its Discontents* (New York: Columbia University Press, 2015).

101 Schoenberg, 'How One Becomes Lonely' (1937), in *Style and Idea*, 53.

102 Schoenberg, 'Criteria for the Evaluation of Music' (1946), in *Style and Idea*, 135.

103 Kutschke, 'Aesthetic Theories and Revolutionary Practice', 80.

104 Cited in Michael Nyman, *Experimental Music: Cage and Beyond*, 2nd ed. (Cambridge: Cambridge University Press, 1999), 131.

105 Taruskin, 'The Musical Mystique', 340.

106 Diepeveen, *The Difficulties of Modernism*, 42.

107 Ibid., 237.

108 Richard Taruskin, 'The Poietic Fallacy', in *The Danger of Music*, 307.

109 Ibid., 304–5.

Modernism: the people's music?

110 Prévost, *No Sound Is Innocent*, 181–82.

111 Theodor Adorno, 'Vers une musique informelle', in *Quasi una fantasia: Essays on Modern Music*, trans. Rodney Livingstone (London: Verso, 1992), 322.

112 Richard Taruskin, 'How Talented Composers Become Useless', in *The Danger of Music*, 90.

113 Mattin 'Against Representation', http://www.mattin.org/essays/Against_Representation.html. For a description of a Mattin performance built on these stipulates, see Graham, *Sounds of the Underground*, 146–47.

114 Jeremy Gilbert, *Common Ground: Democracy and Collectivity in an Age of Individualism* (London: Pluto Press, 2014), 2.

115 Jim Samson, 'Instrumental Music since 1958', in *The Blackwell History of Music in Britain: The Twentieth Century*, ed. Stephen Banfield (Oxford: Blackwell, 1995), 342.

116 Susan McClary, 'Terminal Prestige: The Case of Avant-Garde Music Composition', *Cultural Critique* 12 (1989), 80. Memory and corporeality have hardly been absent from the preoccupations of modernist musicians, but the point about the different value systems of different musical communities stands.

117 Georgina Born, 'On Musical Mediation: Ontology, Technology and Creativity', *Twentieth-Century Music* 2, no. 1 (2005), 12; 'Music and the Materialization of Identities', *Journal of Material Culture* 16, no. 4 (2011), 377–78. As Born herself implies, her argument adds texture to the well-known claims of reader response theory in literary criticism, in which meaning is always constituted by the circumstances of reading: 'an indeterminate "sharing" between writer and reader'; or an encounter in which 'the writer and reader do not share an intent posited originally with the writer; they share their discontinuity [. . .] their difference'; Ben Etherington, cited in Born, 'Listening, Mediation, Event: Anthropological and Sociological Perspectives', *Journal of the Royal Musical Association* 135, no. 1 (2010), 88.

118 For more on these see the chapter by Stephen Graham in the present volume.

119 See Mark Wollaeger and Matt Eatough, eds., *The Oxford Handbook of Global Modernisms* (Oxford: Oxford University Press, 2012).

120 Toth, 'Noise Theory', 27.

121 Raymond Williams, 'Base and Superstructure in Marxist Cultural Theory', in *Culture and Materialism: Selected Essays* (London: Verso, 2005), 40.

122 Ibid., 42.

123 Mathias Spahlinger, 'This Is the Time of Conceptive Ideologues No Longer', *Contemporary Music Review* 27, no. 6 (2008), 592; Prévost, *No Sound Is Innocent*, 119.

124 Elizabeth G. Traube, '"The Popular" in American Culture', *Annual Review of Anthropology* 25 (1996), 130.

125 Nadia Urbinati, *Democracy Disfigured: Opinion, Truth, and the People* (Cambridge, MA: Harvard University Press, 2014), 134.

126 Kieran O'Connor, '"Don't They Represent Us?" A Discussion between Jacques Rancière and Ernesto Laclau' (2015), http://www.versobooks.com/blogs/2008-don-t-they-represent-us-a-discussion-between-jacques-ranciere-and-ernesto-laclau (accessed 15 September 2017); Jacques Rancière, *Hatred of Democracy* (London: Verso, 2009), 49.

Bibliography

Adlington, Robert, ed. *Sound Commitments: Avant-Garde Music and the Sixties*. New York: Oxford University Press, 2009.

———. *Composing Dissent: Avant-Garde Music in 1960s Amsterdam*. New York: Oxford University Press, 2013.

Adorno, Theodor W. 'Vers une musique informelle'. In *Quasi una fantasia: Essays on Modern Music*, translated by Rodney Livingstone, 269–322. London: Verso, 1992.

Albright, Daniel, ed. *Modernism and Music: An Anthology of Sources*. Chicago: University of Chicago Press, 2004.

Allen, Graham. *Intertextuality*. London: Routledge, 2000.

Anderson, Iain. *This Is Our Music: Free Jazz, the Sixties, and American Culture*. Philadelphia: University of Pennsylvania Press, 2007.

Andriessen, Louis. 'Brief History of De Volharding' (1972). In *Louis Andriessen: The Art of Stealing Time*, edited by Mirjam Zegers, 128–36. Todmorden: Arc, 2002.

Ashby, Arved, ed. *The Pleasure of Modernist Music: Listening, Meaning, Intention, Ideology*. Rochester, NY: University of Rochester Press, 2004.

Auner, Joseph, ed. *A Schoenberg Reader: Documents of a Life*. New Haven, CT: Yale University Press, 2008.

Babbitt, Milton. 'Who Cares If You Listen?' *High Fidelity* 8, no. 2 (1958): 38–40 and 126–27.

Beal, Amy C. '"Music Is a Universal Human Right": Musica Elettronica Viva'. In *Sound Commitments*, edited by Adlington, 99–120.

Born, Georgina. 'On Musical Mediation: Ontology, Technology and Creativity'. *Twentieth-Century Music* 2, no. 1 (2005): 7–36.

———. 'Listening, Mediation, Event: Anthropological and Sociological Perspectives'. *Journal of the Royal Musical Association* 135, no. 1 (2010): 79–89.

———. 'The Social and the Aesthetic: For a Post-Bourdieuian Theory of Cultural Production'. *Cultural Sociology* 4, no. 3 (2010): 171–208.

———. 'Music and the Materialization of Identities'. *Journal of Material Culture* 16, no. 4 (2011): 376–88.

Boulez, Pierre. 'Putting the Phantoms to Flight'. In *Orientations: Collected Writings*, edited by Jean-Jacques Nattiez and translated by Martin Cooper, 63–83. London: Faber and Faber, 1986.

Bourdieu, Pierre. *Distinction: A Social Critique of the Judgement of Taste*. Translated by Richard Nice. New York: Routledge, 1984.

Brecht, Bertolt. 'Against Georg Lukács', in *Aesthetics and Politics*, edited by Taylor, 68–85.

Bürger, Peter. *Theory of the Avant-Garde*. Translated by Michael Shaw. Minneapolis: University of Minnesota Press, 1984.

Cage, John. 'Goal: New Music, New Dance'. In *Silence: Lectures and Writings*, 87–88. Cambridge, MA: MIT Press, 1961.

Cooper, John Xiros. *Modernism and the Culture of Market Society*. Cambridge: Cambridge University Press, 2004.

Cottington, David. *The Avant-Garde: A Very Short Introduction*. Oxford: Oxford University Press, 2013.

Crow, Thomas E. *Modern Art in the Common Culture*. New Haven, CT: Yale University Press, 1998.

Curran, Alvin. 'On Spontaneous Music'. *Contemporary Music Review* 25, nos. 5–6 (2006): 483–90.

DeNora, Tia. *After Adorno: Rethinking Music Sociology*. Cambridge: Cambridge University Press, 2003.

Diepeveen, Leonard. *The Difficulties of Modernism*. New York: Routledge, 2003.

Earle, Ben. *Luigi Dallapiccola and Musical Modernism in Fascist Italy*. Cambridge: Cambridge University Press, 2013.

Eisler, Hanns. *A Rebel in Music: Selected Writings*. New York: International Publishers, 1978.

Falck, Robert. 'Emancipation of the Dissonance'. *Journal of the Arnold Schoenberg Institute* 6, no. 1 (1982): 106–11.

Franklin, Peter. 'Modernismus and the Philistines'. In 'Round Table: Modernism and Its Others', edited by Tunbridge, 183–87.

Frost, Laura. *The Problem with Pleasure: Modernism and Its Discontents*. New York: Columbia University Press, 2015.

Garda, Michela. 'Da Venezia all'Avana: Nono, la politica e le tradizioni musicali'. In *Presenza storica di Luigi Nono*, edited by Angela Ida De Benedictis, 27–53. Lucca: LIM, 2011.

Gay, Peter. *Modernism: The Lure of Heresy*. New York: Norton, 2007.

GegenSichKollektiv. 'Anti-Self: Experience-Less Noise'. In *Reverberations: The Philosophy, Aesthetics and Politics of Noise*, edited by Michael Goddard, Benjamin Halligan and Paul Hegarty, 193–206. London: Bloomsbury, 2012.

Gendron, Bernard. 'After the October Revolution: The Jazz Avant-Garde in New York, 1964–65'. In *Sound Commitments*, edited by Adlington, 211–31.

Gibbons, Tom. 'Modernism and Reactionary Politics'. *Journal of Modern Literature* 3, no. 5 (1974): 1140–57.

Gilbert, Jeremy. *Common Ground: Democracy and Collectivity in an Age of Individualism*. London: Pluto Press, 2014.

Graham, Stephen. *Sounds of the Underground: A Cultural, Political and Aesthetic Mapping of Underground and Fringe Music*. Ann Arbor: University of Michigan Press, 2016.

Grainger, Percy. 'Democracy in Music' (1931). In *Grainger on Music*, edited by Malcolm Gillies and Bruce Clunies Ross, 217–22. Oxford: Clarendon Press, 1999.

Harper-Scott, J. P. E. *The Quilting-Points of Musical Modernism: Revolution, Reaction, and William Walton*. Cambridge: Cambridge University Press, 2012.

Harrison, Charles, and Paul Wood, eds. *Art in Theory 1900–2000: An Anthology of Changing Ideas*. Oxford: Blackwell, 2003.

Modernism: the people's music?

Heble, Ajay. *Landing on the Wrong Note: Jazz, Dissonance, and Critical Practice*. New York: Routledge, 2000.

Hentea, Marius. *Ta Ta Dada: The Real Life and Celestial Adventures of Tristan Tzara*. Cambridge, MA: MIT Press, 2014.

Higgins, Hannah. *Fluxus Experience*. Berkeley: University of California Press, 2002.

Huber, Nicolaus A. 'Critical Composition'. *Contemporary Music Review* 27, no. 6 (2008): 565–68.

Huyssen, Andreas. *After the Great Divide: Modernism, Mass Culture, Postmodernism*. Bloomington: Indiana University Press, 1986.

Iles, Anthony, and Mattin, eds. *Noise and Capitalism*. Gipuzkoa: Arteleku, 2009.

Jameson, Fredric. *Postmodernism, or: The Cultural Logic of Late Capitalism*. London: Verso, 1991.

———. *A Singular Modernity: Essay on the Ontology of the Present*. London: Verso, 2013.

Kutschke, Beate. 'Aesthetic Theories and Revolutionary Practice: Nikolaus A. Huber and Clytus Gottwald in Dissent'. In *Sound Commitments*, edited by Adlington, 78–96.

Lachenmann, Helmut. 'The "Beautiful" in Music Today'. *Tempo*, no. 135 (1980): 20–24.

———. 'Zur Frage einer gesellschaftskritischen (-ändernden) Funktion der Musik'. In *Musik als existentielle Erfahrung: Schriften, 1966–1995*, edited by Josef Häusler, 98. Wiesbaden: Breitkopf & Härtel, 1996.

Levenson, Michael. *A Genealogy of Modernism*. Cambridge: Cambridge University Press, 1986.

Levitz, Tamara. *Modernist Mysteries: Perséphone*. New York: Oxford University Press, 2012.

Lukács, Georg. 'Realism in the Balance'. In *Aesthetics and Politics*, edited by Taylor, 28–59.

Mahnkopf, Claus-Steffen, ed. *Critical Composition Today*. Hofheim: Wolke, 2006.

Mao, Douglas, and Rebecca L. Walkowitz. 'The New Modernist Studies'. *PMLA* 123, no. 3 (2008): 737–48.

Mattin. 'Against Representation', 2010. http://www.mattin.org/essays/Against_Representation.html.

———. 'Improvisation and Communisation' (2013). http://www.mattin.org/essays/Improvisation_and_Communisation.html.

Maxwell, William J. 'Ralph Ellison and the Constitution of Jazzocracy'. *Journal of Popular Music Studies* 16, no. 1 (2004): 40–57.

McClary, Susan. 'Terminal Prestige: The Case of Avant-Garde Music Composition'. *Cultural Critique* 12 (1989): 57–81.

Monson, Ingrid. *Freedom Sounds: Civil Rights Call out to Jazz and Africa*. New York: Oxford University Press, 2007.

Murphy, Timothy S. 'The Negation of a Negation Fixed in a Form: Luigi Nono and the Italian Counter-Culture 1964–1979'. *Cultural Studies Review* 11, no. 2 (2005): 95–109.

Nelson, Amy. *Music for the Revolution: Musicians and Power in Early Soviet Russia*. University Park, PA: Pennsylvania State University Press, 2004.

Nonnemann, Rainer. 'The Dead End as a Way Out – Critical Composition: A Historical Phenomenon?' In *Critical Composition Today*, edited by Mahnkopf, 88–109.

Nono, Luigi. 'Il musicista nella fabbrica' (1966). In *Scritti e colloqui*, 1: 206–9.

———. 'La musica è uno strumento di lotta: Intervista di Gabor Hallasz' (1975). In *Scritti e colloqui*, 2: 217–19.

———. *Scritti e colloqui*. Edited by Angela Ida De Benedictis and Veniero Rizzardi. 2 vols. Lucca: Ricordi, 2001.

———. 'Die Ermittlung: un'esperienza musicale teatrale con Weiss e Piscator' (1966). In *La nostalgia del futuro: Scritti scelti, 1948–1986*, edited by Angela Ida De Benedictis and Veniero Rizzardi, 129–33. Milan: Saggiatore, 2007.

———. 'Une lettre de Luigi Nono: "Je suis un musicien militant"' (1971). In *Écrits*, edited by Laurent Feneyrou, 347–48. Geneva: Éditions Contrechamps, 2007.

Nyman, Michael. *Experimental Music: Cage and Beyond*. 2nd ed. Cambridge: Cambridge University Press, 1999.

O'Connor, Kieran. '"Don't They Represent Us?" A Discussion between Jacques Rancière and Ernesto Laclau' (2015). http://www.versobooks.com/blogs/2008-don-t-they-represent-us-a-discussion-between-jacques-ranciere-and-ernesto-laclau (accessed 15 September 2017).

Ohana, David. *The Futurist Syndrome*. Brighton: Sussex Academic Press, 2010.

Oja, Carol J. *Making Music Modern: New York in the 1920s*. New York: Oxford University Press, 2003.

Parrino, Francesco. 'Alfredo Casella and "The *Montjoie!* Affair"'. *Repercussions* 10, no. 1 (2007): 96–123.

Piekut, Benjamin. *Experimentalism Otherwise: The New York Avant-Garde and Its Limits*. Berkeley: University of California Press, 2011.

Pleasants, Henry. *The Agony of Modern Music*. New York: Simon and Schuster, 1955.

Potter, Rachel. *Modernism and Democracy: Literary Culture 1900–1930*. Oxford: Oxford University Press, 2006.

Prévost, Edwin. *No Sound Is Innocent*. Matching Tye: Copula, 1995.

Rabaté, Jean-Michel. *Jacques Lacan: Psychoanalysis and the Subject of Literature*. Basingstoke: Palgrave Macmillan, 2001.

Radano, Ronald M. *New Musical Figurations: Anthony Braxton's Cultural Critique*. Chicago: University of Chicago Press, 1993.

Ramsey, Guthrie P. *Race Music: Black Cultures from Bebop to Hip-Hop*. Berkeley: University of California Press, 2004.

Rancière, Jacques. *Hatred of Democracy*. London: Verso, 2009.

Riley, Matthew, ed. *British Music and Modernism, 1895–1960*. Aldershot: Ashgate, 2010.

Ross, Alex. *The Rest is Noise: Listening to the Twentieth Century*. London: Fourth Estate, 2007.

Rudhyar, Dane. 'Dissonant Harmony – A New Principle of Musical and Social Organization' (1928), online at Rudhyar Archival Project website. http://www.khaldea.com/rudhyar/dissonantharmony.html.

Samson, Jim. 'Instrumental Music since 1958'. In *The Blackwell History of Music in Britain: The Twentieth Century*, edited by Stephen Banfield, 278–342. Oxford: Blackwell, 1995.

———. 'Either/Or'. In *Rethinking Musical Modernism*, edited by Dejan Despić and Melita Milin, 15–26. Belgrade: Serbian Academy of Sciences and Arts, 2008.

Schoenberg, Arnold. 'Opinion or Insight' (1926). In *Style and Idea*, 258–63.

———. 'How One Becomes Lonely' (1937). In *Style and Idea*, 30–53.

———. 'Criteria for the Evaluation of Music' (1946). In *Style and Idea*, 124–36.

———. 'New Music, Outmoded Music, Style and Idea' (1946). In *Style and Idea*, 113–24.

———. *Style and Idea: Selected Writings*, edited by Leonard Stein. London: Faber and Faber, 1975.

———. *Theory of Harmony*, translated by Roy E. Carter. London: Faber and Faber, 1978.

Sheppard, Richard. 'The Problematics of European Modernism'. In *Theorizing Modernism*, edited by Steve Giles, 1–51. London: Routledge, 1993.

———. *Modernism – Dada – Postmodernism*. Evanston, IL: Northwestern University Press, 2000.

Spahlinger, Mathias. 'This Is the Time of Conceptive Ideologues No Longer'. *Contemporary Music Review* 27, no. 6 (2008): 579–94.

Stravinsky, Igor. *Poetics of Music in the Form of Six Lessons*. Translated by Arthur Knodel and Ingolf Dahl. Cambridge, MA: Harvard University Press, 1942.

Taruskin, Richard. 'The Dark Side of the Moon'. *New Republic*, 5 September 1988, 28–34. Revised and reprinted in *The Danger of Music*, 202–16.

———. *Music in the Early Twentieth Century*. Vol. 4 of *The Oxford History of Western Music*. New York: Oxford University Press, 2005.

———. *The Danger of Music and Other Anti-Utopian Essays*. Berkeley: University of California Press, 2009.

———. 'How Talented Composers Become Useless'. In *The Danger of Music*, 86–93.

———. 'The Musical Mystique: Defending Classical Music against Its Devotees'. In *The Danger of Music*, 330–53.

———. 'The Poietic Fallacy'. In *The Danger of Music*, 301–29.

Taylor, Ronald, ed. *Aesthetics and Politics: Theodor Adorno, Walter Benjamin, Ernst Bloch, Bertolt Brecht, Georg Lukács*. London: Verso, 1977.

Toronyilalic, Igor. 'Theartsdesk Q&A: Composer James Dillon'. *The Arts Desk*, 31 October 2010. http://www.theartsdesk.com/classical-music/theartsdesk-qa-composer-james-dillon (accessed 15 September 2017).

Toth, Csaba. 'Noise Theory'. In *Noise and Capitalism*, edited by Iles and Mattin, 24–37.

Traube, Elizabeth G. '"The Popular" in American Culture'. *Annual Review of Anthropology* 25 (1996): 127–51.

Tunbridge, Laura, ed. 'Round Table: Modernism and Its Others'. *Journal of the Royal Musical Association* 139, no. 1 (2014): 177–204.

Urbinati, Nadia. *Democracy Disfigured: Opinion, Truth, and the People*. Cambridge, MA: Harvard University Press, 2014.

Van den Berg, Hubert F. 'Avant-Garde: Some Introductory Notes on the Politics of a Label'. In *Sound Commitments*, edited by Adlington, 15–33.

Watson, Ben. *Derek Bailey and the Story of Free Improvisation*. London: Verso, 2004.

Williams, Raymond. *The Politics of Modernism: Against the New Conformists*. London: Verso, 1989.

———. 'Base and Superstructure in Marxist Cultural Theory'. In *Culture and Materialism: Selected Essays*, 31–49. London: Verso, 2005.

Wollaeger, Mark, and Matt Eatough, eds. *The Oxford Handbook of Global Modernisms*. Oxford: Oxford University Press, 2012.

10

MODERNISM FOR AND OF THE MASSES?

On popular modernisms

Stephen Graham

Experiments in modern music: modernism and popular music

The stories of modernist and modern popular music are intertwined. Pieces like Charles Ives' 'From Hanover Square North, at the End of a Tragic Day, the Voices of the People Again Arose' (1919, taken from the Orchestral Set no. 2) and songs like Rodgers and Hart's 'Manhattan' (1925) have much in common. Not only products of the same city and the same historical moment, these two examples of modern music both in their own way prioritized technical innovation and aesthetic experiment. Both also gave voice to a particular kind of observing urban sensibility, something akin to Georg Simmel's disinterested 'city type', which might be characteristic of the early decades of the massifying, urbanizing Western twentieth century.[1] Casting our net further afield, we can hear other significant connections, whether we think of the political theatre of Schoenberg and Weill, the sprung rhythms, extended tonality and style pastiches of Stravinsky and Gershwin, or, later, the modal trancing of Coltrane and Riley and the politicized improvisation of the Black Arts Movement and groups like Musica Elettronica Viva. Modern music can be seen as a broad church rather than simply a series of sects. This is not to erase important tensions and differences; it is merely to point out that this music emerged at the same times, dealt with some of the same creative, technical and political problems, and used some of the same tools.[2]

The potential intimacy of the relationship between modernist and popular music is reflected in a growing body of revisionist literature that examines agreement between the two forms.[3] This is in addition to humanities literature from outside musicology that similarly looks at or tries to unearth convergences of popular culture and modernism.[4] These various projects, musicological or otherwise, refashion stereotypical conceptions of modernism (and, in some cases, the avant-garde) as primarily elitist and popular culture as primarily entertainment focused by shining a light on previously unheralded connections between the two. This literature, as we shall see, looks at things like Tin Pan Alley, Broadway and the blues through a modernist lens and, on the other hand, considers figures such as Erik Satie in terms of their relationship with popular culture.

But it would be naïve to see this revisionist scholarly trend as representing a timely postmodern deconstruction of now outmoded but formerly rigid boundaries. One way or another, figured in positive or negative terms, modernism and mass culture have been intimately connected from the get-go. As Robert Adlington points out in this volume, via Rachel Potter, it is possible to identify 'two genealogies' even within classic 'high' modernism. Each of these genealogies is defined in terms of its relationship with mass culture; the one anxious and elitist and the other critical but expansionary. The first of these is 'marked by hostility to a mass public and everyday life' and is populated by 'cultural aristocrats' toiling away in a 'sacred realm' fearful of contamination. Adlington embodies this attitude in musical figures such as Arnold Schoenberg and Milton Babbitt. The second genealogy is seen to 'champion democracy and the popular voice' and, following Raymond Williams, to view 'art as the liberating vanguard of popular consciousness'. Adlington identifies groups such as the Futurists and the Constructivists and individuals such as Nikolai Roslavets and Luigi Nono as engaging with the people and/or mass culture through a modernist lens (even if avant-garde might be a better label, at least for the two groups).

By exploring this second genealogy Adlington shows how even within classic 'anti-hegemonic' modernism we can identify the presence 'of a democratizing or popular-revolutionary urge', either directly in figures like Nono or adjacently in historical avant-garde groups. But the importance of the relationship between modernism and the popular in both cases shows that it is not just revisionist critical accounts written from or in the direction of popular culture that are able to identify important links between modernism and mass culture. Such links can be found all the way down, both in practices of and literature on modernism. For instance, theorists such as Peter Bürger and Andreas Huyssen have attempted to frame the historical avant-garde as a mediating faction existing somewhere between high modernism and mass culture.[5] More polarized Frankfurt School accounts likewise rest on some notion of complicity. Adorno's famous description of mass and classical music as 'torn halves of an integral freedom' is typical in emphasizing dialectical entanglement.[6] Despite what he saw as a 'volatile relationship', for his part Huyssen identified a 'persistent complicity of modernism and mass culture'.[7] Adorno further underlined the intertwinement of the two forms in his suggestion that 'the diverse spheres of music must be thought of together' since 'in both there appear, however distantly, the changes of the whole'.[8]

But to be intertwined is not to be the same. Notwithstanding the convergences identified in recent literature and the complicities threaded through all sorts of classic accounts, modernism and popular culture have usually been defined in more or less antagonistic terms. Modernism, for one, has invariably been seen to emphasize anti-hegemonic innovation, complexity and affective estrangement, providing through this, in Daniel Albright's words, 'a testing of the limits of aesthetic construction'.[9] Björn Heile, similarly, has homed in on criticality as a key modernist contribution: 'the dialectical critique advocated by modernism is something one gives up at one's peril'.[10] This focus on anti-hegemonic critique, expressed both in implicit (largely the first genealogy) and explicit (largely the second) political and aesthetic terms in modernist art, potentially places it in something of an oppositional relationship to popular culture.

Going further along this track of divergence between modernism and mass culture, other writers emphasize modernism's formalism and its consequent rejection of the mass appeal of popular culture. For example Georg Lukács described modernist literature's 'exclusive emphasis on formal matters'.[11] This emphasis, seen as a negative by Lukács, for its advocates actually allows modernism to embody progressivist, critical ideals in both aesthetic and political registers.[12] Form is content in this understanding, as Brecht responded in not so many words to Lukács, since form can of course easily be deployed for strategic semiotic and political purposes; for example to embody oppression or liberation allegorically. This likewise distinguishes modernist art from what stereotypes would suggest are the text- and image-laden discourses of popular music.

Modernism for and of the masses?

Lukács, meanwhile, also connected modernism's formalism to a kind of 'negation of outward reality', something that we can relate to Clement Greenberg's and Arnold Schoenberg's praise for what they saw as modernism's disdain for popular appeal. Again what was a negative for Lukács, a supposed turning away from the world, was reframed in positive terms as a rejection of commercialism by supporters of modernism. In this spirit Greenberg balked at the 'gigantic apparition of popular art' in urbanized modernity, which he labelled in a broad critical sweep as 'kitsch'. Greenberg suggested that this 'ersatz culture' was 'mechanical and operate[d] by formulas' that only offered 'faked sensations' to audiences.[13] Schoenberg, for his part, famously said that 'if it is art it is not for everybody; if it is for everybody it is not art'.[14] Modernism is seen by these figures as neither 'for' everybody nor as 'operating by formula'. Popular music, by contrast, with its mass market mediations and its basis in a shared rhythmic, timbral and tonal language that is generally more immediately culturally readable than the musical languages of classic modernism, is seen to be hopelessly compromised by its commodity status and therefore as largely dumb with respect to modernism's dialectical critiques.

So we are in a bifurcated situation. On the one hand a narrative of convergence built on or at least framed in response to Frankfurt School accounts of dialectical complicity can be seen to be in the emergence, both in musicology and other disciplines. On the other an oppositional narrative that emphasizes a fundamental disparity between popular and modernist culture retains its classic explanatory power.[15] The rest of this chapter considers literature and music that have something to say to this debate. In contrast to Adlington, who looks at modernism *for* the people but not necessarily *of* the people – in other words looks at classic 'high' modernism directed in one way or another 'towards' the people – I pay particular attention to so-called popular modernism, a form that might be seen as being both *of* and *for* the people. I aim to provide a critical synthesis of existing literature as well as to explore the concept in the context of various musical examples.

Arising out of all of this is a threefold argument about the viability of musical popular modernism. In the next section, I explore a range of potentially 'popular modernist' music from the first half of the twentieth century, and argue that something is lost when we ignore important qualities of modernism's classic form. The section that follows it ('Post-1960s popular modernism') suggests, on the other hand, that popular modernism might be a useful concept in helping us to contextualize and understand various (and variously) exploratory, exigent examples of popular music from across the later twentieth and twenty-first centuries. Both sections begin by examining apposite theoretical literature before moving on to musical examples. Finally, and partly contrarily to the argument put forward in the post-1960s section, I suggest in the conclusion that the concept of 'popular modernism' potentially betrays something of a lack of faith in the popular on its own terms.

Golden Age popular modernism

The central place of so-called Golden Age American popular music in the modern urban moment in the West is fairly clear. Recent scholars have attempted to go beyond the general sense of mutual influence and co-extension that exists between the two, however. They argue that this music might be seen not just as both part and productive of the modern moment, but as being part of modern*ism* too. This argument, reflective of the literature emphasizing convergences between modernism and popular culture mentioned earlier, relies to some degree on an amended version of modernism that nevertheless finds key tenets of classic modernism in the music. In this section I shall survey arguments from Ronald Schleifer and Ulf Lindberg on this topic while also looking at other potential examples of popular modernism from the first half of the twentieth century.

Ronald Schleifer's 2011 book *Popular Music and Modernism* corresponds very closely with Ulf Lindberg's 2003 *Popular Music* article 'Popular Modernism? The "Urban" Style of Interwar Tin Pan Alley'. Schleifer and Lindberg use slightly different language but both look at the way that the lyrics of Golden Age pop songs describe particular modern subjectivities and lives, and at how the form and style of those lyrics and the music through which they are delivered variously embody modernist techniques of formal play, destabilization and innovation.

Schleifer, for his part, attempts 'to locate popular music within a working comprehension of twentieth-century modernism'.[16] In doing so, he points to what he sees as the 'enormous transformations in the lived life of the early twentieth century' through processes such as mass urbanization and the growth of the consumer society.[17] Schleifer's modernism tries to respond to the sheer variety of these transformations, incorporating pleasure and suggesting, in contrast to 'high' modernist alienation, that 'there are other ways of inventing other realities'.[18] Schleifer's approach is to read key figures in terms of a tailored analytical framework based broadly on a quartet of modernist concepts: semantic formalism, defamiliarization, montage and dialectical wholeness. The music discussed by Schleifer 'semanticizes' its abstract laws through these various means, as seen in the 'ensembled' performance-compositions of Billie Holiday and the layered signifyin' and patter of Fats Waller.[19] Meanwhile Schleifer locates Cole Porter's work within a Lacanian nexus of pleasure, desire and enunciation, where Porter's materialized lyrics, his dislocated forms and his shifting chord patterns, for example, use 'metonymic displacement' (where, as for Lacan, desire is always slipping away onto another object) to express fundamentally modernist qualities of transience and disconcertion.[20]

Lindberg takes a similar tack to Schleifer in that he argues that we can identify classically modernist strategies of defamiliarization and estrangement in Golden Age popular music. In order to do so Lindberg develops his own theoretical vocabulary of 'derealisation', self-reflexivity and irony, and as noted draws heavily on Georg Simmel's 1903 notion of a 'city type', a particular modern kind of subjectivity consisting of an 'intellectual, reserved, blasé attitude'.[21] Comparing Golden Age pop to literary modernism, Lindberg suggests that,

> When looked for [. . .] the uncertainties of living in modern times become equally visible in interwar consumer culture (which, like high culture, should be thought of as stratified). The Alley greats were revisionists in their idiom, not iconoclasts; but so were, after all, a great deal of the high literary modernists.[22]

Lindberg expands on this claim, suggesting 'that the renegotiation of the terms of romance, which characterizes the work of the period's top lyricists, should be seen against the backdrop of a developed urban sensibility', and that it 'makes sense to consider the rise of "unsentimental, even anti-romantic" standards for writing song lyrics in terms of a popular modernism'.[23]

Lindberg argues that various songs inhabit and creatively respond to these new social mores. 'Manhattan', for example, is seen to 'pastoralise' and therefore 'ironically re-present' the metropolis, introducing 'the big city as a hybrid between a home and an amusement park – simultaneously place (inhabitable territory) and space (explorable territory)'.[24] Lindberg expands his case using extended analyses of tracks such as Johnny Mercer's 1937 'Too Marvellous for Words' and the Gershwins' 'Embraceable You' (1930), where he hears their lyrics, operating across multiple stylistic levels and registers, as modernist 'meta-texts' using hybrid language to destabilize boundaries between lover and loved, subject and object.[25] Lindberg fleshes out his case by discussing the touristic lenses in Cole Porter songs such as 'Let's Do It', which he thinks help push realist aesthetics 'into modernist uncertainty'.[26]

Modernism for and of the masses?

Both Schleifer and Lindberg have much to say about American popular music that is insightful in terms of its relationship to modernism. The same is true of writers such as Edward Comentale, who has argued that genres such as blues and rock 'n' roll in the pre-/post-war periods embodied through their form and their affect a kind of 'new modernity' and as such can be identified with modernism.[27] But in the end none of these accounts are fully convincing, I think, since modernism needs to transform to such a degree for them to hold water. It is potentially fruitful to see modernism as being as much about urbanity and the urban, or about Comentale's new modernity, as about abrasive criticality – if for no other reason than that the shock often attributed to modernism in this respect is so easily absorbed into bourgeois cultural life and therefore muted. I am also not against making room for pleasure in the modernist project, in line with the efforts of Arved Ashby.[28] But something is surely lost by giving up the aesthetic and/or cultural criticality that has been so central to classic formulations of modernism, or by de-emphasizing affects of estrangement and alienation.

Adding 'popular' to modernism would, as I have said, surely modify the concept's meaning. But it shouldn't fundamentally transform it or water it down so that it becomes tasteless and hollow. Modernist art, at least in its classic form, presents a kind of disunity. It doesn't just re-frame conventions and confound expectations but also tries to present some kind of broken image of the world, maybe to shock audiences or at least simply to embody or critique current conditions. As Adorno suggested of modernist art, 'with equal necessity it [turns] its back on conventional surface coherence, the appearance of harmony, the order corroborated merely by replication'.[29] I don't see Cole Porter or his ilk doing that, however much they can be seen to be engaged in modernistic strategies of defamiliarization and semanticization. Of course, however, Golden Age American popular music doesn't tell the whole story of popular modernism in this era. I shall look at a few potential further examples before moving to my conclusion.

Marxist musical theatre, for one, might merit the label of popular modernism. Kyle Gann has described the Broadway composer Marc Blitzstein as 'at the same time a determined populist and determined modernist', drawing attention to how 'smoothly' Blitzstein 'integrated feisty modernisms into the accompaniment' of his 1937 labour movement musical *The Cradle Will Rock*.[30] Those 'feisty modernisms', which Gann hears in the irregular pulse groups, polyrhythms and chromatic root progressions of songs such as 'There's Something So Damn Low About the Rich', match up with the critical class politics that Blitzstein attempts to braid into the work through its text and narrative.

All these elements in Blitzstein – the wonky, jerky rhythms, the mordant chromaticism and the politics – build clearly on theatrical practices established by Kurt Weill in collaboration with Bertolt Brecht in the late 1920s and early 1930s in Germany, and developed by Weill in America in the ensuing two decades. Though the classic account of Weill is a dualistic one, with the German works seen as modernist but the American ones as trading novelty off for commercial gain, recent scholarship has offered a different perspective. Stephen Hinton, for example, sees a continuous line through Weill's music, arguing of Weill that 'the adjective *new* was as indispensable to his artistic vocabulary as it was to Busoni'.[31] Running throughout Weill's varied career was what Hinton calls a desire for 'reform', as can be seen in everything from the socialist epic theatre of *Die Dreigroschenoper* (1928) to the formally daring albeit highly tuneful psychoanalytical Broadway musical *Lady in the Dark* (1941), and from the hybrid opera-musical *Street Scene* (1946) to the anti-apartheid show *Lost in the Stars* (1949). As Hinton suggests, 'it is Weill's self-appointed role as theatrical reformer that arguably supplies the key to his relatively short but intense creative life.' Moreover, this 'reform', thinks Hinton, 'is not merely a technical or formal matter; it is a moral one as well.'[32] Hinton's continuous vision of Weill's creative life builds on Kim H. Kowalke's 1995 article 'Kurt Weill, Modernism, and Popular Culture: *Öffentlichkeit als*

Stil'. For Kowalke, Weill's music after 1925 'tried to break out of New Music's splendid isolation, to attract a non-specialist audience, to dismantle the barricades that the "art-for-art's-sake" wing of modernism had erected against mass culture'.[33] Speaking of Busoni's 'post-war attempts to reconcile past and present', Kowalke ultimately thinks that Weill's work can be seen in a similar way, as 'characteristic of what Martha Bayles calls "extroverted modernism", whose attitude toward accessibility/popularity differentiates it from its "introverted" and "perverse" kin'.[34]

Does all this make Weill a modernist, popular or otherwise? The political and theatrical reforms of his work seem to problematize simple oppositions of mass culture and modernism, but its sheer tunefulness and accessibility seem to put any modernist credentials in question. Weill innovated profoundly within context, dealt directly with concepts like alienation in his epic theatre works and likewise consistently endorsed critical politics. But the degree to which his music presents disunity and dissension is limited, and as such Weill should only partially be seen to participate in modernism.

We can examine other pre-1960s music in this context. Cabaret has often been cited as a seeding ground of modernist culture, a place where, in the case for example of the famous Le Chat Noir in Paris, composers such as Claude Debussy and Erik Satie could rub shoulders with artists, writers and popular singers such as Aristide Bruant.[35] The cabaret, in this spirit, has been cited as a fertile meeting place of high and low, a place where, in Bernard Gendron's words, 'popular music joined forces with art and literature in a synthesis of high and low cultures that has since rarely been equalled'.[36] But while we can certainly think of examples of art and music that embody this synthesis, for various reasons the direction of the influence was often one-way. This is such that, for example, Erik Satie's music could explore humour, farce and popular music styles, as for example in the ragtime of a short piece like *Le Piccadilly* (*c*1904, pre-echoing the Debussy of *Le petit nègre*, 1909) or the gunshots, typewriters and tottering oom-pah of his ballet *Parade* (1924), or on the other hand entertain with the conceptual hi-jinks of something like *Vexations* (1893), without ever getting beyond the feel of a cross-cultural encounter. The same could be said of the composer-members of Les Six in the 1920s and 1930s, where cabaret and jazz aesthetics come together (creatively, but perhaps uneasily) with modernist sounds and ambitions in pieces like Darius Milhaud's *La création du monde* (1922–23) and Francis Poulenc's Concerto for Two Pianos (1932).

We are only ever really hearing high perspectives in this music. The borrowed syncopations and parodic air in Satie speak to us of a popular-infused modernism rather than anything more organically fused or more authentically popular, notwithstanding the amount of music Satie wrote directly in popular idioms early in his career. In these cases, the distinction between classic characteristics of modernism – difficulty, estrangement, cultural illegibility – and of popular music – commercial appeal and cultural legibility – is upheld through deviation. Similar (albeit reversed) issues of acculturation face other cases of potential popular modernism, from jazz musicians such as Duke Ellington and Louis Armstrong to cabaret singers like Bruant.[37] Despite clear modernist qualities of innovation and urbanity in their work, these artists do not explore criticality or disunity to a fundamental degree.

A whole host of pre-1960s popular, classical and jazz songwriters, composers and musicians can therefore be seen to be working in modernistic and populist ways without fitting comfortably into the popular modernist category. Their work draws on modernism and on popular culture without clearly moving into the liminal territory implied by my use of the popular modernism label. Satie and composer colleagues seem to me only to flirt with the popular. Cole Porter is 'too' popular. Kurt Weill problematizes this binary, but even in his case the work feels too populist, too whole, to count comfortably as modernist. Popular music can therefore be seen to verge onto modernism in many of these Golden Age and pre-1960s cases, but in only a few seem to justify the popular modernist label. We can in the end reasonably describe much popular culture in modernistic terms, as trucking in one or other modernist technique or strategy, but examples of work that is both genuinely popular and genuinely modernist – of popular modernism, in short – are fairly rare. But they do exist. In order to show this, the next section goes back a little and lays some theoretical groundwork with Frankfurt School and Frankfurt-derived arguments, before exploring various potentially more viable examples of popular modernist music.

Post-1960s popular modernism

Theodor Adorno's arguments about mass culture are far more layered than we might expect given the impression we get of him as a humbugging naysayer from figures such as Charles Rosen and Lukács.[38] This caricatured version of Adorno, not wholly inaccurate but nevertheless reductionist, sees him as an irremediably sour figure fixated on *Kulturindustrie* standardization and 'new music' authenticity, subscribing to what Thomas Y. Levin has called 'a myopic mandarinism blind to the utopian and progressive dimensions of mass media'.[39] But Adorno's theories present a much more complicated picture than this caricature allows; I expand on this point here as a way of setting up a theoretical context for popular modernism.

While arguments about standardization and related concepts such as the social substitution of exchange-value for use-value pervade much of Adorno's work, taken in blunt terms these concepts obscure a complex array of evolving dialectical positions. In fact, Adorno can be seen to lay the groundwork for a version of popular modernism we can tie to familiarly modernist notions of criticality. He did this by providing a model of critique which, despite parochialism, was fundamentally malleable. Nothing was beyond criticism; what mattered was concrete expression, not some abstract schema of high/low value. Adorno was after all as willing to criticize high culture and new music as he was mass culture.[40] And in any case the sting of Adorno's dismissive and reductive comments about mass culture should not blind us to how richly developed, comprehensive and indeed dialectical his views actually were. In the letter to Walter Benjamin that the famous 'torn halves' statement comes from, Adorno outlines a complex argument that undermines both 'high' mandarin and 'low' celebrant positions.[41] In *Aesthetic Theory* Adorno again twists away from comfortable Leavisite elitism in suggesting that while 'the distinction between entertainment and autonomous art points to a qualitative difference that must be retained', this is so only 'provided one does not overlook the hollowness of the concept of serious art or the validity of unregimented impulses in lowbrow art'.[42] If everything is compromised then everything can also be free, or at least speak of freedom. This is not to ratify postmodern relativism but merely to recognize the natural variations of value and affinity found in all musical forms.

Adorno's panoramic rulings, then, do not easily reduce to a recognizable or conventional scale of cultural value, instead insisting on specificity with regards both to commodification and critique. As Frederic Jameson suggested in this vein: 'the Adorno-Horkheimer theory of the Culture Industry provides a theoretical description of mass cultural experience which can scarcely be reduced to sheer opinionated or elitist vituperation against "bad art"'.[43] Because of all this, Adorno's work can be treated as a toolkit that helps one to locate critical value in potentially unexpected places; and this kind of treatment of Adorno has indeed become more and more common.[44]

One of the strongest voices raised through Adorno in this kind of way has been the British writer Ben Watson. Watson sees Adorno's 'hysterical' disposition, his rejection of middlebrow classical culture and the 'radical psychosis' of his style in a line with the surrealists, the beats and the punks (echoing Greil Marcus in drawing this kind of line through the twentieth century, if obliquely):[45]

> Adorno is at one with the Surrealists in celebrating the grotesqueries on the edge of the culture industry – he's a video nasty fan, not a moralist [. . .]. Gratitude for the 'culture' handed down to us by the authorities merely paves the way to manipulation. Adorno's revulsion to that kind of top-down, patronizing programme anticipates the sneers punk hurled at 'lovely music'.[46]

In 'Adorno, Plato, Music', Watson expands these links between Adornian cultural critique and popular culture. Discussing Adorno's participation in and encouragement of an 'institutional avant-garde' at Darmstadt in the 1950s and 1960s, Watson connects Adorno to non-institutional or mass cultural practices. He draws particular attention to the 'free jazz, free improvisation and progressive rock movements which exploded in the 60s' and are 'currently [in 2001] urgent objects of debate and inquiry among a new generation of radical musicians and listeners':

> Understanding them requires appreciation of the intimate and tense relationship between possible community, political consciousness, commercial restraints and the noise of negation. Adorno's insights can really help. Attention to how musicians argue about music and freedom shows that the controversies which surrounded a high modernist like John Cage also appear inside demotic genres like rock. Focus on musical actualities can provide an exit from the defeatist paradoxes of postmodernist cultural theory trapped in 'high/low' and 'pro-Adornian/anti-Adornian' binaries.[47]

This last point about postmodern traps of high and low – categories that get reinforced every time a theorist suggests they are traversed in postmodern culture – turns out to be key for Watson. Instead of characterizing music based on 'inert' categories born of market behaviour (e.g. 'popular'), Watson rejects out of hand the 'postmodern empirical sociology' or 'sociology of manners' that he thinks slots music into a static high/low spectrum. This approach is represented most directly for Watson by writers such as Simon Frith and Georgina Born.[48]

Watson instead sees music as a materialist practice where such stratifications of high and low and such commercially defined, nonmusical descriptions will not do:

> A materialist study of music, one that looks at the actual problems facing people engaged in music-making, immediately discovers conflicts over ideological compromise, musical standardization, and audience misunderstanding. It finds antagonism and '*avant-garde*' postures at every level. Only by exclusive focus on the 'consumer' – a putative concept with no ground in social class and a material relationship to the means of production – can popular studies evade the dialectical role of the unpopular in the genesis of Pop.[49]

For Watson, neither popular nor avant-garde/unpopular labels should be seen to designate static or 'watertight' musical practices cordoned off from one another 'as if they describe particular styles', or as if they map neatly on to some abstract high/low distinction. This kind of (in Watson's eyes) music-sociological approach 'obscures the fact that music' is a 'material process in which abstract antinomies are in continual interpretation and transformation'.[50]

Watson therefore tries to draw attention to the ways in which all musical forms contain the possibility of conformity and instability, and to how all are more or less mediated by a social/

cultural nexus of commercial imperatives and capitalist capture. This is as true of new classical composition as it is of noise music or black metal or bluegrass. All music genres are embroiled all the way down in both conforming and confrontational gestures. Of course degree matters: slipping in an unconventional harmony to a bluegrass song or writing a new orchestral piece using combinatorial harmonic principles *may* not be as confrontational as, say, putting a noise act on the main stage at a large popular music festival. But the point is that the possibility exists in each genre or cultural context for profound confrontation and challenge. In laying out this analytical scheme Watson can be seen to expand Adorno's critical project beyond Paul Whiteman jazz and Schoenbergian new music, while nevertheless building on ideas of equal opportunities critique, where any musical form retains the possibility of confronting its own conditions, in doing so.

It is through this expansive, potentially inclusive gesture that we can start to see how Adorno's work could inspire a popular modernism based on criticality. Examples of Watson reading popular music against the grain in this way, as assuming both commercial and antagonistic/avant-garde postures for its audience, abound. Watson's whole project around Frank Zappa, for example, is based on an Adornian framework of negative dialectics (and poodle play).[51] Meanwhile in 'Semen Froth' Watson rails against the class basis of the high/low distinction, and describes the ways in which everything from various entry points of black music into Britain (Lol Coxhill playing with Rufus Thomas; Jimi Hendrix visiting London with Chas Chandler) to the KLF's 'pranks', Sinéad O'Connor's 'politics' and Sonic Youth's 'noisecore raids' communicate an antagonism that equates in many ways to an avant-garde transformation of the status quo.[52]

While Watson is in danger of idealizing these moments of perceived authenticity, and indeed of staging personal taste as historical imperative ('my innovation is better than yours!'), the expansive organizing gesture of his argument about avant-garde postures being visible in all music is valuable nonetheless. Although there is some distance between 'avant-garde' and 'modernism' as concepts,[53] in this case it's not too much of a stretch to identify in Watson's arguments a set of blueprints for how we might read details of specific examples of popular music in popular modernist terms.

And it is here that we finally arrive at the motivating topic for the chapter, popular modernism. This notion of popular modernism, where popular music might be seen to embody modernist techniques and affects of estrangement, critique and alienation to such a degree that it demands (or at least warrants) recontextualization and reconceptualization, is a tantalizing one. Popular modernism, I argue, should be seen as an intermediate region along a spectrum linking popular music at one side and modernism at the other. Popular modernism, in this understanding, would not necessarily operate as a fixed concept with clear and straightforward real-world referents. It would instead be seen as a regional frame through which we might contextualize the interaction and overlapping of popular music and modernism. It does not have one singular definition but instead embodies a set of tendencies in interaction and flux. Concrete examples of music may fit into the frame as clear examples of *popular modernist music*. Or they might exist at its edges, as examples of *modernist popular music* (i.e. as popular music with modernist dimensions). The point, as I shall show, is that enough examples exist of supposedly popular music drawing directly on modernist techniques and goals that using the category of popular modernism to describe them, or at least to provide a context with which they more or less overlap, is both useful and instructive.

I will look at some writing from Mark Fisher in this area as a bridge into more direct discussions of potentially popular modernist, or modernist popular, music. Fisher has been a strong recent advocate for his own version of popular modernism. Working somewhat within the Adorno-infused language of Watson insofar as he endorses criticality and avant-garde postures as existing within all forms of music – in other words, insofar as he subscribes to a version of modernism which insists on its progressive capacities while relativizing these at the same time – Fisher differs even from Watson in his embrace of truly *popular* music.

In a 2006 piece, 'From 1984', Fisher laid out his vision of modernist culture:

> Modernism is not an advocacy of the current or the contemporary. It would be better to say that it is the exact opposite of such a stance. Modernism is about breaks with current conditions. The modernist event is the moment when what appeared to be a seamless 'pre-sent' (Burroughs) breaks open; the Possible shatters into a million previously unimaginable possibilities. [. . .] Each modernist artifact is significant not for what it 'is' but for the possibilities it points to but which itself is not.[54]

This kind of framing of modernism as a negation of the present, as a shattering of the possible and a resetting of current conditions, chimes with more traditional accounts mentioned earlier. But in an untimely (and therefore perhaps essentially modernist) gesture, Fisher identifies these criteria in examples of popular music, from post-punk and no wave in the late 1970s and early 1980s to jungle in the 1990s.[55] Fisher additionally praises the ability of this sort of music to communicate challenging ideas and to shock in this way even while speaking to a broad public. This music, according to Fisher, embodied in its public nature top-down postwar social democratic paternalism's concern for the public good over consumers and market-mediated desire.[56]

Fisher underscores the importance of public impact on what he identifies as popular modernist music:

> The Jam thrived in public space, on public service broadcasting. It mattered that they were popular; the records gained in intensity when you knew that they were number one, when you saw them on Top of the Pops – because it wasn't only you and fellow initiates who heard the music; the (big) Other heard it too.[57]

Fisher makes a similar point when writing in a separate piece about the Bristolian post-punk act The Pop Group, whose music's jerky, prime number union of dub, funk and punk templates within a political programme of Marxist critique, as heard on inflammatory songs such as 'We are all Prostitutes' (1979) and albums like *For How Much Longer Do We Tolerate Mass Murder?* (1980), might be seen to represent a particularly ripe example of popular modernism:

> How could a sound like this ever have been made? A whole secret history of the 20th century is oneirically compressed into this lugubrious, delirious sonic anarchitecture. This incandescent condensation of Stockhausen, Duchamp, King Tubby, Albert Ayler, Guy Debord. [. . .] A polymorphous punk-funkadelia predeconstructed by dub, flirting with collapse and chaos, [. . .] a euphoric shattering of the social in the name of a dream collectivity, a dreaming we, a dreamed we. And not skulking on the margins, but exploding in the heart of the commodity. On the front of the *NME*. 1979 – a different world.[58]

In these arguments Fisher's project shows its Watsonian dimensions most clearly: modernism might applaud and pursue criticality, but popular music can be as critical and as progressive on its own terms as high modernism can on its. In fact, Fisher asserts, popular modernism is in some ways superior to and even justifies 'high' modernism: 'In popular modernism, the elitist project of modernism was retrospectively vindicated'.[59]

Modernism for and of the masses?

This last point is obviously a contentious one, not least because it seems to be based on what some would see as a fundamental contradiction: the inability to be critical of a system when speaking from comfortably within that system. At least, traditional modernists might argue, high modernist culture is somewhat removed from the marketplace and therefore less compromised than the examples Fisher lauds. This is a valid point. But the charge of elitism levelled by Fisher points to its own unanswerable contradiction (attempting to provide an all-encompassing critique of society but from a necessarily limited vantage point), while his argument about popular modernism being able to speak critically for and to the public with a much stronger mandate than high modernism seems to me at least to resolve some of the tension within the second genealogy of modernism quite convincingly.

Watson and Fisher in any case argue in support of a version of popular modernism that equates classic modernist criticality with popular culture. In order to explore and test this point further I will now explore different examples in more depth. One of Fisher's go-to reference points when describing popular modernism is post-punk. I therefore focus initially on no wave, which was a localized movement within post-punk that built on some of the values of punk, chiefly its DIY emphasis and its anti-establishment politics, and claimed to radicalize these.

No wave had a scorched-earth mentality. The music, born amidst the scuzzy venues, low rents and thriving art scene of late 1970s Downtown New York and consecrated by the Brian Eno-produced compilation *No New York* (1978), expressed disdain for the musical grammar and performing etiquette of rock and pop.[60] No wave presented itself as an 'aggressively Year Zero project'.[61] Simon Reynolds suggested that 'no wave groups acted as if they had no ancestors at all'. Teenage Jesus and the Jerks' leader Lydia Lunch indeed ridiculed the idea of links between punk and no wave, saying, 'I hated almost the entirety of punk rock. [...] I don't think No Wave had anything to do with it'.[62]

Like other modernist movements, then, no wave saw itself as a self-consciously critical site of struggle against the conventional limitations of popular music as such. The antagonizing force at the movement's core, the 'no' that tried to refuse new wave, punk and popular norms, displaced punk's musical conciliation with the rock 'n' roll-derived principle of 'three chords and the truth' by installing modernistic appeals to Year Zero novelty, leaning into permanent and clean-slate renewal as a driving force. However, also like other modernist movements, the music's claimed distance from preceding and parallel movements was not so clear-cut as it was often made out to be. The cross-media nature of no wave (where film was as prominent as music), in addition to its challenging performance aesthetics, tied it to previous Downtown scenes.[63] Likewise the musical similarities between no wave and other musical forms are palpable, from Albert Ayler and Ornette Coleman's free jazz in the 1960s to the Stooges' 'LA Blues' in 1970 to punk or proto-punk acts such as Suicide in the later 1970s, all of whose sonic wildness, freedom and abrasion no wave can be seen to mirror.[64]

In this way, no wave clearly emerged from a lineage and existed in a context. But even though the distance from something like punk to no wave was not always as vast as was claimed, we can hear clear differences nonetheless. Punk's simplicity was here fringed with a strong degree of sonic chaos and aggression that seemed to push affect and technique into deeply unconventional territories. No wave songs, at their extreme, could be made almost exclusively of shards of guitar feedback and indistinct noise, as heard on a track like Mars' brutal, rock-slide, almost freeform noise-screed 'N.N. End' (1980). Other songs are dominated by shouted vocals, the most primitive of drum beats and detuned and distorted guitars played with scant regard for conventional chords, as heard on Teenage Jesus's 'The Closet' and 'Orphans' (both 1978). The noise-squall distortion of these songs prioritized dense, metallic sheets of feedback and leaden low-end sounds over the lightly distorted power chords and buoyant rhythm section of punk.

But this doesn't tell the whole no wave story. The music of DNA and the Contortions sounded out a bony, gawky roughness that contrasted somewhat with the squall of Mars or Teenage Jesus, even though noise and aggression were likewise important here. Arto Lindsay's crunchy guitar and unkempt vocals, Tim Wright's skulking bass and Ikue Mori's pulverizing drums in DNA songs such as the irregularly phrased and noise-full 'New Fast' and '32123' (both 1981), or the wild skeletal funk of 'Egomaniac's Kiss' (1978), are exemplary of the screaking, collapsingly angular vocal and instrumental gestures of this end of no wave. As are James Chance's saxophone skronks for the Contortions, which can be heard on wound-tight, brittle shout-songs such as their version of James Brown's 'I Can't Stand Myself' (1978) and, most famously, 'Contort Yourself' (1979). Post-punk angularity – irregular hypermetrical patterns, for instance, or spread-wide guitar riffs – is skewed here to a point of near-collapse.

No wave music therefore emphasized aggression, noise and instability in a manner that separated it from punk (and this isn't even mentioning subsequent and even less punk-like acts often connected to the style, from Swans to Magik Markers). Where punk played with cultural identifiers, from catchy sloganeering to blunt expressions of political antagonism, which allowed it to be read as the culminating point of a radical historical lineage, no wave implied a similar historical trajectory but deduced seemingly different conclusions from it.[65] The clearest path to the future, no wave seemed to suggest, lay in new sounds, not merely in dressings-up of rock 'n' roll conventions. 'N.N. End' or something like the rough, shuddering, trebly sounds of DNA's typically scratchy 'Not Moving' (1978) could never have been made by the Sex Pistols.

It seems clear that no wave provides a strong case of a popular form of music – popular in the sense of working clearly in a pop lineage and in pop contexts, if not in having huge popular appeal – whose aggression, criticality and emphasis on innovation well recommends it as modernist. Of course these aren't the only qualities we might identify as modernist, but they're important nonetheless. The kind of investment in confrontation found in the music and indeed across no wave as a movement – Lunch has referred to herself as a 'confrontationalist' for years, while no wave concerts often accentuated aggression and disorder – as well as its relative innovation within context emblematizes its modernistic credentials. No wave's popular modernism as based on criticality and subversion of localized genre norms is surely an untimely and potentially denatured modernism, but, unless we were either to bar entry to music existing in the marketplace or to treat modernism as a closed historical period, that doesn't necessarily preclude it from the club. The former idea seems to be unreasonable in any case, since nothing is pure in the sense desired by this claim, and the latter, while potentially compelling, would likely serve to inhibit modernism to an unhelpful degree.

Once we accept supposedly 'popular' music as potentially fitting the bill of modernism, we start to see many other examples working in this kind of way. Popular music criticality and abrasion can be heard throughout the twentieth and twenty-first centuries, just as innovation and exploration. I mentioned degree earlier: it would be very easy here to slide down a slippery slope and acclaim any local instance of perceived innovation or abrasion as modernist. Against this tendency, it is important to hold on to some core defining features of modernism. I suggest that criticality; a challenge to normal procedures; and affects of estrangement, shock and alienation are of paramount importance in this context.

By these criteria, no wave and some examples of post-punk would certainly count as popular modernist music. They pull apart musical norms of their time and their immediate contexts, sometimes unite these with critical artistic and/or political programmes, and in doing this challenge audiences profoundly. We can identify similar achievements in many other popular musical forms, from jungle, grime and wonky in Britain in the 1990s, 2000s and 2010s, to related experimental techno in Germany and the United States and finally to noise/free jazz in Italy,

Modernism for and of the masses?

the Netherlands and many other places (not to mention underground and fringe forms such as extreme metal and noise among many others). All these musics place an emphasis on future-facing sounds and reflect evolving and distinctive urban modernities through their lyrics and the technologies they employ. Alongside this emphasis on innovation and experiment, shock and criticality play a lesser or greater role in each of them. Taken together, these genres put traditional separations of modernism and popular culture into question.

In the last category (affects of estrangement, shock and alienation), an act like the Dutch group The Ex – whose album *Catch My Shoe* draws on the aggression and distortion of punk, the scaly, brittle grooves of post-punk and the pulverizing, frenzied attack of free jazz musicians like Peter Brötzmann, among other elements – seeks to challenge and to destabilize in a recognizably modernist way. The aforementioned grime and wonky are just two of a series of 1990s and 2000s club or urban styles of British music hailed by writers in futurist, even modernist terms.[66] Not all may comfortably fulfil the criteria set up above, but they all respond to aspects of popular modernism. Many techno and electronic acts, from those signed to Basic Channel or Raster-Noton in Germany in recent years to Kraftwerk in the 1970s and 1980s, likewise play or played with topoi of futurity while also seeking to make music in unexpected, challenging ways.

Kraftwerk is an interesting example here. On songs such as 'Geiger Counter' (1975), 'Showroom Dummies' (1977), 'The Robots' (1978), 'Neon Lights' (1978) and 'Computer Love' (1981) – songs whose titles and lyrics served as programmatic invocations of the group's conceptual investments – the synthesized sounds, lyrics and even the musicians themselves become projections of a *Gesamtkunstwerk* modernity interested in the automatization of subjectivity and the subjectivation of machines. Kraftwerk's cyborgian modernism clearly expressed a futurist sensibility. But this was nevertheless anchored in postmodern references to and a melancholic longing for past modernisms and past styles of music, evident both in the beauty, proportion and polish of their machinic sounds and in the anchoring of their project in a kind of nostalgia for 1920s and 1930s modernism.[67] So Kraftwerk might be seen as postmodern modernists, if not fully as popular modernists.

But other forms of electronic music played with futurity in a much less ambivalent way. As Kodwo Eshun argues, the various linguistic, sonic and conceptual innovations found across techno, trip hop and electronic music from the likes of Cybotron, Tricky and Drexciya speak of posthuman, alien sound worlds that intimate an 'AfroDiasporic futurism', which Eshun describes as a 'webbed network of computerhythms [sic], machine mythology and conceptechnics which routes, reroutes and criss-crosses the Black Atlantic'.[68] Though the variety of the music Eshun discusses works against its collapse into any neat Black Atlantic modernism, the emphasis on innovated futurity suggests a vibrant strain of popular modernism.

The weird geometries and cyborg sounds of late twentieth and twenty-first century acts and producers such as Timbaland, Missy Elliott, Rodney Jerkins and others *might* place their work into a similar kind of sympathy with popular modernism. Both Destiny Child's 'Get on the Bus' (1998, produced by Timbaland) and Missy Elliott's 'Get Ur Freak On' (2001, co-produced and written by Timbaland) contain characteristic techniques that sounded a clear pop future for audiences. From the importance of the minor second as grounding melodic interval, to interpolated samples that (timbrally and rhythmically) cut against the context, to tight, sprung grooves made of lattice layers of skittering percussion, vocal sounds and synthesizers, these tracks are machines built to speed pop into the future. But despite that, they don't seem critical in any way, nor do they feel abrasive or likely to cause estrangements of perception in audiences. On the other hand, hyper-real future-pop from the likes of PC Music and Yen Tech seems to rest on (ambivalent) criticality, but leans too much towards populist appeal to feel truly modernist. For these reasons, though all of these examples might reasonably be seen to draw directly on modernist techniques and as such to earn the label of modernist popular music, I don't think they or other similarly commercial tracks can be seen in popular modernist terms.

Examples like this might help us to see where a line might be drawn between such clearly critical, challenging and future-facing music as no wave or noise jazz on the one hand, and future-facing but consensual music by the like of Missy Elliott and Destiny's Child and by certain grime, wonky and electronic artists likewise on the other. A more recent case such as Kanye West's coruscating 2013 album *Yeezus* would problematize such a line, however.[69] Commercially successful and publicly appealing despite its modernistic aggression and alienation, this album forces together industrial, techno, pop and electro sounds with fissures intact, form and tone intentionally fragmented amidst lacerating riffs and drums that rip apart as soon as they start to groove. West's lyrics are similarly charged up as they range across slavery, materialism and intensely wrought biography. The fragments and tears of the sounds and the words on *Yeezus* could even be said to evoke Adorno's late Beethoven: instead of building narrative progress through combination they repeat, recur, revolve blankly, mute in their broken shapes. This is a critical and exploratory project if there ever was one, both in a musical sense and in terms of wider political arguments about race in the United States in the twenty-first century. But it is nevertheless dressed in much more recognizably commercial clothes than even jungle or no wave. This album, then, matches the musical futurity of Timbaland and Missy Elliott but frays things with a harsh critical edge even while adding commerciality at the same time. Its modernist and its 'popular' statuses are therefore continually in question as a result.

These are in any case just some examples from a potentially long list of popular modernist acts and styles. Looking at even this small sample it becomes clear that it would be very difficult to draw a straight line that might separate 'popular modernist' music from popular music that might simply draw on modernist values. But examples of styles such as no wave and noise jazz seem to me to vindicate the popular modernist category at least to some degree. Despite the danger of stretching the concept of modernism too far, it seems to me that popular modernism preserves the criticality and alienation of modernism, while at the same time lending it some vitality.

Concluding thoughts on the desire for a modernist popular culture

Though each of the modern musical practices I have discussed are maintained by cultural frameworks of a very different character, they have clearly had much to say to each other. In many cases they even take on characteristics traditionally seen as belonging to the other. So the 'popular modernist' label responds to actually existing mutuality (or, to use my term from earlier, liminality) in demonstrating links that might have been concealed otherwise. It is not, a supporter of this label might argue, about lifting up or dragging down music from one 'sphere' to another, it is about reframing debate. As I have argued throughout this chapter I would go along with this up to a point. I identified many examples that might be seen in popular modernist terms, including borderline cases. Popular modernism, in this twofold argument, is both a fruitful term that shines a light on emergent stories of modernist criticality and exploration in popular music and also a potentially problematic concept whose application to music needs to be handled with care.

In conclusion, I want to add a third layer to my argument. Although in the preceding sections I tried to be careful in describing any popular practices as modernist, I nevertheless recognized the usefulness of a term like popular modernism (as well as the aptness of seeing some examples simply as popular music that draws on modernism). But I did so fully aware that critical projects can easily 'elevate' even when they try not to. In employing such a loaded term as 'modernism' to describe popular music we might be playing into top-down dynamics that indeed elevate. Why is

Modernism for and of the masses?

'popular' (or any of sundry subcategories or styles) not enough? Does 'modernism' secure a prestige for popular music that might have been unavailable otherwise? Does its use conceal enduring cultural prejudices that see popular music as in need of 'conversion' into a serious art form?

Buried within some accounts of popular modernism seems to be a set of prejudices that might give pause in the kinds of ways suggested by these questions. Schleifer, for one, discusses only the 'best' popular music and is stuffily anxious to prioritize 'achieved' over 'banal' popular music as worthy of study.[70] Steven Moore Whiting, in writing about Satie's cabaret modernism, suggested that 'Satie managed to convert popular music into a serious art'.[71] Andreas Huyssen's postmodern account connecting the avant-garde with mass culture ends up time again and again condescending to the latter. On a number of occasions Huyssen even links mass culture and fascism, saying for example of Adorno and Greenberg that they were trying to 'save the dignity and autonomy of the art work from the totalitarian pressures of fascist mass spectacles, socialist realism, and an ever more degraded commercial mass culture in the West'.[72]

All of these perspectives seem to suggest a familiar and tired critical trope that frames popular music as in need of – or being beyond – rescue. Other views are available of course. But whether we have faith in the popular as such or not, I would like to close with a potentially polemical thought. Attempts at loading up popular music with modernist credentials, however much they might make sense in specific examples, risk weakening popular music by playing into outmoded hierarchies of cultural value. Modernism as a concept is alive and well. But it will always be anchored in a particular period of time and a particular set of aesthetic and cultural values. Popular music has, despite its hegemonic commercial and social presence, perhaps struggled to gain the kind of cultural prestige that rightfully infuses modernist art. The way to secure that prestige is potentially not to reach for labels like modernist but instead to look at popular music's own processes and idioms and to develop critical languages of value in response. Popular modernism seems to me to be a useful term to some degree. But even better would be a self-sufficient conception of the popular that could comfortably incorporate both criticality and commercialism.

Notes

1 Ulf Lindberg's 2003 article on the purported popular modernism of Tin Pan Alley analyses the 'city type' and other modernist tropes in songs like 'Manhattan'; 'Popular Modernism? The "Urban" Style of Interwar Tin Pan Alley', *Popular Music* 22, no. 3 (2003), 283–98.

2 My connective gesture here echoes David Clarke in 'Elvis and Darmstadt, or: Twentieth-Century Music and the Politics of Cultural Pluralism', *Twentieth-Century Music* 4, no. 1 (2007), 3–45.

3 In addition to Lindberg, see e.g. Edward P. Comentale, *Sweet Air: Modernism, Regionalism, and American Popular Song* (Urbana: University of Illinois Press, 2013); Mary E. Davis, 'Modernity à la mode: Popular Culture and Avant-Gardism in Erik Satie's *Sports et divertissements*', *Musical Quarterly* 83, no. 3 (1999), 430–73; Bernard Gendron, *Between Montmartre and the Mudd Club: Popular Music and the Avant-Garde* (Chicago: University of Chicago Press, 2002); Keir Keightley, 'Tin Pan Allegory', *Modernism/Modernity* 19, no. 4 (2012), 717–36; Ronald Schleifer, *Modernism and Popular Music* (Cambridge: Cambridge University Press, 2011).

4 See, e.g. Karen Leick, 'Popular Modernism: Little Magazines and the American Daily Press', *PMLA* 123, no. 1 (2008), 125–39, and Juan A. Suárez, *Pop Modernism: Noise and the Reinvention of the Everyday* (Urbana and Chicago: University of Illinois Press, 2007).

5 Peter Bürger, *Theory of the Avant-Garde*, trans. Michael Shaw (Minneapolis: University of Minnesota Press, 1984); Andreas Huyssen, *After the Great Divide: Modernism, Mass Culture, Postmodernism* (London: Macmillan, 1986).

6 Theodor Adorno, 'Letters to Walter Benjamin', *New Left Review* I/81 (1973), 74–80.

7 Huyssen, *After the Great Divide*, vii and 17.

8 Theodor Adorno, 'On the Fetish-Character in Music and the Regression of Listening', in *Essays on Music*, ed. Richard D. Leppert and trans. Susan H. Gillespie (Berkeley and Los Angeles: University of California Press, 2002), 293.

Stephen Graham

9 Daniel Albright, ed., *Modernism and Music: An Anthology of Sources* (Chicago: University of Chicago Press, 2004), 11.
10 Björn Heile, 'Introduction', in *The Modernist Legacy: Essays on New Music*, ed. Björn Heile (Farnham and Burlington, VT: Ashgate, 2009), 2.
11 Georg Lukács, 'The Ideology of Modernism', in *Realism in Our Time: Literature and the Class Struggle*, trans. John and Necke Mander (New York: Harper and Row, 1962), 19 and 25.
12 Martin Scherzinger, 'In Memory of a Receding Dialectic: The Political Relevance of Autonomy and Formalism in Modernist Musical Aesthetics', in *The Pleasure of Modernist Music: Listening, Meaning, Intention, Ideology*, ed. Arved Ashby (Rochester, NY: University of Rochester Press, 2004), 68–101.
13 Clement Greenberg, 'Avant-Garde and Kitsch' (1939), in *Art and Culture: Critical Essays* (London: Beacon Press, 1989), 9–10.
14 Schoenberg, cited in Richard Taruskin, *Music in the Early Twentieth Century*, rev. ed., vol. 4, *The Oxford History of Western Music* (Oxford and New York: Oxford University Press, 2009), 353.
15 See, for example, Georgina Born, *Rationalizing Culture: IRCAM, Boulez, and the Institutionalization of the Musical Avant-Garde* (Berkeley and Los Angeles: University of California Press, 1995).
16 Schleifer, *Modernism and Popular Music*, xv.
17 Ibid., 60 and 10.
18 Ibid., 13.
19 Ibid., 156–61 and 148–49.
20 Ibid., 110–32 and 75.
21 Lindberg, 'Popular Modernism?' 285.
22 Ibid., 284.
23 Ibid., 283.
24 Ibid., 288–89.
25 Ibid., 289–92.
26 Ibid., 292 and 289.
27 Comentale, *Sweet Air*.
28 Ashby, *The Pleasure of Modernist Music*.
29 Theodor Adorno, *Minima Moralia*, trans. E. F. N. Jephcott (London: Verso, 2005), 218.
30 Kyle Gann, 'The Modernist Populist', *PostClassic*, 4 May 2014, http://www.artsjournal.com/postclassic/2014/05/the-modernist-populist.html (accessed 23 October 2015).
31 Stephen Hinton, *Weill's Musical Theater: Stages of Reform* (Berkeley and Los Angeles: University of California Press, 2012), x.
32 Ibid., x–xi.
33 Kim H. Kowalke, 'Kurt Weill, Modernism, and Popular Culture: *Öffentlichkeit als Stil*', *Modernism/Modernity* 2, no. 1 (1995), 30.
34 Ibid., 58.
35 Steven Whiting gives an overview of the French cabaret and popular music scene in the 1890s and 1900s in *Satie the Bohemian: From Cabaret to Concert Hall* (Oxford: Oxford University Press, 2002), 9–10.
36 Gendron, *Between Montmartre and the Mudd Club*, 29.
37 Alfred Appel Jr would disagree with this assessment, particularly as regards Ellington and other jazz artists, whom he regards as participating in modernism; *Jazz Modernism: From Ellington and Armstrong to Matisse and Joyce* (New Haven, CT: Yale University Press, 2004).
38 This incisive reply from Larson Powell to an article by Rosen for the *New York Review of Books* gives a succinct overview of some such attempts to caricature Adorno; 'Adoring Adorno', *New York Review of Books*, 13 February 2002, http://www.nybooks.com/articles/archives/2003/feb/13/adoring-adorno/ (accessed 16 October 2015).
39 Thomas Y. Levin, 'For the Record: Adorno on Music in the Age of Its Technological Reproducibility', *October* 55 (1990), 23.
40 See, for instance, Theodor Adorno, 'The Aging of the New Music' and 'On the Social Situation of Music', in *Essays on Music*, 181–83 and 391–95.
41 Adorno, 'Letters to Walter Benjamin'.
42 Theodor Adorno, *Aesthetic Theory*, trans. Christian Lenhardt (London: Routledge, 1984), 432.
43 Fredric Jameson, *Late Marxism: Adorno, or, The Persistence of the Dialectic* (London and New York: Verso, 1990), 145.
44 Bernard Gendron, 'Theodor Adorno Meets the Cadillacs', in *Studies in Entertainment: Critical Approaches to Mass Culture*, ed. Tania Modleski (Bloomington: Indiana University Press, 1986), 18–36; Jameson,

Modernism for and of the masses?

Late Marxism; Renée Heberle, ed., *Feminist Interpretations of Theodor Adorno* (University Park, PA: Pennsylvania State University Press, 2006).

45 Greil Marcus, *Lipstick Traces* (Cambridge, MA: Harvard University Press, 1989).

46 Ben Watson, 'Adorno and Mass Culture', in *Adorno for Revolutionaries* (London: Unkant, 2011), 8–9.

47 Ben Watson, 'Adorno, Plato, Music', in *Adorno for Revolutionaries*, 13.

48 Ben Watson, 'Born to Die' and 'Semen Froth', in *Adorno for Revolutionaries*, 122–23 and 134–35.

49 Watson, 'Semen Froth', 134–35.

50 Ibid., 135.

51 Ben Watson, *Frank Zappa: The Negative Dialectics of Poodle Play* (London: St Martin's Press, 1993); also see 'Born to Die', in *Adorno for Revolutionaries*, particularly 118–19.

52 Watson, *Adorno for Revolutionaries*, 135 and 141.

53 See Stephen Graham, '(Un)Popular Avant-Gardes: Underground Popular Music and the Avant-Garde', *Perspectives of New Music* 48, no. 2 (2010), 5–20; and Andreas Huyssen, *After the Great Divide*, vii–viii and 8–15.

54 Mark Fisher, 'From 1984', *k-punk*, 14 February 2006, http://k-punk.abstractdynamics.org/archives/007364.html (accessed 22 October 2015).

55 Mark Fisher, *Ghosts of My Life* (Winchester, UK: Zero Books, 2014), 2–29.

56 Mark Fisher, 'Marxist Supernanny', in *Capitalist Realism: Is There No Alternative?* (Winchester, UK: Zero Books, 2009), 71–81.

57 Mark Fisher, 'Going Overground', *k-punk*, 5 January 2014, http://k-punk.org/going-overground/ (accessed 24 October 2015).

58 Mark Fisher, 'How the World Got Turned the Right Way Up Again', *k-punk*, 29 May 2009, http://k-punk.abstractdynamics.org/archives/011150.html (accessed 7 February 2015).

59 Fisher, *Ghosts of My Life*, 22.

60 Various, *No New York*, Antilles AN-7067 (1978).

61 Sam Davies, 'Thurston Moore and His Precursors', *zone styx travelcard*, 7 May 2009, http://zonestyxtravelcard.blogspot.co.uk/2009/05/thurston-moore-and-his-precursors.html (accessed 31 October 2015).

62 Quoted in Simon Reynolds, *Rip It Up and Start Again* (London: Faber and Faber, 2005), vii.

63 Kyle Gann gives an overview of Downtown music and the Downtown Greenwich Village and Soho scene in *Downtown Music: Writings from the Village Voice* (Berkeley and Los Angeles: University of California Press, 2006), 1–16.

64 This 'scronk' lineage is outlined by Lester Bangs in 'A Reasonable Guide to Horrible Noise', *Village Voice*, 30 September–6 October 1981.

65 Marcus, *Lipstick Traces*; Reynolds, *Rip It Up and Start Again*, vi.

66 Dan Hancox has framed grime as an Afrofuturist practice, for instance. Similarly, Owen Hatherley references jungle, grime and bassline house in a discussion of modernism, and Adam Harper has considered the avant-garde, modernist aspects of wonky. See Dan Hancox, *Stand Up Tall: Dizzee Rascal and the Birth of Grime* (London: Amazon Kindle, 2013); Owen Hatherley, *Militant Modernism* (Winchester, UK: Zero Books, 2008); and Adam Harper, 'Loving Wonky', *Rouge's Foam*, 1 June 2009, http://rougesfoam.blogspot.co.uk/2009/06/loving-wonky.html (accessed 2 November 2015).

67 Robert Fink discusses the structural vestiges of classical music and the use of 1930s imagery and ideas in Kraftwerk in 'The Story of ORCH5, or, the Classical Ghost in the Hip-Hop Machine', *Popular Music* 24, no. 3 (2005), 339–56.

68 Kodwo Eshun, *More Brilliant Than the Sun: Adventures in Sonic Fiction* (London: Quartet Books, 1998), 6.

69 Kanye West, *Yeezus*, Def Jam Recordings B0018653–02 (2013).

70 Schleifer, *Modernism and Popular Music*, 9.

71 Whiting, *Satie the Bohemian*, 4–5.

72 Huyssen, *After the Great Divide*, ix and 8.

Bibliography

Adorno, Theodor W. 'Letters to Walter Benjamin'. *New Left Review* I/81 (1973): 74–80.

———. *Aesthetic Theory*. Translated by Christian Lenhardt. London: Routledge, 1984.

———. *Essays on Music*. Edited by Richard D. Leppert. Translated by Susan H. Gillespie. Berkeley and Los Angeles: University of California Press, 2002.

———. *Minima Moralia*. Translated by E. F. N. Jephcott. London: Verso, 2005.

Albright, Daniel, ed. *Modernism and Music: An Anthology of Sources*. Chicago: University of Chicago Press, 2004.

Appel, Alfred, Jr. *Jazz Modernism: From Ellington and Armstrong to Matisse and Joyce*. New Haven, CT: Yale University Press, 2004.

Ashby, Arved, ed. *The Pleasure of Modernist Music: Listening, Meaning, Intention, Ideology*. Rochester, NY: University of Rochester Press, 2004.

Bangs, Lester. 'A Reasonable Guide to Horrible Noise'. *Village Voice*, 30 September–6 October 1981.

Born, Georgina. *Rationalizing Culture: IRCAM, Boulez, and the Institutionalization of the Musical Avant-Garde*. Berkeley and Los Angeles: University of California Press, 1995.

Bürger, Peter. *Theory of the Avant-Garde*. Translated by Michael Shaw. Minneapolis: University of Minnesota Press, 1984.

Clarke, David. 'Elvis and Darmstadt, or: Twentieth-Century Music and the Politics of Cultural Pluralism'. *Twentieth-Century Music* 4, no. 1 (2007): 3–45.

Comentale, Edward P. *Sweet Air: Modernism, Regionalism, and American Popular Song*. Urbana: University of Illinois Press, 2013.

Davies, Sam. 'Thurston Moore and His Precursors'. *zone styx travelcard*, 7 May 2009. http://zonestyxtravelcard.blogspot.co.uk/2009/05/thurston-moore-and-his-precursors.html (accessed 31 October 2015).

Davis, Mary E. 'Modernity à la mode: Popular Culture and Avant-Gardism in Erik Satie's *Sports et divertissements*'. *Musical Quarterly* 83, no. 3 (1999): 430–73.

Eshun, Kodwo. *More Brilliant Than the Sun: Adventures in Sonic Fiction*. London: Quartet Books, 1998.

Fink, Robert. 'The Story of ORCH5, or, the Classical Ghost in the Hip-Hop Machine'. *Popular Music* 24, no. 3 (2005): 339–56.

Fisher, Mark. 'From 1984'. *k-punk*, 14 February 2006. http://k-punk.abstractdynamics.org/archives/007364.html (accessed 22 October 2015).

———. 'How the World Got Turned the Right Way Up Again'. *k-punk*, 29 May 2009. http://k-punk.abstractdynamics.org/archives/011150.html (accessed 7 February 2015).

———. 'Marxist Supernanny'. In *Capitalist Realism: Is There No Alternative?* 71–81. Winchester, UK: Zero Books, 2009.

———. *Ghosts of My Life*. Winchester, UK: Zero Books, 2014.

———. 'Going Overground'. *k-punk*, 5 January 2014. http://k-punk.org/going-overground/ (accessed 24 October 2015).

Gann, Kyle. *Downtown Music: Writings from the Village Voice*. Berkeley and Los Angeles: University of California Press, 2006.

———. 'The Modernist Populist'. *PostClassic*, 4 May 2014. http://www.artsjournal.com/postclassic/2014/05/the-modernist-populist.html (accessed 23 October 2015).

Gendron, Bernard. 'Theodor Adorno Meets the Cadillacs'. In *Studies in Entertainment: Critical Approaches to Mass Culture*, edited by Tania Modleski, 18–36. Bloomington: Indiana University Press, 1986.

———. *Between Montmartre and the Mudd Club: Popular Music and the Avant-Garde*. Chicago: University of Chicago Press, 2002.

Graham, Stephen. '(Un)Popular Avant-Gardes: Underground Popular Music and the Avant-Garde'. *Perspectives of New Music* 48, no. 2 (2010): 5–20.

Greenberg, Clement. 'Avant-Garde and Kitsch' (1939). In *Art and Culture: Critical Essays*, 9–10. London: Beacon Press, 1989.

Hancox, Dan. *Stand Up Tall: Dizzee Rascal and the Birth of Grime*. London: Amazon Kindle, 2013.

Harper, Adam. 'Loving Wonky'. *Rouge's Foam*, 1 June 2009. http://rougesfoam.blogspot.co.uk/2009/06/loving-wonky.html (accessed 2 November 2015).

Hatherley, Owen. *Militant Modernism*. Winchester, UK: Zero Books, 2008.

Heberle, Renée, ed. *Feminist Interpretations of Theodor Adorno*. University Park, PA: Pennsylvania State University Press, 2006.

Heile, Björn. 'Introduction'. In *The Modernist Legacy: Essays on New Music*, edited by Björn Heile, 1–11. Farnham and Burlington, VT: Ashgate, 2009.

Hinton, Stephen. *Weill's Musical Theater: Stages of Reform*. Berkeley and Los Angeles: University of California Press, 2012.

Huyssen, Andreas. *After the Great Divide: Modernism, Mass Culture, Postmodernism*. London: Macmillan, 1986.

Jameson, Fredric. *Late Marxism: Adorno, or, The Persistence of the Dialectic*. London and New York: Verso, 1990.

Keightley, Keir. 'Tin Pan Allegory'. *Modernism/Modernity* 19, no. 4 (2012): 717–36.

Modernism for and of the masses?

Kowalke, Kim H. 'Kurt Weill, Modernism, and Popular Culture: *Öffentlichkeit als Stil*'. *Modernism/Modernity* 2, no. 1 (1995): 27–69.

Leick, Karen. 'Popular Modernism: Little Magazines and the American Daily Press'. *PMLA* 123, no. 1 (2008): 125–39.

Levin, Thomas Y. 'For the Record: Adorno on Music in the Age of Its Technological Reproducibility'. *October* 55 (1990): 23–47.

Lindberg, Ulf. 'Popular Modernism? The "Urban" Style of Interwar Tin Pan Alley'. *Popular Music* 22, no. 3 (2003): 283–98.

Lukács, Georg. 'The Ideology of Modernism'. In *Realism in Our Time: Literature and the Class Struggle*, translated by John and Necke Mander, 17–46. New York: Harper and Row, 1962.

Marcus, Greil. *Lipstick Traces*. Cambridge, MA: Harvard University Press, 1989.

Powell, Larson. 'Adoring Adorno'. *New York Review of Books*, 13 February 2002. http://www.nybooks.com/articles/archives/2003/feb/13/adoring-adorno/ (accessed 16 October 2015).

Reynolds, Simon. *Rip It Up and Start Again*. London: Faber and Faber, 2005.

Scherzinger, Martin. 'In Memory of a Receding Dialectic: The Political Relevance of Autonomy and Formalism in Modernist Musical Aesthetics'. In *The Pleasure of Modernist Music*, edited by Ashby, 68–101.

Schleifer, Ronald. *Modernism and Popular Music*. Cambridge: Cambridge University Press, 2011.

Suárez, Juan A. *Pop Modernism: Noise and the Reinvention of the Everyday*. Urbana and Chicago: University of Illinois Press, 2007.

Taruskin, Richard. *Music in the Early Twentieth Century*. Rev. ed. Vol. 4, *The Oxford History of Western Music*. New York: Oxford University Press, 2009.

Watson, Ben. *Frank Zappa: The Negative Dialectics of Poodle Play*. London: St Martin's Press, 1993.

———. *Adorno for Revolutionaries*. London: Unkant, 2011.

Whiting, Steven. *Satie the Bohemian: From Cabaret to Concert Hall*. Oxford: Oxford University Press, 2002.

Discography

Various. *No New York*. Antilles AN-7067 (1978).

West, Kanye. *Yeezus*. Def Jam Recordings B0018653–02 (2013).

11

TIMES LIKE THE PRESENT

De-limiting music in the twenty-first century

Charles Wilson

In 2015 Douglas Coupland, author of the 1980s bestseller *Generation X*, joined Shumon Basar in hailing the twenty-first century as 'the age of earthquakes'. Their book, with illustrations selected by art curator Hans Ulrich Obrist, offers a breathless sequence of fractured reflections on what its subtitle calls the 'extreme present'.[1] Its chief preoccupation is with the effects of new technologies on the perception of time and space, presenting metaphors and images of 'digital anxiety' self-consciously mingled with those of environmental panic: melting icecaps, floods, earthquakes, tsunamis. The book's memes and soundbites both mirror and actively solicit the instantaneous responses associated with tweeting and internet surfing, such that the collation of the whole between the covers of a printed book seems almost a self-conscious gesture of irony.

A gesture of irony – but also, it soon emerged, a gesture of homage. While trailed as encapsulating the unprecedented experiences of a digital generation, this compact paperback turned out to have an earlier analogue, dating from the analogue age. The book's prototype, as Coupland freely acknowledged, was Marshall McLuhan's punningly titled *The Medium is the Massage*, published almost half a century earlier in 1967.[2] It and its successor are both of pocket-book size; both are monochrome black-and-white throughout (anachronistically so, as regards the later book's graphic invocation of the normally multicoloured palettes of Instagram and Pinterest); and both emphasize their ominous messages of time-space collapse in the same forbiddingly oversized headlines of sans serif font. The earlier book experimented no less daringly with typography, layout and photomontage – although what McLuhan's illustrator did with pop-art-style multiples of photographic headshots, Obrist (for Basar and Coupland) now does with emoticons. Beyond that, the cyclicity of themes is obvious. McLuhan's prophecies concerning the massaging of the brain by new technology ('the medium [...] is reshaping and restructuring patterns of social interdependence and every aspect of our personal life')[3] is one of a number that find themselves rewritten, and further banalized, by Basar and Coupland ('we haven't just changed the structure of our brains these past few years. We've changed the structure of our planet').[4] The all-pervasive media that 'leave no part of us untouched, unaffected, unaltered' may have changed, but their effect is still to create that post-literate society of 'allatonceness',[5] in which memory either atrophies spontaneously or is outsourced to technology itself, 'offload[ed] onto hard drives and into the Cloud'.[6] The 'simultaneous happening' of McLuhan's famous 'global village' is summed up in Basar and Coupland's platitudinous reassurance that 'everybody on Earth is feeling the same way as you'.[7] Regardless of ethnicity or nationality, age or generation, we are all 'contemporaries' now.

Reviewers mostly found *The Age of Earthquakes* inferior to its precursor, one lambasting it as 'stupid for stupid's sake' and as 'reading like a teenager's Twitter account'.[8] But its status as a modified recapitulation of McLuhan should give pause for reflection. Both books assert with equal confidence the uniqueness of their present historical moments. This begs further questions: whether the early twenty-first century is indeed a 'present without precedent', in which digital communications, the internet and Web 2.0 have transformed our lives beyond all recognition; or whether (as with Basar and Coupland's refashioning of McLuhan) we are experiencing simply a digital-age remake, a remediation of those analogue forms of communication that burst onto the scene in the mid-twentieth century; or, further still, whether we are dealing with something inherently cyclical in nature – modernity as 'a constantly recurring trope' that, in Fredric Jameson's words, 'projects its own rhetorical structure onto the themes and contexts in question'.[9] Such a notion of cumulative iterations of technological modernity casts doubt on whether any of them, our own present included, might constitute a genuine break. And, somewhere in the midst of all this, have we definitively abandoned the values and aesthetics of modernism?

McLuhan's book marks the moment that a number of later commentators identified with the onset of postmodernism.[10] By the time Basar and Coupland's sequel emerged in 2015, however, postmodernism, whether as perceived phenomenon or mere descriptor, appeared to be in decline.[11] The question of a break with modernism remains, therefore, unresolved. On the contemporary art music scene, modernism thrives in the work of many living composers – and, indeed, a number of the most prominent and widely performed. While this chapter might have opted to chart the survival of recognizably modernist tendencies in recent music, it resists doing so, as there exist other notable contributions to that debate, elsewhere and in this volume.[12] Rather it focuses on those aspects of music and its culture that appear to question modernist ideals and practices – much as they might turn out to be dependent on them after all. For not all those values dismissed as hangovers of aesthetic modernism are easy to shake off, a number of them appearing, on reflection, vital to sustaining notions of art and 'art music' in general. Hence the self-conscious 'de-limiting' of my title. The English language has no convenient active verb form for the removing or unthinking of boundaries or limits. 'Delimiting', despite the negation that the 'de-' prefix often implies, means of course the very opposite: establishing boundaries or confirming them. This auto-antonymic ambivalence between 'de-limiting' as removing limits and 'delimiting' as asserting them will therefore emerge as crucial to what follows, instances of the former often turning out to implicate fresh instances of the latter.

No time like the present

Both McLuhan's message and that of Basar and Coupland half a century later might be succinctly paraphrased with the English-language commonplace 'no time like the present', an expression graspable in at least two different but related senses: first, that of the ethical priority of the present and, second, that of the historiographical uniqueness of the present time, namely the question of whether we are entering a new period, era or epoch – or indeed coming under a new paradigm that would render such designations irrelevant.

The first of these senses – the urgency and ethical priority of the present within the present – equates essentially with the French historian François Hartog's notion of 'presentism', a 'regime of historicity' predicated on 'the sense that only the present exists' – a present characterized paradoxically by both speed and stasis, by 'the tyranny of the instant and by the treadmill of an unending now'.[13] Presentism in its turn is just one characteristic of the 'contemporary', in the sense theorized of late in fields such as art history (Terry Smith), philosophy (Peter Osborne) and comparative literature (Lionel Ruffel).[14] In the words of Terry Smith, the idea of the 'contemporary' or 'contemporaneousness' is notable for 'its immediacy, its presentness, its instantaneity, its prioritizing of the moment over the time, the instant over the epoch, of direct experience of multiplicitous complexity over the singular simplicity of distanced reflection'.[15]

On one hand, the panicked sense of time's acceleration captured in Basar and Coupland's notion of the 'extreme present' is hardly new. The notion of a world outrunning itself goes back quite literally to the Dark Ages;[16] post-Enlightenment thinkers commented on it, especially in the wake of the French revolution;[17] and it is associated especially with the increased pace of industrial and technological modernity at the start of the twentieth century. Yet, on the other hand, the sense of acceleration in our own present might not be wholly without empirical foundation. It may well be endemic to a post-industrial society in which the velocity of transactions and shorter time horizons that are a feature of the financial (and especially the secondary financial) markets make long-term projections volatile and increasingly tenuous.[18] For individual consumers too, now has always been the time for a marketplace that wants people neither to stick with yesterday's technology nor to wait for tomorrow's. With the uninterrupted connectivity provided by mobile electronic devices, Hartog's 'unending now' merges with Joseph Schumpeter's notion of 'unsleeping capitalism' to create a '24/7' world in which, as Jonathan Crary argues, no moment is immune from becoming 'work time, consumption time or marketing time'.[19] With this blandly uniform rhythm of existence and its 'shapeless continuity' comes an 'abandonment of the pretense that time is coupled to any long-term undertakings', let alone to 'fantasies of "progress" or development'.[20] While opportunities for unprecedented mobility can be capitalized on by those with the readiness and 'fitness' to 'move swiftly where the action is', others (migrants, the unemployed) experience its negative underside, deprived of the opportunity to plan ahead or imagine a future.[21] Symptomatic of this, perhaps, is the recent revival of a WWII British Ministry of Information slogan: 'Keep Calm and Carry On'. If our present is characterized by an inability to think beyond the present, then that may be because, as Hartog notes, the future is often 'perceived as a threat, not a promise'.[22] In a present seemingly cut off at both ends, any narrative promoting continuity between past and future may find itself disavowed or repressed.

Questioning the nature of the present's relationship to both past and future is also fundamental to a second possible apprehension of 'no time like the present', one that suggests the uniqueness of the present in terms of not just its qualities as an era but also its status as such – the question, namely, of whether it constitutes an era at all. Where the term 'contemporary' is concerned, problems of periodization are self-evident. Not only does the contemporary signify 'moving with the times', it itself 'moves with the times', dependent like all so-called linguistic shifters (such as 'now' and 'then') on the time and context of its utterance.[23] It is, in Claire Bishop's words, a 'moving target par excellence'.[24] Some have suggested that a solution to this problem is to abandon periodization altogether. To Lionel Ruffel the contemporary 'appears less as a period than as the critique of a certain kind of knowledge that has made periodization its cornerstone'.[25] Far from the latest stage in the 'modern representation of historical temporality' the contemporary signifies not just 'copresence' but a 'cotemporality' of all times, 'a palimpsestic or layered representation of time', in which 'the present is not a sequence but a point of metabolization of all pasts and all futures'.[26]

In stressing that the historian's present is the only true vantage point for historical observation, Ruffel follows the Benjaminian tradition which favours archaeology as its preferred mode of investigation. Such an approach has a natural affinity with histories of art and music, preoccupied as they are with the traces left by works and artefacts and their afterlife in reception and performance practice – objects, in other words, that are 'polychronic, heterochronic, anachronistic' and 'traversed by multiple times'.[27] Still, the perception of 'anachronism' is something that itself requires a nuanced and astute perception of chronology, and while writers such as Ruffel and Hartog resist the epochal understanding of the present, both involuntarily let slip references to the 'contemporary period'.[28]

Simply abandoning a sense of chronology and chronological boundaries is perhaps, therefore, not the answer. First, periodization was never quite the matter of straightforward sequentiality and succession that Ruffel suggests: historians have long seen the same present as incorporating different historical modalities, for instance in Wilhelm Pinder's concept of the non-contemporaneity of the contemporaneous (*Ungleichzeitigkeit des Gleichzeitigen*).[29] Second, even if the contemporary is to be understood, as Hartog suggests, as a 'regime' rather than a 'period', much of what he and Ruffel regard as characteristic of the present regime is bound up inextricably with either technological developments or forms of global awareness scarcely thinkable before the late twentieth and early twenty-first centuries. Just as terms like 'the Third Republic' (and indeed 'the Third Reich') derive much of their ideological power from their putative designation of both a regime and an era – the one coterminous with the other, rendering the associated ideology as inescapable as the historical moment – so the potency of Ruffel's contemporary would seem to arise from its status as a purportedly ahistorical 'mode of being' allied with its very insistence on *being* about all those things (networked communications, hypermediatized environments and so on) whose enabling conditions would appear time-bound, bound indeed to 'the present age' or, as we should apparently resist saying, 'the contemporary period'. Problematic as the 'epochal contemporary' may be, thinking one's way out of it altogether remains a challenging task. A future 'future', designated as 'contemporary' or whatever else, will doubtless embody its own distinctive character and 'regime of historicity', and hence the potential to constitute a new era – if in all but name. To suggest that our own moment marks the 'end of all epochs' seems in any case uncomfortably redolent of some kind of Hegelian finality or 'end state' – the idea, in Stuart Hall's words, that 'history stops with us'.[30]

Entgrenzung: the 'de-limited' present

In 1993 the French historian Pierre Nora identified four fundamental phenomena that have 'profoundly transformed th[e] contemporary itself, its history and its historiography': these he identified as acceleration, democratization, globalization and mass mediatization.[31] It is striking that subsequent theorists of the contemporary have alighted on broadly similar categories, albeit with a dimension of vectorial movement to suggest traversal, the crossing of boundaries, often marked by the prefix 'trans-'. Indeed, Peter Osborne sums up the contemporary sensibility in terms of an act of *Entgrenzung* or 'de-bordering'.[32] For Osborne, contemporary art is transnational and transcultural, shadowing and modelling processes such as global migration and the flows of capital; it is transmedial, using various different and above all new media (such as the virtual worlds of video and the internet); and it is transcategorial, crossing boundaries of critical discourse and thought. Terry Smith likewise has use for the transnational and the transmedial, adding to them a third category reflecting retrospective tendencies of various kinds: retrosensationalism (seen as involving a repetition of avant-garde shock tactics), spectacularism (the hubristic extravagance and scale of such works as Matthew Barney's *Cremaster* cycle, exhibited at the New York Guggenheim in 2003), and 'remodernism' (the persistence and recasting of the modernist aesthetic).

In the following I shall focus on interrogating borders and limits related to four key notions: access (both Nora's democratization and the 'accessibility' of music more generally), medium (not only Nora's mass mediatization but mixed media and the concomitant challenges regarding the ontology of music), location (less Nora's globalization per se than issues concerning the locatedness and embeddedness of music more broadly) and subjectivity (as linked to, though by no means coterminous with, the virtual). At face value all this might sound like a celebratory dismantling of modernism's limitations and prohibitions: modernism as exclusive and esoteric, barring access to all but a privileged few; modernism as myopically 'medium specific' (though such a judgement would not stand prolonged scrutiny); modernism as a securely grounded and located phenomenon, and not just in the geographical terms of Western Europe and North America; and modernism as dominated by strongly individualistic and, at times, self-consciously prophetic creative subjects. But the issues are not quite so simple. First, not all these boundaries characterize all modernisms, and many aspects of musical production in the present, such as mixed media and cosmopolitanism, have identifiably modernist roots.[33] (Presenting these things as new and independent of their origins is, of course, yet a further manifestation of presentism.) Second, much of the rhetoric that surrounds 'de-bordering' is ideological and designed to mask ongoing exclusions and inequalities. As already noted, any act of 'de-limiting' tends to involve one of 'delimiting' at the same time. Commenting on the work of Peter Sloterdijk, Slavoj Žižek observes that while the global reach of capitalism seems borderless and unlimited, it also 'introduces a radical class division across the entire globe, separating those protected by the entire sphere from those left vulnerable outside it'.[34] Third, moreover, not all de-bordering is liberating and not all limits inherently bad. Žižek recalls how Lenin ('an internationalist if ever there was one') opposed the slogan 'Down with frontiers', stating rather that 'we maintain that the state is necessary, and a state presupposes frontiers'.[35]

To begin with, the issue of borders affects our field of study. If a state presupposes frontiers, so a discipline presupposes some kind of boundaries. And yet the far-reaching transformations wrought by modernism in terms of materials and technique made 'art music' increasingly hard to define on purely, or even primarily, stylistic grounds. More recently, categories such as algorithmic music, soundscape and other forms of media art have further stretched the ontological limits of what music might be. Where stylistic or material definitions fail, it is perhaps to social and institutional ones that we should turn. One of the most persuasive, still after forty years, remains that of Harold S. Powers, a scholar versed in a number of world traditions.[36] Powers's four principal criteria can be reformulated broadly as follows: 1) a tradition of music *making*, whether through the performance of oral tradition, a combination of 'original' composition and performance (as in the Western classical tradition), or composition without the mediation of performance (as, for instance, in electronic music); 2) a corresponding tradition of theory or other professional discourse; 3) an autonomy of definition that allows it to be 'conceived as an independent domain that can stand on its own', even when 'linked to other domains in the high culture'; and 4) a tradition of reception or, as Powers puts it, an elite 'connoisseurship'. All these four categories – a tradition of making, a theoretical or otherwise exegetical discourse, an autonomy of (disciplinary) definition and a tradition of educated reception – have potential implications in terms of access, medium, location and subjectivity. And while all have been subject to challenge in the past half century, they are nonetheless still to exhaust their relevance.

Interleaved with these discussions are case studies of three twenty-first century works: Anna Clyne's orchestral composition *Night Ferry* (2011–12), James Bulley and Daniel John Jones's installation *Living Symphonies* (2014) and Alvin Curran's radiophonic montage *Vindobona Blues* (2005). I have deliberately avoided the best-known composers and, indeed, the best-known compositional tendencies, such as minimalism, spectralism or 'new complexity' (which is not to suggest that the work of my chosen composers would be resistant to any such categories, only that it is not my purpose here). The seeming openness of the contemporary music scene is perhaps in part a result of the sheer number of composers active today (noted ambivalently by John Cage in his 1992 mesostic 'Overpopulation and Art')[37] and the fact that no individual commentator could lay claim to any kind of synoptic vantage point.[38] Few nowadays harbour much nostalgia for a 'one true path' vision of the musical future, if that were ever a genuine proposition. Still, to conclude that ours is an age of unbounded pluralism would be too hasty a conclusion. First, every age appears pluralistic to itself, and second, the power of such rhetoric to mask ongoing politics of exclusion should not be underestimated. The putative borderless zone of the musical present – even the 'extreme present' – is never quite what it seems.

Access

One of the most striking features of the musical present is the widespread availability of an unprecedented amount of music. What began with the advent of recording and other mechanical reproduction technologies has, with digitalization, shed its obligatory reliance on physical media and sound carriers. But problems of access are not thereby resolved. If contemporary art music remains the preserve of a minority of the listening public (as, indeed, does art music in general), this would appear to be not primarily by reason of its putatively disagreeable nature – nor, according to a commentator such as William Weber, was it ever.[39] Though there are composers who have achieved significant public success over the past three decades – among them John Adams, John Tavener and, at one exceptional moment in reception history, Henryk Górecki[40] – it is for the most part not open hostility that composers risk but something arguably far worse: indifference.

The latter half of the twentieth century saw moves to increase access to new music as part of the general drive towards the democratization of culture following WWII. The new Arts Council of Great Britain set out its agenda in 1946,[41] the US National Endowment for the Arts following somewhat later in 1965; in 1948 article 27 of the United Nations Universal Declaration on Human Rights enshrined not only the intellectual property rights of creators but also 'the right freely to participate in the cultural life of the community, to enjoy the arts and to share in scientific advancement and its benefits'.[42]

In Britain the early phases of cultural democratization held that the arts, including modernist art music, set their own standards and imposed their own demands, demands to which audiences could accede through education. Such thinking reached its visionary apex during the tenure of BBC chairman Hugh Carleton Greene in the 1960s, with his distaste for the 'tyranny of ratings',[43] and that of his Controller of Music William Glock, who believed that broadcasting should march in advance of public taste, favouring less what the public enjoyed than what they might one day come to appreciate.[44] Glock's policy of programming new works alongside established modern(ist) works and still older repertoire – doubtless influenced by practices at the Domaine Musical in Paris under Boulez, who later worked alongside Glock as principal conductor of the BBC Symphony Orchestra – persisted in such initiatives as the Arts Council's regional concert touring programme the Contemporary Music Network, which began in 1971. The CMN was notable especially for its policy of touring not premiere performances of newly commissioned works but second and subsequent performances, again alongside established modern classics. The explicit intention of the Network's founder, Annette Morreau, was to 'embed' them not only in the performers' repertoire (through repeated and, with luck, increasingly accomplished performances) but also within a historical (and potentially canonical) lineage.[45]

The 1980s and 1990s, however, saw not just the cultural authority of modernism challenged but also the very notion of cultural authority itself. While attitudes such as those of Glock and

Morreau became regarded increasingly as paternalistic, more drastic still were the consequences of the increasing privatization and marketization of the state infrastructure in European economies. By 2001 the newly appointed director of the Contemporary Music Network, Beverley Crew, was reporting that, owing to the need to be 'publicly accountable', it had to 'forgo the high-risk expensive productions that were a feature of the past' and to reach out 'to a far more diverse audience': 'the arts are funded by everyone in this country and it would be unfair of us to tailor our output solely to any one group of people'.[46] From the late 1990s, under the British 'New Labour' government, the arts found themselves increasingly promoted for their instrumental value as arms of the 'creative industries' in stimulating economic growth and cultural tourism.[47] In line with Hartog's 'tyranny of the instant', organizations found themselves at the mercy of changing policy directives and increasingly contracted funding cycles, which endangered the long-term planning required for ambitious artistic enterprises and seemed to discourage risk-taking in general.

It is not easy to assess the practical impact of such considerations on the horizons of musicians themselves. A 2016 report from the UK development agency for new music found that commissions for composers, while holding up in sheer number, were becoming less remunerative. More tellingly, 49% of composers reported 'less rehearsal/preparation time for new works', with a potential impact 'on the type of work produced' in terms of scale and technical ambition.[48] Some years earlier the composer Simon Emmerson had noted a 'great divide' opening up between 'those who maintain a strong relation with the concert hall and those who have moved out of it'.[49] Music without access to large venues and generous funding streams thus finds itself increasingly restricted to the peer networks of contemporary music festivals and specialist concert series and tends, out of logistical and economic necessity, to be composed for modest performing forces.

There are consequences for cultural memory too. Music that exists on the fringes of public life may somehow be preserved – and may even be more 'accessible' in literal terms than before, locatable in a few clicks for downloading or streaming, rather than through recourse to a library, sound archive or music information centre. But while so much is archived, what of it is remembered?[50] Modernism engaged in relentless struggles with the past, perceiving tradition as an adversary to be overcome, and fighting against it for legitimacy and longevity, the right to survive. Modernism was often charged with preaching a ruthless doctrine of innovation and obsolescence, by which works passed either into a canonical past, rewarded for responding fully to the aesthetic demands of a particular historical conjuncture, or were otherwise set aside as irrelevant.[51] Under a presentist regime, by contrast, the past is neither sifted nor discarded. Neither allowed to remain new, being rapidly replaced by the ever newer, nor permitted to become old, it remains part of a continuous present, an 'unending now' that has yet to recede into the past, into 'history'. The no-longer-brand-new is thus at a double disadvantage: not yet accessible *as* past but rather only as the faded retentions of a constantly extended and all-absorbing present.[52] In the culture of contemporary music this manifests itself in a stark polarization of the brand new on the one hand and an increasingly stable canon on the other – a gap that the Contemporary Music Network had, in its heyday, attempted to bridge.[53] Hence the irony that the very presentist ideology which privileges the new, touting above all its immediacy and relevance, may ultimately be what renders uncertain its cultural longevity.

Case study 1: Anna Clyne, *Night Ferry* (2011)

In line with these trends, contemporary music in the symphony concert hall has suffered a mixed fate. On the one hand, presentist thinking favours newly commissioned music, making it if anything a more established feature of concert life. On the other, the terms under which new music enters the concert hall have become more exacting. Above all, in the United Kingdom and the United States especially, a large commission needs to be an attractive proposition in marketing terms, and where the reputation of the composer proves an insufficient draw, context – or else paratext – is all. That is to say, it helps if the new is also newsworthy.

From the 1990s especially, when the rhetoric of 'crossover' was at its height, high-profile British and American concert commissions were often tethered to topical subjects, contemporary popular culture, or both.[54] *Night Ferry* (2011–12), composed by British-born Anna Clyne during her period of residency with the Chicago Symphony Orchestra, refers to neither.[55] But it more than compensates by offering its listeners especially rich paratexts: visual (a series of collage-based canvases produced in the course of the composition process, reproduced in the online study score) and poetic (a lengthy programme note with epigraphs from Dante and Byron, which describes the work as 'a sonic portrait of voyages [. . .] from stormy darkness to enchanted worlds [. . .] voyages within nature and of physical, mental and emotional states').[56]

The composer's note divides the work into seven sections, each headed with what could be either a performance direction or a poetic description: 'Turbulent darkness with moments of light', 'With tenderness and warmth', 'Quiet and ominous', and so on. The sections intercut one another, often unpredictably, with their characteristic music. These contrasts register strongly thanks to a tendency to favour consistency of texture, harmonic stasis and clearly identifiable melodic materials. While not functionally tonal, the music conveys unambiguous pitch centres composed out over long spans. The opening section is focused on D, the slow ascent of the minor tetrachord providing the dragging undertow to the swirling currents above it. D as focal pitch is later juxtaposed with F, as at the start of the second section, before settling on E (with dragging undertow duly transposed) in the final section. Motives are modal-diatonic: for instance, the five-note mixolydian idea that circles in the echo chamber of the second section, and the work's most extensive 'theme' introduced in the third (still a mere four bars in length). The 'turbulent darkness' of the opening section oscillates between 'Ukrainian' dorian (dorian with raised fourth) and 'Hungarian' minor (harmonic minor likewise with raised fourth), each thickened by minor thirds to create the cascading diminished chords whose topical associations with storm and tempest extend back to Rossini and Liszt. Chromaticism otherwise extends no further than the octatonic, which features at the 'dissolve' preceding the first general pause at bars 33–35 and again in the transition to the second section (bars 89–95).

But even more striking than its modal centricity is the work's continuity of pulse. While metre is often irregular, the surface is nearly always dominated by a consistent unit pulse: the semiquaver swirls of the opening section; the quaver ostinato in harp and piano of the second, holding together the heterophonically echoing layers of the same melodic fragment in the woodwind; the barcarolle rhythm at letter J ('Melting into water'), redolent of Charon's oars; and then the grinding 12/8 pulse of the fifth section ('With drive and grit'), resembling more the relentless chugging of a chain ferry, foghorns (French horns and trombones) to boot.

A reading of *Night Ferry* in terms of the *Materialstand* would doubtless observe that it employs no harmonic or rhythmic resource unavailable a century ago, even though it is in no sense nostalgic or hieratic.[57] Perhaps, therefore, we need to look elsewhere for its contemporaneity. While not explicitly programmatic, the work, along with its multiple paratexts, seems to identify itself with a journey or quest, such as those of fantasy adventure novels or video games. Clyne's score, with its virtuoso orchestration, would for many listeners be reminiscent of a film soundtrack,[58] its brooding, ostinato-driven texture connoting a tension-infused heroic narrative. While, as noted earlier, *Night Ferry* contains no discernible references to popular music, it is perhaps no coincidence that surface pulse and modality – increasingly prominent features of contemporary orchestral music, above and beyond distinctions such as 'minimalism'/'maximalism' or even the obvious stylistic differences between, say, a Lowell Liebermann and a Magnus Lindberg – are likewise a consistent feature of commercial rock and pop. While much has been made of the 'return to tonality' in recent concert music (even if this tonality only rarely equates to common-practice major–minor diatonicism), the return to pulse is if anything still more striking. Indeed, the often rapid alternations of static, rhythmically suspended passages with pulsed sections in works by, for example, Boulez or Lutosławski might prove still more disconcerting to contemporary audiences than their level of dissonance.

Night Ferry is an effective piece of orchestral writing, but it has clear strategies for meeting its stakeholders halfway. With stringent limitations imposed on rehearsal time and instrumental forces, the mainstream concert environment has increasingly become one in which genuine risk cannot be tolerated. The imperative to commission new music has never been greater for classical music institutions, obliged to demonstrate their cultural relevance under the regime of presentism. But, given the level of investment it requires, a major orchestral or operatic commission becomes truly too big to fail. The quest for the tried and tested might take another form, one established already in the second half of the twentieth century, when figures such as Boulez and Maxwell Davies began their careers running independent, counter-cultural concert-giving enterprises before being co-opted into the mainstream. (A more recent case in point is Gabriel Prokofiev, whose international commissions followed in the wake of his celebrated Nonclassical club nights, with their live remixes of contemporary classical music.)[59] Risk is so to speak 'contracted out', and there is a sense in which mainstream performing networks use the specialist festivals and concert series as their 'research and development' arm, investing only when a sufficient track-record of success has been established.[60] In the meantime much innovative music finds itself pushed to the margins.

Medium

Whereas contemporary art seems preoccupied with immediacy, presence, an unmediated sense of the 'real' (even when that 'real' is more the virtual invocation of the 'hyper-real'), twentieth-century modernism tended to emphasize medium and 'mediacy', the visibility of the mediation brought by the artist. In his broadcast lecture 'Modernist Painting' (1961) the art critic Clement Greenberg wrote that while 'naturalistic art had dissembled the medium, using art to conceal art', modernism had 'used art to call attention to art', which meant focusing on 'all that was unique in the nature of its medium'. This 'medium specificity' sought to 'eliminate from the specific effects of each art any and every effect that might conceivably be borrowed from or by the medium of any other art', such as the 'sculptural' illusion of three-dimensional space: 'because flatness was the only condition painting shared with no other art, modernist painting oriented itself to flatness as it did to nothing else'.[61]

While Greenberg's notion of medium specificity represents perhaps a partial and partisan view of aesthetic modernism, it has parallels in modernist musical production. Both before and after the two world wars, composers effected many of their most radical explorations of the categories of musical space and time through the medium of standard pitched instruments such as the piano (whether, for instance, in Schoenberg's Op. 11 or Stockhausen's *Klavierstücke*). Post-WWII composers initially sought a similar specificity and purity in the synthetic, artificial timbres of electronic music. But this was always just one half of the dialectic. The medium-specific ideal of the Cologne school of electronic composers vied with the notion of *musique concrète* and, later, works of *musique mixte* that combined electronics with traditional instruments (Luciano Berio's *Différences* of 1958–59 being among the earliest examples). The next two decades witnessed the still more permeable boundaries of music theatre and John Cage's multimedia 'happenings', both of which, rather than segregating singers or actors and pit musicians, combined all manner of performers, and often audiences too, in the same physical space. The works of Fluxus went one stage further, extending the notion of music 'beyond sound' altogether (or, perhaps, to purely imagined sound), and in doing so stretching the ontological boundaries of music close to their limits.[62]

In his 'Statement on Intermedia' of 1966, Dick Higgins, a former student of Cage's at the New School for Social Research, explained 'the impact of Happenings, event pieces, mixed media films' as 'a new way of looking at things', one that allows 'immediacy, with a minimum of distractions'. He announced that 'the media have broken down in their traditional forms, and have become merely puristic points of reference', useful only 'as critical tools, in saying that such-and-such a work is basically musical, but also poetry'. 'This', he continued, 'is the intermedial approach, to emphasize the dialectic between the media. A composer is a dead man unless he composes for all the media and for his world.'[63] For Terry Smith this 'mobility as to media' stands as 'the most obvious marker for any art that is contemporary'.[64] Just as the American art critic Rosalind E. Krauss wrote of 'Sculpture in the Expanded Field' to refer to sculpture's embrace of quasi-architectural structures, including those created in the natural environment, some are now speaking, by analogy, of 'contemporary music in the expanded field', in that music, long part of *multi*media creations such as opera and the sound film, now becomes *transmedial*, part of representations whose 'musical' components are ambiguous or otherwise hard to extricate or isolate from the whole.[65]

Characteristic of such transmedial representations is the 'sound installation', a term coined in 1967 by Max Neuhaus for a work that is usually site-specific, 'installed' in a particular location, though frequently involving mobile elements.[66] The installation can be seen as thematizing various kinds of boundary crossing, both in terms of medium (in that it might include elements such as sculpture, lighting, projections, video and live electronics) and in terms of space. Unlike standard works of music, installations enjoy 'simultaneous existence in both space and time'.[67] This means, first, that viewers/listeners are no longer either passive or rooted to the spot, being able not only to walk around and through the installation but also to trigger sound events, hence moving from the status of mute receivers to that of performers or co-composers. Another spatial limit breached is that of functional space. Not only does an installation frequently subsume the entire space of the gallery or other building adapted for the purpose; it can also take place in an unbounded space, encroaching upon and potentially colonizing the urban or rural environment to disruptive and politically charged effect.[68] At the more quiescent end of the scale, such unboundedness signifies too that the relatively disinterested aesthetic contemplation of sound is no longer restricted to dedicated social spaces such as concert halls. Such contemplation can take place anywhere, including the natural environment, as R. Murray Schafer's conceptions of the 'soundscape' and 'soundwalk' testify.[69] (Indeed the technological mediation of these and similar projects raises the further question of human versus non-human listening.) Finally, bringing the notions of medium and space together, the sound installation raises questions of 'disciplinary space'. Where does sound art belong as a professional discipline, whether situated 'between' art and music or at a still more complex intersection?[70] Such questions, as the next case study will show, are by no means purely theoretical.

Case study 2: James Bulley and Daniel John Jones, *Living Symphonies* (2014)

Living Symphonies was a work of landscape sound art, a 'site-specific symphony',[71] created by James Bulley and Daniel John Jones. The aim of the project, in Jones's words, was to 'create a piece of music which portrays in real time the huge web of interactions that make up a forest ecosystem'.[72] It was first installed, using loudspeakers concealed in the undergrowth and tree canopy, in Thetford Forest, Suffolk, in May 2014, before touring three further forests over the following three months. The composers presented the work as modelling the interactions of flora and fauna contained within a defined area of Thetford Forest, a model that was articulated musically by attaching melodies and musical motifs to different organisms and their behaviours or 'activity states'. These musical elements were then played back in a location and (where applicable) with a pattern of motion typical of the organism concerned. In this way, the composition process for *Living Symphonies* proceeded in four stages: extracting data from the environment, modelling it, 'musicalizing' the model, and then inserting it back into the natural environment.

Two aspects of *Living Symphonies* as a transmedial, site-specific project should therefore be noted. First, while drawing on information from the environment for which it was conceived, it remains in essence a musical composition: it is formalized, in that its melodies and motifs are ordered on the basis of an abstract, data-driven model, but the musical elements themselves neither constitute straightforward sonifications of the environmental data nor replicate or imitate the soundscape.[73] Second, *Living Symphonies* is not an interactive work, in that neither the humans visiting it nor the non-human organisms inhabiting it trigger any sounds. Yet for those entering the installation, a sense of interacting with the environment – with 'nature' – is created.

Not for nothing does Boris Groys consider installation as 'the leading form in the framework of contemporary art', occurring as it does in the 'fixed, stable, closed context of a topologically well-defined "here and now"'.[74] The notion of the site-specific installation embodies many symptomatically presentist values: presence, immediacy and bodily immersion on the one hand, ephemerality and transience on the other. Terry Smith writes of the 'triumph of the exhibition over the collection',[75] the gallery director now less the curator of a permanent display of artefacts than an impresario for staged events. Although the staged event is hardly a novel concept for musicians, the sound-art installation nonetheless represents something quite unlike the standard work of music, its very location in time and place often a symbol of its impermanence. While the virtual work of music has an ongoing, portable manifestation in the score or recording, the uniqueness of the installation means – paradoxically and despite its concrete materiality – that when it's gone, it's gone.

In an environment in which art and art music exist in constant competition with entertainment culture, such uniquely 'present' events have particular value. For promoters, the liveness of the site-specific spectacle has one significant advantage over those forms of music consumed in commodity form and 'on demand' through streaming technology. Simply put, to hear, to experience *Living Symphonies* requires a trip to the forest. It is no surprise to find that the work was a 'coproduction' with the environmental conservation body Forestry Commission England, exemplifying not just transmediality but also the blurring of boundaries between art, 'heritage' (including environmental heritage) and cultural policy that now characterizes the political landscape in many Western European countries.[76]

How, then, does all this fit with our third Powers-derived art music category, that of 'autonomy of definition'? *Living Symphonies* had another co-producer alongside Forestry Commission England, namely Sound and Music, the UK Development Agency for new music. The involvement of Sound and Music in the project revived issues aired publicly in the British press just two years earlier. Sound and Music had been formed in 2008 from a merger of four organizations, including the Society for the Promotion of New Music (the former British ISCM section) and the Sonic Arts Network (whose focus was electroacoustic work, including sound art).[77] Four years later, in 2012, an open letter to Sound and Music and its principal funder Arts Council England attracted 250 signatures from leading UK musicians.[78] The letter accused Sound and Music of having abandoned 'the long-established and constructive activities' of the organizations merged to form it. In particular, it castigated Sound and Music for adopting the role of 'producer' for specific projects instead of seeking to provide a supportive infrastructure for 'young and unestablished composers (and the musicians working with them)', and for its 'bland and unfocused endorsement of "sound art"' at the expense of what the authors of the letter called 'notated and modern composition'.[79]

Sound and Music was therefore charged with privileging isolated, staged events rather than upholding art music's wider 'tradition of making' and, what is more, with supporting a particular 'tradition of making', namely sonic art, that the authors of the letter saw as other than their own, forced together as their respective bodies had been by the 2008 merger. While the letter drew wide support, others would no doubt have viewed it as an overt act of protectionism on the part of a compositional 'establishment'. But it was also quite clearly a debate about funding and resources: one need not deny multimedia installations the right to exist in order to question the kind of organization, music or art based, that should be funding them. Sound art in the United Kingdom may have a weaker institutional 'tradition of making' than 'notated and modern composition', but it increasingly has its own (albeit distinctly pluralistic and contested) discourse, a developing disciplinary identity and a growing tradition of reception.[80] Rather than constituting a purely protectionist move, perhaps the letter was indicative of a wider concern – namely that, under a presentist regime which sees synergies such as 'music–environment' as offering not just topicality but also potential economies of scale, there is a genuine risk that works produced with today's ever-cheaper and more portable technologies will be favoured over those involving more complex and costly performance infrastructures.

Location

Contemporary art of all kinds remains both stimulated and problematized by the 'globalized imaginary': for Peter Osborne 'the inter- and transnational characteristics of art space have become the primary markers of its contemporaneity'.[81] Still, this globalized imaginary is the source of many myths. Clearly problematic – indeed false – is the idea that geographical location is no longer a factor in a musician's quest for self-fulfilment. At the same time the politics of cultural appropriation that postcolonial theory brought to wider consciousness are reproblematized by both migration patterns and digital technologies.

In any conception of a global musical modernism the spectre of colonialism looms large. As Björn Heile writes, 'Any study of the global dimension of musical modernism has to contend with the fact that it is inextricably connected with one of the darkest chapters in the history of the world', without which 'Western music would not have been adopted so widely'.[82] There remains no doubt whatsoever that music infrastructures (those of both education and performance) remain unevenly distributed across continents. Of the forty-nine national sections of the International Society for Contemporary Music (ISCM), thirty-two are European (including those representing the former Eastern bloc).[83] As of 2017, just ten of the previous forty ISCM festivals had taken place outside Europe. In terms of those composers on the lists of the major classical music publishers, the picture yet again displays a strong centripetal pull to the historic centres of musical training and performance: composers of African and Asian origin who enjoy an exclusive publishing arrangement are nearly all based in Europe or the United States, some having settled for political reasons but by no means all.[84]

Much of the celebratory rhetoric around globalization is bound up with the global reach opened up by technological mediation. But the power of such mediation to level inequalities should not be overestimated. Of all the utopian projects aimed at a kind of technology-driven global synchronicity, the YouTube Symphony Orchestra was perhaps the best publicized as well as the most anticlimactic, and not only because the work commissioned for the occasion, Tan Dun's *Internet Symphony no. 1 'Eroica'* was closer to a concert overture in dimension and was panned for its 'episodic nature and clichéd quoting from Beethoven'.[85] As Shzr Ee Tan notes in her study of the project, YouTube made much of its 'aspiration to create a new utopian playing field engineered through the global, participatory and democratic reach of the internet'.[86] But notwithstanding an open online audition process, the resulting orchestra reinforced a standard demographic, with eighty-five percent of the chosen musicians having been either brought up or educated in North America or Europe.[87] Meanwhile the technological dimension of the project remained rudimentary: while its headline event was a concert at Carnegie Hall, for which successful audition candidates were flown in to rehearse and perform together, its most ambitious product was a virtual 'mashup' performance of Tan Dun's symphony, produced by synchronizing and combining renderings of individual orchestral parts sent in for audition.[88]

In an interconnected world in which technology has failed to simply conjure away long-standing inequities, the dilemmas for musicians remain acute, especially in terms of the ever-problematic boundary between homage and theft. Musicians and composers risk the double bind whereby they avoid intercultural engagement altogether and risk charges of cultural chauvinism or attempt such an engagement and court accusations of exoticist appropriation. Three issues add acuity to these questions. First, a younger generation's sense of disengagement from a colonial history in which they themselves feel no complicity (even if colonialist adventures can, alas, by no means be safely relegated to the past). Second, the realities of multicultural societies and successive waves of migration, which break once and for all what had long been a tenuous link between culture and territory: cultural otherness is as likely to be encountered next door as halfway round the world. Third, the fact that music is often discovered and consumed in environments lacking paratextual indicators of any kind. Musicians of the 1980s and 1990s were criticized for knowingly appropriating ethnographic field recordings, with all the cultural injustices such practices perpetuate.[89] But today many 'ripped' or downloaded music tracks inhabit the world of the contextless acousmatic, bearing nothing but cryptic filenames as vague clues to their origins. To this end Steve Savage has recently spoken of the need to move beyond what he calls the 'stigma of appropriation'. In an environment in which a good deal of music is practically as well as theoretically deterritorialized, the 'complexity and fragmentation' that characterize processes such as audio sampling 'will continue to render so-called notions of appropriation more inappropriate to cultural understanding'. Instead Savage advocates use of the term 'repurposing' as 'a more accurate and less pejorative term for such reuse'.[90] Harking back to Roland Barthes's notion that 'a text's unity lies not in its origin but in its destination',[91] he argues that the term 'repurpose' puts 'the emphasis on the audio's new environment, its newly imagined purpose, and not so much on the lifting (or appropriation) of its previous significance, transference of which is not truly possible anyway'.[92]

Sumanth Gopinath and Jason Stanyek have commented on how 'metasignifiers' such as 'global', 'cosmopolitan' and 'postmodern' have now been supplanted to some degree by the 'mobile', in terms of (quoting Phillip Vannini) 'social practices centered upon the movement of people and objects, as well as their imaginative and virtual movement'.[93] Like Savage, they highlight the way in which music now operates in a constant play of disembedding and reembedding, of deterritorialization and reterritorialization, detached from one set of surroundings and reinserted elsewhere. In the age of the Cloud and the bit torrent, the question of location becomes especially problematic, the phrase 'everywhere and nowhere' seeming for once not wholly misplaced. Some would argue that the wheel has simply turned once more: just as music, once subordinate to ritual and social function, asserted its autonomy and separateness under modernism, it is now reabsorbed, albeit differently, into specific functions and locations, whether

Times like the present

the multimedia installation or the urban landscapes it traverses in its privatized mobile uses on iPods and mobile phones. As the sound artist Claudia Molitor has put it, the idea that music can be 'just free of everything' is 'maybe a little modernist bubble that is bursting'.[94] And yet these new contexts, thanks to their own malleable and indeterminate nature, suggest that music in its relationship to culture remains promiscuous and inherently provisional, perhaps retaining a significant measure of its autonomy after all.

Case study 3: Alvin Curran, *Vindobona Blues* (2005)

Vindobona Blues by Alvin Curran, the American composer and founder member of Musica Elettronica Viva, is perhaps an example less of virtual motion than of virtual locatedness. It appeared first as an installation in the Tonspur (Soundtrack) series curated by Georg Weckwerth and Peter Szely in Vienna's museum quarter (Vindobona being the name for the Celtic and, later, Roman settlements on the site of the modern city); Curran subsequently made a surround-sound radiophonic version for Ö1, Austrian Radio's classical station, and it is on that later version that my observations are based.[95]

In Curran's words, *Vindobona Blues*

> is in theory a sound portrait of the extremely lively and multi-faceted contemporary music scene in present-day Vienna. In practice, it is a vast and subtle sound landscape that involves the acoustic 'essences' of 10 very different artists, essences which, as in a bizarre chess game, re-emerge as moving objects in a 10-track sound installation.[96]

The ten musicians consisted variously of composers in the art tradition (Diether de la Motte and Olga Neuwirth), improvising instrumentalists (Mia Zabelka and Uli Fussenegger), sound and media artists (Robert Adrian, Andrea Sodomka and Bernhard Leitner) and composers of electronica (Erdem Tunakan and Christian Fennesz), in addition to the jazz musician Franz Hautzinger, the Attwenger duo, and Georg Nussbaumer, Austria's 1996 Eurovision entrant. But, with just a few notable exceptions, the sound sources consist of anything but their actual music. Curran sought precisely 'to avoid the conventional kind of collage', preferring conversations and ambient sounds, including de la Motte's parrot and objects rolled along Zabelka's parquet floor.[97] Of the musical excerpts used, most are likewise ambient in character, belonging audibly to the diegesis of the interview, among them a bar-long snatch of a recording of Chaikovsky's Violin Concerto, and the Internationale played on a music box. The relatively few non-diegetic examples of music woven into the texture are Hautzinger's blues, Tunakan's electronic dance music and the folk-inflected contributions of Attwenger. The only other contribution of 'original' material consists of de la Motte reading aloud one of his Musik-Geschichten, 'Das schönste Spiel', a tale about a king's attempts to marry off his reluctant daughter, in which names of characters are replaced by sung notes and short motifs (written into the text in staff notation and here realized with aplomb by the composer).[98]

The inclusion of de la Motte's music-tale is possibly no coincidence, since the abstract musical scaffolding that frames the work's found objects likewise consists of sung notes representing human subjects. Curran asked each of the musicians 'to sing just one long note', his intention being 'to make it a kind of free-floating chorale, an absolutely unconventional and yet democratic musical self-representation of the individual artists'.[99] These vocal performances are amplified, manipulated with glissandos and pitch bends, and combined. At times they act as drones or pedal notes 'tuned' to other music in the sound picture, while at others they form ear-splittingly dissonant and piercing combinations, often at extremes of register. It is as if Curran is seeking to destabilize or even to parody the fetishized notion of 'the composer's voice' and, in a gesture tantalizingly open to interpretation, to bring the otherwise barely commensurable diversity of the different musicians' work to some form of common denominator. The aforementioned exceptions apart, the composers' actual creative voices are for the most part silenced, while they are put in the meantime through an exercise that makes them sound fragile, uncomfortable and, as the copious laughter testifies, not a little ridiculous.

Symptomatic, too, are the audible fragments of the interviews, which are not only literally anonymous (the speakers remain unidentified and, while spatially separated in the ten-track realization, unidentifiable to anyone unfamiliar with their spoken voices), but also metaphorically, in that they reflect generic themes in contemporary composers' discourse: biography, the relationship to the audience ('I want to touch people with my work'), the 'whole burdensome nature of tradition' ('die ganze Traditionslästigkeit'), the approach to musical material ('Basically I treat sound as an object'), the conditioning nature of sound environments ('How do you listen to space?') and historical determinism ('1600, 1700, Mozart, Beethoven, Schubert, Debussy? Who is right? Who is wrong? [. . .] This idea of progress is false.')[100] The irony of Curran's 'acoustic portrait of contemporary Vienna'[101] is that no precise traces of location survive. Any of the musicians could be practically anyone, anywhere.

In this way *Vindobona Blues* problematizes issues of both location and subjectivity. While the work draws its sound sources from a single city, its status as a virtual assemblage means that a similar montage – a 'virtual city' – could just as easily have been created using sounds drawn from far and wide. Beyond site-specific artifices such as Bulley and Jones's *Living Symphonies*, any notion of a 'located' music rubs ultimately up against this notion of the 'always already' virtual.[102] In terms of subjectivity, the work speaks in different voices, but they are voices that emerge as the very opposite of individual, despite being represented on the one hand by their literally unique instrument (their singing voice) and on the other by their most 'personal' utterances regarding their individual creativity – utterances that nonetheless seem reduced to manifestations of a generic, intertextual species of composers' discourse.

Subjectivity

The networked society of the twenty-first century seems to promise an unbridled liberation of the self, what Margaret Wertheim has called a 'cyber heaven' in which the potential for instantaneous and intimate connection across distance allows subjects to imagine themselves, like angelic beings, 'freed from the limitations of physical embodiment'.[103] Whereas McLuhan posited the 'global village' as a 'return to premodernity' ('the tribal emotions from which a few centuries of literacy divorced us'),[104] the virtual replica of community provided by the internet is not so much unified within a singular apprehension of time as superimposed in multiple times – temporalities, even – albeit often retaining an illusion of proximity and intimacy.

At the time of McLuhan's *Medium is the Massage*, the effect of television was felt as both centralizing and synchronizing. Thomas Mathiesen characterized this powerful hold over a 'viewer society' as a 'synopticon', by analogy with Jeremy Bentham's well-known model of surveillance, the 'panopticon': those who, in Bentham's model, were compelled to be watched were, in the television age, seduced into watching.[105] While neither the compulsion towards 'viewing' nor the standardization of content in the mass media have been entirely superseded with the advent of the internet, 'interactivity' has now become the expectation at all levels of culture, blurring the boundaries between actors and spectators, producers and consumers, observers and the observed and, perhaps most radically of all, the human actor and the non-human elements of actor networks. The Deleuzian idea of the 'man-machine assemblage', in which the human

Times like the present

acquires machine-like characteristics in a kind of bio-cybernetic prosthesis or even synthesis, has elicited talk of a transsubjective, or even 'postsubjective', ontology.[106]

On the surface the new environments for musical creativity and its dissemination look uncannily like the utopian notion that Jacques Attali elaborated in his 1977 book *Bruits*, which he termed, somewhat confusingly, 'Composition'.[107] Composition in Attali's terms is a form of *musica practica*, an active form of musical creation that goes beyond ritual, public spectacle and commodification (the three phases of music that precede Composition, and which Attali treats under the headings of 'Sacrificing', 'Representing' and 'Repeating'). In their pursuit of Composition, musicians (including those who might not hitherto have regarded themselves as such) seize back the means of production in order to make music for their own sake and for its own sake ('outside of any operationality, spectacle or accumulation of value'). 'The listener is the operator', calling 'into question the distinction between worker and consumer'. Composition of this kind is non-commodifiable and hence cannot be stockpiled (as can objects like LPs and CDs).[108] The pleasure is therefore in process rather than product, in a music 'produced by each individual for himself, for pleasure outside of meaning, usage, and exchange'.[109]

In its styling of Composition as 'a network within which a different kind of music and different social relations can arise',[110] Attali's vision seems ripe for co-option by the proselytizers of the digital economy. But it is worth asking what kind of 'Composition' is fostered by these new networks.[111] While Attali notes that Composition contains the seeds of the disappearance of composers and musicians as 'specialists', Susan McClary, in her afterword to the 1985 English translation, prophesied a future of participatory, intermedial creation, one neither policed by cultural gatekeepers and intermediaries nor restricted to the schooled and formally trained.[112] At one level this prophecy has come to pass, in that platforms such as MySpace, SoundCloud and YouTube allow the peer-to-peer exchange of all manner of musical content with only rudimentary forms of (mainly user-initiated) censorship. Yet relatively little on these platforms amounts to an antinomian disregard of established musical practices. The majority of 'user-generated content' mimics mainstream mass culture and recycles its content, hence the ubiquity of the cover, the remix and the mashup. Jaron Lanier has complained of this 'nostalgic malaise', this culture of 'reaction without action'.[113] As Attali himself observed, 'the self-management of the repetitive is still repetitive'.[114]

Lanier considers the 'mashup' to be just one manifestation of the phenomenon he calls 'metaness', the notion that the focus has shifted from content to presentation: 'a mashup is more important than the sources who were mashed'.[115] This resonates strongly with David Balzer's idea of 'curationism', the kind of second-order creativity practised not only by art curators, but also concert programmers, club DJs and even individuals managing playlists on their own mobile devices.[116] There is an increasingly fine line between 'creator' and 'curator', enabling curators to become significant power brokers in the creative industries. This has the further effect of strengthening the dominance of the network over its nodes of 'content'. As musicians make increasing use of social media to announce performance events, releases and publications, it is the second-order function of these communications that soon takes over. In line with industry commentator Andrew Dubber's maxim 'forget product, sell relationship',[117] their ulterior aim is to further the reach of the personal or institutional network and – through facilities such as 're-tweeting' – strengthen the user's perceived association with more prestigious actors in the field. In that way the use of social media tools, far from breaking down the pyramidal hierarchies of the creative industries, attempts to deploy those very inequalities to temporary advantage.

And those inequalities quickly become magnified. Online platforms are, to coin a phrase, a panopticon in the guise of a synopticon. By constantly gathering granular data regarding listening habits and preferences and feeding it back, they gradually prise open the tiniest niches for their monetizing potential, refreshing the parts of the market that the blunter instruments of mass entertainment culture could not reach. Meanwhile those whose creativity sustains these platforms have little prospect of sustainable earning power. The result is what Martin Scherzinger describes as a form of 'labor degradation', forcing the creation of a 'digital proletariat' and hence risking 'the obliteration of an entire creative class of people', those Lanier calls the 'musical middle class'.[118] There are clear parallels here with Simon Emmerson's 'great divide' in contemporary art music,[119] between on the one hand those who benefit from traditional mediators (the leading publishers, promoters, orchestras, ensembles and concert halls) and, on the other, the do-it-yourself informal networks, whether offline (small festivals, self-publishing operations) or purely online.

There is debate too as to whether the online environment is necessarily the ideal one for meaningful and memorable cultural encounters. Much ink has been split on 'economies of attention' in the online world, itself a chronotopic zone of impatience in which the smallest addition to connection or uploading time is resented.[120] Websites such as SoundCloud are paratextually impoverished, blandly uniform compared to copiously annotated LPs, CDs or other physical counterparts, a 'non place' in terms of stimulus and affect.[121] By crowding out the user's visual field with advertising and other diversions – including other, perhaps still more enticing offerings from the same source – and offering the ever-present temptation of the 'progress bar', these audio and video platforms seem to promote distraction.[122] While on-demand availability takes the 'waiting out of wanting', it may also, in Zygmunt Bauman's apt formulation, take the 'wanting out of waiting',[123] devaluing cultural products by reducing them to a seemingly ephemeral equivalence.

For value judgement becomes a contested issue. While interactivity is constant and comment copious, genuinely dialogical debate is rare. Rather, raw data ('plays', 'views' and 'likes') convert qualitative, interactive sharing of experience into quantitative indexes of value, which then become fodder for data aggregation. So while opinion is constantly solicited, judgement resides elsewhere. In 2017 the British music critic Norman Lebrecht reported with some indignation that the Arts Council of England had invited tenders for a £2.7 million computer monitoring system designed to 'measure the artistic quality of its National Portfolio Organizations'. His contention that 'Mortal intelligence has been rendered redundant' – 'Computer says yes or no' – would doubtless be countered by assurances that the software merely processes responses from human beings.[124] Still, it is hard not to see in such moves a smokescreen for the often secretive machinations of cultural policy – a way of ensuring that judgements, rather than being the object of accountable and reasoned debate, are apotheosized as hard data and hence passed off as objective. We have clearly travelled some distance from the Arnoldian ideals of the Council's founding chairman John Maynard Keynes, and in particular his belief that the artist 'leads the rest of us into fresh pastures and teaches us to love and to enjoy what we often begin by rejecting'.[125] Such was the vision of those who saw emancipatory potential in modernism: the emancipation offered by the network society starts to seem a matter less of pastures new than of already well-beaten paths.

Conclusion

There seems little doubt that contemporary music as both institution and practice has sought to break with many of the 'bad old' values associated with modernism: its exclusivism and elitism, its restrictions as to medium and mediation, its locatedness and ethnocentricity, and its weddedness to the idea of the stable, authorial human subject. And yet, as we have seen, the transcendence of such limits is not quite effortless or straightforward. Not all de-bordering is liberating, and not all transgression necessarily transgressive. The drive towards accessibility may mean that new music in the concert hall no longer elicits the degree of hostility it once did, but it may also mean restricted access for the general public to risky, innovative musics that are thereby shunted to the margins. Likewise, breaking down the barriers of 'mediacy' – the notion that somehow the more transparent the mediation the more 'real' the result – sits ill with a tradition of art (and not just modernist art) that has traditionally valued the skill of artifice and the types of mediation characteristic of distinct disciplines.

In the world of new media and networked communication, music is arguably no more or less 'material' or 'virtual' – and no more or less 'located' or 'mobile' – than it ever was, though the ubiquitous rhetoric of internet democracy artfully conceals the persistence of global inequities. And while music has always called forth a variety of 'subject positions', malleable personae analogous to today's web avatars and other multiple-choice identities,[126] there remains, above all in legal terms, a finitude to most creative works in terms of their ownership and the definition of their material, virtual or conceptual boundaries. Nor is there any less of a need for ongoing critical discourse and discrimination. As Karol Berger writes, the 'only reprehensible kind of discrimination is that which silences certain voices before they have been heard'. Otherwise, the

> refusal to discriminate among the voices one hears, to compare and evaluate them, is not only a practical impossibility, it is also [. . .] a form of aestheticist detachment whereby we allow the voices we hear to entertain us, but not to challenge our most fundamental assumptions.[127]

What is needed, in other words, is not the static, atomistic paradigm that characterizes the internet community, where conflicting opinions reside in inert juxtaposition, but rather a dynamic dialogism, in which issues are open to debate, people open to persuasion and the landscape, as a result, open to change.

There are still other values that art of the present cannot so easily renounce, values that constitute arguably less categories of modernism than categories of artistic creativity pure and simple. Despite the protean changes in nature that contemporary music has undergone over the past half century, there are many who would be reluctant to break with the notion of an art music that resists instrumentalist demands. While this notion is constantly under siege from neoliberalist calls for relevance and accountability, its presence as a motivating ambition for art music composers remains undimmed. Art music is no more autonomous in practice than it ever was: but, to paraphrase Adorno, perhaps it is less a matter of the autonomous itself than the striving for the autonomous.

What Adorno actually wrote was: 'The new is the longing for the new, not the new itself'.[128] Hence yet another putatively 'modernist' value proves surprisingly persistent. Postmodern scepticism notwithstanding, the striving after newness and innovation continues unabated, and not only in art. Modernism always favoured the rare and the rarefied – and, regardless of changes in style, medium and aesthetic, those aspirations remain not only resilient but also arguably structural to art as an institution, even in an age in which some are heralding the 'death of scarcity'.[129] Art remains about creating what does not already exist. Ezra Pound's injunction to 'make it new' is often cited as a modernist rallying cry. But, as Thomas Osborne writes, 'it would be a mistake to regard this principle as exclusive to *avant-garde* movements', in that 'the will to produce the new' is 'problematically at stake in all art that distinguishes itself from "culture" or entertainment more generally'.[130] The impulse towards rarity, towards the occupation of an as-yet-unoccupied position in the field of creative practice, seems an ineradicable one. And with it – and here, above all, is the ongoing legacy of aesthetic modernism – the need to mediate that moment (materially, virtually or conceptually) in some distinctive and recognizable way.

At the same time, newness is not created *ex nihilo* or in a vacuum. It is differentially defined, and therefore predicated inevitably on a stocktaking of the past. While modernists have fantasized about the burning of the museum – the 'imaginary museum of musical works' included[131] – it is that relationship to the museum that enables the new to be distinguished from fashion, from a purely discursive or media-simulated novelty. The museum thus acts, in Boris Groys's words, as a 'site of systematic historical comparison', acting not merely 'to collect the past but also to generate the present through the comparison between old and new'.[132] As 'a machine that produces and stages the new', it breaks the tyrannical power of the present and resists 'the dictatorship of contemporary taste'.[133]

If art music needs its past tense then it needs its future tense as well. Dick Hebdige once quipped of postmodernity that it seemed rather like modernity but 'without the hopes and dreams which made modernity bearable'.[134] Somehow the notion has arisen that artists or composers commit some unpardonable hubris by aspiring towards a future or afterlife for their work. Richard Taruskin, writing of post-war serial composers, borrows Daniel Bell's phrase 'the megalomania of self-infinitization';[135] and there are doubtless those who would cheerfully throw any idea of the 'epoch-making' out with the 'epoch'. But it is surely fitting that musicians aspire to some degree of longevity for themselves and posterity for their creations, wishing no more to be prisoners of their own present moment than of their national or cultural identity. Transcending space and time is what any kind of art attempts to do. One could go further and say that is it is what any genuine act of communication actually *does*.

Presentism is therefore an agenda inadequate to any artistic or musical present. There is yet a third meaning for that expression 'no time like the present' – the commonest, perhaps. It is a metaphor for seizing the moment, that 'propitious moment' of either decision or grace. To view the present not as a flat, undifferentiated *chronos* but as a punctual *kairos* is to recognize a present conjuncture shaped by unique and unrepeatable historical forces – a present that is 'extreme' more in terms of human urgency than apocalyptic *emergency*, one in which creative artists undertake actions they perceive as necessary and, if at times wishfully, charged with future implications. The concept of necessity – often invoked by modernist composers – has fallen somewhat out of favour in contemporary thinking, associated as it has come to be with rigid and occult doctrines of historical inevitability.[136] Ultimately, though, all creative activity – 'de-limited' or 'delimited' in whatever way – is predicated on precisely that notion that there is something to do and that now is the time to do it. Such a sense of the timeliness of the present – timely by virtue of its very fragility and transience – rehabilitates both past and future and offers what the current phase of our 'unending modernity' might profitably recapture.[137]

Notes

1 Shumon Basar, Douglas Coupland and Hans-Ulrich Obrist, *The Age of Earthquakes: A Guide to the Extreme Present* (New York and London: Random House and Penguin Books, 2015); Douglas Coupland, *Generation X: Tales for an Accelerated Culture* (New York: St Martin's Press, 1981).

2 Marshall McLuhan and Quentin Fiore, *The Medium Is the Massage: An Inventory of Effects* (Harmondsworth, UK: Penguin Books, 1967). The connection is acknowledged by Coupland in Amelia Abraham, 'Predicting the Digital Apocalypse: An Interview with Douglas Coupland', *Vice*, 18 April 2015, http://www.vice.com/en_uk/read/douglas-couplands-favourite-books (accessed 27 April 2017).

3 Ibid., 8.

4 Basar, Coupland and Obrist, *The Age of Earthquakes*, 14–15.

5 McLuhan and Fiore, *The Medium Is the Massage*, 26 and 63 ('Ours is a brand-new world of allatonceness').

Times like the present

6 Basar, Coupland and Obrist, *The Age of Earthquakes*, 90.

7 Ibid., 117.

8 M. H. Miller, 'Disaster Writing: New Book by Douglas Coupland and Hans Ulrich Obrist Wreaks Havoc on Original Thought', *ARTnews*, May 2015, 28, http://www.artnews.com/2015/04/14/disaster-writing-age-of-earthquakes-wreaks-havoc-on-original-thought/ (accessed 27 April 2017).

9 Fredric Jameson, *A Singular Modernity* (London and New York: Verso, 2002), 34.

10 In particular, 1968 is seen by many as a watershed moment. One commentator goes so far as to claim that '[a]s a social theory, postmodernism was born in 1968', with its cultural manifestations following thereafter. Agnes Heller, 'Existentialism, Alienation, Postmodernism: Cultural Movements as Vehicles of Change in the Patterns of Everyday Life', in *A Postmodern Reader*, ed. Joseph P. Natoli and Linda Hutcheon (Albany, NY: SUNY Press, 1993), 503.

11 For more on this point, see the introduction to this volume.

12 See especially David Metzer, *Musical Modernism at the Turn of the Twenty-First Century* (Cambridge: Cambridge University Press, 2011), and the chapters by Edward Campbell and Arnold Whittall in this volume.

13 François Hartog, *Regimes of Historicity: Presentism and Experiences of Time*, trans. Saskia Brown (New York: Columbia University Press, 2015), xv.

14 See Terry Smith, *What Is Contemporary Art?* (Chicago: University of Chicago Press, 2009); Peter Osborne, *Anywhere or Not at All: Philosophy of Contemporary Art* (London: Verso, 2013); Lionel Ruffel, *Brouhaha: Les mondes du contemporain* (Paris: Verdier, 2016); see also Sarah Collins's chapter in this volume.

15 Terry Smith, 'Contemporary Art and Contemporaneity', *Critical Inquiry* 32, no. 4 (2006), 703.

16 Anthony Giddens opened his 1999 Reith Lectures by quoting one such manifestation of apocalyptic panic from Archbishop Wulfstan in 1014: 'The world is in a rush and is getting close to its end'; Anthony Giddens, *Runaway World: How Globalisation Is Reshaping Our Lives* (London: Profile, 2002), 1.

17 Hartog quotes both Chateaubriand on his experiences during the French Revolution – 'I was writing ancient history, while modern history was knocking at my door' – and Lorenz von Stein half a century later in 1843: 'it is as though historical writing is no longer able to keep up with history' (*Regimes of Historicity*, 101).

18 Colin Crouch, *The Strange Non-Death of Neoliberalism* (Cambridge: Polity Press, 2011), 99.

19 Jonathan Crary, *24/7: Late Capitalism and the Ends of Sleep* (London and New York: Verso, 2013), 15.

20 Ibid., 9.

21 Zygmunt Bauman, *Postmodernity and Its Discontents* (Cambridge: Polity Press, 1993), 79. This distinction characterizes the difference between those Bauman describes, respectively, as 'tourists' and 'vagabonds', those who move because they choose to do so, and those who move because they have no choice.

22 Hartog, *Regimes of Historicity*, viii.

23 The term 'shifter' is that of Otto Jespersen, later adopted by Roman Jakobson. Fredric Jameson (*A Singular Modernity*, 19) uses the idea of the 'shifter' to characterize the Latin word *modernus*, which (as Raymond Williams pointed out) is closer in meaning to the present-day usage of 'contemporary' than that of 'modern'; see Raymond Williams, *Keywords: A Vocabulary of Culture and Society* (London: Fontana, 1976), 208.

24 Claire Bishop, *Radical Museology: Or, What's Contemporary in Museums of Contemporary Art?* (London: Koenig Books, 2014), 16.

25 Ruffel, *Brouhaha*, 140.

26 Ibid., 20.

27 Ibid., 178.

28 For instance, Ruffel, *Brouhaha*, 130; Hartog, *Regimes of Historicity*, 11.

29 This was an expression later adopted by Ernst Bloch (who reversed Pinder's formulation as *Gleichzeitigkeit des Ungleichzeitigen*) and Carl Dahlhaus, for instance in *Foundations of Music History*, trans. J. B. Robinson (Cambridge: Cambridge University Press, 1989), 143. For Reinhart Koselleck's discussion of the term, see *Futures Past: On the Semantics of Historical Time*, trans. Keith Tribe (New York: Columbia University Press, 2004), 95.

30 Lawrence Grossberg, 'On Postmodernism and Articulation: An Interview with Stuart Hall', *Journal of Communication Inquiry* 10, no. 2 (1986), 47.

31 Pierre Nora, 'De l'histoire contemporaine au présent historique', in *Présent, nation, mémoire* (Paris: Gallimard, 2011), 81.

32 Osborne, *Anywhere or Not at All*, 28: 'on the one hand, the de-bordering of the arts as mediums, and on the other, the de-bordering of the national social spaces of art'.

33 On cosmopolitanism, for instance, see the chapters of Björn Heile and Eva Moreda Rodríguez in this volume.

34 Slavoj Žižek, *Against the Double Blackmail: Refugees, Terror, and Other Troubles with the Neighbours* (London: Allen Lane, 2016), 6. See also Peter Sloterdijk, *In the World Interior of Capital* (Cambridge: Polity Press, 2013), 8.

35 Ibid., 116n57. For the quotation, see http://www.marxists.org.archive/lenin/works/1917/7thconf/29d.htm (accessed 10 June 2017).

36 Harold S. Powers, 'Classical Music, Cultural Roots, and Colonial Rule: An Indic Musicologist Looks at the Muslim World', *Asian Music* 12, no. 1 (1980), 5–39. Powers proposes that art music is 1) 'purveyed by performers who [...] regard themselves and are regarded as highly skilled specialists, who must be [...] taught and indoctrinated into their specialty by their seniors'; 2) 'said to conform to a music-theoretical norm'; 3) 'culturally grounded, in that it is both a) connected with and supportive of cultural performances to which it is ancillary, and at the same time b) conceived as an independent domain that can stand on its own as the centerpiece of a cultural performance'; and 4) is 'patronized by individuals or groups [...] who profess connoisseurship' (ibid., 11).

37 John Cage, 'Overpopulation and Art', in *John Cage: Composed in America*, ed. Marjorie Perloff and Charles Junkerman (Chicago: University of Chicago Press, 1994), 14–17.

38 That said, a formidable attempt at the impossible has recently appeared in the form of Tim Rutherford-Johnson's *Music After the Fall: Modern Composition and Culture since 1989* (Oakland: University of California Press, 2017).

39 William Weber, 'Consequences of Canon: The Institutionalization of Enmity between Contemporary and Classical Music', *Common Knowledge* 9, no.1 (2003), 78–99. Weber argues that it was principally the accumulation of canonical repertoire rather than the difficulty of new music that made the 'enmity' between contemporary and classical music a common feature of institutionalized concert life, causing a good deal of modernist music to be hived off into the specialist domains of dedicated concert series and festivals.

40 See Luke B. Howard, 'Production vs. Reception in Postmodernism: The Górecki Case', in *Postmodern Music/Postmodern Thought*, ed. Judy Lochhead and Joseph Auner (New York and London: Routledge, 2002), 195–206.

41 John Maynard Keynes, 'The Arts Council: Its Policy and Hopes', *The Listener*, 12 July 1945, 31–32.

42 United Nations, Universal Declaration of Human Rights, http://www.un.org/en/universal-declaration-human-rights/ (accessed 28 April 2017).

43 See David Addison, 'Politics, Patronage and the State in British Avant-Garde Music, c1959–c1974', *Twentieth-Century British History* 27, no. 2 (2016), 260.

44 Glock set out his principle of 'creative unbalance' in his 1963 lecture 'The BBC's Music Policy', reprinted in Glock, *Notes in Advance: An Autobiography in Music* (Oxford: Oxford University Press, 1991), 200–213. See also Addison, 'Politics, Patronage and the State', 244.

45 See the interview with Annette Morreau in *Changing Platforms: 30 Years of the Contemporary Music Network*, ed. Chris Heaton (London: Unknown Public, 2001), 67.

46 See the interview with Beverley Crew in *Changing Platforms*, ed. Heaton, 76 and 74.

47 Chris Smith, Secretary of State in the newly created Department for Culture, Media and Sport in Tony Blair's first administration, declared in his book *Creative Britain* (London: Faber and Faber, 1998) that 'the creative industries are big business' and that 'the intrinsic cultural value of creativity' operates 'in synergy with economic opportunities' (ibid., 26). His immediate successor, Tessa Jowell, retreated from this position somewhat in a pamphlet of 2004, questioning the tendency 'to debate culture in terms only of its instrumental benefits to other agendas'; see 'Government and the Value of Culture', https://shiftyparadigms.wordpress.com/images/Cultural_Policy/Tessa_Jowell.pdf (accessed 27 April 2018). I am grateful to Samuel Murray for drawing that document to my attention.

48 Sound and Music, *Commissioning Report* (London: Sound and Music, 2014), 8.

49 Simon Emmerson, 'The Electroacoustic Tours', in *Changing Platforms*, ed. Heaton, 59.

50 As Pierre Nora writes, 'What we call memory is in fact a gigantic and breathtaking effort to store the material vestiges of what we cannot possibly remember, thereby amassing an unfathomable collection of things that we might someday need to recall'; Nora, 'General Introduction: Between Memory and History', in *Realms of Memory: Rethinking the French Past*, ed. Pierre Nora and trans. Arthur Goldhammer (New York: Columbia University Press, 1996), 8. For a further, illuminating discussion of the

Times like the present

relationship of hypermnesia and amnesia in modernity, see Paul Connerton, *How Modernity Forgets* (Cambridge: Cambridge University Press, 2009).

51 For a discussion of this historical dynamic, with reference to Theodor W. Adorno and Carl Dahlhaus, see Metzer, *Musical Modernism*, 3–4.

52 These points are indebted to Peter Osborne's discussion of retention and recollection in the phenomenology of Edmund Husserl; see *The Politics of Time: Modernity and the Avant-Garde* (London: Verso, 1995), 50.

53 Interestingly an attempt has recently been made to revive the (now defunct) CMN's policy of repeat performances, specifically in the area of British orchestral music. The Resonate project, promoted by the PRS Foundation (the charitable arm of the United Kingdom's principal music licensing organization) in partnership with the Association of British Orchestras, offers funding to orchestras prepared to give second performances of works commissioned in the previous twenty-five years, on the basis that 'single performances of new music do not give audiences the chance to become familiar with important, and ultimately rewarding works [. . .]. Neither does this situation enable substantial pieces of music to develop and improve as they are performed again by different musicians and for the benefit of different audiences.' See 'PRS Foundation: Resonate', http://www.prsformusicfoundation.com/resonate/ (accessed 27 August 2017).

54 Examples include Mark-Anthony Turnage's orchestral work *Hammered Out* (2009–10), with its reference to the song *Single Ladies* by the American R&B singer Beyoncé, and his Royal Opera House commission *Anna Nicole* (2010), based on the life of playboy model Anna Nicole Smith; for a discussion, see Rutherford-Johnson, *Music After the Fall*, 51–53. An article by Timothy D. Taylor ('Music and Musical Practices in Postmodernity', in *Postmodern Music/Postmodern Thought*, ed. Lochhead and Auner, 93–118) addresses borrowings from popular culture in the music of Mikel Rouse, but the issues could just as fruitfully be examined in the music of his compatriot and namesake Christopher Rouse, with regard to works such as *Bonham* (1988), a tribute to John Bonham, the drummer of Led Zeppelin.

55 *Night Ferry* has been recorded by the Chicago Symphony Orchestra on the orchestra's own record label, CSO Resound (CSOR9011401). The coupling is another orchestra commission, *Alternative Energy* by Mason Bates. For a discussion of Bates's music that touches upon issues similar to those raised here, see Marianna Ritchey, '"Amazing Together": Mason Bates, Classical Music, and Neoliberal Values', *Music & Politics* 11, no. 2 (2017), https://quod.lib.umich.edu/m/mp/9460447.0011.202?view=text;r gn=main (accessed 18 August 2017).

56 Clyne describes the piece as 'weaving together many threads of ideas and imagery', and the programme note presents a bewildering web of literary and biographical associations. While the Dante epigraph consists of the words of Charon the ferryman, the title itself is drawn from Seamus Heaney's 'Elegy for Robert Lowell', in which Lowell himself is apostrophized as a 'night ferry' ('You were our Night Ferry / thudding on a big sea, / the whole craft ringing / with an armourer's music'). Clyne recalls that Riccardo Muti, the music director of the Chicago Symphony, suggested that she 'look to Schubert for inspiration', given that the work was to be premiered on an otherwise all-Schubert programme. Clyne makes the connection to Lowell by pointing out that the poet, 'like Schubert, suffered from manic depression', proceeding to offer a symptomatic description of Schubert's supposed cyclothymia and its influence on the visual imagery created alongside the music. Such arguably overdetermined paratexts, while doubtless sincere, nonetheless amount to effective strategies for capturing different kinds of literate audience member, whether of an artistic, literary or medical-scientific bent. Anna Clyne, composer's note to *Night Ferry*, http://www.boosey.com/cr/music/Anna-Clyne-Night-Ferry/56273 (accessed 28 April 2017). These rich associations no doubt also stimulated the adoption of *Night Ferry* for the BBC's UK-wide education project, Ten Pieces, in 2015.

57 The striking resemblance of the theme of the third section (introduced in D minor) to the F♯ minor flute theme from the third movement of Shostakovich's Fifth Symphony may be coincidental, and is certainly not acknowledged anywhere amidst the welter of other named references in the programme note.

58 On the renewed public interest in film music over the past two decades, driven in large measure by the power and sophistication of surround-sound systems in cinema and soon replicated by high-end multichannel systems for home listening, see Andrew Blake, 'To the Millennium: Music as Twentieth-Century Commodity', in *The Cambridge History of Twentieth-Century Music*, ed. Nicholas Cook and Anthony Pople (Cambridge: Cambridge University Press, 2004), 502–3. More recently this enthusiasm has fuelled the popularity of live performances of both film and video-game scores, seen by many orchestras as a promising new avenue for audience development.

59 For a discussion of Gabriel Prokofiev's work, see Rutherford-Johnson, *Music After the Fall*, 41–42.
60 Umberto Eco wrote of the avant-garde, in literature especially, as a testing ground for potential innova-
    tion in the mass market. Though Eco speaks of the avant-garde 'refusing to serve as an experimental
    laboratory for an ever-growing cultural industry', he acknowledges how the latter continues to 'process'
    the former 'according to its commercial standards'; Eco, 'The Structure of Bad Taste', in *The Open Work*,
    trans. Anna Cancogni (London: Hutchinson Radius, 1989), 187–88. For an example of the comparable
    process in popular music, see David Hesmondhalgh, 'Indie: The Institutional Politics and Aesthetics of
    a Popular Music Genre', *Cultural Studies* 13, no. 1 (1999), 34–61.
61 Clement Greenberg, 'Modernist Painting' (1961), in *Art in Modern Culture: An Anthology of Critical Texts*,
    ed. Francis Frascina and Jonathan Harris (London: Phaidon, 1992), 309.
62 For discussions of this twenty-first century transcendentalism, see especially Seth Kim-Cohen, *In the
    Blink of an Ear: Toward a Non-Cochlear Sonic Art* (New York: Continuum, 2009) and G. Douglas Barrett,
    Beyond Sound: Toward a Critical Music (New York and London: Bloomsbury, 2016). With Cage himself
    it is easy – and not only in discussions of *4'33″* (1952), the far from silent piece – to lose track of the
    continued importance of sound. It is often forgotten that the well-known injunction of *0'00″* (1962)
    to 'perform a disciplined action' is preceded by the qualification 'in a situation provided with maximum
    amplification'. See M. J. Grant's comments on the piece in chapter 12 of this volume (299–300).
63 Dick Higgins, 'Statement on Intermedia' (1966), in *Theories and Documents of Contemporary Art: A Source-
    book of Artists' Writings*, ed. Kristine Stiles and Peter Howard Selz (Berkeley and Los Angeles: University
    of California Press, 1996), 729.
64 Smith, *What Is Contemporary Art?* 224.
65 Rosalind Krauss, 'Sculpture in the Expanded Field' (1979), in *Postmodern Culture*, ed. Hal Foster (London
    and Sydney: Pluto Press, 1985), 31. A panel at the Royal Musical Association 53rd Annual Conference
    (Liverpool, 13–15 September 2017) entitled 'Expanded Musicologies: Fields and Frames' took as its
    premise the observation that Krauss's essay 'has proved richly suggestive for other art-forms in recent
    years' (conference programme).
66 For a description of *Drive-In Music* (1967) by Max Neuhaus, the 'sound installation' to which the term
    itself was first applied, see Gascia Ouzounian, 'Sound Installation Art: From Spatial Poetics to Politics,
    Aesthetics to Ethics', in *Music, Sound and Space: Transformations of Public and Private Experience*, ed. Geor-
    gina Born (Cambridge: Cambridge University Press, 2013), 81–82. Ouzounian's insights have helped
    shape a number of the observations in this paragraph.
67 Helga de la Motte-Haber, 'Space – Environment – Shared World: Robin Minard's Sound Installations',
    in *Robin Minard: Silent Music/Between Sound and Acoustic Design*, ed. B. Schulz (Heidelberg: Kehrer,
    1999), 41; quoted in Ouzounian, 'Sound Installation Art', 73.
68 Ouzounian discusses one such example, Rebecca Belmore's sound installation *Ayum-ee-aawach Oomama-
    mowan: Speaking to Their Mother* (1991), which represented a response to (and a sonic intervention in)
    the land crisis between the Canadian government and the Mohawk community in the town of Oka,
    Quebec.
69 R. Murray Schafer, *The Tuning of the World* (New York: Knopf, 1977).
70 For a volume that addresses that very question, see Thomas Gardner and Salomé Voegelin, eds., *Col-
    loquium: Sound Art – Music* (Winchester, UK, and Washington, DC: Zero Books, 2016).
71 See the documentary filmed for *Nature News*, the news feed of the international science journal *Nature*;
    'Living Symphonies', https://www.youtube.com/watch?v=_7qXCzxXTXs at 0:52 (accessed 28
    April 2017).
72 Ibid. (at 0:59).
73 The musical idiom, indeed, almost seems to hanker after an English pastoralism in its modality and lyri-
    cism. In the video documentary Bulley illustrates the buzzard's idea: an Aeolian melody, which can also
    be doubled (in predominantly perfect fourth intervals) to illustrate the paired flight of two such birds
    (ibid. at 4:05).
74 Boris Groys, 'The Topology of Contemporary Art', in *Antinomies of Art and Culture: Modernity, Post-
    modernity, Contemporaneity*, ed. Terry Smith, Okwui Enwezor and Nancy Condee (Durham, NC, and
    London: Duke University Press, 2008), 74.
75 Smith, *What Is Contemporary Art?* 9.
76 Bulley readily admits the project's instrumentalist agenda, expressing the hope that the work's audiences
    'will treat it as a platform for exploring the forest and the ecosystems within it, and learning more about
    it through the piece'; 'Living Symphonies', https://www.youtube.com/watch?v=_7qXCzxXTXs at
    7:05 (accessed 28 April 2017).

Times like the present

77 The other two organizations were the British Music Information Centre (the English member of the International Association of Music Information Centres, whose former activities have since been partly taken over by the British Music Collection at Huddersfield) and the Contemporary Music Network, discussed earlier in this chapter.

78 The open letter was signed by, among others, the composers Sir Harrison Birtwistle, Sir Peter Maxwell Davies, Oliver Knussen, Thea Musgrave and Judith Weir, the cellist Steven Isserlis and the conductor Martyn Brabbins. It is archived at http://www.rhinegold.co.uk/classical_music/archive-1311/ (accessed 22 May 2018).

79 The letter stated that Sound and Music had shown 'no sign of recognition of or apology for the extent of its failure to live up to its original plans' but had instead, 'in self-regarding fashion, promised more of the same'. It went on to quote a list of music genres issued by the organization – 'Electronic and Improvised; Noise and Art Rock; Notated and Modern Composition; Sonic Art; Multimedia and Cross Art Form; Jazz, World and Folk; and Alternative Rock & Dance' – describing them as 'areas of music which have many virtues but are for the most part entirely different from those for which Sound and Music was created' (ibid.).

80 See Gardner and Voegelin, eds., *Colloquium: Sound Art – Music*.

81 Osborne, *Anywhere or Not at All*, 27.

82 Heile, this volume, 177.

83 There are just three full sections from South America, three from the Middle East (Israel, Egypt and Turkey) and one from Africa (South Africa). Other than the four Chinese sections, South East Asia is represented by Japan, South Korea and Taiwan (Chinese Taipei). These national sections are indexed, and tellingly plotted on a world map, at http://www.iscm.org/about/members (accessed 28 April 2018).

84 Of the two living South East Asian composers published by Boosey and Hawkes, the Chinese composer Quigang Chen is resident in Paris and the South Korean Unsuk Chin in Berlin. Japanese composers, who, as Björn Heile's chapter points out, have a strong institutional infrastructure to rely on, are rare in having tended not to emigrate. Of the Asian- and African-born composers published by Music Sales Classical, Tan Dun, internationally the most successful Chinese composer, settled in New York as did his compatriot Bright Sheng. South-African born Kevin Volans and Indian-born Param Vir have adopted, respectively, Irish and British citizenship.

85 Shzr Ee Tan, '"Uploading" to Carnegie Hall: The First YouTube Symphony Orchestra', in *The Oxford Handbook of Music and Virtuality*, ed. Sheila Whiteley and Shara Rambarran (New York: Oxford University Press, 2016), 350.

86 Ibid., 335.

87 Ibid., 339.

88 Ibid., 350–51.

89 See David Hesmondhalgh, 'Digital Sampling and Cultural Inequality', *Social and Legal Studies* 15, no. 1 (2006), 53–75.

90 Steve Savage, *Bytes and Backbeats: Repurposing Music in the Digital Age* (Ann Arbor: University of Michigan Press, 2013), 190.

91 Roland Barthes, 'The Death of the Author', in *Image – Music – Text*, trans. Stephen Heath (London: Fontana, 1977), 148.

92 Savage, *Bytes and Backbeats*, 190.

93 Phillip Vannini, 'Mobile Cultures: From the Sociology of Transportation to the Study of Mobilities', *Sociology Compass* 4, no. 2 (2010), 111; quoted in Sumanth Gopinath and Jason Stanyek, 'Anytime, Anywhere? An Introduction to the Devices, Markets, and Theories of Mobile Music', in *The Oxford Handbook of Mobile Music Studies*, ed. Sumanth Gopinath and Jason Stanyek (New York: Oxford University Press, 2014), 1: 3.

94 Claudia Molitor, discussion contribution in *Colloquium: Sound Art – Music*, ed. Gardner and Voegelin, 155.

95 This 35-minute version is available for streaming at http://www.kunstradio.at/2005B/02_10_05.html (accessed 28 April 2017).

96 Curran, composer's note (dated 20 September 2005), http://www.kunstradio.at/2005B/02_10_05.html (accessed 28 April 2017).

97 Ibid.

98 'Das schönste Spiel' is published in de la Motte's pedagogical collection of 'stories, games, enchantments and improvisations' entitled *Musik ist im Spiel*, 2nd ed. (Kassel: Bärenreiter, 1990).

99 Curran, composer's note.

100 'Sechszehnhundert, siebzehnhundert, Mozart, Beethoven, Schubert, Debussy. Wer ist richtig? Wer ist falsch? [...] Diese Fortschreitung ist falsch.' The speaker, identifiable from his contributions elsewhere, is Diether de la Motte.

101 Introductory note (unsigned), http://www.kunstradio.at/2005B/02_10_05.html (accessed 28 April 2017).

102 Umberto Eco saw television as creating this artificial unity by bringing together 'within the same field' images and events that need not 'be in close contact with one another'; 'Chance and Plot: Television and Aesthetics', in *The Open Work*, 110. The existence of the musical work is often seen as a 'virtual' one; see Sally Macarthur, *Towards a Twenty-First-Century Feminist Politics of Music* (Aldershot: Ashgate: 2010), 11–12. Mark Grimshaw writes that 'terms such as "virtual worlds", "virtual environment", "virtual character", and "virtual reality" and their application and usage may well be ingrained in the modern digital consciousness, but thinking about virtuality has a history almost as long as that of Western civilization itself. Digital technology simply provides new ways to conceptualize, to use, and to experience that virtuality.' Mark Grimshaw, 'Introduction', in *The Oxford Handbook of Virtuality* (New York: Oxford University Press, 2014), 2.

103 Margaret Wertheim, 'The Pearly Gates of Cyberspace', in *Architecture of Fear*, ed. Nan Elin (New York and Princeton, NJ: Architectural Press, 1997), 296.

104 McCluhan and Fiore, *The Medium Is the Massage*, 63.

105 Thomas Mathiesen, 'The Viewer Society: Michel Foucault's "Panopticon" Revisited', *Theoretical Criminology* 1, no. 2 (1997), 215–32; the title refers to Foucault's discussion of Bentham's panopticon in *Discipline and Punish: The Birth of the Prison*, trans. Alan Sheridan (London: Allen Lane, 1977), especially 200–209.

106 Gilles Deleuze writes of the 'man-machine assemblage' in, inter alia, *Cinema II: The Time Image*, trans. Hugh Tomlinson and Robert Galeta (London: Athlone Press, 1989), 263.

107 Jacques Attali, *Noise: The Political Economy of Music*, trans. Brian Massumi (Minneapolis: University of Minnesota Press, 1985). In order to distinguish Attali's definition from more commonplace historical notions of music composition, I shall follow the lead of other commentators in capitalizing Attali's term.

108 Ibid., 135.

109 Ibid., 137.

110 Ibid.

111 McClary saw Composition as removing musical creation 'from the rigid institutions of specialized musical training in order to return it to all members of society'. She saw it emerging in performance art, neo-tonality and, perhaps most surprisingly, minimalism – a music as securely embedded in the practice of repetition (in Attali's or any other sense) as could be imagined: 'The traditional taxonomic distinction between high and popular culture becomes irrelevant in the eclectic blends characteristic of this new music.' See Susan McClary, 'Afterword: The Politics of Silence and Sound', in Attali, *Noise*, 157–58.

112 The 'egalitarianism' proposed by McClary is therefore double-edged. On the one hand, it offers the prospect of participation for all; on the other, it appears to disavow the need for specialist musical skill and expertise, hence offering a potential legitimation for the increasingly restricted access to high-level music education experienced in many Western countries over the past three decades. For an articulate discussion of this issue, see Ian Pace, 'Deskilling and Musical Education', *Desiring Progress* (blog), https://ianpace.wordpress.com/2016/08/21/ (accessed 27 April 2018). I am grateful to Björn Heile for the reference and the encouragement to emphasize this point.

113 Jaron Lanier, *You Are Not a Gadget*, 2nd updated ed. (London: Penguin Books, 2011), 20; quoted in Martin Scherzinger, 'Divisible Mobility: Music in an Age of Cloud Computing', in *The Oxford Handbook of Mobile Music Studies*, ed. Sumanth Gopinath and Jason Stanyek (New York: Oxford University Press, 2014), 1: 92.

114 Attali, *Noise*, 137. One might almost believe that Attali foresaw something resembling YouTube when he wrote of the 'essential use of the image recorder' as being 'in its private use for the manufacture of one's own gaze upon the world, and first and foremost upon oneself. Pleasure tied to the self-directed gaze. Narcissus after Echo' (ibid., 144). Eric Drott notes how, in the second edition of *Bruits* from 2001, Attali 'recognized the likelihood that some corporate entity – be it the record industry, internet service providers, or an emergent sector of the information economy – might yet succeed in enclosing the virtual commons opened up by computer technologies, (re)commodifying the virtual goods that threaten to slip through the market's grasp'; Eric Drott, 'Rereading Jacques Attali's *Bruits*', *Critical Inquiry* 41, no. 4 (2015), 751.

Times like the present

115 Lanier, *You Are Not a Gadget*, 79; quoted in Scherzinger, 'Divisible Mobility', 79.

116 David Balzer, *Curationism: How Curating Took Over the Art World and Everything Else* (London: Pluto Press, 2015).

117 Andrew Dubber, 'The 20 Things You Must Know about Music Online' ([n.p.]: New Music Strategies, 2008), 89, http://newmusicstrategies.com/wp-content/uploads/2008/06/nms.pdf.

118 Scherzinger, 'Divisible Mobility', 96.

119 Emmerson, 'The Electroacoustic Tours', 59.

120 See, for instance, Nicholas Carr, *The Shallows* (New York: W. W. Norton, 2010), especially chapter 7. The scientific evidence would appear as yet inconclusive: for a recent literature review, see Kep Kee Loh and Ryota Kanai, 'How Has the Internet Reshaped Human Cognition?' *Neuroscience* 22, no. 5 (2014), 506–20.

121 Marc Augé, *Non-Places: Introduction to an Anthropology of Supermodernity*, trans. John Howe (London and New York: Verso, 1995). Augé posits the idea of 'non-places' as spaces decoupled from both time and geography, not only places characterized by transit and transience (such as motorways and airports) but architectures (real or, as here, virtual) that display no markers of particularity or location.

122 'The Net is, by design, an interruption system, a machine geared for dividing attention. [. . .] It's possible to think deeply while surfing the Net, just as it's possible to think shallowly while reading a book, but that's not the kind of thinking the technology encourages and rewards' (Carr, *The Shallows*, 131 and 116).

123 Zygmunt Bauman, *Globalization: The Human Consequences* (New York: Columbia University Press, 1998), 79.

124 Norman Lebrecht, 'Council of Despair', *The Spectator*, 1 July 2017, 42.

125 Keynes, 'The Arts Council', 32.

126 An early and seminal discussion on subject positions in music is Lawrence Kramer, 'The Mysteries of Animation: History, Analysis and Musical Subjectivity', *Music Analysis* 20, no. 2 (2010), 153–78. Here Kramer holds that the subject 'is a disposition to incessant and multiple relationship that assumes concrete form in the positions it can occupy, fantasise, or aspire to' (ibid., 156).

127 Karol Berger, *A Theory of Art* (New York: Oxford University Press, 2000), 240.

128 Theodor W. Adorno, *Aesthetic Theory*, trans. Robert Hullot-Kentor (Minneapolis: University of Minnesota Press, 1997), 32.

129 Dubber, 'The 20 Things You Must Know', 46.

130 Thomas Osborne, *Aspects of Enlightenment: Social Theory and the Ethics of Truth* (London: UCL Press, 1998), 113.

131 See, for instance, Pierre Boulez, 'The Vestal Virgin and the Fire-Stealer: Memory, Creation and Authenticity', trans. Susan Bradshaw, *Early Music* 18 (1990), 355–58.

132 Boris Groys, *Art Power* (Cambridge, MA: MIT Press, 2008), 21–22.

133 Ibid., 29, 22. The notion of resisting the 'dictatorship of contemporary taste' is similar to the position articulated by Mark Fisher, quoted in Stephen Graham's chapter (this volume, 248), who writes that 'Modernism is not an advocacy of the current or the contemporary', but is rather 'about breaks with current conditions'.

134 Dick Hebdige, *Hiding in the Light: On Images and Things* (New York and London: Routledge, 1988), 195.

135 Daniel Bell, *The Cultural Contradictions of Capitalism* (New York: Basic Books, 1976), 49; quoted in Richard Taruskin, 'Back to Whom? Neoclassicism as Ideology', *19th-Century Music* 11, no. 3 (1993), 301. Taruskin does not explicitly name those individuals susceptible to megalomania, mentioning simply the institutional centres of 'Darmstadt and Donaueschingen'.

136 For Liam Cagney's nuanced discussion of this concept in the thinking of Pierre Boulez, see chapter 17 in the present volume.

137 The term 'unending modernity' is that of Robert B. Pippin; see *Modernism as a Philosophical Problem: On the Dissatisfactions of European High Culture*, 2nd ed. (Malden, MA: Blackwell, 1999).

Bibliography

Abraham, Amelia. 'Predicting the Digital Apocalypse: An Interview with Douglas Coupland'. *Vice*, 18 April 2015. http://www.vice.com/en_uk/read/douglas-couplands-favourite-books (accessed 27 April 2017).

Addison, David. 'Politics, Patronage and the State in British Avant-Garde Music, c1959 – c1974'. *Twentieth-Century British History* 27, no. 2 (2016): 242–65.

Adorno, Theodor W. *Aesthetic Theory*. Translated by Robert Hullot-Kentor. Minneapolis: University of Minnesota Press, 1997.

Attali, Jacques. *Noise: The Political Economy of Music*. Translated by Brian Massumi. Minneapolis: University of Minnesota Press, 1985.

Augé, Marc. *Non-Places: Introduction to an Anthropology of Supermodernity*. Translated by John Howe. London and New York: Verso, 1995.

Balzer, David. *Curationism: How Curating Took Over the Art World and Everything Else*. London: Pluto Press, 2015.

Barrett, G. Douglas. *Beyond Sound: Toward a Critical Music*. New York and London: Bloomsbury, 2016.

Barthes, Roland. 'The Death of the Author'. In *Image – Music – Text*, translated by Stephen Heath, 142–48. London: Fontana, 1977.

Basar, Shumon, Douglas Coupland, and Hans-Ulrich Obrist. *The Age of Earthquakes: A Guide to the Extreme Present*. New York and London: Random House and Penguin Books, 2015.

Bauman, Zygmunt. *Postmodernity and its Discontents*. Cambridge: Polity Press, 1993.

———. *Globalization: The Human Consequences*. New York: Columbia University Press, 1998.

Bell, Daniel. *The Cultural Contradictions of Capitalism*. New York: Basic Books, 1976.

Berger, Karol. *A Theory of Art*. New York: Oxford University Press, 2000.

Bishop, Claire. *Radical Museology: Or, What's Contemporary in Museums of Contemporary Art?* London: Koenig Books, 2014.

Blake, Andrew. 'To the Millennium: Music as Twentieth-Century Commodity'. In *The Cambridge History of Twentieth-Century Music*, edited by Nicholas Cook and Anthony Pople, 378–505. Cambridge: Cambridge University Press, 2004.

Boulez, Pierre. 'The Vestal Virgin and the Fire-Stealer: Memory, Creation and Authenticity', translated by Susan Bradshaw. *Early Music* 18 (1990): 355–58.

Bourdieu, Pierre. *Distinction: A Social Critique of the Judgement of Taste*. Translated by Richard Nice. London and New York: Routledge, 1984.

Cage, John. 'Overpopulation and Art'. In *John Cage: Composed in America*, edited by Marjorie Perloff and Charles Junkerman, 14–17. Chicago: University of Chicago Press, 1994.

Carr, Nicholas. *The Shallows*. New York: W. W. Norton, 2010.

Clyne, Anna. 'Composer's note to *Night Ferry*'. http://www.boosey.com/cr/music/Anna-Clyne-Night-Ferry/56273 (accessed 28 April 2017).

Connerton, Paul. *How Modernity Forgets*. Cambridge: Cambridge University Press, 2009.

Coupland, Douglas. *Generation X: Tales for an Accelerated Culture*. New York: St Martin's Press, 1981.

Crary, Jonathan. *24/7: Late Capitalism and the Ends of Sleep*. London and New York: Verso, 2013.

Crouch, Colin. *The Strange Non-Death of Neoliberalism*. Cambridge: Polity Press, 2011.

Curran, Alvin. 'Composer's note to *Vindobona Blues*'. http://www.kunstradio.at/2005B/02_10_05.html (accessed 28 April 2017).

Dahlhaus, Carl. *Foundations of Music History*. Translated by J. B. Robinson. Cambridge: Cambridge University Press, 1989.

Deleuze, Gilles. *Cinema II: The Time Image*. Translated by Hugh Tomlinson and Robert Galeta. London: Athlone Press, 1989.

Drott, Eric. 'Rereading Jacques Attali's *Bruits*'. *Critical Inquiry* 41, no. 4 (2015): 721–57.

Dubber, Andrew. 'The 20 Things You Must Know about Music Online'. [n.p.]: New Music Strategies, 2008. http://newmusicstrategies.com/wp-content/uploads/2008/06/nms.pdf (accessed 28 April 2017).

Eco, Umberto. *The Open Work*. Translated by Anna Cancogni. London: Hutchinson Radius, 1989.

Emmerson, Simon. 'The Electroacoustic Tours'. In *Changing Platforms*, edited by Heaton, 58–59.

Foucault, Michel. *Discipline and Punish: The Birth of the Prison*. Translated by Alan Sheridan. London: Allen Lane, 1977.

Gardner, Thomas, and Salomé Voegelin, eds. *Colloquium: Sound Art – Music*. Winchester, UK, and Washington, DC: Zero Books, 2016.

Giddens, Anthony. *Runaway World: How Globalisation Is Reshaping Our Lives*. London: Profile, 2002.

Glock, William. 'The BBC's Music Policy'. In *Notes in Advance: An Autobiography in Music*, 200–213. Oxford: Oxford University Press, 1991.

Gopinath, Sumanth, and Jason Stanyek. 'Anytime, Anywhere? An Introduction to the Devices, Markets, and Theories of Mobile Music'. In *The Oxford Handbook of Mobile Music Studies*, edited by Sumanth Gopinath and Jason Stanyek, 1: 1–34. New York: Oxford University Press, 2014.

Greenberg, Clement. 'Modernist Painting' (1961). In *Art in Modern Culture: An Anthology of Critical Texts*, edited by Francis Frascina and Jonathan Harris, 308–14. London: Phaidon, 1992.

Times like the present

Grimshaw, Mark, ed. *The Oxford Handbook of Virtuality*. New York: Oxford University Press, 2014.

Grossberg, Lawrence. 'On Postmodernism and Articulation: An Interview with Stuart Hall'. *Journal of Communication Inquiry* 10, no. 2 (1986): 45–60.

Groys, Boris. *Art Power*. Cambridge, MA: MIT Press, 2008.

———. 'The Topology of Contemporary Art'. In *Antinomies of Art and Culture: Modernity, Postmodernity, Contemporaneity*, edited by Terry Smith, Okwui Enwezor, and Nancy Condee, 71–80. Durham, NC, and London: Duke University Press, 2008.

Hartog, François. *Regimes of Historicity: Presentism and Experiences of Time*. Translated by Saskia Brown. New York: Columbia University Press, 2015.

Heaton, Chris, ed. *Changing Platforms: 30 Years of the Contemporary Music Network*. London: Unknown Public, 2001.

Hebdige, Dick. *Hiding in the Light: On Images and Things*. New York and London: Routledge, 1988.

Heller, Agnes. 'Existentialism, Alienation, Postmodernism: Cultural Movements as Vehicles of Change in the Patterns of Everyday Life'. In *A Postmodern Reader*, edited by Joseph P. Natoli and Linda Hutcheon, 497–509. Albany, NY: SUNY Press, 1993.

Hesmondhalgh, David. 'Indie: The Institutional Politics and Aesthetics of a Popular Music Genre'. *Cultural Studies* 13, no. 1 (1999): 34–61.

———. 'Digital Sampling and Cultural Inequality'. *Social and Legal Studies* 15, no. 1 (2006): 53–75.

Higgins, Dick. 'Statement on Intermedia' (1966). In *Theories and Documents of Contemporary Art: A Sourcebook of Artists' Writings*, edited by Kristine Stiles and Peter Howard Selz, 728–29. Berkeley and Los Angeles: University of California Press, 1996.

Howard, Luke B. 'Production vs. Reception in Postmodernism: The Górecki Case'. In *Postmodern Music/Postmodern Thought*, edited by Lochhead and Auner, 195–206.

Jameson, Fredric. *A Singular Modernity*. London and New York: Verso, 2002.

Jowell, Tessa. 'Government and the Value of Culture'. https://shiftyparadigms.wordpress.com/images/Cultural_Policy/Tessa_Jowell.pdf (accessed 27 April 2018).

Keynes, John Maynard. 'The Arts Council: Its Policy and Hopes'. *The Listener*, 12 July 1945, 31–32.

Kim-Cohen, Seth. *In the Blink of an Ear: Toward a Non-Cochlear Sonic Art*. New York: Continuum, 2009.

Koselleck, Reinhart. *Futures Past: On the Semantics of Historical Time*. Translated by Keith Tribe. New York: Columbia University Press, 2004.

Kramer, Lawrence. 'The Mysteries of Animation: History, Analysis and Musical Subjectivity'. *Music Analysis* 20, no. 2 (2010): 153–78.

Krauss, Rosalind. 'Sculpture in the Expanded Field' (1979). In *Postmodern Culture*, edited by Hal Foster, 31–42. London and Sydney: Pluto Press, 1985.

Lanier, Jaron. *You Are Not a Gadget*. 2nd updated ed. London: Penguin Books, 2011.

Lebrecht, Norman. 'Council of Despair'. *The Spectator*, 1 July 2017, 42.

Lochhead, Judy, and Joseph Auner, eds. *Postmodern Music/Postmodern Thought*. New York and London: Routledge, 2002.

Loh, Kep Kee, and Ryota Kanai. 'How Has the Internet Reshaped Human Cognition?' *Neuroscience* 22, no. 5 (2014): 506–20.

Macarthur, Sally. *Towards a Twenty-First-Century Feminist Politics of Music*. Aldershot: Ashgate, 2010.

Mathiesen, Thomas. 'The Viewer Society: Michel Foucault's "Panopticon" Revisited'. *Theoretical Criminology* 1, no. 2 (1997): 215–32.

McClary, Susan. 'Afterword: The Politics of Silence and Sound'. In Attali, *Noise*, 149–58.

McLuhan, Marshall, and Quentin Fiore. *The Medium is the Massage: An Inventory of Effects*. Harmondsworth, UK: Penguin Books, 1967.

Metzer, David. *Musical Modernism at the Turn of the Twenty-First Century*. Cambridge: Cambridge University Press, 2011.

Miller, M. H. 'Disaster Writing: New Book by Douglas Coupland and Hans Ulrich Obrist Wreaks Havoc on Original Thought'. *ARTnews*, May 2015, 28. http://www.artnews.com/2015/04/14/disaster-writing-age-of-earthquakes-wreaks-havoc-on-original-thought/ (accessed 27 April 2017).

Motte, Diether de la. *Musik ist im Spiel: Geschichten, Spielen, Zaubereien, Improvisationen*. 2nd ed. Kassel: Bärenreiter, 1990.

Nora, Pierre. 'General Introduction: Between Memory and History'. In *Realms of Memory: Rethinking the French Past*, edited by Pierre Nora and translated by Arthur Goldhammer, 1: 1–20. New York: Columbia University Press, 1996.

———. 'De l'histoire contemporaine au présent historique'. In *Présent, nation, mémoire*, 79–84. Paris: Gallimard, 2011.

Osborne, Peter. *The Politics of Time: Modernity and the Avant-Garde*. London: Verso, 1995.

————. *Anywhere or Not at All: Philosophy of Contemporary Art*. London: Verso, 2013.

Osborne, Thomas. *Aspects of Enlightenment: Social Theory and the Ethics of Truth*. London: UCL Press, 1998.

Ouzounian, Gascia. 'Sound Installation Art: From Spatial Poetics to Politics, Aesthetics to Ethics'. In *Music, Sound and Space: Transformations of Public and Private Experience*, edited by Georgina Born, 73–89. Cambridge: Cambridge University Press, 2013.

Pace, Ian. 'Deskilling and Musical Education'. *Desiring Progress* (blog). https://ianpace.wordpress.com/2016/08/21/ (accessed 27 April 2018).

Pippin, Robert B. *Modernism as a Philosophical Problem: On the Dissatisfactions of European High Culture*. 2nd ed. Malden, MA: Blackwell, 1999.

Powers, Harold S. 'Classical Music, Cultural Roots, and Colonial Rule: An Indic Musicologist Looks at the Muslim World'. *Asian Music* 12, no. 1 (1980): 5–39.

Ritchey, Marianna. '"Amazing Together": Mason Bates, Classical Music, and Neoliberal Values'. *Music & Politics* 11, no. 2 (2017). https://quod.lib.umich.edu/m/mp/9460447.0011.202?view=text;rgn=main (accessed 18 August 2017).

Ruffel, Lionel. *Brouhaha: Les mondes du contemporain*. Paris: Verdier, 2016.

Rutherford-Johnson, Tim. *Music After the Fall: Modern Composition and Culture since 1989*. Oakland: University of California Press, 2017.

Savage, Steve. *Bytes and Backbeats: Repurposing Music in the Digital Age*. Ann Arbor: University of Michigan Press, 2013.

Schafer, R. Murray. *The Tuning of the World*. New York: Knopf, 1977.

Scherzinger, Martin. 'Divisible Mobility: Music in an Age of Cloud Computing'. In *The Oxford Handbook of Mobile Music Studies*, edited by Sumanth Gopinath and Jason Stanyek, 1: 75–102. New York: Oxford University Press, 2014.

Sloterdijk, Peter. *In the World Interior of Capital*. Cambridge: Polity Press, 2013.

Smith, Chris. *Creative Britain*. London: Faber and Faber, 1998.

Smith, Terry. 'Contemporary Art and Contemporaneity'. *Critical Inquiry* 32, no. 4 (2006): 681–707.

————. *What Is Contemporary Art?* Chicago: University of Chicago Press, 2009.

Sound and Music. *Commissioning Report*. London: Sound and Music, 2014.

Tan, Shzr Ee. '"Uploading" to Carnegie Hall: The First YouTube Symphony Orchestra'. In *The Oxford Handbook of Music and Virtuality*, edited by Sheila Whiteley and Shara Rambarran, 335–54. New York: Oxford University Press, 2016.

Taruskin, Richard. 'Back to Whom? Neoclassicism as Ideology'. *19th-Century Music* 11, no. 3 (1993): 286–302.

Taylor, Timothy D. 'Music and Musical Practices in Postmodernity'. In *Postmodern Music/Postmodern Thought*, edited by Lochhead and Auner, 93–118.

Weber, William. 'Consequences of Canon: The Institutionalization of Enmity between Contemporary and Classical Music'. *Common Knowledge* 9, no. 1 (2003): 78–99.

Wertheim, Margaret. 'The Pearly Gates of Cyberspace'. In *Architecture of Fear*, edited by Nan Elin, 296–302. New York: Princeton Architectural Press, 1997.

Williams, Raymond. *Keywords: A Vocabulary of Culture and Society*. London: Fontana, 1976.

Žižek, Slavoj. *Against the Double Blackmail: Refugees, Terror, and Other Troubles with the Neighbours*. London: Allen Lane, 2016.

12

THE COMPOSER AS COMMUNICATION THEORIST

M. J. Grant

We cannot *not* communicate: this principle will be familiar to anyone who has ever attended a workshop, or picked up a self-help manual, on effective communication. Whenever we are in any sort of aural, visual, tactical or technical proximity to one another, we send out and receive any number of signals regarding our emotional states, our identities, our possible intentions and probable actions. So essential is communicating to human beings that being forced into a position where we *cannot* communicate can have a devastating effect on our psychological well-being.[1]

Communication does not automatically imply understanding, of course: otherwise, there would be no need for all those workshops and self-help manuals. For many twentieth-century composers this issue of necessity became a central preoccupation, for several reasons. First, there was the frequent criticism levelled at composers that they were not interested in communicating with audiences. Second, many of the theoretical and technical strategies employed by composers forced them to confront the realities of how we communicate, musically and otherwise. Third, both these issues led to composers' increasing recourse to nonmusical forms of communication to explore and explain their thinking. Such endeavours were themselves often lambasted as demonstrating that the music 'itself' could not be understood as such by an audience, though, as will be discussed, exploring artistic ideas and motivations in writing is a common feature of modernism in the arts.

This chapter will argue that how modernist composers addressed the issue of musical communication is important not only for an understanding of musical modernism, but for an understanding of human musicality more generally. Although I will focus to a large extent on European and American composers active in the period following the Second World War, these tendencies can also be found in the work of other composers; moreover, the impact of these new perspectives continues right up to the present day. The chapter is divided into seven sections. The first raises the issue of what we mean by 'communication', while the second focuses more specifically on the emergence of a scientific discourse around communication – including in relation to music – in the nineteenth and twentieth centuries. Perhaps the single most important development in this regard – the rise of electronic music – is discussed in the third section, while the fourth shows how these developments also impacted upon a renewed fascination for the human voice. The trend towards conceptions of music as process rather than as 'work' is dealt with in the fifth section, with a particular focus on how composers theorized the status of the score. The role of different media in musical communication is also dealt with in the sixth section, which looks more specifically at how modernist approaches led to a new appreciation of the implicit multimodality of all musical communication. The seventh section demonstrates the interplay of many of these concerns in practice via an extended discussion of John Cage's *Variations IV*. There follows a conclusion which considers some of the implications of these developments for thinking about music in more general terms, and up to the present day.

What do we mean by 'communication'?

Let us begin by thinking ourselves back into our training session on effective communication, and a game developed for use in such contexts. One person is given the task of getting another to draw a particular object. The person giving the command cannot, however, describe what the object actually is – for example, a tall block of flats – only the steps for drawing it; they are also unable to see what the other person is actually drawing, and thus can't correct them. For example, they could give the command 'draw a large rectangle'; but if they neglect to say that the short sides must be parallel to the horizontal, the block of flats may end up long rather than tall. The command 'inside the rectangle, draw pairs of smaller rectangles' may lead to the appearance of windows, but could also result in randomly arranged pairs of differently sized rectangles. And so on.

What type of communication are we dealing with here? For one thing, verbal communication, but a very specific type, namely giving commands. Moreover, this verbal communication is being used to communicate something that is visual, so a translation of sorts is taking place. The set-up excludes the possibility of feedback for clarification; thus it is a linear, unidirectional system. In this way, although the point of the game is primarily to make people more aware of all the parameters involved in effectively communicating even simple tasks, the game also draws attention to the most typical ways in which we think about communication theoretically. The main medium of communication here is verbal language, just as many discussions of communication (perhaps most) are predicated on verbal language: the result of the game would be very different if, instead of speaking, instructions were given by physically moving the drawer's hands, or by miming the desired shapes and their relationship to one another. Moreover, not all communication – verbal or otherwise – has the purpose of transmitting a command. When the drawer frowns while considering the information received, or onlookers collapse into convulsions of laughter when viewing the results, they are communicating something about their emotional state, not issuing a command to be followed or a problem to be solved. Finally, the exclusion of any possibility of checking or clarifying is typical of how communication is often thought of in terms of technical systems for communication at a distance.

Because of the tendency to think about communication primarily in terms of verbal language – written or spoken – there is a concomitant tendency to focus on types of communication at which language is particularly effective (at least in theory), such as giving complex commands or exchanging opinions. The way we understand the media of communication likewise demonstrates the influence of verbal communication – think, for example, of words such as *text* or *discourse* that are standard parlance in contemporary cultural studies. Because communication theory has been heavily influenced by the question of technical aids to communication as well, we also tend to underestimate the role that apparently unrelated sensory information has on our interpretation of the communication in question. Recently, however, the dominance of these tropes has been challenged in academic discourse, as can be seen in extensive discussions around such ideas as performativity, embodiment and space, but also in the attention now being paid to material culture (previously the particular realm of archaeologists, who have long recognized

The composer as communication theorist

that artefacts communicate important information – often the only extant information – on past cultures). Moreover, against the grain of equating 'media' with 'mass media', and of reducing 'communication' to individual acts of direct communication, there has long been an alternative tradition of understanding communication as encompassing all of the ways in which human interaction is structured, and of defining media more broadly as 'any vessel of cultural storage, transmission, or expression'.[2] Researchers have also argued for more awareness of the multiplicity of ways in which humans make sense of and interact with both other humans and the world around them. In this chapter, too, I will approach communication as a dynamic and multimodal process in the sense advocated by Ruth Finnegan and others, who have also drawn attention to the myriad resources for communication, and their merits and demerits relative to certain tasks. Finnegan's classic text on the subject takes the senses sound, sight, smell, taste and touch as well as the creation of artefacts as starting points for an exploration that moves beyond the verbal and technical bias of much thinking around communication; in the most recent edition, she also considers the question of telepathy and dreams.[3] Using a slightly different approach, Judee K. Burgoon and Laura K. Guerrero list seven modes of 'nonverbal' communication that are not limited to particular innate senses: proxemics (using distance and space to communicate); haptics (touch); chronemics (time); kinesics (visual aspects of bodily movement); physical appearance; vocalics (aspects of the voice beyond verbal language); and artefacts.[4] It is worthwhile reflecting on how each of these modes can and does play a significant role in musical activities and practices, including taking into consideration apparently peripheral aspects such as how musicians' visual appearance and gestural language affects our judgement of their performance, what spaces are allocated to musicians and audience respectively, the strong links between music and dance, and so on. Such an approach can help us critique the assumptions we sometimes make about musical communication and how it functions, particularly when we consciously or unconsciously take modern Western ideas about music, and particularly Western art music, as our starting point. And as I shall discuss in this chapter, many of the most challenging, revolutionary and influential aspects of musical modernism relate directly to how composers similarly confronted the question of what musical communication is, has been and can be.

A communications revolution

No matter how we periodize the rise of modernism in music, we will note a striking simultaneity with key developments in sound recording and transmission technologies. If, with Paul Griffiths, we take 1890 as our starting point,[5] we are in the midst of a period that saw Alexander Graham Bell's invention of the telephone (patented 1876), Thomas Edison's first voice recording using the phonograph (1878), Emil Berliner's invention of the gramophone (1887), the advent of film (Edward Muybridge's experiments took place in the 1870s, while the 1890s saw advances leading to the first film studios), and Guglielmo Marconi's first patents in the field of wireless communication (from 1897). If we take the Great War as the turning point, we coincide with the period in which the commercial uses of these technologies come into their own, for example with the establishment of radio broadcasting services from 1920. The period sometimes referred to as high or late modernism, meanwhile, would have taken a very different course without two technologies developed from the 1930s and 1940s, namely magnetic tape and the computer.

It is a truism that innovations in communication technologies and media tend to have far-reaching implications for society as a whole, but as the history of musical composition in the twentieth century demonstrates, envisioning what *might* be achieved through technology is just as important. This is evident in a text such as Busoni's *Sketch of a New Aesthetic of Music* (1911), which clearly reflects the era of wireless transmission when it exclaims that music 'floats on air! It touches not the earth with its feet. It knows no law of gravitation. It is well nigh incorporeal. Its material is transparent. It is sonorous air.'[6] At a later point, Busoni refers to Thaddeus Cahill's invention of the Dynamophon, an electrical musical instrument which Busoni suggested could help overcome the strictures of conventional tuning systems. Busoni's essay is an early but by no means unique example of how composers looked to new technology as a way of expanding music beyond the limitations of conventional instruments and conventional music theory. Microtonality was a frequent topic for discussion, but some composers went further and imagined wholly new types of musical sound – including Edgard Varèse, whose works from the 1920s used expanded musical ensembles to compensate for technologies as yet to be developed. Varèse would live long enough to see this revolution take flight in the 1950s, and his late *Poème électronique*, created for the Philips Pavilion designed by Le Corbusier (with assistance from Iannis Xenakis) for the 1958 Brussels World's Fair, is one of the most important pieces of early electronic music, frequently cited in writing on the history of site-specific music and sound art.

Scientific advances and discourses more generally, and not only applied technology, also proved highly influential for musical modernism. Western music theory has always been drawn to mathematical and physical explanations for musical 'laws', with the explanations frequently being adapted in line with the latest scientific paradigms, to use Thomas Kuhn's famous term.[7] The second half of the nineteenth century saw significant scientific developments that influenced how musical modernists theorized their art as well. Among the most important is Hermann von Helmholtz's psychoacoustic development of overtone theory, published in the 1860s. Helmholtz developed Fourier's theory that complex periodic vibrations can be understood in terms of simple harmonic vibrations, arguing that the human ear itself performed such a Fourier analysis in order to discriminate between different sounds.[8] In the 1950s the idea that all sounds are basically composites of particular frequencies provided a theoretical basis (albeit a questionable one) for the idea of serially determined sound synthesis starting from individual sine tones: if the laws of tonality were related to the harmonic series found within tones themselves – an idea that had dominated theories of consonance and dissonance since the seventeenth century – then a rigorous rejection of the tonal system also necessitated a return to first principles of how musical sounds are constructed. Ultimately this theory proved too simplistic, and in any case too difficult to realize using the technology of the time; but taking this discourse to its (logical or absurd?) conclusion was a learning curve which ultimately liberated composers from this centuries-old discourse.

Just as important were contemporary endeavours to uncover underlying and universal rules of human social organization and communication. The idea that societies and cultures could be studied scientifically, leading ultimately to the development of the modern disciplines of sociology and social and cultural anthropology, is itself connected to developments in ideas about communication, and to an extent depended methodologically on communication technology as well.[9] By the early twentieth century, recording sound was an essential tool for the anthropologist, the first step to analysing the language and music of remote (to Europe) or isolated cultures. The notion of the instant availability of all cultures – an idea by turns utopian or apocalyptic in the prognoses attached to it – would later become a central tenet of media theory, thanks not least to Marshall McLuhan and his deftness with catchphrases such as the 'global village'. As Björn Heile has noted, the impact on later musical modernists of globalization, but also their own contributions to emerging ideas around 'world music', has only rarely been reflected in scholarly discourse outside of the writings of composers themselves.[10] On the other hand, it is standard practice in music histories to point to the influence of foreign or 'folk' music cultures on earlier modernist composers, who found in these repertoires new resources for thinking

The composer as communication theorist

about tonality, rhythmic organization and timbre: well-known examples include the impact on Claude Debussy of gamelan music, and the inspiration Béla Bartók derived from materials collected wearing his other, ethnomusicological hat. Such references to music of 'other' cultures were often popular with audiences, not least given a general fashion for such things among the European élite (as Jonathan Cross has discussed in the case of Stravinsky's early works).[11]

While the recourse to musical materials from folk traditions and other cultures was often at best superficial, at worst racist, the move in anthropology and linguistics was increasingly towards uncovering deeper structures, as is reflected in the name of the critical discourse under which many of these approaches were subsumed: structuralism. This is not the place to enter into a detailed critique of structuralist thought: I merely want to draw attention to certain prerequisites of structuralism that are essential for understanding developments in a number of different fields, including compositional theory. In this regard, the semiotic aspects of structural linguistics as developed by Ferdinand de Saussure – such as his distinction between the signifier and the signified – are less immediately important than the urge to find a way of comparing and understanding languages as such. Later, in the work of Claude Lévi-Strauss and others, this was extended to the analysis of cultures as a whole on the basis of structural features far removed from actual content, be this content the medium of the communication or what this communication aims to represent.

This type of thinking also proved essential for the development of information theory in the mid-twentieth century. Information theory is predicated on the idea that information – in the most general sense – can be understood in quantifiable terms: hence the title of one of the most famous publications in the field, Claude Shannon and Warren Weaver's *The Mathematical Theory of Communication* from 1948.[12] The practical point of the theory is to establish the optimum amount and type of information to be transmitted via a medium in order for the message to be properly decoded, while also being as efficient as possible, since all communication technologies have to filter the message in some way.[13] Shannon and Weaver famously reduced their model to a simple diagram that shows the sender–message–receiver model and the potential for the detrimental impact of disturbance or 'noise' on the message in transit. Like the theory as a whole, the diagram is designed specifically with telecommunications in mind. Technical models such as Shannon and Weaver's have not always been understood as such, however: simplified versions of the sender–message–receiver model have frequently been applied to musical communication as well, despite their obvious limitations.[14] For one thing, the model is linear and unidirectional, with no room for interaction or feedback. Although there have been several highly sophisticated attempts to apply cybernetic concepts and models to the study of social organization and communication, often very useful in clarifying relationships and information flows, such models can quickly become overly deterministic.

The developing sciences of communication had a major impact on musical modernism for a more direct reason, however: they provided the technology and, in some cases, the personal impetus for the establishment of electronic music studios in the period after World War II.

The rise of electroacoustic music

As stated previously, the rise of electroacoustic music is linked closely to the development of magnetic tape. Compared to gramophone records – still used by Pierre Schaeffer in his earliest works in *musique concrète* – tape offered unparalleled flexibility when it came to manipulating and combining, literally cutting and splicing a wide range of different recorded sounds. Thus, though throughout the earlier twentieth century composers had been moving in this direction with the technologies then available, it was the rise of tape which saw the real dawning of a new world of musical sound and the start of a revealing journey into the inner life of sounds as well.

Tape is only a tool, however: composers needed a shot of nonmusical theory to help them master this new medium. The wedding gift of a tape recorder, combined with ideas garnered from Norbert Wiener's influential book on *Cybernetics* (published in 1948, the same year as Shannon and Weaver's theory), proved inspirational for American composers Bebe and Louis Barron.[15] The Barrons are primarily remembered today for their score to the film *Forbidden Planet*, but the home studio they built and their pioneering technological expertise was also the backdrop for John Cage's first forays into composing with tape. Cage had long recognized the potential of sound recording for music, but his attempts to gain funding for intensive research had been unsuccessful. It is significant, then, that the Barrons' studio was an independent initiative and also that demand for their expertise came from the film industry. In Europe, the two pioneering studios in the field of electroacoustic music were based in radio stations: at the RTF in Paris, under the direction of Pierre Schaeffer (who had trained in telecommunications), and at the NWDR, later WDR, in Cologne, where the studio's financing was originally justified by its utility for incidental music and sound for radio programmes. Early supporters of the WDR studio included Robert Beyer, who had been writing on a potential future world of electronically generated sounds since the 1920s;[16] the scientific impetus came from Werner Meyer-Eppler, then one of Europe's foremost figures in the field of communication theory. As professor of phonetics at the University of Bonn, he was particularly interested in speech synthesis and saw in the concomitant theories and technologies great potential for music as well.[17] The timing and even the geography could hardly have been better: Herbert Eimert of the WDR, a modern music polemicist as well as theorist and composer, similarly recognized the promise and in due course became the studio's first director. Eimert was also an early champion of the young Karlheinz Stockhausen, freshly returned from his own first experiments in Schaeffer's studio in Paris.[18] The WDR studio became a focal point for young composers, including those drawn in by the station's regular broadcasts of new music and commentary. Other studios quickly followed, including the Studio di Fonologia set up in Milan by the composers Bruno Maderna and Luciano Berio and the ethnomusicologist Roberto Leydi, among others,[19] and the Siemens studio in Munich, co-founded and for a time led by Josef Anton Riedl, who had gathered experience in Schaeffer's Paris studio, in the studio in Gravesano established by the conductor Hermann Scherchen in 1954, and at the WDR. Gottfried Michael Koenig, a pioneer in the field of computer music in Europe who had previously worked for several years in the WDR studio, led the Studio for Electronic Music at Utrecht University from 1964; this studio had its origins in the Philips studio in Eindhoven and went on to become the Institute of Sonology at The Hague Conservatory. In the United States, almost a decade of work by composers including Vladimir Ussachevsky and Otto Luening led to the establishment, in 1959, of the Columbia-Princeton studio, especially well known for its development of the RCA synthesizer. One of the most important such institutions at present is the Parisian Institut de Recherche et Coordination Acoustique/Musique (IRCAM), set up in the 1970s under the direction of Pierre Boulez with funding from the French government.

Electronic music technology nurtures an approach to sound very different from that of conventional composition. The actual tools of composition also differed from what composers were used to: paper, pencils and pianos being replaced by tape recorders, sound generators and filters. These new media introduced new types of mediation between idea and sounding result, and generally necessitated the assistance of people with the corresponding technical backgrounds. Not least for this reason, studios themselves became centres of communication and exchange, laboratories for musical thinking in the technical but also intellectual sense.[20]

Despite their undeniable importance, studios are only one side of the story. Like all institutions, studios tended not to be open to all comers. By preference or necessity, many composers developed their own technologies and approaches. Building such systems can be regarded both as a contribution to applied communication theory and as a creative act itself: Gordon Mumma, for example, regarded his circuits for live electronic performance as themselves constituting an act of composition.[21] The question of input, manipulation and output through a technical system is clearly every bit as much an act of composition as creating sets of guidelines for musicians to follow in some open and variable form works, such as Stockhausen's and Cage's compositions based on input from radio and other sources.[22] And where electronic systems are used in live performance, they not only showcase the technology used as such, but raise a whole host of new issues regarding interfaces and interactivity. Ultimately, these considerations led to new contexts for music: when no live performance by a musician is necessary, compositions need not be time-limited to a one-off concert, though the technology required may limit the piece to a specific period of time and a specific venue. The development of sound installations and sound art, including systems that require the real-time input of visitors, presents us with quite different modes of communication than conventional forms of performance.[23] This is just one way in which the rise of electronic music, along with other developments, was related to fundamental changes in how composers thought about musical form and the aesthetic status of the musical 'work', as will be discussed in more detail in later sections of this chapter. It is also one of the reasons why, to return to Burgoon and Guerrero's seventh mode, musical communication through proxemics – space as a compositional parameter – became increasingly important at this point.

Music, speech, voice

As we have seen, many of the techniques used in early electronic music were derived from research into the transmission and reproduction of speech. The relationship between music and verbal language, through the common medium of the human voice, proved inspirational in other ways as well. In the aesthetics of absolute music, instrumental music had become the ideal to which not only all music but all art aspires. At the same time, however, the human singing voice remained the sonic ideal to which other instruments must aspire. Modernist composers, on the other hand, realized that the voice can do much, much more than simply sing.

An exploration of the extended expressive qualities of the human voice, and proto-musical aspects of human speech, is already evident in Schoenberg's use of *Sprechgesang* in *Pierrot Lunaire* (1912), and – from a very different perspective – in Dadaist poet Kurt Schwitters's work for solo speaker, *Ursonate* (first version 1923). The latter can be viewed as a precursor of many works in the field of new and experimental music which focus on speech, utterance and other aspects of human vocality, and which become increasingly prevalent from the early 1960s onwards. The name of Riedl in particular is almost synonymous with speech and utterance as musical material, including but not limited to his electroacoustic compositions. Further examples include György Ligeti's *Aventures* (1962, revised 1963) and *Nouvelles Aventures* (1962–65), and Dieter Schnebel's *Glossolalie* (1959–61), one of the most ambitious works in this line. In *Glossalie*, and even more so in *Maulwerke* (1968–74), Schnebel systematically explored the diverse sound-making capacities of the human vocal apparatus, developing techniques that would inspire many others as well.

Both Ligeti and Schnebel were strongly influenced by post-war serialism in the early stages of their careers, especially by developments in Cologne, where Riedl, too, had worked.[24] A systematic exploration of the human voice and the medium of speech is a recurring preoccupation in the work of many post-war serialists, and for other composers such as Luciano Berio who acknowledged the influence of serialism. Stockhausen's *Gesang der Jünglinge* (1955–56) presents a paradigmatic example of the serial principle in practice in the way it mediates not only between what from an acoustic perspective are the simplest and most complex sound sources – electronically produced sounds and the human voice, respectively – but also between different degrees of comprehensibility of the biblical text that forms the basis for the vocal material of the composition. Theorizing the distinction between musical and verbal language in this way echoes the approach taken to aesthetic communication by thinkers inspired by information theory, such as Max Bense and Abraham Moles; Moles's writings on the subject drew extensively on his experience with the work of Schaeffer's group in Paris.[25] Boulez dealt with similar issues, but with very different methods, in *Pli selon pli*, especially in the three *Improvisations sur Mallarmé*, which proceed from a largely syllabic through increasingly melismatic setting of the text up to a point where only the textless, singing voice remains. Boulez's piece is thus a fitting musical counterpart to Mallarmé's poetics, where semantic meaning gives way to a play of concepts and their carrier sounds. James Joyce, in particular *Finnegans Wake*, was another major source of inspiration for composers and for similar reasons. The many works which take Joyce as their starting point include Berio's *Omaggio a Joyce* (1958–59), which Nicola Scaldaferri places at the start of a development from the use of recorded voice in a piece for tape (the *Omaggio*) through a work for live voice and percussion (*Circles*, 1960) to, finally, a work for solo voice without tape (*Sequenza III*, 1965).[26] Berio, discussing the composition of *Sequenza III*, described segmenting the basic text by Markus Kutter at the phonemic level but also at the level of expressive indicators given in the text.[27] Segmentation of this kind is reminiscent of procedures used in phonology and phonetics and also shows the influence of serial techniques. The work was written for Cathy Berberian, whose performances of it inspired a number of other composers to explore the extraordinary possibilities for the voice thus demonstrated.

Scaldaferri notes that the approach to the human voice in such works is often directly related to the experience of working with the voice in the electronic studio.[28] The recorded, disembodied voice, subject to modifications and analysis in a manner never before possible, actually draws attention back to the embodied voice, and away from the notion of language and speech as 'text'. In the specific case of the Milan studio, a further factor may have been the numerous interactions with ethnomusicologists and anthropologists, including the American Alan Lomax, whose 'cantometrics' system of analysing and comparing music of different cultures was itself reminiscent of the approaches composers were taking to the voice.[29] In their explorations of the extraordinarily varied, complex and flexible capabilities of the human voice, modernist composers thus provided a unique if largely overlooked perspective on developing debates around performativity, highlighting the phonetic and phenomenological dimensions of speech communication often granted only secondary status by theorists of language.

From 'music as work' to 'music as process'

The distinction between text and performance is crucial for understanding musical modernism in a more general sense as well. Here, the relationship between sound and action becomes important – so important, in fact, that it will be discussed from a different angle in the next section of this chapter. The relationship between sound and action had crucial theoretical implications deriving from two related developments: first, the ability provided by recording to remove a sound from the action that produces it, and to reproduce the sound without repeating the action itself; and second (conversely, or so it would appear), a resurgent interest in giving the action back to the sound, reaffirming the fundamental relationship between movement or event and sound both in the way that composers notated their music, and also in the way that performance itself, the act of creating sound and creating meaning through that sound, increasingly becomes a parameter of musical composition rather than just a necessary corollary of turning the score into sounding music.

The composer as communication theorist

The idea of the score is, in many ways, crucial here, and is also the reason why what began as questions raised over the best way to notate complex musical structures ultimately led composers in the direction of what is often termed 'open form'. It is probably no exaggeration to say that this aspect of musical modernism – what Eco described as 'the considerable autonomy left to the individual performer in the way he [sic] chooses to play the work'[30] – represented the biggest challenge of all to the entire *Weltanschauung* of Western musical aesthetics. At the heart of that *Weltanschauung* is a particular communicative technology, namely writing, and an aesthetic concept whose emergence was linked closely to the possibilities offered by writing, namely the work concept.

In order to understand how writing and the work concept are related, we need to reflect on the purposes served by musical notation, as evidenced by the development of mensural notation from the early fourteenth century. This form of notation, Wolfgang Fuhrmann argues, is no longer an *aide mémoire*, no longer a mere transcription of a sounding form into a visual form for the purposes of study or storage; rather, notation becomes a way of thinking, a way of forming music of unprecedented complexity due to the possibilities it opens for the exact temporal and thus harmonic coordination of many individual musical voices.[31] Thus emerged a music which, in its very complexity, necessitated the written score for its performance, required that performers follow this score exactly if the whole sonic edifice were not to come tumbling down, and which therefore was independent of individual performances to a very high degree.

This system of communication between the composer and the public through the medium of the score and its executants, the performers, began to break down in the serial music of the early 1950s, however. In part, this had to do with early modern modifications to the way time values were notated, with a unit-based system for counting musical time replacing the context-based system of medieval mensural notation.[32] It was exactly this unit-based approach that created great problems for composers who were in the process of extending the serial principle into the realm of duration, presenting performers with note values of a complexity that neither they nor the audience could accurately follow. This and other features of early total serial method – such as the tendency of some voices to momentarily cancel out others – is often presented in terms of a contradiction within the serial system itself. While this is true to an extent – at least for very early serialism – the real contradiction was between the music and the system used to notate it.[33]

There is a certain beautiful symmetry in the fact that the solutions first developed by composers such as Stockhausen and Pousseur to deal with this issue effectively turned the clock back several centuries to the time when musical notation first came into its own, with the resurgence of methods of rhythmic notation guided by proportion rather than counting, and the relative temporal independence of individual voices within a carefully defined field (as, for example, in Stockhausen's *Zeitmaße* (1955–56), where it is the start and/or end points that are coordinated rather than every single step along the way). Seen from this perspective, it begins to make more and more sense that these apparently micro-theoretical issues, these questions of media and communicative technology, should in turn call the whole concept of the musical work into question – at least to the extent that 'work' implies a type of musical practice predicated on a form fixed on both macro- and microlevels in advance of performance and which requires performers at best to interpret or recreate, but not themselves to create or improvise. Another interesting point of comparison concerns the actual look of written music. This is the period in which, after several hundred years of standardized and mostly functional scores, both composers and publishers begin to experiment with formats whose visual appearance also conveyed something more direct about the aesthetics and style of the music concerned.[34] In some cases these developments were unavoidable, since composers were now using materials for which there was no standard notation, but they also include trends such as leaving individual and currently active staves 'hanging' on an otherwise blank page vacated by voices currently silent; this trend, famous from Universal Edition scores of the period, effectively conveys how silence (or absence) and contrapuntal density are often central parameters in this repertoire. Thus, simultaneously with the creation of musical structures whose openness and variability called the whole heritage of written music into question, attention is drawn to the score as a visual medium for an aural phenomenon to an extent rarely seen since the medieval period, an age in which the writing down of music was still rare enough to warrant celebration as such. Indeed, Jane Alden has suggested a specific influence of early forms of music notation on Earle Brown, whose scores of the early 1950s are possibly the most famous of all in this regard, and practically *de rigueur* in music history textbooks when they talk about notation in post-war music.[35]

Clearly, these developing attitudes to the status of the musical work of art were not only attributable to a crisis in notation. Cage in particular had called into question more or less everything of relevance to this topic in his works of the early 1950s, and especially in *4'33"*, which shows the influence of developments in the visual arts such as Robert Rauschenberg's white paintings.[36] The idea of openness in form and interpretation had decades previously been explored in the literary arts, including in the work of Joyce and of Mallarmé, who as we have seen exerted a particular influence on Boulez. Mallarmé's *Le Livre*, his (necessarily?) incomplete project for a book of structure so flexible that it would encapsulate all literature and all reality, provided the title for Boulez's *Livre pour cordes* (1948–49), one of his earliest works and written far in advance of his own explorations of and responses to open form and chance, including in the essay 'Alea'.[37] Scientific discourse, too, provided several points of contact, and not only in quantum theory's uncertainty principle: the idea of statistical processes and the calculation of probability were a linchpin of information theory, as Werner Meyer-Eppler explored in an essay published posthumously in *die Reihe*.[38] The developments in musical form during the 1950s and 1960s can therefore be related to similar tendencies in the other arts and science as well as more specific compositional problems. These in turn affected philosophical aesthetics and semiotics, notably Umberto Eco's *Opera aperta* (*The Open Work*) of 1962, which takes its cue from modernist compositions of this era.[39]

With the freeing of musical form from its previous strictures, the role of performers and indeed the status of performance as a whole also began to change. In many cases, the score became less a set of instructions through which musicians communicate the intentions of the composer, and increasingly a set of instructions to enable creative communication among musicians themselves. Christian Wolff, writing in 1984, stated that his aim for notation was to make each performance as direct as if it was taking place for the first time, but also direct in the sense that 'the playing is not so much an expression of the player (or composer) as a way of connecting, making a community'.[40] More recently, the pianist Philip Thomas has drawn attention to David Tudor's distinction between music that requires 'feelings' and music that requires 'actions'; most experimental music, Thomas suggests, requires an approach that is 'stylistically non-interventionist' but that also creates a stronger sense in the performer of the physicality and materiality of the very act of creating sound.[41] This itself flags up an important level in any musical communication that involves mediation through, for example, a written score, namely the question of what musicians are supposed to be communicating, and how.

The frequent use of the word 'event' to describe both individual and distinct moments within a piece of music, but also – particularly in experimental music – in the title of compositions, captures the way in which, both at the macrolevel of form and the microlevel of the piece's unfolding, the unforeseeable and unrepeatable become central aesthetic categories uniting what are, in fact, often very different composers and compositional styles. To an extent, this tendency towards the unmediated and even 'unmediatable' is also a response to the inverse situation provided by electronic music (and recording generally), which offered composers the chance to fix their music for posterity and simultaneously to cut out the middleman of the musician. In this way, live performance became more than ever something to be celebrated in all its multimediality and multimodality.

The multimodality of musical communication

There is a famous picture taken in Cologne in 1956 which shows rows of people sitting in a concert hall, facing a stage on which two large loudspeakers are placed. The occasion was the premiere of Stockhausen's *Gesang der Jünglinge*, originally intended as part of an electronic mass to be performed in Cologne Cathedral; the church authorities, however, had stated that loudspeakers had no place in a church. Whether or not they had a place in a concert hall was also very much a moot point, and it is not insignificant that the further development of electronic music put increasing focus on integrating live performance and perfecting spatialization techniques.

'Where do we go from here?' asked Cage a year later, albeit in a different context. 'Towards theatre. That art more than music resembles nature. We have eyes as well as ears, and it is our business while we are alive to use them.'[42] In actual fact, the move towards the theatrical – implying not musical drama, but the implicit theatricality of all musical performance – was already well underway. In *4'33"*, Cage himself had set the scene for a musical performance featuring everything except intentional, organized sound. The loudspeaker performance in Cologne was in a way the negative imprint of that set-up: highly organized, intentional sound, but no musical instrument, no body. But Stockhausen, whose works from the 1960s moved more clearly into the realm of theatre, had also envisioned a return to ritual and ceremonial contexts for musical practice; ultimately, he would go further than any of his contemporaries by composing not just sound, text and movement but in *Düfte-Zeichen* (2002) even the use of particular incenses.

Histories of the post-war avant-garde often point to the importance of theatricality in works around 1960. Key figures in this development also include Mauricio Kagel, in whose work the idea of music as an audiovisual phenomenon taking place not only in time but also in space is as much a trademark as his irreverence towards musical and other conventions. Like the fool who is uniquely permitted to speak truth to power, Kagel's music often leaves us asking: which is more absurd, the breaching of the convention, or the convention itself? This tendency is not limited to the works of Kagel. In many works of the time, self-explanatory forms of musical behaviour, such as the audience sitting still, or musicians marking a clear boundary between 'the work' and everything around it (the physical entry of the musicians onto the stage, the tuning-up, the applause), even the spaces in which 'music' is allowed to happen – all these and more were consciously flagged up as part of a much bigger question: what *is* music?

This question is of course fundamental to musical modernism in very many ways, and one of the reasons why another mode of musical communication – writing *about* music – became so important. Forerunners of this trend can be seen in Robert Schumann's co-founding of the *Neue Zeitschrift für Musik* in the 1830s as a way to discuss the music of newer composers. In twentieth-century modernism, however, written proclamations and commentary gained a whole new status. Manifestos are a common feature of all the modernist arts as well as the social and political movements that have been aligned with or have inspired modernism. In many cases, they were a necessary correlate to those questions about the nature of art and the position of the artist relative to society that modernist arts had thrown up: Luca Somigli noted that 'since at least the sixteenth century the manifesto documents the experience of a rupture within a society or a culture that had hitherto considered itself cohesive';[43] this also helps explain the oftentimes close connection between artistic and political revolutions, and their recourse to the same medium, the manifesto, for communicating their ideas.

Early examples of modernist manifestos relating to music famously include Luigi Russolo's *The Art of Noise* (1913). Following the First World War, declarations of artistic intent, and discussions about the future of music, began to snowball, as did contrary opinions (here, the most famous example is the spat between the arch-conservative Hans Pfitzner and Alban Berg following the publication of Pfitzner's *Die neue Ästhetik der musikalischen Impotenz* in 1920;[44] Pfitzner had previously attacked Busoni's *Sketch of a New Aesthetic of Music*). After the Second World War, journals such as the short-lived *die Reihe* and *Incontri musicali* and the still-extant *Perspectives of New Music* gave composers further forums for the presentation of their newest ideas; the legacy of figures including Boulez, Cage and Stockhausen is also dependent in part on the significance of their writings.

Writing about their music did not, however, necessarily lead to greater understanding: in many cases, the opposite was the case. The polemical and often iconoclastic tone taken in some essays, most notably Boulez's 'Schoenberg Is Dead' (1951)[45] and the highly complex explorations of compositional thinking characteristic of many in *die Reihe*, became another stick with which to beat modernist music. One of the most famous and controversial essays of musical modernism is in fact notorious for the name given it by subeditors rather than its author: 'The Composer as Specialist' by Milton Babbitt, renamed 'Who Cares if You Listen?' when it appeared in *High Fidelity* magazine in 1958. The magazine's chosen title is misleading in many respects, not least since much of the essay is about economics rather than communication: Babbitt argues for composers to be given access to the same type of institutional resources as researchers in other fields. But Babbitt certainly does discuss communication as well, often using concepts derived from information theory, such as his use of redundancy in describing the tonal 'efficiency' of recent music (modern music, he says, has significantly less redundancy than other forms), or when noting that 'Like all communication, this music presupposes a suitably equipped receptor'.[46] Babbitt argues that music, as a form of research, has to set its own limits rather than be guided by the desires of the public at large. This is quite a different attitude to that taken by several of his European contemporaries, whose writings of the 1950s often reveal their interest in musical perception as a guiding principle for musical composition – as reflected in Stockhausen's development of the concept of moment form (inspired in part by listeners' experiences at the first performance of *Kontakte*),[47] and Pousseur's references to gestalt theory in some of his early writings.

Such considerations were important not least because, from the very beginning, musical modernism had revolved around a quest for new ways of organizing music, and new sources of musical material, that directly challenged prevailing discourses. While some composers were concerned with increasingly fine distinctions of pitch material, others moved in the opposite direction: towards non-harmonic sounds, and what is often called 'noise'. Except in the narrowly defined acoustical sense, 'noise' is a relative term which, like 'dissonance', is almost always used with negative implications. In terms of information theory, it signifies something that disrupts the message; and in the olden days of analogue broadcasting, the quickest way to explain what 'noise' means in acoustic terms was to use the example of a television set with its aerial unplugged. Noise, then, is taken to mean the opposite of, or even a threat to, significant sound.[48]

This background gives us a new take on Henri Pousseur's decision, in *Scambi*, to use noise (defined in the physical sense) as the basis for one of the few examples of pure electronic music to use open form.[49] As John Dack has discussed, Pousseur's instructions for the piece demonstrate the importance of realizing that 'noise' is never simply 'noise': there is a way to bring order into it, to find elements which in this context are significant, be they the relative pitch of a sequence or the relationship between sound and silence within a sequence.[50] Pousseur was of course neither the first to use noise as the basis for a composition – noise generators were standard equipment in most studios – nor the first to engage in the musical ordering of 'nonmusical' sounds. Other composers, too, had invited us to hear a whole new array of sounds musically, by putting them into a musical context or subjecting them to basic musical techniques such as repetition, variation or polyphony. In this way, the sounds themselves reveal elements that can be understood in musical terms: pitch, intensity, gesture, rhythm. There is a necessary correlate to all of this, however. For when we appreciate the potential musicality of all sounding objects, we also become aware of how, when we hear a sound, we hear the object likely to have made the sound. As Pousseur wrote,

> sounds are not independent entities, detached from the rest of reality and that can somehow be used without taking that reality into account. Like light vibrations, they carry the *image* of things, information on certain of the things' properties: their weight, for example, their tension, their elasticity, the potential mechanical energy which they contain and which they could discharge under certain conditions.[51]

Exactly this connection between sound and its source, real or implicit, was theorized in the writings of Pierre Schaeffer, whose *Traité des objets musicaux* is the most ambitious attempt yet to analyse and categorize sounds on the basis of their qualities.[52] Schaeffer introduced the term 'acousmatic' to distinguish the heightened attention promoted by recorded sound. The term derives from the work of Pythagoras, where it described a situation in which a speaker would be visually separated from their audience, who would thus be forced to focus on the actual words and not be influenced by the speaker's visual appearance or gestures. In the early *Étude aux chemins de fer* (1948), for example, Schaeffer loops the sound and creates a situation where, eventually, we begin to hear it on a level far removed from the immediate connotation of 'steam train'. A different situation arises, however, when the source of the sound is not obvious. In music for conventional musical instruments, it is easy for us to draw a line between the sound and the source. The less obvious the nature of the sounding body, the more we analyse the sound itself for keys to that nature. Effectively, a process that normally takes place without us ever thinking about it is put under the microscope, and even where the sound is completely unfamiliar, a suitable sounding object, or at least the characteristics thereof (such as its size and material), tends to present itself. Or, to put it another way: even where there is nothing to see or touch, we still see or feel the music.[53]

In a way, this brings us back to the very start of this discussion. We cannot not communicate, simply because we never stop trying to make sense of the world around us. Even when we try to resist claims such as Cage's that the whole world can be heard musically, we can only do so by engaging in a form of musical communication – by determining that this sound, or this event, is *not* music. Music, in this sense, is everything we perceive as music and everything we try to perceive as music. And this brings us to a final musical example, as a way to draw many of these strands together and explore how they work and interact in practice.

By means of an example: John Cage's *Variations IV*

Cage's *Variations IV* (1963) is one of a total of eight compositions using that basic title, and also, in Cage's words, the 'second of a group of works of which *Atlas Eclipticalis* is the first and *0'00"* is the third'.[54] *Atlas Eclipticalis* (1962) for orchestra was based on a map of the stars which Cage, by overlaying it with transparencies, used as the basis for the score; the version of *0'00"* referred to here (also 1962), subtitled *4'33" No. 2*, is a 'solo for any player', the score of which provides the instruction 'in a space provided with maximum amplification (no feedback), perform a disciplined action':[55] Cage's premiere performances saw him operating an amplified typewriter, in one case complemented by a squeaky chair and by taking drinks of water, both also amplified.[56] The idea of maps, of using transparencies and chance operations, and of questioning the boundaries between musical and other activities all feature in *Variations IV*. Like those of other pieces in the *Variations* group, the work's score consists of written instructions and a transparency on which are printed nine dots and three circles; in addition, performers require a map or plan of the performance venue. In advance of the performance, they cut out seven of the dots and two of the circles (the others are spares), and place one of the circles somewhere on the plan. The other cut-out circle and the dots are to be dropped onto the plan; straight lines are then to be drawn from the placed circle towards and through each of the dots and the other circle where they fall. At any point along the axes thus created, but outside the venue as such (for example, in the foyer of a concert hall rather than the auditorium), sounds are to be created; there is no further specification as to the exact nature of this sounding material. Each performer is free to start and to stop participating in the performance at any time, and they may also do something completely different (for example, perform a different piece).

Like many other pieces by Cage, the composition moves between precise and detailed instructions (I have summarized only the most salient points here), while giving significant freedom of choice to the performers. *Variations IV* is in fact one of the least complicated of these scores to understand and put into practice, but even here the multifarious implications for reflections on musical communication are apparent.

First, this composition is about space, the spaces in which musical performances are staged and the relative space between performers and audience: it thus invites reflection on spatial organization as a musical parameter and on the binary distinction inside/outside that is so central to the piece. Second, the sounds created in the piece are certainly intentional, but their exact nature is determined not by the composer but by the performer. Third, by not specifying the length of the performance and in this particular case also allowing individual performers to enter and leave the piece at their own pace, Cage goes further even than in *0'00"* towards what Helga de la Motte-Haber, commenting on that piece, called 'dissolving the temporal frame of music'.[57] Fourth, given the freedom granted performers to stop creating sounds and do something else, or indeed do nothing, the composition is also about decision-making on the part of performers as to whether and how to participate in a group activity. We should note as well, however, that these freedoms are explicitly written into the score: contrary to a common misconception that 'anything goes' in Cage's works, which can lead to interpretations (and audience reactions) that are more about abusing than celebrating freedom, there are actually quite specific instructions on what is to be done. De la Motte-Haber has used the phrase 'rules of play' to describe the content of scores such as this,[58] which captures well the type of communicative system we are dealing with – not least since the playful aspect of the score is as apparent as the rules. (I have worked with a group of children to create a performance of this piece; they had few problems getting to grips with it.)[59]

Last but not least, *Variations IV* is clearly about the score and its relationship to performance. The unusual preparatory stages – the tactile cutting and throwing and drawing – is reserved for the performers (although the score does give the option of performers returning to the plan and rethrowing the dots and circle during the performance and presumably in view of the audience). The relationship between score and performance is direct in the sense that carrying out the instructions in the score leads to the performance, but unlike with conventional scores, the reverse is not possible: it is not possible, on the basis of the performance-as-experience, to know

The composer as communication theorist

what instructions Cage gave to performers in the score. The audience can only know this if they have or have had previous access to the score itself or specific knowledge of it, such as via a programme note. In other words, the sender–message–receiver model and its variants do not work for this composition. But this means neither that the composition has no distinct identity (which it does, starting with the title) nor that nothing is 'communicated' in a performance of it. Clearly, at all stages in the process of performing this piece, multiple communications are taking place, communications that in fact are always part and parcel of musical composition and performance even if we have become accustomed to thinking about 'music' in very different terms.

Writing in 1967 about David Tudor's recording of *Variations IV*, Joseph Byrd suggested that Cage's interest in 'music-as-experience' presents a direct challenge to a view of art which restricts it to 'the initiated aesthete, the elite of the sensitive and cultured. And so the principle by which the "in" group has always exalted itself – the understanding of an art too intricate for lesser mortals – this is denied them.' He continues, 'Cage and Tudor are not propagating some mystical code to be deciphered by the knowing listener', adding Cage's (unsourced) comment to the effect that the clearest way to communicate is via words.[60] While exploding many frames of reference, however, Cage and others maintained other frames precisely in order that we recognize this explosion for what it is. It is not about giving up the idea of the score, or the role of the composer, or even the idea of 'composition', but drawing attention to these elements, these roles, these media, these frames *as such*. This making visible of what, conventionally, is supposed to remain invisible, is one of the most important and revolutionary features not only of modern music but of modernism as a whole.[61]

Conclusion

This chapter has explored several ways in which modernist composers reflected but also influenced contemporary ideas about musical communication. Some of these approaches developed theoretical and aesthetic tenets long familiar in Western art music, such as privileging the sense of hearing, and the act of listening, as the main domains for music. Others, however, questioned these assumptions, sometimes as a direct result of problems arising in the act of composition and performance. The range of interconnected issues that emerged covered every possible aspect of musical communication, whether the spatial aspect of musical performance, the role of media, the influence of the visual on musical perception or the fundamental question of what music actually is.

The role of the composer as communication theorist is probably clearest in the post-WWII avant-garde, not only because electronic sound production and reproduction brought these composers into contact with information and communication science, but also because in pushing the boundaries of the 'musical' through electronic and other means, they so radically called into question many of the assumptions and conventions that had arisen around musical practice and the 'nature' of music. Thus, we witness a new awareness of the implicit multimediality and multimodality even of those musical practices which promoted themselves as presenting the exact opposite. Many of these developments spring from a kind of hypermodernism – the logical further development of Enlightenment models of rational inquiry – but these years also mark an increasing realization of the limits of this model, which is why this period sees a growing interest in the unforeseeable and in aleatory processes.

Many of the theoretical issues discussed in this chapter are of course not unique to modernist music. What is different is that they become conscious: the media really do become the message. In the work of composers from many very different strands of musical modernism, the conditions and conventions of (all) musical communication are highlighted by centre-staging the media that are supposed to disappear behind the 'message' which these media convey. This centre-staging applies not only to things that we conventionally think of as media, such as the score or the tape, but also to the medium of sound itself and the inherent 'message' that sounds carry quite independently of any function they fulfil in a musical structure.

Describing composers as communication theorists also implies something about the relationship of their work to the social. The idea that the social relationships fostered, modelled, attempted and celebrated through music are fundamental to how societies function – that music is not merely the icing on the cake of human life, but part of what holds the cake together (and may even, to extend the analogy, have helped that cake rise in the first place) – has recently developed into one of the most exciting and potentially significant fields of music research.[62] Reflections on how humans relate to the sounding world around them and to each other through the ordering of sound and movement were, however, already fundamental to the work of many musical modernists. Moreover, whether we are discussing the serial concept as a model of how to mediate difference without effacing it, or the creation of different types of social relationship between composers, musicians and audiences, we see composers not merely reflecting the social world but also thinking through alternatives to the status quo. It is often thus: artists do not merely reflect the society around them, but are often predictors of change; they are movers and shakers and not merely commentators on social, political and intellectual life. In this sense, the term 'avant-garde' often used to describe these movements suggests itself again, unexpectedly, as highly appropriate.

Notes

1 Many modern methods of torture were specifically devised to exploit this: see, for example, Alfred W. McCoy, *A Question of Torture: CIA Interrogation from the Cold War to the War on Terror* (New York: Metropolitan Books, 2006). Campaigners against the use of prolonged solitary confinement have likewise flagged up this issue.

2 John Durham Peters and Jefferson D. Pooley, 'Media and Communications', in *The Wiley-Blackwell Companion to Sociology*, ed. George Ritzer (Chichester, UK: Wiley-Blackwell, 2012), 404.

3 Ruth Finnegan, *Communicating: The Multiple Modes of Human Communication*, 2nd ed. (London and New York: Routledge, 2014).

4 Judee K. Burgoon and Laura K. Guerrero, 'Nonverbal Communication', in *Nonverbal Communication: The Unspoken Dialogue*, ed. Judee K. Burgoon, et al., 2nd ed. (New York: McGraw Hill, 1996); cited here from the discussion in Finnegan, *Communicating*, 36–37.

5 Paul Griffiths, *Modern Music: A Concise History* (London: Thames and Hudson, 1978). Specifically, Griffiths takes the opening flute melody of Debussy's *Prélude à l'après-midi d'un faune* as his point of departure.

6 Ferruccio Busoni, 'Sketch of a New Aesthetic of Music', trans. T. Baker, in *Three Classics in the Aesthetics of Music* (New York: Dover, 1962), 77. First published in German in 1907 as *Entwurf einer neuen Ästhetik der Tonkunst*.

7 Thomas Kuhn, *The Structure of Scientific Revolutions* (Chicago: University of Chicago Press, 1962).

8 See Burdette Green and David Butler, 'From Acoustics to *Tonpsychologie*', in *The Cambridge History of Western Music Theory*, ed. Thomas Christensen (Cambridge: Cambridge University Press, 2002), 246–71.

9 John Durham Peters and Jefferson D. Pooley in fact argue that 'communication is not simply a specialty in sociology; it is in many ways the historical precondition of modern social theory' ('Media and Communications', 22).

10 Björn Heile, '*Weltmusik* and the Globalization of New Music', in *The Modernist Legacy: Essays on New Music*, ed. Björn Heile (Farnham and Burlington, VT: Ashgate, 2009), 101–19.

11 Jonathan Cross, *Igor Stravinsky (Critical Lives)* (London: Reaktion Books, 2015). This history can actually be traced back at least as far as the fashion for *turquerie* in the late eighteenth and early nineteenth centuries; the development of a 'centre and periphery' model of music history, in which Germany, France and Italy formed the core, is also relevant as one of the key factors in promoting musical nationalism, and composers' interest in 'folk' music, over the course of the nineteenth century.

12 Claude Shannon and Warren Weaver, *The Mathematical Theory of Communication* (Urbana: University of Illinois Press, 1949).

13 To take a familiar example: modern audio compression technologies filter out certain frequencies that cannot in any case be perceived by human ears.

14 On these limitations, see Finnegan, *Communication*, chapter 1.

15 Jane Brockman, 'The First Electronic Filmscore – *Forbidden Planet*: A Conversation with Bebe Barron', *The Score* 7, no. 3 (1992), 5, 12–13, http://www.janebrockman.org/BebeBarron/BebeBarron.html#scoreintervw (accessed 15 December 2015).

16 For more on this 'prehistory' of electronic music, see M. J. Grant, *Serial Music, Serial Aesthetics: Compositional Theory in Post-War Europe* (Cambridge: Cambridge University Press, 2001), 50–54.

17 For more information, see Elena Ungeheuer, *Wie die elektronische Musik 'erfunden' wurde. . . : Quellenstudien zu Werner Meyer-Epplers Entwurf zwischen 1949 und 1953* (Mainz: Schott, 1992).

18 Schaeffer's developments will be discussed further below.

19 On the history and technical set-up of this studio see Maria Maddalena Novati and John Dack, eds., *The Studio di Fonologia: A Musical Journey 1954–1983. Update 2008–2012* (Milan: Ricordi, 2012).

20 See, for instance, Thomas Neuhaus, 'Wozu noch Studios?', in *Elektroakustische Musik*, ed. Elena Ungeheuer (Laaber: Laaber Verlag, 2002), 176–82.

21 Michael Nyman, *Experimental Music: Cage and Beyond*, 2nd ed. (Cambridge: Cambridge University Press, 1999), 91.

22 For example, Cage's *Imaginary Landscape No. 4* (1951), and Stockhausen's *Kurzwellen* and *Spirale* (both 1968).

23 See here especially Helga de la Motte-Haber, ed., *Klangkunst* (Laaber: Laaber Verlag, 1999).

24 The composer Georg Heike was likewise part of this circle and later became professor of phonetics at Cologne University: his reflections on this topic are therefore particularly interesting. See Heike, *Musiksprache und Sprachmusik: Texte zur Musik 1956–1998* (Saarbrücken: Pfau, 1999).

25 See Grant, *Serial Music, Serial Aesthetics*, chapter 5.

26 Nicola Scaldaferri, 'The Voice and the Tape: Aesthetic and Technological Interactions in European Studios during the 1950s', in *Crosscurrents: American and European Music in Interaction, 1900–2000*, ed. Felix Meyer, Carol J. Oja, Wolfgang Rathert and Anne C. Schreffler (Woodbridge and Rochester, NY: Boydell Press, for the Paul Sacher Foundation, 2014), 349.

27 Interview with Rossana Dalmonte, in Luciano Berio, *Two Interviews with Rossana Dalmonte and Bálint András Varga*, trans. David Osmond-Smith (New York and London: Marion Boyars, 1981), 94–97.

28 Scaldaferri, 'The Voice and the Tape', 344–49.

29 Ibid.

30 Umberto Eco, *The Open Work*, trans. Anna Cancogni (London: Hutchinson Radius, 1989), 1.

31 Wolfgang Fuhrmann, 'Notation als Denkform', in *Musiken: Festschrift für Christian Kaden*, ed. Katrin Bicher, Jin-Ah Kim and Jutta Toelle (Berlin: Ries & Erler, 2011), 114–35.

32 Ibid., 122–25.

33 I discuss these issues in more detail in Grant, *Serial Music, Serial Aesthetics*, esp. chapter 5.

34 The result has also been several publications focusing specifically on notation, including John Cage, ed., *Notations* (West Glover, VT: Something Else Press, 1969), and more recently Torsten Möller, Kunsu Shim and Gerhard Stäbler, eds., *Sound Visions* (Saarbrücken: Pfau, 2005).

35 Jane Alden, 'From Neume to Folio: Mediaeval Influences on Earle Brown's Graphic Notation', in *Contemporary Music Review* 26, nos. 3–4 (2007), special issue *Earle Brown: From Motets to Mathematics*, 315–32.

36 David Ryan has suggested that *4'33"* and Rauschenberg's white paintings 'have remained touchstones for artistic practices ever since, precisely because they have actively called into question the relation of the creation and reception of the art-event, but have also pointed to a fluidity, and called into question, the time and space considerations of their respective mediums'; David Ryan, '"We Have Eyes as Well as Ears": Experimental Music and the Visual Arts', in *The Ashgate Research Companion to Experimental Music*, ed. James Saunders (Farnham and Burlington, VT: Ashgate, 2009), 203.

37 Pierre Boulez, 'Alea' (1957), in *Stocktakings from an Apprenticeship*, ed. Paule Thévenin and trans. Stephen Walsh (Oxford: Oxford University Press, 1991), 26–38.

38 Werner Meyer-Eppler, 'Informationstheoretische Probleme der musikalischen Kommunikation', *die Reihe* 8 (1962), 7–10.

39 Eco, *The Open Work*.

40 Christian Wolff, 'Before the Fact: On Notation' (1984), in *Cues: Writings and Conversations / Hinweise: Schriften und Gespräche*, ed. Gisela Gronemeyer and Reinhard Oehlschlägel (Cologne: Edition Musik-Texte, 1998), 154.

41 Philip Thomas, 'A Prescription for Action', in *The Ashgate Research Companion to Experimental Music*, 77–98. Thomas's article deals largely with more recent experimental music, but roots these tendencies and practices in the period in focus here.

42 John Cage, 'Experimental Music', in *Silence: Lectures and Writings* (Middletown, CT: Wesleyan University Press, 1973), 12.

43 Luca Somigli, *Legitimizing the Artist: Manifesto Writing and European Modernism, 1885–1915* (Toronto: University of Toronto Press, 2003), 38.

44 Hans Pfitzner, *Die neue Ästhetik der musikalischen Impotenz: Ein Verwesungssymptom?* (Munich: Verlag der süddeutschen Monatshefte, 1920). Berg's response begins by returning the insult: 'Die musikalische Impotenz der "neuen Ästhetik" Hans Pfitzners', *Musikblätter des Anbruchs* 2, nos. 11–12 (1920), 399–408; English translation by Cornelius Cardew as 'The Musical Impotence of Hans Pfitzner's "New Aesthetic"', in Willi Reich, *Alban Berg* (New York: Harcourt, Brace & World, 1965), 205–18.

45 Pierre Boulez, 'Schoenberg Is Dead' (1951), in *Stocktakings from an Apprenticeship*, 209–14.

46 Milton Babbitt, 'The Composer as Specialist', in *The Collected Essays of Milton Babbitt*, ed. Stephen Peles (Princeton, NJ: Princeton University Press, 2003), 49–50.

47 Karlheinz Stockhausen, 'Momentform: Neue Beziehungen zwischen Aufführungsdauer, Werkdauer und Moment', in *Texte zur Musik*, vol. 1, ed. Dieter Schnebel (Cologne: DuMont Schauberg, 1963), 189–210.

48 Thus also its frequent use to describe the music or speech of 'others' and outsiders: see, for example, Ruth HaCohen, *The Music Libel against the Jews* (New Haven, CT: Yale University Press, 2011).

49 Three different recent versions can be accessed at http://www.scambi.mdx.ac.uk/listenScambi.html (accessed 15 December 2015).

50 John Dack, '"Scambi" and the Studio di Fonologia: A Musicological Perspective', in *The Studio di Fonologia: A Musical Journey 1954–1983. Update 2008–2012*, ed. Maria Maddalena Novati and John Dack (Milan: Ricordi, 2012), 123–39.

51 '[L]es sons ne sont pas des entités indépendantes, détachées du restant de la réalité et utilisables sons tenir compte de celle-ci. Comme les vibrations lumineuses, ils nous apportent *l'image* des choses, une information sur certaines de leurs propriétés: leur poids, par exemple, leur tension, leur élasticité, l'énergie mécanique potentielle qu'ils contiennent et peuvent dégager à certaines conditions.' Henri Pousseur, *Musique – semantique – société* (Tournai: Casterman, 1972), 7–8. My translation.

52 Pierre Schaeffer, *Traité des objets musicaux* (Paris: Seuil, 1966).

53 For further discussion on these points, see Simon Emmerson, 'The Relation of Language to Materials', and Trevor Wishart, 'Sound Symbols and Landscapes', in *The Language of Electroacoustic Music*, ed. Simon Emmerson (London and New York: Macmillan and Harwood Academic Publishers, 1986), 17–39 and 41–60.

54 John Cage, *Variations IV* (New York: Henmar Press, 1963), title page.

55 Cited in James Pritchett, *The Music of John Cage* (Cambridge: Cambridge University Press, 1993), 138. Pritchett notes that the very first performance actually consisted in the writing of that sentence, to which Cage subsequently added certain other provisos, including that the action performed should not be the performance of a piece of music.

56 Helga de la Motte Haber, '"Invade Areas Where Nothing's Definite" (John Cage): Kunst jenseits des goldenen Rahmens', in *Cage & Consequences*, ed. Julia H. Schröder and Volker Straebel (Hofheim: Wolke, 2012), 15–22.

57 Ibid., 17.

58 Ibid.

59 This was one of several pieces by Cage performed by these children, and probably the most successful, perhaps because of the way in which creativity and independence is fostered through the instructions contained in the score. The performance took place at the University of Göttingen in 2010.

60 Joseph Byrd, 'Variations IV', in *Writings about John Cage*, ed. Richard Kostelanetz (Ann Arbor: University of Michigan Press, 1993), 135. The irony of this comment – as Björn Heile has pointed out to me in a personal communication – is that Cage, like several of his contemporaries, has in the meantime attracted something of a 'cult' following and that many interpretations of the meaning and significance of his works arguably purvey a new form of the elitism critiqued by Byrd. On the other hand, and in my own experience, few composers continue to attract the opprobrium and, often, blatant disrespect by concert-goers that music by Cage does, which suggests that the iconoclasm of his approach continues to ruffle feathers.

The composer as communication theorist

61 See especially Boris Groys, *Unter Verdacht: Eine Phänomenologie der Medien* (Munich and Vienna: Carl Hanser, 2000); English translation by Carsten Strathausen, *Under Suspicion: A Phenomenology of the Media* (New York and Chichester, UK: Columbia University Press, 2012); specifically on Cage, also Rolf Grossmann, 'Medienreflex in der Musik im Anschluss an John Cage', in *Cage & Consequences*, 35–43.

62 See, for example, Stephen Malloch and Colwyn Trevarthen, eds., *Communicative Musicality: Exploring the Basis of Human Companionship* (Oxford: Oxford University Press, 2010); Ian Cross, 'Musicality and the Human Capacity for Culture', *Musica Scientiae* 12, no. 1 (2008), 147–67.

Bibliography

Alden, Jane. 'From Neume to Folio: Mediaeval Influences on Earle Brown's Graphic Notation'. *Contemporary Music Review* 26, nos. 3–4 (2007): 315–32.

Babbitt, Milton. 'The Composer as Specialist'. In *The Collected Essays of Milton Babbitt*, edited by Stephen Peles, 48–54. Princeton, NJ: Princeton University Press, 2003.

Berg, Alban. 'Die musikalische Impotenz der "neuen Ästhetik" Hans Pfitzners'. *Musikblätter des Anbruchs* 2, nos. 11–12 (1920), 399–408; English translation by Cornelius Cardew as 'The Musical Impotence of Hans Pfitzner's "New Aesthetic"'. In Willi Reich, *Alban Berg* (New York: Harcourt, Brace & World, 1965), 205–18.

Berio, Luciano. *Two Interviews with Rossana Dalmonte and Bálint András Varga*, translated by David Osmond-Smith. New York and London: Marion Boyars, 1981.

Boulez, Pierre. *Stocktakings from an Apprenticeship*. Edited by Paule Thévenin. Translated by Stephen Walsh. Oxford: Oxford University Press, 1991.

Brockman, Jane. 'The First Electronic Filmscore – *Forbidden Planet*: A Conversation with Bebe Barron'. *The Score* 7, no. 3 (1992): 5, 12–13.

Busoni, Ferruccio. 'Sketch of a New Aesthetic of Music', translated by T. Baker. In *Three Classics in the Aesthetics of Music*, 75–102. New York: Dover, 1962.

Byrd, Joseph. 'Variations IV'. In *Writings about John Cage*, edited by Richard Kostelanetz, 134–36. Ann Arbor: University of Michigan Press, 1993.

Cage, John. *Variations IV*. New York: Henmar Press, 1963.

———, ed. *Notations*. West Glover, VT: Something Else Press, 1969.

———. 'Experimental Music'. In *Silence: Lectures and Writings*, 7–12. Middletown, CT: Wesleyan University Press, 1973.

Cross, Ian. 'Musicality and the Human Capacity for Culture'. *Musica Scientiae* 12, no. 1 (2008): 147–67.

Cross, Jonathan. *Igor Stravinsky (Critical Lives)*. London: Reaktion Books, 2015.

Dack, John. '"Scambi" and the Studio di Fonologia: A Musicological Perspective'. In *The Studio di Fonologia: A Musical Journey 1954–1983. Update 2008–2012*, edited by Maria Maddalena Novati and John Dack, 123–39. Milan: Ricordi, 2012.

Eco, Umberto. *The Open Work*. Translated by Anna Cancogni. London: Hutchinson Radius, 1989.

Emmerson, Simon. 'The Relation of Language to Materials'. In *The Language of Electroacoustic Music*, edited by Simon Emmerson, 17–39. London and New York: Macmillan and Harwood Academic Publishers, 1986.

Finnegan, Ruth. *Communicating: The Multiple Modes of Human Communication*. 2nd ed. London and New York: Routledge, 2014.

Fuhrmann, Wolfgang. 'Notation als Denkform'. In *Musiken: Festschrift für Christian Kaden*, edited by Katrin Bicher, Jin-Ah Kim and Jutta Toelle, 114–35. Berlin: Ries & Erler, 2011.

Grant, M. J. *Serial Music, Serial Aesthetics: Compositional Theory in Post-War Europe*. Cambridge: Cambridge University Press, 2001.

Green, Burdette, and David Butler. 'From Acoustics to *Tonpsychologie*'. In *The Cambridge History of Western Music Theory*, edited by Thomas Christensen, 246–71. Cambridge: Cambridge University Press, 2002.

Griffiths, Paul. *Modern Music: A Concise History*. London: Thames and Hudson, 1978.

Grossmann, Rolf. 'Medienreflex in der Musik im Anschluss an John Cage'. In *Cage & Consequences*, edited by Julia H. Schröder and Volker Straebel, 35–43. Hofheim: Wolke, 2012.

Groys, Boris. *Unter Verdacht: Eine Phänomenologie der Medien*. Munich and Vienna: Carl Hanser, 2000. English translation by Carsten Strathausen, *Under Suspicion: A Phenomenology of the Media*. New York and Chichester, UK: Columbia University Press, 2012.

HaCohen, Ruth. *The Music Libel against the Jews*. New Haven, CT: Yale University Press, 2011.

Heike, Georg. *Musiksprache und Sprachmusik: Texte zur Musik 1956–1998*. Saarbrücken: Pfau, 1999.

Heile, Björn. '*Weltmusik* and the Globalization of New Music'. In *The Modernist Legacy: Essays on New Music*, edited by Björn Heile, 101–19. Farnham and Burlington, VT: Ashgate, 2009.

Kuhn, Thomas. *The Structure of Scientific Revolutions*. Chicago: University of Chicago Press, 1962.

Malloch, Stephen, and Colwyn Trevarthen, eds. *Communicative Musicality: Exploring the Basis of Human Companionship*. Oxford: Oxford University Press, 2010.

McCoy, Alfred W. *A Question of Torture: CIA Interrogation from the Cold War to the War on Terror*. New York: Metropolitan Books, 2006.

Meyer-Eppler, Werner. 'Informationstheoretische Probleme der musikalischen Kommunikation'. *die Reihe* 8 (1962): 7–10.

Möller, Torsten, Kunsu Shim and Gerhard Stäbler, eds. *Sound Visions*. Saarbrücken: Pfau, 2005.

Motte-Haber, Helga de la, ed. *Klangkunst*. Handbuch der Musik im 20. Jahrhundert, vol. 12. Laaber: Laaber Verlag, 1999.

———. '"Invade Areas Where Nothing's Definite" (John Cage): Kunst jenseits des goldenen Rahmens'. In *Cage & Consequences*, edited by Julia H. Schröder and Volker Straebel, 15–22. Hofheim: Wolke, 2012.

Neuhaus, Thomas. 'Wozu noch Studios?' In *Elektroakustische Musik*, Handbuch der Musik im 20. Jahrhundert, vol. 5, edited by Elena Ungeheuer, 176–82. Laaber: Laaber Verlag, 2002.

Novati, Maria Maddalena, and John Dack, eds. *The Studio di Fonologia: A Musical Journey 1954–1983. Update 2008–2012*. Milan: Ricordi, 2012.

Nyman, Michael. *Experimental Music: Cage and Beyond*. 2nd ed. Cambridge: Cambridge University Press, 1999.

Peters, John Durham, and Jefferson D. Pooley. 'Media and Communications'. In *The Wiley-Blackwell Companion to Sociology*, edited by George Ritzer, 402–17. Chichester, UK: Wiley-Blackwell, 2012.

Pfitzner, Hans. *Die neue Ästhetik der musikalischen Impotenz: Ein Verwesungssymptom?* Munich: Verlag der süddeutschen Monatshefte, 1920.

Pousseur, Henri. *Musique – semantique – société*. Tournai: Casterman, 1972.

Pritchett, James. *The Music of John Cage*. Cambridge: Cambridge University Press, 1993.

Ryan, David. '"We Have Eyes as Well as Ears": Experimental Music and the Visual Arts'. In *The Ashgate Research Companion to Experimental Music*, edited by James Saunders, 193–237. Farnham and Burlington, VT: Ashgate, 2009.

Scaldaferri, Nicola. 'The Voice and the Tape: Aesthetic and Technological Interactions in European Studios during the 1950s'. In *Crosscurrents: American and European Music in Interaction, 1900–2000*, edited by Felix Meyer, Carol J. Oja, Wolfgang Rathert and Anne C. Schreffler, 335–49. Woodbridge and Rochester, NY: Boydell Press, for the Paul Sacher Foundation, 2014.

Schaeffer, Pierre. *Traité des objets musicaux*. Paris: Seuil, 1966.

Shannon, Claude, and Warren Weaver. *The Mathematical Theory of Communication*. Urbana: University of Illinois Press, 1949.

Somigli, Luca. *Legitimizing the Artist: Manifesto Writing and European Modernism, 1885–1915*. Toronto: University of Toronto Press, 2003.

Stockhausen, Karlheinz. 'Momentform: Neue Beziehungen zwischen Aufführungsdauer, Werkdauer und Moment'. In *Texte zur Musik*, vol. 1, edited by Dieter Schnebel, 189–210. Cologne: DuMont Schauberg, 1963.

Thomas, Philip. 'A Prescription for Action'. In *The Ashgate Research Companion to Experimental Music*, edited by James Saunders, 77–98. Farnham and Burlington, VT: Ashgate, 2009.

Ungeheuer, Elena. *Wie die elektronische Musik 'erfunden' wurde . . . : Quellenstudien zu Werner Meyer-Epplers Entwurf zwischen 1949 und 1953*. Mainz: Schott, 1992.

Wishart, Trevor. 'Sound Symbols and Landscapes'. In *The Language of Electroacoustic Music*, edited by Simon Emmerson, 41–60. London and New York: Macmillan and Harwood Academic Publishers, 1986.

Wolff, Christian. 'Before the Fact: On Notation' (1984). In *Cues: Writings and Conversations / Hinweise: Schriften und Gespräche*, edited by Gisela Gronemeyer and Reinhard Oehlschlägel, 154. Cologne: Edition MusikTexte, 1998.

13

HOW DOES MODERNIST MUSIC MAKE YOU FEEL?

Between subjectivity and affect

Trent Leipert

How does modernist music make one feel? We don't typically associate modernism with emotional effusiveness. After all, was modernism not a reaction to the expressive excesses of Romantic individualism? Partly, perhaps, although we would have to ignore not only Expressionism but also a surprisingly vast number of modernist works throughout the last century. So already we know that feeling is not the real problem; nor is modernism, whatever its perceived degrees of emotional indifference. Rather, the issue is twofold, for there is little agreement on the meaning of the last two words in the question posed at the beginning of this chapter: who is the subject in question and what does it mean to feel? The first of these is not a question about the identity of the audience or an individual listener. It is instead a question about what the subject is in the first place. The unpacking of the second question might begin by asking why we should talk of feeling and not some other phenomenon or process that belongs to that complicated cluster of what we consider the 'emotional' aspects of musical experience. Finally, the 'how' remains an important component of the question not only as an outcome – as in the feelings that modernist music produces – but also as a pathway to be explored, one that runs from the immediacy of sonic phenomena to degrees and types of reflection upon them.

There exists an important corollary to the medium-specific self-reflexivity that has often been seen as a hallmark of modernism: a critical reflection on the notion of the self against a growing scepticism in the transcendent subject. Perhaps most evident in the modernist literature, this important aspect of modernist culture has been given few sustained and comparative studies within the history of musical modernism specifically. This chapter will focus on the connection between subjectivity and the under-analysed affective qualities of advanced composition that might be said to belong to a late (i.e. post-1945) modernist tradition. There is, after all, a close relationship between the structuring of affective (or, for the time being, let me say 'emotional'; the distinctions will be explained in the following section of this chapter) features in the music of late modernity and structures of the subject. Yet both of these paths of inquiry – the 'feelings' that modernist music did and might continue to generate and the nature of the subject who is meant to feel a certain way – present certain challenges. Because of the considerable diversity of theoretical and methodological approaches to musical affect and emotion – and the fact that they have often been overlooked or undertheorized in the context of musical modernism – many new and potentially productive avenues of scholarship present themselves. Before returning to the question of the subject in the final portion of this chapter, it is necessary to untangle the ways in which the diversity of 'affective' experience may be approached theoretically.

Emotion, affect, feeling

Marie Thompson and Ian Biddle observe the methodological and theoretical diversity around affect and the existence and necessity of a 'large church' approach when applying such theory to sonic experiences.[1] While I do not disagree with this assessment, part of this theoretical and methodological confusion can in fact be confronted and disentangled through one of affect studies' most important contributions: that is, its emphasis on the distinctions between affect, emotion and feeling (as well as other states such as moods or sentiments). Bringing these distinctions into focus can contribute to the study of musical modernism in several ways: they clarify aspects of musical experience, they reveal the under-examined and under-appreciated role of affective components in modernist aesthetics and poetics, and they indicate ways in which subjecthood is implicated therein. I will pursue these three issues in the remaining sections of this chapter. First, however, it is necessary to clarify some terms. Within the growing body of affect studies we find a range of definitions for affect, emotion and feeling. Simply sorting through these various definitions has at times occupied a considerable portion of the scholarship on affect. This confusion is not only limited to affect studies; as we will see, it pervades music studies and is further complicated by linguistic differences. Eric Shouse provides a useful and succinct distinction which I will employ throughout the remainder of this chapter: 'Feelings are *personal* and *biographical*, emotions are *social* and affects are *prepersonal*'.[2]

Let me begin with *emotion* as there is perhaps surprisingly the least to say here with regard to music and modernist music in particular. Emotions are considered social as they fall into a limited range of categorical types and are a representational or outwardly directed aspect of personal feelings. An important addition to their biological components is the accompaniment of attitudes pertaining to an object outside of the subject. This emotional object is recognized as the cause or focus of the particular emotion. It is no doubt this very condition of falling into socially recognized categories and being easily communicable that has contributed to the (actual or perceived) anti-emotional bent of certain streams of modernist culture. Writing from the perspective of literary studies, Charles Altieri argues, however, that the rejection of emotional expression among certain modernists did not mean they were uninterested in feeling. Rather, emotions were tarnished by centuries of rhetorical codification and, as they largely relied upon narrative (or at least, contextual) situations to arise, came to be seen as increasingly self-theatricalizing.[3] Although emotion remains a favoured and frequently encountered term in many discussions of music, it may in fact be the least appropriate in most discussions of musical modernism, where often the compositional aim was precisely the avoidance, disruption or overturning of conventional emotions and of their codified means of musical representation.

As with many terms pertaining to the complexity of what is generally called 'emotional experience', *affect* is employed in a number of different ways, often used interchangeably with emotion and feeling. Nevertheless, two more precise uses of affect are frequently encountered in contemporary cultural criticism. One of these comes from the mid-century work of the American psychologist Silvan Tomkins, which received renewed interest beginning in the 1990s through the work of queer theorist and literary scholar Eve Kosofsky Sedgwick.[4] Tomkins's theory of affect combines a series of strongly physiological responses along with attitudes. This might suggest something akin to emotion, yet Tomkins considered affects as the more basic and primary responses to situations and events, the six most important being interest-excitement, enjoyment-joy, surprise-startle, distress-anguish, anger-rage and fear-terror.[5] The other and by far more prominent understanding of affect is that which has been elaborated by Brian Massumi, following Spinoza and Gilles Deleuze, who define affect as a pre-personal or extra-personal intensity that involves a host of bodily responses but exists outside of or before consciousness.[6] While this would suggest a considerable discrepancy with Tomkins's primary affects, the latter also suggests that these primary affects have external sources that are largely beyond the subject's control. Affect in this sense constitutes that which affects the body; affectivity is the latter's capacity towards this stimulus which brings about a change of state.

Given affect's suspended ontology between subjects, events and material, the question of how to bring affect into the study of culture is problematic and is necessarily dictated in part by the context and nature of the media involved. For example, according to Deleuze and Guattari, affect is certainly a feature of art but belongs less clearly to the subject:

> the aim of art is to wrest the percept from perceptions of objects and the states of a perceiving subject, to wrest the affect from affections as the transition from one state to another: to extract a bloc of sensations, a pure being of sensations.[7]

This de-subjectivized aspect of affect accounts for its popularity among scholars dealing with postmodern conceptions of the subject; it also opens it up to critique for those critics such as Slavoj Žižek, who either do not wish to cast aside the subject completely or point out the dangers of valorizing the already variously dispersed and decentred subject under the conditions of contemporary capitalism.[8] Affect scholar Lauren Berlant notes that 'on the face of it, affect theory has no place in the work of literary, or any, history. Gilles Deleuze writes, after all, that affects act in the nervous system not of persons, but of worlds.'[9] Yet, in noting the shared nature of affective atmospheres, Berlant suggests that 'affect, the body's active presence to the intensities of the present, embeds the subject in an historical field, and that its scholarly pursuit can communicate the conditions of an historical moment's production as a visceral moment.'[10] This particular orientation allows Berlant to address the problem of how to discuss and chart the paths of affects that seem to exist outside of individual subjects and their reflections on affect's accompanying sensations. In this case, literature provides *documentation* of a particular affective historical field and not necessarily an object or event of affective engagement in the manner of, say, music.[11] Rebecca Wanzo notes that such a methodological move is appealing for cultural scholars whose often Marxist, feminist or post-colonialist orientation tends to overlook, downplay or dismiss the biological aspects of affect. But it often comes with the cost of terminological obfuscation and a critical focus that is always about something in addition to affect:

> Such work is understandably skeptical of biological claims and most invested in the relationship between affect and ideology. Cultural studies projects about affect are thus always about emotion or feeling plus: plus liberalism, plus biopower, plus nationalism, plus any articulation of ideology in action. As affect in cultural studies work is a complex of emotion plus structure, affect can be a bit of a moving target, making the relationship between texts about affect hard to discern given the vastly different objects of study and methodologies.[12]

In pointing out the methodological muddiness of affect, Wanzo too conflates emotion and feeling, or at least suggests that affect scholarship is often as much about emotion and feeling as affect proper. In either case, her observations are apt: given that the applicability of the term affect rests on the pre-subjectivity of individuals and de-subjectized contexts, most studies of affect are concerned with contemporary cultural and social issues, particularly the condition and place of the subject in late or post-modernity. Cultural studies that deal with affect thus tend to either use the term in some other sense (i.e. as synonymous with emotion or feeling) or else, when employing the term in its 'stricter' (Deleuzian) sense, deal with the contexts, climates, functions and operations of social practices or cultural production and less their outcomes and artefacts. The circulation of pre-personal affect may indeed form a part of the focus in such studies, yet emotion and feeling are usually present even if not explicitly parsed.

Steve Goodman's *Sonic Warfare: Sound, Affect, and the Ecology of Fear* is an example of such a study and one of the few which considers music and affect exclusively in the sense proposed by Deleuze and further developed in the work of Massumi.[13] Goodman examines the ways in which the deployment and manipulation of sound contribute to a contemporary atmosphere of anxiety rooted in the political and socio-economic structures of the twentieth century and of the present. The author finds affect widely dispersed, deeply infused, and omnipresent in the contemporary societies organized by the military-industrial complex. According to Goodman, such administered uses and misuses of sound in the present age modulate affect in various ways. It is a powerful pre-personal force but one which oddly results in a relatively narrow cluster of emotions in his account: dread, fear and anxiety.[14] So once again we encounter the situation described by Wanzo in which feeling and emotion *plus* . . . become the real focus. Dread, fear and anxiety all may take objects and are thus more accurately described as emotions; only the anxiety may be said to be at times 'generalized' enough to forego a single or even several objects.

I raise this point not so much as a criticism of Goodman's scholarship but in order to point to some of the challenges in bringing affect into discussions of modernist music. This particular approach to affect encounters difficulties when applied to modernist music for several reasons. First, the focus on the direct linking of sound with physiological responses tends to privilege frequency, amplitude and rhythm at the expense of the more complicated and more difficult to describe parameters and idiomatic features of modernist music, which, even if taken as theoretical and cultural constructs, remain central to the ways in which we talk and think about it. Nevertheless, the blurring of the ontological distinction between noise and music frequently encountered in late modernist musical aesthetics may allow for a productive interrogation of the relationship between affect and feeling among a wide range of composers. Second, the marginal position of late modernist music in terms of the economics of present-day media (including social media) and entertainment industries means that the role of affect in its social networks is less significantly registered or perhaps registered in less recognizable ways. Modernist music largely avoids or is excluded from the types of diffusion and circulation that critics such as Massumi or Goodman consider; thus the affect + ideology or affect + society route described by Wanzo may require additional paths of investigation or theoretical manoeuvring. This is one place where musical analysis – as a discipline already heavily imbricated in the creation and discourse of modernist music – can contribute to discussions of affect in addition to feeling and emotion.

Although there has been much recent work on the application of Deleuzian concepts to music, affect remains something ubiquitous yet difficult to elaborate. Considering affect as a potentiality-intensity between and around subjects, we may begin to understand the use of the term affect in much music literature – where it is usually taken in its more historical sense to be an emotional representation or the conveyance of an emotion – as both too vague and too narrow. Too vague because affect is only one part in the overall course of the development of a feeling or the expression of an emotional condition. Too narrow because its nascent energy can lead to a potentially wide range of emotional and physiological responses.

A somewhat similar conclusion has been reached by Klaus Scherer in an article summarizing the handful of cognitive studies that compare changes in musical parameters with proprioceptive changes.[15] Rather than initiating the path from perceived intensity to emotional state, Scherer considers affects to be a 'peripheral route', as opposed to the cognitive, primary route, to emotion. In this sense, affect in music, somewhat like the Deleuzian sense, characterizes a fluctuation in bodily states arising from changes in particular musical features. Scherer's characterization of affect as 'peripheral' is initially puzzling, although the reason why affect provides a peripheral *route* becomes more apparent when we take into account Scherer's definition of emotion as something requiring an object or attitude. Even without requiring an external object as the cause of a specific emotion, affect reveals itself in Scherer's model as just one aspect of an 'emotional episode'. Rather than as a peripheral component of an emotional experience, we are more likely to think of affect as an integral part of the catalyst of feeling.

Further studies of affect and music could be cited, but a number of issues can already be anticipated if we want to bring affect further into the study of modernist music. First, although affect helps to separate the emotional aspects of listening away from (intentional) models of expression, affect on its own does not always lend the listener much in the way of agency. While we have seen that this is part of affect's theoretical allure, this absence becomes problematic as it may tend to imply that affective responses are somehow biologically automatic and in no way culturally contingent. Second, studying affect in the manner of cognitive psychology has been mainly limited to more traditional or popular repertories. Nevertheless, part of the usefulness of thinking in terms of affect apart from expression and emotion is that it sets up a route towards the feelings experienced by the subject, even though one or several affects will not necessarily lead to the feelings or more codified emotions intended by the artist or composer. Nor can the category of expression satisfy what the listener will make of certain affects. Shouse suggests that 'music provides perhaps the clearest example of how the intensity of the impingement of sensations on the body can "mean" more to people than meaning itself.'[16] Yet in order to investigate how this meaning of 'meaningfulness' is established, we need to establish how the listener would reflect upon these 'impingements of sensation on the body'; in other words, the process of *feeling*.

If it were not already apparent from my title, I have singled out feeling as a productive – but also problematic – mediating term for discussions of the range of affective aspects (and not only affect) that might attend one in listening to modernist music. The term feeling can function as a verb or noun. Most definitions of feeling describe it as emerging from an initial sensation or a prolonged experience that is subject to reflection – and, as such, reflected upon by a subject. As Charles Altieri defines it, '[f]eelings are elemental affective states characterized by an imaginative engagement in the immediate processes of sensation.'[17] So, feeling is like affect in its elemental nature and its close relationship to immediate sensation, but, crucially, involves the imaginative engagement which we can assume can only come about through something resembling a consciousness or a provisional subject. Along similar lines, cognitive psychologist Antonio Damasio confirms this interpretation of feeling:

> It is through feelings, which are inwardly directed and private, that emotions, which are outwardly directed and public, begin their impact on the mind; but the full and lasting impact of feelings requires consciousness, because only along with the advent of a sense of self do feelings become known to the individual having them.[18]

The interrogation of the self and of the subject that has occurred within intellectual history and within modernism must therefore also be taken into consideration along with feeling: just as feeling is a sort of midway point between affect and emotion, the consciousness of the subject remains our imperfect mediator between sensations and ideas. (It is to this question of the subject in relation to these issues that I will return in the final section of this chapter.)

Additional arguments for re-evaluating the role of feeling in music studies arise through certain shortcomings in research on music and emotion. Scherer has further argued, for example, that many studies of the ways in which music might induce emotions are impoverished by relying on lists of basic emotions, valence-arousal dimensions, and eclectic emotion inventories. More importantly in the present context, Scherer notes a similar widespread tendency to treat 'emotions' and 'feelings' as synonymous. He echoes recent accounts in literary studies and philosophy and proposes that feeling 'can be profitably conceptualized as a central component of emotion, which integrates all other components and serves as the basis for the conscious representation of emotional processes and for affect regulation.' He further adds that 'affect produced by music should be studied as (more or less conscious) feelings that integrate cognitive and physiological effects, which may be accounted for by widely different production rules.'[19] The 'more or less conscious' dimension is actually quite important, as that is where feeling is felt, reflected upon and made meaningful. It is precisely this 'more or less conscious' quality of engagement that raises the presence of the subject and the necessity of having some account of its status and make-up. Scherer suggests that feeling has likely been replaced with emotion to lend validity and verifiability to research into the affective states experienced when listening. It is easy to see why this would be given the subjective vagueness that may arise when speaking of personal feeling. A consensus about an emotion also lends us a sense of certainty, particularly when we consider it to be an expressive intention. However, Scherer also urges us to distinguish between the perception of expressed emotion and actual felt emotion. Talking about feeling is difficult and potentially imprecise; it risks relativity and subjectivity – a subjectivity that, as I will further discuss below, has been historically undermined and increasingly called into question in later modernity.

Modernist music studies and the 'emotional turn'

Before turning to some examples of how the delineation of affect, emotion and feeling that I have outlined may be applied to the study of the music of specific composers, I would like to mention some of the recent contributions to enriching our understanding of the affective diversity and richness of musical modernism. In tandem with the broader 'emotional turn' in the humanities there have appeared in recent years a number of critical reappraisals of modernism.[20] Unsurprisingly, several scholars of modernist music have begun turning attention to the frequently overlooked affective aspects of this music, though, as I discuss, their work might be further developed and nuanced by some of the points that I have outlined in the previous section.

David Metzer provides one of the more direct engagements with such aspects in late modernist music in his study *Musical Modernism at the Turn of the Twenty-First Century*. In making a case for the continued vitality of musical modernism, Metzer argues that late twentieth-century composers sustain and reinterpret the modernist tradition by remaining committed to certain expressive capabilities and compositional 'states' first cultivated by earlier generations of modernists.[21] This expression takes the form of a real or metaphorical 'voice' which is often placed in precarious situations, most notably 'sonic states' that include the fragmentary, purity, flux, silence and the lament. Already we might recognize a parable of the late modern subject in this interpretive scheme: the supposedly direct sonic trace of the subject – the voice – imperilled (but also intensified in the case of the 'lament state' that he describes) by structural instabilities in its acoustic environment. The result is a relatively thriving millennial modernist musical culture in which the listener often encounters 'a mediated emotion or idea' which struggles, questions or reflects on the very notion of expression itself.[22] Although his focus is ostensibly on the processes

How does modernist music make you feel?

and content of subjective expression rather than the contours of sensation and feeling, Metzer nevertheless suggests in his introduction that:

> The tensions created by hindrances to the act of expression often translate into sensations of intensity. It should be acknowledged that intensity is hardly a new sensation for modernist music. Some critics of modernism have claimed that it is one of the few effects created by the music, so limited is its expressive palette. Intensity, though, can offer a rich palette, one full of different effects and gradations. [. . .] A range of other emotions and effects emerge in these pieces, including cold and warmth (Lachenmann), imposing weight (Saariaho), lyricism (Ligeti and Nono), emptiness (Lachenmann), loss (Nono), madness (Sciarrino), repose (Harvey), and sensuality (Neuwirth).[23]

Interestingly, in reversing the typical path from sensation to feeling, Metzer's model proposes that the *impediment* of the expressive voice leads to various sensations. The particular nature of the intensity comes after a reflection on its expressive and emotional power or, as is more often the case following his thesis, its vulnerability. The 'mediated emotions or ideas' are therefore placed in already meaningful situations which allow them to be amplified through deliberate frustrations of what might otherwise be their expressive or felt immediacy. Here we encounter the 'content theory' of emotion, which holds that while emotions combine both corporeal sensations and ideational reflection, the nature of the individual emotion arises principally from the beliefs and desires involved. As Rei Terada writes of this theory, '[a]lthough emotions are presented as blends of feelings and ideas, ideas are supposed to do the primary work of coloring emotions.'[24] In other words, initial sensations are vague or general, and it is the specific ideational content associated with contexts and/or objects of cognition that allows the emotion to be distinguished. Unlike the definitions of emotion we encountered earlier, here the emphasis is on ideas rather than the subject simply taking an external object as the focus for feelings. It is understandable that this particular theory of emotion should arise in discussions of music; after all, it is difficult to think how external objects would apply to musical listening beyond cases which involve the intentional representation of extra-musical phenomena.[25]

Metzer would appear to confirm his adherence to the content theory approach when he notes that 'intensity' is one of the few sensations supposedly offered up by late modernist music of the sort he discusses (or, conversely, one of the few 'affective' responses that remain in a musical tradition that has routinely sought to purge itself of codified emotional associations). Intensity is, however, more accurately described as a *degree* of sensation. It is also underdetermined without the necessary context in which its resulting feelings are made meaningful. The problems of affective terminology appear once again in the qualities that Metzer isolates, which range from actual emotions (loss, emptiness) and sensations (imposing weight) to more 'structurally' significant psychological conditions (madness), and other aesthetic qualities imbued with strongly embodied dimensions, whether the voice or touch (lyricism, sensuality). I would suggest that rather than being an initial physiological response to the act of listening, the intensity that Metzer describes – and which is perhaps best understood properly as affect in the sense outlined earlier – is one component, or at the very least a by-product, of expression. That the expressive content is privileged is understandable, however, given that Metzer focuses on a number of highly thematic modernist works including music theatre, vocal works with text, and pieces with relatively detailed programmes proffered by the composer. These 'modern states' also provide their own ready-made associations and meanings, which are heightened through what we might consider the 'tragic' nature of the hindered expressive 'voice' in each example. Metzer's focus on 'strained expression' suggests that the works in question belong to their own particular

313

strain of modernism. The composers in this particular study no doubt participate in the broader cultivation of an important and meaningful mood, and the author has certainly further enriched our understanding of this stream of late modernist music. Taking this observation further, we might even add that, despite his focus on music composed since 1980, Metzer's formulation of a specifically late modernist aesthetics nevertheless continues a longer-running modernist dialectic of expressive abstention and attrition. This point further reinforces his argument that modernism has persisted into the present and that musical modernism from 1980 onwards increasingly thematizes the difficulty of expression. We might press harder on the question of *why* expression is rendered difficult beyond the individual aims and programmes of these various composers. One reason is surely the intensification of the uncertainty surrounding the status of the subject that lies behind such expression. Metzer suggests that 'much more work needs to be done before we can appreciate the range of expressive positions in post-World War Two music and get beyond preconceived ideas of coldness and mechanism.'[26] I would take this further and say there remains much more work to be done on all affective aspects of later modernist music. As I suggest throughout this chapter, one way of approaching this is through asking what sort of subject is being mediated in various cases. Another is to excavate feeling from the embarrassment or terminological confusion with which it is often dealt in aesthetic statements and accounts of musical modernism; I provide a few examples of this in the following section of this chapter.

First, however, I would like to address the role of affect in another addition to late modernist studies. *The Pleasure of Modernist Music: Listening, Meaning, Intention, Ideology*, edited by Arved Ashby, makes a collective and concerted effort to re-evaluate entrenched understandings of modernist repertoires and formulate new meanings for modernist music. Although unable to fully engage all of its relevant contributions here, I would like to examine the role of pleasure that Ashby discusses in his introduction, as it offers a counterpoint to Metzer's focus on expressive 'hindrances'. Despite its title, this volume offers less a sustained inquiry into the emotional operations of modernist music than a collection of 'postmodern approaches', 'sketching out the possible significance of a repertory that in past discussions has been deemed either evasive or iconic, meaningless or beyond describable structural meaning'.[27] This interest in tracking and perhaps tacking down meaning within and around modernist music derives from the hermeneutic enterprises that helped reinvigorate the 'new musicology' of previous decades as well as more recent attempts to refute claims of modernism's inscrutability and indifference to listeners. Ashby's introduction reveals a somewhat ambivalent stance towards meaning despite its appearance in the subtitle of the collection. While several contributions seek to articulate new meanings for modernist music (the logic being that greater understanding brings greater enjoyment), Ashby holds out for its ineffable quality. This is achieved through the promise of 'pleasure', more precisely, the Lacanian jouissance that modernist music as such engenders. Despite acknowledging some of the challenges in ascribing a term developed for linguistic and psychoanalytic operations to music, Ashby suggests that

> because it is not a language, and also because it inspires unique feelings of empathy or even ownership [...] music is able to conquer the Real of jouissance, it offers a way of touching on and dislocating the jouissance that might otherwise invade us.[28]

Such 'affective capture' (to use a term of Massumi) is a tall order for modernist music, or for that matter any music, to fulfil. I agree that empathy and ecstasy are under-explored aspects of (late) modernism. But while jouissance can be a useful and popular concept it can be both too particular and too uncertain. Lacanian jouissance emerges – when and if it ever truly does 'appear' – primarily from drives. Sedgwick notes the distinction offered by Tomkins's affect theory in comparison to psychoanalysis, which relies on motivating drives: unlike the drives, 'any affect may have any "object". This is the basic source of complexity of human motivation and behavior.'[29] While the contexts which precede or accompany the irruption of jouissance can be infinitely inflected by various emotions and feelings which accompany the overt or sublimated expression of these drives, the result tends to revert to the on–off switch of desire and release. This points to another reason why Sedgwick seems to have been drawn to the work of Tomkins. When she was writing in the 1990s, in what now seems like a period of growing post-structural and psychoanalytic fatigue, affect opened up, in Sedgwick's words, 'the conceptual space between two and infinity'.[30] Therefore when Ashby writes that, '[c]ourtesy of obscurity and novelty, modern music becomes a bottomless well of possibility: a good compositional example offers new discoveries with each visit, always promising and never entirely satisfying any listener',[31] he wants to have it both ways: modernism offers unlimited possibilities but only one feeling remains at the end – that of not getting enough. (Incidentally this characterization of 'good' modernist composition may equally apply to 'good' Baroque, Classical or Romantic composition.) I am particularly sympathetic to Ashby's attempt to resurrect pleasure as a basis for discussions of modernist music and to his suggestion that modernist music is a 'bottomless well of possibility'. Yet framing it in terms of a desire and fulfilment binary, one which is hardly unique to modernism, tends to limit the possible responses to these two poles.

If these two studies seek out new meanings for modernist music, the growing interest in musical meaning in recent decades has begun to raise its absent supplement: experiences at the limits of, or beyond, linguistically formulated meaning.[32] Such a tension is revealed in Ashby's shuttling between meaning and the 'beyond' of jouissance. We find this back-and-forth repeated in Thompson and Biddle's introduction to *Sound, Music, Affect*, where the conjunction of sound and affect covers everything 'between the signifying and the sublime'.[33] This particular theoretical tension can be seen to have intensified more recently and more broadly across cultural discourses, animating debates during the last decade or so within musicology and the humanities, whether framed in terms of metaphysics versus presence, or hermeneutics and meaning versus performance and ineffability.[34] Feeling (as opposed to emotion or affect) reveals its problems and potential within such debates: feeling triangulates meaning and experience, belonging completely to neither one nor the other. Emotions can be meaningful and offer socially mediated codes of communication, but they are articulated after experience through aesthetics, or before, as part of the poetics of a work. Affects are the stuff of experience and circulate in the physiological and psychological space before conscious reflection and understanding but require a suspension or disavowal of the subject. Feeling mediates doubly: it allows us a space of experience between affect and emotion; and it also offers a way to shift between the immediacy or even memories of our experiences and the ways in which we think, feel and communicate them. Yet because of this concept's requirement of consciousness it also reintroduces the subject and all its attendant concerns.

Finding feeling in late modernist music

As I discussed in the preceding section, one of the ways to begin the work of addressing the aporias, challenges and complexities of affective issues in modernist music is through composers' writings on the topic. Despite an awareness of the 'poietic fallacy', when it comes to the affective dimension of their music, I believe the hesitancies and torsions around the discussion of affective experience readily demonstrate composers' own uncertainty. These moments therefore become productive sites for critically engaging the composer's own (textual) voice with our thoughts and experiences. In this section, I will briefly examine some of the ways in which affect, emotion and feeling operate in the compositional conception of two later modernist composers: Tristan Murail and Iannis Xenakis. Taken together their compositional output spans the second half of the twentieth century. Each has single-handedly cultivated or has become strongly identified with a particular modernist idiom – spectralism and stochastic music, respectively. Each has also written extensively on musical matters and on his own music in some detail. As neither tends to stress personal *expression* in compositional statements and writings, their writings provide an opportunity to excavate the role and operation of affect and feeling in later musical modernism.

Murail's essay 'Questions de cible' (translated as 'Target Practice') outlines many general and specific features of the composer's approach to composition. Early in the essay, Murail writes that his

> material is not a musical note, nor even a sound, but the *sensation* (*sentiment*) created by that note or sound. The material is not, for example, the harmonic spectrum (an object), but the harmonicity of that spectrum (a sense) and, further, the possibilities of transformation that it contains (the flight of the arrow).[35]

Here we encounter one of the frequent challenges in discussing 'affective qualities' in music when dealing with translation – something that can complicate interpretations of historical pieces and statements, as well as discussions of contemporary music. In this case, for example, *sentiment* can indeed mean sensation, as the translator has chosen, but it more commonly translates as 'feeling' or even simply 'sentiment'. Murail himself finds it necessary to clarify in a footnote what he means by 'sentiment'. The translator renders this as: 'Very generally, that which is sensed [*senti*], in other words, perceived and interpreted.'[36] This might seem like a very minor quibble, as feeling and sensation both involve similar, overlapping processes; many would consider the two to be synonymous. Translation inevitably involves making such decisions. Yet in a subtle but cumulative way, these decisions contribute to the gradual denigration of the affective dimensions (feeling in this case) of modernist music. I do not wish to impute too much intention to the translator's choice of words in this particular instance, but one can easily imagine that in this context the somewhat more impersonal blending of corporeality and consciousness involved with 'sensation' would be generally more acceptable to many readers than the subjective murkiness of 'feeling'. There are, nonetheless, grounds to suggest that Murail does in fact mean something closer to feeling precisely because of the additional component of interpretation that follows perception in his definition. Were it 'mere' sensation that Murail were talking about, perception would be a sufficient response. (Of course, what Murail considers to be involved in 'interpretation' is another important question; the 'perceived' seems straightforward enough in the above context.) The sense of amplification of the richness of sound is therefore transferable as well to an amplification of feeling.

Consider the beginning of Murail's seminal spectralist composition, *Gondwana* (1980) for orchestra, in which a single chord is gradually transformed. In adapting the principles of frequency modulation – a method of tone-production often used in digital synthesizers – to orchestral composition, the composer creates complex, bell-like sonorities. The slowly evolving structure of the piece provides a parallel to the massive geological processes which led to the formation of the ancient super-continent of Gondwana. I do not think the intention is to depict or represent this geological process but rather to create for the listener both the impression of 'heightened' listening (i.e. bringing to the 'surface' the normally barely perceptible inharmonic elements of a sound) and the feeling of slow, 'tectonic' shifts. We might again recall Altieri's earlier discussion of how modernist writers sought to establish a close continuity between

How does modernist music make you feel?

sensation and interpretation, but one in which feeling would be separated from specific emotions and affective states could be developed that were uncontaminated by social and historical baggage.[37] As he writes, 'feelings could be honored for a subtlety and fluidity impossible to stage within socially approved abstractions. When feelings did involve intentionality, they contoured the imagination to the sensation and not the sensation to gesture and posture and belief.'[38]

If we accept that Murail indeed means something closer to this conception when he writes of 'feeling' (*sentiment*), we can also recognize the compositional techniques of Murail's early works such as *Gondwana* – as well as those of other so-called spectral composers – as continuing and enriching modernist aesthetics not only through their scientism and their exploration of the qualities of sound, but also because of their close focus on a type of pathway towards feeling, one that closely tracks sensation and indeed grows directly out of it. At the same time, we might also note that even if Murail's understanding of 'feeling' were closer to perception, he still retains, implicitly, the category of the subject. While it may be less obvious in the case of *Gondwana*, it becomes especially evident in more recent pieces like *Serendib* – whose title refers, according to Julian Anderson's note on the work, to 'the mythical name given by Sindbad the Sailor to the Island of Ceylon' – in which we are not far from the aesthetics of programme music.[39] Here the listener is clearly meant to be a phenomenological subject, and the experience of this piece enacts a transposition of a discontinuous journey through a quasi-mythological, entirely exoticized South Asian landscape.

Murail's retention of the subject contrasts with the lack of an implied subject – or, perhaps more accurately, an ambiguously collectivized or evacuated subjectivity – in the work of Iannis Xenakis. Xenakis's 1963 monograph, *Formalized Music*, is devoted to the mathematical and stochastic formulas employed in the creation of his own compositions. Its opening pages provide a number of fascinating pronouncements, musings and metaphors for thinking about late modernist music of the sort he created. He begins by merging aesthetics and psychology with a dose of nineteenth-century Idealist philosophy:

> Art, and above all, music has a fundamental function, which is to catalyze the sublimation that it can bring about through all means of expression. It must aim through fixations which are landmarks to draw towards a total exaltation in which the individual mingles, losing his consciousness in a truth immediate, rare, enormous, and perfect. If a work of art succeeds in this undertaking even for a single moment, it attains its goal. This tremendous truth is not made of objects, emotions, or sensations; it is beyond these, as Beethoven's Seventh Symphony is beyond music. This is why art can lead to realms that religion still occupies for some people.[40]

I will pass over issues of translation in this particular passage, as well as the general theory of art expounded (sublimation), Xenakis's theory of musical content and the echoes of Wagner and of Wagner's own philosophical forebears. Despite claiming that the substance of a 'successful' work is beyond objects, emotions and sensations, Xenakis nevertheless notes that natural events may provide a pathway to this 'tremendous truth': 'the collision of hail or rain with hard surfaces, or the song of cicadas in a summer field'.[41] From here, he cuts to a very different example: an anecdote evidently drawn from his experience in the Greek Resistance during the Second World War and one which he would repeat or allude to in interviews and writings throughout his career.

> Everyone has observed the sonic phenomena of a political crowd of dozens or hundreds of thousands of people. The human river shouts a slogan in a uniform rhythm.

Then another slogan springs from the head of the demonstration; it spreads towards the tail, replacing the first. A wave of transition thus passes from the head to the tail. The clamor fills the city, and the inhibiting force of voice and rhythm reaches a climax. It is an event of great power and beauty in its ferocity. Then the impact between the demonstrators and the enemy occurs. The perfect rhythm of the last slogan breaks up in a huge cluster of chaotic shouts, which also spreads to the tail. Imagine, in addition, the reports of dozens of machine guns and the whistle of bullets adding their punctuations to this total disorder. The crowd is then rapidly dispersed, and after sonic and visual hell follows a detonating calm, full of despair, dust, and death. The statistical laws of these events, separated from their political or moral context, are the same as those of the cicadas or the rain. They are the laws of the passage from complete order to total disorder in a continuous or explosive manner. They are stochastic laws.[42]

The subtraction of the 'political and moral context' from the scene described by Xenakis is remarkable given its extreme violence. His equivocation of warfare, cicadas and rain relies upon understanding each as phenomena, as something essentially a-human or, at the very least, eschewing individual agency in favour of a swarming collectivity. This de-subjectivation seems echoed in his earlier somewhat extreme comments about the individual mingling with a mass and of losing consciousness. Yet the image is powerful precisely because of the human emotions – political opposition and eventually despair – that accompany and animate the scene. In turn, Xenakis attempts to translate or transmit something of the *intensity* of this experience – although perhaps not its precise emotions – in his music. This is accomplished through a deliberately ambivalent approach to referentiality on the part of the composer. Consider, for example, the opening of *Pithoprakta* (1955–56), scored for forty-six string instruments, two trombones, xylophone and woodblock. The piece utilizes the stochastic approach described by the composer and introduces several questions about which affects, feelings and emotions the listener experiences. *Pithoprakta* begins with string players striking the backs of their instruments to produce wooden, percussive sounds whose distribution and attack within fixed time units is treated statistically. The progression of events is unpredictable but overall shapes and tendencies emerge: there is an initial burst of activity which dissipates and then intensifies as the string players gradually introduce *glissandi* alongside the knocks and *battuti*. Through the course of the piece, a number of different techniques are employed and layered in a similar manner.[43] If the first set of events – wooden knocks and *battuti* – suggest rain or hail, as in Xenakis's own analogy, how do we respond to the *glissandi*, which seem to mimic human voices or gestures? Alternatively, one might imagine, in light of Xenakis's comments regarding political crowds, that the percussive sounds that open *Pithoprakta* recall gunshots. Clearly part of the appeal of these stochastic works by Xenakis is the way in which they invite certain analogies – analogies that are even provided by the composer in his writings. But how, then, should a listener respond when these analogies move beyond benign forces of nature (rain) to deadly human force?

Taking Jacques Attali's controversial thesis that forms of musical organization predict those of future socio-political organization, Xenakis's experiments in shaping musical intensity might be understood to anticipate aspects of the more recent military projects in sound warfare that Steve Goodman, following a Deleuzian model of pre-personal affect, has described. On the other hand, in an essay by Milan Kundera, 'Xenakis, "prophète de l'insensibilité"', the exiled Czech novelist describes the 'bizarre solace' that he experienced upon hearing the composer's music after arriving in France. One assumes he deems it necessary to qualify this feeling as *bizarre* given Xenakis's predilection for dynamic sound masses, violent gestures and multisensory environments. Kundera's title itself refers to an essay by Carl Jung on James Joyce's *Ulysses*.

How does modernist music make you feel?

Jung offers a further dimension, as his own response strikes a somewhat ambivalent tone by suggesting that the 'insensibility' he finds in *Ulysses* is hardly an ideal but rather a compensatory stance for the populist bellicosity stoked by war-time propaganda. Likewise, Kundera traces his aversion to artistic 'hypersensibilité' (as with the Murail example, one could translate this simply as 'hyper-sensibility' or, perhaps more accurately in English, 'extreme feeling'; the difference in my opinion is negligible in this instance) to the legacies of the Communist regime and to the Prague Spring of 1968. We can see with Xenakis's stochastic compositions and the sorts of sonic events encountered in *Pithoprakta* that the transition from affect to emotion is very much dependent on what sorts of references the listener brings to the experience. This is hardly a remarkable observation with regard to modernist music. More interesting is the curious parallel between Xenakis's and Kundera's accounts of stochastic music: both must subtract the individual subject in order to 'sanitize' their own listening. They remove actual emotions, whether resulting from personal memories or based on codified musical signifiers, in order to create a 'properly' aesthetic experience and in order that this experience not be co-opted by other subjects with instrumental intentions (such as in the case of the propaganda that Kundera mentions).

Ultimately what we find in both the Xenakis and the Murail examples is that both affect and feeling play a rather important role for both composers and one that is seldom if ever remarked upon. This is not immediately apparent but is nonetheless revealed through examining their writings, specific compositions and our responses to them. We can also recognize a continuation of the modernist impulse to seek relatively direct pathways to feeling – the 'contouring' of feeling to sensation rather than to an emotional object – such as Altieri has observed in the case of modernist poetry. Yet this often underplayed affective dimension simultaneously reveals an anxiety around the subject that no doubt contributes in part to the neglect that has been paid the former. The particular approach I have briefly demonstrated in this section is, however, just one among many possible routes for approaching the link between subjectivity and the affective qualities of modernist composition. No doubt pursuing any number of other issues raised in the preceding sections may lead down other fruitful paths towards understanding this link. What we encounter in the two brief examples I have discussed – and no doubt a great deal many other compositions in a later modernist tradition – is not a question of what Richard Taruskin has described as the avant-garde's 'impersonal' mode of composition (I suspect that, for Xenakis in particular, mediating the experience of armed conflict *was* rather personal), or even a case of feeling versus 'non-feeling': Murail's *sensible* versus Kundera's *insensible*.[44] You are clearly meant to feel something listening to these pieces; quite a few things, I suspect. But don't expect a modernist to tell you exactly *how* you are supposed to feel.

The declining yet inextinguishable subject

As I have stressed, one of affect studies' most productive contributions to music studies is its attention to the specific categories and valences of affective experiences. Scholarship on musical modernism, specifically, stands to benefit from its perceived lack of emotional interest, intention and outcome, and from the evident confusion which attends the terms used to talk about these aspects. I have chosen to frame this chapter with an appeal to the question of the subject, however, for this problematic though unavoidable concept lingers behind any attempts to first parse and then elaborate the components of affective phenomena. One of the most significant and widespread – though not always theoretically coordinated – intellectual developments of the last century and a half has been the scepticism of the subject of the Cartesian cogito and of the division of body and mind implied therein. While alternately premodern and postmodern critiques can be readily proffered, we can single out the triumvirate of Nietzsche, Marx and Freud – whom Paul Ricoeur

319

famously described as the 'school of suspicion' – for their role in undermining the notion of the transcendent subject during the late nineteenth and twentieth centuries.[45] Ricoeur suggested that each of these three figures of modernity teaches us to regard with suspicion our conscious understandings, judgements and experiences. Elizabeth Grosz singles out the last of these three as especially consequential to the uncertainty of the transcendent subject:

> More directly or explicitly than either Nietzsche or Marx, Freud challenges Descartes' conflation of consciousness with subjectivity. His understanding of the unconscious, sexuality, psychical representations, and the processes involved in the constitution of the subject challenges the Cartesian subject's status as the foundation and source of knowledge.[46]

Though mainstream psychology has not been kind to Freud over the last several decades, relegating him, whether rightly or, more likely, wrongly to this history of ideas, the subject remains in peril by the rise of neuroscience and its focus on revealing the preconscious mechanisms in an ever-increasing number of social and cultural practices.

Another more recent source of uncertainty surrounding the subject has been the result of historical research, particularly that of Michel Foucault, who illuminated the historical specificity of the discursive formation of the concept of Man.[47] If we look further afield, we can also locate a sceptical stance towards the subject cutting across other forms of cultural expression, and not only intellectual disciplines such as history, philosophy and psychology. In asking *what comes after the subject?*, Alain Badiou reminds us of poetry's contribution to this philosophical question:

> on the basis of the hypothesis that modern thinking requires its continuation: what concept of the subject succeeds the one whose trajectory can be traced out from Descartes to Husserl, and which wore thin and fell into ruin between Nietzsche and Heidegger, as well as throughout the whole of what should be called 'the age of the poets' (Hölderlin, Hopkins, Mallarmé, Rimbaud, Trakl, Pessoa, Mandelstam, Celan)?[48]

The present essay might be considered as one response to this inquiry from the perspective of modernist music studies, albeit one that does not provide a direct answer to Badiou's question so much as it asks whether and how the question might not also be applied to the aesthetic programmes of later modernist composers and the listener responses to their music.

Given the lack of a ready answer to Badiou's question, we might, following Gianni Vattimo, accept that the present-day subject is – in whatever possibly myriad ways – *weakened*. For Vattimo it is not so much that we have abandoned the subject completely but that, following Heidegger, it and so many other metaphysical concepts simply don't hold sway in late modernity as they once did. In the introduction to the 1981 collection of essays, *Weak Thought (Pensiero debole)*, Vattimo, like many philosophers of the twentieth century, recognizes the compromised history of the Enlightenment and the structure of the subject that emerged in its wake. Rather than urging a conservative resistance to the diminishment of metaphysical concepts or a postmodern exuberance in their elimination, he encourages us to accept this strangely sustained condition of permanent decline: 'Rationality must de-potentiate itself, give way; it should not be afraid to draw back toward the supposed area of shadow, it should not let itself be paralyzed by the loss of the luminous, stable, Cartesian point of reference'. As he goes on to explain,

> 'Weak thought' is thus certainly a metaphor and, to some extent a paradox. [. . .] It points out a path, it indicates a direction of the route; it is a way that forks from the no

How does modernist music make you feel?

matter how masked hegemonic rationality [*ragione-dominio*] from which, nevertheless, we all know a definitive farewell is impossible.[49]

If the human subject as we know or once knew it has slipped further from immediate view, Vattimo's conception of 'hermeneutical Being' proposes, if not a replacement, at least an orientation to the world and to history that can take account of this *receding* but, for the time being, seemingly indestructible humanist subject. In other words, the concept of the subject is weakened but it is not eliminated altogether. For Vattimo as previously for Heidegger, the decline of the Cartesian and Christian subject is related to the crisis of humanism, itself tied to the crisis of metaphysics. According to Vattimo, for Heidegger, humanism becomes synonymous with metaphysics. As Vattimo writes elsewhere,

> inasmuch as it is only in the perspective provided by metaphysics as a general theory of the Being of entities – which is thought of in 'objective' terms, thus forgetting ontological difference – that humanity can discover a definition on the basis of which it can 'construct' and educate itself through a *Bildung*. [. . .] There is no humanism without bringing into play a metaphysics in which the human subject determines a role for itself which is necessarily central or exclusive.[50]

At the same time, according to Vattimo, we are unable to give a final farewell to metaphysical thought; we accept metaphysics as long as its reduction of everything to the human subject itself remains hidden from view. When instead the reductive nature of metaphysical thought is revealed explicitly, as happens in the work of Nietzsche, 'metaphysics has arrived at the moment of its decline, and with it – as can be seen every day – humanism has also arrived at the moment of its decline'.[51] So along with the subject, humanism and metaphysics find themselves in this strangely suspended state. Vattimo's position is, I believe, an important one to keep in mind for, unlike, say, the work of many French poststructuralists who often sought to think in terms already beyond these concepts, Vattimo reminds us that outside the academy – and even in its few remaining humanist nooks – it remains this 'weakened' but not yet eliminated or surpassed condition of the subject through which we continue to live and function.

Vattimo's notion of the weakened subject is, nonetheless, already more than thirty years old. Has the subject's situation changed much? The rise of affect studies during the last decade or so has been an important development in addressing – often obliquely – questions of the subject's status, constitution and necessity as a concept. Part of my intention in this chapter has been to redirect the lessons of affect studies back towards these questions. This seems to me to be pressing, given that we can detect an ongoing trend in much humanities and social science research: a sort of bifurcation in critical discourses between on the one hand wholly supplanting the subject in favour of pre-subjective affect and, on the other hand, reinstating the subject (perhaps inadvertently at times) through conjunctions of identity, subjectivity and 'subject positions'. Although by now many have contributed to overviews of the so-called affective turn and the reasons for its emergence, relevance and popularity, I suggest that one broad way of conceiving the import of a focus on affect is as a way of productively sidestepping the otherwise unresolved questions of the subject's ontological and epistemological status in late modernity.[52] Just as the subject persists, however problematically, feeling, as a point between pre-subjective affect and socially expressed emotion, also reveals itself as a concept that is both challenging and necessary – a way to understand forms of *attachment* to the subject and what these attachments might mean. As Vattimo reminds us, such metaphysical attachments, however tired or strained, continue to characterize the condition of late modernity.

Trent Leipert

Notes

1 Marie Thompson and Ian Biddle, 'Introduction: Somewhere Between the Signifying and the Sublime', in *Sound, Music, Affect: Theorizing Sonic Experience*, ed. Marie Thompson and Ian Biddle (London: Bloomsbury, 2013), 23.
2 Eric Shouse, 'Feeling, Emotion, Affect', *M/C Journal* 8, no. 6 (2005), http://journal.media-culture.org.au/0512/03-shouse.php (accessed 16 January 2016).
3 Charles Altieri, *The Particulars of Rapture* (Ithaca, NY: Cornell University Press, 2003), 50.
4 Eve Kosofsky Sedgwick, *Touching Feeling: Affect, Pedagogy, Performativity* (Durham, NC: Duke University Press, 2003).
5 Silvan Tomkins, 'What Are Affects?' in *Shame and Its Sisters: A Silvan Tomkins Reader*, ed. Eve Kosofsky Sedgwick and Adam Frank (Durham, NC: Duke University Press, 1995), 33–74.
6 See for example, Brian Massumi, *Parables for the Virtual: Movement, Affect, Sensation* (Durham, NC: Duke University Press, 2002).
7 Gilles Deleuze and Félix Guattari, *What Is Philosophy?* trans. Graham Burchell III (New York: Columbia University Press, 1994), 167.
8 See, for example, Slavoj Žižek, *Organs Without Bodies: On Deleuze and Consequences* (London: Routledge, 2004). A similar critical impulse runs throughout his critiques of Hardt and Negri's use of Deleuzian concepts to mount counter-capitalist movements.
9 Lauren Berlant, 'Intuitionists: History and the Affective Event', *American Literary History* 20, no. 4 (2008), 846.
10 Ibid., 846–47.
11 This is not to say that a musical work may not be considered a type of documentation or that engagement with literature may not be considered a type of affective event. But I think the ontological and epistemological differences in the two art forms makes the above point fairly uncontroversial as do the important points raised by Wanzo.
12 Rebecca Wanzo, 'Against Proper Affective Objects', *American Quarterly* 61, no. 4 (2009), 967–68.
13 Steve Goodman, *Sonic Warfare: Sound, Affect, and the Ecology of Fear* (Cambridge, MA: MIT Press, 2010).
14 Ibid., 1–11.
15 Klaus R. Scherer, 'Which Emotions Can Be Induced by Music? What Are the Underlying Mechanisms? And How Can We Measure Them?' *Journal of New Music Research* 33, no. 3 (2004), 239–51.
16 Shouse, 'Feeling, Emotion, Affect'.
17 Altieri, *The Particulars of Rapture*, 2.
18 Antonio Damasio, *The Feeling of What Happens: Body and Emotion in the Making of Consciousness* (New York: Harcourt Brace, 1999), 36.
19 Scherer, 'Which Emotions?' 239.
20 See for example Björn Heile, ed., *The Modernist Legacy: Essays on New Music* (Farnham: Ashgate, 2009).
21 David Metzer, *Musical Modernism at the Turn of the Twenty-First Century* (Cambridge: Cambridge University Press, 2009).
22 Ibid., 21–26.
23 Ibid., 26.
24 Rei Terada, *Feeling in Theory: Emotion after the 'Death of the Subject'* (Cambridge, MA: Harvard University Press, 2001), 19.
25 I am ignoring here the complicated case of music that is associated by the listener with personal memories.
26 Metzer, *Musical Modernism*, 19.
27 Arved Ashby, 'Introduction', in *The Pleasure of Modernist Music: Listening, Meaning, Intention, Ideology*, ed. Arved Ashby (Rochester, NY: University of Rochester Press, 2005), 2.
28 Ibid., 4.
29 Eve Kosofsky Sedgwick and Adam Frank, 'Shame in the Cybernetic Fold', *Critical Inquiry* 21, no. 2 (1995), 503. As Sedgwick further observes, 'in a refusal of the terms of behaviorism, Tomkins describes the affect system as a whole as having "no single 'output'"; and also unlike the drives, "affective amplification is indifferent to the means–end difference". It is these specifications that make affect theory such a useful site for resistance to the teleological presumptions of the many sorts historically embedded in the disciplines of psychology.'
30 Ibid., 512.
31 Ashby, 'Introduction', 5.

How does modernist music make you feel?

32 Although not articulated in terms of the affective supplement to linguistic signification, calls for attention to music's presence rely indirectly on a typical poststructural understanding of music as a limit case for signification.

33 See Thompson and Biddle, 'Introduction', 24–25.

34 See Carolyn Abbate, 'Music: Drastic or Gnostic?' *Critical Inquiry* 30, no. 3 (2004), 505–36.

35 Tristan Murail, 'Target Practice', trans. Joshua Cody, *Contemporary Music Review* 24, nos. 2–3 (2005), 149–50. The original French reads: 'Il me semble que similairement mon matériau n'est pas la note de musique, ni même le son musical, mais le sentiment créé par cette note ou par ce son. Le matériau n'est pas le spectre harmonique (objet), mais l'harmonicité de ce spectre (sentiment), et plus encore, les possibilités de changement qu'il recèle (le mouvement de la flèche).' Tristan Murail, 'Questions de cible', in *Modèles et artifices*, ed. Pierre Michel (Strasbourg: Presses Universitaires de Strasbourg, 2004), 46.

36 Murail, 'Target Practice', 170.

37 Altieri, *The Particulars of Rapture*, 50.

38 Ibid., 50–51.

39 Julian Anderson, disc notes, *Tristan Murail: Serendib – L'esprit des dunes – Désintégrations*, Ensemble Inter-Contemporain, conducted by David Robertson. CD, Accord 465 3052 (1996), 17; http://www.tristan-murail.com/en/oeuvre-fiche.php?cotage=27525 (accessed 9 May 2018).

40 Iannis Xenakis, *Formalized Music: Thought and Mathematics in Composition* (Bloomington: Indiana University Press, 1971), 1.

41 Ibid., 1.

42 Ibid., 1–2.

43 For a formal and technical overview of *Pithoprakta*, see also James Harley, *Xenakis: His Life in Music* (New York: Routledge, 2004), 13–16.

44 Richard Taruskin, *Music in the Late Twentieth Century*, rev. ed., vol. 5, *The Oxford History of Western Music* (New York: Oxford University Press, 2010), 41 and 64.

45 Paul Ricoeur, *Freud and Philosophy*, trans. Denis Savage (New Haven, CT: Yale University Press, 1970), 32.

46 Elizabeth Grosz, *Jacques Lacan: A Feminist Introduction* (New York: Routledge, 1990), 2.

47 As Foucault famously and controversially stated in *The Order of Things*, 'It is not so long ago when the world, its order, and human beings existed, but man did not'; Michel Foucault, *The Order of Things* (New York: Random House, 1994), 322.

48 Alain Badiou, 'On a Finally Objectless Subject', in *Who Comes After the Subject?* ed. Eduardo Cadava, Peter Connor and Jean-Luc Nancy (London: Routledge, 2001), 24.

49 Gianni Vattimo, 'Dialectics, Difference, Weak Thought', in *Weak Thought*, ed. Gianni Vattimo and Pier Aldo Rovatti and trans. Peter Carravetta (Albany: SUNY Press, 2012), 41.

50 Vattimo, 'The Crisis of Humanism', in *The End of Modernity: Nihilism and Hermeneutics in Postmodern Culture*, trans. Jon R. Snyder (Baltimore: Johns Hopkins University Press, 1988), 32.

51 Ibid.

52 For an excellent overview and critique of the 'affective turn' see Ruth Leys, 'The Turn to Affect: A Critique', *Critical Inquiry* 37, no. 3 (2011), 434–72.

Bibliography

Abbate, Carolyn. 'Music: Drastic or Gnostic?' *Critical Inquiry* 30, no. 3 (2004): 505–36.

Altieri, Charles. *The Particulars of Rapture*. Ithaca, NY: Cornell University Press, 2003.

Ashby, Arved, ed. *The Pleasure of Modernist Music: Listening, Meaning, Intention, Ideology*. Rochester, NY: University of Rochester Press, 2005.

Berlant, Lauren. 'Intuitionists: History and the Affective Event'. *American Literary History* 20, no. 4 (2008): 845–60.

Cadava, Eduardo, Peter Connor and Jean-Luc Nancy, eds. *Who Comes After the Subject?* London: Routledge, 2001.

Damasio, Antonio. *The Feeling of What Happens: Body and Emotion in the Making of Consciousness*. New York: Harcourt Brace, 1999.

Deleuze, Gilles, and Félix Guattari. *What Is Philosophy?* Translated by Graham Burchell III. New York: Columbia University Press, 1994.

Foucault, Michel. *The Order of Things*. New York: Random House, 1994.

Goodman, Steve. *Sonic Warfare: Sound, Affect, and the Ecology of Fear*. Cambridge, MA: MIT Press, 2010.

Grosz, Elizabeth. *Jacques Lacan: A Feminist Introduction*. New York: Routledge, 1990.

Harley, James. *Xenakis: His Life in Music*. New York: Routledge, 2004.

Heile, Björn, ed. *The Modernist Legacy: Essays on New Music*. Farnham and Burlington, VT: Ashgate, 2009.

Kundera, Milan. 'Xenakis, "prophète de l'insensibilité"'. In *Regards sur Iannis Xenakis*, edited by Hugues Gerhards, 21–24. Paris: Stock, 1981.

Leys, Ruth. 'The Turn to Affect: A Critique'. *Critical Inquiry* 37, no. 3 (2011): 434–72.

Massumi, Brian. *Parables for the Virtual: Movement, Affect, Sensation*. Durham, NC: Duke University Press, 2002.

Metzer, David. *Musical Modernism at the Turn of the Twenty-First Century*. Cambridge: Cambridge University Press, 2009.

Murail, Tristan. 'Target Practice', translated by Joshua Cody. *Contemporary Music Review* 24, nos. 2–3 (2005): 149–71.

Ricoeur, Paul. *Freud and Philosophy*. Translated by Denis Savage. New Haven, CT: Yale University Press, 1970.

Scherer, Klaus R. 'Which Emotions Can Be Induced by Music? What Are the Underlying Mechanisms? And How Can We Measure Them?' *Journal of New Music Research* 33, no. 3 (2004): 239–51.

Sedgwick, Eve Kosofsky. *Touching Feeling: Affect, Pedagogy, Performativity*. Durham, NC: Duke University Press, 2003.

Sedgwick, Eve Kosofsky, and Adam Frank, eds. *Shame and Its Sisters: A Silvan Tomkins Reader*. Durham, NC: Duke University Press, 1995.

Shouse, Eric. 'Feeling, Emotion, Affect.' *M/C Journal* 8, no. 6 (2005). http://journal.media–culture.org.au/0512/03-shouse.php (accessed 16 January 2016).

Taruskin, Richard. *Music in the Late Twentieth Century*. Rev. ed. Vol. 5. *The Oxford History of Western Music*. New York: Oxford University Press, 2010.

Terada, Rei. *Feeling in Theory: Emotion after the 'Death of the Subject'*. Cambridge, MA: Harvard University Press, 2001.

Thompson, Marie, and Ian Biddle, eds. *Sound, Music, Affect: Theorizing Sonic Experience*. London: Bloomsbury, 2013.

Vattimo, Gianni. *The End of Modernity: Nihilism and Hermeneutics in Postmodern Culture*. Translated by Jon R. Snyder. Baltimore: Johns Hopkins University Press, 1988.

Vattimo, Gianni, and Pier Aldo Rovatti, eds. *Weak Thought*. Translated by Peter Carravetta. Albany, NY: SUNY Press, 2012.

Wanzo, Rebecca. 'Against Proper Affective Objects'. *American Quarterly* 61, no. 4 (2009): 967–78.

Xenakis, Iannis. *Formalized Music: Thought and Mathematics in Composition*. Bloomington: Indiana University Press, 1971.

Žižek, Slavoj. *Organs Without Bodies: On Deleuze and Consequences*. London: Routledge, 2004.

PART 3

Practices

14

BETWEEN MODERNISM AND POSTMODERNISM

Structure and expression in John Adams, Kaija Saariaho and Thomas Adès

Alastair Williams

To adapt a term coined by Theodor W. Adorno, modernism and postmodernism might be understood as the 'torn halves' of a music that combines structural innovation with expressive meaning – torn because the two halves are seldom neatly divided.[1] At a particular stage in the mid-1990s, postmodernism seemed to have become the dominant discourse, whether in confrontation or in dialogue with post-war modernism. Although postmodernism as a historical moment has now passed, it survives as a pressure that operates within modernism to ensure that innovation and communication work together. Understood as a reconfiguration or expansion of post-war modernism, postmodernism exists alongside (or within) modernism as the possibility for structural invention to gain increased social meaning. One of the ways in which postmodernism has fulfilled this potential is by rewriting post-war modernism in a manner that includes its own early twentieth-century history, which itself includes the legacy of Romanticism. This chapter considers postmodernism both as a historical moment and as a potential force that acts within modernism to expand its range of expression.

There is not much agreement about when postmodernism, as a historical moment, started, and this chapter does not aim to resolve that question. However, in the influential article that became the first chapter of his landmark book on postmodernism, Fredric Jameson, who is as definitive on this undefinitive subject as anyone, indicates that the idea can be traced back to the early 1960s.[2] This view remains valid, though it is worth noting the extent to which the social unrest of 1968 served to channel an emerging politics of the individual. By the time that Jameson's book appeared in 1991, postmodernism had become such a dominant discourse that it seemed as if modernism might fade away. However, that was not what happened: postmodernism turned out to be a corrective to modernism instead of its replacement, allowing modernism to become a more inclusive and flexible aesthetic.[3] Modernism, therefore, lives on, but in a transformed state.[4]

Historically, there is music that might be labelled 'postmodernist'. Yet the need to establish what is modernist or postmodernist now seems less urgent, for the simple reason that postmodernism has provided modernism with the means to broaden its own self-definition. Discussing the music of John Zorn, which combines jazz improvisation with an eclectic mix of musical genres in a style that evokes the rapid disjunctions of television channel-hopping, Richard Taruskin comments: 'The contradiction, the seesaw between social alienation and social communion, was as old as Romanticism itself. Postmodernism seems to have encouraged communion to reassert its rights.'[5] Put differently, a postmodernist willingness to engage with the semantics of music has equipped modernism to communicate more widely by looking beyond matters of construction.

This expanded communication is a central concern in the present chapter, which addresses the relationship between modernism and postmodernism in four areas. The first is postminimalism, as represented particularly by John Adams's *Harmonielehre*, a work symbolic, in style and date, of the age of postmodernism. Specifically, postminimalism seeks to combine the perception of process with expanded harmonic resources and to access the semiotics of affect. Hence it reconfigures the minimalist preoccupation with process while rejecting the interiority of expressionist emotion. The second topic is spectralist music, for which Kaija Saariaho's *Lichtbogen* serves as an example. Spectralism seeks to combine technological progress with discernible textural transformation, in an attempt to move away from what, in Gérard Grisey's view, is the industrial abstraction of serialism.

The third focus is historical reference, as explored through the distinctly non-confrontational kind of pluralism – more a simultaneity or an intertextuality – found in Thomas Adès's *Asyla*. This is music that revisits both Romanticism and early modernism so as to reconfigure pre-existing meanings. A topic that runs through all three of these sections is a re-emergence of the individual, through an emphasis on perception in the case of postminimalism and spectralism, and through a stress on perception and subjectivity in the case of Adès. The fourth section of the chapter is devoted to musicology and considers how it has expanded its understanding of social meaning in music. Here again subjectivity is a primary consideration, in terms of how people interact with music and what it means to them.

Minimalism and postminimalism: process and affect

In an essay from 1952, John Cage described the compositional process of the large-scale piano score *Music of Changes* (1951), conveying the aesthetic outcome as follows: 'It is thus possible to make a musical composition the continuity of which is free of individual taste and memory (psychology) and also of the literature and "traditions" of the art.'[6] The merit of this approach is that its intention to rid music of established conventions creates an opportunity for the unexpected to happen. The price it pays for this aim, though, is that a preoccupation with construction depletes music of subjectivity. Although Cage's proposition is extreme, it represents a certain strand of musical modernism in the 1950s. Traces of it are to be found in the emphasis on process in minimalism, namely the idea of putting a procedure in place and then letting it run its course. Such a notion is expounded by Steve Reich in his 1968 essay 'Music as a Gradual Process', where he writes: 'musical processes can give one a direct contact with the impersonal and also a kind of complete control'.

In the same essay Reich criticizes the *I Ching* method Cage deployed in *Music of Changes*, because 'the processes he used were compositional ones that could not be heard when the piece was performed'. By contrast, Reich writes, 'I am interested in perceptible processes. I want to be able to hear processes happening throughout the sounding music.'[7] The phase shifts and the repeating patterns can indeed be detected in an early score such as *Piano Phase* (1967). Reich in 1968 would not have been able to draw on postmodernism as a developed aesthetic, since it remained nascent at that stage. Nevertheless, although his idea of enhancing communication is conceived structurally, it does at least carry the potential for a more reciprocal interaction between composer and listener.

Keith Potter has argued that 'the early phases of American musical minimalism' can 'be interpreted as essentially modernist, along the radical, "alternative" lines developed by Nyman's definition of an "experimental" aesthetic'.[8] Whatever the strengths of this perspective, there is merit also in the view that all minimalism is postmodernist, because of the emphasis it places on the perception of structure.[9] Either way, there is a degree of consensus that 'classic' American minimalism had run its course by around 1975, after which pivotal figures such as Steve Reich and Philip Glass set about expanding and diversifying its practices.[10] In accordance with this framework, John Adams has stated: 'what sets me apart from Reich and Glass is that I am not modernist. I embrace the whole musical past, and I don't have the kind of refined, systematic language that they have.'[11] In adopting this position, Adams implicitly aligns himself with postmodernism, though he does not use the term, and he simultaneously offers a distinctive view of modernism.

Adams is right to distinguish between his own practice and the aims of an earlier stage of minimalism, for his music is both less systematic than earlier manifestations of minimalism and embraces the past more readily. Jonathan Bernard puts the matter rather more critically, by arguing that 'born ten years later than Glass and Reich, John Adams encountered minimalism principally as a style, having missed the formative years of the aesthetic in downtown New York during the mid- to late 1960s.' The result, for Bernard, is that Adams deploys minimalism 'as a technique, divorced from any aesthetic basis',[12] and because it is merely a style, rather than an ingrained aesthetic, he is able to modify it at will and to blend it with neo-Romantic harmony. It would be easy to recast that perspective so that the minimalism of the 1960s emerges as authentic and modernist, while the later minimalism of Adams becomes less genuine and therefore postmodernist. What such a dichotomy would obscure, though, is that it may well have been Adams's lack of attachment to the minimalist aesthetic that permitted him to create a more hybrid form of it. The quality that most clearly distinguishes Adams's music from the early minimalist style is its use of the expressive gestures of Romantic harmony. Therefore, if minimalism pre-1975 is considered (despite its modernist attributes) to be postmodernist on account of its interest in detectable structures, then the expressive qualities of Adams's music mark a second stage in postmodernism, one that might be associated with a broader willingness to engage with the past.

Moreover, the idea of a shift within postmodernism receives support from the term 'post-minimalism', with which Adams is often associated. According to Kyle Gann, the critic John Rockwell may well have coined the term, having used it first in 1981 and applied it specifically to John Adams in 1983.[13] For Gann himself, postminimalism as a category evokes music that is of a fixed duration rather than consisting of an unspecified number of cycles, on the basis that works of a defined length (such as those of Glass and Reich in the 1980s) are more easily assimilated into the environment of 'concert music'. He notes, furthermore, that in such music 'the phase-shifting and additive processes found in Steve Reich's and Philip Glass's early compositions were often taken over as structural devices' used alongside others, instead of functioning as the primary focus of attention.[14]

Although Adams is the present focus of this discussion relating to postminimalism, Reich and Glass themselves both changed styles at this time as well. The first movement of Glass's *Glassworks* (1982), titled simply 'Opening' and scored for solo piano, features tonal triads as broken chords, played in a hemiola pattern, whose top notes outline a melody over a sustained bass line that frequently implies functional harmonic progressions. Thus it meets Gann's criteria for postminimalism both by dint of its fixed duration and by virtue of the basic tonal shapes and cyclical repetitions that remain recognizably minimalist while now also alluding to the semiotic apparatus of the nineteenth century. As Susan McClary has written: 'Before us glimmers once again the Romantic soul, decked out with all its requisite emotional trappings: alienation, memories of lost arcadia, and longing for utopia.'[15] But, as she also notes, the mechanical repetitions and the lack of direction in the harmony on a larger scale undermine the apparatus of subjective interiority, with the result that the inner self starts to look like something that is dependent on semiotic conventions. Paradoxically, therefore, 'Opening' alludes to an idiom that is about emotional depth but does so in a depthless manner, in keeping with what Jean Baudrillard has dubbed 'simulacrum'.[16]

Even though Adams's scores can also be classified as concert music, and they do indeed use minimalist devices to provide structural support, they offer a wider expressive range than Glass's postminimalist model. *Harmonielehre* (1985) is a case in point: like the first movement of *Glassworks* it mixes minimalist and Romantic idioms, but unlike that example it does so by engaging with the genre of the symphony. Adams is not an obvious successor to György Ligeti in terms of musical style, but he is an equal when it comes to being persuasive at interpreting his own music and providing ways to talk about it.[17] Certainly he provides images, almost programmes, for the three parts of *Harmonielehre*, which contextualize the piece, are easy to assimilate and have become part of its discourse.

Harmonielehre marks a transition in Adams's career, since it is the point at which he started to break away from the limitations of minimalism, notably by using an enlarged tonal vocabulary. Such an enriched vocabulary is suggested by the title, for *Harmonielehre* is also the title of the harmony textbook, translated as *Theory of Harmony*, that Schoenberg completed in 1911, along with the mighty *Gurrelieder*, ironically at the very time when he was moving away from tonal conventions.[18] Adams remarks that 'the harmonies brush up against many totemic works of the preceding hundred years, from *Parsifal*, to *Pelléas et Mélisande* through the Mahler of the Tenth Symphony to Sibelius (particularly his Fourth Symphony) and the luminescent, crepuscular tone-painting of Schoenberg's *Gurrelieder*.'[19]

In a more contemporary vein, he refers to an image that gave rise to the opening E minor chords: 'I'd had a vivid dream in which I was crossing the San Francisco Bay Bridge. In that dream I looked out to see a huge oil tanker sitting in the water. As I watched, it slowly rose up like a Saturn rocket and blasted out of the bay and into the sky.'[20] Adams has described Part I of *Harmonielehre* as 'a single-movement symphony in itself',[21] and it is accordingly characterized by an energetic opening section, a slower lyrical section, and a return to the pulsed character of the opening section, which ends with a climactic restatement of the opening chords. In fact, the structure of Part I mirrors that of the larger score, in which two outer movements that are comparable in character frame a more lyrical middle movement.

As Richard Powell has indicated,[22] the momentum of the opening chords is achieved by changes of metre, not of tempo, and this principle is important for the whole of Part I, though tempo changes are certainly used. Its busy arpeggios contribute a minimalist momentum and create the pulse, but they have a harmonic role as well. Adams modifies harmonies by adding additional notes so as to transform them gradually from within, until the music reaches a point where, in keeping with minimalist phasing, it suddenly switches to another chord. What is unexpected about this music is the way it combines minimalist and symphonic aspirations, for it is end-driven in a way that is more in keeping with the Romantic symphony than with the cyclic patterns of minimalism; and at the end of Part I Adams deploys the different metric layers not only to create cross-rhythms but also to intensify the sense of conclusion. Adams's dream of a space-bound tanker, with its strand of magic realism, provides an intriguing vision for the way in which the last section takes off (see Example 14.1).

Between modernism and postmodernism

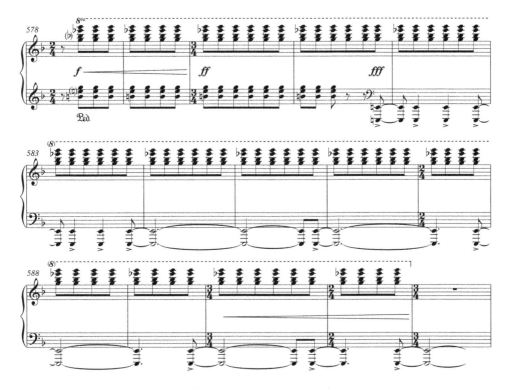

Example 14.1 John Adams, *Harmonielehre* (1985), Part I: piano part, bars 578–92
© Boosey & Hawkes, Inc. All rights reserved

Adams remarks:

> I don't work with identifiable motifs, as much as with forward motion that's colored by its harmonic atmosphere. And I use large, powerful blocks – perhaps I should say 'images', since I think this music is more pictorial or cinematographic than it is developmental.[23]

While this description is one with which it is easy to agree, it is not one that is easy to reconcile with the end-driven music that equally characterizes Part III. Adams has commented about the latter:

> The end of the last movement culminates in a vast harmonic struggle that breaks through into an emphatic release on E-flat major. I was certainly not unaware of the models that existed in earlier music, from the Beethoven *Eroica* and *Emperor* up through the Sibelius Fifth Symphony.[24]

However, these models are developmental and their sense of telos is achieved through structural schemes that are not 'cinematic' in Adams's sense. Furthermore, Adams goes on to disclose that the final eighty bars constitute a reworking of another piece of his called *Light over Water*[25] – a fact that, while not in itself problematic, runs counter to the symphonic ideal of through-composition. That said, there is an overarching key scheme to the score. Part I begins and ends in E minor, though it wins through over the persistent E♭ harmony of the slow middle section as much by force as by tonal resolution (see Example 14.1); and Part III finishes in a triumphant E♭ major.

In the conclusions of Parts I and III, Adams offers a gesture that is distinctly conclusive and organic, but in a way that cuts it off from the structural unfolding it is supposed to represent, thereby rendering it a euphoric non-synthesis. In an inherently postmodernist contradiction, it takes the idea of end-driven music but does so in the absence of the expected hierarchical supporting structure. So instead of encoding a traditional, integrated subjectivity, this evocation of synthesis now presents the experience of intensity. Viewed historically, such culminations have the somewhat subversive effect of implying that the impact of a tonal symphony might rely less on structural unfolding than might otherwise be thought.

If the outer movements of *Harmonielehre* are expressive they are nonetheless not expressionist, because they offer a heightened experience of the present instead of anxiety and alienation. The music engages with subjectivity in the sense that its emphasis is on feeling rather than on recognition of structure, but it is not about the inner self. One reason for this might be that the symphony is a public form, which articulates the socialized self rather than the sort of personalized self evoked by Glass in the solo piano 'Opening' from *Glassworks*. However, for all their largesse and sense of conclusion, Adams's movements do not fully articulate the socialized self, for they are about an environment – an environment through which the self wanders, without creating a reflection, other than by facilitating an elevated mood. This is a landscape in which tonal symbols function by being brightly illuminated rather than subordinated to functional progressions.

Despite its references to European music, and to Schoenberg in particular, *Harmonielehre* is rooted in an American tradition that – as, for example, in Cage's *Variations IV* – is more interested in articulating a soundscape than in creating a connected feeling, though Adams is less willing than Cage to relinquish the authorial grip on form. This difference becomes evident when Adams's perceptions of self and nature are compared with the orientation of the German composer Wolfgang Rihm (who, like Adams, is sometimes dubbed a neo-Romantic). Rihm's chamber opera *Jakob Lenz* (1978) follows a Romantic tradition according to which nature provides a mirror of the inner self, in this case a self that is ill at ease with social and institutional expectations. While Rihm in the opera uses tonal symbols outside their functioning context, so that they become intensities in their own right, unlike Adams he does so to convey psychological instability rather than to generate a euphoric state.

The middle movement of *Harmonielehre* is somewhat different from the outer ones. Although it is repetitive, it makes limited use of established minimalist devices; it is also the section of the score that is most obviously indebted to the vocabulary of late-Romantic harmony. Adams entitled it 'The Amfortas Wound', in a direct allusion to Wagner's *Parsifal*, and it has an expressionist dimension, building to two peaks of anxious dissonance. For Adams, however, what he views as the 'spiritual sickness' in this movement is something to be worked through and dispelled before the grace of Part III.[26]

Adams had stopped being a practising Christian by the age of sixteen.[27] Nevertheless, religion is an explicit topic in his turn-of-the-millennium oratorio *El Niño*, which explores the topic of the Nativity; and it is present in much of his other music, including *Harmonielehre*. Speaking about the choice of title, Adams comments: 'I also thought about harmony in the human, the psychological sense, about living with oneself, about balance in life.' The work also pursues an ideal of art 'which touches you in spirit, which touches you in the center of your soul and affects you.'[28] Modernist encounters with religion tend to take a ritualistic form, as exemplified by Stravinsky, so Adams's free-floating, non-aligned approach to spirituality might indeed be read as postmodernist.

In the interview from 1985, Adams compares *Harmonielehre* with the AT&T building in New York City which, he says, 'is an example of sensuousness, reminiscence, and sentiment; but it also feels like a part of our contemporary experience'.[29] Although Adams does not refer to the architectural critic Charles Jencks, his comment is remarkably close to Jencks's influential concept of double-coding, defined as 'the combination of modern techniques with something else (usually traditional building) in order for architecture to communicate with the public'.[30] Over twenty years later Adams regrets inviting comparisons between his music and postmodernist architecture,[31] which is not surprising when one reads that 'the building [1978–82] first branded as a Chippendale-Highboy became a monumental focus of Post-Modern loathing'.[32]

The validity of the association with the AT&T building is not important, but the terminology that Adams uses in drawing the parallel is significant, since it shows him knowingly using the language of postmodernism in a way that does indeed fit *Harmonielehre* well, in that the score combines allusions to the past with emotional affect and with a contemporary feel. Take that image of the bridge, the bay and the tanker: the vastness of the sea evokes the Romantic sublime on a scale worthy of Caspar David Friedrich, but the car and the space-bound oil tanker transfer it to modern California, not least because the tanker is relieved of its industrial heaviness. Like the music, the image turns to the past but somewhat undercuts its reference points. Although it is often not productive to allocate works to modernist or postmodernist categories, the discourse and historical location of *Harmonielehre* make a strong case for it to be placed in the postmodernist camp.

Spectralism: perception and postindustrialism

Another trend to have emerged in the 1970s, like postminimalism, was spectral music. This approach has a number of precursors, including Ligeti's texture-based scores such as *Atmosphères* (1961) and *Lontano* (1967), which are characterized by the gradual transformation of a sound mass, though it is somewhat ironic that at the time when these scores were exerting an influence on pioneering figures such as Gérard Grisey and Tristan Murail, Ligeti himself was turning from texture-based composition to music with stronger references to the historical past. Karlheinz Stockhausen's *Stimmung* (1968), in which vocalists modify the spectral characteristics of a single chord, was another influence, as was his *Mantra* (1970), for two pianists and live electronics, through the way in which individual pitches on the pianos relate to electronic sine tones, both of which are passed through two ring-modulators.[33] For, as Julian Anderson has indicated with regard to the opening and closing sections, 'the ring-modulation sound loses its "exotic", unfamiliar quality and it becomes possible to hear inside the timbres, to hear them as real harmony.'[34]

With its move from the structural preoccupations of serialism to the perceptual preoccupations of timbral transformation, spectral music would at first appear to be worth ranging under the banner of postmodernism. Eric Drott has examined the ways in which the pioneers of spectral music sought to position themselves in the sphere of cultural production, largely through what he calls 'the rhetoric and metaphoric language employed in artistic commentary'.[35] In doing so, he argues that 'the effects of late capitalism – along with its specific "cultural logic", postmodernism – have been less acutely felt in France than elsewhere'.[36] So, with postmodernism excluded from the picture, he is free to describe the discourse of spectral music in terms of a homology between progressive modernism and progressive politics – a point that is well made.

Nevertheless, it should be remembered that one of the most influential texts on postmodernism, Jean-François Lyotard's *La condition postmoderne*, was by a French author,[37] and that a number

Alastair Williams

of the poststructuralist theorists who were writing in France in the aftermath of 1968 became central to postmodernist thought, whatever their own equivocal beliefs about the term. Ihab Hassan's influential list of 'schematic differences between modernism and postmodernism', for example, includes an opposition between 'totalization' and 'deconstruction'.[38] This polarization is itself too rigid, however, for deconstruction is focused on what is suppressed by arguments or systems, not on simply replacing them with a plurality of particulars. It is more fruitful to understand poststructuralism as a continuation of the modernist project in the realm of theory, which allowed modernism to explore and challenge its own theoretical axioms at the point when it had become less confident of its aims as an aesthetic practice. In this vein, Andreas Huyssen argues,

> if poststructuralism can be seen as the *revenant* of modernism in the guise of theory, then that would also be precisely what makes it postmodern. It is a postmodernism that works itself out not as a rejection of modernism, but rather as a retrospective reading which, in some cases, is fully aware of modernism's limitations and failed political ambitions.[39]

Over thirty years later (Huyssen's essay was first published in 1984), what once looked like a retrospective reading now looks more like an active expansion of modernism.

From this perspective, Drott moves onto the territory of poststructuralism's contribution to postmodernism when he draws attention to 'Grisey's imagination of an "ecology of sound"; [and] the spectralists' shared interest in "difference" and "hybridity"'.[40] Drott also notes that 'the idea that serialism's treatment of sound proceeds in a fashion analogous to technological modernity's exploitation of the natural environment is key to understanding the spectralists' argument.'[41] The Green movement, which is invoked by Grisey's reference to ecology, has its roots in the social turmoil of 1968 as well, even though its environmental critique of technocratic capitalism turns away from traditional socialism. And if the Green movement does not map directly onto postmodernism, the two are not inimical, since both share a suspicion of industrialization and linear notions of progress. When Grisey invokes ecology, however, he comes close to the problematic claim that the musical exploration of the harmonic series is rooted in nature. So he is really trying to have it both ways: on the one hand eschewing industrialization in order to create something more 'natural', but on the other hand using technology, softly, in order to achieve this aim. Although this paradoxical goal may not in itself be problematic, it starts to become so when it is used as a discursive strategy to suggest that other approaches are more artificial.

The discourse of spectral music is postmodernist in the specific sense that it actively seeks to detach itself from what it portrays as the abstract logic of serialism characteristic of post-war modernism. In his article 'Zur Entstehung des Klanges' Grisey attempts to distance himself not only from serialism but also from neo-tonal alternatives to it, using somewhat political language in the process: 'between tonal or neo-tonal hierarchy and serial or neo-serial egalitarianism [*Egalitarismus*] there exists a third way: to recognize and accept difference. Ultimately we seek to avoid both levelling and "colonization".'[42] There is so much happening in these two sentences that they require unpacking. First, in France at that time the word 'difference' was strongly associated with the work of Jacques Derrida. By using it Grisey was therefore aligning himself with poststructuralism, if not postmodernism. Derrida uses the meaning of the French word 'différence', not surprisingly, to invoke both difference and the process of deferring, and this idea is indeed illuminating in relation to Grisey's music, in which one chord both differs from the next and defers to it temporally, in a gradual process of transformation.[43] Second, Grisey's remark attempts to contrast the idea of a music of difference to competing models such as neo-tonality and neo-serialism, linking the first to the structure of class society and the second to the 'levelling' of mass society.

So there is a sequential, historical aspect to the argument as well: tonal music, representative of hierarchical bourgeois society, is followed by the serialist flattening that is characteristic of industrial society, and then by spectralist music with its more nuanced postindustrial (postmodernist) politics. Although serial music is not literally industrial music, because it is not directly connected to polluting technology such as coal-burning power stations, it can be understood in terms of centralized production, since an underlying structure pervades the music. A more direct metaphor, though, for the idea of a move from centralized to decentralized production might be the battle fought at IRCAM (Institut de Recherche et Coordination Acoustique/Musique) between advocates, mainly Boulez, of the mainframe 4X computer and supporters, mainly younger staff, of the new desktop computers.[44] Moreover, such a parallel is in keeping with Jameson's alignment of postmodernism with what he refers to as 'the arrival and inauguration of a whole new type of society, most famously baptized "postindustrial society" (Daniel Bell) but often also designated consumer society, media society, information society, electronic society or high tech, and the like'.[45] Grisey's vision of postindustrial music and society starts to look somewhat idealistic when confronted with the mundane social reality described by Jameson.

Grisey's 'Zur Entstehung des Klanges' was delivered as a lecture at the Darmstadt summer course of 1978, the year that was dominated by a new generation of composers, with Hans-Jürgen von Bose and Rihm both active participants.[46] So, by distancing himself from serialism, Grisey was part of a wider trend at Darmstadt that year, with von Bose in particular being critical of technological progress, but arguing (differently from Grisey) that tradition offers a refuge from the industrialized world.[47] Von Bose's idea of music as a response to environmental damage is in accordance with the new trend of Green politics in West Germany in the 1970s, which departed from the socialist politics of the student movement, partly in reaction to the development of nuclear power.[48] Despite the distrust of serialism being common to Grisey and the new generation of German composers that year, the connection Grisey made between neo-tonality and social hierarchy might have been interpreted as a swipe at this group, whether intended as such or not.

By separating himself from neo-tonality, Grisey was also detaching himself from the category of the 'neue Einfachheit', a term that became part of the debate about postmodernism in West Germany but that was resisted by the generation of composers represented at Darmstadt in 1978. Linking Rihm in particular to the kind of tonality that is emblematic of a hierarchical society is, however, somewhat misguided, because he tends to use tonality as a repository of meanings instead of as an organizing system, and consequently does not simply evoke bourgeois values as if all the associated class structures remained in place. With the term 'neo-serial', Grisey may well have been interpreted, again justifiably or not, as alluding to composers such as Helmut Lachenmann and Brian Ferneyhough, who were becoming prominent at the time and who remained influenced by the serialist legacy.

Despite this anti-serialist stance, there is a distinctly modernist dimension to the notion of using a computer, or a spectrogram in the early days, to analyse a sound spectrum, and then employing the results of the investigation to create a timbre-based composition – a process that is suggestive of scientific research and its associated institutions. Grisey, in particular, made a claim to have taken over the lead from serialism, and he thereby endorsed the idea of progress and the concomitant modernist value of historically advanced material. The approach is commensurate with what Carl Dahlhaus, in an essay published in 1970, called 'problem history'. According to Dahlhaus,

> Karlheinz Stockhausen's development from pointillist technique via group form [*Gruppenform*] and statistical technique to moment form can serve as an example, showing clearly that difficulties which at first seemed insoluble provided the stimulus for works at a second level on which earlier problems were solved.[49]

With this modernizing impulse, along with its other preoccupations, spectral music avoids many of the defining features of postmodernism: it is not interested in creating new meanings from pre-existing ones, except maybe in dissociating texture from serial technique; it is not intertextual, other than by engaging with scores in the same genre; it is not pluralistic; and it is definitely not about engagement with popular culture. Furthermore, it is concerned with social meanings only in the narrow sense of absorbing them into the material.[50]

Spectralism produces a blurring of harmony, in which the individual notes can be identified, and timbre, in which the individual partials fuse instead of being heard individually. By analysing the spectromorphology of a sound it becomes possible to resonate its strongest partials, a process by which what were once partials become more akin to notes in a chord. However, the result is not exact, because acoustic instruments have their own timbral spectra, which influence the resulting sound; and this lack of exactness is possibly, in part, what Grisey means by 'difference'. The opening of *Partiels* (1975), from Grisey's cycle of scores *Les espaces acoustiques*, often serves as the model for spectral music because it clearly shows, aurally and visually, how a low E on trombone and double bass is resonated by strings and wind,[51] though this procedural description does little justice to music in which a jabbing, atavistic bass note is spatially thrown to the ensemble, in a gesture that is repeated a number of times.

Writing about *Modulations*, another score in the same cycle, Grisey commented: 'I think I have got somewhere closer to essential time, not chronometric time but psychological time and its relative value.'[52] The term 'essential time' is not well chosen and is a symptom of an ideology of music that strives towards the status of 'nature' and the 'natural'. Nevertheless, what Grisey wants to convey by using it is that the transformations in *Modulations* take place on a timescale that can be perceived – even if the listener is envisaged to exist in the limited capacity of one who hears transformations but does not necessarily create meanings.

Another innovative feature of spectralism is the blurring of the categories and sounds of instrumental and electronic music. Scores such as *Partiels* or *Modulations* do not attempt this interface literally, since they are purely instrumental; instead they use techniques such as spectral filtration, developed in the field of electroacoustic music, to generate harmonies subsequently realized by conventional instruments. On the one hand, spectral music endeavours like electroacoustic music to work directly with sounds rather than, like serialism, through the abstraction of separate parameters; on the other hand, it remains dependent on the medium of notation to create the desired sonorities. Spectral music, therefore, is situated very much at the intersection of modernism and postmodernism: its experimental aspect is modernist in character, while its emphasis on difference and perception is more postmodernist in orientation.

Just as postminimalism expanded the range of minimalism, so the initial aims of spectralism gave way to post-spectralism. Kaija Saariaho is normally considered to be a post-spectralist, because she takes the intersection of timbre and harmony as something to be worked into wider considerations, such as form.[53] *Lichtbogen* (Arcs of Light, 1986), for nine musicians and live electronics, offers a good example of a score in which research on the qualities of sound produces music with readily noticeable qualities.[54] The title alludes to the northern lights, a spectacle that is connected to the stillness and gradual transformations in the score. Saariaho has commented: 'Those who have experienced them know the feeling of eternity when seeing the lights moving across the arc of sky gently challenging our perceptions.'[55] The arc of the title refers to the form of the piece, but on a smaller scale it also refers to the action of a bow-stroke on a cello; indeed it was her study of the latter that provided the impetus for the work. Two gestures are used: the first increases bow pressure so as to take the sound from a defined pitch to a noise; the second has the cello perform a glissando between two string harmonics, producing noise on the way. Indeed Saariaho uses this duality to create a larger feature of the score:

> The transitions which here are the basis of the harmony again arise from an application of the sound/noise axis. This time the string harmonics correspond to the 'consonance' end of this axis, whereas 'dissonance' is represented by noisy sounds broken up into multiphonics.[56]

It was computational spectral analysis of different phases of the two bow-stroke actions that also produced the harmony of the score, which is characterized by slow transformation.

The instrumental sounds are fed through a mixing desk, so that they can be amplified, subjected to reverberation, and then processed by a harmonizer, which expands the bandwidth of pitches by a quarter-tone either way and thus thickens the harmonies to make them more cluster-like.[57] Amplification is especially important at the end of the work, where the focus is on the breathy sounds of the flautist, who is asked to whisper phonemes into the instrument while sustaining a pitch. (These phonemes are taken from a French translation of 'The World', a seventeenth-century poem by Henry Vaughan, which embraces the topic of eternity.)[58] The harmonizer is used above all in those passages in which the strings move from pitch to noise and back again by means of bow pressure, magnifying the sense of shifting between transparent sounds and noise (see Example 14.2).

The emphasis on extended instrumental techniques in *Lichtbogen*, particularly the focus on cello bow pressure, brings to mind Lachenmann, a composer normally associated neither with Saariaho nor with spectralism in general for that matter. Saariaho's use of the word 'noise' carries resonances of Lachenmann's employment of the German word *Geräusch*, which does not have the negative connotations of intrusion associated with the English word. Since Saariaho visited the Darmstadt summer course of 1980, it is probable that she was aware of Lachenmann's style over the following decade. Nevertheless, unlike Lachenmann, she does not view extended technique as a potential form of social critique, and her idea of using electronics to magnify details of sound clearly bears little relation to his use of mainly instrumental resources.

Lichtbogen is decisively modernist in its progressive blending of instrumental and electronic timbres, and there is an element of idealism in the putative links between micro and macro form: first, the concept that a spectral analysis of a cello bow-stroke provides the harmony; second, that the same gesture features in the score; and, third, that it is reflected in the overall form. Nevertheless the transformations of sonority, colour and timbre do have a perceptual aspect to them, even if a listener's perceptions are unlikely to relate directly to the abstraction of the underlying scheme. These elements may well be as much French (Saariaho is a long-time resident of Paris) as postmodernist, but they do at least sit at the postmodernist end of the spectrum.

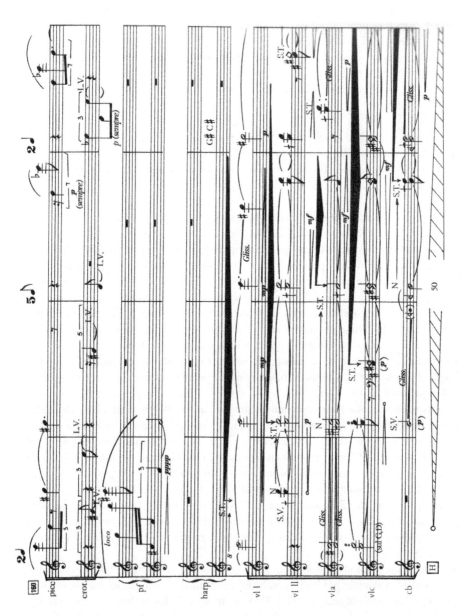

Example 14.2 Kaija Saariaho, *Lichtbogen* (1986), bars 160–63 (the modified crescendo and decrescendo signs underneath the stave lines indicate use of the harmonizer)

© Edition Wilhelm Hansen, Helsinki. All rights reserved

Thomas Adès: abundance and intertextuality

In addition to being a forerunner of spectral music, *Mantra* (1970) is the first score in which Stockhausen used the formula technique – as a way of linking small-scale and large-scale structures – that was to feature in all his music from that time onwards.[59] The choice of the term 'mantra', a repeated word or sound that is used to focus meditation, to designate the underlying formula indicates that the music does not just unfold a structure but addresses a state of mind as well. The formula idea additionally offers a way of combining melodic material with serial organization, in order to provide orientation for the listener. Furthermore, although this concession hardly amounts to a postmodernist realignment, it acknowledges the role of reception and creates opportunities for tonal allusions.

In Europe during the 1970s and 1980s modernism started to include historical allusions, though few composers chose to describe this shift as postmodernist, and it is no coincidence that this reorientation was roughly synchronous with the emergence of postminimalism and spectral music. György Ligeti, Mauricio Kagel, Luciano Berio, Peter Maxwell Davies and even Lachenmann all composed music with a wider historical frame of reference than they had drawn upon previously. Furthermore, although Pierre Boulez did not embrace this trend as a composer, it is arguable that he did so as a conductor, becoming more active in that role and in a repertoire that encompassed, among other nineteenth-century and turn-of-the-century composers, Mahler and Wagner.

Ligeti traversed three different styles in the course of his career: the first was socialist-realist, folk-oriented music; the second texture-based approaches; and the third a late style that was in part characterized by a return to the Hungarian influences of his early style and in part by a reconsideration of devices derived from the tonal tradition. All rather postmodernist, one might think, but not so according to Ligeti – even though the second of his Three Pieces for Two Pianos (*Monument–Selbstportrait–Bewegung*, 1976) has the overtly inclusive title of 'Self-Portrait with Reich and Riley (and Chopin is there too)'. Ligeti remarked, in the context of his piano Études, that what he composed is 'in no way postmodern, as the ironic theatricalizing of the past is quite foreign to me'.[60] One reason for this stance would have been the hostile reception that postmodernism received in West Germany, a reception strongly influenced by the prominent interventions of social theorist Jürgen Habermas. Another, as Charles Wilson has argued, is that Ligeti was highly skilled at describing his music in ways that emphasize originality over more general trends such a postmodernism, though it is true that his late style retained a modernist emphasis on construction.[61] The Horn Trio is the major score that initiated Ligeti's third style, its departure from avant-gardism marked by its idiosyncratic references to the horn fifths (a topic theory favourite) of Beethoven's *Les Adieux* Sonata, to Balkan rhythms, to Transylvanian folk music, and to the descending *lamento* motif of the Baroque.[62]

Habermas considers postmodernism to be a neo-conservative attempt to escape the modern world – a criticism that might justifiably be applied to music that simply reverts to historical styles or produces a montage of them, but less so to music that actively engages the past.[63] Broadly speaking, the reorientation that took place in the 1970s and 1980s was one in which modernism returned to its early twentieth-century roots and cast off a formalist discourse. This trend was recognized by Huyssen: 'Postmodernism is far from making modernism obsolete. On the contrary, it casts a new light on it and appropriates many of its aesthetic strategies, inserting them and making them work in new constellations.'[64] Writing in 2006, he has offered a complementary but retrospective evaluation:

> Despite or perhaps because of its claims to radical innovation, postmodernism has made visible those dimensions of modernism itself that had been forgotten or repressed by

the institutional and intellectual codifications of the modernism dogma of the Cold War: issues related to the semiotic anarchism of the avant-garde, to figuration and narrative, to gender and sexuality, race and migration, the uses of tradition, the tension between the political and the aesthetic, the mixing of media, and so forth.[65]

Born in 1971, the British composer Thomas Adès emerged after the end of the Cold War in 1989, a point that signalled the end of a privileged funding pattern, as support for the arts became more marketized and diversified, and one that marked the start of an internet era, in which music from the past became more readily available.[66] Because he is too young to have been part of the response in the 1970s and 1980s to the post-war avant-gardes, he has from the earliest stages of his career been able to write music in an eclectic range of styles without concerning himself much with the polemics that agitated a previous generation. That said, Ligeti's off-centre modernism has exerted an influence on Adès, most notably in his use of polyphony and pulsing rhythms, and in his liking for combinations of extreme registers. At the same time he shares with Adams a predilection for clearly defined orchestral layers, albeit not the explicit defiance of modernism that characterized the latter's postminimalism.

What might be called Adès's three essays to date in the genre of the symphony are *Asyla* (1997), *Tevot* (2007) and *Polaris* (2010), all of which involve the idea of a journey. *Asyla* is a large orchestral score from 1997 that was premiered by Simon Rattle and the City of Birmingham Symphony Orchestra; Rattle also programmed it in his first concert as artistic director of the Berlin Philharmonic in 2002. In an enthusiastic review of the recording from 1999, Taruskin places it at the communicative end of modernism, though for him it is a surrealist modernism. He argues that 'Mr Adès was thus able to buck sterile utopia while avoiding the opposing pitfall of ironic pastiche,'[67] which is a pointed way of saying that the score manages to bypass the excesses of both modernist abstraction and postmodernist pluralism.

Although there is no pressing need to assign *Asyla* to the category of either modernism or postmodernism, it is nevertheless worth indicating that its polystylistic qualities are in keeping with the latter. The score contains allusions to Béla Bartók, François Couperin, César Franck, Gustav Mahler, Richard Wagner and, more surprisingly, to the genre of electronic dance music. The Bartók quotation, for example, is taken from the opera *Bluebeard's Castle*, but is here presented more as an absorbing instrumental texture than as a sinister reference. However, with the exception of the house music, these stylistic references are not placed in conspicuous quotation marks but instead come and go as part of the larger fabric; whether recognized by listeners or not, they do not register as pluralist, anti-modernist transgressions. In an understated way, it is taken for granted that the music is referential and intertextual. *Asyla* also alludes to the genre of the symphony, since it is written in four movements, with a slow second movement, a dance-form third movement and two related outer movements. Again, the gesture of evoking this established genre is one neither of restoration nor of contravention. For Arnold Whittall, *Asyla* is a 'symphonic process in which the functional contrast between clear-cut basic ideas and richly inventive orchestral presentation can be appreciated at first hearing'.[68]

Along similar lines, the programme note for the premiere of *Asyla* has provided the coordinates by which the score tends to be navigated.[69] It points out that the word 'asyla', the plural of asylum, contains the dual meanings of madhouse and sanctuary, and adds: 'Reflecting these themes, the first movement evokes a sense of motion across open spaces, the inner two movements take place as if in an enclosed setting, and the finale bursts these confines to provide a final, unexpected release.'[70] These ideas encourage speculation on how the topics of confinement and refuge play out in the score, whether as an escape from overbearing instrumental reason or as a more peaceful sense of release, with the genre of the symphony offering both safety

Between modernism and postmodernism

and confinement. Since Adès claims that 'I don't see the distinction between abstract music and programme music',[71] this type of inquiry is not secondary to the way in which the composer, at least, views his own music. By and large, the score is more concerned with the topic of sanctuary than with that of madness; and when madness is presented, it is of the getting-out-of-yourself type that is associated with the electronic dance music gestures of the third movement rather than the type of expressionist outburst that can be traced back to Schoenberg.

Asyla includes parts for six percussionists, and most of the writing is for instruments with metallic qualities, including the tuned cowbells that are heard prominently at the opening of the score (see Example 14.3). Adès says of the cowbells:

> They've been a symbol of 'elsewhere' in symphonic music. 'Elsewhere' is a most important word for me. It was André Breton who said, 'Life is elsewhere'. The cowbells in *Asyla* become a metaphor for Elsewhere, as in Mahler or Webern, although the cowbells are not tuned.[72]

While this comment from the composer is helpful and insightful, it only serves to confirm an association that is already available to the listener, not least because the cowbells are frequently heard alongside an upright piano tuned a quarter-tone flat, which serves to extend the sense of 'elsewhere' through a timbral rather than structural use of microtones. The cowbells are a regular presence in the score, such that the 'elsewhere' idea is not confined to one type of mood or material: they introduce the melodic material of the first and second movements; they are present though less prominent in the raucous third movement; and, along with the two upright pianos (including the mistuned one), they estrange the second statement of the main melodic idea of the fourth movement (rehearsal letter B).

As mentioned above, the evocation of 1990s electronic dance music in the third movement, entitled 'Ecstasio' in a reference to the recreational drug ecstasy, is the most likely candidate for the depiction of madness in this score. Like house music, it facilitates a loss of self through excessive repetition – a trait that is sometimes seen as postmodernist, because instead of the projection of self that is so characteristic of rock it offers a more collective sense of identity.[73] That collective identity is evidently less overt in the case of an orchestral score played to a seated audience than at a rave. There is a humorous aspect to this clunky dance music as well, since the clarity of the medium becomes cumbersome when transmitted through the creaky technology of a traditional orchestra. Still, this somatic music is at one with the sanctuary aspect of the score, since dispersal of self can function as a refuge from day-to-day responsibilities, and the idea of madness as a refuge is a familiar modernist theme. As Edward Venn summarizes it,

> The music remains forever poised, sometimes delicately, sometimes violently, between numerous conflicting impulses: between symphonic development and the repetitions of dance; between directed motion and kinetic impulses; between the evocation of the concert hall and the club; and between madness and sanctuary.[74]

On the intertextual front, Stravinsky's *Rite of Spring* offers a precedent for dance music that is built from layers of rhythmic motifs, yet the influence of electronic dance music renders the result *in Asyla* less ritualistic than that earlier model. At the other end of the spectrum Adès notes that the conclusion of this movement is derived from the end of Act II of *Parsifal*, specifically from the moment when the character Parsifal turns away from the pleasures of Klingsor's enchanted garden, having identified with the plight of Amfortas.[75] The moment does not evoke the sound world of *Parsifal*, so if the reference implies a rather moralistic denial of the sensuality

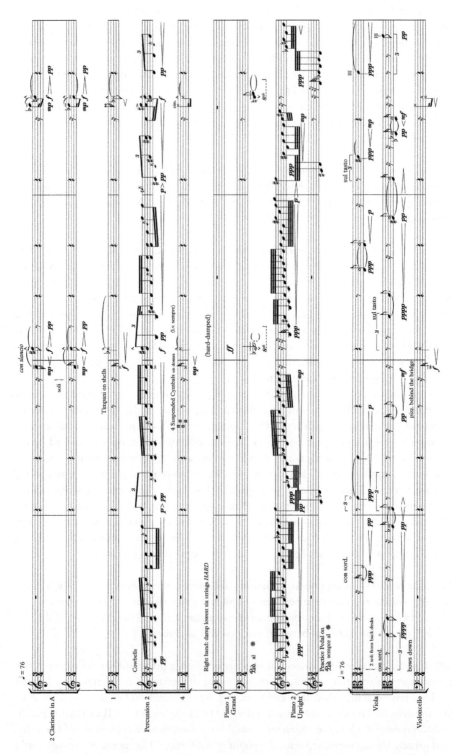

Example 14.3 Thomas Adès, *Asyla*: first movement, bars 1–4
© Faber Music Ltd. All rights reserved

Between modernism and postmodernism

of electronic dance music, then it remains something of a private joke.[76] Nonetheless, the music does become audibly more dramatic in a traditional sense at this point.

Interviewed in 2011, Adès remarks: 'And my orchestral piece *Asyla* has a couple of endings, some in a row and some on top of each other – I can't remember how many. When they are all in place I can sense the equilibrium.'[77] If the term 'a couple' is not taken too literally, there are three endings. The first (rehearsal letters G to H) is where materials from movements I, II and III are superimposed, so it offers a jumbled synthesis, with the blurred Bartók and the fake electronic dance music the most easily recognized elements.

The second ending (letter I) is based around the choral theme from the Finale. Adès comments: 'Everything rushes in from the rest of the piece and then it has one huge statement of this [choral] idea: it's as though you are released at the end. That's what I was aiming to do, anyway.'[78] However, it is announced by a massive chord that is as much an intrusion as a structural goal; if it sounds Mahlerian, that is because it is taken from the end of the Scherzo in Mahler's Third Symphony.[79] In the context of his folksy Scherzo (with its *Wunderhorn* background) Mahler considered this chord to be an incursion of inorganic nature into the animal kingdom – and it is certainly heard as an outside event. Indeed it remains an external event in *Asyla*, resulting in the contradiction that what the composer intended as a moment of release is approached by a dramatic intervention.

The third ending (letter J) is the coda, in which there are recollections of the opening of the score and hence of the associated sense of 'elsewhere'. As Venn has indicated, the return in the coda to material from the opening of the first movement makes the conclusion of the score somewhat enigmatic.[80] For his part Adès notes: 'One way I tried of ending things – I did this as early as my Chamber Symphony – is suddenly to have an aerial view of the whole thing. *In Seven Days* also pulls the camera out at the end. *Tevot* does that, *Asyla* does that.'[81] In another interview Adès has also commented: 'in the last 30 seconds of the piece, there's a sense that a window is thrown open, or suddenly light appears'.[82] So these remarks provide a framework for the way in which the choral theme fades out and the cowbells return, providing a sense of distant resolution, or of dwindling recapitulation.

More broadly, the idea of three juxtaposed endings is one that has some affinities with chance-influenced scores that offer the performer, or indeed listener, a range of options to navigate. It takes from aleatorism, therefore, the idea that recognized codes can be challenged. The difference here, though, is that the combined approaches that Adès offers amount not to a menu of abstract choices but to a collection of devices that create a multidimensional expressive effect. Thus he explores the idea of a symphonic conclusion in a less goal-directed manner than Adams.

Adès's hybridity invokes the programmatic idea of nineteenth-century music, if not the programmatic content. It also refers to the first phase of modernism, yet without the trappings of expressionist anxiety. In addition, it draws on post-war modernism, if to a lesser extent: modernism now functions as another historical style, rather than imposing a set of values. These derivations all mingle in a style that is neither a forced synthesis nor an obvious pluralism, and the presence of club music in a symphonic genre indicates that the once-powerful divide between modernist and popular musics is one that is no longer in force (though the movement does retain a sense of transgression). Although *Asyla* is conspicuously low tech, it is representative of an internet age, or the digital era, in which a range of music is there for the taking – or the sampling. Unlike *Music of Changes*, it is full of memory and tradition, but its meanings are malleable, not the prefabricated ones that Cage aimed to eradicate. As Dominic Wells puts it, 'the tension between tradition and modernism is simply not an issue for him'.[83] Although this sense that different meanings do not have to clash with one another is not necessarily beyond postmodernism, it is beyond an established boundary between a modernist distrust of tradition and a postmodernist reassertion of it.

Musicology: subjectivity and meaning

Adams, Grisey and Adès are all musicologists in more than a trivial sense, because their activities as composers are so firmly embedded in strong discourses that the two aspects – music and discourse – are inseparable. Musicology is, of course, the medium through which the music that has been considered in this chapter is discussed, so to turn now to the topic of musicology and postmodernism is not such a change of direction. One area of confusion in discussions of the modernism–postmodernism nexus is the use of the same terminology to refer to musicological and compositional practice, even though editing, say, a Handel manuscript and composing a serial score are obviously not closely related activities. What unites the two areas, according to the most strident critiques of modernism, is a preference for facts and systems over interpretations. What brings the two areas together, from a more up-to-date perspective, is a recognition that the discourses of music affect both areas, apart from the more obvious point that musicology examines the contemporary as well as the historical.

In his 1995 book *Classical Music and Postmodern Knowledge*, Lawrence Kramer advocated a musicology strongly influenced by critical theory – one known at the time as 'new musicology' – and aligned it with the values of postmodernism.[84] In a later text, *Interpreting Music*, he responded to an article in the *New York Times* from 2002, which had hailed the new musicology as the new norm. 'By then', Kramer comments, 'the once-heady label had become obsolete. It looked like the new musicology was just what musicology is.'[85] He proceeds to outline the ongoing project of new musicology as follows: 'The idea is to combine aesthetic insight into music with a fuller understanding of its cultural, social, historical, and political dimensions than was customary for most of the twentieth century.'[86] Such an intention is now unlikely to be regarded as particularly provocative, which rather confirms the point that new musicology has become mainstream. Indeed the sentiment is remarkably close to Taruskin's stated aim in writing his history of Western music, despite his unease with new musicology: 'I would single out social contention as embodied in words and deeds – what cultural theorists call 'discourse' (and others call 'buzz' or 'spin') – as the paramount force driving this narrative'.[87]

What is notable about Kramer's definition in his later book is that, although it could just as well have appeared in *Classical Music and Postmodern Knowledge* two decades earlier, it no longer reads as especially postmodern.[88] In part this is the case because just as new musicology has been absorbed into general musicology, so postmodernism has been absorbed into general cultural practice; yet it is also the case because a musicology influenced by critical theory need not be postmodernist. If formalist discourse ever became excessive, so did its postmodernist rejection. We now no longer need to make binary choices between centred and decentred subjectivity, grand and micro narratives, structure and surface, or progress and stasis. These pairings are better understood as interactive fields than as alternatives.

Since not all musicologists are actively influenced by critical theory in the same way as Kramer, a name is still needed for the kind of practice that retains links with the theoretical origins of new musicology; and Kramer reflects a common view when he suggests that what was 'new musicology' has now become 'critical musicology', though he acknowledges that they are not identical terms.[89] Indeed there is a difference, because new musicology in the United States was strongly indebted to poststructuralism, whereas critical musicology in the United Kingdom was, and is, influenced not only by poststructuralism but also by the traditions of European Marxism, as represented by figures such as Adorno, Antonio Gramsci and Raymond Williams, so it was never as closely aligned with postmodernism as the American version. There is, nevertheless, a consensus that such a musicology is one that is prepared to venture beyond facts, whether positivist or formalist, to explore the cultural work done by music, to acknowledge the discourses in which music is embedded, and to understand music as a mode of human subjectivity.

The study of performance practice is, of course, one area in which such an approach plays out, not least because historically informed performance (what used to be called 'authentic performance') is one way of addressing the status and practice of classical music in the modern age. Historically informed performance, like postmodernism, emerged in the 1960s, and it was an attempt to break away from a nexus of canonical reception, an affluent recording industry and a smooth, finessed style of playing, all of which served to use classical music as a signifier of social prestige. (This configuration, especially the prestige part of it, is addressed in Kagel's 1970 film *Ludwig van.*) The enterprise is located at the intersection of modernism and postmodernism: on the modernist side, the idea of the *Urtext* is based on notions of textual authenticity and accurate preservation that sought to remove the excesses of Romanticism.[90] On the postmodernist side, it is historically reflective and willing to experiment with an often unfamiliar instrumentarium; and in this capacity it finds a certain parallel in the post-war avant-garde's efforts to re-engage with the past.

Arguing for a view of historically informed performance that is more postmodernist than modernist, and one than is specifically influenced by Jameson's view of postmodernism, John Butt writes: 'however cynical it might sound to suggest that the historicist imperative behind HIP is basically a compensation for a waning history, there is not necessarily any choice in the matter.'[91] For Butt, historically informed performance is an attempt to think Early Music in an age that has forgotten how to think historically, but it nonetheless brings with it new intensities and resonances that are relevant for us in ways that would not have been available to the 'original' performers in history. By this measure, although historically informed performance remains a construction, it is one that is nevertheless suited to the modern age. It is also one in which the score as 'text' plays a less dogmatic role.[92]

Deliberations about historically informed performance could seem somewhat quaint at a time when classical music has lost its prestige, with the consequence that there is no longer any need for politicians and other public figures to even pretend that it interests them. The other side of this coin, though, is that classical music, like other genres of music, is now available in abundance through the internet, which facilitates the choices of style and identity valued by postmodernism, even though postmodernism itself peaked before the internet came into widespread public use.

The topic of music in everyday life is also one that has developed in the aftermath of postmodernism's dominance – but, with its emphasis firmly on reception, it is certainly more postmodernist than modernist. The theme harks back to Cage, since one of his aims was to collapse the distance between art and life, so that music simply became the everyday, as is demonstrated by his famous *4′33″*, which encourages an audience to listen to whatever is happening in the performance space. This approach has the advantage of acknowledging the range of sonic spaces around us, which is offset by the disadvantage that, encountered from Cage's perspective, they are detached from expressive human subjectivity.[93]

The study of music in everyday life, by contrast, does not encourage us to appreciate, for example, traffic noise; instead it examines how people actively engage with music in order to enhance and articulate their lives – perhaps even by shutting out traffic noise. There are two main intersecting areas for this type of study: the first is music in public situations, such as a concert where people share emotions, or a shared lift where piped music serves to alleviate the social awkwardness of strangers finding themselves in a confined space together.[94] The second area is the way in which people use music as a technology of self to regulate their own emotions and to create meanings for themselves: individuals know the kind of response that a track or piece will elicit and will turn to it either to alter a mood, perhaps to build up excitement before a social event, or to enhance one, for instance through reflective relaxation.[95] It is worth balancing this perspective with Simon Frith's observation that 'What music does (all music) is put into play a sense of identity that may or may not fit the way we are placed by other social forces.'[96] The advantage of this viewpoint is that it elevates music – whether created, performed or received – to a more critical role than that of a lifestyle choice.

Whether focusing on the public or the private sphere, studies of music in everyday life deal with the ways in which recorded music is used: how people listen to music in a particular circumstance to regulate mood or to change environment, perhaps via headphones on a train to create an individual space, or in a busy city to block out traffic noise, or maybe through speakers at home to raise spirits while undertaking a tedious task in the house. In this way individuals create a soundtrack to their own lives, though they are undoubtedly responding to the semiotic cues built into the music they choose. Of course, they can employ downloading and live streaming to facilitate this soundtrack – technologies that intensify the postmodern emphasis on lifestyle. Furthermore, there is no reason why modernist music could not be used in this capacity: Stockhausen's *Stimmung* is a hippie-inspired score that is intended to create a contemplative state, so it might work well for someone wishing to erase the memory of a bad day at the office.

If *Stimmung* can be employed in this way, then modernism need not be taken on its own terms, because for all its insistence on autonomy and for all its fetishization of structure, it can be embedded historically and, in that way, appreciated as more than just structure. Indeed the music of the 1950s now sounds more like the characteristic culture of an era than the product of a still-dominant aesthetic. And even though the emphasis on construction that characterized that era jettisons aesthetic considerations, that resistance to hermeneutics is itself meaningful, precisely because it is intended to weaken Romantic associations, and because it is part of Cold War culture, however much it might deny a historical perspective. On the positive side, serially derived styles of composition may be unduly formalist, but they do at least have the capacity to overturn the established patterns of behaviour that are associated with the bourgeois subject. Finally, although the public funding that modernism received in Europe has been criticized for creating elitism, an age in which new music was valued that highly now looks enviable.

★★★

Modernism, having lost its institutional power and prestige, is no longer something that needs to be fought; postmodernism, consequently, no longer has an adversary.[97] Just as postmodernists confronted the previous generation, so it might be expected that postmodernism too might find itself challenged. Yet such a co-ordinated form of resistance has been conspicuous by its absence, mainly because modernism and postmodernism have continued as the two, now less torn, halves of a discourse that retains its potential to be innovative and communicative. Instead of replacing modernism, postmodernism brought out a suppressed side of it and helped it to expand and to mutate. Postminimalism, spectralism, historically reflective modernism, critical musicology, and historically informed performance practice are all, in their different ways, products of the way in which postmodernism has succeeded in recasting modernism over recent decades.

Notes

1 Theodor W. Adorno, 'Letter to Walter Benjamin', in *Aesthetics and Politics*, ed. Ronald Taylor (London: Verso, 2007), 123. The context for Adorno's remark, from 1936, is a comparison of Schoenberg with American film.

Between modernism and postmodernism

2 Fredric Jameson, *Postmodernism, or, the Cultural Logic of Late Capitalism* (London: Verso, 1991), 1. The article in question is 'Postmodernism, or, the Cultural Logic of Late Capitalism', *New Left Review* 146 (1984), 53–92.

3 I make a similar argument in 'Ageing of the New: The Museum of Musical Modernism', in *The Cambridge History of Twentieth-Century Music*, ed. Nicholas Cook and Anthony Pople (Cambridge: Cambridge University Press, 2004), 506–38.

4 Björn Heile has argued that postmodernism is the 'extension or complement' of modernism; *The Music of Mauricio Kagel* (Aldershot: Ashgate, 2006), 106.

5 Richard Taruskin, *Music in the Late Twentieth Century*, rev. ed. (New York: Oxford University Press, 2010), 508. Zorn also features in Kenneth Gloag's *Postmodernism in Music* (Cambridge: Cambridge University Press, 2012).

6 John Cage, 'Composition: Describe the Process of Composition Used in *Music of Changes* and *Imaginary Landscape No. 4*', in *Silence: Lectures and Writings* (London: Marion Boyars, 1978), 59.

7 Steve Reich, 'Music as a Gradual Process', in *Writings on Music*, ed. Paul Hillier (New York: Oxford University Press, 2002), 34–37.

8 Keith Potter, *Four Musical Minimalists: La Monte Young, Terry Riley, Steve Reich, Philip Glass* (Cambridge: Cambridge University Press, 2000), 10.

9 See Gloag, *Postmodernism in Music*, 122–23. He makes the argument particularly in relation to Philip Glass, though for slightly different reasons.

10 Potter, *Four Musical Minimalists*, 16.

11 Quoted in Arnold Whittall, *Exploring Twentieth-Century Music: Tradition and Innovation* (Cambridge: Cambridge University Press, 2003), 181.

12 Jonathan Bernard, 'Minimalism, Postminimalism and the Resurgence of Tonality in Recent American Music', *American Music* 21, no. 1 (2003), 117.

13 Kyle Gann, 'A Technically Definable Stream of Postminimalism, Its Characteristics and Its Meaning', in *The Ashgate Research Companion to Minimalist and Postminimalist Music*, ed. Keith Potter, Kyle Gann and Pwyll ap Siôn (Farnham: Ashgate, 2013), 40.

14 Ibid.

15 Susan McClary, *Conventional Wisdom: The Content of Musical Form* (Berkeley: University of California Press, 2000), 142–43.

16 Jean Baudrillard, 'Simulacra and Simulations', in *Jean Baudrillard: Selected Writings*, ed. Mark Poster (Cambridge: Polity Press, 1988), 166–84.

17 For an examination of the performative function of Ligeti's accounts of his own music, see Charles Wilson, 'György Ligeti and the Rhetoric of Autonomy', *Twentieth-Century Music* 1, no. 1 (2004), 5–28.

18 Arnold Schoenberg, *Theory of Harmony*, trans. Roy E. Carter (London: Faber and Faber, 1978).

19 John Adams, *Hallelujah Junction* (London: Faber and Faber, 2008), 130–31.

20 Ibid., 130.

21 Jonathan Cott, 'An Interview with John Adams, June 1985', disc notes, *John Adams: Harmonielehre*, CD, Nonesuch CD 79115-2 (1985), 1.

22 Richard Powell, 'Accessible Narratives: Continuity in the Music of John Adams', *Contemporary Music Review* 33, no. 4 (2014), 396–97.

23 Cott, 'An Interview with John Adams', 4.

24 Adams, *Hallelujah Junction*, 129–30.

25 Ibid., 130.

26 Cott, 'An Interview with John Adams', 2.

27 Adams, *Hallelujah Junction*, 239.

28 Michael Steinberg, '*Harmonielehre* (1984–85)', in *The John Adams Reader: Essential Writings on an American Composer*, ed. Thomas May (Newark: Amadeus Press, 2006), 103.

29 Cott, 'An Interview with John Adams', 5.

30 Charles Jencks, *What Is Post-Modernism?* (London: Academy Editions, 1986), 14. The quotation is taken from the first edition (1978) of Jencks's *The Language of Post-Modern Architecture* (London: Academy Editions, 1978).

31 Adams, *Hallelujah Junction*, 131.

32 Jencks, *What Is Post-Modernism?* 13.

33 For an account of early influences on spectral music, and the role of Stockhausen's *Stimmung* in particular, see Cagney in this volume.

34 Julian Anderson, 'A Provisional History of Spectral Music', *Contemporary Music Review* 19, no. 2 (2000), 14.
35 Eric Drott, 'Spectralism, Politics and the Post-Industrial Imagination', in *The Modernist Legacy: Essays on New Music*, ed. Björn Heile (Aldershot: Ashgate, 2009), 44.
36 Ibid., 45.
37 Jean-François Lyotard, *La condition postmoderne: rapport sur le savoir* (Paris: Minuit, 1979).
38 Ihab Hassan, *The Postmodern Turn: Essays in Postmodern Theory and Culture* (Columbus: Ohio State University Press, 1987), 91–92.
39 Andreas Huyssen, *After the Great Divide: Modernism, Mass Culture and Postmodernism* (London: Palgrave Macmillan, 1986), 209.
40 Drott, 'Spectralism, Politics', 46.
41 Ibid., 50.
42 Gérard Grisey, 'Zur Entstehung des Klanges', *Darmstädter Beiträge zur Neuen Musik* 17 (1978), 74; trans. in Drott, 'Spectralism, Politics', 57.
43 Derrida's essay 'Différance' was published in the historic year 1968; his reason for modifying the spelling of the word 'différence' is not significant for the present chapter. Jacques Derrida, 'Différance', in *Margins of Philosophy*, trans. Alan Bass (Chicago: University of Chicago Press, 1982), 3–27.
44 This dispute is discussed in Georgina Born, *Rationalizing Culture: IRCAM, Boulez, and the Institutionalization of the Avant-Garde* (Berkeley and Los Angeles: University of California Press, 1995).
45 Jameson, *Postmodernism*, 3.
46 For more on this topic, see Alastair Williams, *Music in Germany since 1968* (Cambridge: Cambridge University Press, 2013), 205–14.
47 Hans-Jürgen von Bose, 'Suche nach einem neuen Schönheitsideal', *Darmstädter Beiträge zur Neuen Musik* 17 (1978), 34–39.
48 For more on the nascent green movement in West Germany, see Hans Kundnani, *Utopia or Auschwitz? Germany's 1968 Generation and the Holocaust* (London: Hurst, 2009), 147–65.
49 Carl Dahlhaus, 'Progress and the Avant Garde', in *Schoenberg and the New Music*, trans. Derrick Puffett and Alfred Clayton (Cambridge: Cambridge University Press, 1987), 20.
50 A range of publications attribute such features to postmodernism in music. An example would be Jonathan D. Kramer, 'The Nature and Origins of Musical Postmodernism', in *Postmodern Music/Postmodern Thought*, ed. Judy Lochhead and Joseph Auner (New York: Routledge, 2002), 13–26.
51 It serves as an example for instance in Robert Hasegawa, 'Gérard Grisey and the "Nature" of Harmony', *Music Analysis* 28, nos. 2–3 (2009), 350–52. However, François-Xavier Féron doubts, from study of source materials, that the beginning of *Partiels* 'is based upon the transcription of the spectrum or spectrogram from the analysis of a trombone sound sample'. See 'The Emergence of Spectra in Gérard Grisey's Compositional Process: From *Dérives* (1973–74) to *Les espaces acoustiques* (1974–85)', *Contemporary Music Review* 30, no. 5 (2011), 363.
52 Gérard Grisey, '*Modulations* (1978) for thirty-three musicians', disc notes, *pour l'ensemble*, CD, Erato 0630-15993-2 (1991), 29.
53 See Damien Pousset, Joshua Fineberg and Ronan Hyacinth, 'The Works of Kaija Saariaho, Philippe Hurel and Marc André Dalbavie – Stile Concertato, Stile Concitato, Stile Rappresentativo', *Contemporary Music Review* 19, no. 3 (2000), 67–110.
54 The scoring is for flute (also piccolo and alto flute), a range of mainly tuned percussion (one player), piano, harp, two violins, viola, cello and double bass.
55 Quoted in Pirkko Moisala, *Kaija Saariaho* (Urbana and Chicago: University of Illinois Press, 2009), 32.
56 Kaija Saariaho, 'Timbre and Harmony: Interpolations of Timbral Structures', *Contemporary Music Review* 2, no. 1 (1987), 130.
57 For a more detailed consideration of the electronics used in *Lichtbogen*, see James O'Callaghan and Arne Eigenfeldt, 'Gesture Transformations through Electronics in the Music of Kaija Saariaho', *Proceedings of the Seventh Electroacoustic Music Studies Network Conference Shanghai, 21–24 June 2010*, http://www.ems-network.org.
58 See Moisala, *Kaija Saariaho*, 32.
59 The formula idea is explained in Karlheinz Stockhausen, '*Mantra* für 2 Pianisten (1970)', *Texte zur Musik 1970–1977*, ed. Christoph von Blumröder (Cologne: DuMont, 1978), 154–56.
60 György Ligeti, 'Études', trans. David Feurzeig and Annelies McVoy, disc notes, *György Ligeti Edition: Works for Piano*, CD, Sony SK62308 (1998), 11–12.
61 Charles Wilson, 'György Ligeti and the Rhetoric of Autonomy'.

Between modernism and postmodernism

62 For a more detailed discussion of the Horn Trio, see Amy Bauer, *Ligeti's Laments: Nostalgia, Exoticism, and the Absolute* (Aldershot: Ashgate, 2011), 160–74. For a study of post-war modernism in its second stage, see David Metzer, *Musical Modernism at the Turn of the Twenty-First Century* (Cambridge: Cambridge University Press, 2009).

63 Jürgen Habermas, 'Modernity – An Incomplete Project', trans. Seyla Benhabib, in *Postmodern Culture*, ed. Hal Foster (London: Pluto Press, 1985), 3–15.

64 Huyssen, *After the Great Divide*, 217–18.

65 Andreas Huyssen, 'Introduction: Modernism after Postmodernity', *New German Critique* 33, no. 3 (2006), 3.

66 For a study of music that takes 1989 as its point of departure, see Tim Rutherford-Johnson, *Music After the Fall: Modern Composition and Culture since 1989* (Oakland: University of California Press, 2017).

67 Richard Taruskin, 'A Surrealist Composer Comes to the Rescue of Modernism', in *The Danger of Music and Other Anti-Utopian Essays* (Berkeley and Los Angeles: University of California Press, 2009), 149.

68 Arnold Whittall, 'Thomas Adès', in *The New Grove Dictionary of Music and Musicians*, ed. Stanley Sadie and John Tyrrell, vol. 1 (London: Macmillan), 156.

69 The comments echo those made by the composer in the Radio 3 interval discussion at the world premiere on 1 October 1997, http://www.youtube.com/watch?v=28v6oBv37K0 (accessed 8 May 2016).

70 Mathias Tarnopolsky, programme note to *Asyla*, first performance, 1 October 1997, http://brahms.ircam.fr/works/work/21709/ (accessed 27 August 2017).

71 Thomas Adès, *Full of Noises: Conversations with Tom Service* (London: Faber and Faber, 2012), 5.

72 Ibid., 71.

73 See Jason Toynbee, *Making Popular Music: Musicians, Creativity and Institutions* (London: Arnold, 2000), 131–32.

74 Edward Venn, 'Thomas Adès's "Freaky, Funky Rave"', *Music Analysis* 33, no. 1 (2014), 92.

75 Adès, *Full of Noises*, 58.

76 It is most likely a coincidence that Adams and Adès both allude to *Parsifal*. Nevertheless in his late music drama Wagner stepped back from the process of modernization by going back to diatonic writing, and thereby provided a model for a non-linear understanding of music history.

77 Adès, *Full of Noises*, 5.

78 Quoted in Edward Venn, 'Asylum Gained? Aspects of Meaning in Thomas Adès's *Asyla*', *Music Analysis* 25, nos. 1–2 (2006), 93.

79 See ibid., 104.

80 Ibid., 115–16.

81 Adès, *Full of Noises*, 14.

82 Adès, Radio 3 interval discussion, 1 October 1997.

83 Dominic Wells, 'Plural Styles, Personal Style: The Music of Thomas Adès', *Tempo*, no. 66 (2012), 2–14.

84 Lawrence Kramer, *Classical Music and Postmodern Knowledge* (Berkeley: University of California Press, 1995).

85 Lawrence Kramer, *Interpreting Music* (Berkeley: University of California Press, 2011), 63.

86 Ibid., 64.

87 Taruskin, 'Introduction', in *Music in the Late Twentieth Century*, xiv. (The same introduction serves all five volumes of his *Oxford History*.)

88 I have argued previously that the hermeneutic turn taken by musicology in the 1990s extends beyond the confines of postmodernism. See Alastair Williams, *Constructing Musicology* (Aldershot: Ashgate, 2001).

89 Kramer, *Interpreting Music*, 64.

90 This is the aspect that Taruskin has pursued: see Richard Taruskin, *Text and Act: Essays on Music and Performance* (New York: Oxford University Press, 1995).

91 John Butt, *Playing with History* (Cambridge: Cambridge University Press, 2002), 163.

92 See Nicholas Cook, 'Music as Performance', in *The Cultural Study of Music: A Critical Introduction*, ed. Martin Clayton, Trevor Herbert and Richard Middleton (London: Routledge, 2003), 204–14. For an alternative view of the relationship of modernism to historical and other performance practice, see Knapik in this volume.

93 For more on this topic, see Alastair Williams, 'Cage and Postmodernism', in *The Cambridge Companion to John Cage*, ed. David Nicholls (Cambridge: Cambridge University Press, 2002), 227–41.

94 See Simon Frith, 'Music and Everyday Life', in *The Cultural Study of Music: A Critical Introduction*, ed. Clayton, Herbert and Middleton, 92–101.

95 See Eric Clarke, Nicola Dibben and Stephanie Pitts, *Music and Mind in Everyday Life* (New York: Oxford University Press, 2010), 81–92.

96 Simon Frith, *Performing Rites: Evaluating Popular Music* (Oxford: Oxford University Press, 1996), 276–77.

97 A recent publication by Susan McClary offers a more forgiving reading of modernism than she has hitherto advocated. See 'The Lure of the Sublime: Revisiting the Modernist Project', in *Transformations of Musical Modernism*, ed. Erling E. Guldbrandsen and Julian Johnson (Cambridge: Cambridge University Press, 2015), 21–35.

Bibliography

Adams, John. *Hallelujah Junction*. London: Faber and Faber, 2008.

Adès, Thomas. *Full of Noises: Conversations with Tom Service*. London: Faber and Faber, 2012.

Adorno, Theodor W. 'Letter to Walter Benjamin'. In *Aesthetics and Politics: Theodor Adorno, Walter Benjamin, Ernst Bloch, Bertolt Brecht, Georg Lukács*, edited by Ronald Taylor, 120–26. London: Verso, 1977.

Anderson, Julian. 'A Provisional History of Spectral Music'. *Contemporary Music Review* 19, no. 2 (2000): 7–22.

Baudrillard, Jean. 'Simulacra and Simulations'. In *Jean Baudrillard: Selected Writings*, edited by Mark Poster, 166–84. Cambridge: Polity Press, 1988.

Bauer, Amy. *Ligeti's Laments: Nostalgia, Exoticism, and the Absolute*. Aldershot: Ashgate, 2011.

Bernard, Jonathan. 'Minimalism, Postminimalism and the Resurgence of Tonality in Recent American Music'. *American Music* 21, no. 1 (2003): 112–33.

Born, Georgina. *Rationalizing Culture: IRCAM, Boulez, and the Institutionalization of the Avant-Garde*. Berkeley and Los Angeles: University of California Press, 1995.

Bose, Hans-Jürgen von. 'Suche nach einem neuen Schönheitsideal'. *Darmstädter Beiträge zur Neuen Musik* 17 (1978): 34–39.

Butt, John. *Playing with History*. Cambridge: Cambridge University Press, 2002.

Cage, John. 'Composition: Describe the Process of Composition Used in *Music of Changes* and *Imaginary Landscape* No. 4'. In *Silence: Lectures and Writings*, 57–59. London: Marion Boyars, 1978.

Clarke, Eric, Nicola Dibben and Stephanie Pitts. *Music and Mind in Everyday Life*. New York: Oxford University Press, 2010.

Clayton, Martin, Trevor Herbert and Richard Middleton, eds. *The Cultural Study of Music: A Critical Introduction*. London: Routledge, 2003.

Cook, Nicholas. 'Music as Performance'. In *The Cultural Study of Music*, edited by Clayton, Herbert and Middleton, 204–14.

Cott, Jonathan. 'An Interview with John Adams, June 1985'. Disc notes, *John Adams: Harmonielehre*, San Francisco Symphony Orchestra, conducted by Edo De Waart. CD, Nonesuch 79115-2 (1985): 1.

Dahlhaus, Carl. 'Progress and the Avant Garde'. In *Schoenberg and the New Music*, translated by Derrick Puffett and Alfred Clayton, 14–22. Cambridge: Cambridge University Press, 1987.

Derrida, Jacques. 'Différance'. In *Margins of Philosophy*, translated by Alan Bass, 3–27. Chicago: University of Chicago Press, 1982.

Drott, Eric. 'Spectralism, Politics and the Post-Industrial Imagination'. In *The Modernist Legacy: Essays on New Music*, edited by Björn Heile, 39–60. Aldershot: Ashgate, 2009.

Féron, François-Xavier. 'The Emergence of Spectra in Gérard Grisey's Compositional Process: From *Dérives* (1973–74) to *Les espaces acoustiques* (1974–85)'. *Contemporary Music Review* 30, no. 5 (2011): 343–75.

Frith, Simon. *Performing Rites: Evaluating Popular Music*. Oxford: Oxford University Press, 1996.

———. 'Music and Everyday Life'. In *The Cultural Study of Music*, edited by Clayton, Herbert and Middleton, 92–101.

Gann, Kyle. 'A Technically Definable Stream of Postminimalism, Its Characteristics and Its Meaning'. In *The Ashgate Research Companion to Minimalist and Postminimalist Music*, edited by Keith Potter, Kyle Gann and Pwyll ap Siôn, 39–60. Farnham: Ashgate, 2013.

Gloag, Kenneth. *Postmodernism in Music*. Cambridge: Cambridge University Press, 2012.

Grisey, Gérard. 'Zur Entstehung des Klanges'. *Darmstädter Beiträge zur Neuen Musik* 17 (1978): 73–9.

———. '*Modulations* (1978) for thirty-three musicians'. Disc notes, *pour l'ensemble*, Ensemble Intercontemporain, directed by Pierre Boulez. CD, Erato 0630-15993-2 (1991): 29.

Habermas, Jürgen. 'Modernity – An Incomplete Project', translated by Seyla Benhabib. In *Postmodern Culture*, edited by Hal Foster, 3–15. London: Pluto Press, 1985.

Between modernism and postmodernism

Hasegawa, Robert. 'Gérard Grisey and the "Nature" of Harmony'. *Music Analysis* 28, nos. 2–3 (2009): 349–71.

Hassan, Ihab. *The Postmodern Turn: Essays in Postmodern Theory and Culture.* Columbus: Ohio State University Press, 1987.

Heile, Björn. *The Music of Mauricio Kagel.* Aldershot: Ashgate, 2006.

Huyssen, Andreas. *After the Great Divide: Modernism, Mass Culture and Postmodernism.* London: Palgrave Macmillan, 1986.

———. 'Introduction: Modernism after Postmodernity'. *New German Critique* 33, no. 3 (2006): 1–5.

Jameson, Fredric. 'Postmodernism, or, the Cultural Logic of Late Capitalism'. *New Left Review* 146 (1984): 53–92.

———. *Postmodernism; or, the Cultural Logic of Late Capitalism.* London: Verso, 1991.

Jencks, Charles. *The Language of Post-Modern Architecture.* London: Academy Editions, 1978.

———. *What Is Post-Modernism?* London: Academy Editions, 1986.

Kramer, Jonathan D. 'The Nature and Origins of Musical Postmodernism'. In *Postmodern Music/Postmodern Thought*, edited by Judy Lochhead and Joseph Auner, 13–26. New York: Routledge, 2002.

Kramer, Lawrence. *Classical Music and Postmodern Knowledge.* Berkeley: University of California Press, 1995.

———. *Interpreting Music.* Berkeley: University of California Press, 2011.

Kundnani, Hans. *Utopia or Auschwitz? Germany's 1968 Generation and the Holocaust.* London: Hurst, 2009.

Ligeti, György. 'Études', translated by David Feurzeig and Annelies McVoy. Disc notes, *György Ligeti Edition: Works for Piano.* CD, Sony SK62308 (1998): 11–12.

Lyotard, Jean-François. *La condition postmoderne: rapport sur le savoir.* Paris: Minuit, 1979. Translated by Geoff Bennington and Brian Massumi, *The Postmodern Condition: A Report on Knowledge.* Minneapolis: University of Minnesota Press, 1984.

McClary, Susan. *Conventional Wisdom: The Content of Musical Form.* Berkeley and Los Angeles: University of California Press, 2000.

———. 'The Lure of the Sublime: Revisiting the Modernist Project'. In *Transformations of Musical Modernism*, edited by Erling E. Guldbrandsen and Julian Johnson, 21–35. Cambridge: Cambridge University Press, 2015.

Metzer, David. *Musical Modernism at the Turn of the Twenty-First Century.* Cambridge: Cambridge University Press, 2009.

Moisala, Pirkko. *Kaija Saariaho.* Urbana and Chicago: University of Illinois Press, 2009.

O'Callaghan, James, and Arne Eigenfeldt. 'Gesture Transformations through Electronics in the Music of Kaija Saariaho'. *Proceedings of the Seventh Electroacoustic Music Studies Network Conference Shanghai, 21–24 June 2010.* http://www.ems-network.org.

Potter, Keith. *Four Musical Minimalists: La Monte Young, Terry Riley, Steve Reich, Philip Glass.* Cambridge: Cambridge University Press, 2000.

Pousset, Damien, Joshua Fineberg and Ronan Hyacinth. 'The Works of Kaija Saariaho, Philippe Hurel and Marc André Dalbavie: Stile Concertato, Stile Concitato, Stile Rappresentativo'. *Contemporary Music Review* 19, no. 3 (2000): 67–110.

Powell, Richard. 'Accessible Narratives: Continuity in the Music of John Adams'. *Contemporary Music Review* 33, no. 4 (2014): 390–407.

Reich, Steve. 'Music as a Gradual Process'. In *Writings on Music*, edited by Paul Hillier, 34–37. New York: Oxford University Press, 2002.

Rutherford-Johnson, Tim. *Music After the Fall: Modern Composition and Culture since 1989.* Oakland: University of California Press, 2017.

Saariaho, Kaija. 'Timbre and Harmony: Interpolations of Timbral Structures'. *Contemporary Music Review* 2, no. 1 (1987): 93–133.

Schoenberg, Arnold. *Theory of Harmony.* Translated by Roy E. Carter. London: Faber and Faber, 1978.

Steinberg, Michael. '*Harmonielehre* (1984–85)'. In *The John Adams Reader: Essential Writings on an American Composer*, edited by Thomas May, 101–5. Newark: Amadeus Press, 2006.

Stockhausen, Karlheinz. '*Mantra für 2 Pianisten* (1970)'. In *Texte zur Musik 1970–1977*, edited by Christoph von Blumröder, 154–56. Cologne: DuMont, 1978.

Tarnopolsky, Mathias. Programme note to Adès, *Asyla*, first performance, 1 October 1997. http://brahms.ircam.fr/works/work/21709/ (accessed 27 August 2017).

Taruskin, Richard. *Text and Act: Essays on Music and Performance.* New York: Oxford University Press, 1995.

———. 'A Surrealist Composer Comes to the Rescue of Modernism'. In *The Danger of Music and Other Anti-Utopian Essays*, 142–52. Berkeley and Los Angeles: University of California Press, 2009.

———. *Music in the Late Twentieth Century*. Rev. ed. Vol. 5, *The Oxford History of Western Music*. New York: Oxford University Press, 2010.

Toynbee, Jason. *Making Popular Music: Musicians, Creativity and Institutions*. London: Arnold, 2000.

Venn, Edward. 'Asylum Gained? Aspects of Meaning in Thomas Adès's *Asyla*'. *Music Analysis* 25, nos. 1–2 (2006): 89–120.

———. 'Thomas Adès's "Freaky, Funky Rave"'. *Music Analysis* 33, no. 1 (2014): 65–98.

Wells, Dominic. 'Plural Styles, Personal Style: The Music of Thomas Adès'. *Tempo* no. 66 (2012): 2–14.

Whittall, Arnold. 'Thomas Adès'. In *The New Grove Dictionary of Music and Musicians*, edited by Stanley Sadie and John Tyrrell. Vol. 1, 156. London: Macmillan, 2001.

———. *Exploring Twentieth-Century Music: Tradition and Innovation*. Cambridge: Cambridge University Press, 2003.

Williams, Alastair. *Constructing Musicology*. Aldershot: Ashgate, 2001.

———. 'Cage and Postmodernism'. In *The Cambridge Companion to John Cage*, edited by David Nicholls, 227–41. Cambridge: Cambridge University Press, 2002.

———. 'Ageing of the New: The Museum of Musical Modernism'. In *The Cambridge History of Twentieth-Century Music*, edited by Nicholas Cook and Anthony Pople, 506–38. Cambridge: Cambridge University Press, 2004.

———. *Music in Germany since 1968*. Cambridge: Cambridge University Press, 2013.

Wilson, Charles. 'György Ligeti and the Rhetoric of Autonomy'. *Twentieth-Century Music* 1, no. 1 (2004): 5–28.

15

FOUNDATIONS AND FIXATIONS

Continuities in British musical modernism

Arnold Whittall

Foundations, fixations, continuities – the implications of certainty and stability in such words seem unambiguous. Yet in writing about music it is a familiar strategy to claim that to embrace modernism is the best way for a composer to supplant classicism's governing tonal stabilities and continuities with post-tonal instabilities and discontinuities. The further, ironic implication is that modernism itself continues, flourishes, by becoming familiar in its consistent, foundational use of instability and discontinuity – not just by setting the 'exploding' against the 'fixed',[1] but by ensuring that the fixed, the relatively stable, is kept subordinate to disintegrative forces.

Two recent books dramatize some of the most basic ways in which musical modernism, and its particular manifestations in Britain, are understood: *The Quilting Points of Musical Modernism: Revolution, Reaction, and William Walton* by J. P. E. Harper-Scott, and *British Musical Modernism: The Manchester Group and their Contemporaries* by Philip Rupprecht.[2] The differences between them are profound. Harper-Scott believes that 'all the music of Western modernity' since at least 1789 is modernist: and although he provides much detailed technical analysis of passages from compositions by Walton, his book is not primarily about Britain, or even about music, but about modernism as a 'contested aesthetic category and a powerful political statement'. It involves philosophers – Heidegger, Badiou, Žižek, Agamben – more intensively than musicologists, with the ultimately explicitly Leftist objective of outlining 'a vision of the community to come'.[3]

Rupprecht follows a more traditional musicological pathway, focusing on the recent twentieth-century past, and elaborating the 'modernism' in his title in precise technical terms. The composers he considers in depth are responding to 'radical avant-garde developments in mainland Europe', and to 'the serial-structuralist preoccupations of mid-century internationalism' as well as to the 'exuberant theatricality' of the 1960s and to aspects of 'pop, minimalism and live electronics' which emerged in the early 1970s.[4] Nevertheless, the approaches of Harper-Scott and Rupprecht are not totally disparate. Both allow for the presence of renewal within musical modernism, and what Rupprecht identifies (in an earlier publication) as 'Britten's triadic modernism' can be paralleled by Walton's 'reactionary novelties', in Harper-Scott's formulation.[5] After all, both Walton and Britten made use of a fundamental modernist technique, the emancipation of dissonance from its consistent subordination to consonance in classical tonality.

Technical initiatives like the emancipation of the dissonance, associated in particular with the progressive theories expounded by Arnold Schoenberg in the early twentieth century,[6] might create a strong desire among commentators a century later to think beyond the actualities of the present and to further the cause of that 'community to come'. Alternatively, such initiatives might be judged sufficiently fruitful in their own right, and therefore deserving to endure, in a steady-state modernism, for the foreseeable future. It is against the background of perceptions about how reinforced continuities fail to suppress all doubts about the viability of the kind of modernist methods used in recent years that my own narrative will unfold. I will not attempt a summary survey of British musical modernism in all its aspects. Nor will I deal with compositions by such leading figures as Harrison Birtwistle, Peter Maxwell Davies, Brian Ferneyhough and James Dillon, on whom relevant literature is already extensive.[7] Instead, after a frankly autobiographical explanation of how my own understanding of modernism has come to take its present form, I will use a brief comparison of compositions by Michael Finnissy (b. 1946) and Thomas Adès (b. 1971) to introduce an account of recent pieces by James Clarke (b. 1957) and Morgan Hayes (b. 1973).

Personal contexts

Even if, as is often argued, the earliest phase of musical modernism belongs to the post-classical Romanticism of the nineteenth century, its fullest, high-modernist manifestation as post-tonal music has occurred in the years since 1900. But its presence in Britain has only been extensive and decisive since 1950, so it is to be expected that a national, British strain of modernism will have much to do with reactions to earlier manifestations in both Europe and America. In turn, this creates the possibility that elements of continuity between those earlier manifestations and the examples of British modernism discussed here might have evolved logically into continuities within British modernism itself – continuities amounting to 'fixations'.

'Modernism' was not a word I often needed to use during the 1960s and 1970s.[8] At a time when the academic disciplines of music theory and analysis tended to be based in very specific concepts involving all-embracing technical procedures (whether Schenkerian for tonal music or set-theoretic for post-tonal music), modernism, like classicism and Romanticism, belonged to the separate spheres of music history and aesthetics – if it belonged at all. In the mid-twentieth century too little time had passed since 1900 for it to seem necessary to interfere with the sequence progressing from Romanticism to late-Romanticism and on to contemporary or avant-garde.

By the 1960s it was clear that art music had not been subject to a permanent and total change as a result of the emergence of 'atonality' during the century's first decade. That this apparent non-tonality could coexist with a continuing tonality – Schoenberg and Webern alongside Sibelius and Rachmaninoff, Boulez and Stockhausen alongside Britten and Shostakovich – meant that Romanticism and even classicism could coexist with those non-tonal alternatives whose primary aesthetic and technical motivation appeared to involve rejecting, or distorting, earlier compositional styles and methods. But boundaries were inevitably breached from the beginning, and the prefix 'neo', as especially with 'neo-classical', was used in recognition of the kind of confrontations between older and newer that could be heard in a work like Stravinsky's Violin Concerto (1930).[9] It suited the expansive and progressive academic spirit of the mid-twentieth century to emphasize the technical riches and expressive ambiguities of such music, relishing the possibility that the secrets of something neither tonal in traditional classical terms nor atonal in more contemporary terms could still be made manifest by theorizing about the kinds of modality – often octatonic – to be found in Bartók and Messiaen as well as Stravinsky. And even though comparisons between the 'cubist' qualities of Stravinsky and Picasso have a long history, the need to propose a separate aesthetic category or historical periodization to account for this was not immediately perceived by commentators. Looking back from the 1960s to the 1930s, violin concertos by Stravinsky, Schoenberg, Bartók and Berg seemed to require acknowledging

Foundations and fixations

the separation between the non-Germanic nationalism of one pair and the Teutonically twelve-tone preoccupations of the other. To say then that all four exemplified different, even conflicting aspects of musical modernism appeared at that time to add little to critical interpretation, and even to retreat into relatively bland generalizations that undervalued difference and originality.

Whether or not through dissatisfaction with attempts to drive old and new ever further apart in explorations of music theory that were seeking broader perspectives once the subject itself had moved closer to the musicological centre during the 1960s and 1970s, the adoption of modernism as a useful, even necessary interpretative term seems to have coincided with those initiatives thought of as representing a 'new' musicology.[10] A crucial aspect of these initiatives was dissatisfaction with a forced, would-be absolute separation of tonal and atonal, coupled with the realization that theoretical systems prioritizing their differences created a strong desire to find ways of allowing for their similarities. This was emphatically not to seek out ways of downgrading tensions and erasing conflicts within musical styles and techniques. But the impulse to search for similarities and common ground also owed something to the perception that commentators on the other arts had moved further in usefully defining modernism than commentators on music. In my own case it was reading Malcolm Bradbury's and James McFarlane's 'Guide to European Literature' *Modernism, 1890–1930*, first published in 1976, that suggested possible analogies.

For Bradbury and McFarlane, modernist art was unashamedly anti-autonomous, embedded in and engaged with the worlds of politics and science. Modernism was designated

> the one art that responds to the scenario of our chaos. It is the art consequent on Heisenberg's 'Uncertainty principle', of the destruction of civilization and reason in the First World War, of the world changed and reinterpreted by Marx, Freud and Darwin, of capitalism and constant industrial acceleration, of existential exposure to meaninglessness or absurdity.[11]

Such an open celebration of art's wider relevance, while not immediately identifying a single modernist technique, was refreshing for a reader concerned that the progressive arts of the later twentieth century were self-consciously detaching themselves from the real world and, if not risking inevitable decline and extinction as a result, were courting increased irrelevance in face of the robust transformations taking place in the parallel, commerce-driven sphere of popular music. Yet there was little support for the argument that a relevant modernist music could be predominantly conservative, prioritizing techniques that had flourished before any of the political and scientific developments that were used in the comparison. If anything, the prospect was being raised of a necessary antagonism between such techniques and those of authentic modernism.

As a glance at their bibliographies and index underlines, Bradbury, McFarlane and their various contributors were not in the business of challenging their readers with much in the way of philosophical or psychoanalytic theorizing. But even at the time their eloquent advocacy of progressiveness seemed to risk excluding all but the most intransigent attributes from modernism as an aesthetic force, while not considering that renewal itself might be radical. In due course I made several attempts to provide plausible outlines for a 'modernist mainstream' in music, as with my 1985 tribute to Tippett on his eightieth birthday.[12] Some years later I even proposed a distinction between this and a 'moderate mainstream' for the years 1945–70, embracing a well-varied team from Strauss and Vaughan Williams to Britten and Shostakovich,[13] in order to reinforce the idea that modernism proper, even when in the mainstream rather than on the avant-garde margins, might always involve the distinction between something 'immoderate', if not frankly chaotic, and something tending to the opposite. Reduced to the simplest formula, emancipation of the dissonance interacted with 'higher' consonance – chords that were not purely triadic but were rooted in the most basic consonant intervals – to create inherently unstable yet still (in some respects) hierarchic musical processes.[14]

In an essay published in 1995 I quoted Bradbury and McFarlane as part of a discussion of twentieth-century British composers, and by then the possibility of interpreting the documentary evidence for European and American influence on the pioneering British modernists born in the 1930s, as well as their successors, was incontrovertible.[15] By the 1990s it was no longer plausible, as it had been around 1950, to contrast the reverence of Schoenberg for Brahms (and of Babbitt for Schoenberg) with Boulez's contempt for the twelve-tone Schoenberg in particular and neo-classicism in general. Boulez had long seen continuities between himself and Debussy. In the 1970s he began to describe continuities between Debussy and Wagner, in music that 'places the emphasis for the first time on uncertainty, on indetermination. It represents a rejection of immutability, an aversion to definitiveness',[16] bringing his appreciation of this alongside the more overtly 'chaotic', or disruptively expressionistic kind of modernism tried out by Webern and Schoenberg in the years between 1908 and 1914. The immense conceptual weight invested in these years by later twentieth-century commentators on early twentieth-century radicalism – boosted as it was by the increase in authoritative performances and recordings of this repertory after 1960 – inevitably implicated the emergence of atonal or post-tonal modernism in the steady but sure erosion of classical stabilities that provided the core of the Wagner style, whose own roots could be found as much if not more in the questing formal experiments of the later Beethoven as in the free-and-easy constructions of German and French opera. If modernism (not just 'modernity') required a root-and-branch critique of the multi-layered but well-integrated designs of classical sonatas and symphonies, the concept of an early, nineteenth-century modernism giving unprecedented emphasis to centrifugal forces, yet in which elements of all-embracing tonal construction were nevertheless maintained (as was the case even in *Tristan und Isolde* or *Boris Godunov*), leading to the 'high' modernism of *c*1908–70 and to 'late' (or post-) modernism thereafter seemed a logical one.

As already suggested, transformations in musicology and music theory were as much a part of twentieth-century musical life after 1950 as changes in compositional style. But the failure of unambiguously absolute atonality to achieve dominance in compositional technique matched the failure of theories involving pitch-class set transformation to achieve dominance in musical pedagogy. For example, both Schoenberg's Wind Quintet Op. 26 (1923–24) and Webern's Symphony Op. 21 (1928) can be dissected in terms of their twelve-tone constructions, yet the greater closeness of Schoenberg's Quintet to classical formal models, and its hierarchic approach to serial technique, suggests either that Schoenberg's modernism was more moderate than Webern's – so much so as to amount to moribund neo-classicism in the young Boulez's scathing assessment[17] – or that Webern could only achieve freedom from the Schoenbergian kind of classical allusions by maximizing the integrative potential of the twelve-tone method, both with respect to the intervallic organization of basic series forms and to ways of building movement structures from series-form successions. Neither Schoenberg nor Webern ever completely lost contact with pre-twelve-tone kinds of expressionistic turbulence in their serial music; so seeing both, along with Stravinsky's post-tonal, modal neo-classicism, as under the aegis of modernism is not a sign of this term's impossible looseness but a positive indication of how fundamental the resistance of modernist composers was to the specifics of tonal and formal integration in truly classical tonality, as expounded during and after the inter-war years by Heinrich Schenker and his followers. That Schenkerians were also commonly resistant to atonality is especially significant for

Foundations and fixations

musicologists concerned to consider what more forward-looking forms of compositional practice might legitimately involve.

By the 1990s theory-based musicology had evolved the kind of steady-state approach to interpretation in terms of modernism – whether early, high or late – as resistance to classical integration (if not invariably described as such). Well-contrasted examples are John Daverio's *Nineteenth-Century Music and the German Romantic Ideology*, with its concept of a musico-dramatic form emphasizing the 'art of transition' whilst no less intensively exploring the abrupt juxtapositions of what Wagner himself called 'rhetorical dialectics',[18] and Anthony Pople's monograph on Berg's Violin Concerto, with its closing image of 'a work which simultaneously, and indeed similarly, celebrates both reconciliation and confrontation' that 'might be said at the same time to have reconciled – and yet not reconciled – those two inseparable and eternal opposites'.[19] In-depth studies with a modernist dimension began to flourish after the 1970s, buttressed by the validation that could be found in writings by and about T. W. Adorno and Carl Dahlhaus in Europe and by Lawrence Kramer and James Hepokoski in the United States.[20] When Hepokoski later joined forces with Warren Darcy in a spectacularly expansive study of *Elements of Sonata Theory: Norms, Types, and Deformations in the Late-Eighteenth-Century Sonata*, it might have been expected that he would have given way to the kind of focus on unifying, connecting, classicizing qualities notable in Darcy's earlier quasi-Schenkerian work on Wagner.[21] In the event, however, the collaborative outcome was a teasingly ambivalent exploration involving the possibility that modernism – as a technical tendency to introduce convergence against a more prominent divergence – was already being foreshadowed during the years of Haydn and Mozart (in Mozart's piano concertos, especially) as well as Beethoven.

That the play of general and particular possible when 'modern' – as of now, the present day – is put alongside 'modernist' aesthetics and compositional techniques was strongly in evidence during the 1990s is shown by the proceedings of the International Symposium of the Paul Sacher Stiftung (Basel, April 1996) under the overall German title *Die klassizistische Moderne in der Musik des 20. Jahrhunderts*. Just as Stephen Hinton spoke about 'Kurt Weill's "Modern Classical Art"', while allowing 'modernism' a place in his terminology, my own 'Peter Maxwell Davies and the Problem of Classicizing Modernism' couldn't avoid a simple 'modern' in the actual text.[22] Rather than struggling vainly in the twenty-first century to enforce impermeable divisions between modernist and non-modernist, therefore, it seems more worthwhile to try to clarify what is modernist even when something classical, or classicizing, might also be present; and having recently explored this theme in an essay focusing on the music of five British-born contemporary composers not widely written about in the specialist literature,[23] I now offer a related but significantly different exercise, with implications for further work in the field.

An initial comparison

Using an earlier composer's name in the title of a work that is not simply an arrangement of the earlier composer's music but alludes to that music in ways that might be far from straightforward, combines homage and distancing, and creates tensions between two quite different impulses in a way that is typically modernist. Using a familiar generic label for something remote from its pre-modernist source, as Webern did with his Symphony Op. 21 (1928), or making esoteric reference to chant materials, as Peter Maxwell Davies did in early compositions like *Alma Redemptoris Mater* (1957) and *Te Lucis Ante Terminum* (1961), are other ways of dramatizing the distance between past and present. But there is something even more directly confrontational, representing modernism in its later phases, about the quality of many works by Michael Finnissy: for example, the three movements from his *Second Political Agenda* for piano called 'Erik Satie like anyone else' (2000–01), 'Mit Arnold Schoenberg' (2002) and 'Skryabin in itself' (2007–8). These are not so much portraits-in-sound of the named composers that seek to represent them through consistently literal imitations of their actual musical idioms, but dramatic encounters between Finnissy and those idioms as he hears and understands them. Something similar might be said of Thomas Adès's *Brahms* (2001) for baritone and orchestra, setting a poem by Alfred Brendel that does not merely allude to the composer of *Ein deutsches Requiem* and *Vier ernste Gesänge* but uses his name over and over again. As Edward Venn writes at the beginning of an extended analysis of Adès's short piece, 'the familiar figure of Brahms is made alien in this new guise', and this effect is all the more successful not only for involving elaborate allusions to Brahms's own music which depend on distancing from the kind of extended and literal quotation that might be easily identifiable, but also for what Venn plausibly interprets as Adès's response to the ideas and analyses of one of Brahms's most perceptive and radical disciples, Arnold Schoenberg.[24]

Venn believes that in Adès's *Brahms* 'the music of the past is rendered strange in its new context' by means of 'organizational principles [. . .] far removed from those of common-practice tonality', as when a motivic cell 'implies an octatonic background at odds with the tonal implications of the Brahmsian foreground'.[25] The result might nevertheless involve pleasurable allusions to that 'suspended' tonality that Schoenberg occasionally invoked when seeking to defend his own later – post-tonal – music from the common accusation that it embraced atonality (for Schoenberg, a logical impossibility).[26] Indeed, I argue here that one reason why modernism has continued to survive and even to flourish up to the present relates to its capacity to adapt to survivals from the common-practice past in ways which the more intransigent avatars of the avant-garde have sought to reject. No less resourcefully – some might say quixotically – modernism has found new ways of setting modern against ancient and thereby involving memory along with other qualities suggesting broader continuities – even when 'atonal' seems a more plausible term than 'post-tonal' for the musical language in question. In the twenty-first century, musical modernism's strongest suit is not to embrace the avant-garde fantasy of a way of writing that manages to sever all conceivable connections with the past, but to follow the path of what Pierre Boulez, discussing what Alban Berg learned from Wagner in his operas, termed 'radical renewal'.[27] The remainder of this chapter considers the usefulness of this concept in relation to recent works by James Clarke and Morgan Hayes.

James Clarke: titles and techniques

In 2011 I published a short study of James Clarke's music focusing on five of the six compositions that then comprised his *Untitled* series, written between 2006 and 2010. In that essay I noted that:

> in opting for title as non-title, Clarke (who is a painter as well as a composer) cites comments by the American abstract expressionist Clyfford Still (1904–1980), about wanting 'no allusions' to interfere with or assist the viewer/listener, explaining that 'my paintings have no titles because I do not wish them to be considered illustrations or pictorial puzzles'. [. . .] Nevertheless, Clarke has also stated that his compositions 'may be read [. . .] as an example of modernist thought, as a modest statement of man's value and dignity, and the pursuance of the expression of our humanity through art': even more directly, he has said that his own 'purpose in composition is to express the human in music'.[28]

Foundations and fixations

A more explicit affirmation of belief in the link between modernism as disturbing and the human subject would be difficult to find, aligning Clarke with another British composer, Richard Barrett (b. 1959), who has written that 'I'm much more optimistic about humanity than many people who write happy music', and has declared his uncompromising belief in 'abandoning all affirmation save that the work of art exists, as a token of the *possibility* of human dignity'.[29]

With Barrett, the rejection of affirmation is obvious in titles like *No, Lost* and *Adrift*, and with composers like Barrett and Clarke, who might be placed in the more radical quadrant of the modernist spectrum, there is another aspect to rejection. Because of the technical challenges to performers, compositions involving a substantial orchestra are relatively rare, and since a particularly important example of such a composition in Clarke's *Untitled* series that I passed over briefly in 2011 is *Untitled no. 2 for Piano and Orchestra* (2006/2008), I will discuss it more fully here.[30]

This 28-minute, single-movement work is dedicated to the memory of Clyfford Still, and it is soon clear that the dramatic rhetoric of the traditional concerto is being set aside as firmly as the concerto's most familiar formal principles. Nevertheless, in some brief comments the composer has not discouraged thinking of his music in terms of a metaphorical landscape: 'the piano is not at the forefront of the musical texture but should be heard as one layer within it, rather like one of several rock strata in a canyon'.[31] So, at the outset, the orchestra assembles a dense chord – a higher consonance involving the total chromatic but rooted by E♭ and B♭ octaves, which is soon made denser by microtonal inflections. Meanwhile the piano elaborates and reinforces its own E♭/B♭ rooted sonority with a contribution to the texture that is both distinct and integral. Example 15.1(a) shows the basic, interactive disparity between the orchestral strings and solo piano in the first two bars (further chordal doublings in the woodwind and brass – with harp and tubular bells – are not shown).

In its use of immediate and persistent repetition, *Untitled no. 2* has affinities with some of the more experimental varieties of musical minimalism – a quality it shares with other pieces in the *Untitled* collection. But this is less a retreat from complexity than a way of dramatizing the turbulent forces that can be harnessed when tension-accumulating reiterations explode or collapse into contrast. Almost from the start slower, single-note repetitions begin to negate the florid music's capacity for developmental forward motion and to reinforce the significance of Clarke's observation in 2006 that 'aspects of repetition are becoming more prominent in my work'. After about four minutes (bar 55) the texture seems thoroughly becalmed, the piano punctuating the orchestra's more static layers rather than striking sparks off them, and avoiding any E♭/B♭ emphasis. After around seven minutes there is something like a new start: the E♭-based chord from the opening returns (bar 112), functioning as a recurrent point of focus as the mood grows steadily more aggressive. But the monolithic orchestral material drives the piano away from decorative flourishes into chordal repetitions that are eventually absorbed into the orchestral strata, and the music reaches its central point of crisis (bar 187f).

After about fourteen minutes (bar 196) the solo piano introduces relatively restrained, decorative figuration for a third time, and the alternation of this with sustained chordal material gradually re-energizes the atmosphere, to the extent (bar 245f, around eighteen minutes in) that a spirit of almost heroic enterprise threatens to break through. This spirit turns more anxiously aggressive as the separate strata become more confrontational, and the piano loses most of its separate identity at the music's point of maximum crisis (bars 271–74). Then, after about twenty minutes, the final phase of *Untitled No. 2* begins (bar 277). A sustained yet pulsating chord in the strings – avoiding E♭ – provokes similar material from the rest of the ensemble. Initially,

359

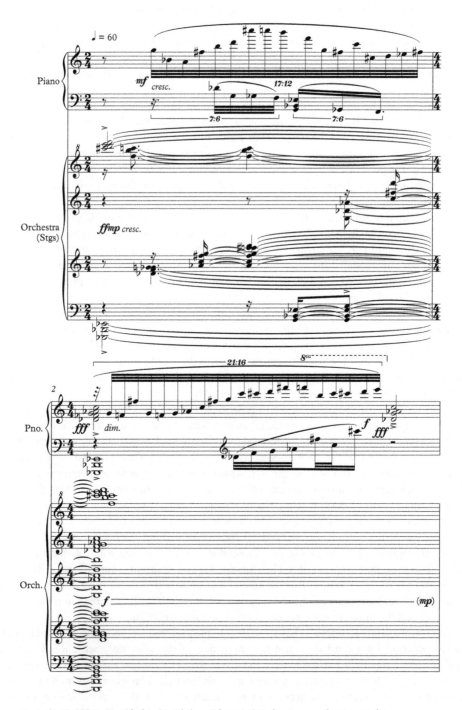

Example 15.1(a) James Clarke, *Untitled no. 2*, bars 1–2 (solo piano and strings only)
Copyright © James Clarke 2008. All rights reserved. Used by permission

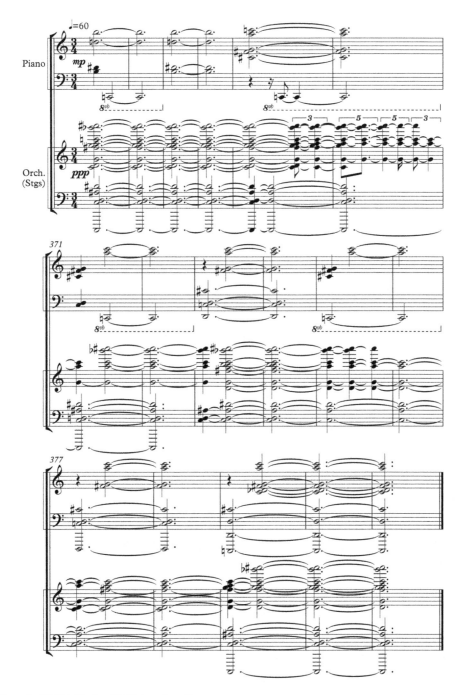

Example 15.1(b) Clarke, *Untitled no. 2*, ending

Copyright © James Clarke 2008. All rights reserved. Used by permission

the mood remains aggressive, the texture over the next four minutes or so ever more strongly polarized between fracturing and fixity. The last three or four minutes (bar 347f) then provide a counterweight with a much calmer atmosphere. The material for both piano and orchestra becomes more stable, the orchestral stratum pared down to very soft strings underpinning the piano's more widely spaced closural sonorities (Example 15.1(b)). The mood is one of relative repose, but without any resolution back onto the initial E♭-based chord. This chord, it is clear, is not a guarantor of overall stability but rather a starting point to be consistently, if not completely, negated over the composition's twenty-eight-minute span.

Clarke since 2007

For Clarke himself, it is *Untitled no. 5* (2007) – the second for solo piano – which begins 'the reintroduction of more complex patterns and textures (referring also to bell patterns...)',[32] after the less elaborate processes used earlier, and especially in the orchestral parts of *Untitled no. 2*. Seven years later, though still working with degrees of convergence and divergence involving stability and instability, *Untitled no. 7* revisited solo piano writing and E♭-centred harmony to explore very different processes – processes that have something to do with the piece's close proximity to the String Quartet No. 3.

Clarke's Third Quartet was 'written for and dedicated to the Arditti Quartet on the occasion of their fortieth anniversary' in 2014. Appropriately, therefore, this five-minute piece celebrates that ensemble's capacity for the projection of unanimity within the most fiercely fragmented of contexts: and it also celebrates the survivability – the indestructibility, even – of a particular modernist formal archetype, the one embodied in the familiar Boulezian binary of ' . . . explosante/fixe. . . '. The first pair of musical States, A (bars 1–4) and B (bars 5–11), represent very different gestural explosions, the first centring on heavily accented fragments and glissandos with different (but related) rhythmic patterns in each instrument, the second an exuberantly uniform melodic outpouring, doubled across four octaves and in consistent rhythmic unison (Example 15.2(a)). The third State (bars 12–18) then projects a much more 'fixed' impression – very soft and chorale-like, and ending with a similarly restrained chord to cut short the attempted reassertion of a more explosive manner in bars 15–16.

These eighteen bars are all preliminary to the four longer episodes which follow: State D (bars 19–42) can be thought of as developing associations with both A (mainly in second violin and viola) and B (mainly in first violin and cello), but calling the work's initial exploration of unanimity into question in the interests of a more evolved, stratified kind of musical discourse. Conversely, State E (bars 43–51) is even more reductively chorale-like than State C, interrupting the expressionistic aura which is then reasserted by the conclusion, State F (bars 52–65). State F is initially more connected to State A's melodic fragments and glissandos, but then restores State B's kind of melodic unisons (viola and cello from bar 60, the two violins from bar 66), by which time viola and cello are initiating reiterations of a single pitch, B♭. The two upper instruments join in with this from bar 72 in a short coda that follows the 'fixed-exploding-fixed' pattern in a collective descent down a whole tone from B♭ to A♭, as each instrument contributes independently to the continuous semiquaver rhythm (Example 15.2(b)). This – 'As' as the German for A♭ but also short for the Ardittis? – could be the music's ultimate tongue-in-cheek tribute to that redoubtable ensemble.

The Third Quartet's modernist strategy – in which inherently unstable textural states (whether 'exploding' or 'fixed') acquire degrees of stability and thereby become familiar to the ear by being extended and reiterated – is also to be found in *Untitled no. 7* for solo piano

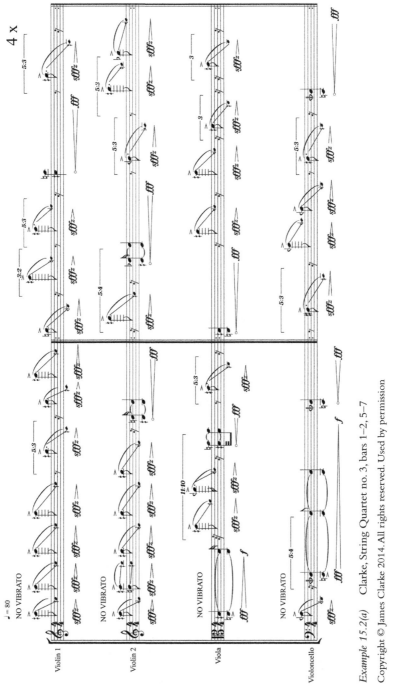

Example 15.2(a) Clarke, String Quartet no. 3, bars 1–2, 5–7
Copyright © James Clarke 2014. All rights reserved. Used by permission

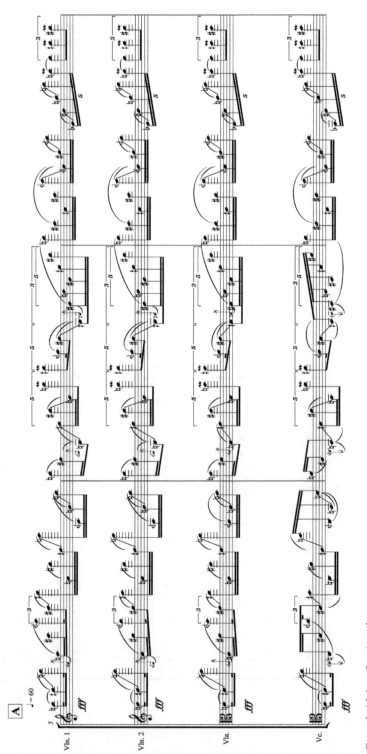

Example 15.2a Continued

Example 15.2(b)   Clarke, String Quartet no. 3, bars 74–78

Copyright © James Clarke 2014. All rights reserved. Used by permission

(2014–15). In an email to me, Clarke commented that this was 'the first work in which [he had used] retrogrades' since he was fifteen. He continued:

> Now that I have a more visually influenced approach, as opposed to directional or literary, retrograde forms make logical sense. Before I found the idea of playing the music backwards inconsistent with the forward-moving transformational approach. Now I think of receiving music in similar ways to the observation of a painting: information is placed in front of the observer and it is not dependent on a narrative interpretation.

Clarke has no need to spell out the obvious paradoxes inherent here. Spending ten minutes listening to a performance of *Untitled no. 7* is scarcely comparable to spending ten minutes in front of (say) one of Richard Diebenkorn's 'Untitled' canvases – though the types of experience might converge to some extent if the listener to the musical performance already has a good sense of what *Untitled no. 7* as a whole is like. Knowing what to expect as a listener to a textless piece of music might well – as Clarke suggests – be judged analogous to processing information

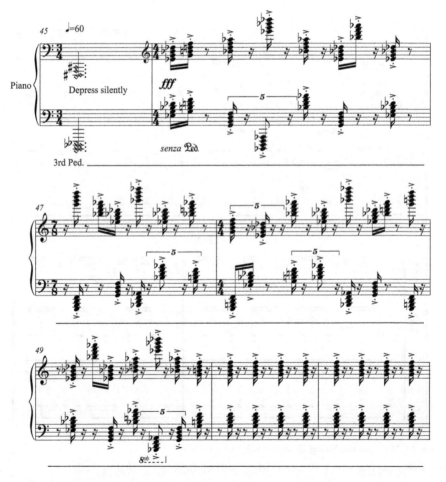

Example 15.3(a)   Clarke, *Untitled no. 7*, bars 45–51

Copyright © James Clarke 2015. All rights reserved. Used by permission

Foundations and fixations

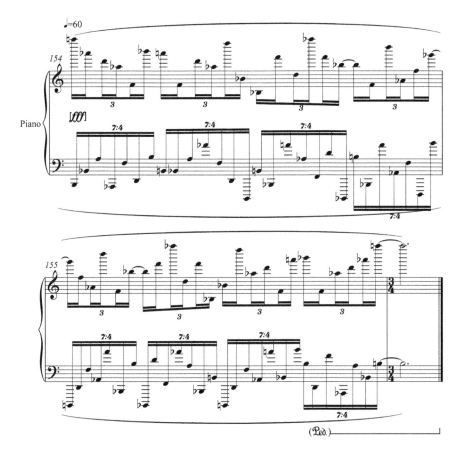

Example 15.3(b)   Clarke, *Untitled no. 7*, bars 154–56
Copyright © James Clarke 2015. All rights reserved. Used by permission

presented complete from the outset when studying an abstract painting. As it happens, *Untitled no. 7* is not quite free of text associations: Clarke has revealed that the piece's initial flourish derives from a much earlier composition from 1989–90 for bass clarinet, cello and piano called *Verstörung*, a German word meaning roughly 'disturbance', and the title of a 1967 novel by Thomas Bernhard – *Gargoyles* in the 1970 English translation.[33] The version of this that begins *Untitled no. 7* can be said (and heard) to distort the earlier version by greatly extending the intervallic span, changing simple into compound intervals.

A contrasting element of stability is retained, by way of pitch as well as pitch-class repetition, but the predominant effect of such a revisiting of twenty-four-year-old material is that of the music itself intensifying the emotional and physical state originally spelled out for the listener in a title, and the intensity is further intensified by the polarity of projecting this febrile and refracted statement against the resonating aura of the initial, silently depressed E♭ major triads. Clarke's notes on *Untitled no. 7* refer to such chords as 'tonal', not merely as 'consonances', and although their presence in the piece is rather more peripheral than would be the case in a properly tonal structure, they serve – like the initial higher consonance of *Untitled no. 2* – to dramatize the music's pervasive negation of such structures. Simply because history has shown that such consonant sonorities cannot easily be completely forgotten or excluded from a listener's sensibility, the most effective modernist strategy is to confront them and in so doing to demonstrate their irreducible otherness. In *Untitled no. 7* the fierce or hushed presentations of E♭ major elements in the earlier stages (Example 15.3(a)) are ultimately negated by the splintering symmetries of the quasi-minimalist permutational and palindromic techniques that dominate the final pages, discussed further in the closing section of this chapter (Example 15.3(b) shows the last three bars). This 'absence in presence' seems the very essence of a late-modernist understanding of suspended – consonant – tonality. Here, suspended tonality has the quality of a destabilized hierarchy, of classicism reduced to a trace of its most elemental substance.

The 'otherness' for which the major triad stands in *Untitled no. 7* cannot usefully be equated with the placement of small, precisely rendered 'real' objects in abstract paintings, or even with the insertion of such actual objects in a cubist collage. Rather, it serves to reinforce the autonomously musical materials in use, materials that are not telling a story, even though they have unavoidable associations with older and newer musical elements. Clarke's non-story in *Untitled no. 7* is a musical unfolding in which the unambiguously synthesis-rejecting modernist resists the elementally classical. This kind of challengingly uningratiating music provides endless food for thought, as do its uneasy parallels with the work of a younger British modernist, Morgan Hayes – uneasy in that Hayes cleaves closer to the modernist mainstream than does Clarke, while avoiding most of the risks of dumbing down and dilution that might emerge in the implied comparison.

Morgan Hayes: distressed surfaces and delicate balances

In a short study first published in 2012, I wrote that 'like his mentor Michael Finnissy, Hayes relishes multiple allusions, while not invoking connections with expressionistic melancholia or with "new" complexity as directly as British modernists of earlier generations.' Echoes of British new complexity can be heard from time to time, and 'as recently as 2005, in *Strip*, a BBC Proms commission for full-sized orchestra'.[34] Since then, Hayes has avoided large-scale orchestral forces, with even his sixteen-minute Violin Concerto (2006) using only a fifteen-strong accompanying ensemble.

Hayes's penchant for satire and irony – with a hint that the comic can be even more unsettling and subversive than the tragic – has always been a vital strand in his compositional output and helps to define his distinctive take on the possibilities of modernist music drama. There are qualities of exuberance and delicacy here which, as I wrote in 2012, 'represent Hayes's aversion to unmitigated "angst" in music: though they are not incompatible with the kind of hectic or febrile moods [. . .] of certain scores by Birtwistle, including *Panic* and *Theseus Game*'.[35] Like a host of British composers born several decades after Birtwistle, however, Hayes is as wary of being hypnotized by British modernist precursors as composers of Birtwistle's generation were of non-British precursors such as Schoenberg, Stravinsky and Varèse. And in Hayes's case it is no less necessary to avoid abject dependence on both the 'complex' modernists, including Finnissy, and composers often defined as 'experimental', many of them in both categories born in the 1940s – especially when 'experimental' involves a new angle on modernism rather than attempts to reject it out of hand.

James Clarke's avoidance of explicit associations with political or cultural subject matter – an affinity with abstract expressionist painting aside – is complemented by Hayes's relish for such connections. That Hayes's musical thinking might have more to do with exuberantly fanciful futurism and surrealism than with melancholic Germanic expressionism is openly acknowledged in his eight-minute *Futurist Manifesto* (2007) for string orchestra, which celebrates – but perhaps also questions – what the composer's note in the score describes as the 'excitable, breathless tone

Foundations and fixations

of voice: a celebration of the machine age, aeroplanes, war and a plea to dispense with all traces of the past' that the manifestos of Filippo Marinetti and Umberto Boccioni so extravagantly propose. It was nevertheless a much more immediately contemporary, locally British topic that provided the basis for the short operatic scena called *Shirley and Jane* with which Hayes concluded a period as composer-in-association with Music Theatre Wales in 2008. Shirley (soprano) is the controversial one-time head of Westminster City Council, Dame Shirley Porter, and Jane (mezzo) a (fictional) domestic servant or secretary-housekeeper.[36]

A touch political

If it is rare for a British composer to name a leading political figure as Finnissy does in his 'You Know What Kind of Sense Mrs Thatcher Made' (*First Political Agenda* no. 3) – the music is an alienated meditation on Parry's 'Jerusalem' – it is even rarer for a leading political figure to be given a voice, at least without the kind of temporal distancing found in Prokofiev's *War and Peace*, where the 'real' people seem scarcely more contemporary in character than Julius Caesar does in Handel's opera. The text for *Shirley and Jane*, by playwright Gary Owen (b. 1972), makes no attempt to mythify or poeticize the straightforward generic concept of a dialogue between two characters as a duet in which similarities ultimately override differences. Hayes's music characteristically combines the quirky with the matter-of-fact, and the role of the accompanying piano is crucial in dictating the atmosphere and shape of the dialogue. The spare, very quiet two-part texture of the opening defines the nature of the duet as a blend of difference and similarity – rhythmic unison, pitch materials which share some common notes (Example 15.4(a)). At first Jane is smoother, Shirley more hectoring. But in the scena's main section, which the piano launches with forceful march rhythms (marked 'brutal'), both characters use rhetorical emphasis to assert identities that embody a strong sense of responsibility whose sinister overtones are revealed at the end.

While Shirley turns expressionistic in her assumption that those she is responsible for prefer to 'leave the dirty work to me', Jane is more reticent in acknowledging that 'I know I soak up the filth of your life then carry it away'. The march boils over as Shirley proclaims 'my vision takes in the grander scheme', as against Jane's 'my duties include soiled sheets'. Both rather breathlessly define the sheer hard work involved in their lives, and at the very end both agree that the 'people' (Jane) or 'peasants' (Shirley) with whom they deal on a daily basis are simply 'fools': not a comfortable conclusion for those expecting a resolution in terms of stark contrasts between a sinner and a saint (Example 15.4(b)). Instead, both women appear to find fulfilment in alienation and in exasperation with those they serve – though Jane's contempt for Shirley is more acceptable than Shirley's visceral dislike of her multiple Westminster 'constituents'.

Such uncompromising representations of the contemporary demand to be offset by the kind of stark portrayals of ancient forces of nature (again, like *Futurist Manifesto*, with special relevance to Italy) that Hayes provided in 2010 in *E Vesuvio monte*, a six-minute setting for eight solo voices of an extract from Pliny the Younger's account of his uncle's death as a result of the eruption of the Mount Vesuvius volcano in 79 AD. Hayes's piece involves persistent contrasts between the fragmentary and the sustained, a simple but potent metaphor for the ironic awareness of 'our assumptions about human progress when confronted with the raw power of nature' that the composer notes in the score, comparing the Vesuvius eruption with that in Iceland in April 2010. 'Human progress' explains the anguished eloquence of the music while the 'raw power of nature' bites back in the explosive textural layout.

Example 15.4(a)   Morgan Hayes, *Shirley and Jane*, bars 1–9
Copyright © Morgan Hayes 2008. All rights reserved. Used by permission

Foundations and fixations

Example 15.4(b) Hayes, *Shirley and Jane*, bars 158–65

Copyright © Morgan Hayes 2008. All rights reserved. Used by permission

Stressful subjects

Both the 'ancient' *E Vesuvio monte* and the 'modern' *Shirley and Jane* are unambiguously modernist in offering mordantly destabilized representations of reality, and in Hayes's music there is more than a hint of the aesthetic stance that argues for satire, whether gentle or savage, as a more effective aesthetic weapon against pomposity and corruption than mythic distancing or solemn sermonizing. Equally, the stance might embody a rueful acceptance of an inescapable status quo. But, to counter the ever-present risks of complacency, there is also a relish for the disturbingly absurd that comes to the fore in an instrumental diptych comprising the multi-sectioned piano work *Elemental* (2013–17) and the eight-strong ensemble composition *The Unrest-Cure* (2013–15).

In the diptych, the absence of verbal text results in a more abstract form of music drama than is the case with the hyper-literal *Shirley and Jane*. At the outset of *Elemental* (though this

Arnold Whittall

music was not actually written first) Hayes seems to equate elemental with elementary, with textures a world away from the post-Xenakisian turbulence of Clarke's *Untitled no. 7*, though it soon emerges that one note at a time, or consistent two-part homophony (as with the opening of *Shirley and Jane*), can be rhythmically complex and require a considerable degree of digital dexterity. The beginnings of both *Shirley and Jane* and *Elemental* confirm that Hayes's version of late modernism involves resistance to anything transparently systematic, with the distinction between what is 'invariant' and 'deviant' ambiguously indefinite. In particular, the sense of consistently destabilized hierarchies leaves any selection of pitch-centre to individual choice: there is no definitive 'key', but no absolute negation of 'key' either. In the short piano introduction to *Shirley and Jane* (shown in Example 15.4(a)), a systematic scaffolding built from the complementary trichords A, E, B and E♭, B♭, F might be deduced. B♭ is the pitch on which the voices converge, and one of the piano's final pitches too (Example 15.4(b)), but the music's directed motion shrugs off serial constraints as gleefully as it sidesteps tonal voice-leading. As for the 21-bar first movement of *Elemental* (Example 15.5), the pitch-class A recurs often and prominently enough to suggest pivotal centrality, and the repetitions of A/F/E♭ build on that centrality to add a further sliver of structural stability. As the final section of this chapter will underline, the enveloping contexts are centrifugal, anti-centric – the kind of entertainment that keeps the listener guessing and refuses to be pinned down.

In the final moments of its third part, *Elemental* turns robustly virtuosic, as if to acknowledge the essential ambiguity of a title suggesting both the primitive and the sublime. Such hints of the uneasy and the strange can explain the link to *The Unrest-Cure*, which follows. But *Elemental* itself best sketches in such attributes in the way its melodic lines resist the shapely regularity of traditional, classical melody. Even if a tidily systematic background were to be revealed, the first part's ever-changing capriciousness, answered by the second part's edgily mysterious constraints (occasionally exploded by a forceful cadence), leaves little doubt that the approach to the third part through the progress from 'timid' to 'more confident' is a risky enterprise, consistency virtually guaranteeing an ultimate instability. Part Three's gigue-like velocity seems designed to threaten disintegration, then to recover not just velocity but elegance. Yet the brittle showmanship of Part Three's ending (echoed as this is at the end of the work's final, ninth section) might be most relevant to the sardonically manipulative persona of the character central to *The Unrest-Cure* – the luridly named Clovis Sangrail.

'The Unrest-Cure', a short story by Saki (the pen name of H. H. Munro) included in *The Chronicles of Clovis*, was first published in 1911.[37] It tells how the deceptively un-Mephistophelian Clovis meets the bored and disaffected Huddle (Saki's names are nothing if not nudgingly redolent) and diagnoses the need for a radical and catastrophic 'unrest-cure', that is, to engineer 'a blot on the twentieth century' that is nothing less than a massacre of Jews. This gleeful inversion of all that, even in 1911, would have been thought proper and possible, works though the economy and polish of its elegantly witty prose. Associations are often made between Saki and Wilde, and a brief episode in Hayes's piece recalls the vehemently cod-militaristic anti-Germanism of Gerald Barry's opera *The Importance of Being Earnest* (2012). The one musical reference in Saki's story is the suggestion that another effective unrest-cure would be 'to give lectures in Berlin to prove that much of Wagner's music was written by Gambetta' – a curious allusion (presumably) to the French statesman from the time of the Franco-Prussian War in 1870. In any event, Hayes's music in 2015 was still more in tune with eerie understatement than overtly expressionistic anguish.

Within the instrumental octet of alto flute, oboe, bass clarinet, horn, piano, violin, viola and cello the viola seems to lead, though reticently rather than aggressively – the marking is 'delicato' – as if representing the voice and thought of the insidiously diabolical Clovis.

The initial melodic line is *Elemental*-like, shared with a shadowing piano, and with atmospheric punctuations from the other instruments, prompting the texture to become increasingly febrile. The first major change (from bar 90) comes when the piano provides a regularly patterned accompaniment to transitional material that 'rests' the viola, but this leading voice returns with a relatively direct and decisive melodic statement (bars 55–59), the immediate response to which is the outburst of what might be called 'the idea of massacre' march. This soon becomes both more insistent and more diverse, running out of steam and leading to a 'desolato' coda. The viola (muted, 'murmurando') again stands for regularity, though the initial pattern of fourteen quavers is eroded on attempted repetition and yields prominence to the cello in a reversal of roles that manages its own fourteen-quaver succession before the final dissolution.

At about six minutes and twenty seconds, Hayes's piece emulates Saki's subversively elegant economy, superimposing its own subversiveness in the way its possible connections to narrative explicitness are deflected by music's innate inability to speak. If the solemn moral of the story is that it is addiction to routine and aversion to change which are the real dangers to civilization, as well as the most effective triggers for an outrage like the massacre of any religious or national group, then the idea of the civilized as itself something potentially sublime comes through as deserving of respect as much as of mockery. In this spirit, Hayes's music – like that of any number of outwardly very different contemporaries, in Britain and elsewhere – can be construed as embodying and actually strengthened by modernism's disdain for classicism's utopian certainties. Saki's tales, the paintings of Clyfford Still and the music of the composers discussed in this chapter might be transparently detached from naturalistic reality, but that is the source of their appeal, the basis of what they can mean for real people contemplating them and considering their place in the real world.

A relatively theoretical conclusion

In post-tonal pitch-class set theory, hexachords like [012369] and [012469] allow for very particular perspectives on basic tonal harmonic elements like the major triad [037] and dominant seventh [0258]. Aspects of Clarke's *Untitled no. 7* and Part One of Hayes's *Elemental* illustrate what is involved. In Clarke's piece the early stages draw particular attention to the B♭/D/F/A♭ collection in an E♭ major context, and the piece's conclusion presents a spectacularly dispersed toccata-like texture in which both hands – groups of six semiquavers per beat in the right, of seven semiquavers per beat in the left – spend most time with palindromic permutations of B♭ dominant-seventh patterns. As Example 15.3(b) shows, the right-hand music is confined to these four pitch classes, countered only by a disruptive G♭ at the centre of a palindrome in bars 154–55 and an A at the extremities. The left-hand septuplets add both A and B to the invariant dominant seventh on B♭, with the B that is missing from the right-hand music marking both the centre and the extremities of the palindrome. Omitting the disruptive G♭, the entire passage therefore focuses on the hexachord 0 (B) 1 (B♭) 2 (A) 3 (A♭) 6 (F) 9 (D).

The twenty-one bars of Hayes's *Elemental 1* (Example 15.5) divide into four segments defined by tempo – crotchet = 65 (bars 1–11), crotchet = 50 (12–13), crotchet = 65 (14–19), crotchet = 50 (20–21). The first of the two crotchet = 50 segments has the quality of a generative core: if the decorative pitches are omitted, the music comprises two tetrachords – [0126] in bar 12, [0258] in bar 13 – and conflated (A and E♭ occur in both) the whole deploys the 0 (E♭) 1 (E) 2 (F) 4 (G) 6 (A) 9 (C) hexachord, in ways that offer fresh perspectives on the diatonic scale's capacity for projecting such diverse features as the [016] and [037] trichords. The

Example 15.5 Hayes, *Elemental 1*

Copyright © Morgan Hayes 2015. All rights reserved. Used by permission

second two-bar segment begins as a restatement of the first with the same three crotchets A, F and E♭ an octave higher, but with the addition of C in place of the earlier E♮ (cf. bar 1) the tetrachord is (again) [0258]: the next four melody notes also form [0258] (B, A, F♯, E♭), and the piece's final tetrachord (including the F♯ that spans the flourish in bar 21) is equivalent to the first segment's first group – 0 (F♯) 1 (F) 2 (E) 7 (B). In these terms the music can be thought to progress from an emphasis on the melodic trichord A, F, E♭ ([026] to the F, E, B trichord [016]), countering the piece's prevailing tendency to cycle round A♮ as a pitch focus.

Foundations and fixations

An analysis of this kind involves strings of data whose musical plausibility must then be assessed, and whose tendency to prioritize connections is only useful to the extent to which it implicitly urges taking positive note of differences. With both Clarke and Hayes it seems clear that any tendency to the systematic, the consistently invariant, is usually countered by the spontaneously divergent. But this is not to argue that, as modernists, Hayes and Clarke neatly converge on similar moods and identical techniques. While Clarke's manner is unfailingly serious, though never sentential, Hayes's is more playful, mordantly reflecting on the kind of generic and stylistic qualities that come into the strongest focus when the music is laid out on a rather small scale. Overall, then, the two composers diverge, but within the capacious properties that the modernist aesthetic, as defined here, is able to supply. In turn, this suggests that a systematic post-tonal theory (not actually used by the composers themselves) can never be as all-explanatory for such music as voice-leading analysis or sonata-theory segmentation can be for classical tonal music. What theory-based analysis of post-tonal music that is not systematically based on such theories can usefully accomplish is to suggest how the kinds of consistency provided by the extrapolation of invariants interact with elements that resist or negate such invariant features in ways that reinforce the sense of a modernist aesthetic at work.

Earlier, I noted that modernism's apparent capacity for survival has to do with its ability to acknowledge certain 'survivals from the common-practice past'. As the twenty-first century advances, there is nevertheless a shift of emphasis away from the style of modernism most palpable in the musics of composers born during the lifetimes of Webern and Schoenberg – in Britain including Maxwell Davies, Birtwistle, Harvey, Ferneyhough and Finnissy. As those composers reach the ends of their careers, and other influences emerge, it is becoming evident that a genuine postmodernism – it might loosely be dubbed 'the John Adams phase' – is gaining ground. 'Genuine postmodernism' would seem to involve a renewal of classical continuities without direct reference to traditional tonal music and thereby to open up certain affinities with the otherwise very different stylistic and technical qualities of minimalism and spectralism. It remains to be seen for how long new examples of genuinely modernist music will appear alongside such more immediately accessible compositions: but in the context of a performance culture which has not thus far brought the more challenging examples of modernism composed since 1900 into the mainstream, a pessimistic prediction seems justified.

Notes

1 Pierre Boulez took the title of ... *explosante/fixe*... from André Breton's *L'amour fou* (1937). Beginning in 1971 as a tribute to Stravinsky, the composition evolved into a thirty-six-minute work for MIDI flute solo and instrumental ensemble, first performed in 1995.

2 J. P. E. Harper-Scott, *The Quilting Points of Musical Modernism: Revolution, Reaction, and William Walton* (Cambridge: Cambridge University Press, 2012); Philip Rupprecht, *British Musical Modernism: The Manchester Group and Their Contemporaries* (Cambridge: Cambridge University Press, 2015).

3 Harper-Scott, *The Quilting Points of Musical Modernism*, 252.

4 Rupprecht, *British Musical Modernism*, cover material.

5 Philip Rupprecht, 'Among the Ruined Languages: Britten's Triadic Modernism, 1930–1940', in *Tonality 1900–1950: Concept and Practice*, ed. Felix Wörner, Ullrich Scheideler and Philip Rupprecht (Stuttgart: Steiner, 2012), 223–45; Harper-Scott, *The Quilting Points*, 252.

6 In his 1926 essay 'Opinion or Insight?' Schoenberg placed the expression 'emancipation of the dissonance' in quotes, adding that dissonance 'came to be placed on an equal footing with the sounds regarded as consonances'; Arnold Schoenberg, *Style and Idea: Selected Writings*, ed. Leonard Stein and trans. Leo Black (London: Faber and Faber, 1975), 260.

7 Of my own contributions I would list especially '"Let it Drift": Birtwistle's Late-Modernist Music Dramas', in *Harrison Birtwistle Studies*, ed. David Beard, Kenneth Gloag and Nicholas Jones (Cambridge: Cambridge University Press, 2015), 1–25; '"A Dark Voice from Within": Peter Maxwell Davies and

Modern Times', in *Peter Maxwell Davies Studies*, ed. Kenneth Gloag and Nicholas Jones (Cambridge: Cambridge University Press, 2009), 1–20; and 'Theory, History, Analysis: Exploring Contemporary Complexity', *Theory and Practice* 37–38 (2012–13), 241–61.

8 In this respect, compare its absence from my *Music since the First World War* (London: Dent, 1977) with its prominence in this text as revised and expanded in *Musical Composition in the Twentieth Century* (Oxford: Oxford University Press, 1999).

9 For a comprehensive discussion of this topic, see Gretchen Horlacher, *Building Blocks: Repetition and Continuity in the Music of Stravinsky* (New York: Oxford University Press, 2011).

10 Among many texts, Lawrence Kramer's *Music as Cultural Practice (1800–1900)* (Berkeley, Los Angeles and Oxford: University of California Press, 1990) is an influential demonstration of the new-musicological emphasis on context.

11 Malcolm Bradbury and James McFarlane, 'The Name and Nature of Modernism', in *Modernism, 1890–1939*, ed. Malcolm Bradbury and James McFarlane (Harmondsworth, UK: Penguin Books, 1976), 27.

12 Arnold Whittall, 'Tippett and the Modernist Mainstream', in *Michael Tippett O.M.: A Celebration*, ed. Geraint Lewis (Tunbridge Wells: Baton Press, 1985), 109–15.

13 Arnold Whittall, 'Individualism and Accessibility: The Moderate Mainstream, 1945–75', in *The Cambridge History of Twentieth-Century Music*, ed. Nicholas Cook and Anthony Pople (Cambridge: Cambridge University Press, 2004), 364–94.

14 For an early discussion of this topic, see my *The Music of Britten and Tippett: Studies in Themes and Techniques* (Cambridge: Cambridge University Press, 1982), 5–6. See also George Perle's concept of 'twelve-tone tonality', which 'seems to combine two contradictory forces, the equality of the twelve distinct notes in twelve-tone music and the focus on tone centers characteristic of tonality'; Dave Headlam, 'Introduction', in George Perle, *The Right Notes: Twenty-Three Selected Essays on Twentieth-Century Music* (Stuyvesant NY: Pendragon Press, 1995), xii.

15 Arnold Whittall, 'British Music in the Modern World', in *The Blackwell History of Music in Britain: The Twentieth Century*, ed. Stephen Banfield (Oxford: Blackwell, 1995), 9–26.

16 Pierre Boulez, 'Approaches to Parsifal', in *Orientations*, ed. Jean-Jacques Nattiez and trans. Martin Cooper (London: Faber and Faber, 1986), 254.

17 For this argument at its most extreme, see Pierre Boulez, 'Schoenberg Is Dead' (1952), in *Stocktakings from an Apprenticeship*, ed. Paule Thévenin and trans. Stephen Walsh (Oxford: Oxford University Press, 1991), 209–14.

18 John Daverio, *Nineteenth-Century Music and the German Romantic Ideology* (New York: Schirmer, 1993) 189.

19 Anthony Pople, *Berg: Violin Concerto* (Cambridge: Cambridge University Press, 1991), 102.

20 Among a host of English-language titles, see Lawrence Kramer, *Classical Music and Postmodern Knowledge* (Berkeley, Los Angeles and London: University of California Press, 1995); Theodor W. Adorno, *Essays on Music*, ed. Richard Leppert (Berkeley, Los Angeles and London: University of California Press, 2002); Max Paddison, *Adorno's Aesthetics of Music* (Cambridge: Cambridge University Press, 1993); James Hepokoski, *Sibelius: Symphony No. 5* (Cambridge: Cambridge University Press, 1993); Carl Dahlhaus, *Schoenberg and the New Music*, trans. Derrick Puffett and Alfred Clayton (Cambridge: Cambridge University Press, 1987); Carl Dahlhaus, *Between Romanticism and Modernism: Four Studies in the Music of the Later Nineteenth Century*, trans. Mary Whittall (Berkeley, Los Angeles and London: University of California Press, 1980).

21 For example Warren Darcy, *Wagner's Das Rheingold* (Oxford: Clarendon Press, 1993); James Hepokoski and Warren Darcy, *Elements of Sonata Theory: Norms, Types, and Deformations in the Late-Eighteenth-Century Sonata* (New York: Oxford University Press, 2006).

22 Stephen Hinton, 'Kurt Weill's "Modern Classical Art"'; Arnold Whittall, 'Peter Maxwell Davies and the Problem of Classicizing Modernism', in *Die klassizistische Moderne in der Musik des 20. Jahrhunderts*, ed. Hermann Danuser (Winterthur: Amadeus, 1997), 115–22 and 143–51.

23 Arnold Whittall, 'Expressionism Revisited: Modernism beyond the Twentieth Century', in *Transformations of Musical Modernism*, ed. Erling E. Guldbrandsen and Julian Johnson (Cambridge: Cambridge University Press, 2015), 53–73.

24 Edward Venn, 'Thomas Adès and the Spectre of Brahms', *Journal of the Royal Musical Association* 140, no. 1 (2015), 163.

25 Ibid., 167 and 171.

26 For a summary discussion of the debate around the term 'suspended tonality', see my *Cambridge Introduction to Serialism* (Cambridge: Cambridge University Press, 2008), 110–11; see also Matthew Arndt, 'Schoenberg on Problems, or, Why the Six-Three Chord Is Dissonant', *Theory and Practice* 37–38 (2012–13), 1–62.

Foundations and fixations

27 Pierre Boulez, 'The *Ring*: Time Re-Explored', *Orientations*, 272.
28 Arnold Whittall, 'Affirmative Anger: James Clarke and the Music of Abstract Expressionism', *Musical Times* 152 (Summer 2011), 21.
29 Richard Barrett, 'Tracts for Our Times?' *Musical Times* 139 (Autumn 1998), 23; see also comments from an unpublished interview cited in Arnold Whittall, 'Resistance and Reflection: Richard Barrett in the 21st Century', *Musical Times* 146 (Autumn 2005), 61.
30 Parts of this discussion derive from a note on the work I provided for a London performance by Nicolas Hodges and the BBC Symphony Orchestra, conductor Ilan Volkov (BBC Programme Book, BBC Symphony Concerts, Barbican Hall, London, 29 April 2011).
31 Whittall, 'Affirmative Anger', 26.
32 Ibid., 23.
33 Thomas Bernhard, *Verstörung* (Frankfurt am Main: Insel, 1967); Eng. trans. *Gargoyles* (New York: Knopf, 1970).
34 Arnold Whittall, 'Distressed Surfaces: Morgan Hayes and 21st-Century Expressionism', *Musical Times* 153 (Autumn 2012), 1–25.
35 Ibid., 9.
36 For scores and recordings of relevant works, see Morgan Hayes's website, http://www.morganhayes.com.
37 H. H. Munro, 'The Unrest-Cure', in *Saki: The Complete Short Stories* (London: Penguin Books, 2000), 127–33.

Bibliography

Adorno, Theodor W. *Essays on Music*, edited by Richard Leppert. Berkeley, Los Angeles and London: University of California Press, 2002.
Arndt, Matthew. 'Schoenberg on Problems, or, Why the Six-Three Chord Is Dissonant'. *Theory and Practice* 37–38 (2012–13): 1–62.
Barrett, Richard. 'Tracts for Our Times?' *Musical Times* 139 (Autumn 1998): 21–24.
Bernhard, Thomas. *Verstörung*. Frankfurt: Insel, 1967. Translated into English by Richard and Clara Winston as *Gargoyles*. New York: Knopf, 1970.
Boulez, Pierre. 'Approaches to *Parsifal*'. In *Orientations*, edited by Jean-Jacques Nattiez and translated by Martin Cooper, 245–59. London: Faber and Faber, 1986.
———. 'The *Ring*: Time Re-Explored'. In *Orientations*, edited by Jean-Jacques Nattiez and translated by Martin Cooper, 260–77. London: Faber and Faber, 1986.
———. 'Schoenberg Is Dead' (1952). In *Stocktakings from an Apprenticeship*, edited by Paule Thévenin and translated by Stephen Walsh, 209–14. Oxford: Oxford University Press, 1991.
Bradbury, Malcolm, and James McFarlane, eds. *Modernism, 1890–1939*. Guides to European Literature. Harmondsworth, UK: Penguin Books, 1976.
Dahlhaus, Carl. *Between Romanticism and Modernism: Four Studies in the Music of the Later Nineteenth Century*, translated by Mary Whittall. Berkeley, Los Angeles and London: University of California Press, 1980.
———. *Schoenberg and the New Music*, translated by Derrick Puffett and Alfred Clayton. Cambridge: Cambridge University Press, 1987.
Danuser, Hermann, ed. *Die klassizistische Moderne in der Musik des 20. Jahrhunderts*. Winterthur: Amadeus, 1997.
Darcy, Warren. *Wagner's Das Rheingold*. Oxford: Clarendon Press, 1993.
Daverio, John. *Nineteenth-Century Music and the German Romantic Ideology*. New York: Schirmer, 1993.
Harper-Scott, J. P. E. *The Quilting Points of Musical Modernism: Revolution, Reaction, and William Walton*. Cambridge: Cambridge University Press, 2012.
Hepokoski, James. *Sibelius: Symphony No. 5*. Cambridge: Cambridge University Press, 1993.
Hepokoski, James, and Warren Darcy. *Elements of Sonata Theory: Norms, Types, and Deformations in the Late-Eighteenth-Century Sonata*. New York: Oxford University Press, 2006.
Horlacher, Gretchen. *Building Blocks: Repetition and Continuity in the Music of Stravinsky*. New York: Oxford University Press, 2011.
Kramer, Lawrence. *Music as Cultural Practice (1800–1900)*. Berkeley, Los Angeles and Oxford: University of California Press, 1990.
———. *Classical Music and Postmodern Knowledge*. Berkeley, Los Angeles and London: University of California Press, 1995.

Munro, H. H. 'The Unrest-Cure'. In *Saki: The Complete Short Stories*, 127–33. London: Penguin Books, 2000.

Paddison, Max. *Adorno's Aesthetics of Music*. Cambridge: Cambridge University Press, 1993.

Perle, George. *The Right Notes: Twenty-three Selected Essays on Twentieth-Century Music*. Stuyvesant, NY: Pendragon Press, 1995.

Pople, Anthony. *Berg: Violin Concerto*. Cambridge: Cambridge University Press, 1991.

Rupprecht, Philip. 'Among the Ruined Languages: Britten's Triadic Modernism, 1930–1940'. In *Tonality 1900–1950: Concept and Practice*, edited by Felix Wörner, Ullrich Scheideler and Philip Rupprecht, 223–45. Stuttgart: Steiner, 2012.

———. *British Musical Modernism: The Manchester Group and Their Contemporaries*. Cambridge: Cambridge University Press, 2015.

Schoenberg, Arnold. 'Opinion or Insight?' In *Style and Idea: Selected Writings*, edited by Leonard Stein and translated by Leo Black, 258–64. London: Faber and Faber, 1975.

Venn, Edward. 'Thomas Adès and the Spectre of Brahms'. *Journal of the Royal Musical Association* 140, no. 1 (2015): 163–212.

Whittall, Arnold. *Music since the First World War*. London: Dent, 1977.

———. *The Music of Britten and Tippett: Studies in Themes and Techniques*. Cambridge: Cambridge University Press, 1982.

———. 'Tippett and the Modernist Mainstream'. In *Michael Tippett O.M.: A Celebration*, edited by Geraint Lewis, 109–15. Tunbridge Wells: Baton Press, 1985.

———. 'British Music in the Modern World'. In *The Blackwell History of Music in Britain: The Twentieth Century*, edited by Stephen Banfield. Oxford: Blackwell, 1995.

———. *Musical Composition in the Twentieth Century*. Oxford: Oxford University Press, 1999.

———. 'Individualism and Accessibility: The Moderate Mainstream, 1945–75'. In *The Cambridge History of Twentieth-Century Music*, edited by Nicholas Cook and Anthony Pople, 364–94. Cambridge: Cambridge University Press, 2004.

———. 'Resistance and Reflection: Richard Barrett in the 21st Century'. *Musical Times* 146 (Autumn 2005): 57–70.

———. *The Cambridge Introduction to Serialism*. Cambridge: Cambridge University Press, 2008.

———. '"A Dark Voice from Within": Peter Maxwell Davies and Modern Times'. In *Peter Maxwell Davies Studies*, edited by Kenneth Gloag and Nicholas Jones, 1–20. Cambridge: Cambridge University Press, 2009.

———. 'Affirmative Anger: James Clarke and the Music of Abstract Expressionism'. *Musical Times* 152 (Summer 2011): 19–30.

———. 'Distressed Surfaces: Morgan Hayes and 21st-Century Expressionism'. *Musical Times* 153 (Autumn 2012): 1–25.

———. 'Theory, History, Analysis: Exploring Contemporary Complexity'. *Theory and Practice* 37–38 (2012–13): 241–61.

———. 'Expressionism Revisited: Modernism Beyond the Twentieth Century'. In *Transformations of Musical Modernism*, edited by Erling E. Guldbrandsen and Julian Johnson, 53–73. Cambridge: Cambridge University Press, 2015.

———. '"Let it Drift": Birtwistle's Late-Modernist Music Dramas'. In *Harrison Birtwistle Studies*, edited by David Beard, Kenneth Gloag and Nicholas Jones, 1–25. Cambridge: Cambridge University Press, 2015.

16

THE BALINESE MOMENT IN THE MONTREAL NEW MUSIC SCENE AS A REGIONAL MODERNISM

Jonathan Goldman

Introduction: on regional modernism

Historians of musical modernism have lately shown an interest in exploring the diversity of modernist musical practice in different sites of its production.[1] By refusing to accept the binary opposition 'centre/periphery' that classical modernist historiography imposes, they have demonstrated the ways in which sites of modernist musical production can be studied for their specificity, rather than as emanations from a notional aesthetic centre. As Shmuel Eisenstadt has noted, 'The idea of multiple modernities presumes that the best way to understand the contemporary world – indeed to explain the history of modernity – is to see it as a story of continual constitution and reconstitution of a multiplicity of cultural programs.'[2] Indeed, a relatively recent strand of research into modernism seeks to elucidate the relationship between local scenes of modernist musical creativity and the international currents in which they can be inscribed. These scholars call into question a persistent myth that treats all modernist practice as a monolithic whole that employs a common musical lingua franca (whether atonal, serial, statistical, spectral or whatever). Far from envisaging the modernist current as a geographically and temporally homogeneous unit, these scholars emphasize the specificities of musical manifestations of modernism in different locales, and take seriously historical, linguistic and cultural differences, inspired by the burgeoning field of cultural geography.[3] Creative practices do not necessarily emanate from a single, central source and then get 'implanted' in various peripheral regions. They can also arise spontaneously in various particular regions through a mixture of sociocultural conditions and the presence of certain strong personalities (such as Juan Carlos Paz and Alberto Ginastera in Buenos Aires, Nadia Boulanger or Olivier Messiaen in Paris, Gilles Tremblay in Montreal etc.). Comparing regional hubs of musical effervescence not only brings to the fore the similarities and differences of each but also throws into relief the networks that each of them shares.

This chapter examines one such site of regional modernist practice, that of composers of concert music in Montreal who, beginning in the early 1970s, became spellbound by the gamelan musical traditions of Bali and Java. Composers such as Claude Vivier (1948–83), among others, produced a small but significant corpus of works inspired by the structure and sonorities of gamelan repertoire. A number of these works will be examined here in order to see how the transcription/assimilation process has been shaped by regionally specific narratives – narratives that in part explain the intercultural turn taken by modernist music in Quebec.

The Quebec–Bali moment and its inscription into the history of modernist music in Quebec

The most common narratives about artistic production in French Canada (specifically the province of Quebec) see a particularly thriving community taking root after the Second World War or, more specifically, the era of secularization and modernization that is known in Quebec as the 'Quiet Revolution' (*La révolution tranquille*).[4] Of course, to view history in this way is to ignore the impressive artistic activity in Quebec that goes back, in the European tradition, at least to the seventeenth century[5] and in First Nations traditions, of course, much further.[6] But it is nonetheless clear that in the 1950s a particularly thriving period of artistic experimentation, theoretical reflection and intense production began among Quebec writers, artists and musicians. One has only to think of the famous anti-clerical manifesto 'Refus global', launched by figures such as the painter Paul-Émile Borduas, the poet Claude Gauvreau and the choreographer Jeanne Renaud in 1948.[7] In parallel with this, young composers like Gilles Tremblay, Serge Garant and François Morel wanted to expose concert audiences to modernist repertoire much as, at exactly the same time, Pierre Boulez was inaugurating the Domaine Musical in Paris. In fact, in the year that the Domaine had its first concert, Tremblay, Garant and Morel organized what would be the first concert of avant-garde contemporary music in Quebec, on 2 May 1954 at the Montreal Conservatory, featuring music of Webern and Boulez in addition to new works by the three co-organizers.[8] This activity was also bolstered by the arrival in Quebec of immigrants seeking refuge from Nazism, as was the case for the German-Jewish composer Otto Joachim (1910–2009), who in the mid-1950s built what was to be the first electronic music home studio in Canada, in which he produced the electronic music that would be played continuously in the Canadian pavilion of Expo '67 in Montreal.[9] Hungarian-born István Anhalt (1919–2012), a post-war immigrant, founded the electronic music studio at McGill University in Montreal, the first of its kind in Quebec.[10] A watershed for the development of contemporary music in Quebec occurred in August 1961, when the composer and radio-television producer Pierre Mercure, one of the most important figures in the Quebec contemporary music scene at the time, organized the Semaine Internationale de Musique Actuelle (SIMA, International Contemporary Music Week), which allowed audiences to hear works by new music luminaries such as John Cage, Morton Feldman, Earle Brown, Mauricio Kagel, Luigi Nono, Pierre Schaeffer, Karlheinz Stockhausen and Edgard Varèse, and involved collaborations with visual artists and choreographers.[11] SIMA provided the momentum for the establishment of the first contemporary music organizations in Quebec, in particular the Société de Musique Contemporaine du Québec (SMCQ), which exists to this day.[12]

Building on the foundations laid in the 1950s and 1960s, a new generation of composers began to come to the fore in the 1970s. It is on these composers, born around 1945, that this chapter will focus. Their engagement with non-Western musical traditions, gamelan in particular, seemed in part an escape from the strictures of (serialist) high modernism. But it is also possible that the widely shared interest in other cultures, of which the Quebec–Bali musical moment was but one manifestation, was partly attributable to Quebec's growing awareness of its own distinctness as a culture or nation, reflected in the political sphere by the gain in momentum of the independence movement spearheaded by the Parti Québécois, founded in 1968.

Of course, the attraction of this younger generation of Montreal composers to gamelan bears many similarities to the comparable encounters of other twentieth-century figures (Cage,

The Balinese moment in Montreal new music

Messiaen, Harrison, Cowell, Reich etc.), which, in turn, are usually traced back to the demonstration of Javanese music at the Exposition Universelle in Paris in 1889, famously visited by Claude Debussy.[13] Quebec composers who travelled to the region and engaged in a study of the local music to varying degrees include Serge Garant (1929–86), Gilles Tremblay (1932–2017), John Rea (b. 1944), José Evangelista (b. 1943), and the best-known composer of their cohort, the aforementioned Claude Vivier. Works inspired by the structure and sonorities of gamelan repertoire subsequently produced by these composers and others included Vivier's *Pulau dewata* (1977) and *Cinq chansons* (1980), Evangelista's *Ô Bali* (1989) and *Ô Java* (1993), John Rea's *Médiator* (1981) and Walter Boudreau's *Le matin des magiciens* (1995–96): representative examples will be discussed later in this chapter. The 1992 CD *Bali à Montréal* documents some of the works that emerged from this encounter.[14] These works consciously channel the achievements of Montreal-born composer Colin McPhee (1900–64), who lived in Bali throughout the 1930s, notably composed the orchestral suite *Tabuh-Tabuhan* (1936) in a Balinese style, and authored a memoir entitled *A House in Bali*. McPhee's posthumously published analytical study of Balinese music, *Music in Bali* (1966), remained for a long time the only available English-language volume on the subject.[15] The burst of creativity experienced by composers of different generations in Montreal was productive of a variety of objects, including musical compositions, the establishment of a concert society and the founding of gamelan classes at the Université de Montréal. Cultural exchange also travelled in the other direction when, for example, Evangelista was named composer-in-residence of the Indonesian STSI Academy in 1986.

Tracing the chronology of this 'school' (even if the tendency described here is neither widespread nor uniform enough to deserve that overused moniker) involves both personal milestones and collective ones shared not only by the composers discussed here but also by an entire generation of composers in North America and Europe. Thus, the release of the 1967 LP *Music for the Morning of the World* on the Nonesuch label, derived from field recordings in Bali and Java by David Lewiston, formed part of the soundscape of countless university students in the late 1960s, and was for most of them their first encounter with the sounds of these islands.[16] In a similar fashion, the presence of many music examples transcribed into Western notation in McPhee's *Music in Bali* rendered them instantly accessible for adaptation by any number of composers into Western compositions.

Other chronological milestones are specific to the geographical and linguistic community of Quebec. One of the earliest references to Balinese music by a Quebec composer comes from Pierre Mercure (1927–66), who, in 1961, lamented the fact that

> The music of Bali is not taught at the conservatory. [. . .] But the music of Bali is more a question of sonorities, of sounds, often of space, of sensations other than those conveyed by the tonal or even modal system that is taught at the conservatory.[17]

Certainly Mercure did not engage seriously with Bali, as the quotation suggests, since it rehearses intact the old canard according to which gamelan is all timbre and no structure. However, it is impossible to predict the direction that the music of this amazingly Protean composer might have taken had he not been killed in a car accident in France at the age of 38, as a comparison of works as diverse as his *Cantate pour une joie* (1955) and the *Structures métalliques I* and *II* (1961) suggests. Serge Garant (1929–85), the father of Quebec post-war modernism, travelled to Bali in 1972 on vacation, possibly the first Quebec composer after McPhee to do so, but he returned convinced that however attractive the music he heard there, the idea of seeking inspiration in Balinese gamelan was unthinkable, apparently for ethical reasons: 'I returned with a kind of certainty that that music could not be taken out of the island, that it belonged to Bali

Jonathan Goldman

and that almost none of its elements could be of use to us'.[18] His contemporary Gilles Tremblay travelled to South East Asia shortly after him, in the summer of 1972, and four years later, in the summer of 1976, composers José Evangelista and John Rea travelled with their families to Indonesia, staying in Bali for several weeks. They were followed by Claude Vivier, who stayed in Bali from December 1976 to February 1977.[19] The following year, on 28 January 1978, the first performance of Vivier's *Pulau dewata*, the first work by a Quebecois composer explicitly inspired by Balinese gamelan, was heard in Toronto. Two years later, Vivier followed it up with another Balinese-inspired work, *Cinq chansons pour percussion* (1980), in which Balinese bossed gongs play a central role.

Then, in 1986, at the World Fair in Vancouver, the Indonesian government organized the First International Gamelan Festival and Symposium in the Expo's Indonesia Pavilion.[20] It was the Indonesian custom, spearheaded by the chairman of the event, musicologist I Made Bandem, to donate the gamelan to the host country after events at which it had been showcased. After negotiations, the Indonesian delegation donated the Javanese gamelan to Simon Fraser University in Vancouver, where the composer Martin Bartlett (1939–93) had had an interest in gamelan; the Balinese gamelan (in fact two sets, a *gamelan gong kebyar* and a *gamelan angklung*) was given to the Université de Montréal, thanks to the efforts of José Evangelista. Consequently, SFU in Vancouver has a thriving Javanese gamelan programme to this day, and the Université de Montréal has included Balinese gamelan in its curriculum for more than twenty-five years, overseen by a musician-in-residence, a position held by major Balinese musicians such as I Wayan Suweca and I Komang Astita, recruited from the STSI School for Advanced Studies in Music and Dance in Yogyakarta (Java), and later the Institut Seni Indonesia (ISI) in Denpasar (Bali).[21] In 1994, the Giri Kedaton gamelan ensemble was formed as an offshoot of the Université de Montréal's gamelan workshop.

Examples of gamelan-inspired modernist musical works from Quebec

Gilles Tremblay, Oralléluiants

The composer Gilles Tremblay (1932–2017) taught from 1962 to 1998 at the Montreal Conservatory (today the Conservatoire de Musique du Québec), where he trained several generations of composers, including many of those most active in Quebec's musical life, such as Michel Gonneville, Silvio Palmieri, Serge Provost and André Villeneuve. Tremblay's music takes its cue from his former teacher Olivier Messiaen, but also from Boulez, Varèse and Xenakis.[22] The prominent Quebec composer's composition class was without doubt modelled on Messiaen's famous analysis classes at the Paris Conservatoire, in that it too emphasized analysis of a somewhat poetic sort, and chose to study wide-ranging, sometimes eclectic repertoire. Michel Gonneville (b. 1950), who studied with Tremblay from 1973, gives a sense of the breadth of Tremblay's classes by recalling having studied Gregorian alleluias, Machaut's *Messe de Notre-Dame*, the fourth Brandenburg Concerto, three Mozart concertos (K467, K488 and K595), Haydn's Piano Sonata in E-flat major, Beethoven's Symphony no. 3 'Eroica', Berlioz's *Symphonie fantastique*, Debussy's *La mer*, Stravinsky's *The Rite of Spring*, Messiaen's *Livre d'orgue* and Varèse's *Intégrales*, as well as works by Webern, Boulez and Stockhausen, and certain non-Western musics including Japanese *gagaku*, music from *nô* and *bunraku* theatre, and Balinese gamelan.[23]

Tremblay himself first discovered Balinese music as a child, as a young flute pupil studying with the French flautist Marcel Moyse (1889–1984) at the Marlboro Music School and Festival. Moyse introduced him to recordings of gamelan music.[24] Later, he heard Balinese music on a

382

The Balinese moment in Montreal new music

Folkways record of gamelan.[25] In 1971, Tremblay, then a composition teacher at the Montreal Conservatory, received an open artistic travel grant from the Canada Council for the Arts to allow him to 'live the music of Bali and Java through tangible experience.'[26] He set out in the summer of 1972 on a voyage that would last several months and take him to Japan, South Korea and the Philippines, before arriving in Indonesia, where he visited Java and Bali. During his travels, he studied the music in each of those countries, made recordings and took photographs, which he later used in a lecture entitled 'À l'écoute de l'orient' (Listening to the Orient), delivered after his return to Montreal in December 1972. In his lecture, he describes the *gamelan angklung* of Bali in terms of its approach to time:

> During ceremonies in the (family or village) temples of Bali★ (★where the main religion is a Hindo-Buddhist fusion) one often hears the so-called 'Anklung' gamelan that ritually plays relatively short pieces separated by long pauses, as if dusting time with its colour so fresh.[27]

But it must have been his experience of Javanese music that marked him most profoundly, owing perhaps to the fact that he was guided while there by Dutch-born musicologist and impresario Bernard Suryabrata. In any event, it was Javanese gamelan that he chose to evoke in the work that he began during his stay abroad, *Oralléluiants*. In his lecture, Tremblay again emphasizes the rhythmic aspects of the music he heard in Java:

> Although the Javanese gamelan (*Surakarta*) is the source of Balinese gamelan, it possesses a totally different character, made of more rhythmic sounds in which the tempo is constantly fluctuating and in which the rhythmic cycles are punctuated by the deepest of all gongs that sometimes ring for a very long time (more than five minutes). Besides the metallic orchestra there is a rebab (type of violin). The long durational cycles and the impression of the infinite that arise from them corresponds very well with the Buddha and the architecture of the Borobudur Temple [...] and the landscape that surrounds it. Although the temple dates back to the eighth century and the current dominant religion is no longer Buddhism, this music nevertheless comes out of the same civilization. The Javanese gamelans are less narrowly associated with religion than those of Bali, but are used wherever there is a ceremony, ritual or sacred dance.[28]

Tremblay shows himself here to be more attracted to the Buddhist/Hindu roots of Javanese culture or, more precisely, his preconceived notion of Buddhism in which, as he writes, 'art and life are one'. This is supported by the conclusions he draws in his final report about his trip: reflecting on the differences between Western and Eastern cultures, he notes that

> there are nevertheless many domains and regions of thought that intersect, touch and recognize each other, especially for people on either side who have antennae that are sensitive to the other. *In every Westerner there is a dormant Orient, and vice versa.*[29]

But Tremblay's attachment to the music of Java may also be linked to a personal experience he had while there, which he describes in the report he filed to the Canada Council upon his return to Montreal:

> In Central Java, after Bali, I sojourned successively in Surakarta and in Yogyakarta where I took classes with teachers. One day, when I was playing a very simple melody

Jonathan Goldman

that I had learned to play very quickly on the *sarong* (which is one of the gamelan instruments), in order to help me grasp the fluctuation of tempi (which is typical of Java), my master started to play on some drums, behind my back. To my great amazement, I followed him very naturally. I played and 'was played' at the same time. At that moment, a group of musicians came in, out of curiosity, to see who was there, and then they sat down beside various gamelan instruments, playing a constellation of rhythmic counterpoints. This was one of the most intense musical experiences that I have ever had. I almost lost my sense of gravity; I was literally lifted up by so much beauty and also by non-verbal human communication. A communication owing to the fact that I was a musician among other musicians![30]

It may be the memory of this musical experience that Tremblay tried to evoke in a particular passage of *Oralléluiants*,[31] which he completed upon his return to Quebec. *Oralléluiants* is one of his few works to explicitly display the influence of (Javanese) gamelan, a rarity from this composer who admitted after his Asian voyage that 'making exoticist music never attracted me'.[32] And yet, commenting in the liner notes to a recording of the work, premiered in 1975, Tremblay noted that it

> was written after my return from the Far East, and the influence this had was, I believe, by no means superficial, such as that acquired as a tourist or from a postcard or storybook. Yet even though I was still steeped above all in Javanese music at the time I wrote the work, the whole of the last sequence – notwithstanding the fact that my temperament has occasionally led me to write some rather violent works, ablaze with rapid, virtuosic passages – this whole last sequence is on the contrary one of serenity and gentleness.[33]

Oralléluiants is a vocal work scored for solo soprano and the unusual combination of flute, bass clarinet, horn, three double basses (the harmonic fields of the piece are derived from the harmonic series of the open strings of the double bass), and two percussionists playing a variety of instruments, including amplified sheets of aluminium foil and wrapping paper. Tremblay uses the text of the first alleluia of the Pentecost Mass, and makes use of a theme directly inspired by Gregorian chant, marked 'Psalmodie' at its first appearance at rehearsal figure 14.[34] The combination of plainchant with a certain (indirect) evocation of gamelan music is in keeping with Tremblay's and many Western admirers' understanding of gamelan.[35] Tremblay, like McPhee himself, saw a close parallel between the way a sacred motet is structured around a Gregorian cantus firmus and the way a gamelan composition is derived from its melodic skeleton. Indeed, McPhee evidently regarded the parallel between gamelan and Gregorian chant to be so salient that he refers, in his seminal *Music in Bali*, to the core melody as a 'cantus firmus'.[36] The percussion section also includes a set of Balinese *cengceng*, the small cymbals used in most Balinese gamelan ensembles.

The passage that Tremblay describes as evoking the music of Java occurs at rehearsal figure 60 (Example 16.1), and is marked 'Lent, très serein'. It is scored for soprano, one double bass and two percussionists, the first playing a variety of instruments (crotales, metal plate etc.) and the second playing exclusively on what he describes as a 'tambour javanais', that is the two-sided kendang drum found in Javanese and Balinese gamelan. As can be seen in Example 16.1 (Perc. II), Tremblay inscribes the traditional stroke names onto the percussion line.

Despite the 'serene' atmosphere, which for Tremblay may well have evoked either the improvised jam session that he described as 'one of the most intense musical experiences that I have ever had' or

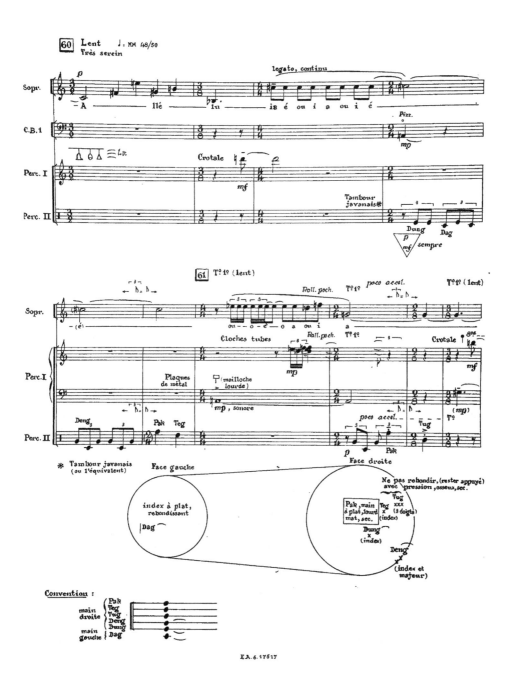

Example 16.1   Gilles Tremblay, *Oralléluiants* (1974–75), rehearsal figure 60
© 1980. © Éditions Salabert. All rights reserved

some other impression of Surakarta Javanese gamelan, most listeners would not immediately register a musical reference to gamelan in the ending of *Oralléluiants*. Indeed, most critics registered the sacred dimension of the music rather than any exotic accents. Writing a review in *Le Devoir*, Gilles Potvin described the work as 'mystical', adding that 'true to his line of thought, Tremblay dreams of leaving the earthly world in order to rise up to the summit and to take his listener with him'.[37] But of course this listener had heard 'correctly', since Tremblay's foray into South East Asian music was guided from the start by a wholly mystical desire to unify the divided realms of art and life.

Claude Vivier, Pulau dewata

The striking compositional style of Claude Vivier (1948–83) fuses many of the dominant currents of twentieth-century art music, from serialist practices to the structural melodies of what was sometimes called the New Simplicity, to the techniques associated with spectral composition. Like other composers of his generation working in Montreal at the time, he had a deep and durable fascination with the musical cultures of mostly Asian locales. Completed in June 1977, Vivier's *Pulau dewata* is cast as a tribute to Bali, whence the Quebecois composer, a student of Gilles Tremblay as well as of Karlheinz Stockhausen, had recently returned. While in Bali, Vivier studied at the music academy and performed ceremonial music in temples.[38] He also took notes on the structure of Balinese music, recording his findings in his diary (Figure 16.1) and in a letter sent to a friend and later published.[39]

In his writing from Bali, Vivier tries to give expression to an experience that he considers to be fundamentally ineffable, and warns himself against the lure of stylistic imitation:

> It is impossible for me to analyse my behaviour at the moment but I have become a little Balinese I laughed, cried and got frightened just as I found it inconceivable that tourists bathe naked on the beach even though I didn't even notice that the older Balinese women walked around with their breasts showing or those entire families that bathe in the rivers. What is Claude Vivier the composer to do? Well, he shuts his mouth and listens, records impressions and also he describes as technically as possible, as in my first letter. To say that this experience was easy would be a lie because I must admit that learning Indonesian and two dialects of Balinese was rather arduous and terribly exhausting! But what I retained can be little described through words because, as in the story of the master who asks his pupil what he has learned, and the pupil repeats feverishly by heart everything that the master had said, upon which the master responds by slapping him in the face and telling him to return when he understands, I don't want to get a slap in the face, and most of all I don't want to write Balinese music![40]

To a large extent, Vivier heeded this warning against succumbing to 'exoticist' imitation in the Balinese tribute work that he composed shortly after his return to Montreal. In *Pulau dewata*, a piece originally composed for a percussion ensemble but scored for unspecified instruments, which has resulted in its performance on a dizzying variety of instruments from saxophone quartet to string quartet to ondes martenot, Vivier only explicitly quotes gamelan music in one passage, at the very end of the work (Example 16.2). In this passage, Vivier alludes to the *norot* texture that Michael Tenzer defines as

> a common and elegant orchestral texture used in a variety of musical contexts and tempi. [...] Norot is considered simple and basic because of the close emulation of the shape of the *pokok* [i.e. the nuclear tones] observable in all melodic strata.[41]

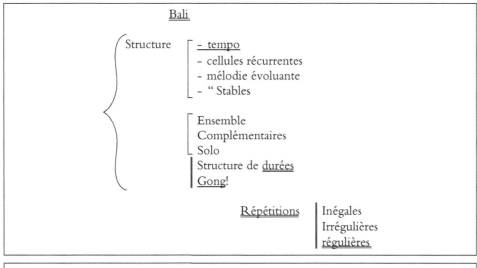

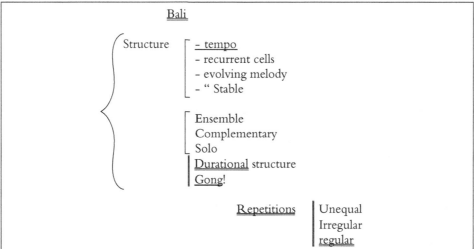

Figure 16.1 Excerpt from Claude Vivier's notebooks written during his stay in Bali (December 1976–March 1977), Claude Vivier Fonds, Université de Montréal Archive

Example 16.2 Claude Vivier, *Pulau dewata* (1977), end

© 1977, 2006 by Boosey & Hawkes (Canada) Ltd, a Boosey & Hawkes company. Reprinted by permission of Boosey & Hawkes, Inc.

And yet this is but one explicit paraphrase found in a catalogue that bristles with the flavour of the extra-European, and finds in these sources a kind of justification for its melodicism and its long rhythmic cycles.

But over and above specific references or quotations of gamelan in Vivier's music, which are extremely rare, Vivier was drawn to gamelan because of the appeal of the communal music-making in which he participated while in Bali, and especially by the so-called colotomic structure, in which large sections are signalled by gongs. Vivier often articulates the form of his later works through these gong-like signals, sometimes intoned on the rin (Japanese bowl), for example in one of his best-known works, *Lonely Child*.

José Evangelista, Ô Bali

José Evangelista (b. 1943), who was born in Valencia, Spain, and settled in Montreal in the early 1970s, is one of a group of composers in the city who, during that decade, became deeply committed not only to gamelan but also to the learned musics of many non-Western cultures. He enrolled as a student in the Faculty of Music of the Université de Montréal in 1970, eventually being appointed professor of composition in 1978. In the same year he co-founded the concert series Traditions Musicales du Monde, co-produced by the Montreal Museum of Fine Arts, which put on concerts by acclaimed interpreters of non-Western musical traditions, beginning with Ali Akhbar Khan; in 1979 the series notably invited a Javanese troupe led by Sumursam to present traditional shadow theatre (*wayang kulit*) for what was possibly the first time in Montreal. Later, as was previously mentioned, he was instrumental in procuring a gamelan for the University. Significantly, Evangelista also co-founded Les Événements du Neuf, in 1979, along with Vivier, Lorraine Vaillancourt (who would go on to found the Nouvel Ensemble Moderne) and John Rea. Les Événements was a concert society that presented recent new music often either inspired by music of extra-European traditions or composed by musicians hailing from countries in the East or the South.[42] In 1979 the society notably produced a concert tribute to Colin McPhee at which the latter's *Balinese Ceremonial Music* was performed.

Much of Evangelista's compositional output explores a kind of expanded monody or, to be more precise, the space between monody and polyphony, namely heterophony. Gamelan, which Evangelista characterizes as 'stratified heterophony', has remained a lasting source of inspiration for him.[43] While Evangelista sometimes casts his works as tributes to gamelan traditions, as in the trio of works *Ô Bali* (1989), *Ô Java* (1993) and *Ô Gamelan* (2013), other works are indirectly inspired by gamelan textures, such as *Clos de vie* (1983), the piece he wrote in memory of Vivier, whose untimely death occurred that same year.[44]

Ô Bali was commissioned by Radio Canada as a way to commemorate a hundred years since 'the West's first contact with Indonesian music at the World Fair in Paris in 1889'.[45] Evangelista decided for the occasion to compose a tribute to the 'extraordinary music of Bali' by 'conceiving the piece according to the principles of Balinese music but in a free manner'. As he remarks in the preface to the score:

> My piece is based on two melodies played by the flutes that are at the same time orna-
> mented and punctuated by the other instruments. This technique of instrumentation,
> very essential to gamelan, is as a matter of fact the source of the heterophonic writing
> I have used in my music since 1982. However, the melodies themselves have nothing

to do with Bali: they make use of the twelve tones of the tempered scale rather than five- or seven-note systems, as is the case with Balinese music.[46]

Evangelista uses these two core melodies as sources for the musical material of Ô Bali. Like Tremblay and indeed McPhee, Evangelista calls this main melody the 'cantus firmus' (Example 16.3). Once the cantus firmus is composed, Evangelista restricts all chordal simultaneities in Ô Bali to groups of adjacent notes in the cantus firmus – segments of between two and four notes, of which Example 16.4 illustrates one of countless examples.

Example 16.3   Cantus firmus melody from José Evangelista, Ô Bali (1989), measured version
© Editions Salabert. All rights reserved

Example 16.4   Evangelista, Ô Bali, bar 160: harmony derived from adjacent notes of cantus firmus
© Editions Salabert. All rights reserved

Just as Evangelista suggests gamelan without literally employing the traditional modes of gamelan melodies, so he tried to evoke the instrumental colour of gamelan without using traditional Balinese instruments. Evangelista chooses an instrumentation consisting of two flutes, piano, vibraphone and four strings (two violins, cello and double bass). One of the provisional titles for the piece was *Gambuh*, an allusion to the eponymous centuries-old tradition of danced Balinese classical theatre.[47] *Gamelan gambuh*, the music that accompanies *gambuh* theatre, uses four sulings and a rebab, a timbre not dissimilar to that of the two flutes and two violins of *Ô Bali*.

The most striking aspect of the instrumental writing of *Ô Bali* is the interaction between the piano and vibraphone parts, which play elaborate ornamentations of the core melody inspired by *kotekan*, the figuration patterns characteristic of gamelan. Formally speaking, the eleven minutes of *Ô Bali* are performed without interruption, but the work has a sectional form in which each part corresponds to a genre or piece typical of Balinese gamelan. The piece makes use of gamelan formal units such as *pengawit*, *pengawak* and *pengechet*, as well as the rhythmic breaks known as *angsel*.[48]

John Rea, Médiator (Pincer la musique aujourd'hui)

In the case of the composer John Rea, his relationship with non-Western musical traditions is more difficult to encapsulate. His fascination in the 1980s and 1990s with musical postmodernism led him to theorize the way in which artists can allude to other identities in their works in either a naïve or a critical manner, noting that the former often ends up as kitsch. His attraction to artists who play with their identities has led him to explore the dizzying world of Fernando Pessoa's orthonyms (in his 1999 incidental music to the play *Urfaust*, staged by Denis Marleau), Velázquez's famously self-reflexive painting *Las Meninas* (in his piano work of the same name, an extended set of variations from 1990–91 on Schumann's *Kinderszenen*) and M.C. Escher's paradoxical geometries (in *Treppenmusik* of 1982). He invokes the non-Western other only in rare instances, such as *Reception and Offering Music* (1975), his orchestral arrangement of Vivier's *Pulau dewata* (1986), and the piece discussed here, *Médiator* (1981). Along with Evangelista, he co-founded the Événements du Neuf and the Traditions Musique du Monde concert series. He also visited Bali in the summer of 1976 in the company of Evangelista. And yet he consciously decided not to make music inspired by this experience. This decision is also doubtless rooted in his sceptical stance in respect of artistic projects based on any kind of imitation, which he associates with the most uncritical strains of postmodernism. As he writes:

> That a composer would knowingly and wilfully produce a simulacrum or a counterfeit bespeaks as much about the art of composition itself as it does about the perpetrator of the facsimile and the listener for whom the art-like object is intended. An audience that accepts a likeness in place of the real thing is either uneducated and thus being duped, or perhaps purposefully disingenuous about cultural matters, preferring to affirm traditionalist values by avoiding new and often disturbing modes of expression, the ones that may be threatening to community standards, that are iconoclastic, and that are usually associated with modernist poetics.[49]

Speaking about so-called world music, Rea goes so far as to claim that

> this trend appears to involve the following research strategy: musical cultures of the non-Western world, both high classical as well as popular, are examined at some level,

The Balinese moment in Montreal new music

in part it would seem in order to help bring about a New Age, and then ingested like so many possible cures. So much so that one often gets the impression that the Western artists and composers assimilating such influences may soon perish from an overdose of exoticism.[50]

Rea goes on to invoke a familiar postcolonial critique of musical appropriation:

> There is, moreover, something embarrassing in all of this. For one is again witnessing cultural interactions which seem linked to the ancient principles of colonialism: occidentals readily assimilating world musical traditions as if they were consuming other people's possessions. If, however, this trend were not to be considered like yet another deferred level of colonialism, it might be useful to view it as a psychological condition: this very consumption reveals a form of projection as it exposes an involuntary type of melancholia that probably owes its origin to our dynamic – and modernist – capitalist societies wherein, in order to move forward and progress, one must discard things, that is, one must accept their ineluctable obsolescence, a behaviour with which musically sensitive people have much difficulty it would seem. And so one associates oneself with counter-irritant strategies by linking up with the eternal and pre-modern features found in numerous cultures of Asia, South America and Micronesia, etc.

Unsurprisingly, a musical project by John Rea that references other musical cultures does so critically, ironically and through a clear thematization of the appropriative mechanisms themselves, namely the process of mediation. His work *Médiator* (1980) alludes humorously in its subtitle, 'Pincer la musique aujourd'hui', to the title of Pierre Boulez's monograph *Penser la musique aujourd'hui*, since one of the meanings of the verb 'pincer' in French is 'to pluck', and *Médiator* is scored for instruments with plucked strings. The word 'médiator' refers in music to a plectrum, the tool that mediates between the player's body and the vibrating body, namely the musical instrument, and thereby acts as a metaphor for the mediation between (Western) musical minds and the artefacts of human culture. *Médiator* was composed to form part of a concert produced on 9 March 1981 by the Événements du Neuf concert series, on the theme 'Carnets de voyage' (travel notebooks), as a way of exploring the interests of three of the society's co-founders in Asian learned musics. The other two works on the programme were Evangelista's heterophonic *Immobilis in mobili* (1976) and Vivier's *Love Songs* (1977). The concert combined readings of excerpts of travel notes and snatches of recorded music. The original programme note to *Médiator* makes the connection to non-Western musics explicit:

> As in art, so in travels: in the past as in the present, artists have tried to be travellers in other ethnic realities, to grasp distant worlds and their exoticism, and to make them serve as sources of inspiration.
>
> *Médiator* (. . . *pincer la musique aujourd'hui* . . .) [plectrum, plucking music today] is, among other things, a musical 'travel book', the testimony of an admiration for the musics of the Far East, which can be found in other works of mine.
>
> Just as the plectrum mediates between the hand and the string, *Médiator* is a friendly attempt at communication between musical instruments of our tradition and certain sounds and gestures of east Asian musics.

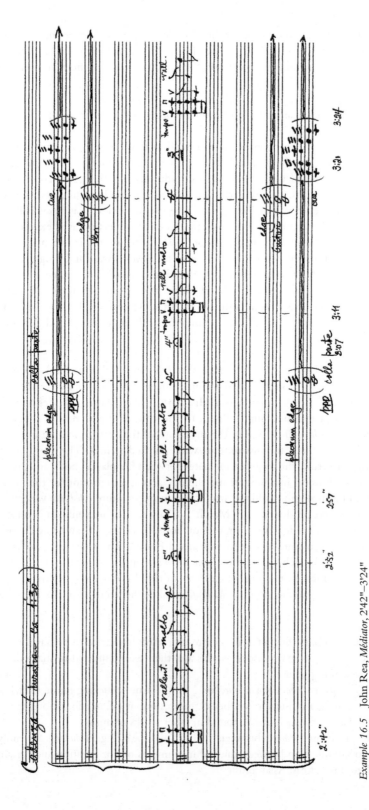

Example 16.5 John Rea, *Médiator*, 2'42"–3'24"

© 1980. Published by the Canadian Music Centre/Centre de Musique Canadienne. All rights reserved

By focusing on the mediations that make the borrowings from non-Western traditions possible, something that neither Tremblay's, Evangelista's nor Vivier's works do in an explicit manner, Rea stages as it were his own postcolonial critique of exoticist borrowing, even if it is couched in mild tones of irony. The work is scored for a 'soloist/conductor' who plays the violin or the viola, and eight other instruments, consisting of guitar, cello, piano, violin and four unspecified plucked instruments, all tuned at the performers' discretion. All the instruments are played with a plectrum and on open strings only, the score being written in a tablature in which the open strings are represented by the spaces in a standard five-line stave. The 'soloist/conductor' holds the violin horizontally in his lap 'somewhat "à la shamisen"' and 'plays in a ceremonial-ritualistic fashion making broad and slow gestures with the right hand and arm'. The music alternates soloistic gestures played by the soloist/conductor and rhythms that fan out to the four instruments on either side of him or her. As John Rea noted in conversation, at the pre-concert talk before a Vancouver performance of the work in 1985, it was

> a kind of an ethnological composition, if you wish. I'm making a kind of direct reference to court music of, you might say, Japan or China, or any of the Far East nations that have a kind of court music where there may or may not be soloists and where often string instruments are played with plectrums: many, many Japanese instruments, for example – the biwa or the shamisen are played, in fact, with large plectrums, and my role as the conductor soloist is to lead and to perform and to give an overall, you might say, tone to the quasi-ritual of this work.[51]

Nevertheless, at times, *Médiator* seems to aspire to imitation, as in the first soloist's cadenza, which really does take on the air of a shamisen solo in gagaku (Example 16.5). One suspects, however, that, like Mauricio Kagel in his *Exotica* (1972), in which Western musicians perform on a vast array of non-Western instruments, singing all the while with affected 'foreign-sounding' accents, Rea seeks through these inexact imitations to 'expose the rather relative term "exoticism"'.[52]

And yet imitation seems beside the point in a work that gives pride of place to the mediations that make it possible: these mediations sometimes favour communication and understanding, sometimes the opposite. Indeed, emphasizing the aporias of intercultural exchange seems to be the very content of the work.

Interpretations

The types of musical practices discussed here are associated not only with a specific locality (Quebec) but also with a specific timespan (roughly the last quarter of the twentieth century) – both factors that set them apart from most generalized accounts of musical modernism. Associating the late twentieth century with a modernist practice sometimes very narrowly associated with developments that occurred around 1910 aligns with a growing tendency to move beyond a historical narrative that sees modernism as having been supplanted by postmodernism. David Metzer, for example, describes certain works written after 1980 by composers such as György Kurtág, Kaija Saariaho, Helmut Lachenmann, Gérard Grisey or Brian Ferneyhough as 'late modernism', claiming that at the turn of the twenty-first century, modernism 'has not been supplanted'.[53] Similarly, Alastair Williams characterizes certain works composed since 1970 in terms of 'transformed modernism',[54] while Claus-Steffen Mahnkopf sees the practices of certain composers born around 1960 as an aesthetic return to the foundations of the first generation of musical modernists. Transposing to music a taxonomy proposed by Heinrich Klotz with respect to the visual arts, Mahnkopf refers to a 'second modernity', explaining that:

> The second modernity does not define itself merely negatively as a rejection of post-modernism, however, but also positively, by expressing solidarity with the tenets of classical modernism and the avant-garde. These are above all the belief in experimentation and innovation, and the conviction that construction, i.e., the technical validation of the musical discourse, is indispensable.[55]

Indeed, the compositional practices of Tremblay, Vivier, Evangelista and Rea from the 1970s onwards have been described here in terms that might bring them into a conversation about other twentieth-century composers' encounters with non-Western music. Recent work by Martin Scherzinger on the African-inspired compositions of Reich, Ligeti and Berio has highlighted the complex questions that arise from any musical project predicated on cultural exchange.[56] And yet, it seems possible to grasp something of the regional specificity of a particular manifestation of musical modernism by examining the ways in which composers inscribe other musical cultures into their compositions. These works become sites in which the construction of the self is mirrored in or even engendered by the construction of other musical cultures, whose social, political and cultural implications can then be studied. As Georgina Born and David Hesmond-halgh have noted in their landmark volume from 2000, *Western Music and Its Others*:

> It is perhaps a truism to point out that those modernist and postmodernist composers who have drawn upon or made reference to other musics (non-Western, folk, or urban popular) are not producing that music but drawing upon it in order to enrich their own compositional frame. They are transforming that music through incorporation into their own aesthetic: appropriating and re-presenting it. Crucially, in doing so, they intend not only to evoke that other music, but to create a distance from it and transcend it.[57]

The gamelan moment in the Quebec of the 1970s through to the 1990s is a classic site of this kind of re-presentation, replete with all of its complexities.

Notes

1 Other recent additions to scholarship on regional modernism include David Bernstein's *The San Francisco Tape Music Center: 1960s Counterculture and the Avant-Garde* (Berkeley and Los Angeles: University of California Press, 2008) and Benjamin Piekut's study of experimental music in 1960s New York, *Experimentalism Otherwise: The New York Avant-Garde and Its Limits* (Berkeley and Los Angeles: University of California Press, 2011).
2 Shmuel N. Eisenstadt, 'Multiple Modernities', *Daedalus* 129, no. 1 (2000), 2.
3 Adam Krims, *Music and Urban Geography* (New York: Routledge, 2007).
4 See Dale C. Thomson, *Jean Lesage and the Quiet Revolution* (Toronto: Palgrave Macmillan, 1984).
5 See Élizabeth Gallat-Morin and Jean-Pierre Pinson, *La vie musicale en Nouvelle-France* (Montreal: Septentrion, 2003).
6 See Tara Browner, ed., *Music of the First Nations: Tradition and Innovation in Native North America* (Champaign: University of Illinois Press, 2009).
7 See, for example, André-G. Bourassa and Gilles Lapointe, *Refus global et ses environs* (Montreal: Éditions de l'Hexagone, 1988).
8 Marie-Thérèse Lefebvre, *Serge Garant et la révolution musicale au Québec* (Montreal: Éditions Louise Courteau, 1986), 54.

The Balinese moment in Montreal new music

9   Anne Marie Messier, 'Ticket pour la liberté: Entretien avec Otto Joachim', *Circuit: musiques contemporaines* 19, no. 3 (2009), 38–47.

10 Matt Rogalsky, 'Finger Exercises for Oscillators: István Anhalt on Electronic Music', *Circuit: musiques contemporaines* 19, no. 3 (2009), 77–84.

11 See Claudine Caron and Jonathan Goldman, eds., 'Musique automatiste? Pierre Mercure et le *Refus global*', special issue, *Circuit: musiques contemporaines* 21, no. 3 (2011).

12 See Réjean Beaucage, *La SMCQ: Histoire à suivre* (Montreal: Septentrion, 2011).

13 See Annegret Fauser, *Musical Encounters at the 1889 Paris World's Fair* (Rochester, NY: University of Rochester Press, 2005).

14 On the CD *Bali à Montréal* (UMMUS 104, 1992), Lorraine Vaillancourt and the Nouvel Ensemble Moderne (NEM), along with the Atelier de gamelan de l'Université de Montréal, perform works by I Wayan Suweca (then the director of the gamelan ensemble, and often referred to as Wayan Suweca from Batubulan in order to distinguish him from the musician with the same name who was the first director of the gamelan atelier), Colin McPhee, Evangelista, Vivier and Robert Valin.

15 Colin McPhee, *A House in Bali* (New York: John Day, 1946; repr., Boston: Periplus, 2002); and McPhee, *Music in Bali: A Study in Form and Instrumental Organization in Balinese Orchestral Music* (New Haven, CT: Yale University Press, 1966). On Javanese gamelan, Jaap Kunst's *De toonkunst van Java* (The Hague: M. Nijhoff, 1934), translated into English in 1949 as *Music in Java: Its History, Its Theory and Its Technique*, 3rd ed. (The Hague: Nijhoff, 1973), was for decades the only available reference work. Kunst also wrote a book on Balinese music, *De toonkunst van Bali* (Weltevreden: Druk G. Kolff, 1925), but because it was never translated, it had little impact outside of the Netherlands.

16 Later, field recordings made by the French ethnologist Jacques Brunet became well known among Quebec musicians, for example the LP *Java: Une nuit de Wayang Kulit / Légende de Wahju Tjakraningrat*, CBS 65440, 1973.

17 'La musique de Bali, on ne l'enseigne pas dans un conservatoire. On nous enseigne à peine les notions d'acoustique. On nous enseigne un solfège qui est entièrement relatif à la gamme bien tempérée; la gamme bien tempérée ayant apporté ces magnifiques deux siècles de . . . ou trois siècles plutôt, de musique. Mais la musique de Bali est plutôt une question de sonorités, de sons, d'espace souvent, de sensations autres que celles apportées par le système tonal, ou même modal, qu'on apprend dans ce conservatoire.' Mario Gauthier, ed., 'Table ronde de 1961 autour d'*Incandescence* de Pierre Mercure', *Circuit: musiques contemporaines* 21, no. 3 (2011), 91–92.

18 'Je suis revenu de là avec cette espèce de certitude qu'on ne pouvait pas sortir cette musique de l'île, qu'elle appartenait à Bali et qu'à peu près aucun des éléments ne pouvait nous servir'. Comment in interview with Maurice Fleuret ('Rencontre avec Serge Garant', *Cahiers canadiens de musique*, no. 9, 1974), quoted in Lefebvre, *Serge Garant*, 63.

19 Audio recording of an interview of Claude Vivier by Kevin Volans, March 1977 in Cologne; courtesy of the Fondation Vivier.

20 Bill Cotter, *Vancouver's Expo '86* (Charleston: Arcadia, 2009), 73.

21 The first concert of the Université de Montréal Atelier de gamelan took place in May 1988, led by I Wayan Suweca.

22 See Danick Trottier, 'Enquête: Gilles Tremblay pédagogue vu par ses anciens élèves – questionnaire réalisé par courriel', *Circuit: musiques contemporaines* 20, no. 3 (2010), 73–90.

23 Silvio Palmieri, in Trottier, 'Enquête', 74.

24 Gilles Tremblay, interviewed by the author on 19 December 2012 in Montreal.

25 From a Radio Canada programme on the music of Indonesia produced by Gilles Tremblay and broadcast in 1973. The Folkways album to which Tremblay refers is probably *Music of Indonesia, vol. 2: Bali*, recorded by Phil and Florence Walker and edited by Henry Cowell, Ethnic Folkways Library FE 4537 D.

26 'vivre par expérience tangible la musique de Bali et de Java'; taken from application found in Fonds Gilles Tremblay, Université de Montréal Archives Division.

27 'Lors des cérémonies dans les temples de Bali* (*où la religion principale est une synthèse hindo-boudhiste) (soit familiaux, soit du village) on entend souvent le gamelan dit "Anklung" qui joue rituellement des pièces assez courtes séparées de longues pauses, comme parsemant le temps de sa couleur si fraîche'; Lecture notes from 'À l'écoute de l'orient', delivered at the Faculty of Music, Université de Montréal on 14 December 1972 (Fonds Gilles Tremblay, Université de Montréal Archives Division, P0392 D4 0006).

28 'Le Gamelan javanais (Surakarta) s'il est à l'origine du gamelan de Bali possède un tout autre caractère, fait de sons plus rythmique où le tempo est sans cesse fluctuant où les cycles rythmiques ponctués par le plus profond de tous les gongs durent parfois très longtemps (plus que 5 minutes). À l'orchestre de métal s'ajoute ici le rebab (sorte de violon). Ces longs cycles de durées, et l'impression d'infini qu'ils dégagent, s'apparentent très bien avec les buddha et l'architecture du Temple de Borobudur [. . .] et le paysage qui l'entoure. Bien que le temple date du 8e siècle et que la religion actuelle répandue ne soit plus le bouddhisme, cette musique procède néanmoins d'une même civilisation. Les gamelans javanais sont moins étroitement liés à la religion que ceux de Bali, mais ils sont utilisés partout où il y a céré-monie, rite, danse sacrée.' Ibid.

29 'Il y a cependant beaucoup de domaines et de régions de la pensée qui se croisent, se touchent, et se reconnaissent, surtout pour des hommes qui ont de part et d'autre des antennes sensibles à l'autre. Il y a dans chaque occidental un orient qui sommeille, et inversement.' Ibid.

30 'Dans le Java-central, après Bali, je séjournai successivement à Surakarta et à Jogdjakarta où je pris des cours avec des professeurs. Un jour, alors que je jouais une mélodie très simple mais que j'appris très vite sur un "sarong" (qui est un des instruments du gamelang), mon maître pour me faire saisir la fluctuation des tempi (qui est typique de Java), se mit à jouer les tambours, derrière mon dos. À mon grand étonnement je suivais très naturellement. Je jouais et étais joué en même temps. À ce moment un groupe de musiciens vint voir par curiosité qui était là, puis s'installèrent aux différents instruments du gamelan, jouant une constellation de contrepoints rythmiques. Ce fut une des expériences musicale les plus intenses que j'ai vécue. J'en perdis presque la notion de la pesanteur, littéralement soulevé par tant de beauté et aussi par une communication humaine qui ne passe pas par la parole. Communica-tion donnée par le fait d'être musicien avec d'autres musiciens!' Final report to the Canada Council (addressed to Jules Pelletier) in a letter dated 26 October 1974 (Université de Montréal Archives divi-sion, Fonds Tremblay P0392 D4, 0006).

31 *Oralléluiants* (1974–75), CBC commission, premiered on 8 March 1975 in Toronto by New Music Concerts, Gilles Tremblay (conductor); Quebec premiere: 9 December 1976, Salle Pollack, Serge Garant (conductor), Pauline Vaillancourt (soprano).

32 'faire de l'exotisme musical ne m'a jamais attiré' (ibid.).

33 Gilles Tremblay in interview with Maryvonne Kendergi, in album booklet, *Anthologie de la musique canadienne*, RCI, ACM 12, 1983.

34 Vincent Ranallo, 'Une célébration sonore de l'Esprit: À propos d'*Oralléluiants*', *Circuit: musiques contem-poraines* 20, no. 3 (2010), 50.

35 In an interview with the author, 19 December 2012.

36 McPhee, *Music in Bali*, 57 and 375.

37 'Fidèle à sa ligne de pensée, Tremblay ne songe qu'à quitter le monde terrestre pour s'élever vers les cimes et y entraîner du même coup son auditeur'; Gilles Potvin, 'Une superbe fête musicale marque le 10ème anniversaire de la SMCQ', *Le Devoir*, 13 December 1976.

38 Vivier interviewed by Kevin Volans in Cologne in March 1977. Tape recording at the archive of the Fondation Vivier, Contrecoeur, Québec.

39 Claude Vivier, 'Trois lettres de Bali', *Circuit: musiques contemporaines* 2, nos. 1–2 (1991), 70–79.

40 'Il m'est actuellement impossible d'analyser mon comportement mais je suis devenu un peu balinais j'ai ri, pleuré et ai eu peur tout comme j'ai trouvé inconcevable que les touristes se baignent nus sur la plage et pourtant je n'ai même pas remarqué les balinaises âgées se promenant les seins nus ou les familles complètes se baignant dans les rivières. Que fait Claude Vivier le compositeur? Hé bien, il se ferme la gueule et écoute, enregistre les impressions et aussi techniquement un peu ce que dans la première lettre, il a décrit. Dire que cette expérience fut facile serait mentir car je dois avouer que l'apprentissage de l'indonésien et de 2 niveaux de Balinais est une chose plutôt ardue et terriblement fatigante! Mais ce que j'ai pu en retenir se décrit assez peu avec des mots car, comme dans l'histoire où le maître demande à l'élève ce qu'il a appris et l'élève de répéter fébrilement par cœur ce que le maître lui a dit sur quoi le maître répond par une gifle et demande à l'élève de revenir quand il aura compris, je ne veux pas recevoir de gifle et ne veux surtout pas écrire de la musique balinaise !' From Vivier's travel notebooks, 26 December 1976; published in 'Les écrits de Claude Vivier', *Circuit: musiques con-temporaines* 2, nos. 1–2 (1991), 73.

41 Michael Tenzer, *Gamelan gong kebyar: The Art of Twentieth-Century Balinese Music* (Chicago: University of Chicago Press, 2000), 63.

42 By way of example, the first season of concerts programmed pieces including a work by Luis de Pablo with tanpura, a work by Ecuadorian composer Mesías Maiguashca, and compositions by Japanese composers Jo Kondo and Yūji Takahashi.

43 Eight of Evangelista's works to date have been inspired by gamelan music: *Motionless Move* (1980), for fifteen musicians, commissioned by L'Itinéraire; *Labyrinthe* (1988), for harp; *Ô Bali* (1989), for two flutes, piano, vibraphone and strings, with a later version for orchestra (2000), commissioned by the Canadian Broadcasting Corporation; *Balinese Scherzo* and *Slow Song*, from *Monody Quartet* (1989), for string quartet, commissioned by the Kronos Quartet; *Ô Java* (1993), for orchestra; *Concerto Kebyar* (1998), for ondes martenot and gamelan *gong kebyar*, commissioned by Jean Laurendeau and the Evergreen Gamelan Club; *Bali Symphony* (2004), for gamelan *gong kebyar* and orchestra (with I Nyoman Windha); and *Ô Gamelan* (2013), for orchestra, commissioned by the Esprit Orchestra (Toronto).

44 *Clos de vie* (1983), for piano, harp, harpsichord, electric guitar, banjo and vibraphone and four stringed instruments, commissioned by the Société de Musique Contemporaine du Québec (SMCQ).

45 From the preface to the published score (Paris, Salabert, EAS 19020): '"Ô Bali" a été commandée par Radio-Canada pour commémorer le centenaire du premier contact important de l'Occident avec la musique indonésienne lors de l'Exposition universelle de 1889 à Paris.'

46 From the preface to the published score: 'Ma pièce est basée sur deux mélodies jouées par les flûtes qui sont en même temps ornementées ou ponctuées par les autres instruments. Cette technique d'instrumentation, très essentielle au gamelan, est par ailleurs à l'origine de l'écriture hétérophone que j'emploie dans ma musique depuis 1982. Cependant, les mélodies en soi n'ont rien à voir avec Bali: elles emploient les douze sons de la gamme tempérée et non pas des systèmes de cinq ou sept, comme c'est le cas dans la musique balinaise'.

47 McPhee, *Music in Bali*, 355.

48 A lengthier discussion of *O Bali* can be found in Jonathan Goldman, 'A House in Bali/Une maison à Montréal: José Evangelista's *Ô Bali*', in *Texts and Beyond: The Process of Music Composition from the 19th to the 20th Century*, ed. Jonathan Goldman (Bologna: UT Orpheus Edizioni and Ad Parnassum, 2015), 241–69.

49 John Rea, 'Post-modernisme(s)', in *Musiques: Une encyclopédie pour le XXIe siècle*, ed. Jean-Jacques Nattiez, vol. 1 (Arles: Actes Sud, 2003); quotations taken from the unpublished English original version.

50 Ibid.

51 From a recording of a pre-concert radio interview on 29 September 1985, recorded at the Vancouver East Cultural Centre, Vancouver New Music; see 'Composer showcase – John Rea', http://www.music-centre.ca/centrestreams/swf?mode=play_by&opt=composer&id=679 (accessed 6 September 2017).

52 Björn Heile, '*Weltmusik* and the Globalization of New Music', in *The Modernist Legacy: Essays on New Music*, ed. Björn Heile (Aldershot: Ashgate, 2009), 111.

53 David Metzer, *Musical Modernism at the Turn of the Twenty-First Century* (Cambridge: Cambridge University Press, 2009), 1–3.

54 Alastair Williams, *New Music and the Claims of Modernity* (Aldershot: Ashgate, 1997), 148; quoted in Metzer, *Musical Modernism*, 2.

55 Claus-Steffen Mahnkopf, 'Second Modernity – An Attempted Assessment', in *Facets of the Second Modernity*, ed. Claus-Steffen Mahnkopf, Frank Cox and Wolfram Schurig (Hofheim: Wolke, 2008), 9; Heinrich Klotz, *Kunst im 20. Jahrhundert: Moderne – Postmoderne – Zweite Moderne* (Munich: Beck, 1994).

56 Martin Scherzinger, 'Curious Intersections, Uncommon Magic: Steve Reich's "It's Gonna Rain"', *Current Musicology* 79–80 (2005), 207–44; Scherzinger, 'György Ligeti and the Aka Pygmies Project', *Contemporary Music Review* 25, no. 3 (2006), 227–62; Scherzinger, 'Luciano Berio's *Coro*: Nexus between African Music and Political Multitude', in *Luciano Berio: Nuove prospettive/New Perspectives*, ed. Angela Ida de Benedictis (Florence: Olschki, 2012), 399–432.

57 Georgina Born and David Hesmondhalgh, eds., *Western Music and Its Others: Difference, Representation, and Appropriation in Music* (Berkeley and Los Angeles: University of California Press, 2000), 15.

Bibliography

Beaucage, Réjean. *La SMCQ: Histoire à suivre*. Montreal: Septentrion, 2011.

Bernstein, David. *The San Francisco Tape Music Center: 1960s Counterculture and the Avant-Garde*. Berkeley and Los Angeles: University of California Press, 2008.

Born, Georgina, and David Hesmondhalgh, eds. *Western Music and Its Others: Difference, Representation, and Appropriation in Music*. Berkeley and Los Angeles: University of California Press, 2000.

Bourassa, André-G., and Gilles Lapointe. *Refus global et ses environs*. Montreal: Éditions de l'Hexagone, 1988.

Browner, Tara, ed. *Music of the First Nations: Tradition and Innovation in Native North America*. Champaign: University of Illinois Press, 2009.

Caron, Claudine, and Jonathan Goldman, eds. 'Musique automatiste? Pierre Mercure et le *Refus global*'. Special issue, *Circuit: musiques contemporaines* 21, no. 3 (2011).

Cotter, Bill. *Vancouver's Expo '86*. Charleston: Arcadia, 2009.

Eisenstadt, Shmuel N. 'Multiple Modernities'. *Daedalus* 129, no. 1 (2000): 1–29.

Fauser, Annegret. *Musical Encounters at the 1889 Paris World's Fair*. Rochester, NY: University of Rochester Press, 2005.

Fleuret, Maurice. 'Rencontre avec Serge Garant'. *Cahiers canadiens de musique*, no. 9 (1974): 13–32.

Gallat-Morin, Élizabeth, and Jean-Pierre Pinson. *La vie musicale en Nouvelle-France*. Montreal: Septentrion, 2003.

Gauthier, Mario, ed. 'Table ronde de 1961 autour d'*Incandescence* de Pierre Mercure'. *Circuit: musiques contemporaines* 21, no. 3 (2011): 87–98.

Goldman, Jonathan. 'A House in Bali/Une maison à Montréal: José Evangelista's *Ô Bali*'. In *Texts and Beyond: The Process of Music Composition from the 19th to the 20th Century*, edited by Jonathan Goldman, 241–69. Bologna: UT Orpheus Edizioni/Ad Parnassum, 2015.

Heile, Björn. '*Weltmusik* and the Globalization of New Music'. In *The Modernist Legacy: Essays on New Music*, edited by Björn Heile, 101–19. Aldershot: Ashgate, 2009.

Kendergi, Maryvonne. 'Interview with Gilles Tremblay'. Disc notes, *Anthologie de la musique canadienne*, RCI, ACM 12 (1983).

Klotz, Heinrich. *Kunst im 20. Jahrhundert: Moderne – Postmoderne – Zweite Moderne*. Munich: Beck, 1994.

Krims, Adam. *Music and Urban Geography*. New York: Routledge, 2007.

Kunst, Jaap. *De toonkunst van Bali*. Weltevreden: Druk G. Kolff, 1925.

———. *De toonkunst van Java*. The Hague: M. Nijhoff, 1934. English translation, *Music in Java: Its History, Its Theory and Its Technique*, edited by E. L. Heins. 3rd ed. The Hague: Nijhoff, 1973.

Lefebvre, Marie-Thérèse. *Serge Garant et la révolution musicale au Québec*. Montreal: Éditions Louise Courteau, 1986.

Mahnkopf, Claus-Steffen. 'Second Modernity – An Attempted Assessment'. In *Facets of the Second Modernity*, edited by Claus-Steffen Mahnkopf, Frank Cox, and Wolfram Schurig, 9–16. Hofheim: Wolke, 2008.

McPhee, Colin. *Music in Bali: A Study in Form and Instrumental Organization in Balinese Orchestral Music*. New Haven, CT: Yale University Press, 1966.

———. *A House in Bali*. New York: John Day, 1946. Reprint, Boston: Periplus, 2002.

Messier, Anne Marie. 'Ticket pour la liberté: Entretien avec Otto Joachim'. *Circuit: musiques contemporaines* 19, no. 3 (2009): 38–47.

Metzer, David. *Musical Modernism at the Turn of the Twenty-First Century*. Cambridge: Cambridge University Press, 2009.

Piekut, Benjamin. *Experimentalism Otherwise: The New York Avant-Garde and Its Limits*. Berkeley and Los Angeles: University of California Press, 2011.

Potvin, Gilles. 'Une superbe fête musicale marque le 10ème anniversaire de la SMCQ'. *Le Devoir*, 13 December 1976.

Ranallo, Vincent. 'Une célébration sonore de l'Esprit: À propos d'*Oralléluiants*'. *Circuit: musiques contemporaines* 20, no. 3 (2010): 43–58.

Rea, John. 'Post-modernisme(s)'. In *Musiques: Une encyclopédie pour le XXIe siècle*, edited by Jean-Jacques Nattiez. Vol. 1. Arles: Actes Sud, 2003.

Rogalsky, Matt. 'Finger Exercises for Oscillators: István Anhalt on Electronic Music'. *Circuit: musiques contemporaines* 19, no. 3 (2009): 77–84.

Rogers, Stephen. 'Travelogue pour un Marco Polo [My Travels with Claude?]: A Journey through the Composer's Life and Work in 10 Days'. *Circuit: musiques contemporaines* 18, no. 1 (2008): 27–51.

Scherzinger, Martin. 'Curious Intersections, Uncommon Magic: Steve Reich's "It's Gonna Rain"'. *Current Musicology* 79–80 (2005): 207–44.

———. 'György Ligeti and the Aka Pygmies Project'. *Contemporary Music Review* 25, no. 3 (2006): 227–62.

———. 'Luciano Berio's *Coro*: Nexus between African Music and Political Multitude'. In *Luciano Berio: Nuove prospettive/New Perspectives*, edited by Angela Ida de Benedictis, 399–432. Florence: Olschki, 2012.

Tenzer, Michael. *Gamelan gong kebyar: The Art of Twentieth-Century Balinese Music*. Chicago: University of Chicago Press, 2000.

———. *Balinese Gamelan Music*. Rutland: Tuttle, 2011.

Thomson, Dale C. *Jean Lesage and the Quiet Revolution*. Toronto: Macmillan, 1984.

Trottier, Danick. 'Enquête: Gilles Tremblay pédagogue vu par ses anciens élèves – questionnaire réalisé par courriel'. *Circuit: musiques contemporaines* 20, no. 3 (2010): 73–90.

Vivier, Claude. 'Les écrits de Claude Vivier'. *Circuit: musiques contemporaines* 2, nos. 1–2 (1991): 39–135.

———. 'Trois lettres de Bali'. *Circuit: musiques contemporaines* 2, nos. 1–2 (1991): 70–79.

Williams, Alastair. *New Music and the Claims of Modernity*. Aldershot: Ashgate, 1997.

17

VERS UNE ÉCRITURE LIMINALE

Serialism, spectralism and *écriture* in the transitional music of Gérard Grisey

Liam Cagney

In July 1980 Gérard Grisey sent Hugues Dufourt a letter from Berlin, where Grisey was at the time living as a DAAD fellow.[1] Grisey's letter concerned the imminent Darmstadt Summer Courses, at which performances of their music had been programmed and Grisey, Dufourt and Tristan Murail were to give presentations. This would be the first major international presentation of their collective musical aesthetic – it was for Darmstadt 1980, for example, that Murail's classic orchestral work *Gondwana* was commissioned – and, being aware of the importance of first impressions, and considering it important that they present a strong united front, Grisey wrote to Dufourt with two purposes: to get Dufourt's feedback on the text of one of his lectures (a lecture on musical time, which after further development was published as 'Tempus ex machina: A Composer's Reflections on Musical Time')[2] and to solicit Dufourt's approval of the name Grisey thought they should use to denote their collective musical aesthetic: *liminal music*.

In presenting their music to a German audience, Grisey wrote, the three composers ran the risk of being saddled with some 'derisory adjective' or other.[3] 'I propose therefore for Darmstadt the adjective LIMINAL', he writes. '*Liminal* (limen: the threshold, that which concerns the threshold, *taking place on the threshold*) is only used, as far as I know, in psychology. *Liminaire* seems to have the sense of "that which remains ahead".' Grisey's choice of this term is informed by the fact that, for him, it crystallizes the salient feature shared by his music, that of Dufourt and that of Murail: not a focus on frequency spectra but a focus on acoustical *thresholds*.

> The threshold is what joins all of us; it is our common denominator. It can have a dynamic sense (only a retrograde person rests on a threshold!). It implies at least two fields, and it encourages movement. We play with thresholds as others play with series.

In proposing this name, Grisey rejects two other candidates: vectorial (too much like Xenakis) and spectral ('too static, too vague: *Stimmung* and Tibetan music are spectral musics').

Dufourt was quick to respond. Although, due to other work commitments, he would unfortunately not be able to come to Darmstadt, he did have some views on Grisey's theoretical and aesthetic concerns. 'Use the adjective "liminal" if you wish,' Dufourt writes, 'but I am not very warm, for it is too restrictive, too "reductive".'[4] Dufourt then makes a remark that, from our standpoint in history, might come as a surprise: 'I've given up on "spectral" since a while back – much too narrow as well. But it doesn't matter; I have more pressing things to talk about.'

Vers une écriture liminale

This epistolary exchange opens a window onto that transitional moment when the music of a group of young Paris-based composers started to shift towards becoming a wider international institution. That transition was effected in part through the invention of a common identity: not, in the end, *écriture liminale* but spectral music, an act of naming that brought with it, alongside a prescribed set of compositional techniques, an inevitable conceptual homogenization and a partial obscuring of the process by which the movement came to emerge. This initial historical brittleness of a concept that is nowadays so well established in our discourse gives us pause for thought. That the composer who by most accounts invented the current and the composer who named it each considered the concept misleading is certainly worth remarking in charting the history of the movement. For these reasons the correspondence functions here as a means of entering into this chapter's focus: a revised examination of both the formative influences behind the French spectral current and its channelling of those influences into a music that emphasized becoming over being, processes over fixed forms, and thresholds over entities.

The causes for the emergence of French spectral music are various: the early 1960s establishment of an acoustics laboratory at the Université Paris VI with the installation there of France's first sonograph; the development of unprecedentedly accurate psychoacoustic models of audition and of computer sound synthesis (by Jean-Claude Risset and others); a growing dissatisfaction during the 1960s with serialism; the appearance of a group of like-minded young composition students in Messiaen's class around the same time; the Ministry of Culture's funding of new music initiatives, in particular from 1973 onwards of L'Itinéraire, the collective that was spectral music's institutional platform; Grisey and Murail's being Prix de Rome scholars together in 1972–73, during which time they had discussions on acoustics and composition; the 1975 addition to L'Itinéraire's *bureau* of the theoretical and political adeptness of Hugues Dufourt; the need for the group to define itself and its work strongly in the face of threatened funding cuts following the establishment of IRCAM; and so on. Properly elucidating these multiple factors in spectral music's emergence would take a book in itself. This chapter therefore restricts its focus to one of the most important and least studied areas: Grisey's early development of the techniques and concepts that would define his mature compositional framework, the framework that would later be generalized under the name spectral music. To privilege Grisey is not to subscribe to a 'great man' view of history; it is simply to observe historical fact. Grisey's final two works composed whilst a student, *Vagues, Chemins, le Souffle* and *D'eau et de pierre*, though not always idiomatically characteristic of spectral music, established the route along which spectral music would pass. Moreover, focusing on this early moment in Grisey's development and on these two works has the advantage in this book from a large historiographical perspective of addressing – albeit still in a provisional manner – how spectral music's development was fostered by the post-serial compositional environment and the enduring desire in this period to coin a new, generalizable compositional system. Showing how spectral music arose from a critique and reformulation of this serial aim affords us a fuller picture of the legacy of this post-war modernist current and its continuity down to the present day.

Serialism in France in the late 1960s

Given how often serialism is invoked as a bugbear in accounts of how spectral music arose, what exactly was serialism's status in France in the late 1960s, when Grisey, Murail and Dufourt were composition students? How did Grisey engage with serialism in the process of establishing his mature musical style? A student of Helmut Degen at the Trossingen Conservatoire, Messiaen at the Paris Conservatoire and Dutilleux at the École Normale de Musique,

Grisey arrived in French new music at a choice moment, when, although serialism was still the main reference point for young composers, its status was changing. By the 1960s the generation of 1925 – Boulez, Stockhausen, Barraqué et al. – had each creatively transformed the method in line with their own particular aesthetic aims. In the same period a younger group of composers emerged, the generation of 1935 – Amy, Guézecs, Méfano and others – which, in finding its feet, used the serial method in a less adventurous, more conservative way. Their figurehead was Boulez, who by now was the most influential composer in France. In a 1966 interview with the *New York Review of Books*, Stravinsky was aware enough of this to note: 'There is a new French school, and a good one, judging by levels of skill. Boulez is the father figure, naturally.'[5] These young composers had for the most part undertaken Boulez's composition masterclass in Basel (which ran between 1960 and 1963); there they got a grounding in Boulez's version of serialism. In Basel Boulez gave his students the same tone row, instructed them in techniques such as isomorphism and chord multiplication, and oversaw their subsequent composition of faintly Boulezian works.[6] The best of those works were then promoted through Boulez's Domaine Musical concert series. Alongside the publication of two books of Boulez's writings in 1963 and 1966 (supplementing or supplanting Leibowitz's earlier guides to the twelve-tone method), this saw serialism in France reach peak visibility in the mid- to late 1960s through Boulez's influence on younger composers (despite the fact he no longer lived in his native country).[7]

The exact sense of the term serialism, though, was equivocal. In discussing serialism in France at this time, one must distinguish between a more open concept of serialism and a more academic, closed concept of serialism. Jean Boivin highlights how, when it began to be taught at the Paris Conservatoire, serialism became academicized:

> It was thus strangely at the moment when composers were beginning to give up on serialism, at least in its 'hard' form, that the enclosure of the [Paris] Conservatoire, formerly rather sealed against modernity, showed itself capable of being permeated. In the footsteps of Boulez, whose *Penser la musique aujourd'hui* appeared in 1964 [sic], a new group of students insisted on the incontrovertible character of this mode of thought. Grudgingly, one would think, the *écriture* professors let them say so.[8]

Tristan Murail, who studied at the Conservatoire from 1967 to 1971, recalls a peer pressure among composition students to compose in this authoritatively sanctioned avant-garde idiom.[9] This was more a question of having a certain kind of superficial atonal idiom than of the means used to compose it (which didn't have to be serial).[10] One of the few places where Murail adhered to the serial idiom is in certain parts of *Couleur de mer* (1969) for ensemble (in particular the second movement). Murail took leave of this in *Altitude 8000* (1970) for string orchestra, a Ligeti- and Xenakis-influenced work. When it was premiered in January 1971 at a Conservatoire composition concert, a section of the audience booed, disapproving of the work's occasional overt consonances and moments of unabashed harmonic beauty. This signified for Murail that, although Boulez had traded places with Fauré as the sanctioned compositional model, the underlying corseted academicism remained.[11]

In contrast to this, a serial composer exploring the more adventurous approach to serialism in this period was Jean-Claude Eloy. After having won prizes at the Conservatoire, where his composition teacher was Milhaud, Eloy was taken under Boulez's wing (he has left the best account of Boulez's teachings in Basel).[12] While Boulez gave instruction in his own version of the serial method, Eloy says he was more interested in Boulez's recent ensemble writing, which

Vers une écriture liminale

gave unprecedented breadth to static harmonic complexes, notably in the work *Pli selon pli* (1957–62, rev. 1984, 1989):

> In listening to *Pli selon pli* I was struck by a phenomenon that was compositionally new in that period. Zones of relative stability frequently seemed to be established for quite long periods, creating these sorts of 'polarizations', the sudden discovery of which fascinated me. I had, indeed, become more and more bothered by the permanence and rapidity of information in the earlier serial works. [. . .] This obsession with a dimension that would be capable of organizing the mobile and the immobile, 'stasism' and 'dynamism', became essential for me.[13]

Eloy's first successful orchestral work, *Étude III* (1962), while rooted in the serial method Boulez taught in Basel, tentatively moves away from the post-Webernian idiom towards a style occasionally incorporating colouristic blocks of harmony sustained for extended durations; punctual events are framed against that static harmonic backdrop, which functions in the manner of a harmonic pole or auditory frame of reference. Jésus Aguila notes that in taking as his compositional focus simply the types of sonority he wished to hear, Eloy had begun to relegate the serial method to second place in compositional precedence; the ear had begun definitively to dictate to the page.[14] This augured what Grisey, Murail and Dufourt would explore, and that connection is evident in the terms used for Eloy's music at the time, which faintly pre-echo what would be said of spectral music. Messiaen, for example, in his 1967 book of conversations with Claude Samuel praised Eloy's music as moving towards a new concept of musical time as facilitated by this exploration of extended static harmonies: 'We're witnessing a change in the notion of time, and I believe that one of the composers most sensitive to this change is Jean-Claude Eloy';[15] this can be compared to Grisey's oft-repeated remark that spectral music has a temporal origin.[16] In Eloy's case this would lead in the 1970s to extended sound canvases such as *Kâmakalâ* (1971), *Shânti* (1972–73) and *Fluctuante-immuable* (1977). Certain aspects of *Kâmakalâ* in particular – its slowness, its static elements, and its periodic repetition and variation of audibly distinct sound figures – correspond to elements of Grisey's style as it developed slightly later. Eloy's case shows that this adventurous approach to serial thought in the mid-to-late 1960s was bringing about changes to the serial idiom.[17]

This was also, of course, the case with Boulez's 1960s music. It is no accident that works such as *Pli selon pli, Figures, Doubles, Prismes* (1963–64, rev. 1968) and *Cummings ist der Dichter* (1970, rev. 1986) at times can sound similar to works by Grisey and Murail. By the early 1960s Boulez was giving more scope to harmonic beauty (of a highly complex type) and admitting that the initial post-war serialist project had been overly dogmatic and naïve: that it had privileged an image of 'what might seem to be a perfect "technological" rationality but was in fact a monumental absurdity'.[18] In his Darmstadt lectures from this time Boulez frequently takes aim at technicism, the reduction of the musical work to a nuts-and-bolts abstraction; against this tendency, like Schoenberg before him, Boulez promoted *thought* and *idea* as categories of primary import in analysis and artistic creation. He considered that 'juggling with numbers surely reveals a lack of confidence, an impotence and a lack of imagination'; that the instant of imagination comes, rather, from 'an indestructible kernel of darkness' (a phrase adapted from André Breton's 'infracassable noyau de nuit'); and that '[a]ll reflections on musical technique must be based on sound and duration, the composer's raw material'.[19] Such should be the aims of the contemporary composer engaging serialism in a creative, properly artistic way, he suggested. An important, scattered nexus within *Relevés d'apprenti* charts Boulez's reflections over the period from *Le marteau sans maître* ('Recherches maintenant') to *Pli selon pli* ('Tendences de la musique récente'). In these essays, while still referring to Webern as the 'threshold' whose music passes onto 'a new mode of musical being',[20] Boulez had begun to give greater emphasis to sound complexes,[21] to chordal sound blocks whose internal organization is modelled on resonance (after Varèse, the 1954 premiere of whose *Déserts* in Paris seems to have influenced Boulez as well as Dutilleux),[22] to the sequential generation of chords of variable density one from another,[23] to the notion of *l'objet sonore* – recently coined by Abraham Moles and adopted by Pierre Schaeffer – and the pivotal importance for its identity of its specific surrounding context,[24] and, in general, to the priority of perception over abstraction. The application of these ideas is clear in the acoustical character of *Le marteau* (particularly the last movement, 'Bel édifice et les pressentiments'), *Poésie pour pouvoir* (1958, since withdrawn), and the *Improvisations sur Mallarmé* (later incorporated into *Pli selon pli*).[25] Following a performance of the latter on BBC television sometime in 1964, asked how audiences should understand his musical language, Boulez replied, 'Just forget all about explanations and just hear'; and a couple of years later, when, again on the BBC, discussing *Éclat*, Boulez gave a similar insight on his aesthetic:

> When I am hearing a combination of tones which sounds good I can just let the sound die, and I can appreciate the sound until the last moment. One is not in a hurry to hear the music, but one can just wait his own pleasure [sic].[26]

These empirical views are far from the rationalism with which Boulez is often stereotyped, and are similar to remarks made around the same time by Murail.[27] They further suggest how elements of Grisey's style would develop through Grisey's engagement with Boulez's music and writings.

Boulez's analytic attitude encouraged composition students not simply to ape but to re-interpret creatively compositional approaches past, including his own.[28] It was through analysing a composition as closely as possible that a composer realized the 'NECESSITY' – or otherwise – of the decisions made therein and of the techniques the composer had used.[29] This is how Boulez himself had approached Schoenberg,[30] and though he may have been ambivalent about it, this is how he expected his students to approach him, not as epigones but as creative artists: the composer as seer, scouring the past's bloody entrails and envisioning therein the future.[31] While Boulez knew by this stage that the utopian ideal of serialism as a general compositional language was untenable, he nonetheless considered that the next stage of music could only be an outgrowth of serialism (Messiaen held a similar view).[32] To some extent Grisey bore out that intuition. If the motivating ethos of Boulezian serialism was the bracketing out from composition of everything that was unnecessary, and the derivation of one's compositional framework from the internal nature of sound itself, Grisey simply applied this principle more deeply than Boulez himself. In this regard, as someone adhering to certain elements of Boulez's music while doing away with those that he deemed superfluous, Grisey was faithful to Boulez as teacher through being unfaithful to Boulez as compositional model.[33]

In his early journal Grisey had characterized serial music critically as *bavardage*, a too-voluble chatter in which little was said. It was too intellectual, and the serial musician too much a savant, not enough a poet.[34] This did not preclude Grisey, as a student of Messiaen's, composing several works in the serial idiom and engaging closely with serial thought (as well as the aleatorism that was modish at that time in France). He read books by Leibowitz, Boulez and Stockhausen in detail, studied serially composed scores, analysed works such as Stockhausen's *Kreuzspiel* (1951) and *Zeitmaße* (1955–56) and, following this, in the manner typical of an apprentice composer seeking to keep up with the main composers of the day, emulated the music in question.[35] In

Vers une écriture liminale

short, Grisey as a student was a serial composer, and a talented one. Works such as *Charme* (1969) for clarinet solo, *Mégalithes* (1969) for fifteen brass, and *Perichoresis* (1969–70) for twelve players, by and large idiomatically serial, are accomplished works. But whilst these works are broadly 'serial' in sound, they also at times exhibit a drive to attain a different expressive register. In this respect three characteristics stand out as significant for Grisey's preliminary efforts towards his mature style: 1) the use of *personnages sonores*, audibly distinct musical archetypes, particularly the case in *Charme* and a principle that would significantly inform the conception of Grisey's first stylistically mature work, *D'eau et de pierre* (1972), as will be seen; 2) an increasing prominence given to sustained sonorities and to resonance chords (in evidence, for example, at the end of *Perichoresis*); and 3) in keeping with his spiritual ideals, a view of the musical artwork as something existing essentially beyond language, something transcendental, which the categories of representational thought cannot capture. Each of these characteristics prioritizes perceptibility over the intellectual rationale in which contemporary art music was often swathed.

In an interview in later years, Grisey summed up his earlier attitude to serial thought:

> [F]or a number of my contemporaries the blackness and complexity of a score is as determinant for their judgment as the ear. This is what I call the perverse effect of written composition [*l'écriture*]. My generation was brutally confronted with this dilemma: should we continue along the path of extreme combinatorial complexity of our elders or rather search for more comprehensibility and transparency? The taste for combinatorial games and abstraction, alongside a certain intellectual elitism, had very naturally brought the 1950s towards perversion: 'the map for the territory'. In music nothing prevents a composer from multiplying structures on to infinity, for one can always accumulate; all that's needed is a bit of patience. What will make us stop? Nothing, unless the listener rightly feels ridiculous at the 'fourth retrograde inversion of a fragment of the series multiplied by itself'. From the 1970s, my obsession was: what do I actually perceive out of all that? What remains out of that complexity? I always had this desire to imagine what I called 'the skin of time', this immediate zone of contact between the listener and the music, in searching for an extreme limpidity. My ideal is that the complexity of structures does not serve to detract from audibility, but to underlie an event that is simple in appearance.[36]

As has been seen, in 1960s France Grisey was not alone in this. After Boulez had begun to put more emphasis on harmonic lustre, some younger composers like Eloy followed suit. This was in line with Boulez's own observations on how composition evolves:

> I am convinced that however perceptive the composer, he cannot imagine the consequences, immediate or ultimate, of what he has written, and that his perception is not necessarily more accurate than that of the analyst (as I see him). Certain procedures, results and types of invention will become obsolete or else will remain completely personal, even though the composer may consider them fundamental when he discovered them; observations which later turn out to be of great consequence may have seemed to him negligible or of secondary importance. It is very wrong to confuse the value of a work, or its immediate novelty, with its possible powers of fertilisation.[37]

These comments certainly apply to Boulez's own *Pli selon pli*. Grisey's effort towards developing a distinctive style – a complex method that would produce an apparently simple surface, music that would be 'intellectual without that intellectualism being apparent' – began nascently to develop during the 1969–70 academic year, as he made a concerted effort to expand his technical abilities and broaden his musical knowledge.

Boulez, Xenakis, Messiaen and Marie, and their influence on nascent spectralism

In May 1969 Boulez brought the BBC Symphony Orchestra to Paris for the second French performance of *Pli selon pli*. Maurice Fleuret's review of the concert in *Le Nouvel Observateur* indicates the impression the work made on many. Describing *Pli selon pli* as a decisive move beyond 'post-Webernian rarefaction', Fleuret wrote:

> Nothing is gratuitous: not the durations, not the attacks, not the volumes, not the dynamics, not the timbres. All participate in the perfect, fragile equilibrium that the work succeeds in maintaining for more than an hour on the clock. [...] It is as if sound, in being forced to discover the hard heart of its substance, opened up a universe truer and more vibrant than the real.[38]

Whether Grisey attended this performance of *Pli selon pli* or was influenced by it indirectly (through discussion in Messiaen's composition class and/or the concert's broadcast on French radio), it seems to have spurred him towards exploring resonance chords and other germinal features of spectral music in more detail; for around this time Grisey bought the score of Boulez's *Don* (1960–62, revised 1989) for soprano and orchestra, the opening movement of *Pli selon pli*.[39] Grisey's copy of *Don* has been preserved and bears witness to his study and analysis of the work, an analysis conducted not in terms of the composition's discreet serial process but in terms of its surface resonant sonorities and the interactions between the subdivisions of the ensemble: just the type of creative analysis that Boulez as teacher prescribed. At different passages on pages 10, 18 and 19 of the score Grisey notes: '*Klangfarbenmelodie* issuing from the resonance of a melody'. These sections (which include the opening line sung by the soprano) feature blocks of colour that bleed across the ensemble in reaction to the 'pressure' of a melodic line. On page 2 of the score, where the ensemble is divided into three groups, Grisey notes some of the characteristics of how the groups interact: 'The high and low groups imitate the principal instrument of the central group (attack and resonances).' In other words, a sub-ensemble of players produce a complex sonority – a type of harmony-timbre – in imitation of, and in reaction to, a strike on one of the resonant instruments of the central group. Grisey would adapt this principle of micro/macro simulation in the closing section of his next major work, *Vagues, Chemins, le Souffle*, and with further development it would eventually lead to the famous opening of *Partiels*, in which an ensemble plays a synthetic chord modelled on a low trombone note. Grisey also analysed this attack-and-resonance pattern in *Domaines* (1961–68) for clarinet and ensemble.[40]

Another impetus for development at this time was Grisey's studies in electroacoustics and applied maths. Having decided to complement his composition classes with Messiaen with studies elsewhere, Grisey enrolled at the Schola Cantorum for a year-long course in 'radiophonic production, sound engineering, applied acoustics, and the analysis of experimental music' run by the composer Jean-Étienne Marie (1917–89), probably his first introduction to the physics of sound and electronic composition. Although Grisey never mentioned his studies with Marie in later interviews, Marie's approach and ideas are likely to have had a crucial impact on him at the time. For instance, he studied the different types of sound wave (sine, saw-tooth, square), signal processing effects (such as filtering), ring modulation (RM), reverb, tape loops and tape delay, the multi-oscillator synthesizer, frequency modulation (FM) and amplitude modulation (AM). This overview of studio techniques set the ground for a future instrumental music using several of them as models; in *D'eau et de pierre*, for instance, Grisey conceives changes to the work's spectral chord in terms of formants and filtering. When Grisey gave his first presentation on his mature music, at Darmstadt in 1978, he notably referred to the new current in France of which he was a part as one based on the application to instrumental composition of ideas and techniques from the electronic music studio.[41]

During this time, Grisey also made a concerted effort to improve his mathematical knowledge and abilities, covering, for example, mathematical sequences and series, arithmetical and geometrical progressions of rhythmic values (and the distinction between their respective representations as curves on X–Y axis graphs), logarithms, exponentials and the application of the golden section to durations. In this, too, Marie's classes were instrumental: in one of them, for instance, Marie had demonstrated how he had used Pascal's Triangle in his recent composition *Tlaloc* (1967), the opening section of which, a progressively densifying orchestral texture, is a clear antecedent of Grisey's own process forms.[42] This training doubtless encouraged Grisey towards the later (sometimes onerous) calculation of tables of frequency spectra and resultant tone harmonies, as for instance in his *Jour, contre jour* or *Tempus ex machina*, the sketches for which illustrate the high degree of mathematical calculation in Grisey's mature method.[43]

After Boulez, Xenakis was the second most prominent composer in France at this time, providing another example of the significance of mathematics for advanced composition at the time. Grisey became interested in Xenakis's music around the time of the October 1968 festival Journées de Musique Contemporaine de Paris, at which many of the Greek composer's works were performed.[44] A specific concept of Xenakis's that Grisey adopted was that of the *métabole* or sound 'metabolism', a key factor in planning some of the process-based aspects of *Vagues, Chemin, le Souffle* and *D'eau et de pierre*.[45]

Finally, during the same period, Grisey also started reading up on acoustics and perception, particularly gestalt theory, purchasing brief introductions to these topics in the iconic *Que sais-je?* series. The gestaltist distinction between synthetic and analytic attitudes appears to be behind Grisey's later description of his music as *synthetic* as opposed to the *analytic* music of serialism.[46] Arguably even more crucial for the development of spectralism was the concept of *figure* in gestalt theory. In works such as *Charme* Grisey was already using a modified version of Messiaen's *personnages sonores*, and a renewed effort to compose perceptually distinct auditory figures would underpin the composition of his first idiomatically spectral work, *D'eau et de pierre*.

Although Jean-Étienne Marie is typically regarded as a comparatively minor figure, it is clear that his interest in mathematics, acoustics, electroacoustics and perception provided a vital impulse for the genesis of spectralism.

Nascent spectralism: *Vagues, Chemins, le Souffle* (1970–72)

In the summer of 1970, shortly after finishing his studies with Marie, Grisey began work on an ambitious composition for two orchestras and amplified solo clarinet incorporating many of the currents in vogue at the time – aleatorism, spatialization, post-serialism, a dash of music theatre, some mixed electroacoustics. He worked on it for a year and a half and, through Messiaen, secured a high-profile premiere for the work at the 1972 Festival International d'Art Contemporain de Royan.[47] Typically for a student composer, the work that eventually emerged, *Vagues, Chemins, le Souffle*, tries to do too many things at once, and the over-elaborate score – two conductors, players distributed all around the hall, coordinated spatial movements of sound and unwieldy aleatory elements – may well have played a part in the Orchestre Philharmonique de l'ORTF going on strike and the concert being cancelled.[48] But despite its failure, and despite its being for the most part uncharacteristic of Grisey's mature style, *Vagues, Chemins, le Souffle* marks the tentative introduction of certain key elements he would carry forward and subsequently develop: 1) schematic precompositional planning by way of the acoustical parameters; 2) the composition of auditory processes; 3) the sequential repetition and variation of an audibly distinct sound figure; 4) chords modelled on harmonic spectra; and 5) the composition of a 'timbral mirror', whereby an ensemble chord is conceived as a macroscopic simulation of a microscopic instrumental tone. I treat each of these now in turn in charting the elements of Grisey's nascent spectral style in *Vagues, Chemins, le Souffle*.

Schematic precompositional planning by way of the acoustical parameters

In mid-to-late 1970, when he was beginning work on his as yet untitled orchestral composition, Grisey took technical notes on composing on the basis of what is 'directly perceptible'.[49] One way such perceptibility could occur was when a sound parameter was pushed to its limit, such that it was transformed into a different parameter and required an equivalent conceptual reformulation. The 'harmonic hypertrophy' of Wagner and Debussy, for example, eventually led to dissolution in the notion of colour and timbre (as in Schoenberg's *Farben*), while the rhythmic hypertrophy of the post-war music of Boulez and others led to dissolution into the notion of rhythmic density (as Xenakis was the first to observe).[50] In this way traditional concepts came to be revised in light of acoustical evidence and replaced by more appropriate ones: musical concepts were reformulated to be brought closer to perception. Grisey later called one of the chief starting points of his music the wish to find greater adequation between concept and percept, and it is not difficult to see how Grisey adhered to this principle in leading the colouristic harmonic complexes of Boulez towards spectral organization. In *Vagues, Chemins, le Souffle* this line of thought manifests itself in the thorough schematization of the composition. In planning the work, Grisey charted the concurrent activity at any given time of the various parameters of the orchestral sound: for example, rhythm, rhythmic density, density of instrumental timbre, space, dynamic of intensities, pitches, and general dynamic curve. Following this planning and calculation, Grisey would then write the notes in the score. Though at this point the method was not refined, it laid the ground for his mature approach. The focus on the statistical character of the ensemble sound shows the influence of Xenakis and Marie.

The composition of auditory processes

As previously mentioned, *Vagues, Chemins, le Souffle* features a spatialized orchestra, and its main models in this regard were Xenakis's *Terretektorh* and Marie's Concerto 'Milieu Divin' (named after a book by Pierre Teilhard de Chardin). *Terretektorh* was premiered at the Royan Festival in 1966, and like Grisey's composition it features the orchestra distributed around the hall among the audience. This orchestral layout in *Vagues, Chemins, le Souffle* allows the composition of processes of sound movement: 'numerous forms of sound shifting (continuous–discontinuous, at even speed, accelerating or decelerating) as well as the superimposing of different speeds and the variability of spatial density (in other words, the breadth of the sonic layer being shifted).'[51] One of Grisey's aims in this way was to create a hypnotic effect on the audience; to this end he considered calling the work *Transe* before opting for its eventual tripartite title (which reflects its tripartite structure).[52] Grisey's score also makes liberal use of mass string glissandos, whose trajectory he mapped out using the same orange A3 graph paper favoured by Xenakis. Grisey's plotting of vectors passing through registral space over time, in combination with his plotting of the speed and trajectory of each sound movement throughout the three-dimensional space of the hall, evinces a desire towards a totally 'comprehensive' composition of sound experience. These spatial ideas are at once of historical interest in illustrating an aspect of the milieu of French new music at this time (a time when Xenakis's music was becoming more and more popular) and of theoretical interest with regard to Grisey's oeuvre. They are the source in Grisey's music of the composition of process, perhaps the salient attribute of his mature 1970s style. Baillet states the matter succinctly: 'In Grisey's music processes of transformation are omnipresent, constituting the foundation of his compositional methods. These processes are easily perceptible, systematic and quasi-mechanical in character, single-handedly outlining the formal architecture of the work.'[53] While Grisey would for the most part subsequently abandon sound spatialization, with occasional exceptions, such as *Tempus ex machina* (1979), he would retain the approach of composing musical processes. This continuity is underlined by comments Grisey makes about Xenakis's music in his unpublished 1972 lecture 'Music and Space':

> Seen under a microscope, certain sections of Xenakis's works tend towards conjuration; or if one prefers, they try to hypnotize the listener. Taking off from a precise material, they generate a totally other material in a few seconds. This metamorphosis is very progressive, without any rupture; if one abandons oneself to its play, it is sometimes very difficult to become aware of it. [...] This is an instance of the method of continual transformation.[54]

In his 1978 lecture 'The Becoming of Sound', Grisey goes so far as to state that such continuous transformation is *the* core principle of his music: 'The different processes of mutation of one sound into another sound or of a group of sounds into another group constitutes the very base of my compositional method – the primary idea, the germ of all composition.'[55]

The sequential repetition and variation of an audibly distinct sound figure

The form of *Vagues, Chemins, le Souffle* is ternary. The aforementioned microscopic/macroscopic simulation – a precursor of spectralism's technique of instrumental synthesis – is found in the relation between the work's beginning and ending. The first movement opens with the solo amplified clarinet playing a series of long, swelling notes, the 'Waves' of the title, which gradually become more dissonant and noisier over successive iterations; the last movement, 'Breath', ends with a series of antiphonal, swelling chords sounding over and back across the hall on winds, brass and percussion, as the strings play glissandos that move in waves across the two orchestral sections. In this way the ending is conceived as an orchestral simulation of the solo clarinet beginning. The closing antiphonal swelling chords alternately sound two major third dyads: a C and an E followed by a G♭ and a B♭, the overlap of which creates a chord that in tonal harmony might be classified as an inverted French sixth chord or a dominant seventh with a flattened fifth. The chord is thus analogous to the chord that ends *Dérives* (a chord, in that work, modelled on the harmonic spectrum); and that characteristic of the *Dérives* chord that Féron calls 'prismatic revelry' – a sensuous lounging within a spectrally rich harmony – is also applicable to 'Le Souffle'.[56] Grisey's programme note states: 'The third movement, "Breath", is a sort of timbral mirror of the first [movement], being likewise made up of swaying motion; this time, waves of breath.'[57] Grisey's sketches show that his idea for this gradual evolution of a synthetic sound is a 'metabolism of timbre'. Although the word *métabole* also served (in the plural) as the title of one of Dutilleux's orchestral works, Grisey was here using the term in the sense that Xenakis employed it (albeit doing so in a looser way), to denote the process of mutation of a parametrically defined sound complex.

Chords modelled on harmonic spectra and the composition of a 'timbral mirror'

These final two germinal spectralist features return us to the influence of *Pli selon pli*. Resonance chords feature midway through Grisey's second movement, 'Chemins' (Paths), and at the opening of the third movement, 'Le Souffle'. The sketches show that in 'Le Souffle' the chords are conceived as imitating the internal structure of the clarinet intonations at the opening of the piece, and Grisey writes 'spectre harmonique' beside the initial sketch for the chords.[58] Grisey's study around this time of resonance chords in Boulez's *Don* seems to have inspired the idea. Example 17.1 shows an extract from the opening of 'Le Souffle': the first of a series of

Example 17.1   Opening of 'Le Souffle' from Gérard Grisey, *Vagues, Chemins, le Souffle*, featuring a resonance chord

© 1974 Copyright Gérard Billaudot Editeur SA, Paris. Reproduced by kind permission of the publisher

ensemble chords which sound as if resonating from a brief attack on a percussion instrument. In the given chord the attack comes from a tubular bell and the ensemble comprises the strings of one orchestral unit. The idea is the same as the opening bars of *Don*. Grisey's borrowing from Boulez is even clearer when one compares the respective opening chords of *Don* and *Dérives* (1973–74) for orchestra and amplified ensemble. The opening ideas are identical: a *tutti* strike at the top of the dynamic range, followed by a resonant chord; but whereas in *Don* the resonant chord dies out within seconds, in *Dérives* it is extended for several minutes. In this way we see how Grisey fashioned core elements of his style through creatively modifying elements of Boulez's music.[59] That lineage would later be obscured in the consistent theoretical antithesis of serialism and spectralism.

Towards the 'absolute sound': *D'eau et de pierre* (1972)

D'eau et de pierre is Grisey's first idiomatically spectral work. Where *Vagues, Chemins, le Souffle* drew in part on elements from Boulez and Xenakis, *D'eau et de pierre* augmented this with elements drawn from Stockhausen. *D'eau et de pierre* came about after Royan's departing artistic director Claude Samuel offered Grisey another commission for an ensemble work to be premiered in late 1972 at Samuel's new festival, the Rencontres Internationales de Musique Contemporaine Metz. The commission arrived around the same time as Grisey won the Prix de Rome and was readying to attend for the first time the Darmstadt Summer Courses. By the time of the premiere Grisey had moved to Rome as a Prix de Rome scholar. There, newly inspired to study acoustics, he read treatises by Emile Leipp and Fritz Winckel and discussed his ideas with Murail. This period would produce *Périodes*, the first work composed in his *Les espaces acoustiques* cycle.

Compared to Grisey's previous works, *D'eau et de pierre* is radically stripped down. Like *Charme* it is based on the interrelation of two antithetical, audibly distinct musical *personnages*, here two instrumental groups. The first group plays a static, synthetic chord modelled (in a rudimentary way) on the harmonic spectrum with 'coloration' high above the chord in the form of string harmonics modelled on resultant tones (see Example 17.2). The second, antithetical group appears at intervals playing sporadic, aggressive rhythms that 'disturb' the static surface of the first group (like the surface of a pool disturbed by a projectile stone).[60] As the work progresses, each aggression by the second group disturbs the first group more and more, making the chord more and more inharmonic, until in a chaotic middle section the two groups fuse in a squall of sound. Eventually the calm, static chord of the outset returns. The work thus has a ternary form, and it lasts around twenty minutes in performance. Here we find several formal features characteristic of spectral music: a well-defined auditory figure based on the harmonic spectrum; a process of gradual deviation by which a given sound figure changes in appearance; a dualistic conception whereby one sound figure influences another sound figure; and a ternary form, starting here from relative harmonic simplicity, moving into harmonic complexity, then returning once again to harmonic simplicity. Needless to say, when the Ensemble Européen de Musique Contemporaine, conducted by Michel Tabachnik, premiered *D'eau et de pierre* on 26 November 1972 at Metz's Théâtre Municipal, nobody, least of all Grisey, considered it as the beginning of a new current in composition – but so it proved to be.

D'eau et de pierre's compositional process shows how Grisey came to hit upon this new style. His initial sketches in spring 1972 were for a work for clarinet and tape, the tape part of which comprised pre-recorded clarinet tracks made at the studio of the Conservatoire in Pantin; with the Metz commission Grisey transposed his ideas to an ensemble format. The earliest sketches show that Grisey's dualistic conception (which, again, followed the earlier example of *Charme*)

Example 17.2 First page of the score of Gérard Grisey, *D'eau et de pierre*, showing the first, 'calm' musical group. The piece is an exercise in reduction, a striking lack of events, other than shifting harmonic colour, in evidence here

© 1972 Casa Ricordi. Reproduced by kind permission

Vers une écriture liminale

was as much guided by a conception of ontological sound types as by their actual acoustical make-up. Before deciding to model the first instrumental group on a harmonic spectrum, Grisey simply had the idea for what he termed – in a faintly metaphysical fashion – an 'absolute sound':

1 Take off from the principle of an absolute sound without any event, which directs itself a little

[. . .]
4 Think the progressive separation [*éloignement*] of an absolute sound in one or several parameters simultaneously
5 The sections are determined by the action on one or more given parameters and by the degree of separation from the absolute sound[61]

Grisey elsewhere in the sketches refers to the proposed absolute sound as a 'coloured silence' (a term taken from Stockhausen). These notions of silence and of an acoustical absolute evince the search for something purer and more essential than the stereotype of serial *bavardage*.[62]

This notion of silence, although arcane, is instructive here. A music of silence would be one whose constitution is unavailable to linguistic representation. Although it is never explicitly developed, the concept of silence appears throughout Grisey's *Écrits*. The idea has spiritual, metaphysical roots, related to his theological leanings. Some notes Grisey took in 1969 in Siena upon viewing an Annunciation painting by Lorenzetti are instructive with regard to the notion of silence embodied in his initial concept for *D'eau et de pierre*. Grisey describes the '[m]arvellous distance between two figures [*personnages*]. [. . .] The empty space [*vide*], the silence, separating and attracting two forms, seemingly made to be directly interlinked and blended.' Grisey's note ends by invoking 'Silence as a droplet of the great Silence of the Love of God fallen in the middle of the "work"'.[63] Silence here describes the invisible relation between the painting's two figures or *personnages*, and Grisey considers that he should look for a musical correspondence: 'Silence would not be conceived there as a *caesura* or as arsis and thesis [that is, as having a straightforward metrical function] but as the tearing-apart imposed upon two objects each dependent upon the other and as if magnetic.' This describes accurately enough the nature of the relation between *D'eau et de pierre*'s two figures: two distinct figures with a quasi-magnetic relation that is in itself imperceptible. In this sense, the use of an extended spectral harmony in the piece stems from an initial desire to explore the progressive deviation of an acoustical absolute, the correlate of which was coloured silence.

Once Grisey received Samuel's commission for an ensemble work, he modified his plans. Again he thoroughly schematized the ensemble sound, creating tables that chart the concurrent action over time of the different parameters of the collective sound. This time, though, there is a crucial addition: the application to that collective sound state of the notion of 'the degree of change'. Grisey's use of the degree of change as a means of progressively modifying his sound complex came following a guest lecture given by Stockhausen to Messiaen's composition class during the 1971–72 academic year. In a later interview Grisey underlined the impression Stockhausen's presentation made on him:

What is happening when I inscribe on the paper a timbre or chord? I had to go back to zero, make a sort of *tabula rasa* of all my knowledge. When one questions oneself on the foundations of perception, one very quickly arrives at the phenomenon that Stockhausen called the degree of change, which originates in Information Theory. Stockhausen had spoken about it at length when he came to Messiaen's class to analyse

Carré. He said: 'when I have written one chord, then another, I wonder what has changed between the two.' In other words, what is important is not that the chord be constituted by such and such an interval but that it engenders the degree of change.[64]

In Grisey's mature spectral music the use of the degree of change in formal terms corresponds to the use of the harmonic spectrum to determine acoustical material. The harmonic spectrum and the degree of change each adhere optimally to the principle of perceptibility: that one's compositional concept be clearly perceptible to the listener.[65] The degree of change allows the temporal animation of the harmonic spectrum. This compositional framework is the basis for a music based on difference, transience and the liminal (the three epithets Grisey initially favoured over spectral).[66] Through the use of the degree of change a figure constituted through a fragment of the harmonic spectrum alters, deviates, changes and does so imperceptibly. Having decided on the presentation of a perceptually distinct absolute sound, Grisey achieves the gradual alteration of that sound through a controlled variation of the acoustical parameters that are used, in a post-serial manner, to define that sound. Some parameters remain unchanged whilst others alter. Alongside the presentation of a static auditory surface modelled on the harmonic spectrum, it is the technique of measuring degrees of change that gives *D'eau et de pierre* the distinctive auditory quality of Grisey's mature ensemble music; the technique would be used in a similar way, for example, to compose the gradual deviation of the famous opening chord of *Partiels*.[67]

In *Vagues, Chemins, le Souffle* Grisey's use of resonance chords stems from Boulez, but harmonicity was always something Grisey was drawn to. Grisey's first prominent use of harmonic centricity is in *Perichoresis*, which contains a section featuring repeated minor triads and which ends on a long, static perfect fifth. This openness to consonance is expanded in *Vagues, Chemins, le Souffle* into an ending based on a prolonged consonant chord. Given this past engagement with harmonicity, and given that Grisey had recently used resonance chords in *Vagues, Chemins, le Souffle*, it is not entirely surprising that in his next composition Grisey would be open to exploring harmonicity in much more detail through the use of the harmonic spectrum to embody his absolute sound. Moreover, by mid-1972, consonance and harmonicity had begun to feature more frequently in art music, particularly evident in the *musique répétitive* of Riley, Reich and Glass that was beginning to be heard in France.[68] On the level of concrete influence, however, Grisey's use of an extended spectral chord in *D'eau et de pierre* was influenced by either one or two specific sources to which he was exposed in the summer of 1972: La Monte Young's drone music and Stockhausen's *Stimmung*.

Given the many shared characteristics of minimal and spectral music, it is unsurprising that they might have shared sources. In late May 1972 – around the time Grisey was considering how to embody his concept of an absolute sound – La Monte Young had the first presentation of his music in Paris. The programme for Young's 1972 Paris Sound and Light concert, given with his regular collaborator Marian Zazeela, featured tape recordings of The Theatre of Eternal Music's mid-1960s overtone-based drone music and of Young and Zazeela's more recent music featuring singing over synthesizer drones.[69] Whether or not Grisey attended this Sound and Light concert, given the size of the Paris new music scene he was surely aware of it; in the *Nouvel Observateur* the event had prominent billing, for example, a photograph of Young appearing with the words 'the most esoteric of contemporary music's sorcerers'. A special issue of the magazine *Chroniques de l'art vivant* was also published to coincide with the visit. Featuring discussions of Young's aesthetics, it described the complex mathematical basis of Young's ostensibly simple music, in which the combination of extended durations and a flux of acoustic identity is based on close attention to and manipulation of the mechanics of human auditory perception.[70] Certain of Young's Fluxus compositions were reproduced – including the famous *Composition 1960*

Vers une écriture liminale

No. 7, a graphic of a perfect fifth with the instruction 'to be held for a long time' – as well as a fragment of Young's 'Lecture 1960', the final lines of which discuss the notion of 'entering into the interior of sound', a phrase that would subsequently be adopted by the young *courant spectral* composers.[71] The magazine also featured an interview with John Cage, who stated that Young's music had 'changed the way I hear' and which dwelt on the discreet complexity under this music's surface simplicity. One of Grisey's main harmonic techniques – used for the first time in *D'eau et de pierre* – is the modelling of ensemble harmonies on sum and difference tones. Such resultant-tone harmonies characterize the 'coloration' of the static spectral chord in *D'eau et de pierre*. It is thus notable that, in the long interview between Caux and Young published in the May 1972 issue of *Chroniques de l'art vivant*, Young talks in detail about the sum and difference tone principle and its systematic exploration in his music.[72] The harmonic system that proceeds from Young's use of sum and difference tones is close to that discussed by Grisey in his unpublished Darmstadt lecture 'Ombre du son' (1980), which focuses on the systematic exploitation of such harmonies in ensemble composition. While Grisey was introduced to resultant tones during his studies with Marie, that he should first apply the idea just after Young's visit is certainly suggestive and possibly telling.

A definite influence on *D'eau et de pierre* is Stockhausen's *Stimmung* (a work itself, of course, inspired by Young).[73] In June 1972 Grisey attended the Darmstadt Summer Courses. There, as well as attending seminars by Xenakis and Ligeti – and, notably, a concert of Romanian music at which was performed music that would later be considered Romanian spectral music[74] – Grisey attended Stockhausen's seminars. Stockhausen's analytic focuses that year were *Mantra* (1972) and *Stimmung*. *Mantra* left Grisey decidedly unimpressed. Beside the details he copied from Stockhausen on the expansion, contraction and repetition of the thirteen original forms of the mantra – procedures similar to orthodox serialism – Grisey wrote: 'Voir relation réalité < – > œuvre'.[75] Here, in four words and a symbol, the young composer delivers pithy judgement on what he considers Stockhausen's overly abstract compositional apparatus, symptomatic of those problems with serialism he was trying to resolve. It is tempting to read this little note as the moment Grisey decisively crossed a personal Rubicon from the post-serial approach to his distinctive mature spectral compositional framework.

Grisey was much more taken with *Stimmung*. He, Boudreau and Vivier lay on the floor during the evening performance by the Collegium Vocale Köln and they subsequently almost got kicked off the Darmstadt tram for doing an impromptu rendition each day when travelling.[76] Grisey's notes from Stockhausen's *Stimmung* seminar illustrate how certain elements of Grisey's subsequent compositional practice derive from this *Stimmung* analysis. A first element is Grisey's use, from *Dérives* on, of the intervallic proportions of the harmonic spectrum to determine at once both a work's harmonic content and its durational proportions:[77] in *Stimmung*, as Grisey notes, the small portion of the harmonic spectrum used by Stockhausen determines both the relation between the sung pitches and the relations between tempos. A second element is a more fundamental tenet of Grisey's mature music: the view that the harmonic series and periodicity are the same principle applied to different domains. A third element is the notion of a work as auto-engendering itself, which Baillet correctly notes as one of the basic attributes of Grisey's style.[78] For Grisey the latter will create, from *D'eau et de pierre* on, a style in which sound is always in flux, in which, as he writes in his *Modulations* programme notes, 'all is movement'; a music of dynamism and radical transience.[79] This auto-engendering of form from material is also something achieved by Chowning's FM Synthesis (to spectacular effect in Chowning's work *Stria*). It should be noted that this was already one of the underlying formal aims for the projected clarinet and tape piece sketched in the spring (albeit expressed in different terms), and so the influence came not only from *Stimmung* (Figure 17.1).

415

Liam Cagney

---

2. 3. 4. 5. 7. 9 : même rapport 1) entre les tempi★ qu'entre les harm.

　　　　　　　　　　　　2) entre le nombres [. . .]

　　　　　　　　　　　　d'unités d'un certain tempo ''''

[. . .]

★ tempi = battements périodiques = hauteurs = harmoniques

Élargissement des domaines compositionnelles par accel. ou rall. des matériaux, dont le résultat sera un timbre nouveau. L'oeuvre s'engendre elle-même par condensation.

---

2. 3. 4. 5. 7. 9 : same relationship 1) between the tempos★ as between the harm[onics]

　　　　　　　　　　　　2) between the numbers [. . .]

　　　　　　　　　　　　of units of a certain tempo ''''

[. . .]

★ tempos = periodic beats = pitches = harmonics

Broadening the range of compositional possibilities by means of the accel. [speeding up] or rall. [slowing down] of materials, the result of which will be a new timbre. The work engenders itself by means of compression.

Figure 17.1 Reproduction of a section of Gérard Grisey's notes on Karlheinz Stockhausen's *Stimmung*, in which the composer links periodicity and the harmonic spectrum, as he would in his own works from *Dérives* onwards, and links form and material via the idea of auto-engenderment, pinpointing some of the relations between *Stimmung* and Grisey's mature style

Reproduced by kind permission of the Paul Sacher Foundation, Basel, Switzerland

From the 1960s Grisey had been seeking a musical style that would be more perceptually based, and *Stimmung* became a point of reference for him in this regard. The terms in which he speaks of *Stimmung* in his Darmstadt lecture 'Tempus ex machina' show the role it played for him in validating the use of relatively simple, perceptually immediate periodic rhythms: '*Stimmung* for six vocalists by Stockhausen (1969) shows us that only some elementary, even primary rhythms give us the very clear possibility of perceiving the tempo of these rhythms.'[80] This was an intuition Grisey had already had since 1970, as his journal shows.[81] *Stimmung*'s perceptibility, encompassing harmony and rhythm alike, suggested a whole 'other approach' to composition, as Grisey would say in a 1974 radio interview: '*Stimmung* [. . .] leads us to listen to the interior of sound.'[82] Nevertheless, as seen at the outset of this chapter, in his 1980 epistolary exchange with Dufourt Grisey was at pains to distinguish his own dynamic 'liminal music' from the static 'spectral music' of *Stimmung*.

Conclusion: style and *écriture*

This is a natural endpoint for our study of the beginnings of Grisey's spectral style. From the preceding it should be clear why Grisey, in the letter quoted at the start of this chapter, might have sought alternatives to an epithet that risked reducing his music to the construction of

Vers une écriture liminale

harmonies on the basis of spectral analysis. Grisey's style developed through his concertedly directing the post-serial framework towards perceptibility of material, transience of motion and dynamism of form. These three attributes equate, respectively, to statistically defined spectral harmonies, the degree of change as measure of moment-to-moment temporal evolution and process-focused formal structures. The twin poles, or regulative principles, in this system are harmonicity and periodicity.[83] These focuses express a prioritizing of perception over the objectivist approach Grisey associated with serialism and which, from the time of his early journal entries, he wished to move away from. But if Grisey criticized how the epithet *spectral* reduced fluidity to fixity, that tension was inherent in his project from the start, by its very terms.

In the theoretical explanations of spectral music from Grisey, Dufourt or Murail, a consistent element is how they present their compositional attitude in contradistinction to that of serial music. As late as 1998, in his final theoretical article, this was the pattern Grisey followed:

> No musicians were waiting for spectral music to use or to highlight the use of sonic spectra, just as none waited for dodecaphonic techniques in order to compose chromatic music: but just as the series is not a question of chromaticism, spectral music is not a question of sonic color. [. . .] [I]n serial music, the interplay of permutations becomes an obstacle to memory, it forbids radical renewal along with all the types of surprises, excesses and deviations that tonal music offers to its listeners. In short, serial music neutralizes the parameter of pitch; this involuntary neutralization, however, allows the concentration and emergence of new techniques which have become necessary to avoid monotony. Take, for example, the heterophonies of varying harmonic and temporal densities, the choices of instrumentation and the combinations of timbres, the explosion of registers, or the games of adding and removing ornamentation.[84]

On a straightforward level this passage is about defining how spectral music took leave from serial music. But on closer examination it is apparent that, even while seemingly distancing his music here from serialism, Grisey consistently uses serialism as a frame of reference. This is because in a deeper historical way each partakes of the same project. That project is the elaboration of a new musical language or system of organization the principles of which are derived from the internal substance and behavioural properties of sound. For spectral music as for serial music, it is not only a matter of creating fresh musical material but of establishing a well-defined, self-consistent, acoustically derived mode of organization from which that material derives. Inasmuch as it is conceptually based, that mode of organization is as much a metaphysical system as a set of compositional techniques and guidelines. It is for this reason that Dufourt sees fit to call spectral music 'an epistemological revolution'.

The above passage from Grisey reads like any number of passages from *Boulez on Music Today* or any number of articles from the pages of *die Reihe*. In each case we find the search for rigorous first principles and a consistent conceptual framework. Viewed through the lens of artistic modernism, and the emergence of numerous movements and -isms in the early twentieth century, serialism and spectralism might be regarded as representing two types of constructivism. In one sense this is the case. Spectral music developed more or less directly by way of the serial project (as Dufourt recognized), but as a critique and reformulation of that project.[85] Accordingly, since the early 1980s numerous subsequent composers have, in more or less inventive ways, adopted and applied the basic techniques of Grisey and Murail. To the post-serial generation, mentioned earlier, of Amy, Eloy and Méfano corresponds the post-spectral generation of Saariaho, Dalbavie, Hurel, Leroux and Hervé. Though in the early phases any connection with common-practice tonality was downplayed, in recent years Murail has been more open in suggesting how spectral music's system – which Murail occasionally terms 'frequential harmony' – is a contemporary replacement for the old diatonic system:

> [Frequential harmony] is harmony which is based on frequency and not on pitches – that's what it means. But that makes a big difference; because pitch is organized along discrete scales, while frequencies are continuous. So [now] there is an infinity of different combinations; whereas if you take the chromatic scale, the combinations are many but limited, and that was maybe the big crisis in music in the past decades. People have gone around all of the possibilities with chromatic scales. Lots of people now move on to noises; but it's a way of ignoring the issue. [. . .] It has been like that even from the 50s, I would say. You still have pitches and harmony in serial music, whether you like it or not, and of course Messiaen has lots of beautiful harmonies, but these harmonies are not functional. And that's the big difference [with our music]. I think in the beginning, especially in the 80s, when we were discovering the possibilities of spectral combinations and of frequential harmony [. . .] I thought the basis of my music came mostly from these new and maybe extraordinary new sounds. But in fact I don't think that's true. [. . .] The organization of the musical discourse in time is probably the most important thing, and I'm working more consciously with this now.[86]

Murail's recent exploration of tonal forms and of tropes from the symphonic tradition suggests a view of spectral music as a constructivism that has arrived at the natural end of its initial utopic aim, replenishing the Western classical tradition in a sort of *Aufhebung*.

This constructivist version of spectral music is a limited one. By contrast, Grisey's notion of *écriture liminale* suggests a more obscure view of how we might conceive spectral music as a music-compositional framework derived from a metaphysical system. Inasmuch as the spectral framework is based on certain fundamental principles of auditory perception, it is irreducible to whatever local material is selected to instantiate those principles. Grisey refers to the harmonic spectrum, for example, when he uses it not as a basic unit of construction but rather as the most probable phenomenon: as that which can be used as an auditory reference regulating the music's diverse manifestations and flows. In principle this implies that any material whatsoever, from white noise to sine wave, from a pre-recorded vocal sample to the sound of a raindrop, could function in much the same way depending on the work-specific parameters set by the composer. Within this compositional framework, more primary than stereotypical 'spectral' sounds are force-based processes: deviation, distending, tearing, manipulation, becoming. In the first section of *Modulations* 'the material does not exist in itself',[87] Grisey writes, but only as defined by the immanent trajectory of the dual process driving the music's evolution and form (moving from inharmonic to harmonic sounds and from aperiodic to periodic events). This 'open' version of spectralism is also found in *Tempus ex machina* (1979) for six percussionists, the score of which features no pitched instruments. 'This music forces itself to make time palpable in the "impersonal" form of durations', Grisey writes, using Bergsonian terms. 'Finally, it is sounds and their own materials which generate, through projections or inductions, new musical forms.'[88] This anonymous, pre-personal vision of *écriture liminale* – a music of thresholds rather than things – resonates with Grisey's earlier search for a music that would be beyond language, adhering to something obscurer, more essential. It also contrasts with any simple constructivism.

This chapter took off from Grisey's concern as expressed in his 1980 letter to Dufourt that the name spectral music would encourage a way of thinking about this music that would be overly preoccupied with the technique of designing complex harmonic models through spectral analysis. The scholarly reception of spectral music has to an extent borne out this concern.

Analytically, spectral music has tended to be discussed in a 'static', objectivist manner, with a predominant focus on pitch/frequency aggregates and the bracketing out of the perceptual dimensions of dynamism and transience that were, for Grisey, at the core of his music. It is notable in this regard that a musical aesthetic that grew out of the wish that, in composition, one not confuse the map and the territory – a confusion Grisey and his colleagues squared at serialism – has given rise to an unprecedented exercise in acoustical mapping: the calculation of precise grid references affixing forests of harmonic complexes, mountain ranges of rhythmical configurations and lakes of formal schemata. This has occurred despite Grisey's insistence that transience and liminality are more fundamental to his style than spectra, and Dufourt's characterizing Grisey's music in this regard as paradigmatic of Baudelaire's concept of modernity.[89]

The two views of spectral music just outlined – as constructivist compositional tool-kit and as regulative metaphysical system – are bound together in one key term: *écriture*. *Écriture* is a French musical term with no direct English translation. Though in one sense it can simply mean the practice of notating music, it also signifies the compositional logic that inheres within that notation, guiding the composer's pen. French Conservatoire training in tonal *écriture* entails learning the principles of harmony and voice-leading and techniques of strict counterpoint such as fugue and canon. In a like manner, through the system of *écriture liminale* he developed, Grisey could know what material to write down and how to develop it.

> Allow me to insist on this: herein it is very much the case of a real compositional logic [*écriture*] rather than simply of an amalgamation of new materials. Unfortunately, that aspect still escapes those for whom writing [*écriture*] *is read more than it is heard.*[90]

Écriture encapsulates the inevitable tension in Grisey's compositional outlook between fluidity and fixity, between a music of transience and difference and a discourse of structure and identity. Writing always entails fixity. What we might begin to consider is a different approach to reading: reading musical sound not in terms of appearance but in terms of appearing, not in terms of a language, discourse or grammar but in terms of an originary inscription – Derrida's *archi-écriture* in the domain of musical sound.

Notes

1 The research for this chapter was in part funded by the Paul Sacher Foundation, the Society for Musicology in Ireland and the City University of London. I gratefully acknowledge here the generous assistance of each. Much of the material in this article is covered in more detail in my doctoral thesis: Liam Cagney, 'Synthesis and Deviation: New Perspectives on the Emergence of the French *courant spectral*, 1969–74' (PhD thesis, City University of London, 2015).

2 Gérard Grisey, 'Tempus ex machina: A Composer's Reflections on Musical Time', *Contemporary Music Review* 2, no. 1 (1987), 239–75. The original 1980 version of this paper is published as '[Réflexions sur le temps]' in Gérard Grisey, *Écrits, ou l'invention de la musique spectrale*, ed. Guy Lelong and Anne-Marie Réby (Paris: L'Harmattan, 2008), 39–44. The other lecture Grisey gave at Darmstadt in 1980, 'L'ombre du son', focused on Grisey's technique of resultant tone harmonies and remains unpublished, though the lecture notes are preserved in the Gérard Grisey Collection at the Paul Sacher Foundation (henceforth GGC PSF). All documents from the Gérard Grisey Collection are quoted with the kind permission of the Paul Sacher Foundation.

3 The letter is published as Gérard Grisey, 'Lettre à Hugues Dufourt', in *Écrits*, 281–82. All translations in this article are my own unless otherwise stated. Grisey may have had in mind here the reception he received two years earlier at Darmstadt when he gave a presentation on his music: judging by the audio recording the audience was not particularly receptive, and when at one point the young Frenchman gave examples of influences on his music a wave of laughter broke out in the audience. This presentation was subsequently published as Gérard Grisey, 'Zur Entstehung des Klanges',

Darmstädter Beitrage zur Neuen Musik 17 (1978), 73–79, and is reproduced as 'Devenir du son', in Grisey, *Écrits*, 27–33.

4 Hugues Dufourt, Letter to Gérard Grisey, 9 July 1980, GGC PSF (original in French).

5 'I have heard some striking scores by new French composers: Guézec's *Architectures colorés*, Eloy's *Équivalences*, and Gilbert Amy's double-orchestra *Antiphonies*. There is a new French school, and a good one, judging by levels of skill. Boulez is the father figure, naturally, though he steers clear of the question of Dada.' Igor Stravinsky, 'Stravinsky on the Musical Scene and Other Matters', in *New York Review of Books*, 12 May 1966. Pierre Souvtchinsky was unequivocal as to Boulez's intentions: 'What Boulez has done is to make a school, build a base. It remains intact as a kind of academicism. It is a system he follows but passes around. Still, the school stays.' Quoted in Joan Peyser, *Pierre Boulez: Composer, Conductor, Enigma* (London: Macmillan, 1976), 149.

6 See Jean-Claude Eloy, 'Dix ans après, qu'en reste-t'il?' (1974), *Textuerre*, nos. 17–18 (1979), III–XXXVI.

7 The first monograph published on dodecaphony in French was René Leibowitz, *Introduction à la musique de douze sons* (Paris: Éditions de l'Arche, 1949).

8 Jean Boivin, *La classe de Messiaen* (Paris: Christian Bourgois, 1995), 164. Among Grisey's documents is an exercise instructing the student to compose a piece using a given twelve-tone series, likely from his Paris Conservatoire *écriture* classes. GGC PSF.

9 'Around 1967–68 at the Conservatoire, the serial atmosphere prevailed. [. . .] The academic mindset finally took over serial music. [. . .] It amounted to a sort of peer pressure from students on other students.' Tristan Murail, quoted in Boivin, *La classe de Messiaen*, 164.

10 In a 1987 programme note for a performance of his piece *Couleur de mer*, Murail wrote: 'If in a certain period composers felt the need for a theory, a set of more or less arbitrary rules to free themselves from the domain of tonal music and the compositional habits coming out of that music, for the musicians of my generation, on the other hand, the "serial" language (rightly or wrongly, I use that word to describe a whole style with numerous elements that was the dominant style of the 1950s and 1960s, and for which the "series" was only one of its aspects) was something quite natural, our mother tongue in a way. Our difficulty was having the courage and force to escape from it and to invent a language that truly corresponded to our expressive needs.' Tristan Murail, programme note for *Couleur de mer* at concert by l'Ensemble Musiques Nouvelle, Bordeaux, 2 March 1987, quoted in Thierry Alla, *Tristan Murail: La couleur sonore, métaphore pour la composition* (Paris: Michel de Maule, 2008), 56.

11 Boivin, *La classe de Messiaen*, 164. Murail stuck to this view consistently: 'Fauré had been replaced by Boulez, but the academic spirit remained intact.' Quoted in Eric Dahan, 'Tristan Murail, maître spectral à Marseille', in *Libération*, 22 May 2002, http://next.liberation.fr/culture/2002/05/22/tristan-murail-maitre-spectral-a-marseille_404345 (accessed 4 May 2017).

12 Eloy, 'Dix ans après, qu'en reste-t'il?' On the background to Boulez's time in Basel, see Robert Piencikowski, 'Une expérience pédagogique: Les Cours supérieurs de composition à la Musik-Akademie de Bâle au début des années soixante', in *"Entre Denges et Denezy . . . ": La musique du XXe siècle en Suisse, manuscrits et documents*, ed. Ulrich Mosch and Matthias Kassel (Basel and Geneva: Contrechamps and Paul Sacher Foundation, 2001).

13 Eloy, 'Dix ans après, qu'en reste-t'il?' 11–12.

14 Jésus Aguila, *Le Domaine Musical: Pierre Boulez et vingt ans de creation musicale* (Paris: Fayard, 1992), 296–97.

15 'In recent times we've moved into great spans of long durations which extend beyond not only classical rhythms but even Greek metre, the deçî-tàlas of India and irrational values. We are witnessing a change in the notion of time and I believe that one of the composers for whom this change is most perceptible is Jean-Claude Eloy. Beyond the refinement of timbre and the quality of "heterophony", I discern in Jean-Claude Eloy's music a concept of time that is absolutely at the spearhead of the avant-garde.' Olivier Messiaen, quoted in Claude Samuel, *Conversations with Oliver Messiaen*, trans. Félix Aprahamian (London: Stainer & Bell, 1976), 48, translation modified. A review of Eloy's *Polychronies* (1964, since withdrawn by the composer), although negative, gives some descriptive remarks which call to mind Grisey's initial mature works: '*Polychromies* [sic] by J.-C. Eloy is a study of sonorities in two parts, wherein the parts played by atmospheric effects is capital. The work comprises long sustained instrumental notes, with variations of colours, sorts of vast changeable sonorous spans on which diverse and refined concretions come to be deposited, originating in the percussion. The effect is perhaps not new, and this continuity in slowness, quite current in this genre of research, fatally ends up bringing about a certain monotony.' Jean Durbin, *La Croix*, 7 January 1965; online on the personal website of Jérôme Joy, http://joy.nujus.net/w/index.php?page=DOCELOY (accessed 7 May 2017).

Vers une écriture liminale

16 'For me, spectral music has a temporal origin. It was necessary at a particular moment in our history to give form to the exploration of an extremely dilated time and to allow the finest degree of control for the transition from one sound to the next.' Gérard Grisey, 'Did You Say Spectral?' trans. Joshua Fineberg, *Contemporary Music Review* 19, no. 3 (2000), 1.

17 In another text from around this time, similarly instructive with regard to the transition from serialism, Messiaen discusses how the sense of the term serial has changed. Quoted in 'Enquête d'André Boucourechliev', *Preuves*, no. 179 (January 1966); repr. 'Douze, chiffre puéril et périmé', in *Olivier Messiaen, le livre du centenaire*, ed. Anik Lesure-Devriès and Claude Samuel (Lyon: Symétrie, 2008), 57.

18 Pierre Boulez, 'Putting the Phantoms to Flight', in *Orientations*, ed. Jean-Jacques Nattiez and trans. Martin Cooper (Cambridge, MA: Harvard University Press, 1986), 66.

19 Ibid., 73. Boulez considered Leibowitz such a number-juggler ('imprisoned by academic techniques [. . .] he could see no further than the numbers in a tone row') and in general held such academic composition in low regard; quoted in Peyser, *Pierre Boulez*, 39 and 44.

20 Pierre Boulez, 'Incipit', in *Stocktakings from an Apprenticeship*, ed. Paule Thévenin and trans. Stephen Walsh (Oxford: Clarendon Press, 1991), 215.

21 Pierre Boulez, 'Possibly. . .', in ibid., 135.

22 Pierre Boulez, ' . . . Near and Far', in ibid., 152.

23 Ibid., 153.

24 Pierre Boulez, 'Corruption in the Censers', in ibid., 21.

25 Cf. Robert Piencikowski, 'Introduction', in ibid., xiii–xxix.

26 Both quotations from 'Episode 2: But Is It Music? 1945–1989', *In Their Own Words: 20th Century Composers*, 21 March 2014 (BBC Four, 2014), television broadcast.

27 When advising an audience on how they should listen to *Couleur de mer*, the young Murail said '[o]ne shouldn't try to "understand" the music of today, since it isn't charged with a "message", even one of intellectual pretension'. Instead he stressed the great freedom of the composer in his sound-associations and 'the necessity for the listener [. . .] to receive the work in a "state of abandon", without reference to the framework of previous centuries, the best recipe for welcoming it as an "ear to the world" surrounding us'. [Unsigned], 'Répétition publique et débat autour de "Couleur de mer" de Tristan Murail', *Havre presse*, 14 May 1969.

28 '[A]nalysis is only of interest when it is active, and it can only be fruitful in terms of its deductions and consequences for the future. [. . .] Certain procedures, results and types of invention will become obsolete or else will remain completely personal, even though the composer may have considered them fundamental when he discovered them; observations which later turn out to be of great consequence may have seemed to him negligible or of secondary importance. It is very wrong to confuse the value of a work, or its immediate novelty, with its possible powers of fertilisation.' Pierre Boulez, *Boulez on Music Today*, trans. Susan Bradshaw and Richard Rodney Bennett (London: Faber and Faber, 1971), 16–18. See also Eloy, 'Dix ans après', XI. Boulez's view of history is as that of Nietzsche as stated in the essay 'On the Use and Abuse of History for Life': 'We want to serve history only to the extent that history serves life: for it is possible to value the study of history to such a degree that life becomes stunted and degenerate'; Friedrich Nietzsche, 'On the Use and Abuse of History for Life', in *Untimely Meditations*, ed. Daniel Breazeale and trans. R. J. Hollingdale (Cambridge: Cambridge University Press, 1997), 59.

29 For an overview of Boulez's concept of necessity see 'Second Stage of the Dialectic: *Necessity*', in David Walters, 'The Aesthetics of Pierre Boulez' (PhD diss., University of Durham, 2003), 160–98. Walters examines how '[i]n order to overcome the inherited material, Boulez proposes that the composer must challenge all concepts', relating this to Descartes' method of doubt.

30 That is, by adopting Schoenberg's twelve-tone method while ignoring Schoenberg's inherited tonal forms. 'Schoenberg saw the series as a lowest common denominator which would guarantee the semantic unity of the work, but that the linguistic components generated by this means are organised according to a pre-existent, non-serial, rhetoric.' See Pierre Boulez, 'Schoenberg Is Dead', in *Stocktakings from an Apprenticeship*, 213.

31 A large part of Webern's importance lies in his stripping away all extraneous, inherited discursive elements: along with Debussy, 'he reacts violently against all inherited rhetoric, and aims instead to rehabilitate the power of sound' (Boulez, 'Incipit', 215).

32 See Boulez, 'Putting the Phantoms to Flight', 78–79. For a discussion of the relation between Boulez's writings on music and the generality of otherwise of their compositional application, see Jonathan Goldman, *The Musical Language of Pierre Boulez* (Cambridge: Cambridge University Press, 2011), 54–56.

33 'I shall never tire of saying that personality starts with a robust critical perspicacity that forms part of the gift itself. Any vision of history actually implies, from the first moment of choice, a sharpness of perception in judging "the moment", and that perception is not explainable in exclusively logical terms. It is all part of the faculty which makes the poet a "seer", as Rimbaud used to insist so energetically. It is the gift that enables him to clarify what appears to be a confused situation, to discern the lines of force in any given epoch, to take an overall view, to grasp the totality of a situation, to have an intuitive hold on the present and to apprehend its structure on a cosmic scale – that is what is demanded of any candidate who aspires to the title of "seer". [. . .] When I speak of clarifying the present situation, it is not simplifications of this kind that I have in mind, but a prevision of what the future will show to have been merely seminal and what will have proved truly lasting.' (Boulez, 'Putting the Phantoms to Flight', 68–69.) This attitude is as that of Nietzsche's Zarathustra: 'One repays a teacher badly if one always remains only a pupil.' This can also be considered an example of Harold Bloom's theory of creative misreading.

34 Gérard Grisey, journal entry for 1 March 1964, 'Pages de journal: Journal d'adolescence, 1961–1966', in *Écrits*, 312.

35 The *Zeitmaße* analysis is twenty-seven pages long and comprehensive of all of *Zeitmaße*'s serial aspects, with numerous tables of numerals, series, durations, rhythms and inserts (GGC PSF). It is unclear when Grisey did these analyses; the simpler *Kreuzspiel* analysis might date from Trossingen.

36 Gérard Grisey, 'Les dérives sonores de Gérard Grisey: Un entretien avec Guy Lelong', in *Écrits*, 235–42 (235–36). One of Grisey's regular themes in discussing his music was that it was a music in which compositional complexity is used to produce an ostensibly simple surface; see, for example, Grisey, 'Le simple et le complexe', in '[Réflexions sur le temps]', in *Écrits*, 40–41.

37 Pierre Boulez, *Boulez on Music Today*, trans. Susan Bradshaw and Richard Rodney Bennett (London: Faber and Faber, 1971), 18.

38 Maurice Fleuret, review of *Pli selon pli*, Théâtre National de Chaillot, BBC SO/Boulez, *Le Nouvel Observateur*, 19 May 1969; repr. in Maurice Fleuret, *Chroniques pour la musique d'aujourd'hui* (Le Mas de Vert: Éditions Bernard Coutaz, 1992), 61–64.

39 All references to Grisey's copy of Pierre Boulez, *Don* (London: Universal Edition, 1967), GGC PSF.

40 Jonathan Goldman writes as follows about the role of resonance in Boulez's music: 'The fundamental dichotomy which obtains in Boulez's work [. . .] opposes pulsation to resonance. [. . .] Boulez famously distinguished between "smooth" and "striated" time. An alternation between a pulsed, rhythmic conception of musical discourse and another, in which musical time is undifferentiated and continuous, remains the key to Boulez's sound world. Smooth time amounts to spinning out a sound's resonance in all its unpredictability, from its initial attack through its resonance and ultimate decay. Striated time, on the other hand, is the succession of accents that create sharp, audible discontinuities in the musical fabric. [. . .] Part of Boulez's fascination with these resonating instruments surely lies in a desire to let these instruments "sound" without any human intervention. [. . .] This fascination with resonance is a constant in Boulez's oeuvre, and contains within itself the seeds of aleatoric composition: [. . .] In the moments in which he lets these instruments resonate, the listener can suspend structural or analytical listening, and abandon himself to hearing the sounds produced without human intervention, in an aesthetic experience not unlike the universe of John Cage. This "sono-centrism" is a constant counterpoint in Boulez to his preoccupation with global organization.' Goldman, *The Musical Language of Pierre Boulez*, 12–13.

41 In his 1978 Darmstadt lecture this was how Grisey characterized the common movement of which he was part: 'It seems to me that at the moment the inverse is happening of what was being described a few years ago as a proliferation of styles. We are present at the formation, if not of a group with a label, at least of very fruitful exchanges between composers. [. . .] We have in common the same mistrust of abstraction, the same attention to immediate perception, and a similar research of apparent simplicity as the ultimate stage of a complexity that is internal and hidden; and often an identical material, which is the application to the instrumental domain of the experience of the electronic studio and acoustical research.' Grisey, 'Devenir du son', 342–43 (edited out of the original published essay).

42 GGC PSF.

43 For two indicative accounts of Grisey's working method in this respect see Jérôme Baillet, 'Tempus ex machina', in *Gérard Grisey: Fondements d'une écriture* (Paris: L'Itinéraire and L'Harmattan, 2000), 167–76, and François-Xavier Féron, 'Gérard Grisey: Première section de *Partiels* (1975)', *Genesis*, no. 31 (2010), http://genesis.revues.org/352 (accessed 4 May 2017).

44 Xenakis also visited Messiaen's composition class around this time, as Murail recalls: 'I remember seeing and speaking with [Iannis] Xenakis in Messiaen's class. Xenakis had brought some of his big orchestra

Vers une écriture liminale

pieces – *Metastaseis, Pithoprakta* – and he explained them. I was quite impressed by his approach, which was very different from what you were taught at the conservatories.' Tristan Murail, 'Lecture at Ostrava Days Festival (excerpt)', http://www.ocnmh.cz/days2003_lectures_murail.htm (accessed 1 January 2015).

45 *Metabolae* are discussed in Iannis Xenakis, *Formalized Music: Thought and Mathematics in Composition*, ed. and trans. Sharon Kanach (Stuyvesant, NY: Pendragon Press, 1992), 190–94.

46 'After a long night of the analytic, we are now directed towards a synthetic mode of composition'; Gérard Grisey, 'Vers une écriture synthétique: Entretien à propos de *Dérives* (1974)', in *Écrits*, 224.

47 The festival director Claude Samuel asked Messiaen for suggestions for that year's festival, the theme of which was 'The Young Generation'; one of Messiaen's suggestions was Grisey's 'very extraordinary' work, which could be performed at Royan 'in the same hall where Xenakis's *Terretektorh* was performed'. Oliver Messiaen, Letter to Claude Samuel, 19 June 1971, in Claude Samuel, *Permanences d'Olivier Messiaen: Dialogues et commentaires* (Arles: Actes Sud, 1999), 156–58.

48 One of the conductors, Michel Tabachnik, in an interview conducted at Royan and published shortly afterwards, criticizes orchestral aleatory music: 'Experience proves that aleatory music is not viable. Stockhausen, who was one of its pioneers, these days writes down all of his works. Because what's possible with a little group of players working together, able to create among themselves, no longer is when you pass to ninety musicians.' Quoted in Edith Walter, 'Trois jeunes chefs rencontrés à Royan', in *Harmonie*, no. 76, 18 April 1972. In the same issue Walter says it had been hoped Grisey would be 'the new musician revealed by Royan 1972'. Fleuret discusses the ORTF strike in Maurice Fleuret, 'Musiques du large: À Royan, une nouvelle génération de compositeurs prend le vent en toute liberté', *Le Nouvel Observateur*, no. 386, 1–9 April 1972.

49 Grisey, journal entry for 17 June 1970, 'Pages de journal', in *Écrits*, 315.

50 Iannis Xenakis, 'La crise de la musique sérielle', *Gravesaner Blätter* 1 (1955), 2–4; quoted in Xenakis, *Formalized Music*, 8.

51 Gérard Grisey, programme note, *Vagues, Chemins, le Souffle*, March 1972, *Neuvième festival d'art contemporain de Royan, 1972* programme booklet. On the relation between spatialization and sound movement in Xenakis's spatialized works see the chapter 'Spatial Sound Movement in the Instrumental Music of Iannis Xenakis', in Maria Anna Harley, 'Space and Spatialization in Contemporary Music: History and Analysis, Ideas and Implementations' (PhD diss., McGill University, Montreal, 1994), 279–300. The tripartite title is also reminiscent of Boulez's *Figures, Doubles, Prismes* (1963–64, rev. 1968), an allusion Robert Piencikowski considers deliberate (private conversation with the author).

52 GGC PSF. Jonathan Harvey, reviewing the premiere (the first discussion of Grisey's music in English), described the effect of Grisey's spatial shifting of sound as creating 'a sensation of musical dizziness with string glissandos turning round a false axis as if in a distorting mirror, the wind instruments taking off from the glissandos' point of arrival with their own material'; Jonathan Harvey, 'The ISCM Festival', *Musical Times* 117 (1976), 33. Harvey and Grisey first met on this occasion (GGC PSF).

53 Jérôme Baillet, 'Des transformations continues aux processus de transformation', in *Iannis Xenakis, Gérard Grisey: La métaphore lumineuse*, ed. Makis Solomos (Paris: L'Harmattan, 2003), 237–44; also published on Baillet's personal website, https://jeromebaillet.files.wordpress.com/2011/10/baillet_transformations.pdf (accessed 4 May 2017). See also Jérôme Baillet, 'Processus et forme', in *Gérard Grisey: Fondements d'une écriture*, 65–74.

54 Grisey, *Musique et espace* (manuscript GGC PSF, original in French).

55 Grisey, 'Devenir du son', 27.

56 François-Xavier Féron, 'The Emergence of Spectra in Gérard Grisey's Compositional Process: From *Dérives* (1973–74) to *Les espaces acoustiques* (1974–85)', *Contemporary Music Review* 30, no. 5 (2011), 354–56.

57 Grisey, programme note, *Vagues, Chemins, le Souffle*, Théâtre de la Ville, Festival d'Automne, Paris, October 1975.

58 See Liam Cagney, 'On *Vagues, Chemins, le Souffle* (1970–72) and the Early Use of Resonance Chords in Grisey's Oeuvre', *Mitteilungen der Paul Sacher Stiftung* 28 (2015), 49–54.

59 As a student Grisey also studied *Domaines* and the Third Piano Sonata, and his orchestral work's tripartite title would have brought to mind Boulez's recent *Figures, Doubles, Prismes* (see note 51 above). It is also worth noting that Grisey's next work, *D'eau et de pierre*, was programmed at the Domaine Musical in January 1973, and that he was one of the first French composers commissioned by Ensemble InterContemporain, a commission resulting in *Modulations* (1976–77).

60 Ligeti and Cerha had both explored this type of form before. Grisey's formal conception is similar to that described in György Ligeti, 'States, Events, Transformations', trans. Jonathan W. Bernard, *Perspectives of New*

Music 31, no. 1 (1993), 164–71: 'The musical form that is built from the ideas and principles mentioned here originates in a continuous reciprocal relationship between states and events. The states are broken up by suddenly emerging events and are transformed under their influence [. . .]. Because the degree of state alteration is approximately proportional to the attack strength of events, the impression is created of a causal relationship between event and state alteration.' The original publications of this essay are György Ligeti, 'Zustände, Ereignisse, Wandlungen: Bemerkungen zu meinem Orchesterstück *Apparitions*', *Bilder und Blätter* 11 (1960), 50–57, and György Ligeti, 'Zustände, Ereignisse, Wandlungen', *Melos* 34 (1967), 165–69.

61 GGC PSF (folder *D'eau et de pierre*, original in French).

62 In a journal entry Grisey states what he thought should be his key precepts as a composer: to 'make the synthesis between the cerebral and the emotional'; to avoid 'useless vociferation [*bavardage*] and especially [. . .] dryness'; to 'remain natural above all'; to 'aim for the precision and brightness of Ravel'; and – most presciently for his future style – to create music that would be 'intellectual without that intellectualism being apparent'. Grisey, journal entry for 17 March 1966, 'Pages de journal: Journal d'adolescence, 1961–1966', 312. Grisey's sketches from this time show that he still used serial procedures in determining pitch content; in *D'eau et de pierre* he experimented with vertical mirror arrangements of intervals (GGC PSF).

63 Grisey, journal entry for 18 December 1970, 'Pages de journal: Fragments 1967–1974', in *Écrits*, 316.

64 Quoted in Danielle Cohen-Levinas, 'Gérard Grisey: Du spectralisme formalisé au spectralisme historisé', in *Vingt-cinq ans de création musicale contemporaine: L'Itinéraire en temps réel* (Paris: L'Itinéraire and L'Harmattan, 1998), 53. A lecture delivered by Stockhausen around the same time as this at the ICA in London and recorded as a video gives an idea of what Grisey heard Stockhausen say in Messiaen's class: 'the degree of change is a quality that can be composed as well as the characteristics of the music that is actually changing. I can compose with a series of degrees of change, or we can call them degrees of renewal. Then I can start with any musical material and follow the pattern of change, and see where it leads, from zero change to a defined maximum.' Quoted in 'Stockhausen Edition no. 7 (Momente)', http://www.sonoloco.com/rev/stockhausen/07.html (accessed 4 May 2017). Grisey refers to Stockhausen's use of the degree of change in 'Tempus ex machina: A Composer's Reflections on Musical Time', 258.

65 Grisey underlined the importance for him of finding the optimal correspondence between concept and perception: 'The second statement of the spectral movement – especially at the beginning – was to try to find a better equation between concept and percept – between the concept of the score and the perception the audience might have of it.' See also the introductory remarks in Gérard Grisey, 'La musique: le devenir des sons' (1982), in *Écrits*, 45.

66 Grisey introduces these epithets in 'La musique: le devenir des sons', a 1982 Darmstadt lecture that is structured around the three categories.

67 On Grisey's use of the degree of change in *Partiels*, see François-Xavier Féron, 'Gérard Grisey: première section de *Partiels* (1975)'.

68 Some idea of the growth in interest in this new American music in the early 1970s is given in the fact that when Cathy D'Arcy, head of Shandar Records, organized a concert of Steve Reich's music in 1971 in Cannes, three hundred people came, whereas when Reich performed at a festival in the south of France in 1973, the audience numbered three thousand. 'Ode to Gravity: Shandar Records', *Other Minds Audio Archive*, 23 May 1973, https://archive.org/details/OTG_1973_05_23 (accessed 4 May 2017).

69 See Marian Zazeela, 'Light Performances – *Ornamental Lightyears Tracery*', http://www.melafoundation.org/liteperf.htm (accessed 4 May 2017). The programme was likely similar or identical to the presentation at Rhode Island School of Design a few months earlier, which featured an excerpt from *Map of 49's Dream The Two Systems of Eleven Sets Of Galactic Intervals Ornamental Lightyears Tracery*, a Drift Study and recordings of The Theatre of Eternal Music among other items.

70 Daniel Caux, 'La Monte Young: Créer des états psychologiques précis', *Chroniques de l'art vivant* 30 (May 1972), 27–30.

71 La Monte Young, 'Lecture 1960', in *Chroniques de l'art vivant*, no. 30 (May 1972), 25. In the context of spectralism, the phrase is used, for example, in an essay in L'Itinéraire's 1976 season programme guide, *Les nouvelles dimensions de la pensée musicale*, and in a couple of Murail's programme notes.

72 Caux, 'La Monte Young', 28.

73 See Keith Potter, *Four Musical Minimalists* (Cambridge: Cambridge University Press, 2002), 89. On Stockhausen's borrowings from Young see Peter Niklas Wilson, 'Stockhausen, der Epigone? Karlheinz Stockhausen und die amerikanische Avantgarde', *Neue Zeitschrift für Musik* 149, no. 5 (1988), 6–11.

74 A performance of Octavian Nemescu's *Concentric* (1969) is of particular interest, since, along with Corneliu Cezar, Nemescu is one of the founders of the spectral current in Romanian music, which

Vers une écriture liminale

developed prior to and independently of the spectral current in France. *Concentric* is scored for ensemble (clarinet, violin, viola, cello, piano) and tape. It opens with a recording of a resonant gong strike, immediately followed by the entry in the tape part of a pedal drone of harmonic overtones entering and disappearing over a continuous fundamental. When I asked Nemescu if much discussion took place at Darmstadt after this concert of the new strand of music emanating from Romania, he answered in the affirmative. 'On the same occasion Stockhausen presented and extensively commented his piece "Stimmung". This is a work raised around a major seventh and ninth chord, which can be seen as spectral music, too. Many comments were made on the resemblance but mainly on the differences between the 2 works. It seemed like a new aesthetic direction appeared: the recovery, from a different position, of something long forgotten (the consonance).' Octavian Nemescu, email to the author, 22 June 2014. Some remarks on Nemescu's spectralism are found in Thomas Beimel, 'Suche nach dem Einklang: Octavian Nemescus "Stundenbuch"', *MusikTexte*, no. 141 (2014), 55–58.

75 All references to Grisey's 1972 Darmstadt notes, GGC PSF.

76 Walter Boudreau, email to the author, 5 July 2013.

77 For a description of Grisey's method in this regard see Féron, 'The Emergence of Spectra'.

78 Discussed by Baillet in 'La musique comme auto-engendrement', in *Fondements d'une écriture*, 43–45.

79 Gérard Grisey, 'Écrits sur ses oeuvres: *Modulations*', in *Écrits*, 138–39.

80 Grisey, 'Tempus ex machina', 242. Eloy also uses simple, periodic rhythms in *Kâmakalâ*.

81 'Concerning form: Never construct a form solely on abstract rhythmical structures, but also on *directly perceptible* sonorous impacts (rhythm, intensity, timbre etc.).' Gérard Grisey, journal entry for 17 June 1970, 'Pages de journal: Fragments 1967–1974', 315.

82 Gérard Grisey, 'Vers une écriture synthétique', in *Écrits*, 224. Again, this phrase is almost identical to that used by La Monte Young about his own music, as quoted earlier.

83 A clear account of how Grisey developed these principles in his oeuvre is Jérôme Baillet's *Fondements d'une écriture*.

84 Grisey, 'Did You Say Spectral?' 1. In the same passage Grisey alludes negatively to Xenakis's concept of in-time and outside-time, again showing the legacy of this late 1960s/early 1970s apprenticeship for his mature musical thought.

85 'Spectral music has its basis in a theory of functional fields and an aesthetic of unstable forms. It marks, on the path traced out by serialism, a progression towards immanence and transparency.' Hugues Dufourt, 'Musique spectrale', in *Musique, pouvoir, écriture* (Paris: Christian Bourgois, 1991), 338.

86 Tristan Murail, in conversation with the author, Salzburg, 15 January 2014.

87 Gérard Grisey, 'Écrits sur les œuvres: *Modulations*', in *Écrits*, 138–39.

88 Grisey, 'Did You Say Spectral?' 2.

89 '[Grisey's] subjectivism was the basis for his [music's] capturing those fleeting, ephemeral, transient phenomena that constitute the basis of the modern outlook.' Hugues Dufourt, *La musique spectrale: une révolution épistémologique* (Paris: Delatour, 2014), 23.

90 Gérard Grisey, 'Structuration des timbres dans la musique instrumentale', in *Écrits*, 90; italics added.

Bibliography

Aguila, Jésus. *Le Domaine Musical: Pierre Boulez et vingt ans de creation musicale*. Paris: Fayard, 1992.

Alla, Thierry. *Tristan Murail: La couleur sonore, métaphore pour la composition*. Paris: Michel de Maule, 2008.

Baillet, Jérôme. *Gérard Grisey: Fondements d'une écriture*. Paris: L'Itinéraire and L'Harmattan, 2000.

———. 'Des transformations continues aux processus de transformation'. In *Iannis Xenakis, Gérard Grisey: La métaphore lumineuse*, edited by Makis Solomos, 237–44. Paris: L'Harmattan, 2003.

Beimel, Thomas. 'Suche nach dem Einklang: Octavian Nemescu "Stundenbuch"'. *MusikTexte*, no. 141 (2014): 55–58.

Boivin, Jean. *La classe de Messiaen*. Paris: Christian Bourgois, 1995.

Boulez, Pierre. *Boulez on Music Today*. Translated by Susan Bradshaw and Richard Rodney Bennett. London: Faber and Faber, 1971.

———. *Orientations*. Edited by Jean-Jacques Nattiez. Translated by Martin Cooper. Cambridge, MA: Harvard University Press, 1986.

———. *Stocktakings from an Apprenticeship*. Edited by Paule Thévenin. Translated by Stephen Walsh. Oxford: Clarendon Press, 1991.

Cagney, Liam. 'Synthesis and Deviation: New Perspectives on the Emergence of the French *courant spectral*, 1969–74'. PhD thesis, City University, London, 2015.

425

Liam Cagney

———. 'On *Vagues, Chemins, le Souffle* (1970–72) and the Early Use of Resonance Chords in Grisey's Oeuvre'. *Mitteilungen der Paul Sacher Stiftung* 28 (2015): 49–54.

Caux, Daniel. 'La Monte Young: Créer des états psychologiques précis'. *Chroniques de l'art vivant* 30 (May 1972): 27–30.

Cohen-Levinas, Danielle. 'Gérard Grisey: Du spectralisme formalisé au spectralisme historisé'. In *Vingt-cinq ans de création musicale contemporaine: L'Itinéraire en temps réel*, edited by Danielle Cohen-Levinas, 51–66. Paris: L'Itinéraire and L'Harmattan, 1998.

Dufourt, Hugues. 'Musique spectrale'. In *Musique, pouvoir, écriture*, 335–40. Paris: Christian Bourgois, 1991.

———. *La musique spectrale: une révolution épistémologique*. Paris: Delatour, 2014.

Eloy, Jean-Claude. 'Dix ans après, qu'en reste-t'il?' (1974). In *Textuerre*, nos. 17–18 (1979): III–XXXVI.

Féron, François-Xavier. 'Gérard Grisey: Première section de *Partiels* (1975)'. In *Genesis*, no. 31 (2010). http://genesis.revues.org/352 (accessed 4 May 2017).

———. 'The Emergence of Spectra in Gérard Grisey's Compositional Process: From *Dérives* (1973–74) to *Les espaces acoustiques* (1974–85)'. *Contemporary Music Review* 30, no. 5 (2011): 343–75.

Fleuret, Maurice. 'Musiques du large: À Royan, une nouvelle génération de compositeurs prend le vent en toute liberté'. *Le Nouvel Observateur*, no. 386, 1–9 April 1972.

———. *Chroniques pour la musique d'aujourd'hui*. Le Mas de Vert: Éditions Bernard Coutaz, 1992.

Goldman, Jonathan. *The Musical Language of Pierre Boulez*. Cambridge: Cambridge University Press, 2011.

Grisey, Gérard. 'Zur Entstehung des Klanges'. *Darmstädter Beitrage zur Neuen Musik* 17 (1978): 73–79. Original French version, 'Devenir du son'. In Grisey, *Écrits*, 27–33.

———. 'Tempus ex machina: A Composer's Reflections on Musical Time'. *Contemporary Music Review* 2, no. 1 (1987): 239–75. Original French version, '[Réflexions sur le temps]'. In Grisey, *Écrits*, 39–44.

———. 'Did You Say Spectral?' translated by Joshua Fineberg. *Contemporary Music Review* 19, no. 3 (2000): 1–3.

———. *Écrits, ou l'invention de la musique spectrale*. Edited by Guy Lelong and Anne-Marie Réby. Paris: L'Harmattan, 2008.

Harley, Maria Anna. 'Space and Spatialization in Contemporary Music: History and Analysis, Ideas and Implementations'. PhD diss., McGill University, Montreal, 1994.

Harvey, Jonathan. 'The ISCM Festival'. *Musical Times* 117 (1976): 33.

Leibowitz, René. *Introduction à la musique de douze sons*. Paris: Éditions de l'Arche, 1949.

Lesure-Devriès, Anik, and Claude Samuel, eds. *Olivier Messiaen, le livre du centenaire*. Lyon: Symétrie, 2008.

Ligeti, György. 'States, Events, Transformations', translated by Jonathan W. Bernard. *Perspectives of New Music* 31, no. 1 (1993): 164–71. Originally published as 'Zustände, Ereignisse, Wandlungen: Bemerkungen zu meinem Orchesterstück *Apparitions*'. *Bilder und Blätter* 11 (1960): 50–57. Also as 'Zustände, Ereignisse, Wandlungen'. *Melos* 34, no. 5 (1967): 165–69.

Murail, Tristan. 'Lecture at Ostrava Days Festival (Excerpt)'. http://www.ocnmh.cz/days2003_lectures_murail.htm (accessed 1 January 2015).

Nietzsche, Friedrich. 'On the Use and Abuse of History for Life'. In *Untimely Meditations*, edited by Daniel Breazeale and translated by R. J. Hollingdale, 57–123. Cambridge: Cambridge University Press, 1997.

Peyser, Joan. *Pierre Boulez: Composer, Conductor, Enigma*. London: Macmillan, 1976.

Piencikowski, Robert. 'Une expérience pédagogique: Les Cours supérieurs de composition à la Musik-Akademie de Bâle au début des années soixante'. In *"Entre Denges et Denezy . . .": La musique du XXe siècle en Suisse, manuscrits et documents*, edited by Ulrich Mosch and Matthias Kassel. Basel and Geneva: Contrechamps and Paul Sacher Foundation, 2001.

Potter, Keith. *Four Musical Minimalists*. Cambridge: Cambridge University Press, 2002.

Samuel, Claude. *Conversations with Oliver Messiaen*. Translated by Félix Aprahamian. London: Stainer & Bell, 1976.

———. *Permanences d'Olivier Messiaen: Dialogues et commentaires*. Arles: Actes Sud, 1999.

Stravinsky, Igor. 'Stravinsky on the Musical Scene and Other Matters'. *New York Review of Books*, 12 May 1966.

Walters, David. 'The Aesthetics of Pierre Boulez'. PhD diss., University of Durham, 2003.

Wilson, Peter Niklas. 'Stockhausen, der Epigone? Karlheinz Stockhausen und die amerikanische Avant-garde'. *Neue Zeitschrift für Musik* 149, no. 5 (1988): 6–11.

Xenakis, Iannis. *Formalized Music: Thought and Mathematics in Composition*. Edited and translated by Sharon Kanach. Stuyvesant, NY: Pendragon Press, 1992.

Young, La Monte. 'Lecture 1960'. *Chroniques de l'art vivant*, no. 30 (May 1972): 25.

18

CONTEMPORARY OPERA AND THE FAILURE OF LANGUAGE

Amy Bauer

Opera after 1945 presents what Robert Fink has called 'a strange series of paradoxes to the historian'.[1] The second half of the twentieth century saw new opera houses and companies proliferating across Europe and America, while the core operatic repertory focused on nineteenth-century works. The collapse of touring companies confined opera to large metropolitan centres, while Cold War cultural politics often limited the appeal of new works. Those new works, whether written with political intent or not, remained wedded historically to 'realism, illusionism, and representation', as Carolyn Abbate would have it (as opposed to Brechtian alienation or detachment).[2] Few operas embraced the challenge modernism presents for opera. Those few early modernist operas accepted into the canon, such as Alban Berg's *Wozzeck*, while revolutionary in their musical language and subject matter, hew closely to the nature of opera in its nineteenth-century form as a primarily representational medium. As Edward Cone and Peter Kivy point out, they bracket off that medium of representation – the character singing speech, for instance, in an emblematic translation of her native tongue – to blur diegetic song, 'operatic song' and a host of other conventions.[3] Well-regarded operas in the immediate post-war period, by composers such as Samuel Barber, Benjamin Britten, Francis Poulenc and Douglas Moore, added new subjects and themes while retreating from the formal and tonal challenges of Berg and Schoenberg. As Björn Heile notes, we are left with few examples of contemporary opera that acknowledge the crisis of representation and the challenge of modernism, especially when faced with the 'apotheosis of realism' in current cinema.[4] Arnold Whittall agrees that contemporary operas continue to revisit the two broad categories of 'realist and mythic', but calls on musicologists and theorists for critical interpretations that determine opera's contribution to the continuing evolution of modernism.[5]

To be sure, there are important outliers: composers and works that radically rethought the relations between music, text and dramaturgy in the late 1950s and 1960s. Many compositions by Mauricio Kagel, from *Anagrama* (1958) onwards, treat text itself as musical material, while his theatrical works, among them *Sur scène* (1960) and *Phonophonie* for solo bass (1964), treat instruments and sounds as elements of the drama. *Anagrama*'s 'Babylonian mix of different existing languages' alongside nonsense leave scraps of meaning stranded, as Heile notes, like 'small islands in an ocean of incomprehensible babbling'.[6] *Staatstheater* (1970) presents a full-blown parody of grand opera, subverting every aspect – libretto, plot, pit orchestra, staging, focal roles – while retaining the distinction between solo, chorus, tutti and prop-based dramatic action. The collage

427

that results resembles 'a do-it-yourself *opera povera*', prioritizing the relation between sounds and visual elements over narrative sense.[7]

Solo works for voice such as John Cage's *Aria* (1958), perhaps the first work to introduce 'unmusical' vocal noises and bodily actions into a dramatic performance,[8] greatly influenced the 1960s avant-garde. György Ligeti's *Aventures* (1962) and *Nouvelles aventures* (1965) retrace the mythical steps of sound discovery through the invention of a new language (sketched with reference to the International Phonetic Alphabet) that often blends with the accompanying instrumental ensemble. In each work three singers employ a carefully delimited repertoire of human affects to essay over a dozen virtual characters, enacting simultaneous 'plots' that rely on mimetic behaviour patterns to identify strands of the polyphonic drama. Henri Pousseur's *Votre Faust* (1961–68, rev. 1980), a 'variable fantasy in the style of an opera' (as it is subtitled) composed with librettist Michel Butor, combines an aleatory, mobile structure and a division of labour among actors, singers and instrumentalists with a vast collection of existing musical and literary materials based on the Faust legend.[9]

Such theatrical experiments were brought more closely, and self-consciously, into line with opera as genre in the 1970s. Luciano Berio's *Opera*, for ten actors, soprano, tenor, baritone, vocal ensemble and orchestra (1970, rev. 1977), intertwines three narrative layers that comment upon the theme of death (Alessandro Striggio's libretto for Monteverdi's *Orfeo*, a documentary on the sinking of the Titanic, and the spoken play *Terminal*, which deals with the treatment of the terminally ill). Rather than the individual singer displaying a wealth of extended techniques, *Opera* relies on a huge range of vocal styles and mannerisms. The work's proliferating styles complement its three narrative levels, as well as its relation to past and present opera history. Although *Opera* lets listeners chart several independent paths through its tissue of allusions, those paths are foreclosed with the death of two children at the end of the work.[10] Morton Feldman wrote his only opera *Neither* (1977), on sixteen lines by Samuel Beckett, as a monodrama for solo soprano; the soprano elongates words to such an extent that they not only lose all meaning but seem to freeze in the air (both recorded performances to date last nearly an hour).[11] Georges Aperghis, a Greek composer who worked in France with Pierre Schaeffer and Iannis Xenakis, created a series of theatre works positioned between play and opera. The comic flair of his work is reminiscent of Kagel's vocal experiments, but Aperghis's works address more general aspects of human experience and, specifically, human communication. *Récitations* for solo voice (1978) recombines French syllables and phonemes, which often seem to be chosen for sound quality over sense.[12] *Die Hamletmaschine-Oratorio* (1999–2000), based on Heiner Müller's eponymous 1977 play, salts the violent German text with English phrases (although none are taken from Shakespeare), and demands that its singers act and perform on instruments.

During the same period, John Cage's series of five *Europeras* (1987–91) took on the operatic tradition directly. All five *Europeras* rely on fragments of the existing operatic tradition, mixing the real-time performance of original and transcribed excerpts with pre-recorded music. Furthermore, all five maintain a strict separation among musical, dramatic, visual (scenery and costumes) and textual elements. Over almost five hours of stage time, Cage gradually reduces the number of singers and instrumentalists while adding pianists (playing transcriptions) and, in *Europeras* 3 and 4, Victrolas; *Europera* 5 introduces radio, television and a lighting system. Philip Glass's monumental *Einstein on the Beach* (1976) was the first of a trilogy that would include *Satyagraha* (1979) and *Akhnaten* (1983), yet *Einstein*, as Fink avers, was an opera in name only, 'a five-hour abstraction with no plot, no characters, no arias, no trained singers, no orchestra, and no intermissions'.[13] The succession of minimalist operas that followed, from both Glass and Michael Nyman (that latter's first opera was *The Man Who Mistook His Wife for a Hat*, 1986), met with a success that stemmed largely from their comforting adherence to earlier operatic

Contemporary opera and the failure of language

protocols: all featured clearly etched protagonists, narrative arcs and sumptuous settings (at least in the case of Glass). The 'continued vitality of opera as a public art'[14] hence followed from the public nature of opera as either a lavish spectacle or one with the potential to resonate with current affairs or events.

The fortunes of so-called CNN operas – John Adams's *Nixon in China* (1987) and *The Death of Klinghoffer* (1991) – rose and fell on their contemporary themes and staging. Adams's *Doctor Atomic* (2005) appeared as the culmination of such ambitions, yet it is fascinating that in Fink's gripping study of the opera's reception history, the perceived gulf between its libretto and its music – the text versus the text-setting – surfaces time and again as an impassable barrier to its entry into the canon.[15] As at other familiar flashpoints in the long and storied history of music and drama from the Renaissance onwards, words and music stand at cross purposes. This brings Fink back to Boulez's famous interview on music theatre, in which the French composer rejects any operatic expression but the ideal: an opera in which music and language emerge together from a single creative impulse.[16]

If we agree with Fredric Jameson that language remains 'at the center of an essentially modernist "system of the fine arts"',[17] then that challenge to representation – especially with regard to opera – must begin with language and its vexed relation to music. This problematic, of course, is central to the history of opera as a genre, but I wish to tease it out from other contemporary explorations of voice, language and music, before exploring that challenge in a circumscribed manner. My scheme stages music 'overcoming' its historical subservience to language in four late twentieth-century operas and one from the turn of the century. Each has as its premise an embrace of the problem of representational language and its relation to truth, the law and subjectivity. There are other works I might have chosen: for instance, Brian Ferneyhough's opera on Walter Benjamin, *Shadowtime* (1999–2004), or George Benjamin's *Written on Skin* (2012). But the five operas selected for discussion each present a similar dilemma – the loss of the self, life or even world – as bound to the failure of language. Each treats this failure in a different way, yet in each the collapse of the representational function of the word can only be overcome, or affectively illustrated, by resorting to music and the sonic dimension of language. Each opera poses a unique challenge to this crisis of representation, one that marks it as modernist in both a material and an ethical sense: the ethics of the sensual and the particular as bulwarks against totalitarian rationalism, fear of the Other and the rule of capital.

Music, voice, philosophy, language

Andrew Bowie calls for a philosophy that rather than speaking 'of' music emerges 'from' it, one that takes music's expressive, symbolic and non-representational resources seriously as challenges to philosophy, especially to analytic traditions that address metaphysical questions via a strict, representational language.[18] The problem is, as Abbate remarks in her gloss on nineteenth-century transcendental claims for music, that even Nietzsche understood that this 'linguistically pure object [. . .] must still be described in words'.[19] The paradoxical need to couch music's philosophy in pre-existing philosophical terms proves the major obstacle to Bowie's goal, even as it illustrates philosophy's repression of music, in all its subjective freedom and concrete particularity. Any philosophical statement is above all about language itself, and is therefore only a view of language. In the words of Giorgio Agamben, philosophy 'can lead thought only to the boundaries of the voice: it cannot say the voice (or at least, so it seems)'.[20] We may admit, along with Christopher Norris, that the experience of music is unique in its combination of the 'sensory-perceptual with analytically informed and sociopolitically aware modes of listener-response'.[21] But how music might help philosophy retrieve something it has lost remains largely an open question. As Norris reminds us, music's mode of existence falls within the remit of intersubjective disciplines.[22] As such, it seems inherently wrong to even attempt to specify the normative criteria which would need to be met in order for a musical response to count as veridical, competent or indeed properly 'musical'.[23]

Recent work on the voice struggles with separating metaphorical, functional, psychoanalytic and transcendent notions of voice with its instantiation as a material object, a distinction that Adriana Cavarero develops from the Greek notion of phōnē onwards.[24] Cavarero turns to literature (Italo Calvino in particular) to find the musicality of song acknowledged as a reflection of the musicality of the word.[25] But Barthes's famous 'grain' of the voice is a mere distraction where true communication is concerned: it is mediated everywhere by language, but cannot itself be transmitted, except obliquely.[26] Singing, therefore, is patently 'bad communication' in Mladen Dolar's view, a bearer of surplus meaning as such. The musical voice becomes another abstraction without purchase in the concrete, adding to the mystique of the voice an illusion of double transcendence.[27] Simon Porzak thus lauds Cavarero for not losing herself within idealizing or fetishizing tendencies regarding the pre-semantic character of voice, by directing it towards a destination: one 'absolutely particular other' to which that voice is directed.[28] In this, Porzak finds an echo of Stanley Cavell's description of the perlocutionary act, which may communicate more effectively when stripped of semantic meaning.[29]

This notion of a perlocutionary act stripped of logos returns us to the material basis of language. Roman Jakobson wrote of the multifarious babbling of the infant, the vast library of sounds that seem to be drastically, irrevocably discarded as the child acquires language.[30] These buried sonic treasures surface in adulthood as onomatopoeias or interjections, the latter constituting breaches of language as a representative system which, Nikolai Trubetskoy argued, pass beyond a single tongue 'into an indistinct region of sound that belongs to no one language – and that often seems, in truth, not to belong to any human idiom at all'.[31] Interjections and onomatopoeias lie on the boundaries of language as utterances: they are neither metalinguistic nor do they, in line with Agamben's futile plea, say language itself and show its limits.[32] Agamben hazards that what actually unifies us as a race is not a nature, nor a divine voice, nor even the common imprisonment of signifying language, but this experience of the boundaries of language, 'of its end'.[33]

We might begin to experience this boundary where music flips its historically subservient relation to representational language and, instead of being spoken by verbal language, speaks for it in purely musical terms. I argue that the five operas discussed below forge a new aesthetic for opera by questioning both the medium of representation and language itself as a site of stable meaning. Four of the operas stage the failure of language, as it is performatively subsumed by a musical discourse that 'speaks' in the place of a verbal text, while the fifth and most recent, I argue, employs sparing musical accompaniment to underline the collapse of meaning. Their composition ranges from 1977 to 2001: the brief *Prologue pour un Marco Polo* by Claude Vivier, *Le Grand Macabre* by György Ligeti, *Das Mädchen mit den Schwefelhölzern* by Helmut Lachenmann, *Luci mie traditrici* by Salvatore Sciarrino and *The Difficulty of Crossing a Field* by David Lang. Vivier's one-act *Prologue* invokes the historical Marco Polo as a symbolic stand-in for the traveller in constant transformation, with no immediate precedents, while in Ligeti's opera each aria and one duet represent general number types familiar from eighteenth- and nineteenth-century opera, types often associated historically with just such a rhetorical enactment of the battle between music and language for supremacy. Lachenmann's *Das Mädchen* includes intertextual citations yet is grounded in the composer's high modernist techniques, which highlight the musical material and its means of production. Sciarrino's opera is a highly stylized gloss on the tradition, taking its cues from a Renaissance topic and a Baroque libretto. In David Lang's *The*

Difficulty of Crossing a Field (2001), Mac Wellman's repetitive libretto dissolves into banal music suspending logic and time like the unknowable absence that drives its narrative. Each work is rooted in a specific historical context – whether that be the references of Ligeti, Lachenmann and Sciarrino to both operatic and modernist tradition, or the mythic summoning of Marco Polo (in Vivier) and the antebellum American South (Lang). But the concrete, if idiosyncratic, nature of each evokes a universal experience: that point at which representation breaks down, and what is sayable gives way to what is beyond words, and irreducible to nonmusical expression.

Le Grand Macabre

Ligeti's *Le Grand Macabre* introduces us to the mythical realm of Breughelland on the eve of its destruction. As it opens, we meet our hapless everyman protagonist Piet the Pot. Upon encountering the demonic, otherworldly Nekrotzar and his homicidal rage, the drunken Piet begins an aria with all the signifiers of an eighteenth-century mad scene. His plaint begins lucidly in first person with 'Just had a bit too much to drink, have now and then hallucinations, hear horrible music', accompanied by a broken music box. As Nekrotzar reveals a coming reign of terror, Piet shifts to a paranoid third person, singing a highly disjunct line punctuated by screams of terror, and triple *forte* chords in the orchestra that grow ever more dissonant. Piet's aria ends with 'here in Breeu—ghel, ghel-la-la-la', splintering into meaningless, melismatic syllables drawn out by periodic repetitions of the musical line, over the infamous Petrushka chord, with its maximum number of dissonant tritones, as shown in the reduction of Example 18.1. His cries ascend chromatically, exploring divisions within the outer bounds of shifting intervals as note values decrease and the dynamics cycle from *pianissimo* to *sforzando* with each ascent, marked by the performance indication 'Piet has gone completely mad'. Upon reaching a falsetto trill in the fifth octave at triple *forte*, he is thrust to the ground like a puppet, at which point Nekrotzar 'springs into action, as if a film which had come to a standstill suddenly carries on'.[34]

Music and madness have been associated from the earliest Greek myths, threaded together, as John Hamilton notes, through the third term of language.[35] Hamilton views music and madness as opposing limits on language: the silence beyond either may indicate the complete breakdown of the subject – Piet as lifeless marionette – or act as a sign of transcendence into a realm beyond concepts. Madness may drag us down to an atavistic state, while music lifts us up, but both manifest themselves with an immediacy that is lost in language, with its inherent bias towards reflection. Either term may be co-opted by language as an abstract sign. Yet the 'mad aria' seems explicitly designed to thwart that impulse: it binds music and madness in a redoubled dissolution of sense, allowing voice to speak in language's stead and the audience to revel in senseless sound. Piet's mad aria goes one step further, by taking a toponym – a synecdoche for the world

Example 18.1   Piet's drunken aria. György Ligeti, *Le Grand Macabre*, revised version, Scene 1

© 1996 Schott Musik GmbH & Co. KG, Mainz, Germany. All rights reserved

of the opera – and dismantling it, syllable by syllable, until only a gasp is left. All of Breughelland in essence becomes 'horrible music', expressing an imagined fate beyond words for its citizens. That the music does not stop with Piet's collapse clues us in to Breughelland's unlikely survival, which, given all that has transpired, also transcends the bounds of sense.

Scene 3 of the opera introduces the reigning Prince Go-Go's quarrelling black and white ministers. Their tenor–baritone duet reflects the dark, comic themes of many a *buffa* aria and Gilbert and Sullivan patter song, in which the opulence of language seems ever on the verge of escaping the singer's grasp. Yet the duet's construction as a series of escalating insults more immediately evokes the tradition of the dozens in its scatological content. It reduces that tradition to the rote recitation of bare invective, constrained mechanically by the alphabet, as the ministers begin at A and exhaust the blasphemous potential of each letter before continuing, as if in a demented parody of a Sesame Street skit. The ministers' routine was merely hinted at in the play by Michel de Ghelderode that formed the basis for the opera's libretto.[36] In their original context these characters prefigured the Smiths and Martins of Ionesco's *The Bald Soprano*, as the indistinguishable but archetypal pair of absurdist comedy, whose contrasting appearance is belied by their uniform discourse. Their farce, in good Oulipo fashion, is constrained by several juxtaposed 'machines'.[37] While the libretto cycles through the alphabet, a steady waltz in 3/4 is interrupted every third bar by duple time, which stops the dance dead in its tracks, punctuated by a chromatic chord orchestrated differently at each break.

The sung insults mimic the oom-pa-pa waltz rhythm with a compound melody; the upper voice descends by semitone, with each minister allotted two notes (and two curses) before shifting to the next letter in the alphabet. This broken waltz outlines a Bavarian *Zwiefacher*, a folk dance that typically alternates 3/4 waltz and 2/4 pivot steps, albeit an abbreviated version that accompanies the serial tune to shape a tipsy twelve-bar period.[38] The pitch cycle continues on repeat, at odds with both the alphabetical and the rhythmic cycle, as shown in Example 18.2. After the second period the letter cycle breaks down ('ha, can't think of anything with "I"', rehearsal figure 279), and shifts into double time: one 'insult' per minister (rehearsal figure 280). The letter 'O' halts the proceedings again, and the pitch series begins to decay. Melismatic elaborations are prompted by the profusion of abuse available under 'S' in the dictionary, but 'U' and 'V' bring the volley of abuse to a standstill, with 'X, Y, Z' serving as a coda to the withered strophic form.

In an opera characterized up to this point by surreal but still intelligible discourse, the duet strips the libretto of narrative and syntactic function. Language performs a musical role, serving merely as another layer of the polyphonic fabric, each serial curse punctuating the sequence like a dissonant orchestral chord. As the duet cycles towards entropy, language surrenders even its semantic content, its failure coinciding with a diatonic cadence composed of quintal chords. If language here has capitulated to music, one might also say that music has given up its vaunted freedom. The duet's serial construction mocks the arbitrary, pre-subjective automatism inherent in language, stripped of the pretence of meaningful content and reduced to a ritual, a catalogue aria of convention disguised as a vaudeville slapstick routine.

Both the madness of Piet and the serial joust of the ministers are revived and expanded in the three arias sung by Breughelland's secret police chief, Gepopo. Gepopo's arias resemble those sung by Mozart's Queen of the Night in their fearsome difficulty and fevered pitch. Gepopo's avian disguise and obsequious demeanour seem to conflate two characters in *The Magic Flute*: Papageno and the Queen, the obsequious male servant and the patrician female harridan. Gepopo moves with the dance-like rhythms of Papageno but acts with unthinking authority, a perfect conflation of Carolyn Abbate's reading of Papageno as a 'mechanist chimera' and the Queen of the Night's aria as representing 'soulless birdsong'.[39] As a confluence of man and

Contemporary opera and the failure of language

Example 18.2 Zwiefacher of the black and white minister. Ligeti, *Le Grand Macabre*, Scene 3
© 1996 Schott Musik GmbH & Co. KG, Mainz, Germany. All rights reserved

woman, of bird catcher and queen, Gepopo embodies a contradiction: the mechanical, senseless voice of authority, of the Law, from her entrance uttering the nonverbal imperative 'Psssst!' to her paranoid recitation of random warnings. Her second aria begins backstage when, mute with terror, she enters as a pure voice on high B, revealed only as the orchestral masking subsides. The held B gradually turns into a wobbling trill and crescendos to quadruple *forte*, as the orchestra abruptly halts and the soprano begins again a semitone lower, before launching into a virtuoso cadenza sung *staccatissimo*. When Gepopo again engages with language, she hovers on a precipice of intelligibility, shouting 'Secret cipher! Code-Name: Loch Ness Monster!'.

The orchestra cycles mechanically through twelve-tone rows in an equally mechanical Latin dance rhythm, as shown in Example 18.3, while the alternate screams of 'yes!' and 'no!' are amplified by offstage whispers. Here the libretto's language slips beyond mysterious nonsense to

Example 18.3 Gepopo's second aria. Ligeti, *Le Grand Macabre*, Scene 3
© 1996 Schott Musik GmbH & Co. KG, Mainz, Germany. All rights reserved

Contemporary opera and the failure of language

blatant paradox – a shift that reveals the crippling deadlock of language as a symbolic machine which, like the secret police chief herself, wields an ersatz authority with utter contingency and no connection to truth. Gepopo's final tirade begins with cries of 'Coming!' and devolves into nonsense syllables – a stew of hard consonants and rotating vowels – that cycle more rapidly as she continues (according to the directions in the score) 'insanely', 'completely insanely' and in 'a paroxysm of excitement, confusion and panic'. With syntax and meaning forsworn, her otherworldly voice becomes the sole, irrational support for her position. Wide leaps, repeated accents and extreme dynamics communicate a state beyond horror and beyond the reach of the symbolic. Her final rational phrase and final exercise of authority – 'Where's the guard?' – is gradually stripped of phonemes as it repeats, until she is left shouting the paternal signifier 'Da!' (or 'there') sixty times before returning to the high B she came in on almost six minutes earlier.

Prologue pour un Marco Polo

'The importance of the human voice to Vivier's output cannot be overstated', writes Jonathan Goldman.[40] Vocal compositions such as *Lonely Child*, *Bouchara*, *Trois airs pour un opéra imaginaire* and *Kopernikus* were the outcome of automatic writing sessions inspired by the surrealists, and often resulted in a kind of private language, even when those texts did not stray from French. But Vivier's own invented language dates back to his very first vocal work, *Ojikawa* (1968), in which it is treated as a kind of sound poetry, a string of colourful phonemes: 'O-ji-ka-wa/ Ah! . . . Ni-ê-do-ka-wa. . . '.[41] Laurent Feneyrou places such imaginative constructions in a Jakobsonian childlike world without grammar, syntax, meaning and/or Law, falling somewhere between Benveniste's categories of the semiotic and the semantic. Influenced by Stockhausen's focus on acoustic colour in *Stimmung*, they operate as a playful '*experimentum linguæ*, the pure fact that one speaks and there is language', before discourse proper.[42] This desire to flee representation has a whiff of the utopian, yet Vivier retains a playful and direct address that prompts an empathetic response from the listener.

This process is heightened by the juxtaposed and expanded forms found in *Prologue pour un Marco Polo* from 1981, which takes a historical avatar of cosmopolitan travel and adventure and focuses on his human loneliness and isolation. According to György Ligeti, the air of decadent sensuality and heightened pathos found in Vivier's earlier work was tempered in *Prologue* by its brilliant sonic synthesis, unique forces (six voices join a chamber ensemble composed of clarinets, strings and percussion, in addition to tape) and command of large form.[43] At only twenty-two minutes, the piece is sometimes performed as part of an 'opera fleuve', consisting of companion works suggested by the composer. Yet *Prologue* is self-contained, encompassing the journey of a 'misunderstood seeker' from the obscure towards a lucid apotheosis.[44] Vivier engaged the Quebec poet Paul Chamberland to write part of the libretto in French. Yet what literary French populates the work 'speaks more of Polo than it speaks [itself]';[45] the majority of *Prologue* is composed in Vivier's *langue inventée*, intended to symbolize Polo's general incomprehension as he moves through each alien landscape. The simple phonemes that characterize this imaginary language are of a piece with both the childlike mysticism of the work and the clear diatonic allusions found in all of the late works.[46] Yet they are enhanced in *Prologue* by spectral harmonies that thicken a primarily homophonic line.

Bryan Christian refers to this late practice with the term *grammelot*, derived from the use of nonsense by French *commedia* players and popularized by the playwright Dario Fo.[47] A grammelot in this sense functions not as but rather in place of natural language, relaying the sense of meaning with the aid of gestures, rhythms and sounds. If, as Christian asserts, Vivier's *langue inventée* represents a constant striving to express the ineffable, this ineffable is given a material shape in *Prologue*. Here *langue inventée* stands in not for a specific foreign tongue but for the complete opacity of the 'other' in any incarnation. As a non-functional text that bears only the appearance of language, it represents anything and nothing, pointing towards the profound leap of faith that represents every true attempt at discourse.

A Sage who abuses the searcher speaks the first text in French, over *langue inventée* sung by the chorus, further obscured by techniques that include singing through tubes, tremolos at different speeds and locations, and phonemic colour changes. A single intelligible word recurs like a refrain throughout *Prologue*: 'Zipangu', a transliteration of the Chinese word for Japan in Polo's era. In the midst of nonsense 'Zipangu' marks a familiar unknown, a fabled isle that Polo never reached. When French text is heard again, it is on the lips of the Greek chorus, urging a rapt Polo, in the person of a soprano, to 'Seek out your true friends in the shadow of the mountains and the peace, the peace of the deserts', before subsiding once again into babble. The 'solo de solitude' comes in the middle of *Prologue*, spoken not by the soprano standing in for Polo but by a bass with the most elaborate text yet, as shown in Figure 18.1. If Polo began not comprehending his surroundings, now he himself cannot be understood. Polo does not receive the

---

(g)
Bouchara sneu von t(r) euss
kiordou jreu yos Flietkloss
kata-i nouss trâ yess dja vieu niou jtoustiè
ga nieu stou vlâ
o-i jtiè zneu Kakroustikia
ne tièotebrou tcheé ka keuss ties kouch
nor tiou chfleu kiardos dio krénélokio
kâtâro-i kátáro-i chiflu miardus do kou
    (mouillé)
ne-u-ille jdu fleukrinia yo frichtchia
stoy kiatchko neu la-i freu kiet chkovrou
v(r)i boy yak leu jniè

(r): r roulé [rolled r]
(g)
ch: ch dur guttural (voir 'g' hollandais) [hard guttural ch (as in the Dutch 'g')]
o-i: passage de o vers i [transition from o towards i]

Dans ce texte toutes les consonnes sont dures. On peut aussi utiliser un larynx artificiel, dans ce cas les consonnes seront prononcées fortes et les voyelles très douces. Le laryngophone sera silencieux pendant les arrêts du texte.

[In this text all the consonants are hard. An artificial larynx can also be used, in which case the consonants will be produced loudly and the vowels very softly. The laryngophone should be silent during the breaks in the text.]

durée totale: ±80 secondes [Total duration: ±80 seconds]

Figure 18.1 'Solo de solitude', from Claude Vivier, *Prologue pour un Marco Polo*

Contemporary opera and the failure of language

gift of intelligible speech until his final 'testament', in which the soprano climbs ever higher to approximate, in Vivier's words, 'the voice of God, almost the voice of madness'.[48] He is ultimately understood only in death, singing the refrain 'darkness over darkness . . . only in death will I find the ultimate language'.

Das Mädchen mit den Schwefelhölzern

Helmut Lachenmann's *Das Mädchen mit den Schwefelhölzern* may be the most famous contemporary opera to address the problem of language and representation, a problematic attacked on several levels of narrative, musical and visual structure. Commissioned in 1988 but not premiered until 1996, it was immediately hailed for its 'astonishing range, freshness, and grace'.[49] The opera seems to accord musical elements independence from the narrative burden of its accompanying libretto, even while that combination addresses weightier political and social issues. *Das Mädchen's* innovative treatment of narrative, voice and text seems to belie its subtitle: music with images. Which images, a listener might ask? How do these images arise (are they literal or figurative?), and in what sense are they 'with' music (alongside? entwined?)? Music 'with' images suggests a doubled presentation, one we might read through a temporal lens: voices that *speak* of past events are reconstructed as *images* in the present. The narrated past, mediated through language, opposes 'the deictic gesture of the here and now'.[50]

And there is more than one reconstruction. While the Hans Christian Andersen story of the little match girl forms the work's basis, that narrative is split and refracted throughout the opera; texts from Lachenmann's childhood acquaintance, the Red Army Faction member Gudrun Ensslin, and the *Codex Arundel* of Leonardo da Vinci appear as extended excerpts, while musical quotations and programmatic episodes float in and out of the minimal libretto. The libretto cites not only Leonardo and Ensslin, but Ernst Toller, Friedrich Nietzsche, Mozart's *Magic Flute* and Humperdinck's *Hansel and Gretel*, in such a way as to position the original fairy tale, in Christian Kemper's reading, at the 'crossroads of archetypical, mythical, utopian, and critical moments' given body by the conflicting images that arise from the texts.[51] Adult concerns about the relationship between the individual and society, art and knowledge, and the responsibility of political action are 'broken' (one might also say brokered) by the 'prism of childlike experience'.[52] The introduction of each subsequent story appears to upend the bare semantic elements of the previous one as a basic principle: cold inverts to warmth, light replaces dark, and the flux of society becomes the solitude of a prison cell, deserted street or Leonardo's cave. The first section of Ensslin's letter summarizes this conflict *inter vivos*: 'The criminal, the lunatic, the suicide, they embody this contradiction; they are annihilated by it.'[53] On the level of plot Andersen's original tale operates, as Matthias Schmidt notes, as a 'forgotten memory', momentarily illuminated or animated by its intertexts.[54] Such a structure exemplifies Lachenman's oft-stated dictum 'I hate – not only in art – the Messiah and the buffoon. One of them is a distortion of the other. Therefore I love Don Quixote, and I believe in the little Match Girl.'[55]

If Lachenmann writes music as 'ideological criticism from the outset',[56] that criticism reaches beyond psychological and sociological concerns to vivify archetypal human experiences by means of particular instrumental playing techniques (wiping, plucking, rubbing, striking, stroking, and so on). His concept of *musique concrète instrumentale* presumes that sound carries a 'message of its origin', one that mediates between itself and narrative meaning, even in the context of opera as an art dependent on language.[57] Thus we need look no further than the musical material itself for insight. Hence, when Lachenmann sets himself the task of illuminating the opera's structure through semantic means, he refers to the semantics of musical gesture as well as language.[58] Periodic movement becomes an involuntary physical reaction to the cold, which

437

becomes an expression of freezing. Likewise, the 'cold' tone colour of the 'Queen of the Night' citation – a toneless whistle with diaphragmatic accents – equates meteorological with social frigidity.[59] But musical semantics complement, and complicate, the verbal: the match girl is an 'it', Gudrun Ensslin speaks of 'us', and Leonardo's researcher says 'I'. We move from the existential word of the girl to her world – a world she is powerless to change – to Ensslin, who acts upon the world, to Leonardo, who seeks to understand it.[60]

Alienated speechlessness

'I always paid familiar genres special attention – in a paradigmatically modified context. [. . .] "What do you think of voice?" [. . .] has remained a traumatic one to me', states Lachenmann.

> A musical understanding that eludes the voice, or even excludes singing is somehow not quite right. I knew that, it was gnawing at me. When we speak of the girl's genesis, then this includes the fact that this opera came to be thanks also to my – still unfinished – occupation with the singing voice.[61]

If singing, as a direct expression of emotion, has always stood for truth,[62] then noises, indecipherable text, and the sonic artefacts of voice comment on its indivisible assertion: they alienate it and express 'enlightened' irony, as in the hidden chorale 'O du fröhliche'.[63]

Lachenmann states that 'I try to make a precise definition of that which can be defined by language, to keep the mind free for what cannot be expressed by language. [. . .] The irrational, the transcendental, all the things we cannot define.'[64] The breadth of this sonic reach includes the sound of words, how musical sounds relate to those of language, and the 'non-sound of words, the "speechlessness" where words used to be or should be'.[65] Such sonic precision demands that listeners make a greater perceptual effort, an effort not normally associated with opera, a genre in which the confluence of language, music and dramaturgy may purposively overwhelm the senses and thwart concentrated listening. Yet many of Lachenmann's sounds – framed by silence or timbral halos – speak eloquently in place of a suspended text: the friction of each of the girl's matches as it is struck, or the two sopranos audibly rubbing their hands to create a non-pitched rhythmic expression of their frigid state. These nonverbal 'semantics' are augmented by a mild shock when elemental elements of language pop out of the texture, most notably the 'ich' that pierces the enigmatic surface of the work to signal the match girl's emotional depths and heights. And each intertext offers language at a different level of discourse: Gudrun Ensslin's statement appears as a tape overlay, while the Leonardo text is divided primarily into syllables, and recited in a hocket-like, pointillistic manner by two characters.[66] David Metzer traces Lachenmann's depiction of speechlessness in *Das Mädchen* as a concerted act to resist the various losses of speech experienced by the voices threaded throughout.[67] As an example, I present brief analyses of two passages that demonstrate the fraught relation between tone and text that characterizes the opera and its attempt to articulate what one reviewer called a pervasive 'alienated speechlessness' in place of sung language.[68]

The 'Chorale prelude' on 'O du fröhliche' (Joyous night) that opens the opera – in *flautando* strings, on a sustained A♭ chord with added sixth – plays the role of an anti-overture. As Daniel Kötter notes, before the music has begun at all, it is ready to stand still.[69] That A♭ marks the beginning of the chorale tune in D♭ major. The tune is then slowly deconstructed, its syllables merely implied by isolated phonemes – on discrete beats – in a slow, augmented rhythm marked by antique cymbals. This shadow chorale is further obscured by pitches related to B minor, distributed as harmonics in violas, cymbals, guitar, horns and pizzicato strings. Pitchless sounds

Contemporary opera and the failure of language

connoting the chill surround the chorale as it slips down gradually from C major to B major over the course of the first ninety-nine bars. Individual instruments separate specific chorale pitches from rhythms, but the harmonization defeats any recognition of the melody. We sense the rawness in the air, the struggle to express joy, the difficulty in moving forward, rather than merely remaining in place; hence the fragility of the subject in the opera's existential landscape.

Scene 12 in the opera's second act, titled 'Ritsch 1' (Stove) (bars 96–165), expresses the elusiveness of the hot, bright match, against the pervasive cold and dark to which all warmth must succumb. The passage begins in silence; 'ich' enters, divided into a percussive 'i' sounds followed by a sustained 'ch'. This fading phoneme joins the resonance of rolled cymbals and a cushioned dôbachi (large Japanese gong). Similarly, 'hol-' (from 'streichholz') is succeeded by a longer 'z' to onomatopoeically evoke the strike of a match and its hissing flame. Here identity, material object, action, temperature and image coalesce in one event. In a sense, the simple sound of a match being struck connotes life in the void, a 'sound as a message of its origin' that operates on several levels of meaning.[70] As instruments enter and expand the metallic corona, a huge waxing and waning orchestral sound evolves, and shifting tone colours and dynamics build to a sonorous equivalent of the blazing oven. Consonant harmonies emerge from the texture, dragging the two sopranos with them. The fragmented words are completely subsumed by the mass of sound, a climactic point of the opera that suddenly dies off. The oven's image – of a piece with its sonorous representation – vanishes with the dead match, while the next scene returns us to its antithesis: the sound of styrofoam blocks rubbed together against a frigid wall. The dry, white noise and unvaried pace of the styrofoam part mock the acoustic richness of the glorious cluster, and build to a kind of anti-climax that gives way to anticipation of the second match.

Luci mie traditrici

The plot of Sciarrino's opera *Luci mie traditrici* (1996–98) reflects the most flagrant melodrama: it moves swiftly from professions of eternal love between a Duke and his wife to the brutal murder of the Duchess, her lover and the servant who betrayed them. Following the provenance of its Baroque libretto, the music draws on stylized Baroque writing, while a 1608 elegy by Claude Le Jeune provides implicit commentary during the prologue and the three intermezzos. Yet contrary to the conventions of grand opera, passionate dialogues between characters are conducted in short, stunted recitative that barely rises above a whisper, while a twenty-piece ensemble surrounds their discourse with ambient punctuation that hovers between noise and tone. Christian Utz notes the discrepancies between text and music in his semiotic analysis of vocal lines and their contribution to a 'spiral form'.[71] In contrast, I view the opera as a challenge to language itself on three levels: 1) as the text and voice of the Le Jeune lament are replaced with instruments in its three repetitions; 2) in metalinguistic terms, in the way language is used in the libretto to undermine its own stability and inherent danger, and finally 3) by the sheer materiality of the vocal entreaties and their instrumental accompaniment, which eclipse the text by not simply signifying affect but also by embodying it and its psychological context. *Luci mie traditrici* pays homage to opera's longstanding staging of music's subservient relation to representational language, but there are good reasons to accept its creator's assertion that it represents an 'out-and-out assertion of a reform of the theatre'.[72]

The Le Jeune elegy opens as a monophonic lament emerging from darkness, with the soprano slowly appearing as she reaches the second verse. It marks an appropriate introduction to a work inspired by Gesualdo, both for its chromatic genus, so beloved by the composer, and its sombre theme. Example 18.4 provides an annotated comparison of the first phrase in the prologue and each intermezzo. Intermezzo 1 brings back the elegy in its original, three-voice

Example 18.4 Salvatore Sciarrino, *Luci mie traditrici*: comparison of the prologue and three intermezzos
© 1998 Casa Ricordi, Milan. All rights reserved

harmonization, but with cello and alto saxophone taking the soprano part, bassoon and trumpet the alto, and viola the low voice. A direction for false unisons in the alto saxophone and a flourish of harmonics in the violin lends the slightest air of instability to this appearance, as morning turns to noon within the garden. Intermezzo 2 paraphrases the original elegy, with ghostly flute harmonics and *flautando* in the strings. Winds and brass have vanished, with the melody now

Contemporary opera and the failure of language

held aloft in the fifth register by *divisi* violas. This version also marks a transition within the same space, as dusk becomes evening within the manor. The fourth and final appearance of the elegy occurs in Intermezzo 3. By now only a skeleton of *Qu'est devenu*, it appears mainly *pianissimo* through string harmonics and faint rustlings in brass and percussion as the drama withdraws even further to the bedchamber late at night. As Marcelle Pierson notes, 'Le Jeune's elegy has crumbled into ruins'.[73]

The plot references the true tale of the Renaissance prince-composer Gesualdo, as portrayed in a later *roman à clef*, Giacinto Andrea Cicognini's 1664 play *Il tradimento per l'onore* (Betrayal for Honour's Sake).[74] In *Il tradimento* the Duchess Armidea succumbs to her former lover and is betrayed by a scorned servant. Duke Federico sets up a rather elaborate scheme to exact vengeance, involving a dinner party with murder for dessert and the reading of *Il pastor fido* that forecasts her death. Sciarrino both compacts and expands the original text: the players lose their proper names, and the plot is whittled down to an archetypal tale of revenge honour killing sans garish melodramatic confrontations. But, in another homage to the work's early seventeenth-century inspirations, he retains *Il tradimento*'s stichomythic couplets, often pared down further to one- and two-word oblique retorts.

From the opening scene, in which the Duchess pricks her finger on a symbolic thorn, the stilted parlance suggests that language is not to be trusted: 'Too high a price is your blood. Not if from that blood the rose was born.'[75] This is but the first of many freighted conversations conducted in riddles, feints and outright contradiction. In Scene 4 the Guest and the Duchess implore each other to speak, to tell, while the eavesdropping servant cries 'I wish I had no ears'. As the scene ends, the Duchess murmurs 'Let silence protect me', foreshadowing a tragedy compelled by language. For when the servant promptly reveals all as Scene 5 opens, the Duke's answers 'I was not dishonoured as long as you were silent'.

The opera's vocal writing adopts a pitched declamatory style and a technique Sciarrino calls *sillabazione scivolata* (gliding syllable articulation), which combine to suggest a stylized form of High Renaissance freedoms with the unstressed syllables of text. But *sillabazione scivolata* clearly serves Sciarrino's modernist aesthetic, favouring the sensuous aspects of text over sense. These measured glissandos move more quickly than actual speech, often over a long-held note that quickly breaks off. The stilted replication of text pairs is framed by a silence that thwarts connection, and points both inwards and outwards to the instrumental cues that carry the emotional weight of the exchange. The background noise created by the instrumental ensemble becomes another character in the drama: constructed of tiny rotating modules lifted imperceptibly from the opening chanson, the instrumental web that buoys the action undergoes a continual transformation, one that keeps pace with the large-scale temporal, emotional and spatial motion of the opera, from morning to night, outside to inside, and tranquillity to horror.

Scenes 1–4 are set in the garden, where the rippling, overlapping dialogue is framed by the mimetic sounds of birds, insects and wind that animate the scene, performed using high harmonics and a full palette of extended techniques in the chamber accompaniment. When the action moves indoors and the sun sets, the orchestra comes indoors as well, sketching the interior landscape of characters in hushed tones. The undulating speech of earlier scenes is here replaced by a parlando, rapidly descending speech, and the Duke makes his fateful decision. The final scene will span the entire gamut of vocalities: whispering, soft pleading and singing at all dynamic levels. Yet the drama as an essentially static cycle is underlined by a return to the sounds and pacing of the first scene.

Two brief passages from separate points in the opera illustrate the dominance of pure sound over textual meaning, as the focus shifts from the external environment to animate the inner drama of the characters. In Scene 3 the Duchess meets her lover, the Guest. Gripped by a mutual

Guest	Taci, lingua	Be silent, my tongue
Duchess	Chiuditi, o bocca	Be closed, my mouth
Guest	Lingua presuntuosa	Presumptuous tongue
Duchess	Bocca temeraria	Rash mouth
Guest	Non parlo più, o Signora	I will speak no more, my Lady
Duchess	Nel silenzio mi profondo	In deep silence I fall
Guest	Parto, o Duchessa	I must leave, Duchess
Duchess	A Dio, o Marchese	With God, my Lord
Guest	Sentite	Hear (feel)
Duchess	Uditemi	Hear me...
Guest	Che?	What?
Duchess	Cosa?	What?
Guest	Nulla	Nothing.
Duchess	Niente	Nothing.
Guest	Ohimè	Alas!
Duchess	O Dio	O God!
Guest	Che confusione	What confusion...
Duchess	Che sconvolgimento	What turmoil...

Figure 18.2 Text of the duet between the Duchess and her lover in Salvatore Sciarrino, *Luci mie traditrici*, Scene 3

passion, they fuse into one entwined vocal entity, sharing the same vocal register, rhythms, images and rhetorical figures. An excerpt from the libretto at the end of the scene highlights its obsession with speaking and sounding (Figure 18.2).

Harmonics in flutes and high strings, tongued percussive punctuation in the saxophone, and tremolandos in the lower strings swell and subside with the voices without replicating their lines, as though the lovers had been absorbed into nature. Such is the absence of normal instrumental musical discourse – identifiable melodies and harmonic progressions – that the merest hint of a third motive, answering the Duchess's pleas for the Guest to 'hear' her, captures our attention as silence and confusion overtake language. The penultimate scene ends with the Duke having made his decision, while the Duchess leaves believing that she has been forgiven. Here the crickets, frogs and rustling wind of the garden scenes become a physiological sketch of the Duke's torment, his pulsing heart, laboured breathing and stifled sobs, before giving way to the final intermezzo as the ghost of the original elegy signals his resolve.

The Difficulty of Crossing a Field

In his *Los Angeles Times* review of the Long Beach Opera production, Mark Swed declared that David Lang's *The Difficulty of Crossing a Field* was about the 'difficulty of existence [...] a hybrid opera/play, unlike any other I know'.[76] Based on a one-page story by Ambrose Bierce (1842–c1914), Lang's 'opera' concerns a plantation owner in the antebellum South who – in full view of witnesses – disappeared into thin air while crossing a field. As a 'hybrid opera/play', the work's form thus matched its subject. Words, music and drama fold into one another, mimicking the way in which each character's view of the opera's central mystery collapses into the unknowable absence that drives its narrative. Although Mr Williamson's disappearance remains ambiguous,

Contemporary opera and the failure of language

the work's setting does not: the thoughts of his slaves, neighbours and family reflect different existential viewpoints even as the relations between slaves and owners, and among Williamson and his wife and daughter, fix the story squarely in 1854.

Based on the anecdotal report of a man's disappearance with no immediate rational, poetic or allegorical import, Lang's *Difficulty of Crossing a Field* could glibly be said to be about nothing. Yet the entire music-theatrical experience creates a sense of profound unease. Mac Wellman's libretto makes deft use of the seven hundred words in Bierce's restrained account to illustrate the suspension of logic and time, while Lang's string quartet lines circle literally and figuratively around the hypnotic spoken and sung exhortations. Andreas Mitisek's novel staging for the Long Beach Opera further emphasized the gap between observation and reason by putting the audience on stage, while singers and actors moved forward and back, and up and down, from various locations in the fog-shrouded and dimly lit auditorium.

The opera's narrative, such as it is, is explicitly, almost didactically, structured around an absence that cannot be explained, or even named. Thus Wellman's libretto proceeds as a series of seven numbered 'tellings' removed from chronological time, but positioned to comment on each other through hidden repetitions and associative connections, aided by the almost subliminal effect of the subdued string quartet that accompanies most of the stage action. Each telling recounts the central event from a different viewpoint, one informed by the memories, psychology and ideologies of those for whom Mr Williamson's disappearance exerted such a strange and troubling power. In a previous study of the opera I attempted to account for its compelling affect through a series of seven 're-tellings', envisioning it as a convergence of seven entwined narratives that work together.[77] Here I focus on the minimal musical score and its accompanying libretto as independent, if complementary, narratives that structure the opera's surface.

Ambrose Bierce, a minor figure of nineteenth-century American letters, and one of its most notorious investigative journalists, was an almost postmodern 'literary hippogryph', who conjoined elements from realism and impressionism, naturalism and surrealism, while rejecting wholesale the sentimental and ideological assumptions of his contemporaries.[78] Bierce is popularly known for his Civil War tales and the cynical witticisms of *The Devil's Dictionary* (1911).[79] Yet Bierce's stories moved far beyond standard tales of the war and the macabre. Riddled with gaps and ambiguous details, they often challenge the reader's perceptions of events and characters, exploring the limits of the narrative as a mode of expression.[80] His varied tales share a singular obsession with time and the fallibility of human psychology. Bierce's narratives often focus on an arrested moment, a kind of hallucinatory tableau vivant that, paradoxically, is always in motion, while the act of reading recapitulates the doomed strategies that his protagonists employ to understand their predicament.

Bierce's tale *The Difficulty of Crossing a Field* is the slightest of a particular subgenre in his oeuvre, one in which an inexplicable event is left unexplained by either rational or supernatural means. Despite its brevity and presentation, the story could therefore be seen as the prototypical Biercean tale. A journalistic report of the disappearance is followed by one of Bierce's favourite tropes: a trial or, in the words of the *Devil's Dictionary*, 'A formal inquiry designed to prove and put upon record the blameless characters of judges, advocates and jurors'.[81] We could turn to Bierce's *Dictionary* for further subtext, from his satirical take on 'inadmissible evidence' (that of slaves), down to the property across which Mr Williamson strides, the notion of land 'considered as property' being described by Bierce as something that, 'carried to its logical conclusion, [...] means that some have the right to prevent others from living'.[82]

In his original play Mac Wellman greatly expanded Bierce's text through repetition and the explicit incorporation of seven 'tellings'.[83] Wellman's attraction to Bierce follows from his fascination with dated language, stemming from his concerns regarding a lost richness in the American vernacular, one that has led to a concomitant flattening of affect and meaning. Wellman's politics and aesthetics are expressed materially by his concern with the physicality of language – words as 'objects flying around the room'.[84] This embodied aesthetics may be best illustrated in the play by those scenes in which slaves appear to spout nonsense, but betray a kind of understanding beyond sense. Wellman calls these passages 'moments of transcendence, moments of being absolutely spiritually naked'.[85] In the repetition of simple words and phrases ('crutch, crane'), the language transforms and interacts with the music, which has a life of its own.

Mrs Williamson's singular, troubled voice is closely identified with the central erasure at the play's centre: the gaps in a language that cannot name what is 'more than a mere disappearance'. Inasmuch as she has no name other than 'Mrs Williamson', her identity has been effaced along with that of her husband. The chorus of slaves that follow her introduction exist on a different ontological plane, their proper names replaced by mundane objects and qualities such as Round, Juniper, Crabgrass, Clock, Nuisance and Doorbell. The women in the Williamson household share affinities with the field hands as members of two classes whose speech is ignored. Meanwhile the presiding magistrate opens the second and fifth tellings in a closed room, where he interrogates Selma planter Armour Wren and the overseer, Andrew. Wren's testimony draws liberally on Bierce's richly detailed language, yet within each telling, events are retold several times, highlighting the 'gaps [...] in the factual evidence'. Andrew's testimony includes a manifesto on slave management, but when confronted with his ignorance of the matter at hand his discourse dissolves.

Lang agreed to use Wellman's *Difficulty of Crossing a Field* as a libretto as it already seemed to adopt 'premusical strategies' of recycling, repetition and permeable characters,[86] given its truncated source text. Yet there is little variability in Lang's monotonous score, which relies on two basic harmonic/voice-leading models and their variations. The opera begins with an introduction in E minor, which provides material for a series of chorale variations. A related series of four-bar (or slightly longer) ostinato figures arises from a simple contrapuntal framework: a four-note descending tetrachord set against a descending step-neighbour, as shown in the harmonic reduction of Example 18.5. This pattern appears in different modes and voices, opposed to a simple two-chord progression whose root motion descends by step. This vamp will be vocalized in several octaves, be altered to produce a more emphatic i–v progression, or at times be pared back to a barely perceptible harmonic tic. The brilliant heterogeneity of Wellman's surreal language pops out from its pale musical setting: the true music of the opera comes from the sound and poetry of language performing its impasse with meaning and history. The final scene opens with the opera's only true aria: an unabashed, unaccompanied ABA, compound ternary form for Mrs Williamson, with recursive aspects that emphasize the circularity of the narrative.

Example 18.5 Descending tetrachord that pervades David Lang, *The Difficulty of Crossing a Field*

© 2002 Red Poppy, Ltd. Administered by G. Schirmer. All rights reserved

Contemporary opera and the failure of language

Bierce's politically astute, dispassionate and succinct treatment of race, class and history commented wryly on American politics in 1854, after the Kansas-Nebraska Act had repealed the antislavery clause of the Missouri Compromise. But writing about slavery directly, claims Wellman, would rob those characters 'of their cunning silence, patience, their terse and succinct truth-telling. Their irony.'[87] The chorus of slaves makes no more conventional sense than the mad character of Mrs Williamson. As 'it is not the purpose of [their] narrative', owners and authority figures eventually depart the stage, leaving the dispossessed, whose voices have been stricken from the official record. Those same dispossessed suffer a double loss. The disappearance of 'Mr Williamson' is also the loss of the signifier that knit them to their symbolic universe. *The Difficulty of Crossing a Field* acknowledges that truth – that 'ingenious compound of desirability and appearance' in Bierce's words – is a burden to be questioned.[88] The minimal musical score works to deny the redemptive power of narrative while underlining the musicality of the libretto, offering repetition, remembrance and re-reading as an ethical act.

The failure of language and 'anti-(anti-)opera'

Music interrogates the libretto in the first four operas presented above – as a site of stable meaning in Lachenmann and Sciarrino, or as a discourse even intelligible as language in Ligeti and Vivier. In Lang, meanwhile, I argue that the score merely highlights the inherent musicality of the libretto, released from its habitual duty to communicate rational meaning and drive the plot forward. Brief assertions, long passages and breathless imperatives are all rendered mute when they fail to ground us in narrative sense. Hence these works embody the fear of being struck dumb that haunts all investments in voice and opera, as Jeremy Tambling asserts.[89] Words and their constituents become voluble music, a process that reflects in microcosm the failure of representation and the triumph of musical meaning described by all five operas as a whole. Ligeti's 'anti-anti-opera' eschews a master narrative in which evil is defeated by good, yet *Le Grand Macabre* retains an ethical charge. The apocalyptic destruction promised by Nekrotzar – 'All do now as I say: when Death speaks, men obey!' – was nothing more, it would seem, than a verbal construction, mere death by description. Thus the citizens of Breughelland elude their obscene fate by escaping the 'bitter word' of the *Grand Macabre*'s tidings. They reject the pathological demands of language, so as to live experientially in music alone.

But for the emotional peaks of the opera – Piet's and Gepopo's arias – *Le Grand Macabre* rests on a comprehensible libretto that merely subverts what appeared to be a predetermined outcome. But the libretto of *Prologue pour un Marco Polo* dispenses with any pretence of a rational plot. Here we are privy to Marco Polo's struggle for mutual understanding through the scrim of *langue inventée*, which functions as a kind of delirious bridge between the demands of language and music. Vivier's text fits Jean-Jacques Lecercle's notion of *délire* as a discourse founded in the material side of language, its origin in the human body and desire – a discourse no longer bound by its abstract function as a means of communication.[90] As Lecercle reminds us, nonsense words structure the text: 'The function of nonsense is to create sense, to make sense.'[91] *Langue inventée* exists on the frontier between language and music, lacking meaning but not sense: its orderly appearance expresses an exaggerated respect for the form of language combined with a repudiation of its goals. The only intelligible language in *Prologue* is that which points beyond language – to the lands and people Polo cannot reach, and eventually beyond life to an 'ultimate language' which resists even musical expression.

Prologue pour un Marco Polo, with its quasi-mystical, almost utopian appreciation for the sonic and expressive properties of language, stretches the boundaries of opera as traditionally

Amy Bauer

understood. Yet *Das Mädchen mit den Schwefelhölzern* arrived on the scene explicitly heralded as an 'anti-opera'. A large portion of the literature devoted to *Das Mädchen* reflects on its 'polymorphic manipulation' of opera as genre.[92] Kötter asserts that what begins as pure negation is gradually converted into an opera that establishes its own standards.[93] But many scholars are sceptical. Laurence Osborn, for instance, asks how 'a composing philosophy based on the predicate that sound can only truly express its own existential conditions [can] be reconciled with a genre whose proclivity is to establish a perceptible relationship between music and dramatic narrative'.[94] If Lachenmann was concerned with 'images in which observation – like listening in music – comes to its own senses, in which one looks with one's ears and listens with one's eyes', is anything left of the traditional dramatic conflicts and representational arcs that constitute opera as we know it?[95] Metzer sees the opera as mired in an outdated 'rhetoric of autonomy and purity', while Wolfgang-Andreas Schultz cautions that Lachenmann, 'who puts claim on his reflection of the material, has not himself reflected how historical his material has become'.[96]

Das Mädchen may stand as a historical model of late modernist 'autonomy and purity', but many would consider it a belated acknowledgement of modernist ideals within the hidebound walls of the opera house. Its ambitions – creating new myths out of old, reflecting contemporary injustice – stretch far beyond issues of language and representation. Still, *Das Mädchen* stands as a monument to the attempt to transcend verbal representation with sound, 'to keep the mind free for what cannot be expressed by language'.[97]

In contrast to the surreal *Macabre*, the Dadaist *Prologue*, and the high modernist *Das Mädchen*, *Luci mie traditrici* revels in a kind of hypernaturalism that intensifies the irregular tempos, dynamics and inflections of speech. Representation is in a sense wrested from recitative, with verbal sense supplanted by pure material immediacy: sounds that, in Sciarrino's words, 'only the characters can hear'.[98] The unnatural speech rhythms, melodies, and hushed volume of its sung text enact time and again that point at which representation breaks down. As an allegory of a world in which language kills, the opera's aesthetic invokes an ethics of the particular that privileges what is unsayable, irreducible to nonmusical expression and hence beyond the dangers of representation. It reflects the operatic past without dwelling on it; *Luci* is neither anti-opera nor anti-anti-opera but a 'reform of the theatre, because the use of the voices, the invention and the maturation of the vocal style allow us to do theatre again, not just sing generically on the stage.'[99]

As befits a modern provenance (as opposed to the postmodern minimalism of its score), *The Difficulty of Crossing a Field* emphasizes the central mystery of the modern subject as a lack laid bare, replacing a central figure with a central lack, and a conventional plot with a circular, almost motionless narrative. If the music emphasizes this theme with a heavy hand, Wellman's libretto celebrates the infinite variations through which language indicates lack, and performs Lecercle's four stages of language. Language first speaks without a subject: 'in the beginning was the text'. Speech then possesses its speaker, and interpellates the subject, yet *délire* rules the text, which remains empty, and has no object other than to fulfil a sense of urgency that can never end.[100] Mr Williamson has exited both the material world and the roles he played as patriarch, landholder and overseer. Yet he is not categorically dead, and thus cannot be memorialized or put to rest in his proper symbolic place. The 'undeadness' of Mr Williamson, a kind of zombie signifier with no material remnant, is but the first of the opera's revelations. For the work reminds us, as Hegel wrote about the Egyptians, that 'the mysteries of Selma, Alabama' are mysteries for the Alabamians themselves and, by proxy, their audience: the 'objective riddle par excellence', whose meaning remains obscure to all who witness it.[101]

Such is the nature of language, which 'is equally certain and incomprehensible'.[102] Hence Cavell's sense that opera, in its uniquely intimate address, is capable of reinscribing an ethics

Contemporary opera and the failure of language

of revelation that functions outside of language.[103] It is in that spirit that I offer *The Difficulty of Crossing a Field*, *Le Grand Macabre*, *Prologue pour un Marco Polo*, *Das Mädchen mit den Schwefelhölzern* and *Luci mie traditrici* as five completely different operatic attempts at foregrounding the failure of language as representation. Not only the ambiguity but the threat of language becomes germane to the actual plots of *Macabre* and *Luci*, while *Das Mädchen* puts language under the microscope, splitting it into affective atoms of sound dispersed into the musical fabric of the whole. *Difficulty* and *Prologue* revel in language as *délire*, its meaning remaining forever just out of reach while compelling our attention. The challenge of modernism is met head on in these works by musicalizing language, turning it into a particularity that must be experienced, a task for which opera is uniquely suited. As Bowie avers, it is because music is musical that it can speak to us of things that are not strictly musical, with a voice whose very opacity demands our engagement. It is this aspect of all five operas which – more than their staging, narrative openness and self-referential historicism – points towards a new operatic practice that engages fully with a modernist aesthetic.

Notes

1 Robert Fink, 'After the Canon', in *The Oxford Handbook of Opera*, ed. Helen M. Greenwald (New York: Oxford University Press, 2014), 1066.

2 Björn Heile, review of *The Cambridge Companion to Twentieth-Century Opera*, ed. Mervyn Cooke, in *Music & Letters* 88, no. 3 (2007), 347. The reference is to Carolyn Abbate, *Unsung Voices: Opera and Musical Narrative in the Nineteenth Century* (Princeton, NJ: Princeton University Press, 1991). See also Arnold Whittall, 'New Opera, Old Opera: Perspectives on Critical Interpretation', *Cambridge Opera Journal* 21, no. 2 (2009), 181–98.

3 Peter Kivy, 'Speech, Song, and the Transparency of Medium: A Note on Opera Metaphysics', *Journal of Aesthetics and Art Criticism* 52, no. 1 (1994), 63–68; Edward T. Cone, 'The World of Opera and Its Inhabitants', in *Music, A View from Delft: Selected Essays*, ed. Robert P. Morgan (Chicago: University of Chicago Press, 1989), 125–38.

4 Heile, review of *Twentieth-Century Opera*, 347.

5 Whittall, 'New Opera, Old Opera', 182.

6 Björn Heile, *The Music of Mauricio Kagel* (Aldershot: Ashgate, 2006), 24.

7 Heile, *The Music of Mauricio Kagel*, 58. Paul Griffiths labels *Staatstheater* the first anti-opera, in *Modern Music and After*, 3rd ed. (New York: Oxford University Press, 2010), 201. For Paul Attinello, the rhetorical deconstructions evinced by *Anagrama* – and the non-hierarchical works of *Staatstheater* – mark both as postmodern. See 'Imploding the System: Kagel and the Deconstruction of Modernism', in *Postmodern Music/Postmodern Thought*, ed. Judy Lochhead and Joseph Auner (New York: Routledge, 2002), 263–85. See also Karl-Heinz Zarius, *Staatstheater von Mauricio Kagel* (Vienna: Universal Edition, 1977).

8 Francesca Placanica, '"Unwrapping" the Voice: Cathy Berberian and John Cage's *Aria*', in *Transformations of Musical Modernism*, ed. Erling E. Guldbrandsen and Julian Johnson (Cambridge: Cambridge University Press, 2015), 264–78.

9 See Pascal Decroupet, 'Citation et collage dans *Votre Faust* d'Henri Pousseur et *Die Soldaten* de Bernd Alois Zimmermann', *Art et Fact* 6 (1987), 70–82; also André Brégégère, 'L'harmonie revée: An Analysis of Henri Pousseur's *Votre Faust* and *Les litanies d'Icare*' (PhD diss., City University of New York, 2014). See also Eric Salzman and Thomas Dési's account of the reception of *Votre Faust* in *The New Music Theater: Seeing the Voice, Hearing the Body* (New York: Oxford University Press, 2008), 153–55.

10 See Raymond Fearn's discussion of the work in *Italian Opera since 1945* (Abingdon: Routledge, 2013), 121–30, and Claudia Di Luzio, 'Opera on Opera: Luciano Berio's *Opera*', in *"Music's Obedient Daughter": The Opera Libretto from Source to Score*, ed. Sabine Lichtenstein (Amsterdam: Rodopi, 2014), 463–82.

11 Morton Feldman and Samuel Beckett, *Neither*, hat[now]ART 102 (1997) and Col Legno WWE 1CD 20081 (2000).

12 See Daniel Durney, 'Quelques repères d'analyse pour les récitations de Georges Aperghis', *Musurgia* 2, no. 1 (1995), 52–60; also Erin Gee, 'The Notation and Use of the Voice in Non-Semantic Contexts:

Phonetic Organization in the Vocal Music of Dieter Schnebel, Brian Ferneyhough, and Georges Aperghis', in *Vocal Music and Contemporary Identities: Unlimited Voices in East Asia and the West*, ed. Christian Utz and Frederick Lau (Abingdon: Routledge, 2013), 175–97.

13 Fink, 'After the Canon', 1068.

14 Ibid.

15 Ibid., 1070–81.

16 Felix Schmidt and Jürgen Hohmeyer, '"Sprengt die Opernhäuser in die Luft! *Spiegel*-Gespräch mit dem französischen Komponisten und Dirigenten Pierre Boulez', *Der Spiegel*, 25 September 1967, 166–74.

17 Fredric Jameson, *The Modernist Papers* (London: Verso, 2007), 6.

18 Andrew Bowie, *Music, Philosophy, and Modernity* (Cambridge: Cambridge University Press, 2007).

19 Abbate, *Unsung Voices*, 17.

20 Giorgio Agamben, 'The Idea of Language: Some Difficulties in Speaking about Language', *Graduate Faculty Philosophy Journal* 10, no. 1 (1984), 144–45.

21 Christopher Norris, *Platonism, Music and the Listener's Share* (London: Continuum, 2006), 3.

22 Ibid., 27.

23 Ibid., 28.

24 Adriana Cavarero, 'The Vocal Body', trans. Matt Langione, *Qui Parle* 21, no. 1 (2012), 73. See also Adriana Cavarero, *For More Than One Voice: Toward a Philosophy of Vocal Expression*, trans. Paul A. Kottman (Stanford, CA: Stanford University Press, 2005), Mladen Dolar, *A Voice and Nothing More* (Cambridge, MA: MIT Press, 2006), Jean-Luc Nancy, *Listening*, trans. Charlotte Mandell (New York: Fordham University Press, 2007), and Simon Porzak, 'Zerbinetta's Laughter: An Introduction to the Marginality of Song', *Qui Parle* 21, no. 1 (2012), 3–69.

25 Cavarero, 'The Vocal Body', 79.

26 Roland Barthes, 'The Grain of the Voice', in *Image – Music – Text*, trans. Stephen Heath (New York: Hill and Wang, 1977), 179–89; see also Porzak, 'Zerbinetta's Laughter', 56.

27 Dolar, *A Voice and Nothing More*, 30.

28 Porzak, 'Zerbinetta's Laughter', 42.

29 Stanley Cavell, 'Performative and Passionate Utterance', in *Philosophy the Day after Tomorrow* (Cambridge, MA: Harvard University Press, 2005), 173; cited in Porzak, 'Zerbinetta's Laughter', 43–44.

30 Roman Jakobson, *Child Language, Aphasia, and Phonological Universals*, trans. Allan R. Keiler (The Hague: Mouton, 1968), 21; cited in Daniel Heller-Roazen, *Echolalias: On the Forgetting of Language* (New York: Zone Books, 2005), 9–11.

31 Nikolai Sergeevich Trubetskoi, *Principles of Phonology*, trans. Christiane A. M. Baltaxe (Berkeley: University of California Press, 1969), 207–9; cited in Heller-Roazen, *Echolalias*, 17.

32 Agamben, 'The Idea of Language', 148.

33 Ibid., 149.

34 György Ligeti, *Le Grand Macabre*, rev. version, ED 8522 (Mainz: Schott, 1996), 35 (rehearsal figure 51). Peter Edwards analyses the 'leit characteristics' of Piet's first aria in chapter 3 of *György Ligeti's* Le Grand Macabre: *Postmodernism, Musico-Dramatic Form and the Grotesque* (Abingdon: Routledge, 2017), 51–62.

35 John T. Hamilton, *Music, Madness, and the Unworking of Language* (New York: Columbia University Press, 2008), 5.

36 Michel de Ghelderode, *La balade du Grand Macabre* (Paris: Gallimard, 1952).

37 Oulipo was a French literary group founded in 1960 that used mathematical and other arbitrary constraints as goads to inspiration and formal invention; see Warren F. Motte, ed. and trans., *Oulipo: A Primer of Potential Literature* (London: Dalkey Archive Press, 1998).

38 The majority of *Zwiefacher* follow two waltz bars with two Dreher, or pivot bars, although there are infinite variations (see http://www.folkdancing.com/Pages/seattle/Zwie-Patn.html). Many thanks to Björn Heile for pointing out this connection.

39 Carolyn Abbate, *In Search of Opera* (Princeton, NJ: Princeton University Press, 2001), 76–77.

40 Jonathan Goldman, 'Claude Vivier at the End', in *Contemporary Music and Spirituality*, ed. Sander van Maas and Robert Sholl (Abingdon: Routledge, 2016), 205.

41 Claude Vivier, 'Les écrits de Claude Vivier', *Circuit: musiques contemporaines* 2, nos. 1–2 (1991), 48.

42 Laurent Feneyrou, 'Claude Vivier: parcours de l'œuvre', *IRCAM Brahms Composer Database*, http://brahms.ircam.fr/claude-vivier#parcours (accessed 5 September 2017).

43 Louise Duchesneau, 'Sur la musique de Claude Vivier: György Ligeti – Propos recueillis par Louise Duchesneau', *Circuit: musiques contemporaines* 2, nos. 1–2 (1991), 7–16; ed. and trans. Monika Lichtenfeld

as György Ligeti, 'Zur Musik Claude Viviers', in *Gesammelte Schriften*, ed. Monika Lichtenfeld (Mainz: Schott, 2007), 1: 497–501.

44 Claude Vivier, *Prologue pour un Marco Polo* (1981), composer's note, http://www.boosey.com/cr/music/Claude-Vivier-Prologue-pour-un-Marco-Polo/47759 (accessed 16 May 2017). Bob Gilmore reads *Prologue pour un Marco Polo* as partly autobiographical; see *Claude Vivier: A Biography* (Woodbridge: Boydell & Brewer, 2014), 181–82.

45 Vivier, 'Les écrits', 111.

46 See Patrick Levesque, 'L'élaboration du matériau musical dans les dernières œuvres vocales de Claude Vivier', *Circuit: musiques contemporaines* 18, no. 3 (2008), 104–5.

47 Bryan Christian, 'Automatic Writing and Grammelot in Claude Vivier's *langue inventée*', *Tempo*, no. 270 (2014), 15–30.

48 Vivier, *Prologue pour un Marco Polo*, composer's note.

49 Griffiths, *Modern Music and After*, 394.

50 Barbara Zuber, 'Die doppelte ästhetische Differenz und noch einmal die Frage: Was heißt "Musik mit Bildern"? Zu Helmut Lachenmanns *Mädchen mit den Schwefelhölzern*', in *Helmut Lachenmann: Musik mit Bildern?* ed. Matteo Nanni and Matthias Schmidt (Munich: Wilhelm Fink, 2012), 187.

51 Christian Kemper, 'Repräsentation und Struktur in einer "Musik mit Bildern": Überlegungen zu Helmut Lachenmanns Musiktheater', *Musik und Ästhetik* 5 (2001), 105.

52 Ibid., 106.

53 Libretto in booklet for *Das Mädchen mit den Schwefelhölzern*, CD, Kairos 0012282 (2002), 39–40 (translation modified). See also the interview with Peter Szendy, 'Paradiese auf Zeit', in Lachenmann, *Musik als existentielle Erfahrung: Schriften 1966–1995*, ed. Josef Häusler (Wiesbaden: Breitkopf & Härtel, 1996), 210.

54 Matthias Schmidt, 'Schöpferische Bilderinnerung: Geschichtliches Sehen und Hören in Helmut Lachenmanns *Mädchen mit den Schwefelhölzern*', in *Helmut Lachenmann: Musik mit Bildern?* ed. Nanni and Schmidt, 201.

55 Helmut Lachenmann, 'Selbstportrait 1975', in *Musik als existentielle Erfahrung*, 154.

56 Christian Grüny, '"Zustände, die sich verändern": Helmut Lachenmanns *Musik mit Bildern* – und anderem', in *Helmut Lachenmann: Musik mit Bildern?* ed. Nanni and Schmidt, 41.

57 Daniel Kötter, 'Die Irreführung der Oper: Sprachlosigkeit und -fertigkeit in Helmut Lachenmanns "Das Mädchen mit den Schwefelhölzern"', *MusikTexte*, no. 105 (2005), 45.

58 Helmut Lachenmann, '"Klänge sind Naturereignisse": Helmut Lachenmann im Gespräch mit Klaus Zehelein und Hans Thomalla', in *Das Mädchen mit den Schwefelhölzern*, programme book (Stuttgart: Staatsoper, 2001), 20–35.

59 See Matthias Schmidt, 'Schöpferische Bilderinnerung', 203, and Stephanie Jones, 'The Cruelty of Coldness: An Interpretive Analysis of *Das Mädchen mit den Schwefelhölzern* by Helmut Lachenmann' (MMus thesis, University of Leeds, 2012).

60 Frank Hilberg discusses the movement from one point of view to another in 'Die erste Oper des 21. Jahrhunderts? Helmut Lachenmanns *Das Mädchen mit den Schwefelhölzern*', *Neue Zeitschrift für Musik* 1997, no. 4, 19.

61 Lachenmann, 'Sounds Are Natural Phenomena' (interview with Klaus Zehelein and Hans Thomalla), disc notes, *Das Mädchen mit den Schwefelhölzern*, CD, Kairos 0012282 (2002), 41.

62 As cited in Peter Kivy, 'Speech, Song, and the Transparency of Medium'.

63 Discussed in Max Nyffeler, 'Helmut Lachenmann und die Transzendenz', http://www.beckmesser.info/helmut-lachenmann-und-die-transzendenz/ (accessed 28 April 2018); from Nyffeler, 'Himmel und Höhle: Transzendenz der Musik von Helmut Lachenmann', in *Der Atem des Wanderers: Der Komponist Helmut Lachenmann*, ed. Hans-Klaus Jungheinrich (Mainz: Schott, 2006), 79–89.

64 Paul Steenhuisen, 'Interview with Helmut Lachenmann – Toronto, 2003', *Contemporary Music Review* 23, nos. 3–4 (2004), 13.

65 David Metzer, *Musical Modernism at the Turn of the Twenty-First Century* (Cambridge: Cambridge University Press, 2009), 205.

66 See Piotr Grella-Możejko's analysis in 'Helmut Lachenmann – Style, Sound, Text', *Contemporary Music Review* 24, no. 1 (2005), 57–75.

67 Metzer, *Musical Modernism*, 220–21; see also Helmut Lachenmann, 'Les Consolations (1967/78)', in *Musik als existentielle Erfahrung*, 391, and Zuber, 'Die doppelte ästhetische Differenz', 176.

68 Ute Schalz-Laurenze, 'Radikales Wahrnehmungsspektakel – "Das Mädchen mit den Schwefelhölzern" in Frankfurt', *Neue Musikzeitung*, 20 September 2015, http://www.nmz.de/online/

radikales-wahrnehmungsspektakel-das-maedchen-mit-den-schwefelhoelzern-in-frankfurt (accessed 5 September 2017).

69 Kötter analyses the slow transformation of pitch material and shifting orchestration of this section in 'Die Irreführung der Oper', 42–44.

70 Kemper, 'Repräsentation und Struktur', 119.

71 Christian Utz, 'Statische Allegorie und "Sog der Zeit": Zur strukturalistischen Semantik in Salvatore Sciarrinos Oper *Luci mie traditrici*', *Musik & Ästhetik* 14, no. 1 (2010), 37–60.

72 'Luci mie traditrici voleva essere la vera e propria affermazione di una riforma del teatro'; Anna Maria Morazzoni, 'Luci di uno spirito sottile: Conversazione con Salvatore Sciarrino', in *Aspern: Singspiel in due atti, musica di Salvatore Sciarrino*, programme book (Venice: Fondazione Teatro La Fenice, 2013), 30.

73 Marcelle Pierson, 'The Voice under Erasure: Singing, Melody and Expression in Late Modernist Music' (PhD diss., University of Chicago, 2015), 44.

74 This libretto is traced in Edward T. Norris, 'The Italian Source for Ravenscroft's Italian Husband', *Review of English Studies* 10 (1934), 202–5.

75 'Troppo gran prezzo il vostro sangue / No, se dal sangue la rosa ebbe il natal'; Salvatore Sciarrino, *Luci mie traditrici* (1998), score (Milan: Ricordi, 2000), Scene 1.

76 Mark Swed, 'Portal to a Realm of Eerie Ambiguity: An Ambrose Bierce Tale Becomes a Haunting Musical Question in the New "The Difficulty of Crossing a Field"', *Los Angeles Times*, 25 March 2002, F14.

77 Amy Bauer, '"The Mysteries of Selma, Alabama": Re-telling and Remembrance in David Lang's *The Difficulty of Crossing a Field*', in *In Search of the Great American Opera: Tendenzen des amerikanischen Musiktheaters*, ed. Gregory Herzfeld and Frédéric Döhl (Münster: Waxmann, 2016), 219–34.

78 Cathy N. Davidson, *The Experimental Fictions of Ambrose Bierce* (Lincoln: University of Nebraska Press, 1984), 1–4.

79 Ambrose Bierce, *The Unabridged Devil's Dictionary*, ed. D. E. Schultz and S. J. Joshi (Atlanta: University of Georgia Press, 2001).

80 Martin Griffin, *Ashes of the Mind: War and Memory in Northern Literature, 1865–1900* (Amherst, NY: University of Massachusetts Press, 2009), 137.

81 Bierce, *The Unabridged Devil's Dictionary*, 229.

82 Ibid., 74.

83 Mac Wellman, 'The Difficulty of Crossing a Field', in *The Difficulty of Crossing a Field: Nine New Plays* (Minneapolis: University of Minnesota Press, 2008), 123–70.

84 Marc Robinson, 'Figure of Speech: An Interview with Mac Wellman', *Performing Arts Journal* 14 (1992), 49.

85 Shawn-Marie Garrett and Mac Wellman, 'Werewolves, Fractals, and Forbidden Knowledge', *Theater* 27, nos. 2–3 (1997), 88.

86 Mac Wellman, David Lang and Erika Munk, 'The Difficulty of Defending a Form', *Theater* 30, no. 2 (2000), 35.

87 Garrett and Wellman, 'Werewolves, Fractals', 90.

88 Bierce, *The Unabridged Devil's Dictionary*, 230.

89 Jeremy Tambling, 'Towards a Psychopathology of Opera', *Cambridge Opera Journal* 9, no. 3 (1997), 277.

90 Jean-Jacques Lecercle, *Philosophy through the Looking-Glass: Language, Nonsense, Desire* (La Salle, IL: Open Court, 1985).

91 Lecercle, *Philosophy*, 104.

92 Eberhard Hüppe, 'Rezeption, Bilder und Strukturen: Helmut Lachenmanns Klangszenarien im Lichte transzendenter Gattungshorizonte', in *Helmut Lachenmann: Musik mit Bildern?* ed. Nanni and Schmidt, 70, and Kötter, 'Die Irreführung der Oper', 38.

93 Kötter, 'Die Irreführung der Oper', 47.

94 Laurence Osborn, 'Sound, Meaning and Music-Drama in Lachenmann's *Das Mädchen mit den Schwefelhölzern*', *Tempo*, no. 268 (2014), 24.

95 Helmut Lachenmann, 'Klänge sind Naturereignisse', 27; see also Hilberg, 'Die erste Oper des 21. Jahrhunderts?', 19.

96 Metzer, *Musical Modernism*, 202; Wolfgang-Andreas Schultz, 'Der Tod der Musik – Der historische Ort von Helmut Lachenmann', unpublished paper, http://www.wolfgangandreasschultz.de/Lachenmann.pdf.

97 Paul Steenhuisen, 'Interview with Helmut Lachenmann – Toronto, 2003', *Contemporary Music Review* 23, nos. 3–4 (2004), 12.

98 Salvatore Sciarrino, cited in Alan Riding, 'An Opera Just as Unconventional as Its (Anti) Hero', *New York Times*, 8 July 2001.

99 Morazzoni, 'Luci di uno spirito sottile', 30.

100 Lecercle, *Philosophy through the Looking-Glass*, 76–78.
101 G. W. F. Hegel, *Lectures on Fine Art*, vol. 1, trans. T. M. Knox (Oxford: Oxford University Press, 1988), 360.
102 Agamben, 'The Idea of Language', 144.
103 Cavell, 'Performative and Passionate Utterance', 180.

Bibliography

Abbate, Carolyn. *Unsung Voices: Opera and Musical Narrative in the Nineteenth Century*. Princeton, NJ: Princeton University Press, 1991.

———. *In Search of Opera*. Princeton, NJ: Princeton University Press, 2001.

Agamben, Giorgio. 'The Idea of Language: Some Difficulties in Speaking about Language'. *Graduate Faculty Philosophy Journal* 10, no. 1 (1984): 141–49.

Attinello, Paul. 'Imploding the System: Kagel and the Deconstruction of Modernism'. In *Postmodern Music/Postmodern Thought*, edited by Judy Lochhead and Joseph Auner, 263–85. New York: Routledge, 2002.

Barthes, Roland. 'The Grain of the Voice'. In *Image – Music – Text*, translated by Stephen Heath, 179–89. New York: Hill and Wang, 1977.

Bauer, Amy. '"The Mysteries of Selma, Alabama": Re-telling and Remembrance in David Lang's *The Difficulty of Crossing a Field*'. In *In Search of the Great American Opera: Tendenzen des amerikanischen Musiktheaters*, edited by Gregory Herzfeld and Frédéric Döhl, 219–34. Münster: Waxmann, 2016.

Bierce, Ambrose. *The Unabridged Devil's Dictionary*, edited by D. E. Schultz and S. J. Joshi. Atlanta: University of Georgia Press, 2001.

Bowie, Andrew. *Music, Philosophy, and Modernity*. Cambridge: Cambridge University Press, 2007.

Brégégère, André. 'L'harmonie revée: An Analysis of Henri Pousseur's *Votre Faust* and *Les litanies d'Icare*'. PhD diss., City University of New York, 2014.

Cavarero, Adriana. *For More Than One Voice: Toward a Philosophy of Vocal Expression*. Translated by Paul A. Kottman. Stanford, CA: Stanford University Press, 2005.

———. 'The Vocal Body', translated by Matt Langione. *Qui Parle* 21, no. 1 (2012): 71–83.

Cavell, Stanley. 'Performative and Passionate Utterance'. In *Philosophy the Day after Tomorrow*, 155–91. Cambridge, MA: Harvard University Press, 2005.

Christian, Bryan. 'Automatic Writing and Grammelot in Claude Vivier's *langue inventée*'. *Tempo*, no. 270 (2014): 15–30.

Cone, Edward T. 'The World of Opera and Its Inhabitants'. In *Music, A View from Delft: Selected Essays*, edited by Robert P. Morgan, 125–38. Chicago: University of Chicago Press, 1989.

Davidson, Cathy N. *The Experimental Fictions of Ambrose Bierce*. Lincoln: University of Nebraska Press, 1984.

Decroupet, Pascal. 'Citation et collage dans *Votre Faust* d'Henri Pousseur et *Die Soldaten* de Bernd Alois Zimmermann'. *Art et Fact* 6 (1987): 70–82.

Di Luzio, Claudia. 'Opera on Opera: Luciano Berio's *Opera*'. In *"Music's Obedient Daughter": The Opera Libretto from Source to Score*, edited by Sabine Lichtenstein, 463–82. Amsterdam: Rodopi, 2014.

Dolar, Mladen. *A Voice and Nothing More*. Cambridge, MA: MIT Press, 2006.

Duchesneau, Louise. 'Sur la musique de Claude Vivier: György Ligeti – Propos recueillis par Louise Duchesneau'. *Circuit: musiques contemporaines* 2, nos. 1–2 (1991): 7–16.

Durney, Daniel. 'Quelques repères d'analyse pour les Récitations de Georges Aperghis'. *Musurgia* 2, no. 1 (1995): 52–60.

Edwards, Peter. *György Ligeti's* Le Grand Macabre: *Postmodernism, Musico-Dramatic Form and the Grotesque*. Abingdon: Routledge, 2017.

Fearn, Raymond. *Italian Opera since 1945*. Abingdon: Routledge, 2013.

Feneyrou, Laurent. 'Claude Vivier: parcours de l'œuvre'. *IRCAM Brahms Composer Database*. http://brahms.ircam.fr/claude-vivier#parcours (accessed 5 September 2017).

Fink, Robert. 'After the Canon'. In *The Oxford Handbook of Opera*, edited by Helen M. Greenwald, 1065–86. New York: Oxford University Press, 2014.

Garrett, Shawn-Marie, and Mac Wellman. 'Werewolves, Fractals, and Forbidden Knowledge'. *Theater* 27, nos. 2–3 (1997): 87–95.

Gee, Erin. 'The Notation and Use of the Voice in Non-Semantic Contexts: Phonetic Organization in the Vocal Music of Dieter Schnebel, Brian Ferneyhough, and Georges Aperghis'. In *Vocal Music and Contemporary Identities: Unlimited Voices in East Asia and the West*, edited by Christian Utz and Frederick Lau, 175–97. Abingdon: Routledge, 2013.

Ghelderode, Michel de. *La balade du Grand Macabre*. Paris: Gallimard, 1952.

Gilmore, Bob. *Claude Vivier: A Biography*. Woodbridge: Boydell & Brewer, 2014.

Goldman, Jonathan. 'Claude Vivier at the End'. In *Contemporary Music and Spirituality*, edited by Sander van Maas and Robert Sholl, 202–23. Abingdon: Routledge, 2016.

Grella-Możejko, Piotr. 'Helmut Lachenmann – Style, Sound, Text'. *Contemporary Music Review* 24, no. 1 (2005): 57–75.

Griffin, Martin. *Ashes of the Mind: War and Memory in Northern Literature, 1865–1900*. Amherst: University of Massachusetts Press, 2009.

Griffiths, Paul. *Modern Music and After*. 3rd ed. New York: Oxford University Press, 2010.

Grüny, Christian. '"Zustände, die sich verändern": Helmut Lachenmanns *Musik mit Bildern* – und anderem'. In *Helmut Lachenmann: Musik mit Bildern?* edited by Nanni and Schmidt, 39–68.

Hamilton, John T. *Music, Madness, and the Unworking of Language*. New York: Columbia University Press, 2008.

Hegel, G. W. F. *Lectures on Fine Art*. Vol. 1. Translated by T. M. Knox. Oxford: Oxford University Press, 1988.

Heile, Björn. *The Music of Mauricio Kagel*. Aldershot: Ashgate, 2006.

———. Review of *The Cambridge Companion to Twentieth-Century Opera*, edited by Mervyn Cooke. *Music & Letters* 88, no. 3 (2007): 347–48.

Heller-Roazen, Daniel. *Echolalias: On the Forgetting of Language*. New York: Zone Books, 2005.

Hilberg, Frank. 'Die erste Oper des 21. Jahrhunderts? Helmut Lachenmanns *Das Mädchen mit den Schwefelhölzern*'. *Neue Zeitschrift für Musik*, 1997, no. 4: 14–23.

Hüppe, Eberhard. 'Rezeption, Bilder und Strukturen: Helmut Lachenmanns Klangszenarien im Lichte transzendenter Gattungshorizonte'. In *Helmut Lachenmann: Musik mit Bildern?* edited by Nanni and Schmidt, 71–96.

Jakobson, Roman. *Child Language, Aphasia, and Phonological Universals*. Translated by Allan R. Keiler. The Hague: Mouton, 1968.

Jameson, Fredric. *The Modernist Papers*. London: Verso, 2007.

Jones, Stephanie. 'The Cruelty of Coldness: An Interpretive Analysis of *Das Mädchen mit den Schwefelhölzern* by Helmut Lachenmann'. MMus thesis, University of Leeds, 2012.

Kemper, Christian. 'Repräsentation und Struktur in einer "Musik mit Bildern": Überlegungen zu Helmut Lachenmanns Musiktheater'. *Musik und Ästhetik* 5 (2001): 105–21.

Kivy, Peter. 'Speech, Song, and the Transparency of Medium: A Note on Opera Metaphysics'. *Journal of Aesthetics and Art Criticism* 52, no. 1 (1994): 63–68.

Kötter, Daniel. 'Die Irreführung der Oper: Sprachlosigkeit und -fertigkeit in Helmut Lachenmanns "Das Mädchen mit den Schwefelhölzern"'. *MusikTexte*, no. 105 (2005): 37–48.

Lachenmann, Helmut. '"Klänge sind Naturereignisse": Helmut Lachenmann im Gespräch mit Klaus Zehelein und Hans Thomalla'. In *Das Mädchen mit den Schwefelhölzern*, programme book, 20–35. Stuttgart: Staatsoper, 2001. English translation, 'Sounds Are Natural Phenomena'. Disc notes, *Das Mädchen mit den Schwefelhölzern*, Staatsoper Stuttgart, conducted by Lothar Zagrosek. CD, Kairos 0012282 (2002): 39–41.

———. *Musik als existentielle Erfahrung: Schriften, 1966–1995*. Edited by Josef Häusler. 2nd ed. Wiesbaden: Breitkopf & Härtel, 2004.

Lecercle, Jean-Jacques. *Philosophy through the Looking-Glass: Language, Nonsense, Desire*. La Salle, IL: Open Court, 1985.

Levesque, Patrick. 'L'élaboration du matériau musical dans les dernières œuvres vocales de Claude Vivier'. *Circuit: musiques contemporaines* 18, no. 3 (2008): 89–106.

Ligeti, György. *Gesammelte Schriften*. Edited by Monika Lichtenfeld. 2 vols. Mainz: Schott, 2007.

Madlener, Frank. 'Georges Aperghis: A Talk with Frank Madlener'. Disc notes, *Aperghis: Die Hamletmaschine-Oratorio*, SWR Vokalensemble Stuttgart, Ictus Ensemble, conducted by Georges-Elie Octors. CD, Cyprès CYP5607 (2001): 24–28. http://www.ictus.be/hamletmaschine (accessed 7 September 2017).

Metzer, David. *Musical Modernism at the Turn of the Twenty-First Century*. Cambridge: Cambridge University Press, 2009.

Morazzoni, Anna Maria. 'Luci di uno spirito sottile: Conversazione con Salvatore Sciarrino'. In *Aspern: Singspiel in due atti, musica di Salvatore Sciarrino*, programme book, 23–36. Venice: Fondazione Teatro La Fenice, 2013.

Motte, Warren F., ed. and trans. *Oulipo: A Primer of Potential Literature*. Normal, IL: Dalkey Archive Press, 1998.

Nancy, Jean-Luc. *Listening*. Translated by Charlotte Mandell. New York: Fordham University Press, 2007.

Nanni, Matteo, and Matthias Schmidt, eds. *Helmut Lachenmann: Musik mit Bildern?* Munich: Wilhelm Fink, 2012.

Norris, Christopher. *Platonism, Music and the Listener's Share*. London: Continuum, 2006.

Norris, Edward T. 'The Italian Source for Ravenscroft's Italian Husband'. *Review of English Studies* 10 (1934): 202–5.

Nyffeler, Max. 'Himmel und Höhle: Transzendenz der Musik von Helmut Lachenmann'. In *Der Atem des Wanderers: Der Komponist Helmut Lachenmann*, edited by Hans-Klaus Jungheinrich, 79–89. Mainz: Schott, 2006.

Osborn, Laurence. 'Sound, Meaning and Music-Drama in Lachenmann's *Das Mädchen mit den Schwefelhölzern*'. *Tempo*, no. 268 (2014): 20–33.

Pierson, Marcelle. 'The Voice under Erasure: Singing, Melody and Expression in Late Modernist Music'. PhD diss., University of Chicago, 2015.

Placanica, Francesca. '"Unwrapping" the Voice: Cathy Berberian and John Cage's *Aria*'. In *Transformations of Musical Modernism*, edited by Erling E. Guldbrandsen and Julian Johnson, 264–78. Cambridge: Cambridge University Press, 2015.

Porzak, Simon. 'Zerbinetta's Laughter: An Introduction to the Marginality of Song'. *Qui Parle* 21, no. 1 (2012): 3–69.

Riding, Alan. 'An Opera Just as Unconventional as Its (Anti) Hero'. *New York Times*, 8 July 2001.

Robinson, Marc. 'Figure of Speech: An Interview with Mac Wellman'. *Performing Arts Journal* 14, no. 1 (1992): 43–51.

Salzman, Eric, and Thomas Dési. *The New Music Theater: Seeing the Voice, Hearing the Body*. New York: Oxford University Press, 2008.

Schalz-Laurenze, Ute. 'Radikales Wahrnehmungsspektakel – "Das Mädchen mit den Schwefelhölzern" in Frankfurt'. *Neue Musikzeitung*, 20 September 2015. http://www.nmz.de/online/radikales-wahrnehmungsspektakel-das-maedchen-mit-den-schwefelhoelzern-in-frankfurt (accessed 5 September 2017).

Schmidt, Felix, and Jürgen Hohmeyer. '"Sprengt die Opernhäuser in die Luft! *Spiegel*-Gespräch mit dem französischen Komponisten und Dirigenten Pierre Boulez'. *Der Spiegel*, 25 September 1967, 166–74.

Schmidt, Matthias. 'Schöpferische Bilderinnerung: Geschichtliches Sehen und Hören in Helmut Lachenmanns *Mädchen mit den Schwefelhölzern*'. In *Helmut Lachenmann: Musik mit Bildern?* edited by Nanni and Schmidt, 195–218.

Schultz, Wolfgang-Andreas. 'Der Tod der Musik – Der historische Ort von Helmut Lachenmann'. Unpublished paper. http://www.wolfgangandreasschultz.de/Lachenmann.pdf.

Steenhuisen, Paul. 'Interview with Helmut Lachenmann – Toronto, 2003'. *Contemporary Music Review* 23, nos. 3–4 (2004): 9–14.

Swed, Mark. 'Portal to a Realm of Eerie Ambiguity: An Ambrose Bierce Tale Becomes a Haunting Musical Question in the New "The Difficulty of Crossing a Field"'. *Los Angeles Times*, 25 March 2002, F14.

Tambling, Jeremy. 'Towards a Psychopathology of Opera'. *Cambridge Opera Journal* 9, no. 3 (1997): 263–79.

Trubetskoi, Nikolai Sergeevich. *Principles of Phonology*. Translated by Christiane A. M. Baltaxe. Berkeley: University of California Press, 1969.

Utz, Christian. 'Statische Allegorie und "Sog der Zeit": Zur strukturalistischen Semantik in Salvatore Sciarrinos Oper *Luci mie traditrici*'. *Musik & Ästhetik* 14, no. 1 (2010): 37–60.

Vivier, Claude. 'Prologue pour un Marco Polo' (1981), composer's note. http://www.boosey.com/cr/music/Claude-Vivier-Prologue-pour-un-Marco-Polo/47759 (accessed 16 May 2017).

———. 'Les écrits de Claude Vivier'. *Circuit: musiques contemporaines* 2, nos. 1–2 (1991): 39–135.

Wellman, Mac. *The Difficulty of Crossing a Field: Nine New Plays*. Minneapolis: University of Minnesota Press, 2008.

Wellman, Mac, David Lang and Erika Munk. 'The Difficulty of Defending a Form'. *Theater* 30, no. 2 (2000): 34–43.

Whittall, Arnold. 'New Opera, Old Opera: Perspectives on Critical Interpretation'. *Cambridge Opera Journal* 21, no. 2 (2009): 181–98.

Zarius, Karl-Heinz. *Staatstheater von Mauricio Kagel*. Vienna: Universal Edition, 1977.

Zuber, Barbara. 'Die doppelte ästhetische Differenz und noch einmal die Frage: Was heißt "Musik mit Bildern"? Zu Helmut Lachenmanns *Mädchen mit den Schwefelhölzern*'. In *Helmut Lachenmann: Musik mit Bildern?* edited by Nanni and Schmidt, 171–94.

19

'ES KLANG SO ALT UND WAR DOCH SO NEU!'

Modernist operatic culture through the prism of staging *Die Meistersinger von Nürnberg*

Mark Berry

Reflection on opera: the 'emotionalization of the intellect'

Reflection on opera – upon what it is, what it might be, what it ought to be – is as old as opera itself. One might even claim, not entirely nonsensically, that it is older still; for opera as we know it has its roots in an intellectual discussion concerning how best to perform ancient tragedy. Almost as old is hostility towards such reflection, whether from those who disdain opera or from those who would prefer it to be just 'entertainment', whatever that might be. Wagner, an inescapable figure for any understanding of musical, let alone operatic, modernism, sometimes veered dangerously close in some of his theorizing, though never in his dramas, to (highly mediated) insistence upon immediacy, upon a lack of mediation – although we should always bear in mind that his celebrated phrase in *Opera und Drama*, 'Gefühlswerdung des Verstandes' ('emotionalization of the intellect'), does not imply abdication of that intellect.[1] Whether in composition or stage direction – he more or less invented the role of the modern opera *Regisseur* – Wagner was, almost irrespective of intention, perhaps the single most important godfather to a critical, modernist tradition of staging and interpretation that has been unavoidably, if problematically, linked to the word *Regietheater* (director's theatre). Without wishing entirely to elide 'modernist' and 'critical', let alone to elide either or both with *Regietheater*, whose caricatured binary opposition to 'traditionalism' has generated plenty of heat but little light, it is to that world of still raging, if all too often threadbare, controversy that I shall attend.

Let us first, though, take several steps further back to one of the multiple dawns of Western musical drama, in order to travel beyond Wagner in the opposite direction. What is opera, or perhaps better operatic culture, concerned with? How does it relate to modernist culture? One of the principal themes to be explored in this chapter is the importance of that reflexivity to our understanding of an operatic culture we can reasonably consider to be modernist in nature, without embarking too far down upon the hopeless, if tempting, path of tick-box definitions.

In the beginning, or close to the beginning, was Orpheus: a mythical 'truth', or at least believed to be so, repeated persistently through Western musical culture, and especially throughout operatic history. What did Orpheus do, and why did it matter? He sang, to the accompaniment of his lyre. Every scene in his legend relates in some sense to music, both in the ancient, broader understanding of *mousikē* (all that emanated from the Muses) and in our own, more restricted sense. The Muses, it may be worth reminding ourselves, were traditionally nine: Clio (Muse of history), Euterpe (lyric), Thalia (comedy), Melpomene (tragedy), Terpsichore (dance), Erato (love poetry), Polyhymnia (hymns), Urania (astronomy) and, first among equals, Calliope (epic), who in turn submitted to their true leader, Apollo Mousagētēs. Orpheus was Calliope's son, and according to some tellings of his legend (Pindar is ambiguous) Apollo's too.[2] He tamed animals and resisted the Sirens, even charmed Hades itself, through performance on his lyre. His purview – and that of *mousikē* – was far greater than that which we, in an age labouring under the curse of specialization, might consider to be 'music': he was poet, enchanter and prophet; he communicated the qualities of all the Muses, not in addition to but through his very identity as a musical performer.

If not the first opera, what has often been considered to be the first great opera – a value judgement modernism has never relinquished – was Claudio Monteverdi's 1607 *Orfeo*, its roots traditionally understood to have lain in the sixteenth-century Florentine Camerata's belief that Attic tragedy had been sung. When Christoph Willibald von Gluck and his librettist, Ranieri de' Calzabigi, believed opera to have strayed too far from its dramatic purpose, to have degenerated too far into an opportunity for commercially inspired vocal display, their first 'reform opera' would be *Orfeo ed Euridice*. After tragedy, there should come a satyr play; and what better example, knowingly so, might one give than Jacques Offenbach's *Orphée aux enfers* (discussed elsewhere in this volume by James Currie)? In *The Mask of Orpheus*, Harrison Birtwistle composed what many have regarded as the greatest twentieth-century English opera; at the very least it marked a new level in English musico-dramatic complexity.

Reflection has thus not been only, or even primarily, external. It has, at the very least, been intrinsic to those composers and works most central to what we might characterize as the modernist operatic canon. (Re-)traced back now to Monteverdi, it has some points of contact with what we might call the 'actually existing' practical canon or, perhaps better, working repertoire of opera houses. It also, though, stands apart from that working repertoire – which, admittedly, varies considerably over time and place – and criticizes it. The two stand in a dialectical relationship to one another, neither capable of existence without the other: on the one hand the modernist and, on the other, the non-, anti- or counter-modernist. And yet perhaps both partake of modernism in one way or another. We are brought, whether we like it or not, to the thorny, insoluble question of definitions. There is no need, however, to lament the lack of solutions. If there were some definitive solution somewhere, we should arguably have no need of art, nor indeed of writing upon it. We can reach for it, and it is perhaps in that act of reaching, in that act of trying to understand, that we find something of what it is or was to be modernist, or to partake or to have partaken in modernism.

Opera and modernism

In the introduction to a recent collection of essays on musical modernism, Julian Johnson and Erling E. Guldbrandsen write:

> Modernism is neither a style nor an epoch; it has neither imploded nor come to a historical end. Rather, musical modernism is an attitude of musical practice – in composition, performance and listening – that involves an increased awareness of its own historical situation [...]. As soon as music starts reflecting upon its own language – its means of expression – it takes on a historical self-awareness that amounts to modernist, critical reflection. From this view, musical modernism simply [?] involves a heightened consciousness of the relations between present and past, between present and future

and between continuity and discontinuity in the history of music; in brief, it provokes an acute awareness of the condition of historicity that has always been embedded in the present moment of musical experience.[3]

Forestalling one immediate possible rejoinder, the writers continue: 'such a historical awareness was already a characteristic of Beethoven's world and of the modernity that erupts with the French Revolution and the philosophy of Hegel'.[4] One might, of course, trace it further back, to the disintegrative whirlwind of competing dances and to those distended cries into (or from) the abyss of 'Viva la libertà!' heard in the first act of *Don Giovanni*, or to Gluck's or indeed to Monteverdi's *Orfeo*.

Perhaps the point is, then, that tendencies and examples – which might be made to stretch back further and further, even to the very beginning – reach at some point a critical mass. Once that moment has been reached, critical reflection, whether consciously articulated or not, seems necessary on the part of the general musical (and, in this case, musico-dramatic) culture, if not altogether ineluctably on the part of creators themselves. There will be anti-modernist currents, or at least tendencies we may consider as such, just as the Enlightenment, for Isaiah Berlin in a celebrated and still highly valuable article, met a counter-Enlightenment neither to be directly associated with nor directly dissociated from 'early' or 'pre'-Romanticism.[5] Whether we consider them to be 'modernist', to partake of 'modernism' to some degree, or to be downright 'anti-modernist' is perhaps not so very important beyond the particular terms of our particular endeavour. There remains – however unfashionable such Hegelianism may have become in certain, often 'anti-modernist', even neoliberal quarters – something of a spirit of the age to such thinking. That seems unavoidable: take the opposing conception and you also witness a *Zeitgeist*, almost a mirror image. As Jacques Derrida warned following the events of 1989, Marx and, by extension, Hegel are far from dead; they have rather become, like the modernism with which they stand so inextricably interlinked in cultural terms, all the more indispensable in a world of (neo)liberal triumphalism, a world which at the time of writing seems considerably less secure than it did in 1993.[6]

Whatever modernism might 'be' or 'have been' – ontological inquiry is unlikely to be of assistance – it neither refers to nor even concerns itself with style. Individual examples may well do so. (Stravinsky's neoclassicism certainly does, though that is another matter.) But works such as Schoenberg's *Moses und Aron* and Debussy's *Pelléas et Mélisande* – or even Schoenberg's tone-poem *Pelleas und Melisande* – do not share a fundamental style, which is neither to say that one cannot find certain musical features in common, nor to say that one cannot learn much from discovery and analysis of such features. Nor, by the same token, does an idea or framework of modernism prescribe stylistic identity or even proximity between, say, the 'modernist' Kroll Opera's production of *Der fliegende Holländer*, directed by Jürgen Fehling and conducted by Otto Klemperer, and a Berlin 'modernist' or 'modernistic' successor, directed by Harry Kupfer and conducted by Daniel Barenboim. Stylistic kinship may be present, yet it need not be; indeed, there is nothing more pernicious than a tick-box approach to such matters. 'The modernist may dispense with "atonality", so long as (s)he includes some compensating developing variation' is as absurd a proposition as it sounds, perhaps more so. None of that is to say that every opera written or produced during this period 'is' modernist, or can be helpfully understood as 'modernist', although it may well be the case that every opera written or produced might be helpfully understood within a modernist frame of reference. The relative 'abstraction' of the concept is part of its point. In that respect, but not only that respect, it has a good deal in common with 'Renaissance', 'Enlightenment', 'Classicism', 'Romanticism', and so on.

The director as modernist: Wagner and his successors

Wagner has stood at the forefront of musico-theatrical experiment since he burst onto the operatic scene, not just as composer but as conductor, director, aesthetician and cultural phenomenon. His was in many ways an experimental, critical approach that we should be hard put, indeed perverse, not to consider modernistic. Uncomfortably for those, from the bizarre 'Bayreuth Idealists' onwards, who would protect his work against transgression, the 'Master' had no compunction in treating other composers' works in a way that would have today's operatic reactionaries scream 'Eurotrash', 'desecration', or – still worse to many of their ears – *Regietheater*. In his autobiography, Wagner tells of his work in Dresden on Gluck's *Iphigénie en Aulide* (or *Iphigenie in Aulis*, since it was performed in German). His 1847 staging – 'wherein I had to prove myself as a stage director as well; indeed, I was even obliged to lend the most urgent aid to the scene-painters and the machinists' – revealed Wagner not only as conductor but as imaginative editor and composer, even musicologist.[7] He presented Gluck's opera in a new edition, providing preludes, postludes and transitions, in order, as he saw it, to aid the dramatic flow of a number opera, while also bringing to Gluck's orchestration the advantages or otherwise of a mid-nineteenth-century hue. 'I had to find new ways,' Wagner would recall, 'to enliven the staging, for the problem seemed to me to lie largely in the conventional treatment of such scenes prevailing at the Paris Opera during Gluck's time.'[8]

Wagner additionally attempted a return beyond Racine to Euripides when he transformed the ending, ridding Gluck's work of its conventional concluding marriage between Iphigénie and Achille. In just the same way, Jürgen Flimm and Daniel Barenboim would in 2016 rid Gluck's *Orfeo* of its *lieto fine*, both criticizing the work and attempting a restoration of a superior version that never was (but 'should' have been), very much in the tradition of Wagner. In their Berlin production of the original Vienna version, following the expected choral and balletic rejoicing, the performance returned to the Parisian number (that is, for the later *Orphée et Eurydice*) that many would have missed most of all: the 'Dance of the Blessed Spirits'. Euridi/yce vanished once again, somewhere between the cracks of competing versions, yet without forsaking insistence (indeed arguably inciting still greater insistence) on an ideal version, thereby maintaining adherence to a Wagnerian work concept against the more haphazard tendencies he denounced in his own Paris and elsewhere. Orfeo's fevered, grieving imagination seemed to have conjured hope only for it to dissipate. The vision of a happy ending such as Adorno excoriated in his vituperative critique of Wagner was lain bare for what it was: the protagonist's desperate, unrealizable fantasy.[9] Fire and its heat, emptiness, and loneliness return. Awaiting him now were only the Maenads – or perhaps Jupiter, an additional Wanderer-like figure introduced by Flimm, who observes events but never intervenes, although he would presumably be capable of doing so.

Moreover, Wagner's own works, his widow Cosima's understandable role as Bayreuth protectress notwithstanding, have always been at the forefront of critical intervention on the stage (as well as, arguably, in the pit, Boulez complementing Chéreau in the most celebrated instance of all, the 1976 'Centenary *Ring*').[10] The highly influential ideas of the Swiss designer Adolphe Appia, who had aimed at a drastic simplification of the stage clutter by which he had felt so distracted in *Parsifal* at Wagner's own Bayreuth staging in 1882, were bitterly opposed by Cosima. Houston Stewart Chamberlain's attempts to persuade his mother-in-law that Appia's ideas might hold some validity came to naught. Wagner had, to quote Patrick Carnegy, 'wanted to establish a "fixed tradition" because he needed to defend his own imaginings against misunderstanding and perversion'.[11] So, rightly or wrongly, do many creators. We might think of Samuel Beckett, in his attempt to prevent a Boston staging of *Endgame* of which he disapproved:

> Any production of *Endgame* which ignores my stage directions is completely unacceptable to me. My play requires an empty room and two small windows. The American Repertory Theater production which dismisses my directions is a complete parody of the play as conceived by me. Anybody who cares for the work couldn't fail to be disgusted by this.[12]

Beckett's decision to bring an injunction against the Berlin production was somewhat puzzling in the light of his earlier disinclination to do so in similar cases, true to the belief that such action was not within the rights of the playwright. Still, the injunction failed, upon which outcome Beckett proceeded to amend the contract licensing his plays for performance, so as to include a clause forbidding deviation not only from the script but also from his stage directions.[13] Closer still to operatic home, we might think of György Ligeti, always a strenuous taskmaster to musical performers of his work, dissociating himself from Peter Sellars's nuclear-age premiere production of the revised version of *Le Grand Macabre*, whose extremely detailed stage directions have never been 'faithfully' observed, and perhaps never will be. And yet, as Carnegy also remarks, 'what Cosima forgot to say was' that Wagner, like Shakespeare and Goethe, 'had also built and run theatres, and that they and Wagner all recognized that performance had its own active, ultimately protean role in the completion of the written text'. Carnegy continues: 'In "fixing" a tradition he most surely did not intend', as Cosima, Fafner-like, did, 'to imply a ban on the freedom of intelligent performers and stage directors to contribute their own artistry and make lively contribution to the challenges he had flung down.'[14]

Ultimately, Appia's vision would win out across Europe and the world, and eventually even at Bayreuth under Wagner's – and Cosima's – grandson Wieland, whose post-WWII 'New Bayreuth' not only saved the Festival from extinction following its close association with National Socialism, but also proved so influential as a modernistic trailblazer for operatic culture more generally. There was in Wieland's work good ideological reason for dissociating his new Wagner from what had come before, both immediately and in the longer term. John Deathridge once commented that when Wieland 'spoke of "the clearing away of old lumber" (*Entrümpelung*), [. . .] [he produced] stage pictures bereft of their "reactionary" ethos – and, as sceptics were prone to add, most of their content as well.'[15] Wieland's *Die Meistersinger* 'ohne' rather than 'von' *Nürnberg* was perhaps the most celebrated, or notorious, case in point there. Yet, quite apart from the dramatic advantages that might be won by scenic minimalism (less can often be more), that *Entrümpelung* paved the way for subsequent stagings, which proceeded to engage more directly with the critical content and potentialities of operatic works (not that Wieland ignored those elements entirely – far from it). That renewed critical engagement extended far beyond Wagner, of course, but the concentration here on modernist, reception-focused Wagner will, I hope, be forgiven, given that it is impossible to discuss everything within the confines of an essay such as this.

Die Meistersinger

I shall consider four productions of *Die Meistersinger von Nürnberg*, the first three in their different ways very much modernistic in the critical sense I have outlined, the fourth almost defiantly not so, and yet unable to resist – just as, say, Rachmaninoff's music cannot resist comparison with Stravinsky or Schoenberg – being considered in their light. (That, I hasten to add, is intended

Modernist operatic culture

neither to denigrate Rachmaninoff's music nor to claim that it possesses no 'modernist' features.) Why, though, *Meistersinger*? Partly it is a matter of picking up from Wieland Wagner, and partly a matter of not repeating themes I have discussed elsewhere.[16] However, there is more to it than that. There are specific, rather than accidental, reasons for paying attention to *Meistersinger* too.

The work's concern with the mediated nature of art, its production and its performance makes it perhaps Wagner's most self-reflective work. Its deliberate anachronisms pave the way, or at least have been seen to do so since the Second World War, for similar playing with history and with its retelling, rewriting, relistening. Pierre Boulez, whose plans to conduct a new production of this work and of others (such as *Wozzeck, Elektra, Ariadne auf Naxos, Boris Godunov* and *Don Giovanni*) with Wieland were forestalled by the latter's death, once noted, very much in this connection:

> The Romantics rediscovered the Gothic style. At the end of the nineteenth century there were Gothic churches in profusion. This was the most striking example of stylistic reference. On the other hand, although in *The Mastersingers* there is no end of references to the Minnesänger, and to the forms of sixteenth- and – even more so – fifteenth-century music, Wagner's music actually has nothing to do with the historical truth about the town of Nuremberg. This is why I feel really ill at ease when people try to depict the historical town on the stage when it is absent from the music.[17]

If Hans Sachs says of Walther's Prize Song, 'It sounded so old, and yet was so new' ('Es klang so alt und war doch so neu'), we should also both guard against eliding the multiple varieties of ancient and modern: the celebrated *quérelle* between the two should perhaps be pluralized. Boulez, as one of Wagner's foremost modernist interpreters and successors – composer, conductor, polemicist, revolutionary, although never actually as opera composer – offers a powerful, *musical* case against slavish adherence to stage directions, just as Appia had to Cosima. Yet, as Carnegy writes, in speaking of Wagner as 'the creator of drama from the spirit of music', Cosima

> was, unknowingly, on the same ground as Appia, whose point was that the production must derive from the music and not from the stage instructions. The crucial difference was that while Cosima believed that music and stage instructions told the same story [always an unwise assumption], Appia maintained that the latter were an aberration [to be fair, something of an exaggeration] and that, in Schopenhauerian spirit, only the music was to be trusted.[18]

There was mysticism, then, to be rid of, or at least to be questioned, in Appia's conception too, and he was not merely prefiguring a successor when saying that the 'contrast' in *Meistersinger* 'between the external events and the inner meaning is central to Wagner's intention'.[19] Nevertheless, the idea that the music might stand closer to the drama than Wieland Wagner's 'lumber' has certainly offered critical possibilities to performance and to operatic culture more generally. Boulez would explore them more fully in his work with Chéreau on the *Ring*. We shall now, however, turn to those promised stagings of the one Wagner 'music drama' Boulez never had the opportunity to conduct.

Harry Kupfer: old and new/*alt und neu*

Harry Kupfer, director of one of the two most successful overall (certainly, prior to Frank Castorf's post-dramatic treatment, the most celebrated) post-Chéreau Bayreuth *Rings*, also directed the nine 'canonical' Wagner operas, from *Der fliegende Holländer* to *Parsifal*, for Berlin's Staatsoper Unter den Linden, in collaboration with one of the performing musicians closest to Boulez, Daniel Barenboim. I mention that since Barenboim may, in certain cases, be understood to have picked up the baton (had Boulez used one) from the French composer-conductor in a number of modernist operatic projects, not least *Tristan und Isolde* at La Scala with Chéreau (long postponed, but originally suggested as a Boulez-Chéreau Bayreuth reunion). Modernism has its own traditions, which, as Boulez remarks (in a comment that simultaneously acknowledges their existence), 'a strong personality will inevitably transform'.[20]

Kupfer's *Meistersinger*, his second staging of the work, ran through the second half of the 1990s and the following decade until what seems to have been its final appearance in 2008. Kupfer did not go so far as to present a *Meistersinger ohne Nürnberg*. Indeed, Nuremberg was present throughout, replete with Cranach, stained glass and banners (including King David and his harp), although never with quite such exuberant delight as, say, in Graham Vick's roughly contemporaneous Breughelesque production for Covent Garden. What perhaps better served that general point from Boulez concerning a mismatch between work and history was a staired centrepiece (see Figure 19.1), serving in different guises as the Katharinenkirche, as the balcony of Act Two, as a staircase to Sachs's workshop, and so forth. The city whose absence from the stage Boulez had advocated was reinstated, albeit in mediated, critical fashion. That centrepiece's shape suggested a ruined tower, perhaps even an image of Berlin's own celebrated Kaiser-Wilhelm-Gedächtniskirche, and thereby seemed to allude to the devastation of Friedrich Meinecke's 'German catastrophe', the course of German history to which even the most studiously uncritical

Figure 19.1 Richard Wagner, *Die Meistersinger von Nürnberg* (dir. Harry Kupfer, Staatsoper Unter den Linden, Berlin). *Festwiese* scene (Act 3, scene 5), with staired centrepiece visible

Photo © Monika Rittershaus, for Staatsoper Berlin. Used by permission

Modernist operatic culture

of *Meistersinger* stagings will struggle to avoid reference entirely.[21] An impression of the modern city was superimposed, by virtue of a skyscraper backdrop to the second act and the first part of the third, suggesting, like an affectionate Adorno (if such a figure can be imagined), tension between Wagner's thoroughgoing adoption of modern technical and technological means and his harking back to a pre-modern age of guilds and corporations, an age prior to excessive division of labour. A guiding principle of the production, not obsessively emphasized yet certainly present and productive (generative, one might say, in parallel to the developmental qualities in Wagner's score), was that of conflict between old and new, with due reference to those shades in between.

Moreover, a utopian quality to that lost age was gently suggested by the joy of the *Festwiese* scene and its processions, replete with giant figure of Death, flamethrowers, acrobats, and all. To be utopian cuts both ways, for a utopia cannot exist – and certainly has not existed. Kupfer's staging did not travel very far down the deconstructionist route, but the presentation was finely nuanced. There was, however, a nice touch to Sachs's inability, following Walther's refusal (see Figure 19.2), to find someone on whom to bestow the *Festwiese* garland. It was eventually placed on the floor. A sentimental path might have been simply to present it to Beckmesser. Instead, with considerable poignancy, the defeated town clerk walked over, looked at the abandoned garland, and imagined what might have been. The way in which Beckmesser was excluded from the general rejoicing without being entirely ostracized was both faithful to and yet critical of the broad dramatic thrust of Wagner's drama and its reception.

Figure 19.2 Die Meistersinger (dir. Kupfer, Staatsoper Unter den Linden, Berlin). Eva offers the *Festwiese* garland to Walther (Act 3, scene 5)

Photo © Monika Rittershaus, for Staatsoper Berlin. Used by permission

Mark Berry

Stefan Herheim: dreaming, reimagining, performing tradition

Next for consideration is the staging by the Norwegian director Stefan Herheim, first seen at the Salzburg Festival for the bicentenary of Wagner's birth in 2013 and then again at the Paris Opéra in 2016. I shall not attempt firmly to distinguish between the two, for the 'revival', if we might call it that, was very much an extension of the first outing, and, in Bayreuth *Werkstatt* tradition, a Herheim production tends to be an ongoing, developing artwork rather than something set in stone.

The production opened, during the opening Prelude, in Hans Sachs's nineteenth-century workshop. Sachs was seen dreaming, like Wagner, of a Nuremberg which, like the 'traditional' productions of 'traditionalists', never was, and for Appia and Boulez never should have been. We proceeded to see – and to hear – how Sachs and, by implication, Wagner created rather than exhumed before themselves and us a Nuremberg of their own time(s). They invited, perhaps even required, us to do the same, for the historical distance between us and the designs on stage – between directorial reflection and all-too-beautiful, more-than-a-little-knowing designs – was brought to the forefront of our self-consciousness by what we saw and heard. It might be worth reiterating here that it could not be further from the truth – a dividing line, if an unstable one, between many conceptions of modernism and postmodernism – to confuse Wagner, that theoretician of the 'emotionalization of the intellect', with someone who would have us abdicate that intellect. Indeed, brazen 'infidelity' to Wagnerism will most clearly be found in the 'traditionalism' of latter-day Nietzschean 'Wagnerians', those who would 'protect' the composer's works from the very development to which Wagner subjected works of earlier composers, whether as performer, composer or theorist.[22]

Still more than Mendelssohn before him and (Adorno's) Second Viennese School after him, Wagner took the modernist route for Bach: to quote Adorno in his celebrated Bach essay, he 'calls his music by name in producing it anew'.[23] Not for nothing did Wagner decline in his score to employ even the most cursory stylistic – as opposed to formal – reference to Renaissance music. His guiding spirit here was his very own creation of Bach, the 'history of the interior life of the German spirit', according to the contemporaneous essay 'What Is German?'[24] Invention of tradition was seen throughout the production, just as it was heard throughout the musical performance. The Masters' Nuremberg – seen at a time (post French Revolution) of renewed crisis for guilds and other corporate institutions – was shiny, new, a little insistent, a little desperate. Echoes, visual and verbal, were to be experienced of that *Tand* both of Sachs's peroration and, earlier in Wagner's oeuvre, of Loge's description of the Rhinegold. All that glistened, were it in the Rhine or at a guild meeting, was not necessarily gold. Indeed Sachs, rightly or otherwise, would, at the close of the work, condemn it as the very thing the Masters insist it is not: 'wälsche[r] Tand', foreign vanity.

A key feature of Wagner's Romantic conception of Sachs and indeed of Nuremberg concerned overcoming the division of labour – or, the more cynical, perhaps Marxist, commentator might respond, never having reached it in the first place. In that sense, at least, we might consider Wagner pre-modernist. Yet Marx and Engels too had their poetic flight of fancy in a celebrated passage from *The German Ideology*:

> In communist society, where nobody has one exclusive sphere of activity but each can become accomplished in any branch he wishes, [. . .] it [is] possible for me to do one thing today and another tomorrow, to hunt in the morning, fish in the afternoon, rear cattle in the evening, criticise after dinner, just as I have a mind, without ever becoming hunter, fisherman, shepherd, or critic.[25]

Wagner and Herheim portrayed Sachs in more post-Nazarene fashion; there was something of later German Romantic painting to this dream. Yet Sachs remained a polymath and, more than that, a rebuke to involuntary specialization: cobbling, writing verse, singing, indeed painting too. Not only did he dream at the opening; he continued to do so, Herheim reminding us of Schopenhauer, of Freud, of fairy tales and, of course, of the centrality of dreams to the work 'itself'.

The 'real' world – shades of Schopenhauer, modernistically read back into Freud, himself strongly influenced by Schopenhauer – both disappeared and yet remained, projected onto the curtain as it was opened and closed, with increasing difficulty, by a night-capped Sachs at the beginnings and ends of the first two acts. And when he dreamed, objects in his workshop grew, like the Christmas Tree from Chaikovsky's *Nutcracker*; or was it that he and the characters of his dreams shrank? Still more than in Salzburg's Grosses Festspielhaus – Herbert von Karajan's vast, modernist stage – there was, in the Bastille amphitheatre of the Paris Opéra, a strong sense of toy-town, even before the toys came out to play. Yet the dream world, initiated erotically by Sachs's sexual approach to Eva in the church, was made up of what he knew, and of what his – and Wagner's – culture knew. A painting was transformed into Eva herself. Sachs's writing bureau, magnified, became the organ (Figure 19.3), as indeed the furniture generally offered another *Nutcracker*-like magnification and intensification for the *Wahn* of the second-act riot. Did the organ, resplendent as a nineteenth-century, Leipzig Gewandhaus-like invention of tradition, become Sachs's bureau, and thus nourish via tradition, in a proper sense, his creations, whether artistic or social? It was not either/or: this was a dialectical world, for composer,

Figure 19.3 Die Meistersinger (dir. Stefan Herheim, Salzburger Festspiele, 2013). Act 1, scene 1, with Hans Sachs's writing desk having expanded to become the interior of Nuremberg's Katharinenkirche

Photo © Salzburger Festspiele/Forster. Used by permission

director and intelligent audience. A bust of Wagner made its ambiguous, multivalent point, without undue exaggeration.

The Prelude over, and the curtain once again drawn back, the back of the writing desk became the church and indeed the municipal organ. The green of the surface became, crucially, the arena for contest, never more so than in the remarkable *agon* – intensified in Paris from Salzburg – between Walther and Beckmesser. In Paris there was to be heard in the person of Bo Skovhus an undeniably charismatic Beckmesser.[26] He had to fight for the Masters' support, they having been initially enraptured by Walther's song. They swayed, literally and metaphorically. Such seemed a contest as political as it was aesthetic, and we are of course very much in the realm of Walter Benjamin's aestheticization of politics, an idea which did not spring from nowhere but was very much rooted in ideas which, if not Wagner's as such, were similar and historically related.[27] All but the most historically ignorant of audience members would know, however regretfully, where such ideas might lead – and what role Nuremberg would come to play in them, just as Wieland did with his *Entrümpelung*. Dancing in concentric circles around Walther, even after Beckmesser's apparently successful intervention, the Masters – and, in front of them, the Apprentices – might yet have decided in either direction. They looked outwards, though, not at Walther but perhaps at the audience, in the hope that it too might play its part in the artistic production of self-reflection. It was anything but a benign scene, whatever the prettiness-on-steroids. The violence, more or less sublimated, when Sachs came close to striking Beckmesser caused visible, audible intakes of breath when I saw it.

Books featured heavily. In the first act *Des Knaben Wunderhorn* proved the (neo-)Romantic inspiration. Towering above the characters, a giant volume was opened to reveal, as such volumes often do, pressed flowers. They came to life as visual instantiations of David's tones: 'deeds of music made visible', one might say – as indeed did the composer to whom Cosima and Appia, Wieland Wagner and Boulez, and not least Herheim himself have all made their appeals.[28] In the second act it was the Brothers Grimm whose 'characters' came to life, inciting and participating in the *Prügelfuge*, that splendidly dialectical creation of dramatic chaos out of musical, fugal order, as if to remind us that 'fuga' means flight. There was madness, delusion, illusion – Wagnerian *Wahn* aplenty, however we translate that elusive, Schopenhauerian concept – in that dream of Sachs. By the third act Sachs's whole library was on offer: a clear offer of interpretative freedom, the director following Wagner as man of the theatre rather than a forbidding dispenser of rules (via his widow). And it was in this act that old Meister Wagner came visibly, not just audibly, on stage – *ersichtlich gewordene Taten der Musik* indeed.

All good, and bad, things must come to an end, however. The action began to unravel with Sachs's shocking refusal to shake Beckmesser's proffered hand. Beckmesser had been humiliated, bruised in every sense, and yet seemed willing to meet Sachs half way. Was Sachs actually, then, the proto-fascist that some, often unable to distinguish between two different German words for 'master', *Meister* and *Herr*, have claimed him to be? As the action froze, the unravelling proper gathered pace. There was yet another awakening: that of Beckmesser as *alter ego*. Who had dreamed whom? It was not Sachs who, for the final time, drew the curtain. Or was it? Beckmesser emerged for his curtain call – that strange, liminal zone both part of and yet beyond the performance 'itself' – in night dress, matching that of his antagonist. It was a move alert equally to the comedy and to the darkness at the heart of a work whose depths lie in precisely those matters *faux* 'traditionalists', from the Nazi period (or even further back) up to the present day, would ignore and preferably bury. The problem with such 'tradition' from a modernist standpoint is not that it is invented, for what is not? It is rather that it refuses to consent to the truth content, as Adorno might have put it, whether of Wagner's world, of our own, or of the

Modernist operatic culture

Figure 19.4 Die Meistersinger (dir. Herheim, Salzburger Festspiele, 2013). Act 2, scene 7: the *Prügelfuge*, with busts (left to right) of Goethe, Wagner and Beethoven at the front of the stage

Photo © Salzburger Festspiele/Forster. Used by permission

world in which both of those worlds, perhaps others too, collide, corrode, self-criticize: that of the artwork in performance.

Perhaps most telling on a structural level was the way in which Herheim's staging traced, or rather instigated, Sachs-like manipulation of *Wahn* – and doubtless *Wahn*'s manipulation of Sachs. Just as Walther, his song, and Nuremberg's public are guided, so too were Sachs's dream and Sachs's reality – not least by the score. Yes, there were proto-fascist undertones there for those wishing to find them, as suggested by the chilling lighting of a semi-crazed Sachs during his final peroration. The glow worm who could not find its mate, to whom Sachs would refer in the following act, could be seen in the mêlée of the *Prügelfuge* (Figure 19.4) desperately – graphically – trying to find a replacement. This was no world of idealized Romantic or even sexual love; it was clear-eyed, brutal as Schopenhauer's Will itself. And so the creation of the third act, Wagner's and Sachs's, both broke with and incorporated what had gone before, like the Prize Song itself. Opera took more than a few steps towards music drama, perhaps even towards a reimagined form of music theatre.

David Bösch: the violence of reconstruction

David Bösch's staging for the Bavarian State Opera, with designs by Patrick Bannwart and Meentje Nielsen, was first seen in 2016. It proved far more than a vehicle for Jonas Kaufmann as Walther, although that was not unreasonably an attraction for much of the audience, just as was Kirill Petrenko's conducting. If less all-encompassing than Herheim's staging – much German theatre since the Second World War, and not just its most post-dramatic reaches, has understandably recoiled from neo-Hegelian claims to 'totality' – it intrigued by virtue of an unusually feminist standpoint, criticizing and revivifying the work in a different but no less valid fashion. To look more closely at Eva's standpoint and her treatment is something staging and scholarship alike might usefully, fruitfully attend to. No more than Romanticism or most other 'isms' does modernism gain a feminist pass, although it may well offer us some potentially useful critical tools (as well as the contrary). Eva Rieger's observations that 'so little has been written about Eva Pogner', and that what has been written tends to correspond 'to all the stereotypes of the traditional bourgeois woman', offers a critical challenge that did not go unheeded here, whether consciously or otherwise.[29] Bösch's staging also arguably offered one of the most intriguing treatments yet – I shall not say a 'solution', for surely there is none – to the perennial 'Beckmesser problem': how to justify, or to deal with, the undeniable cruelty to this Malvolio figure, who may or may not be a victim of sublimated anti-Semitism.

Bösch took his audience to the 1950s: an interesting move for a work concerned with reconstruction, set in a city which, more than most, has had to be concerned with reconstruction. The relationship between provincialism and post-war reconstructionalism was to be explored here. (Lest we forget, 1955 was the year in which the West German Army was (re)founded, denying its origins in what had gone before.) 'They say Bach, [but] mean Telemann', as Adorno unforgettably put it.[30] For there is nastiness as well as homeliness in provincialism; Bösch drew out the former, in a useful corrective to the norm. What might initially have seemed an almost philistine nostalgia for the period and its 'popular culture' – similarly in Bösch's Munich staging of L'Orfeo, to take us back to where we began – was revealed to be far more complicated than that, that slight sense of nostalgia more a way of drawing in the audience member only to confound him or her. For one thing, what does 'popular culture' mean? That problem lies at the heart of the opera, at the heart of relationships between the Masters and the populace and of Sachs's suggestion that the rules be tested. Such has arguably become still more so, given the rise of what some of us are old-fashioned enough still to regard, with Adorno et al., as the Culture Industry. If resistance is to come, it will be more likely to come from Helmut Lachenmann than from the world of commercial music, successfully masquerading as 'of the people'. And so, when microphones and various other paraphernalia of the recording industry – 'Classical' in the deadly marketing-speak of that world, then as well as in the twenty-first century – were put in place, we sensed an act of domination over our 'administered' world and lives.

Although the Personenregie of Bösch's staging was detailed throughout, it was only really – as in the work itself – towards the end of the third scene, in the Singschule, that things came closer into conceptual focus. As befits the modern, administered state, the means by which this was accomplished was violence – violence that implicitly criticized and yet perhaps also helped salvage the darker provincialism of the work. David had already come across as a vainer, indeed more interesting character than usual, with the strong implication that his penchant for small-scale violent behaviour was owed in part not only to provincialism but also to his inability to be a true creator. (The two of course may well be related.) Walther had tried to defend David when the apprentices, at the beginning of the scene, attacked him, but he would have none of it: outsiders were not to be welcomed. Would David prove to be a second Beckmesser? That remained to be seen; for it was the first Beckmesser who provided the shock – literally.

The electric shocks administered by the Marker to Walther, forcibly restrained in his chair, were the work of what Gudrun Ensslin would soon call the Auschwitz generation. As Ensslin would continue, there could be no arguing with them – something that came across strongly in Bösch's production despite, or perhaps because of, Beckmesser's – and Pogner's – relative attractiveness (relative to how we usually see them, and indeed to the definitely older-school Kothner). Who, after all, had not occasionally found something of attraction in the discipline of fascism, especially when emboldened, as there, by readily available bottles of Meisterbräu? The guilds had never been as stable as nostalgia suggested – that was surely part of Wagner's meaning here – and Bösch was merely bringing already existing divisions to the foreground. Indeed, it seemed no mere accident that some Masters looked (costumes are crucial here) and acted with greater modernity, or at least closer to the dictates of fashion than others. If the Guild were keeping things together – and such was the crux of nineteenth-century Romantic and Hegelian

Modernist operatic culture

defences in the face of liberal attacks upon them – then it was not clear whether it would succeed for much longer. 'Reconstruction' has a tendency to incite – as any Stolzing, Ensslin or, indeed, Lachenmann would tell you. Consider the latter's open letter to Hans Werner Henze, during their angry confrontation over the claims of modernism. Lachenmann definitely takes the 'Wagner' role here, quoting from a lecture he had given the previous year:

> that outbreak of the muzzled subject into a new emotional immediacy will be untrue, and degenerate into self-deception, wherever the fat and comfortable composer, perhaps slightly scarred structurally and therefore the more likely to complain, sets up house again in the old junk-room of available emotions. The temptation to do this is great, and the impression cannot simply be dismissed out of hand that after so much lamentable stagnation, the recent teeming abundance of powerfully emotional music exists thanks to the degenerate fruitfulness of maggots having a good time on the fat of the tonal cadaver.[31]

Sachs's van – 'Sachs' read the neon, definitely not of a Fifth Avenue variety – captured our attention at the beginning of the second act. The *mise-en-scène* was clearly of a grimmer 1950s: a product in part, presumably, of the cost of war. But this, one felt, had never been a suburb of joy. It was not the Munich we see in the second *Heimat* of Edgar Reitz, teeming with modernist life; nor was it the Nuremberg the tourist would see. In its reassertion, Beckmesser's virtuosity came to the fore. He was not a fraud, unimaginative though he may have been; he had craft if not art, to employ a (neo-)Romantic formulation. He was, moreover, certainly no mere figure of fun. His *piccolo* guitar to Walther's full-size version invited a number of reflections. And yet his song worked, in its way: perhaps of another age, another age that perhaps never was. But such is – and was – reconstruction. Anti-modernism, then, was granted its voice, even its dignity.

The violence of the *Prügelfuge*'s staging eclipsed any I have seen. David's deeds with baseball bat marked him out as every inch the neo-fascist, to be greeted with open arms by Pegida or its predecessors. At its close, the Night Watchman (in modern policeman's garb) was dealt with by the remaining small gang of young townsfolk. They took him back to his car and sent him on his way, but it was clear that he had no choice; this was *their* manor. Crossing themselves beforehand, they had mimicked the (deliberately?) incongruous religious procession at the opening: they knew how to use traditional forms, visual and musical, when it served their purpose. The final punishment beating took place as the curtain – and one of the thugs' baseball bats – fell.

The final *Festwiese* scene posed questions of the work very different from those in Herheim's staging. Who owned the guild or at least its 'products', symbolic of that ever-present, ever-powerful, even omnipotent Culture Industry? A corporation, albeit in the modern rather than the archaic sense: 'Pognervision'. The early televisual variety show we saw might initially have seemed 'popular' but, as with most of what loudly proclaims itself to be 'of the people', it was deeply – and indeed shallowly – manipulative. Falko Herold's video work provided 'titles' for each Master ('individual', or styled to be corporate?) as he came on stage, just 'like on the television'. (Adorno would have had something to say about that.) There was something for all the family – within strict limits. David and a troupe of camp dancers suggested the reality of 'deviance', which might be tolerated as a 'harmless' joke, yet would certainly be rejected if it were to offer any serious attack to patriarchy. In any case, David was not in on the joke and was once again humiliated, a proto-Beckmesser: violence bred violence. When compelled ('peer pressure') to drink too many shots in order to prove his real 'masculinity', he fell paralytic, unable to perform his social and sexual functions.

The cruelty meted out to Beckmesser would be even worse. However, we were reminded that he wished essentially to buy Eva, a fully fledged bartered bride. Indeed, he made very clear his desire to possess her, even against her will. Bedecked in gaudy 'variety' gold, anything but comfortable, he had been set up to fail. 'Entertainment' was, as a game show host might have put it, the name of the game; more broadly, the audience was reminded of the cruelty of a work in which the comedy, in the common sense at least, pertains to characters laughing at another – comedy at which we should feel uncomfortable. Eva, who had learned a great deal during the course of the work, was increasingly disgusted by what she saw. When she thought that Sachs had fallen in with her father's plan to sell her off – this 'show', with related 'philanthropy', never forgot its roots in the commercialism Wagner claimed so to abhor – she could not bear to look at him any more. While the crowd, manipulated by the 'event', sang his praises, not only did she turn away; from her balcony she cast the contents of her glass in his direction. No one noticed on stage, but the audience did. If, to quote Rieger, 'German musicologists still condescendingly use the diminutive "Evchen" as if they identified themselves with Sachs', Bösch – and, in some sense, the material of Wagner's drama – redirected us so as to rectify his and the male guild's disinclination to 'take her particularly seriously'.[32]

Yet otherwise, Sachs remained wiser than most, realizing that all had gone awry at the moment when most – whether on stage or in the typical audience – complacently believe that it has been resolved. He remained deeply troubled rather than triumphant. Then Beckmesser returned, desperately trying to shoot dead the presumed author of his misfortunes, yet falling before being able to carry that out. Things never worked out as 'intended', then, whether for Beckmesser, for 'reconstruction', or for attempts to 'protect' Wagner's works from the implications of his own standpoint and from the unavoidable – even should one wish to avoid it – path of historical reception.

David McVicar: anti-modernism and entertainment

And so, to consider, more briefly, largely for the sake of contrast, a staging that could not really be considered as partaking of the modernist operatic culture we have been considering, and might even be thought of as anti-modernist. Enter David McVicar, latterly a darling of operatic reactionaries online, such as the notorious 'Against Modern Opera Productions' Facebook group and its harder-line German sister-group, 'Gegen Regietheater in der Oper'.[33] McVicar had earlier presented himself as offering a 'third way' – in what, perhaps not entirely coincidentally, had been the era of New Labour – between so-called *Regietheater* and backward-looking musico-theatrical inertia. His work had indeed seemed to be just that: a keen sense of theatre allied to a visual aesthetic generally acceptable to even such timid opera audiences as those of London's Royal Opera House and New York's Metropolitan Opera. Latterly, though, he has adopted an explicitly anti-modernist stance, veering close to the overblown vulgarity of the later Franco Zeffirelli or the determinedly 'anti-interpretative' kitsch of the Vienna State Opera's house favourite, Otto Schenk. (Schenk's *Meistersinger* remains in the Met's repertoire, a bold attempt to have a reworking of Herheim's staging replace it having been safely seen off by the house's patrons.)

A fawning interview with McVicar in 2009 in *The Independent* seems both to have reflected and perhaps even to have heralded some part of that transformation. Having admired the director's biceps, the journalist interviewing him gushed: 'Actually, he [McVicar] laughs quite a lot,' continuing:

> One of the things he laughs at (but not in a good way) is the way operas can be produced in Germany. 'There'll be combat physiques,' he says, 'and balaclava helmets, and

Modernist operatic culture

machine guns, and there'll be neon strip-lighting, and everything will be antiseptic and everyone will over-react madly and the audience will sit there, taking it all incredibly seriously, and I'll be sitting there stuffing my fist in my mouth, because I'm trying so hard not to laugh.'[34]

So far, so unamusingly caricatured, especially coming from one who, in several earlier productions, had taken care to deal with history, reception and indeed other conceptual, critical matters, albeit in a relatively unthreatening way for conservative or reactionary audiences. The Teutonophobia, which seems perhaps more a reflection of anti-modernism than actual xenophobia, becomes sharper with the following:

> What he hates most of all is a 'concept' ('das Koncept' [sic] he says in a forbidding German accent), anything that sticks a work of art in a straitjacket and tries to 'tie up the ends'. 'Art,' he says, 'comes from a much more instinctive, intuitive place.'[35]

Thus we return to the realm of the allegedly unmediated.

And yet it seemed, at least to start with, as though there might actually prove to be some kind of *Konzept* to McVicar's Glyndebourne staging, first seen in 2011. The action certainly did not take place in sixteenth-century Nuremberg, idealized or otherwise, but rather in the earlier nineteenth century, presumably at around the time Wagner was growing up. There are many things to be said for such an idea, looking at influences upon the young Wagner that helped shape his worldview (from a more hostile standpoint, his ideology). It would not have been so very distant from what Herheim was doing at more or less the same time in Salzburg and Paris. For instance, German guilds and corporations came under concerted post-Enlightenment attack at this time; Hegel, generally supportive of the Prussian reform movement, opposed the removal of their monopolies as an attack on partial association, on civil society.[36] The guild in Nuremberg, then, might well be portrayed as under attack; such is surely in part the meaning of Walther's intrusion, a typical Wagnerian move of introducing a charismatic leader to a society from without – a move which might itself be subjected to criticism.

There was, unfortunately, no evident attempt to do any such thing with the updating. It was difficult to rid oneself of the suspicion that the principal point, or at least principal result, of the updating was simply to present an audience uninclined to criticism, whether of artworks or itself, with a host of 'pretty' designs. The Culture Industry, one might say, was offering more of the same through carefully 'curated' variety. Vicki Mortimer's handsome designs might have done so much more, just as those Heike Scheele and Gesine Völlm most certainly did for Herheim, yet they were granted no opportunity to do so.

Drama, moreover, was determinedly reduced to mere 'entertainment'. There is, of course, nothing wrong with art being entertaining; it would often be failing, in some sense, if it were not. However, McVicar's playing to the gallery – not in a metatheatrical sense, imitating or leading Wagner's dialectical relationship between Masters and people – became wearying. 'Amusing' interpolations, which served little or no dramatic purpose other than to make those who have partaken of a few too many glasses of champagne erupt into apparently helpless laughter, were too often the order of the day. Downright silly, seemingly quite irrelevant dances, especially painful at the opening of the second act, seemed present more to give the choreographer something to do than to make any dramatic point. Perhaps most bizarrely of all, Beckmesser became a preening figure of high camp. Unlike, say, the intrusions of carefully manufactured camp into Bösch's staging, there was no obvious (or even less obvious) reason for this other than to make certain of those audience members once again laugh uproariously. It was uncomfortable, though, for anyone who might be concerned with the cruelty inflicted upon that most problematic of characters. Doubtless that was not the intention, but such is perhaps one of the problems with an anti-critical stance that 'simply' wishes to 'entertain'.

In modernist conclusion: to Beckett, Stockhausen and beyond

A dramatist such as Beckett could never justly have been accused of that. And yet he was notoriously no fan of 'alternative' or, as we might say, critical approaches to the staging of his dramas. Indeed, the Beckett estate adamantly pursues a policy of mortmain. So there is certainly an alternative modernism, or at least a stance taken by those we should consider modernists in their creative work, one which insists ever more strongly upon the letter. (Perhaps we might call it Stravinskyan, given that composer's notorious, if personally inconsistent, disdain for interpretation.) Beckett seems to have felt similarly when it came to opera, despising Chéreau's staging of Berg's *Lulu* for its three-act premiere under Boulez. As Duncan Scott related:

> He had been very upset by Patrice Chéreau's design for Berg's *Lulu* in Paris [actually Richard Peduzzi's]. He said he couldn't understand how Boulez could 'let somebody fuck such an opera about' except that Boulez and Chéreau were 'cronies'. A water-closet on the set particularly upset him. He called it a 'Lulu loo'.[37]

A stress on the performative, or at least the interpretative, such as I have offered may lay itself open to the charge of having missed the modernist point. And yet I do not think it does so completely. There has always been tension between 'creators' of artworks and those who would perform, criticize, interrogate them. What I have wished to show is that the more strongly critical approach of an operatic culture we might consider modernist has been one of its most important and interesting developments – not that it has been its only one, nor that it has not been challenged, even from 'within'.

For modernism retains, even at this late – some might say too late – juncture, some hope, however despairing, of the emancipatory, especially when considered in contrast to the conservative-reactionary and to the postmodern. It retains something of a post-Romantic appreciation of the crucial importance of structure, while pouring new wine into new and old bottles alike (with apologies to Liszt). That holds even in the case of Adorno, for the practice and theory of relentless criticism without hope – it is never quite so straightforward as that, as Adorno's discovery of a sliver of hope even in *Tristan* would suggest – remains predicated upon the emancipatory.[38] That is, one cannot dash hope where hope does not or cannot exist; the idea of an administered society makes no sense without an alternative. Postmodernism, by contrast, tends to mock any idea of truth content, of emancipation. Thus, in our particular operatic world, a staging in which criticism is predicated upon, say, revolutionary transformation, however hopeless a prospect that might seem, however tragic the denouement, may be distinguished from one in which it is all a bit of a game and nothing should be taken too seriously. We might actually, tentatively, reinstate *a* distinction, although certainly not mutual exclusion, between 'art' and 'entertainment'.

Part of that battle, and one of the principal reasons I have chosen to look at responses to Wagner, lies in a critical determination to take seriously the claims of music to be – not simply to enhance, let alone to prettify – drama. By the same token, part of that battle is to continue to engage critically with artworks from the past, to refuse to let the museum door close behind us. It is no coincidence, I think, that those tendencies and some of the others considered above have been prevalent in an age haunted by the coming, in the 1960s and 1970s, of music theatre as a critical alternative to 'opera' – as, indeed, Wagnerian 'music drama' had been a century earlier.

Modernist operatic culture

I am far from suggesting that we should elide music theatre and *Regietheater* (for want of a better term). They denote broadly different, although not mutually exclusive, things. However, it may well be worth considering the latter, as it emerged from roughly the 1970s onwards, as part of an operatic response to the former; it may even be worth considering the former as part of a response to earlier twentieth-century manifestations of the latter. At any rate, further consideration of the dialectical relationship between the two would be valuable. Operas such as Stockhausen's *Licht* works – and we seem to call them operas – incorporate a good deal of the music-theatre approach. One might think, for instance, of the trombonist's seduction, provocation, serenade, whatever it may be, in *Mittwoch*'s 'Michaelion', of Luzicamel, Bactrian 'emanation' of Lucifer. Given the paucity of performances, we have not yet reached the stage of a *Regietheater* reassessment or deconstruction of Stockhausen, estimable though Graham Vick's Birmingham Opera 2012 staging and indeed all aspects of that *Mittwoch* performance were. It will come, though – and it would not be entirely surprising to see it resisted by the keepers of the Stockhausen flame, following in the footsteps of the Beckett Estate or indeed Cosima Wagner. A Wieland, however, will most likely come thereafter, or maybe she or he is already here, awaiting a 2019 'semi-staged' performance – no longer, alas, the initially promised *intégrale* – in Amsterdam.

Who knows? The future is ours, but it is not for us to know, or we should be doing it now. One may or may not be able to make some better sense of *Licht* via, for instance, *Originale*; however, one certainly could not predict the former from the latter. As Marx put it, declining to play the utopian parlour game of outlining the nature of communist society, he was not in the business of 'writing receipts (Comtist ones?) for the cook-shops of the future'.[39] Such is perhaps as close to a modernist lesson, even a modernist truth, as we shall come. Alternatively, as a modernist composer once asked:

> New German opera houses certainly look very modern – from the outside; on the inside, they have remained extremely old-fashioned. To a theatre in which mostly repertoire pieces are performed one can only with the greatest difficulty bring a modern opera – it is unthinkable. The most expensive solution would be to blow the opera houses into the air. But do you not think that that might also be the most elegant solution?[40]

Notes

1 Richard Wagner, *Oper und Drama*, ed. Klaus Kropfinger (Stuttgart: Reclam, 1994), 215. For a recent, revealing treatment of this idea, see Christian von Goldbeck, 'Wagner's Emotional Understanding: A Critical Appraisal of the Concept of Leitmotiv' (DPhil thesis, University of Oxford, 2016).

2 'And from Apollo's home came Orpheus, the lauded lyrist, king of song' (Pythian IV, lines 175–77); *Pindar's Odes*, trans. and ed. Roy Arthur Swanson (Indianapolis: Bobbs-Merrill, 1974), 89. Pindar's scholiast (writer of marginalia) cites authorities for Apollo as father, and notes the (deliberate?) ambiguity in the Greek text.

3 Erling E. Guldbrandsen and Julian Johnson, introduction to *Transformations of Musical Modernism*, ed. Guldbrandsen and Johnson (Cambridge: Cambridge University Press, 2015), 1–2.

4 Ibid., 2.

5 Isaiah Berlin, 'The Counter-Enlightenment', in *Against the Current: Essays in the History of Ideas*, ed. Henry Hardy (London: Hogarth, 1979), 1–24.

6 Jacques Derrida, *Spectres de Marx: L'état de la dette, le travail du deuil et la nouvelle Internationale* (Paris: Galilée, 1993).

7 Richard Wagner, *My Life*, trans. Andrew Gray and ed. Mary Whittall (Cambridge: Cambridge University Press, 1983), 338.

8 Ibid.

9   On Adorno and the 'Happy End', see Theodor Wiesengrund Adorno, *Versuch über Wagner* (Frankfurt: Suhrkamp, 1981); also Mark Berry, 'Adorno's *Essay on Wagner*: Rescuing an Inverted Panegyric', *Opera Quarterly* 30, nos. 2–3 (2014), 217.

10 See Jean-Jacques Nattiez, *Tétralogies – Wagner, Boulez, Chéreau: Essai sur l'infidélité* (Paris: Christian Bourgois, 1983).

11 Patrick Carnegy, *Wagner and the Art of the Theatre* (New Haven, CT: Yale University Press, 2006), 149.

12 Natka Bianchini, 'Bare Interiors, Chicken Wire Cages and Subway Stations – Re-thinking Beckett's Response to the ART *Endgame* in Light of Earlier Productions', in *Samuel Beckett's 'Endgame'*, ed. Mark S. Byron (Amsterdam and New York: Rodopi, 2007), 136.

13 Ibid., 121–22.

14 Carnegy, *Wagner and the Art of the Theatre*, 149.

15 John Deathridge, 'A Brief History of Wagner Research', in *Wagner Handbook*, ed. Ulrich Müller, Peter Wapnewski and John Deathridge (Cambridge, MA: Harvard University Press, 1992), 217.

16 In *After Wagner: Histories of Modernist Music Drama from 'Parsifal' to Nono* (Woodbridge and Rochester, NY: Boydell & Brewer and University of Rochester Press, 2014), I devoted chapter 7 to Stefan Herheim's Bayreuth staging of *Parsifal* (2008–12) and chapter 8 to stagings of *Lohengrin*.

17 Pierre Boulez, *Conversations with Célestin Deliège* (London: Eulenburg, 1976), 32. Translation slightly modified.

18 Carnegy, *Wagner and the Art of the Theatre*, 148.

19 Quoted in ibid., 180.

20 Pierre Boulez, 'The Vestal Virgin and the Fire-Stealer: Memory, Creation and Authenticity', trans. Susan Bradshaw, *Early Music* 18 (1990), 356.

21 Friedrich Meinecke, *Die deutsche Katastrophe: Betrachtungen und Erinnerungen* (Wiesbaden: Brackhaus, 1946).

22 Friedrich Nietzsche, 'Der Fall Wagner', in *Sämtliche Werke: Kritische Studienausgabe*, ed. Giorgio Colli and Mazzino Montinari (Berlin and New York: De Gruyter, 1987–88), 6: 29.

23 Jean Vermeil, *Conversations with Boulez: Thoughts on Conducting*, trans. Camille Naish (Portland, OR: Amadeus, 1996), 79; Theodor Wiesengrund Adorno, 'Bach gegen seine Liebhaber verteidigt', in *Gesammelte Schriften*, ed. Rolf Tiedmann and Gretel Adorno (Frankfurt: Suhrkamp, 1971–86), 10: 151.

24 Richard Wagner, 'Was ist deutsch?' in *Sämtliche Schriften und Dichtungen*, ed. Richard Sternfeld and Hans von Wolzogen (Leipzig: Breitkopf & Härtel, 1912–14), 10: 65.

25 Karl Marx and Friedrich Engels, *The German Ideology, Including Theses on Feuerbach and Introduction to the Critique of Political Economy* (Amherst, NY: Prometheus, 1998), 53.

26 That, rather than spurious, unearned dignity, is perhaps the best way to have a character now, rightly or wrongly, seen as problematical, taken seriously. For a summary of some of the issues, see Hans Rudolf Vaget, '"Du warst mein Freund von je": The Beckmesser Controversy Revisited', in *Wagner's 'Meistersinger': Performance, History, Representation*, ed. Nicholas Vazsonyi (Woodbridge and Rochester, NY: Boydell & Brewer and University of Rochester Press, 2003), 190–208.

27 See Ansgar Hillach, 'The Aesthetics of Politics: Walter Benjamin's "Theories of German Fascism"', trans. Jerold Wikoff and Ulf Zimmermann, *New German Critique* 17 (1979), 99–119.

28 Wagner, 'Über die Benennung, "Musikdrama"', in *Sämtliche Schriften*, 9: 306.

29 Eva Rieger, '"I Married Eva": Gender Construction and *Die Meistersinger*', trans. Nicholas Vazsonyi, in *Wagner's 'Meistersinger'*, ed. Vazsonyi, 209.

30 Adorno, 'Bach gegen seine Liebhaber verteidigt', 150.

31 Helmut Lachenmann, 'Open Letter to Hans Werner Henze', trans. Jeffrey Stadelman, *Perspectives of New Music* 35, no. 2 (1997), 191.

32 Rieger, 'I Married Eva', 210.

33 For a brief placing of such groups' ideology within broader cultural and political milieux, not least that of National Socialism, see my review of Bernd Weikl's *Swastikas on Stage: Trends in the Productions of Richard Wagner's Operas in German Theaters Today*, trans. Susan Salms-Moss (Berlin: Pro-Business, 2015), in *Wagner Journal* 10, no. 22 (2016), 78–82.

34 Christina Patterson, 'David McVicar: "I'm good because I care so much"', *The Independent*, 10 September 2009, http://www.independent.co.uk/arts-entertainment/interviews/david-mcvicar-im-good-because-i-care-so-much-1784901.html.

35 Ibid.

36 Georg Friedrich Wilhelm Hegel, *Elements of the Philosophy of Right*, trans. H. B. Nisbet and ed. Allen W. Wood (Cambridge: Cambridge University Press, 1991), 273 (§255).

Modernist operatic culture

37 Quoted in *Beckett Remembering/Remembering Beckett: Uncollected Interviews with Samuel Beckett and Memories of Those Who Knew Him*, ed. Elizabeth Knowlson and James Knowlson (London: Bloomsbury, 2006), 215.
38 Adorno, *Versuch über Wagner*, 143.
39 Karl Marx, *Capital: A Critical Analysis of Capitalist Production*, part II, vol. 9 of *Karl Marx – Friedrich Engels Gesamtausgabe* (Berlin: Dietz, 1990), 22.
40 Felix Schmidt and Jürgen Hohmeyer, '"Sprengt die Opernhäuser in die Luft!"': *Spiegel*-Gespräch mit dem französischen Komponisten und Dirigenten Pierre Boulez', *Der Spiegel*, 25 September 1967, 172.

Bibliography

Adorno, Theodor Wiesengrund. 'Bach gegen seine Liebhaber verteidigt'. In *Gesammelte Schriften*, edited by Rolf Tiedemann and Gretel Adorno, 10: 138–51. Frankfurt: Suhrkamp, 1977.

———. *Versuch über Wagner*. Frankfurt: Suhrkamp, 1981.

Berlin, Isaiah. 'The Counter-Enlightenment'. In *Against the Current: Essays in the History of Ideas*, edited by Henry Hardy, 1–24. London: Hogarth, 1979.

Berry, Mark. 'Adorno's *Essay on Wagner*: Rescuing an Inverted Panegyric'. *Opera Quarterly* 30, nos. 2–3 (2014): 205–27.

———. *After Wagner: Histories of Modernist Music Drama from 'Parsifal' to Nono*. Woodbridge and Rochester, NY: Boydell & Brewer/University of Rochester Press, 2014.

———. Review of *Swastikas on Stage: Trends in the Productions of Richard Wagner's Operas in German Theaters Today*, by Bernd Weikl. *Wagner Journal* 10, no. 2 (2016): 78–82.

Bianchini, Natka. 'Bare Interiors, Chicken Wire Cages and Subway Stations – Re-thinking Beckett's Response to the ART *Endgame* in Light of Earlier Productions'. In *Samuel Beckett's 'Endgame'*, edited by Mark S. Byron, 121–43. Amsterdam and New York: Rodopi, 2007.

Boulez, Pierre. *Conversations with Célestin Deliège*. With an introduction by Robert Wangermée. London: Eulenburg, 1976.

———. 'The Vestal Virgin and the Fire-Stealer: Memory, Creation and Authenticity', translated by Susan Bradshaw. *Early Music* 18 (1990): 355–58.

Carnegy, Patrick. *Wagner and the Art of the Theatre*. New Haven, CT: Yale University Press, 2006.

Deathridge, John. 'A Brief History of Wagner Research'. In *Wagner Handbook*, edited by Ulrich Müller and Peter Wapnewski, with English translation edited by John Deathridge, 202–23. Cambridge, MA: Harvard University Press, 1992.

Derrida, Jacques. *Spectres de Marx: L'état de la dette, le travail du deuil et la nouvelle Internationale*. Paris: Galilée, 1993.

Goldbeck, Christian von. 'Wagner's Emotional Understanding: A Critical Appraisal of the Concept of Leitmotiv'. DPhil thesis, University of Oxford, 2016.

Guldbrandsen, Erling E., and Julian Johnson, eds. *Transformations of Musical Modernism*. Cambridge: Cambridge University Press, 2015.

Hegel, Georg Friedrich Wilhelm. *Elements of the Philosophy of Right*. Edited by Allen W. Wood. Translated by H. B. Nisbet. Cambridge: Cambridge University Press, 1991.

Hillach, Ansgar. 'The Aesthetics of Politics: Walter Benjamin's "Theories of German Fascism"', translated by Jerold Wikoff and Ulf Zimmermann. *New German Critique* 17 (1979): 99–119.

Knowlson, Elizabeth, and James Knowlson, eds. *Beckett Remembering/Remembering Beckett: Uncollected Interviews with Samuel Beckett and Memories of Those Who Knew Him*. London: Bloomsbury, 2006.

Lachenmann, Helmut. 'Open Letter to Hans Werner Henze', translated by Jeffrey Stadelman. *Perspectives of New Music* 35, no. 2 (1997): 189–200.

Marx, Karl. *Capital: A Critical Analysis of Capitalist Production*. Part II. Vol. 9 of *Karl Marx – Friedrich Engels Gesamtausgabe*. Berlin: Dietz, 1990.

Marx, Karl, and Friedrich Engels. *The German Ideology, Including Theses on Feuerbach and Introduction to the Critique of Political Economy*. Amherst, NY: Prometheus Books, 1998.

Meinecke, Friedrich. *Die deutsche Katastrophe: Betrachtungen und Erinnerungen*. Wiesbaden: Brackhaus, 1946.

Nattiez, Jean-Jacques. *Tétralogies – Wagner, Boulez, Chéreau: Essai sur l'infidélité*. Paris: Christian Bourgois, 1983.

Nietzsche, Friedrich. 'Der Fall Wagner'. In *Sämtliche Werke: Kritische Studienausgabe*, edited by Giorgio Colli and Mazzino Montinari 6: 9–53. Berlin and New York: De Gruyter, 1987–88.

Patterson, Christina. 'David McVicar: "I'm Good Because I Care So Much"' (interview). *The Independent*, 10 September 2009. http://www.independent.co.uk/arts-entertainment/interviews/david-mcvicar-im-good-because-i-care-so-much-1784901.html.

Rieger, Eva. '"I Married Eva": Gender Construction and *Die Meistersinger*', translated by Nicholas Vazsonyi. In *Wagner's 'Meistersinger'*, edited by Vazsonyi, 209–25.

Schmidt, Felix, and Jürgen Hohmeyer, '"Sprengt die Opernhäuser in die Luft! *Spiegel*-Gespräch mit dem französischen Komponisten und Dirigenten Pierre Boulez'. *Der Spiegel*, 25 September 1967, 166–74.

Swanson, Roy Arthur, trans. and ed. *Pindar's Odes*. Indianapolis: Bobbs-Merrill, 1974.

Vaget, Hans Rudolf. '"Du warst mein Freund von je": The Beckmesser Controversy Revisited'. In *Wagner's 'Meistersinger'*, edited by Vazsonyi, 190–208.

Vazsonyi, Nicholas, ed. *Wagner's 'Meistersinger': Performance, History, Representation*. Woodbridge and Rochester, NY: Boydell & Brewer/University of Rochester Press, 2003.

Vermeil, Jean. *Conversations with Boulez: Thoughts on Conducting*. Translated by Camille Naish. Portland, OR: Amadeus, 1996.

Wagner, Richard. 'Über die Benennung, "Musikdrama"'. In *Sämtliche Schriften und Dichtungen*, edited by Richard Sternfeld and Hans von Wolzogen, 9: 302–7. Leipzig: Breitkopf & Härtel, 1912–14.

———. 'Was ist deutsch?' In *Sämtliche Schriften und Dichtungen*, edited by Richard Sternfeld and Hans von Wolzogen, 10: 36–53. Leipzig: Breitkopf & Härtel, 1912–14.

———. *My Life*. Translated by Andrew Gray. Edited by Mary Whittall. Cambridge: Cambridge University Press, 1983.

———. *Oper und Drama*. Edited by Klaus Kropfinger. Stuttgart: Reclam, 1994.

Weikl, Bernd. *Swastikas on Stage: Trends in the Productions of Richard Wagner's Operas in German Theaters Today*. Translated by Susan Salms-Moss. Berlin: Pro-Business, 2015.

20

THE MODERNISM OF THE MAINSTREAM

An early twentieth-century ideology of violin playing

Stefan Knapik

Since the late 1980s Richard Taruskin has repeatedly attacked what he regards as the positivistic and dehumanizing ideology of the Early Music movement, contrasting it, whether explicitly or implicitly, with the subjectivist ideology of interpretation that characterizes discourses of 'mainstream' performance.[1] Whereas 'interpretation' implies a high degree of creative autonomy on the part of the performer, the 'authenticity' movement's faith in historical evidence suggests that its practices are to a large extent prefigured prior to the act of performance, based on 'objective' evidence of how performers played around the time of a work's composition. This chapter, however, will demonstrate that interpretation and authenticity are ideologies arising from similar aesthetic trajectories, both of which are rooted in modernism: at least from an ideological perspective, 'mainstream' classical performance can be as dogmatic and prescriptive as the Early Music movement in its approach; and conversely the Early Music movement has given rise to instances of creativity the like of which it would be hard to imagine having arisen in mainstream cultures of performance. The ideals and practices of the Early Music movement have received extensive cultural contextualization at the hands of Taruskin, John Butt and Laurence Dreyfus; less so the practices of earlier, mainstream performance, however. In this chapter I aim to show how certain modernist ideals gave rise to concrete aims and solutions to the challenges of performance in the early twentieth century.

I argue here that, while high-art interpretation purports to champion individualized performance choices, it is not a matter of untrammelled self-expression but rather of a self-conscious prefiguring of the performing subject. Such an ideology of subjectivity stems from the same modernist aesthetic that Taruskin believes to underpin the Early Music's movement's suppression of free engagement between present-day performers and the past. I draw here on the work of John Butt to indicate that modernism did not so much reject the past as attempt to articulate the subject's relationship with it. Moreover, it is this acute yet uneasy awareness of the past that produces an anxious attempt to preserve the present vitality of the living performer. I thus aim to overturn the dichotomy of Early Music/modernism and mainstream/vitalism, as well as Taruskin's assumption that modernism made a belated appearance in the field of classical performance. Indeed, the iconic discourses and artworks associated with modernism arguably have more in common than is often supposed with the performance discourses that emerged chronologically alongside them.

Stefan Knapik

My focus in this chapter is on texts relating to string playing, including not only those of central figures in late nineteenth- and early twentieth-century high-art performance, such as Joseph Joachim (1831–1907), Leopold Auer (1845–1930) and Carl Flesch (1873–1944), but also those of the American librettist and writer Frederick Martens (1874–1932) and the Polish violinist Bronisław Huberman (1882–1947). Drawing on Andrew Bowie's work on Nietzsche, and Laurence Dreyfus's work on the interpretation metaphor, I identify the early twentieth-century penchant for a strong model of artistic vitality, one that is nonetheless limited in its engagement with both wider society and the past, and highlight the incorporation of that model into texts that largely eschew an engagement with the past even as they show an awareness of it. I show the way in which texts by Auer, Huberman and Martens, reflecting Nietzschean and wider modernist tendencies towards elitism, transcend the generic classifications of pedagogical treatise and biography to posit a model of greatness in violin playing to which students are expected to aspire.

The kind of performance gestures that emerged under the banner of the Early Music movement sounded novel, of course, against the background of mainstream classical performance. But my aim here is to show that mainstream classical performance style is not a stable norm, let alone a timeless one, but rather a culturally contingent phenomenon. I show that the abstract ideal of artistic vitality gains material form when writers equate it with the older, Romantic ideal of endless melody. These writers are more afraid, however, of threats to vitality, which – in keeping with contemporaneous cultural mores, and reflecting a modernist preoccupation with disease – include the dangers of nervous exhaustion, and of the physiological and moral ills that cause it. In previous work I have shown that such anxieties shape approaches to vibrato, portamento and dynamics.[2] Here I show that they also underpin writers' concerns over performers' general lifestyles and practice regimens, which in turn prompt the suggestion of both preventative and curative remedies for nervous exhaustion.

History and the living performer

Within musicology, a field of study previously dominated by composers and musical works, the ideals and anxieties underpinning the burgeoning Early Music movement constituted the first ideology of performance to attract attention across the discipline as a whole. Richard Taruskin has argued that the Early Music movement did not so much restore the past, in the way that it claimed, as sound the present. In a series of polemical essays dating from the late 1980s and early 1990s (collected in *Text and Act*), Taruskin questions the underlying tenets of what had by then become a commercially successful movement, and was posing a serious challenge to the aesthetics of mainstream classical performance. How is it possible, Taruskin asks, that even before hearing performers play a critic can openly chastise them for not performing on original instruments? This is 'a spectacular instance', he writes, 'of what has become an obnoxious fallacy: taking the instrument for the player', and hence valuing the 'hardware' involved in the act of historical reconstruction over the agents who operate it.[3] Depersonalization is not necessarily what the composers and players of past music would have wanted, and the rhetoric of authenticity, Taruskin argues, is in fact the product of more recent tastes: 'I hold that "historical" performance today is not really historical' and 'that a specious veneer of historicism clothes a performance style that is completely of our own time, and is in fact the most modern style around'.[4] Referencing the work of T. E. Hulme, as well as Ortega y Gasset's *The Dehumanization of Art*, he goes on to claim that depersonalization is a facet of modernism. By noting a parallel between the movement's predilection for strict tempos and motor rhythms, and similar performance traits exemplified in recordings and comments made by Stravinsky in his neo-classical

The modernism of the mainstream

phase (of which one of the best-known of the high modernists, T. S. Eliot, approved), Taruskin further vouches for authenticity's roots in modernism by dint of its penchant for what he calls 'the geometrical in twentieth-century performance practice'.[5]

John Butt has contended, however, that framing Early Music as modernism in disguise does not explain why it needed the veneer of historical authenticity in the first place.[6] The answer to this question, Butt argues, is that modernism itself took history seriously. Butt notes that early strains of modernism frame the subject as playing an active role in making the past live. In his influential essay 'On the Use and Abuse of History for Life' (1874), Nietzsche rejected antiquarianism, or the view that history is readily intelligible based on fossilized evidence of bygone days; yet he allowed for a 'critical' mode of historical inquiry in which the historian assembles past facts into a living narrative. Butt further notes that a dialogue between past and present is the cornerstone of the hermeneutical philosophy of Wilhelm Dilthey.[7]

Modernism developed its reputation for being ahistorical, however, through a conscious belief in its own historical import and, to that extent, a desire to pre-empt the way in which its own history would be written. These tendencies in turn caused it to assert or even impose its new ideology over and against open-ended dialogue with the past. Butt observes a divergence between on the one hand writers who derive from historicism a sense of their own contingency as historically situated beings, and hence a sense of the ultimate transience of their interpretations of the past, and on the other hand those who with 'shameless certainty' assume 'the mystical connection with the past that is guaranteed by the universal world spirit'.[8] Kant's and Hegel's penchant for systematic philosophies of *Geist* had, by the end of the nineteenth century, given way to the dynamic, rhetorical prose of Nietzsche; yet a failure to constantly keep in mind the ephemerality of the subject can lead to the emergence of a new kind of fixed ideology of the subject, one that assumes its own superiority over the past as opposed to entering into dialogue with it. Butt notes Ezra Pound's shift from existential historicism to a 'classicist' historicism, whereby an earlier engagement with history as multiple in kind became replaced with a primary focus on an interpretation of the past according to a fixed set of beliefs and ethics. T. S. Eliot, Butt notes, goes as far as to insist that the historian be 'neutral' when assessing past facts, a tenet that almost returns modernism to the positivistic antiquarianism that it tried to escape.[9]

Butt goes on to portray a more complex picture of historically informed performance and its cultural underpinnings, arguing that the movement draws on modernism as well as a separate tradition of positivism, which has its roots in Romanticism. Although Early Music became commercially viable in the 1970s, its roots extend much further back (if one remembers that Arnold Dolmetsch, a pioneer in the field, became active in the 1880s): source studies in music became popular in Germany in the latter half of the nineteenth century and can trace their emergence back to the Romantics' reverence for past composers (for example, Mendelssohn's revival of Bach's music).[10] Moreover, Butt observes, modernism places a high premium on technique, whereas historically informed performance (HIP), in its early stages especially, embraced amateurism.[11] Nevertheless, HIP has absorbed something of the variegated and sometimes ambiguous relationship to the past displayed by modernism: to be sure, it has engaged with historical evidence, but one cannot imagine the transformation of such material into living recordings and performances without the 'inspired antiquarians' who made it live, as Butt describes them. He notes how figures such as Nikolaus Harnoncourt, Thomas Binkley and William Christie seem to convince us that we have been transported back to the past by virtue of their charisma as much as by the techniques and hardware they employ.[12]

It may be that, far from dehumanizing classical music, HIP has in fact freed up living performers to be more creative than they might previously have been. Laurence Dreyfus argues that proponents of Early Music believe its practitioners to be eschewing the vagaries of self-expression for trust in historical treatises and original instruments; yet some of the more noteworthy performers associated with the movement, he suggests, are seeking not so much to establish historical conditions as facts beyond scrutiny and for their own sake, as to furnish 'weapons' with which they could force mainstream classical performance to engage creatively once again with history.[13] Moreover, Dreyfus suggests that the mainstream has neglected such a dialogue for the sake of upholding what it believes to be 'metaphysical universals' which function as ideals of classical performance.[14] For Dreyfus, however, such ideals do not of themselves awaken a true subjective agency: rather, he suggests, only an open engagement with history can once again allow a 'hitherto silenced subject to speak'.[15] Such an assertion raises the question, which I attempt to answer in this chapter, of the extent to which practitioners of mainstream performance may previously have been silenced, despite being seen as free and spontaneous individuals, creatively interpreting the music they play.

For Taruskin, in comparison, there is still some life left in the performing traditions of the mainstream. Like Dreyfus he acknowledges the stranglehold of the mainstream, observing that its practices seem to be inculcated in its practitioners ('a performer schooled in the mainstream (any mainstream) receives his basic training before he has reached the age of consent') but he equally contends that a pluralistic society such as ours requires choices consciously formed on the part of the performer ('such an approach will seek to bring to consciousness, and thereby transcend the constraints [...] imposed [...] by conventional training').[16] Taruskin suggests that the mainstream's faith in tradition resulted in a homogeneity of practices: an uncritical passing on of practices, he argues, was fine for the relatively homogeneous musical culture that existed up until World War I, but not for the pluralism of what Western culture has become.[17] Yet later he diverges from his framing of tradition as leading to homogeneity when promoting it as an antidote to the doctrine of objectivity that HIP (or 'modernism' under his definition) tries to impose: tradition is 'cumulative, multiply authored, open, accommodating, above all *messy*, and therefore human'.[18] There is not much in the way of a discussion in *Text and Act*, however, of the pitfalls of engaging with tradition in a society in which the only way to be authentic, in the best sense, is to painfully account for all of one's decisions (as Taruskin himself here seems to argue).[19]

More difficult to accept is Taruskin's implied argument in the essay 'The Pastness of the Present and the Presence of the Past' – albeit not explicitly stated – that mainstream performance, at least up until the final decades of the twentieth century, allowed for greater subjective input than HIP. Taruskin rightly notes performers' aspirations towards vitality, from the late nineteenth century onwards. But he seems to imply that such an ideal really did allow for greater freedom on the part of performers, and he fails to subject expressions of such an ideology to the same scrutiny that he applies to the rhetoric of HIP. Taruskin seems to wish to rescue vitality from everyday uses of the term to give it a somewhat more elevated position as a source of musical meaning. He quotes Susanne K. Langer's notion of music as reflecting the 'morphology of feeling' and as sounding 'the way moods feel', as well as Roger Sessions' explicit severing of vitality from the 'consciously formulated purpose of the composer' (in other words, from the ideology of *Werktreue*) to realign it with 'the nature of our existence', 'our emotions [...] [and] our every impulse and action'.[20] Vitality in mainstream performance thus seems to come close to the non-authoritarian, democratic model of performance generally upheld by Taruskin. Such a view is reinforced by moments of verbal slippage in *Text and Act*, where Taruskin could have easily replaced 'vital' with the more neutral terms 'important' or 'crucial' when promoting his ideal of multiple, open-ended human performance.[21] Taruskin further suggests that a vitalist, and therefore truly liberating, idyll of performance aesthetics existed before World War I, a view with which I contend directly in this chapter. In his defence of vitalism, Taruskin proceeds straight to identifying what it sounded like: vitalism's emphasis on dynamism and

The modernism of the mainstream

ever-fluctuating intensities is why 'Romantic music – and Romantic performance practice – are more richly endowed than any other kind with crescendos and diminuendos, accelerandos and ritardandos, not to mention tempo rubato and a highly variegated timbral palette'.[22] Yet, he goes on to argue, the conductor Leopold Stokowski's 'didactic'-sounding allargandos, in a 1961 recording of Bach's Fifth Brandenburg Concerto, are what 'we can all agree to call "mannered"', the reason being that the extensive use of flexible tempos had 'lost its connection with the vitalist aesthetic that had provided its justification', since Stokowski had 'reached his majority by the First World War'.[23] Similarly, Wilhelm Furtwängler's 'vitalist' recording of the same piece in 1950 is an 'anachronism', since Furtwängler had also come of artistic age by 1914.[24] Can we be sure, however, that vitalism was less didactic before the First World War? Taruskin evokes an era of harmonious relationships existing between performers, audiences and practices, all safely bound by the aesthetics of vitalism – an assumption that I wish to challenge.

To give Taruskin credit, a concise yet distanced critique of the kind produced by Dreyfus in 1983 is clearly not Taruskin's goal, and much of his vibrant discourse is born of longsuffering and bittersweet experiences of engaging with performers and critics at the chalk face. Indeed, Taruskin's writings have proven to be fertile soil for the development of later cultural and discursive studies of musical performance, including my own. Yet I aver that a facile distinction can be gleaned from *Text and Act*, between HIP/modernism/limitation of the performer's input and mainstream/vitalism/untrammelled freedom for the performer's input. The duality is further encouraged by the ease with which one can imagine the sounds representative of the two: the motor rhythms of the one contrasted by the fluid tempos of the other; the terraced dynamics of the one compared to the modulatory dynamics of the other. In a more recent article, '"Alte Musik", or "Early Music"?', Taruskin demonstrates that twentieth-century vitalist performance embodies an ideology of its own, yet he stops short of asking how this ideology colonized the practices of the era.[25] He argues that while Stravinsky and like-minded composers and performers located themselves in an imagined present of past music (to which they nonetheless applied their own ideological frameworks) the *Wiener Schule* conceived of the historical music it so venerated as 'old', as belonging to a past regarded from the vantage point of an 'actual or conceptual present'. Webern's and Schoenberg's reworkings of past music reflect this notion of an unbroken, Germanic musical tradition that culminates in a present, living form.[26] Taruskin goes on to show, however, that Schoenberg's defence of the vital tradition of German music is deeply ideological, built on strong opposition to its perceived others (including popular music of the day) as well as anxieties typical of the wider culture of the era. In a 1948 essay entitled 'Today's Manner of Performing Classical Music', Schoenberg complains that many conductors have succumbed to a rigidity of tempo (the 'geometrical' performance style that, according to Taruskin, gave rise to the Early Music aesthetic), and compares American dancehall culture to a drug that prevents performers from feeling the true lifeblood of music, namely flexible tempo.[27] The dichotomy Taruskin draws between the approaches of 'early music' and *alte Musik* is striking, but the question surely arises, if not for Taruskin then for future research, of how the practices of the largely Germanic vitalist school, with its opposition to geometrical performance styles, became established, spearheaded as they were by representatives just as influential as Stravinsky. How exactly were vitalist tendencies shaped by these influential figures and the ideologies they propounded? And can one then begin to see both the geometrical and the vitalist ideologies of performance, for all their differences, as having been to an equal extent products of modernist trends?

Taruskin's critique of HIP nonetheless seems to have achieved the status of received wisdom among musicologists. For example, in their entry on modernism in *Musicology: The Key Concepts*, David Beard and Kenneth Gloag make a brief nod to modernism in performance, adopting Taruskin's critique of it as the sole voice on the topic.[28] What is now needed, however, is greater critical attention towards the aesthetics of the mainstream. What exactly is vitalism? Is vitalism at odds with modernism or does it join with modernism's quest to articulate an appropriate relationship with the past? HIP may well have constituted a belated flourishing of modernist aesthetics in musical performance, but surely it is unlikely that a culture of performance at the heart of bourgeois, Western civilization remained immune to the influence of a major aesthetic movement for an entire century. If vitalist discourses of performance resemble those of modernism, then the ultimate questions are the ones that Taruskin and Butt pose with reference to HIP: How does the discourse negotiate authority? Do early twentieth-century discourses of mainstream performance suppress agency, as Taruskin says of HIP discourses, or do they better enable the performing subject to speak?

Modernist strains of vitalism: the unquestionable authority of the performing subject

It is often Pound's and Eliot's depersonalized and objectivist models that readily spring to mind in connection with the period of high modernism. Yet, as Butt notes, it is easy to forget modernism's incorporation of vitalist strains of thought. The cultural reception of Nietzsche's work was widespread in the early twentieth century, and his ideas were particularly appealing to those artistic and literary figures who found in his work a potent rallying cry for the artistic cause. 'Art is the great stimulus to life', Nietzsche wrote, and a recurring theme in his work is art's ability to reverse the depleting effects of scientific knowledge on modern culture.[29] Noting his influence on Strauss, Mahler, Delius, Mann, Rilke and Yeats, among others, Aaron Ridley argues that Nietzsche's greatest influence, in the decades following his death, was not on philosophy but on art and literature: 'if Nietzsche's thoughts about art can be said to have left a legacy behind them', Ridley writes, 'it has not been to philosophical aesthetics. It has, rather, been to two areas much more central to his own concerns: to art itself, and to Wagner criticism.'[30]

Aspects of Nietzsche's work reflect the rise of historicism in the latter half of the nineteenth century, but Nietzsche ultimately rejects an open dialogue with history in favour of a reductive model of artistic vitality. Nietzsche dispenses with the system-building approach of his predecessors Kant and Hegel, choosing instead to articulate vitality's dynamism, with the fittingly dynamic, rhetorical prose characteristic of his major texts. Yet Andrew Bowie has argued that, despite this, Nietzsche disregards the possibility that history – but also ethics, audience reception, and any imagined, autonomous aesthetic realm itself – might act as externally moderating agents on artistic intuition.[31] Whereas, as Bowie demonstrates, the early Idealists favoured cosmopolitan diversity, Nietzsche prefers a model of self-expression that essentializes according to origins: German myth, the Dionysian, and the notion of the will to power, which Nietzsche portrays as inevitably gaining ascendancy, in the hands of the producers of art, over the weak. As Nietzsche asserts in 'On the Use and Abuse of History', the handling of history should be solely entrusted to the 'strong artistic spirits [...] [who] alone are capable of learning from that history in a true, that is to say life-enhancing sense'.[32] What Nietzsche posits in this text is not a dialogue with history but a prescription for an ahistorical philosophy, which privileges artistic vitality above all else. Small wonder, then, that artists, largely cut loose from former ties to churches and courts, saw in Nietzsche's work a means of justifying their now isolated societal position and of protecting their endeavours from wider scrutiny: the very act of creativity is justification enough for what it produces.

A number of early twentieth-century modernists favoured such a model of artistic vitality in musical performance, among them the German critic Paul Bekker, a prominent advocate of the *Neue Musik* of Schoenberg, Hindemith and others. In his essay 'Improvisation und

The modernism of the mainstream

Reproduktion' (1922), Bekker lamented the way in which the performing artist was now forced, in the interests of a 'sham objectivity [*Sachlichkeit des Scheines*]', to 'emphasize his physical talents at the cost of his humanity', in the process becoming 'ever more reduced to the level of a mechanical functionary'.[33] Bekker was convinced that even the Baroque musician 'would not have been bound by rigorous demands with regard to the correctness of the text', but rather by an ideal of 'improvisation' that aimed 'to illuminate the musical work through the intimate, creative fusion of composer and performer, as if in the moment of its first sounding, thus bringing it into harmony with the composer's original creative impulse'.[34] This ideal of improvisation stood, in Bekker's view, contrary to that of 'reproduction', the desire to be 'fully at the service of the composer [...] in order to give a true likeness or rather reproduction of the will of the creator' – an ideal that he considered 'virtuous' but 'in reality unrealizable'. Ultimately, he concluded, a 'monstrous presumptuousness [...] lies behind the concept of an objectively note-faithful reproduction'.[35] This 'objectively founded and nonetheless personally unhampered improvisation' would be 'the easier to find, the more the performing artist occupies himself with the creative art of his own time. Out of the latter, not out of the historical sciences, stem the laws of performance style, also for older music.'[36]

In one of the earliest articles to explore twentieth-century ideologies of mainstream performance, Laurence Dreyfus observed the way in which absolute authority was invested in the interpreting artist. Dreyfus attempts to dislodge the assumption that 'interpretation' is a 'neutral synonym for performance', arguing instead that to interpret is to 'elevate the act of music-making, to invest it with high, even philosophic, value'.[37] Dreyfus suggests that to 'play' music, with the connotation that one is playing *with* something else, gave way, in the course of the nineteenth century, to a preoccupation with authority – to the question of who, or what, has the final say when it comes to making performance choices. The issue became particularly pressing for performers, he argues, when historical musicology, established as an academic discipline at the end of the nineteenth century, began to present itself increasingly as the ultimate source of authority on performance practice issues. Whereas late nineteenth- and early twentieth-century performers such as Arnold Dolmetsch and Wanda Landowska were prepared to revise their models in response, Dreyfus notes in others, such as the German violinist Leopold Auer and the Catalan cellist Pablo Casals, a 'sense of irritation' towards the increasingly prevalent view that fidelity to the composer might entail historical inquiry into what can be known about his intentions.[38] Dreyfus perceives a parting of ways between historical inquiry and previously common and untroubled affirmations of the performer's 'spiritual' or 'vital' connection with the composer or artwork. Auer, for example, rejects historical inquiry as 'material' and endorses a 'mental' or 'spiritual' affinity between performer and artwork. Indeed, Casals' repeated insistence that the performer vitally recreate the artwork ('the essential problem is to produce a vital creation') begs the question of exactly what is being interpreted.[39]

The parting of ways between historical inquiry and the subjectivist art of interpretation had begun around the turn of the twentieth century. The subjectivism of the German violinist and musicologist Andreas Moser in *Violinschule* (1905) offers a foretaste of the headstrong vitalism of Auer and Casals. Yet still, as Dreyfus notes, Moser reports in a biography of 1899 his former teacher's belief that to enter the 'spirit' (*Geist*) of an artwork was to simply 'reproduce' it (*reproduzieren*).[40] Dreyfus surmises, however, that the rise of photography and sound recording soon afterwards cast a shadow over a 'mere' rendering of the score. Moser's essay 'Vom Vortrag' ('On Interpretation', 1905), in the third volume of *Violinschule*, displays a strident blend of subjectivism with German nationalism, which is all the more striking considering that by this time Moser was already a seasoned scholar of musical source studies.[41] 'On Interpretation' certainly displays the breadth of Moser's knowledge, with detailed references to the historical treatises of C. P. E.

Bach, Quantz and Leopold Mozart on the topic of ornaments; yet Moser continually halts the flow of his discussion (sections 7–9 of the 10 sections of the essay) with reminders that 'individual taste', a sense of what is 'artistic' and 'personal choice', should always take precedence over 'a timid anxiety to hold true to the letter'. History's role as an externally moderating agent is dropped towards the end of the discussion, however, especially in the essay's final section. There Moser constructs a flawed history, which attempts to vouch for the authenticity of German violin playing on the basis of its putative origins in the Italian *bel canto* tradition (widely seen at the time as an ideal of musical performance). This discussion is shot through with uncomfortable insinuations regarding the sincerity of German self-expression versus the superficiality of the Franco-Belgian school.[42]

By the 1920s, Auer and Carl Flesch were confidently asserting the autonomy of the performer's vitality, but were careful not to imply that this entailed a departure from the dictates of the score. Moser talks of the spirit of the artwork itself, not of the interpretative act. Joachim 'always strove to lose himself, heart and soul, in the spirit of the artwork', and the need to capture this spirit is assumed from the outset of the essay on interpretation: 'for the performance of a musical composition in the spirit of its creator, two conditions must necessarily be fulfilled'.[43] For Auer, however, vitality essentially requires the act of performance, although there is also the suggestion that it is latent in the score or the composer: inspiration 'merely lies dormant in the printed page until we make it live and glow and radiate in tone'.[44] The Hungarian violinist Carl Flesch (1873–1944) goes further, in his treatise *Die Kunst des Violinspiels* (1923, vol. 2, 1928), to assert that performance is an act of re-creation that deliberately resists the influence of the composer. He condones an 'active' (*aktive*) approach to violin playing, since players possessing such a temperament 'have a powerful inner urge which enables them to achieve their task with an enthusiasm that is independent of the object they recreate [the musical work]'; 'passive types, however, lacking this powerful impulse, cannot stand on their own, and [are] driven without will of their own on the waves of the creator's emotion.'[45]

Whereas Auer takes refuge in a reductive model of subjectivity, however, Flesch seeks to substantiate this new power invested in the living performer with the nascent psychiatric and physiological beliefs of the age. In his text *Violin Playing as I Teach It* (1921), Auer devotes a whole chapter to asserting that 'style' is pure individuality, and should not be weighed down by historical treatises or traditions of performance: 'let them [violinists] not hamper that most precious individual quality the artist has', Auer writes, 'with the dusty precepts handed down from times gone by';[46] and 'if respect for tradition were carried to its logical conclusion we should still be living in the Stone Age, doing as our forefathers had done before us'.[47] This is a text that mostly promotes an abstracted ideal of violin playing, however, and other, notable interpreters (for example, Mischa Elman and Jascha Heifetz) appear in it *in nomine* only. As Dreyfus suspects, to acknowledge the worth of historical treatises would have 'threatened the powerful authority vested in the author of *Violin Playing as I Teach It*'.[48] What Auer really means by individuality is the collective sensibility of the here and now, however; and not even a democratically formed collective, since Auer subscribes to the Nietzschean ideal of the artist as the powerful imposer of meaning over the crowd:

> For the violinist whose technique is assured, and who possesses that peculiar magnetism which exerts irresistible and convincing charm, is able to sway the greatest audience with compelling power – like the Hebrew prophets and the great masters of the plastic arts, like the great poets of ancient and of modern days, the public speakers of all ages – in a word, like all other artists whose appeal is addressed to the multitude.[49]

The modernism of the mainstream

While not denying the performer's power, Flesch turns the focus inwards to consider what makes performers fit to undertake their high calling. Reflecting the emerging discipline of psychiatry, the second volume of *Die Kunst des Violinspiels* considers various kinds of 'hindrances' (*Hemmungen*) to the psyche, and Flesch recommends techniques of auto-suggestion developed by Emil Coué in order to boost self-confidence.[50]

More general aspects of the early twentieth-century literature on violin playing indicate that its primary aim is to idealize a model of the living, performing subject. The genre most prevalent in this period's violin-playing literature is that of the pedagogical treatise, which by the early twentieth century was part of a well-established tradition that dated back to the French *méthodes* of the 1800s and, in common with music source studies, had gathered pace during the latter half of the nineteenth century. One can draw an even closer parallel, however, with the Nietzschean, more subjectivist strains of modernism in that the texts under consideration try to inculcate performance practices not by simply issuing instructions that regulate isolated bodily mechanisms, as do earlier texts, but by trying to regulate the whole violinist, both mind and body.

The amount of prose and the lack of notated exercises in early twentieth-century manuals of violin playing are telling signs of this approach. Earlier texts try to instruct largely by providing daily exercises, which of course are designed to help the player develop a consistent set of bodily mechanisms. Both earlier and later texts contain straightforward and practical descriptions of how to execute a certain device or score marking – yet in the early twentieth-century literature these are buried in extensive prose devoted to extolling an ideology of vitality. Indeed, Huberman's *Aus der Werkstatt*, Martens's *Violin Mastery* and *String Mastery* and Auer's *Violin Playing as I Teach It* are almost entirely composed of text. There are more notated examples in Flesch – perhaps around twenty percent of the material – but the amount of prose is by no means small given that the second volume of Flesch's text (in Ries and Erler's first edition) alone totals 222 pages. A mere practising of bodily mechanisms is exactly what early twentieth-century writers wish to prevent their readers from doing: as noted above, Huberman does not believe that 'mechanical exercises' lead to progress; Auer, meanwhile, insists that 'the question of tone production is not primarily a matter of [...] change of bow on the strings, nor of change of position by means of the fingers of the left hand' but requires 'all the mental and spiritual concentration of which he [the student] is capable'; and Martens, in his turn, speaks of the 'purely soulless and mechanical system' for which the Czech violinist Otto Sevčik was (and still is) well known.[51]

Despite its outward promise of letting its readers in on the craftsman's ways, Huberman's *Aus der Werkstatt des Virtuosen* is by no means a straightforward manual of violin playing. The cursory browser may have taken the title as an indication of purely didactic content, the word 'workshop' perhaps promising gnostic knowledge of how the virtuoso has achieved such an uncommonly high level of technical expertise. The virtuoso in this particular workshop, however, prefers to recount his life story. While Huberman spends much of the text tracking his own rise to success, there are nonetheless many tips given on specific aspects of violin playing, such as how to approach runs, how to deal with nerves and the importance of developing an artistic personality over and above a reliance on technique and tools.

The other major genre of the period, the biography, is equally committed to extolling a high model of violin mastery, and indeed all texts from this period borrow to a lesser or greater extent from each other's generic classification, devoted as they are to positing an ideal of greatness. In fact, Martens's *Violin Mastery* and *String Mastery* can be said to be neither biographies nor pedagogies, seamlessly blending, as they do, advice with biographical anecdotes. The figure of the celebrated and then recently deceased Joachim (1833–1907) looms large in many texts as the embodiment of – or perhaps a metonym for – greatness, even featuring prominently in Auer's *Violin Playing* and Huberman's text of 1912. Having performed the Mendelssohn Concerto

Stefan Knapik

with the composer at the age of twelve, Joachim was certainly a prodigy, yet the biographies of Moser (*Joseph Joachim: Ein Lebensbild*, 1899) and J. A. Fuller-Maitland (*Joseph*) are relentless in their emphasis on Joachim's genius reflected at every stage of his career. Joachim's genius, along with a tacit implication of Auer's genius, features prominently in Auer's text: 'those among us who were able to understand him', Auer writes, 'benefited enormously', whereas 'others, less fortunate, stood with wide-open mouth uncomprehending'.[52] Auer is particularly candid about his wish to limit violin playing to the elites, or the 'elect', as he calls them in his *Violin Works and their Interpretation*: he complains that students unaware of their inherent lack of talent and their physical deformities are better off taking up 'some other career', for they 'do not know that to genius alone the brilliant firmament of promise opens wide'.[53]

There is a similar implication of inherited genius in Huberman's praise for Joachim in *Aus der Werkstatt*. Yet the unbending sycophantism is tempered somewhat by the sensuous allure of the high places to which Huberman's hardened fingers traversing perilous tracks led him:

> What I loved most was to follow him into those highest regions of the music, the opening up of which is one of his everlasting services [to music]. Where one had previously expected only ice and rocks he plucked the most beautiful alpine roses and Edelweiss, and he opened up the most magnificent view of blue lakes, softly stirred by the balmy air, and surrounded by sun-drenched meadows filled with flowers.[54]

Huberman's Joachim is Nietzsche's Zarathustra: 'let us live above them like strong winds', Nietzsche has Zarathustra utter, 'neighbours of the eagles, neighbours of the snow, neighbours of the sun. Their bodies and their spirits would call our happiness a cave of ice.'[55]

The model of greatness at the centre of these texts is peculiar to a particular strain within modernism: elitist, retreating, scornful of society. As Robert Currie explains in his study of genius, the Romantic genius aspires to magnanimity whereas the modernist genius becomes somewhat self-serving:

> A romantic posits a higher order which is, in general estimation, a better world, and which can be attained. A modernist doubts, almost to the point of disbelief, that the higher order can be attained; and he interprets the higher order in terms so ascetic, or even so objectionable, as to repel all but those who can rise to the austerity of his creed.[56]

In comparison with performance discourses dating back to Romanticism, the shift is away from the notion of artistic talent or inspiration as occurring in a more unexpected or fortuitous fashion to more prescriptive models of interpretation. Mary Hunter sets out to demonstrate that, contrary to the tendency of the better-known Romantic and Idealist authors (for example, Hegel, Fichte, E. T. A. Hoffman, Novalis, Wackenroder) to obliterate agency in their celebration of an all-consuming artistic genius manifest in the work, string pedagogical treatises from the period promote a somewhat more active working of the performer to cultivate genius, or *Geist*.[57] Nevertheless, as Hunter shows, such texts continue to advocate the idea that genius can equally be serendipitous – easily acquired, in comparison to Auer's portrayal of the tortuous road to success.

Regardless of how they portray their projected ideal violinist, it is clear that these highly influential players hold the living performing subject as the central locus of musical meaning. The question now is how the formation of this idealized performer is to take place. How must such a performer train? What are the goals to be striven towards and the pitfalls to be avoided?

The rhetoric appears to legitimate the autonomous will of the interpreting artist, but these pedagogues nevertheless proceed to prefigure what actions he or she will take.

The prescriptions of vitalism: disciplining the performing subject

Vitality's foil – morbidity – is as important a facet of Nietzschean and modernist discourses as is life itself. Nietzsche's preoccupation with sickness is well known: for example, in *The Gay Science* he asks 'whether we can dispense with sickness', and asserts that 'being sick can even become an energetic stimulus for life'.[58] Disease is a common theme in much modernist art and philosophy, embodied in the characters of the morbid residents of the sanatorium in Mann's *The Magic Mountain*, the mental decline of the character Septimus in Wolff's *Mrs Dalloway*, or Edvard Munch's painting *The Scream*, for example. Similarly, discourses of violin playing develop not just out of stout defences of subjectivity as from anxieties over what happens when its outworking in performance is undermined.

As writers working beyond the walls of academia, violinists displayed a keen awareness of wider social anxieties over disease and contagion, particularly surrounding the nervous system, whose vulnerability was blamed for a wide range of perceived medical, moral and social ills. Anxieties over nervous exhaustion were widespread during the *fin de siècle*: doctors diagnosed neurasthenia (the medical term for physical exhaustion coined by the American physician George Miller Beard in 1888) as the condition underlying a range of common ailments.[59] There is evidence that writers on violin playing saw undesirable performance practices as resulting from nervous exhaustion, as when Auer surmises that the continuous use of vibrato, as opposed to selective use of the device on a limited number of notes, 'may be traced to a group of sick or ailing nerves'.[60] More common in the literature is the tendency to reflect the wider societal tendency to blame malfunctioning nerves for a plethora of social ills: thus Flesch reflects the wider notion that a lack of masculinity results from nervous decline when he describes the over-use of vibrato as 'effeminate', and Achille Rivarde echoes the widespread linkage between hysteria, a condition thought to mostly affect women, and nervous exhaustion in his characterization of the over-use of vibrato as 'hysterical'.[61]

In order to understand how pathological anxieties shaped an ideology of violin playing more deeply in the twentieth century, it is first necessary to outline writers' ideals of melody. A number take their cue from Wagner's influential 1869 essay 'On Conducting' ('Über das Dirigiren', 1869; Moser and Flesch had read it), in which Wagner argues that *melos* is the basis of all musical execution. The concept, however, refers to something far more basic and all-encompassing than simply unbroken, legato phrases: Michael Spitzer, who traces the ideal of song or melody as a basic metaphor for music throughout the nineteenth century and into the twentieth, argues that the nineteenth- and early twentieth-century idea of melody 'operates beneath the level at which the literal distinction between rhythm and melody applies, a level denoting dynamic, energetic flow'.[62]

Reflecting the ubiquity of pathological anxieties in the late nineteenth and early twentieth centuries, the principle of continuous melody in this era is often discussed in connection with factors that might threaten to destroy it. Moser thus compares the violinist who undermines the principle of continuous melody to an 'asthmatic singer [. . .] whose breath fails him at the most important moment'.[63] In Frederick Martens's interview with Bronisław Huberman, recorded in his *String Mastery* (1923), a highly distinctive set of ideas about realizing continuous melody in performance is presented, particularly with regard to how the violinist should prepare beforehand in order to ensure its constant presence. On a bowed string instrument, the further one's bow is placed from the bridge while it is being drawn across a string, the faster one will need to move it in order to keep the string vibrating continuously: failure to do causes the sound to 'crack', whereas if the bow veers too close to the bridge the tone becomes thin and metallic-sounding. Naturally, the margin of error becomes much smaller when one shortens the string by stopping it high up the fingerboard with the left hand. Huberman, according to Martens, targets the problem of maintaining a continuous sound with full volume when playing in higher positions on the E (the highest) string:

> I have developed a special technique of power and endurance in the high registers on long notes. Why? Because, as I have already mentioned, violinists usually fall short of the fullness of tone and power needed when a climaxing phrase or a climaxing melody occurs in a high position. I admit that it is difficult to gain lyric breadth and fullness of tone high up on the E string, but it can be done. Caruso made his high climaxing notes gloriously powerful: the violinist can do the same.[64]

Huberman boldly states what he means by a 'special technique':

> As regards virtuoso violin playing, two great technical factors are required: a colossal reserve of tonal and technical power and strength, built up by endurance study; and absolute purity of intonation.[65]

One should not build up strength through repetitive exercises, however, but through the repeated playing of difficult passages from the music itself. Huberman suggests the unusual remedy of practising such passages at a faster tempo than one would play them in concert:

> As to daily mechanical exercises, I do not believe very much in them. For what might be called daily 'technical baths' I think the scales in thirds are excellent, especially for endurance. But the best thing to do is to pick out entire difficult sections and practice them, whether you think you need them or not. I do this myself because endurance training in the highest sense can only be developed by innumerable repetitions of difficult passages at a rapid tempo.[66]

This might involve up to twenty renditions, and might involve playing the entire piece, not just passages from it. Huberman takes as an example the third movement of Paganini's second violin concerto (Op. 7), the *Rondo 'La campanella'*, commonly nicknamed *La clochette* ('The Little Bell'), or *Les clochettes*, as Huberman calls it:

> In order to bring his technique to the point that he is able to play 'Les Clochettes' just *once* on the concert platform, the violinist must be able to play it through *twenty* times without interruption at home![67]

I shall return later to the question of why Huberman insists on playing musical works themselves and not simply practising technical exercises. First, I want to try to contextualize Huberman's assumption that one can build up strength through extensive, prior physical exertion. One can view Huberman's comments as a reflection of the therapeutic dimension of pathological discourses – namely the question of how to treat exhaustion as an ailment afflicting the individual body. The belief was widespread at the time that the body operates on an economy of nervous energy. Anson Rabinach has demonstrated a shift, in the late nineteenth century, from

The modernism of the mainstream

a prior optimism surrounding the unlimited potentials of industrialization to the limits on productivity presented by 'the human motor'.[68] The debate thrived off two opposing approaches, much as it does today: prevention and cure. By the 1920s a general shift seems to have occurred away from a culture of neurasthenia to a politically charged debate about degeneration: when the American physician George Miller Beard published his seminal texts on the condition in the 1880s, nervous exhaustion was largely seen as a problem in the domestic context, for which doctors prescribed remedies. With the heightened militarism and chauvinism of the early twentieth century, however, nervous exhaustion seems to have taken centre stage as governing the fate of entire nation states, and preventative measures were taken: alongside mass exercise programmes, film footage of which continues to capture the contemporary imagination, eugenics was implemented as public policy in several Western countries.[69] There is still evidence of attempts to cure, though: Joachim Radkau's research on patient records from around the turn of the twentieth century in Germany has found that they continue to display a '"soft", humane tendency', perhaps suggesting that 'there is more than one single story of neurasthenia'.[70] This tendency remains contrasted, however, with 'the polemical use or rather abuse of "nervousness" as a reproach', which Radkau continues to recognize as a central attribute of cultures of the nerves in the early twentieth century. In such a culture, nervous fatigue is not to be accommodated but is to be prevented through engagement with vigorous physical regimes.

Martens's chapter on Huberman shows a distinctive preference for a preventative approach to exhaustion in violin playing. He appeals to the way in which the Norwegian explorer Fridtjof Nansen was commonly thought to have prepared for his polar expeditions thirty years earlier (1893–96):

> The violinist should have, in reality, twice as much technical power and strength at his disposal in order to play a given composition as he *thinks* necessary. And this he can only get by endurance study, the true key to violin virtuosity. Before Nansen undertook his Polar expeditions he trained himself to sleep in the open under conditions as nearly as possible approaching those he was to encounter.[71]

A publication penned by Huberman himself shows that he embraced the idea of endurance training even earlier in his career: in *Aus der Werkstatt des Virtuosen* (1912) Huberman favours a building up of strength through training, appealing to a similar metaphor:

> Nobody would expect their legs to carry them straight up Montblanc after several weeks of lying in bed, and tourist legs are to Montblanc what the violinist's hands are to the fingerboard, with the difference that the tracks of the fingerboard are much narrower and more perilous.[72]

Huberman's earlier comments vouch for the fidelity of Martens's later 'reporting': indeed, among Martens's interviewees, Huberman's comments are unique – no other performer stresses the need to take preventative measures against exhaustion, let alone develop a formalized practice method out of it. In fact, several violinists explicitly advise against excessively vigorous practice. From his reported comments, it is hard to imagine the young Jascha Heifetz, for example, practising Paganini's aforementioned concerto movement twenty times through without stopping, especially given that the movement is around eight minutes in length:

> In the first place I have never believed in practicing too much – it is just as bad as practicing too little! [...] I have never believed in grinding. In fact I think that if one

has to work very hard to get his piece, it will show in the execution. To interpret music properly, it is necessary to eliminate mechanical difficulty; the audience should not feel the struggle of the artist with what are considered hard passages. I hardly ever practice more than three hours a day on an average.[73]

Here is the violinistic equivalent of Radkau's 'humane' culture of the nerves, then: the equivalent of the famous 'rest cures', often prescribed for neurasthenia in the late nineteenth and early twentieth centuries.

Whereas Huberman advocates strenuous physical activity, other writers recommend a deliberate abstention from it through greater mental concentration on the musical work. In a similar warning over succumbing to physical exhaustion during practice, Auer refers vaguely to the principle:

'How long should the advanced pupil practice?' Professor Auer was asked. 'The right kind of practice is not a matter of hours,' he replied. 'Practice should represent the utmost concentration of brain. It is better to play with concentration for two hours than to practice eight without.'[74]

The idea that careful application of thought can save hours of labour is hardly groundbreaking, of course, but there is evidence from the early twentieth century of a belief that this is not just a case of making the right decisions to avoid unnecessary physical work, but that the process of turning decisions into actions is directly physiological in kind. There is an interesting account of how mental concentration directly prevents bodily exhaustion in a 1908 violin treatise written by an Austrian physician, named as S. Mittelmann on the cover, and the Czech violinist František Ondříček (1857–1922). The writers argue that by entertaining a wide variety of ideas, the brain can share the efforts of doing so among a greater number of nerves, and subsequently delay the onset of nervous exhaustion. Demonstrating an awareness of wider cultural debates surrounding economies of energy among the workforce, the writers note that the use of a greater number of muscles delays the onset of exhaustion:

Experience teaches that if a machine pre-determines labour in such a way that only the hands are employed, fatigue occurs much more quickly than if the same work performed on such a machine also engages the lower extremities.[75]

The rather unscientific assumption made at the next stage of their argument is that the nerves behave in the same way as the muscles, for which the writers plead innocence based on lack of scientific knowledge of how the nerves work. This then allows them to assert that if a greater number of nerves are used there is a greater capacity to store the waste products that lead to fatigue, resulting in its delayed onset:

The consumption of usable material and the storing of products of decomposition are distributed in the latter case among a greater number of muscles, so that the moment of fatigue sets in later. Of course the processes of activity of the nerve cells are not clear, but from their mode of reaction (they are capable of stimulus summation, and with continual irritating finally get into a state of exhaustion) the above mentioned can be applied also to the nervous system.[76]

The solution is to invoke a large quantity of varied ideas, which, for these defenders of high-art interpretation, naturally results from meditating on the musical work itself:

The modernism of the mainstream

In the study of the great composers' works the master helps the pupil to capture the spiritual (*geistig*) value of them through presenting word- and speech-pictures, with which the thought processes of the composer might have been filled. The labour becomes varied because large complexes of ideas will be brought into motion.[77]

Ondříček and Mittelmann's suggested remedy for fatigue offers insight into deeper cultural motivations for what David Milsom has a called a 'doctrine of diversity' in ideals of violin playing.[78] The writers' detailed analysis of mental and bodily workings is absent from the writings of violinists who lacked access to a medical consultant (the treatise goes into substantial detail regarding the workings of the skeletal and muscular movements of the violinist's body). Yet what Mittelmann and Ondříček provide is some insight into what may have been a pathologically grounded impetus for the widespread notion of variety, among early twentieth-century violinists, as an ideal in violin playing. The notion that mental variety is essential to violin playing prompted Auer to declare nuance as 'the soul of interpretation', the subject of which forms the basis of an entire chapter (the tenth) of his *Violin Playing as I Teach It*.[79] In the first paragraph of his chapter on nuance Auer explains:

A genius of Beethoven's calibre excels in teaching us how to shade, how to develop nuance. Study his quartets, his trios, his violin sonatas – not to forget his symphonies! – and you will find them replete with the greatest imaginable abundance of nuances.[80]

In keeping with Moser's German-nationalist agenda in his essay on interpretation in the third volume of the *Violinschule*, he suggests that the ideal of tonal variety is what Franco-Belgian players fail to realize in their playing: what is missing, Moser writes, is a 'modulation-rich manner of tone production, which has all nuances of expression on the palette'.[81] When discussing a passage containing a succession of rhythmically identical figurations in Beethoven's Violin Concerto, Flesch recommends using varying emphases for the notes in each figuration, for the reason that 'an all too even and continuous [. . .] tone production greatly taxes the listener's attention'.[82] Hans Wessely recommends that 'single slides should vary so as not to become monotonous and distasteful'.[83]

The equation of mind/spirit with the musical work, advocated in both the work of Auer and that of Mittelmann and Ondříček, and their notion that it directly alleviates physical exhaustion in a physiological manner, explains why Huberman, according to Martens, insists on practising by means of playing through actual pieces rather than technical exercises. The idea is also present in Huberman's 1912 text:

A run which singularly serves as a means to an end, i.e. for the higher purposes of musical expression, requires much subtler control than the same run, as an end in itself, would require. [When playing] a run that serves as a means to this end, namely the higher purpose of musical expression [. . .] the mind of the player must nevertheless bring about the free joining together of each note of the run, and at great speed: for example, [this will incorporate] hardly perceptible stresses of the thematic notes, if the melody is embellished or a kind of variation, or individual accents, crescendos etc., according to the requirements of the melodic or harmonic expression.[84]

One notes that Huberman preserves the principle of continuous melody ('must nevertheless bring about the free joining together of each note') yet this is tempered by the 'mind' or 'spirit' (*Geist*), the results of which might also suggest that Huberman has applied the principle of variety/diversity, since doing so results in varied stresses of thematic notes and/or accents and small-scale dynamics that could potentially be varied and numerous if, as Huberman says, they arise out of melodic and harmonic activity (and not just the markings provided by the composer).

Conclusion

While the practices of early twentieth-century violin playing are far removed from those of the Early Music movement, the two ultimately come across as not fundamentally at odds with each other in terms of ideology. Both, in their different ways, created idealized models, whether of historical fidelity or of artistic vitality, in order to discipline the performing subject and hence, to some degree, prefigure the act of performance. Whereas the Early Music movement made history an unquestionable source of authority, the early twentieth-century ideology of interpretation sought to suppress history and instead inculcate an ideology of self, both through claims regarding the elite status of that self and through warnings of its potential pathological downfall (accompanied by prescribed remedies for prevention or cure). This would seem to problematize Taruskin's assumption that pre-World War I performers enjoyed greater creative freedom than those active later in the century, notwithstanding the possible argument that it took time for the theories of influential violinists to become common practice, and that only after World War II did the practices of the mainstream become predictable and sterile.

A further complicating issue, not explicitly addressed in this chapter, is the extent to which an ideology of *Werktreue* has bound interpreters since the nineteenth century to obligations concerned with the accurate reproduction of the score. Earlier I noted Dreyfus's suggestion that whereas Auer and Flesch laid emphasis on the ultimate authority of the performing artist in terms of creative content, such an emphasis was less important to Andreas Moser, writing twenty years earlier, when anxieties over the mechanization induced by the advent of sound recordings were less pronounced. The authority of the performing artist might have become still less of an urgent issue for all performers concerned, however, had the ideology of *Werktreue* been understood not as the realization of a spatially conceived, frozen score, but rather as a theory concerned with the performer's and listener's cognition of the musical work, such as appears to have developed in the late nineteenth and early twentieth centuries.

Musicological scholarship is increasingly drawing attention to such a psychological account of the work, which prevailed alongside the concept of the musical work as the frozen or pre-articulate contents of the score. As Nicholas Cook and Mine Doğantan-Dack have separately argued, this model held live performer and listener cognition to be vital to ascertaining the meaning of the musical work. As Cook has shown, such an understanding of a musical work was embraced by no less a figure than Schenker, whose analyses were previously misunderstood as laying out a frozen, underlying architecture of the work, but which rather, Cook argues, identify cognitive focal points in the music towards (or away from) which the listener works, or is drawn, during the live act of listening.[85] Doğantan-Dack has similarly identified a psychological account of the work in the writings of Mathis Lussy, Tobias Matthay and Stewart Macpherson, and even those of that supposed arch-formalist Eduard Hanslick.[86] Lee Rothfarb's work on the energeticists also shows the importance of subjective listener experience in the work of analysts such as August Halm, Arnold Schering, Hans Mersmann and Ernst Kurth, who conceive of musical motives as possessing constantly fluctuating meaning as they are experienced temporally by the listener.[87]

The main point to be appreciated here, though, is that subjective expression and reception, as discussed in the late nineteenth and early twentieth centuries, is not to be taken at face value:

The modernism of the mainstream

it was extensively theorized, pre-empted and circumscribed. Far from offering fewer constraints than those implicit in the practices of the Early Music movement, not to mention their representation by Taruskin, the vitalistic traditions of mainstream classical performance turn out to have been just as didactic and prescriptive, only in a different way. And in that different way – in particular their elevation of the ascetic, austere and essentially self-serving image of the artistic genius – they constitute what is arguably an equally important part of modernism's legacy to performance practice.

Notes

1 See Richard Taruskin, *Text and Act* (Oxford: Oxford University Press, 1995), a collection of essays written in the late 1980s and early 1990s. A particularly extensive essay in this collection, 'The Pastness of the Present and the Presence of the Past', was previously printed in a volume containing the writings of other prominent critics of Early Music, including Nicholas Kenyon, Howard Mayer Brown, Will Crutchfield, Robert Morgan, Philip Brett and Gary Tomlinson. See *Authenticity and Early Music*, ed. Nicholas Kenyon (Oxford: Oxford University Press, 1988).
2 See Stefan Knapik, 'Vitalistic Discourses of Violin Pedagogy in the Early Twentieth Century', *19th-Century Music* 38, no. 2 (2014), 169–90; also 'The Master(ed) Violinist: Carl Flesch's Pedagogical Treatise and Memoirs', *Music & Letters* 96, no. 4 (2015), 564–601.
3 Taruskin, *Text and Act*, 299.
4 Ibid., 102.
5 Ibid., 111. For further discussion, see Taruskin, *Text and Act*, 107–51; also John Butt, *Playing with History: The Historical Approach to Musical Performance* (Cambridge: Cambridge University Press, 2002), 137–38, for a discussion of Eliot's view of Stravinsky.
6 See Butt, *Playing with History*, 132.
7 Ibid., 133–35.
8 Ibid., 135.
9 Ibid., 135–39.
10 Ibid., 134–35.
11 Ibid., 132.
12 Ibid., 139.
13 Laurence Dreyfus, 'Early Music Defended Against Its Devotees: A Theory of Historical Performance in the Twentieth Century', *Musical Quarterly* 69, no. 3 (1983), 304.
14 Ibid.
15 Ibid.
16 Taruskin, *Text and Act*, 77.
17 Ibid., 77–78.
18 Ibid., 192.
19 'All this means, ultimately, cultivating an essentially sceptical frame of mind that will allow no "truth" to pass unexamined' (ibid., 77).
20 Susanne K. Langer, *Philosophy in a New Key* (New York: Mentor Books, 1948), 193 (Langer, in turn, drawing on the work of Carroll C. Pratt); Roger Sessions, *Questions about Music* (New York: Norton, 1971), 45. Both cited in Taruskin, *Text and Act*, 109.
21 For example, ibid., 169, 237 and 334.
22 Ibid., 109.
23 Ibid., 109–10.
24 Ibid., 109.
25 Richard Taruskin, '"Alte Musik", or "Early Music"?' *Twentieth-Century Music* 8, no. 1 (2011), 3–28.
26 Ibid., 11.
27 Arnold Schoenberg, 'Today's Manner of Performing Classical Music' (1948), in *Style and Idea: Selected Writings*, ed. Leonard Stein (London: Faber and Faber, 1975), 320–22.
28 David Beard and Kenneth Gloag, *Musicology: The Key Concepts* (Abingdon and New York: Routledge, 2005), 85.
29 Friedrich Nietzsche, *Twilight of the Idols*, trans. R. J. Hollingdale (Harmondsworth, UK: Penguin Books, 1968), 24. Ernst Behler has charted Nietzsche's widespread reception across Europe and the United

Stefan Knapik

States from the 1890s onwards. Behler notes an 1888 edition of *The Gay Science* which includes an extensive list of publishers of multiple European nationalities. Russian dissidents produced a pre-revolutionary 'Nietzschean Marxism', and English intellectuals such as George Bernard Shaw saw in Nietzsche a source of subversion to stifling Victorian morality. In France and Germany Nietzsche's thought was critiqued by authors such as André Gide and Thomas Mann. Ernst Behler, 'Nietzsche in the Twentieth Century', in *The Cambridge Companion to Nietzsche*, ed. Bernd Magnus and Kathleen M. Higgin (Cambridge: Cambridge University Press, 1996), 281–322.

30 Aaron Ridley, *Routledge Philosophy Guidebook to Nietzsche on Art* (New York and London: Routledge, 2007), 141–42.

31 Andrew Bowie, *Aesthetics and Subjectivity from Kant to Nietzsche* (Manchester: Manchester University Press, 1990).

32 Friedrich Nietzsche, *Untimely Meditations*, ed. Daniel Breazeale and trans. R. J. Hollingdale (Cambridge: Cambridge University Press, 1997), 71 and 75–76.

33 Bekker, 'Improvisation und Reproduktion' (1922), in *Klang und Eros* (Stuttgart and Berlin: Deutsche Verlags-Anstalt, 1922), 294–307; extracts trans. Robert Hill as appendix to Hill, '"Overcoming Romanticism": On the Modernization of Twentieth-Century Performance Practice', in *Music and Performance during the Weimar Republic*, ed. Bryan Gilliam (Cambridge: Cambridge University Press, 1994), 56–58.

34 Ibid., 56.

35 Ibid., 57.

36 Ibid., 58.

37 Laurence Dreyfus, 'Beyond the Interpretation of Music', *Dutch Journal of Music Theory* 12, no. 3 (2007), 253.

38 Ibid., 267.

39 Josep M. Corredor, *Conversations with Casals* (London: Hutchinson, 1956), 182–84; Dreyfus, 'Beyond the Interpretation of Music', 268–69.

40 Dreyfus, 'Beyond the Interpretation of Music', 262.

41 Joseph Joachim and Andreas Moser, *Violinschule/Violin School*, 3 vols, parallel Eng. trans. Alfred Moffat (Berlin: Simrock, 1905). The use of the verb *vortragen* (which can mean to 'recite' or 'present' as well as 'express' or 'perform') supports Dreyfus's observation, in 'Beyond the Interpretation of Music', that while most countries were widely using the verb to 'interpret' by the turn of the twentieth century, *vortragen* was still widely used in Germany (before *interpretieren* gained currency). The shift in vocabulary correlates with a distancing from the idea of high-art performance as 'reproduction' and a move towards a view that defended the performer's creative role.

42 See Knapik, 'Vitalistic Discourses', 177–80.

43 Andreas Moser, *Joseph Joachim: Ein Lebensbild* (Berlin: Behr, 1900), 50. Translation adapted from Andreas Moser, *Joseph Joachim: A Biography*, trans. Lilla Durham (London: P. Wellby, 1901), 54. 'Der Vortrag einer musikalischen Komposition im Geist ihres Schöpfers ist an die Erfüllung zweiter Bedingungen geknüpft' (Joachim and Moser, *Violinschule*, 3: 5).

44 Leopold Auer, *Violin Playing as I Teach It* (New York: Frederick A. Stokes, 1921), 160.

45 'Die im vorhergehenden besprochen vier Temperamente kann man der Einfachheit halber auch in bloß zwei Gruppen teilen: in die aktiven und die die passiven Temperamente, die ihrerseits wider die Veranlassung für eine aktive oder passive Spielweise bilden// Choleriker und Sanguiniker besitzen einen starken inneren Antrieb, der sie ihre Aufgabe mit einer vom nachzuschaffenden Objekt unabhängigen Begeisterung vollbringen heißt [. . .] Melancholiker und Phlegmatiker, die Passiven, entbehren hingegen des kraftvollen inneren Antriebes, lassen sich nicht von des eigenen, sondern von des Schöpfers Gefühlswogen willenlos treiben, um bestenfalls in den lauen Wässern einer musikalisch korrekten, jedoch unpersönlichen Wiedergabe zu landen.' Carl Flesch, *Die Kunst des Violinspiels* (Berlin: Ries & Erler, 1923, 1928), 2: 61–62; Carl Flesch, *The Art of Violin Playing*, trans. Frederick H. Martens (New York: Carl Fischer, 1930), 2: 69.

46 Auer, *Violin Playing as I Teach It*, 176.

47 Ibid., 175.

48 Dreyfus, 'Beyond the Interpretation of Music', 268.

49 Ibid., 137–38.

50 The section on auto-suggestion occupies pages 98–102 of the second volume of *Die Kunst des Violinspiels* and pages 110–14 of the corresponding volume of *The Art of Violin Playing*. The entire section on hindrances fills 23 pages out of a total of 222 in the second volume of *Die Kunst des Violinspiels* and 37 pages out of a total of 237 in the same volume of *The Art of Violin Playing*.

The modernism of the mainstream

51 Martens, *Violin Mastery* (New York: Frederick A. Stokes, 1919), 262; Auer, *Violin Playing as I Teach It*, 51–52.

52 Auer, *Violin Playing as I Teach It*, 23.

53 'There are only a few of the elect who are able to correctly grasp the character of the music which they interpret.' Leopold Auer, *Violin Works and their Interpretation* (New York: Carl Fischer, 1925), vii; Auer, *Violin Playing as I Teach It*, 8.

54 'Am liebsten folgte ich ihm in jene höchsten Regionen der Musik, in deren Erschließung eines seiner unvergänglichen Verdienste liegt. Wo man bis dahin nur Eis und felsiges Gestein vermutete, da pflückte er die schönsten Alpenrosen und Edelweiß, und eröffnete den herrlichsten Fernblick auf blaue, von linden Lüften sanft bewegte Seen, umrahmt von blumengeschmückten, im Sonnenschein erstrahlenden Fluren.' Bronislaw Huberman, *Aus der Werkstatt des Virtuosen* (Leipzig and Vienna: Heller, 1912), 61.

55 Friedrich Nietzsche, *Thus Spoke Zarathustra*, trans. R. J. Hollingdale (Harmondsworth, UK: Penguin Books, 1961), 196.

56 Robert Currie, *Genius: An Ideology in Literature* (London: Chatto and Windus, 1974), 12.

57 Mary Hunter, '"To Play as if from the Soul of the Composer": The Idea of the Performer in Early Romantic Aesthetics', *Journal of the American Musicological Society* 58, no. 2 (2005), 357–98.

58 Friedrich Nietzsche, *The Gay Science, with a Prelude in Rhymes and an Appendix of Songs*, ed. and trans. Walter Kaufmann (New York: Random House, 1974), 177 and 224.

59 The American neurologist George Miller Beard coined the term 'neurasthenia' in the 1880s, a 'catch-all' disease which accounted for all kinds of maladies and shortcomings, including physical and mental exhaustion, poor appetite, and the inability to perform sexually: doctors and writers in many European countries sought to spread awareness of the malady, such as Henry Maudsley, William Playfair and T. A. Ross in England, Gerbrandus Jelgersma in the Netherlands and Paul Julius Möbius, Richard von Krafft-Ebing and Emil Kraepelin in Germany.

60 Auer, *Violin Playing as I Teach It*, 49.

61 Achille Rivarde, *The Violin and Its Technique as a Means to the Interpretation of Music* (London: Macmillan, 1921), 28. Flesch, *The Art of Violin Playing*, 1: 102; *Die Kunst*, 1: 76. Auer, *Violin Playing as I Teach It*, 33–34.

62 Michael Spitzer, *Metaphor and Musical Thought* (Chicago: University of Chicago Press, 2004), 281.

63 'Wer hier [...] durch Aufheben des Bogens eine Luftpause verursacht, ruft den Eindruck eines asthmatischen Sängers hervor, dem in entscheidenden Moment der Atem ausgeht' (Joachim and Moser, *Violinschule*, 3: 14). See Knapik, 'Vitalistic Discourses' for a fuller discussion of the negotiation of pathological anxieties in early twentieth-century discourses of string playing.

64 Frederick, H. Martens, *String Mastery: Talks with Master Violinists, Viola Players and Violoncellists* (New York: Frederick A. Stokes, 1923), 68.

65 Ibid., 65.

66 Ibid., 66.

67 Ibid.

68 Anson Rabinach, *The Human Motor: Energy, Fatigue, and the Origins of Modernity* (New York: Basic Books, 1990).

69 Volker Roelcke has charted a shift away from curative and towards preventative solutions in the work of the influential German psychiatrist Emil Kraepelin, who by 1896 had replaced the term 'neurasthenia', as a medically classified disease, with 'disorders of exhaustion'. Roelcke notes the increasing inclusion, in Kraepelin's work, of the ideas of social Darwinism, which Kraepelin used to provide hereditary accounts of the spread of nervous afflictions. Kraepelin's work contributed to the implementing of eugenics policies in many Western countries throughout the twentieth century. Volker Roelcke, 'Electrified Nerves, Degenerated Bodies: Medical Discourses on Neurasthenia in Germany, circa 1880–1914', in *Cultures of Neurasthenia from Beard to the First World War*, ed. Marijke Gijswijt-Hofstra and Roy Porter (Amsterdam and New York: Rodopi, 2001), 177–98.

70 Radkau, 'The Neurasthenic Experience', in *Cultures of Neurasthenia*, ed. Gijswijt-Hofstra and Porter, 214–15.

71 Martens, *String Mastery*, 65.

72 'Kein Mensch würde nach einem mehrwöchigen Zubettteliegen seinen Beinen zumuten, ihn schnurstracks auf dem Montblanc zu tragen und was Touristenbeinen der Montblanc, das bedeutet Geigerhänden das Griffbrett, mit dem Unterschied, daß des Griffbretts Wege nur noch viel enger und halsbrecherischer sind' (Huberman, *Aus der Werkstatt*, 22–23).

73 Martens, *Violin Mastery*, 79.

Stefan Knapik

74 Ibid., 18.

75 'Die Erfahrung lehrt, dass, wenn die Arbeit an einer Maschine derart eingerichtet ist, dass z.B. nur die Hände in Anspruch genommen sind, die Ermüdung viel rascher eintritt, als wenn die gleiche Arbeit an einer derart konstruierten Maschine vollführt wird, an welcher auch die unteren Extremitäten beteiligt sind.' Franz Ondricek and S. Mittelmann, *Neue Methode zur Erlangung der Meistertechnik des Violinspiels auf anatomisch-physiologischer Grundlage* (Vienna: Nickau und Welleminsky, 1909), 73. The English translation is given side by side with the German original but the translator is not named. All translations adapted from the original.

76 'Der Verbrauch von nutzbarem Material und die Anhäufung von Zersetzungsprodukten verteilt sich ihm letzteren Falle auf eine größere Anzahl von Muskeln, weshalb der Moment der Ermüdung später eintritt. Freilich sind die Vorgänge in der Tätigkeit der Nervenzellen nicht klar, aber aus der Reaktionsweise derselben, da sie die Fähigkeit der Reizesummation besitzen und bei fortgesetzter Reizung nach Entfaltung intensiver Wirkungen schließlich in den Zustand der Erschöpfung geraten, läßt sich das oben Gesagte auch auf das Nervensystem beziehen' (ibid., 73–74).

77 'Beim Studium der Werke großer Komponisten hilft der Meister dem Schüler, den geistigen Wert derselben zu erfassen, durch Vorführung von Wort- und Klangbildern, mit denen der Gedankengang des Komponisten erfüllt gewesen sein konnte. Die Arbeit wird abwechslungsreich, weil große Vorstellungskomplexe in Bewegung gebracht werden' (ibid., 74).

78 See David Milsom, *Theory and Practice in Late Nineteenth-Century Violin Performance: An Examination of Style in Performance, 1850–1900* (Aldershot: Ashgate, 2003), 189.

79 Auer, *Violin Playing as I Teach It*, 141.

80 Ibid., 141–42.

81 Joachim and Moser, *Violinschule*, 3: 32 ('modulationsreichen Art der Tongebung, die alle Nuancen des Ausdrucks auf der Palette hat').

82 Flesch, *Die Kunst des Violinspiels*, 2: 12. Flesch, *The Art of Violin Playing* (1930), 2: 13 ('allzu gleichmäßige und andauernde [. . .] Betonung bewirkt leicht eine, die Aufmerksamkeit des Hörers auf eine harte Probe stellende Monotonie').

83 Hans Wessely, *A Practical Guide to Violin-Playing* (London: Joseph Williams, 1913), 85.

84 'Ein Lauf, der nur als Mittel zum Zweck, nämlich zum höheren Zwecke des musikalischen Ausdrucks dient [. . .] muß der Geist des Spielers auch in der größten Geschwindigkeit sich noch immer die freie Verfügung über jedes Tönchen des Laufes vorbehalten, z. B. kaum wahrnehmbare Betonung der thematischen Noten, wenn es sich um Variationen oder Fiorituren handelt, oder einzelne Akzente, Crescendi usw., je nach den Geboten des melodischen oder harmonischen Ausdrucks' (Huberman, *Aus der Werkstatt*, 29). Huberman undertook light periods of training (among others, with Joachim's assistant, Markees) before winning acclaim at an early age. Through his teenage years he courted fame across Europe, performing at Adelina Patti's farewell concert and gaining Johannes Brahms's approval with his performance of the composer's Violin Concerto. In 1903 Huberman was invited to play the Guarneri violin that Paganini once owned.

85 Nicholas Cook, *Beyond the Score: Music as Performance* (New York: Oxford University Press, 2014), 56–90.

86 Mine Doğantan-Dack, '"Phrasing – the Very Life of Music": Performing the Music and Nineteenth-Century Performance Theory', *Nineteenth-Century Music Review* 9, no. 1 (2012), 7–30.

87 See Lee Rothfarb, 'Energetics', in *The Cambridge History of Western Music Theory*, ed. Thomas Christensen (Cambridge: Cambridge University Press, 2002), 927–55.

Bibliography

Auer, Leopold. *Violin Playing as I Teach It*. New York: Frederick A. Stokes, 1921.
———. *Violin Works and Their Interpretation*. New York: Carl Fischer, 1925.
Beard, David, and Kenneth Gloag. *Musicology: The Key Concepts*. Abingdon and New York: Routledge, 2005.
Behler, Ernst. 'Nietzsche in the Twentieth Century'. In *The Cambridge Companion to Nietzsche*, edited by Bernd Magnus and Kathleen M. Higgins, 281–322. Cambridge: Cambridge University Press, 1996.
Bekker, Paul. 'Improvisation und Reproduktion' (1922). In *Klang und Eros*, 294–307. Stuttgart and Berlin: Deutsche Verlags-Anstalt, 1922.
Bowie, Andrew. *Aesthetics and Subjectivity from Kant to Nietzsche*. Manchester: Manchester University Press, 1990.

The modernism of the mainstream

Butt, John. *Playing with History: The Historical Approach to Musical Performance*. Cambridge: Cambridge University Press, 2002.

Cook, Nicholas. *Beyond the Score: Music as Performance*. New York: Oxford University Press, 2014.

Corredor, Josep M. *Conversations with Casals*. London: Hutchinson, 1956.

Currie, Robert. *Genius: An Ideology in Literature*. London: Chatto and Windus, 1974.

Doğantan-Dack, Mine. '"Phrasing – the Very Life of Music": Performing the Music and Nineteenth-Century Performance Theory'. *Nineteenth-Century Music Review* 9, no. 1 (2012): 7–30.

Dreyfus, Laurence. 'Early Music Defended Against Its Devotees: A Theory of Historical Performance in the Twentieth Century'. *Musical Quarterly* 69, no. 3 (1983): 297–322.

———. 'Beyond the Interpretation of Music'. *Dutch Journal of Music Theory* 12, no. 3 (2007): 253–72.

Flesch, Carl. *Die Kunst des Violinspiels*. 2 vols. Berlin: Ries & Erler, 1923, 1928. Translated into English by Frederick H. Martens as *The Art of Violin Playing*. 2 vols. New York: Carl Fischer, 1930.

Gijswijt-Hofstra, Marijke, and Roy Porter, eds. *Cultures of Neurasthenia from Beard to the First World War*. Amsterdam and New York: Rodopi, 2001.

Hill, Robert. '"Overcoming Romanticism": On the Modernization of Twentieth-Century Performance Practice'. In *Music and Performance during the Weimar Republic*, edited by Bryan Gilliam, 37–58. Cambridge: Cambridge University Press, 1994.

Huberman, Bronislaw. *Aus der Werkstatt des Virtuosen*. Leipzig and Vienna: Heller, 1912.

Hunter, Mary. '"To Play as if from the Soul of the Composer": The Idea of the Performer in Early Romantic Aesthetics'. *Journal of the American Musicological Society* 58, no. 2 (2005): 357–98.

Joachim, Joseph, and Andreas Moser. *Violinschule / Violin School*. 3 vols. With parallel English translation by Alfred Moffat. Berlin and London: Simrock and Schott, 1905.

Kenyon, Nicholas, ed. *Authenticity and Early Music*. Oxford: Oxford University Press, 1988.

Knapik, Stefan. 'Vitalistic Discourses of Violin Pedagogy in the Early Twentieth Century'. *19th-Century Music* 38, no. 2 (2014): 169–90.

———. 'The Master(ed) Violinist: Carl Flesch's Pedagogical Treatise and Memoirs'. *Music & Letters* 96, no. 4 (2015): 564–601.

Langer, Susanne K. *Philosophy in a New Key*. New York: Mentor Books, 1948.

Martens, Frederick H. *Violin Mastery*. New York: Frederick A. Stokes, 1919.

———. *String Mastery: Talks with Master Violinists, Viola Players and Violoncellists*. New York: Frederick A. Stokes, 1923.

Milsom, David. *Theory and Practice in Late Nineteenth-Century Violin Performance: An Examination of Style in Performance, 1850–1900*. Aldershot: Ashgate, 2003.

Moser, Andreas. *Joseph Joachim: Ein Lebensbild*. Berlin: Behr, 1900. Translated into English by Lilla Durham as *Joseph Joachim: A Biography*. London: P. Wellby, 1901.

Nietzsche, Friedrich. *Thus Spoke Zarathustra*. Translated by R. J. Hollingdale. Harmondsworth, UK: Penguin Books, 1961.

———. *Twilight of the Idols*. Translated by R. J. Hollingdale. Harmondsworth, UK: Penguin Books, 1968.

———. *The Gay Science, with a Prelude in Rhymes and an Appendix of Songs*. Edited and translated by Walter Kaufmann. New York: Random House, 1974.

———. *Untimely Meditations*. Edited by Daniel Breazeale. Translated by R. J. Hollingdale. Cambridge: Cambridge University Press, 1997.

Ondricek, Franz, and S. Mittelmann. *Neue Methode zur Erlangung der Meistertechnik des Violinspiels auf anatomisch-physiologischer Grundlage*. Vienna: Nickau & Welleminsky, 1909.

Rabinach, Anson. *The Human Motor: Energy, Fatigue, and the Origins of Modernity*. New York: Basic Books, 1990.

Radkau, Joachim. 'The Neurasthenic Experience'. In *Cultures of Neurasthenia*, edited by Gijswijt-Hofstra and Porter, 199–218.

Ridley, Aaron. *Routledge Philosophy Guidebook to Nietzsche on Art*. New York and London: Routledge, 2007.

Rivarde, Achille. *The Violin and Its Technique as a Means to the Interpretation of Music*. London: Macmillan, 1921.

Roelcke, Volker. 'Electrified Nerves, Degenerated Bodies: Medical Discourses on Neurasthenia in Germany, circa 1880–1914'. In *Cultures of Neurasthenia*, edited by Gijswijt-Hofstra and Porter, 177–98.

Rothfarb, Lee. 'Energetics'. In *The Cambridge History of Western Music Theory*, edited by Thomas Christensen, 927–55. Cambridge: Cambridge University Press, 2002.

Schoenberg, Arnold. 'Today's Manner of Performing Classical Music' (1948). In *Style and Idea: Selected Writings*, edited by Leonard Stein, 320–22. London: Faber and Faber, 1975.

Stefan Knapik

Sessions, Roger. *Questions about Music*. New York: Norton, 1971.
Spitzer, Michael. *Metaphor and Musical Thought*. Chicago: University of Chicago Press, 2004.
Taruskin, Richard. *Text and Act*. Oxford: Oxford University Press, 1995.
———. '"Alte Musik", or "Early Music"?' *Twentieth-Century Music* 8, no.1 (2011): 3–28.
Wessely, Hans. *A Practical Guide to Violin-Playing*. London: Joseph Williams, 1913.

INDEX

Note: Page numbers in *italic* indicate a figure or example on the corresponding page.

AACM 222–23
Abbate, Carolyn 427, 429, 432
acousmatic 299
acoustics 407, 411
Adams, John 2, 236; and postmodernism 14, 21–22, 328–29, 330–33, 340, 344, 349n76, 375; WORKS: *The Death of Klinghoffer* 429; *Doctor Atomic* 429; *El Niño* 332; *Harmonielehre* 328, 330–33, *331*; *Light over Water* 331; *Nixon in China* 429
Adams, John Luther 190, 194n74
Adès, Thomas 339–44, 349n76, 354, 358; and postmodernism 21, 328, 340–43, 344; WORKS: *Asyla* 328, 340–43, *342*; *Brahms* 358; *Polaris* 340; *In Seven Days* 343; *Tevot* 340, 343
Adorno, Theodor W. 7, 15, 25n38, 50n14, 127n43, 161, 162, 170, 172n12, 327, 344, 357, 457, 461, 462, 464, 466, 467, 470; on Auschwitz 43; autonomy vs identity 206; and Baudelaire 26n48; and the beautiful 133–35; and Berg 117; and Boulez 112, 122, 123, 125; and Debussy 112–14, 120, 121, 127n35; and history 18, 109, 110–15, 117–18, 120–21, 125, 127n32, 127n43; on ISCM name 62, 72; on mass vs autonomous art 240, 243, 245–46, 247, 252, 253; and *Materialstand* 6; and new music (*Neue Musik*) 71–74, 111–12, 133–34, 275; and resistance in music 222, 226, 227, 228; on Strauss 37; on Stravinsky 113, 114, 123, 127n35; and the sublime 141–42, 148; and Taruskin 15, 115, 117, 118, 120, 121, 123–24; WRITINGS: *Aesthetic Theory* 26n39, 114, 134, 245; 'The Aging of the New Music' 71, 134; *Dialectic of Enlightenment* 5; *In Search of Wagner* 36, 457; 'Music and New Music' 71, 134; *Philosophy*

of New Music (*Philosophie der Neuen Musik*) 9, 26n39, 112, 113, 122, 172n3, 189; 'Sacred Fragment: Schoenberg's Moses und Aron' 141–42; 'Stravinsky: A Dialectical Portrait' 113, 114; 'Vers une musique informelle' 112, 114, 227
aesthetics 11, 157, 158; Adorno on 74, 134; of the beautiful and the sublime 233–48; vs institutional theory 18, 93, 100, 102, 103, 106n83
affect 21, 307–21; definition 308–9; and emotion, feeling 308–12; in late modernist music 315–19
affective turn in modernist studies 321, 323n52
Against Modern Opera Productions (Facebook group) 468
Agamben, Giorgio 58, 80n67, 429, 430
Agawu, V. Kofi 79n35, 178, 192n27
agency 162, 311, 484
Agrupación Nueva Música 183
Aguila, Jésus 403
Albèra, Philippe 142–43
Albright, Daniel 41, 240
Alden, Jane 296
aleatory techniques and chance 42, 296, 299–300, 343, 404
Alford, Robert R. 94, 95
alienation 68, 243, 244
Allanbrook, Wye Jamieson 50n3
Altieri, Charles 308, 311, 316, 319
AMM 225
amplification 4, 13, 337
Amy, Gilbert 402, 417
Andersen, Hans Christian 437
Anderson, Benedict 175
Anderson, Julian 317, 333

Index

Andriessen, Louis 225
Anhalt, István 380
Ankersmit, Frank 157
Antheil, George, *Ballet mécanique* 13, 220
anthropology 290, 291
anti-hegemonic music 218–23, 224–30, 240
Aperghis, Georges: *Die Hamletmaschine-Oratorio* 428; *Récitations* 428
Apollinaire, Guillaume 40
Appadurai, Arjun 179, 180
Appel Jr, Alfred 254n37
Appia, Adolphe 457, 458, 459, 462, 464
Appiah, Anthony 190
appropriation 179, 220, 223, 269–70, 391, 394; and 'masculine sublime' 137, 147
archaeology 260, 288
Arditti Quartet 362
Argentina 182–83, 186, 187, 200, 209, 210
Argerich, Martha 182
Armstrong, Louis 225, 244
art: Adorno and 72, 111, 134, 135; artworld and institutional theory 99–100, 102, 103; Baudelaire on 124–25; the beautiful and sublime 133, 134, 135, 136, 139; Cage and 301, 345; contemporary art 58–61, 72–73, 77, 261, 266, 268; Deleuze and Guattari on 309; vs entertainment/mass culture 217, 226, 469–70; and history 117, 118; modern(ist) art 58, 68, 72, 134, 243, 355; Nietzsche on 480; revolutionary and anti-hegemonic art 220, 226, 227, 240; Schoenberg on 135
art history 72, 117, 128n60
art music: boundaries and definitions 262, 269, 276, 278n36, 301; and indigenous traditions 123–24, 202, 204, 379–94; question of autonomy in 275, 278n47; under colonialism and postcolonialism 177–91; Western art music vs popular culture 4, 161, 268, 278n54
Arts Council: Arts Council England 268, 274; of Great Britain 263
artworld 18, 99–100, 101–3, 105n68, 105n74
Ashby, Arved 224, 243, 314, 315
Asian Composers League 187
Association of British Orchestras 279n53
atonality 7, 56, 61, 136, 207, 354, 356, 358, 456; Schoenberg and 39, 112, 220
Attali, Jacques 273, 282n107, 282n114, 318; *Bruits (Noise)* 273, 282n114
Attinello, Paul 447n7
Attwenger duo 271
Auer, Leopold 476, 481–85, 488–89, 490; *Violin Playing as I Teach It* 482, 483, 484, 489; *Violin Works and their Interpretation* 484, 493n53
Augé, Marc 283n121
Auschwitz 128n56, 466
Austria 59, 62, 64, 142, 206
authenticity 345, 475, 476, 477, 482

authority: anti-hegemonic music 218, 230; claim of modernism to cultural authority 1–2, 40, 56, 263; legitimation crisis and cultural authority 69; and the performing subject 481, 490; tacit authority of colonial discourse 179, 188
autonomy: in art/modernist music 1, 16, 68, 115, 179, 199, 206–11, 228, 245, 253, 270–71, 275, 346, 355, 446; creative autonomy of composer/performer 94, 295, 480–85; as criticality 1, 19, 222, 253, 275
auto-suggestion 483, 492n50
avant-garde 14, 21, 39, 77n10, 125, 232n28, 239; and affect 319; and the anti-hegemonic 216–18, 223–24, 228; in Argentina 183; and the beautiful 136; in Britain 59; and comedy 42; and communication 301, 302; and the contemporary 57, 76; Eco on 280n60; and faithful/reactive modernism 155; in Finland 185; free improvisation 223; in Japan 186; Kagel and 101, 297; and mass culture 240, 247, 253; and postmodernism 50n9, 345; and the sublime 139–40
Avanti! 185
Ayler, Albert 249

Babbitt, Milton 57, 217, 240, 298, 356; 'The Composer as Specialist'/'Who Cares if You Listen?' 298
Bacarisse, Salvador 19, 201–2
Bach, C. P. E. 481–82
Bach, J. S. 56, 462, 477, 479
Badiou, Alain 19, 21, 36, 50n15, 158, 160, 171, 320; *The Century* 36;
Baillet, Jérôme 409, 415, 423n53
Baird, Tadeusz 95
Baker, Geoffrey 178, 180
Bakhtin, Mikhail, *Rabelais and His World* 40
Bali à Montréal (CD) 381, 395n14
Balinese music 22, 379–94; Kunst on 395n15
Bal y Gay, Jesús 202–3, 210, 211; *Serenata para orquesta de cuerda* 210
Balzer, David 273
Bangs, Lester 255n64
Bannwart, Patrick 465
Barber, Samuel 427
Barenboim, Daniel 182, 456, 457, 460
Barnby, Sir Joseph 81n78
Barney, Matthew 261
Barrett, Richard 359
Barron, Bebe 292
Barron, Louis 292
Barry, Gerald 372
Barthes, Roland 80n66, 94, 270, 430
Bartlett, Martin 382
Bartók, Béla 7, 10, 70, 79n38, 83n111, 120, 121, 340, 343, 354; Adorno on 120, 189; and ethnomusicology 186, 291; and exile 204, 208; WORKS: *Bluebeard's Castle* 340; *Music for Strings, Percussion and Celesta* 121

Index

Basar, Shumon 258, 259, 260
Basic Channel 251
Bates, Mason 279n55
Baudelaire, Charles 18, 109, 124–25, 131n107,
419; Adorno on 26n48; and Boulez 121–22,
123–25; *Les fleurs du mal* 7; 'The Painter of
Modern Life' 125; 'Le voyage' 125–26
Baudrillard, Jean 330
Bauhaus movement 220
Bauman, Zygmunt 274, 277n21
Bautista, Julián 200
Bayles, Martha 244
Bayreuth 457, 458, 462
BBC (British Broadcasting Corporation) 1, 70,
204, 205, 263, 404, 406
Beard, David 479
Beard, George Miller 485, 487, 493n59
beauty in music 18, 102, 133–48; Adorno on
133–35; Lachenmann and 135–38; and the
sublime 139–40; Schoenberg and 135
Becker, Howard 99, 100, 101, 102, 103
Beckerman, Michael 200
Beckett, Samuel 10, 43, 48, 428, 458, 470, 471
Beckles Willson, Rachel 178, 207
Bedford, Herbert 80n59
Bedrossian, Franck 145
Beethoven, Ludwig van 7, 112, 159, 160, 162–63,
165, 270, 272, 317, 356, 357, 456; Adorno
on 252; and Rihm 138; and Wagner 147,
356; WORKS: Piano Concerto no. 5 in E-flat
'Emperor' 331; Sonata in E-flat 'Les Adieux'
339; Symphony no. 3 in E-flat 'Eroica' 165, 331;
Symphony no. 7 in A 317; Symphony no. 9 in
D minor 162–63; Violin Concerto in D 489
Béhague, Gerard 194n64
Behler, Ernst 491n29
Bekker, Paul 12, 480–81
Bell, Alexander Graham 289
Bell, Daniel 276, 335
Belmore, Rebecca 280n68
Benjamin, George 429
Benjamin, Walter 7, 36, 71, 111, 245, 429, 464
Bennett, Arnold 4
Bense, Max 294
Bentham, Jeremy 272, 282n105
Benveniste, Émile 435
Berberian, Cathy 294
Berg, Alban 65, 117, 133, 298, 354, 358, 427;
Altenberg Lieder 134; *Lulu* 65, 470; Violin
Concerto 205, 357; *Wozzeck* 142, 427
Berger, Karol 8, 9, 275
Bergman, Erik 185, 186, 187, 193n43
Bergson, Henri 33, 45, 47
Berio, Luciano 94, 97, 292, 293, 294, 339, 394,
428; *Circles* 294; *Différences* 266; *Omaggio a Joyce*
294; *Opera* 428; *Sequenza III* 294
Berlant, Laurent 33, 309

Berlin 44, 62
Berlin, Isaiah 456
Berliner, Emil 289
Berman, Marshall 108, 111
Bernard, Jonathan 329
Bernhard, Thomas, *Gargoyles* 367
Bernstein, David 394n1
Beyer, Robert 292
Beyoncé 279n54
Bhabha, Homi 179, 188, 189, 191
Bick, Sally 207
Biddle, Ian 308, 315
Bierce, Ambrose 442, 443, 444, 445
Binkley, Thomas 477
Birtwistle, Harrison 1, 281n78, 368, 375; *The Mask
of Orpheus* 455; *Panic* 368; *Theseus Game* 368
Bishop, Claire 260
Bistoen, Gregory 171
Bizet, Georges 119
Black Arts Movement 218, 239
Blake, Andrew 279n58
Blast Theory 106n83
Blitzstein, Marc 243
Bloch, Ernst 44, 277n29
Blonay, André de 67
blues 239, 243
Boccioni, Umberto 368
Bohlman, Andrea 201, 208
Boivin, Jean 402
Bolaño, César 183
Bonaparte, Louis-Napoléon *see* Napoleon III
Bonnard, Pierre 127n32
Bons, Joël 144
Borduas, Paul-Émile 380
Borges, Jorge Luis 183
Borio, Gianmario 206–7
Born, Georgina 91–92, 228, 235n117, 246, 394
Bösch, David 23, 465–68
Bose, Hans-Jürgen von 335
Boston Manifesto 58
Botstein, Leon 201
Boudreau, Walter 415; *Le matin des magiciens* 381
Boulanger, Nadia 203, 379
Boulez, Pierre 1, 10, 15–16, 57, 95, 220, 263,
266, 339, 354, 382, 429; and Adorno 112, 122,
123, 125; and Argentina 183; and Baudelaire
7, 121–22, 123–25; on Berg 358; and Cage
42; and Darmstadt 97; and Debussy 7, 122–23,
124, 356; and the Domaine Musical 263, 380,
402; and history 7, 18, 108–10, 112, 113, 115,
121–25, 128n52; and IRCAM 91, 292, 335;
and Mallarmé 296; and Schoenberg 356; and
opera production 457, 459, 460; and spectralism
22, 402–9, 411, 421–22; and Wagner 356, 459,
460, 462, 464, 470; on Webern 112, 356, 404,
421n31; WORKS: *Cummings ist der Dichter* 403;
Domaines 406, 423n59; *Don* 406, 410, 411; *Éclat*

404; . . . *explosante/fixe*. . . 375n1; *Figures, Doubles, Prismes* 403, 423n59; *Improvisations sur Mallarmé* 95, 294, 404; *Livre pour cordes* 296; *Le marteau sans maître* 404; *Pli selon pli* 294, 403, 404, 405, 406, 410; *Poésie pour pouvoir* 404; *Répons* 147; *Structures* 42, 94, 95, 97; WRITINGS: 'À la limite du pays fertile' 123; 'Alea' 296; 'La corruption dans les encensoirs' 123–24, 130n103; 'Eventuellement. . .' ('Possibly. . .') 121; *Penser la musique aujourd'hui* (*Boulez on Music Today*) 108, 390, 402, 403, 417, 421n28; 'Recherches maintenant' 404; *Relevés d'apprenti* (*Stocktakings from an Apprenticeship*) 403; 'Schoenberg est mort' 121, 298; 'Stravinsky demeure' ('Stravinsky Remains') 123; 'Tendances de la musique récente' 404

Bourdieu, Pierre 1, 221, 233n53
bourgeoisie: in Catalonia 208, 209; and Futurism 217–18; and 'inauthentic' beauty 133, 134, 136; modernist music as critique of 68, 221–23, 225–27, 335, 346; Offenbach's *Orphée* as critique of 35, 37; and 'popular modernism', 243
Bowie, Andrew 429, 447, 476, 480
Boys, Henry 79n38, 81n89
Brabbins, Martyn 281n78
Bradbury, Malcolm 21, 355, 356
Brahms, Johannes 8, 56, 356, 358, 494n84
Braudel, Fernand 117
Brecht, Bertolt 44, 45, 219, 224, 225, 232n33, 240; *Die Dreigroschenoper* (*The Threepenny Opera*) 44, 243
Brendel, Alfred 358
Breton, André 341, 375n1, 403
Brinkmann, Reinhold 211n7
British musical modernism 353–75; and the ISCM 58–59, 62, 69–70, 76
British Music Information Centre 281n77
Britten, Benjamin 3, 170, 353, 355, 427
broadcasting 4, 13, 82n90, 178, 289
Broadway 204, 239, 243
Brodsky, Seth, *From 1989* 6, 25n38
Brötzmann, Peter 251
Brown, Earle 296, 380
Brown, James 250
Browning, Robert 155
Bruant, Aristide 244
Brunet, Jacques 395n16
Buenos Aires 182, 379
Bugs Bunny 47–49; *The Rabbit of Seville* 48, 49; *What's Opera, Doc?* 49
Bulley, James 20, 262, 267–68, 272, 280n73, 280n76; *Living Symphonies* 20, 262, 267–68, 272
bunraku theatre 382
Buñuel, Luis 200
Bürger, Peter 232n28, 240
Burgoon, Judee K. 289, 293
Burke, Edmund 133, 139, 140, 146, 147

Busoni, Ferruccio 243, 244, 298; *Sketch of a New Aesthetic of Music* 289–90, 298
Butler, Judith 16
Butor, Michel 428
Butt, John 8, 345, 475, 477, 480
Byrd, Joseph 301

cabaret 204, 244, 253
Cabaret Voltaire 217
Cage, John 13, 95, 186, 220, 263, 266, 292, 293, 296–99, 304n60, 380, 415; at 1954 Donaueschingen Festival 102–3; and humour 38, 42, 47, 51n29; and popular music 246; and the sublime 147; WORKS: *0'00"* 280n62, 299, 300, 304n55; *4'33"* 38, 280n62, 296, 297, 303n36, 345; *Aria* 428; *Atlas Eclipticalis* 299–301; *Concert for Piano and Orchestra* 103; *Europeras* 428; *Music of Changes* 328, 343; *Solo for Piano* 103; *Variations IV* 299–301, 332, 304n59
Cahill, Thaddeus 290
Calvino, Italo 52n31, 430
Calvocoressi, Michel-Dimitri 67, 80n59
Calzabigi, Ranieri de' 455
Canetti, Elias 44
cantometrics (Lomax) 294
capitalism 222–23, 225–26, 260, 262, 309, 334
Carnegy, Patrick 457, 458, 459
Carter, Chandler 11
Carter, Elliott 1
Cartesian subject 319, 320, 321
Casals, Pablo 481
Casella, Alfredo 83n111, 218
Castorf, Frank 459
Castro, José Maria 182
Castro, Juan José 182
Caux, Daniel 415
Cavarero, Adriana 430
Cavell, Stanley 430, 446
CDMC *see* Centre de Documentation de la Musique Contemporaine
Celan, Paul 43
Cendo, Raphaël, *Rokh* 145
centre and periphery model 59, 176–77, 181–82, 184, 187–89, 302n11, 379
Centre de Documentation de la Musique Contemporaine (CDMC) 145
Cézanne, Paul 127n32, 140
Cezar, Corneliu 424n74
Chaikovsky, Pyotr Ilyich 128n56, 271, 463
Chalk, Bridget T. 213n36
Chamberlain, Houston Stewart 457
Chamberland, Paul 435
chance *see* aleatory techniques and chance
Chance, James 250
Chandler, Chas 247
Chang, Ha-Joon 89, 90, 104n9
chant *see* Gregorian chant

Index

Chat Noir, Le 244
Chávez, Carlos 187, 193n42, 193n43; *El fuego nuevo* 184
Chen, Qigang 281n84
Chéreau, Patrice 457, 459, 460, 470
Chernilo, Daniel 191
Childs, Peter 5, 6
Chin, Unsuk 281n84
China 186, 187, 194n58, 281n83, 281n84, 393
Chou Wen-chung 186
Chowning, John, *Stria* 415
Chowrimootoo, Christopher 3
Christian, Bryan 435
Christie, William 477
Cicognini, Giacinto Andrea 441
cinema 131n105, 204, 207, 267, 279n58, 289, 427
city type (Simmel) 239, 242, 253n1
CLAEM (Centro Latinoamericano de Altos Estudios Musicales) 183, 193n39
Clark, Edward 72, 80n65
Clark, T. J. 7, 10; *Farewell to an Idea* 6
Clarke, David 60, 69, 78n23, 79n35, 253n2
Clarke, James 21, 354, 358–62, 363–68, 375; String Quartet no. 3 362, *363–65*; *Untitled no. 2 for Piano and Orchestra* 359–62, *360*, *361*, 367; *Untitled no. 5* 362; *Untitled no. 7* 362, 366–68, *366*, *367*, 372, 373; *Untitled* series 358–59; *Verstörung* 367
classical music (Western): and non-Western traditions 123–24, 177–91, 202, 204; and performance practice 477–79; and popular culture 240; status and cultural currency 266, 345, 466
classicism 3, 9, 353–54
Claudel, Paul 124
Clifford, James 190
Clyne, Anna 279n56; *Night Ferry* 20, 262, 264–66, 279n55
CMN *see* Contemporary Music Network
CNN operas 429
cognition 310–11, 313, 490
Cohen, Bridget 207
Cohen, Ted 102, 106n82, 106n83
Coleman, Ornette 249
Cologne school 101, 266
colonialism 60, 177–80, 187–89, 223, 269, 270, 391
coloured silence (Stockhausen) 413
Columbia-Princeton studio 292
Comédie Française 35
comedy 33–49; and anti-Romanticism 34, 37, 40; Bergson on 45; bridging 'high' and 'low' culture 44–45; in Cage 38, 42; comic indifference 45, 48; and cruelty 43–44; in Hayes 368; and humourlessness 42; in Ligeti 39–40, 432; and Nietzsche 38, 39, 40, 43; in Offenbach's *Orphée* 34–36, 37, 47; and postmodernism 33–34; in

Poulenc 40–42, 49; in Schoenberg 39; in Strauss 37–38; in Stravinsky 36, 46, 47, 49; in Verdi 39; and Webern 42
Comentale, Edward 243
commercialism 204, 253; modernism's disavowal of 226, 241, 468
commissioning (of new music) 264, 265, 266
communication 224, 253, 287–302, 384, 393; and language in opera 430, 445; multimodality of 297–99; in postmodernism 327–28
computer technology 13, 274, 289, 292, 334, 335, 401
conceptual imperialism 124, 125
Conciertos de la Nueva Música 183
Cone, Edward T. 427
Connor, Steven 68, 81n70
Conrad, Peter 7
consciousness: political 224, 225, 229, 240, 246; and subjectivity 311, 315, 316, 320
conservatism: vs modernism 10, 11, 14, 16, 23; and nationalism 182, 187
conservatoires 178, 192n12
consonance: vs dissonance 135, 163, 170, 290, 337, 353; 'higher' consonance 356, 359, 367; and suspended tonality 267–68; in spectralism 402, 414, 424n74
constitutive outside (Derrida) 16, 162
constructivism 217, 228, 234n86, 240, 417, 418
consumer culture 228, 248, 260, 268, 272–73, 335; Adorno and 222, 226, 246; modernist antipathy to 217, 222–23, 226
contemporary art 58–61, 72–73, 77, 261, 266, 268
contemporary: as category 56–61, 68–70, 259–61; as distinct from modern and new 62–63, 72–73; in the ISCM 56–77; 'international contemporary' 58, 64–66, 74–76
Contemporary Music Centre, London 72, 75, 78n21
Contemporary Music Network (CMN) 263, 264, 279n53, 281n77
Contemporary Music Review (journal) 56–57
Contortions, The 250
Cook, Nicholas 180, 191n3, 490
Cooksey, Douglas 138
Copland, Aaron 183, 184
cosmopolitanism 74, 82n102, 190–91, 262, 278n33
Coué, Emil 482
counterpoint (Edward Said) 178, 188, 192n11
Couperin, François 340
Coupland, Douglas 258, 259, 260, 276n2; *Generation X* 258
Coxhill, Lol 247
Craps, Stef 171
Crary, Jonathan 260
Crew, Beverley 264
cricket, indigenization of 180

501

Index

criollo identity 182, 184
critical composition 221
criticality 19, 221–22, 240, 243, 245, 247, 250, 251
critical musicology 344, 346
critical theory 25n38, 110–11, 115, 123, 222, 344
Cross, Jonathan 291
Crow, Thomas E. 233n66
cubism 113, 354, 368
Culkin, John 92
culture industry 162, 222, 245–46, 466, 467, 469
curationism (Balzer) 273
Curran, Alvin 218; *Vindobona Blues* 20, 262, 271–72
Currie, Robert 484

Dack, John 298
Dada movement 38, 217, 220, 228
Dahlhaus, Carl 37, 50n6, 277n29, 357; on history
109, 116, 117, 127n32, 128n52, 128n60; on the
modern and the new 3, 7, 25n23, 63
Dalbavie, Marc-André 417
Dallapiccola, Luigi 83n111, 183
Dalmayer, Fred 191
Damasio, Antonio 311
Danto, Arthur 61, 72–73, 99, 102, 103, 106n83
Danuser, Hermann 208
Darcy, Warren 357
Darmstadt International Summer Courses 1,
18, 42, 82n90, 88–89, 95–99, 110, 182, 183,
185, 187, 337, 403; 'Darmstadt School' as
institutionalized avant-garde 60, 97, 248,
283n135; Grisey and 335, 400, 407, 411, 415
Daverio, John 357
David, Jacques-Louis 7
Davies, Peter Maxwell 221, 266, 281n78, 339, 357,
375; *Alma Redemptoris Mater* 357; *Te Lucis Ante
Terminum* 357
De Volharding *see* Orkest De Volharding
Deathridge, John 458
Debussy, Claude 7, 10, 12, 18, 109, 112–14, 119,
121, 244, 272, 408; and Adorno 112–14, 120,
121; and Boulez 122–23, 124, 356; and gamelan
music 189, 291, 381; and Ortega 12, 118,
119, 120, 121; Taruskin on 118–23, 129n64,
129n68, 129n77; WORKS: 'Fêtes' (*Nocturnes*) 118;
'Golliwog's Cakewalk' (*Children's Corner*) 51n30,
120, 130n82; *Jeux* 122; *mélodies* 119, 121; *La mer*
113, 141; *Pelléas et Mélisande* 12, 456; *Le petit
nègre* 244; *Pour le piano* 113; *Prélude à l'après-midi
d'un faune* 7, 109; *Préludes*, book 1 117–19;
decolonization 179, 180, 188
deconstruction 334
Degen, Helmut 401
degree of change (Grisey) 413–14, 417, 424n64,
424n67
dehumanization (Ortega) 11–12, 118, 119–21,
129n77, 476
Deleuze, Gilles 190, 282n106, 309, 310

délire 445, 447
democratic modernism 19, 216, 227–30, 240, 261,
263
Denis, Maurice 127n34
Dent, Edward 58, 61–64, 66, 75, 76, 78n21, 79n48
Derrida, Jacques 418, 456; constitutive outside 16;
différence/différance 42, 334–35, 348n43; and the
sublime 133, 141, 146, 147; *The Truth in Painting*
146
Descartes, René 319, 320
Destiny's Child 251, 252
Dickie, George 99–100, 102, 105n68, 106n82
Dickinson, Emily 125
Diebenkorn, Richard 366
Diepeveen, Leonard 219, 227; and 'difficulty' in
modernism 227–28
différance (Derrida) 42, 348n43
digital technology 60, 79n28, 258–59, 263,
269–70, 273–74, 282n102
Dillon, James 222
Dilthey, Wilhelm 477
discrimination 2, 222, 275
displacement 19, 199, 201, 203, 205–7, 210, 211;
see also emigration, exile, migration
dissonance 63, 135, 208, 266, 290, 298;
emancipation of 10, 19, 159, 163, 165, 170–71,
220, 232n39, 353, 356, 375n6
distant reading (Moretti) 175
Dixon, Bill 220
DNA (band) 250
dodecaphony *see* twelve-tone technique
Doğantan-Dack, Mine 490
Dolar, Mladen 52n52, 430
Dolmetsch, Arnold 477, 481
Domaine Musical, Paris 263, 380, 402
Donaueschingen Festival (Donaueschinger
Musiktage) 18, 61, 62, 102, 283n15
Dreyfus, Laurence 475, 477–78, 479, 481, 482,
490, 492n41
drives (psychoanalysis) 315
Drott, Eric 282n114, 333, 334
Dubber, Andrew 273
Duchamp, Marcel 102, 106n83
Dufourt, Hugues 22, 400, 401, 403, 416, 417–19,
425n85
Dutilleux, Henri 22, 401, 404, 409
dynamic sublime 147
Dynamophon 290

Earle, Ben 2, 217
Early Music movement 345, 475, 476, 477–78,
479, 490, 491
Ears Open (Korvat Auki) association 185
Eco, Umberto 280n60, 282n102, 295, 296; *Opera
aperta* (*The Open Work*) 296
écriture 22, 405, 419; *écriture liminale* 401, 418
Edison, Thomas 289

502

Index

Eimert, Herbert 292

Eisenstadt, Shmuel 379

Eisler, Hanns: anti-hegemonic music 221, 225, 232n29; exile 201, 202, 207, 208; ISCM 64, 66, 67; WORKS: *Hollywooder Liederbuch* 208; *Reisesonate* 208

electroacoustic music 336, 406–7; rise of electroacoustic music 291–93; *see also* electronic music

electronic dance music 251, 252, 271, 340, 341, 343

electronic music 13, 183, 266, 290, 291–93, 294, 297, 298, 301, 380; and spectralism 333–37, 406–7

Elgar, Edward 3, 8

Eliot, T. S. 4, 14, 216, 477, 480

elitism 58, 121, 221, 226, 227, 228, 230, 239, 248, 249, 274, 304n60, 346, 476, 484; Ortega and 11–12

Ellington, Duke 244, 254n37

Elliott, Missy 251, 252

Elman, Mischa 482

Eloy, Jean-Claude 402–3, 405, 417, 420n15; *Étude III* 403; *Fluctuante-immuable* 403; *Kâmakalâ* 403; *Polychronies* 420n15; *Shânti* 403

emancipation of dissonance 10, 19, 163, 165, 170, 171, 220, 353, 356; Schoenberg origin 375n6

emigration 49; *see also* displacement, exile, migration

Emmerson, Simon 264, 274

emotion: and affect, feeling 21, 307–12; and comedy 41, 45–46. 47; and communication 287–88; 'emotionalization of the intellect' 454, 462; emotional turn in modernist music studies 312–15; Lachenmann on 467; in Murail 316–17; in performance 478, 482; and postmodernism 330, 333; and rationality 16, 47, 89; and the sublime 146; and the voice 438, 441; in Xenakis 317–19

emotional turn in modernist studies 312–15

empire 177, 178, 180, 188, 189, 190

empiricism 60, 172n5

Engels, Friedrich 462

Enlightenment 143, 162, 163, 165, 191, 301, 320, 456

Eno, Brian 249

Ensslin, Gudrun 437, 438, 466, 467

entertainment: industry 1, 274, 310; and operatic production 454, 469–70; vs art 222, 226, 239, 245, 275, 469

Entgrenzung (Osborne) 261

Erlmann, Veit 188

Escher, M. C. 390

Eshun, Kodwo 251

esthesis 10, 116, 123, 128n56

Estrada, Julio 184

ethnomusicology 110, 175, 176, 178, 291

eugenics 487, 493n69

Evangelista, José 22, 381, 382, 390, 393, 394, 397n43; *Clos de vie* 388, 397n44; *Immobilis in mobili* 391; *Ô Bali* 381, 388–90, *389*, 397n48; *Ô Gamelan* 388; *Ô Java* 381, 388

Evans, Edwin 73, 75, 78n21

Evans, Richard J. 108, 109, 115, 116, 128n56

Événements du Neuf, Les 388, 390, 391

event (Badiou) 62, 158–62, 170–71; modernist event (Fisher), 248

Everett, Yayoi Uno 181

Evers, Megdar 43

Ex, The (group) 251

exclusivity of modernism 1, 2

exile 47, 65, 199–211; *see also* displacement, emigration, migration

exoticism 124, 125, 185, 187–88, 190, 230, 270, 317, 384, 386, 391, 393

Experimental Studio of Polish Radio 95

Exposition Universelles 130n103, 381

expression in modernism (Metzer) 312, 313, 314

expressionism 7, 94, 128n52, 307, 368

extreme present (Basar and Coupland) 258, 260, 263

extroverted modernism (Bayles) 244

faithful modernism, faithful subject 19, 155, 157–60, 162, 163, 170, 171

Falla, Manuel de 203, 210

fascism 2, 11, 46, 208, 217, 218, 231n9, 253, 466

Fauré, Gabriel 161, 402

Federation of Newly Rising Composers (Japan) 186

feeling 296, 478; definition 308, 311–12; and emotion, affect 308–12; emotional turn 314, 315; in late modernist music 315–19; and subjectivity 21, 307, 319, 321

Fehling, Jürgen 456

Feldman, Morton 143–44, 380, 428; *For Philip Guston* 144; *Neither* 428

feminine sublime (Freeman) 147

Feneyrou, Laurent 435

Ferneyhough, Brian 99, 144, 147, 190, 335, 375, 393, 429; *Shadowtime* 429; *Time and Motion Study III* 144; *Unity Capsule* 144

Féron, François-Xavier 348n51, 409

figure (gestalt theory) 407

film music 129n77, 131n105, 162, 200, 204, 207, 265, 267, 279n58, 289, 292

Fine, Robert 82n102

Fink, Robert 255n67, 427, 428, 429

Finland 184–85, 187

Finnegan, Ruth 289

Finnissy, Michael 21, 190, 191, 194n74, 354, 357–58, 368, 375; *English Country Tunes* 190; *First Political Agenda* 368; *Second Political Agenda* 357–58

First World War *see* World War I

Index

Fischer, David Hackett 128n53, 128n60
Fisher, Mark 247–49, 283n126
Flaubert, Gustave 94
Flesch, Carl 476, 482–83, 485, 489, 490; *Die Kunst des Violinspiels* 482, 483, 492n50
Fleuret, Maurice 406
Flimm, Jürgen 137, 457
Fluxus 40, 221, 267, 414
Fo, Dario 435
folk music: Adorno and 189; in Argentinian modernism 182–83; and Bartók 204; and Catalan *modernisme* 208; in Debussy 130n82; in Ligeti 339, 432; in Mahler 343; and modality 63; in modernist historiography 290–91
Forbidden Planet (film) 292
Forestry Commission England 268
formalism 188, 240, 241
Formes software 91
formula (Stockhausen) 339, 348n59
Forster, E. M. 4
Foster, Hal 61
Foucault, Michel 4, 57, 131n108, 282n105, 320, 323n47
Fourier, Joseph 290
fragment 34
Franck, César 182
Frank, Alan 72, 73
Frankfurt School 5, 6, 25n38, 110, 240, 241
Franklin, Peter 217, 223, 231n7
free improvisation 218, 223, 224, 229, 234n93, 246
free jazz 218, 219, 246, 249, 250, 251
Freeman, Barbara Claire 147
Freud, Sigmund 42, 162, 319, 320, 463
Friedland, Roger 94, 95
Friedrich, Caspar David 333
Frith, Simon 246, 346
Fry, Roger 7
Fuente, Eduardo de la 5
Fuhrmann, Wolfgang 295
Fujii, Kiyomi 186
Fuller-Maitland, J. A. 484
funding of new music 264, 269, 279n53, 346
Furtwängler, Wilhelm 77n6, 479
Futurism 47, 217, 220, 228, 240, 368

gagaku 186, 382, 393
Galsworthy, John 4, 9
gambuh theatre 390
gamelan 22, 189, 379–82, 394, 395n15; Boulez on 123; and Debussy 189, 291; in Evangelista's *Ô Bali* 388, 389–90; in Tremblay's *Oralléluiants* 382–86; in Vivier's *Pulau dewata* 386, 388
Gann, Kyle 243, 255n63, 329
Garant, Serge 380, 381
García Ascot, Rosa 19, 202–3, 204, 212n23
Gaudí, Antoni 208
Gauguin, Paul 113, 127n32

Gavreau, Claude 380
Gay, John, *The Beggar's Opera* 44
Geist 477, 481, 484, 489
gender: in colonialism 180; in modernism 2, 15, 38; in Wagner criticism 468; Woolf on gender relations 5
Gendron, Bernard 244
genius 484, 491
George, Stefan 39
Gerhard, Roberto 200, 213n33; and exile 200, 205–6, 208, 210, 211; WORKS: *Adventures of Don Quixote* 205; *La Dueña* 210, 211; Violin Concerto 205, 212n30
Gershwin, George 51n22, 239, 242
gestalt theory 298, 407
Ghelderode, Michel de 432
Gibson, William 108
Giddens, Anthony 277n16
Gide, André 492n29
Gielen, Michael 182, 183
Gilbert, Jeremy 228
Gillies, Malcolm 204
Ginastera, Alberto 183, 184, 185, 186, 187, 379
Giri Kedaton gamelan ensemble 382
Glass, Philip 161, 414, 428, 429; and postmodernism 329–30, 332, 347n9; WORKS: *Akhnaten* 428; *Einstein on the Beach* 428; *Glassworks* 329–30, 332; *Satyagraha* 428
Gloag, Kenneth 24n17, 347n9, 479
globalization 59, 60, 79n28, 190, 261, 269, 290
global musical modernism 175–91, 269; Argentina 182–83; colonialism and postcolonialism 177–82; cosmopolitanism as procedural ethics 190–91; Finland 184–85; global diffusion and musical modernism 188–89; Japan 185–86; Mexico 184; overview 19, 175–77
global village (McLuhan) 258, 272, 290
Glock, William 263, 278n44
Gluck, Christoph Willibald von: *Iphigénie en Aulide* 457; *Orfeo ed Euridice* 35, 455, 456, 457
Goehr, Lydia 126n8, 202
Goethe, Johann Wolfgang von 38, 119, 458, *465*
Goldbeck, Frederick 81n89
Golden Age of American popular song 241–45
Goldman, Jonathan 422n40, 435
Gonneville, Michel 382
Goodman, Steve 310, 318
Gopinath, Sumanth 270
Górecki, Henryk 263
Graham, Stephen 233n76
Grainger, Percy 220
grammelot 435
gramophone 289, 291
Gramsci, Antonio 224, 344
Granados, Enrique 203
Gravesano studio 292
Great War *see* World War I

Index

Greenberg, Clement 241, 253, 266
Greene, Hugh Carleton 263
Green movement 334, 335, 348n48
Gregorian chant 357, 384
Griffiths, Paul 289, 447n7
grime 250, 251, 252, 255n66
Grimley, Daniel 3
Grimshaw, Mark 282n102
Grisey, Gérard 99, 143, 344, 393, 400–419; and Boulez 22, 402–9, 411, 421–22; and serialism 401–2, 403, 404–5; spectralism 22, 143, 328, 333, 334–35, 336, 400–419; and the sublime 143; WORKS: *Charme* 405, 407, 411; *D'eau et de pierre* 401, 405, 407, 411–16, *412*, 423n59; *Dérives* 409, 411, 415; *Les espaces acoustiques* 336, 411; *Jour, contre jour* 407; *Mégalithes* 405; *Modulations* 336, 415, 418, 423n59; *Partiels* 336, 348n51, 406, 414, 424n67; *Perichoresis* 405, 414; *Périodes* 411; *Tempus ex machina* 407, 409, 418; *Vagues, Chemins, le Souffle* 401, 406, 407–11, *410*, 414; WRITINGS: 'Tempus ex machina' (lecture) 400, 416, 424n64; 'Zur Entstehung des Klanges' 334, 335, 419n3
Gropius, Walter 217
Grosz, Elizabeth 320
group form (*Gruppenform*) 336
Groys, Boris 268, 276
Gruber, Franz Xaver 163, 164
Grupo de los Ocho (Group of Eight) 201, 202, 203, 210, 212n10
Grupo Renovación 182–83
Guattari, Felix 190, 309
Gubaidulina, Sofia: *Allelujah* 138; *Offertorium* 138; *Seven Words* 138
Guerrero, Laura K. 289, 293
Guevara, Ernesto 'Che' 137
Guldbrandsen, Erling E. 10, 455–56
Gumbrecht, Hans Ulrich 158, 172n6
Guston, Philip 143
Guys, Constantin 125, 131n107

Haas, Georg Friedrich 144
Hába, Alois 112
Habermas, Jürgen 68, 90, 92–94, 100, 109, 339
Haefeli, Anton 63, 66, 83n110, 193n30
Halffter, Rodolfo 19, 184, 185, 200, 210; *Sonatas de El Escorial* 210
Hall, Peter A. 92
Hall, Stuart 16, 261
Halm, August 490
Hamilton, John 431
Hancox, Dan 255n66
Hannerz, Ulf 191
Hanslick, Eduard 490
Harnoncourt, Nikolaus 477
Harper, Adam 255n66
Harper-Scott, J. P. E. 3, 8, 16, 234n99, 353–54

Hart, Lorenz 239
Hartmann, Karl Amadeus 122
Hartog, François 259, 260, 261, 264, 277n17
Harvey, Jonathan 423n52
Hasegawa, Robert 348n51
Hassan, Ihab 334
Hatherley, Owen 255n66
Hautzinger, Franz 271
Haydn, Joseph 140, 148, 357; *The Creation* 148
Hayek, Friedrich 89, 96–97
Hayes, Morgan 21, 354, 368–75; *Elemental* 371–72, 373–74, *374*; *E Vesuvio monte* 369, 371; *Futurist Manifesto* 368–69; *Shirley and Jane* 369–71, *370–71*, 372; *Strip* 368; *The Unrest-Cure* 371, 372–73; Violin Concerto 368
Heaney, Seamus 279n56
hearing *see* listening
Hebdige, Dick 276
Hegel, Georg Wilhelm Friedrich 35, 50n15, 124, 134, 142, 146, 446, 456, 469, 477, 480, 484; *The Phenomenology of Spirit* 42
hegemony 224, 228, 230
Heidegger, Martin 99, 160, 320, 321
Heifetz, Jascha 482, 487–88
Heike, Georg 303n24
Heile, Björn 2, 101, 240, 269, 290, 304n60, 347n4, 427
Heininen, Paavo 185
Helmholtz, Hermann von 290
Helsinki Music Institute 184
Helsinki Philharmonic Society 184
Hemingway, Ernest, *A Moveable Feast* 199
Hendrix, Jimi 247
Henze, Hans Werner 136, 138, 467
Hepokoski, James 3, 357
Herd, Judith Ann 186
Herheim, Stefan 23, 462–65, 468, 469
Herold, Falko 467
Hervé, Jean-Luc 417
Hesmondhalgh, David 394
Hess, Carol A. 187, 194n64
heterophony 388
Het Leven 225
Higgins, Dick 267
'high' and 'low' cultures *see* mass culture and 'high' culture
'high' modernism 57, 240, 241, 242, 248, 249, 289, 480
Hilberg, Frank 449n60
Hind, Rolf 145
Hindemith, Paul 61, 81n89, 116–17, 135, 208
Hinton, Stephen 44, 200, 243, 357
HIP *see* historically informed performance
historical institutionalism 88, 90–92
historically informed performance (HIP) 345, 346, 476, 477, 478, 479, 480
historical musicology 176, 481

505

Index

historiography of music 8, 14, 60, 108, 109, 112, 125, 158, 176, 179, 379
history 108–26; Adorno and 110–15; Boulez and 121–25, 421n28, 422n33; and the canon 126n8; Dahlhaus on 'problem history' 128n60, 336; evental model of 158–59; fictive nature of 157–58; global history of music 175–76; periodization and historical breaks 6–10, 25n26, 56, 260–61; Marx on world history, 35; Nietzsche on 421n28, 422n33, 477, 480; and performance practice 476–80, 482, 490; and postmodernism 328, 339, 346; Taruskin and 115–21; universal and particular histories (History and history) 18, 108–9, 124
Hockings, Elke 137
Hoffman, E. T. A. 484
Hofmannsthal, Hugo von 37
Holiday, Billie 242
Hollywood 204
Holocaust 43, 128n56, 143
Honegger, Arthur, *Pacific 231* 13
Horkheimer, Max, *Dialectic of Enlightenment* 5
Hosokawa, Toshio 186
house music 340, 341
Huber, Nicolaus A. 221, 226; *Harakiri* 226
Huberman, Bronisław 476, 483–90, 494n84; *Aus der Werkstatt des Virtuosen* 483, 484, 487
Hullot-Kentor, Robert 113, 127n36
Hulme, T. E. 476
humanism 220, 321
human nature 6, 10–12
Hunter, Mary 484
Hurel, Philippe 417
Husserl, Edmund 279n52
Hutcheon, Linda 36
Huyssen, Andreas 16, 50n14; and the avant-garde 231n7, 232n28, 240, 253; 'great divide' 44, 217, 221, 231n7; on postmodernism 334, 339–40
hybridity 334, 343

Ichiyanagi, Toshio 186
Idealism 120, 317, 457, 480, 484
identity 191, 206–11, 321, 346, 390
I Komang Astita 382
Iles, Anthony 222, 225
I Made Bandem 382
imitation 390, 393
immanent critique 111–12, 114, 123
immanent sublime 147
immersive art 106n83
imperialism 179, 188, 189
Impressionism 112, 113, 118, 119, 129n64
improvisation 223, 225, 234n93, 239, 246, 481
Incontri musicali (journal) 298
India 176, 180, 420n15
indifference 45, 46, 48
indigenismo 184

indigenous culture 178, 179, 181
individuality: and institutions 91–98; in performance 482; and the social 162–63
industrialization 220, 260, 334, 335, 487
ineffable, the 141–42, 314, 386, 435
information theory 291, 294, 296, 297–98
installation 267, 268, 269, 280n66, 293
Institut de Recherche et Coordination Acoustique/Musique *see* IRCAM
institutions 86–103; and artworld 99–100, 101–2; Darmstadt 88–89, 97, 98–99; Donaueschingen Festival 102–3; historical institutionalism 88, 90–92; institutional change 97–98, 102; IRCAM 91–92; Kagel and 101; Ligeti and 94; new institutionalism 87; norms 93–94, 95–98, 100, 101; overview 18; rational choice institutionalism 88, 89–90; rational myths 95–97; social institutionalism 88, 90, 92; symbolic aspects 94–95; theory of 86–88; Warsaw Autumn 95–96
Institut Seni Indonesia (ISI) 382
intensity 313, 318
interactivity 272, 274, 293
intermediality 267, 273
International Association of Music Information Centres 281n77
International Composers' Guild 184
internationalism 58, 60, 61, 74, 193n30
International Society for Contemporary Music (ISCM) 18, 58–83, 182, 183, 186, 187, 193n30, 205, 206, 269, 281n83; foundation 61–62; and notion of 'international contemporary' 58, 74–76; naming of 61–67
internet 270, 272, 275, 283n122, 345
interpretation: and sensation 316, 317; in performance 475, 476, 481, 482, 489, 490, 492n41
intertonality 209, 213n53
intonarumori (Russolo) 13
Ionesco, Eugène 38; *The Bald Soprano* 432
IRCAM (Institut de Recherche et Coordination Acoustique/Musique) 57, 91–92, 292, 334, 401
Irving, David 177, 178, 179, 188
ISCM *see* International Society for Contemporary Music
Isserlis, Steven 281n78
Italy 39, 76, 217, 218
Ives, Charles 26n44, 147; *Central Park in the Dark* 7; 'From Hanover Square North, at the End of a Tragic Day, the Voices of the People Again Arose' (*Orchestral Set* no. 2) 239
I Wayan Suweca 382, 395n14, 395n21

Jakelski, Lisa 96
Jakobson, Roman 277n23, 430
Jalowetz, Heinrich 65
Jam, The 248

Index

Jameson, Fredric 1–2, 4, 25n26, 188, 191n8, 245, 259, 277n23, 429; and postmodernism 327, 334, 345
Janáček, Leoš 47, 120, 189; *The Cunning Little Vixen* 47
Jankélévitch, Vladimir 140–41; *Music and the Ineffable* 141
Japan 179–81, 185–86, 187, 194n58
Jarocinski, Stefan 113
Jarvie, I. C. 93, 94
Javanese music 379, 381, 383, 384, 386, 388, 395n15
jazz 207, 218, 219, 222, 244, 247, 254n37, 327
Jencks, Charles 333, 347n30
Jenkins, Keith 157
Jepperson, Ronald L. 92
Jesperson, Otto 277n23
Joachim, Joseph 476, 482, 483–84
Joachim, Otto 380
Johnson, Julian 8, 9, 10, 455–56
Jones, Daniel John 267–68, 272; *Living Symphonies* 20, 262, 267–68, 272
jouissance 224, 227, 314, 315
Jowell, Tessa 278n47
Joyce, James 4, 294, 296, 318–19; *Finnegans Wake* 294; *Ulysses* 318–19
Jung, Carl 318–19
jungle 250, 255n66

Kafka, Franz 190
Kagel, Mauricio 97, 101, 136, 339, 380; and comedy 39, 42; and theatricality 221, 297; WORKS: *Anagrama* 427; *Exotica* 393; *Ludwig van* 345; *Phonophonie* 427; *Staatstheater* 427, 447n7; *Sur scène* 427
Kahneman, Daniel 89–90
Kandinsky, Wassily 112, 135, 136, 139
Kant, Immanuel 133, 140, 146, 147, 477, 480
Karajan, Herbert von 463
Karlsbad: aborted 1935 ISCM festival 65–66
Katz, Mark 27n74
Kaufmann, Jonas 465
Keller, Hans 56, 57, 69, 77n4, 78n17, 81n67
Kemper, Christian 437
Keynes, John Maynard 274
Khan, Ali Akhbar 388
Kivy, Peter 427
Klee, Paul 10, 123, 124
Kleiber, Carlos 182
Klemperer, Otto 456
KLF, The 247
Klotz, Heinrich 394
Knussen, Oliver 281n78
Koelbe, Thomas A. 90
Koellreutter, Hans-Joachim 183, 186
Koenig, Gottfried Michael 292
Kolisch, Rudolf 65

Kondo, Jo 397n42
Korngold, Erich Wolfgang, *Das Wunder der Heliane* 117
Korvat Auki (Ears Open) association 185
Koselleck, Reinhart 277n29
kotekan 390
Kötter, Daniel 438, 446, 450n69
Kowalke, Kim H. 243–44
Kracauer, Siegfried 34, 35, 50n12
Kraepelin, Emil 493n69, 493n59
Kraftwerk 251, 255n67
Kramer, Lawrence 172n5, 283n126, 344, 357, 376n10; *Classical Music and Postmodern Knowledge* 344; *Interpreting Music* 344; *Music as Cultural Practice* 376n10
Kranichstein 88
Kranichsteiner Musikpreis 99
Krasner, Stephen 97, 98
Kraus, Karl 36, 37
Krauss, Rosalind E. 267, 280n65
Krenek, Ernst 57, 61, 67, 80n60, 135; Adorno on 112; and exile 204, 206, 208
Kristeva, Julia 191, 224
Kroll Opera 456
Kröpfl, Francisco 183
Kubrick, Stanley 148
Kuhn, Thomas 290
Kundera, Milan 49, 318–19
Kunst, Jaap 395n15
Kupfer, Harry 23, 456, 459–61
Kurtág, György 393
Kurth, Ernst 490
Kuspit, Donald 110, 111
Kutschke, Beate 226
Kutter, Markus 294
Kvalbein, Astrid 80n64

Lacan, Jacques 224, 242, 314
LaCapra, Dominick 128n56
Lachenmann, Helmut 19, 23, 190, 335, 337, 339, 393, 466, 467; and the beautiful 133, 135–38, 139, 140, 145, 148; and contemporary opera 430, 431, 445, 446; and 'critical composition' 218, 221; and Darmstadt 99; WORKS: *Ausklang* 137; *Das Mädchen mit den Schwefelhölzern* 23, 430–31, 437–39, 446, 447
Laclau, Ernesto 16
Landowska, Wanda 481
Lang, David 430–31, 445; *The Difficulty of Crossing a Field* 23, 430–31, 442–45, *444*, 446, 447
Langer, Susanne K. 478
language: in contemporary opera 427–29, 430–32, 435–39, 445–47; failure of 23, 430, 445–47; in Lachenmann's *Das Mädchen mit den Schwefelhölzern* 437, 438; in Ligeti's *Le Grand Macabre* 431, 432, 435; in musical communication 288, 294; in Vivier's *Prologue*

Index

pour un Marco Polo 435–36; and voice 293–95, 429–31, 435, 438
langue inventée 435, 436, 445
Lanier, Jason 273, 274
late modernism 22, 68, 289, 315–19, 393
Latin America 182–83, 184, 186
Latour, Bruno 60
Lau, Frederick 187
laughter 33, 40, 43, 45, 48, 52n52, 52n60; Bergson on 45
Lawrence, D. H. 4
Lebrecht, Norman 274
Lecercle, Jean-Jacques 445, 446
Le Corbusier 290
legitimation crisis 61, 68, 69, 74
Lehár, Franz 44
Leibowitz, René 402, 404, 421n19
Leipp, Emile 411
Le Jeune, Claude 439
Lenin, Vladimir Ilyich 262
Leninism 220
Leonardo da Vinci 437, 438
Leone, Sergio 145
Leroux, Philippe 417
Levenson, Michael 231n2
Levi, Primo 43
Levin, Thomas Y. 245
Lévi-Strauss, Claude 291
Lewiston, David 381
Leydi, Roberto 292
Liebermann, Lowell 266
Ligeti, György 1, 23, 101, 136, 148, 221, 293, 313, 394, 415, 423n60; comedy in 39–40, 42; contemporary opera 428, 430, 431–35, 445; and postmodernism 330, 333, 339, 340, 347n17; and self-representation 94, 339, 347n17; WORKS: *Artikulation* 39; *Atmosphères* 39, 148, 333; *Aventures* 40, 293, 428; *Le Grand Macabre* 23, 430, 431–35, *431*, *433*, *434*, 445, 447, 458; Horn Trio 339, 349n62; *Lontano* 148, 333; *Lux Aeterna* 148; *Nouvelles Aventures* 40, 293, 428; opera 458; *Poème symphonique* 40, 52n39; Three Pieces for Two Pianos 339; *Trois Bagatelles for David Tudor* 40; *Die Zukunft der Musik* 40
liminal music 400, 414, 416, 418, 419
Lindberg, Magnus 184, 185, 266
Lindberg, Ulf 241, 242, 243, 253n1
Lindsay, Arto 250
linguistics 291
listening 267, 301, 490
Liszt, Franz 119, 141, 265
literary modernism 4–5, 7, 9, 21, 188, 199, 240, 242
literature: and aesthetic modernism 5, 9; 21; affect in 308–9; and cosmopolitanism 190; and discontinuity in exile 202; 'high' modernism in 480; 'late modernism' in 68; Mallarmé and *Le Livre* 296; 'minor literature' (Deleuze and

Guattari) 190; modernist literary studies 3, 21, 224, 280n60, 355; peripheral and postcolonial 179, 181, 188, 190; progressive politics in 240; 'world literature' (Moretti) 176, 181
L'Itinéraire 401
Llano, Samuel 213n33
lokale Musik (local music) 190, 194n74
Lomax, Alan 294
London 59, 62, 75, 188, 204; 1938 ISCM festival in 73, 81n89; London Contemporary Music Centre 72, 75, 78n22
Longinus 139
Lorenzetti, Ambrogio 413
'low' culture 45, 204–6, 244, 246, 247
Lowell, Robert 279n56
Loy, Mina 216
Luening, Otto 292
Lukács, Georg 111, 222, 240, 241, 245
Lunch, Lydia 249, 250
Lussy, Mathis 490
Lutosławski, Witold 96, 266
Lyotard, Jean-François: and postmodernism (*La condition postmoderne*) 333; and the sublime 133, 139–41, 145, 147, 148

Machaut, Guillaume de 162, 382
Machover, Tod 57
Macpherson, Stewart 490
McClary, Susan 24n16, 130n100, 228, 273, 282n111, 282n112, 330, 350n97
McFarlane, James 21, 355, 356
McGill University, Montreal 380
McLuhan, Marshall 92, 258, 259, 272, 290; *The Medium is the Massage* 258–59, 272
McPhee, Colin 381, 384, 388; WORKS: *Balinese Ceremonial Music* 388; *Tabuh-Tabuhan* 381; WRITINGS: *A House in Bali* 381; *Music in Bali* 381, 384
McVicar, David 23, 468–70
Maderna, Bruno 97, 292; *Musica su due dimensioni* 97
madness 340, 341, 431, 432
Madrid, Alejandro L. 181, 187, 193n42, 193n43
Maeterlinck, Maurice 129n69
magnetic tape 289, 291–92
Mahler, Gustav 134, 140, 339, 340, 343
Mahnkopf, Claus-Steffen 57, 220, 393
Maiguashca, Mesías 397n42
mainstream: mainstream performance (vs Early Music movement) 475, 478, 480, 481, 491; mainstream vs specialist/resistant cultures 94, 218, 219, 223, 228, 266, 273, 375; moderate mainstream in composition 155, 355, 375; modernist mainstream 355, 368
Malevich, Kazimir 139
Mallarmé, Stéphane 118, 127n32, 294, 296; *Le Livre* 296
Manet, Édouard 7, 34, 140

508

Index

manifestos 297–98

Manila 178, 179

man-machine assemblage (Deleuze) 272, 282n106

Mann, Thomas 120, 492n29; *The Magic Mountain* 485

March, James G. 92, 97

Marco, Tomás 201

Marconi, Guglielmo 289

Marcus, Greil 246

Marie, Jean-Étienne 22, 406, 407, 408, 415; Concerto 'Milieu Divin' 408; *Tlaloc* 407

Marienhöhe, Darmstadt 88

Marinetti, Filippo 368

Marion, Jean-Luc 144–45; *In Excess* 144

Marleau, Denis 390

Mars (band) 249, 250

Martens, Frederick 476, 483, 485–87, 489; *String Mastery* 483, 485; *Violin Mastery* 483

Marx, Karl 50n7, 221, 319, 320, 456, 462, 471; *The Communist Manifesto* 47; *The Eighteenth Brumaire of Louis Bonaparte* 35, 50n7; *The German Ideology* 462

Marxism 6, 108, 220, 221, 225, 243, 248, 309, 344, 462, 492n29

masculinity 485

mashups 273

mass culture: and anaesthetization 219, 222; as anti-hegemonic 224; vs bourgeois taste 221; and 'high' culture 15, 44–45, 162, 204–6, 216, 217, 244, 246, 247, 273, 274; hostility towards 220

mass mediatization 261, 262, 289

Massumi, Brian 309, 310, 314

material culture 288

Materialstand 6, 189, 265, 335–36

mathematics 42, 217, 290, 317, 406, 407; mathematical sublime 147

Mathiesen, Thomas 272

Matisse, Henri 101, 127n35, 127n32

Matthay, Tobias 490

Mattin (noise artist) 228

maximalism 7, 8, 266

Maxwell Davies, Peter *see* Davies, Peter Maxwell

Mayuzumi, Toshiro 186; *Essay for String Orchestra* 180

meaning: and affect 311, 314, 315, 343, 430; beyond semantic meaning in modernism 294, 427–28; conventions of 71, 137; excess of 141, 145, 147; and intentionality 118, 128n56; in postmodernism 327, 328, 335, 336, 343–44, 345–46

mechanization 11, 161, 490

media 258, 261, 262, 267, 290, 301–2, 310; mass mediatization 261, 262, 289

mediacy 266, 275

medium (in contemporary music) 261, 262, 266–67

Méfano, Paul 402, 417

Meiji Restoration 181, 185

Meinecke, Friedrich 460

melody, ideals of in performance 476, 485, 489

memory 203–4, 235n116, 258, 264, 278n50, 315

Mendelssohn, Felix 129n78, 462, 477

mensural notation 295

Mercer, Johnny 242

Mercure, Pierre 380, 381; *Cantate pour une joie* 381; *Structures métalliques I* and *II* 381

Merikanto, Aarre 184

Merleau-Ponty, Maurice 140

Mersmann, Hans 490

Messager, André 161

Messiaen, Olivier 29, 354, 379, 382; and spectralism 401, 403, 404, 406, 407, 413, 418, 420n15, 421n17, 422n44, 423n47

mestizaje 184

métabole 407, 409, 423n45

metaness (Lanier) 273

metaphysics 320, 321

metropolis 5, 46, 189

Metzer, David 312–14, 393, 438, 446

Metzger, Heinz-Klaus 103

MEV *see* Musica Elettronica Viva

Mexico 184, 200, 203

Meyer, John W. 95, 96

Meyer, Richard 60

Meyer-Eppler, Werner 292, 296

Michel, Louise 137

microtonality 144, 290

migration 269, 270; *see also* displacement, emigration, exile

Miki, Minoru 187, 190

Milhaud, Darius 244, 402; *La création du monde* 244

Miller, Stephen Paul 4, 7

milonga 182

Milsom, David 489

mimicry (Bhabha) 179, 187

minimalism 161, 375, 414, 428; and postmodernism 22, 328–33, 336

minor literature (Deleuze and Guattari) 190

Mitisek, Andreas 443

Mittelmann, S. 488, 489

mixed media 262

mobile devices 260, 271

moderate modernism 2, 3, 14, 19, 21, 155, 162; *see also* reactive modernism

modernism, modernism in music: aspects of modernism in music 12–14; British musical modernism 354, 355; and comedy 17, 41, 42, 44–45, 47, 49; and the contemporary 68, 70; critical debates 1–3, 15; definitions 3, 4; and exile 208; genealogies of 216–19, 220, 225–29, 240, 249; global musical modernism 175–91, 269; 'high' modernism 57, 240, 241, 242, 248, 249, 289, 480; and history 108–26; literary modernism 4–5, 7, 21, 188, 199, 240, 242;

Index

and opera 455–56, 470–71; origins of 14–17; overview 17–24; and popular music 239–41; and postmodernism 327–28, 333, 334, 339; reactive modernism 155, 162–63, 379–80; regional modernism 16–17, 19, 22, 179, 187, 190–91, 379–80, 394; revolutionary modernism 161, 219–20, 224, 225, 229; and rupture/shock 5–8, 12, 140, 207; subjectivity and affect 307, 314; theories of 3–12; and trauma 162–63; and twenty-first century music 262, 263–64, 266–67; vitalism and performance 475, 476–77, 480–85

modernisme (Catalan) 208, 209

modernist event (Fisher), 248

modernity: alienation and disenchantment of 13; Berman on 111; distinguished from modernism 3, 5, 8–10, 12; global modernity 176–77, 181; Habermas on 109; instability and trauma of 42, 47–48, 49, 162, 171; iterative modernity 259; 'new modernity' (Comentale) 243; sublime as response to 133, 139–40, 147–48

Mohanty, Satya P. 79n35

Moles, Abraham 294, 404

Molino, Jean 116

Molitor, Claudia 271

moment 26n42

moment form 298, 336

Mondrian, Piet 139

Monet, Claude 127n32, 129n64

Monteverdi, Claudio 65; *Orfeo* 428, 455, 456, 466

Montreal 379–94

Moore, Christopher 41

Moore, Douglas 427

Moreau, Gustave 127n32

Morel, François 380

Moretti, Franco 176, 178, 181, 188; 'distant reading' 176

Mori, Ikue 250

Morillo, Roberto García 193n43

Morley, Simon 139

Morley College 204

Morón, Ciríaco 11

Morreau, Annette 263, 264

Morricone, Ennio 145

Mortimer, Vicki 469

Moser, Andreas 481–82, 484, 485, 489, 490; *Joseph Joachim* 484; *Violinschule* 481, 489; *Vom Vortrag* 481

Mosolov, Alexander 13

Motte, Diether de la 271, 281n98

Motte-Haber, Helga de la 300

Mouffe, Chantal 16

mousikē 454, 455

Moyse, Marcel 382

Mozart, Leopold 482

Mozart, Wolfgang Amadeus 56, 77n4, 357; *Così fan tutte* 9; 'Jupiter' Symphony 147; *The Magic Flute* 432, 437; *The Marriage of Figaro* 41; *Ein musikalischer Spaß* 163

Müller, Heiner 428

multimedia 142, 266, 267, 269, 271, 297, 301

multimodality 288, 289, 297, 301

Mumma, Gordon 293

Munch, Edvard, *The Scream* 485

Munro, H. H. *see* Saki

Munslow, Alan 157

Murail, Tristan: and affect 21, 316–17, 319, 323n35; and spectralism 333, 400–404, 411, 417–18, 420n11, 422n44; and the sublime 143; WORKS: *Altitude 8000* 402; *Couleur de mer* 420n10, 421n27; *Gondwana* 316, 317, 400; *Serendib* 317

Murray, David 138

Muses 454–55

museum: as canon, cultural repository 126n8, 276; Danto on 73

Musgrave, Thea 281n78

Musica Elettronica Viva (MEV) 218, 225, 226, 239, 271

musical appropriation *see* appropriation

musical communication *see* communication

musical modernism *see* modernism (in music)

musicals, musical theatre 204, 243

'Music and Life' Congress 73

music drama 368, 371, 465, 470

Music for the Morning of the World (LP) 381

music historiography *see* historiography of music

music history *see* history

musicology 2, 15, 33–34, 86, 110, 241, 315; historical musicology 157, 176, 481; and theory 356–57; *see also* new musicology, postmodernism: in musicology

music theatre 266, 313, 407, 429, 465, 470–71

Music Today (ISCM journal) 65

musikalische Moderne 3, 7, 62–63

Musiktexte (journal) 225

musique concrète 266, 291, 437

musique liminale see liminal music

musique mixte 266

musique répétitive see minimalism 414

Musorgsky, Modest Petrovich, *Boris Godunov* 356, 459

Mussolini, Benito 11, 46, 217, 218

Muti, Riccardo 279n56

Muybridge, Edward 289

Myers, Rollo 65, 75, 76

MySpace 273

Nancy, Jean-Luc 146, 147

Nansen, Fridtjof 487

Napoleon III (Louis Napoleon) 35, 37

National Endowment for the Arts (USA) 263

nationalism 184, 187, 190, 209; cultural nationalism in the ISCM 64, 76

Nazism 122, 134, 160, 185, 217; and the ISCM 65, 66, 67, 74; exiles from 201, 380; and Wagner 458, 464, 472n33

510

necessity 121–22, 135, 159, 276, 404, 421n29
Neff, Severine 207
negative dialectics 109, 170, 173n21, 247
NEM *see* Nouvel Ensemble Moderne
Nemescu, Octavian, *Concentric* 424n74
neo-classicism 45, 49, 232n29, 354, 356, 456
neo-serialism 334, 335
neo-tonality 334, 335
Nettl, Bruno 175, 176, 177, 178
neue Einfachheit 335
Neue Musik see new music
Neue Zeitschrift für Musik 297
Neuhaus, Max 267, 280n66
neurasthenia 485–88, 493n59, 493n69
neuroscience 320
Neves, Maria João 11
Newcomb, Antony 9
new complexity 99, 144, 368
new institutionalism 87
New Left 217, 229
Newman, Barnett 139, 140; *Here I, Here II, Here III*
139; *Vir heroicus sublimis* 139
Newman, Ernest 69, 70, 81n89
new modernist studies 3, 229
new modernity (Comentale) 243
new music (*Neue Musik*) 57, 59, 67, 70, 116, 219,
244; Adorno and 71–74, 111–12, 133–34, 275;
and the beautiful 135–37; vs 'contemporary' in
ISCM 62–64; vs modern/modernism 3, 7; and
the sublime 140–45, 148
New Music Days (ISCM) 182
new musicology 1, 115, 118, 314, 344, 355
newness 6, 56, 275, 276
New Simplicity 386
New York 218, 249
Ngai, Sianne 33
Niedermayer, Franz 129n76
Nielsen, Meentje 465
Nietzsche, Friedrich 38, 80n67, 429, 437, 462,
476, 477, 480, 482, 484, 485; reception of
491n29; and subjectivity 319, 320, 321; and
Wagner 38, 119; WRITINGS: *The Case of Wagner*
38; *Ecce Homo* 40; *The Gay Science* 485, 492n29;
'On the Use and Abuse of History for Life'
421n28, 477, 480; *Thus Spake Zarathustra* 38,
422n33
Nilsson, Bo 95
Nobre, Marlos 187, 190
Noh drama 180, 382
noise: as anti-hegemonic 223–24, 226; as distinct
from musical sound 249, 298, 310, 337, 428,
438; in electroacoustic composition 298–99;
in industrial modernity 14; noise jazz 252; in
no wave 249–50, 252; noise music (as genre)
223–24, 228, 229, 247, 251–52; and subjectivity
223–24, 234n77, 345–46; and the sublime 138,
144, 145; white noise 298, 418, 439

No New York (recorded compilation) 249
Nono, Luigi 94, 97, 136, 137, 183, 207, 380; and
anti-hegemonic music 218, 219, 221, 224, 240;
WORKS: *Al gran sole carico d'amore* 137; *La fabbrica
illuminata* 224
nonverbal communication 289
Nora, Pierre 261, 262, 278n50
Norman, Richard 90
Norris, Christopher 429, 430
nostalgia 207, 208, 216, 251, 466; and exile 202, 203
notation, musical 103, 144, 181, 295–96, 336, 419
Nouvel Ensemble Moderne (NEM) 388, 395n14
novels 6, 9, 34, 176
no wave 249–50, 252
'now' moment (of the sublime) 139–40, 143, 147
nuance (in musical interpretation) 46, 489
Nuss, Steven 180
Nussbaumer, Georg 271
NWDR studio, Cologne *see* WDR studio
Nyman, Michael 329, 428; *The Man Who Mistook
His Wife for a Hat* 428

objet sonore 404
Obrist, Hans Ulrich 258
obscure modernism, obscure subject 160–61
Ocampo, Victoria 182
O'Connor, Sinéad 247
Offenbach, Jacques 4, 7, 34–37, 44, 45, 47, 51n22;
Orphée aux enfers (*Orpheus in the Underworld*) 7,
34–36, 37, 44, 455
Olsen, Johan P. 92, 97
Ondříček, František 488, 489
open form 293, 295–96, 298; *see also* aleatorism
opera 23, 34–38, 39, 48–49, 121, 131n105, 178,
185, 267, 356, 369–71; contemporary opera
427–47; director as modernist 457–58; and
modernism 23, 455–56, 458–59, 470–71;
productions 454–71
orientalism 123, 187
Orkest De Volharding 225
Ortega y Gasset, José: and Debussy 12, 118, 119,
120, 121; dehumanization 11–12, 118, 119–21,
476; *The Dehumanization of Art* 476
Osborn, Laurence 446
Osborne, Peter 59, 60, 74, 260, 269, 275, 279n52
Oulipo 432, 448n37
Ouzonian, Gascia 280n66, 280n68
Owen, Gary 368

Pablo, Luis de 397n42
Pace, Ian 8
Paddison, Max 57, 110, 111, 114, 115, 206
Paganini, Niccolò 487, 494n84; *Rondo 'La
campanella'* (*La clochette*) 486
Pahissa, Jaume 19, 208–11, 213n53; *Dos canciones*
210, 211; *Quomodo sedet sola* 210; *Suite intertonal*
209

511

Index

pain 146
painting 100, 112, 113, 114, 118, 127n35, 139, 140; as medium 266
Palmer, Anthony 187
Palmieri, Silvio 382
panopticon (Bentham) 272, 282n105
parergon 146
Paris 7, 17, 22, 36, 67, 188, 379
Paris Conservatoire 382, 402
Parker, Robert 193n43
parody 36, 37, 39, 40–41, 223, 427, 432
Parsons, James 208
Pärt, Arvo 2, 13
Parti Québécois 380
Patkowsi, Józef 95
Patti, Adelina 494n84
Paz, Juan Carlos 182, 183, 185, 187, 379
PC Music 251
Pedrell, Felipe 203
Penderecki, Krzysztof 13, 136
PEN International 72, 82n91
perception 316, 317, 328, 407, 417
performance: extended vocal techniques 428; historically informed performance (HIP) 345, 349n92, 475–85, 490–91; live performance vs technology 4, 13, 82n90, 264, 269, 279n58, 293; opera 454–71; performance challenges of new music 144, 147, 359; relationship of text/notation to 294–97, 343, 345, 490; repeat performance of new works 263, 279n53; spatial dimension of 266–67, 297, 300, 345; theatricality/multimodality of 297, 300–301; twentieth-century styles of 129n62, 475–85, 489–91; vitalism in 23, 475, 485–90; Western classical performance culture 181, 375
performativity 288, 294
Perle, George 376n14
perlocutionary act 430
Permanent Council for the International Cooperation of Composers 66, 80n60
Perón, Juan 183
personnages sonores 405, 407
Perspectives of New Music (journal) 57, 298
Pessoa, Fernando 390
Peters, John Durham 302n2
Petrenko, Kirill 465
Pfitzner, Hans 298
phonograph 27n74, 289
Picasso, Pablo 101, 140, 354
Piekut, Benjamin 394n1
Pierson, Marcelle 439
Pinder, Wilhelm 261, 277n29
Pippin, Robert B. 283n137
pitch class set theory 356, 373–75
Pla, Joan Baptista 210
plainchant *see* Gregorian chant

pleasure: and affect 314, 315; and anti-hegemonic music 226–27, 228; and desire 242, 243; and noise 224; and the sublime 139–40, 146; *see also* jouissance
pluralism 2, 60, 61, 69, 77, 78n23, 228, 263, 328
poetry 43, 319, 320
poiesis 10, 116, 123, 124, 128n56; 'poietic fallacy' (Taruskin) 116, 315
Polanyi, Karl 87, 88, 104n4
Polin, Claire 138
Polish Composers' Union *see* Związek Kompozytorów Polskich
Polish Radio *see* studios
Pollock, Jackson 139
Polo, Marco 430, 431, 435
Ponce, Manuel 184
Pooley, Jefferson D. 302n2
Pope, Alexander 143
Pop Group, The 248
Pople, Anthony 357
popular culture, popular music: and authenticity 15, 51n22, 244, 245, 247; critical and/or modernist strains of popular music 1, 19–20, 43–44, 239–53; modernism and/as popular resistance 19–20, 216–30; opera and popular culture 466, 467; represented in art music 2, 14–15, 38, 51n30, 120, 130n82, 265, 279n54, 291, 341, 343; technology in 13; tension between popular and elitist 4, 14–15, 120–21, 161, 199, 202, 216–7, 282n111, 282n112, 343, 479
Porter, Cole 242, 243, 244
Porter, Peter 43, 48
Porter, Shirley 368
Portoghesi, Paolo 50n9
Porzak, Simon 430
postcolonialism 179, 188, 192n15, 269, 391, 393
postminimalism 21, 22, 328–33, 336, 339, 340, 346
postmodernism, postmodernity 21–22, 23, 26n61, 50n9, 191, 218, 239, 246, 251, 253, 270, 276, 277n10, 327–46; Adams and 329–33; Adès and 339–43; and comedy 33, 34, 43, 49; German reception 339; and Hayes 375; and history 108–9, 128n56, 158, 172n5; and Lang 446; and minimalism 328–33; in musicology 110, 115, 344–46, 349n88; in opera 447n7, 462, 470; Rea on 390–91; as response to modernism 2, 4, 16, 259, 275, 276, 375, 393; Saariaho and 336–38; and spectralism 21–22, 333–38; and the subject 309, 319–20, 344–46
post-punk 248–51
poststructuralism 321, 323n32, 334, 344
post-tonality 358, 375
Potter, Rachel 19, 216, 220, 229, 230, 231n2, 240
Potvin, Gilles 386, 396n37
Poulenc, Francis 19, 40–42, 49, 165–71, 427; Concerto for Two Pianos 244; *Les mamelles de Tirésias* 40, 41, 42; *Stabat Mater* 41; *Trois*

Index

mouvements perpétuels no. 1 19, 165–70, *166, 167, 168, 169*
Pound, Ezra 6, 216, 275, 477, 480
Pousseur, Henri 295, 298–99, 428; *Scambi* 298; *Votre Faust* 428
Powell, Larson 254n38
Powell, Richard 330
Powers, Harold S. 262, 278n36
practice techniques, instrumental 486, 487, 488, 489
Prague 66, 67, 95, 319
presentism (Hartog) 259, 262, 276
Prévost, Eddie 218, 223, 225, 227
Pritchett, James 304n55
Prokofiev, Gabriel 266, 280n59
Prokofiev, Sergey, *War and Peace* 368
Proms (Promenade concerts) 69, 368
Provost, Serge 382
proxemics 289, 293
PRS Foundation 279n53
psychoanalysis 163, 171, 315
Punchdrunk 106n83
punk 246, 249, 250, 251
Puvis de Chavannes, Pierre 127n32
Pythagoras 299

quantum theory 296
Quantz, Johann Joachim 482
Quebec 17, 22, 380–82, 393, 394
queer aesthetics 41
Querelle des bouffons 121

Rabaté, Jean-Michel 224
Rabinach, Anson 486
race 2, 15, 38, 180, 222, 252
Rachmaninoff, Sergey 3, 354, 458–59
Radano, Ronald 222, 223
radio 205, 289, 292, 293
Radkau, Joachim 487, 488
Rancière, Jacques 19, 230
Raster-Noton 251
rational choice institutionalism 88, 89–90
rationality 88–90, 93, 104n9, 162, 320, 321
rational myths 95, 96, 97
Rattle, Simon 340
Rauschenberg, Robert 296, 303n36
Rautavaara, Einojuhani 185, 187
Ravel, Maurice, *L'enfant et les sortileges* 47
RCA synthesizer 292
Rea, John 22, 381, 382, 388, 390–93, 394; *Médiator* 381, 390–93, *392*; *Reception and Offering Music* 390; *Treppenmusik* 390
reactive modernism, reactive subject 155–71; history, aesthetics and the event 157–62; modernism and trauma 162–63; overview 14, 19, 155–57, 171; Poulenc 165–71; Schnittke 163–65

reader response theory 235n117
realism 6, 12, 34, 36
reconstructionalism 466, 467
recorded sound *see* sound recording
Refus global 380
Regietheater 454, 457, 468, 471
regional modernism 16–17, 19, 22, 179, 187, 190–91, 379–80, 394; in Quebec 379–94
Reich, Steve 381, 394, 414, 424n68; 'Music as a Gradual Process' 328; *Piano Phase* 328; and postmodernism 328, 329
Reihe, die (journal) 298, 417
Reitz, Edgar 467
religion 13, 41, 60, 141, 332
Renaud, Jeanne 380
Renaud-Barrault theatre company 183
Renoir, Pierre-Auguste 127n35
repetition 163, 171, 341
repurposing (Savage) 270
resonance 414, 422n40
Resonate project 279n53
Réti, Rudolf 61, 62
retrosensationalism 261
revolutionary modernism 161, 219–20, 224, 225, 229
Reynolds, Simon 249
Richter, Hannah 16
Ricoeur, Paul 319–20
Ricordi Americana 209, 210
Ridley, Aaron 480
Riedl, Josef Anton 292, 293
Rieger, Eva 465, 468
Rihm, Wolfgang 13, 99, 138, 145, 332, 335; *Fremde Szenen I–III* 138; *Jakob Lenz* 332
Riley, Matthew 63, 79n43, 414
Rings, Steven 173n19
Risset, Jean-Claude 401
Ritchel, Charles Frances 35
Rivarde, Achille 485
Robin, Yann 145
Robinson, J. Bradford 63
Rochberg, George 14
rock music 243, 246, 249, 250, 266, 341
Rockwell, John 329; *All American Music* 60, 126n8
Rodgers, Richard 239
Roelcke, Volker 493n69
Romanian music, spectral current in 415, 424n74
Romanticism: 3, 7, 9, 12, 26n47, 34, 50n6, 128n56, 131n105, 217, 226, 227, 307, 354; and postmodernism 327, 328, 329, 345; and the sublime 139, 146, 147; and vitalism in performance 477, 479, 484
Rosen, Charles 122, 245
Rosenblum, Robert 139
Roslavets, Nikolai 217, 225, 240
Ross, Alex 144
Rossini, Gioachino 48, 265

Index

Rothfarb, Lee 490
Rothko, Mark 139
Rouse, Christopher 279n54
Rouse, Mikel 279n54
Rowan, Brian 95, 96
Royal Shakespeare Company 200
RTF, Paris 292
Rudhyar, Dane 220
Rufer, Josef 194n73
Ruffel, Lionel 260, 261
Rupprecht, Philip 68, 353
Russolo, Luigi 13; *The Art of Noise* 298
Rutherford-Johnson, Tim 278n38
Ryan, David 303n36
Ryle, Gilbert 86–87

Saariaho, Kaija 21, 22, 184, 185, 393; and
    postmodernism 336–38; and spectralism 328,
    336–38, 417; *Lichtbogen* 328, 336–38, *338*,
    348n57
Saavedra, Leonora 187, 193n42, 193n43
Said, Edward 37, 123, 130n101, 178, 188, 189,
    192n11, 201; *Culture & Imperialism* 188
Saki (H. H. Munro) 372, 373
Salazar, Adolfo 203, 210
Salonen, Esa-Pekka 184, 185
Salzburg Festival 61, 62, 75, 76, 462, 463
sampling 270
Samson, Jim 218, 228
Samuel, Claude 403, 411, 423n47
Sargent, Malcolm 74
Satie, Erik 38, 118, 239, 244, 253; *Parade* 244; *Le
    Piccadilly* 244; *Vexations* 244
satire 35, 36, 44, 368, 371
saturated music 145
Saussure, Ferdinand de 291
Savage, Steve 270
Scaldaferri, Nicola 294
Scarlatti, Domenico 210
Schaeffer, Pierre 291, 294, 299, 380, 404; *Étude aux
    chemins de fer* 299; *Traité des objets musicaux* 299
Schafer, R. Murray 267
Scheding, Florian 201, 204, 208
Scheele, Heike 469
Schenk, Otto 468
Schenker, Heinrich 356, 490
Scherchen, Hermann 61, 65, 292
Scherer, Klaus 310–11
Schering, Arnold 490
Scherzinger, Martin 274, 394
Schleifer, Ronald 241, 242, 243, 253
Schmidt, Matthew 437
Schnebel, Dieter: *Glossolalie* 293; *Maulwerke* 293
Schnittke, Alfred 14, 19; *Stille Nacht* 19, 163–65,
    164
Schoenberg, Arnold 10, 56, 63, 79n38, 96, 159,
    161, 183, 189, 194n73, 209, 239, 341, 353, 354,

356, 358, 368, 427, 458; Adorno on 9, 112,
    114; on beauty and pleasure 133–35, 148, 226;
    Boulez and 112, 121–22, 403, 404, 421n30; on
    the elite and the popular 51n22, 217, 220, 240,
    241; and 'emancipation of the dissonance' 19,
    375n6; and exile 207–8, 211n7; and Gerhard
    205; and Kandinsky 112; and Kraus 36, 37; on
    performance style 479, 480; and religion 13;
    and the sublime 141–42, 147; WORKS: *Das
    Buch der hängenden Gärten* 161; Five Orchestral
    Pieces Op. 16 no. 3 'Farben' 408; *Gurrelieder* 330;
    Moses und Aron 141, 142, 456; *Ode to Napoleon
    Buonaparte* 37; *Pelleas und Melisande* 456; *Pierrot
    lunaire* 37, 39, 70, 293; Second Chamber
    Symphony 207; Second String Quartet 7, 39,
    156–57, *156*, 161; Six Little Piano Pieces Op.
    19 70; Three Piano Pieces Op. 11 70, 266;
    Variations for Orchestra Op. 31 65; Wind
    Quintet Op. 26 356; WRITINGS: *Harmonielehre*
    (*Theory of Harmony*) 135, 220, 330; 'Opinion or
    Insight?' 375n6; 'Today's Manner of Performing
    Classical Music' 479
Schopenhauer, Arthur 463, 465
Schorske, Carl E. 36
Schubert, Franz 56, 130n86, 163, 279n56
Schultz, Wolfgang-Andreas 446
Schumann, Robert 119, 138, 297; *Kinderszenen*
    390
Schumpeter, Joseph 260
Schwitters, Kurt, *Ursonate* 293
Sciarrino, Salvatore 430, 431, 445, 446; *Luci mie
    traditrici* 23, 430, 439–42, *440*, *442*, 446, 447
score, musical: layout and format 295–96;
    relationship to musical performance 300–301;
    as 'text' 345, 490
Scott, Duncan 470
Scott, W. Richard 91
Scriabin, Alexander 13; *Prometheus* 7
scronk 255n64
sculpture 267
second modernity (Mahnkopf) 22, 57, 394
Second Viennese School 63, 185, 209, 462
Second World War *see* World War II
Sedgwick, Eve Kosofsky 308, 315, 322n29
Sehnsucht 146
self (subjectivity) 162, 163, 307, 311
Sellars, Peter 458
Semaine Internationale de Musique Actuelle
    (SIMA, International Contemporary Music
    Week) 380
semiotics 291, 296, 328
sensation 311, 313, 316, 317, 319
serialism 1, 56, 63, 137, 160, 183, 187, 199, 293,
    294, 295; in 1960s France 401–6; Boulez and
    42, 122, 402, 404; multiple/integral serialism
    42, 101, 185; neo-serialism 334, 335; and
    spectralism 22, 328, 333–36, 401–5, 415, 417,

514

Index

419, 421n17, 425n85; *see also* twelve-tone
technique
seriousness in modernism 17, 41–43, 47–48
Sessions, Roger 478
Seurat, Georges 113, 127n32
Sevčik, Otto 483
Sex Pistols 250
shadow theatre (*wayang kulit*) 388
shakuhachi 181
Shannon, Claude 291, 292
Shaw, George Bernard 492n29
Sheng, Bright 281n84
Sheppard, Richard 216
shō 181
Shostakovich, Dmitri 171, 279n57, 355
Shouse, Eric 21, 308, 311
Shreffler, Anne 65, 66, 67
Sibelius, Jean 3, 73, 147, 171, 184; Symphony no. 5
in E-flat major 3, 331
Sibelius Academy 184, 185
Siemens studio, Munich 292
Signac, Paul 113, 127n32
silence 296, 299, 312, 431, 438; and Cage 38,
280n62; in Grisey 413; and the ineffable/
sublime 141, 143; as supplement to comedy 43
Silverberg, Laura 207
SIMA *see* Semaine Internationale de Musique
Actuelle
Simmel, Georg 46, 47, 111, 239, 242; 'The
Metropolis and Mental Life' 46; and Weber 5
Simone, Nina, 'Mississippi Goddam' 43–44
Simon Fraser University (SFU), Vancouver 382
simulacrum (Baudrillard): in postmodernism 330,
390
singing *see* song
Sisley, Alfred 127n32
Sisman, Elaine 147
Sistema, El 181, 192n24
Six, Les 244
Skovhaus, Bo 464
Sloterdijk, Peter 262
SMCQ *see* Société de Musique Contemporaine
du Quebec
Smith, Anna Nicole 279n54
Smith, Chris, *Creative Britain* 278n47
Smith, Terry 59, 60, 79n28, 260, 261, 267, 268
social institutionalism 88, 90, 92
socialism 6, 216, 334
socialist realism 67, 74, 253, 339
social media 273, 310
Société de Musique Contemporaine du Quebec
(SMCQ) 380
Society for the Promotion of New Music 268
Socrates 42, 53n60
Somigli, Luca 297
song: in opera 427; as truth/communication 430,
438; as ideal in instrumental performance 485

sonic art 268, 269, 293
Sonic Arts Network 268
sonic states 312
Sonic Youth 247
sonograph 401
sound: and affect 310, 315; and communication
289, 294, 298–300, 302; and noise music
223–24; sound spectrum 335, 336; and the
sublime 140, 143–45, 147
Sound and Music 268–69, 281n79
sound art 267, 268, 269, 293
SoundCloud 273, 274
sound installation *see* installation
sound recording 4, 13, 289–92, 294, 299, 346, 481,
490
sound warfare 318
space, spatiality 112, 267, 289, 300
Spahlinger, Mathias 221
Spain 200–204, 205–6, 208–11
Spanish Civil War 183, 200, 201, 202, 205
spectacularism 261
spectralism 17, 21, 22, 99, 143; Grisey and
400–419; Murail and 317; and postmodernism
328, 333–38, 339, 346, 347n33; Saariaho and
336–38; and serialism 328, 333–35, 401–5, 415,
417, 419, 421n17; Stockhausen and 143, 333,
415
spectrogram 335, 348n51
speech as communication 293, 294, 438; speech
synthesis 292
Spinoza, Baruch 309
Spitzer, Michael 485
Spivak, Gayatri Chakravorty 2
Sprechgesang 141, 293
Stalling, Carl 48
Stanyek, Jason 270
Steege, Benjamin 11
Stein, Gertrude 125, 130n104, 216
Stein, Lorenz von 277n17
Steinecke, Wolfgang 97
Steinmo, Sven 90, 91, 98, 102, 104n18
Steuermann, Eduard 65, 70, 183
Still, Clyfford 139, 358, 359, 373
stochastic music 317, 318, 319
Stockhausen, Karlheinz 13, 19, 57, 103, 133,
134, 136, 248, 298, 354, 380, 382, 386, 402; at
Darmstadt 94, 95, 97, 99; electroacoustic music
292, 293; influence on spectralism 333, 336, 411,
413–16, 424n64, 424n73; WORKS: *Düfte-Zeichen*
297; *Gesang der Jünglinge* 95, 159, 293, 297;
Klavierstücke 95, 266; *Kontakte* 298; *Kreuzspiel*
97, 404; *Kurzwellen* 303n22; *Licht* cycle 471;
Mantra 333, 339, 348n59, 415; *Mittwoch aus Licht*
471; *Originale* 471; *Spirale* 303n22; *Stimmung* 22,
143, 333, 346, 347n33, 414–16, 435; *Zeitmaße*
95, 295, 404, 422n35; *Zyklus* 95, 103
Stokowski, Leopold 479

515

Index

Stooges, The 249

Strachey, Lytton 4

strategic essentialism (Spivak) 2

Strauss, Richard 7, 37–38, 63, 66, 80n59, 209, 355; *Der Rosenkavalier* 37; *Salome* 5, 37–38

Stravinsky, Igor 10, 36, 57, 63, 76n39, 96, 125, 140, 155, 161, 171, 183, 209, 239, 291, 354, 356, 368, 456, 458; Adorno and 9, 112–14, 123, 127n35; Boulez and 122, 123, 375n1, 402, 420n5; and exile 47, 49, 208; and humour 46; Kundera on 49; Ortega on 119; and performance style 129n62, 476, 479; and politics 11, 217, 220, 232n29; and religion 13, 333; WORKS: *Firebird* 7; Octet 12, 46; *Petrushka* 7; *Rite of Spring* 7, 14, 17, 47, 122, 123, 140, 134, 341, 382; Violin Concerto 354

Striggio, Alessandro 428

string playing *see* violin playing

structuralism 291

studios: Columbia-Princeton 292; Gravesano 292; Polish Radio 95; Siemens, Munich 292; NWDR, later WDR, Cologne 292; Studio di Fonologia, Milan 292

studio techniques 292–93, 406–7

subjectivity 12, 21, 272–74, 307–21; automatization of subjectivity 251, 272–74; creative/immanent subjectivity 112, 122, 162, 228; and dehumanization 12; of historian 109, 158; music as mode of subjectivity 223, 224, 225, 234n77, 242, 274, 283n126, 344–46; and postmodernism 328, 332; subjectivity of performer 475, 481, 482, 485, 490; subjective responses to modernist event 159–62, 171

sublime: aesthetic qualities 18; affect 315; and the beautiful 133, 137, 138, 145–48; masculine/feminine 147; and modernity 139–40; and new music 140–45

Subotnik, Rose Rosengard 57, 81n69, 110, 114, 127n43

Suicide (band) 249

Sumarsam 388

Sur (magazine) 182

surrealism 40, 245, 246, 340, 368, 435, 443

Suryabrata, Bernard 383

Swed, Mark 442

Szakolczai, Arpad 45

Szely, Peter 271

Tabachnik, Michel 411, 423n48

Takahashi, Yūji 397n42

Takemitsu, Toru 186, 187

Tambling, Jeremy 445

Tan, Shzr Ee 270

Tan Dun 186, 270, 281n84; *Internet Symphony no. 1 'Eroica'* 270

tape recording 289, 291–92

Taruskin, Richard 36, 130n94, 131n105, 217, 226, 231n9, 234n99, 276, 319; on Adès 340; and

Adorno 15, 115, 117, 118, 120, 121, 123–24, 226; on Boulez and Baudelaire 121–25, 127n50; and Cage 51n29; on Chaikovsky 128n56; and chronologies of musical modernism 7, 8, 10, 128n51, 131n105, 232n29; on Debussy 118–23, 129n64, 129n69, 129n71, 129n77, 130n84; and Early Music movement 23, 475–80, 490, 491; and history 18, 109, 115–20, 121–24, 125, 127–31; and Ortega 11–12, 120, 129n77; on pleasure and modernist music 226–28, 232n29; on postmodernism 327–28; and Rosen 122; WRITINGS: '"Alte Musik," or "Early Music"?' 479; 'Back to Whom?' 283n135; *Oxford History of Western Music* 10, 11, 109, 115, 116, 118–22, 128n53, 344; 'The Pastness of the Present and the Presence of the Past' 51n19, 478, 491n1; 'The Poietic Fallacy' 116; *Text and Act* 476, 478, 479

Tavener, John 263

Taylor, Timothy D. 279n54

Tchaikovsky, Pyotr Ilyich *see* Chaikovsky, Pyotr Ilyich

technology 5, 12, 13–14, 27n74, 139, 222, 223, 224; communications revolution 258–60, 269–70, 289, 290, 291–93, 295; in contemporary music 57, 60, 91, 114; digital technology 258, 259, 260, 269, 270, 282n105, 283n122; music as 'technology of self' 345; spectralism and 334–35

Teenage Jesus 249, 250

Teilhard de Chardin, Pierre 408

telephone 289

television 272, 282n102

Tenzer, Michael 386

Terada, Rei 313

theatre 100, 208; epic theatre 243–44; *see also* music theatre

Theatre of Eternal Music, The 414

Thelen, Kathleen 90, 91, 98, 102, 104n18

Thieme, John 179

Thomas, Ernst 99

Thomas, Philip 296

Thomas, Rufus 247

Thompson, Marie 308, 315

Tiessen, Heinz 185

Timbaland 251, 252

timbre 172n15, 291; in spectralism 333, 335, 336, 337, 408, 409, 413, 416, 425n81

time 336, 403

Tin Pan Alley 239, 242, 253n1

Tippett, Michael 355

Toller, Ernst 437

Tomkins, Silvan 308, 309, 315, 322n29

Tomlinson, Gary 119, 129n77, 130n100

tonality 6, 10, 71, 266, 290, 291, 353, 354, 356, 358, 376n14; Lachenmann and 137; Pahissa and 209, 213n53; and obscure modernism 155, 161,

516

Index

173n20; and reactive modernism 157, 159, 160, 162–65, 170; Schoenberg and 37, 157, 209, 220; spectralism and 334–35, 417
Tonspur (Soundtrack) series 271
Toop, Richard 40
torture 302n1
totalitarianism 218, 253
Tovey, Donald 73
Traditions Musicales du Monde (concert series) 388
transcendence 34, 217
trans-culturalism 181
transformed modernism (Alastair Williams) 57, 393
transmediality 261, 267, 268
Traube, Elizabeth A. 230
trauma 162–63, 171
Tremblay, Gilles 379, 380–82, 394; and Balinese music 22, 380–86, 393; *Oralléluiants* 383, 384–86, *385*
Trier, Lars von 10
Trotsky, Leon 109, 225
troubadour poetry 162
Trubetskoy, Nikolai 430
Trump, Donald 45, 49
Tsurukame (Noh drama) 180
Tudor, David 95, 102, 103, 296, 301
Tunakam, Erdem 271
Turnage, Mark-Anthony 279n54
twelve-tone composition 71, 73, 183, 184, 185, 189, 199, 207, 208, 356, 376n14; Adorno, 112; Leibowitz 402; Schoenberg 63, 135; *see also* serialism
Tzara, Tristan 217

underground music 233n76, 251
United Nations 72, 263; Universal Declaration on Human Rights 263
Universal Edition 296
universalism 181, 190, 191
Ussachevsky, Vladimir 292
Utz, Christian 439

Vaillancourt, Lorraine 388, 395n14
Valls, Manuel 209, 210
Van den Berg, Hubert 216
Van Gogh, Vincent 113, 124, 127n32
Vanheule, Stijn 171
Vannini, Phillip 270
Varèse, Edgard 10, 117, 184, 187, 290, 368, 380, 382; *Déserts* 404; *Intégrales* 382; *Poème électronique* 290
Vasconcelos, José 184, 187, 193n43
Vattimo, Gianni 21, 320–21
Vaughan, Henry 337
Vaughan Williams, Ralph 74, 355
Velázquez, Diego, *Las Meninas* 390
Venn, Edward 341, 343, 358

verbal communication 288, 293, 294
Verdi, Giuseppe 39, 40; *Falstaff* 39; *Un giorno di regno* 39
vernacular cosmopolitanism 191
vibrato 476, 485
Vick, Graham 471
Vienna 36, 44, 62, 188, 271
Villeneuve, André 382
violin playing 476, 480–91
Vir, Param 281n84
virtuality 282n102
virtuosity 487
vitalism 475–91; modernist strains of 23, 480–85; and the performing subject 485–90
Vivier, Claude 22, 379, 381, 382, 388, 391, 393, 394, 415; and Balinese music 381, 382, 386–88; and contemporary opera 430, 431, 445; notebooks 387, 396n40; WORKS: *Bouchara* 435; *Cinq chansons pour percussion* 381, 382; *Kopernikus* 435; *Lonely Child* 388, 435; *Love Songs* 391; *Ojikawa* 435; *Prologue pour un Marco Polo* 23, 430, 435–37, 445, 447; *Pulau dewata* 381, 382, 386–88, 387, 390; *Trois airs pour un opéra imaginaire* 435
Vogel, Wladimir 65, 185
voice 293–95, 429–31, 435, 438; in music post-WWII 293–94; pre-semantic character of 429–31, 435, 438
Volans, Kevin 281n84
Völlm, Gesine 469

Wade, Bonnie C. 179, 186, 187
Wagner, Cosima 457, 459, 464, 471
Wagner, Richard 8, 38, 124, 135, 140, 161, 209, 317, 339, 340, 357, 358, 372, 408; and Beethoven 147, 356; and Debussy 51n30, 121; and Mendelssohn 129n78; music drama 454, 457–58, 470; and Nietzsche 119; and performance 480, 485; WORKS: *Der fliegende Holländer* 456, 460; *Die Meistersinger von Nurnberg* 23, 458–70; *Parsifal* 332, 341, 349n76, 457, 460; *Ring* cycle 119, 457, 459; *Tristan und Isolde* 51n30, 165, 356, 460, 470; WRITINGS: *Oper und Drama* 454; 'Über das Dirigiren' ('On Conducting') 485
Wagner, Wieland 458, 459, 464, 471
Waller, Fats 242
Walton, William 3, 8, 171, 353
Wanzo, Rebecca 309, 310
Warsaw Autumn 95–96
Watson, Ben 245–46, 247, 249
WDR studio, Cologne 292
Weaver, Warren 291, 292
Weber, Max 5, 6, 12, 13, 111
Weber, William 263, 278n39
Webern, Anton 42, 65, 79n38, 96, 341, 354, 356, 357, 375, 380; Adorno on 71, 112, 133; and *alte Musik* 479; in Barcelona 205; Boulez on

Index

112, 404, 421n31; and Nazism 217; WORKS: Concerto for Nine Instruments Op. 24 65; Symphony Op. 21 356, 357

Weckwerth, Georg 271

Weill, Kurt 44, 45, 200, 204, 208, 243–44; *Die Dreigroschenoper* (*The Threepenny Opera*) 44, 243; *Lady in the Dark* 243; *Lost in the Stars* 243; *Street Scene* 243

Weinbaum, Wiktor 96

Weir, Judith 281n78

Wellesz, Egon 61, 65, 73, 75, 78n21

Wellman, Mac 431, 443–44, 445, 446

Wells, Dominic 343

Wells, H. G. 4

Werbeck, Walter 63

Wertheim, Margaret 272

Wessely, Hans 489

West, Kanye 252

West Indies 180

White, Hayden 157

Whiteman, Paul 247

Whiting, Steven Moore 253, 254n35

Whittall, Arnold 3, 7, 57, 155, 162, 340, 427

Widmann, Jörg, *Lied* 138, 147

Wiener, Norbert 292

Wilde, Oscar 38, 372

Williams, Alastair 57, 115, 393

Williams, Alberto 182

Williams, Christopher 130n84

Williams, Raymond 68, 78n24, 216, 220, 221, 222, 229, 240, 344

Wilson, Charles 94, 339, 347n17

Winckel, Fritz 411

Wire, The (magazine) 225

wireless communication 289, 290

Wittgenstein, Ludwig 130n86; *Tractatus* 46

Wolff, Christian 95, 219, 296

Wolpe, Stefan 207

wonky 250, 251, 252, 255n66

Woolf, Virginia: 'Character in Fiction' 4–5, 6, 9, 10, 25n28; *Mrs Dalloway* 485; and theories of modernism 6, 7, 8, 12, 125, 216

'world literature' (Moretti) 176

'world music' 72, 290, 390–91

World War I 116, 120, 143, 289

World War II 1, 42, 72, 74, 75, 183, 287, 301, 314; as historical watershed 57–58, 68; music as response to experiences in 143, 208, 317–18

Wright, Joseph 9

Wright, Tim 250

writing *see* manifestos, notation

Wurth, Kiene Brillenburg 143, 144, 145–46, 147

WWI *see* World War I

WWII *see* World War II

Xenakis, Iannis 1, 21, 145, 183, 290, 372; and spectralism 22, 407–9, 415, 422n44, 425n84; subjectivity and affect 21, 316, 317–19; and Tremblay 382; WORKS: *Pithoprakta* 318, 319; *Terretektorh* 408; *Tracées* 145; WRITINGS: *Formalized Music* 317

Yamada, Kosaki 186

Yeats, W. B., 'The Second Coming' 43

Yen Tech 251

Young, La Monte 22, 414–15, 424n73, 425n82; *Composition 1960 No. 7* 414–15; 'Lecture 1960' 414–15

YouTube 269–70, 273, 282n114

Yun, Isang 186

Zabelka, Mia 271

Zappa, Frank 247

Zazeela, Marian 414

Zeffirelli, Franco 468

Zemlinsky, Alexander von 209

Zenck, Claudia Maurer 204

Zimmermann, Bernd Alois 142–43; *Requiem for a Young Poet* 142; *Die Soldaten* 142, 143

Zimmermann, Walter 190, 191, 194n74

Žižek, Slavoj 43, 262, 309, 322n8

ZKP *see* Związek Kompozytorów Polskich

Zola, Émile 34, 129n66

Zorn, John 327

Zucker, Lynne G. 96

Związek Kompozytorów Polskich (ZKP; Polish Composers' Union) 95–96

Zwiefacher (folk dance) 432, 448n38